Kenya

written and researched by

Richard Trillo

this edition researched and updated by

Okigbo Ojukwu and Daniel Jacobs

with additional contributions from

Doug Paterson

**ROUGH
GUIDES**

www.roughguides.com

ii

EQUATOR (0°)

Metres
4000
3000
2000
1500
1000
500
200
0

Liboi

Garissa

MERU NATIONAL PARK

Meru

Isiolo

LAIKIPIA

Nanyuki

Mount Kenya

Embu

Nyeri

Murang'a

Thika

ABERDARES NATIONAL PARK

Nyahururu

Nakuru

Lake Bogoria

Lake Nakuru

Lake Naivasha

Naivasha

MAU ESCARPMENT

Narok

RIFT VALLEY

Ngong

NAIROBI

Kajiado

Magadi

Lake Magadi

LOITA HILLS

Kitui

Machakos

Kibwezi

TSAVO NATIONAL PARK

Voi

Taveta

Moshi

Mount Kilimanjaro

AMBOSELI NATIONAL PARK

Namanga

Arusha

TANZANIA

TARANGIRE NATIONAL PARK

Lake Manyara

Lake Natron

MAASAI MARA NATIONAL RESERVE

SERENGETI NATIONAL PARK

Migori

Homa Bay

Kisumu

Mumias

Busia

Lake Victoria

Kakamega

KAKAMEGA FOREST

Kapsabet

Kericho

Sotik

Kisii

Lamu Island
Pate Island
Lamu

Garsen

Malindi

Watamu

Mombasa

Diani Beach

Shimoni

SHIMBA HILLS NATIONAL PARK

INDIAN OCEAN

Tanga & Dar es Salaam

Dar es Salaam

Kampala

Mwanza

AFRICA

KENYA

INDIAN OCEAN

ATLANTIC OCEAN

iii

Introduction to

Kenya

Lying on the equator, with the glaciated peaks of Mount Kenya – second highest mountain in Africa – rising from a natural environment of exceptional beauty, Kenya is a hugely rewarding place to travel. The country's dramatically diverse geography has resulted in a great range of natural habitats, while its history of migration and conquest has brought about a complex social panorama. But if the world-famous national parks, colourful ethnic mix and superb beaches lend an exotic image, the glossy hype of the tourism industry ignores Kenya's post-colonial poverty and deep political tensions.

In any case, treating Kenya as a succession of tourist sights isn't the most stimulating way of experiencing the country. Travelling independently, or at least with eyes open (something this book is designed to facilitate), you can enter the very different world inhabited by most Kenyans: a ceaselessly active landscape of farm and field, of streams and bush paths, of wooden and corrugated-iron shacks, tea shops and lodging houses, of crammed buses and pick-up vans, of overloaded bicycles, and of streets wandered by goats, chickens and toddlers. Off the more heavily trodden tourist routes, you'll find a rewarding degree of warmth, openness and curiosity in Kenya's towns and villages. And out in the wilds, there is an abundance of superb scenery – vistas of rolling savannah dotted with **Maasai** and their herds, high **Kikuyu** moorlands, dense **forests** bursting

Fact file

- At 582,000 square kilometres Kenya is about two and a half times the size of Britain and nearly one and a half times the size of California. The **population**, which, for many years had a growth rate faster than that of any other country in the world, is now around 30 million, and the rate of increase has at last begun to slow.

- Kenya regained **independence** in 1963 after nearly eighty years of British occupation and colonial rule. Although the Republic is a multi-party democracy, the opposition is hamstrung by internal divisions and by the ruthless power hunger of the ruling party.

- Kenya has a huge **debt burden**, currently (2002) running at a little under $7 billion, or roughly $230 for every man, woman and child. Every month, Kenya spends as much on servicing this debt as it does on health care for the whole year.

- Most Kenyans scrape a living by subsistence agriculture, and with no oil or natural gas and few mineral resources, most of the **foreign currency** needed for vital imports is earned from coffee and tea exports and tourism.

- Kenyan society consists of a huge, impoverished underclass, a small but growing middle class and a tiny, rich elite whose success often owes much to nepotism and graft. **Corruption** percolates every corner of the country and most official transactions.

with bird song and insect noise, and stony, shimmering **desert** – all of which comes crisply into focus when experienced in the context of an economically beleaguered African nation four decades after Independence.

Where to go

The **coast** and major **game parks** are the most obvious targets, and if you come to Kenya on an inclusive tour you're likely to have your time divided between these two attractions. Despite the impact of human population pressures, Kenya's **wildlife spectacle** remains a fascinating and addictive experience and most visitors are enchanted by their safaris. Kenya's million-odd annual visitors are easily absorbed in such a large country, and there's nothing to prevent you escaping the predictable tourist bottlenecks: even on an organized tour, you should not feel constrained to follow the prescribed plan.

Kenya's peoples

Although urban growth and inter-marriage are blurring distinctions, certain language groups remain easily identifiable through dress and lifestyle. The brilliantly beaded and closely related Maasai and Samburu peoples are associated with the parks named after them, but they herd their animals across vast reaches of savannah and, when access to water demands it, even into the big towns. Many Turkana and members of some of the other remote northern groups also retain their traditional garb and rather tooled-up appearance, with spears much in evidence. However, Kenya's biggest language groups, the Kikuyu in the highlands, the Akamba east of Nairobi, and the Luo in the west, rarely wear traditional dress these days. They have had a largely West-ernized orientation for three genera-tions and their economic, if not political, influence is notable. For more details on language and eth-nicity, see p.67.

The vast majority of the population live in the rugged **highland areas** in the **southwest** quarter of the country, where the ridges are a mix of *shamba* smallholdings and plantations. Run-ning through the heart of these high-lands sprawls the **Great Rift Valley**, an archetypal East African scene of dry, thorn tree savannah, splashed with lakes and studded by volcanoes. It's great walking country, as are the high forests and moors of the **Central Highlands** and **Mount Kenya** itself – a major target and a feasible climb for most people. **Nairobi**, the capital, on the highlands' southern edge, is generally used only as a gateway to Kenya, but has plenty of diversions to occupy your time while arranging an onward trip. The **national parks and reserves**, watered by seasonal streams, are mostly located in savannah coun-try on the highland fringes.

Further west, towards **Lake Victo-ria**, lies gentler countryside, where you can travel for days without seeing another foreign visitor and get per-haps the best immersion in Kenyan life and culture. Beyond the rolling tea plantations of Kericho and the hot plains around the port of Kisumu lies the steep volcanic massif of **Mount Elgon**, astride the Ugandan border. The little-known **Kakamega Forest** rainforest reserve, with its unique wildlife, is here too, and more than enough reason to strike out west.

In the north, the land is **desert** or semi-desert, broken only by the high-light of **Lake Turkana** in the north-west, almost unnaturally blue and gigantic in the wilderness. Although northeast Kenya, towards the Somalian border, is currently unsafe for travellers, the routes up to Turkana are still open, and you can even get there by public transport. For serious adventure, it is one of the most spectacular and memorable of all African regions.

Separating Kenya's interior – or "up-country" – from the Indian Ocean, the arid Maungu Plains form a barrier which accounts in large part for the separate history and culture of **the coast**. Here, a distinct Islamic **Swahili** civilization exists with a long historical record in its mosques and tombs and the ruins of several ancient towns cut from the jungle, while along the length of the coast, beyond the white sandy beaches – invariably shaded by coconut palms or casuarina trees – runs an almost continuous coral reef, protecting a shallow, safe lagoon from the Indian Ocean.

When to go

Kenya has complicated and rather unpredictable **climatic shifts**. Broadly, the pattern is that January to March is hot and dry, while from April to June it is hot and wet, a period known as the "long rains". From July until October the weather is very warm and dry, and then come the "short rains", making November and December warm and wet. At high altitudes, however, it may rain at almost any time. Western Kenya has a scattered rainfall pattern influenced by Lake Victoria, while the eastern half of the country, and especially the coast itself, are largely controlled by the Indian Ocean's monsoon winds – the dry northeast monsoon (*kaskazi*) blowing from December to March and the moist southeast monsoon (*kusi*) from April to November, which normally brings the heaviest rain in May. **Temperatures** are determined largely by altitude: you can reckon on a drop of 6°C (or 11°F) for every 1000m you climb from sea level. Nairobi, for example, (at 1600m, higher than the Cairngorms or the Appalachians) has a moderate climate, and can get down to 5°C (41°F) at night.

The main **tourist seasons** tie in with the rainfall patterns: the biggest influxes are in December and January and, to a lesser extent, July and August. **Dry-season** travel has a number of advantages, not least of which is the greater visibility of wildlife as animals are concentrated along the diminishing watercourses. July and August are probably the **best months**, overall, for game-viewing. October to January are the months with the clearest seas for **snorkelling** and **diving** – especially November. In the "long rains", the mountain parks are sometimes closed, as the muddy tracks are undrivable. But the **rainy seasons** shouldn't deter travel unduly: the rains usually come only in short afternoon or evening cloudbursts, and the landscape is strikingly green and fresh even if the skies may be cloudy. There are bonuses, too, in the lack of tourists: hotel and other prices are reduced and people generally have more time for you.

"Kenya" or "Keenya"?

Although you'll hear "Kenya" most of the time, the second pronunciation is still used, and not exclusively by the old settler set. The colonial pronunciation was closer to the original name of Mount Kenya, Kirinyaga. This was abbreviated to "Ki-nya", spelt Kenya. With the arrival of modern orthography, this spelling came to be pronounced with a short "e" and when Jomo Kenyatta became president after Independence, the pure coincidence of his surname was exploited.

Kenya's climate

	Jan	Feb	Mar	Apr	May	June	July	Aug	Sept	Oct	Nov	Dec
Nairobi (Alt 1661m)												
Av day temp (°C)	25	26	25	24	22	21	21	21	24	24	23	23
Av night temp (°C)	12	13	14	14	13	12	11	11	11	13	13	13
Days with rainfall	5	6	11	16	17	9	6	7	6	8	15	11
Rainfall (mm)	38	64	125	211	158	46	15	23	31	53	109	86
Mombasa (sea level)												
Av day temp (°C)	31	31	31	30	28	28	27	27	28	29	29	30
Av night temp (°C)	24	24	25	24	24	23	22	22	22	23	24	24
Days with rainfall	6	3	7	15	20	15	14	16	14	10	10	9
Rainfall (mm)	25	18	64	196	320	119	89	66	63	86	97	61
Kisumu (Alt 1135m)												
Av day temp (°C)	29	29	28	28	27	27	27	27	28	29	29	29
Av night temp (°C)	18	19	19	18	18	17	17	17	17	18	18	18
Days with rainfall	6	8	12	14	14	9	8	10	8	7	9	8
Rainfall (mm)	48	81	140	191	155	84	58	76	64	56	86	102

25

things not to miss

*It's not possible to see everything Kenya has to offer in one trip –
and we don't suggest you try. What follows is the author's selection
of some of the highlights, ranging from remarkable events to natural
wonders and compelling sights and activities. Arranged in five
colour-coded categories, you can browse through to find the very best
things to see, do and experience. All highlights have a page reference
to take you straight into the guide, where you can find out more.*

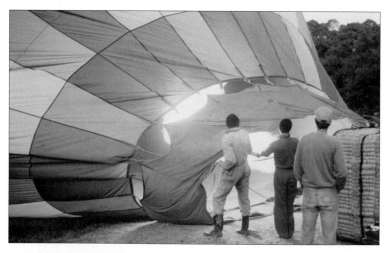

01 Balloon safaris Page **428** • Not a real safari, and madly expensive, balloon safaris are almost worth every cent of the US$400 or so you'll pay to be aloft over the plains at dawn (that's around five bucks a minute): an unforgettable experience.

02 Lake Bogoria hot springs
Page **274** • Geysers on the shores of Lake Bogoria, in the northern Rift Valley, erupt with fierce clouds of steam across a bleached landscape. Beware of accidents as the area is remote.

04 Turkana overland safaris
Page **590** • Remote Turkana is most easily visited on a camping safari from Nairobi, involving days of bumping through arid wilderness and encounters with local people, wildlife and swollen rivers all on the cards.

03 Crocodiles hatching
Page **597** • Central Island, in Lake Turkana, is an important breeding place for Nile crocodiles. Visit at the right time of year, and you can see hundreds of baby crocs breaking out.

05 The tea country
Page **323** • Kericho, Kenya's tea capital and the most important centre for the bush in the whole of Africa, is surrounded by an endless rolling sea of brilliant green plantations.

06 Light aircraft flights Page 139
• Flying is a good way to get around. The country is well served by small operators and short sightseeing flights can be arranged in many places, with unparalleled opportunities for a bird's-eye view.

07 Fort Jesus Page 460
• Mombasa's Fort Jesus was the site of gruesome battles between Portuguese and Arab colonizers and local people, but today, the fort's spacious leafy interior houses an excellent historical museum.

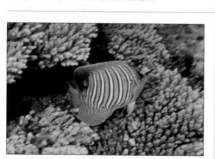

08 Diving and snorkelling Page 59
• Kenya's coral reef has superb underwater opportunities, with diving schools in all the main centres, and snorkelling equipment widely available to rent for a couple of hours. Wasini, Watamu and Kiwaiyu are outstanding sites but note that water clarity tends to be seasonal as swollen rivers bring silt into the sea.

09 Lamu Page 554
• Lamu is a relaxing and welcoming island getaway with no shortage of things to do and a variety of low-key facilities. It also has some of Africa's best preserved ancient town architecture, many of the houses dating back hundreds of years.

10 Mzima Springs Page **394** • A remarkable oasis in Tsavo West National Park, bubbling with crystal-clear water, Mzima is inhabited by hippos, crocodiles and a diversity of smaller species. Check out the walkways and underwater viewing chamber.

11 Climbing Mount Kenya Page **179** • An extinct volcano straddling the equator, glacier-topped Mount Kenya is Africa's second highest peak. You can hike the lower slopes at will, but if you attempt the 5200m summit you need to go slowly enough to acclimatize to the altitude.

12 Gedi ruins Page **526** • These eerily atmospheric ruins, of a Swahili town abandoned in the seventeenth century, are easily visited from Watamu or Malindi. Take time to wander the jungle-shaded lanes away from the main site.

13 Cave of skulls Page **380** • The Taita keep the exhumed skulls of their deceased in concealed rock niches – an example of traditional religious practice that is becoming increasingly rare. With sensitivity, you can visit.

14 **Agricultural shows** Page **54** • Every large town has its annual farm show, based on the British tradition, but infused with Kenyan style.

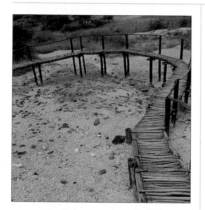

15 **Olorgasailie Prehistoric Site** Page **227** • A stark site in the southern Rift Valley, where you can commune with nature by camping or staying in a *banda*, and examine the fossil evidence of one of our hunting ancestors preserved in situ along a guided trail through the scrub.

16 **Nyama choma** Page **47** • Kenya's most popular big meal out is *nyama choma* or roast meat – goat, mutton or beef – and lots of beer. Nyama choma bars are to be found throughout the country.

17 **Hell's Gate National Park** Page **243** • A hop away from Lake Naivasha, the scene changes dramatically under the sheer, red cliffs of this winding gorge. A national park you can walk, cycle, ride or drive through, it's home to a selection of less threatening plains game.

19 Arabuko-Sokoke Forest Page 523 •
The largest area of indigenous coastal forest in Kenya harbours a range of wildlife, including forest elephants, several rare mammals and multitudes of birds and butterflies. Guided walks are available from the visitor centre near Watamu.

18 Makindu Handicrafts Co-operative Page 375 •
Wooden carvings are the stock-in-trade of Kenya's curio-sellers. Makindu, on the Nairobi-Mombasa Highway, has an excellent small co-operative, where you can often pick up discarded "failures" as well as finished articles at good prices.

20 Live music Page 57 •
Any weekend it's easy to find live music in the towns. Nairobi is the biggest focus, with dozens of clubs and bands, mostly guitar-based, but wherever you are, taxi drivers or hotel staff can help point you in the right direction.

21 Saiwa Swamp National Park Page 339 •
Home to the unusual sitatunga, a partially aquatic antelope, several interesting species of monkey, and a wide variety of birds, Saiwa Swamp offers peaceful camping and the chance to explore on foot.

23 **Maulidi** Page **567** • The annual Muslim celebrations to mark the prophet's birthday are an important event on the coast, best witnessed in Lamu. Book a place to stay well in advance.

24 **Shimba Lodge** Page **495** • For an atmospheric splurge, stay in the only tree hotel on the coast, Shimba Lodge, in Shimba Hills National Park, a mere hour from Mombasa, where you'll share your arboreal abode with wildlife, from bats to bushbabies — and leopards if you're lucky.

22 **Maasai Mara wilde-beest migration** Page **428** • Observing the cacophonous herds from the banks of the flood-swollen Mara River – especially at one of the deadly, crocodile-infested crossing points – is one of nature's most awe-inspiring experiences. The migration takes place between July and October, varying from year to year.

25 **Kakamega Forest** Page **354** • An isolated patch of the equatorial forest that once girdled the breadth of Africa, Kakamega is a haven for hundreds of species that exist nowhere else in Kenya.

contents

Using the Rough Guide

We've tried to make this Rough Guide a good read and easy to use. The book is divided into six main sections, and you should be able to find whatever you want in one of them.

colour section

The front colour section offers a quick tour of Kenya. The **introduction** aims to give you a feel for the place, with suggestions on where to go. We also tell you what the weather is like and include a basic country fact file. Next, our author rounds up his favourite aspects of Kenya in the **things not to miss** section, followed by a wildlife spotter's guide. Right after this comes a full **contents** list.

basics

The Basics section covers all the **pre-departure** nitty-gritty to help you plan your trip. This is where to find out which airlines fly to your destination, what paperwork you'll need, what to do about money and insurance, about internet access, food, security, public transport, car rental – in fact just about every piece of **general practical information** you might need.

guide

This is the heart of the Rough Guide, divided into user-friendly chapters, each of which covers a specific region. Every chapter starts with a list of **highlights** and an **introduction** that helps you decide where to go, depending on your time and budget. Likewise, introductions to the various towns and smaller regions within each chapter should help you plan your itinerary. We start most town accounts with information on arrival and accommodation, followed by a tour of the sights, and finally reviews of places to eat and drink, and details of nightlife. Longer accounts also have a directory of practical listings. Each chapter concludes with **public transport** details for that region.

contexts

Read Contexts to get a deeper understanding of what makes Kenya tick. We include a **history**, articles about **music** and **wildlife**, literature extracts and a detailed further reading section that reviews dozens of **books** relating to the country.

language

The **language** section gives useful guidance for speaking Swahili and pulls together all the vocabulary you might need on your trip, including a comprehensive menu reader. Here you'll also find a glossary of words and terms peculiar to the country.

index + small print

Apart from a **full index**, which includes maps as well as places, this section covers publishing information, credits and acknowledgements, and also has our contact details in case you want to send in updates and corrections to the book – or suggestions as to how we might improve it.

chapter map of **Kenya**

contents

colour section   i–xxxii

basics   7–80

the guide   81–630

contexts   631–734

language   735–748

index & small print   749

map symbols

maps are listed in the full index using coloured text

Regional Maps

———	Minor roads (mostly unpaved)
═══	Main roads (mostly paved)
- - - - -	Footpath
▬▬▬	Railway
— —	Ferry route
———	River
▬▬▬▬	International border
———-	Chapter division boundary
⌃⌃⌃	Mountain range
▲	Mountain peak
⟨⟨	Escarpment
⟫	Cliff
⟋	Hill
⟋⟋	Viewpoint
⊕	Crater
⌂	Cave
𝑥	Waterfall
⩊	Marshland
⩕	Spring
◆	General point of interest
⚡	Lighthouse
卅	Picnic area
⌐	Golf course
⊠—⊠	Gate
⌂	Lodge
⌂	Park HQ
⚊	Campsite

⊙	Monument
✈	Airport
✈	Airstrip
▦	Park/reserve
⁂	Forest
▦	Beach
▦	Glacier

Town Maps

═══	Roads
★	Bus stop
▯	Petrol station
@	Internet access
ⓘ	Information office
ⓒ	Telephone
⊠	Post office
P	Parking
♰	Monastery
✡	Synagogue
☪	Mosque
♠	Temple
✚	Church
▮	Building
⬭	Stadium
✝	Cemetery
▦	Park

basics

basics

Getting there

Flying is really the only practicable way of getting to Kenya. Apart from scheduled flights to Nairobi, an inclusive package holiday (usually using a charter flight to Mombasa) can make a lot of sense as some, based around mid-range coast hotels, are very cheap, and if you choose carefully, you shouldn't feel too packaged. Some of the tour brochures contain quite interesting safari itineraries and a number of independent companies specialize in adventure packages. Overland routes to Kenya are currently only feasible from southern Africa and, with difficulty, from Egypt via Sudan and Ethiopia. Conflicts have effectively closed routes from West Africa for the time being.

Types of ticket

Round-trip tickets are generally of three types – short excursions (usually one month), three-month excursions and one year. A one-way fare (valid one year) is normally half the relevant "yearly" fare. You may be able to fly out to Nairobi and back from somewhere else (an "open jaw" flight), depending on the airline and the agent's contract.

Passing through immigration at the airport is always smoother if you have a flight out again, but if you want to travel onwards from Kenya and only need a **one-way flight**, check the cancellation charge for cashing in the unused half of a return ticket.

If Kenya is only one stop on a longer journey, you might want to consider buying a **round-the-world (RTW) ticket**. Some travel agents can sell you an "off-the-shelf" RTW ticket that will have you touching down in about half a dozen cities (Nairobi is on several itineraries); others will have to assemble one for you, which can be tailored to your needs but is apt to be more expensive. As a general rule you must decide your itinerary and stopover cities in advance, travelling in a single direction, either eastbound or westbound with no backtracking. You set a date for the first outbound flight in advance, and then reserve the others as you go, completing the entire journey within either six months or a year. Figure on £1500–2000 ($2000–2800) for a RTW ticket including Kenya.

Buying a ticket

You can often cut costs by going through a specialist flight agent – either a consolidator, who buys up blocks of tickets from the airlines and sells them at a discount, or a **discount agent** (listed on pp.11, 12, 14 and 16), who in addition to dealing with discounted flights may also offer special student and youth fares and a range of other travel-related services such as travel insurance, rail passes, car rentals, tours and the like. From Britain or Europe, you can also get **charter flights**, which are often cheaper, but there's usually a maximum stay of four or six weeks, with the price depending on the number of days you stay, and you won't be able to change your dates. These are not comfortable flights – the seating is tight, and most refuel en route (and you can't get off the plane), which adds a couple of hours to the journey time.

Always ask what **refund** you'll get if anything goes wrong and find out how easy it will be to change your reservation dates once you've got your ticket. You can sometimes leave a return ticket "open-dated" on its return portion, but in that case you'll have to make a seat reservation yourself with the airline in Kenya. It's just as easy, and more prudent, to have a confirmed seat and change the date if necessary (and if seats are available).

Airline **seasons** for Kenya vary a little but generally departures from late June to mid-August and mid-December to mid-January will be the most expensive. The majority of airlines have low-season rates from February to June, and often again from October to early December.

If you're a **student**, academic or under 32, ask if the agent has special fares – some of the better airlines grant various **restricted eligibility fares** to certain selected agents which are not available in theory to the general public. Note that the advantage of some of these discretionary fares may lie more in the length of stay they offer and an easing of booking regulations than purely in their price. They are not automatically cheaper than anything else, but they may, all things considered, be much better value.

Book as far **in advance** as you can. Six months isn't too long, and that's when you can pick up the cheapest scheduled tickets. Airlines can be full to capacity at peak periods, especially Christmas, and discounted seat availability is often snapped up quickly. On the other hand, if you find early on that flights seem to be "full", check the same outlets again nearer your departure date – assuming you haven't got something by then – for reservations not taken up.

Booking flights online

Many airlines and discount travel websites offer you the opportunity to book your tickets online, cutting out the costs of agents and middlemen.

Online booking agents and general travel sites

Ⓦ **www.cheapflights.com** Flight deals and travel agents for the UK and Ireland, plus links to other travel sites.

Ⓦ **www.cheaptickets.com** and **.co.uk** Discount flights.

Ⓦ **www.deckchair.com** Bob Geldof's online venture, drawing on a wide range of airlines from the UK.

Ⓦ **www.etn.nl/discount.htm** A hub of consolidator and discount agent web links, maintained by the nonprofit European Travel Network.

Ⓦ **www.expedia.com** and **.co.uk** Discount airfares, all-airline search engine and daily deals.

Ⓦ **www.flyaow.com** Online air travel info and reservations site for the US.

Ⓦ **www.hotwire.com** Bookings from the US only. Last-minute savings of up to forty percent on regular published fares. Travellers must be at least 18 and there are no refunds, transfers or changes allowed.

Ⓦ **www.lastminute.com**

Ⓦ **www.priceline.com** and **.co.uk** Name-your-own-price website that has deals at around forty percent off standard fares. You cannot specify flight times (although you do specify dates) and the tickets are non-refundable, non-transferable and non-changeable.

Ⓦ **www.geocities.com/Thavery2000** Has an extensive list of airline toll-free numbers and websites in the USA.

Ⓦ **www.skyauction.com** Bookings from the US only. Auctions tickets and travel packages using a "second bid" scheme. The best strategy is to bid the maximum you're willing to pay, since if you win you'll pay just enough to beat the runner-up regardless of your maximum bid.

Ⓦ **www.smilinjack.com/airlines.htm** Links to airline websites.

Ⓦ **www.travelocity.com** and **.co.uk** Destination guides, hot web fares and best deals for car rental, accommodation and lodging as well as fares. Provides access to the travel agent system SABRE, the most comprehensive central reservations system in the US.

Ⓦ **www.travelshop.com.au** Australian website offering discounted flights, packages, insurance and online bookings.

Flights from Britain and Ireland

London is by far the best departure point for Kenya from the British Isles, with **direct flights** to **Nairobi** seven times a week from Heathrow with both Kenya Airways and British Airways, taking around nine hours. **Fares** start at around £400 return with BA if booked early (you can book up to twelve months in advance), £420 with Kenya Airways. A cheaper option is an **indirect flight**, with prices starting from as little as £250 return. Airlines worth considering include Egyptair via Cairo, Ethiopian Airlines via Addis Ababa, El Al via Israel, and Gulf Air, Emirates or Saudia via the Gulf, as well as KLM via the Netherlands. There are no direct scheduled flights from any British airports other than Heathrow, your choice from most regional airports being either BA via London or KLM via Amsterdam.

There are also several **charter operators** with whom you can get seats – only to Mombasa – out of London or Manchester from around £350. These normally come with accommodation, which at the budget end doesn't affect the price much, but you can also get "seat only" deals. Any travel agent will have details.

Flying from Ireland, there are convenient

through-connections from Dublin on British Airways (daily via London Gatwick, overnight) and KLM via Amsterdam (Mon, Wed & Fri). From **Belfast**, the only good connections are on British Airways (daily via London Gatwick, overnight).

Because of the small time difference – Kenya is two hours ahead of the British Isles in summer, three in winter – you won't experience any jet lag.

Airlines

Air Mauritius ☎020/7434 4375–7, ⓦwww.airmauritius.com. From Heathrow via Mauritius. Twice weekly service to Nairobi, but requiring a stopover in Mauritius both ways.

British Airways UK ☎0845/773 3377, ⓦwww.britishairways.com, Ireland ☎0141/222 2345. From Heathrow direct, with connecting flights from Dublin and from most UK airports.

Egyptair ☎020/7734 2395, ⓦwww.egyptair.com.eg. From Heathrow via Cairo.

El Al ⓦwww.elal.co.il, UK ☎020/7957 4100, Ireland ☎01/670 4731. From Heathrow via Tel Aviv.

Emirates ☎0870/243 2222, ⓦwww.emirates.com. From Gatwick via Dubai.

Ethiopian Airlines ☎020/8987 7000, ⓦwww.flyethiopian.com. From Heathrow via Addis Ababa.

Gulf Air UK ☎0870/7771 717, ⓦwww.gulfairco.com, Ireland ☎01/285 8643. From Heathrow via Bahrain and Abu Dhabi.

Kenya Airways ☎01784/888222, reconfirmations ☎01784/888333, ⓦwww.kenya-airways.com. From Heathrow.

KLM UK ☎0870/507 4074, ⓦwww.klmuk.com, Ireland ☎0345/445588. From Heathrow, Gatwick, London City, Stansted, Aberdeen, Birmingham, Bristol, Cardiff, Glasgow, Edinburgh, Humberside, Leeds/Bradford, Manchester, Newcastle, Norwich and Teesside, via Amsterdam.

Lufthansa UK ☎0845/773 7747, ⓦwww.lufthansa.com, Ireland ☎01/844 5544. From Heathrow, connecting in Munich or Frankfurt for weekly Condor flights to Mombasa.

Saudia ☎020/8995 7777, ⓦwww.saudiairlines.com. From Heathrow via Jeddah.

Discount agents in Britain

Africa Travel Centre ☎020/7387 1211, ⓕ7383 7512, ⓦwww.africatravel.co.uk. Helpful and resourceful.

Air Travel Guide ☎020/7434 1523, ⓕ7494 3560, ⓦwww.airtravelguide.com. General discount agent.

Bridge the World ☎020/7911 0900, ⓦwww.bridgetheworld.com. Specializing in round-the-world tickets, with good deals aimed at the backpacker market.

Brightways Travel ☎020/8574 2622, ⓕ8621 8880, ⓦwww.brightways.co.uk. Good fares to Nairobi via Brussels.

Destination Group ☎020/7400 7000, ⓦwww.destination-group.com. Good discount airfares.

Flightbookers ☎020/7757 2444, ⓦwww.ebookers.com. Low fares on scheduled flights.

Flynow ☎020/7835 2000, ⓦwww.flynow.com. Large range of discounted tickets; official South African Airways agent.

The London Flight Centre ☎020/7244 6411, ⓦwww.topdecktravel.co.uk. Long-established agent dealing in discount flights.

North South Travel ☎ & ⓕ01245/608291, ⓦwww.northsouthtravel.co.uk. Friendly, competitive travel agency, offering discounted fares worldwide, with profits used to support projects in the developing world, especially the promotion of sustainable tourism.

Quest Worldwide ☎020/8547 3322, ⓦwww.questtravel.com. Small, personal agent. Recommended.

Soliman Travel ☎020/7244 6855, ⓕ7835 1394, ⓦwww.solimantravel.co.uk. Particularly good on Egyptair flights via Cairo.

Somak Travel ☎020/8903 8526, ⓕ8902 8434, ⓦwww.somak.co.uk. Good deals on BA, Kenya Airways and KLM.

STA Travel London ☎0870/1606070, Aberdeen ☎0122/465 8222, Bristol ☎0117/929 4399, Edinburgh ☎0131/226 7747, Glasgow ☎0141/338 6000, Leeds ☎0113/244 9212, Liverpool ☎0151/707 1123, Manchester ☎0161/834 0668, Newcastle ☎0191/233 2111, ⓦwww.statravel.co.uk. Worldwide specialists in low-cost flights and tours for students and under-26s, though other customers welcome.

Superstar Holidays ☎020/7957 4300, ⓕ7957 4399, ⓦwww.superstar.co.uk. Official consolidator for El Al tickets, with special six-month fares and free Tel Aviv stopovers.

Tradewings ☎020/7631 1840, ⓕ7636 1705. Happy to shop around for good deals to Nairobi.

Trailfinders London ☎020/7628 7628, Birmingham ☎0121/236 1234, Bristol ☎0117/929 9000, Glasgow ☎0141/353 2224, Manchester ☎0161/839 6969, ⓦwww.trailfinders.com. Respected discount flights agency with a convenient range of other services.

Some reasonable fares, but not especially geared up for Africa.

Travel Cuts ☎020/7255 2082,
ⓦwww.travelcuts.co.uk. Canadian company specializing in budget, student and youth travel and round-the-world tickets.

Wexas ☎020/7589 3315, ⓕ7589 8418,
ⓦwww.wexas.com. This membership-only organization handles everything competently by post. Detailed brochures and fare and airline information.

World Express Travel ☎020/7434 1654,
ⓕ7734 2550, ⓔsales@world-express.demon
.co.uk. Official UK consolidators for Kenya Airways, Alliance Air and Ethiopian Airlines.

Discount agents in Ireland

Apex Travel ☎01/671 5933,
ⓦwww.apextravel.ie. Long-haul flights, including Africa.

Aran Travel International ☎091/562595,
ⓦhomepages.iol.ie/~arantvl/aranmain.htm. Good value flights to all parts of the world.

CIE Tours International ☎01/703 1888,
ⓦwww.cietours.ie. General flight and tour agent.

Co-op Travel Care ☎028/9047 1717, ⓕ9047 1339. Flights and holidays around the world.

Joe Walsh Tours Dublin ☎01/872 2555 or 01/676 3053, Cork ☎021/427 7959,
ⓦwww.joewalshtours.ie. General budget fares agent.

Lee Travel ☎021/427 7111, ⓦwww.leetravel.ie. Flights and holidays worldwide.

McCarthy's Travel ☎021/427 0127,
ⓦwww.mccarthystravel.ie. General flight agent.

Premier Travel ☎028/7126 3333,
ⓦwww.premiertravel.uk.com. Discount flight specialists.

Rosetta Travel ☎028/9064 4996,
ⓦwww.rosettatravel.com. Flight and holiday agent.

Trailfinders ☎01/677 7888,
ⓦwww.trailfinders.ie. One of the best-informed and most efficient agents for independent travellers.

Twohigs ☎01/648 0800, ⓕ01/648 0899. Long-haul flights including Africa.

USIT Now Dublin ☎01/602 1777 or 677 8117, Belfast ☎028/9032 7111, Cork ☎021/427 0900, Derry ☎028/7137 1888, Galway ☎091/565177, Limerick ☎061/415064, Waterford
☎051/872601, ⓦwww.usitnow.ie. Student and youth specialists.

World Travel Centre ☎01/671 7155, ⓕ677 7155, ⓦwww.farebank.net. Long-haul flights including Africa.

Package holidays

Package holidays of flight and two weeks' dinner and bed and breakfast (half-board) in a beach hotel can cost as little as £499. You don't have to stick with the crowd all the time – or even stay at the hotel – and you could make several short independent trips around the country.

Coast hotels vary greatly in price, atmosphere and amenities. Find out as much as possible about the establishment, and beware of spending hundreds of pounds more on a place that isn't actually a lot nicer than the one next door.

A **safari** component in a package tour will knock up the price to around £750 minimum, inclusive of flight. Whilst you'll pay more for a safari this way than organizing it in Kenya, the convenience is well worth it on a short trip. If booking independently, see the section on organizing safaris from Nairobi (p.139) or Mombasa (pp.468–9) and see "Safaris" on p.61. If you're looking for a package, see "Overland and adventure tour operators" on p.17.

UK package tour operators

Abercrombie and Kent ☎020/7730 9600,
ⓦwww.abercrombiekent.com. Very upmarket long-haul specialists, with unusual offerings, a dedicated and very flexible manner and a wide knowledge of Kenya, where the company originated. Busy Nairobi operation.

About Africa ☎020/8747 0177,
ⓦwww.southerncrosssafaris.com. Sales agents for Southern Cross Safaris in Nairobi (p.142), a reputable mid-range safari and tailor-made holiday package company.

Africa Archipelago ☎020/8780 5838,
ⓦwww.africaarchipelago.com. General operator which takes bookings for some upmarket lodges.

Art of Travel ☎01285/650011,
ⓦwww.artoftravel.co.uk. Innovative travel stylists with a personal approach, specializing in tailor-made trips. Tempting combinations of game driving, walking, horse riding and beach lounging, with accommodation in luxury lodges or off-the-beaten track farmhouses.

British Airways Holidays ☎0870/242 4245,
ⓦwww.baholidays.co.uk. Impressive range of safari and beach combinations; some keen prices but you'll find certain hotel packages offered for less elsewhere.

Elite Vacations ☎020/8864 4431,

@ www.elite-vacations.co.uk. Numerous holiday options including the combination of a classic Kenyan safari with four to seven nights spent in Mauritius or the Seychelles.

Hayes & Jarvis ☎ 0870/898 9890,
@ www.hayes-jarvis.com. Long-established, experienced operator, originally from Kenya, whose wide-ranging options stretch from budget self-catering and no-frills safaris to luxury escorted tours.

The Imaginative Traveller ☎ 020/8742 8612,
@ www.imaginative-traveller.com. Inspired range of hotel/lodge-based and camping safaris in Kenya alone, or Kenya and Tanzania. Also offers a fifty-day overland trip Cape Town to Nairobi

Kuoni ☎ 01306/742888, @ www.kuoni.co.uk. Reputable long-haul holiday operator, with a flexible approach and lots of experience. Good choice of safaris and coastal destinations.

Safari Consultants ☎ 01787/228494,
@ www.safari-consultants.co.uk. Tailor-made itineraries including less usual destinations and arrangements.

Somak Holidays ☎ 020/8423 3000,
@ www.somak.co.uk. Long-established Kenyan company with busy offices in Nairobi PO Box 48495 ☎ 02/557832, ℱ 535175 and Mombasa PO Box 90738 ☎ 011/486197, ℱ 487324. Wide selection of safaris including tailor-mades. Good-value charter flights, BA and Kenya Airways flights. Recommended.

Thomson ☎ 0870/550 2554, @ www .thomson-holidays.com; late availability offers on Teletext. The big one as far as British visitors are concerned. Lots of choice, spread over two comprehensive brochures (*Faraway Shores* and *Worldwide*).

Tropical Places ☎ 01342/330777,
@ www.tropicalplaces.co.uk. Good-value coast packages using a choice of scheduled or charter flights from London or Manchester to Nairobi and Mombasa. Run the excellent Porini Camp near Amboseli with Maasai involvement, only bookable through them (@ www.porini.com).

Wildlife Discovery ☎ 01737/223903,
@ www.travelshop.com/operators/wldop.shtml. Individual operator with a firm emphasis on high-quality safaris using good accommodation. Tailor-made arrangements, or fixed-itinerary safari including BA flight and professional guides. Excellent value. Office in Nairobi.

Worldwide Journeys and Expeditions ☎ 020/7381 8638,
@ www.worldwidejourneys.com. Tailor-made trips with unusual emphases, including "homestead" safaris, staying on private estates as the guests of experienced guides and wildlife experts.

Flights from the USA and Canada

There are no direct flights from the USA or Canada to East Africa: you have to change planes and, quite possibly, airlines. The **fastest routes** to Nairobi are from New York via London, either on British Airways or a combination of Virgin Atlantic and Kenya Airways. Alternatively, you can fly via various European hubs. Note that if you break your journey in Europe the regular international baggage limit of 20kg will apply on your flight on to Kenya.

Fares from the US, purchased direct from the airline and flying mid-week in the low-season, extend upwards from $1300 out of New York, and from $2600 out of Los Angeles ($1100 and $1300 respectively for students and under-26s); travelling on week-ends will increase this fare by $100–200. Going through a discount broker (see p.14) can cut this somewhat.

From **Canada**, the airlines' Toronto–Nairobi Apex fares start at around CDN$4000, but if you book through a Canadian travel agent you can cut the rate to as low as CDN$1450.

Airlines

Air Canada ☎ 1-888/247 2262,
@ www.aircanada.ca.
British Airways ☎ 1-800/247 9297,
@ www.british-airways.com.
EgyptAir @ www.egyptair.com.eg, US ☎ 1-800/334 6787, Canada ☎ 1-800/263 2899. New York to Nairobi via Cairo (also from Montreal, but requiring a Cairo stopover).
El Al ☎ 1-800/223 6700, @ www.elal.com. New York to Nairobi via Tel Aviv.
Ethiopian Airlines ☎ 1-800/445 2733,
@ www.flyethiopian.com. New York and Washington DC to Nairobi via Addis Ababa.
Gulf Air ☎ 1-800/553 2824,
@ www.gulfairco.com. New York to Nairobi via London, Bahrain and Abu Dhabi (also from Chicago and Miami, but requiring a stopover on route).
KLM/Northwest @ www.klm.com, US ☎ 1-800/447 4747, Canada ☎ 514/397 0775.
Lufthansa ☎ 1-800/645 3880, in Canada ☎ 1-800/563 5954, @ www.lufthansa-ca.com.
Saudia ☎ 1-800/4-SAUDIA,
@ www.saudiairlines.com. New York and Washington DC to Nairobi via Jeddah.

Swissair ☎1-800/221 4750,
Ⓦwww.swissair.com.

Discount agents

Air Brokers International ☎1-800/883 3273 or
415/397 1383, Ⓦwww.airbrokers.com.
Consolidator and specialist in RTW tickets.
Council Travel ☎1-800/226 8624 or 617/528
2091, New York ☎212/822 2700, San Francisco
☎415/421 3473, Los Angeles ☎310/208 3551,
Boulder ☎303/447 8101, Washington DC
☎202/337 6464, Chicago ☎312/951 0585,
Boston ☎617/266 1926, Minneapolis ☎612/379
2323, Austin ☎512/472 4931, Seattle
☎206/632 2448, Ⓦwww.counciltravel.com.
Nationwide organization that mostly, but by no
means exclusively, specializes in student/budget
travel.
Educational Travel Center ☎1-800/747 5551
or 608/256 5551, Ⓦwww.edtrav.com.
Student/youth discount agent.
Flytime ☎212/760 3737,
Ⓔflytimetravel@usa.net. Discounted tickets for
scheduled flights with Ethiopian, KLM and Northwest.
High Adventure Travel ☎1-800/350 0612 or
415/912 5600, Ⓦwww.airtreks.com. Round-the-
world specialists. The website features an interactive
database that lets you build and price your own RTW
itinerary.
Interworld ☎305/443 4929,
Ⓔmtocabens@traveleaders.com. Discounted
tickets for the Virgin Atlantic/Kenya Airways route.
Magical Holidays ☎1-800/228 2208 or
212/486 9600. Air tickets on the Northwest/KLM
route.
Pan Express Travel New York ☎1-800/518
7726 or 212/719 9292, San Francisco ☎415/989
8282, Ⓦwww.panexpress.com. Air tickets and
package tours.
Sendant Travel International ☎1-800/221
8139.
Skylink US ☎1-800/AIR-ONLY or 212/573 8980,
Canada ☎1-800/SKY LINK. Consolidator.
STA Travel ☎1-800/777 0112 or 1-800/781
4040, New York ☎212/627 3111, Los Angeles
☎310/824 1574, San Francisco ☎415/391 8407,
Florida ☎352/338 0068, Washington DC
☎202/887 0912, Boston ☎617/266 6014,
Philadelphia ☎215/568 7999, Ⓦwww.sta-travel
.com. Specialists in independent travel.
TFI Tours International ☎1-800/745 8000 or
212/736 1140. Consolidator.
Travac New York ☎1-800/872 8800 or 212/563
3303, Orlando ☎407/896 0014,
Ⓦwww.thetravelsite.com. Consolidator and charter
broker.

Travel Avenue ☎1-800/333 3335,
Ⓦwww.travelavenue.com. Full-service travel agent
that offers discounts in the form of rebates.
Travel Cuts toll-free in Canada ☎1-800/667
2887, Toronto ☎416/979 2406, Calgary
☎403/282 7687, Edmonton ☎403/488 8487,
Halifax ☎902/494 2054, Montreal ☎514/843
8511, Ottawa ☎613/238 8222, Quebec City
☎418/654 0224, Saskatoon ☎306/975 3722,
Vancouver ☎604/659 2830, Winnipeg ☎204/269
9530, in US ☎416/979 2406,
Ⓦwww.travelcuts.com. Canadian student travel
organization.
UniTravel ☎1-800/325 2222 or 314/569 2501,
Ⓦwww.unitravel.com. Air tickets on the
Northwest/KLM route.
Worldtek Travel ☎1-800/243 1723,
Ⓦwww.worldtek.com. Discount travel agency for
worldwide travel.
Worldwide Discount Travel Club ☎305/993
1713. Discount travel club.

Inclusive tours

A large number of tour operators offer inclusive vacation and safari packages to Kenya.
When checking with them, remember that
most of the quotes you'll be given are for the
land arrangements only, with flight extra
(which may be purchased from the travel
operator or from another source). Prices, not
including flights, start at around $1000 per
week, with most of the tour spent on safari.
Hotel-based beach extensions work out
somewhat cheaper and are more subject to
seasonal variation.

Most agents are representatives not only
for North American companies but also for
many of the adventure travel operators
whose head offices are in Britain (see
pp.17–18).

US tour operators and agents

Abercrombie & Kent ☎1-800/323 7308 or
630/954 2944, Ⓦwww.abercrombiekent.com.
Leading upscale operator with over thirty years of
experience organizing African safaris. Comprehensive
and professional programme in Kenya; offices in
Nairobi.
Africa Tours ☎1-800/235 3692 or 516/264
2800, Ⓦwww.africasafaris.com. A variety of Kenya
safaris.
African Adventure Company ☎1-800/88 WILD
or 954/491 8877. One of the best agencies in the
business, offering over a hundred programs to Africa
and thousands of safari options.

David Anderson Safari Consultants ☎1-800/927 4647, ⓦwww.davidanderson.com. No expense spared here: escorted wildlife safaris and first-class accommodation.

Geo Expeditions ☎1-800/351 5041 or 209/532 0152, ⓦwww.geoexpeditions.com. Eleven-day Kenya safaris and combination Kenya/Tanzania safaris.

Holbrook Travel ☎1-800/451 7111 or 352/377 7111, ⓦwww.holbrooktravel.com. Top-quality natural history tours and safaris led by experts.

Journeys ☎503/226 7200, ⓔtravel@journeys1.com. Tailor-made trips for individuals and groups, plus flights through consolidators.

Journeys International ☎1-800/255 8735, ⓦwww.journeys-intl.com. Eight- and fifteen-day safari trips.

Ker & Downey ☎1-800/423 4236 or 713/917 0048, ⓦwww.kerdowney.com. Renowned upmarket safaris under canvas in style, with an "Edwardian feel". Also runs to South Africa, Botswana and Tanzania.

Micato Safaris ☎212/545 7111 ⓦwww.africansafari.org/micato/.Very highly regarded and long-established tour operator.

Mountain Travel–Sobek ☎1-888/687 6235 or 510/527 8100, ⓦwww.mtsobek.com. Mountaineering, hiking, white-water rafting and other activity tours.

Nature Expeditions International ☎1-800/869 0639 or 954/693 8852, ⓦwww.naturexp.com. Education and adventure in travel, offering wildlife, natural history and cultural expeditions.

Safari Center ☎1-800/223 6046 or 310/546 4411, ⓦwww.safaricenter.com. Deluxe, economy or adventure safari options, as well as off-the-beaten track safaris.

Somak Safaris ☎310/642 3700 or 1-800/757 6625, ⓦwww.somaksafaris.com. A wide range of safaris to Kenya and all of Africa with frequent cost-cutting special promotions.

Spector Travel ☎617/338 0111 or 1-800/TRY AFRICA, ⓦwww.spectortravel.com. African specialist with a good record.

Tamsin & Cooke ☎201/337 6151, ⓦwww.tamsinandcooke.com. Customized itineraries based on thirty years' residence in Africa, with emphasis on luxury, away-from-it-all accommodation and safaris on foot, horseback and by camel.

Wilderness Travel ☎1-800/368 2794, ⓦwww.wildernesstravel.com. Small-group expeditions to the great game parks of Kenya, led by an experienced Maasai guide.

Canadian tour operators and agents

Adventure Center ☎1-800/228 8747 or 403/439 9118, ⓦwww.adventure-center.com. Hiking and "soft adventure" specialists.

Blyth & Co ☎1-800/387 1387 or 416/964 2569. Custom tours to Kenya.

Worldwide Quest Adventures ☎1-800/387 1483, ⓦwww.worldwidequest.com. Natural history safaris.

Flights from Australia and New Zealand

There are no direct flights from Australia or New Zealand – all require a stopover either in Asia, southern Africa, or in the carrier's home city. The **most direct flights** from **Australia** are via Johannesburg with SAA, via Harare with Quantas and Air Zimbabwe, or via Singapore and Mauritius with Qantas and Air Mauritius (from A$2950 out of Sydney, Brisbane or Melbourne and A$2635 out of Perth). Gulf Air via Bahrain, Emirates via Dubai, and Egyptair via Cairo also offer similar prices. In the high season (mid-Nov to mid-Jan) expect to pay an extra A$300 or so.

From New Zealand, your most direct route is via Johannesburg with SAA. Alternatively, you can travel via the Middle East with Emirates or Egyptair, or via Sydney and Harare with Qantas and Air Zimbabwe. Expect to pay NZ$2500–3000 for the cheapest tickets.

Airlines in Australia and New Zealand

Air Mauritius Australia ☎02/9267 7199, ⓦwww.airmauritius.com.

Egypt Air Australia ☎02/9267 6979, ⓦwww.egyptair.com.

Emirates Australia ☎02/9290 9700 or 1300/303 777, New Zealand ☎09/377 6004, ⓦwww.emirates.com.

Gulf Air Australia ☎02/9244 2199, New Zealand ☎09/308 3366, ⓦwww.gulfairco.com.

South African Airways Australia ☎02/9223 4402 or 1800/221 699, New Zealand ☎09/379 3708, ⓦwww.saa-usa.com.

Sri Lanka Airlines Australia ☎02/9244 2234, New Zealand ☎09/308 3353, ⓦwww.srilankan.com.

Qantas Australia ☎13/1313, New Zealand ☎09/357 8900 or 0800/808 767, ⓦwww.qantas.com.au.

Tour operators & travel agents

Many of these agents are representatives not only for Australian and New Zealand companies but also for adventure travel operators whose head offices are in Britain (see opposite).

Australia

Abercrombie & Kent ☎03/9536 1800, ⓦwww.abercrombiekent.com. Long-established, upmarket operator selling its own exclusive holidays.
Adventure World ☎02/9956 7766 or 1300/363 055, ⓦwww.adventureworld.com.au. Accommodation, car rental, discounted air fares and a varied selection of tours from city mini-stays in Nairobi and Mombasa to camping and overland safaris.
Africa Bound Holidays ☎08/9361 2047, ⓔafricabound@citysearch.com.au. Travel consultant covering the whole of Africa.
Africa Travel Centre ☎02/9249 5444 or 1800/000 447, ⓦwww.travel.com.au. Accommodation, self-drive, Nairobi and Mombasa stop overs and a comprehensive range of safaris.
Africa Wildlife Safaris ☎03/9696 2899. Specialists in upmarket camping and lodge-based safaris.
Anywhere Travel ☎02/9663 0411 or 018/401 014, ⓔanywhere@ozemail.com.au.
Flight Centres ☎02/9235 3522 or for nearest branch 13/1600, ⓦwww.flightcentre.com.au.
Northern Gateway ☎08/8941 1394, ⓔoztravel@norgate.com.au.
Peregrine ☎03/9663 8611, ⓦwww.peregrine.net.au. Beach stays, overland trips and all-inclusive game safaris; offices in Melbourne, Sydney, Brisbane, Adelaide and Perth.
STA Travel ☎13/1776 or 1300/360 960, ⓦwww.statravel.com.au.
Student Uni Travel Australia ☎02/9232 8444, ⓔAustralia@backpackers.net.
Trailfinders ☎02/9247 7666.

New Zealand

Abercrombie & Kent ☎09/523 2966, ⓦwww.abercrombiekent.com.
Adventure Travel Shop ☎09/303 1805.
Adventure World ☎09/524 5118, ⓦwww.adventureworld.co.nz. Agents for Exodus Expeditions and Peregrine, Australia.
Budget Travel ☎09/366 0061 or 0800/808 040, ⓦwww.budgettravel.co.nz.
Destinations Unlimited ☎09/373 4033.
Flight Centres ☎0800/243544, Auckland ☎09/358 4310, Christchurch ☎09/379 7145,

Wellington ☎04/472 8101, ⓦwww.flightcentre.co.nz.
STA Travel ☎0508/782872, Auckland ☎09/309 0458 or 09/366 6673, Wellington ☎04/385 0561, Christchurch ☎03/379 9098, ⓦwww.statravel.co.nz.
Usit Beyond ☎09/379 4224 or 0800/874833, ⓦwww.usitbeyond.co.nz.

Flights from South Africa

There are **direct flights** from Johannesburg (the only departure point) to Nairobi operated by South African Airways (Tues, Wed, Thurs, Fri & Sun ☎011/978 1111, ⓕ773 8988, ⓦwww.flysaa.com) and Kenya Airways (daily ☎011/881 9747, ⓕ881 9749, ⓦwww.kenya-airways.com). Booking direct with the airlines, fares start at R2800 for a fixed-date one-month trip booked at least three days in advance; open yearly returns start at R6430. For details on **overland travel** from South Africa, see below.

Tour operators and travel agents

Adventures ☎011/465 1288, ⓔfsal@global.co.za. Exclusive package tours.
African Outposts ☎011/884 6848, ⓦwww.tourism.co.za/af-out. Specialists in "environmental education through tourism".
African Safari Shop ☎011/888 6364, ⓦwww.safarishop.co.za. Wide range of options for many budgets.
Africa Travel Centre ☎021/423 5555, ⓦwww.backpackers.co.za. Local branch of the London-based Africa overland specialist.
Student Travel Centre ☎011/447 5551, ⓔinfo@statravel.co.za. Good youth and student fares.
Wild Frontiers ☎011/315 4838, ⓦwww.wildfrontiers.com. A range of mid-priced tours.

Getting there overland

With unlimited time and a sense of adventure, **travelling overland** can be an exciting and rewarding way of getting to Kenya, though opportunities to travel this way are subject to change as Africa's borders open and close in the wake of political and military conflicts. It's still possible to get there from Egypt – taking a boat from Aswan to Wadi Halfa in Sudan, crossing into Ethiopia at Humera or Metema, and entering Kenya at Moyale, but the route is not an easy one, and currently the only **advisable route** is from southern Africa. From **Harare**, you can take the train through Zambia and Tanzania, go overland by local transport, or hook up with any number of foreign-operated overland trips from Harare, Cape Town or Johannesburg to Nairobi, most of which are very good value for money and take a month or two for the trip.

Overland and adventure tour operators

As well as the operators listed below, check the listings of operators and agents on pp.12, 14–15 and 16, and "Discount agents" on pp.11–12, 14 and 16. Many of the latter are agents for companies detailed here. When getting quotes, find out whether flights are included, and how much your contribution to the communal "kitty" is, as this can add up to thirty percent to the total cost.

Check out the company as much as possible. Most operators run occasional evening slide and video sessions, when you can decide if a packaged adventure is for you. Otherwise, scrutinizing their blurb gives a good indication of their probable preparedness and real know-how; if the blurb looks cheap or hasty, you should forget it.

Most of the following operators offer five- to eight-week Nairobi–Harare–Cape Town runs, which are usually possible in the other direction too, and most also offer shorter trips covering Kenya and either Uganda, Tanzania or both (game parks in Kenya and gorillas in Uganda is a favourite). Most operators are based in the UK, but many of them sell their trips internationally via the internet. Prices are given here in sterling and include the "kitty", but exclude flights into or within Africa, and of course are subject to change.

Absolute Africa UK ☎020/8742 0226, Ⓦwww.absoluteafrica.com. Eight weeks Nairobi–Cape Town (£920), or eleven weeks via Uganda (£1360).

Africa Travel Centre UK ☎020/7387 1211, Australia ☎02/9249 4444 or 1800/000 447, New Zealand ☎09/520 2000, South Africa ☎021/423 5555, Ⓦwww.africatravel.co.uk. Helpful agents for several overland companies.

African Routes South Africa ☎031/569 3911–2, Ⓦwww.africanroutes.co.za. Overland operator and agent for northbound trips from South Africa.

African Trails UK ☎020/8742 7724, Ⓦwww.africantrails.co.uk. Various trips from two weeks in Kenya, Uganda and Tanzania (£525) to an eight-week Nairobi–Cape Town trip (£1015), plus trans-Africa trips when conditions permit.

Bukima Africa UK ☎0870/757 2230, Canada c/o Go-Active Vacations ☎1-800/649 3629 or 604/606 1830, Australia c/o Living Adventure ☎1800/882 103 or 08/8223 2955, New Zealand c/o Waiuku Travel ☎0800/388488 or 09/235 9614, Ⓦbukima.com. Long-established overlanders, pricier than most, running the usual trips from Nairobi including three weeks around East Africa (around £600), seven weeks to Cape Town (around £1050), or eleven weeks to Victoria Falls (around £1100).

Dragoman UK ☎01728/861133, USA c/o Adventure Center ☎1-800/227 8747 or 510/654 1879, Canada c/o Trek Holidays ☎1-888/456 3522 or 780/439 9118, Australia c/o Adventure World ☎02/9956 7707, New Zealand c/o Adventure World ☎09/524 5118, Ⓦwww.dragoman.co.uk. Personal and creative with notably good trucks and competitive prices. Regular East, southern and trans-African departures (fly-over from Cameroon to Nairobi). Trips range from seventeen days in Kenya and Uganda (around £1000) to ten and a half weeks Nairobi–Cape Town (just under £3000).

Drifters South Africa ☎011/888 1160, Ⓦwww.drifters.co.za. Fortnightly overland departures to Nairobi, at around £1470.

Encounter Overland UK ☎01768/862222, Ⓦwww.encounter-overland.com. Well-respected operator offering three- to eight-week trips through East and southern Africa. Straightforward no-extras pricing. Three weeks in East Africa from £575, eight weeks Nairobi–Cape Town from £1760.

Exodus UK ☎020/8675 5550, Ireland c/o Colette Pearson Travel ☎01/677 1147, USA c/o Gap Adventures ☎914/278 9899, Canada c/o Gap Adventures ☎416/260 0999, Australia c/o Peregrine ☎03/9662 2700, Ⓦwww.exodus.co.uk. Long-established outfit, offering a seventeen-day trip exploring the Maasai Mara, Rift Valley and Uganda (from £1306), and a seventeen-day camping safari in Kenya and Tanzania including three days by the beach in Zanzibar (from £1297).

Explore Worldwide UK ☎01252/760000, Ireland c/o Maxwells Travel ☎01/679 3948, USA c/o Adventure Center ☎1-800/227 8747 or 510/654 1879, Canada c/o Trek Holidays ☎1-888/456 3522 or 780/439 9118, Australia c/o Adventure World ☎02/9956 7707, New Zealand c/o Adventure World ☎09/524 5118, Ⓦwww.explore.co.uk. Highly respected small groups operator which runs an interesting seventeen-day Kenya and Tanzania tour including Amboseli and Maasai Mara plus a walk in the Loita Hills (from about £1550), or an eighteen-day trip including Samburu, Lake Nakuru, Tsavo East and Zanzibar (from about £1440).

Footloose Adventure Travel UK ☎ 01943/ 604030, ⓦ www.footlooseadventure.co.uk. Small, enthusiastic independent outfit offering a classic Mount Kenya–Kilimanjaro trek for mountain enthusiasts; they'll tailor-make a safari to fit your budget and interests, offer advice on overland travel options, and track down good-value flights.

Guerba Expeditions UK ☎ 01373/826611, ⓦ www.guerba.co.uk. The acknowledged African experts, running a string of Kenya trips, including an eight-day camping safari for around £445 (you can find cheaper in Nairobi) and an eight-day lodge safari for £890, plus longer East African trips. Office in Nairobi ☎ 02/544165 or 352430.

Kumuka Expeditions UK ☎ 020/7937 8855,

Australia ☎ 02/9279 0491, ⓦ www.kamuka.com. An assortment of trips including Kenya and other countries in East and southern Africa, from eighteen days in Kenya and Uganda for around £720 to a nine-week Nairobi–Cape Town overlander for around £2460.

Phoenix Expeditions UK ☎ 01509/881818, ⓦ www.phoenixexpeditions.co.uk. Well-equipped outfit offering three weeks in Kenya, Uganda and Tanzania for around £500, an eight-week trip from Kenya to the Cape for around £1200, or a twenty-week overland (plus the odd flight) expedition from Istanbul to Cape Town or vice-versa, via Nairobi from £1575.

Truck Africa ⓦ www.truckafrica.com. Personal but professional long-haul overland tour company enthused over by past clients, offering a twenty-week expedition from London to Nairobi for £1650, and an eight-week extension to Cape Town for around £1210.

Visas and red tape

Check that your passport will remain valid for at least six months beyond the end of your projected stay in Kenya, and ensure it has plenty of spare pages for stamps if travelling further afield in Africa. Nationals of the UK, USA, Canada, Australia, New Zealand, South Africa, all EU countries and Japan all need visas to visit Kenya. Requirements change however, and you should always check in advance with a Kenyan embassy, consulate or high commission to confirm the current situation.

Visas and visitor's passes

Visas can be obtained in advance from any Kenyan embassy, consulate or high commission (sometimes from a British embassy in countries where Kenya has no diplomatic representation). Visas normally take 24–48 hours to process, require two passport-size photos and usually an **air ticket** out of the region (not just to Uganda or Tanzania). This requirement is usually waived if the embassy is satisfied of your alternative arrangements or financial responsibility. A single-entry visa costs £35/$50 and is valid for three months.

Multiple entry visas cost roughly double that. Remember that Kenyan diplomatic missions are closed on Kenyan public holidays (see p.54 for a list of holidays). Transit visas (valid for seven days) can be bought on arrival for $20. Visas are normally valid for entry within three months of the date of issue.

It's possible to get a **visa on arrival** at the airport (sterling or dollars cash only), though it's best avoided if you're arriving at night. Although this is generally a hassle-free formality, it does leave you open to potential problems caused by corrupt officials preying on your fear of being refused a visa. It also generally requires you to stand in line and can take up to an hour, so if you do decide to take this option, get off the plane quickly.

On arrival in Kenya you'll be issued with a **visitor's pass** usually limiting the length of stay to three months, though various factors may determine the length of time granted, including your appearance, how much money you have and (fortunately) how long you actually want to stay.

Your visa allows **re-entry** to Kenya after visits to Uganda or Tanzania (assuming of course you have a visa for these countries). For other trips outside Kenya, you'll need to reapply for a visa to get back in.

Kenyan embassies, consulates and high commissions

Australia 33 Ainslie Ave, PO Box 1990, GPO Canberra ☏ 02/6247 4788; also serves New Zealand.

Belgium 208 Av Winston Churchill, 1180 Brussels ☏ 02/3401040.

Canada 415 Laurier Ave East, Ottawa, Ontario K1N 6R4 ☏ 613/563 1773.

Congo D.R. Plot 5002, ave de l'Ouganda, BP 9667, Zone Gombe, Kinshasa ☏ 012/30117.

Egypt 7 Sharia Mohandes Galal, PO Box 362, Dokki, Cairo ☏ 02/345 3628.

Ethiopia Hiher 16, Kebelle 01, Fikre Mariam Rd, PO Box 3301, Addis Ababa ☏ 01/610303.

France 3 rue Freycinet, 75116 Paris ☏ 01/5662 2525.

Germany Markgrafenstr 63, 10969 Berlin ☏ 030/2592660

India E-66 Vasant Marg, Vasant Vihar, New Delhi 110 021 ☏ 011/614 6537.

Italy Via Archimede 164, 00197 Rome ☏ 06/808 2714.

Japan 3–24–3 Yakumo, Meguro-Ku, Tokyo 152–0023 ☏ 03/3723 4006.

Netherlands Nieuwe Parklaan 21, 2597 LA The Hague ☏ 070/350 4215.

Nigeria PO Box 6464, 53 Queen's Drive, Ikoyi, Lagos ☏ 01/261 4929.

Russia Bolshaya Ordinka, Dom 70, Moscow ☏ 095/237 4702.

Rwanda Blvd de Nyabugogo, PO Box 1215, Kigali ☏ 82774.

Saudi Arabia PO Box 95458, Riyadh 11693 ☏ 01/488 2484.

South Africa 302 Brooks St, Menlo Park, Pretoria 0081 ☏ 012/362 2249.

Sudan Street 3, Amarat, PO Box 8242 Khartoum ☏ 011/40386 or 43758.

Sweden Birger Jarlsgatan 37, 2nd floor, PO Box 7694, 11141 Stockholm ☏ 08/21 83 00.

Tanzania 4th floor, NIC Investment House, Samora Machel Ave, PO Box 5231, Dar es Salaam ☏ 051/112955.

Uganda 60 Kira Rd, PO Box 5220 Kampala ☏ 041/258235.

United Arab Emirates PO Box 3854 Abu Dhabi ☏ 02/666300.

United Kingdom 45 Portland Place, London W1N 4AS ☏ 020/7636 2371.

USA 2249 R St NW, Washington, DC 20008 ☏ 202/387 6101, ⊛ www.kenyaembassy.com.

Zambia 5207 United Nations Ave, PO Box 50298, Lusaka ☏ 01/250722.

Zimbabwe 95 Park Lane, PO Box 4069, Harare ☏ 04/790847.

Extending your stay

It's important to remember the time limit that's been stamped on your visitor's pass when you arrive, and to renew well in advance. You'll certainly have to renew after three months. Confusion can arise if, for example, you can't decipher KVP5W/H ("Kenya Visitor's Pass 5-Week Holiday") – if in doubt, ask. There have been a number of cases of travellers overstaying the limits of their visitor's passes by a few days and finding themselves invited to spend the night behind bars while a suitable fine was discussed – anything up to the equivalent of £100/$150).

Extensions to visitor's passes and visa renewals can be done at the immigration offices in Nairobi, Mombasa, Lamu or Kisumu. Addresses for these are given in the relevant "Listings" sections in the guide (pp.150, 302, 471 and 573). You can only renew your pass for a further three months (giving a six-month maximum stay in all), after which you'll have to leave East Africa.

For neighbouring countries' embassies in Nairobi see "Nairobi Listings" on p.146.

Customs

Duty free allowance is one bottle of spirits or wine, and one carton of 200 cigarettes or 50 cigars or half a pound of tobacco.

If you're stopped at the customs benches, you will normally be asked if you have any photographic equipment, video camcorders, cassette players and so on. Unless you're some kind of professional, with mountains of specialist gear, there shouldn't be any question of paying duty on personal equipment, though some customs officers like to make notes of it all in your passport to ensure it is re-exported. If you have friends in Kenya, however, and are taking presents for them, you are likely to have to pay duty if you

declare the items. Even if you have nothing to declare, corrupt customs officers may ask you for a bribe before clearing you: you can of course refuse, and they will usually give up on you after half an hour; alternatively, you can kick up a fuss.

Information, websites and maps

The Kenya Tourist Board (KTB) has recently been revamped and promises more professional marketing and efficient diffusion of information. Their offices abroad, franchized to private marketing companies in each country, are not really walk-in, but they can supply brochures and answer queries. They also publish a 1:2,400,000 tourist map of Kenya, with insets of Lamu, Mombasa, Nairobi and the coast, which is fine for navigation if you intend sticking to the main routes. More detailed maps of the country are best bought at home as, with the exception of the inexpensive Kenya Survey maps, they're usually cheaper and better than those available inside the country. As for what you can learn about Kenya from surfing the web, the picture is not a very exciting one, but a few sites are worth a look.

Kenya Tourist Board offices abroad

As well as the individual tourist offices listed below, the Kenya Tourist Board also has a general website, ⓦ www.magicalkenya.com.
Canada c/o Discover the World, Suite 100, 1599 Huronatario St, Mssissauga, ON L5G 4S1 ☏ 905/891 0093, ⒺToronto@discovertheworld.ca.
France c/o Express Conseil, 5bis rue du Louvre, 75001 Paris ☏ 01/4477 8806, Ⓕ 4260 0545, Ⓔ marina@ecltd.com.
Germany c/o Mangum, Herzogspiltalstrasse 5, D-80331 Munich ☏089/236 6210, Ⓕ 2366 2192, Ⓔ k.mangum@mangum.de.
Italy c/o Adam & Partner Italia, Via Salaino 12, 20144 Milan ☏02/4810 2361, Ⓕ 4331 8385, Ⓔ kenya@adams.it.
Netherlands c/o TMC, Leliegracht 20, 1015 DG Amsterdam ☏ 020/421 2668, Ⓕ 670 5357, Ⓔ kenia@travelmc.com.
Spain c/o CS Développement, c/Tuset 10, 3º, 4ª, 08006 Barcelona ☏93 292 0655, Ⓕ93 415 4577, Ⓔ kenya@ketal.com.

UK c/o Interface, 69 Monmouth St, London WC2H 9DG ☏020/7836 7743, Ⓕ7240 1024, Ⓔ kenya@iiuk.co.uk.
USA c/o Carlsons Destination Marketing, 1405 Xenium Lane North, Station 8257, Minneapolis, MN 55441 ☏763/212 6414, Ⓕ212 2533, Ⓔ htodd@carlson.com.

Kenya online

Though the information on Kenya available on the internet is far from comprehensive, if you do have access, it's well worth clicking away at the websites listed below, and also those of the Kenyan newspapers listed on p.53.

Take a look as well at two newsgroups, **rec.travel.africa** and **soc.culture.kenya**, which are genuinely useful information forums and good sources for new websites.
US State Department Travel Advisory ⓦ travel.state.gov/kenya.html. The US State Department's latest advice on travel in Kenya.
British Foreign and Commonwealth Office ⓦ www.fco.gov.uk/travel/countryadvice.asp?KY.

The latest FCO advice on Kenya, increasingly detailed and well researched. The "Before You Go" section, endorsed by Rough Guides, is well worth reading through.

Child's Eye Project
Ⓦ www.piac.org/childseye/zibf98/index.html
Give cameras to a group of Mathare valley slum kids, and this is what they come up with. In a class of its own.

Kenya Tourist Board
Ⓦ www.magicalkenya.com. Very useful and informative, with fact files on Kenya's wildlife and historical sites, lists of safari companies, and even advice for photographers.

Africa On Line
Ⓦ www.africaonline.com/site/ke/index.jsp. Latest news about Kenya, not very good listings, but a lively discussion forum/notice board, with everything from comments on the latest political controversy to lonely hearts seeking partners.

Ministry of Tourism and Wildlife
Ⓦ www.africaonline.co.ke/AfricaOnline/karibu.html
Nicely packaged in the USA, with information that is useful but official ("Kenya is a stable and peaceful country..").

Konaka's Website Ⓦ africa.u-shizuoka-ken.ac.jp.
Lovingly put together "haiku ethnography" by Japanese friends of the Samburu. Great pictures of daily life and ritual, plus downloadable sounds, music and essays.

Tim's and Lara Beth's Kenya Pages
Ⓦ www.blissites.com/kenya.
An excellent cultural site, with long pieces on Kenya's people, a linguistic map, stamps,coins, riddles and proverbs, Kenyan recipes, and pleasing oddities like practical advice on how to make traditional musical instruments.

Bwana Zuia's Kenya Travel Guide
Ⓦ www.bwanazulia.com/kenya.
Practical stuff with good links.

Kenyaweb Ⓦ www.kenyaweb.com. A very wide-ranging site with information in varying degrees of usefulness on transport, media, entertainment and sport, plus surveys of the country's economy, geography, politics and ethnography.

Representing The Real
Ⓦ www.lclark.edu/~soan/alicia/rebensdorf.101 .html. Top marks for totally arcane PhD research: "Exploring appropriations of Hip-Hop Culture in the Internet and Nairobi".

Traditional Music and Cultures
Ⓦ www.bluegecko.org/kenya. An excellent site, absolutely chocker with information on Kenya's peoples, their cultures and beliefs, but most of all their music, of which there are soundclips for each of Kenya's main peoples, put together by *Rough Guide*

toTanzania author Jens Finke.

Visit Kenya Ⓦ www.visit-kenya.com.
A very useful site, with information, listings and travel tips for anyone visiting Kenya.

Rich Bowen's Kenya Site
Ⓦ www.rcbowen.com/kenya. Tends to be a bit out of date, but has useful information, and a page entitled "What's a Matatu", featuring not only an explanation, but also links to other pages of matatu-related interest.

Amnesty International
Ⓦ web.amnesty.org/ai.nsf/countries/kenya.
Amnesty's latest reports on the human rights situation in Kenya.

Yahoo! weather report
Ⓦ weather.yahoo.com/regional/Africa/Kenya.html.
The latest weather conditions and five-day forecast for each of twenty locations around the country.

Maps

You'd do well buying a good, large-scale map of Kenya before leaving home, possibly two if you're planning to head off on less-trodden roads (though none of the maps listed below are completely accurate). In **Nairobi**, there's a good selection of maps at the **Public Map Office** (see p.148 for details on how to obtain the Survey maps, which you might want to do months in advance) and it's really worth getting hold of the Survey of Kenya park maps before taking off for the wilds (at the park gates they're usually either out of stock or twice the price) – with the aid of the numbered junctions, you can actually find your way around. The best maps for each national park are mentioned at the start of the relevant sections.

If you're doing more in Africa than visiting Kenya alone, you probably want one or more of the **Michelin series**, nos. 953, 954 or 955, still the best all-purpose travel maps for Africa. Kenya comes out small at this scale but with surprising detail.

Freytag & Berndt 1:1,500,000. Rather cluttered and not easy to read.

GeoCenter World Map 1:1,000,000.

ITMB 1:2,800,000. Quite detailed, despite the small scale, showing relief as well as roads.

Macmillan 1:1,750,000. Clear and fairly tough, with Nairobi and Mombasa plans on the reverse, but it could be more detailed. Macmillan also does park maps for Amboseli, Tsavo and Maasai Mara, but these are now well overdue for updating.

Nelles Verlag 1:1,100,000. German, but published

in English, and detailed (though poor on minor road numbers and missing various highways built in the last ten years). Includes a good chunk of Northern Tanzania and some inserts, together with mostly accurate annotations.

Shell/Marco Polo 1:1,000,000. The best of the lot, largely up to date and easy to read, with road surfaces clearly distinguished (if not always correctly), and plenty of topographical detail (hill peaks, obscure wells, dunes and so on).

Map and book outlets in the UK and Ireland

Belfast Waterstone's, Queens Bldg, 8 Royal Ave, BT1 1DA ☎028/9024 7355, ⓦs1.waterstones.co.uk.
Bristol Stanfords, 29 Corn St, BS1 1HT ☎0117/929 9966, ⓦwww.stanfords.co.uk.
Cambridge Heffer's Map Shop, 3rd floor, 19 Sydney St, CB2 3HL ☎01223/568467, ⓦwww.heffers.co.uk.
Cardiff Blackwell's, 13–17 Royal Arcade, CF1 2PR ☎029/2039 5036, ⓦwww.bookshop.blackwell.co.uk.
Cork Waterstone's, 69 Patrick St ☎021/276522.
Dublin Easons Bookshop, 40 O'Connell St, Dublin 1 ☎01/873 3811, ⓦwww.eason.ie; Fred Hanna's Bookshop, 27–29 Nassau St, Dublin 2 ☎01/677 1255; Hodges Figgis Bookshop, 56–58 Dawson St, Dublin 2 ☎01/677 4754, ⓦwww.hodgesfiggis.com; Waterstone's, 7 Dawson St, Dublin 2 ☎01/679 1415.
Glasgow John Smith and Sons, 27 Colquhoun Ave, G52 4PJ ☎0141/552 3377 ⓦwww.johnsmith.co.uk
Inverness James Thin Melven's Bookshop, 29 Union St, IV1 1QA ☎01463/233500, ⓦwww.jthin.co.uk.
Leicester The Map Shop, 30a Belvoir St, LE1 6QH ☎0116/247 1400.
London Africa Bookcentre, in the Africa Centre, 38 King St, London WC2E 8JT ☎020/7240 6649; Daunt Books, 83 Marylebone High St, W1M 3DE ☎020/7224 2295 & 193 Haverstock Hill, NW3 4QL ☎020/7794 4006; National Map Centre, 22–24 Caxton St, SW1H 0QU ☎020/7222 2466, ⓦwww.mapsworld.com; Nomad Books, 781 Fulham Rd, London SW6 5HA ☎020/7736 4000; Stanfords, 12–14 Long Acre, WC2E 9LP ☎020/7836 1321, ⓦwww.stanfords.co.uk, also in the USIT Campus shop at 52 Grosvenor Gardens, SW1W 0AG ☎020/7730 1314, and in the British Airways shop at 156 Regent St, W1R 5TA ☎020/7434 4744; The Travel Bookshop, 13–15 Blenheim Crescent, W11 2EE ☎020/7229 5260, ⓦwww.thetravelbookshop.co.uk.

Manchester Waterstone's, 91 Deansgate, M3 2BW ☎0161/837 3000, ⓦs1.waterstones.co.uk.
Newcastle Newcastle Map Centre, 55 Grey St, NE1 6EF ☎0191/261 5622.
Oxford Blackwell's Map and Travel Shop, 53 Broad St, OX1 3BQ ☎01865/792792, ⓦwww.bookshop.blackwell.co.uk.
Worcestershire The Map Shop, 15 High St, Upton-upon-Severn, WR8 0HJ ☎01684/593146, ⓦwww.themapshop.co.uk.
Maps by **mail or phone order** are available from Stanfords ☎020/7836 1321, ⓔwww.stanfords.co.uk and several of the other listed suppliers.

Map and book outlets in the USA and Canada

Burlington Adventurous Traveler Bookstore, PO Box 64769, Burlington, VT 05406 ☎1-800/282 3963, ⓦwww.adventuroustraveler.com.
Chicago Rand McNally, 444 N Michigan Ave, IL 60611 ☎312/321 1751, ⓦwww.randmcnally.com; The Savvy Traveller, 310 S Michigan St, Chicago, IL 60602 ☎312/913 9800.
Minneapolis Latitudes Map & Travel Store, 4811 Excelsior Blvd, St Louis Park, MN 55416 ☎952/927 9061.
Montreal Ulysses Travel Bookshop, 4176 St-Denis, PQ H2W 2M5 ☎514/843 9447, ⓦwww.ulysses.ca.
New York The Complete Traveler Bookstore, 199 Madison Ave, NY 10016 ☎212/685 9007; Oceanie Afrique-Noire Books (OAN), 15 W 39th St, 2nd floor, New York, NY 10018 ☎212/840 8844; Rand McNally, 150 E 52nd St, NY 10022 ☎212/758 7488, ⓦwww.randmcnally.com; Traveler's Choice Bookstore, 22 W 52nd St, NY 10019 ☎212/941 1535, ⓔtvlchoice@aol.com.
Ottawa World of Maps, 1235 Wellington St, ON K1Y 3A3 ☎613/724 6776, ⓦwww.worldofmaps.com.
Palo Alto Phileas Fogg's Books & Maps, #87 Stanford Shopping Center, CA 94304 ☎1-800/533-FOGG, ⓦwww.foggs.com.
San Francisco The Complete Traveler Bookstore, 3207 Filmore St, CA 92123 ☎415/923 1511; Rand McNally, 595 Market St, CA 94105 ☎415/777 3131, ⓦwww.randmcnally.com; Sierra Club Bookstore, 730 Polk St, CA 94110 ☎415/977 5653, ⓦwww.sierraclubbookstore.com.
Santa Barbara Map Link, 30 S La Petera Lane, Unit #5, CA 93117 ☎805/692 6777, ⓦwww.maplink.com.
Seattle Elliott Bay Book Company, 101 S Main St, WA 98104 ☎206/624 6600,

Ⓦ www.elliottbaybook.com.

Toronto Open Air Books and Maps, 25 Toronto St, ON M5R 2C1 Ⓣ416/363 0719.

Vancouver World Wide Books and Maps, 552 Seymour St, BC V6B 3J5 Ⓣ604/687 3320, Ⓦ www.itmb.com.

Washington DC ADC Map and Travel Center, 1636 I St NW, DC 20006 Ⓣ202/628 2608.

Rand McNally has stores across the US; call Ⓣ1-800/333 0136 (ext 2111) for the address of your nearest store, or for direct mail maps.

Map and book outlets in Australia and New Zealand

Adelaide The Map Shop, 6 Peel St, SA 5000 Ⓣ08/8231 2033, Ⓦ www.mapshop.net.au.

Auckland Specialty Maps, 46 Albert St Ⓣ09/307 2217.

Brisbane Worldwide Maps and Guides, 187 George St, Qld 4000 Ⓣ07/3221 4330, Ⓦ www.worldmaps.com.au.

Christchurch Mapworld, 173 Gloucester St Ⓣ03/374 5399, Ⓦ www.mapworld.co.nz.

Melbourne Mapland, 372 Little Bourke St, Vic 3000 Ⓣ03/9670 4383, Ⓦ www.mapland.com.au.

Perth Perth Map Centre, 884 Hay St, WA 6000 Ⓣ09/9322 5733, Ⓦ perthmap.com.au.

Sydney Travel Bookshop, Shop 3, 175 Liverpool St, NSW 2000 Ⓣ02/9261 8200.

Magazines and periodicals

Good Africa-centred magazines, worth checking through for news before you go, include the following:

Africa Confidential Fortnightly eight-page newsletter with solid inside info on politics and other matters. Subscription only (Miramoor Publications, 73 Farringdon Rd, London EC1M 3JB Ⓣ020/7831 3511, Ⓦ www.africa-confidential .com). Not to be taken into Kenya.

African Business Good general coverage, issued monthly, available worldwide.

BBC Focus on Africa News, general-interest features, and information from the BBC World Service.

New African This is a monthly news and lifestyle magazine after the style of the French Jeune Afrique, with quarterly special supplements. Available internationally.

Libraries and resource centres in London

If your trip to Kenya takes you via London, there are some worthwhile places to check out for further information on the country.

Africa Centre 38 King St, London WC2E 8JT Ⓣ020/7836 1973. Office and reading room open Mon–Fri 10am–5.30pm. Britain's best independent charity institute for African affairs, open to all: reading room with magazines and newspapers, exhibitions, music, theatre, cinema, language teaching (good Swahili classes), bar and restaurant open all week. A good place to meet people.

Commonwealth Institute Kensington High St, London W8 6NQ Ⓣ020/7603 4535. Large centre offering library and resource services, shop, exhibitions, workshops. Performance venue.

Royal Geographical Society 1 Kensington Gore, London SW7 2AR Ⓣ020/7591 3000. Helpful Expedition Advisory Service provides a wealth of information, including maps and technical guides.

School of Oriental and African Studies Library Thornhaugh St, Russell Square, London WC1H 0XG Ⓣ020/7637 2388, Ⓦ www.soas.ac.uk/library. A vast collection of books, journals and maps in a modern building. Day visits are allowed (£7/day) but long-term membership is expensive, especially if you want the right to borrow books, and requires a reference.

Insurance

You'd do well to take out an insurance policy prior to travelling to cover against theft, loss and illness or injury. Before paying for a new policy, however, it's worth checking whether you are already covered and that you won't duplicate the coverage of any existing plans which you may have or be covered by. For example, some all-risks home insurance policies may cover your possessions when overseas, and many private medical schemes include cover when abroad.

Travel facilities paid for with credit cards are routinely insured, but this won't help you if your camera is stolen or your jeep is rammed by a buffalo. In Canada, provincial health plans usually provide partial cover for medical mishaps overseas, while holders of official student/teacher/youth cards in Canada and the US are entitled to meagre accident coverage and hospital in-patient benefits. Students will often find that their student health coverage extends during the vacations and for one term beyond the date of last enrollment.

After exhausting the possibilities above, you might want to contact a specialist travel insurance company, or consider the travel insurance deal we offer (see box). A typical travel insurance policy usually provides cover for the loss of baggage, tickets and – up to a certain limit – cash or cheques, as well as cancellation or curtailment of your journey.

Most of them exclude so-called dangerous sports unless an extra premium is paid: in Kenya this could mean scuba-diving, windsurfing and climbing, though not jeep safaris. Many policies can be chopped and changed to exclude coverage you don't need – for example, sickness and accident benefits can often be excluded or included at will. If you do take medical coverage, ascertain whether benefits will be paid as treatment proceeds or only after return home, and whether there is a 24-hour medical emergency number. When securing baggage cover, make sure that the per-article limit – typically under £500 – will cover your most valuable possession. If you need to make a claim, you should keep receipts for medicines and medical treatment, and in the event you have anything stolen, you must obtain an official statement from the police.

Rough Guide Travel Insurance

Rough Guides offers its own travel insurance, customized for our readers by a leading UK broker and backed by a Lloyds underwriter. It's available for anyone, of any nationality and age, travelling anywhere in the world.

There are two main Rough Guide insurance plans: **Essential**, for basic, no-frills cover; and **Premier** – with more generous and extensive benefits. Alternatively, you can take out **annual multi-trip insurance**, which covers you for any number of trips throughout the year (with a maximum of 60 days for any one trip). Unlike many policies, the Rough Guides schemes are calculated by the day, so if you're travelling for 27 days rather than a month, that's all you pay for. If you intend to be away for the whole year, the Adventurer policy will cover you for 365 days. Each plan can be supplemented with a "Hazardous Activities Premium" if you plan to indulge in sports considered dangerous, such as scuba-diving or climbing.

For a policy quote, call the Rough Guide Insurance Line: freefone from the UK ☏0800/015 09 06; toll-free from the US ☏1-866/220 5588; from elsewhere ☏+44-1243/621046. Alternatively, get an online quote or buy your policy online at ⓦ www.roughguides.com/insurance.

Health

Disease is an ever-present threat to people in Kenya, most of whom have no access to clean water, and not enough money to afford a doctor if they do fall ill. As a visitor it's wise to take precautions – wash and dress all cuts, and avoid food that has been left lying around after cooking.

Malaria is endemic to the country, as are other diseases such as bilharzia, and rates of HIV infection are high. If you're going to be on the road for a long time, it may be worth considering taking some vitamin tablets with you, though these are no substitute for a balanced diet with plenty of fresh fruit and vegetables. One of the biggest hazards though, is the fierce heat of the tropical sun, against which you would be wise to take protection.

For a comprehensive, and extremely useful, account of the health problems which travellers encounter worldwide, consult the pocket-format *Rough Guide to Travel Health* by Dr Nick Jones.

If you're interested in homeopathy, look at the very impressive Abha Light Health Centre's website ⓦ http://home1.pacific.net .sg/~rucira/alf/. The centre is in Kariobangi, east Nairobi and has ambitious aims.

Medical resources for travellers

Your first source of advice and probable supplier of jabs and prescriptions is your general practitioner. Family doctors are often well informed and are likely to charge you a (relatively low) flat fee for routine injections. For yellow fever and other exotic shots you'll normally have to visit a specialist clinic, often in the next large town if you live in the country, although city-dwellers should have no difficulty finding a vaccination centre that has supplies.

Britain and Ireland

British Airways Travel Clinics 28 regional clinics call ☎ 01276/685040 for the nearest, or consult ⓦ www.britishairways.com. Several branches in London (Mon–Fri 9.30am–5.15pm, Sat 10am–4pm), including 156 Regent St, London

W1 ☎ 020/7439 9584, no appointment necessary. There are appointment-only branches at 101 Cheapside, London EC2 ☎ 020/7606 2977; and at the BA terminal in London's Victoria Station ☎ 020/7233 6661. All clinics offer vaccinations, tailored advice from an online database and a complete range of travel healthcare products.

Communicable Diseases Unit Brownlee Centre, Glasgow G12 0YN ☎ 0141/211 1074. Travel vaccinations including yellow fever.

Dun Laoghaire Medical Centre 5 Northumberland Ave, Dun Laoghaire, Co. Dublin ☎ 01/280 4996, ⓕ 280 5603. Advice on medical matters abroad.

Liverpool School of Tropical Medicine Pembroke Place, Liverpool L3 5QA ☎ 0151/708 9393. Walk-in clinic Mon–Fri 1–4pm, appointment required for yellow fever but not for other jabs.

Malaria Helpline 24-hour recorded message (☎ 0891/600350; 60p per minute).

MASTA (Medical Advisory Service for Travellers Abroad) London School of Hygiene and Tropical Medicine. Operates a pre-recorded 24-hour Travellers' Health Line (☎ 0906/822 4100, 60p per min; Republic of Ireland ☎ 01560/147000, 75p per minute), giving written information tailored to your journey by return of post.

Nomad Pharmacy surgeries 40 Bernard St, London WC1; and 3–4 Wellington Terrace, Turnpike Lane, London N8 ☎ 020/7833 4114 to book vaccination appointment (Mon–Fri 9.30am–6pm). They give advice free if you go in person, or their telephone helpline is ☎ 09068/633 414 (60p per minute). They can give information tailored to your travel needs.

Trailfinders Immunization clinics (no appointments necessary) at 194 Kensington High St, London ☎ 020/7938 3999 (Mon–Fri 9am–5pm except Thurs to 6pm, Sat 9.30am–4pm).

Travel Health Centre Dept of International Health and Tropical Medicine, Royal College of Surgeons in Ireland, Mercers Medical Centre, Stephen's St Lower, Dublin ☎ 01/402 2337. Expert pre-trip advice and inoculations.

Travel Medicine Services PO Box 254, 16 College St, Belfast 1 ☎028/9031 5220. Offers medical advice before a trip and help afterwards in the event of a tropical disease.

Tropical Medical Bureau Grafton Buildings, 34 Grafton St, Dublin 2 ☎01/671 9200, ⓦwww.iol.ie/-tmb.

USA and Canada

Canadian Society for International Health 1 Nicholas St., Suite 1105, Ottawa, ON K1N 7B7 ☎613/241 5785, ⓦwww.csih.org. Distributes a free pamphlet, *Health Information for Canadian Travellers*, containing an extensive list of travel health centres in Canada.

Centers for Disease Control 1600 Clifton Rd NE, Atlanta, GA 30333 ☎1-800/311 3435 or 404/639 3534 ⑤1-888/232 3299, ⓦwww.cdc.gov. Publishes outbreak warnings, suggested inoculations, precautions and other background information for travellers. Useful website plus International Travelers Hotline on ☎1-877/FYI-TRIP.

International Association for Medical Assistance to Travelers (IAMAT) 417 Center St, Lewiston, NY 14092 ☎716/754 4883, ⓦwww.sentex.net/~iamat and 40 Regal Rd, Guelph, ON N1K 1B5 ☎519/836 0102. A non-profit organization supported by donations, it can provide a list of English-speaking doctors in Kenya, climate charts and leaflets on various diseases and inoculations.

International SOS Assistance Eight Neshaminy Interplex Suite 207,Trevose, USA 19053-6956 ☎1-800/523 8930, ⓦwww.intsos.com. Members receive pre-trip medical referral info, as well as overseas emergency services designed to complement travel insurance coverage.

Travel Medicine ☎1-800/872 8633, ⑤1-413/584 6656, ⓦwww.travmed.com. Sells first-aid kits, mosquito netting, water filters, reference books and other health-related travel products.

Travelers Medical Center 31 Washington Square West, New York, NY 10011 ☎212/982 1600. Consultation service on immunizations and treatment of diseases for people travelling to developing countries.

Australia and New Zealand

Travellers' Medical and Vaccination Centres 27–29 Gilbert Place, Adelaide, SA 5000 ☎08/8212 7522.
1/170 Queen St, Auckland ☎09/373 3531.
5/247 Adelaide St, Brisbane, Qld 4000 ☎07/3221 9066.

5/8–10 Hobart Place, Canberra, ACT 2600 ☎02/6257 7156.
147 Armagh St, Christchurch ☎03/379 4000.
5 Westralia St, Darwin, NT 0800 ☎08/8981 2907.
270 Sandy Bay Rd, Sandy Bay, Hobart, Tas 7000 ☎03/6223 7577.
2/393 Little Bourke St, Melbourne, Vic 3000 ☎03/9602 5788.
5 Mill St, Perth, WA 6000 ☎08/9321 1977, plus branch in Fremantle.
7/428 George St, Sydney, NSW 2000 ☎02/9221 7133, plus branches in Chatswood and Parramatta.
Shop 15, Grand Arcade, 14–16 Willis St, Wellington ☎04/473 0991.

Inoculations

For arrivals **by air** from Europe, Australia and New Zealand, or North America, Kenya has no required inoculations. Entering overland, though, you may well be required to show International Vaccination Certificates for both yellow fever and cholera.

If you fly on an airline that stops en route in Africa, you should have the yellow fever shot before you leave and preferably get a cholera vaccination exemption stamp in case some border official thinks that you need a cholera vaccination stamp to enter the country (the cholera shot is widely considered completely ineffective, and not officially required for entry into Kenya or any other East African country, although border officials may not be aware of this). You may otherwise be subjected to them at the airport. Plan ahead and start organizing your jabs at least six weeks before departure. Remember that a yellow fever certificate only becomes valid ten days after you've had the jab. You should also start taking malaria tablets before departure and don't forget to continue taking them for the prescribed time after you return.

Tetanus and **polio** boosters are necessary and doctors usually recommend **typhoid** jabs (beware that these can take you out of action for a couple of days). For **hepatitis A**, Havrix is now commonly prescribed, and needs a booster after six months to knock up your immunity to ten years. The much cheaper gamma-globulin (or immunoglobulin) shots are only effective for a few months.

To reduce the risk of contracting hepatitis, be extra careful about cleanliness and in particular about contamination of water – a problem wherever a single cistern holds the whole water supply in a cockroach-infested toilet/bathroom, as often happens in Lamu.

Malaria

Though in Nairobi and the highlands, the **malaria** risk is low, on the coast, mosquito bites are assured and protection against the disease is absolutely essential.

Caused by a **parasite** carried in the saliva of female Anopheles mosquitoes, malaria is endemic in tropical Africa and has a variable **incubation period** of a few days to several weeks meaning you can get it long after being bitten. Though not infectious, the disease can be very dangerous and sometimes fatal if not treated quickly. The destruction of red blood cells by the falciparum type of malaria parasite can lead to **cerebral malaria** (blocking of the brain capillaries) and is the cause of a nasty complication called **blackwater fever** in which the urine is stained by excreted blood cells.

Prevention

The best and most obvious method of prevention is to **avoid being bitten** – sleeping under a **mosquito net** and burning **mosquito coils** (readily available in Kenya) ensure a peaceful night. If you're carrying your own mosquito net, it's worth impregnating it with pyrethrum or Deet. Electronic buzzers don't work. Anopheles mosquitoes prefer to **bite** in the evening (they can be distinguished by their eager, head-down position as they settle to bite) so keep arms, legs and feet covered as much as possible after dusk, and always cover exposed parts with a strong repellent. **Deet** (the insecticide diethyltoluamide) works well, or if you prefer **natural alternatives** a particularly effective formulation is X-Gnat skin gel. Strangely, one of the most effective mosquito repellents is said to be Avon "Skin-so-soft" bath oil – not that they market it as such; try the "Lightbouquet" version. Some people also swear by vitamin B tablets, though medical authorities in general do not, and citronella oil is considered much less effective as a repellent than the alternatives, and has the disadvantage that elephants are attracted to the smell, and have been known to break into cars and tents to get at it.

It's also normally considered vital to take **anti-malaria tablets** (the oft-promised vaccine has yet to materialize), and your doctor will advise which pills to take and what the various side effects can be. It's important to maintain a careful routine and cover the period before and after your trip with doses.

Going down with malaria

If you do contract malaria, you'll soon know about it: the fever, shivering and headaches are something like severe flu and come in waves. If a child gets malaria, however, you might not realise, so take any fever very seriously indeed. If you suspect anything go to a hospital or clinic immediately. Delay is very risky.

If you suspect malaria but cannot get to a doctor and need a **cure**, take 20–25mg of Lariam (mefloquine) per kilo of body weight in one or two doses, four Malarone tablets daily for three days, or 200mg of doxycycline daily for a week (always finish the course). An alternative, easily available in Kenya, is quinine – 600mg twice a day for five days, and then three Fansidar tablets. If you notice no improvement after the first dose of quinine, it's a safe bet that your malaria is quinine-resistant – take three Fansidar tablets straight away. Of these drugs, however, use only quinine if you are pregnant, and Malarone is not suitable for infants of less than 11kg body weight. Mefloquine, Fansidar and quinine are all available in Kenya.

Other diseases

Bilharzia (medical name schistosomiasis) is a dangerous disease. It comes from tiny flukes (the schistosomes) that live in freshwater snails and which burrow into animal (or human) skin to multiply in the bloodstream. The snails only favour stagnant water and the chances of picking up bilharzia are small. The usual recommendation is never to swim in, wash with, or even touch, lake water that can't be vouched for. Most lakes and rivers harbour bilharzia, to some extent, but the possible danger of crocodile attack means you are unlikely to want any close contact with inland waters. If you feel major fatigue and pass blood – the first symptoms of bilharzia – see a doctor: it's curable.

Medicine bag

Various items worth taking on a trip include:

- ☐ **Alcohol swabs** Invaluable for cleaning minor wounds or insect bites.

- ☐ **Antihistamine cream** Apply immediately after insect bites to reduce itchiness.

- ☐ **Anti-malaria tablets** Enough for prevention, plus extra for a cure if necessary.

- ☐ **Antibiotics** If you are likely to be far from medical help for any length of time, your doctor should be able to prescribe you suitable antibiotics in case you need to treat a serious lower bowel crisis or dysentery.

- ☐ **Antiseptic cream** Avoid metal tubes, which tend to puncture.

- ☐ **Aspirin or paracetamol** for pain or fever relief.

- ☐ **Iodine tincture, with dropper, or water purifying tablets** If you can't get clean water, these will do the trick.

- ☐ **Lens solution/eye drops** If you wear contacts, take a good supply.

- ☐ **Lip-salve/chapstick**

- ☐ **Thermometer** Get a plastic one that sticks on your forehead. Ideally you'll be 37 ° C or 98.4°F

- ☐ **Zinc oxide powder** Useful anti-fungal powder for sweaty crevices.

Sexually transmitted diseases (STDs), including the **HIV** virus, are rife in Kenya. Four out of five deaths among 25 to 35 year olds are AIDS-related. It goes without saying that casual sex without a condom is a deadly gamble and you should assume any sexual contact to be HIV positive (see "Prostitution" p.78). Using a condom will also protect you from other sexually transmitted diseases, including **Hepatitis B**

(HBV), which is quite widespread in Kenya and if anything even more contagious, though rarely fatal if treated. Both HIV and HepB are very easily passed between sexual partners suffering from relatively minor, ulcerous STDs, and the very high prevalence of these is thought to account for the high incidence of heterosexually transmitted HIV. These diseases are also quite easily transmitted by shared syringe or body-piercing or tattooing equipment.

Water and bugs

Kenya's once fairly safe **tap water** is increasingly unfit to drink and the supply can be particularly suspect during periods of drought or heavy flooding. If your stay is brief, you might as well stick to the widely available bottled water (buy in bulk from supermarkets, not from your hotel). Be very cautious of rain-or well-water where there is no mains supply and always purify it first if in any doubt.

In truth, serious stomach upsets don't afflict a large proportion of travellers. If you're only staying a short time, it makes sense to be very scrupulous: if bottled water isn't available, then purifying tablets or, better, iodine (six drops per litre of water, then wait for half an hour), or boiling it for thirty minutes kills most things. For longer stays, think of **re-educating your stomach** rather than fortifying it; it's virtually impossible to travel around the country without exposing yourself to strange bugs from time to time. Take it easy at first, don't overdo the fruit (and wash it in clean water), don't keep food too long, and be very wary of salads served in cheap restaurants. It is also wise to eat food that is freshly cooked and piping hot, rather than things that have been lying around for hours hatching germs.

Should you go down with **diarrhoea**, it will probably pass of its own accord in 24–48 hours without treatment. In the meantime, and especially with children, for whom it may be more serious, it's essential to replace the fluids and salts you are losing, so drink lots of water with oral rehydration salts (if you can't get them – usually in sachets from pharmacies – use half a teaspoon of salt plus eight of sugar in a litre of water). It's a good idea to avoid greasy food, heavy spices, caffeine and most fruit and dairy products, though some say bananas and pawpaws are good. Plain rice or ugali with boiled vegetables is the best diet if you can stick to it, with maybe weak black tea if you can't survive without it. Yoghurt or a soup made with Marmite or Vegemite (the former available in Kenya) are forms of protein that can be easily absorbed by your body while you have the runs. Drugs like Lomotil and Immodium simply plug you up – undermining the body's efforts to rid itself of infection – though they can be useful if you have to travel. Stay right away from the popular Kaomycin, which isn't particularly safe to use and can even encourage diarrhoea. Avoid jumping for antibiotics at the first sign of trouble: they annihilate what's nicely known as your "gut flora" and will not work on viruses. If you continue to feel bad, seek medical help. Also note that having diarrhoea can make drugs less effective if taken orally, as they can pass straight through your system without being absorbed – this can apply to malaria pills for example, and women using **the pill** should note that diarrhoea can make it less reliable.

Heat and altitude

It's important not to underestimate the power of the **equatorial sun** at the equator and overdose on rays in the first week or two. A hat and sunglasses are strongly recommended at all times to combat the heat and bright light.

The sun can quickly **burn**, or even cause **sunstroke**, and a high-factor sunblock is vital on exposed skin, especially when you first arrive. Finally, be aware that overheating can also cause **heatstroke**, which is potentially fatal. Signs are a very high body temperature, without a feeling of fever but accompanied by headaches and disorientation. Lowering body temperature (by taking a tepid shower for example) and resting in a cool place is the first step in treatment.

The sun's radiation is stronger at higher altitudes, but the biggest risk if you climb to over 2500m above sea level can be **altitude sickness**, which may affect climbers on Mount Kenya, and even walkers in the Cherangani Hills. For further advice on altitude sickness, see pp.181–182.

Many people get occasional **heat rashes**, especially at first on the coast. A warm shower, to open the pores, and loose cotton clothes should help, as can zinc oxide powder. **Dehydration** is another possible prob-

lem, so make sure you are drinking enough fluids (but not alcohol or caffeine), especially when hot or tired. The main danger sign is irregular urination (only once a day for example). Dark urine definitely means you should drink more. Excessive sweating can also lead to the body losing a lot of **salt**. If this applies to you, sprinkle extra on your food.

Cuts and bites

Take more care than usual over minor **cuts and scrapes**. In the tropics, the most trivial scratch can quickly become a throbbing infection if you ignore it. Take a small tube of antiseptic with you, or apply alcohol or iodine.

Dogs are usually sad and skulking, posing little threat, but rabies does exist in Kenya, and can be transmitted by a bite or even a lick, so it's best to avoid playing with pets unless you know the owner and are sure they are safe. **Scorpions and spiders** abound, but are hardly ever seen unless you deliberately turn over rocks or logs: scorpion stings are painful but almost never fatal, while spiders are mostly quite harmless, even the really big ones. **Snakes** are common but, again, the vast majority are harmless. To see one at all, you'd need to search stealthily; walk heavily and they obligingly disappear. For more on other, potentially dangerous, animals, see p.46.

Hospitals

For serious treatment there's a frightening lack of well-equipped hospitals and drugs, and in most you're routinely expected to pay for treatment, syringes, plastic gloves, cotton wool, drugs and other medical equipment. The Consolata Sisters' hospitals – the Nazareth Hospital on Riara Ridge, outside Nairobi (☎02/335684), and another in Nyeri (☎020/772032) – are well-run and modestly priced. Nairobi itself is fairly well provided: the Nairobi Hospital in Argwings Kodhek Road is reasonably good (☎02/722160). We've mentioned the best local hospitals throughout the text in the "Listings" sections.

Teeth

Get a thorough **dental check-up** before leaving home and take extra care of your teeth while in Kenya. Stringy meat, acid fruit and sugary tea are some of the hazards. A freshly cut "toothbrush twig" (*msuake*) is a useful supplement –

some varieties contain a plaque-destroying enzyme; you can buy them at markets.

Flying doctors

Kenya's flying doctor **Air Ambulance service** (which also operates in Tanzania) offers free evacuation by air to a medical centre – very reassuring if you'll be spending time out in the wilds. Annual tourist membership costs $50 per person. The income goes back into the service and the African Medical Research Foundation (AMREF) behind it. You can contact them in advance (PO Box 30125 Nairobi; membership/information ☏02/501301–3, ℻609518, ⓦwww.amref .org) or buy their insurance on arrival; they have an office at Wilson Airport, from where most of their rescue missions set out. Similar services are offered by AAR Health Services (☏02/715318–26) and Mediplus (☏02/714060 or 712502), both in Nairobi.

Costs, money and banks

Kenya's currency, the Kenyan shilling (Ksh), is a colonial legacy based on the old British currency. People often talk in "bob", meaning shillings, and occasionally in "pounds", meaning Ksh20 (you'll also hear "quids" for pounds). There are Ksh1000, 500, 200, 100 and 50 notes, and coins of Ksh20, 10, 5, 1, 50 cents (half a shilling), 20 cents, 10 cents and 5 cents, though in practice you will rarely come across coins of less than Ksh1. Some foreign banks stock shillings should you wish to buy some before you leave, but at rates about ten percent less than what you might find in Kenya. For information on bargaining, see p.56.

At the time of writing, the rates of exchange were approximately Ksh110: £1 and Ksh78: $1. Street money changers in Nairobi and Mombasa may offer slightly higher rates, but the black market is illegal, and most of them (certainly in Nairobi) are just muggers aiming to lure you into a dark alley and rob you, so you are very strongly advised not to change money on the street.

Costs

Most **prices** in this guide are given in Kenyan shillings, however, we've given prices in US$ for those establishments, especially **tourist services** such as safaris and car rental, which still quote their rates in the "hard" **dollar**. Almost all the more expensive hotels and lodges also charge non-Kenyans in dollars, though you are legally entitled to pay in Ksh, usually at inferior rates of exchange.

Kenya can be **expensive** if you want to rent a car or go on organized safaris, especially in high season (see p.40). But by staying in the more economical hotels, eating in local places and using public transport, you can get by easily enough on £12/$17 a day. On a daily average budget of £25/$35, you would be living very well most of the time, even staying in the occasional more luxurious tourist hotel.

Staying put you'll find it much easier to live cheaply: a week or so in Lamu on the coast or Lake Naivasha in the Rift Valley need not cost you much more than £10/$14 a day. For more on accommodation costs and seasonal variations, see p.40.

Getting around by bus and matatu is very cheap (rarely more than £5/$7 for the longest journey), but the main disadvantage is that they can't drive you around the game parks. Renting a vehicle – and paying for fuel – will add at least £50/$70 a day to your costs, though shared between two or more this isn't massively expensive for a week or so; see "Car rental and driving" on p.35. You can also find all-inclusive camping safaris from around £50/$70 a day, sometimes even less, but many of the very cheap ones are organized by disreputable companies and undermine legitimate operators and the preservation of wildlife – for more information see the "Safaris" section on p.61.

Money

You can **exchange** hard currencies in cash or travellers' cheques (passport and sometimes receipt required) at banks and foreign exchange bureaux ("forex") all over the country, and at most large hotels for a substantially poorer rate. US dollars and British pounds sterling are always the most acceptable and will cause the least delay; always ask first what commission and charges will be deducted, as they vary mysteriously even within branches of the same bank (it shouldn't be more than one percent, plus Ksh15 per cheque). Cash invariably attracts better rates than travellers' cheques. Comparative tables of bank and forex bureau rates are published daily (except Sun) in the *Nation* newspaper.

Carrying money

It's wise to carry valuable hard currency (as opposed to Kenyan shillings), as well as passport and air ticket, in a very **safe place**, ideally in a leather pouch or money belt under your belt or waistband, but wrap your things in a plastic bag to avoid damage by sweat. Pouches hanging around your neck are easy targets for grab-and-run robberies and ordinary wallets are a disaster with the proliferation of pickpockets. Similarly, the voluminous "bum bags" worn back to front by many tourists over their clothing invite a mugging. As for Kenyan shillings, you'll be carrying around large quantities of coins and paper money. Be aware that, except in the towns, Ksh1000 bills can be hard to change (few people have that sort of money) – so make sure you have a safe purse or secure zip pocket to stuff all the small denominations in.

Travellers' cheques can be worth carrying as a back up to plastic (see below). Despite the marginally lower rates, and the exchange fee charged by banks (forex bureaux do not usually charge it), they have the major advantage over **cash** of being replaceable if lost or stolen. In theory you should keep the receipt separate from the

cheques themselves, but in practice banks and forex bureaux may demand to see it when changing cheques, so keep an extra record of the serial numbers separately too. If your cheques are lost or stolen, the issuing company will expect you to report the loss immediately; most companies claim to replace them within 24 hours.

Credit cards and cash machines

As for **plastic**, Visa and American Express are widely accepted for tourist services such as upmarket hotels and restaurants, flights, safaris, and car rental; MasterCard and Diners' Card are more limited. There's usually a two- to five-percent mark-up on top of the price for the cost of the transaction to the company. A credit card can be very useful for leaving a deposit for car rental (frequently tens of thousands of shillings).

Most branches of Barclays Bank and Standard Chartered give **cash advances** in shillings (no charge), US dollars or sterling (one percent charge) on Visa and MasterCard, whilst some post offices do cash advances in shillings, slapping on a hefty seven percent commission. The maximum amount you can withdraw is usually your card limit, although large withdrawals may entail an interrogation to screen for potential fraud.

Also useful are the 24-hour **ATM cash machines** at many branches of Barclays and Standard Chartered, where you can use your PIN (make sure before leaving that it can be used abroad) to withdraw cash up to a maximum of Ksh80,000 (about £800 or $1000) per day. The machines accept cards with Visa, Visa Electron, MasterCard, Plus or Cirrus symbols. Obviously, **security** is a concern if you're using ATMs (you're a tempting target with your back turned to the street), so if you're wary, get a friend to come along and look out for you. Some branches have machines inside the building or armed guards on the street. The **exchange rate** you'll be charged for ATM withdrawals varies, but is usually slightly better than the rate you'd get for cash in a bank. However, ATMs sometimes cease working for a day or two, and Standard Chartered's, in particular, have a reputation for swallowing cards when that happens.

Abuse of credit cards is not uncommon in Kenya. If you're paying a sum in shillings by credit card, make sure that the voucher specifies the currency before you sign. If it doesn't, it's all too easy for the vendor to fill in a dollar sign in front of the total after you've left. Also fill in the leading digits with zeroes. Be especially careful not to let the card get out of your sight (for example in hotels and restaurants), to ensure that only one slip is filled in.

A compromise between traveller's cheques and credit cards is **Visa TravelMoney**, a disposable pre-paid debit card with a PIN which works in all ATMs that take Visa cards. You load up your account with funds before leaving home, and when they run out, you simply throw the card away. You can buy up to nine cards to access the same funds – useful for couples or families travelling together – and it's a good idea to buy at least one extra as a back up in case of loss or theft. In such an emergency, you can also make a collect call to Visa in Baltimore on ☎410/581 3836. The card is available in most countries from branches of Thomas Cook and Citicorp. For more information, check the Visa website at ⓦ www.visa.com.

Wiring money

Having **money wired** from home is never convenient or cheap, and should be considered a last resort. The easiest way is with Western Union to branches of Kenya Post Bank, or with MoneyGram to branches of the Co-op Bank. The transfer is instantaneous, and fees depend on the amount being transferred but, as an example, wiring £700/$1000 will cost around £40/$60. Avoid drafts and money orders, as they cannot be cashed but have to be credited to a Kenyan bank account, and telexed draft orders can take weeks to reach you at the counter, even though the normal delay should be four or five working days.

Money-wiring companies

Moneygram UK ☎0800/018 0104; Ireland ☎1800/205800; US and Canada ☎1-800/926 9400; Australia ☎1800/230 100; New Zealand ☎0800/262 263 or ☎09/379 8243; ⓦ www.moneygram.com.
Western Union UK ☎0800/833833; Ireland ☎1800/395395; US and Canada ☎1-800/325 6000; Australia ☎1800/649 565; New Zealand ☎09/270 0050; ⓦ www.westernunion.com.

Banks

Banks in cities are usually open Monday to Friday (9am–3pm) and on the first and last Saturday of the month from 9 to 11am. Rural banks, and those in small towns, are generally open Monday to Friday (8.30am–2.30pm), and every Saturday (8.30–10.30am).

Branches of Barclays and the Commercial Bank of Africa, as well as forex bureaux (which are open longer hours), are normally fastest, and Standard Chartered is also reasonable. The Kenya Commercial Bank (KCB) is ubiquitous but usually slow and in places charges outrageous commission (fifteen percent). In out-of-the-way places, you may have to wait till 10am to change money, as the rates take ages being sent up from Nairobi. Lastly, if a clerk is being unhelpful or otherwise difficult, a polite but firm demand to see the manager can work miracles.

Getting around

A quick reference round-up of regional travel details is given at the end of each chapter. Details refer both to routes within the chapter and to routes from towns covered in the chapter to places in other chapters. Bus and train telephone booking numbers are given in the "Practicalities" or "Moving on" section for each town.

Be aware that Kenya's minibuses (known as matatus), and to a lesser extent buses, have a bad **safety record** and certain companies are worse than others. Among bus companies, Tawfiq and the associated firms of Takrim and Interstate 2000 are notorious for frequent crashes, while matatu routes especially prone to crashes include Nairobi–Meru and Nairobi–Mombasa. The most dangerous matatu are those billed as "express" (they mean it). Buses are always safer if you have the choice, and Akamba has the best safety record among bus companies. If you feel unsafe, don't hesitate to ask to get out of the vehicle and demand a partial refund – which will usually be forthcoming. Lastly, if you're driving yourself, beware of buses and matatus and keep your distance from them.

Buses, matatus and taxis

There's a whole range of public transport vehicles on Kenya's roads. Alongside the flashy "**video coaches**" tearing up one or two of the main highways, you'll find smaller "**country bus**" companies operating a single battered Leyland. In towns of any size, a whole crowd of **minibuses**, **pick-ups** and **Peugeot taxis** hustle for business constantly.

Fares vary a great deal according to the competition and the condition of the road. There is also great variation in fares between the speed and comfort of a Peugeot 504 station wagon and the grinding progress of a clapped-out country bus. But fares in the latter type of vehicle can still be little more than Ksh1 per kilometre and shouldn't be above Ksh3 per kilometre in a Peugeot except on short routes. This

means that most journeys of up to a day in length will cost under Ksh500 (£5/$7) and quite often half this. Rarely will anyone attempt to charge you more than the going rate. Baggage charges should not normally be levied unless you're transporting a huge load, though enough touts will try and convince you otherwise: if you get stuck, talk to other passengers (away from the touts, who will usually intervene in Swahili and bribe the passenger) to find out how much they paid.

It's worth considering your general direction through the trip and which side will be **shadier**. This is especially important on dirt roads when the combination of a slow, bumpy ride, dust and fierce sun through closed windows can be horrible.

Urban transport

Nairobi has city bus services, and all big towns have taxi companies. The taxis are about the only means of getting around late at night, but always settle on a fare before getting in because the meters hardly ever work. Taxis around town usually cost Ksh100–200, though drivers will invariably try to overcharge you – haggle hard, and if you get nowhere, try another driver.

Buses

Ordinary **buses** cover the whole country, getting you close to almost everywhere. Some, on the main runs between Nairobi and Mombasa, and to a lesser extent the west, are fast, comfortable and keep to schedules; you generally need to **reserve** seats on these a day in advance. The large companies – in particular Akamba Public Road Services – have ticket offices near the bus stations in most towns, where they list their routes and prices, but their parking bays are rarely marked and there are no published timetables. The easiest procedure is to mention your destination to a few people at the bus park and then check out the torrent of offers. Keep asking – it's virtually impossible to get on the wrong bus. Once you've acquired a seat, the wait can be almost a pleasure if you're in no hurry, as you watch the throng outside and field a continuous stream of vendors proffering wares through the window. (If you want something, ask one of them to get it for you; there'll be a tiny mark-up.)

Matatus and shared taxis

Public vehicles at the smaller end of the spectrum have a gruesome safety record and their drivers, on the whole, a breathtaking lack of road sense; this is especially true of **matatus** – usually white Nissan minibuses along main routes, or pick-up trucks fitted with wooden benches and a canvas roof for rural trips. The Nissans are especially dangerous: try to sit at the back (to avoid too graphic a view of blind overtaking), and it's a good idea to avoid sitting near a front window – they sometimes shatter.

Some of the matatus are clearly falling apart: they break down often and travel terrifyingly fast when they're able to. But on occasions they can be an enjoyable way of getting about, giving you close contact (literally) with local people, and some hilarious encounters. They are also often the most convenient and sometimes only means of transport to smaller places off the main roads, and they're cheap – a trip within town will rarely cost you more than Ksh20–30, and even the longest journey should not cost you more than Ksh300–400. You should not be charged for any baggage, though people will try.

Peugeot taxis operate mainly from Nairobi to the highlands and the west, are faster and more expensive than matatus, and usually drive directly from one point to another with a full complement of passengers. This should consist of one passenger in the front (who sometimes pays a supplement), four in the middle and three in the back, which is only marginally less uncomfortable than matatus. Any more and they're overloaded and on long runs may be stopped by police along the route, paying in bribes any extra fares they may have collected.

If your destination doesn't lie on a standard shared taxi route, or if you don't want to wait for a car to fill up (or, indeed, if you just want to travel in style), drivers will happily negotiate a price for the rental of their whole car. The amount will normally be the same as all the fares they would receive from the passengers in a full taxi over an equivalent distance.

Always choose a vehicle that's full and about to leave or you'll have to wait inside until they are ready to go – sometimes for hours. Beware of being used as bait by the driver to encourage passengers to choose his car, and equally of a driver filling his car with young touts pretending to be passengers (spot them by the newspapers and lack of luggage), who mysteriously disappear when you've bought a ticket. Competition is intense and people will lie unashamedly to persuade you the vehicle is going "just now".

In particular, don't hand over any money before you set off and, when the taxi does get going, wait until you've left town. This isn't a question of being ripped off (though discreetly noting the licence plate of the vehicle is never a bad idea), but too often the first departure is just a cruise around town rounding up passengers and buying petrol (with your money) and then back to square one.

Lastly, some matatu terminology: "stage" or "stand" is the matatu yard; manamba or "turnboy" is the one whose job it is to tout for business, take the fares and hang on dramatically; "dropping" is what you do when you're getting off, as in "I'm dropping here".

Boda-bodas

For journeys around small towns, particularly in the west of the country, there are also **bicycle taxis** known as *boda-bodas*, consisting of a bicycle with a padded seat on the back. These are often the easiest way to get around, and an alternative to walking if you don't know the way, but they can be tricky if you're heavily laden with baggage.

Trains

In the wake of a catastrophic train crash in March 1999 along the Nairobi–Mombasa line, possibly caused by brake failure, the future of passenger services on Kenya Railways was for a time uncertain. The **railways** have been underfunded (or funds have been siphoned off) for years, with the result that all passenger trains were halted in 2001 with the exception of the Nairobi–Mombasa service, which was reduced to four trains a week. Services may be restored at some time in the future between Nairobi and Kisumu, Kisumu and Butere, and even Nairobi and Eldoret, but at present none are running, and there are no longer any connections into Tanzania or Uganda (and not much remaining of their rail services either).

The main draw for travellers is the four-times-weekly overnight **Nairobi–Mombasa** run, which leaves in either direction at 7pm, to arrive anytime between 8am and 10am the following morning. Frustrating though the (almost routine) delays are, they at least mean you are likely to have a couple of hours of morning light to watch the passing scene: approaching Nairobi, the animals on the Athi Plains; approaching Mombasa, the sultry crawl down from the Maungu Plains to the ocean. See "Moving on" in Nairobi chapter, p.152, for further details.

If you need to check train schedules before leaving home, they can be found in *Thomas Cook's Overseas Train Timetable* (the blue volume), available at branches of Thomas Cook, and in most reference libraries.

Planes

Kenya has a number of reasonably priced **internal services**, and it's well worth seeing the country from the air at least once; the flight from Lamu to Malindi is an especially exotic and exhilarating one over reefs and jungle. There are details at the end of each chapter and in the relevant "Moving on" sections.

Baggage allowances on internal flights, apart from Kenya Airways, are usually under 20kg and may be as little as 10kg. Fortunately, the excess baggage charges are nominal. There is an airport tax of Ksh300 on all domestic flights, plus Ksh200 compulsory insurance, all usually included in the fare.

Lastly, note that ordinary **connecting times** shouldn't be relied on if you're flying to catch an international departure. Many of the cheaper flight tickets to Europe cannot be endorsed to another airline if you miss your flight, and domestic services are often delayed.

Ferries

There are no regular ferries up and down the coast, other than those connecting the islands of the Lamu archipelago, but dhow journeys can be negotiated, in particular between Shimoni and Pemba (Tanzania). On Lake Victoria, the network of steamer routes was suspended when the lake became clogged up with water hyacinth (which snarls up the propellers). With the clearance of the hyacinth, services have resumed between Kisumu, Homa Bay and Mbita, but there are no passenger services to Uganda or Tanzania.

Hitching

This is how the majority of rural people get around – by **waving down a vehicle** – but they invariably pay, whether it's a bus, a matatu, a lorry or a private vehicle with a spare place. Private vehicles, except on the main Kisumu–Nairobi–Mombasa artery and one or two other routes, are comparatively rare and usually full. Because of the cheapness of buses, travellers don't try it much, but hitching can be a good change of pace, enabling you to cover distances fast and usually in safety. Along the coast, where there are relatively fewer matatus and more private cars, it's often easy. More calculatingly, if you're on a low budget, hitching rides with private cars can throw you in with Asians and Europeans, often resulting in opportunities to visit national parks and reserves.

Hitching **techniques** need to be fairly exuberant; a modest thumb is more likely to be interpreted as a friendly, or even rude, gesture than a request for a lift. Reckon the driver to stop with your palm. And if you genuinely can't afford to pay, say so right away; generosity will often provide you a lift anyway.

Car rental and driving

Renting a car has advantages over any other means of transport, which makes it seriously worth considering for a week or two. All the parks and reserves are open to private and rented vehicles (as well as organized tours), and there's a lot to be said for the freedom of choice that having your own wheels gives you. Unless there are more than two of you, though, it won't save you money over one of the cheaper camping safaris. The minimum age is 23, sometimes 25.

Prices vary greatly, with some quoted in Kenyan shillings, though most in dollars. It's often **cheaper** to rent by the week if you do enough kilometres – reckon on driving an average of 1000km per week (around 600–700 miles).

Shop around for the best deals (making sure you're quoted the inclusive price, including the minimum daily mileage) and try to negotiate as you might with any purchase, bearing in mind the season (July, August and Christmas are busy, so you might want to book ahead) and how long you're renting. This is easier with independent companies than the big-name franchises. Check the insurance details and always pay the daily **collision damage waiver (CDW)** premium, sometimes included in the price; even a small bump could be very costly otherwise. **Theft protection waiver (TPW)** should also be taken. However, even with these, you'll still be liable for **excess liability**, usually averaging $500–1000, exceptionally as low as $75–100, and sometimes an astronomical $2000 (avoid these companies), so always check the amount before taking a car. You're also required to leave a hefty deposit, roughly equivalent to the anticipated bill – credit cards are useful for this. Lastly, always check whether VAT (eighteen percent) has to be added to the cost.

Choosing a vehicle

Four-wheel drive (4WD) is always useful, but, except in mountainous areas and on some of the marginal dirt roads during periods of heavy rain, is not essential. **High clearance**, however, is, thanks to the dire state of many roads, even in dry weather. However, few, if any agencies will rent out non-4WD vehicles for use in the parks, and most park rangers will turn away such cars

at the gate, regardless of season. This does depend on the park: Maasai Mara and the mountain parks (Mount Elgon, Mount Kenya and the Aberdares) are the most safety-minded.

Four-wheel-drive **Suzuki jeeps** are the most widely available vehicles and they make ideal safari transport: light, rugged and capable of amazing feats of negotiation. Don't expect them to top more than their legal limit of 80kph (50mph), however, and beware their notorious tendency to fall over on bends or on the dangerously sloping gravel hard shoulders that line many Kenyan roads. They also tend to stall on rocks or boulders on exceptionally steep inclines. Long-wheel-base Suzukis, with luggage space behind the rear seats, three doors and enough room for four, or five at a pinch, are more stable and easier to drive. It would be wise to avoid driving the flashier four-wheel drives like Mitsubishi Pajeros and Freelanders; they are much in demand in Somalia and there's a risk of hijack. They're also much less controllable on mud than the Suzukis.

Don't automatically assume the vehicle is roadworthy. Have a good look at the engine and tyres, and don't set off without checking the spare (preferably two) and making sure you have a few vital tools. Ideally, always carry a tow rope, spare water and fuel. You might also take a spare fan belt, brake pads, and brake fluid. Check that your vehicle's PSV status (see p.38) is displayed. You are, of course, responsible for any ongoing **repair and maintenance work** that needs doing while you're renting the vehicle, but keep any receipts as the company should reimburse you. Try to get a list of recommended service stations from the rental company; to avoid bogus repairs some of them will insist you use certain garages. Always bargain hard before work begins.

Booking car rental in advance

It's quite easy to book a vehicle before you even set foot in Kenya, pay for it at home, then pick it up when you arrive. It costs much more doing this than tracking down a good deal locally – and prices are extremely variable – but if time is short (or money no object) you may find it preferable.

Car rental reservation numbers

Avis Australia ☎ 1800/225 533; Canada ☎ 1-800/879 2847; Ireland ☎ 01/605 7555; New Zealand ☎ 0800/655 111 or ☎ 09/526 2847; UK ☎ 0870/606 0100; US ☎ 1-800/331 1212; ⓦ www.avis.com.
Budget Australia ☎ 1300/362 848; Ireland ☎ 1850/575767; New Zealand ☎ 0800/652 227 or 09/375 2222; UK ☎ 0800/973159; US & Canada ☎ 1-800/527 0700; ⓦ www.budgetrentacar.com.
Europcar Australia ☎ 03/9330 6161; Ireland ☎ 01/614 2800; UK ☎ 0870/607 5000; US & Canada ☎ 1-877/940 6900; ⓦ www.europcar.com.
Hertz Australia ☎ 1800/550 067; Canada ☎ 1-800/263 0600; Ireland ☎ 01/676 7476; New Zealand ☎ 0800/654321; UK ☎ 0870/848 4848; US ☎ 1-800/654 3131; ⓦ www.hertz.com.
National Australia ☎ 13/1908; Ireland ☎ 1800/301401; New Zealand ☎ 0800/800115 or 09/537 2582; UK ☎ 0870/536 5365; US & Canada ☎ 1-800/CAR RENT; ⓦ www.nationalcar.com.

Buying a secondhand car

If you're going to be in Kenya for some time, or you're planning to travel more widely, **buying** a secondhand vehicle in Nairobi, though prices are inflated, is a realistic possibility if you're confident about engines. Rental companies sometimes have vehicles to dispose of, and the *Nation* and *Standard* carry lots of ads. Langata Road in Nairobi (see p.139) has a weekly used-car sale, on Sunday mornings, and you can sell back fairly easily in Nairobi too.

Driving in Kenya

You can drive in Kenya with either a valid driving licence from your home country, or an international one. In theory you **drive on the left**, though in reality vehicles keep to the best part of the road until they have to pass each other.

Petrol (gasoline) costs about Ksh55 per litre (50p or 70¢), which is about $2.80 per US gallon. You should get 12–15km per litre out of a Suzuki (which holds about 38 litres). That's around 33mpg (US) or 38mpg (imperial). Keep an eye on the fuel gauge and top up whenever possible. All towns and villages (except the very smallest) have petrol for sale, but if you're intending to do a lot of driving in a remote area you should definitely carry spare fuel in cans. If you plan to pay by credit card, check that you can use it; some places only accept Kenyan-issued cards. When refilling, check the petrol pump gauge is set to zero and anticipate how many litres your tank will need – fixing the pumps is not unknown.

Parking in towns, you should obviously never leave your vehicle with anything of value in it. Apart from that, finding somewhere to park is rarely a problem, even in Nairobi or Mombasa. There are parking meters in Mombasa and over-eager traffic wardens in Nairobi from whom you can buy a ticket for the day (Ksh50). If you don't, your car will either be clamped or towed away (find it at City Hall – the fines are around Ksh750).

On most of the main paved highways you can make good time, but as soon as you leave them, **journey times** are very unpredictable. We've tried to give some idea of road conditions in various places throughout the book, but they can change radically in half a year. The north and highland regions are the worst, particularly during periods of heavy rain when districts may become virtually cut off. The devastating 1997–98 El Niño rains washed away a good portion of the main Mombasa to Nairobi road as well as dozens of others.

Signposting in Kenya, while generally useful, is haphazard – especially on dirt roads. If a junction appears to lack a sign, it's assumed you'll keep to the busiest track. Beware of **speed bumps**. Although occasionally you'll see a sign like "Rumble strips ahead", usually the first you'll know of them is when your head hits the roof. They are found both in rural areas, wherever a busy road has been built through a village, and on the roads in and out of nearly every large town.

A **useful book** for driving around Kenya, which has some good routes and lots of useful detail, is *On Safari* by Phillippe Oberlé, which was widely available in Kenya, but was out of print at last check.

Driving etiquette

When driving, **beware** of unexpected rocks, ditches and potholes – and animals and people – on the road. It's accepted practice to honk your horn stridently to warn pedestrians.

It's **common practice** to flash oncoming vehicles (especially if they're leaving you little room or the headlights are blinding you) and to signal right to indicate your width and deter drivers behind you from overtaking. You may find both practices disconcerting at first. Left-hand signals are used to say "Please overtake me", but you shouldn't assume the driver in front of you can really see that it is safe for you to pass. In fact, never assume anything about other drivers.

Driving at night

Try to **avoid driving at night**, especially in a Suzuki, as its lights are hopeless (though remember if you've been off the road and you can't seem to see 10m in front, your headlamps may be caked in mud). Be especially careful when passing heavy vehicles, and even more so when passing lorries groaning uphill in the opposite direction. Sometimes a line of them churning out diesel fumes can cut off your visibility without warning – extremely dangerous on a narrow mountain road. If you're driving in a city at night (especially Nairobi and Mombasa), keep your doors locked and windows rolled up to avoid grab-and-run incidents at traffic lights or in heavy traffic. You may feel safer doing this during the day, too. Incidentally, **car-jackings** are common in Nairobi and in remote parts of the northeast. However, tourists and rental cars are generally not a target, at least not unless you're in a flashy, high-powered cruiser. The puny Suzuki jeeps are quite the safest in this respect.

Accidents and the police

Driving test examiners are not incorruptible, and Kenya's **accident** statistics are horrifying. Counting the casualties is a national obsession. There was recently a campaign – which failed miserably – to keep the annual death toll below 2000 (it's currently around 3000). Police records suggest that an average of eight to nine people die on Kenya's roads every day.

Should you have the misfortune to have an **accident** or a **breakdown**, the first thing to do is pile bundles of sticks or foliage 50m or so behind and in front of the car. These are the universally recognized "red warning triangles" of Africa, and their placing is always scrupulously observed (as is the wedging of a stone behind at least one wheel). When you get a flat tyre, as you will, get it mended straight away – it costs very little (Ksh50–80) and can be done almost anywhere there are vehicles. Local mechanics are usually very good and can apply creative ingenuity to the most disastrous situations. But spare parts, tools and proper equipment are rare off the main routes. Always settle on a price before the work begins. And beware of scams and con-artists; the "oil leak" under your parked car still catches many people out (see p.251).

Being **stopped by the police** – even when they can see you're likely to be a tourist – is becoming increasingly common (one or two regular checkpoints are mentioned in the text). Checkpoints are generally marked by low strips of spikes across the road with just enough room to slalom round. You should always stop if signalled. The usual reason given is that you were speeding (and they do indeed have one or two radar traps), but that is not why they stop cars. Don't reach into your purse: apologize, agree that it's a pity you will have to go to court, and wait to be sent on your way with a caution (court appearances are just work for all concerned). It's worth knowing that you may be asked to produce evidence that your rented car has a **PSV licence** as a "passenger service vehicle". You should have a windscreen sticker for this as well as the letters "PSV" written somewhere on the body, and you're strongly advised to check it out with the company before you leave.

Cycling

Kenya's climate and varied terrain make it challenging **cycling** country. If it appeals to you – whether you're a lycra-laminated pro or just use a bike once in a while – it's one of the best ways of getting around. With a bike, given time and average determination, you can get to parts of the country that would be hard to visit by any other means except perhaps on foot, and what would take several days to hike can be cycled in a matter of hours. It's also one way you will get to see wildlife outside the confines of the game parks. Most towns have bicycle shops which sell both mountain bikes and the trusty Indian three-speed roadsters – we've

Cycling holidays

The energetic might like to try an organized **bicycle tour** of Kenya. In Britain, Leisure Activity Safaris (☎01626/777903), offers various long and short bike safaris. In North America, try Bicycle Africa of Seattle (☎206/767 0848 ⓦwww.ibike.org/bikeafrica/), which offers mountain-bike trips with a pioneering spirit and a wide variety of accommodation.

You can fix up similar arrangements in Kenya through a number of agents and operators (see p.142) and book short jaunts to Hell's Gate and lakes Naivasha, Nakuru, Baringo and Bogoria.

mentioned some of these in the Mombasa and Nairobi "Listings" sections.

Practical considerations

Whatever you take – and a mountain bike is certainly best – it will need low gears and strongly built wheels and you should have some essential spare parts. If you have a sympathetic local bike shop, you might consider leaving a deposit with them so they could send you **spare parts** if and when necessary.

If you're taking a bike with you, then you'll probably want to carry your gear in **panniers**. These are fiendishly inconvenient when not attached to the bike, however, and you might consider sacrificing ideal load-bearing and streamlining technology for a backpack you can lash down on the rear carrier. An arrangement like this is probably what you'll have to do if you buy a bike in Kenya. With light wood, or the kind of cane used to make cane furniture, plus lashings of inner tube rubber strips, you can create your own highly unaerodynamic **carrier**, with room for a box of food and a gallon of water underneath.

With a bike from home, take a battery **lighting system** – it's surprising how often

you'll need it. The front light doubles as a torch, and getting the large-sized U2 batteries is no problem. Also take a **U-bolt cycle lock**. In situations where you have to lock the bike, you'll always find something to lock it to. Out in the bush it's less important. Local bikes can be locked with a padlock and chain in a length of hosepipe which you can buy and fix up in any market.

Cycling won't restrict your travel options. Buses and matatus with roof-racks will always carry bicycles for about half-fare – even if flagged down at the roadside – and trucks will often give a lift. The trains take bikes, too, at a low fixed fare. You need to consider the **seasons**, however; you won't make much progress on dirt roads during the rains when chain sets and brakes become totally jammed with sticky mud. Obviously, you also need to be cautious when cycling on **main roads**. A mirror is essential and, if the road surface is broken at the edge, give yourself plenty of space and be ready to leave the road if necessary. That said, cycle tourists are still a novelty in Kenya – drivers often slow down to look and you'll rarely be run off the road.

Accommodation

Accommodation in Kenya exhibits a fine diversity, ranging from campsites and local lodging houses for $3–5 a night to genuinely excellent, luxury hotels costing fifty or a hundred times as much. Beds can also be found in "tented camps" and "tree hotels" at the expensive end of the spectrum, and bandas and a clutch of youth hostels at the budget end.

Seasons

If you're planning a trip to Kenya using moderate or expensive accommodation, it's useful to know that a lot of money can be saved by not going in the high **season**. With slight variations on date, resort hotels and safari lodges have separate low-, mid- and high-season rates (it applies much less to town hotels). The seasons of many of the coastal, cottage-type establishments are tied closely to the school year, with the Easter and Christmas holidays, plus July and August, being considered "high". **Low-season rates** can be anything from a third to a half of the high-season tariff.

Low season: After Easter to June 30 or July 15 (coinciding with the "Long Rains").

Mid season: July 1–16 to November 30 or December 15 (coinciding with the "Short Rains").

Accommodation price codes

Most accommodation rates in this guide have been price-coded according to the categories below. The prices indicated are non-resident (tourist) rates for standard **double** or **twin** rooms. For **cottages**, even if they sleep more than two people, the price code system has been used. For dormitory accommodation, hostels and campsites (which charge per person), exact prices have been given where possible. Where there are **seasonal differences**, as in some park lodges and in all tourist- or luxury-class accommodation on the coast, the high- and low-season price codes are given. All Nairobi hotels, most up-country hotels and most places in the ❶–❹ categories have non-seasonal tariffs.

Cheap hotels quote their rates in **Kenyan shillings**, while hotels in categories ❺ and above tend to quote their rates in **dollars**. You should still be able to pay at these establishments in Ksh, although often at an inferior rate of exchange. Special rates for **Kenya residents** (typically discounts of fifteen to thirty percent, sometimes much greater) are offered at some establishments in category ❹ and above.

The facilities you can expect in each category are as follows, unless otherwise specified in the guide's reviews. The rates of exchange used in the following conversions is approximately Ksh78 to $1.

❶ Under Ksh500: very basic B&L with shared facilities.
❷ Ksh500–1000: B&L with elementary comforts (s/c) or cheap hotel; B&B basis.
❸ Ksh1000–2000: adequate hotel with s/c rooms; B&B.
❹ Ksh2000–4000: mid-range local hotel or modest tourist-class hotel; B&B.
❺ Ksh4000–6000: tourist-class hotel; B&B or HB.
❻ Ksh6000–9000/$80–120*: tourist-class hotel or cheap lodge; HB or FB.
❼ Ksh9000–12,000/$120–150*: luxury hotels and lodges; FB.
❽ Ksh12,000–16,000/$150–215*: luxury hotels and lodges with special facilities; FB.
❾ Over Ksh16,000/$215*: as preceding category.

* usually priced in dollars

Accommodation terms and abbreviations

AC air-conditioned, usually only on the coast.

banda thatched cottage or chalet, sometimes round and dubbed "*rondavel*", generally cheap, occasionally furbished into upmarket "bush" accommodation for tourists.

B&B bed and breakfast.

B&L Boarding and Lodging house.

cube sometimes used to refer to a small room in a B&L.

FB full board, meaning all meals included.

HB half board, meaning dinner, bed & breakfast.

hoteli or sometimes just "hotel", a cheap restaurant or greasy spoon; rarely with accommodation.

lodge designer hotel or country house, usually in the game parks.

long-drop self-explanatory; the kind of non-flushing toilet found in some B&Ls, and in most *bandas* and campsites.

s/c "self-contained", with private shower and toilet.

tented camp hotel in the bush, or in a game park, using large tents and *bandas*, often with all the usual hotel facilities plumbed into a solid bathroom at the back.

tree hotel an animal-viewing hotel in the trees, or on stilts, after the style of *Treetops*.

High season: December 1–16 to Easter (hot and sunny weather until March).

Boarding and lodgings

In any town, down to the very smallest, you'll always find **Boarding & Lodgings** (for which we've coined the abbreviation "B&Ls"). These can vary from a mud shack with water from the well, to a little multi-storey building of self-contained rooms ("s/c") with washing facilities, a bar and restaurant. B&Ls tend to be noisy; they're sometimes rather airless and often double unofficially as brothels, but the better ones are clean and comfortable. For those unaccustomed to, or not interested in, budget travel, they can nonetheless come as something of a shock.

Prices of rooms aren't always a good indication of the standard, though you should rarely have to pay more than Ksh600 for a double (Ksh400 for a single), often much less. Always try to bargain for a good price. It's worth checking several places, testing the hot water (if any) as well as cold (buckets in the bathrooms mean it has to be carried up and chances are it'll be cloudy) and asking to see the toilets; you won't cause offence by saying no thanks. Bringing toilet paper, a towel and soap is a good idea. And, if the place seems noisy in the afternoon, it will probably become cacophonous during the night, so ask for a room away from the source of the din. This applies especially to Wednesday, Friday and Saturday nights, when most discos operate.

Security is also an important factor. Obviously, the more the establishment relies on its bar for income, the less guarantees you have. You can leave valuables with the owner, though you'll need to use your judgement. Leaving valuables in rooms is usually safe enough, especially if things are not left lying around too temptingly – better still, if they allow you, would be to take your key with you.

Boarding & Lodgings are covered in detail through the regional chapters; there's nearly always at least one good example in every town.

If you're driving, some lodgings have lock-up yards where you can park – helpful in avoiding mysteriously deflated tyres and lost wing-mirrors and wipers. Obviously, don't leave anything inside an unattended car, especially during the night.

Hotels and lodges

More **expensive hotels** are a variable commodity. At the top end of the range are the big tourist establishments, many in one of the country's four or five chains. In the game parks, they are known as **lodges**. Some

Hotel reservations

Local addresses and telephone numbers for most hotels are included in the guide. Many are part of chains or management groups and rooms can be reserved by phoning or writing to the head offices. Some chains don't have overseas offices, but travel agents will often make the reservations.

Alliance Hotels

Ⓦ www.alliancehotels.com

Small, highly rated group with very pleasant package-tour hotels, noted for their good food and experienced management.

Kenya College House, University Way, PO Box 49839 Nairobi Ⓣ 02/337501 or 337508, Ⓕ 219212 or c/o *Safari Beach Hotel*, Diani, PO Box 90690 Mombasa Ⓣ 0127/2726, Ⓕ 2357;
Ⓔ alliance@africaonline.co.ke

Lodges

Naro Moru River Lodge, Naro Moru, Mount Kenya

Coast

Africana Sea Lodge, Diani Beach
Jadini Beach Hotel, Diani Beach
Safari Beach Hotel, Diani Beach

Block Hotels

Ⓦ www.blockhotelske.com

Generally good, sometimes excellent, package-tour establishments, popular with Kenya residents too.

Kenya Block House, Lusaka Rd, off Uhuru Highway, PO Box 40075 Nairobi Ⓣ 02/535412–9, Ⓕ 545954,
Ⓔ blockreservations@net2000ke.com

Lodges and tented camps

Keekorok Lodge, Maasai Mara National Reserve
Lake Baringo Club, Lake Baringo
Lake Naivasha Country Club, Lake Naivasha
Larsens Tented Camp, Samburu National Reserve
Ol Tukai Lodge, Amboseli National Park.
Outspan Golf and Country Club, Nyeri
Samburu Lodge, Samburu National Reserve
Shimba Hills Lodge, Shimba Hills National Park
Treetops, Aberdares National Park

Nairobi

Landmark Hotel, Westlands

Coast

Indian Ocean Beach Club, Diani Beach
Nyali Beach Hotel, Mombasa

Bush Homes of East Africa

Ⓦ www.bush-homes.co.ke

The marketing company for over a dozen small, very exclusive privately owned tented camps and ranch houses in less accessible corners of Kenya (guests usually arrive by air). Around $500 for two people.

Kenya Argwings Kodhek Rd, PO Box 56923 Nairobi Ⓣ 02/571647, 571649 or 571661, Ⓕ 571665,
Ⓔ bush-home@africaonline.co.ke.

Wilderness Trails, Lewa Downs, Laikipia
Ol Malo, Laikipia
Rekero, outside Maasai Mara National Reserve
Patrick's Camp, Solio Estate, Laikipia
Kitich Camp, Mathews Mountain Range, Northern Kenya
Lokitela Farm, Mount Elgon
Mundui, Lake Naivasha
Ol Jolai, Soysambu Ranch, Elmenteita
Ol Kanjau, by Amboseli National Park

Coast

Tana Delta Camp, Tana River (access from Malindi)
Takaungu House, Takaungu

Governors' Camps

Ⓦ www.governorscamp.com.

Expensive, and not as exclusive as they pretend.

Kenya Musiara Ltd, 3rd floor, International House, Mama Ngina St, PO Box 48217 Nairobi Ⓣ 02/331871 or 337344, Ⓕ 726427,
Ⓔ reservations@governorscamp.com.

Lodges and tented camps

Governors' Camp, Maasai Mara National Reserve
Governors' Ilmoran Camp, Maasai Mara National Reserve
Governors' Private Camp, Maasai Mara National Reserve
Little Governors' Camp, Maasai Mara National Reserve
Loldia House, Lake Naivasha
Mfangano Island Camp, Lake Victoria

Heritage Hotels
Ⓦ www.heritage hotels.co.ke
Formerly *Prestige Hotels*, this group has also taken over Siana Springs in the Maasai Mara. The *Intrepids* are highly rated.
Kenya Office located between David Osieli Rd and Mvuli Rd, off Waiyaki way, Westlands, Nairobi.
P.O. Box 74888, Nairobi
Ⓣ 02/446651/447929
Ⓕ 02/446600/446533
Lodges and tented camps
Mara Explorer Camp,
Mara Intrepids Camp,
Siana Springs Intrepids Camp,
Voyager Safari Lodge (formerly *Mara Paradise*), all in Maasai Mara National Reserve
Samburu Intrepids Camp, Samburu National Reserve
Voyager Safari Camp (formerly *Ziwani*), Tsavo West National Park
Great Rift Valley Lodge & Golf Resort, Lake Naivasha
Coast
Voyager Beach Resort, Nyali Beach
Kipungani Explorer, Lamu

Kenya Safari Lodges & Hotels
Rump of the collapsed AT&H chain, but may expand in future. The three present properties are old (1970s) but well-maintained and superbly positioned package-tour places.
Kenya *Mombasa Beach Hotel*, PO Box 90414 Mombasa Ⓣ 011/471861–5, Ⓕ 472970.
Mombasa Beach Hotel, North Coast
Ngulia Safari Lodge, Tsavo West National Park
Voi Safari Lodge, Tsavo East National Park

Kilimanjaro Safari Club
Mid-range lodges covering the main game parks of Tsavo East and Amboseli.
Kenya 3rd floor, IPS House, Kimathi St, PO Box 30139 Nairobi Ⓣ 02/33888–90, Ⓕ 219982, Ⓔ ksc@africaonline.co.ke
Lodges
Amboseli Lodge, Amboseli National Park

Kimana Lodge, between Amboseli and Tsavo West
Tsavo Inn, Mtito Andei, Mombasa Highway
Tsavo Safari Camp, Tsavo East National Park

Lonrho Hotels
Ⓦ www.lonrhohotels.com
Busy upmarket package tour refuges, with excellent standards across the board.
Kenya *Norfolk Hotel*, Harry Thuku Rd, PO Box 58581 Nairobi Ⓣ 02/216940, Ⓣ 216796, Ⓔ lonhotsm@form-net.com
UK Ⓣ 01926/844034, Ⓕ 844035
USA Ⓣ 1-800/845 3692 or 941/951 1155
Lodges and tented camps
Aberdare Country Club, Mweiga, north of Nyeri
The Ark, Aberdares National Park
Mara Safari Club, Maasai Mara National Reserve
Mount Kenya Safari Club, Nanyuki/Mount Kenya
Ol Pejeta Ranch House, Laikipia, near Nanyuki
Sweetwaters Tented Camp, Laikipia, near Nanyuki
Nairobi
Norfolk

Msafiri Inns
A group formed to look after some of the Kenya Tourist Development Corporation's less successful hotels. Standards vary, but the lodges, at least, are in fine locations.
Kenya 11th floor, Utalii House, Uhuru Highway, PO Box 42013 Nairobi Ⓣ 02/330820, 229751 or 222661, Ⓕ 227815
Lodges
Marsabit Lodge, Marsabit (currently closed)
Mount Elgon Lodge, Mount Elgon
Town hotels
Golf Hotel, Kakamega

continued overleaf

Izaac Walton Inn, Embu, Mount Kenya
Tea Hotel, Kericho

Sarova Hotels
ⓦ www.sarovahotels.com
Mostly high quality and good service at competitive (for the luxury level) prices.
Kenya *Panafric Hotel*, PO Box 72493 Nairobi ☎02/713333, ⓕ715566, ⓔreservations@sarova.co.ke
USA ☎410/563 6331, ⓕ563 6323
Lodges and tented camps
Sarova Lion Hill Lodge, Lake Nakuru National Park
Sarova Mara Camp, Maasai Mara National Reserve
Sarova Shaba Lodge, Shaba National Reserve
Nairobi
Panafric Hotel
The Stanley
Coast
Whitesands Hotel, Mombasa North Coast

Savannah Camps and Lodges
ⓦ www.savannahcamps.com
Small, upmarket camps and lodges in less frequented corners, mostly on private land. These are some of Kenya's most delightful lodges, and most have great bird-watching interest.
Kenya 11th floor, Fedha Towers, Standard St, PO Box 48019 Nairobi ☎02/331191 or 335935, ⓕ330698, ⓔeaos@africaonline.co.ke
Lodges and tented camps
Delamere's Camp, Soysambu Wildlife

Sanctuary, Lake Elmenteita
Galla Camp, Taita/Rukinga Ranches, near Tsavo East
Indian Ocean Lodge, Malindi
Lerai Tented Camp, Lewa Downs Conservancy
Mara River Camp, Maasai Mara National Reserve
Sangare Ranch, Aberdares National Park

Serena Hotels
ⓦ www.serenahotels.com
Some of Kenya's (and Tanzania's) most comfortable and well-managed hotels, combining strong architectural themes with harmonious local blending. Mostly recommended.
Kenya 4th floor, Williamson House, 4th Ngong Ave, PO Box 48690 Nairobi ☎02/711077–8, ⓕ718103, ⓔcro@serena.co.ke
Tanzania 6th floor, AICC Ngorongoro Wing, PO Box 2551 Arusha ☎057/6304 or 8175, ⓕ4155, ⓔreservations@serena.co.tz
Lodges
Amboseli Serena Safari Lodge, Amboseli National Park
Mara Serena Safari Lodge, Maasai Mara National Reserve
Mountain Lodge, Mount Kenya
Samburu Serena Safari Lodge, Samburu National Reserve
Nairobi
Nairobi Serena Hotel
Coast
Mombasa Serena Beach Hotel, Mombasa North Coast

---

establishments are extremely good value – a night in a good hotel can be tremendously fortifying if you're usually roughing it. Others are shabby and overpriced, so check carefully before splurging. If possible, you should try to reserve the more popular establishments in advance (see the box above), especially for the busiest season from December to February.

As a rule, expect to pay anything from Ksh800–3000 for a decent double or twin room in a **town hotel**, with attached bathroom (self-contained, or "s/c"), electricity, hot water and breakfast included. Singles usually cost around seventy percent of a double. Out of the towns and on the coast, hotels and lodges in the top price brackets are normally quoted in dollars and on a half- or full-board basis, and prices can go right into orbit ($80–3000 is usual, with the exceptions reaching over $1000 for a double). Most of these hotels cut their prices in the low season, April–June, and many have much lower rates for Kenyan residents (sometimes citizens).

Between the hotels featured in the glossy brochures and the cheap lodging-houses, come all the **medium-priced**, middle-class places. Some of them were once slightly grand, others are old settlers' haunts that don't fit modern Kenya, and some newer ones cater for the black middle class. A few are fine – delightfully decrepit or bristlingly smart and efficient. Most are boozy and uninteresting, and it adds more colour to your travels to mix the cheapest B&Ls with the occasional night of luxury.

Cottages, villas and homestays

Increasingly, it's possible to book **self-catering apartments**, **villas** or **cottages**, especially on the coast. Home from Home, ⓦ www.kenyasafarihomes.com/ in the offices of Langata Link on the Langata South Road PO Box 15097, ☏02/891314, and Holiday Homes Ltd, Lavington Green Shopping Ctr, James Gichuru Rd, Waiyaki Way, Westlands, PO Box 10723 ☏02/574795, are agents for a wide range of holiday homes. Another style of accommodation on the increase is **homestays** – inclusive accommodation in a (usually Anglo-Kenyan) household in the countryside. Meals and drinks are generally part of the package, and excursions and safaris with generous helpings of local insight, or occasionally prejudice, are optional. Let's Go Travel (address p.141) have details of some.

Youth hostels

Disappointingly, only three **youth hostels** are affiliated to the International Youth Hostel Association (IYHA) – Nairobi and Naro Moru. Non-members normally have to join the association first (Ksh540), though this can be done by buying Ksh90 "stamps" on each of your first six overnights, which then qualifies you for international membership. The hostels can be booked from outside Kenya through the IYHA, or in Kenya through KYHA (*Nairobi Youth Hostel*, Ralph Bunche Rd, PO Box 48661 Nairobi ☏02/721765, ⓕ724862). There's also an unaffiliated hostel in Nanyuki.

There are **YMCAs and YWCAs** in Kisumu, Nairobi and Mombasa, and **church-run hostels** and dormitories in a number of small towns in which the atmosphere can be a stark contrast to the sleazier lodging-houses.

Camping

There are enough **campsites** in Kenya to make it worthwhile carrying a tent, and camping rough is often a viable option, too. Bring the lightest tent you can afford and remember the main point of a tent is to keep insects out. You might consider making your own tent: nylon netting with a sewn-in groundsheet is the basic tent. A rip-stop nylon fly sheet adds privacy. Outside poles back and front can be used for guys and tension, but you'll probably resort to trees if there are any. A tube of **ant-killer** comes in handy if you're camping, particularly on the coast.

Campsites and camping rough

Campsites, wherever they exist, are mentioned in the main body of the guide. Those in the parks are usually very cheap and equally basic. The mysterious "special campsites" in a number of parks are, in reality, simply restricted sites which you can reserve on an exclusive basis for private use – and they cost a lot more. Some of them are especially attractive – so they draw film crews and the like – but they are all quite devoid of facilities. To book them, either write to the warden or visit/write to Special Campsite Reservations, Kenya Wildlife Service, Langata Rd, PO Box 40241 Nairobi ☏02/501081–2, ⓕ505866, ⓔkws@kws.org; this office is one of those right by Nairobi National Park main gate. On top of the flat advance booking fee of Ksh5000, you have to pay daily camping charges at the prevailing rates (see p.60).

A handful of privately owned sites have more in the way of facilities. In rural areas, hotels are often amenable if you ask to camp discreetly in their grounds.

Camping rough depends on whether you can find a suitable space. In the more heavily populated and farmed highland districts, you should ask someone before pitching in an empty spot. Out in the wilds, hard or thorny ground is likely to be the only obstacle (a foam sleeping-mat is a good idea if you don't mind the bulk). During the dry seasons, you'll rarely have trouble finding wood for a fire so a stove is optional, but don't burn more fuel than you need. You're not allowed to collect firewood in the mountain parks. Camping gas cartridges and packaged, dried food is available in variety in Nairobi, but the easiest and cheapest camping food is *ugali* (see "Eating and drinking" below), flavoured with curry powder or sauce mixes if you like.

Safety

Camping out is generally pretty **safe**, although in populated areas you should ask beforehand. Be aware also of areas where there are ethnic tensions (these are mentioned in the text), or where cattle-rustling is prevalent. A fire may worry local people and delegations armed with *pangas* sometimes turn up to see who you are, and might want to stay and chat. Camping right by

the road, in dried-out river beds, or on trails used by animals going to water, however, is unwise.

On the subject of **animals**, lions and hyenas, which are occasionally curious of campfires, rarely attack unprovoked. More dangerous are buffalos: you should steer well clear of solitary bulls. In the vicinity of lakes and slow-moving rivers you should watch out for hippos, which will attack if you're blocking their route back to water, and crocodiles, which can be found in most inland waters and occasionally attack swimmers. Lake and river-swimming is not advised.

An important exception to the safety of rough camping is the Indian Ocean coast. Almost anywhere between Malindi and the Tanzanian border, sleeping out on the **beaches** should be counted as an invitation to robbery. North of Malindi, there are fewer tourists and the risks are correspondingly reduced, although the region is prone to banditry which sometimes makes getting to the beaches a more risky business.

Eating and drinking

Not surprisingly, perhaps, Kenya has no great national dishes. The living standards of the majority of people don't allow for frills, and food is generally plain and filling. Eating out is not a Kenyan tradition. Still, in the most basic local restaurant, decent meals can be had for less than Ksh100 (£1/$1.30). For fancier meals in touristy places, expect to pay up to Ksh1500 (£14/$19) – rarely more – for a large meal of international-style dishes. For culinary culture, only the coast's long association with Indian Ocean trade has produced distinctive regional cooking, where rice and fish, flavoured with coconut, tamarind and exotic spices, are the dominant ingredients.

For food terms and help translating Swahili menus, see pp.743–745.

Breakfast

The first meal of the day varies widely. Standard fare in a *hoteli* (a small restaurant) consists of a cup of sweet **chai** (tea) and a chapati or a doorstep of white bread thickly spread with margarine (on both sides, and often the edges too). At the other extreme, if

you're staying in a **luxury hotel** or lodge, breakfast is usually a lavish acreage of hot and cold buffets that you can't possibly do justice to. In the average **mid-priced hotel**, you'll get "full breakfast", like something from an English B&B – greasy sausage, bacon and eggs, with tea or instant coffee (in a pot) and soggy "toast" (which is rarely in fact toasted).

Home-style cooking

If meals are unlikely to be a lasting memory, at least you'll never go hungry. In any *hoteli* there's always a number of predictable dishes intended to fill you up at the least cost. Potatoes, rice and especially **ugali** (a stiff, cornmeal porridge) are the national staples, eaten with chicken, goat, beef, or vegetable stew, various kinds of spinach, beans and sometimes fish. Portions are usually gigantic; half-portions (ask for *nusu*) aren't much smaller. But even in small towns, more and more cafés are appearing where most of the menu is fried – eggs, sausages, chips, fish, chicken and burgers.

Snacks, which can easily become meals, include samosas, chapatis, paratha, miniature kebabs, roasted corncobs, *mandaazi* (sweet, puffy, deep-fried dough cakes) and "egg-bread". *Mandaazi* are made before breakfast and served until evening time, when they've become cold and solid. Egg-bread (misleadingly translated from the Swahili *mkate mayai*) is a light wheat-flour "pancake" wrapped around fried eggs and minced meat, usually cooked on a huge griddle. While you won't find it everywhere, it's a delicious Kenyan response to the creeping burger menace. Snacks sold on the street include cassava chips and, if you're very lucky, termites (which go well as a bar snack with beer).

The standard blow-out feast for most Kenyans is a huge pile of **nyama choma** (roast meat). *Nyama choma* is usually eaten at a purpose-built *nyama choma* bar, with beer and music (live or on a jukebox) the standard accompaniment, and *ugali* and greens optional. You go to the kitchen and order by weight (half a kilo is plenty) direct from the butcher's hook or out of the fridge. There's usually a choice of goat, beef or mutton. After roasting, the meat is brought to your table on a wooden platter and chopped to bite-size with a sharp knife. *Kuku choma* is roast chicken.

Restaurant meals

Indian restaurants in the larger towns, notably Nairobi and Mombasa, are generally excellent (locally, there's often a strong Indian influence in *hoteli* food as well), with *dal* lunches a good stand-by and much fancier regional dishes widely available too.

When you splurge, apart from eating Indian, it will usually be in **hotel restaurants**, with food often very similar to what you might be served in a restaurant at home. It will rarely cost more than Ksh1000 a head, though there's a handful of classy establishments in Nairobi and on the coast which take delight in charging, for Kenya, outrageous prices for lavish meals – up to Ksh3000 – generally with some justification.

Kenya's seafood and meat are renowned and they are the basis of most serious meals. **Game meat** is a bit of a Kenyan speciality, supposedly farmed on ranches, though there is a fair amount of illegal poaching still going on to supply the trade. Giraffe, zebra, impala, crocodile and ostrich all regularly appear at various restaurants, and often on a weekly basis in hotel buffets. Gazelle and impala is especially good, as is zebra; not the horse meat you might imagine. *Carnivore* in Nairobi (see p.129) is one of the best places to try game meat.

The **lodges** usually have buffet lunches at about Ksh800–1000, which can be great value if you're really hungry, with table-loads of salads and cold meat. Among Kenya's exotic cuisines, you'll find Italian restaurants and pizzerias, various Chinese options, and French, Japanese, Thai, and even Korean food.

Vegetarians

If you're a **vegetarian** staying in tourist-class hotels, you should have no problems, as there's usually a meat-free pasta dish, or else the usual omelettes. Vegetarians on a strict budget don't have an easy time because meat is the conventional focus of any kind of special meal – in other words, any meal not eaten at home – and *hotelis* seldom have much else to accompany the starch. Even vegetable stew is normally cooked in meat gravy. Nor are salads and green vegetables served much in the cheaper *hotelis* (and if they are, make sure they're fresh). Eggs, at least, can be had almost anywhere, and fresh milk is distributed widely in wax paper tetra-packs, as well as UHT or fresh in thin plastic packs. With bread and tinned margarine, two more staples available everywhere, you won't starve. Look out for Indian vegetarian restaurants where you can often eat remarkably well at a very low cost.

Fruit

Fruit is a major delight. Bananas, avocados, pawpaws and pineapples are in the markets all year, mangoes and citrus fruits more seasonally. Look out for passion fruit (the familiar shrivelled brown variety, and the sweeter and less acidic smooth yellow ones), cape gooseberries, custard apples and guavas – all highly distinctive and delicious. On the coast, roasted cashew **nuts** are cheap, especially at Kilifi where they're grown and processed (never buy any with dark marks on them), while coconuts are filling and nutritious, going through several satisfying changes of condition (all edible) before becoming the familiar hard brown nuts.

Drinking

The national beverage is **chai** – tea. Universally drunk at breakfast and as a pick-me-up at any time, it's a weird variant on the classic British brew: milk, water, lots of sugar and tea leaves, brought to the boil in a kettle and served scalding hot. It must eventually do diabolical dental damage, but it's addictive and very reviving. Instant **coffee** – fresh is rare – is normally available in *hotelis* as well, but it's expensive (ironically, as the country is a large coffee producer), so not as popular as tea. The main tea-producing region is around Kericho in the west, but the best tea is made on the coast. Upcountry it's all too often a tea bag in a cup of vaguely warm water or milk.

Soft drinks (sodas) are usually very cheap, and crates of Coke, Fanta and Sprite find their way to the wildest corners of the country where, uncooled, they're pretty disgusting. Krest, a bitter lemon, is a lot more pleasant. Krest also makes a ginger ale, but it's watery and insipid; instead go for Stoney Tangawizi (ginger beer) which has more of a punch. Sometimes you can get Vimto (a mixed-fruit concoction), and occasionally plain soda water. There are fresh fruit **juices** available in the towns, especially on the coast (Lamu is fruit juice heaven). Passion fruit, the cheapest, is excellent, though nowadays it's likely to be watered-down

concentrate. Some places serve a variety: you'll sometimes find carrot juice and even tiger milk – made from tiger nuts (which are actually a type of tuber). Bottled Picana mango juice is also available at some shops that sell sodas.

Bottled **mineral or spring water** is relatively expensive but widely available. Mains water (see "Water and bugs", p.28) may be drinkable, but it's safer to stick with bottled.

Beer

Kenyan **lager beer** is generally good, and prices vary according to where you drink it, from Ksh65 in local dives up to Ksh150 in posher establishments. Of the normal beers, Tusker, White Cap, Pilsner (a little stronger) and the South African Castle Lager are the main brands, sold in half-litre bottles, or in one-third-litre sizes at fancier places and hotel bars. White Cap seems to be the old colonials' brew and Tusker is the biggest seller, though the aggressively marketed Castle Lager may make inroads there. A recent addition is Pilsner Ice, in third-litre bottles, which promises Kenyan men – somewhat unconvincingly – of their ability to stagger back home without reeking of stale beer. There are also two **stouts**: a head-thumping version of Guinness at over seven percent, and Castle Milk Stout, a milder competitor.

There are two points of beer **etiquette** worth remembering. First, never take your bottle out of the bar (bottles carry deposits and this is considered theft – surprisingly ugly misunderstandings can ensue). Secondly, in small places out of the cities (especially in western Kenya), men buy each other beers and accumulate them on the table in a display of mutual generosity. When he's drunk enough, each customer takes his unopened presents back to the bar and stores them for the next day.

Other alcoholic drinks

Kenya Cane (white rum) and **Kenya Gold** (a gooey, coffee-flavoured liqueur) deserve a try perhaps, but they are expensive and nothing special.

More interesting is **papaya wine**, Kenya's desperate solution to its shortage of vineyards. This – ostensibly in medium or dry, white and rosé – is certainly an acquired taste, but it's one you might acquire quickly. The stuff is potent and much cheaper than imported wine. A whole range of fruity wines has recently appeared, including passion and mango. But there are now several quite drinkable **white wines** made from Kenyan grapes – notably the products of Naivasha Wineries – and reasonably priced South African wine is widely available.

You won't often find **cocktails** except in expensive hotels and restaurants. One Kenyan mix to try is a *dawa* ("medicine") – vodka, white rum, honey and lime juice.

There's a battery of laws against **home brewing** and distilling – perhaps because of the loss of revenue in taxes on legal booze – but these are central aspects of Kenyan culture and they go on. You can sample *pombe* (bush brews) of different sorts all over the country. It's as varied in taste, colour and consistency as its ingredients: basically fer-

mented sugar and millet or banana, with herbs and roots for flavouring. The results are frothy and deceptively strong.

On the coast, where the coconuts grow, merely lopping off the growing shoot produces a naturally fermented **palm wine** (*mnazi* or *tembo*), which is indisputably Kenya's finest contribution to the art of self-intoxication. There's another variety of palm wine, tapped from the doum palm, called *mukoma*. Though there's usually a furtive discretion about *pombe* or *tembo* sessions, consumers rarely get busted.

Not so with spirits. Think twice before accepting a mug of **chang'aa**. It's treacherous firewater, and is also frequently contaminated, regularly killing drinking parties en masse, and filling a niche in the Kenyan press. Sentences for distilling and possessing *chang'aa* are harsh, and police (or vigilante) raids common.

Communications

Keeping in touch by post, telephone and email is generally easy, but not fantastically reliable. Mail takes a few days to Europe and around ten days to North America, Australia and New Zealand; times from these places to Kenya are slightly longer, and things go missing frequently enough – keep photocopies of letters you don't want to lose, and don't send valuables. Kenya's telephone system is improving, though lines are often busy, while emailing is becoming more and more useful as a means of communication.

Receiving and sending mail

Stamps can be bought only at post offices and large hotels. There are main post offices in all the towns and, except in the far north, sub-post offices throughout the rural areas. City **post offices** are usually open Mon–Fri 8am–5pm, Sat 9am–1pm, while those in the country generally open Mon–Fri 8am–12.30pm & 2–5pm. Prepaid "**aerograms**" are the cheapest way of writing

home, but they tend to sell out quickly. If you want speedy delivery, pay a little extra for express. The internal service, like the international one, is steadily getting less efficient and things do go missing.

Poste restante (general delivery) is free, and fairly reliable in Nairobi, Mombasa, Malindi and Lamu. Have your family name marked clearly, but look under any combination of initials and be ready to show your passport. Smaller post offices will also hold mail but your correspondent should mark the letter "To Be Collected". Parcels can be received, too, but expect to haggle over import-duty payment when they're opened. Ask the sender to mark packages "Contents To Be Re-exported From Kenya".

When posting things home, out of Kenya, airmail packages are expensive but **surface mail** (up to a maximum of 20kg) is good value, reliable and worth considering if you've accumulated things on your travels. Parcels must be no more than 105cm long and the sum of the three sides less than 200cm, and must be wrapped in brown paper and tied with string. They are usually examined in advance, so everything has to be checked, in the post office, before you wrap it. Cheaper for large consignments (over 10kg) is to get yourself and the parcel to the British Airways cargo counter at Jomo Kenyatta International Airport in Nairobi (p.153). BA can send it to any airport they serve – rapid and efficient to London, but can take weeks to anywhere else.

Addresses in Kenya

All addresses in Kenya have a post office box number, except out in the sticks where some are just given as "Private Bag", or "PO", followed by the location of the post office. There's no home delivery service. In large towns, business and office addresses are usually identified by the "House" or "Building" in which they're situated.

Telephones

The local **telephone** service is generally dependable and inexpensive; not so long distance, which gets close to international rates. Outside the big towns, you can spend a long time waiting for a connection or passing the time of day with the operator. Phonecards are a help, if you find any (no easier outside large towns than finding a working phone that will take them).

To make **local calls** from a call box you need a good handful of Ksh1, 5 and 10 coins. When you pick up any pay phone you'll hear a sustained tone and, in the background, a series of beeps. After five beeps you dial (you can dial before that, but you might lose your money). Use the area code or dial 900 for the operator.

The easiest and most economical way to make an **international call** is to dial direct from a **cardphone** (most commonly found outside Telekom offices and post offices). The prepaid, credit-card-sized plastic phonecards used in them can often be bought at newsstands, Telekom offices and post offices, but are often unavailable. Cardphones are also useful for using a **charge card** from your own telephone company (they don't take ordinary credit cards). You dial ☏0800/44 for the UK or ☏0800/10 for the USA or Canada and get through to an international operator in your country. The operator should be able to tell you how much the call – charged to your account – will cost; the Kenyan Telekom people have no idea.

In the absence of a cardphone it's possible to make **operator-assisted** international calls from a main post office ("station-to-station"). Charges are about £10 ($14) for three minutes to Europe, more to North America or Australasia. Shorter calls are now possible, but cost more per minute (about £6/$9). When you ask for a station-to-station connection, you pre-pay for a specified number of minutes, and you get your money back if you fail to get through, but not if the conversation ends up taking less time than you expected, for example if you get through to an answering machine. If you want more minutes you have to specify how many – all very user-unfriendly. You can also usually phone from large hotels, but you could pay well over twice the usual price for this facility.

Collect calls can also be made, but not from call boxes. Three minutes' worth costs about £13 ($20). It works out cheaper overall if you call your correspondent briefly and ask them to call you back at a hotel.

Larger post offices and some internet or telecommunications offices have **fax** machines – the international rate is around £5/$7 per page – or you can use a private fax bureau, where the rate will sometimes be cheaper. Charges for receiving faxes, however, are nominal.

Mobiles

If you want to use your **mobile phone** in Kenya, you'll need to check with your phone provider whether it will work abroad, and what the call charges are. In the UK, for all but the very top-of-the-range packages, you'll have to inform your phone provider before going abroad to get international access switched on. You may get charged extra for this depending on your existing package and where you are travelling to. You're also likely to be charged extra for incoming calls when abroad, as the people calling you will be paying the usual rate. If you want to retrieve messages while you're away, you'll have to ask your provider for a new access code, as your home one is unlikely to work. For further information about using your phone abroad, check out your provider's website, call them, or have a look at Ⓦwww.telecomsadvice.org.uk/features/using_your_mobile_abroad.htm. More people in Kenya have mobiles than land lines, and most of the country has coverage.

Internet and email

One of the best ways to keep in touch while travelling is to sign up for a free internet email address which can be accessed from anywhere, for example YahooMail or Hotmail – accessible through Ⓦwww.yahoo.com and Ⓦwww.hotmail.com. Once you've set up an account, you can use these sites to pick up and send mail, but Hotmail in particular can be painfully slow, and often seizes up altogether after about 10am, so if you have a Hotmail account, try to use it before that time. Internet offices are reasonably widespread in Kenya, but they can be thin on the ground in small places, and also much more expensive due to the cost of long-distance calls to the nearest server. The cheapest places to use the internet are Nairobi and Mombasa, where you can pay less than a shilling a minute. The price can be as much as ten times more than that elsewhere.

Dialling codes

To call Kenya, dial the international access code (00 from the UK, Ireland or New Zealand, 011 from North America, 0011 from Australia, 09 from South Africa) followed by 254 for Kenya, the area code (omitting the initial 0), and then the number itself. If you have to be connected by the operator, call your own international operator and quote the exchange and number.

Plans are afoot for nationwide numbering changes by December 2002, with all landlines having seven-digit numbers and two-digit codes (after the initial zero). Nairobi's code, for example, will change from 02 to 020. The code for Safaricom mobile numbers is expected to change from 072 to 0722.

Calling out of Kenya, dial 000 then:
Australia 61
Canada 1
Ireland 353
Netherlands 31
New Zealand 64
South Africa 27
UK 44
USA 1

Useful numbers
International operator/directory enquiries 0196
Line problems 980
Emergency (fire, police, ambulance) 999

The media

English tends to predominate over Swahili in public life; higher education and parliament get by almost exclusively on it, and the media uses it heavily. Although most television is in Swahili, most newspapers are in English, as are most radio stations. The press in Kenya is pretty lively and provides reasonable coverage of international news, while CNN, the BBC and European sports stations are increasingly available on satellite TV.

Radio and TV

KBC **radio** has three services, broadcasting in English, Swahili and local languages, as well as an FM station, Metropolitan FM, competing with the independent Capital FM (which also broadcasts BBC World Service programmes in English, Swahili and Somali). *The Nation* newspaper also has a news station, Nation Radio on 96.4FM. The BBC World Service is on shortwave kHz 6005, 11860 and 11940, and in Nairobi on 93.7FM (for latest schedules and frequencies check their website at ⓦ www.bbc.co.uk/worldservice). You'll find the Voice of America (ⓦ www.voa.gov) on kHz 909, 1530, 15240 and 17895 among other frequencies, and Radio Canada (ⓦ www.rcinet.ca) on kHz 7425, 9805 and 11600.

Kenyan **television**, much of it imported, is in English and Swahili. There are three main channels: the stuffy and hesitant KBC (which used to carry BBC's World Service TV until it pulled out over government censorship; KBC is now apparently making moves to distance itself from the establishment); the upbeat, mainly urban KTN, which carries CNN for much of the morning, and the South African "Channel O" music channel for most of the night; and *The Nation* newspaper's channel, Nation TV, which also sometimes carries CNN. In addition to these, KBC operates a pay channel, KBC2, which is run in conjunction with South Africa's M-NET, and there is also a Christian Channel called Family TV. An increasing number of homes, and certainly bars and hotels, now have satellite dishes, which give them access to Britain's Sky TV, Eurosport and other foreign channels.

The press

Kenya is a nation absorbed in its **press**. Despite continued suppression (and blatant threats to curb press freedom from KANU party bigwigs, see p.666), the Kenyan press has enjoyed a renaissance since the unbanning of the opposition in 1992, and there are many magazines and occasional papers, all of which carry interesting articles from time to time and often surprise their readers with their outspokenness.

The leading quality daily is the *Daily Nation* (and *Sunday Nation*), part-owned by the Aga Khan (45 percent; the remaining 55 percent by shareholders), which has meaty news coverage (international, too, as well as European football results), a daring editorial line, and a letters page full of insights into Kenyan life. Its main competitor, the *East African Standard*, is dull and lightweight in comparison, but usually carries more international news. *The People*, whose logo "Fair, Frank and Fearless" is about right, and which verges on the scurrilous, looks a lot scrappier and arrives later on the newsstands than *The Nation* and the *Standard*, but is more incisive and carries more international news than both, though less sport. Less worthwhile is the *Kenya Times*, a stodgy KANU organ, partly owned by Britain's Mirror Group Newspapers. The Nation Group also publishes the excellent and highly recommended *The East African* on Mondays, a relatively weighty, conservatively styled round-up of the week's news in Kenya, Uganda and Tanzania, shot through with an admirable measure of justified cynicism. Its own reporting is consistently incisive, intelligent and thought-provoking, and it also carries the cream of the foreign press news features. All are available from street vendors.

Of other papers, *Taifa Leo* and *Kenya Leo*, are in Swahili. The *Weekly Review* is always worth picking up (as are *Society*, *Law* and *Finance* – if you can find any copies that haven't been confiscated for one crime of the pen or another). In similar vein, *Kenya Confidential* (on blue paper) is not easy to come by outside Nairobi, and features painfully detailed exposés on corruption and the manifold misdeeds of Kenyan politicians. Its editor really should consider moving his office to Nairobi prison, as he gets thrown in there with alarming frequency.

Of the **foreign press**, the UK *Daily Telegraph* gets to all sorts of settler-ish bastions, as does the *Daily Express* – both have weekly editions that are often available. Other British papers and the *International Herald Tribune* can usually be found in Nairobi or, a few days old, at one or two stores around the country. They tend, however, to be unavailable when Kenya's internal affairs make international news. British tabloids are usually available, several days late.

Time and *Newsweek* are hawked widely and, together with old *National Geographic*s and copies of *The Economist*, filter through many hands before reaching the second-hand booksellers.

Newspapers online

The Nation is at
ⓦ www.nationaudio.com.
The East African is at
ⓦ www.nationaudio.com/News/East African/current.
The *East African Standard* is at
ⓦ www.eastandard.net.
The regional weekly *Coastweek* is at both
ⓦ www.africaonline.co.ke/coastwk and ⓦ www.net2000.com/coastwk.

Opening hours, public holidays and festivals

Both Christian and Muslim religious holidays are observed, as well as secular national holidays. Local seasonal and cyclical events, peculiar to particular ethnic groups, are less well advertised.

Opening hours

Standard **opening hours**, where there are any, follow familiar patterns. In larger towns, the major stores and tourist services will be open Monday to Saturday from 8am to 5 or 6pm, often with a break for lunch. Offices and museums open at similar times, though offices will usually be closed on Saturdays. In rural areas and out in the bush, small shops can be open at almost any hour, and may double as *hotelis* or *chai* kiosks.

In Muslim areas, opening hours will vary during **Ramadan** (see p.54), when eating places may be closed during the day, while shops and businesses will close in time for sunset, to break the daily fast.

Bank opening hours in cities are Mon–Fri 9am–3pm, and on Saturdays (or sometimes just the first and last Saturday of the month) 9–11am. Larger **post offices** usually open Mon–Fri 8am–5pm, Sat 9am–1pm, with smaller ones, especially in rural areas, open Mon–Fri 8am–12.30pm & 2–5pm.

Public holidays

1 Jan	New Year's Day
Mar–April (movable)	Good Friday
Mar–April (movable)	Easter Monday
10 Dhu'l Hijja (see below)	Tabaski
1 May	Labour Day
1 June	Madaraka Day (celebrating 1960 granting of self-government)
10 Oct	Moi Day
20 Oct	Kenyatta Day (anniversary of his imprisonment)
1 Shawwal (see below)	Id ul Fitr
12 Dec	Jamhuri (Independence) Day
25 Dec	Christmas Day
26 Dec	Boxing Day

Note: if a holiday falls on a Sunday, the following Monday is usually declared a public holiday.

Islamic festivals: approximate dates

	2002	2003	2004	2005
Beginning of Ramadan (1st Ramadan)	Nov 5	Oct 25	Oct 13	Oct 2
Id ul Fitr/Id al-Saghir (1st Shawwal)	Dec 5	Nov 24	Nov 12	Nov 1
Tabaski/Id al-Kabir (10th Dhu'l Hijja)	Feb 22	Feb 11	Jan 31	Jan 19
Muslim New Year (1st Moharem)	March 15	March 4	Feb 21	Feb 10
Ashoura (10th Moharem)	March 24	March 13	March 1	Feb 19
Maulidi/Mouloud (12th Rabia I)	May 24	May 13	May 1	April 20

The Islamic calendar

On the coast, throughout the northeast, and in Muslim communities everywhere, the lunar **Islamic calendar** is used for religious purposes. The Muslim year has 354 days, with 355 days eleven times every thirty years, so dates recede against the Western calendar by an average of eleven days each year. Only the month of fasting called **Ramadan**, and Id ul Fitr – the feast of relief at the end of it which begins on the first sighting of the new moon – will have much effect on your travels. During Ramadan, most stores and *hotelis* are closed through the daylight hours in smaller towns in Islamic districts. Public transport and official business continue as usual. **Maulidi**, the celebration of the prophet's birthday, is worth catching if you're on the coast at the right time, especially if you'll be in Lamu.

Agricultural shows

The annual **agricultural shows** put on by the Agricultural Society of Kenya (ASK) are lively, revealing occasions, borrowing a lot from the British farming show tradition, but infused with Kenyan style. As well as stock and produce competitions, and the usual beer and snack tents, there are often some less expected booths: women's groups, family planning, beekeeping, soil conservation and herbalism. Large towns have an ASK fairground (sometimes reasonable places to camp, incidentally) and the shows happen at roughly the same time each year. Many smaller towns have annual district shows as well.

ASK shows

Eldoret	Early March
Nanyuki	First week in May
Meru	Early June
Nakuru	Early July
Kisii	July
Garissa	Third week in July
Kisumu	First week in Aug
Embu	Second week in Aug
Mombasa	Last week in Aug
Nyeri	Early Sept
Nairobi	Late Sept/early Oct
Kitale	Late Oct/early Nov
Kakamega	Last week in Nov

Shopping

Kenya is a good place to buy carvings and textiles in particular, the former usually made specifically for the tourist market. Basketwork, beadwork and traditional utensils made from gourds are also popular. Other good buys include music (usually on cassette, sometimes on CD), and musical instruments. Whatever you're buying, aside from groceries, bargaining is usually the order of the day, and in places that see tourists and travellers, prices of souvenirs, like those of hotels (see p.40), can vary considerably through the year.

Arts and crafts

Sculptures and carvings in wood and soapstone (*kisii*-stone) are cheap and ubiquitous. The most striking carvings are in the dramatically vertical and delicate **makonde style** (after the Makonde people of Mozambique and Tanzania), ostensibly carved in ebony, but in Kenya usually made of blackened rosewood or something similar. This shouldn't deter you – it saves on ebony forests' stocks and looks just as wonderful on your mantelpiece.

The familiar **sisal baskets** (*chondo*, or *vyondo* in the plural) come in a huge variety of patterns and can be made from cheap nylon string as well as sisal and, much more rarely, baobab bark twine, with beads woven in. They're all light and functional.

Beadwork (*ushanga*, *mkufu*) and tribal **regalia** – weapons, shields, drums (*ngoma*), musical instruments, stools, headrests and metal jewellery – are common as well, but much more expensive when authentically used rather than made for the tourist industry.

Masks are mostly imported from west and central Africa (they're not a feature of traditional Kenyan art) and by no means sure to be old or "authentic" no matter how much congealed cow dung appears to fill the crevices.

Textiles, notably a profusion of printed women's wraps in cotton (**kanga**) and heavier-weave men's loincloths (**kikoi/vikoi**) are really good buys on the coast, and older ones represent collectable items worth seeking out. Kangas are always sold in pairs and are printed with intriguing Swahili proverbs. They're usually found to have been manufactured in the Far East. Local tailors will make them into garments for you at very reasonable prices.

Music **cassettes** make good souvenirs, but the tapes themselves are often low quality, and it may be worth transferring the music onto a different medium when you return home. **CDs** are harder to come by as few Kenyans own a CD player. Musical **instruments** make good buys too. Drums can be rather bulky (some people even buy them to use as tables), but those designed to be held under one arm, more common on the coast, are more practical as souvenirs. Lamu has its own wind instrument called a *siwa*.

Whether or not you have children or are buying presents for kids, the **toys** you can come across from time to time are highly recommended souvenirs. Most worthwhile are the beautifully fashioned, and sometimes large and intricate, wire buses, cars and lorries, fitted with stick-up steering wheels, that lucky boys in rural areas get given by older brothers and uncles. These are not often for sale, except on the coast in Malindi, but you might commission one, if you have time (Kariokor market in Nairobi is the place for this). More widely available are various push-along bikes, birds and monkeys, and pottery matatus, these latter for the tourist market.

Other local specialities are mentioned through the guide. In the end, what you take home is going to depend partly on how much you can carry. It's easy, with attractive items and low prices, to get quite carried away, but carvings (especially ebony makonde) and soapstone are extremely heavy.

Ivory, incidentally, carved or otherwise, and in any quantity, is strictly illegal. Most countries have banned all ivory imports. It will be seized and, in many countries, the carrier is subject to a heavy fine. You may also wish to avoid buying things made of woods such as ebony and mahogany whose existence is threatened by logging. Carvings made of neem and acacia are more environmentally friendly.

Bargaining

Bargaining is an important skill to acquire, and you'll need to get into it quickly. Every time you pay an unreasonable price for goods or services, you contribute to local inflation, so be cautious at first over your purchases, until you've established the value of things. Once you start, it's surprising how little is sold at a strictly fixed price; it's nearly always worth making an offer. You're expect-

ed to knock most negotiable prices down by at least half. Souvenirs are sometimes offered at first prices ten times what the vendor is prepared to accept. You can avoid the silly first prices by having a chat first and establishing your streetwise credentials. The bluffing on both sides is part of the fun; don't be shy of making a big scene. Where prices are marked, they are generally fixed – which you'll quickly discover if you walk out and aren't called back. Once you get into it, you'll rarely end up paying more than the going rate for food, transport or accommodation, although as a tourist, your earning power will be much higher than that of most local people, so while you don't want to pay over the odds for things, you can afford to be relaxed about it, and you don't always need to seek the absolute lowest price you can get.

Entertainment and sport

Kenya's espousal of Western values has belittled much traditional culture, so only in remote areas are you likely to come across traditional dancing and drumming which doesn't somehow involve you as a paying audience. If you're patient and reasonably adventurous in your travels, however, you'll be able to witness something more authentic sooner or later – though most likely only by accident or if you stay somewhere off the beaten track long enough to make friends. Kenyan popular music, gospel, and spectator sports are more accessible. For more information on the Nairobi arts scene, see "Cultural venues and art galleries" on p.132.

Dance

The hypnotic swaying and displays of effortless leaping found in **Maasai and Samburu dancing** are the best known forms of Kenyan dance. Similar dance forms occur widely among other non-agricultural peoples, while foremost among exponents of **drumming** are the Mijikenda on the coast (the Akamba have sadly all but forgotten the art). **Mijikenda dance troupes** (notably from the Giriama people) perform up and down

the coast at tourist venues. As with the Maasai dancing, it's better to ignore any purist misgivings you might have about the authenticity of such performances and enjoy them as distinctive and exuberant entertainments in their own right.

Music

As for **popular music**, apart from what your ears pick up on the street and in buses (often amazingly loud), the live spectacle is limited to Nairobi, coastal entertainment spots, and a fair scattering of up-country **discos** and "**country clubs**". The indigenous music scene seems overshadowed by foreign influences: British and American soul and jazz-funk, reggae (especially in the sacred image of Bob Marley) and a vigorous contribution from Congo predominating on radio and in record shops. The guide to the Nairobi club and music scene (p.137) includes a detailed rundown on where to hear the home-grown product. The article in Contexts at the end of the book (pp.713–733) gives a condensed history of music in Kenya and a current discography.

If you're lucky enough to be invited to a coastal Swahili wedding with all the trimmings, a **tarabu** band may be playing. Tarabu (or Taarab) music, especially the older music (modern tarabu relies heavily on synthesizers) is hauntingly beautiful, an effervescent blend of African, Arabic and Indian musical influences. Steady drumbeat, tambourines, accordions, an instrument called the *udi* – like a lute – and plaintive Swahili lyrics are the traditional components, while electric guitars, fiddles and microphones are modern additions.

Theatre and film

Theatrical performances are effectively limited to one or two semi-professional clubs in Nairobi and Mombasa and a handful of up-country amateur dramatic groups. African actors and scripts tend to be rare but things are improving, at least in Nairobi, where there are a number of groups performing in English.

Indigenous theatre was dealt a severe blow in 1978 when the innovative Kamiriithu Community Education and Cultural Centre in Limuru put on a Kikuyu language play by Ngugi wa Thiongo and Ngugi wa Mirii (*I Will Marry When I Want*), which, after seven weeks of playing to packed houses, was banned. The authorities mistrusted the play's power to mobilize people and question the status quo in Kikuyu rather than English. Ngugi wa Thiongo, one of the country's most eminent writers, was detained without trial for a year as a result. In such a climate – which doesn't appear to have altered much – the notion of popular, issue-raising theatre gets automatically labelled as subversive and

hasn't much hope of emerging again. Kamiriithu's brief but spectacular success only shows the potential.

Cinema in Kenya revolves almost entirely around imports. The big towns have cinemas and a few drive-ins, while smaller towns may have one cinema with the occasional screening. American and Indian box-office hits are the staple fodder.

Sports

Sports received encouragement from Kenya's much-vaunted – if financially disastrous – hosting of the 1987 All Africa Games. The country's Olympic successes are indisputable, with a regular clutch of gold and silver in the **track events**. Kenya's athletes are the continent's leaders and the country's long-distance runners are the best in the world, with Moses Kiptanui, from Kapcherop in the Cherangani Hills, the most dazzling recent record-breaker. Recently, it has been suggested that certain Kalenjin communities may have a gene which makes them more likely to be stronger athletes, but Kalenjins as much as anyone else have played down this idea.

Kenya has possibly the most successful athletics training school in the world in St Patrick's High School, Iten, in the Rift Valley. You'll also find evidence of keen amateur involvement – joggers, martial arts enthusiasts and road cyclists in training.

Football is wildly popular. Kenya was to have hosted the Nations Cup finals in early 1996 and it was a major disappointment when they had to pull out due to insufficient funds. A lot of people, in fact, support English Premiership teams, and there are even matatus decorated with the colours of Arsenal and Manchester United. Kenya's national team, known as the Harambee Stars, wins the East and Central Africa Challenge Cup frequently and, in the Premier League, Nairobi's AFC Leopards and Gor Mahia rank with the best clubs on the continent, although the last time a Kenyan club won an African competition was in 1987 when Gor Mahia took the Cup Winners' Cup. Crowds are pretty well behaved, perhaps because forking out for the modest gate fee precludes getting drunk as well.

Car rallies

The only regular national event that gets much international attention is the three-day **Safari Rally**, in late February or early March. From the beginning of the year, the Kenyan papers wax eloquent about this "toughest motor rally in the world", the teams and drivers who will be entering, and the cost of their preparations. While the whole country seems gripped with rally fever, the costs are prohibitive for most Kenyans and no African driver has yet won – Asian and European entrants predominate. Unless you're a rally buff, however, it's really nothing to get excited about. The route has become monoto-

nous of late, invariably starting with a one-day "special" show stage around Nairobi, followed by two days south and west of the capital in Maasai-land. Information can be had from the Automobile Association at North Airport Rd, Embakasi, Nairobi PO Box 40087 ☎02/825060. If you're into this kind of thing, look out also for the **Caltex Equator Rally**, which takes place in early October, and the annual fund-raising **Rhino Charge** rally in the Rift Valley, which is a ten-hour spin across tough, unmarked terrain to find checkpoints. Information and advance booking (you can get in as part of a safari) from Rafiki ☎02/884238 ✉safarico @arcc.or.ke.

Outdoor activities

Kenya is a country with huge untapped potential for outdoor activities. The following brief notes suggest the possibilities for walking, riding, fishing, golf, diving, climbing and rafting. Cycling is covered under "Getting Around" (p.38). Safaris are covered in a separate section on p.61.

Walking

Walking, if you have plenty of time and the relevant Survey of Kenya maps (see p.148 for details on how to obtain them), is highly recommended and gives you unparalleled contact with local people. In isolated parts, it's often preferable to waiting for a lift, while in the Aberdares, Mau and Cherangani ranges, and on mounts Kenya and Elgon, it's the only practical way of moving away from the main tracks. You will sometimes come across animals out in the bush, but buffalos and elephants (the most likely dangers), unless solitary or with young, usually move off. Don't ignore the dangers, however, and stay alert. You'll need to carry several litres of water much of the time, especially in lower, drier regions.

Before plunging off into the bush, though, you might prefer to go on an organized **walking safari**, at least as a starter. Walking

safaris are offered by a number of safari companies in Nairobi (see p.140).

Mountain Walking in Africa: Kenya by David Else (McCarta, London 1991) is a useful book. For hill and mountain hiking, *The Mountains of Kenya: A Walker's Guide*, by Paul Clarke (Mountain Club of Kenya, Nairobi 1989) is also recommended, with step-by-step route details for almost one hundred hills and mountains.

Riding

There are good opportunities for **horseback riding** in the Central Highlands and an active equestrian community in Nairobi. Safaris Unlimited (see p.143) offers riding safaris near the Maasai Mara National Reserve. **Camel safaris** are popular too, though the best operators to contact tend to change from year to year. Contact any of the addresses under "Special activity safaris" on p.142.

Fishing

Many of the highlands' streams are well stocked with **trout**, which were imported early in the twentieth century by British settlers. A few local fishing associations are still active and the usual rules about seasons and licences apply. Naro Moru River Lodge and the Izaac Walton Inn in Embu offer rods for rent. The Fisheries Department headquarters, next to the National Museum in Nairobi, can supply details (1-year licence: Ksh500). For **lake fishing**, it's possible to rent rods and boats at lakes Baringo, Naivasha and Turkana, and there are luxury fishing lodges on Rusinga, Mfangano and Takawiri islands on Lake Victoria.

The Indian Ocean offers excellent sport fishing opportunities. Enthusiasts have the chance to land an impressive tally of species including sailfish, marlin, swordfish, barracuda and shark. Kenya's superb stretch of offshore coral reef, with its deepwater drop-offs and predictable northerly currents, is ideal for **near-shore angling**. Watamu, Malindi and the resorts around Mombasa are the most popular centres for **ocean fishing**.

Golf

Kenya has almost forty **golf clubs**, mostly patronized by the European and Asian communities, notably around the old colonial centres of Nairobi, Naivasha, Thika, Nanyuki and Nyeri in the Central Highlands, and Kisumu and Kitale in the west. There are also a number on the coast, and – incontestably the most bizarre – on the scorched moonscape shore of Lake Magadi. Green fees vary widely, usually from about US$30 per person per day. Details for all of these from the Kenya Golf Union, PO Box 49609 Nairobi ☎02/763898, ℗765118, ⓦwww.kgu.or.ke. For organized upmarket **golfing safaris**, contact Tobs Golf Safaris Ltd, PO Box 20146 Nairobi ☎02/721722 or 727790, ℗722015, ⓦwww.kenya-golf-safaris.com.

Diving and snorkelling

Kenya's coastal waters are warm all year round so it's possible to **dive** without a wetsuit and have a rewarding dip under the waves almost anywhere.

Most of the diving bases are located at Malindi, Watamu or on the coast south of Mombasa; Diani Beach is probably the most popular area. There are centres here which will provide training to PADI leader level (for details see pp.506, 535 and 544). For underwater photographers, in particular, the immense coral reef is a major draw – the landscape is spectacularly varied, with shallow coral gardens and blue-water drop-offs sinking as deep as 200m and, as there are few rivers to bring down sediment, visibility is generally excellent. *The Dive Sites of Kenya and Tanzania*, by Anton Koornhof (New Holland, London 1997) is highly recommended, and also covers sites suitable for snorkelling. For fish identification, *A Guide to Common Reef Fishes of the Western Indian Ocean and Kenyan Coast* by Kenneth Bock (Macmillan, London 1992) or *Coral Reef Fishes – Indo-Pacific & Caribbean* by Ewald Lieske and Robert Myers (Collins, London 1994) are the obvious choices.

If you plan to do a fair bit of **snorkelling**, it makes sense to bring your own mask and snorkel though they can always be rented.

Climbing

Apart from Mount Kenya, there are **climbing** opportunities at all grades in the Aberdares, Cheranganis, Mathews Range, Hell's Gate and Rift Valley volcanoes – including Longonot and Suswa. If you have time to get acquainted with it, the Mountain Club of Kenya (PO Box 45741 Nairobi; ⓦwww.mck.or.ke; club house at Wilson Airport; club night Tues 8pm ☎02/501747) is a good source of advice and contacts, not just for climbing, but for outdoor pursuits in general. If you intend to do any serious climbing in the country, you should make early contact in writing. Don't expect them to answer detailed route questions, however; leave that until you arrive. If you want to go climbing with a guide, safari companies in Nairobi offer everything from a simple hike to technical ascents of Batian and Nelion (see pp.140–143).

Rafting

Both the Tana and Athi rivers have sections which can be **rafted** when they're in spate. Approximate dates are early November to mid-March, and mid-April to the end of August. Savage Wilderness Safaris is the main operator (see p.143), and most trips are for one day only.

National parks and reserves

The national parks are administered by the Kenya Wildlife Service (KWS) in Nairobi as total sanctuaries where human habitation (apart from the tourist lodges) is prohibited. Things seem to be gradually changing, however, as the benefits of readmitting traditional pastoralists begin to be appreciated (humans and wildlife lived in equilibrium before the British arrived). National reserves, run by local councils, tend to be less strict on the question of human encroachment.

Parks and reserves are not fenced in (except Nakuru National Park, parts of the Aberdares and the north side of Nairobi National Park), and the **animals** are free to come and go, though do tend to stay within the boundaries, especially in the dry seasons when cattle outside compete for water.

Most parks and reserves are open to **private visits** (though it's worth noting that foreign-registered commercial overland vehicles are not allowed in). A few parks have been heavily developed for tourism with graded tracks, signposts, lodges and the rest, but none has any kind of bus service at the gate for people without their own transport. You may be able to hitch a lift at the park gate with visitors in a private vehicle, but this can never be counted on, so in general, without your own transport, you'll have to go on an organized safari. The largest and most frequently visited parks are covered in depth in Chapter Five. An introduction to the main game parks, giving you some idea of what to expect from them and the best times to visit, is given on pp.386–390. Details about smaller and lesser-known parks and reserves, some of which can be visited on foot, are included in the rest of the guide.

Entry fees

Park entry fees are charged per person per day (24 hours, so you only pay for one day if you arrive in the afternoon, stay overnight and leave at midday). Prices are fixed in dollars, though you can also pay in shillings, at a bad rate. You pay in advance at the park gate, though in practice it's possible to pay for extra days on leaving if you've stayed longer than you originally intended. Children get reduced rates, and these apply to anyone under 18,

but students over that age only get a reduction if they are in an organized group from their place of learning. Fees vary according to the popularity of the park: the Aberdares, Amboseli and Lake Nakuru cost $27 ($10 children), Tsavo East and West cost $23 ($8 children), Nairobi, Shimba Hills and Meru cost $20 ($5 children), Mount Kenya charges $10 ($5 children), and other parks $15 ($5 children). The marine parks are very cheap ($5, or $2 children). Maasai Mara and Samburu national reserves have their own fees. If you want to camp, you have to stay in a recognized campsite and pay extra ($2–15, depending on the park and whether it's a "special" campsite). Details of these are given in the text.

Entry to some parks – currently Nairobi, Lake Nakuru, Aberdares, Tsavo East and West, and Amboseli, but eventually it will be all of them – is paid for by **smart card**. You can buy this and "load" it with payment at the main gates of the parks using it, and at one or two other places such as the KWS offices in Mombasa and Malindi. Although you can just pay enough to enter the park you are visiting, you could also load it with extra payment to use later. The advantage of doing this is that you can then use it to enter any of the parks it covers by any entrance. Otherwise, you will have to go to the main gate to buy or load your card.

Kenyan citizens and residents are eligible for massively reduced rates (you won't pay more than Ksh250). If you qualify, you must have ID to prove it, and KWS is now very strict about enforcing the regulation. If you don't qualify, it's strongly recommended that you pay the proper fee and get the right receipt. KWS, and thus the future of Kenya's national parks, depends heavily on gate money. If you defraud them, you're ultimately contributing to the destruction of Kenya's wildlife. High as they are compared to residents' rates, the fees are a small price to pay.

For **Kenyan residents** only, there used to be a one-year "**National Parks Pass**" (Ksh6600 per adult or Ksh11,000 per couple; Ksh1000 per child under 16) allowing unlimited access to KWS national parks, other than the Maasai Mara and the Samburu complex. At last check, this pass had been suspended, but it may be brought back, and if so, should be available from the licensing section at the parks headquarters on Langata Road in Nairobi (Mon–Fri 8am–1pm & 2–5pm), or you can contact them at PO Box 40241 Nairobi ☎02/501081, 506671 or 602345, ℱ501752, ℯtourism@kws.org.

Vehicles of less than 6 seats are charged at Ksh200 per day, 6–12 seats Ksh500, 13–24 seats Ksh1000. A **guide service** costs, per person per guide, Ksh500 for a day, Ksh300 for half a day (4hr). Prices, gate opening times, regulations and information on maps are given at the start of the relevant sections in the guide.

Park and reserve considerations

Limiting human impact on the parks and reserves is vital, and with large numbers of visitors to the better-known sites, it's important to bear in mind some simple facts to ensure you leave the place and the animals as you found them and for others to enjoy.

Harassment of animals disturbs feeding, breeding and reproductive cycles, and too many vehicles surrounding wildlife is not only unpleasant for you, but will also distress the animals. Cheetah, for example, only hunt during the day and, if hemmed in by vehicles, including yours, could end up deprived of a meal. Be quiet when viewing, switch off your engine (or ask your driver to) and keep a minimum distance of 20m. Never, under any circumstance, get out of your vehicle, and don't feed animals as it upsets their diet and leads to unnecessary dependence on humans. Habituated baboons, especially, can become violent if refused handouts.

Off-road driving causes irreparable damage to the vegetation. Stay on the designated tracks (even if it means you won't get the best photograph), and if you have a driver, ask him to do the same.

If you **smoke** while on your visit, tip all ash in an ashtray. Carelessly discarded cigarettes start numerous unnecessary bush fires every year, which cause great damage to vegetation and wildlife.

Safaris

Before arranging a safari, think about whether you want comfort or a more authentic experience, and whether you want the convenience of having it pre-booked as part of a package holiday, or the independence of picking and choosing once in Kenya itself. Remember, too, that the parks and reserves can also be visited privately, allowing you to set your own itinerary – sometimes an attractive alternative to an organized trip.

Types of safari

Air safaris, using internal flights to get around, will add enormously to the cost and comfort of your trip and give you spectacular views but a much less intimate feel of Africa.

On the other hand, long bumpy **drives** to meet the demands of an itinerary can be completely exhausting (and impossible for the physically infirm) while hours of your time are eaten away in a cloud of dust. Note that the "**balloon safaris**" you see advertised are short balloon flights, not complete tours. They take place at dawn and last a couple of hours at most. They can be done in several parks, most popularly in the Maasai Mara, and the bill is a big one – around £250/$360. There are more details on pp.428–429.

Many safaris take you from one game park hotel (known as **lodges**) to another, using **minibuses** with lift-up roofs for taking pictures. Make sure you have a window seat and ask about the number of passengers and whether the vehicle is shared by several operators or is for your group only.

The alternative to a standard lodge safari is a **camping safari**, also in a minibus, where the crew – or you, if it's a budget trip – pitch your tents each day. With this kind of trip you have to be prepared for a degree of discomfort along with the self-sufficiency: insects can occasionally be a menace, you may not get a shower every night, the food won't be so lavish and the beer not so cold.

It's common on camping safaris to spend the hot part of the day at the campsite. While some are shady and pleasant, that's not always the case and, where there are lodges with swimming pools, cold beer and the rest nearby, there's no reason not to spend a few hours in comfort. Similarly, if you want to go on an early game drive, don't be afraid to suggest you skip breakfast, or take sandwiches. In too many companies, interpretations of what customers want are passed from management to drivers and cooks and rarely questioned.

On the best camping safaris, you travel in a fairly **rugged vehicle** – a four-wheel-drive land cruiser or even an open-sided lorry – giving more flexibility about where you go and how long you stay. The more expensive camping safaris come very expensive indeed and tend to model their style on images culled from *Out of Africa*; they can easily cost over £200/$280 a day.

Pre-booking at home

Most travel agents can fix you up with brochures for the more **mainstream tour operators** whose packages generally (though not always) fall into the more expensive lodge and minibus category. For more **off-beat adventure trips**, or a better selection of camping safaris, you should contact the operator directly. Note that the **single-person supplement** tends to be high on conventional beach and safari packages and somewhat less (or you can share) on the more adventure-spirited trips, where prices are per person, but depend also on the size of the group, which can make things extremely expensive if there are only two or three people.

The minibus safaris fitted into most of the inexpensive Mombasa-based charter packages venture no further afield than the three national parks easily accessible from the coast – Tsavo East, Tsavo West and Amboseli (trips up to Samburu or west to Maasai Mara are more expensive, and therefore cheaper if arranged from Nairobi).

Booking in Kenya

Independently choosing a **safari company** to spend your money on can be fairly hit or miss. Unless you have the luxury of a long stay, your choice will probably be limited by the time available. Remember, though, that you may be able to use this to your advantage; if you ask, many companies are willing to discount a trip in order to fill unsold seats if you're buying at the last minute. Some outfits will also give student discounts if you ask. In fact, any angle you can employ to get a good deal, you should use.

This is not to recommend the very cheapest outfits. As the competition in Nairobi becomes more cut-throat, some budget camping operators, not all of them licensed, are pushing safaris at the very bottom of the market in a price war which completely undercuts the legitimate firms. Any safari which is offered at less than £40/$60 per day is likely to be cutting corners. The easiest way for disreputable operators to cut costs is to avoid paying park entry fees, which threatens the preservation of wildlife in Kenya. Give these fly-by-night companies a miss.

A number of **recommended operators** are given in the Nairobi account on pp.140–143 but it's notoriously difficult to find a company that's absolutely consistent (if they're a member of KATO – see opposite – that's a good sign, and at least you have somewhere to complain to). Group relations among the passengers can assume surprising significance in a very short time and other unpredictables such as weather, illness and visibility of animals all contribute to the degree of success of the trip. More controllable factors like breakdowns, food, equipment and competence of the drivers and tour leaders, really determine reputations. The companies we've listed all have pretty good records and get regularly mentioned in readers' letters, but even they turn up the occasional duff trip. Give them a try unless an alternative sounds especially good and reliable. The Nairobi grapevine is probably your best guide on this.

If anything **goes wrong**, reputable companies will do their best to compensate on the spot (an extra day if you broke down, a night in a lodge if you didn't make it to a campsite, partial refunds without demur). If your grievance is unresolved, you might want to contact the Kenya Association of Tour Operators (KATO), PO Box 48461, 3rd floor, Hughes Building, Kenyatta Ave, Nairobi ☏02/225570, ⑤218402, ⑥kato@africaonline.co.ke, who can intercede with their members.

Staff relations and tipping

When on your trip, it's important not to take a passive attitude. Although some of the **itinerary** may be fixed, it's not all cast in stone, and daily routines may be altered to suit the clients easily enough if you ask.

As long as they know there will be reasonable **tips** at the end of the trip, most staff will go out of their way to help. Tipping on budget trips, however, can often cause days of argument and misunderstanding between the clients, who are usually expected to organize themselves to give collective gratuities on the last day. Good companies make suggestions in their briefing packs. Something like Ksh1000–1500 per employee per week from the whole group is not excessive and would be greatly appreciated.

Photography

Kenya is immensely photogenic and with any kind of camera you'll get beautiful pictures. If you take photography seriously, you'll probably want a single-lens reflex (SLR) camera and two or three lenses, but remember, these are heavy, relatively fragile and eminently stealable. Except in the game parks (where some kind of telephoto is essential if you want pictures of animals rather than savannah), you don't really need cumbersome lenses. It's often easier and less intrusive to take a small compact and keep your money for extra film.

Whatever you decide to take, **insure** the camera (if ordinary travel insurance won't cover it, check the insurers who advertise in photo magazines), and make sure you have a dust-proof bag to keep it in, as film gets scratched otherwise. Take spare batteries – they can be outrageously expensive in Nairobi, and flashy hyper-automated cameras are completely useless without juice (SLRs in contrast will often work without a battery, it's just the light meter that goes dead). **Film** is no longer especially expensive, but try to bring all you'll need just the same, particularly if you use colour transparency film or black and white. Try to keep it cool by stuffing it inside a sleeping bag, or wrapping it in newspaper. If you're away for some time, posting film home seems a good idea but is still risky, even if registered – better to leave it with a reliable hotel or friend in Nairobi or Mombasa. **Digital cameras** have an obvious advantage in that respect because you can simply email your snaps home. Processing in Kenya has improved with the introduction of automatic machines (four-hour service is not uncommon), and is not particularly expensive, but be aware that even machines can screw up your film, especially when mounting slides. A few places in Nairobi have a decent enough reputation (see p.149).

Subjects

As for subjects, **animal photography** is a question of patience and not taking endless pictures of nothing happening; if you can't get close enough, don't waste your film. While taking photos, try keeping both eyes open and, in a vehicle, always turn off the engine.

The question of **photographing people** is more prickly. Though most people are amazingly tolerant of the camera's harassment, sensitivity on your part is essential. The Maasai and Samburu – Kenya's most colourful and photographed people – are usually prepared to do a deal (at Monopoly prices), and in some places you'll even find professional posers making a living at the roadside. If you're motivated to take a lot of pictures of people, you might seriously consider lugging along a Polaroid camera and as much film as you can muster – most people will be very pleased to have a snap. Or you could have a lot of photos of you and your family printed up with your address on the back, which should at least raise a few laughs when you try the exchange.

One thing is certain: if you won't accept that some kind of **interaction and exchange** are warranted, you won't get many pictures. Taking the subject's name and address and sending a print when you get home is an option that some people prefer, but it's less popular with subjects who look on the photo call as work and have

fixed the rates they're prepared to accept. Blithely aiming at strangers won't make you any friends and it may well get you into trouble.

On the subject of sensitivity, it's a bad idea to take pictures of anything that could be construed as strategic, including any military or police building, prisons, airports, harbours, bridges and His Excellency the President.

Technical business

Getting (slightly) **technical**, use skylight or UV filters to block haze and protect your lens and yellow filters for dramatic black and white shots. Take several speeds of film (don't let anyone tell you it's unnecessary to have fast film) in rolls of 20 or 24, so you don't get stuck at the wrong speed too long. And, if you feel it's worth taking a camera bag of lenses for your SLR, then it really makes no sense not to take two camera bodies as well – less lens changing, more film speeds available, and you could shoot the same subject in (say) fast black and white and slow, fine-grain colour.

Early morning and late afternoon are the **best times** for photography. At midday, with the sun almost directly overhead, the light is flat and everything is lost in a formless glare. In the morning and evening, the contrast between light and shade can be huge, so be careful to expose for the subject and not the general scene. And, if you are used to photographing mainly white people, then remember, as you negotiate for your next Maasai masterpiece, that black skin usually needs a little more exposure (think of people as always back-lit); a half stop is normally enough. The rainy seasons are rewarding, especially when the first rains break: months of dust are settled, greenery sprouts in a few hours, the country has a lush, bold sheen, and the sky is magnificent.

The environment and ethical tourism

In many African countries, Kenya included, tourism plays an important part in maintaining indigenous cultures, and also provides an invaluable source of foreign currency. However, along with these benefits, there are also some irreversible and detrimental consequences.

Tourism's growth in Kenya has been spectacular, from 36,000 visitors in 1955 to over half a million in 2000. It has been a boon for the economy, but with serious and potentially disruptive effects environmentally, socially, culturally and economically. Environmental and land degradation as a direct consequence of tourists is evident in Maasai Mara, Samburu and Amboseli, as well as on the beaches.

Local issues have been covered throughout this book. If you're at all concerned about the impact of tourism or environmental matters, get in touch with the organizations mentioned in the text, or the ones listed below. Read also the boxes "Responsible snorkelling, diving and fishing" (p.443) for the coast, and "Environmental concerns" for information on game parks (p.389).

Forests and land-grabbing

The rate of clearance of Kenya's remaining areas of indigenous **forest** is alarming, worsening the problem of soil erosion, and the consequent siltation of lakes, rivers and estuaries. Illegal "land grabbing" made headlines for much of 1998 and 1999 and sparked off countless demonstrations, legal moves and protests. The government responded with the 1999 Environment Conservation Management Act, which protects forest areas that are officially gazetted, and allows members of the public to oppose degazettement. This did not stop the government in early 2001 from announcing the excision of 67,000 hectares from gazetted forests for development, resulting in widespread protests by environmentalists, and attempts in the High Court to halt the move. The area most affected by the latest move is the Mau Forest in the Rift Valley (see p.267), but areas also threat-

ened by land grabbing and illegal logging include Kakamega Forest (pp.354–360), parts of Mount Kenya Forest with its near extinct camphor plant, the coastal mangroves, and Arabuko-Sokoko Forest (pp.523–526).

Contacts

African Wildlife Foundation ☎ 02/710367 or 710369–70. A long-running study of Amboseli's elephants. Produces many films on the subject.

Centre for Environmentally Responsible Tourism (CERT) PO Box 4246, London SE21 7ZE ⓦ www.c-e-r-t.org. Lobbies to educate tour operators and tourists on a sensitive approach to travel, focusing on immediate practical ways in which the environment can be protected.

East African Wildlife Society PO Box 20110 ☎ 02/574145, Ⓕ 570335, Ⓔ eawls@elci.sasa.unon.org. Influential group, strongly involved in the movement to ban the ivory trade (achieved 1989), and remaining active in other areas, recently raising awareness about forest and mangrove protection. Individual membership, which entitles you to annual subscription of their quarterly magazine, *Swara*, and use of their library, costs £35 (£45 airmail) in the UK, $50 in the US.

Ecotourism Society of Kenya PO Box 10146 Nairobi ☎ 02/225570 or 331286, Ⓕ 218402, ⓦ www.esok.org. A Kenyan organization working to promote sustainable tourism that contributes to rather than destroys local communities and the environment.

Friends of Conservation Kenya: PO Box 74901 Nairobi ☎ 02/442048 or 442075, Ⓕ 332106; UK: 1st floor, 22 Chapter St, London SW1P 4NP ☎ 020/7559 4790, Ⓕ 7559 4792; USA: 1520 Kensington Rd, Suite 201, Oak Brook, IL 60521 ☎ 630/954 3388, Ⓕ 954 1016. Concerns itself with raising awareness of the detrimental consequences of tourism in eastern and southern Africa. In return for membership (£10/$15 student/senior citizen; £15/$25 and up for adults), you receive their newsletter, *Survivor*.

The Friends of Nairobi National Park PO Box 42976 Nairobi ☎ 02/607974, ⓕ 600324. Group which strives to keep the migratory routes to the park open, and aims to raise awareness among Nairobi citizens about the park. Members (adults $25, students $5, families $50) receive a monthly newsletter.

Greenbelt Movement Adams Arcade, Ngong Rd, PO Box 67545 Nairobi ☎ 02/603867 or 571223. The movement attempts to stop the illegal expropriation and development of public land, notably the controversial Karura Forest development saga.

The Kenya Forests Working Group (KFWG) ☎ & ⓕ 02/571335. Concerned with conserving and managing Kenya's forests, and has a "Forest Hotline" for up-to-date information on current issues.

Kenya Tourism Concern PO Box 22449 Nairobi ☎ 02/535850, ⓕ 557092. Kenyan sister organization to the UK's Tourism Concern.

Partners in Responsible Tourism P.O. Box 237, San Francisco, CA 94104–0237 ☎ 415/675 0420, ⓦ www.pirt.org/about.html. An organization of individuals and travel companies promoting responsible tourism to minimize harm to the environment and local cultures. Their website features a "Traveler's Code for Traveling Responsibly".

Save the Rhino 16 Winchester Walk, London SE1 9AQ ☎ 020/7357 7474, ⓦ www.savetherhino.org.

Tourism Concern Stapleton House, 277–281 Holloway Rd, London N7 8HN ☎ 020/7753 3330, ⓦ www.tourismconcern.org.uk. Campaigns for the rights of local people to be consulted in tourist developments affecting their lives, and produces a quarterly magazine of news and articles.

Tusk Trust 19 Amner Rd, London SW11 6AA ☎ 020/7978 7100, ⓦ www.tusk.org. Organization aimed at conserving the wildlife of Africa.

Worldwide Fund for Nature (WWF) Panda House, Weyside Park, Godalming, Surrey GU7 1XR ☎ 01483/426444.

Peoples, languages and religions

Whether called peoples, ethnic groups or tribes (the term still used officially and in casual conversation), Kenyans have a multiplicity of racial and cultural origins. Distinctions would be simple if similarities in physical appearance were shared by those who speak the same language and share a common culture. But "tribes" have never been closed units, and appearance, speech and culture have always overlapped. Families, for instance, often contain members of different tribes, though tradition still dictates whether an individual's "tribe" is determined through their father's line, or through their mother's brother's line.

In the last fifty years, **ethnic identities** have broken down as broader class, political and national ones have emerged. However, a worrying recent development, spurred on by the chaotic general elections of 1992 and 1997, has been the organizing and splitting of political parties along ethnic lines, at the same time as an upsurge in violence. Although small on an African scale, the killings and attacks, mostly in remoter parts of the Rift Valley, pose a much greater problem nationally – the potential disintegration of the nation.

Languages

The most enduring ethnic distinction is **language**. A person's "mother tongue" is still important as an index of social identity, and a tribe is best defined as people sharing a common first language. However, in the towns and among affluent families, language is increasingly unimportant. Many people speak three languages (their own, Swahili and English) or even four if they have mixed parentage. And for a few, English has become a first language (and is, along with Swahili – or Kiswahili as it's correctly known – the offical language of the country).

The history and culture of the main language groups in each region are covered throughout the book.

African language groups in Kenya

What follows is, broadly speaking, the breakdown of Kenya's language groups into separate ethnic identities. You'll find variations on these spellings, and inconsistencies in the use of prefixes (ie Kamba instead of Akamba, Agikuyu instead of Kikuyu, and so on).

Bantu-speaking

Western Bantu Luhya, Gusii, Kuria.
Central Bantu Akamba, Kikuyu, Embu, Meru, Mbere, Tharaka.
Coastal Bantu Swahili, Mijikenda, Segeju, Pokomo, Taita, Taveta.

Nilotic-speaking

Lake-River Nilotic Luo.
Plains Nilotic Maasai and Samburu (Maa-speakers), Turkana, Teso, Njemps, Elmolo.
Highland Nilotic Kalenjin group (Nandi and its dialects), Marakwet, Pokot, Tugen, Kipsigis, Elkony.

Cushitic-speaking

Southern Cushitic Boni.
Eastern Cushitic Somali, Rendille, Orma, Boran, Gabbra ("Oromo" is often used to describe all these language groups except the Somali).

Names and groups

Books continue to use various unwieldy terms. **Bantu** and **Nilotic** are language groups (like Indo-European or Semitic) and, restricted to a linguistic sense, are fair enough. But Hamitic, which still pops up occasionally, is almost meaningless and hedged with racist overtones. "Hamitic influence" has been credited with many technological, social and political innovations in the past. The Biblical origins of the word give it away. It reflects the early European presumption that lighter-skinned people with thinner lips and straighter noses were more intelligent than other Africans. The origins of

67

these people in northeast Africa and their implied association with the well-springs of Mediterranean civilization were further "evidence" of this. The term "Nilo-hamitic" (often used to refer to the Maasai and other pastoralists admired by the Europeans) just confuses the issue further. It implies the cross-cutting cultural, linguistic and racial overlays that most Kenyans have inherited, without abandoning the idea of racially superior influences from the north.

In terms of appearance, members of some ethnic groups have more "Negroid" (wider, flatter) features, while members of others have more "Caucasoid" (sharper, thinner) ones. Such variations obviously indicate different ancestry, but have little to do with people's language or culture, a fact which makes it plainly obvious, as you travel around the country, just how far off the mark the old racist doctrines really were.

Kenya's largest ethnic group are the Kikuyu, based in the central region, who make up about 20 percent of the population, followed by the Luo from the Nyanza region around Kisumu, who are around 14 percent. The Luhya of western Kenya are 13 percent, followed by the Akamba from the eastern region around Machakos who form 11 percent of the population, and President Moi's people, the Kalenjin from the Rift Valley, also 11 percent. Many tourists are surprised that, among smaller ethnic groups, only about 1.4 percent of the population are Maasai.

Apart from indigenous ethnic groups, who make up about 99 percent of the population, Kenya has a considerable and diverse **Asian** population – perhaps over 100,000 – most of whom live in Nairobi, Mombasa, Kisumu and Nakuru. Descendants in part of the labourers brought over to build the railway, they also number many whose parents and grandparents came in its wake, to trade and set up businesses. And some families, notably on the coast, have lived in Kenya for centuries. Predominantly Punjabi and Gujarati speakers from northwest India and Pakistan, they are overwhelmingly dominant in business. There's a dispersed Christian Goan community, too, identified by their Portuguese surnames, who tend to have less formalized relations with other Kenyans. And a persistent, but diminishing Arab-speaking community remains on the coast.

Lastly, there are still an estimated 34,000 **European** residents – a surprisingly motley crew from British ex-servicemen to Italian aristocrats – scattered through the highlands and the rest of the country, some four thousand of whom hold Kenyan citizenship. Some maintain a scaled-down version of the old planter's life, and a few still hold senior civil service positions. Increasingly, though, the community is turning to the tourist industry for a more secure future.

Religion

In the matter of **religion**, the majority of "up-country" Kenyans have converted to Christianity, with most people on the coast professing Islam. Indigenous religion is rapidly disappearing, but it holds on in remoter areas.

Varieties of Catholicism and Protestantism are dominant in the highlands and westwards, and are increasingly pervasive elsewhere. In the Rift Valley and the far west, especially towards Lake Victoria, there are many minor Christian sects and churches – over a thousand denominations – often based around the teaching of local prophets and preachers.

Broad-based, non-fundamentalist **Sunni Islam** dominates the coast and the northeast, and is the fastest growing religion in the country. Many towns have several mosques (or dozens on the coast), but one usually serves as the focal Friday mosque for the whole community. The Aga Khan's **Ismaili** sect is an influential Asian constituency with powerful business interests. **Hindu** and **Sikh** temples are found in most large towns, and there are adherents of **Jainism** and the **Bahai** faith, too.

Indigenous religion (mostly based around the idea of a supreme god and intercession between the living and the spirit worlds by deceased ancestors) survives as an inclusive belief system only in the remotest areas of northern Kenya, among the remaining Okiek (or Ndorobo) hunter-gatherers in a very few forests, and among pastoralists like the Maasai. But, while it is continually under threat from Christian missionaries, its influence over the lives of many nominally Christian or Muslim Kenyans remains powerful.

Etiquette in Muslim areas

Islamic moral strictures tend to be generously interpreted. On the coast, it's always best to **dress** in loose-fitting long sleeves and skirts or trousers in the towns, but shorts and T-shirts won't get you into trouble. People are far too polite to admonish strangers. Malindi, in particular, is very relaxed. Lamu calls more for *kikoi* and *kanga* wraps for both sexes and, because it's so small, more consideration for local feelings. Suitably dressed and hatted men, and often women, can enter **mosques**. Few are very grand, however, and you rarely miss much by staying outside.

Crime and personal safety

There's no denying that petty crime is a problem in Kenya, and you have a far higher chance of being a victim in touristy areas, where pickings are richer. It's important to bear in mind, however, that the number of "attack on tourist" stories that appear in the world press is relative to the large numbers who visit the country each year, most of whom enjoy their trip with no difficulties, and the hundreds of journalists based in Nairobi. For advice on wildlife safety, see p.46.

Avoiding trouble

After **arriving** by air for the first time, an incredible number of people get robbed during their first day or two in Nairobi, before they've had chance to get used to the pace and dangers of the place. You should at first be acutely conscious of your belongings: never leave anything unguarded even for five seconds, never take out cameras or other valuables unless absolutely necessary, and be careful of where you walk, at least until you've dropped off your luggage and you're settled in somewhere. It's hard not to look like a tourist, but try to **dress** like a local – short-sleeved shirt, slacks or skirt and sunglasses – and try not to wear anything brand new. **Sunglasses** make avoiding unwanted eye contact easier. Most importantly, don't carry a **bag**, particularly not the little daypack over your shoulder which will virtually identify you as a tourist. See also the section on security in the Nairobi chapter (p.90).

The only substantial risks outside Nairobi are down at the coast (where valuables often disappear from the beach or occasionally get grabbed), in the other big towns (Nakuru and, to a lesser extent, Kisumu), and in some of the game parks – Samburu and Maasai Mara have had a number of incidents in recent years.

If you're **driving**, it's never a good idea to leave even a locked car unguarded if it has anything of value in it. In towns, there's usually someone who will volunteer to guard it for you for a tip (Ksh20–50 is enough).

All of this isn't meant to induce paranoia, but if you flaunt the trappings of wealth where there's urban poverty, somebody will want to remove them. There's always less risk in leaving your valuables in a locked hotel room or – judiciously – with the management, than in taking them with you. Don't wear dangling earrings or any kind of chain or necklace, and even a cheap wrist watch is tempting. If you clearly have nothing on you, you're unlikely to feel, or be, threatened. In Nairobi, the rush hour at dusk is probably the worst time, but it's a good idea to be alert getting off a night bus early in the morning, too. There are always more pickpockets about at the end of the month too, when people are carrying their pay packet.

When you have to **carry money**, put it in several places if possible. A money belt tucked into your trousers or skirt is invisible and thus usually secure for traveller's cheques, passport and large amounts of cash. Put the rest – what you'll need for your day/walk/night out – in a pocket or somewhere more accessible. Somewhat perversely, you're safer with at least some money to hand, as few muggers will believe you have nothing on you.

Cons and scams

Doping scams seem to be a persistent problem, with individuals on different public transport routes managing to drug tourists and relieve them of their belongings. Don't accept any food or drink on public transport, even at the risk of causing offence.

Approaches in the street from "schoolboys" with sponsorship forms (only primary education is free, and even then, books, uniforms, even furniture have to be bought) and from "refugees" with long stories are not uncommon and probably best shrugged off, even though some, unfortunately, may be genuine.

One scam, almost "traditional" by now, and surprisingly successful to judge by the number of tourists who fall for it, relies entirely on people's belief in the paranoid republic. It involves an approach by a "student", followed by a request for a small sum of money, or sometimes just someone who engages you for a chat and claims to be a Sudanese or Somalian refugee. Shortly after you part company, a group of heavies surround you and claim to be undercover police, interested in the discussion you've been having with that "terrorist", or whatever, and a large fine is demanded, or they may want to "arrest" you and then demand money with menaces. You can ask to see ID, or just tell them to go to hell – such aggressions are never the real thing. Also beware of people offering to change money on the street, especially in Nairobi – it's usually a trick to get you down a dark alley where you can be divested of your cash.

A treat for Nairobi motorists is a small boy popping up and slapping you in the face as you get out after parking. As you make to go after him in outrage, his friends grab what they can from the car. Other car tricks are described in the sections on Nakuru (p.251) and Isiolo (p.618) – where they seem most popular.

Muggings

If you get **mugged**, the usual advice applies: don't resist as knives and guns are occasionally carried. It will be over in an instant and you're unlikely to be hurt. But the hassles, and worse, that gather when you try to do anything about it make it imperative not to let it happen in the first place. Thieves caught red-handed are usually mobbed – often killed – so avoid the usual Kenyan response of shouting "Thief!" ("Mwizi!" in Swahili), unless you're ready to intercede instantly once you've retrieved your belongings.

Usually you'll have no chance to catch the thief, and the first reaction is to go to the **police**. Unless you've lost a lot of money (and cash is virtually irretrievable) or irreplaceable property, however, think twice

---

Would-be helpers

It's very easy to fall prey to **misunderstandings** in your relations with people (usually boys and young men) who offer their services as guides, helpers or "facilitators" of any kind. You should absolutely never assume anything is being done out of simple kindness. It may well be but, if it isn't, you must expect to pay something. If you have any suspicion, it's invariably best to confront the matter head on at an early stage and either apologize for the offence caused by the suggestion, or agree a price. What you must never do, as when bargaining, is enter into an unspoken contract and then break it by refusing to pay for the service. If you're being bugged by someone whose help you don't need, just let them know you can't pay anything for their trouble. It may not make you a friend, but it always works and it's better than a row and recriminations.

about doing this. They rarely do something for nothing – even stamping an **insurance form** will probably cost you, though you will need it to claim – and secondly, you should consider the ramifications if you and they set off to try and catch the culprits. This kind of scenario, with you in the back of a police car expected to point out the thief in the crowds, is a complete waste of time. And, whatever you do, never agree to act as a decoy in the hope that the same thing will happen again in front of a police ambush. Police shootings take place all the time and you may prefer not to be the cause of a cold-blooded murder.

If you have to visit the police in Nairobi, go to the main police station (marked on the map on p.108), rather than the smaller posts and offices.

Dealing with the police

If you have official business with the police (recognizable by their blue uniforms), then politeness, smiles and handshakes always help. If you're expected to give a **bribe** – *chai* is the usual word for it, which means "tea" or *Kitu Kidogo*, meaning "something small" – wait for it to be hinted at and haggle over it as you would any payment; the equivalent of a dollar or so is often enough to oil small wheels. Be aware, of course, that bribery is illegal, no matter what the behaviour of Kenyan politicians. If you know you've done nothing wrong and are not in a rush, refusing a bribe will only cost a short delay until the policeman gives up on you and tries another potential source of income.

In **unofficial dealings**, the police, especially in remote outposts, can go out of their way to help you with food, transport or accommodation. Try to reciprocate. Police salaries are low – no more than a few thousand shillings a month – and they rely on unofficial income to get by. Only a brand new police force and realistic salaries could alter a situation which is now entrenched.

Common ways of exciting police interest are staggering around a city late at night, and drug possession. The first needs lots of humble pie and nothing more, the latter carries a possible long prison sentence, though you may be lucky and be given a large fine and deportation – but don't expect to buy yourself out of this kind of trouble. **Driving**

offences are less serious, though being stopped at the fairly frequent road checkpoints is becoming increasingly common, with the sole purpose of finding fault to elicit a bribe. Insist on a receipt before handing over any money – if he refuses, you can talk yourself out of it. It's worth knowing that some forces have speed-trap radar equipment which they set up outside towns. Drive with caution as speed limits are often vague.

Drugs

Though officially **illegal**, marijuana (*bhang* or *bangi*) is widely cultivated and smoked, and is remarkably cheap. However, with the authorities making efforts to control it and penalties of up to ten years for possession (life and a million-shilling fine for trafficking), its use is not advisable. Official busts result in a heavy fine and deportation at the very least, and quite often a prison sentence, with little sympathy from your embassy. Heroin is becoming a major problem on the coast, but possession of that, or of anything harder than marijuana will get you in a lot worse trouble if you're caught. *Miraa* (qat), a herbal stimulant, is legal and widely available, especially in Meru, Nairobi, Mombasa and in the north. It's traditionally used by people in drought-prone areas, as it suppresses hunger. It also keeps you awake all night, and so is favoured by bus, lorry and matatu drivers. Local police chiefs sometimes order crackdowns on its transport, and it is illegal in Tanzania and many Western countries (see p.200 for more on *miraa*).

Unseemly behaviour

Be warned that failure to observe the following points of **Kenyan etiquette** can get you arrested or put you in a position where you may be obliged to pay a bribe. Stand in cinemas and on other occasions when the national anthem is playing. Stand still when the national flag is being raised or lowered in your field of view. Don't take photos of the flag or His Excellency the President (often seen on state occasions in Nairobi). Pull off the road completely when scores of motorcycle outriders appear, then get out and stand by your vehicle (for it is he). It's also a criminal offence to tear or deface a banknote of any denomination, and to urinate in a public place.

Women travellers

Women travellers will be glad to find that machismo, in its fully fledged Latin varieties, is rare in Kenya and male egos are usually softened by reserves of humour. Women's groups flourish across the country, but are concerned more with improvement of incomes, education, health and nutrition than social or political emancipation, though this is changing.

Travelling alone

Women, whether travelling alone or together, may come across occasional **persistent hasslers**, but seldom much worse. **Drinking** in bars unaccompanied by men, you can expect a lot of male attention, as you can in many other situations. Universal rules apply: if you suspect ulterior motives, turn down all offers and stonily refuse to converse, though you needn't fear expressing your anger if that's how you feel. You will, eventually, be left alone. Really obnoxious individuals are usually on their own, fortunately. These tactics are hardly necessary except on the coast, and then particularly in Lamu.

Travelling on your own you'll usually be welcomed with generous hospitality. On **public transport** a single woman traveller causes quite a stir and fellow passengers don't want to see you badly treated. Women get offers of **accommodation** in people's homes more often than male travellers. And, if you're staying in less reputable hotels, there'll often be female company – employees, family, residents – to look after you.

The way you look and behave get noticed by everyone and they're more important if you don't appear to have a male escort. Your **head** and everything from **waist to ankles** are the sensitive zones, particularly in Islamic regions. Long, loose hair is seen as extraordinarily provocative; doubly so if blonde. Pay attention to these areas by keeping your hair fairly short or tied up (or by wearing a scarf) and wearing long skirts or, at a pinch, very baggy long pants. If you find it's too hot to wear a **bra**, it's unlikely to bother people. If you'll be travelling much on rough roads, however, you'll need a bra for support. Seriously.

Women's rights in Kenya

Women in Kenya are becoming increasingly vocal in their call for political representation at local and national levels. The government-sponsored Maendeleo ya Wanawake Organization (MYWO) started to help women at a very basic level forty years ago. It now encourages economic independence and, with a nominal annual membership fee, almost every woman in Kenya can belong. The umbrella group teaches basic literacy, family planning and nutrition and is also working hard to abolish the practice of ritual **female genital mutilation**, "female circumcision". This is carried out as a rite of passage on an estimated fifty percent of Kenyan girls, and is more prevalent in some ethnic groups (the Kisii and the Maasai for example) than others. Unsurprisingly, it is more common in rural areas and among uneducated people than in cities and among those with schooling. Kenya is a signatory to the UN's Human Rights Convention, which proscribes genital mutilation, and the government promised in 1990 to ban the practice, but a motion calling for its prohibition was heavily defeated in parliament in 1996, and it remains legal. Womens' groups are meanwhile trying to persuade rural communities to accept a mutilation-free "alternative rite of passage", with some limited success.

Kenya is also still used as something of a contraceptive testing ground, with less stringent rules on over-the-counter drugs than many countries. Depo-provera, high-level oestrogen pills and the Dalkon shield have all been foisted on Kenyan women.

For more information and contacts, get in touch with MYWO (Maendeleo House, Monrovia St, Nairobi PO Box 44412

02/222095, (F) 225390), or the much more independent National Council of Women of Kenya (PO Box 43741 Nairobi, 02/224634, (F) 335851, (W) www.ncwk.org/), headed by Wangari Maathai, also the founder of the Greenbelt Movement (see Contexts, p.662).

Travelling with children

Wherever you go, the reaction of local people to families and their children is exceptionally welcoming. However, if you're considering taking young kids, ask yourself if you can really be bothered with all the hassle. It's a good start if they're already enchanted with the idea of Africa and its wildlife.

The following is aimed principally at families with babies and under-fives. For the under-fives, Kenya is a mixture of fun – in the pool, on the beach, with other kids – and tedium – in the car or plane, on a game drive, in a restaurant.

Children's health

Health issues figure most prominently in most people's minds. With the exception of malaria, however, you can discount fears about your children getting tropical diseases in Kenya. Remember how many healthy second-generation expatriate children have been brought up there (the biggest health problem for Kenyan children is poverty).

It can, however, be very difficult to persuade small children to take **malaria pills**, under any guise. Breast-feeding babies will be as protected as their mother. With toddlers you may have to choose between ramming pills down their throats or giving in and risking it. In the latter case, up-country Kenya is much safer territory than the coast, but you should be extremely careful to cover them with Deet repellent early each evening and be sure they sleep under secure nets (take a small net for babies). For more on malaria, see p.27.

You can buy **nappies/diapers** in Kenya, but they are expensive (around Ksh700 for 36), so bring your own supply for a short stay. **Baby foods** are also available in large supermarkets, but here you'll have few problems if you're staying in hotels as there's usually a good variety of fresh food and staff who, given some warning, are happy to prepare it to infants' tastes.

Unless your time is to be spent exclusively on the coast, bring some **warm clothing** for up-country mornings and evenings. Temperatures in some parts drop low and hotels are not heated.

Probably the most important health concern is the **sun**. On the equator, even when the altitude keeps temperatures down, the effect of thirty minutes' ultra-violet on delicate skin can be severe. Keep them thoroughly smothered in factor 40 and insist they wear hats. Children should also wear T-shirts when swimming, and especially if snorkelling. Sunglasses, too, are a good idea, even for babies, to reduce the intense glare – you can always find little novelty ones that will fit. And of course, make sure they drink plenty of clean **water**.

Travelling

Air travel with under-twos (who get no seat for their ten percent fares) can be a nightmare. Make every possible effort to get bulkhead seats and a bassinet (hanging cradle) for a baby. These requests should be a priority in your plans. When you reconfirm 48 hours before flying, double-check you still have them. If you have lively children who won't easily settle, consider the simple drugging method: trimeprazine can be obtained on prescription and they'll sleep right through the flight and wake up refreshed.

For a young family, going on a group safari (whether organized from home as part of a package or booked in Kenya) is probably not on. **Renting a car** is quite feasible, however, and gives you the flexibility and privacy you need for changing nappies, toilet stops and so on. For babies and children too small for seat belts, you'll need a car seat which, if you have the right model, also works as an all-purpose carrier, pool-side recliner and picnic throne.

If you have a light, easily collapsible **buggy**, bring it. Many hotels and lodges have long paths from the central public areas to the rooms or cottages. A **child-carrier** backpack is another very useful accessory.

For flying with all this baggage, remember you have a full luggage allowance for each passenger with a seat.

Safaris and hotels

On **safari** with young children, your driving time is more likely to be spent in getting from one lodge to the next than in purposeful game drives, but if the children are old enough to enjoy spotting the animals, make sure they have their own **binoculars**. Some **parks** are more child-friendly than others. Nairobi National Park is great (if you can

divert their attention from the planes landing at the airport) and Lake Nakuru is a hit as well, as distances are small and the animals close. Equally, Amboseli's small size and the presence of large numbers of elephants make it popular with younger children.

Most **hotels**, lodges and tented camps do not specifically exclude children of any age, but a number of organized tours have a minimum age of 7, while several of the more exclusive tented camps and all four of the "tree hotels" have minimum ages (restrictions are noted in our reviews). The **coast hotels** are on sandy beaches facing a warm sea, safely protected by the reef, and particularly suitable family hotels are mentioned in the text.

Very few places make provision for **babysitters**. The management can usually find a local woman to come in, given a few hours' notice, but they tend to leave the question of payment up to you – Ksh500 for a full evening is the most you should ever pay. Alternatively, if the children are asleep, speak to the restaurant manager and arrange for an *askari* (night watch) to sit outside.

Swimming pools, focus of attention for most children, are only sure to be warm on the coast. In the higher, up-country regions, including Nairobi, the invariably unheated pools are always chilly, which can be a big disappointment for keen splashers.

Gay travellers

Sex between men is illegal in Kenya, and attitudes to gay life are rather hard to pin down. While there is no gay scene as such, male homosexuality is an accepted undercurrent on the coast, where it finds most room for expression in Lamu and Malindi, and to a small extent in Nairobi. The Lake Victoria region has a fairly relaxed attitude, too. Msenge is Swahili for gay man. Homosexuality is still largely a taboo subject in Kenya, lesbianism doubly so, and many Kenyans take the attitude that it's a foreign, un-African practice. Recently, however, more gay Kenyan men have been making themselves known, usually by wearing high-fashion clothes. Lesbians, on the other hand, remain invisible.

Contacts for gay travellers

You'll find a small amount of information on the male gay scene in Kenya in the *Spartacus Gay Guide*, available in most bookshops.

Australia and New Zealand

Gay Travel ☎1800/GAY TRAVEL or 1800/429 8728, ⓦwww.gaytravel.com. Internet-based firm offering an all-gay Kenya safari.
Parkside Travel 70 Glen Osmond Rd, Parkside, SA 5063 ☎08/8274 1222 or 1800/888 501, ⓔhwtravel@senet.com.au. Gay travel agent associated with local branch of Hervey World Travel; all aspects of gay and lesbian travel worldwide.

Kenya

Promote Kenya ☎0123/31951 or 21232, ⓕ31952, ⓦwww.kenya-travel.com. Gay-friendly company offering tailor-made safaris and beach holidays.

USA and Canada

Damron Company ☎1-800/462 6654 or 415/255-0404, ⓦwww.damron.com. Publisher of *Damron Accommodations*, which provides detailed listings of over 1000 accommodations for gays and lesbians worldwide.
Ferrari Publications ☎1-800/962 2912 or 602/863 2408, ⓦwww.ferrariguides.com. Publishes *Ferrari Gay Travel A to Z*, a worldwide gay and lesbian guide; *Inn Places*, a worldwide accommodation guide; the guides *Men's Travel in Your Pocket* and *Women's Travel in Your Pocket*, and the quarterly *Ferrari Travel Report*. Their website features a page on Kenya.

Travellers with disabilities

Although by no means easy for people with disabilities, Kenya does not pose insurmountable problems. While there is little government involvement in improving access, tourist industry staff – not to mention passers-by – are usually prepared to help whenever necessary. For wheelchair-users and those who find stairs hard to manage, many hotels have ground-floor rooms; a number on the coast have ramped access walks to public areas and adapted rooms; and larger hotels in Nairobi have elevators. Safari vehicles can usually manage wheelchair-users.

Getting there

British Airways and Kenya Airways offer the only non-stop **flights** from London to Kenya (note that Kenya Airways "direct" flights to Mombasa require a plane change to a domestic Kenya Airways flight in Nairobi). These airlines, together with KLM, are the best airlines for disabled passengers. They're sometimes more costly, but less physically demanding than the cheapies. If you're flying by charter, you'll arrive at Mombasa, which has very basic facilities, but at least no steps (other than those coming off the plane) or long distances to negotiate.

From **North America to Europe**, Virgin and Air Canada come out top in terms of disability awareness (and seating arrangements) and may be worth contacting first for any information they can provide.

If you're looking for an all-in **tour**, contact the upmarket Kenya specialists Abercrombie & Kent (address in the "Getting There" section on pp.12, 14 and 16) who have some experience in carrying disabled passengers on their regular itineraries.

In Kenya

Attitudes to disabled people are generally good – there are always willing hands to help you over any obstacle. All the international-class **hotels** in Nairobi have elevators, as do several of the cheaper places (details in the text). **Getting around** the city, however, to do some of its limited sightseeing or to book safaris, is difficult in a wheelchair. While distances are short, there is little ramping of pedestrian areas and drivers are not used to wheelchairs crossing the road. The capacious London-style taxi cabs, however, are a boon.

Safari vehicles have superb springing, but taking a pressure cushion is a wise precaution. Even then, off-road trips can be very arduous, especially on the awful roads in and around Maasai Mara, where flying in is recommended. It's perhaps better to use Nairobi as a base, and go on one of the many one-day excursions, to Nakuru, Naivasha or the Outspan near Mount Kenya for example. If you are determined, however, any of the luxury lodges and tented camps should be accessible, with help, making a proper safari quite feasible, especially if you fly. One or two places even have baths (as well as showers), and are mentioned in the guide. Only on the most adventurous trips, with temporary camps set up in the bush, and long-drop toilets, would wheelchair-users really have problems.

The all-night Nairobi–Mombasa **sleeper train** sounds improbable but, again, is possible. On this, though, if completely wheelchair-dependant, you would have to be carried – with some difficulty – from your cabin to the toilets and dining car, as the corridors are very narrow. Your wheelchair would go in the luggage van, too, so expect a delay in retrieving it on arrival. With the exception of the "luxury" coaches plying between Nairobi and Mombasa, other public transport in Kenya is not at all wheelchair-friendly.

Contacts for travellers with disabilities

UK and Ireland

Disability Action Group UK ☎028/9049 1011.

Provides information about access for disabled travellers abroad.

Holiday Care UK ☎01293/774535, Minicom ☎01293/776943, ⓦ www.holidaycare.org.uk. Provides free lists of accessible accommodation. Information on financial help for holidays available.

Irish Wheelchair Association Ireland ☎01/833 8241, ⓕ833 3873, ⓔiwa@iol.ie. Useful information provided about travelling abroad with a wheelchair.

Tripscope UK ☎08457/585641, ⓦwww.justmobility.co.uk/tripscope, ⓔtripscope@cableinet.co.uk. This registered charity provides a national telephone information service offering free advice on UK and international transport for those with a mobility problem.

USA and Canada

Access-Able ⓦwww.access-able.com. Online resource for travellers with disabilities.

Directions Unlimited USA ☎1-800/533 5343 or 914/241 1700. Tour operator specializing in custom tours for people with disabilities

Mobility International USA Voice & TDD ☎541/343 1284, ⓦwww.miusa.org. Information and referral services, access guides, tours and exchange programmes. Annual membership $35 (includes quarterly newsletter).

Society for the Advancement of Travelers with Handicaps (SATH) ☎212/447 7284, ⓦwww.sath.org. Non-profit educational organization that has actively represented travellers with disabilities since 1976.

Wheels Up! ☎1-888/389 4335, ⓦwww.wheelsup.com. Provides discounted airfare, tour and cruise prices for disabled travellers, also publishes a free monthly newsletter and has a comprehensive website.

Australia and New Zealand

ACROD (Australian Council for Rehabilitation of the Disabled) ☎02/6282 4333 or 9743 2699. Provides lists of travel agencies and tour operators for people with disabilities.

Disabled Persons Assembly New Zealand ☎04/801 9100. Resource centre with lists of travel agencies and tour operators for people with disabilities.

Directory

Beggars In touristy parts of Nairobi and Mombasa beggars are fairly common; most are visibly destitute, and many are disabled, lepers or homeless mothers with children. While some have regular pitches, others keep on the move, and all are harassed by the police. Kenyans often give to the same beggar on a regular basis and, of course, to the many Kenyans who are Muslim, alms-giving is a religious requirement, believed to benefit the donor. The hundreds of glue-sniffing boys are a sad development of recent years in most cities and big towns. They're responsible for much of the cities' petty crime, and often pay a swift, final price – if you do want to help them, food is better than money as it cannot be spent on glue, and there are also organizations, in Nairobi particularly, which are dedicated to rehabilitating street kids and always welcome donations.

Body language You are likely to notice a widespread and unselfconscious ease with close physical contact, especially on the coast. Male visitors may need to get used to holding hands with strangers as they're shown around the guesthouse, or guided down the street, and, on public transport, to strangers' hands and limbs draped naturally wherever is most comfortable — which can include your legs or shoulders. Be aware of the left hand rule: traditionally the left hand is reserved for unhygienic acts and the right for eating and touching, or passing things to others. Like many "rules" it's very often broken, at which times you have to avoid thinking about it. Unless you want a serious confrontation, never point with your finger. It's equivalent to an obscene gesture. For similar reasons, beckoning is done with the palm down, not up.

Books Less than fifty percent of Kenyans are literate, but books and reading material have a high profile. Bookstores in Nairobi, Mombasa and in the tourist hotels have imported paperback selections. Locally printed books are sometimes very cheap, and provide insights into Kenyan life you wouldn't otherwise find. Secondhand book stalls are often worth looking at, too. Books by Kenyan and other African authors are much cheaper in Kenya than they would be at home, and Kenya has some fine authors writing in English. For suggestions on reading matter, see pp.686–699 of Contexts.

Clothes Take loose cotton clothes, comfortable sandals (or suede shoes or boots for the highlands), plus at least one really warm sweater or, better still, a soft-lined jacket with pockets. (See the "Mount Kenya" section, p.180, for advice on what you need at high altitudes.) And, even if you're on a shoestring, take some nicer clothes to wear in lodges; access is often difficult for the ragged.

Contraceptives Condoms are available from town pharmacies and supermarkets, and are sometimes even dispensed free in hotels. Family planning clinics in most main towns are helpful (see Nairobi and Mombasa "Listings", pp.145 and 471) and will sometimes provide them and – with a prescription – oral contraceptives, free or for a small charge. But it's far wiser to bring all you'll need. Be aware that oral contraceptives may be rendered ineffective if you go down with a dose of diarrhoea.

Departure tax When leaving Kenya by air there's a departure tax equivalent to US$20, payable in foreign currency or Kenyan shillings, which most airlines now include in their fare (ask when buying your ticket). If you don't have the right money, change will be given only in Kenyan shillings. Departure tax on domestic flights is Ksh300, again mostly included in the airfare. Neither kind of departure tax is payable for infants.

Electricity Kenya's electricity supply is less and less reliable. As in Britain, it uses square, three-pin plugs on 220–240V (the exceptions are Kisii and some older buildings, which use large round two-pin plugs). Only fancier hotels have outlets or shaver points in the rooms. Australian, New Zealand and European appliances will need an adaptor to fit Kenyan sockets (available in Nairobi from major supermarkets), while North American appliances that work on 110V will also need a transformer.

Emergencies For police, fire and ambulance dial ☎ 999. They take ages to arrive.

Gifts Ballpoint pens and postcards are about the only small items worth taking and can always be given to children, but they encourage begging if just handed out of a truck or minibus window. Off the beaten track, these gifts will be appreciated by many adults, too. If you'll be travelling or staying for some time and really want to prepare, get a large batch of photos of you and your family with your address on the back. You'll get lots of mail.

Greetings and conversation Every contact starts with a greeting. This means a handshake followed by polite enquiries, even as you enter a shop. Traditionally, such exchanges can last a minute or two, and you'll often hear them, performed in a formal manner between two men, especially in rural areas. Long greetings help subsequent negotiations. In English or Swahili you can exchange something like "How are you?" "Fine, How's the day?" "Fine, How's business?" "Fine, How's the family?", "Fine, Thank God". It's usually considered polite, while someone is speaking to you at length, to grunt in the affirmative, or say thank you at short intervals. Breaks in conversation are filled with more greetings. Shaking hands upon meeting and departure is normal between all men present. Women shake hands with each other, but with men only in more sophisticated milieux. Soul brother handshakes and other exotic variations are popular among young men, while a common, very respectful handshake involves clutching your right arm with your left hand as you shake or, in Muslim areas, touching your left hand to your chest when shaking hands. Don't be put off by apparent shiftiness in eye contact, especially if you're talking to someone much younger than you. It's normal for those deferring to others to avoid direct looks. Hissing ("Tsss!") is an ordinary way to attract a stranger's attention, though less common in more sophisticated urban situations. You may get a fair bit of it yourself, and it's quite in order to hiss at the waiter in a restaurant. Finally, answering anything in the negative is often considered impolite. If you're asking questions, don't ask yes-no ones. And try not to phrase things in the negative ("Isn't the bus leaving?") because the answer will often be "Yes (it isn't leaving)".

Laundry There are virtually no launderettes/laundromats in Kenya. Hotels, even cheap ones, often run a laundry service for guests, and you'll easily find people offering the same service (*dobi* in Swahili) in most towns. As *dobis* on street stalls and in cheap hotels do not usually accept underwear however, you may have to wash at least some of your own clothes. Washing powder is easy to buy in small packets, and things dry fast in the sun. Beware of New Blue Omo washing powder, however – it's very strong and wrecks clothes if you use it for long. Don't spread clothes on the ground to dry. They might be infested by the *tumbu* fly, which lays its eggs in them for the larvae to hatch and burrow into your skin.

Place names Place names all over Africa (not just Kenya) are remarkably confusing to outsiders. In some parts, every town or village seems to have a name starting with the same syllable. In the Kenya highlands, you'll find Kiambu, Kikuyu, Kiganjo, Kiserian, Kinangop and so on. Further west you confront Kaptagat, Kapsabet, Kabarnet, Kapsowar. As soon as you detect a problem like this, just get into the habit of "de-stressing" the first syllable and remember the second. A more practical problem all over rural Kenya is the vague use of names to denote a whole district and, at the same time, its nucleus, be it a small town, a village, or just a cluster of corrugated-iron shops and bars. Sometimes there'll be two such focuses. They often move in a matter of a few years, so what looks like a junction town on the map turns out to be away from the road, or in a different place altogether. Ask for the "shopping centre" and you'll usually find the local hive of activity and the place with the name you were looking for.

Prostitution and heterosexual attitudes Although there is a certain amount of ethnic and religious variation in attitudes, sexual mores in Kenya are generally hedonistic and uncluttered. Expressive sexuality is a very obvious part of the social fabric in most communities and female prostitution flourishes almost everywhere, with a remarkable number of cheaper hotels doubling as informal brothels, or at least willingly renting rooms by the hour. There are no signs of any organised sex trade and such prostitution appears to merge seamlessly into casual promiscuity. If you're a man, you're likely to find flirtatious pestering a constant part of the scene, especially if you visit bars and clubs, but you should know that HIV infection rates are extremely high (surveys suggest anything up to nine out of ten Nairobi prostitutes are HIV-positive), and even protected sex is extremely inadvisable. If you're a woman who appears to be unattached to a man, you are likely to receive amateur propositions just about anywhere, but approaches by male prostitutes are rare and confined to the coast, particularly Lamu.

Receipts Petty bureaucracy is deeply engrained in Kenya and you will often be given a hand-written receipt after making the most elementary purchase. If you have cause to doubt that the sum you're being asked to pay is officially sanctioned, however – for example, an obscure entrance fee, or a fee for a guide, or in cases where police try to impose an on-the-spot fine – just ask for a receipt and this will often clarify matters.

Student cards If you qualify, get hold of an International Student Identity Card (ISIC) from student unions or student/youth travel agents. In

Kenya, it's no passport to automatic cheap deals, but you may be able to get a few discounted entry fees if you show it. Note that only American ISIC cards provide automatic basic insurance cover for their holders.

Tampons Available in town chemists but expensive, so bring your own supplies.

Time Kenya is three hours ahead of Greenwich Mean Time (UTC) all year round. It's eight hours ahead of North American Eastern Standard Time, and eleven hours ahead of Pacific Standard Time. Take off an hour from these during summer daylight saving time. Kenya is seven hours behind Sydney, five behind Perth, and nine behind New Zealand; add an hour to these during summer daylight saving time. With slight variations east and west, it gets light at 6am and dark at 6pm. If you're learning Swahili, remember that "Swahili time" runs from dawn to dusk to dawn rather than midnight to midday to midnight. 7am and 7pm are both *saa moja* (one o'clock) while midnight and midday are *saa sita* (six o'clock). It's not as confusing as it first sounds – just add or subtract six hours to work out Swahili time (or read the opposite side of your watch). People and things are usually late in Kenya. That said, if you try to anticipate, you're generally caught out. Trains nearly always leave right on time; buses often have punctual departures as well. In more remote areas though, if a driver tells you he's going somewhere "today", it doesn't necessarily mean he expects to arrive today.

Tipping If you're staying in tourist-class establishments, and travelling a lot, you will often be expected to tip staff. In expensive hotels, Ksh100 wouldn't be out of place for portering a lot of luggage, but coins are usually adequate, or small notes at most. For most small services, Ksh20 is adequate (euphemisms for a tip include a *chai* or a soda – an indication of how much is expected; the price of a beer would be generous). Many mid-range hotels have a gratuities box, where you can leave a single tip for all the staff when you leave. With the peculiar, upside-down logic of the world of service industries, in the very humblest establishments, tipping is not the custom. Note that on safaris, tips are considered almost part of the pay and you're expected to shell out at the end of the trip (see p.63).

Toilets Carry toilet paper – which you can buy in most places – as few cheap hotels provide it. Town public toilets (*Wanawake* for Women; *Wanaume* for Men) are invariably disgusting, as are those in cheaper B&Ls. Public buildings and hotels are unlikely to turn you away if you ask.

Weddings Many of the coastal hotels and a few game lodges will lay it on thick if that's what you really want – garlands of flowers, gospel choirs, "complimentary" cakes and tributes, tree-planting ceremonies and so on. The whole experience can feel rather conveyor-belt-driven (you may be just one of half a dozen happy couples getting hitched on the same day at your dream resort hotel), and you might find that being gawped at by holidaymakers in swimming togs as you say "I do" doesn't do much for the solemnity of the occasion. Choose your venue carefully.

Work Unless you've lined up a job or voluntary work (see below) before leaving for Kenya, you have little chance of getting employment. Wages are extremely low – for university lecturers, for example, they start at not much more than the equivalent of £150/$225 per month, whilst school teachers earn about £80/$125 – and there's serious unemployment in the towns. Particular skills are sometimes in demand – mechanics at game park lodges, for example – but the employer will need good connections to arrange the required papers. It's illegal to obtain income in Kenya while staying on a visitor's pass.

Work camps The Kenya Voluntary Development Association is a locally inspired organization, founded in 1962, bringing Kenyans and foreigners together digging irrigation trenches, making roads, building schools, or just producing as many mud bricks as possible. An international work camp is no holiday, and conditions are usually primitive, but they can be a lot of fun, too, and are undoubtedly worthwhile. There's no upper age limit (but volunteers older than 25 are unusual) and the minimum age is 18. The groups are very mixed in terms of nationality. The registration fee is $200 or, if you're very energetic, $300 for two consecutive work camps (they last about three or four weeks). Write to KVDA, PO Box 48902 Nairobi, Kenya ℡ 02/225379.

Since 1998, members of Outreach Kenya Development Volunteers (an Indiana University student organization) have been working with a local group (ICODEI) in Bungoma district implementing sustainable community development projects. The main focuses have been in AIDS awareness, education and women's income generation. They've built a public library and a pre-school and established an education sponsorship programme to assist families who can't afford to send their children to school ($14 covers a child's annual primary school fees). The team has also organized 62 local women's groups, comprising more than 2000 members, into three consortia to establish sewing and tailoring centres. Current and future plans include a health education centre and clinic, to be staffed by expat volunteers alongside local health care professionals. The involvement of visitors is actively encouraged: contact the OKDV through ⓦ www.indiana.edu/~okdv or email Hank Selke at ⓔ hankselke@hotmail.com.

Things to take

In no particular order, and not all essential:

☐ **Sunglasses** are a necessary health precaution, and they're expensive to buy in Kenya.

☐ A **multipurpose penknife** is handy for cutting food and all sorts of things.

☐ A flashlight **torch** can help you navigate unlit roads at night, and is also good to have in case of power cuts.

☐ An **alarm clock** is handy for pre-dawn starts.

☐ For driving around the parks and hiking, a **compass** is immensely useful.

☐ A **padlock** can be useful in lodgings where doors don't lock.

☐ **Binoculars** (the small, fold-up ones) are invaluable for game watching. Without them you'll miss half the action. Take a pair for each person.

☐ **Plastic bags** are invaluable: large bin-liner bags to keep dust off clothes, small resealable ones to protect cameras and film.

☐ On the coast, **plastic sandals** are best for walking on the reef; if you don't have your own to take, you can buy them cheaply in Kenya.

☐ You might want to take your own **flip-flops/thongs** for cheap hotel bathrooms (though a pair is often provided, and they are cheap and easy to buy in Kenya).

☐ A **sheet sleeping bag** (sew up a sheet) is essential if you intend staying in the very cheapest accommodation.

☐ A **compass** is immensely useful when hiking, or driving round the parks.

☐ A **stove** is worth considering, even if you're not camping, to boil water or for simple cooking. Camping gas canisters can be bought in Nairobi and a few other places, or take a Trangia stove that works on methylated spirit (easily available in any town), though this is less reliable at high altitude.

☐ **Earplugs** are a help in some lodgings if you're a light sleeper.

guide

guide

Nairobi and around

SUDAN

ETHIOPIA

UGANDA

⑦

SOMALIA

③

④

Lake
Victoria

②

①

⑤

⑥

N

INDIAN
OCEAN

TANZANIA

0   200 km

CHAPTER 1 # Highlights

✳ **The Thorn Tree** The original acacia has gone, but the newly planted successor continues the tradition of pinning up notices for fellow travellers. See p.107

✳ **National Museum** As good an introduction to Kenya's natural and cultural attractions as you could reasonably expect, and by far the biggest – and best – museum in the country. See p.113

✳ **The Carnivore** Tacky, touristy but fun temple to meat-eating on the outskirts of town. See p.129

✳ **Giraffe Manor** A serious giraffe conservation project with great photo ops. The giraffe-level observation platforms are a big hit with children. See p.103

✳ **Maasai Market** Open Tuesday and Friday mornings at the top of Moi Avenue, and offering an excellent range of beads, baskets and gourds at a fraction of curio shop prices. See p.120

✳ **Nairobi National Park** Where classic telephoto images of plains animals against a backdrop of skyscrapers are taken, this park, on Nairobi's doorstep, is home to most of Kenya's big mammals. See p.155

1

Nairobi and around

asily the largest city in East Africa, **NAIROBI** is also the youngest, the most modern, the fastest growing, the largest and, at 1700m, the highest. The superlatives could go on forever. "Green City in the Sun", runs one tour brochure sobriquet, "City of flowers", another. Less enchanted visitors growl "Nairobbery". The city catches your attention at least. This is no tropical backwater.

Most roads, particularly paved ones, lead to Nairobi and, like it or not, you're bound to spend some time here. But walking down Kenyatta Avenue at rush hour, or up Tom Mboya Street after dark, when the security men armed with whips and clubs cluster around their fires on the pavement, it's perhaps easy to forget how quickly you can leave the city and be in the bush.

Apart from being the **safari** capital of the world, Nairobi is an excellent **base for travel**, just nine hours by road, or an overnight train journey, to the coast; about the same time to the far west; and just a couple of hours northwest to the great trough of the Rift Valley or north to the slopes of Mount Kenya, while a great **day-trip**, and one literally on the city's doorstep, is **Nairobi National Park**, a wild attraction where you'd expect to find suburbs.

Nairobi

NAIROBI is one of Africa's major cities: the UN's fourth "World Centre", East Africa's commercial and aid hub, and a significant capital in its own right, with a population of between a million and a half and three million, depending on how big an area you include. As a traveller, your first impressions are likely to depend on how – and where – you arrive. Coming here overland, some time resting up among the fleshpots can seem a pleasant proposition. Newly arrived by air from Europe, though, you may wonder – amid the rash of signs for *California Cookies*, *Wimpy* and *Oriental Massage* – just how far you've travelled. Nairobi, just a century old in 1999, has real claims to Western-style sophistication but, as you'll soon find, it lacks a convincing heart. Apart from some lively musical attractions – some of East Africa's busiest **clubs** and best **bands** – there's little here of magnetic appeal, and most travellers stay long enough only to take stock, make some travel arrangements and maybe visit the **National Museum**, before moving on.

If you're interested in getting to know the real Kenya, though, Nairobi is as compelling a place as any and displays enormous vitality and buzz. The controlling ethos is commerce rather than community, and there's an almost wilful superficiality in the free-for-all of commuters, shoppers, police, hustlers and tourists. It's hard to imagine a city with a more fascinating variety of people, and almost all of them newcomers. Most are immigrants from rural areas, drawn to the presence and opportunities of money, and Nairobi, on the surface at least, seems to accept everyone with complete tolerance. On any downtown pavement you can see a complete cross-section of Kenyans, plus every variety of tourist and refugees from many African countries.

Nairobi's rapid growth inevitably has a downside however (read any newspaper or talk to any resident and you'll hear some jaw-dropping stories of crime and police shootings), and you should certainly be aware of its reputation for **bag-snatching** and **robbery**, frequently directed at new tourist arrivals (see the box on security on pp.90–91). If you plan to stay for any length of time, learn the art of survival; with the right attitude, you're unlikely to have problems. For the few days that most people spend in Nairobi – if initial misgivings can be overcome – it's a stimulating city.

Some history

Nairobi came into being in May 1899, an artificial settlement created by Europeans at Mile 327 of the East African railway line, then being systematically forged from Mombasa on the coast to Kampala, now the Ugandan capital. It was initially a supply depot, switching yard and campsite for the thousands of Indian labourers employed by the British. Its site, bleak and swampy, was simply the spot where operations came to a halt while the engineers figured out their next move – getting the line up the steep slopes that lay ahead. The name came from the local Maasai word for the area, *enkare nyarobi*, "the place of cold water", though the spot itself was originally called *Nakusontelon*, "Beginning of all Beauty".

Surprisingly, the unplanned **settlement** took root. A few years later it was totally rebuilt after an outbreak of plague and the burning of the original town compound. By 1907, it was so firmly established that the colonists took it as the capital of the newly formed "British East Africa" (BEA). Europeans, encouraged by the authorities, settled in large numbers, while Africans were forced into employment by tax demands (without representation) or onto specially created **reserves** – the Maasai to the Southern Reserve and the Kikuyu to their own reserve in the highlands.

The capital, lacking development from any established community, was somewhat characterless – and remains so. The **original centre** retains an Asian influence in its older buildings, but today it's shot through with glassy, high-rise blocks. Surrounding the commercial hub is a vast area of **suburbs**: wealthiest in the west and north, increasingly poor to the south and especially the east, where they become, in part, out-and-out slums.

Names of these suburbs – Parklands, Lavington, Eastleigh, Shauri Moyo, among others – reflect the jumble of African, Asian and European elements in Nairobi's population, none of whom were local. The term "Nairobian" is a new one that still applies mostly to the younger generation. Although it has a predominance of Kikuyu, the city is not the preserve of a single ethnic group, nor is it built on any distinctively tribal land. Standing as it does at the meeting point of Maasai, Kikuyu and Kamba territories, its choice as capital, accidental though it may have been (Kikuyu **Limuru** and Kamba **Machakos** were also considered), was a fortunate one for the future of the country.

Driving in Nairobi

Driving in **Nairobi** can be a nerve-wracking experience for inexperienced or nervous drivers, though you do tend to get used to it after a few days. The main things to watch out for are matatus, which stop as suddenly as they lurch back into the fray, and roundabouts. These labour under "priority traffic" regulations, which in theory means cars already on the roundabout have priority, but in practice means chaos as no-one is terribly keen to cede right of way. Always stay in lane. If you're worried, you should pick up the car at the airport, which gives you time to get used to the car and the traffic before joining the city centre fray.

Parking in central Nairobi can be difficult during business hours, though there's usually space at the Intercontinental (50 Ksh/hour) or at the Kenyatta International Conference Centre (entrance off City Hall Way).

Arrival

Getting into central Nairobi presents few problems and, once you're there, you'll have little trouble finding your way around. The city has widespread suburbs but its inner area is relatively small: a triangle of stores, offices and public buildings, with the train station on the southern flank and the main bus sta-

Kabete & Kikuyu ▲   Limuru (Country ▲ Route)

GREATER NAIROBI   SPRING VALLEY ESTATE

Highridge Shopping/ Diamond Plaza

THIRD PARKLANDS RD

PARKLANDS

W A I Y A K I   W A Y

GROGANVILLE

RHAPTA ROAD

WESTLANDS

See 'Westlands' map for detail

PARKLANDS ROAD

Kikuyu & Naivasha (Old Road) ▲

Nairobi River

RIVERSIDE DRIVE

CHIROMO

Strathmore College

British Institute   LAIKIPIA RD

MANDERA ROAD

Museum Hill Centre ❸

❺

❹

CHIROMO

ARBORETUM DRIVE

International Casino ❻

National Museum

Kenya High School

The Arboretum

Textbook Centre

KILELESHWA

State House Garden

State House

STATE

MANYAKA ROAD

UHURU HIGHWAY

Central Park

DENIS DRITT ROAD

CHAKA RD

LENANA RD

❼

❽   ❾

MILIMANI ROAD

VALLEY ROAD

❿

Boating Lake

RING RD KILIMANI

ROSE AVE

ARGWINGS KODHEK ROAD

⓬

Hurlingham Shopping Centre ⓫

❸

Uhuru Park

LOWER HILL ROAD

ELGEYO MARAKWET RD

KIRICHWA RD

MENELIK RD

YaYa Centre ⓒ

ⓑ

⓮ ⓭

Ormolu

UPPER HILL ROAD

Karen & Ngong ▲

ⓓ

NGONG ROAD

Nairobi Hospital

NAIROBI HILL

⓰

Adam's Arcade

⓯

Kenyatta National Hospital

HOSPITAL ROAD

Motherland Inn

Uchumi Supermarket

MBAGATHI WAY

KIBERA

SOUTH 'C'

KIBERA

Kisumu ▲

ACCOMMODATION

Bavaria		Ngong Hills	15
Boulevard		Panafric	6
Fairview	11	Plums	3
Heron Court	9	Silver Springs	14
Hurlingham	12	Sirona	4
Ma Roche's Guest House	2	Upper Hill Campsite	16
Nairobi Backpackers	8	Utalii	1
Nairobi Youth Hostel	13	Woodmere Apartments	7

Wilson Airport

Nairobi National Park, Karen, Langata & Olorgasailie ▼

tions to the east. Note that if you're arriving on a Sunday, it will all seem strangely quiet; most shops and many restaurants are closed.

By air

Arriving by air, you'll find yourself at **Jomo Kenyatta International Airport**, 15km out of town to the southeast off the Mombasa highway.

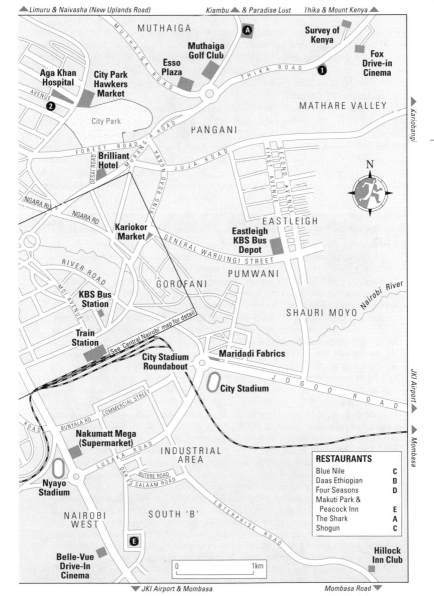

Limuru & Naivasha (New Uplands Road)   Kiambu ▲ & Paradise Lost   Thika & Mount Kenya ▲

MUTHAIGA

A

Survey of Kenya

Muthaiga Golf Club

Esso Plaza

MUTHAIGA ROAD

THIKA ROAD

1

Fox Drive-in Cinema

Aga Khan Hospital   **City Park Hawkers Market**

AVENUE

2

City Park

MATHARE VALLEY

▶ *Kariobangi*

PANGANI

FOREST ROAD

Brilliant Hotel

DESAI ROAD

MURANG'A ROAD

NGARA ROAD

JUJA ROAD

KING'ORI ROAD

FIRST AVENUE

SECOND AVENUE

N

NGARA RD.

NGARA RD

EASTLEIGH

Kariokor Market

Eastleigh KBS Bus Depot

GENERAL WARUINGI STREET

RIVER ROAD

PUMWANI

GOROFANI

MOI AVENUE

KBS Bus Station

SHAURI MOYO

Nairobi River

Train Station

See 'Central Nairobi' map for detail

City Stadium Roundabout

Maridadi Fabrics

JOGOO ROAD

City Stadium

▶ *JKI Airport*

▶ *Mombasa*

COMMERCIAL STREET

Nakumatt Mega (Supermarket)

BUNYALA RD.

LUSAKA ROAD

DAR ES SALAAM ROAD

INDUSTRIAL AREA

BUTERE ROAD

ROAD

Nyayo Stadium

NAIROBI WEST

SOUTH 'B'

ENTERPRISE ROAD

E

RESTAURANTS

Blue Nile	C
Daas Ethiopian	B
Four Seasons	D
Makuti Park & Peacock Inn	E
The Shark	A
Shogun	C

Belle-Vue Drive-In Cinema

0   1km

Hillock Inn Club

▼ JKI Airport & Mombasa   Mombasa Road ▼

Arrivals are normally straightforward, but do beware of **pickpockets**, even inside customs. The **visa desk** is to the right of passport control – obtaining one, if you haven't already done so, should be a simple, form-filling formality (payment in dollars or sterling cash only). Once through passport control, check your **luggage** is intact as soon as you get it off the carousel. If anything appears to be missing go straight to the "Lost Luggage" desk before passing through customs. For customs advice, see pp.19–20. If at any stage someone asks you for a **bribe**, refuse tactfully, pointing out the many signs on the walls concerning the heavy penalties for attempted bribery and corruption. If you really get stuck, kicking up a loud fuss and demanding to see the airport manager usually works. Whilst still in baggage reclaim, take the time to get your luggage in order, hiding cameras, small handbags and other valuables – you'll have rather less privacy to do so in the main arrivals hall. It'd be wise, also, to have decided where you want to go, and how, before facing the taxi touts outside.

There's a **24-hour bank** (in theory) inside customs, and another exchange bureau in the main hall, both with ATM machines. Both refuse traveller's cheques from time to time, so you'd be safer bringing some cash. Examine the receipt and your money carefully – there have been reports of rip-offs. Safer still would be to change some shillings at your airport of departure, though the rate is invariably worse. Also inside customs is a **duty-free shop**, which you're free to use on arrival. The airport has an office of the **Flying Doctors**

Security

First read the "Crime and personal safety" section in Basics, pp.69–71.

An alarming number of new arrivals have to deal with a **robbery** in their first day or two in Nairobi, before they've adjusted to the city's pace and ways. Despite the fact that it usually carries armed undercover police, a lot of people get ripped off within an hour of arriving on the **#34 bus** from the airport. Victims get distracted in conversation or jostled, or have their hands grabbed and shaken by strangers. It's no joke and the best way to avoid unwanted attention is to take exaggerated care of your valuables: stash away cameras, wristwatches and jewellery; tuck your money belt inside your trousers/skirt; keep nothing of value in breast-pockets; and ensure that luggage zips and pockets are closed before you walk out into the main arrivals hall. If anything does start to happen on the bus, make a lot of noise – it's no time to be shy. Sometimes it's enough just to clock the thieves – often young – and let them know you've seen them, which, surprisingly enough, usually stops them, and you can all have a (nervous) laugh.

Once in town, it helps to memorize any route you're walking, as lost-looking tourists are the easiest target of all. Keep your hands out of reach and be – rationally – suspicious of everyone until you've caught your breath. It doesn't take long to get a little streetwise. Every rural Kenyan coming to the city for the first time goes through exactly the same process, and many are considerably "greener" than you, having never been in a city before. Dressing like a local and not carrying a bag will help you avoid ninety percent of unwanted approaches.

Apart from the occasional petty thieving, the younger ubiquitous glue-sniffing **street children** are generally no problem. Giving food is better for them than money, but some charitable organizations advise against hand-outs of any kind as they might encourage others onto the street. However, be aware of the muck-chuckers amongst them who *will* carry out their muck-chucking threats if you don't give them some money – a few shillings is usually enough to keep yourself clean. More serious is the number of teenagers amongst them, some as old as 18, with group muggings by organization, where you can buy their special brand of life-saving insurance if you expect to be out in the wilds a lot. The *Simba Restaurant* at the top of the arrivals building is surprisingly good and reasonably priced.

Invariably, hordes of **taxi** touts assail you once you're through customs. Don't be alarmed by this – just ignore them and walk straight to the waiting cabs lined up outside, or else to the Kenatco office – but if you'd prefer to be met, try contacting Let's Go Travel (address on p.141). For the London-style cabs there's a fixed price to the city centre, currently around Ksh1500, depending on which hotel you want to go to. Other taxis to the city centre should be less than this – they don't have meters, so bargain hard. Don't be afraid to ask several drivers their price. Given that even a good fare is a rip-off, tipping is not necessary.

The local KBS Stagecoach **bus #34** operates roughly every twenty minutes (6am–8pm) and costs just Ksh30. It enters the city through the eastern suburbs (rather than running straight up the proud artery of Uhuru Highway) and stops at the central KBS bus station on Mfangano Street before continuing to the youth hostel on Nairobi Hill. (See the warning about robbery on the #34 bus in the box on security below.)

You will be obliged to take a taxi if your plane arrives **late at night** – British Airways, Kenya Airways, Cameroon Airlines, Emirates and KLM have such flights. You may well feel intimidated by a night-time first contact with central

these street boys not unheard of, so try, particularly at night, to avoid them. It's always a good idea to carry a small amount of money with you in case you do find yourself in a difficult situation and have to negotiate your way out of trouble. A helpful tactic is to act friendly and unafraid, but to keep walking to avoid being surrounded, and to hopefully reach a safer area where there might be more witnesses or a few policemen.

Be aware of the fact that certain areas have acquired **local notoriety** and the carrying of knives and guns is on the increase. Most areas are fine in daylight, but if you're walking at night within the city centre be extra vigilant and don't wander outside the commercial district unless you're really clued in. If you head out from the centre to poorer districts there seems to be less of a threat. If you're **driving**, keep the windows rolled up after dark, especially at traffic lights. Be especially wary in the following areas, which are all parts of the city where tourist pickings are fairly rich – and there are always a few who haven't read a guidebook:

River Road district, which in practical terms means anything east of Moi Avenue, and indeed sometimes including the avenue, has become something of a **no go area for tourists** at night. Even locals avoid walking there and taxi drivers are quite often reluctant to venture into certain parts of the district.

Uhuru Highway, **Uhuru** and **Central parks** are fine during the day but prime muggers' territory at night, with occasional shootings.

The area west of Uhuru Highway from the **Serena Hotel** to the **Youth Hostel** is unsafe at night.

The area near the **Museum** and **Casino** is extremely dangerous at night.

By day, the area between **Kenyatta Avenue** and **University Way**, especially around the **City Market**, is prone to con-merchants and occasional snatch-and-run robberies.

All **main bus** and **matatu stations**. These chaotic places are the ideal place for pickpockets and snatch-and-run robberies. Do not accept food, drinks, sweets or cigarettes from strangers, as doping is common.

Nairobi and you'll find many of the cheapest hotels are already closed before midnight. An obvious alternative is simply to curl up in a corner of the arrivals hall (there are police and soldiers) until morning. Remember, though, this isn't a large airport – comforts and even basic facilities are limited and sleeping in a corner is barely tolerated. Watch out for your bags, too.

By train

Arriving by overnight train from Mombasa, you'll find yourself virtually in the city centre right in front of one of Nairobi's biggest Matatu stages. From the **train station** (watch out for taxi drivers and porters who will more or less kidnap your luggage if you let them), just walk straight out through the station concourse and follow Moi Avenue into town. The only real attention you'll attract is from **safari touts** (see "Safari operators", p.139) – they're persistent, but friendly enough, and useful if you need an escort to one of the cheaper River Road addresses; a small tip (say Ksh50) would be appreciated. If you're worried about wandering about with your bags, there are two **left luggage** facilities at the station.

By bus and matatu

Most **bus companies** have their booking offices or parking areas in the River Road district, just a short walk from the city centre. Many of the matatu stages are here, too. If you've been following the map and know where you are, however, you can generally ask to be dropped off anywhere along the route into town. All the bus company terminals are marked on the map on pp.98–99, and the main bus and matatu routes and their terminals are listed in the box on pp.94–95.

Orientation and city transport

The triangle of **central Nairobi** divides into three principal districts bisected by the main thoroughfares of **Kenyatta Avenue** and **Moi Avenue**.

The grandest and most formal part of town is the area around **City Square**, in the southwest. This square kilometre is Nairobi's heart: government buildings, banks and offices (most of them housed in commercial buildings with names like Jubilee Insurance House and Lonrho House) merge to the north and east with upmarket shopping streets and luxury hotels. The area's big landmarks are the extraordinary **Kenyatta International Conference Centre**, with its huge cylindrical tower and artichoke-shaped conference centre, the blue-glass skyscraper of **Lonrho House**, and the bizarre zebra-striped "legs" of the **Nation Centre**, all visible from miles outside the city. To the south of this area, towards the train station, stands the **Memorial Park** on the site of the bombed Cooperative Bank Building (see the box on p.112).

North of Kenyatta Avenue, there's a shift to smaller scale and lesser finance. The **City Market** is here, surrounded by a denser district of shops, restaurants and hotels. The **Jeevanjee Gardens** are a welcome patch of greenery (though avoid walking through after dark), and a little further north is the university district and Nairobi's oldest establishment, *The Norfolk Hotel*, contemporary with the original rebuilding of the city.

East of Moi Avenue, the character changes more radically. Here, and down towards the reeking Nairobi River, is the relatively poor, inner-city district identified with **River Road**, its main thoroughfare. The River Road quarter is where most long-distance buses and matatus start and terminate, and where you'll find the capital's cheapest restaurants and hotels, as well as the highest concentration of African-owned businesses. It's also a somewhat notorious area, with a traditional concentration of sharks and pickpockets (see "Security" box). You can meet European residents who work five minutes' walk away and in all their years in Nairobi have never been to this part of town.

Getting around central Nairobi is straightforward. By day, most visitors **walk**; by night, they take a **taxi**. Unless you're only here for a day or two, though, it's certainly worth getting to know the city's **public transport** systems.

Taxis

While Nairobi's **taxis** are overpriced by Kenyan standards, at night, when certain parts of the city are definitely not recommended for pedestrians, you'll almost certainly want to make use of them. Grey, London-style taxi cabs (Kenya Taxi Cabs Association ☎02/222953) crowd around key spots in the city – notably outside the *Hilton Hotel* and *680 Hotel* – and have pretty fixed prices, with the current bottom-line fare for any trip in the city centre well known by all (the cheapest ride isn't likely to be less than around Ksh250). Another reliable company is the 24-hour Kenatco, who have their office at Uchumi House on Aga Khan Walk (☎02/225123, 316611 or 230771–2), and a branch at Jomo Kenyatta International Airport (☎02/824248 or 822356). It's really only possible to bargain with the private drivers, who drive sometimes astonishingly battered cars. You'll find them angling for business on Mama Ngina Street, Kimathi Street outside the *Oakwood Hotel*, and at the junction of Standard Street and Muindi Mbingu Street, by the *680 Hotel*.

Tuk-tuks, motorized rickshaws, are also now available, mostly at the corner of Moi Avenue and Kimathi Street. They cost a little less than regular taxis. Bargain hard.

Buses and matatus

The **public transport** – buses and matatus – used by the ordinary people (the *wananchi*) of Nairobi will save you money on getting around, certainly for longer trips out of the city centre, but it takes some figuring out. The KBS Stagecoach **buses** roar around Nairobi all day, usually packed far beyond capacity. They're cheap (Ksh10–30) and very unpredictable. Buses are numbered, but bus stops aren't and routes change frequently. **Matatus** can be slightly easier. They tend to take the same routes as buses and often display the same route numbers. They're generally faster, more dangerous and packed, though bad accidents rarely happen in the city. The confusion in Nairobi is occasionally exacerbated by matatus going on strike, or by clumsy police sweeps in which matatu and bus drivers are "netted" for overloading their vehicles, playing loud music or, latterly, not carrying their ID cards, leaving the passengers stranded – usually at rush hour when it causes maximum chaos. The "stages" (terminuses) are scattered throughout River Road district. The more helpful bus and matatu routes, and where to board them, are listed in the box overleaf.

For national bus, matatu and train services, see the "Moving on from Nairobi" section on pp.150–154).

Local buses are run by KBS Stagecoach, who have their main bus station in the eastern corner of River Road district, between Ronald Ngala, Mfangano and Uyoma streets, beside the bizarre-looking Siri Guru Singh Sabha Temple. This is also a major stage for matatus. Other bus and matatu stops include: outside the **Ambassadeur** hotel on Moi Avenue (mainly eastbound); outside the **Kencom** building facing the *Hilton* on City Hall Way and also outside the **GPO** tower on Kenyatta Avenue (mainly westbound); the **train station** end of Moi Avenue (west and southwest); and **Latema Road** (north and northeast).

1 (bus/matatu) Ngong Road, Dagoretti Corner; from GPO.
2 (bus/matatu) Ngong Road, Dagoretti Corner, Kikuyu town; from KBS bus station or GPO.
3 (bus/matatu) Ngong Road, Adam's Arcade, Dagoretti Corner; from GPO.
4 (bus) Ngong Road, Adam's Arcade, Dagoretti Corner; from Kencom or GPO.
4 (bus) Kariokor market, General Waruinge Road, Eastleigh; from *Ambassadeur*.
6 (bus) Kariokor market and Eastleigh; from Accra Road or Tom Mboya Street.
8 (matatu) Kenyatta National Hospital, Kibera; from railway stage.
9 (matatu) Eastleigh; from corner Accra Road/Tom Mboya Street.
11 (matatu) City Park, Parklands; from Tom Mboya Street by *Mayur* restaurant.
15 (matatu) Langata Road (National Park, Wilson Airport); from Mfangano Street/Ronald Ngala Street.
17B (matatu) Thika Road, Kasarani; from KBS bus station.
18 (bus) Kenyatta National Hospital; from GPO.
20 (bus) Kenyatta National Hospital; from GPO.
21 (bus) National Museum, Westlands; from Kencom.
21 (bus) City Stadium roundabout, Jogoo Road; from *Ambassadeur*.
23 (bus) National Museum; Westlands; from Kencom.
24 (bus/matatu) Langata Road, Bogoni Road, Karen; from Mfangano Street/Hakati Road or GPO.
25 (matatu) Murang'a Road, Thika Road; from Odeon Cinema Latema Road, or Koinange Street.
28 (bus) Eastleigh, Kariobangi; from *Ambassadeur*.
30 (matatu) Murang'a Road, Westlands; from KBS bus station.
31 (bus) Kariobangi; from *Ambassadeur*.
32 (matatu) Kariokor market; Eastleigh; from corner Accra Road/Taveta Road.
34 (bus) Jogoo Road, Jomo Kenyatta International Airport; from *Ambassadeur* and KBS bus station.
34 (bus) *Youth Hostel*, Langata Road, Wilson Airport; from Kencom and KBS bus station.
36 (bus) Jogoo Road, Kariobangi South; from *Ambassadeur* and KBS bus station.
37 (bus) Jogoo Road, Kariobangi South; from *Ambassadeur*.
38 (matatu) Jogoo Road, Kariobangi South; from KBS bus station.

Accommodation

Finding **accommodation** in Nairobi isn't difficult. There's loads of choice, and hotels are rarely full even during the peak season. The main question is which area fits your needs. The city lacks a long-established focus, so travellers end up congregating at a number of different spots determined by budget and requirements. If you're arriving in town very early, beware that most places

39 (matatu) Jogoo Road, Kariobangi South; from KBS bus station.

40 (bus) Kariokor, Kariobangi; from *Ambassadeur*.

41 (bus) Valley Road (*Youth Hostel*), Argwings Kodhek Road; from GPO.

42 (matatu) Kariobangi market, Eastleigh; from corner Accra Road/Tsavo Road.

42 (bus) Kibera; from Kencom or KBS bus station.

44A (matatu) Ngumba Estate, Thika Road; from KBS bus station.

45 (bus) Thika Road (Moi Sports Centre); from Kencom.

46 (matatu) Valley Road, Argwings Kodhek Road; from railway stage and GPO.

46 or **46B** (bus) Valley Road, Argwings Kodhek Road, Gitanga Road; from Kencom.

46 or **46B** (bus) Kariokor market; from *Ambassadeur*.

48 (matatu) Arboretum; from Odeon cinema, Latema Road.

61B (bus) Kenyatta National Hospital; from GPO.

100 (matatu) Kiambu Road, Kiambu; from KBS bus station.

102 (bus/matatu) Ngong Road, Dagoretti Corner, Kikuyu town; from KBS bus station.

103 (bus) Ngong Road, Dagoretti Corner, Kikuyu town; from KBS bus station.

104 (matatu) Westlands; from KBS bus station.

108 (bus) Murang'a Road; Muthaiga Road; Limuru Road; from KBS bus station.

110 (matatu) Kitengela, Athi River (Chapter Five); from KBS bus station (hourly).

111 (bus) Ngong Road, Dagoretti Corner, Karen, Ngong, Kiserian; from KBS bus station.

114 (matatu) Limuru; from Jamia Mosque (Kigali Road) or outside Mayur on Tom Mboya Street.

115 (matatu) Kikuyu town; from railway stage.

119 (bus) National Museum, Westlands, Peponi Road, Wangige; from KBS bus station.

123 (matatu) Thika, from MP station on Ronald Ngala Street.

125 (matatu) Langata Road, Magadi Road, Kiserian; from railway stage.

126 (bus) Langata Road, then either to Karen or Kiserian along Magadi Road; from KBS bus station.

137 (matatu) Thika Road; from Koinange Street.

145 (bus) Thika Road (Moi Sports Centre); from Kencom.

160 (matatu) Thika Road (Moi Sports Centre) to Ruiru via Githurai; from KBS bus station.

237 (matatu) Thika; from Kencom. Other Thika matatus from corner BP station on Ronald Ngala Street.

Un-numbered:

to Enterprise Road, marked "Industrial Area/Hillock"; from Afya Centre, Tom Mboya Street.

to Limuru; from outside *Mayur* restaurant, Tom Mboya Street.

to Parklands and Highridge, marked "Parklands/Aga Khan"; from Latema Road, facing *Iqbal Hotel*, or from along Tom Mboya Street.

won't allow you to take a room before 10am. If you're travelling by rented car and concerned about safe parking, don't panic – the city council and most hotels employ *askaris* (security guards), who can be persuaded to up their workload for a modest tip. Most top-of-the-range places have guarded or enclosed parking anyway. Naturally, leave nothing in, or attached to, the vehicle. To help you aim straight for the best places, the ones in the following shortlist meet with near-universal approval: *Iqbal* and *Planet Safari* (low-budget, popular with travellers, River Road district); the YMCA (cheap, out-of-centre meeting place with a pool, popular with travellers); *Fairview* (peaceful mid-range out-of-centre hotel, great for families); *Boulevard* (reliable mid-range out-of-centre base); *Oakwood* (reliable mid-range city centre base); *The Stanley* and *Grand Regency* (excellent value in the luxury range); and *Safari Park* (totally Kenya-proof luxury resort out of town).

River Road area

The very cheapest lodgings are around **River Road**, the main drag through the city centre's poorest quarter – although in recent years, a number of more expensive hotels have been built here. Despite the constant worry about safety, River Road is the city's most stimulating and animated area, and offers a plunge into a world which would pass you by if you stayed elsewhere in the city centre or out in the suburbs. The cheapest places generally double as rowdy bars and nightclubs (not for lone women), and are neither terribly clean nor secure. Should a modicum of hygiene and perhaps s/c facilities be important to you, you're looking at between Ksh600–1000 for a double room. In several of those listed below you can expect to run into other travellers. If you're genuinely broke, try the welcoming **Sikh Temple** on Gaberone Road: overnights and meals are free, though you're expected to leave a donation. All places below are shown on the "Commercial Centre and River Road Area" map, pp.98–99.

Cheap

Hotel Africana Dubois Rd, PO Box 47827 ℡02/220654, ℻331886. Clean linoleum-floored s/c rooms with telephones and hot water. The single beds are tiny. There's a café downstairs. Recommended if you want to be near the Latema Road area and need a little more comfort, though not as smart as it was. B&B ❷

Al Mansura B&L Munyu Rd, PO Box 22020 ℡02/336338. Cheapest of the cheap, pleasantly characterful and friendly, though hygiene is not high on the management's agenda, and if you're single you may have to share. There are no iron gates to pass, but the place appears secure enough and, being Muslim-run, this is almost the only establishment on Munyu Rd which doesn't have a bar. The restaurant downstairs is simple and good, the smell and smoke drifting up to the rooms more of a bonus than a drawback. ❶

Cana Lodge Hotel Duruma Rd, PO Box 41237 ℡02/223017. Small, clean s/c rooms (with phones) and good security, if a slightly desultory atmosphere. Quieter rooms are at the rear. Hot water mornings and evenings. A good first base in Nairobi, with clean sheets daily and good breakfasts. B&B ❷

Danika Lodge Dubois Rd, PO Box 12840 ℡02/230687. Very secure (the gate is locked at all times) and friendly, quieter than most, with clean and breezy s/c rooms, hot water 24 hours, and the rare luxury of mosquito nets. Good laundry service. Recommended. ❶

Destiny Hotel Duruma Rd, PO Box 72780 ℡02/253123-6. This four-storey block offers good value and is conscientiously run, with clean, airy s/c rooms and hot showers. There is a payphone in the corridor and a laundry service, and a bar and restaurant are planned. B&B ❷

Hotel Emmaccra Accra Rd, PO Box 28172 ℡02/242609. Friendly, with good security and nets over the beds, but the rooms are small with dirty bathrooms. *Nyama choma* available from the bar downstairs; rooms with windows on the street side are quieter (relatively speaking, of course). They're happy to store bags while you go off up-country. B&B ❷

Evamay Lodge River Rd at the junction with Duruma Rd, PO Box 16000 ℡02/216218. Very good value for the price with clean s/c rooms, with phones and nets, and good security. ❷

Hotel Gloria Duke House, corner Ronald Ngala St and Tom Mboya St, PO Box 32087 ℡02/228916. An overpriced and only slightly better-than-basic B&L, with grubby rooms (s/c with nets and baths, but erratic hot water), and "enough security". Not noticeably welcoming, and it's on a noisy, hustly corner. B&B ❷

Iqbal Hotel Latema Rd, PO Box 11256 ℡02/220914. A very friendly place, the rooms are basic and cleanish, but the main advantage is the opportunity to meet other travellers. Rooms are secure (no "guests" allowed, either), but aren't s/c, and those at the front overlooking the matatu stand are noisy. There's temperamental hot water in the mornings, a cheap laundry service, lock-up store, safari booking office and noticeboard. The café upstairs (no food) has a breezy terrace for residents. Although dorm beds are also available, it's often full, so book in advance.

Mercury Hotel Tom Mboya St, PO Box 4445 ☎02/212504. Next door and similar to the *Princess Hotel* (see below), but cheaper and not as well furnished. ❶

New Kenya Lodge River Rd at the top of Latema Rd, PO Box 43444 ☎02/222202. Like the *Iqbal*, a long-established backpackers' haunt with a popular communal area. Friendly, cheap and unhygienic, with little or no hot water, and uncertain security. Don't come here if you've much to lose; we've received persistent reports of thefts from bags left unattended in rooms and in storage. They also organize cheapish safaris (around $50 per day) which, by all accounts, are perfectly reasonable. There's also a book exchange. The "annexe" on Duruma Rd (☎02/338348) is even less tempting (though breakfast is thrown in). ❶

New Swanga Lodge Duruma Rd, PO Box 46387 ☎02/213777 or 213827. The rooms here, though not large, are comfortable and s/c (with telephones and nets), secured behind spectacular, time-consuming, triple locks. Clean sheets daily. Good value, though hardly quiet. Often full. B&B ❷

North Eastern B&L Dubois Rd, ☎02/222554. Basic rooms tucked away like a rabbit warren, the main draw being that it's popular with traders from Cameroon, Senegal and elsewhere in Africa, which makes for some interesting encounters. Not s/c. Reasonable security (the stairway gates are locked at night). ❶

Orchid Hotel Mfangano St, PO Box 45613 ☎02/228663. Clean, friendly, spacious, with hot water and, though not fancy, excellent value. One of the best of the cheapies (breakfast not included), and there's a safe lock-up for luggage when you're on safari (Ksh30/day). ❶

Planet Safari 9th floor, Sonalux House, Moi Ave, PO Box 79347 ☎02/229799, ⒻFax211899, ✉planet@africaonline.co.ke. Just out of River Road district, this is the oddest place in Nairobi – and very popular with backpackers – with six tents pitched on the roof. There's a grubby communal kitchen,

and a safari booking office for its captive market (you can stay free for up to three days if you take them up on a trip). Lift to 5th floor, then stairs. Security appears reasonable, despite some off-putting hangers-on. ❶

Princess Hotel Tom Mboya St ☎02/214640. Very busy, local establishment with bars on all floors. It's Nairobi's main gay rendezvous (rooms by the hour), and much cheaper if you're a couple. Basic but adequate, and it fills up quickly. ❷

Sirikwa Lodge Munyu Rd, at the corner with Accra Rd ☎02/226687 or 318332. Reasonable s/c rooms accessed over a cheerfully blaring music shop, and great for observing the chaos at the Accra Rd matatu stages. Hot water 24 hours, and secure basement parking. Often full. B&B ❷

Sunrise Lodge Latema Rd, PO Box 48224 ☎02/330362. Small, reasonably secure, but not terribly hygienic and lacks running water. Some rooms are exceptionally noisy due to its location next to the *Modern Green Bar*. Don't dawdle after dark in the alley between them or you'll get mugged. ❷

Moderate

Abbey Hotel Gaberone Rd, PO Box 75260 ☎02/243256 or 241562. A noisy, boozy place, rather expensive nowadays, but the rooms have nets and are mostly clean and fresh, with tiled bathrooms (hot showers). Unlovely, but adequate. ❸

Hotel Accra and Fitness Club Accra Rd, PO Box 75862 ☎02/215698. Overpriced for a basic B&L, with small, superficially s/c single rooms (no toilet paper or toilet seats), but perhaps worth it for a night's clubbing in the wild neighbourhood. Sweat out your hangover in its unlikely sauna and steam room (Ksh400), with or without a massage (Ksh300 for half an hour), or punish yourself in their gym (Ksh100). There's *nyama choma* on the second floor. ❸

Hotel Dama Luthuli Ave, PO Box 48031 ☎02/221738. An impressive facade conceals the same old stuff within: small, clean s/c rooms, but good security. They sometimes have (loud) discos downstairs. ❸

Diplomat Hotel Tom Mboya St, PO Box 30777 ☎02/245050, ⒻFax220475. Fifty large, well-kept s/c

---

Drinking water

Nairobi's tap water is unfit to drink. Most people boil their water, even those on very low incomes, and the more affluent drink only bottled water. If in any doubt, or if eating in hotelis where bottled water is not offered, stick to sodas. See "Water and bugs" on p.28.

ACCOMMODATION

Abbey	27		
Hotel Accra and Fitness Club	24		
Hotel Africana	13		
Al Mansura B&L	25		
Ambassadeur	37		
Cana Lodge	7		
Hotel Dama	28		
Danika Lodge	14		
Destiny	5		
Diplomat	40	Grand Holiday	21
Down Town	10	Grand Regency	29
Hotel Embassy	19	Hotel Greton	16
Hotel Emmaccra	22	Hilton	36
Eureka Highrise	38	Inter-Continental	44
Evamay Lodge	6	Iqbal	17
Hotel Gloria	41	Marble Arch	8

Mercury	43	Orchid	39
Meridian Court	3	Oriental Palace	23
Nairobi Safari Club	1	Parkside	2
New Kenya Lodge	4	Planet Safari	32
New Swanga Lodge	11	Princess	42
North Eastern B&L	15	Sagret	20
Oakwood	30	Hotel Salama	33

Samagat	26		
Sirikwa Lodge	18		
680 (Six-Eighty)	35		
Solace Hotel	34		
The Stanley	31		
Sunrise Lodge	12		
Hotel Terminal	9		

**COMMERCIAL CENTRE
AND RIVER ROAD AREA**

0   100 m

KIRINYAGA ROAD

KILOME ROAD

KEEKOROK ROAD

NGARIAMA LANE

Eastleigh
Mattresses
(supermarket)

RIVER ROAD

Matatu
Stage

FIRE STATION LANE

Akamba Bus Station

LAGOS ROAD

Kenya
Cycle
Mart

GOVT LANE

Cycle Land

Assanand's
Music

Nation
Centre

Book
Point

Imenti
House

Victor
House

Barclays
Bank

Nakumatt
Supermarket

Westminster
House

Kimathi
House

Old
Mutual
Building

Zanzibar
Curio Shop

Sonalux House

Eagle
House

Union
Towers

Stanbank
House

Rehema
House

IPS
House

Lonrho
House

Corner
House

Vedic
House

KCS
House

Jubilee
Exchange
House

Norwich
Union
House

Prudencial
Assurance
Building

20th
Century
Plaza

Transnational
Plaza

International
House

Hilton Building

Kencom
House

National
Archives

SHORT STREET

Stewart
Building

California Stars
Butchery

SHEIKH KARUME RD

SHEIKH
KARUME LANE

Sikh
Temple

Monte
Carlo
Club

Lizie Bar

Reke
Marie
B&L

Uchumi
Supermarket

Mombasa
Liners

Kensilver
Express

Friends
Corner Bar

Odeon
Cinema

Modern
Green Bar

Daily
Peugeot
Service

Takrim
Bus

City
Sounds

Goldline
Bus

Arusha
Express

Barclays
Bank

Coast
Bus

Crossline Bus

Caltex

Rajab
Manzal
Building

Tumaini
House

New York
New York

KTDA
Plaza

Florida
2000
Nightclub

Kenya
Cinema
Plaza

Shankardass
House

Rahimtulla
Library

Development
House

Afya
Centre

Church
House

NHC
House

Jeevan
Bharati
Building

HARAMBEE AVENUE

Reinsurance
Plaza

Uchumi
House

Nairobi
Cinema

Law
Courts

Jogoo
House

Kenyatta
International
Conference Centre

DURUMA RD

MOI AVENUE

TOM MBOYA STREET

ACCRA ROAD

RIVER RD

LUTHULI AVE

RONALD NGALA ST

MOI AVENUE

KBS BLs Station

BP

H K 5 L D
4 6 7 11
8 12 S 13 14 15 16 18 20
17 21 22 23 24 25 26 27 28 33 34 37 38 40 41 42 43
30 31 32 36 39

U V W Z d e f

RESTAURANTS, CAFÉS & BARS

Al Hawal	**G**	Coffee House	**d**	Ismailia's	**J**	Paris Metro	**e**	Steers	**M & f**
Ali Baba	**A**	Express Bakery	**a**	K&A Coffee House	**b**	Pre Area Eating House	**L**	Sun Sweet Centre	**D**
Bakers Pie	**X**	Fameland	**K**	Kenchic Inn	**O**	Reata Fish & Chips	**V**	Taj	**T**
Beneve	**c**	Garden Square	**g**	La Taverna	**B**	Silver Sun	**R**	Tickles	**P**
Benrose	**U**	Goldstar	**Q**	Malindi Dishes	**W**	Simmers	**Y**	Trattoria	**Z**
City Fry's	**C**	Hong Kong	**F**	Mayur/Supreme Hotel	**H**	Sno Cream	**I**	Zaïqa New Flora	**S**
				Melting Pot	**N**	Star Delux Fish & Chips	**E**		

rooms (showers) with telephones, and there's lift access. ④

Eureka Highrise Hotel Tom Mboya St, PO Box 28229 ☎02/228935. Three floors up. Slightly overpriced, but with large, clean s/c rooms with hot water for the showers, good security and a calm, vaguely Christian atmosphere. ③

Grand Holiday Hotel Tsavo Rd, PO Box 69343 ☎02/228370 or 211372, ℻243851. Perhaps after the current renovations the place will reflect its name, but at present it has rather spartan rooms with cheap and mangy mattresses – though the more expensive suites have enormous beds, as well as TVs. Tall people beware, the staircase lintels are low. It has a calm, almost posh first-floor restaurant, complete with fish tank. Acceptable at this range, but there's better. ③

Hotel Greton Tsavo Rd, PO Box 55909 ☎02/242891, ℻242892. Rather small rooms, but they have phones and hot showers and it's friendly, with good security and attentive management. A clean, pleasant, value-for-money hotel. Recommended. B&B ③

Marble Arch Hotel Lagos Rd, PO Box 12224 ☎02/245720 or 245656, ℻245724. Totally out of keeping with the generally slummy surrounding accommodation – the plushest of the area's hotels, it even won an architectural design award. The coffee shop, bar and restaurant are replete with polished marble, brass fixtures and tacky fountains. Rooms are of a similar standard: wall-to-wall carpet, direct-dial phone, bath, video, TV, piped music and secure parking. ⑤

Oriental Palace Hotel Taveta Rd, PO Box 72237 ☎02/217600–3, ℻212335. One of the best-appointed hotels in the district. All 106 rooms here have TV (with in-house video), direct-dial phones, and – fortunately – ceiling fans (the *Little India* restaurant on the ground floor generates a ubiquitous curry atmosphere). Overpriced however, especially for the location – you can get much better in the city centre for about the same. B&B ⑤

Sagret Hotel River Rd, PO Box 18324 ☎02/333395. Comfortable and efficiently managed, very clean and very secure, but very loud and too expensive. ④

Hotel Salama Corner of Luthuli Ave and Tom Mboya St, PO Box 28675 ☎02/224784, ℻343960. Characterful and seemingly family run, despite the "massage" service offered by a permanent guest. The rooms themselves (all s/c) are clean and come with nets. B&B ③

Samagat Hotel Park House, Taveta Rd, PO Box 10027 ☎02/217668, ℻220604. A nine-storey former apartment block (lift access). Spacious s/c rooms, upper ones with views over the commercial district's highrises, with kitchen areas but no cooking equipment. There's a ninth-floor dining/TV-room. Good value. Lower end of price bracket. B&B ③

Solace Hotel Tom Mboya St, PO Box 48867 ☎02/331277. The corridors and stairs here are tatty, but the rooms themselves are very decent: clean, with telephones and nets, and reliable hot water to fill the baths. One of the better mid-range choices. ③

West of Moi Avenue

The following listings cover the more monied parts of the city, roughly north as far as the museum and west as far as Central and Uhuru parks. There are a number of **medium-priced places** on the west side of Moi Avenue up near Jeevanjee Gardens and City Market. For the faint-hearted, this may be a better prospect than the River Road area – quieter and possibly safer (at least more salubrious). Central Nairobi also has over twenty **luxury places** and many more trailing close behind. For locations, see "Commercial Centre and River Road Area" map, unless otherwise indicated in the review.

Moderate

Hotel County (see "Central Nairobi" map, pp.108–9) County Lane, off Haile Selassie Ave, PO Box 41924 ☎02/226190 or 220390, ℻213889, ✉aladins@africaonline.co.ke. A very reasonable, functional block and quieter than most. It's the first hotel from the airport, close to the railway museum, but relatively far from the main shopping streets. Popular with African businessmen, and offers email services. Good value. ④

Down Town Hotel Moktar Daddah St, PO Box 3438 ☎02/310485, ℻310435. Just down from the *Terminal*, and not as loud, but nonetheless overpriced in comparison. Rooms are smaller and not especially clean, lack nets, and the hustly atmosphere doesn't feel at all safe. Bed only. ③

Hotel Embassy Tubman Rd, right behind the City Market, PO Box 47247 ☎02/224087, ℻224534, ✉hotel@webwise.ke.com. Scruffy, but clean and quite decent, with ancient telephones lovingly preserved in some rooms (they don't all work) and a nice restaurant, but be wary of leaving valuables in the rooms, or flaunting them in the area. Group bookings are given discounts and breakfast is pretty cheap (Ksh150). ③

Oakwood Hotel Kimathi St, PO Box 40683 ⓣ02/220592, ⓕ332170, ⓔmadahold@kenyaweb.com. An older, two-storey hotel, currently undergoing a gradual renovation, and an endearing oddity lost amidst the skyscrapers rising all around. All wood panelling, very basic telephones and TVs, and a great antique lift which still works. The location is as central as you can get, with good large rooms and excellent clean bathrooms (hot water and real baths), and there's good security. Popular with aid workers as well as tourists, it also has a first-floor bar overlooking the touristy *Thorn Tree Café*. Wed, Fri and Sat nights can be noisy due to *Jax Invitations* disco next door, but it remains good value compared to other city-centre hotels. B&B ④

Parkside Hotel Monrovia St, PO Box 53104 ⓣ02/333329, ⓕ310435. Facing Jeevanjee Gardens, large, secure, reasonably quiet and pleasant with airy s/c rooms, hot water and telephones, but slightly overpriced, and not as glossy as its brochures. The restaurant is nothing special, and breakfast varies in quality. B&B ③

Hotel Terminal Moktar Daddah St, ⓣ02/228817–8, ⓕ220075. A long-time backpackers' favourite, with large, clean, well-kept rooms, all with nets, telephones and hot showers. No guests after 7pm. Good value compared to other city-centre places, and would be recommended if it wasn't for the rowdy bar-restaurant downstairs. Room only ③

Expensive

Hotel Ambassadeur Moi Ave, PO Box 30399 ⓣ02/336803, ⓕ336860; reservations through Sarova, p.44. A modern, adequate, if rather tired international-style hotel, lagging miles behind Sarova's usual standards, but it's cheap. The staff are helpful, and the rooms are large and bright if unspectacular, but it's surprisingly noisy. If possible get a double-glazed, top-floor room, but even these are no match for determined matatu horns and night-time River Road discos. The two bars are calm, and there's a very pleasant coffee house and restaurant on the ground floor, though its food sometimes takes a dive. Guests can use the *Panafric*'s pool. Rates open to discussion. B&B ⑤

Boulevard Hotel (see "Greater Nairobi" map, pp.88–89) Harry Thuku Rd, PO Box 42831 ⓣ02/227567–9, ⓕ334071, ⓔhotelboulevard@form-net.com. Perhaps the best

mid-range address in the city – functional rather than extravagant, well cared for, in a pleasant garden setting and with a good pool (though unfortunately it's on the traffic side of the building), tennis court, TVs in all rooms and ample parking. To overcome Uhuru Highway's noise, get a room at the back in the middle, overlooking the garden. Uhuru Highway is prone to muggings at night. Buses #21, #23 and #119, matatu #104. Room only ⑤

Grand Regency Off Loita St, PO Box 57549 ⓣ02/211199, ⓕ217120, ⓔgrhadmin@african-line.co.ke. Built in 1994, a successful example of modern technology melded to architectural ambition. The interior is gobsmacking to say the least. Built around a cool marble-clad atrium, three glass and gold-lacquer lifts glide up and down one side to the rooms, the more expensive of which have balconies opening onto the atrium. Service is efficient, the clientele mostly businessmen. There's also an expensive pool and health club (Ksh950). ⑧–⑨

Hilton Hotel Mama Ngina St, PO Box 30624, ⓣ02/250000, ⓕ250099, ⓔhilton@africaonline.co.ke. The cylindrical tower is unmistakable, and the lobby impressive, but otherwise an average example of the species, somewhat impersonal and catering mainly for expense accounts. Rooms get better the higher you go, but the "rooftop pool" is down at second-floor level and rather overshadowed. Also offers a health club, Jacuzzi, sauna and steam bath, as well as four restaurants, but nonetheless over-priced compared to *The Stanley*. Room only ⑧

Hotel Inter-Continental City Hall Way, PO Box 30533 ⓣ02/261000, ⓕ210675, ⓦwww.interconti.com. Thirty years old and not as good value as its competitors, but still fairly palatial if you're not a regular in such places. It has some surprisingly secluded corners in the grounds, and many amenities (including a heated pool, health club, casino and a good Mediterranean restaurant, *Le Mistral*). Disabled facilities, and they can pick you up or drop you at the airport. Room only ⑧

Meridian Court Hotel Murang'a Rd, off the top of River Rd, PO Box 30278 ⓣ02/333916, ⓕ333658. Grim position hemmed in by bad drivers and exhaust emissions, but no matter, the *Meridian* is well run and friendly, and offers excellent value for its facilities. All rooms have bath, fridge, a safe, satellite TV and kitchenette (but no cooking facilities), whilst amenities include a rooftop pool (Ksh100 for non-guests) and bar, sauna, 24hr room service, and two good restaurants: the *Khyber* and the *Mandarin* (see "Eating and drinking", pp.127 & 128). Underground parking. Room only ④

Nairobi Safari Club University Way, PO Box 43564 ☎02/251333, ⓕ224625, ⓔnsclub@africaonline.co.ke. A prestigious address, but not as exclusive as you might imagine, despite the copy of the club's bye-laws issued to you at reception and the astronomical rates. It's a twelve-storey block, ill-placed on the loud and fume-filled University Way, but with good service, and seems gradually to be moving away from its suffocatingly pompous club atmosphere. Rooms are well-equipped suites, the quieter ones higher up, but it's still ridiculously overpriced, and even use of the small pool and health club costs extra. Room only ❽

Norfolk Hotel (see "Central Nairobi" map, pp.108–9) Harry Thuku Rd, PO Box 40064 ☎02/250900, ⓕ336742; reservations through Lonrho, p.43. Nairobi's oldest and most historic lodgings, built in mock-Edwardian style. It was, and remains, the traditional haunt of visiting celebrities. Elspeth Huxley once noted the possibility of having "an Italian Count or an Austrian Baron thrown through the window on to your bed in the middle of the night". Still recommended on the whole, but much too pricey for the facilities on offer, limited to a pool, expensive shop, health club and sauna, and a few old cars and rickshaws in the courtyard. The newer accommodation blocks have also cluttered up the grounds somewhat. Room only ❾

Serena Hotel (see "Central Nairobi" map, pp.108–9) Nyerere Rd, off Kenyatta Ave, PO Box 46302 ☎02/725111, ⓕ725184, ⓔnairobi@serena.co.ke; reservations through Serena, p.44. Highly polished and sumptuous place, with impeccable rooms, first-class service, a calming atmosphere and exceptional if expensive food ($25–30 per meal). Amenities include a health club, pool and shops. Unfortunately, the location, fronting onto Central Park, is dangerous at night. The real muggers, however, are at the reception: it's way overpriced. Room only ❾

680 (Six-Eighty) Hotel Corner of Kenyatta Ave and Muindi Mbingu St, PO Box 43436 ☎02/332680, ⓕ332908. Soulless 340-room 1970s towerblock, right in the heart of the city, but comparatively cheap. Safe underground parking and convenient for shopping. Guests can use the *Boulevard's* pool. Room only ❺

The Stanley Hotel (formerly *New Stanley*) Corner of Kimathi St and Kenyatta Ave, PO Box 30680 ☎02/228830 or 333233, ⓕ229388, ⓦwww.sarovahotels.com; reservations through Sarova, p.44). Complete with its famous *Thorn Tree Café* rendezvous, this is the best upmarket choice, and as central as you can get. Originally an Edwardian structure, with touches of Art Deco, it's a popular downtown base for tourists and businessmen alike. The period decor isn't overdone, service is friendly and efficient, and the rooms themselves equipped with satellite TV, minibars and essential double glazing. They have specially designed rooms for disabled guests. Facilities include a modern gym, sauna and steam room, and a pleasant heated rooftop pool and bar. Courtesy bus to the airport. Room only ❼ low, ❽ high.

Out of central Nairobi

Most of Nairobi's better value mid- and upper-range hotels are located out of the city centre, both in the relatively affluent **suburbs** of Westlands and Parklands which are also the main focus for more sophisticated night-time bars and clubs, and along the main roads radiating out of the city. Two of the main focuses for budget travellers, the youth hostel and *Ma Roche's Guest House*, are a short journey away from the city centre in the suburbs, and both have their devotees, while the excellent **YMCA** is within walking distance.

Camping and hostels

Central YMCA (see "Central Nairobi" map, pp.108–9) State House Rd, 300m from Uhuru Highway, PO Box 30330 ☎02/713599, ⓕ728825, ⓔkenyaymca@net2000ke.com. This is an excellent place popular with travellers not quite on a shoestring budget. It's well equipped, with a choice of dorms (Ksh580 per person) and s/c rooms, and isn't markedly different from a modest hotel. There's well-priced if average food, a guarded parking lot, but the clincher is the excellent pool (Ksh40 for day visitors). And no, you don't have to be Christian or male. Open 24 hours; no alcohol (or drunks) allowed. ❸

Ma Roche's Guest House (see "Greater Nairobi" map, pp.88–89) Third Parklands Ave, opposite the Aga Khan Hospital admissions ☎02/562452. A private home, in the predominantly Asian suburb of Parklands. Take a bed either in one of the cabins or in Mrs Roche's bungalow, camp in the garden, or sleep on the verandah. Popular with worn-out overlanders and travellers who really loathe Nairobi. Fall into either category and you should love it. Also a good place to meet people and it's often possible to fix up shared arrangements to drive to the game parks or head on through Africa – use the noticeboard. There's also a laundry and a convenient lock-up store to leave surplus gear while you travel, but there's no *askari* – don't leave valuables in your tent. Take a matatu #11, or one from Latema Rd, opposite the *Iqbal*, asking for "Aga Khan". Ksh300 per person.

Nairobi Backpackers (see "Greater Nairobi" map, pp.88–89) PO Box 9545 ℡02/724827, Ⓔnbobackpackers@yahoo.com. Five mins from *Buffalo Bill's* on Milimani Rd, this newly decorated place has dorm rooms (up to 21 people), email, hot showers and satellite TV. The food is basic but good, and breakfast is included in the rates (Ksh 250 camping per person, Ksh 500 in a dorm for four and Ksh600 in a dorm for two). However, with the owner also living in the small house it does have the feel at times of an international boarding house with a motherly housewife.

Nairobi Park Services Campsite (see "Nairobi outskirts" map, pp.156–7) Magadi Rd, off Langata Rd just past Langata Gate, PO Box 54867 ℡ & Ⓕ892261–2, Ⓔnps@swiftkenya.com. The campsite is one of the best equipped, popular with overland trucks, with single and double rooms and some dorm beds. The site is secure, and if you want to find out about which safari to go on, the bar is the local for a number of operators, including Gametrackers. There's food available, and cable TV. Matatu #125 or bus #126. Camping Ksh250 per person (tent hire Ksh60 per person/night), Ksh200 per vehicle; beds in the dorm Ksh300 per person. Recommended.

Nairobi Youth Hostel (see "Greater Nairobi" map, pp.88–89) Ralphe Bunche Rd, near Nairobi Hospital, PO Box 48661 ℡02/723012, Ⓕ724862. A gentle introduction to the city, and full most of the time, but second best to the YMCA. Not having a IYHF card isn't a problem, as you can pay a daily Ksh90 fee for a stamp, which after six nights (Ksh540) converts to annual international membership. The small compound can get claustrophobic, though, and it's a bad idea to walk into (or back from) town after dark. Still, there are lots of other hostellers to talk to, it also has a few two- and four-bed rooms, and there's a s/c flat (③) available too. Usual YH rules apply, including a (lax) ban on booze. Many buses and matatus, including #34, #41 and #46 pass by one end or the other of Ralphe Bunche Rd. Ksh380–480 per person.

Rowallan Scout Camp (see "Nairobi outskirts" map, pp.156–7) Off Kibera Drive, south of Jamhuri Park, PO Box 41422 ℡02/573799. Set deep in the Ngong Rd forest, the Kenya Scouts Association has the best campsite location in Nairobi, with richly overgrown vegetation, plenty of shade, myriad forest tracks for walks (great for bird-watching), and even a few caves around. You're best bringing your own tent (Ksh100 per person; tent hire Ksh200 per night), as the *bandas* and dorms are filthy and close to collapse. Things aren't helped by the squalid pit latrines and showers, but despite all this it's a beautiful place. You can buy firewood for the outdoor kitchen, and limited supplies from the *duka*. There's a fridge for sodas, and a large, rather green, swimming pool. The huge site is patrolled by police officers and *askaris*, but leave valuables with the helpful warden. Incidentally, you don't have to be a boy scout or girl guide. Get there either from Ngong Road (a two-kilometre walk down Kibera Drive), or on bus #42 or #111, or #8 matatu to Kibera, from where it's a ten-minute walk along the tarmac downhill to the forest's edge, with a signposted left 300m further on.

Upper Hill Campsite (see "Greater Nairobi" map, pp.88–89) Menengai Rd, off Hospital Rd ℡02/720290, Ⓕ719662, Ⓔcampsite @thorntree.com. A newish campsite, already well discovered by the overland trucks, with beds in dorms (Ksh250 per person) and clean double rooms (②) also available. Hot showers, kitchen, a bar, restaurant and relaxed atmosphere; cheap tent hire is possible. Good security. Take matatu #8, or bus #18 or #20 to Nairobi hospital.

Wildlife Clubs of Kenya Hostel (see "Nairobi outskirts" map, pp.156–7) Langata Rd in Nairobi South "C", next to the Bomas of Kenya ℡02/891904. A rather wild, overgrown site, popular with locals, with dormitory-style rooms (Ksh300 per person) and decent facilities. Bus/matatu #24, #34, #125 or #126.

Hotels

Fairview Hotel (see "Greater Nairobi" map, pp.88–89) Bishops Rd, PO Box 40842 ℡02/713993, Ⓕ721320, Ⓔreserv@fairviewkenya.com. A peaceful, rambling country-style place with pleasant grounds (great bird-watching), and a wide variety of accommodation. All rooms have nets and TVs, some have baths, and the deluxe doubles are excellent. Family rooms have bunk beds for kids, but some of the standard rooms are dull and not much better than a decent B&L. Moreover, if you don't look the part the atmosphere can feel stuffy, and they can be awkward about letting you see rooms. Good meals, though, and it's popular with families, so reserve ahead. Bus/matatu #1, #2, #3, #4, #41, #46 or #111 to 3rd Ngong Ave, then a three-minute walk. B&B ⑤

Giraffe Manor (see "Nairobi outskirts" map, pp.156–7) Koitobos Rd, adjacent to the AFEW

Giraffe Centre, Langata ☎02/891078, ℱ890949. If you have serious money to burn, this place rises neck and shoulders above the rest: a wonderfully eccentric set-up in a Scottish-style manor house in the grounds of AFEW Giraffe Centre whose quadrupedal inmates like to share your breakfast through the first-floor dining room windows. It's extremely exclusive, astoundingly expensive ($480 double including drinks), and bookings are by prior arrangement only. Profits go to the centre; closed April. Take a taxi to get there. FB ❾

Hurlingham Hotel (see "Greater Nairobi" map, pp.88–89) Argwings Kodhek Rd, PO Box 43158 ☎02/721920, ℱ726691. A pre-war feeling lingers here which some find charming, others gloomy. Most people enjoy it, though, especially for the excellent cooking, with touches like wholemeal bread. However, most of the seventeen rooms are long overdue for a revamp, and some mattresses badly need replacing – inexcusable at the price. Check the rooms before paying. Prices bargain-able. B&B ❸

Kentmere Club (off the top of "Nairobi outskirts" map, pp.156–7) Limuru Rd, Tigoni, PO Box 39508 ☎0154/3950, ℱ40692, ℮kentclub@net2000ke.com. Situated 16km north of Nairobi amidst the tea and coffee plantations of the Tigoni highlands, *Kentmere* is a small and friendly country inn, pretty much what you might find in the Cotswolds in England, all wooden beams and wooden "slate" roofs. It has sixteen s/c rooms in cottages with beautiful gardens and cosy fireplaces, and a good restaurant which uses mostly locally grown ingredients. Ten minutes' drive away is the Limuru Country Club with its golf course and swimming pool. Matatu #114 or one from outside *Mayur* restaurant on Tom Mboya St. HB ❺

Ngong Hills Hotel (see "Greater Nairobi" map, pp.88–89) Ngong Rd, PO Box 40485 ☎02/571747, ℱ571750, ℮ngonghills @iconnect.co.ke. Helpful mainly if you fancy boogying the night away at the hotel's popular live music venue (see p.138) or around the jumping nightspots of Dagoretti Corner and Ngong Rd, and don't want the hassle of getting back in the wee hours. The ambience is relaxed, and the s/c rooms – off prison-like corridors – are good, with carpets, nets, telephones and proper baths. The green pool is more inviting after a few beers. Bus/matatu #1, #2, #3, #4, #102, #103 or #111. B&B ❹

Panafric Hotel (see "Greater Nairobi" map, pp.88–89) Kenyatta Ave, Nairobi Hill, PO Box 30486 ☎02/720823, ℱ726356; reservations through Sarova, p.44). 500m up the hill west of Uhuru Park, with views over the city. Potentially a good uptown option, but this 1965 concrete block is generally uninspiring and in need of zest (and renovation), despite the refreshing pool and satellite TV. Service is very good and its *Flame Tree Restaurant* (which is very busy and worth a visit at the weekends for its live bands) has garnered a solid reputation for high quality. Bus/matatu #1 to #4, #34, #41, #46 or #111. Room only ❻

Pathway Hotel (see "Nairobi outskirts" map, pp.156–7) Ngong Rd, opposite the racecourse, PO Box 54803 ☎02/577545. A new and well-priced place over a mellow bar (fear of neighbours' complaints keeps the volume down and the pace slow – as yet), with good s/c rooms and hot water. Like the *Ngong Hills Hotel*, a reliable base for exploring the nightlife around Dagoretti Corner and the Ngong Rd. Bus/matatu #1 to #4, #102, #103 or #111. ❷

Safari Park Hotel (see "Nairobi outskirts" map, pp.156–7) Thika Rd, 14km from town, PO Box 45038 ☎02/802493, ℱ802477, ℮safariht@arcc.or.ke; reservations at Kimathi House, Kimathi St ☎02/216070, ℱ217677. A huge, purpose-built "inland resort", offering a wholly sanitized vision of "Real Africa". Although far out of town (there's a regular shuttle bus), it's an attractive base for an upmarket stay, with a large expanse of landscaped gardens, a massive swimming pool, health club, tennis courts, four-poster beds in all rooms, seven excellent and remarkably affordable restaurants, a discotheque, piano bar, horse riding, and faultless service. Everything you could wish for, and certainly should expect at this price. There's also a casino, should you have any money left over. Bus/matatu #45, #137, #145, #160 or #237. Room only ❽–❾.

Silver Springs Hotel (see "Greater Nairobi" map, pp.88–89) Valley Rd/Argwings Kodhek Rd, PO Box 61362 ☎02/722451–6, ℱ720545. A large and rather grey establishment overlooking the hospital (it reeks of antiseptic), with comfortable rooms, pool, health club and massage, but it lacks the class of its competitors. Safe parking. Bus #41 or #46. B&B ❺

Simbayo House (see "Nairobi outskirts" map, pp.156–7) Bogoni East Rd, two compounds down from Utamaduni Crafts Centre, PO Box 15110 ☎02/890921, ℱ890462, ℮utalihotel@insightkenya.com. This is an American-owned homestay run by the same people as the *Jikoni* restaurant at Utamaduni. There are three rooms available (one s/c), each with verandah looking out onto gardens. Singles half price. Bus/matatu #24. B&B ❹, FB ❻ (including lunch at *Jikoni*).

Sirona Hotel (see "Greater Nairobi" map, pp.88–89) Keiyo Rd, off Forest Rd, Parklands

T02/743969, @sirona@bidii.com; bus #108 to Parklands Roundabout. There are single, double and dorm rooms available, all very clean and quiet with spacious bathrooms. The bar, which is always lively with locals as well as travellers, has an open-air BBQ area, and huge satellite screen. Security within the compound is excellent at all times but, even with a police station nearby, don't walk around outside at night. They also arrange transfers to the airport, Arusha and Moshi. Breakfast is included in the price. Recommended. ❸

Utalii Hotel (see "Greater Nairobi" map, pp.88–89) Thika Rd, 6km from town, PO Box 31067 T02/802540/1–7, F803094, @utalii@insightkenya.com. This offers something different, with unbeatable standards. It's run by the Utalii College, Kenya's college of tourism, so you get impeccable, if slightly hesitant, service. Rooms have TVs. Amenities include a large outdoor heated pool, tennis courts and an astonishingly good restaurant (Tues Kenyan buffet lunches; Sat evening poolside BBQ; Sun buffet lunch). Facing it, across the banana tops, sprawls one of Nairobi's worst slums, Mathare Valley. Courtesy bus to city centre, or bus/matatu #45, #137, #145, #160 or #237. B&B ❺

Whistling Thorns (see chapter map on p.85 for the Kiserian–Isinya road) 35km south of Nairobi off the Magadi Rd: turn left after Kiserian (22km) onto the D523 to Isinya for 13km, PO Box 51512 T & F02/350720, @speccampsaf@thorntree.org.

Overlooking the Ngong Hills and the plains south of Nairobi National Park, this place offers homely two-bedroomed cottages and a swimming pool, and the option of walks, cycling (Ksh400 per half-day) and horse-riding (Ksh1000 per hour). Also open daily for food (pizzas and grilled wildebeest). You can camp here too. Very good value if getting out here isn't a problem (bus #126 or matatu #125 to Kiserian, then potluck with matatus headed for Isinya). Credit cards accepted. B&B ❹

Windsor Golf & Country Club (see "Nairobi outskirts" map, pp.156–7) Off Kigwa Rd, Ridgeways, 15km north of the city, PO Box 45587 T02/862300, F802322, @windsor@africaonline.co.ke. Built in 1992, this rather absurd golfers' resort has been styled and fitted entirely in mock-Victorian and Georgian style, complete with landscaped gardens, copper-plate clock tower, gazebos, and even designer creaking floorboards. It's superbly run, with services and amenities second to none. Situated on an old coffee plantation, the conversion to golfer's paradise has been done to a tee; most rooms look out over the manicured course, complete with lakes and bunkers. Facilities include an outdoor heated pool, health club with steam room and massage, tennis and squash courts, a croquet lawn, fishing and riding, and there's a resident ornithologist. Accommodation ranges from rooms and suites to some lovely twin cottages ($570). Take a taxi. Bed only ❽–❾.

Westlands and Parklands hotels

The following hotels are on the "Westlands" map unless otherwise stated. Buses/matatus #21, #23, #30, #104 and #119 go to Westlands. For Parklands (adjacent to Westlands), catch a matatu on Latema Road. Both areas are relatively safe for walking around with luggage during the day.

Bavaria Hotel (see "Greater Nairobi" map, pp.88–89) Chiromo Rd, Westlands, PO Box 31153 T02/741132 or 747394. A *nyama choma*-joint-cum-hotel setup, common "up-country" but unusual for Nairobi, just up from the International Casino. The rooms are nothing flash, but there's a beer garden, a sauna (for a steaming Ksh600/hour), 24hr bar (loud discos Wed, Fri & Sat), Indian/Chinese restaurant, a swimming pool (Ksh100 for non-guests) and safe parking. Room only ❸

Holiday Inn Parklands Rd, PO Box 66807 00623 T02/740920, F748823, @holidayinn@africaonline.co.ke. Classy, well maintained, modern hotel in pastiche Edwardian and Art Nouveau styles (the original structure was a 1930s hotel), with small tropical gardens, and a bar. It's rather

business-oriented, but efficiently run and has good disabled access with some specially designed rooms. There's also a pool, the obligatory fitness centre and sauna, and adjacent Mayfair Casino. Excellent value in its class. B&B ❼

Impala Hotel Parklands Rd, Parklands, PO Box 14144 T02/742346–7, F743258. Not at all touristy, with reasonably priced rooms, good parking and a shaded, leafy bar. ❸

Landmark Hotel Waiyaki Way, Westlands, PO Box 14287 T02/448713, F448977, @landmark@africaonline.co.ke; reservations through Block, p.42. The rooms are a bit small, but all have satellite TV and fans, though the building itself remains charmless, its lawns surrounded by tall fences. Service varies between middling and excellent, and there's a nice pool. Be careful when

Map labels:
Parklands
Sarit Centre
WESTLANDS
0   200 m
WAIYAKI WAY
KARUNA RD
PARKLANDS ROAD
MKUNGU CLOSE
RING ROAD WESTLANDS
Standard Chartered Bank
Agip
Rank Xerox House
MATIA CLOSE
Makson's Plaza
MPAKA ROAD
Mayfair Casino
A104
Barclays Bank
Undungu
Unga House
Apic Centre
PARKLANDS ROAD
Total
WESTLANDS AVENUE
WOODVALE GROVE
Westlands Market
Brick Court
MUTHITHI ROAD
MOGOTIO ROAD
MPESI LANE
THE CRESCENT
Parklands
Mobil
Sound Plaza
RING ROAD WESTLANDS
KASKAZI LANE
Mpaka House
CHIROMO ROAD
The Mall
Bishan Plaza
N
RHAPTA ROAD
Soin Arcade
WESTLANDS CLOSE
CROSSWAY
WESTLANDS ROAD

ACCOMMODATION
Holiday Inn   2
Impala Hotel   3
Landmark Hotel   1

Swan Court

RESTAURANTS & BARS
Addis Ababa   F   Nargis Kapuri Pan A
Clubhouse I   D   Pavement   G
Gipsy/Tropicanna Bar E   West Cafe   B
Grapes Cafe   C

Museum Hill & Uhuru Highway   National Museum

walking in the vicinity at night. B&B ⑥
Plums Hotel (see "Greater Nairobi" map, pp.88–89) Ojijo Rd, Parklands, PO Box 40747 ☎02/745222–3. Pleasant establishment near the museum, with good car security if you're driving, plus an attached *nyama choma* joint playing Kikuyu and *zilizopendwa* oldies weekends (ie it can get loud). ②

Long stays

For long stays in Nairobi, cheap **flats**, **rooms and studios** are advertised in the classified columns of the *Nation* and the *Standard*. Otherwise, contact an apartment agency (Westlands is probably the most promising area), or there's a very useful noticeboard at the supermarket in Karen. Remember, if the place has no *askari* (security guard), the danger of burglary is very real. If your stay is more temporary, the YWCA is your best bet.

Fairview Bishops Rd (same management and details as *Fairview Hotel*, p.103). Three-room flats available for three-month stays or longer at Ksh72,000 per flat per month.
Heron Court Apartment Hotel (see "Greater Nairobi" map, pp.88–89) Milimani Rd, PO Box 41848 ☎02/720740–3, ℱ721698, ℮herco@iconnect.co.ke. Much used by volunteers and their kin, and fine (if a little moth-eaten) especially if self-catering appeals. Reasonable rooms or studio apartments. There's a bleach-filled pool and the dubious benefit of *Buffalo Bill's*, a seedy pick-up bar, which can be rather noisy at night, but is kept separate from the hotel itself. Bus/matatu #1, #2, #3, #4, #34, #41, #46 or #111 to *Panafric*, then a five-minute walk up Milimani Road. Monthly rates Ksh27,500 double (per night ③).
Nairobi Protea Apartments Yaya Centre (see "Greater Nairobi" map, pp.88–89), Argwings

Kodhek Rd, PO Box 76377 ☎02/713360, ℱ561902, ℮protea@africaonline.co.ke. Currently the top luxury option for long stays, with fully furnished and serviced apartments (one to four bedrooms) including kitchens and satellite TV. Amenities include an Olympic-sized pool and two floodlit tennis courts (with resident coach). Safe parking. Bus #41 or #46. One-bedroom $1700, two-bedrooms $1890 per month.
Woodmere Apartments (see "Greater Nairobi" map, pp.88–89) Rose Ave, off Lenana Rd, three blocks from the Yaya Centre, PO Box 74381 ☎02/724080, ℱ720721, ℮woodmere@net2000ke.com. A little bit out of the way: well-guarded premises, daily cleaning included in the price, small pool, sauna, "garden" and space for kids. Accommodation ranges from fully furnished, small, serviced studios with tiny kitchen and "loft" sleeping to spacious one and

two bedroom, tastefully decorated apartments. From about $50 per night, with cheaper weekly and monthly rates. Recommended if you have the cash and are planning to stay in Kenya for a while. YWCA (see "Central Nairobi" map, pp.108–9) Mamlaka Rd, off Nyerere Ave, just west of Central Park, PO Box 40710 ☎02/724699,

ⓔywca@icconect.co.ke. Best value for men as well as women (and couples can share). Rates for room only are in the order of Ksh7000 per month for a double room with washbasin, or about Ksh5000 per month for a single. There are flatlets for about Ksh9000. Write well in advance to reserve.

Around central Nairobi

Kenyatta Avenue is the obvious place to start looking around Central Nairobi. A good initial overview of it can be had from the vertigo-inducing, glass-walled lifts in the **ICEA building**, on the northwest corner of Wabera Street. If the guards at the bottom need an excuse, tell them you're visiting the Japanese Embassy on the fifteenth floor; they may even be persuaded to escort you onto the roof. Tipping (Ksh20–50) might be helpful.

Kenyatta Avenue

Kenyatta Avenue was originally designed to allow a twelve-oxen team to make a full turn, though livestock is nowadays no longer permitted within the city limits. Broad, multi-laned and planted with flowering trees and shrubs, it remains (along with the Kenyatta Conference Centre) the capital's favourite tourist image. The avenue is smartest – and most touristy – on its south side, with would-be moneychangers, itinerant souvenir hawkers and safari touts assailing you from every direction, and wily shoeshiners inspecting each passing pair of feet from their stands (who given half a chance will throw some wax on your shoes and then insist on having to clean it off). The focus of the avenue's eastern end is the *Stanley Hotel's* **Thorn Tree Café**, diagonally opposite Nakumatt supermarket on the corner of Kimathi Street. The *Thorn Tree* is Nairobi's one proper pavement café and, despite its prices and largely *wazungu* and rich businessman clientele, an enduring meeting place. The thorn tree in question was cut down in 1997 and replaced with a new sapling in December 1998 and a smaller message board.

At the other end of Kenyatta Avenue, is the skyscraper of the **General Post Office** (GPO) on the left and, just before it, **Koinange Street**, named after the Kikuyu Senior Chief Koinange of the colonial era. The peculiar caged **Galton-Fenzi Memorial**, just here on the left, is a monument to the man who founded, of all things, the Nairobi branch of the Automobile Association. Fenzi was also the first motorist to drive from Nairobi to Mombasa, back in 1926 when there was only a dirt track.

City Square and Parliament

Heading down Koinange Street and on to Kaunda Street, passing the *Inter-Continental* on your right and Holy Family Cathedral on your left, you cross City Hall Way and enter **City Square**. Jomo Kenyatta's statue sits benevolently, mace in hand, on the far side of the wide, flagstoned court; his mausoleum, with flickering eternal flames, is on the right as you approach the Parliament building. When the flags are out for a conference it all looks very bright and confident.

The legend over the main doors of Kenya's **Parliament** reads: "For a Just Society and the Fair Government of Men". With the government forced by both national and international pressures to allow greater democracy and

The Museum, Casino & Westlands ▲

Kenya National Theatre

Synagogue

St.Paul's Catholic Church

St. Andrew's Church

Lutheran Church

1st Church of Christ Scientist

Hazina Towers

View Park Towers

Utalii House

Maendeleo House

University Campus

HARRY THUKU ROAD

Police Headquarters

Murang'a Roundabout

UNIVERSITY WAY

Nairobi Safari Club

Davanu Shuttle (Windsor House)

See Commercial Centre & River Road Area map for more detail

MONROVIA STREET

Nginyo Towers

Jeevanjee Gardens

MOKTAR DADDAH STREET

NJUGU LANE

BIASHARA STREET

TUBMAN ROAD

KIGALI ROAD

City Market

Jamia Mosque

McMillan Library

Nation Centre

MARKET STREET

BANDA STREET

ICEA Building

KENYATTA AVENUE

KENYATTA AVENUE

All Saints' Cathedral

GPO

STANDARD STREET

STANDARD STREET

Lonrho House

Bruce House

KAUNDA STREET

Nyayo House

KAUNDA

Holy Family Cathedral

MAMA NGINA STREET

Boating Lake

CITY HALL WAY

City Hall

CITY HALL WAY

Uhuru Park

City Square

Kenyatta's Mausoleum

Kenyatta Conference Centre

Law Courts

Reinsurance Plaza

Parliament

Kenya Cinema Plaza

Freemark Capital Pavilion

Continental Towers

Public Map Office

Jogoo House

HARAMBEE AVENUE

HAILE SELASSIE AVENUE

Embassy House

Office of the President

Ministry of Foreign Affairs

National Bank

NHC House

Professional Centre

Agip House

'Extelcoms'

Comcraft House

HAILE SELASSIE AVENUE

7 August 1998 bombsite

Railway Golf Club

Railway Museum

Kenya Railways HQ

Central Park

Minet ICDC House

▲ The Panafric Hotel & Youth Hostel

▲ The Ngong Road

▼ Nyayo Stadium, Airports & Nairobi National Park

accountability in its business, the motto seems finally to be losing its edge of irony. Parliament is open to the public. Talk to the guards at the gate, who will tell you when the next session is taking place (usually Wed & Thurs at 2.30pm; it's in recess mid-July to mid-October) or, when it's not in session, how to get a tour of the building. If you're assigned a guide, make sure both parties are clear about how much you'll pay. To sit in the public gallery you must first reg-

City Park, Ma Roche's & Safari Park Hotel

MURANG'A ROAD

NGARA ROAD

N

WASTELAND

Nairobi River

KIRINYAGA ROAD

KILOME RD

DESAI ROAD

NGARA ROAD

KINSHASA ROAD

KULALU RD

PARK ROAD

MUSLIM RD

QUARRY ROAD

★ Akamba Bus

LAGOS ROAD

LATEMA ROAD

VOI ROAD

ACCRA ROAD

KUMASI ROAD

RIVER ROAD

National Archives

♣ Sikh Temple

LUTHULI AVENUE

Hotel Ambassadeur

MOI AVENUE

RONALD NGALA STREET

MFANGANO STREET

KBS Bus Station

TEMPLE ROAD
★
Transluxe Bus

OTOMASI ST.

HAKATI ROAD

★ KBS Bus Station Matatus

Mang' Hotel

HAILE SELASSIE AVENUE

MOI AVENUE

Railway Station

VGARA ROAD

RACECOURSE ROAD

QUARRY ROAD

Kariokor Market

RING ROAD

RACECOURSE ROAD

QUARRY ROAD

RING ROAD PUMWANI

Nairobi River

Wakulima Market

PUMWANI ROAD

LANDHIES ROAD

Country Bus Station (Machakos Airport)

ACCOMMODATION	
Hotel County	5
Norfolk	2
Serena	4
YMCA	1
YMCA	3

0   250   500 m

CENTRAL NAIROBI

Eastleigh KBS Depot ▶

Mombasa ▶

Maridadi Fabrics ▼

ister at the gatehouse on the corner of Parliament Road and Harambee Avenue, leaving all your belongings with the attendant outside. Once seated, be on your best behaviour. The gallery tends to be full of very well-behaved schoolchildren – which of course is more than can be said of the members of parliament. With the admission of opposition members since 1992, proceedings are livelier now than they have perhaps ever been, with a host of contentious motions being openly debated concerning corruption, ethnic violence and even the occassional vote of no-confidence in President Moi's government. Try to get hold of a copy of the Orders of the Day – there may be a juicy question or two worth anticipating.

Kenyatta Conference Centre

From Parliament, walking down Harambee Avenue along the shady pavement, you come to Nairobi's pride and joy – the **Kenyatta International Conference Centre** (KICC) and its tall brother, "KANU tower", the ruling party headquarters (all enquiries ☎02/332383 or 332760). This, for a long time the tallest building in Kenya, is capped by a mile-high (a mile above sea level that is) formerly revolving restaurant. Confusion has always arisen on the ground floor about whether anyone was allowed up to the 28th. The restaurant has closed, but it's worth making an effort to get as high as possible. If you talk to the security staff in the foyer, assent is usually given for ascent partly because it has become accepted practice to tip the guards who come with you (a mean Ksh200 is the going rate, though nothing's fixed). The view of Nairobi is without equal and a firm reminder of the vastness of Africa. Just 4km to the south, you see the Mombasa Road leave the suburbs behind and take off across the yellow plains. Northwards, hills of coffee – and, at higher altitudes, tea – roll into the distance. If you pick a good day in December or January you really can see Mount Kenya in one direction and Kilimanjaro in the other. Immediately below, the traffic swarms – and Jogoo House is suddenly seen to be built remarkably like a Roman villa.

National Archives

Straight down Harambee Avenue, cut across Moi Avenue and up to the **National Archives** (Mon–Fri 8.30am–4.30pm, Sat 8.30am–1pm;

Saba Saba and the Trees of Peace

The months preceding the December 1997 **general election** were fraught with violence. It all began on July 7, already nick-named Saba Saba Day ("seven-seven day", from the anniversary of a brutal crackdown on a pro-democracy demonstration on July 7, 1990), when history repeated itself. A rally in central Nairobi degenerated into running battles with police, whose brutality was widely reported on Kenyan and international TV. This in turn led to nationwide riots in which thirteen people were killed. Police, chanting *Uua! Uua!* (Kiswahili for "kill") stormed an examination room at Nairobi University and beat up students, others stormed the Anglican Cathedral – a focal point of the pro-reform movement – where many people had taken refuge, while on the streets police dragged passengers out of taxis and beat them up, and TV news bulletins carried pictures of women with their babies strapped to their backs being attacked by policemen.

The effect of all this, together with the spiralling violence of the following months, was to shatter Kenya's previously peaceful international image, and indirectly led to the suspension of an IMF loan to the country, as well as the virtual collapse of Kenya's tourist industry. Hemmed in on all sides, President Moi finally acceded to the demonstrators' demands and promised to institute a set of reformist measures, including the unbanning of Richard Leakey's Safina party, just before the election. A poignant memorial to the many lives lost in political violence over the past decade, can be seen at the roadside verge of Uhuru Park at Kenyatta Avenue ("Freedom Corner"), where the Greenbelt Movement planted a dozen saplings (themselves destroyed and replanted several times) as "Trees of Peace", each bearing a simple wooden cross with the name of a victim and the words "Saba Saba".

02/228959 ext 211, 228027, knarchives@form-net.com). Housed in the striking old Bank of India building on the bend of Moi Avenue across from the *Hilton*, the archives amount to a **museum/art gallery** in the heart of the city which few visitors to Nairobi seem to know about; entry is free and a look around takes an hour or so.

The ground floor is a public gallery with Joseph Murumbi's (briefly vice-president under Kenyatta) oddball collection of paintings dominating the walls. The collection, sold to the government in 1966, ranges from uninteresting dabbles to some beautiful drawings and striking collages, but in a city that's not exactly cluttered with art collections, it does deserve a look. In the centre of the floor there's also a delightfully jumbled collection of African ethnographia – musical instruments, masks, weapons, domestic artefacts. The Senufo masks and figures from the Ivory Coast are especially impressive.

Past the first floor and its photograph library, the second floor houses a **photographic exhibition** of the struggle for **Independence** – compelling not just for its content but because this is almost the only public place in the country where Kenyans can be reminded of the period in their history euphemistically called "The Emergency". There's also a collection of black-and-white press **photos**, highly revealing as a record of the early part of Daniel Arap Moi's presidency, with foreign tours figuring prominently. Also here are a number of fascinating portraits of tribal elders, mostly from the colonial era. If you're around on a Saturday, there are free 10am screenings of films relating to culture, politics or wildlife. The actual archives themselves (mainly books, papers, correspondence and some recordings) are closed to the general public, though if you're interested you can pay a small fee (just Ksh50) for a year's membership.

The Jamia Mosque

The **Jamia Mosque** stands near the City Market, north of Kenyatta Avenue. The ornate green-and-white exterior contrasts strikingly with the simple interior, where the large central dome appears far larger from beneath than it does from the courtyard outside. Although most Kenyan towns now have at least one mosque, often financed by Saudi Arabia, few are as large or as beautiful as the Jamia, which is currently being enlarged. It's highly unlikely that non-Muslims will be allowed in, although polite requests, a genuine interest in Islam, and the usual modesty of attire (limbs covered, feet washed and unshod) may help. So, for an alternative, bird's-eye view of the mosque, the top of the ICEA building is (again) a good vantage point.

The museums and parks

Covered here are the handful of **parks** and **museums** in Nairobi itself. Nairobi National Park gets separate coverage in the "Nairobi Province" section later in this chapter (see p.154), as do the Bomas of Kenya, the Karen Blixen Museum and the Langata Giraffe Centre. Unless you have your own wheels you may be better off joining a tour for them. The following sites, however, are all easily walkable.

The Railway Museum

Now privately run, Nairobi's **Railway Museum** (daily 8.15am–4.45pm; Ksh200, children Ksh100; camera Ksh100, camcorder Ksh200; free guides) is a

It was a Friday morning just like any other, and the Nairobi rush hour was getting into its habitually chaotic swing. As usual, the roundabout next to the **US Embassy** at the junction of Moi and Haile Selassie avenues was packed with vehicles, and the streets were full of people. On Haile Selassie Avenue, a yellow Mitsubishi van made its way into the parking bay at the rear of the embassy.

Some witnesses say that a gunfight ensued, others that a hand-grenade was hurled at the embassy's guards. Whatever, moments later, the van's cargo of 800kg of TNT exploded, gouging a deep crater in the ground, setting fire to the asphalt and propelling the vehicle 10m into the air, where it remained stuck to the side of the embassy in a cloud of black smoke and flame. The force of the explosion was so intense that it was felt over 10km away. In the embassy itself – the intended terrorists' target – some forty people perished (twelve of them Americans) despite the reinforced concrete walls. The brunt of the blast, however, was borne by the adjacent four-storey Ufundi Cooperative House, a commercial building that also housed a secretarial and computer college. It was reduced to a mound of burning rubble. Next to it, the 22-storey Cooperative Bank Building skyscraper had black smoke pouring out from its shattered windows. Altogether, some forty buildings within a 150-metre radius were seriously damaged by the blast. In the packed streets below, thousands of people were showered with flying glass and masonry, as were the buses and cars that were snared up at the roundabout. In their panic, many fled the city on any transport they could find, believing that World War III had started, or that a coup was underway. But many more, even some of the injured, gathered their wits and started to help with the rescue operation.

A few minutes later, a second car bomb exploded outside the US Embassy in Tanzania's capital, Dar es Salaam, killing eleven people. In Kenya, the final toll stood at 263 dead and over 5000 injured, almost all of them Kenyans. Sixty people lost their eyesight, many more were partially blinded, and the material damage was estimated at around $500 million. The Americans were quick to blame Osama bin Laden for the attack, and promptly retaliated by bombing a suspected chemical weapons factory in Sudan and bin Laden's terrorist training base in Afghanistan. The country was plunged into confusion, mourning and grief: why had the terrorists chosen Kenya, which had no quarrel with either the USA or Islam? The answer appears to have been a lethal combination of lax security both at the embassy and at the Tanzanian border (over which the explosives were apparently smuggled), the embassy's central and exposed location, the proximity of the international press corps in East Africa, the United States' covert activities in Sudan, and the fact that Nairobi had been America's second largest CIA and FBI base in Africa.

The mindless cruelty and barbarism of this act was symbolized by what happened to Rose Wanjiku, a tea-lady in one of the Ufundi House offices. After the building collapsed, she remained buried alive for five days as rescuers, including a special unit of Israeli soldiers, worked desperately around the clock in an effort to save her and others. She had communicated constantly with them from beneath the rubble, but died half a day before she was reached. The tragic futility of her struggle for life touched millions across the world, and in Kenya, the long-stemmed rose became the symbol of the bomb blast victims. The National Memorial Service held two weeks after the outrage included Hindu and Muslim speakers, and the papers were full of praise for all Kenyans, whatever their religion or tribe, for having helped rescue victims in the immediate aftermath.

The site of the explosion itself, now a memorial garden (daily 6am–6pm; Ksh20), has become a place of pilgrimage where, every day, individuals, groups and delegations pay their respects to the victims of the bomb whose names are recorded on a plaque which also expresses the hope that those who died in this tragic event may rest in the knowledge that "it has strengthened our resolve to work for a world in which man is able to live alongside each other in peace".

natural draw for rail fans and of more than passing interest for anyone else. It's signposted, ten minutes' walk from the railway station, but be careful, as there was a rash of grab-and-run robberies down here a few years back.

The main hall contains a mass of memorabilia: photos of early stations, of the "Lunatic Express" East African Railway from Mombasa to Kampala being built, and the engineering feats involved in getting the carriages up and down the escarpment, and strange pieces of hardware, such as the game-viewing seat mounted at the front of the train. Passengers who risked this perch were reminded that "The High Commissioner will not be liable for personal injury (fatal or otherwise)". In the museum annexe, the motorized bicycle inspection trolley is quite a sight but, as the write-up explains, the experiment in the 1950s "was not really successful", as the wheels kept slipping off the rail.

The engines

Outside, exposed to the elements, is the museum's collection of old **locomotives**, most of them built in Britain. You can clamber inside any of the cabs to play with the massive levers and switches. The restriction on forward visibility in some of the engines seems incredible; the driver of the *Karamoja Express* couldn't have had any idea what was in front of him while steaming down a straight line. If it all fills you with nostalgic delight, you should also note that Nairobi and Mombasa stations both have locomotive graveyards which, with enthusiastic persistence, you should be able to look around. There are plans to renovate some of the old steam locos, and to have trips hauled by them.

Lions figure prominently in the early history of the Uganda Railway. Look in the shed for first-class coach no.12 to learn the story of Superintendent C. H. Ryall. During the hunt for the "Maneaters of Tsavo" in 1898, Ryall had readied his gun one evening, settled down in the carriage and offered himself as bait. Unfortunately, he nodded off and was dragged from this carriage and devoured while colleagues sat frozen in horror. The coach, together with the repainted loco no.301, took part in the filming of *Out of Africa* at Kajiado.

The National Museum

The **National Museum** (daily 9.30am–6pm; Ksh400, children/students Ksh100; free guides available on request; ☏02/742878,ⓦwww.museums.or.ke) is probably the city's prime sightseeing attraction but surprisingly few travellers make the small effort to get to it. It's the best possible prelude to any tour around the country, and only about a thirty-minute walk from Kenyatta Avenue – or a few minutes by taxi or bus #21, #23 or #119. Allow yourself a morning or afternoon to look around. If museum fatigue hits you, the pleasant *Café Bustani* is open daily until 6pm, and does self-services lunches.

Natural history and geology

The museum's most extensive collections are **ornithological**, with most of Kenya's thousand-plus species of birds represented. Kenya's birdlife usually makes a strong impression, even on non-bird-watchers. Look out for the various species of hornbills, turacos and rollers, and for the extraordinary standard-wing nightjar, which is frequently seen fluttering low over a swimming pool at dusk, hunting for insects. There are also dioramas of Kenyan mammals in the large mammal room, casts of fish, even a whale skeleton, as well as the skeleton and a fibreglass replica of Ahmed, the famous elephant from Marsabit.

Quite useful if you're going anywhere near the Rift Valley, the **Geology Gallery** is a mine of information on plate tectonics and the life-cycle of volcanoes, with a good collection of rocks and minerals which you may see on your travels.

Gallery of Contemporary East African Art

On the second floor, next to the birds, the **Gallery of Contemporary East African Art** is an exhibition space and **showroom** for principally Kenyan, Tanzanian and Ugandan artists to display their work and wares. Everything is for sale and the gallery, although non-profit-making, takes a commission from what's sold and ploughs this back into running the place, and into acquiring work for the museum's own, long-planned Modern Art Gallery. It's also become an increasingly popular venue for foreign embassies in Nairobi to mount exhibitions from their own countries.

Human prehistory

The special interest of Nairobi's museum lies in the cultural, human and quasi-human exhibits. The **Prehistory Gallery**, where the paleontology exhibits are housed, has walls disguised with stunning reproductions of a series of Tanzanian rock paintings. Ahead, on the floor, is a cast of wide-splayed, human-looking footprints – two walking side by side and the third in the prints of one of the others – which were discovered at Laetoli in Tanzania. They belong to *australopithecines* and were squeezed into the mud about 3,500,000 years ago. Down the hall, eerily life-size reconstructions of a family of *Homo erectus* (rather like a scene from *Planet of the Apes*) wolfing down an antelope carcass bring the story of human evolution vividly to life.

There's a separate display telling the story of the Lake Turkana **Koobi Fora excavations** – "The Origins of Man in Kenya" – on the ground floor to the right of the Prehistory Gallery entrance.

Ethnography and history

In contrast, the rather dry second-floor cases of **ethnographic** exhibits aren't particularly illuminating, though you can piece a lot of information together if you've the time. However, they contain some fascinating odds and ends – don't miss the Maasai ear-stretching devices, and the "divining sandals" made of elephant hide tanned in dung and urine. If you're planning on travelling through any of the areas inhabited by pastoral peoples (especially Pokot, Samburu, Maasai or Turkana), then seeing some old and authentic handicrafts beforehand is a good idea. This will also be a big help when you find yourself faced with, for example, an urgent vendor offering you a dozen different carved headrests – not an uncommon experience. The collections indicate the tremendous diversity of Kenya's cultures, a quality impressively evoked by Joy Adamson's series of ethnic portraits mounted on the walls, commissioned by the colonial government and now an impressive record of, in many cases, already vanished cultures. Her beautiful **botanical paintings** are displayed downstairs by the main entrance.

Finally, in the **Lamu Gallery** on the main floor, the excellent exhibition "The Kenya Coast 9th–19th Century", has been refurbished and provides an excellent introduction to Swahili culture and society.

If you want to keep abreast of developments in Kenya's museums and on-going ethnological and archeological research, contact the **Kenya Museum Society** (PO Box 40658 ☎02/750136 or 742131–4 ext 289, Ⓔkms @africaonline.co.ke), who are based in the museum grounds. As well as publishing the excellent annual journal *Kenya Past and Present*, they organize an annual two-week "Know Kenya Course" (Ksh4500), including lectures, films and fieldtrips on Kenyan natural history, prehistory, ethnography, wildlife and conservation, and traditional medicine, towards the end of October to early November. Individual morning lectures can be attended in that period for Ksh500. They also organize an Arts Festival around March which promotes local artists. For research contacts and more on environmental matters, see the "Nairobi listings" section on pp.144–150.

The Snake Park and Aquarium

Opposite the museum and going downhill (in both senses of the word) is the **Snake Park** (same times and price as National Museum). It's only fair to say that you'd have to be very enthusiastic about reptiles to find this interesting, and very insensitive to find it enjoyable. Exhibits take in East African and American snakes, a crocodile or two, some murky terrapins, emaciated monitor lizards and fish tanks (revamped in 1998). But there are much better (and cheaper) snake parks on the coast. There are plans to start a nature walk in the grounds, which would at least provide a nice picnic site.

The city's parks

A colour map of Nairobi suggests a multitude of cool green spaces around the city. However, the two remaining **forests** – Ngong Road in the west and Karura in the north – are currently battlegrounds between environmentalists and those who have illegally expropriated these public lands for private development amid a morass of corruption and government inaction. **Karura Forest** is especially under threat, and there have been several violent confrontations between protesters and the security personnel guarding the illegal plots. (To find out more, contact the Greenbelt Movement, Adams Arcade, Ngong Road, PO Box 67545 Nairobi ☏02/603867 or 571523.) **Ngong Road Forest** is presently much calmer, but don't visit unless you're with someone who knows the area well – you're a long way from help. Much more accessible is the **Arboretum** (gates close at dusk), northwest of Uhuru Park on Arboretum Road (matatu #48). Somewhat overgrown, almost jungly in parts, it's a lovely place to wander or picnic and, of course, a must if you're botanically inclined. There are over 200 varieties of tree alone, and even the odd monkey. There are security notices everywhere, so don't take any valuables. You may be reassured – or unnerved – by the officious plain-clothes policemen who stalk the glades (it backs onto State House). On the last Monday of each month there is a guided walk; be at the gate by 9.30am if you're interested.

Otherwise, Nairobi's **parks** aren't always very inviting, but several are pleasant places to retreat to for a while. Biggest and best is **City Park** in the north, a half-hour stroll from the National Museum down Forest Road and Limuru Road, or by matatu #11. City Park has a wealth of tropical trees and birdlife, several troops of vervet monkeys, a small stream with wooden bridges, gravel paths, shady lawns and, on weekends, families everywhere. During the week it's delightful, though not for women alone. And, as usual, hang onto your possessions. If you're a couple, beware of a recent, apparently completely legal **scam** operated by police. They've made a habit of surprising kissing or canoodling couples, and then promptly charging them with "indecent behaviour in public"; around Ksh200 should be enough to pay them off.

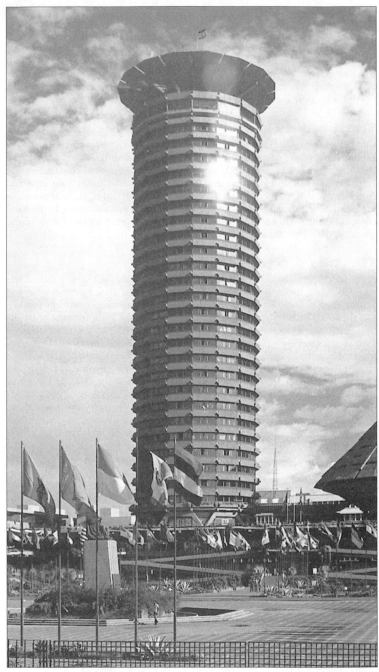

△ Kenyatta Conference Centre, Nairobi

Bird-watching in Nairobi

Bird-watching need not be exclusively a bush pursuit. For any visitor staying in central Nairobi, an impressive sight during the early morning and late evening is that of groups of **black kites** circling over the city as they move between feeding and roosting sites; amongst these are **pied crows**, readily identified black-and-white birds. **Marabou storks, sacred ibises** and **silvery-cheeked hornbills** can sometimes be seen flying over the city, while flocks of **red-winged starlings** call noisily from office buildings.

The leafier areas of the city are likely to produce even more birds. The gardens adjacent to the National Museum are an interesting and relatively safe area to start bird-watching. Here, keen bird-watchers may encounter the **cinnamon-chested bee eater**, a common, small, green bee eater found in open areas with scattered bushes. The plants and flowering shrubs outside the front steps of the museum provide excellent opportunities to observe **sunbirds**; several species, including variable and Hunter's sunbirds can be seen here. Another bird of the gardens is the **African paradise monarch**, a species of flycatcher. In breeding plumage, the rufous males have long tail streamers, which trail behind them like ribbons, as they flit from tree to tree.

Nature Kenya (formerly the East Africa Natural History Society) organizes bird walks from the National Museum every Wednesday morning at 8.45am. They usually proceed to another part of Nairobi. Longer trips are also held at least once a month. For more information, contact Nature Kenya at the museum (PO Box 44486 ☏02/7449303 or 741049).

Uhuru and **Central** parks, on the western side of Uhuru Highway, have the city's worst reputation for muggings, particularly after dark. They're unfenced and never closed but to walk across either park after 6pm is asking for trouble. There are rowing boats for rent in the small murky lake in Uhuru Park, which are very popular, particularly with Indian families, at weekends and holidays.

In a more reputable part of the city (though a night walk even here would be foolish), try **Jeevanjee Gardens**, especially during a weekday lunchtime when you can picnic on a bench and chat with the office workers who aren't thronging the nearby restaurants. You can listen, too, to the preachers who have made Jeevanjee their church and the bemused picnickers their congregation. The park contains a curiously small statue, just about recognizable, of Queen Victoria, presented to Nairobi by nineteenth-century business tycoon A. M. Jeevanjee, founder of the *Standard* newspaper.

Markets and shopping

It doesn't take long to realize that commerce is Nairobi's *raison d'être*. Disappointingly perhaps, the form which trade takes here is not always very exotic. But Nairobi is the best place in East Africa to buy **handicrafts**, with the widest (if not the cheapest) selection and the best facilities for posting the stuff home. The city also has some lavish **produce markets**, enjoyable even if you only want to browse.

Bargaining is expected at all Nairobi's markets and most shops, with the exception of supermarkets and stores selling imported goods. Be aware, however, that the "last price" will vary seasonally and can sky-rocket when a major conference hits town.

Produce markets and food

Though it doesn't offer the city's lowest prices, for a colourful and high-quality range of fruit and vegetables, the **City Market** (Mon–Fri 7.30am–6.30pm, Sat 7.30am–3pm, Sun 8.30am–noon) is the obvious target (beware of bag-snatching in the area). If you're buying, the best-value stalls are in the outside aisle flanking the main hall on the right. Fish and meat are on either side of the main building, and the supermarket at the entrance has a good variety of Kenyan cheeses. The other large produce markets are the **Wakulima** (farmers) market, also known simply as "Marikiti", a cavernous and dank hall at the bottom of River Road, just before the country bus station (fruit and vegetables are pretty cheap here), and the excellent, if totally chaotic, open-air **Kariokor Market** at the north end of Racecourse Road at the junction with General Waruingi Street. There's a smaller, less hassly produce market at the corner of Woodvale Grove and Ring Road Westlands in Westlands (daily 6am–6pm).

There are usually dozens of children and young women selling a few oranges, mangoes, whatever, on street corners. Blink, and they may be gone, tipped off that city *askaris* are about to "swoop", so buy from them while you have the chance.

Supermarkets and grocery stores can be found all over the city. Branches of **Uchumi** (Aga Khan Walk; Kimathi House, Kimathi Street; Market Street; Nkrumah Avenue; Taveta Lane) and **Nakumatt** (Kenyatta Avenue at Kimathi Street; Kenyatta Avenue between Wabera Street and Muindi Mbingu Street) are open Mon–Sat 8.30am–8.30pm and Sun 10am–7pm. They're also good for camping supplies, sleeping bags, and have general household goods and stationery. Samaki & Tilley, on Kaunda Street, are first-class **butchers** and **fishmongers**; there's a good **cheese shop** in the YaYa Centre in Hurlingham, and a number of excellent delicatessens in Lenana Forest Centre on Ngong Road and in most of Westlands' many malls (see "Shopping malls" on p.122). For a good cheap selection of Kenyan and South African **wines**, try Joles Ltd at Hamilton House on Kaunda Street. An excellent **bakery**, with daily supplies of fresh rye and wholemeal bread, is Oscarsson's in 20th Century Plaza, Mama Ngina Street (there's another branch at Rank Xerox House in Westlands).

Crafts

For the exhausting business of buying **crafts and curios**, it's advisable to decide what you want before stepping into a shop or looking at a stall. At some of the more pretentious places you can browse for ages undisturbed, but at the cheaper outlets dilly-dallying is not encouraged and the pressure may be on to part with your money. To browse and to establish comparative values, pay a visit to the excellent Zanzibar Curio Shop on Moi Avenue, which has a huge range of stuff at fixed and very reasonable prices. With the exception of some antique sculptures, masks and xylophones, you'd be hard-pressed to match its prices by bargaining anywhere else.

Curio shops and hawkers

There are dozens of **curio shops** in Nairobi and, depending on any number of factors, you might get a good deal at almost any of them. Never accept their first price, and bargain hard. The upmarket places are clustered on Standard, Kaunda and Mama Ngina streets. Apart from the Zanzibar Curio Shop, African Heritage on Banda Street is the main lure, and has some beautiful things (including great musical instruments like thumb pianos and lyres), but mostly at absurdly inflated prices. If you're mobile, there's a much bigger selection at its branch at Libra House on the Mombasa Road, on the way to JKI Airport, which also has a pleasant café and salad bar. It's the largest curio shop in Kenya, with eager suppliers in many parts of Africa. If you're in no hurry and are after something unique, but not necessarily Kenyan, the warehouse-like Zebra Crafts Centre at the bottom of Koinange Street, near Kenyatta Avenue, is worth a visit, with a great selection of carvings, masks and jewellery from across the continent at very reasonable prices. There's also the good Arki Ethiopian Curio Centre in Barclays Plaza, just the place for Coptic crosses (they also have advice on travel to Ethiopia).

You'll find lots more curio shops in the streets around the **City Market**, mostly overpriced and stubbornly unresponsive to substantial bargaining. Clearly, however, the cheaper prices will usually be at places where they don't have to pay a shop rent – **street stands** and **market booths** – though these are currently an almost extinct species, constantly being harassed and demolished by the city council. The more permanent booths in the enclosure at the back of the City Market off Koinange Street are an obvious choice, especially for soapstone, batiks and basketwork, but the whole area is something of a tourist trap and, while you'll probably find what you're looking for, you're unlikely to knock it down to a good price (some people report good deals by offering clothes in exchange).

For **traditional fabrics and clothes** such as *kikois* and *kangas*, there are around a dozen shops to browse through along Biashara Street. Of these, Haria's Stamp Shop has an excellent and very reasonably priced range (prices around Ksh200–600 per metre). The **traditional masks** you'll see everywhere are imported from elsewhere. Only a handful of Kenyan tribes make masks, the Kikuyu being the best known, and these are exceedingly rare. Mount Kenya Sundries, Vedic House, Mama Ngina Street, have one of the best selections from West and Central Africa, albeit mostly reproductions, and are knowledgeable about their varied significance and use in ritual. For more masks, batiks and outstanding **beads**, a wonderful if expensive place is Kenafro Antiques & Crafts, Olympic House, at the corner of Tubman and Koinange streets, but you'll need to have honed your haggling skills to ruthless perfection.

Buying curios from **strolling vendors** is generally unwise but can occasionally turn up a good deal if you're skilled at bargaining and the vendor's desperate. If you're not interested, say *Sitaki biashara* – "I don't want to do business". Steer well clear of the **elephant-hair bracelets**. Although it's unlikely that they really are made from pachyderm (unless they're from Tanzania, where protection orders are less widely enforced), the vendors are quite perversely adamant about their origin – stating, with bizarre stories to back them up, that the hair is collected, not poached. In fact, most are made either from plastic, tree root fibres or "captured" telephone lines; one resident pleaded with us to mention this, as they were fed up with their line going dead.

Community craft centres

Nairobi has a number of craft shops with charitable status, or based on development or self-help projects. Although sometimes a little expensive – and you can't bargain – they are worthy of support, and often have unusual and well-made stock (some of which finds its way into the Christmas charity catalogues overseas). A few are a little way out of town, but well worth making special journeys to visit – good tonics if you're suffering from curio shop fatigue.

Kamili Designs Langata Rd, Karen (Mon–Fri 9am–4.30pm; bus/matatu #24, #111, or some #126; ☎02/883640). This textile workshop sells locally designed, hand-printed fabrics. The designs are typically bold and colourful, available both by the metre and as cushions, bedspreads and the like.

Kazuri Beads & Pottery Centre Mbagathi Ridge, Karen (workshops Mon–Fri 9am–4.30pm, Sat 8am–noon; shop Mon–Sat 8am–4.30pm, Sun 11am–4.30pm; bus/matatu #24, #111, or some #126; ☎02/883500, ©kazuri@africaonline.co.ke). Kazuri, which means "small and beautiful", employs nearly a hundred formerly destitute women, who make an extraordinary variety of handmade jewellery and beads, principally ceramic, and there's also a pottery showroom. You can watch the whole process from shaping and colouring to firing. It's expensive, but the stuff is lovely. They also have outlets at African Heritage.

Maridadi Fabrics City Stadium roundabout, Landhies/Jogoo Rd (Mon–Fri 8am–5pm; buses #21, #34 or #36; ☎02/554250). Church-based, like Undugu (see below), Maridadi was created in 1966 as an income-generating community project for women in one of Nairobi's oldest slum areas – Pumwani and Shauri Moyo. The main workshop is a delight if you're into making your own clothes. A large screen-printing workshop (on view from the visitors' gallery) produces the wide range of prints for sale in the shop. Especially appealing are the bark cloth prints – a natural weave used for clothing by many East African peoples until the end of the nineteenth century. In the district around the Maridadi workshop, there's a huge diversity of enterprises, with two distinctive market areas – Gikomba (clothes) and Landhies Mawe (scrap metal processing) – both recommended. The latter is deafeningly unmistakable, the place to go to get that handmade tin suitcase. Be careful in either area.

Mikono Craft Shop Opposite Ratna Fitness Studio, Gitanga Rd, Kawangware, just north of Dagoretti Corner (bus #46 or #46B; ☎02/577498). The outlet of the Jesuit Refugee Service, with well-made work (especially beautiful patchwork textiles) from refugees, and superb Mozambican carvings.

Ormolu Chyulu Rd, off Haile Selassie Ave, where it joins Ngong Rd (any Ngong Rd bus or #18 or #61B; ☎02/727484 or 725366). An outlet for naturally dyed sisal baskets and mats woven by rural women.

Spinner's Web 2nd floor, Viking House, Waiyaki Way, Westlands (☎02/440882; any Westlands bus/matatu). A large shop, with a Germanic influence, selling a lot of good stuff – crafts, textiles, woollen goods and jewellery, much of it made by self-help groups and individuals, including Meru's Makena Textile Workshop.

Terra Pottery Centre Opposite the War Cemetery, Ngong Rd (any Ngong Rd bus; ☎02/567636). A pottery shop with a difference: they encourage you to try your hand at casting and turning.

Undugu Woodvale Grove, Westlands, opposite Westlands produce market (Mon–Fri 8.30am–5pm; any Westlands bus/matatu; ☎02/535944, ©undugu@insightkenya.com). This is the Undugu ("fraternity") society's retail outlet, helping raise funds for community self-help programmes, notably for the street children and youth. With its roots in the church, Undugu is the most vigorous society of its kind in the country and the shop sells a good selection of well-priced, high-quality crafts with some more unusual items, such as Ethiopian jewellery, basketwork, and crafts from Congo, Somalia, Tanzania and Uganda. A free booklet about the Undugu society is available and you may be able to have a look around the workshops. They also organize regular guided visits to their slum projects.

Utamaduni Crafts Centre Bogoni East Rd, between the Ostrich Park and Giraffe Sanctuary, Langata (daily 9am–6pm; bus/matatu #24; ☎02/890464). Eighteen individual craft shops in one large house, opened by Richard Leakey in 1991 (a portion of the profits go to the Kenya Wildlife Service). It has everything you might want, much of it made on site or from street-kid projects; quality and prices are high. The attached *Jikoni* restaurant is one of Nairobi's best.

The Maasai Markets

If you're after Maasai traditional and tourist gear, the **Maasai Market** (Tues and Fri 9am–3pm; also known as "Globe Cinema" or "Tuesday" market) is highly recommended. Anything from twenty to fifty Maasai and other women from up-country areas display their wares on the waste ground beside the roundabout connecting Murang'a Road and Kijabe Street (past the *Meridian Court Hotel*). Assuming that they don't get evicted (as they were from all their previous sites), you'll find prices here well below those in any tourist mart, or even in the Narok/Mara area, with especially good deals on the simpler designs of beaded jewellery, and also on baskets and gourds. You can bargain to as little as ten percent of the sort of prices marked in fancy curio stores, if you've the time and energy. Often, items like nail varnish and cheap watches are helpful for bargaining. However, the market now also attracts more aggressive male vendors, which can make for an unpleasant shock early on in a trip. Be sure to buy from a stall rather than them.

If you miss this market, there's a much smaller, "civilized" Maasai crafts market held inside the National Theatre on Harry Thuku Road, opposite the *Norfolk Hotel*, every Thursday (7am–6pm). The Maasai market also convenes every Friday at the Village Market, Limuru Road.

Kariokor Market

A real artisans' market is **Kariokor Market**, between Racecourse Road and Ring Road (bus/matatu #4, #6, #7, #14, #30, #32, #40, #42, or #46/46B). This is without question *the* place in Nairobi to buy **sisal baskets** (*vyondo*). Inside and outside the market there are thousands of baskets available and, since many are made here, you can buy just the basket without the leather pieces or straps which raise the price. Long sisal straps can be bought separately for a few shillings. *Vyondo* come in sisal, coloured with natural or artificial dyes, in garish plastic, or in cord manufactured from the bark of the baobab tree. Some of these last baskets are truly exquisite, occasionally quite old, with tiny beads included in the tight weave.

Kariokor (named after the despised wartime "Carrier Corps") is closer to an oriental bazaar than most markets in Kenya, with permanent booths for the traders. Inside, there's as much manufacture and finishing going on as selling – sisal weavers, leather workers, makers of tyre-rubber sandals ("5000-mile shoes", about Ksh100 a pair and surprisingly comfortable), carpenters, toymakers, tailors, hairdressers, and a row of good, very cheap, amazingly clean eateries, popular at lunchtime with local workers. A number of booths sell vaguely pharmaceutical oddities – snuff, remedies, charms, amulets and so on – where you can pick up anything from feathers to snakeskin. Outside, you'll find the odd African literary gem on the second-hand bookstalls. Note that you may sometimes be mobbed by kids and touts at Kariokor – a hassle.

Embakasi Village Crafts Market

This new market, located on the Mombasa Road, on the way to the airport, second turning on the left, just after *City Cabanas Restaurant* (bus #34B), is perhaps one of the most organized in Kenya: there's definitely less hassle here. As one seller puts it, "Anyone who has come this far to our market is looking to buy something, so we can all wait". Currently there are 120 booths, but the management is hoping to turn the place into the biggest market of its kind in East Africa with a total of 400 booths, a traditional African bar and restaurant, a supermarket, a campsite and a number of *bandas* for rent. Apart from the occasional collection of Central African carvings, Ethiopian and West African beads, you'll find most of what is sold here at much higher prices in the other markets in Nairobi. There is an area where you can watch the carvers in progress (commissioning the individual carvers is allowed as they are mostly affiliated to individual booths in the market) and an open-air market which is busy on Monday, Wednesday and Friday, when traders from the Maasai Market and craft centres from further afield turn up with their wares. If you want to see traditional dancers, call in advance to find out when the next performance will be (☎02/247039).

General merchandise, clothes, shoes and toys

For everyday **general merchandise stores**, the eastern part of the City Market district is the most worthwhile area. **Biashara Street** (*biashara* means commerce) is the street for fabrics and the best place to buy tents and mosquito nets (see "Listings" on p.145). For cheap and not-so-cheap imports, the hangar-like Freemark Pavilion in south **Uhuru Park** has hundreds of stalls. The upper part of Moi Avenue is Nairobi's busiest ordinary shopping street, all colonnaded shop-fronts and antiquated name-boards, fun to wander past. You'll find clothes shops all over, with high-fashion outlets on Standard and Kaunda streets, and more down-to-earth gear on Kenyatta Avenue, Moi Avenue and Kimathi Street. Abdulla Fazal in the Jubilee Exchange House on Mama Ngina Street has a good selection of locally made clothes. Good-value **footwear** is available from the African Boot Co, on Moi Avenue opposite Bookpoint, and even cheaper footwear at Miniprice Footwear Supermarket on River Road, by the *Bull Café*. If you're buying **toys**, the best items are locally made wire-and-fabric contraptions – cars, bicycles, flapping birds – which are sometimes beautiful works of art. Scouring the out-of-centre markets will find you some, but the better ones are usually made at home for sons and nephews and not for sale. The best general toy shop, full of standard imports, is Hobby Centre on Kaunda Street (☎02/222765) in the Jubilee Insurance House.

Shopping malls

Nairobi now has the dubious distinction of having more **shopping malls** – over twenty – than any other African city barring those in South Africa, providing a hassle-free environment for getting on with ordinary shopping and office business. You'll find most of them stuffed into more affluent suburbs like Westlands and Parklands. They cater to the expatriate and middle-class Kenyan markets and many include banks, travel agents, specialist food suppliers and an assortment of cafés and restaurants.

Apic Centre On Mpaka and Parkland Road. This place has shops, a dry-cleaner and a number of fast-food places. For authentic Indian desserts and snacks try *Sweety Sweets* on the ground floor.

The Mall Westlands (buses #21, #25, #29, #30 and many others). Shops and offices including a branch of Let's Go Travel, a sports shop, a French bakery, ice-cream parlour, a Seven-Eleven-style convenience store and numerous fashion and clothing stores.

Mobil Plaza Muthaiga Rd, Muthaiga. This boasts a good health-food shop and the tacky *Celebrities Nightclub*.

Rank Xerox House Not a shopping mall as such, but has a number of cheapish cafés and restaurants. *Oscarsson's Patisserie* on the ground floor does good pastries.

Reliance Centre Woodvale Road (buses as for The Mall). Like Rank Xerox House, cannot be compared with somewhere like the Sarit Centre as a mall, but there are a few reasonable eating places. Rochar Enterprise, on the ground floor, is a flower shop which sells interesting gifts.

Sarit Centre Westlands (buses as for The Mall). A big, established complex, with over sixty shops and offices, including a dry-cleaner, a health-food shop, a watch repairer, a post office, a multiplex cinema, a Uchumi Hypermarket, the Areana Health Club and a large new branch of the Textbook Centre.

Yaya Centre Argwings Kodhek Rd, Hurlingham (bus/matatu #41, #46/46B or #56). There's a good cheese shop here, a useful newsagent with a wide selection of mainly British magazines, a bookshop, supermarket, health-food shop, French bakery, post office, chemist, and a useful "for sale" noticeboard.

Eating

Nairobi has no shortage of **eating places**. Their diversity is one of the city's best points, and eating out is an evening pastime which never dulls. Admittedly, African food is generally not highlighted in the more expensive restaurants which offer a range of Asian and European food, and spectacular quantities of meat.

This bias isn't really a problem. You can save money *and* eat African and Asian food in hundreds of unpretentious places, though to catch the cheap eats you'll have to go out early; by 8pm most of the bargain restaurants have finished the day's food. And if you want a burger or a pizza or a huge steak or totally vegetarian salad, it's all available.

With some exceptions, the following listings are restricted to the city centre; but Nairobi, including the suburbs, has hundreds of restaurants with new ones opening every month. **Westlands**, in particular, is a culinary growth area, with every street and shopping mall containing a handful (we've mentioned a few of the best) and *Vasili & Sons*, on Mpaka Road, an extremely good **bakery**.

Finding restaurants on our maps

To avoid cluttering up the "Commercial Centre and River Road Area" map on pp.98–99, we've omitted those **restaurants** located in commercial buildings which are already marked on the map (eg *Supermac* in Kimathi House). Those not in commercial buildings have been keyed. Restaurants located out of the centre on other maps are noted accordingly, together with directions on how to get there by bus or matatu (the relevant stops are listed in the box on pp.94–95).

Breakfasts

Get up for breakfast. It's the only time of the day to really enjoy *mandaazi* and *chai*. You can get fried eggs, sausages and bread in many cheap places, too (look for Swahili menus saying something like *Mayai kukaanga* or sometimes "Eggs fly"). None of it's healthy, or aims to do anything but inject you with hot calories, but it tastes good.

You can get an excellent **continental breakfast** at the *Goldstar Restaurant* (see p.125). For something heartier, most of the *hotelis* around River Road serve up stacks of well-prepared eggs, sausages, beans and toast. The big hotels do lavish breakfast **buffets**, of which the *Hilton Hotel*'s is highly rated. Alternatively, both the *Meridian Court*'s and the *Ambassadeur*'s are also good, and cheaper (around Ksh350). For something simpler, all the cafés and snack bars listed below cater for early-birds, as do *Pasara* and *Calypso* (see "Salads", p.130).

Cheap eateries and snacks

The **River Road area** has all the very cheap places with one *hoteli* (cheap restaurant) after another on most streets, generally dishing up standard fare of chips or *ugali* with fish or fried chicken. At any of the following you should be able to eat hugely for Ksh200, often for much less. See the "Commercial Centre and River Road Area" map, pp.98–99 for locations.

Al Mansura B&L Munyu Rd (open from 6am). Good for *mandaazi* and *chai* breakfasts, and **Ali Baba** Murang'a Rd, opposite *Meridian Court*

Hotel. Superficially Lebanese (some kebabs, falafel and kibbé), but popular mainly for its filling lunchtime mini-buffets (Ksh280).

Street food

Strictly speaking, **street food** is limited to **roasted corncobs** (which are so tough and take so long to eat you'll feel you've had a whole meal) and **fruit**. But places like the shacks near the Country Bus Station can fill you up with tea and *mandaazi* for next to nothing. On Haile Selassie Avenue by the Agip Garage, women cook up *githeri* which you eat squatting down on the pavement. The best place, though, is **Kariokor Market**, which has an enclosure containing dozens of *chai*, *ugali* and *nyama choma* joints vying for business. The meat and fish is very fresh and sizzling outside on charcoal grills, as reggae music blares. Prime rump steak, brains or sweetmeats, it's all there, and if you're thirsty, several dodgy bars oblige. It's a great little place.

simple but tasty standard Kenyan fare at other times (*ugali*, stews, and goat-meat *nyama choma*).

Benrose Gaberone Rd. Busy and bustling with reasonable *chai* and samosas.

City Fry's Murang'a Rd. Excellent stand'n'eat fish'n'chip shop; very fast service.

Fameland Duruma Rd. Good solid meals (notably *nyama choma* with *ugali*) with excellent music, sometimes live, in this unusually good "day and night club".

Ismailia's River Rd. Very inexpensive, welcoming and comfortable, with a good vegetarian selection.

Kenchic Inn Corner of Moktar Daddah St/Muindi Mbingu St. No-frills halal fish and chicken bar, busier than most and therefore fresher.

Malindi Dishes Gaberone Rd. Mainly snacks – less intimate than *Benrose*, but cleaner and airier. Like a cafeteria, but still welcoming.

Paris Metro Mfangano St. The tiled vault inside is supposed to resemble a metro station, but apart from that it's entirely on the other side of the Channel: chips, fried chicken, sausages and occasionally fish to take away. Noisy and relatively dirty.

Pre Area Eating House Duruma Rd. Snacks, stews and booze – great for breakfast after a long night out.

Reata Fish & Chips Corner of Taveta and Accra roads. A renowned purveyor.

Sun Sweet Centre Ngariama Rd. Vegetarian Indian place, bright and appetizing, with tempting sweets and – for once – open till late.

Sunrise Lodge Latema Rd, across from the *Iqbal Hotel*. Standard *hoteli* fare in a reasonably bright, workaday atmosphere. Take a table at the front and watch street life on Latema Rd.

Supermac Kimathi House, Kimathi St, next to the *Oakwood Hotel*. Quality this ain't, but it is one of the cheapest places in the city centre. Feast on fluorescent mushy peas, chips and soggy burgers.

Swara Imenti House, Tom Mboya St (daily 7.30am–10pm). Cheap and reliable for proper meals (steaks, fish, stews; meals around Ksh200), with good service in a slightly tattered dining room full of velvet-upholstered chairs and dusty textile lampshades. Popular with office workers.

Zaïqa New Flora Tsavo Rd. Used to be extremely popular among locals and travellers alike for very good budget meals with tandoori bread, but the sometimes terrible service is a drawback. The dining room upstairs is more refined. Open for lunch and early dinner.

Cafés, fast-food joints and ice-cream parlours

You'll find most cafés and snack bars as well as a rash of McDonald's–style fast-food joints (at Stateside prices) situated in the upmarket business district **north of City Hall Square**. Most are closed on Sundays after lunch. Passion juice is widely advertised these days, but check whether it's fresh or factory pressed or, worse, just syrup and water. Most of the following are on the "Commercial Centre and River Road Area" map, pp.98–99, unless otherwise indicated.

Bakers Pie The best and cleanest branch is on Kenyatta Ave, near the BP petrol station between Koinange and Loita streets. A cheap filler if you're

on the move. They make excellent *Mbusze* pies.

Bel Canto Bruce House, Standard St. Not exactly gastronomic heaven, but filling and relatively cheap by city-centre standards (meals around Ksh300, cheaper snacks).

Coffee House Mama Ngina St (closed Sat pm & Sun). The Kenya Coffee Board's café, and the best cup in town. Faded murals on the walls hark back to a not-so-distant era of African coffee estate labourers, white overseers and continental café loungers. You can buy the house blends by the kilo for something like a quarter of what you'd pay at home (call in before flying home).

Express Bakery Standard St, next to Let's Go Travel. Always crowded at lunchtime, but otherwise a good place to sit and recoup your energy.

Goldstar Corner of Koinange and Moktar Daddah streets. Excellent breakfasts and cheap, filling meals at other times.

Grapes Café (see "Westlands" map, p.106) Corner of Mpaka and Parklands Road, which serves OK African food and a good selection of beers.

Hooters Hamilton House, Kaunda St. Very smart, chrome and wood café verging on fast-food joint (milkshakes, burgers, pizzas), with music videos on the monitors. Overpriced to keep out the rabble, and good service.

K&A Coffee House Corner of Standard St and Koinange St. Simple little cafeteria with good *brioches,* meat pies, samosas and simple dishes such as pilau rice and beef stew. The coffee is average in comparison to the *Coffee House*'s. Also good for breakfast and lunch.

Kahawa Coffee House Fedha Towers, Kaunda St. An elegant, crowded and notably upmarket setting, filled with delicious smells. Great for breakfast – fried eggs, milkshakes, excellent samosas and iced tea.

Kencake Coffee Shop Jubilee Exchange House, Kaunda St. Good for ice-creams.

Mandy's Restaurant and Take Away Rehani House, Koinange Street. Burgers, hot dogs, interesting tasting ice-creams and decent pizzas.

Melting Pot Next to Nginyo Towers. Original venue, with a mud hut entrance and a menu of African snacks, porridge and meatballs in vegetable soup, which vary in quality from edible to delicious.

Monsoon Bar and Restaurant Sarit Centre, Westlands, a slightly glitzy new place on the ground floor of the shopping mall. Serves light snacks, sandwiches, Mexican and Indian food and a wide selection of milkshakes. It also has a branch called *Café Café* by the Xerox Centre.

Nandos Union Towers, corner of Mama Ngina St and Moi Ave. Three fast-food emporia in one: pizzas, Portuguese snacks, and fried chicken, with a large and spotless dining room upstairs overlooking the busy junction. Same prices as European equivalents, but still busy. Free drinking water. There's also a branch next door to the *New Florida* nightclub on Koinange St.

Plaza Café Barclays Plaza. Spotless and swish café in the similar mall, with good fast food, decent cappuccinos, espressos and Irish coffees.

Sno Cream Corner of Koinange St and Monrovia St. Rather run down but still the best parlour in town, especially after a hot day's walkabout, with amusing retro decor depicting various ice-cream fantasies – most of them available.

Star Delux Fish and Chips Corner of Koinange and University Way. Chewy but tasty kebabs.

Steers Muindi Mbingu St (opposite Jeevanjee Gardens), and at the junction of Tom Mboya and Ronald Ngala streets (both to 9pm). Also at the Apic Centre in Westlands. Halal meets *McDonald's*, yet this potential powder-keg mismatch works surprisingly well. The Islamic South African fast-food chain's first venture into Kenya offers the usual junk food, plus toasted sandwiches, salads, milk shakes, juices (try the passion) and great toffee ice-creams.

Tickles Next to *Hollywood Nightclub* on Moktar Daddah St. Local joint with tasty snacks and a bar upstairs.

Restaurants

The following listings are mostly for more **upmarket** eating houses, at some of which it's a good idea to reserve a table. Many are closed one day a week, often Sunday or Tuesday, and most are closed 2.30–6.30pm. Prices, without drinks, should normally work out at around Ksh400–500 a head, though you can certainly eat more cheaply at several of the curry houses. In the more international league, specializing mainly in meat, prices are higher (say Ksh500–800 a head) and you'll pay up to Ksh1500 at fancy establishments. The city has famously good beef and other fleshy delights so, if you enjoy it, indulge while you're here, as the rest of the country is much less well endowed. All are either marked on the maps noted or can be found in relation to the buildings they're in. You can get to **Westlands** by bus or matatu #21, #23, #30, #104 or #119.

"African", Ethiopian and Swahili

Many hotel restaurants offer an "African night" or lunchtime buffet once a week. These include Tuesday nights at the *Fairview*, *Utalii Hotel*, and *Nairobi Safari Club*, Tuesday lunches at the *Green Corner Restaurant* (see "Live-music venues"), Wednesday evenings at the *Stanley Hotel*, and Friday evenings at *Hotel Inter-Continental*. The *Suncourt Inn* and the *Solace Hotel* both do weekday lunchtime buffets, and the *Hilton* has an eat-all-you-can *nyama choma* barbecue every lunchtime at its poolside restaurant for Ksh795, with live music Sundays.

Addis Ababa Ethiopian Restaurant (see "Westlands" map, p.106) Woodvale Place, Woodvale Grove ☎02/447321. Upmarket Ethiopian, with attentive service, fantastic food, and occasional live entertainment. Worth calling to find out current opening hours.

Al Hawal (see "Commercial Centre and River Road Area" map, pp.98–99) Twiga Towers, Muranga Rd ☎02/253702. Very clean and quiet, they serve African as well as Lebanese food.

Beneve (see "Commercial Centre and River Road Area" map, pp.98–99) Corner of Koinange St and Standard St (lunchtimes only). Off putting from the outside, but clean within. This is a cheap self-service joint popular with office workers, serving well-made Kenyan dishes: fried or stewed tilapia fish, *ugali* and beef stew, *sukuma wiki* and other greens. Under Ksh200.

Blue Nile Ethiopian Restaurant (see "Greater Nairobi" map, pp.88–89) Argwings Kodhek Rd, Hurlingham; no phone; daily; buses #41, #46/46B or #56. Very pleasant, laid-back place, with a good range and a helpful "mix dish" where you can try everything out for Ksh280. Try their *tej* (a mead-like Ethiopian honey beer). Steer clear if you don't like chilli.

Daas Ethiopian Restaurant (see "Greater Nairobi" map, pp.88–89) Lenana Rd, near the Chinese and Nigerian embassies ☎02/712106; matatu #46 to Argwings Kodhek/Woodlands roads, then walk 200m up Woodlands and turn right. A bit of a revelation if you thought you'd eaten traditional African food. The basic staple *njera* "bread" does take some getting used to, but the spicy overall effect of *doro wat* (chicken in a spicy sauce; *wat* means sauce) or *anye* (spinach, cheese and spices), washed down with copious quantities of *tej*, is a fine culinary experience. Food is cooked

on your own table's *jiko* (stove). A little costly, but recommended.

Garden Square Restaurant (see "Commercial Centre and River Road Area" map, pp.98–99) Garden Square, City Hall Way ☎02/226474. Relaxed spacious place, occasionally with live bands. Cheap African buffets lunchtimes, sometimes evenings. Safe parking.

Hornbill Eating House *Ambassadeur Hotel* (see "Commercial Centre and River Road Area" map, pp.98–99). Pleasant Lamu-style decor on the ground floor, with a small selection of of quasi-traditional Kenyan dishes: try the Maasai *mshikaki*. Also good for breakfast.

Makuti Park (see "Greater Nairobi" map, pp.88–89) South "B" Shopping Centre, Mchumbi Rd, South "B" ☎02/531835; matatus from railway stage to South "B". Mellow and entirely free of touristy panderings, this famous music venue has recently started concentrating on Kenyan food. Simple, cheap and very traditional, including dried meat (*aliya*), fire-dried meat (*athola*), liver, *kienyeji* and coastal Swahili dishes. There's also a children's "fun corner".

Seasons Restaurant (see "Commercial Centre and River Road Area" map, pp.98–99) 1st floor, Old Mutual Building, Kimathi St. Breakfast is Ksh100, the same price as a beer. Extremely popular with locals on Friday nights, and as well as a menu there's an African buffet in the evenings at a very reasonable Ksh300.

Wheels Restaurant (see "Westlands" map, p.106) 2nd floor, The Mall. Primarily a cheap *nyama choma* joint (but you can order other local dishes too) with a pleasant verandah overlooking the area, and attracting local business types at lunchtimes during the week.

Chinese, Thai and Korean

The following are closed Saturday unless stated; ring to check.

Bangkok Restaurant (see "Westlands" map, p.106) Rank Xerox House Parklands Rd ☎02/751312/3. Expensive, but fine, Chinese food.

China Jiangsu (see "Westlands" map, p.106) Soin Arcade, Westlands Rd ☎02/446700. This

has all the authentic dishes including jellyfish, shark's fin and green onion pancakes as well as the old sweet and sour favourites. Reasonably priced.

Five Star Chinese Restaurant (see

"Commercial Centre and River Road Area" map, pp.98–99) 1st floor, Loita House, Loita St. The huge sad-looking aquarium with few fish and no vegetation, and the yellowish, dull walls are a far cry from the glitzy atmosphere you might expect from the name, but the food is basic, cheap and tasty enough.

Four Season Restaurant (see "Greater Nairobi" map, pp.88–89) Kamburu Rd, off Ngong Rd ☎02/720292; Ngong Rd matatus. Tasty Korean barbecued meat, with good salads and vegetables in a pleasant compound. Around Ksh800.

Hong Kong (see "Commercial Centre and River Road Area" map, pp.98–99) Kenya House, Koinange St ☎02/228612; closed Mon. Excellent Cantonese, related to the *Hong Kong* in Mombasa, though not particularly friendly.

Kowloon Restaurant (see "Commercial Centre and River Road Area" map, pp.98–99) Nginyo Towers, Koinange St ☎02/318885. The newest of the batch of Chinese eating houses in Nairobi and with its large, well-stocked bar and its extensive menu with lots of vegetarian dishes, it promises to be popular.

Little China (see "Westlands" map, p.106) Rank Xerox House, Muthithi Rd; daily to 10pm. Chinese take-away, under Ksh500 a head. Can deliver around Westlands.

Meridian Mandarin 5th floor, *Meridian Court Hotel* ☎02/333916 (see "Commercial Centre and River Road Area" map, pp.98–99). High quality with a very affordable "business lunch" for around Ksh320.

Siam Thai (see "Westlands" map, p.106) 1st floor, Unga House, Muthithi Rd ☎02/751727. Run by an Indian family in love with Thai food, and it shows – it's probably the best Nairobi Thai restaurant, despite its uninspired decor. The use of herbs and spices is subtle and sometimes unusual. Try the tangy *Tom Yam Goong* soup, spare ribs, or *Larb Gai* – spiced minced chicken with onions, mint leaves and lemon grass. Food around Ksh850, cheaper lunchtime set menus, often under Ksh600. Licensed and open daily.

Silver Sun (see "Commercial Centre and River Road Area" map, pp.98–99) Loita St, opposite Kenindia House ☎02/330858. Good Szechuan and a reasonable selection of Thai dishes. Expensive in the evenings, but a bargain at lunchtime.

Tin Tin (see "Central Nairobi" map, pp.108–9) Kenyatta Conference Centre, entrance off Harambee Ave ☎02/241614. Heavy on the monosodium glutamate, with cheapish business lunches (around Ksh500), but severely overpriced à la carte at other times. Good service, awful muzak.

Winners Pavilion *Safari Park Hotel* ☎02/802493–7 (see "Nairobi outskirts" map, pp.156–7); taxi costs Ksh800, or bus/matatu #45, #137, #145, #160, #237. One of seven equally good restaurants in the vast Thika Road complex, with surprisingly affordable Szechuan cuisine.

French

Alan Bobbe's Bistro (see "Commercial Centre and River Road Area" map, pp.98–99), Cianda House, Koinange St ☎02/224945; Sat dinner only, Sun closed. The manicured poodle logo says it all: a welcome touch of humorous absurdity, with your first impression of high camp pretentiousness soon belied by the genuine interest in seriously good food. And the sheep's brains are actually quite nice. One of the oldest restaurants in the city (since 1962); still devoutly French and devotedly patronized. Around Ksh1200 for dinner with wine is normal, but you'd pay four times more in a European equivalent. Lunchtimes are a deal cheaper (around Ksh650). Recommended.

The Claremont (see "Nairobi outskirts" map, pp.156–7) in Runda, off Limuru Rd ☎02/521308; weekends only; matatu #108, #114 and others to Limuru, get off at the "Village Market". The better of the two restaurants here (the other is the *Conservatory*, open daily), dominated by a hexagonal stained-glass ceiling featuring two women, one black, the other white. A roaring fireplace, candles and heavy silver cutlery complete the scene. Ostentatious, but pulled off with grace, style and panache. Both food and service are excellent, and there's a fine selection of imported wines to go with the classic French menu (snails, and even rock lobster, cooked with wine, mushrooms, mustard and cream, and served in its shell). The bill, presented on a silver platter, is bound to be hefty (Ksh2200–5000, including wine).

West Café (see "Westlands" map, p.106) Woodvale Grove ☎02/446472. Intimate and tastefully decorated restaurant with relaxing jazz music. A good array of desserts. A three-course meal will cost you roughly Ksh1200.

Zéphyr (see "Westlands" map, p.106) 1st floor, Rank Xerox House, Parklands Rd ☎02/750055; closed Mon & Sun dinner. A shade cheaper than *Alan Bobbe's* and still cordon bleu, with a Japanese chef who does some tasty hybrid cooking. Strong on seafood. Under Ksh1000.

Greek

Kebabish Centre (see "Greater Nairobi" map, pp.88–89) Highridge Shopping/Diamond Plaza, 3rd Parklands Ave; matatu from Latema Rd opposite the *Iqbal* to "Aga Khan". Just the place for a Saturday night kebab before throwing back the beers.

Indian

Anghiti (off the "Westlands" map, p.106) New Rehema House, Rhapta Rd ☏ 02/441258. The decor is a bit stark, but this is, along with the *Haandi*, Westland's leading subcontinental gastronomic experience. The *anghiti* is a traditional Indian clay stove which apparently keeps the aroma of foods cooked in it. The speciality is *Raan Anghiti*, whole mutton leg marinated overnight in garlic, ginger, vinegar and chillies before being baked. No beef or pork.

Cheers Bhajia Hotel Under the *New Kenya Lodge* (see "Commercial Centre and River Road Area" map, pp.98–99). Popular south Indian vegetarian. Huge meals and small bills.

Haandi (see "Westlands" map, p.106) The Mall, Westlands ☏ 02/448294. Generally considered Nairobi's best (north) Indian restaurant, if a little expensive (Ksh1000 per head), specializing in masalas. Skip breakfast to make room.

Khyber *Meridian Court Hotel* (see "Commercial Centre and River Road Area" map, pp.98–99). Excellent and very reasonably priced Mughlai cuisine, with good lunchtime set menus (around Ksh700).

La Taverna (see "Commercial Centre and River Road Area" map, pp.98–99) Monrovia St ☏ 02/251403. Cheap and always busy, serving mainly chicken and tandoori.

Mayur/Supreme Hotel (see "Commercial Centre and River Road Area" map, pp.98–99) Corner of Keekorok Rd and Ngariama Lane ☏ 02/3381586; daily noon–2.30pm & 7–9.30pm. South Indian, and the only certified vegetarian restaurant in the city centre, with food so delicious and well presented that to miss eating at the *Mayur* would be a shame. The eat-as-much-as-you-like buffet upstairs (lunch Ksh260, dinner Ksh280 – an absolute bargain, even with a large tip expected) is worth starving all day for. Downstairs, there's a less lavish choice, and you have to put up with maddeningly chirpy muzak, but they have substantially the same dishes, and also a good selection of sweets by the kilo. Takeaway also available. The only downside is the rather somnolent atmosphere.

Minar (see "Commercial Centre and River Road Area" map, pp.98–99) Stanbic Bank Building, Banda St ☏ 02/330168. Slick, north Indian Mughlai with a light Middle Eastern influence, such as kebabs, and a touch of Goan, too, and a first-class reputation. Alcohol available. An à la carte splash costs around Ksh700, and there's a lunchtime buffet for Ksh470. There's a branch in the Yaya Centre, Hurlingham (☏ 02/561676), with occasional Bhangra nights. Open daily. Recommended.

Nargis Kapuri Pan (see "Westlands" map, p.106) Next to "Global Museum" Yoga Centre, Parklands Rd. Small cheap meals, mainly chicken tikka, kebabs and takeaway. Pleasant tables outside, and some colourful child-sized tables and chairs. Safe parking. Daily 1–3pm & 6–10pm.

Slush's Happy Eater (see "Commercial Centre and River Road Area" map, pp.98–99) Kalyan House, Tubman Rd ☏ 02/220745. Indian vegetarian, with a good variety of snacks and takeaways. There's also a branch in Diamond Plaza, Parklands (see "Greater Nairobi" map, pp.88–89).

Taj (see "Commercial Centre and River Road Area" map, pp.98–99) Taveta Rd. Very cheap and filling; good birianis. Open daily.

Top of the Town (see "Commercial Centre and River Road Area" map, pp.98–99) 2nd floor, Hamilton House, corner of Wabera and Kaunda St. One of the few places open late, combining Indian and Chinese food with a live but none-too-exciting band. Moderately priced. Evenings only, from 9.30pm.

Italian

Bon Appetit (see "Commercial Centre and River Road Area" map, pp.98–99) City Hall, Mama Ngina St/Wabera St ☏ 02/217851. In the City Hall garden courtyard. By no means exclusively Italian, and not the greatest cuisine, but wholesome, plentiful and pleasantly relaxing. Mon–Sat 7am–10pm, Sun 7am–3pm.

La Galleria (see "Greater Nairobi" map, pp.88–89) At the International Casino, Westlands Rd, off Museum Hill ☏ 02/744474; bus #21, #23 or #119. Likes to consider itself classy, and is pleasant enough, but the *Toona Tree* in the same complex is much nicer. Mon–Fri lunch and dinner, Sat lunch only, closed Sun.

La Scala Pizzeria (see "Commercial Centre and River Road Area" map, pp.98–99) Phoenix House Arcade, Standard St/Kenyatta Ave ☏ 02/332130. Much cheaper than *Trattoria*, with a simple, uncluttered interior. Pizzas are inexpensive (under Ksh250), small but perfectly formed, salads are large and fresh. Good service, and the lunchtime specials are a bargain. Daily until midnight. Recommended.

Toona Tree (see "Greater Nairobi" map, pp.88–89) At the International Casino, Westlands Rd, off Museum Hill ☏ 02/744477; daily; bus #21, #23 or #119. Very pleasant, open-air place, set among the boughs of the eponymous tree, and majoring on seafood. Playground for kids. Regular live music.

Trattoria (see "Commercial Centre and River Road Area" map, pp.98–99) Corner of Wabera St and Kaunda St ☏ 02/340855. Growing more pretentious with age, this still gets enthusiastic notices from low-budget travellers having a splurge, though it's sometimes too busy for its own good (at lunchtime, full meals only). The pasta dishes and pizzas are the real thing and the cakes and ice-cream – when they come – magnificent. No credit cards. Daily until midnight.

Japanese

Akasaka *Six-Eighty Hotel*, Standard St ☏ 02/220299 (see "Commercial Centre and River Road Area" map, pp.98–99). Without doubt one of Nairobi's best restaurants, with its uncluttered Zen-like interior, impeccable service and delicious food. Its "lunchboxes" at around Ksh500 are good value, especially *sashimi* (raw fish). Highly recommended. Closed Sun and public holidays.

Chiyo *Safari Park Hotel* ☏ 02/802493–7 (see "Nairobi outskirts" map, pp.156–7), taxi costs Ksh800, or bus/matatu #45, #137, #145, #160, #237. Blend steel tables, Chef Song and his minions, several cleavers and a slightly unreal atmosphere, and you get perfect *teppanyaki*-style

Japanese food (whatever that is). It's surprisingly good value, although the taxi there and back (about Ksh800 one way) will add to the night's folly.

Shogun (see "Greater Nairobi" map, pp.88–89) Argwings Kodhek Rd, behind the *Blue Nile* restaurant, Hurlingham ☏ 02/716080; closed Sun lunch; buses #41, 46/46B or 56. Similarly excellent, slightly less formal than *Akasaka* and slightly cheaper (evening meals from Ksh750), though dreadful muzak does rather spoil the atmosphere. There's a huge range of dishes and their *sushi* is excellent. Reservations advisable for traditional Japanese "rooms". Recommended.

Mainly fish

Stavrose (see "Commercial Centre and River Road Area" map, pp.98–99) mezzanine floor, Postbank House, Market Lane ☏ 02/335107. A little-known posh fish restaurant, famed among those in the know for its tilapia fish, cooked any way you want it. They also do good salads. Expensive.

Tamarind (see "Central Nairobi" map, pp.108–9) National Bank Building, Harambee Ave ☏ 02/338959. If you can cope with the location next to the August 7 bomb site, this is Nairobi's largest, best and most expensive seafood restaurant. Highly rated. Reservations essential. Daily Mon–Sat, Sun dinner only.

Mainly meat

Angus Steak House (see "Commercial Centre and River Road Area" map, pp.98–99) Uchumi House, Aga Khan Walk ☏ 02/602775. Excellent steaks, salad bar and beer for around Ksh350.

Carnivore (see "Nairobi outskirts" map, pp.156–7) Langata Rd towards the National Park entrance ☏ 02/602775, ✉ info@carnivore.co.ke; buses/matatus #15, #24, #31, #34, #125, #126 all pass the entrance road, from where it's a 1km walk – overall much easier by taxi. Grossly named and yes, there is a connection – endless supplies of the fauna you thought was carefully protected,

served charcoal grilled. The all-you-can-eat menu (lunch Ksh885, dinner Ksh985) includes impala, giraffe, zebra, ostrich, crocodile, but the less exotic meats are often served first to lessen your appetite. Don't be shy, eat fewer sausages and chicken wings and ask for more game. A meal here has become part of every package itinerary and it's often tacked onto the tour outfits' excursions to Nairobi National Park. It's touristy – with discos at the end of the week and at weekends in the adjoining *Simba Saloon* – but very few people seem to dislike it. There's a good vegetarian buffet, too, and on Saturday afternoons kids can disappear to their Funland which features fairground, donkey and camel rides, games, magic shows, face-painting – enough to keep them happy for a few hours. It's debatable whether the nearby 500-metre Grand-Prix Karting circuit (Wed–Sun; ℡02/501758) aids or hinders digestion. See also "Live-music venues", p.139. Daily noon–3pm & 7–10.30pm.

Nyama Choma Ranch *Safari Park Hotel* ℡02/802561 (see "Nairobi outskirts" map, pp.156–7); taxi costs Ksh800, or bus/matatu #45, #137, #145, #160, #237. At once classy and tacky, with perfectly grilled food served by an assortment of dancers, and wildlife videos to keep you entertained. Better value than *Carnivore*, but you'll need a taxi to get back at night.

Porterhouse (see "Commercial Centre and River Road Area" map, pp.98–99) KCS House, Mama Ngina St ℡02/221829. Great steaks any way you want them.

Professional Centre Restaurant (see "Central Nairobi" map, pp.108–9), Parliament Rd ℡02/220014; closed Sun. Wide choice of well-prepared steaks, as well as a number of decent vegetarian dishes. In the same building as the Phoenix Players (see "Film, theatre and casinos").

Red Bull (see "Commercial Centre and River Road Area" map, pp.98–99) 1st floor, Transnational Plaza, Mama Ngina St ℡02/223332. A very 1970s German/Swiss "theme" restaurant, now aiming more upmarket. Wonderful steaks, game meat, seafood and vegetarian selection. Couples night with fifty percent discount for women on Wed. Dinner only Sat & Sun.

The Shark (see "Greater Nairobi" map, pp.88–89) 1km up Kiambu Rd, Muthaiga North ℡02/513381; taxi or matatu #100. An upmarket *nyama choma* joint (and disco palace at night; see p.139), cheaper than *Carnivore*.

Simmers (see "Commercial Centre and River Road Area" map, pp.98–99) Corner of Muindi Mbingu St and Standard St (daily 7am–midnight). Large and laid-back, central Nairobi's only *nyama choma*-style joint (and so very popular), with an "African lunchtime buffet" for Ksh500. There are live bands nearly every day of the week.

Salads

Calypso (see "Commercial Centre and River Road Area" map, pp.98–99) Bruce House, entry from Standard St or Kaunda St ℡02/335097. Full of smart young business types. Pancakes and waffles, and a fresh salad buffet. Open Mon–Sat.

Pasara (see "Commercial Centre and River Road Area" map, pp.98–99) 2nd mezzanine floor, Lonrho House, Standard St ℡02/338247. Delicious lunches, including sandwiches, muffins and pancakes. Open Mon–Fri.

Zanzebar (see "Commercial Centre and River Road Area" map, pp.98–99) 5th floor, Kenya Cinema Plaza, Moi Ave ℡02/222568. Quiet, lunchtime getaway with an economical salad buffet, KTN television and soft rock in the background. Famous for its "twelve-inch hot dogs". Lively bar in the evening and sometimes live bands. Wed, Fri, Sat are disco nights. Open daily.

Film, theatre and casinos

Nairobi has twelve **cinemas**, including two drive-ins. **Theatre** in the city is gradually improving, with a number of active stage venues and a dedicated local acting community.

Cinema

In the **city centre**, the twin-screen 20th Century on Mama Ngina Street (℡02/338070); the Nairobi, in Uchumi House, Nkrumah Lane just off Harambee Avenue (℡02/241614 or 338058); and the Kenya Cinema on Moi Avenue (℡02/226982; two screens) show fairly recent mainstream releases – usually blockbusters or award winners – when they can get them. Other movie theatres tend to show kung fu, vintage James Bond, old Westerns and, of course, Hindi and Punjabi movies which you don't need to understand to enjoy – the Fox Drive-In on Thika Road and the Belle-Vue Drive-In on the Mombasa Road have gone over pretty well exclusively to the genre. The Odeon on Latema Road near the *Iqbal Hotel* is a cheap fleapit with dire sound and film quality, and there have even been a few muggings. Weekend matinees here are packed. The Cameo on Kenyatta Avenue rarely shows anything watchable. If you go to **Westlands**, you'll find the new multiplex at the Sarit Centre, the best in Nairobi. Seats in the mainstream cinemas cost up to Ksh160, and around Ksh60 in the dives. Daily programmes can be found in the *Nation* and the *Standard* newspapers (the *Nation*'s two-line resumés are often more entertaining than the movie in question).

Theatre

The small theatre in the **Professional Centre**, at the end of Parliament Road (Mon–Fri 10am–5pm; box office and enquiries ☎02/225506), has assumed the mantle of Nairobi's leading playhouse, and is highly recommended. Its energetic repertory company, the **Phoenix Players** (formed in 1948), stage contemporary works by Kenyan or foreign playwrights, or sometimes perform classics adapted for Kenya. Their productions, since the increasingly less self-censoring climate of the 1990s, have always been worth catching and are sometimes excellent. They have some fine actors and superb singers, and the centre is a pleasant, intimate venue.

Under the dynamic directorship of Agatha Ndambuki, the **Kenya National Theatre** in Harry Thuku Road (☎02/2215174), opposite the *Norfolk*, gives considerable emphasis to Kenyan drama and African theatre in general – though with a less hectic schedule than the Phoenix Players.

You should also see what's going on at the University (they often have festivals of African and Caribbean theatre performed in the Education Department Lecture Theatre), and if you're around at the beginning of November, check out the **Kenya Music Festival** at the Kenyatta International Conference Theatre, heavy on choirs but with a lot of other fascinating song and dance. Otherwise, see if the **Serekasi Players** are doing anything in the basement of the conference centre; check out the productions of the **Miujiza Players** at the Rahimtulla Trust Library Theatre in Mfangano Street (☎02/212660); and enquire about the **Tamduni Players**, a long-established group run by a Gambian woman, Janet Young, who do occasional productions.

If you're interested in the state of the theatre in Kenya, the **French Cultural & Cooperation Centre**, **Goethe–Institut**, **Paa Ya Paa** or even **Gallery Watatu** (details for all on pp.132–3), may be able to tell you more, and the first two sometimes host productions. The *Standard*'s Thursday edition and the Friday and Saturday *Nation* carry theatre pages.

Casinos

There are more than enough places in Nairobi in which to unburden yourself of your money. One place that draws fair numbers of tourists is the **International Casino** (☎02/742600; bus #21, #23 or #119) on Westlands Road off Museum Hill, close to the *Hotel Boulevard* and museum. The complex consists of the main gaming room itself (main entrance off Chiromo Road; open from 9pm weekdays, 4pm weekends; smart casual dress code; nominal entrance fee), a couple of restaurants (see *Toona Tree* and *La Galleria* on pp.128–9), a slot machine hall, the Lucky Strike – a bit of a dive but the view is good – and a private member's club (Galileo's, basically just a disco). The whole area around the casino is dodgy – and extremely unsafe after dark – with clusters of prostitutes and drug-hawkers to waylay you, and opportunities for being mugged for your winnings.

Other options include the plush Mayfair Casino, next to the Holiday Inn in Parklands (daily noon–3am, Fri all night), and the rather classier Casino

Paradise at the *Safari Park Hotel*, sumptuous in every respect (no minimum bet, and it stays open, obligingly, until the last bankruptcy), but rather too far to walk back from if you're penniless. Lower down the social gambler's scale are a number of **bingo halls** that have recently appeared in the city centre, complete with nasally intoning callers and slot machines (usual prices are around Ksh500 for five bingo cards, entrance is free). Try Slots of Luck under the *Oakwood Hotel* in Kimathi Street, or the flashier Savoy Casino, above *New York New York* disco in Accra House, at the junction of Tom Mboya Street and Accra Road. Both are currently open 24 hours, despite a number of armed raids.

Cultural venues and art galleries

After years of stagnation, the Nairobi arts scene seems to be finally finding a rhythm of its own, independent of the tourist market which had previously driven much of it. The last few years have seen a very positive and encouraging proliferation of arts and cultural activities which, though still modest by international standards, are infectiously energetic and stimulating, and well worth discovering.

The **Mzizi Arts Center**, 6th floor, Sonalux House, Moi Avenue (☎02/574372, ☎245366, ✉sanaa@insightkenya.com) is the first port of call, and has become the scene's main focus, with a dedicated nucleus of writers, artists and musicians staging exhibitions, concerts, happenings, and innovative theatrical productions often by young Kenyan playwrights. Their offices, though cramped and far from ideal (they'd like to move if they get funding), are a hive of activity and a great source of information and contacts, and also contain an impromptu gallery of modern art and sculpture. They relaunched their library/resource facilities in 2001 as the Mzizi Creative Centre and also publish the fortnightly *Sanaa* freesheet, carrying arts and food reviews, news articles and general information. You can pick up a copy at their office, or at Kenya Cinema on Moi Avenue, the Japanese and French cultural centres, British Council and Goethe-Institut (addresses below), or at the Professional Centre theatre (see "Theatre" on p.131). Annual membership of their Nyungu Cultural Club (Ksh4500, students Ksh2000) gives you discounts and free entry to some performances, but is more a way of supporting their activities. The club organizes highly recommended monthly "Sigana" performances (Ksh300) at the centre which combine narration, song, music, dance, chant, ritual, mask, movement, banter and praise poetry.

The Museum Performing Arts Program (Zamaleo ACT at Museum Performing Arts Program, Museum Studio and Arts Centre, Museum Hill ☎02/751049, ☎751515, ✉aghano@yahoo.com), is an offshoot of the Mzizi group. Their aim is to help develop and popularize African performing arts as a theatrical genre. Currently they entertain various children's homes at the museum on the last Thursday of each month and work with a traditional Luo Band, Kenge Kenge Orutu Systems, which practises lunchtimes at the museum as well as performs at the African Village (Wed), the National Theatre (Thurs), Green House, Chaka Road, near the Yaya Centre (Fri) and at *Selys Restaurant* at the Motherland/Karen Motors (Sat & Sun).

The two other central places which you might not otherwise notice are the **French Cultural** and **Cooperation Centre** in the Maison Française (☎02/336748, ☎336253), and the **Goethe–Institut** in Maendeleo House (☎02/224640, ☎340770), both at the top of Loita Street near Uhuru

Highway. The Goethe-Institut puts on art exhibitions and concerts, both German and Kenyan, and has a monthly programme of subtitled German films. The French Cultural Centre has an equally dynamic programme, offering a space for Kenyan dance and theatre as well as staging events and activities derived from France. Long the most active cultural and intellectual forums in Nairobi, they're well worth checking out during your stay. Other similar venues, with less frequent events, include the British Council, ICEA Building, Kenyatta Avenue (☎02/334855, ☏02/334875, ✉bc.nairobi@bc-nairobib-council.org); the Italian Cultural Institute, Chiromo Court, 3rd floor, Chiromo Road (☎02/746739, ✉hcnbi@form-net.com); and the Japan African Culture Interchange Institute (known as Jacii), Kamburu Drive (☎02/566262). See also the section "Film, theatre and casinos" pp.130–132.

As with permanent exhibition spaces, most of the "galleries" scattered around the central business district are commercial and entirely tourist-oriented, heavy on batiks, *makonde* wood sculpture and paintings of the elephants-in-a-dust-bowl school. The only **art galleries** deserving the name (other than the National Archives, pp.110–111) are the Gallery of Contemporary East African Art (see National Museum), **Gallery Watatu** at Lonrho House on Standard Street (Mon–Sat 9am–6pm, Sun 10am–5pm ☎02/228737), and the **Paa Ya Paa Arts Centre**, way out of town on Ridgeways Road, off Kiambu Road, Ridgeways (☎02/512421, ✉sternjm@maf.org; see "Nairobi outskirts" map on pp.156–7). Gallery Watatu is dedicated to the development and promotion of contemporary African art, mostly painting – exhibitions change monthly, and they've stacks of work for sale at the back. It's also the venue for occasional "alternative" events. If you're at all artistically minded, missing Paa Ya Paa ("the Antelope Rises") would be a great shame. Begun in 1965, the centre suffered a disastrous fire in 1997 which gutted most of its galleries and destroyed countless paintings and sculptures. Starting over more or less from scratch, the idea was to create an artistic space where performers, artists and poets could meet, work, exhibit, live and be inspired. Mrs Njau teaches piano, and plays in the "Bush Bach" ensemble, an eclectic fusion of classical piano and African drum rhythms. There's usually an artist or two in residence, occasional workshops, and many paintings hung or propped up all over the place (some for sale) as well as a few sculptures which survived the fire. Set in overgrown woodland and banana trees, the clutter is wonderfully soothing, as is the informal atmosphere. Essentially, it's up to you to suggest what you'd like to do. Get to Ridgeways Road by #100 matatu, and walk for five minutes, turning left after Ridgeways Supermarket.

Nightlife and music

With the limited range of cultural activities available, it's not surprising that **drinking and dancing** are what a night out in Nairobi is usually about. Entrance fees are low by international standards and prices for drinks are much the same as you'll pay in similar establishments elsewhere in the country. Be warned, however that, male or female, if you're not accompanied by a partner of the opposite sex, you soon will be.

Bars

Although things are gradually getting livelier, central Nairobi is still a bit of a dead loss at night if you just want a **drink**, as most people tend to head off towards **Westlands** for its sleeker, more upmarket bars, or else pack into a number of sweaty discos. The great exception for city-centre revelling is the **River Road area** where, suitably stripped down (to the clothes on your back and a little cash), you can venture out to the land of "**Day & Night Clubs**" (see below). The district vibrates from dawn to dusk and back to dawn again with the sound of beery mayhem and jukeboxes. If you like the sound of it, you might consider taking a room nearby to avoid the hassle of getting back.

Ambassadeur Hotel Moi Ave. Popular with businessmen, and largely hassle free (the prostitutes limit their advances to waving at you).

Buffalo Bill's Milimani Rd, by the *Heron Court Hotel* (take a taxi if you're not staying up Nairobi Hill). A famous and remarkably seedy joint – a cowboy theme bar with a waiting woman in every "covered wagon" drinking booth. Noisy and high-spirited at night, the tone is much gentler by day, with good cheap food (the "hangover plate" is recommended) and occasional live jazz on Saturday and Sunday afternoons. The bar closes at 11.30pm, when the prostitutes head off downtown to either of the *Florida* nightclubs.

Dodi's Food and Drink Kenya Cinema Plaza, Moi Ave. Nice place, shame about the name. A bright and laid back two-level bar overlooking the fun and games and occasional preachers on Moi Ave. Closes around 10pm.

Gipsy Bar (aka *Tropicanna*), Woodvale Grove, Westlands ☎02/440836. Near the *Landmark Hotel*, this is a popular upmarket late-night choice, if a little cliquey. It serves tapas and remains open to the early hours.

Holiday Inn Parklands Rd. This is where the Friday night crowd moved to when the *Norfolk*'s

prices went up. Open to the early hours.

Hurlingham Hotel Argwings Kodhek Rd. This hosts an international working crowd and has darts, but closes at 10pm and can be a bit snooty.

Jockey Club *Hilton Hotel*, City Hall Way, next to Egyptair. This has a more traditional pub feel, but is predictably rather bland.

Norfolk Hotel Sooner or later, a people-watching drink or a snack at the *Norfolk's Lord Delamere Terrace* bar is a must, though at times it can feel like a pub in the City of London. It does, however, offer the full range of Tusker beers, and the snacks aren't as expensive as you might expect.

Six Eighty Hotel Pretty relaxed terrace bar with a good view over Muindi Mbingu Street.

Thorn Tree Café *Stanley Hotel*, Kimathi St. Hard to avoid as it's in the thick of the worst zone for tourist hustling, so a welcome refuge, and a handy meeting place. Snacks (excepting its terrible pizzas) are good, but overpriced. There's a cheesy band in the evenings. Closes around 11pm.

Zanzebar 5th floor, Kenya Cinema Plaza, Moi Ave. A pleasant place to down the beers (or cocktails) in the afternoons or evenings, before it gets disco-feverish. See also "Nightclubs", p.136.

Local dives – River Road district

On **Latema Road**, people contort themselves just to get into the *Modern Green Day and Night Club*. Here, entrance is free, cold beer is not the fashion – though you can get it, from the barman in his security cage – and the floor show is you and the rest of the customers. Just why the place is so popular is hard to say. For the girls, it's partly because of the steady trickle of potential customers from the *Iqbal* and other lodgings nearby. For some of the men, it's a place to chew *miraa* all night for the price of a soda. From the outside, with the usual arguments and hustle going on in the doorway, it might appear a place to avoid, but squeeze inside, drink a beer or two, and soak up the elevated (and very relaxed) atmosphere. People make friends quickly here, though having a conversation over the racket of the throng and the din of the jukebox is exhausting.

If you can't take the pace, try the *New Congoni Day and Night Club* on River Road, off Luthuli Avenue (see "Reggae Discos" opposite), and the excellent *Fameland* on Duruma Road (great music and food). *Habari Day & Night Club*, on Luthuli Avenue, and *Lizie Bar* at the corner of Gaberone Lane and Munyu Road, are both raucous and cheap like the *Modern Green*, but minus the hustling young women. *Reke Marie B&L* on Munyu Road is more fun and full of drunken old men, whilst *Friends Corner*, on the corner of Latema and Tsavo roads, one block up from the *Iqbal*, is also a favourite spot for a drink, though the toilets are horrible. The atmosphere is a characterful mixture of card-playing old-timers and more youthful faces making eyes. Also worth a mention is the *California Stars Butchery* on Gaberone Road, actually a bar and *nyama choma* joint, with tables out on the street opposite the Sikh Temple. There's nothing to keep you from checking out dozens of others – plenty of people do. For a place to start, try **Munyu Road**, which has more bars and clubs per hundred metres than any other place in Kenya.

Local dives – Dagoretti Corner

Aside from the city-centre clubs and the fairly touristy places which draw their custom from a wide area, there are plenty of other nightspots catering for a more local clientele in the outlying communities. Reputations change rapidly enough depending on the state of the neighbourhood and the security situation – asking around River Road's clubs will fill you in pretty quickly about what's in (and safe) and what's not. Currently one of the livelier of such communities, musically or otherwise, is **Dagoretti Corner** (see "Nairobi outskirts" map). Although only a fifteen-minute bus ride from town, it has a completely different look and feel from the modern centre.

Quite a number of bars in and around Dagoretti Corner, at the junction of Ngong Road and Naivasha Road, feature **live music** (another reason to think of staying out there), if not necessarily on a regular weekly schedule. Check out the four-storey *Matigari Bar*, hard to miss as it's painted top to toe with a Guinness ad, between Ngong and Naivasha roads, which sometimes features bands and is an interesting enough place the rest of the time. Heading back to town along Ngong Road, other choices include the **Impala Club**, **Motherland Inn** and *Ngong Hills Hotel* (all covered on p.138), all of which feature fairly regular live music. The best disco at Dagoretti Corner is currently the so-called *Holiday Inn* on Ngong Road past the junction with Naivasha Road, which is wildly packed at weekends. Buses and matatus #1, #2, #3, #4, #102, #103 and #111 run along Ngong Road to Dagoretti Corner.

Discos

Reggae is the popular staple sound of the **cheap discos**, often not much more than "Day & Night Clubs". The government's anti-rasta drive of the early-1990s fizzled out and reggae music is back on the airwaves and in the street. Nairobi also has a scattering of **nightclubs** complete with flashy interiors and the latest dance hits from Europe and America, as well as more danceable tunes from Congo. If this style appeals, try one of the established places below (or *Carnivore*, see p.129). In the glitzy places, men usually pay more than women, around Ksh100–300 as against Ksh50–100. In the rootsier discos, entrance is free or very cheap.

Reggae discos

Hollywood (see "Commercial Centre and River Road Area" map, pp.98–99) Moktar Daddah St ☏ 02/227949. Mostly a drinking club, with dancing and regular fights – something the regulars do to keep from falling asleep. Jah'mbo Soul have their residency here, though the action finishes early. Wed–Sun, live reggae on Sun; Ksh50 entry fee.

Monte Carlo Club (see "Commercial Centre and River Road Area" map, pp.98–99) Accra Rd ☏ 02/223181. A cavernous place with a good atmosphere and music. "No weapons or *miraa*", say the signs – a necessary notice, judging from the few unsavoury types. Daily till dawn; reggae disco Wed from 8pm, Sat from 4pm, Sun from 2pm; Ksh100.

New Congoni Day & Night Club (see

Unpredictable live music, predictably smelly toilets. Reggae discos on Sunday afternoons.

Nightclubs

The big **nightclubs** all put on floor shows for those who stay late enough – gyrating trios, limbo dancing and all – but except for the once-weekly "African Nites", don't come expecting any startling African musical revelations: you're more likely to hear Madonna. Most places charge around Ksh300 to get in.

Central Nairobi

These are all on the "Commercial Centre and River Road Area" map on pp.98–99.

Dolce Club Cianda House, Koinange St ☎ 02/218275. Slick and smooth *soukous* and soul for a glitzy crowd; deafening sound system. Daily.
Florida 2000 1st floor, Commerce House, Moi Ave near the Kenya Cinema ☎ 02/229036. The red-and-black themed *New Florida*'s sister attracts similar clients and offers equally unambiguous entertainment, pumped up with what they call "most exotic floor shows" (nightly 1am). For the local ladies, this means grabbing drunken *wazungu* on the razzle. Wildly popular, and its Sunday afternoon disco is *the* place to keep on swinging if sleep has somehow eluded you. Daily.
L'Ora Blue Corner House, Kimathi St ☎ 02/218953; closed Sun. A brand-new, rather smart dinner-dance place, appealing to grown-up, upmarket smoochers rather than disco freaks. Cabarets some nights. Judging by the lack of clientele, this may very well turn into something else.
New Florida Chai House, Koinange St ☎ 02/334870. Irresistible for its tackiness (with matching floorshows),

this big orange mushroom of a building above the Total filling station is always full of hookers and rather desperate-looking business types, but the atmosphere is merely steamy, not heavy. To go with the beer, there's a traditional English restaurant (ie Chinese). Reggae on Wednesday. Tacky floorshows at 1am.
New York House Savoy Building, junction of Tom Mboya St and Moi Ave ☎ 02/252846. Brand new and already massively popular, connected with the Savoy bingo and casino, cashing in on the rekindled interest in retro 1980s disco with a touch of techno. There's a nightly 1am cabaret, occasional events like beauty contests, and Sunday afternoon jam contests. Daily 9pm–6am.
Zanzebar 5th floor, Kenya Cinema Plaza, Moi Ave ☎ 02/222568. Very swish pinewood and neon club full of trendy types. Tuesday and Thursday are karaoke; Wednesday soul (of the diva sort); Friday disco till dawn; Saturday is turning over to *ndombolo*, sometimes live; and Sunday has a mixture of everything. Daily; free except Fri, Ksh100.

Westlands

See "Westlands" map, p.106.

Klub House 1 Westlands, Corner of Mpaka and Parklands Rd ☎ 02/541608. Relatively new night club with a sports bar, restaurant and a pool room upstairs. The beer garden is pleasant and popular during Happy Hours 5–8pm.

Pavement Westview Centre, Ring Road, Westlands ☎ 02/441711. In-place for the young and funky, but a sizeable crowd of the not-so-youthful and trendy hang on with a vengeance.

Out of town

These are all on the "Nairobi outskirts" map on pp.156–7.

Capital Planet Ngong Racecourse; buses/matatus #1, #2, #3, #4, #102, #103 and #111. Once called *The Barn* and considered to be the best disco around, with a relaxed club atmosphere. It's popular simply for being popular, which makes for a good night out. Safe parking and good security.
Cats Club *Safari Park Hotel*, 14km up Thika Rd; bus/matatu #45, #137, #145, #160 or #237.

Smooth tunes, decent lighting and sound system, but lacking in atmosphere. Get a taxi back.
Psy's Off Langata Rd, opposite the turning for *Carnivore*; buses/matatus #15, #24, #34, #125 or #126. New dance place attracting migratory birds from the *Carnivore*'s Simba Saloon. Wednesday, Friday and Saturday are the main nights, with Friday attracting the flocks disenchanted with rap's

inroads at *Simba Saloon*'s "Soul Nite".

Rhino Club *Park Place Hotel*, Magadi Rd
☏ 02/890456; matatu #125 or bus #126. Relaxed and unhustly, more like a *nyama choma* joint, and no DJ. It's fine for lone women.

Sahara City Mombasa Highway ☏ 02/822933; matatu #110. Arguably Nairobi's top disco with the best sound system – an excellent place for dance freaks, with the best DJ working Wed–Sun. No

tourists and plenty of young affluent Asians dancing *mujurrah*.

Swamp Village Park Inn Kikuyu Rd, Siruta
☏ 02/571361; matatus #2 and #102. A thorough convert to the Congolese *ndombolo* invasion, which is featured Saturday & Sunday, together with tempting extras like beer-drinking competitions, dance contests and hair beauty shows. There are also occasional live acts.

Live-music venues

Given the volatile nature of the music business in Kenya, **venues** and **bands** change at a moment's notice. Although there are a few downtown music places, much of Nairobi's live music action takes place on the perimeter of the city. The following listings include all the places that have been around for some time, plus the latest information on new ones. In addition, you might check out Friday's and Saturday's *Daily Nation* for announcements of one-off gigs. **Starting times** vary considerably for all the clubs. On weekdays, 7.30 or 8pm wouldn't be too early, while weekend warm-ups usually begin around 9–10pm, and some may not get really rolling until midnight. But don't judge any band by their first hour: many run through some pretty dreadful warm-up material to begin with. Remember, too, that many clubs have **Sunday afternoon "jam sessions"** that can be just as lively as the evening shows, and often include acrobats, jugglers, magicians or comedians as well – excellent for families, too, and convenient if you don't want to be taxiing around the city late at night.

Nairobi bands

The big names to watch out for are the Everest Kings, Super Mazembe, Les Mangelepa, Tshackatumba (a mix of Congolese and Kenyan musicians), the Seiko System Band (playing a fusion of benga and rumba), rumba from Bilenge Musica, Golden Sounds Band (featuring fantastic sax players Twahir Mohamed and Rama Athumani), and number-one female benga singers Queen Jane (Nyambura) and Princess Jully. Look for special shows at Safari Park Hotel and The Carnivore, especially the WorldSpace satellite hookup from The Carnivore on the last Thursday of the month. The Panafric Hotel's Saturday night Golden Oldies programmes regularly showcase some of the top names of early Kenyan pop.

Possibly less interesting sounds come from the voices and instruments of a clutch of tourist and international-style pop and rock bands – the Pressmen, Big Matata Band and Hakuna Wafungwa. For nearly a decade there's been a huge gospel trend in Nairobi and you're bound to hear of some of the following artists: Mary Atieno, Augustus Baraza, Wilson Majale, Pete Odera, and Esther Wahome.

Records and cassettes

Pirated cassettes may seem a good deal at under Ksh100 (originals cost Ksh 200) but quality and durability are so bad they're practically worthless. Identify them by the lack of labels on the cassette itself. For CDs and tapes, try Assanand's and Musikland on Moi Avenue, Melodica on Tom Mboya or, better still, any of a host of shops and stalls on and around River Road and Accra Road.

City centre

The following are on the "Commercial Centre and River Road Area" map on pp.98–99, unless otherwise stated.

African Heritage Banda St ☎02/251414. Easy-going, informal, weekend afternoon mixes of reggae, *soukous* and more traditional music. Sat & Sun 1–5pm.

Arturo's Restaurant Tumaini House, Moi Ave ☎02/226940. Not exactly a restaurant (though the food's OK) and not really Italian, but its first-floor verandah has live music (could be anything: Congolese, Kikuyu, Luo) on Wed, Fri and Sat nights. Very danceable, very local, and entrance is free.

Fameland Club Duruma Rd ☎02/248000. Live bands and good DJs weekends in this elegant and cosy joint. Thursdays are African night discos, with plenty of hip-gyrating rhythms to grind to. Don't walk around here unaccompanied.

Green Corner Restaurant Tumaini House, Nkrumah Rd ☎02/219084. The *Cactus Bar* here is handy to fill a dull night but nothing special in itself. There's the obligatory Wed ladies' night, a busy "Friday Jam" (DJs), and live music from the Hot Rod Band on Thurs and Sat.

Mang' Hotel (see "Central Nairobi" map, pp.108–9) Haile Selassie Ave ☎02/224090. An exuberant local venue where *soukous* and Lingala still reign. Mpingo Band play Wed & Fri from 6pm; there's a disco on other nights and more live *soukous* after midnight.

Terrace Hotel Ronald Ngala St. Live music with a chance that the expected band will not turn up, and the only real entertainment will be the sight of you struggling with teeth-wrenching *nyama choma*.

Suburban and out of town

Almost all of the following double as *nyama choma* joints. Except when noted, all can be found on the "Nairobi outskirts" map on pp.156–7.

Calabash Bezique 20km down Thika Rd at Kahawa Sukari, opposite Kenyatta University ☎02/811084; bus/matatu #137 or #237. A large 24hr *nyama choma* place with studenty discos Thurs–Sat and occasional live bands – phone in advance for details.

City Cabanas Mombasa Highway, 3km before the airport turning ☎02/820549 or 820992; matatu #110. A massive entertainments complex rapidly becoming one of the prime venues for visiting international stars (including Congolese *ndombolo* dancesters Koffi Olomide and Le General Defao), as well a lot of home-grown talent – look in the press for details. Big name tickets around Ksh800.

Hillock Inn (see "Greater Nairobi" map, pp.88–89) Enterprise Rd ☎02/544819 or 545668. In the unlovely Industrial Area, this is a long-established venue, with *nyama choma*, several bars, tacky fountains and "Intelligent Band" resident Wednesday, Friday and Saturday (6pm to past midnight), and Sunday afternoons. They have some s/c rooms available (❷) if you feel less than clever for the taxi ride back (Ksh800). Get there on a matatu for "Industrial area/Hillock" outside the Afya Centre, Tom Mboya St.

Impala Club Ngong Rd ☎02/565684; buses/matatus #1, #2, #3, #4, #102, #103 and #111. Occasional live acts on Friday nights.

The Jazz Bar (see "Greater Nairobi" map, pp.88–89) 2nd floor, Yaya Centre, Hurlingham ☎02/711473; bus #41 or #46. A sadly pretentious (and expensive) piano bar rather than the jumpin' jazz joint Nairobi really needs. Still, it hosts smooth US jazz artists from time to time – ring, or check press for details. Daily 10am till late.

Motherland Inn (see "Greater Nairobi" map, pp.88–89) Ngong Rd, opposite Menelik Rd; buses/matatus #1, #2, #3, #4, #102, #103 and #111. Matata Five Band play here regularly.

Ngong Hills Hotel (see "Greater Nairobi" map, pp.88–89, Ngong Rd ☎02/567137, ⓔngonghills@iconnect.co.ke; buses/matatus #1, #2, #3, #4, #102, #103 and #111. One of the best venues, this hotel has Orchestra Malembe Stars resident on Wednesday, Friday and Saturday nights (8pm–3am), and Sunday afternoons (2–8pm). The atmosphere is not at all intimidating and the bands (Kenya's coolest, Tanzania's hottest and some Lingala) uniformly excellent. Sunday afternoons host a very laid-back jam session, complete with dancers, acrobats, tight-rope walkers and *nyama choma* by the green pool to drown your hangover in. Ideal for kids. Ample parking.

Peacock Inn (see "Greater Nairobi" map, pp.88–89) Dai Dai Rd, Nairobi South "B" Shopping Centre ☎02/552639; matatus from railway stage. On Fridays this is well worth checking out for occasional visits by Tanzanian bands, including Arusha's Ngamiani Band.

Roasters Inn Thika Rd, Ruaraka, 2km before

Safari Park Hotel ☎02/861000; bus/matatu #45, #137, #145, #160 or #237. Opposite Kenya Breweries, *Roasters* hosts the resident Forvics Band (playing "oldies") as well as cabaret. Wednesday, Friday and Saturday are the main nights. Take a taxi.

Shark (see "Greater Nairobi" map, pp.88–89) 1km up Kiambu Rd, Muthaiga North ☎02/512439; matatu #100. An upmarket *nyama choma* joint featuring Wamilika and the Ruiru Youngstars live every Wednesday (basically jazz-funk), and pure disco-trash Friday–Sunday am. Cheaper than *Carnivore*, but it's miles out. Take a taxi back.

Simba Saloon *Carnivore Restaurant* (see p.129) ☎02/602764. A successful meld of live music and disco in a pleasant, outdoor environment. Wednesday nights are rock (till 2am; free before 9pm); Thursday is live jazz or rave (6pm–midnight; free before 9pm); Friday is "Africa Nite" with a band called Simba Ngoma; Saturday disco party night (smoochy African and US crooners; 6pm till dawn); and Sunday is Simba Soul (6pm till 2am; free till 9pm). Visiting big-name groups sometimes take the Sunday afternoon slot. Look out for occasional comedy (in English as well as Swahili) on Tuesdays. Thursday (Ngoma Night) is African music. No music Mon or Tues.

Splash! 300m from *Carnivore* (see p.129) ☎02/603777. An uneventful night out but you can go swimming. Ksh150.

Sportsview Hotel Thika Rd, Kasarani, near the Moi Sports Complex ☎02/861648; bus/matatu #17B, #45, #137, #145, #160 or #237, plus 1.5km walk. Another outsize *nyama choma* joint which occasionally books some interesting groups. There are also horse rides and a playground for the kids. Friday and Saturday nights have discos.

Wida Highway Motel Naivasha Rd, Kikuyu ☎0154/32813; bus/matatu #2 or #102. Part beer and *nyama choma* garden with live music (especially Fri), part disco Groove Syde (soul and R&B Sat). The live music is mainly local bands with the odd rowdy beauty contest thrown in for fun. Saturday and Sunday afternoons have family-oriented shows, with R&B disco, some gospel, acrobats and comedy.

Safari transport and operators

Nairobi is the travel hub of Africa, with a mass of opportunities for **safaris** around Kenya and literally hundreds of safari operators, car rental outlets and travel agents to provide you with everything you need for your trip. If you want to make simple hotel and lodge reservations, either do it through a travel agent (see "Listings", p.150) or contact the hotel reservation services in person (addresses and hotel lists on pp.42–44).

The **transport** options available if organizing your own safari meet every taste and budget. One possibility not often considered is **cycling**. Although the big game parks are out of reach, several of the smaller ones allow bikes (Hell's Gate at Naivasha, Lake Bogoria Reserve, Kakamega Forest) and there's a lot of wonderful cycling country besides. The cheapest Chinese and Indian three-speed machines are widely available, as well as large numbers of cheap mountain bikes (from around Ksh8500), and a few lightweight models with good specification. These can be good value, but you'll have trouble reselling. For listings of bike shops, see p.144. For **bicycle rental**, contact Bike Treks (see "Special activity safaris", p.142): it costs Ksh1800 per day, but they prefer you to use them for longer treks to reduce the risk of theft in Nairobi. For further information on cycling, see Basics p.38.

Having a **car** allows the independence to set your own itinerary and explore at your own pace. Details on **renting** a vehicle are in "Car rental and driving" in Basics, p.36, while car rental companies in Nairobi are listed on p.145. If you're looking to **buy** a vehicle in Kenya, scan the classified ads in the papers or visit the stretch of Langata Road opposite Nyayo National Stadium on a Sunday morning, where there's a regular second-hand vehicle sale.

If you're in the market to **charter a plane**, a few small operators, mostly based at Wilson Airport (☎02/501941–3), will oblige. It's not as outrageously expensive as you might assume and the opportunities for photography and seeing the country are without equal. The current standard rate for a Cessna 182 (two passengers) is around $1.60 per mile (1.6km) – the minimum mileage is usually 500 miles (800km or three hours' flying) for $750 – though that takes you a very long way. You shouldn't be charged for *démarrage* (the plane parked on the ground), if you're coming back the same day. See "Airlines, internal", p.144 for charter company details.

Safari operators

You can pick up plenty of leaflets about safaris from touts, or at any travel agent or ticket-booking company. Armed to the teeth with brochures and anxious to take you to operators' offices, **touts** are by no means a bad thing, as they often work for several companies and their commission is never added to the price you pay. Indeed, some are quite knowledgeable and will be able to advise you relatively truthfully about which companies are currently good for what. Bear in mind, however, that because relatively few companies with established reputations give them commission, they are unlikely to take you to them.

The best of the **travel agents** are reputable, but it's always a good idea to meet the company you're travelling with in advance and to try to ensure that it is that company and not you who is paying the agent their commission. You should also check whether the advertised safari is actually run by the company in question, as the practice of one company subcontracting a safari to another is quite common, especially in low season, and gives you less redress if things go wrong. This is especially important for safaris to **Tanzania** and **Uganda** – ensure that the company has at least an office in the relevant country.

For a copy of the operator's code of conduct, as well as a list of companies which adhere to the code, contact the **Kenya Association of Tour Operators (KATO)**, 3rd floor, Hughes Building, Kenyatta Avenue, (PO Box 48461 ☏02/225570, ☎218402, ☒info@katokenya.org). They should also be able to advise you on the reputation of a company you're considering going with. But remember, if you do decide to choose a cheaper company which is not a member of KATO, you'll not necessarily be ripped off. Take your time, ask to see the vehicles, demand everything in writing including a breakdown of the costs, and don't be pressured into making any decisions until you are ready. In the unfortunate circumstance that you have been duped, contact Mr Fred Kaigua, the Chief Executive of KATO who may be able to help. And, contact us to let us know what happened.

The following listings are classified broadly – several operators could be put into more than one bracket. All are members of KATO unless otherwise stated.

Camping safaris

First, read the section on "Safaris" in Basics (pp.61–63). Every other shop seems to belong to a safari outfit and it's obviously impossible to mention more than a few. With so much to go wrong, spotless reputations are hard to maintain, but the following, who run most of their **camping trips** by truck or minibus, are good value and only rarely come in for criticism.

Gametrackers 5th floor, Nginyo Towers, Koinange/Moktar Daddah St, PO Box 62042 ☏02/338927, ☎330903, ⊕www.gametrackers.com. Popular and consistently good operator with some twenty tours, including – apart from game safaris – cycling, camel treks, Aberdares walking and Mount Kenya climbs, as well as trips further afield (they have branches in Tanzania and Uganda). Around $60–80 per day and up. They run an excellent eight-day Turkana safari via Samburu National Reserve, Marsabit National Park and the Chalbi Desert, which is highly recommended ($480).

Guerba Kenya 1st floor, International House,

Mama Ngina St, PO Box 43935 ☎ & ℱ 543244, 🌐 www.gorp.com/guerba. The Kenyan arm of the respected Africa overland specialists, primarily dealing with their overseas clients, but also offering safaris to walk-in customers, usually on a small commission.

Habib's Tours & Travel Agip House, Haile Selassie Ave, PO Box 48095 ☎ 02/220463, ℱ 220985, 🌐 www.habibtours.com. Pricier than most, but reliable and long-established, specializing in tailor-made safaris and packages to suit most price ranges (aided by discount deals with many hotels). From $75 per day for camping safaris, and $110 upwards for the same in lodges or hotels.

Ice Rock & Safari Adventure 4th floor, NCM Building, Tom Mboy St, PO Box 50155 ☎ 02/244608, 🌐 www.climbingclimbingafrica.com. Mainly deals with safaris to Mount Kenya, Kilimanjaro and Hell's Gate. A small professional set up with knowledgeable guides. The owner, who used to be a member of the Mount Kenya rescue team, organizes and leads every expedition. Prices for the four-day Sirimon route up Mount Kenya start from $300 per person. (Not a member of KATO).

Kenia Tours and Safaris 4th floor, Jubilee Insurance House, Kaunda/Wabera streets, PO Box 19730 ☎ 02/223699, out of hours ☎ 02/444572, ℱ 217671, 🌐 www.gorp.com/kenia. Proficient and generally reliable general Kenya camping safaris specialist, keenly priced and conscientious. $70–80 per day for camping safaris, $95–100 for lodge safaris, discounts in low season.

Safari Camp Services Lower ground floor, Barclays Plaza, Loita St, PO Box 44801 ☎ 02/228936, 330130, or after hours ☎ 02/891348, ℱ 212160, 🌐 www.kenyaweb.com/safari-camp. For over twenty years the operators of the original "Turkana

Bus" (a converted Mercedes lorry; $450 for 7 days) and also of a "Wildlife Bus" trip ($578 for 7 days) emulated by many others. Their customer service and experience is second to none, and their limited number of tried-and-tested safaris keeps standards up and prices fairly well down; the combined "Turkana Bus and Camel Trek" in the Mathew's Range and Lake Turkana is great ($910 for 13/14 days). No-frills safaris $60–70 per day; more comfortable, less streamlined, small-group camping safaris, around $150 per day.

Safari Seekers 5th floor, Jubilee Exchange House, Kaunda St, PO Box 9165 ☎ 02/226206, ℱ 334585, 🌐 www.kenyaweb.com/safari-seekers. General operator, offering mountain-bike safaris in cooperation with an American company, Paradise Bicycle Tours. From $70–80 per day.

Savuka Tours & Safaris 4th floor, Pan Africa House, Kenyatta Ave, PO Box 20433 ☎ 02/215256, ℱ 215016, 🌐 www.savukatravels.com. Neither a member of KATO, nor a newcomer, but they do get favorable recommendations from budget travellers. They are generally reliable and the food is surprisingly good.

Scenic Safaris Biashara St, PO Box 49188 ☎ 02/578135, ℱ 571461, ✉ scenic@nbnet.co.ke. Wide range of shorter trips and reasonably priced lodge safaris. Camping from around $60 per day; lodges from $150 per day.

Twiga Tours 4th floor, Victor House, Kimathi St, PO Box 14365 ☎ 02/337332, ℱ 337330, 🌐 www.twiga-tours.com. A relative newcomer with tailor-made tours for as few as two people from $90 to $100 per person per day.

Venture Africa 3rd floor, City House, corner of Standard St and Wabera St, PO Box 8696 ☎ 02/219511, ℱ 219263, 🌐 www.venture-africa.com. Relatively new operator with no bad reports. Camping safaris from $70 per day, lodge safaris between $100 and 200 a day.

Lodge and homestay safaris

The following are all pretty conscientious and helpful operators, catering for those who appreciate their wildlife taken with more than a modicum of luxury. Most have discounted deals with hotel chains (see pp.42–44 for a list of these), which means that their more popular trips are generally better value than less frequently run ones. If you don't mind the effort of driving, renting a car and booking accommodation yourself shouldn't work out much more expensive, but read our hotel and lodge reviews first. All also run half- and full-day trips in and around Nairobi for $35–80.

Let's Go Travel Caxton House, Standard St, PO Box 60342 ☎ 02/340331, ℱ 336890, 🌐 www.letsgosafari.com. Branches in Karen shopping centre ☎ 02/882505, ℱ 882172 or 214713, and ABC, Westlands ☎ 02/441030, ℱ 441690,

which is the head office. Apart from acting as agents for a large number of homestay and ranch-house sites throughout Kenya (and offering some specially negotiated deals on the more expensive hotels), Let's Go also runs its own well-organized budget camping safaris, from $60 to 85 per day. Lodge safaris are $130 to 170 per day, depending on season and group size. One of the few companies to have offices in both Tanzania and Uganda and run trips there.

Pollman's Tours & Safaris Pollman's House, Mombasa Rd, PO Box 84198 ☎02/533140, ℻544544. One of the largest operators, running to all the major parks, though decidedly package-tour in feel (travelling in "convoy" with four or five other Pollman's minibuses isn't unusual). Around $380 for three nights. Popular with German visitors.

Rhino Safaris Rhino Safaris Building opposite the Baptist Church, Ngong Road, PO Box 48023 ☎02/720610, ℻720624, ✉rhinosafarisnbo @kenayweb.com. Highly regarded and long-established firm, founded in 1970, specializing in scheduled lodge, homestay and flying safaris. Customer service is second to none, and they're happy to tailor itineraries to individual needs. Prices start from around $390 for a three day/two night Mara trip, to over $1000 for a six-night tour covering Samburu, the Aberdares, Lake Nakuru, and Maasai Mara or Amboseli. They have offices in Mombasa and Arusha in Tanzania.

Somak Travel 8th floor, Corner House, Mama Ngina St, PO Box 48495 ☎02/330285, ℻218954, ✉somak@form-net.com. Well-regarded, offering a range of scheduled departures to all the main parks.

Southern Cross Safaris Symbion House, Karen Road, PO Box 24584 ☎02/884712–19, ℻884723–24, ✇www.kenya-direct.com/southerncross. Reliable and long-established mid-range operator specializing in overnights in

lodges and luxury tented camps rather than basic camping safaris, including visits to private wildlife sanctuaries as well as the national parks. Fine if you like everything taken care of and are happy to pay for it, but otherwise expensive compared to a DIY combination of car rental and self-booked nights. They have an office in Mombasa, and operate their own vehicles in Tanzania.

Suntrek Tours & Travel Swan Court, off Muthithi Rd, Westlands, PO Box 48146 ☎02/751349, ℻742055, ✉suntrek@form-net.com. Long-established quality outfit happy to tailor itineraries and accommodation style to your needs. Standard trips cover all the major game parks and use reliable lodges. Recommended, if you're short on time, are their five- or six-night trips which cover a combination of different parks and scenery, for example Tsavo West, Amboseli, the Aberdares, Lake Nakuru and Maasai Mara national parks. Lack of regularly scheduled departures means you're unlikely to have other tourists on the same safari, although this makes things more expensive if there are only two of you. They also run trips into Tanzania. From $165 to 185 per night.

Tour Africa Safaris Dennis Pritt Rd, off State House Rd, PO Box 34187 ☎02/729333, ℻723513, ✇www.tourafrica-safaris.com. Well-run travel agency, which also runs its own tailor-made lodge safaris (its camping safaris are arranged through other companies). A five-day jaunt in high-class lodges costs $600–800. They also arrange safaris in Tanzania, including the lesser-known national parks, from $90 to 120 per day camping, or $150–180 in lodges.

Special activity safaris

The following are recommended because they offer unusual, if normally much more expensive, trips – notably safaris on foot (sometimes using pack animals), by bicycle (usually with vehicle back-up), on horseback or camel. Those that don't have walk-in addresses are usually small companies: enquire and book with a large agent like Let's Go Travel (see p.141). For information on balloon "safaris", see pp.428–429.

Bateleur Safaris Ndorobo Rd, Langata, PO Box 42562 ☎02/890454, ℻891007. Specialists in walking safaris for ornithologists.

Bike Treks Kabete Gardens, behind Sarit Centre, off Karuna Rd, Westlands, PO Box 14237 ☎ & ℻02/446371, ✉info@biketrek.co.ke. Truly adventurous trips, tailor-made, with vehicle back-up, led by a veteran mountain-bike enthusiast; the trans-Mara ride during the wildebeest migration is quite something. Minimum three people for guaranteed departures. They can also arrange trekking and

mountain-climbing trips. $95–100 per day.

Desert Rose Camels ☎02/5677251, ℻564945, ✉ras@swiftkenya.com. Expertly guided and flexible camel (or horseback) expeditions in and around the Mathews, Ndoto and Nyiru mountain ranges of Samburu district. Don't come expecting total comfort, but it is a wonderful experience, with plenty of contact with local people. The only, rather minor and unusual, gripe might be the overly romantic view that your hosts have of the tribespeople. Rates vary according to length of safari and number of people participating. $170–210 per person per day. They also run the exquisite *Desert Rose Lodge*, between Baragoi and South Horr (see p.604).

East African Ornithological Safaris
☎02/331191 or 222075, ℻330698 or 216528, ✉eaos@africaonline.co.ke. By no means the cheapest safaris, but with years of experience in bird-watching. It costs $3000 all-in, including accommodation at well-selected lodges and tented camps (and at most of the related Savannah Camps & Lodges chain, p.44).

Ewaso River Camel Hikes (bookings via Southern Cross Safaris, see p.142). Based near Loisaba, 2hr northeast from Rumuruti in Laikipia on the Ewaso Nyiro River. Camel-assisted walks are $205 per person per day, or just camel hire ($35 per camel) if you've got your own wheels to get there (the nearby *Colcheccio Lodge* is one of Kenya's priciest).

Naturetrek Adventure Safaris Imenthi House, Moi Ave, PO Box 34817 ☎02/341188, ℻243572, ⊛www.naturetreksafaris.com. Specialists in walking safaris, notable for a seven-day walk in the Rift Valley and Loita Hills on the Tanzanian border, and a thirteen-day jaunt in Tanzania itself, encompassing Mount Meru, lakes Manyara and Natron, and Ngorongoro. From $150 to 200 per day. Not in KATO.

Safaris Unlimited Ltd 328 Langata Rd, PO Box 24181 ☎02/890435, ℻891113,

⊛www.safarisunlimited.com. Specialists in horse-back safaris, covering the Aberdares, Samburu, the Rift Valley and Maasai Mara. Exclusive and expensive: trips cost around $300–500 per person per day, depending on the length of the trip and group size. They also run *Longonot Ranch House* in Naivasha (p.239).

Savage Wilderness Safaris Thigiri Rd, PO Box 44827 ☎02/521590, ⊛www.whitewaterkenya.com. Excellent, if naturally risky, programme of technical climbing and walking trips on Mount Kenya, "white-water" rafting, and walking safaris in the Chyulu and Loita hills. One-day rafting from $95. Other trips $100 per day and up, depending on numbers. Not in KATO, but in Kenya Professional Safari Guides Association.

Tropical Ice Suite 8, 1st floor, Muthaiga Shopping Centre, Muthaiga Rd, PO Box 57341 ☎ & ℻02/884652, ⊛www.tropical-ice.com. Upmarket walking safaris along the Galana river for $160 per day. Not in KATO.

Yare Safaris Union Towers, Moi Ave, PO Box 63006 ☎ & ℻214099, ⊛www.iconnect.co.ke/~travelkenya/. One of the leaders in North Kenyan travels, offering various off-beat tours and camel treks in the Samburu district from their base in Maralal (see p.604). A seven-day camel safari, with transfer from Nairobi, costs $495 per person.

Upmarket safaris

If you can afford it, the **expensive safari outfits** are mostly operated to very high standards. They often depend heavily on reputations passed by word of mouth among clients and overseas operators. The following firms will give good return for your money if you are in the $300–1000 per day league and want something special. At this level, what you do is entirely "tailor-made" – in other words, it's largely up to you. Transport is usually by land cruiser, accommodation is in luxury lodges or pre-set private campsites, and leader/tour guides tend to be white hunter types who know the ground well and their clients' requirements even better.

Abercrombie & Kent Bruce House, Standard St, PO Box 59749 ☎02/334955, ℻215752, ⊛www.abercrombiekent.com.
Cheli & Peacock PO Box 39806 ☎02/603090, ℻0154/22553, ⊛www.chelipeacock.com.
East African Wildlife Safaris Titan Aviation, Wilson Airport, PO Box 43747 ☎02/605661, ℻605622, ⊛www.kenyaweb.com/eaws.
Glen Cottar Safaris 60 Forest Lane, Karen, PO Box 44191 ☎02/884508, ℻882234,

✉cottars@form-net.com.
Ker & Downey Safaris Busia/Enterprise Rd, Industrial Area, PO Box 41822 ☎02/556466, ℻552378, ✉kerdowneykenya@form-net.com.
Richard Bonham Safaris Nandi Rd, Karen, PO Box 24133 ☎02/882521, ℻882728, ✉bonham.luke@swiftkenya.com.
Tor Allan Safaris 80 Bogani East Rd, PO Box 15114 ☎02/891190, ℻890142, ✉torallan@africaonline.co.ke.

Listings

Air ambulance If you're worried about medical evacuation from the wilds, contact: AAR Health Services ☎02/715318–26; or the Flying Doctors Service (Amref) ☎02/717374, ⨍336886. See p.30.

Airlines, internal Most airline offices are open Mon–Fri 8am or 8.30am–1pm & 2–4.30pm or 5pm, Sat 8.30am–1pm. Aircraft Leasing Services ☎02/500156; Airkenya ☎02/501421–3, bookings ☎02/6605745, ⨍602951; Blue Bird Aviation ☎02/602338; Boskovic Air Charters Ltd ☎02/501210, ⨍609619, ✉boskovic@swiftkenya.com; Eagle Aviation ☎02/822924, ⨍602338; East African Air Charters ☎02/504731, ⨍502358; Fuf Aviation ☎02/505541; Sarman Aviation ☎02/606416; Trackmark ☎02/501263, ⨍504907.

Airlines, international For opening hours see "Airlines, internal" above. Note that Kenya Airways operates jointly with Ethiopian Airlines and Air France. Aero Zambia, ground floor, International House, Mama Ngina St ☎02/246519; Air India, 3rd floor, Jeevan Bharati Building, Harambee Ave ☎02/313300; Air Madagascar, 1st floor, Hilton Building, City Hall Way ☎02/225286; Air Malawi, International House, Mama Ngina St ☎02/248265; Air Mauritius, mezzanine, International House, Mama Ngina St ☎02/229166; Air Tanzania, ground floor, Chester House, Koinange St ☎02/336224; Air Zimbabwe, ground floor, Chester House, Koinange St ☎02/339524; Aeroflot, Corner House, Mama Ngina St ☎02/220746; Balkan Bulgarian Airlines, 2nd floor, Royal Card Centre, Mpaka Rd, Westlands ☎02/445900; British Airways, International House, Mama Ngina St ☎02/244430; Cameroon Airlines, 9th floor, Rehani House, Kenyatta Ave ☎02/224743; Egyptair, Hilton Building, City Hall Way ☎02/226821; El Al, 9th floor, KCS House, Mama Ngina St ☎02/228123; Emirates, 20th floor, View Park Towers, Loita St ☎02/211978; Ethiopian Airlines, Bruce House, Muindi Mbingu St ☎02/330837; Gulf Air, ground floor, International House, Mama Ngina St ☎02/211986; Kenya Airways, 5th floor, Barclays Plaza, Loita St ☎02/229291; KLM, Barclays Plaza, Loita Street ☎02/210771; Olympic Airlines, 12th floor, Ambank House, University Way ☎02/338026; Pakistan International Airlines, ICEA Building, Banda St/Kenyatta Ave ☎02/333901; Royal Swazi National Airways, 4th floor, KCS House, Mama Ngina St ☎02/210670; Saudi Arabian Airlines, mezzanine II, Anniversary Towers, University Way ☎02/240606; South African Airways, 1st floor, Lonrho House, Kaunda St ☎02/227486; Swissair, Ambank House, University Way ☎02/250288.

American Express Express Travel Group, Bruce House, Standard St PO Box 40433 is the main walk-in office (☎02/215916, ⨍334825). There is also one at the *Hilton*. They both provide all the usual services and they'll hold card-holders' mail.

Artists' materials Sciencescope, Victor House, by the Nation Centre, Kimathi St (☎02/210741 or 447920), is the place for professional oils, acrylics, pastels, paper etc. They have a branch at the Yaya Centre, Hurlingham.

Banks There are branches of Barclays every-where, most with ATM cash machines and effi-cient, helpful service, but only Standard Chartered Bank, which also has ATMs, has more abysmal exchange rates. The best bank rates are offered by Stanbic Bank, Stanbic Bank Building, Kenyatta Ave, followed by African Banking Corporation (ABC), Koinange St (also at Woodvale Grove, Westlands). The best overall rates are posted by the numerous competing forex bureaux found throughout the city, whose rates differ only by one percent or so. Worth a mention, though, is the Central Bureau de Change on Wabera St, their rates are one of the best for sterling traveller's cheques (no commission) and they don't ask for proof of purchase. Many of the exchange bureaux are little more than a desk and armed *askari* guard; some don't accept traveller's cheques (or require your proof of purchase), others refuse plastic, but their service is usually fast. If you're worried security-wise about being seen to change money, the Commercial Bank of Africa inside the *Hilton Hotel* (Mon–Fri 1–8pm, Sat 8am–8pm) is out of sight, but has bad rates. There are no banks open on Sundays except the exchange bureaux at the airport, though the larger hotels may oblige with their facilities. Western Union transfers are received by Postbank, Postbank House, Market Lane (☎02/651696, ⨍210593; Mon–Fri 8.30am–4pm, Sat 8.30–11am) – get there early as it could take up to three hours, Fridays are less busy. For details of bank charges and ATMs, see Basics, p.31.

Bike shops Cycle Land, Moi Ave ☎02/223955; Cycle Mart & Exchange Ltd, Kijabe St ☎02/223459; Gitonga Cycle Dealers, OTC Building, Landhies Rd ☎02/214697; Kenya Cycle Mart, Moi Ave ☎02/223417; Sadar Singh Vohra Ltd, River Rd, next to Evamay Lodge ☎02/222715; Westlands Cycle Mart, Old Uchumi Building, oppo-site The Mall, Westlands ☎02/448055.

Books Good downtown bookshops, carrying wide selections of coffee-table books, maps of Kenya and the major game parks, and imported paperbacks, include: Westland Sundries/Nation Bookshop, Kenyatta Ave (entrance also from the *Stanley Hotel*); Bookpoint, Loans House, Moi Ave; Premier Bookshop, corner of Tom Mboya St and Ronald Ngala St (who have the widest range of maps); Prestige, Prudential Assurance Building, Mama Ngina St (also open Sun 9.30am–12.30pm); and Primrose Sundries, 20th Century Plaza, Mama Ngina St. The Textbook Centre, Kijabe St (☎02/330340–5, ☏225779, ✉info@tbc.co.ke) behind the *Norfolk Hotel*, with an excellent branch at the Sarit Centre, Westlands (☎02/747405), also has a good choice, as well as stationery and artists' materials. In River Road district, you'll find a cluster of bookshops at and around the junction of Lagos Rd and Latema Rd. For a good second-hand selection, try Prestige, or the Book Stop, Yaya Centre, Hurlingham. East African Educational Publishers have their sales office on Mpakard St (☎02/4447000).

Bus companies The following terminals and offices are marked on either the "Commercial Centre and River Road Area" or "Central Nairobi" maps. Companies not listed operate from the Country Bus Station ("Machakos Airport"). Akamba Bus, Lagos Rd ☎02/340430 or 221779; Arusha Express, Cross Rd/River Rd ☎02/212083 or 338322; Busscar, Duruma Rd/Kumasi Rd ☎02/229662; Coast Bus, Accra Rd/Duruma Rd ☎02/214819; Colobus Shuttle, Village Market ☎02/581726, ✉sales@colobusenroute.com; Cross Road Travellers, Cross Rd ☎02/331531; Crossline, River Rd ☎02/245358; Daily Peugeot Service (DPS), Dubois Rd ☎02/242824; Davanu Shuttle, Windsor House, University Way ☎02/222002; Eastern Express (no phone) from the Country Bus Station; Goldline, top of Accra Rd/Cross Rd ☎02/225279 or 221963; KBS Stagecoach, KBS bus station, Mfangano St ☎02/246047; Kensilver Express, Dubois Rd ☎02/221839 or 240218; Mombasa Liners, Accra Rd/River Rd ☎02/241564; Mwingi Coach, opposite Eastleigh KBS depot, General Waruinge St ☎02/765763; Sunbird Services (no phone), from the Country Bus Station; Transluxe, opposite OTC (behind the KBS bus station), Temple Rd ☎02/220059.

Camping equipment Atul's, Biashara St (Mon–Fri 9am–1pm & 2.30–5.30pm, Sat 9am–3pm; ☎02/228064), is the only place where you can rent outdoor equipment – especially useful if you're going to Mount Kenya – but the prices can seem excessive to budget travellers (tent rental

from Ksh320 per day). They are also fully equipped for repair jobs. On the same street, but on the other side of Muindi Mbingu St, Kenya Canvas Ltd (Mon–Fri 8am–5pm, Sat 8am–1pm; ☎02/333509) sells tents (from Ksh9000), mosquito nets (Ksh375) and other equipment. Much cheaper than either for basic tents (from Ksh4000), sleeping bags (Ksh3000 and up), kipmats (Ksh800), cooking stoves and gas bottles is the Nakumatt Centrepoint supermarket on Kenyatta Ave, between Koinange St and Muindi Mbuingi St (Mon–Sat 8.30am–8.30pm, Sun 10am–7pm).

Car rental Avis, College House, University Way, ☎02/336704, ☏339111, ✉avis@form-net.com; Budget/Payless, Hilton Building, Simba St, ☎02/223581–2, airport ☎02/822370, ☏223584, ✉payless@kenyaonline.com; Central, ground floor, Fedha Towers, Standard St, ☎02/222888, ☏339666; Concorde, Agip Garage, Waiyaki Way, Westlands, ☎02/448953, ☏448135; Crossways, Banda St, ☎02/220848; Eurodollar, Kenya Woodvale Grove, Westlands, ☎02/440333, ☏552857, airport ☎02/432069, ✉natcarnb@africaonline.co.ke; Europcar Express, Travel Group, Bruce House, Standard St, ☎02/334722–7, ☏334825, ✉expressk@africaonline.co.ke; Hertz/UTC, corner of Kaunda St and Muindi Mbingu St ☎02/248777, ☏216871, airport ☎02/822339, ✉info@herts.utc.co.ke; Kenia Tours and Safaris, 4th floor, Jubilee Insurance House, Kaunda St/Wabera St, ☎02/223699, out of hours ☎02/222513, ☏217671, 🌐www.keniatours.com; Let's Go Travel, Caxton House, Standard St, ☎02/214713, ☏336890; Pola's Car Hire, 1st floor, NCM House, Tom Mboya St, ☎02/334207, ☏337933; Rasuls, Butere Rd, Industrial Area (taxi to Mater Misericordiae Hospital), ☎02/558234, ☏540341; Southern Cross Safaris, *Stanley Hotel*, Standard St, ☎02/225255, ☏216553, ✉sxsnbo@africaonline.co.ke; Suntrek Tours & Travel, Swan Court, off Muthithi Rd, Westlands ☎02/751349, ☏742055, ✉suntrek@form-net.com; Venture Africa, 3rd floor, City House, corner of Standard St and Wabera St, ☎02/219511, ☏219263, ✉ventureafrica@form-net.com.

Car repairs Undugu Motor Garage, near Maridadi Fabrics by the City Stadium roundabout (☎02/76563), is reliable.

Contraceptives Oral contraceptives are available from the Family Planning Clinic, 5th floor, Phoenix House, Standard St (☎02/335775). Condoms are sold in any supermarket or pharmacy.

Dentist Dr Peter Griffiths, Kolloh Rd, Lavington

℡02/448211. Pager 717717 no.283. Up-to-date equipment.

Doctors Dr Sheth, Westlands ℡02/441176 or 582040. Alternatively, ask your embassy for a list. For blood tests, Alliance Health Services, Pioneer House, 5th floor, Moi Ave (℡02/313339) is very good. A malaria check costs about Ksh600. If you prefer homeopathic treatment, consult Dr R. J. S. Panesar, Diamond Plaza, High Ridge, near *Ma Roche's Guest House* (℡02/746772). A recommended chiropractor is Dr Thomas Adagala, mornings downtown at 1st floor, APDC House, Lagos Rd (℡02/330782), afternoons at Vanga Rd, Lavington (℡02/560078).

Email and internet services There are internet cafés practically on every street in Nairobi and most of them are reasonably cheap, though slow and unreliable. If you have a Hotmail account, it's probably better to open an account with another server for the duration of your trip; Hotmail is extremely slow in Kenya. One of the most reliable and fastest places to send email is Safari Surf Café, IPS Building, bottom of Kaunda St, near Kimathi St (Ksh4 per min). Browse Internet Access in Norwich Union House, 4th floor, opposite the *Hilton*, is also reasonably cheap, but it can be slow and over crowded (Ksh25 per 15min). Christos Internet Café, Phoenix House, 2nd floor, Kenyatta Ave, is smaller than Browse and the staff are friendly and helpful, but can also be slow – Ksh4 per min or Ksh1500 monthly membership which entitles you to 15min daily internet access). Other places include: the *Hilton*'s business centre, 2nd floor, *Hilton Hotel* (Mon–Fri 7am–8pm, Sat 8am–4pm; ⓔ hilton@africaonline.co.ke; emails Ksh70 to receive; internet Ksh500 per 30min); Cyber Safaris at *Simmers Restaurant*, corner of Kenyatta Ave and Muindi Mbingu St (emails Ksh100 per 15min; internet Ksh400 per hr); Cybervore Internet Café at *Carnivore* (Mon–Fri 10.30am–11pm, Sat & Sun 11am–11pm; email/internet Ksh150 per 15min; Ksh10 per page printed; Cyberc@fe, Bruce House, Kaunda St (Mon–Fri 8.15am–6pm, Sat 8.15am–1.30pm, ⓔ cybercafe@insightkenya.com; email Ksh65 to send/receive; internet Ksh300 per hr).

Embassies, high commissions and consulates Australia, ICIPE House, Riverside Drive, off Chiromo Road, PO Box 47718 ℡02/445034–9; Austria, 2nd floor, City House, Standard/Wabera Street, PO Box 30560 ℡02/228281–2; Belgium, Muthaiga/Lumuru Road, Parklands, PO Box 30461 ℡02/741564–7; Burundi, 14th floor, Development House, Moi Avenue, PO Box 44439 ℡02/335973; Canada, 6th floor, Comcraft House, Haile Selassie Avenue, PO Box 30481

℡02/214804; China, Woodlands Road, off State House Road, Hurlingham, PO Box 30508 ℡02/722559; Congo, 12th floor, Electricity House, Harambee Avenue, PO Box 48106 ℡02/229771–2; Cyprus, 5th floor, Eagle House, Kimathi Street, PO Box 30739 ℡02/220881; Czech Republic, Embassy House, Harambee Avenue, PO Box 30204 ℡02/210494 or 223448; Denmark, 11th floor, HFCK Building, Kenyatta Avenue/Koinange Street, PO Box 40412 ℡02/331088–90; Egypt, 7th floor, Harambee Plaza, Uhuru Highway/Haile Selassie Avenue, PO Box 30285 ℡02/250764; Eritrea, 2nd floor, New Rehema House, Rhapta Road, PO Box 38651 ℡02/443163; Ethiopia, State House Avenue, Nairobi Hill, PO Box 45198 ℡02/723027; Finland, 2nd floor, International House, Mama Ngina Street, PO Box 30379 ℡02/334777; France, 9th floor, Barclays Plaza, Loita Street, PO Box 41784 ℡02/339978; Germany, 8th floor, Williamson House, 4th Ngong Avenue, PO Box 30180 ℡02/712527–8; Greece, 13th B floor, Nation Centre, Kimathi Street, PO Box 30543 ℡02/340722; Hungary, Ole Odume Road, off Argwings Kodhek Road, PO Box 61146 ℡02/560060; Iceland, Bendera Lane, off Spring Valley Road, PO Box 45000 ℡02/521487; India, 2nd floor, Jeevan Bharati Building, Harambee Avenue, PO Box 30074 ℡02/222566–7; Ireland, Owashika Road, Lavington PO Box 30659, ℡02/578043; Israel, Bishops Road, PO Box 30354 ℡02/724021–2; Italy, 9th floor, International House, Mama Ngina Street, PO Box 30107 ℡02/337777; Japan, 15th floor, ICEA Building, Kenyatta Avenue, PO Box 60202 ℡02/332955-8; Luxembourg, 8th floor, International House, Mama Ngina Street, PO Box 30610 ℡02/224318; Madagascar, 1st floor, Hilton Building, Mama Ngina Street, PO Box 41723 ℡02/225286; Malawi, Mvuli Road/Church Road, off Waiyaki Way, Westlands, PO Box 30453 ℡02/440568–9; Mozambique, HFCK Building, Kenyatta Avenue/Koinange Street ℡02/222446; Netherlands, Riverside Lane, off Riverside Drive, PO Box 41537 ℡02/447412; New Zealand, 3rd floor, Minet ICDC House, Mamlaka Road, PO Box 47383 ℡02/722467; Nigeria, Lenana Road, Hurlingham, PO Box 30516 ℡02/564116–8; Norway, 8th floor, HFCK Building, Kenyatta Avenue, PO Box 46363 ℡02/337121–2; Pakistan, Church Road, off Rhapta Road, Westlands, PO Box 30045 ℡02/443911–2; Poland, Kabarnet Road, off Ngong Road, Woodley, PO Box 30086 ℡02/566288; Portugal, 10th floor, Reinsurance Plaza, Taifa Road, PO Box 34020 ℡02/338990; Russia, next to Army HQ, Lenana Road, PO Box

30049 ☏02/728700; Rwanda, 12th floor, International House, Mama Ngina Street, PO Box 48579 ☏02/240563; Seychelles, 7th floor, Agip House, Waiyaki Way, PO Box 20400 ☏02/441150; Slovakia, Milimani Road ☏02/721896–7; Somalia, 5th floor, International House, Mama Ngina Street, PO Box 30769 ☏02/580165; South Africa, 17th floor, Lonrho House, Standard Street, PO Box 42441 ☏02/215616–8; Spain, 5th floor, Bruce House, Standard Street, PO Box 45503 ☏02/335711; Sudan, 7th floor, Minet ICDC House, Mamlaka Road, PO Box 74059 ☏02/720883; Sweden, 10th floor, International House, Mama Ngina Street, PO Box 30600 ☏02/229042; Switzerland, 7th floor, International House, Mama Ngina Street, PO Box 30752 ☏02/228735; Tanzania, 9th floor, Reinsurance Plaza, Taifa Road, PO Box 47790 ☏02/331056; Uganda, 5th floor, Uganda House, Kenyatta Avenue, PO Box 60853 ☏02/330801; United Kingdom, Upper Hill Road, off Haile Selassie Avenue, PO Box 30465 ☏02/719107 or 719082; USA, Mombasa Road, PO Box30137 ☏02/537800, 🖷537810; Zambia, Nyerere Road, PO Box 48741 ☏02/724796; Zimbabwe, 6th floor, Minet ICDC House, Mamlaka Road, PO Box 30806 ☏02/721049

Flight information ☏02/822111 or 822206 at Kenyatta International Airport.

Football (soccer) Nyayo Stadium, at the junction of Uhuru Highway and Langata Rd. Seats cost Ksh60–120. Highly recommended, whether you're a regular fan or not, but especially for international matches (these may be played at Moi International Stadium on the Thika Rd). Getting back to the town centre afterwards by public transport can be a problem.

Freight Air freight is cheaper than sea freight except for very large items. All companies charge the same per kilo rates (currently $5.32 per kg, with discounts for certain items like books), but shop around for the lowest handling charges. Federal Express, Bruce House, Standard St, PO Box 49707 ☏02/240106 or 240138, 🖷211307) is reliable and charges a minimum fee of $80 which is less than most. Alternatively, much cheaper is simply to bypass the middlemen and send your parcels direct from the British Airways cargo counter at Kenyatta International Airport's international departures lounge (☏02/822172–5; currently $3.50 per kg for any airport in Europe, no handling charges). See also "Post and parcel couriers" p.149.

Golf Bookings for all the following can be done through Tobs Golf Safaris Ltd, PO Box 20146 ☏02/721722, 727790, 🖷722015, @tobsgolf@form-net.com. Windsor Golf & Country

Club, Kigwa Rd, 15km north of the city (☏02/862300) has the best location, in rich lake- and woodland teeming with Sykes monkeys. The 6751-yard par 72 course, with a long 640-yard 5th, is reckoned the most challenging, and there's a resident pro, too. On Muchai Drive, the Royal Nairobi Golf Club's 7021-yard par 72 course is easier, with a cultivated landscape and views of the Ngong Hills (☏02/725769). Muthaiga Golf Club on Muthaiga Rd (☏02/762414, @muthaigagolf@insightkenya.com), has its 6676-yard par 72 on the edge of Karura forest. It boasts a variety of indigenous trees and flowering shrubs, has fast greens, and hosts the Kenya Open. Other clubs include the pretty and very colonial Karen Golf & Country Club (☏02/882801) with a 6893-yard par 72, next to the Blixen Museum; and Limuru Country Club's 6519-yard par 71, in tea country, whose altitude (2130m) provides the rainfall to keep the turf green year-round.

Guides Guides for almost anywhere in Kenya can be arranged through Utalii College, Kenya's college for tourist-oriented trades, though it would be advisable to contact them well in advance (PO Box 31052 ☏02/802540–7).

Hairdressers and barbers Very cheap, no-fuss men's cuts at Boston's, Uganda House Arcade, Kenyatta Ave/Standard St. Manes Unisex Hair Salon, mezzanine floor, Avenue House, Kenyatta Ave, offers bonding weaves, spiral rolls, pedicure, false nails and pussycat, among other mysterious delights.

Health foods Healthier Options, Soin Arcade, Westlands Rd, Westlands. Good range of imported health foods and remedies.

Horse racing Frequent buses on race days (usually Sun) to Ngong Rd Race Course from the KBS bus station.

Horse riding Arifa Riding School, Marula Lane, Karen (☏02/882937), offers lessons and hire. Kitengela Polo Club, Karen (☏02/882782), also has lessons, "game drives", picnic rides and, of course, polo.

Hospitals The Kenyatta National Hospital, Argwings Kodhek Rd (☏02/726300) is the main public hospital for accidents and emergencies, and did miraculous work in the aftermath of the August 7 US Embassy bombing. It's adequate for non-life-threatening problems, but under-staffed and under-funded. The private Consolata Sisters' Nazareth Hospital (☏02/335684), on Riara Ridge Rd, near Limuru, about 25km from Nairobi (bus #117 from bus station), charges reasonable rates and is recommended if you need to be in for some time (assuming you have any choice in the matter). Another private place with a good reputation is the Aga Khan Hospital in Third Parklands Ave (PO Box 30270 ☎ 02/740000). For emergencies, dial ☎ 999 (free calls).

Kenya Wildlife Service (KWS) See also Basics "The environment and ethical tourism", p.65. This is Kenya's National Parks organization, who are in charge of their day-to-day running and security, as well as liaison with local communities. Contacting them is essential if you plan to visit the more remote parks and reserves, or have specialist requests or queries. They are also the only body to give (hard to get) official clearance for entering parks and zones where security is a concern (notably Mount Elgon, and all the parks and reserves in Northeastern Province). KWS Headquarters, Langata Rd, Nairobi National Park Main Gate, PO Box 40241 ☎ 02/501081–2, ℗ 505866 or 501752, ⊛ www.kws.org.

Language schools Trans Africa Language Services, Joseph Kangethe Rd, Adam's Arcade, off Ngong Rd (☎ 02/561160), offers Kiswahili courses individually and in groups. Other languages are also available. A similar service is offered by Makioki Language Services, Kijabi St (☎ 02/242330), and Nairobi Cultural Institute, Ngong Rd (☎ 02/340310). For private teaching, check the noticeboard at Gallery Watatu.

Laundry There are two laundries in Nairobi: Mbuni Dry Cleaners in Westlands at the corner of Chiromo and Mpaka roads; and – better and more expensive – Niki's in Hurlingham Plaza, Hurlingham, Argwings Kodhek Rd (☎ 02/710909). Laundry may be left with the staff to wash and iron for later collection. There are plenty of dry-cleaners: Pearl branches are everywhere and cheap, whilst the equally ubiquitous White Rose is more expensive but has an express service. Hotels and lodgings will always do washing for you.

Left luggage Bags can be left safely at either of the two left-luggage offices at the train station. There are lockers at the side of the 1st/2nd class entrance (daily except Sun 6.30am–noon & 2–6.30pm; Ksh150 per item), whilst larger bags can be left at the third-class hall (daily 7.30am–7.30pm; Ksh300 per item). Given the expense, consider leaving bags in the care of your hotel, if you think you can trust them. There is no left-luggage facility at the airport.

Libraries The British Council, ICEA Building, Kenyatta Ave (Tues–Fri 10am–5pm, Sat 9am–noon; ☎ 02/334875), has British newspapers and magazines, in addition to videos for rent, and film/video screenings on Tues and Thurs at 5.30pm. The McMillan Memorial Library, Banda St (Mon–Fri 9am–5pm, Sat 9.30am–1pm; free; ☎ 02/224281 ext 2253), is the main public library,

with a good "Africana" reading room (Ksh100 for a week's use). For serious research, the British Institute in Eastern Africa, 3km northwest of town at Laikipia Rd (off Arboretum Drive), Kileleshwa (☎ 02/43721 or 43330, ℗ 43365, ℮ britinst@insightkenya.com) is excellent, with a comprehensive collection of books, academic journals, off-prints and theses: membership costs Ksh500 for residents, £12.50 for non-residents, for which you also receive the annual journal *Azania*. Also good for research is the reading room in the National Archives, Moi Ave (see p.110), whose annual membership is a paltry Ksh50. There are also small research libraries at the university's Department for African Studies, based in the National Museum compound, and at the National Museum itself, jointly run with the East Africa Natural History Society.

Maps Game park maps published by the Survey of Kenya (some of which are over a decade out of date), and maps of Nairobi and environs, are available from bookshops; so, too, are the city-wide *A–Z of Nairobi* (Kenway Publications; 1999) and general maps of Kenya. For Survey of Kenya covering other parts of the country, the procedure is complicated to say the least: you first visit the Public Map Office, Harambee Ave (just west of the Conference Centre), to find out which of the sheets you want are available, and note their numbers (they sell all the game park maps, too). Then you go to the Survey of Kenya offices (PO Box 30046) out on the Thika road (see "Greater Nairobi" map, pp.88–89) where you make a formal written request stating which sheets you want, why ("I am a tourist wishing to visit. . ."), and leaving your address. They will, eventually, get back to you, with an authorization to buy the maps. You might want to do all this before even reaching Kenya, though in fact some of the supposedly "sensitive" maps are available to order through stockists in Europe and America. The British Ordnance Survey is one such agent.

Newspapers and magazines Foreign papers such as the *International Herald Tribune* are available from several news stands around Kenyatta Ave, as are *Newsweek* and *Time*, and most of the British dailies and Sundays. The majority of bookshops stock magazines. The best Kenyan daily is the *Nation. The People* on Fridays and the *East African* on Mondays are also good.

Noticeboards The best-known was at the *Thorn Tree Café* at the *Stanley Hotel*, but this disappeared after the eponymous tree was cut down in 1997. There is now a smaller and a less used noticeboard in its place. The *Iqbal's, the Upper Hill Campsite* noticeboards are good for budget travellers, as are those at *Ma Roche's* and the youth hostel. The *Fairview Hotel* has a slightly more upmarket noticeboard, used by travellers.

Opticians All your needs, including contact lenses and solutions, at Eye Masters Ltd, Kenya Cinema Plaza, Moi Ave (Mon–Fri 7.30am–6pm, Sat 9am–2pm; ☎02/222601). Or try the Family Eye Care Centre, Princely House, Moi Avenue (Mon–Sat 8.30am–5pm, Sun 9am–noon; ☎02/337989).

Ornithology The Museum Ornithology Society organizes bird walks or drives around Nairobi. Enthusiastic non-members are welcome if they make a donation. Meet at the museum on Wed at 8.30am.

Passport photos Five-minute passport photo service at Studio One, corner of Moi/Nkrumah avenues, and at Custom Color, Kaunda St. There's a Colour Studio at Vedic House on Mama Ngina St.

Pharmacies Kam Pharmacy, Mpaka Rd, Westlands (☎02/443776), has a branch too on the ground floor of the IPS House on Kimathi St. There's also a chemist in the *Hilton* (Mon–Fri 9am–6pm, Sun 9am–1.30pm).

Photocopying Numerous places throughout Nairobi. MBIM, bottom of consolidated Bank House, corner of Loita and Koinange streets. Xerox, right by the entrance to the *Hilton* is probably the easiest to find.

Photography For camera repairs, try Camera Clinic, Biashara St (☎02/222492). Buying a camera is approximately twice as expensive as in Europe: check Nairobi noticeboards (see under "Noticeboards"). For batteries and to rent cameras and binoculars, the main outlet is Elite Camera House, Kimathi St, south of Kenyatta, but they are not recommended for repairs. Expo Camera, Esso House, Mama Ngina St (next to the Kenya Coffee Board), offers a fast, reliable service for prints and slides and also does good repairs. Any branch of Colorama is likely to be reliable, and there's an efficient one-hour service (2hr for slides) from Spectrum Colour Lab at Rehema House on Standard St.

Post and parcel couriers If you have valuable items to send home contact: DHL, Longonot Place, Kijabe St, PO Box 67577 ☎02/534988, ⓕ339850; TNT Express Worldwide, Kiambere Rd, PO Box 41520 ☎02/723554, ⓕ723077; UPS, Fedha Towers, Kaunda St, PO Box 45422 ☎02/252200, ⓕ333411; or EMS Speedpost on Posta Rd. See also "Freight".

Postal services The GPO (Mon–Fri 8am–6pm, Sat 9am–noon) on Kenyatta Ave has *poste restante*. Letters normally take under a week to arrive from Europe, although 3–4 weeks is not unheard of, and too many things simply never arrive. The parcels office is upstairs. Parcels from home can be addressed to you at *poste restante*: you'll get a note from the Parcels Section. There are smaller branch offices on Moi Ave opposite Tubman Rd, and another nearby on Tom Mboya St. Alternatively, one of the larger hotels may oblige by selling you stamps.

Sports and health clubs (see also "Golf clubs"). The *Norfolk Hotel* sells one-month membership (under $50) of its health club, which includes use of its heated pool and gym, and aerobics. The *Serena Hotel* has a similar deal, which includes its unheated pool and multigym. The *Nairobi Safari Club*'s facilities are ridiculously expensive, as are the *Grand Regency*'s. Much more fun than any of these is Grand-Prix Karting, next to *Carnivore*, with its 500-metre circuit (Wed–Sun; ☎02/501758). There's indoor bowling at the Cosmic Bowling & Pool Centre in Sound Plaza, Woodvale Grove, Westlands.

Swimming pools One of the best pools is at *Hotel Boulevard*, a nice setting with delightful water and better value than the *Norfolk*'s. For the genuinely skint, *Heron Court Hotel* charges a mere Ksh40 for its pool, and the excellent one at the YMCA on the west side of Uhuru Highway costs the same. The pool at the *Panafric* is handy if you're staying at the youth hostel; the pool at *Silver Springs Hotel*, Valley Rd, behind the hostel, is even better. A day by an ordinary pool usually costs around Ksh100–200. If you're staying at *Ma Roche's*, you should certainly check out the modern sports complex behind the Aga Khan Hospital – fantastic pool, diving board, lounging area, snooker rooms, gym and team-sport pitches and courts all for about Ksh60 a day. More central are the pools at the *Stanley Hotel* (including Jacuzzi and steam room), *Meridian Court Hotel*, and *Hotel Inter-Continental* (use of the steam room, Jacuzzi and sauna for Ksh800, though you stay as long as you like). *Safari Park Hotel*'s pool is unfortunately for residents only. For real water-babies, a trip to *Carnivore*'s Splash! water park is a must: water-slides, fountains, ecstatic children and sometimes a disco at night.

Taxis Kenatco ☎02/225123, 316611, 230771–2; JKA airport branch ☎02/824248 or 822356. Kenya Taxi Cabs Association ☎02/222953. Discount Travel, ground floor, 20th Century Plaza, Mama Ngina St (☎02/251203), runs to the airport for Ksh900.

Telephone and faxes (see also "Email and internet services", and read the details in Basics on pp.50–51). The main place is the official Extelcoms on Haile Selassie Ave. There are two entrances: the one on the left is for calls within Kenya (open

24hr); the one on the right is for international calls (daily 7am–midnight). Calls are made through an operator – you fill in a form stating how many minutes you'd like (currently Ksh540 per minute to Europe, or three minutes for Ksh930, then wait for the call to be put through (sometimes immediate, sometimes takes hours). Lines are less busy at weekends. It's easier, if they haven't run out, to buy a phone card (Ksh200 & Ksh500) to use the blue IDD card phones outside the building (or in the Kenyatta International Conference Centre), but the largest card will only last you a couple of minutes. Note that card phones elsewhere in the city are for national calls only. If all else fails, you can make calls from large hotels; you pay through the nose for this (Ksh1500 and up for 3min) but at least you can talk in peace. Faxes can be sent and received at Extelcoms (℗02/330170; Ksh250 to send a page worldwide, Ksh28 to receive); but much cheaper is Win.World, 7th floor, Standard Building, Standard St (Ksh170 per page worldwide). Hotels will receive faxes for a small fee (usually around Ksh50 per page).

Tourist information Nairobi has no official tourist information service – a lamentable state of affairs. The free and widely circulated monthly *What's On in Kenya* is always worth a glance. If you can't find a copy, ask at the Nation Centre, Kimathi St. The *Standard* and *Nation* newspapers are a useful source of current information and special offers.

Travel agents and airline bookings Bankco Tours & Travel, 1st floor, Mulji Jetha Mansion, Latema Rd/Lagos Rd, PO Box 11536 ℡02/336144, ℗331874; Crocodile Travel, Stewart Building, Ronald Ngala St/Tom Mboya St, PO Box 20380 ℡02/335250; Haidery Tours & Travel, 1st floor, Impala House, Tom Mboya St, PO Box 45728 ℡02/335256, ℗211949; Hanzuwan El-Kindy Tours & Travel, Dubois Rd, PO Box 49266 ℡02/227387; Kambo Travel, Tom Mboya St, opposite Latema Rd, PO Box 41819 ℡02/228131, ℗228734; Prince Safaris, ground floor, Kenyatta International Conference Centre, PO Box 51096 ℡02/219499, ℗217692; Tour Africa Safaris, 7th floor, Rehani House, corner Kenyatta Ave and Koinange St, PO Box 34187 ℡02/336767, ℗338271, ℠www.tourafrica-safaris.com; Trade & Travel Ltd, Monrovia St, opposite Jeevanjee Gardens, PO Box 11392 ℡02/227575, ℗228710; Travel Service, Pan Africa House, Standard St, PO Box 45456 ℡02/3221992, ℗214120, ℮info@bunsontravel.co.ke.

Vaccinations Cholera, yellow fever, typhoid and hepatitis jabs can be obtained from City Hall, City Hall Way, or from Dr C.S. Sheth, Sarit Centre, Westlands, who can also advise about malaria.

Visitor's passes/visas Visitor's pass extensions (up to six months in all) can be obtained at Nyayo House, Posta Rd, behind the GPO (Mon–Fri 8.30am–12.30pm & 2–3.30pm; ℡02/332022). This is usually done while you wait. Don't go there if you've overstayed your permit (see Basics, p.19).

Women's movement The Maendeleo ya Wanawake ("Women's Progress") Organization has its main office in Maendeleo House on Monrovia St, PO Box 44412 ℡02/222095, ℗225390. Founded in 1952, the MYWO also has a shop on Muindi Mbingu St, selling crafts without the middle men. The Forum for African Women Educationalists (FAWE, PO Box 53168 ℡02/226590, ℗210709), established in 1992, aims to improve girls' and women's education.

Worship As well as many mosques and temples, Nairobi has a number of churches, two cathedrals, and a synagogue. The four main churches and synagogue are located in the northwest of the city centre and the area is a lively focus for Christians on Sunday mornings. All Saint's Cathedral, a beautiful church behind Uhuru Park, has often been a gathering point for peaceful opposition protest to the government.

Moving on from Nairobi

Getting out of Nairobi by public transport is normally a fairly haphazard business. The following is intended to lend a degree of structure to a chaotic scene, but to make it comprehensive would be a never-ending task. If in doubt, ask. You'll always get where you want to, somehow.

By matatu

If you decide to take a mini-bus **matatu** out of Nairobi, you'll find that vehicles for different destinations congregate in different areas of town, the most useful of which are listed below with reference to chapters in this book. Be warned, however, that their locations change fairly frequently – ask around, and remember, the suicidal reputation attached to matatus is by no means entirely the result of paranoia. Matatus to Nakuru, Naivasha and Thika have a particularly bad reputation. See also p.33 in Basics.

Matatu routes

Chapter Two: The Central Highlands
Embu (2hr–2hr 30min; Ksh200), Accra Road between River Road and Duruma Road; **Karatina** (2hr; Ksh160), Accra Road/River Road, opposite *Crossline*; **Meru** (4hr 30min; Ksh270), Accra Road between River Road and Tsavo Road; **Mwea** (5hr 30min; Ksh170), Accra Road between River Road and Tsavo Road; **Nanyuki** (4hr; Ksh200), Accra Road between River Road and Tsavo Road; **Nyahururu** (3hr; Ksh200), Latema Road; **Nyeri** (3hr; Ksh160), Accra Road/River Road, opposite *Crossline*; **Thika** (40min; Ksh40–50), Ronald Ngala Street by the BP station, or Koinange Street by *New Florida*.

Chapter Three: The Rift Valley
Gilgil (90min; Ksh220), *Nyamakima Bar*, Duruma Road; **Naivasha** (1hr; Ksh110), *Nyamakima Bar*, Duruma Road; **Nakuru** (2hr; Ksh180), *Nyamakima Bar*, Duruma Road.

Chapter Four: Western Kenya
Eldoret (4hr; Ksh330), *Nyamakima Bar*, Duruma Road; **Kitale** (5–7hr; Ksh430), *Nyamakima Bar*, Duruma Road.

Chapter Five: The Mombasa Road and major game parks
Kajiado (90min; Ksh100), Ronald Ngala Street; **Machakos** (1hr; Ksh100), the car park just north of Country Bus Station; **Namanga** (3hr; Ksh180), Ronald Ngala Street; Narok (2hr 30min; Ksh200), *Nyamakima Bar*, Duruma Road.

Chapter Six: The coast
There are no direct matatus to the coast.

Chapter Seven: The north
Isiolo (5hr 30min–6hr; Ksh250), Accra Road between River Road and Tsavo Road.

Buses and express shared taxis

Slower, cheaper and generally safer than matatus are the **bus services** which cover almost all of Kenya. The smaller companies operate out of the Country Bus Station (aka "Machakos Airport"), 1.5km east of the city centre just past Wakulima Market, between Pumwani Road and Landhies Road (bus #4, #18 or #28 from the *Ambassadeur*). The larger companies have booking offices in various locations around River Road (see p.145), from where most of their services operate. Most services will sell seats to towns on the way, when space permits. Seats should, if possible, be reserved in advance at the bus offices. **Shared taxis**, usually Peugeot station wagons, are faster and cost roughly twice as much, and cover all the main towns in the centre and west of the country (chapters two, three and four). They're best caught early in the morning (around 8am) on Accra Road, each displaying boards with their destinations. Addresses and phone numbers for all bus and shared-taxi companies mentioned are given below.

First, a couple of **warnings** about buses and bus stations. Drugging of food, drink, cigarettes and chewing gum is not uncommon – do not accept such gifts, even at the risk of giving offence, nor leave your own stuff unattended. Secondly, as the most useful services often leave at night, getting to the bus station can be a problem (though the buses themselves are considered safe). Needless to say, walking unaccompanied with your luggage at night is the height of folly – take a taxi, hire an *askari* escort from your hotel, or else catch a daytime service.

For details on bus companies, see "Listings" p.145.

Bus services

Chapter Two: The Central Highlands
A continual stream of buses leaves for Thika and destinations in Kiambu district from the Country Bus Station. The most frequent runs are provided by Sunbird Services, with almost hourly departures to Maua via Embu (Ksh120), Chogoria and Meru (Ksh200). Kensilver runs comfortable 25-seater

mini-buses to Meru. Akamba covers all the main destinations, usually only once or twice a day. You'll find smaller companies at the Country Bus Station for Murang'a (Ksh80), Nanyuki (Ksh170) and Nyeri (Ksh140). Arusha Express has a service to Nanyuki and Nyeri. KBS Stagecoach service #231/233 at 7am and 9pm runs to Embu, Meru and Maua.

Chapter Three: The Rift Valley

Akamba's services for Olorgasailie and Magadi leave from their Lagos Road office at 1pm and 3pm. Many buses from the Country Bus Station call at Naivasha en route for points west, but ensure that the bus actually goes into town (Moi Avenue) instead of dropping you at the flyover 1.5km out. The majority of passengers for Nakuru travel by matatu or Peugeot, though there are buses for Nakuru (Ksh130) from the Country Bus Station. The Peugeot 504 station wagons hang out in the Duruma/Accra roads area. Nakuru is also covered by most westbound (Chapter Four) services, but check before buying tickets that the bus actually stops inside the town – otherwise you may have a long walk in.

Chapter Four: Western Kenya

Akamba, Transluxe and KBS Stagecoach are the main companies, with several daily and overnight departures to most locations. Other buses leave from the Country Bus Station for Busia (Ksh500), Kakamega (Ksh400), Kericho (Ksh250), and Kisumu (Ksh300): you'll catch most of them between 7–8am and 8–9.30pm. Eldoret Express have frequent runs to Eldoret (Ksh250) and Kitale (Ksh350) from the Country Bus Station. Faster and roughly twice as expensive (ie Ksh600-800) are the Peugeot shared-taxis, which cover most of the region: Bungoma; Busia; Eldoret; Kakamega; Kericho; Kisii; Kisumu; Kitale; Luanda; Malaba; Mumias; Siaya; Vihiga; Webuye. Services depart early in the morning from Accra Road or Dubois

Road.

Chapter Five: The Mombasa Road and major game parks

Regular services from the Country Bus Station to Machakos (Ksh60) and Kitui (Ksh150).

Chapter Six: The coast

Competition is fierce over the Nairobi–Mombasa route, with reputations tarnished all round and accidents not uncommon. Safest of the lot is Akamba. Coast Bus and Mombasa Liners have newish coaches. Avoid Tawfiq aka Interstate Buses. Busscar, which has more daily runs than any other company, is pretty reckless too. Crossline's twice-daily minibus is extremely fast, whilst Goldline's fleet is astonishingly rickety. Most companies run at least two day buses and one at night. It's hard to decide which is worse – arriving after dark or driving all night (accidents generally occur in daylight, but the occasional hijackings and shootings usually happen at night).

Chapter Seven: The north

With the dangers inherent in travel there, the north sees few buses, with the northernmost limits of services being Isiolo run by Akamba and Eastern Express (daily; Ksh300).

Tanzania

Apart from regular public buses run by Akamba to Arusha and Dar es Salaam, more comfortable (and expensive, around $30–35) coaches to Arusha and Moshi are operated by Davanu Shuttle (2 daily) and Riverside (2 daily; bookings through Tour Africa Safaris, p.142).

Uganda

Malaba is served by buses from the Country Bus Station (Ksh550). Akamba runs both day and night services via Busia to Kampala (Ksh950 standard, Ksh1800 in comfier seats), as do some of the Peugeot companies. Jaguar Shuttle Services has the most comfortable coaches (Ksh2000; Gilfillan House, Kenyatta Avenue – or book through a travel agent).

By train

The **train station** (☎02/221211 ext 2700 or 2701) is at the south end of Moi Avenue, beyond the bustle and confusion of the railway matatu stage. There's a safe **left-luggage service** here if you want to dump your bags (Ksh150 per item per day).

Currently, the only service available is the overnight Nairobi–Mombasa. It's important to make **reservations**, especially if you want a first-class compartment, and while it may be fine to leave this until a couple of hours before departure during the low season, it's advisable to reserve well in advance during the busy Christmas and New Year period when trains are often full. Ticket offices at the stations in Mombasa and Nairobi will take reservations weeks ahead. Travel agents will usually do the work for you, sometimes for a fairly hefty supplement. A number of overseas agents will handle first-class train reservations, too, though expect to pay a little more.

To travel **first class**, you have to take a private two-berth compartment. **Second-class** compartments are shared by four people and are single-sex, though, with the consent of the occupants, this can sometimes be disregarded. The **third-class** carriages have seats rather than bunks and are packed.

Fares for Nairobi–Mombasa are Ksh3000 first-class, Ksh2100 second-class and Ksh300 third-class (all one-way). You can pay by credit card, but there's a surcharge. The first- and second-class fares include reserved berth number, pre-paid dinner, breakfast and bedding vouchers. You have to wait at the sign board at either station for your name to be pinned up with the relevant number, and also need to get one of the white-suited attendants to give you your dinner voucher (for one of four sittings, all rushed). Both dinner and breakfast are hearty cooked meals, and eating in the dining car is an experience in itself (first and second class get the same food and service), but don't expect haute cuisine. Wine, beer and sodas cost extra. If you buy from Kenya Railways direct, you can elect to pay just for your berth.

By plane: Jomo Kenyatta International Airport

International flights and **internal Kenya Airways** services leave from Jomo Kenyatta International Airport, 15km southeast of the city on the Mombasa road (flight arrivals and departures information on ☎02/822111 or 822206). Remember to **reconfirm** your flight reservations and also try to check that the plane is scheduled to arrive on time (addresses and telephone numbers in "Listings", p.144). To get to the airport, take the KBS Stagecoach #34 bus (Ksh20 from the *Ambassadeur Hotel*, Ksh30 from the *Youth Hostel*; every 20min from around 6am to 8pm). See the warning in the "Security" box on p.90 about robbery on the #34 bus. After 8pm you'll have to get a taxi; all hotels will arrange this, or contact one of the companies listed on p.150. The ride is generally cheaper than on the way in, costing around Ksh600–800 if you pick one up on the street. You are allowed to take up to Ksh100,000 out of the country so long as you've kept the exchange receipts. Always check-in with time to spare – overbookings are commonplace.

Bunson Travel Group publishes a free comprehensive **timetable** of all sched-uled national and international flights from Nairobi, while Let's Go Travel has a handy list of flights within Kenya and for Zanzibar; addresses for both below. The *Nation* publishes a timetable of flights in and out of JKI every Friday.

Kenya Airways flights from JKI airport

To Mombasa: at least 8 daily non-stop from 7am to 8pm, extra weekend and high-season flights (1hr–1hr 15min; $85 single).

To Malindi: 2 daily non-stop (1hr 10min; $85 single Kenya Airways; Ksh8400 African Express).

To Kisumu: 1 or 2 daily (1hr; $47 single).

To Zanzibar: 3 weekly (1hr 10min; $141 single; much cheaper from Mombasa).

By plane: Wilson Airport

Wilson Airport has regular **scheduled services** within Kenya (and to the Kilimanjaro region in Tanzania), and unscheduled flights into Somalia and the Democratic Republic of Congo (ex-Zaïre). Get to the airport on bus or matatu #15, #24, #31, #34, #125 or #126, alighting at the BP station (it's on your left). Note that several internal operators have only a 10kg baggage allowance, although a blind eye is sometimes turned. In any case, excess baggage isn't usually charged too highly ($1 per kilo is normal). Internal flights are subject to a Ksh300 departure tax. If you're in the market for **chartering a plane**, see pp.139–140. There are also about a dozen commercial and NGO aviation companies who may also take passengers, all with offices at Wilson Airport. Some flights are advertised in the *Nation* and *The People*. Eagle Aviation flies to Lamu, Mombasa, Malindi and Zanzibar, Tsavo West is served by East African Air Charters and Lokichokio by Trackmark. See "Airlines", p.144 for details.

Scheduled flights from Wilson Airport

Amboseli lodges Airkenya, daily 7.30am (roughly 45min depending on lodge; $135 return).

Kilimanjaro (Tanzania) Airkenya, daily except Mon & Thurs 10.30am (1hr 25min; $135 single).

Kiwaiyu Airkenya, daily 1.15pm (1hr 45min; $182 single).

Lamu (Manda Island) Airkenya and Kenya Airways, daily (1hr 45min; $130–187 single).

Lokichokio Aircraft Leasing Services, Mon, Tues, Wed & Sat 11am (2hr 5min; $245 single).

Maasai Mara lodges Airkenya, daily 10am and 3pm; Aircraft Leasing Services daily 10am and 2.45pm (roughly 45min depending on lodge; $165 return).

Malindi Airkenya, via Mombasa: Tues 8am, Fri 8am & 5pm; direct Sun 3.15pm (1hr 15min–1hr 55min; Ksh5385–8885 single).

Mombasa Airkenya, Mon–Sat 8am & 3.15pm (1hr 15min; Ksh5385–8885 single).

Mwanza (Tanzania) Eagle Aviation, Mon & Fri 9am (1hr 30min; $185 single).

Nanyuki Airkenya, daily 9.15am (45min; $124 return).

Samburu (& Lewa Downs) Airkenya, daily 9.15am via Nanyuki (1hr 35min; 1hr 5min to Lewa Downs; $195 return).

Hitch-hiking

To **Naivasha and beyond** take bus/matatu #2, #102, #103 or #115 as far as the "Kikuyu flyover". To **Thika and beyond** take bus/matatu #17B, #25, #45, #160, #237 as far as Kenya Breweries.

Nairobi Province

NAIROBI PROVINCE stretches way beyond the city suburbs, taking in an area of some 690 square kilometres (270 square miles) and ranging from agricultural and ranching land to jungle and national park.

For visitors, most of the interest lies to the **south**, in the predominantly Maasai land that begins with **Nairobi National Park**, and includes the watershed ridge of the **Ngong Hills**. It's a striking landscape, vividly described in Karen Blixen's *Out of Africa* (see "Books", p.689).

North of the city, the land is also distinctive: narrow valleys twisting down from the Kinangop plateau, some still filled with jungle and, it's said, leopards. In spite of that, the steep slopes here are high-value real estate, still being developed as exclusive suburbs, planted with shady gardens and festooned with security signs. To the **west**, lies largely Kikuyu farmland, densely cultivated with corn, bananas and the cash crop insecticide plant, pyrethrum. **East**, beyond the shanty suburb of Dandora, are the wide Athi plains, which are mostly ranching country.

Nairobi National Park and around

Daily 6am–7pm, no entry after 6.15pm; $20, children $5); 30kph speed limit. Warden PO Box 42076 ☎ 02/500622, ☏ 505866. Maps: the best is the KWS one usually sold at the Main Gate (1997); otherwise, Survey of Kenya SK71 (1990) has loads of detail, but is a little out of date.

Despite the hype, it really is remarkable that the 113-square-kilometre patch of plains and woodland making up **Nairobi National Park**, should exist almost uncorrupted, and complete with more than eighty species of large mammals and the second-largest herbivore migration after that of the Mara/Serengeti, literally within earshot of the downtown traffic. If you have the money and the time, it's worth spending at least a morning or afternoon in the park, giving you the chance to see some of the animals which might elude you in the bigger Kenyan reserves. There are no elephants, but this is a small deficiency among a surprisingly high concentration of animals. For all the low-flying planes and lines of tourist minibuses, you have a greater chance of witnessing a kill here than in any of the other parks. Kenya residents use the park as a route from Karen and Langata to Jomo Kenyatta International Airport – it does make a pleasant way of leaving the country if you can work it into your flight times, though obviously you still have to pay.

Getting there

Without your own transport, the cheapest and most adventurous way in is to **hitch a ride** at the main gate. This is probably easiest on a Saturday or Sunday morning, when Kenyans are most likely to visit. The weekends are also by far the busiest time; during the week you'll find it very quiet. Take bus #125 or matatu 126 at 5.40am from Nairobi's KBS bus station to the main gate, or after that time any bus or matatu which goes down Langata Road.

Alternatively, you should be able to swing a good deal on a **rental car** for a single day – you won't need anything more than a saloon car and kilometre charges won't amount to much. You could compare the cost with that of hiring a taxi for a few hours; if you do that, be dead sure of what you'll get for the agreed price – petrol will cost you.

Lastly, most of the safari shops in town sell three- to four-hour **trips around the park** for around $45–90. The only operator with regularly scheduled trips is the United Touring Co (UTC), Fedha Towers, Muindi Mbingu St (PO Box 42196 ☎ 02/331960, ☏ 331422, ✉ utcn@attmail.co.ke), charging $75, excluding lunch. The problem with organized tours is that they normally leave at 10am and 2pm, which are not ideal times – though late afternoon is better than midday. A trip like this doesn't guarantee anything, but your chances of sighting most of the animals are high. Note that open-topped minibuses provide better vantage points than cars.

If you're looking for a spot to **picnic**, go a couple of kilometres into the park to the first fork. There's a shady site on the left, beside a raised mound of elephant-tusk ash, publicly burned in 1989 by President Moi to mark the start of a major (and astonishingly successful) offensive on ivory poaching and smuggling, led by the director of the Kenya Wildlife Service, Dr Richard Leakey.

Limuru, ① & Naivasha (A104) ▲

LIMURU ROAD

NAIROBI OUTSKIRTS

Naivasha & Nakuru (B3) ▲

ACCOMMODATION
Giraffe Manor	9
Kentmere Club	1
Nairobi Park Services	7
Pathway	4
Rowallan Scout Camp	5
Safari Park Hotel	3
Simbayo House	8
Wildlife Clubs of Kenya Hostel	6
Windsor Golf & Country Club	2

RESTAURANTS
Carnivore	A

Wida Highway Hotel

Kikuyu Flyover

N

KABETE

Kikuyu

NAIVASHA ROAD

SPRING VALLEY

WAIYAKI WAY

WEST

Nairobi River

NAIVASHA ROAD

LAVINGTON

KILELESHWA

Dagoretti Corner

Butterfly Visiting Centre

DAGORETTI ROAD

Lenana Forest Centre

NGONG ④ ROAD

JAMHURI PARK

Impala Club

Karen Shopping Centre (Karen Dukas)

Race Course

St Francis Church

Nairobi War Cemetery

NGONG ROAD FOREST

Nairobi Dam

Psy's (Disco)

⑤

KAREN

Don Bosco Boys Town

Ngong, the Ngong Hills & Narok road (D523) ▲

MARULA LANE

LANGATA ROAD

Bomas of Kenya ⑥

A

Main Gate & KWS HQ

Karen Club

Swedo House

Kazuri Beads

NDEGE ROAD

LANGATA

Langata Gate ⑦

LANGATA ROAD

LANGATA ROAD SOUTH

Mini Animal Orphanage, Nairobi Safari Walk & Rangers Restaurant

BOGONI ROAD

⑧

Karen Blixen Museum

Mizizi Cultural Centre

USHIRIKA RD

Banda Gate

AFEW Giraffe Centre ⑨

ONGATA RONGAI

Mbagathi Gate

0   2km

MAGADI ROAD

Ongata-Rongai Shops

▼ Olorgasailie & Magadi (C58)

Seeing the animals

The first hours of the day are always best for game-watching. Ask any ranger on arrival and you'll get the day's results: "Number 13 for a cheetah; two rhinos at 6; lions at number 4 . . ." – the numbers referring to the road junctions, marked on every map of the park.

Alternatively, just follow your nose. If you're driving around independently,

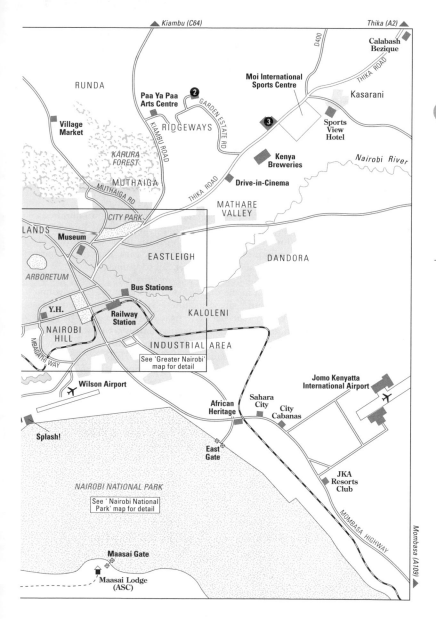

Kiambu (C64)

Thika (A2)

Calabash Bezique

Moi International Sports Centre

Kasarani

RUNDA

Paa Ya Paa Arts Centre

❷

GARDEN ESTATE RD

❸

Sports View Hotel

Village Market

RIDGEWAYS

KIAMBU ROAD

Nairobi River

KARURA FOREST

Kenya Breweries

MUTHAIGA RD

THIKA ROAD

MUTHAIGA

Drive-in-Cinema

CITY PARK

MATHARE VALLEY

LANDS

Museum

EASTLEIGH

DANDORA

ARBORETUM

Bus Stations

Y.H.

Railway Station

KALOLENI

MBAGATHI WAY

NAIROBI HILL

INDUSTRIAL AREA

See 'Greater Nairobi' map for detail

Wilson Airport

Jomo Kenyatta International Airport

Sahara City

African Heritage

City Cabanas

Splash!

East Gate

NAIROBI NATIONAL PARK

See ' Nairobi National Park' map for detail

JKA Resorts Club

MOMBASA HIGHWAY

Maasai Gate

Maasai Lodge (ASC)

go to the western end, near the main entrance, where most of the woodland is concentrated. This is where you are most likely to see giraffe and, just after dawn, if you're very lucky, a leopard – back perhaps from a nocturnal foray into Langata, hunting for guard dogs (apparently quite a problem). The highest point here, known as **Impala Hill**, is also a **picnic site** (with toilets) and a good spot from which to scan the park with binoculars, but **lions**, usually found in more open country, are better located by checking with the rangers at the gate. There are a few families of **cheetahs** in the park, though you have to be lucky, and seasonal long grass will make seeing them very difficult. It's not so difficult to see some of the park's **rhinos**, however, most often found in the forest glades in the west.

Several of the park's seasonal streams are dammed to regulate the water supply. In the dry season, these **dams** – all located on the northern side of the park where the streams come down off the Embakasi plain – draw the heaviest concentrations of animals. Many of the herds cross the Mbagathi every year and disperse across the Athi plains as the rains improve the pasture, returning to the park during the drought. Before 1946, when the park was opened, only the physical barrier of Nairobi itself diverted the northward migration. The erection of fences along the park's northern perimeter has changed that, but the occasional lion still finds its way up as far as the suburb of Karen.

Birdlife in the park is staggering – a count of more than four hundred species. Enthusiasts won't need priming, and will see rarities from European latitudes as well as the exotics. Even if you're fresh off the plane and ornithologically illiterate, the first glimpses of ostrich, secretary bird, crowned crane and the outlandishly hideous marabou stork never fail to impress.

Although the western end has the best cross-section of wildlife, there are two gates out onto the Mombasa road in the east, so you don't have to retrace your route. The lovely **Mokoyeti picnic site** (junction 14B) is near the "Leopard Cliffs" (junction 15), en route to Cheetah Gate near Athi River (p.404). This route gives you a chance to drive through the open savannah country favoured by **zebra** and **antelope**. There are large herds of introduced **buffalo** which you can see – they're hard to miss – out here and almost anywhere in the park. **Hippos** can usually be viewed at a pretty pool at the confluence of the Mbagathi and Athi rivers in the east (junction 12), beyond the Leopard Cliffs, which has the added attraction of a **nature trail** and **picnic site** where you can leave the car and disappear into the thickets for closer communion with nature (there's an armed ranger on guard until around 5.30pm). As you're wandering, look out for crocodiles in the river (to an untrained eye little different from submerged logs), and monkeys in the bushes. The Mbagathi/Athi forms the southern boundary of the park and is its only permanent river. It's fringed with the yellow acacias that early explorers and settlers dubbed "fever trees" because they seemed to grow in the areas where fever (malaria) was most common. Their notions were doubtless encouraged by the sight of the gravity-defying marabou storks and vultures commonly seen sitting on the highest branches.

Mini Animal Orphanage, Nairobi Safari Walk and David Sheldrick Wildlife Trust

If you're fed up with seeing animals only from a distance, the **Mini Animal Orphanage** (daily 8am–6.30pm; $5) by the park's Main Gate is moderately interesting, and mainly intended for children. Here, a motley and shifting collection of waifs and strays, protected from nature, have for some years been allowed to regain strength before being released. That anyway was the idea, though many of the inmates seem to be established residents and it appears doubtful whether "this orphanage is not a zoo", as the sign claims. At least it's a zoo with a difference; there are as many wild monkeys outside the cages as in them. A better alternative is the **Nairobi Safari Walk**, on the right of the Main Gate before entering the park, and at the site of the old Animal Orphanage. Unlike all the other mini wildlife sanctuaries in Nairobi, the Safari

NAIROBI NATIONAL PARK

15 Road junction number

0   2 km

Walk is the closest you come to seeing captive animals behaving as they would in their natural habitat. In fact, if you want a closeup picture of some of the shyer creatures of Kenya such as the leopard, this is the place to cheat a little, the surrounding flora and fauna is authentic enough to convince your friends back home that the image was taken in the wild.

The sanctuary is a show case of Kenya's vast ecological diversity; the wetlands, the savannah and the woodland/forest found across the country is simulated behind concealed safety barriers to create an intimate environment which is both captivating and informative. The boardwalks to the open-air pens, observation points and platforms are clearly signposted and full of useful literature about the animals. The guides are friendly and knowledgable, and there are plans to build a children's corner with a learning laboratory in which young vistors will be able to play at being animals by experiencing what different creatures hear, see and touch. Also accessible through the walk is **Rangers Restaurant**, recommendable if only because of its comfortable verandah, which is partly in the national park and overlooking a floodlit water hole. There is an extensive menu consisting of African, continental and vegetarian dishes here, and the food is usually good, even if it doesn't always reflect its price.

More seriously, the **David Sheldrick Wildlife Trust** elephant and rhino orphanage (daily 11am–noon ☎02/891996, ⓦwww.sheldrickwildlifetrust .org) is run by Daphne Sheldrick in memory of her husband, the anti-poaching warden of Tsavo National Park. Calling beforehand is absolutely essential, especially if in a large group, both to check whether they're open and to get directions (it's usually accessible through the closed-to-the-public Maintenance Gate on Magadi Road). The trust is run on a voluntary basis, so entry is by donation.

The Bomas of Kenya

Forest Edge Road, at the junction with Langata and Magadi Road, 1km past National Park Main Gate; from city centre, bus/matatu #15, #125 or #126; performances Mon–Fri 2.30–4pm, Sat, Sun & holidays 3.30–5.15pm; Ksh600, students/children Ksh30; ☎02/891801–2.

The **Bomas of Kenya** were originally an attempt to create a living museum of indigenous Kenyan life, with a display of eleven traditional homesteads (*bomas*) and an emphasis on regional dances. Unfortunately, the place has always had a heavily touristy feel, not helped by its huge indoor amphitheatre where the dances are performed. Its vitality is channelled mainly into souvenir-selling. The homesteads (a guided tour is included in the price), representing the architectural styles of Kenya's people, are for the most part sadly unkempt. Even so, if you're looking to fill an afternoon, or you want a change from the National Park, they can be enjoyable enough, particularly on weekends when they're crowded and a disco follows the dance show.

Surprisingly, perhaps, the dances are not performed by the appropriate Kenyan nationalities; instead, the **Harambee Dancers** do fast costume changes between acts and present the nation's traditional repertoire as professionals rather than participants. If the sound system were good, the acoustics bearable and the whole place less of an amphitheatre, the impression would undoubtedly be better, but at least you do get a very comprehensive taste of Kenyan dance styles, from the mesmeric jumps and sinuous movements of the Maa-speaking peoples to the wild acrobatics of some of the Mijikenda dances. But this is definitely a theme park, not a living museum.

AFEW Giraffe Centre

Although promoted as a children's outing, the **AFEW Giraffe Centre** (daily 9am–5.30pm; Ksh500, children Ksh250; ☎02/891658) on Koitobos Road, 3km off Langata Road (signposted), and run by the African Fund for Endangered Wildlife, has serious intentions. It has successfully boosted the population of the rare Rothschild's giraffe from the original nucleus of animals which came from the wild herd near Soy (p.334), and educates children about conservation. You'll get some great mug shots from the giraffe-level observation tower, where they push their huge heads through to be fed by pellets offered by the visitors. Try to go in the morning or on a dull day, as afternoon shots into the sun can be tricky. There are various other animals around, including a number of tame warthogs (the original one, named after Walter Cronkite, fell to poachers) and a fine new wooden "Safari Walk". There's also a tea house. If you really like it here, and have money to burn, you can stay overnight at the wonderful, Scottish-style **Giraffe Manor** (p.103).

Mizizi Cultural Centre

Housed in the Utamaduni Crafts Centre, on the corner of Bogoni East Road and Langata South Road (#24 bus or matatu from outside the GPO on Kenyatta Avenue), the **Mizizi Cultural Centre** (daily 9am–6pm; Ksh300, children Ksh150; ☎02/891050) aims to preserve and propagate traditional cultures (mizizi means "roots of culture") as expressed through dance, music, handicrafts, foods and architecture. Intended not so much for tourists (as the Bomas of Kenya plainly are) but for Kenyans themselves, it's particularly a place where schoolchildren can learn about their nation's rich tribal heritage. It's a noble idea, but unfortunately lack of funds has brought its plans to a standstill. It no longer has any guaranteed daily performances or musicians on hand, and seems to function more as a laid-back sort of bar, but it's still worth ringing them a day or two in advance to check whether there will be anything happening, such as hands-on workshops or performances for children. The *Verandah Garden Restaurant* is dull and unenticing, but cheap, with a variety of snacks, sandwiches and pizzas.

Karen

Until recently, **KAREN** was the quintessential white suburb – five-acre plots spaciously set on eucalyptus-lined avenues amid fields grazed by ponies. But the number of African homes is steadily increasing as the middle classes become more affluent and move out of Nairobi itself. The Karen shopping centre, at the crossroads of Langata and Ngong roads, includes the mock-Tudor *Horseman Restaurant*, branches of Barclays and Standard Chartered banks, both with ATMs, a forex bureau with better rates, and an arty riding-tack and gift shop. Still separated from Nairobi by a dwindling patch of dense, bird-filled woodland – the Ngong Road Forest – Karen is a reminder of how completely the settlers visualized and created little Europes for themselves. In Karen you could almost be in the English shires – or, for that matter, northern California.

The *Horseman Restaurant* (daily 11.30am–11pm ☎02/882782) is certainly worth a visit, with several separate speciality kitchens (including Mongolian, fondue and pub-style) and a wide choice of game meat. The food is fresh and imaginative: Zanzibari fish and coconut soup is well worth trying, as is "Beach and Bush" (crab claws, green bananas, *ugali* in coconut, and medallions of Thomson's gazelle). They have real Italian ice-cream, too.

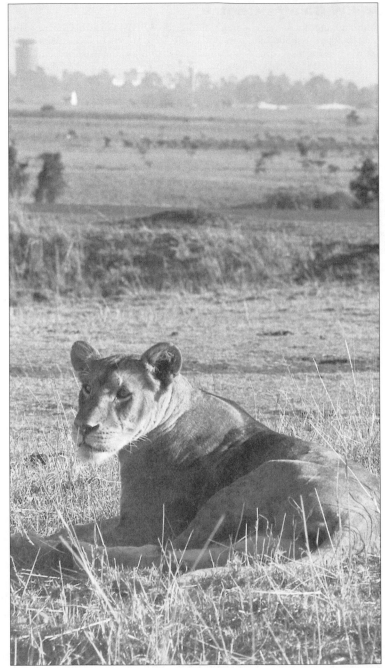

△ Lioness, Nairobi National Park

On the way to Karen, if you're driving the more direct way from the city, along Ngong Road, you pass **Jamhuri Park** (the Agricultural Society of Kenya showground, see p.54), the **Nairobi War Cemetery** and the **Racecourse**. The World War II cemetery is a peaceful and dignified place, set far back from the busy road among shady trees, with pink stone and carefully tended lawns.

Buses to Karen include the #111 (fast) from the KBS bus station and the interminable bus matatu #24 also runs the route.

Karen Blixen Museum and Swedo House

Bus #24 can drop you at the **Karen Blixen National Museum**, Karen Road (daily 9.30am–6pm; Ksh200, children Ksh100), the house where much of the action of Karen Blixen's *Out of Africa* took place. The epitome of colonial Africa, the Danish government presented it to Kenya as an Uhuru gift along with the agricultural college built in the grounds. It's a beautiful, well-proportioned house with square, wood-panelled rooms; the restoration of its original appearance and furnishings has evidently been very thorough. A guided tour is included in the price but can be somewhat rushed, especially at weekends, and there's no guarantee that they'll let you wander around on your own, which is unfortunate.

On weekends, too, you may be suffocated by Mozart and tour groups complaining about how little Denys Finch Hatton resembles Robert Redford, but come during the week and it's more peaceful. The gardens, laid out as in former times, are delightful. If you're a true fan, you can come on an organized tour from town (around $45–70) – often including the *Giraffe Manor*.

The fake-1920s Nairobi that was built nearby for the shooting of *Out of Africa* would have been a more magnetic attraction than the museum house. Strangely, political dictates ensured its demolition once the film crews left. Just up the road towards Karen *dukas* is **Swedo House**, an old Swedish coffee plantation manager's residence, built in 1912 and stuffed with archetypal colonial memorabilia and fittings, but which is usually closed to the public. The grounds are delightful, and there's a bar and restaurant here: the *Karen Blixen Coffee Garden* (daily 9.30am–11pm), with tables in the gardens under the trees. The food is variable, but the Sunday buffet lunch (Ksh700) remains popular. There's also a craft shop, although much better local handicrafts can be bought at the nearby **Kazuri Bead Centre**, behind Hillcrest School (see p.120 for more details). Incidentally, the suburb was not named after Karen Blixen (who went by the name Tania von Blixen when in Kenya) as is popularly supposed, but her cousin, Karen Melchior, whose father was the chairman of the Karen Coffee Company Ltd.

The Butterfly Visiting Centre

The concept behind the **Butterfly Visiting Centre** (daily 9am–4.30pm; Ksh400, children/students Ksh200; ☎02/884972–3), 2.5km from Karen Shopping Centre along the Dagoretti Road (Bus #125 from the KBS bus station), is as bold and original as conservation gets in Africa. It's the second of its kind (the first being in South Africa) and it brings much needed contrast to the big-game-reserve image the continent has been pigeonholed with. Although the centre is generally geared towards teaching children and students about the importance of conservation, it's still worth a visit if you want to gain a better appreciation of the rich biodiversity of Kenya. The beautifully landscaped garden in the greenhouse with its hundreds of brightly coloured butterflies (all of which are Kenyan species) stuttering through the air from plant to plant is enthralling. There are 48 out of the 900 species of butterflies found in Kenya in the centre. As well as caterpillars and the occasional empty pupa case, look out for the chameleons. Plans are afoot to move them to a centre of their own in the near future. There are guided walks, a shop full of butterfly memorabilia and *The Caterpillar Café,* which serves reasonably priced snacks, three course meals (Ksh1000–1300, not including drinks) and tasty homemade desserts.

The Ngong Hills

Ngong village, the jumping-off point for the **Ngong Hills** ahead, is 8km past Karen *dukas* (bus #111 every 30min, every 20min at weekends; sometimes bus #126, but you might have to change at Kiserian). Turn right after the police station in Ngong. If you have the chance, stop on the way at **Bulbul** and take a look at the pretty mosque of this largely Muslim village. As often happened in Kenya, Islam spread through the settlement of discharged troops from other British-ruled territories – this time Sudanese Nubia. Ngong itself is basically just a small junction town with limited shops and services and the rough D523 road trailing out to the right towards the Maasai Mara.

The hills are revered by the Maasai, who have several traditional explanations of how they were formed. The best known says that a giant, stumbling north with his head in the clouds, tripped on Kilimanjaro. Thundering to the ground, his hand squeezed the earth into the Ngongs' familiar, knuckled outline. An even more momentous story explains the Ngongs as the bits of earth left under God's fingernails after he'd finished creating.

The walk along their sharp spine was once a popular day's hike and picnic outing. The views, of Nairobi on one side and the Rift Valley on the other, are magnificent, and the forested slopes are still inhabited by buffalo and antelope. Unfortunately, the number of attacks and robberies of unwary walkers has discouraged people, Kenyans included, and the north side is considered especially dangerous. The route up from the village is now patrolled by police most of the time and they extract a small fee at a barrier before you proceed. Check things out at Ngong police station, where they will provide you with an escort (Ksh500 for half a day). Women travelling without men are, as usual, at a disadvantage. All this is a great pity as the walk, even simply up to the radio relay station above Ngong village, is a fine one.

With a car (4WD if it's been raining), you can get to the summit, **Point Lamwia** (2459m), which offers 360 degrees of view. Down on the lower ridges, almost due east of the highest point, is the **Finch Memorial**, Karen Blixen's tribute to the man who took her flying. It's on privately owned land and there's a Ksh100 entrance fee.

2

The Central Highlands

CHAPTER 2

Highlights

* **Climbing Mount Kenya** Africa's second-highest mountain is a memorable and highly recommended climb, with various routes and diverse flora and fauna. See p.178

* **Laikipia game-viewing camps** With your own transport, visiting one of the private game sanctuaries in this high plains region is highly recommended for seeing rhinos, and even introduced chimpanzees. See p.196

* **Tree-hotels** Three to choose from – the original Treetops, its upstart competitor The Ark, and the less vaunted, more spacious Mountain Lodge, which also has some of the best wildlife. See p.176, 213

* **Aberdares waterfalls** Sensational views and a good chance of seeing large wild animals (including elephants and lions) in a compelling, highland environment. See p.212

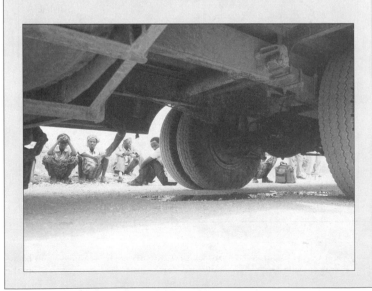

2

The Central Highlands

As the political and economic heartland of the country, the **Central Highlands** stand at the focal point of Kenyan history. Mount Kenya, Africa's second-highest peak, gave the colonial nation its name, and the majority of British and European settlers carved their farms from the countryside around it. Later, and as a direct consequence, it was this region which saw the development of organized anti-colonial resistance culminating in Mau Mau.

Until Independence, the fertile highland soils ("A more charming region is not to be found in all Africa," thought Joseph Thomson, exploring in the 1880s) were reserved largely for Europeans and considered, in Governor Eliot's breathtaking phrase, "White Man's Country". The **Kikuyu peoples** (Kikuyu, Meru and Embu) were skilled farmers and herders who had held the land for centuries before the Europeans arrived. They were at first mystified to find themselves "squatters" on land whose ownership, in the sense of exclusive right, had never been an issue in traditional society. They were certainly not alone in losing land but, by supplying most of the fighters for the Land and Freedom Army (see Contexts, p.643), they were placed squarely in the political limelight. In return, they have received a large proportion of what Kenyans call the "Fruits of Independence".

Today, most of the land is in African hands again, and it supports the country's highest rural population. There's intensive farming on almost all the lower slopes, as well as much of the higher ground, beneath the **national parks** of **Mount Kenya** and the **Aberdares**.

There are considerable rewards in travel through the Highlands. Above all, if you're into hiking, there's the ascent of Mount Kenya. And, while hikes lower down and in the Aberdare range are easier, they are scarcely less dramatic, with the bonus of a chance to see some of the highland **wildlife**. The mountain streams are full of the trout that were introduced early last century, and most tourist lodges will rent out **fishing** tackle even if you're not staying there. Nor is travel itself ever dull in the Highlands, where the range of scenery is a spectacular draw in its own right: primary-coloured **jungle** and **shambas**, pale, windswept **moors**, and dense **conifer plantations**, all with a mountain backdrop. People everywhere are friendly and quick to strike up a conversation, the towns are animated and markets colourfully chaotic.

Prospects for **hitching** are well above average, but **public transport** is good, too, and bus journeys invariably packed with interest and amusement. For **accommodation**, you'll find a handful of tourist hotels and lodges – including the famous *Treetops* – that will give fair return for your cash if you're in the mood to splurge. But there's also a wide range of reasonably priced lodgings. *Hotelis* are plentiful and serve gargantuan portions of food.

Around Mount Kenya: the Kirinyaga ring road

After the main game-viewing areas and the coast, this natural **circuit** is one of the most travelled in Kenya. Not that it's overcrowded, or even really touristy

The Kikuyu peoples

Ancestors of the **Kikuyu** migrated to this region between the sixteenth and eighteenth centuries, from northeast of Mount Kenya. Stories describe how they found various hunter-gatherer peoples already in the region (the **Gumba** on the plains and the **Athi** in the forests), and a great deal of intermarriage, trade and adoption took place. The newcomers cleared the forests and planted crops, giving the hunters gifts of livestock, honey, or wives in return for using the land. As this Bantu-speaking, cultivating, livestock-keeping culture expanded, the indigenous peoples gradually lost their old identities.

Between the Kikuyu and the **Maasai**, however, relations were less easy. They both placed (and still place) high value on the ownership of cattle, the Maasai depending entirely on livestock. During bad droughts, Maasai might raid their Kikuyu neighbours' herds, with retaliation at a later date being almost inevitable. But such **intertribal warfare** often had long-term benefits, as ancient debts were forever being renegotiated and paid off by both sides, thus sustaining the relationship. There was lively trade and **intermarriage** between the two peoples, and married Kikuyu women enjoyed a special immunity enabling them to organize trading expeditions deep into Maasai-land, often with the help of a *hinga*, a Kikuyu of Maasai descent, to oil the wheels.

As well as economic and social relations, the Kikuyu had close **cultural affinities** with the Maasai. Like them, the Kikuyu advanced in status as they grew older, through named age-sets and rituals still important today. A Kikuyu who discovers you're both the same age is likely to say, "We're age mates then!"

Circumcision still marks the important transition into adulthood for most Kikuyu males. Female circumcision (clitoridectomy) is illegal and performed less and less, though reluctance to talk about it makes estimating just how widespread it still is difficult. In the past, the operations were accompanied by changes in dress and ornament. Boys grew their hair and dyed it with ochre in the style of Maasai warriors (in fact, the Maasai got their ochre from the Kikuyu, so it may really be the other way around). They also wore glass beads around their necks, metal rings on their legs and arms, and pulled their ear lobes out with ear plugs. Women wore a similar collection of ornaments and, between initiation and marriage, a headband of beads and discs, still worn today by most Maasai women. Even now, men who haven't been circumcised are not accorded the same respect as those who have, and can be denied the right to marry or to be included in social gatherings.

Traditionally, the Kikuyu had no centralized **authority**, no tribal or clan leaders; "chiefs" were only installed by the colonial administration. When disputes had to be settled or far-reaching decisions made, the elders of a district would meet as a council and the matter would be cleared up in public, with a party to follow. After their deaths, elders – as ancestors – continued to be respected and consulted.

The Kikuyu traditionally believed that *Ngai*'s or *Mwininyaga*'s (God's) most likely abode, or at least his frequent resting place, was **Kirinyaga** (Place of Brightness), Mount Kenya. Accordingly, they used to build their houses with the door always looking out towards the mountain; hence the title of Jomo Kenyatta's book, *Facing Mount Kenya*. Christianity has altered beliefs in the last few decades, though many churchgoers still believe strongly in an **ancestor world** where the dead have powers for good and bad over their living descendants because of their closeness to *Ngai*.

Today, the Kikuyu remain in the forefront of Kenyan development. Despite entrenched nepotism and a growing poverty gap, they are accorded grudging respect as successful business people and formidable politicians – though their political power at national level has been much eroded in recent years and is only starting to return with the legalization of political opposition. There is considerable political rivalry between the **Kiambu Kikuyu** of the tea- and coffee-growing district north of Nairobi (Jomo Kenyatta's district and now a Democratic Party stronghold), and the **Nyeri Kikuyu**, who rely on a more mixed economy and where there is more support for the FORD Asili and FORD Kenya parties.

(such places are few indeed up-country), but there are always a few safari minibuses to be seen somewhere on the road and other signs that the tourist industry up here is growing.

At present, the whole region is wonderfully untouched by anything much more than the steady encroachment of *shambas* up the ridges and the burgeoning of small towns into larger ones. Apart from the high forests, moors and peaks, little of this remains wild country, but the Kikuyu, Meru and Embu have created an extraordinary spectacle of cultivation on the steep slopes, gashed by the road to reveal brilliant red earth.

As you travel, you're also aware of the looming presence of **the mountain**. Its twin peaks are normally obscured by clouds, but early in the morning and just before sunset, the shroud can vanish suddenly, leaving them magically exposed for a few minutes. With a base 80km across, Mount Kenya is one of the largest free-standing volcanic cones in the world, and the peaks – when you can see them from the road – are always distant. To the east and south, the mountain slopes steeply away to the broad expanse of Ukambani (Akambaland) and the Tana River basin. Westward, it drops more gently to the rolling uplands of Laikipia, drier than the east and for the most part treeless.

Getting here is an easy trip from Nairobi up a busy road. If you're not driving, either buy a bus ticket from Nairobi direct to any of the towns in this section, or make **Thika** or **Murang'a** a first destination before heading around the mountain. **Naro Moru**, the usual base for climbing Mount Kenya, lies on the west side some 25km south of **Nanyuki**, an alternative base for a climb from the north. On the eastern slopes, **Chogoria**, between **Meru** and **Embu**, offers arguably the finest route up the mountain.

Thika and around

Despite the literary connections (Elspeth Huxley's *The Flame Trees of Thika*) and being the first major town on the way from Nairobi to Mount Kenya, **THIKA** is a dull little place, not even redeemed by the profusion of flame trees you might expect. These days, it's essentially a satellite of Nairobi.

Pineapples, introduced in 1905, are Thika's contemporary claim to fame. Thousands of acres flourish here, easily confused with the sisal that is also grown in the area. Until 1968, most of the valuable export crop was produced on *shambas*; since then Del Monte has held the lion's share of the plantations.

Thika is off the tourist route – or at least the main road to Mount Kenya (matatu route #237 from the Kencom Building in Nairobi, or others from the BP station on Ronald Ngala Street) – but it's noticeably cheaper than Nairobi and a laid-back, friendly sort of place. There's a Standard Chartered **bank** with an ATM if you need money, and email access at Thika Computer Consultants on Kisi Road (Ksh50 sending & Ksh20 receiving). If you stay, the best-value **accommodation** is *New Fulila Hotel*, Uhuru Street (PO Box 1161 ⊤0151/21840; ➊) which has clean s/c rooms. Other slightly more expensive possibilities include *December Hotel*, Commercial Street (PO Box 156 ⊤0151/22140; ➋), whose enormous rooms are clean and have telephones (ask for s/c), though hot water is erratic, and *White Line Hotel*, Stadium Road (PO Box 290 ⊤0151/22857; ➊), which is fairly acceptable and has a lively bar, but only non-s/c singles.

The **upmarket choice**, out of town on the Nairobi–Murang'a road is *Blue Posts Hotel* (PO Box 42 ⊤ & Ⓕ0151/22241 or 21086; ➌), which is older than

THIKA

ACCOMMODATION
Blue Posts   1
December   3
New Fullia   2
White Line   4

RESTAURANTS & BARS
Brilliant Bar   D
Golden Plate   G
Macuast   F
NK Bar   A
Prismos Hotel   E
Sky Motel Day & Night Club   B
Thika Central   C

Matatus for Ol Doinyo,
Fourteen Falls & Garissa

Stadium

Market Stalls

Market ▲

Garissa Road (0.5 km), Ol Doinyo & Fourteen Falls ▶

STADIUM ROAD

Kangari General Store

Matatu & Bus Stage ★

Thika Computer Consultants

KICI ROAD

KCB Bank

UPPER ROAD

Consolidated Bank of Kenya

UHURU STREET

STREET

Co-op Bank

KCB Bank

Police

KWAME NKRUMAH STREET

STREET

Standard Chartered Bank

Clock Tower

Caltex

KENYATTA HIGHWAY

Town Hall

Sikh Temple

Jain Temple

Hindu Temple

TEMPLE ROAD

◀ C67, ① (1.5 km) & A2 Nairobi-Muranga road

Safeway Hypermarket

COMMERCIAL

Matatus for Nakuru ★

Thika Arcade

Barclays Bank

Total

Agip

▼ Nairobi & Garissa Road

100 m

N

the town itself, dating from 1908. Although you might expect a certain quaint shabbiness, the old place has been refurbished and rooms in the Chania Wing are excellent: en suite with balconies overlooking lush gardens, with glimpses of the Chania Falls. Its restaurant has a sweeping view of the falls, and tea with pastries costs only Ksh120. The *Blue Posts'* grounds contain both the Chania Falls and the Thika Falls – with a five-minute walk between the two. The hotel makes a good stop-off on the road to Murang'a or Nyeri – the food is good, and the terrace is very pleasant for a drink overlooking the garden and Chania Falls. The toilets are clean, and parking is safe.

Restaurants in town include the relatively swish (and expensive) *Prismos Hotel*, MTC Building, Uhuru Street; the *New Fulila's* bar-restaurant, which is a deal cheaper; *Macuast Restaurant* for fish and chips; and good local eats at *Golden Plate* and *Thika Central Restaurant*. Outclassing them all is the restaurant at the *Blue Posts*. For a decent cup of **coffee** (the plantations around Thika are the nearest to Nairobi), the *December Hotel* has a great Parisian-style pavement café which was opened by Kenyatta himself in December 1970. For your own supplies, there's a Safeway **supermarket** in Thika Arcade, with a newer larger branch a few blocks north, and Kangari General Store is off the top of Stadium Road. The **market** is east of town, past the thriving street stalls at the stadium roundabout.

Foot-tappers should try out *NK Bar* on Uhuru Street, which plays **Congolese music** and **reggae**, sometimes live (Wed & Fri–Sun). Otherwise, *Cascades Disco* at the *Blue Posts* entertains Nairobi clubbers, whilst heavy-duty drinkers can fade away at *Sky Motel Day & Night Club* or the decidedly less-than-sparkling *Brilliant Bar*, another good place to meet inebriated locals. More dignified clubbing can be had at Thika Sports Club, Bendor Road (☏0151/21101 or 31088) with its **golf course** set amidst the pineapple and coffee plantations. The clubhouse is unusually rustic, with a large fireplace and wooden beams running along the ceiling.

The Fourteen Falls and Ol Doinyo Sapuk National Park

From Thika, the trip out to tiny **Ol Doinyo Sapuk National Park** and **Fourteen Falls** on the Athi River is a popular one with motorized travellers and Nairobi weekenders. For either site, head for Kilima Mbogo village, some 22km down the Garissa road. There are matatus from Thika's "U Shops" stage by the stadium to here. *Munje Hotel* (PO Box 1510 Thika; ❶) may have rooms. If you're lucky, the matatu might carry on to Ol Doinyo Sapuk village ("Doinyo"), 2.5km off to the right down a dirt track, which passes close to the entrance to the falls and is some 2km from the national park gate. Doinyo village, itself, is surprisingly busy, with dozens of *dukas*, bars and lodges.

Fourteen Falls

Ten minutes' walk from Doinyo village down a very dusty track, **Fourteen Falls** (daily 9am–5pm; Ksh150, children Ksh100, vehicles Ksh200, cameras Ksh150) is a broad cascade of white water which plunges 30m over a precipice with many lips, which give rise to the name. They're especially spectacular after rain when they flood into a single, genuinely impressive thundering red cataract. But a vague, obnoxious smell hangs in the air, presumably caused by effluent from Thika's emerging industries. There are no hotels hereabouts, but you can **camp** or stay in spartan but dirt-cheap *bandas* at the council-run *14 Falls Campsite* on the Athi River, for which you theoretically need YHA membership (camping Ksh25 per person; *bandas* Ksh70 per person). A rash of robberies in the 1990s at the Fourteen Falls explains the presence of two policemen every day until 5pm, but there have been no incidents of late.

Ol Doinyo Sapuk National Park

Daily 6am–6pm; $15, children $5; $4 to camp. Warden: PO Box 1514 Thika. Map: Survey of Kenya SK113, 1990.

Seen from a distance, **Ol Doinyo Sapuk** (Maasai for Big Mountain), or Kilima Mbogo (Kikuyu for Buffalo Mountain), is not the most inspiring of hulks, nor is it high in Kenyan terms, rising to 2146m. Its attractions only become apparent when you approach the gate, as the dry scrubland gives way to redder soil, forest and cooler air. The national park encloses the entirety of the mountain, and surrounding the summit is a primal forest with some of the giant plants, notably the lobelia *giberroa*, associated with the Afro-alpine zones of mounts Kenya, Elgon and Kilimanjaro. Birdlife is diverse, though the mammals – a few leopards, buffaloes, Sykes' and colobus monkeys and porcupines – makes themselves scarce in the thick vegetation. Watch out for snakes, too. At the 7km mark, you come to the grave of Sir William Northrup MacMillan, the fattest of famous settlers, whose intended burial place on the summit had to be abandoned when the modified tractor-hearse's clutch burned out. He rests here with his wife, maid and dog. Views from here are tremendous and you're not likely to get further in a vehicle, even with four-wheel drive, because the final couple of kilometres of track is particularly bad. Between the MacMillans' graves and just below the summit, the track winds through dense forest cover. If you make it to the top, the 360-degree panorama over a huge oxbow in the Athi River, Thika's pineapple fields and mounts Kenya and Kilimanjaro can be wonderful in December and January, when the air is really clear. Long prohibited for security reasons (large numbers of buffalo, and sporadic incidents of banditry up to 1997), **walking** the 9km to the summit is now possible, so long as you take an armed ranger along with you (Ksh300 per person for half a day, Ksh500 per person for a whole day).

The **national park gate** is reached by crossing the Athi River, then taking a (signposted) right turn at the end of Kilima Mbogo village. The gate is 3km further on, and is the only place where you're allowed to camp (park fees are payable, as it's just inside the gate).

Murang'a

Established as the administrative outpost of **Fort Hall** in 1900, **MURANG'A** has since come to be thought of as the "Kikuyu Homeland" because of its proximity to *Mukuruwe wa Nyagathanga*, the "Garden of Eden of the Kikuyu". Here, in Kikuyu mythology, God made husbands for the nine daughters of Gikuyu and Mumbi, spiritual ancestors of all the Kikuyu people. The husbands, who became the ancestors of the nine Kikuyu clans, were found by Gikuyu under a large fig tree. Take a matatu to **Mugeka** and walk from there to Gakuyu village if you'd like to see the site; plans for a museum here are still just that, and the original *mukuruwe* (fig tree) disappeared long ago.

Fort Hall was never a settlers' town. The district was outside the zone earmarked for white colonization and most of it comprised the "Kikuyu reserve".

Richard Meinertzhagen, an officer in the King's African Rifles posted here in 1902, found the time (when not shooting animals – or people) to write:

If white settlement really takes hold in this country it is bound to do so at the expense of the Kikuyu who own the best land, and I foresee much trouble.

Kenya Diary (Kenway Publications, Kenya 1989)

That said, Meinertzhagen helped put down some of this trouble, launching "punitive expeditions" from Fort Hall with his African troops.

There's even a bit of sightseeing. In the **CPK Cathedral** (formerly the Church of St James and All Martyrs) hangs an unusual *Life of Christ* mural sequence by the Tanzanian artist, Elimo Njau. It depicts the Nativity, Baptism, Last Supper, Gethsemane and Crucifixion of an African Christ in an African landscape. The murals were painted in 1955, the year the church was founded by the Archbishop of Canterbury, as a memorial to the thousands of Kikuyu victims of Mau Mau attacks.

Practicalities

At the beginning of the twentieth century, Fort Hall consisted of "two grass huts within a stone wall and a ditch". Present-day Murang'a, perched above the busy main road, remains a small, but expanding commercial centre, strewn with litter. However, there are a number of decent, basic hotels on the steep hillside if you feel like staying – and it's a happy enough place, bustling energetically. Recommended **lodgings** are *Murang'a Mukawa & Lodges* on Uhuru Highway (PO Box 207 Maragua ☏0156/22542; B&B ➌), large and clean with a somnolent bar-restaurant and nets in the bedrooms, and *Murang'a Tourist Lodge*, 2km down the Thika road (PO Box 552 ☏0156/22120; ➋), similar to the

Mukawa with airier rooms and nets, but breakfast costs extra. *Rwathia Bar* on Market Street (PO Box 243 ☎0156/22527; ❶) is very basic but clean with a pleasant courtyard, and is the best of three adjacent day-and-night-club lodgings; the *Manguyo* next door also has rooms and does good *kienyeji*. You might also try the *Forest Bar Restaurant*, 200m up Uhuru Highway from *Murang'a Mukawa* (PO Box 382; ❶).

There's no shortage of **hotelis** either. *Famous Café* on Uhuru Highway has great samosas, while *Marmu Restaurant* on the same street has a good range of snacks. *View Point Inn* on Kenyatta Road serves good *nyama choma* with a great view of the town, and the *Tana View Tavern* at the corner of Uhuru Highway and Kenyatta Road is recommended not only for its fine balcony but for its unusually tender and lightly curried goat dishes (Ksh100 with chips). *Nankas Bakery* is in Ngeka Centre above the Co-op Bank, spicy *chai* is served at the zebra-striped *Friends' Corner Café* by the matatu stage, and there's the Neema Yake **supermarket** at the east end of Market Street. The closest you get to a **nightclub** in Murang'a is *Kahiriga Bar,* on Market Street, a 24hr joint with a juke box, two pool tables, and chess sets behind the counter which, judging from the boozy clientele, must either still be in their original packaging, or be pretty battered. Barclays Bank has an ATM and you can send **emails** at Pentastar Computer Service (Ksh80 per email) on the first floor in the Ngeka Centre.

Moving on from Murang'a

There are three onward travel options from Murang'a: clockwise around Mount Kenya via Karatina and Naro Moru (see below); anti-clockwise around the mountain via Embu (see p.202); or up to Nyeri and the Aberdares (p.207). Nyeri, a few kilometres off the Mount Kenya circuit, is a recommended detour and one which most public transport on the ring road will include.

Routes west into the Aberdare range

If you want to get up into the **Aberdare Forest**, take one of the two minor roads leading out of Murang'a to the west. They join at Kiriani and dip north to Nyeri via Othaya. If you have all day to dawdle, either of them would make a nice, circuitously backwoods route to Nyeri. Matatu availability may determine which you take. If you have your own wheels, the longer of the two, via Koimbi, takes you past the start of a rough, snaking, high-altitude track which climbs as far as Tusha, just 10km from the Aberdare National Park's Kiandongoro Gate, one of the two park entrances above Nyeri.

Towards Mount Kenya: Sagana, Karatina and Mountain Lodge

Heading north, **SAGANA** is a district dotted with rice fields and a place you'll be glad you brought your mosquito repellent to. It lies at the junction for Thika, Nyeri and Embu, but has little to recommend it apart from some basic accommodation options. The pleasant *Sagana Country Hotel* (PO Box 25 Sagana ☎0163/46229; ❷), on the Nairobi road 500m before the junction has singles only, with good solid meals, bar and tables outside under some trees. In town, try *Hotel Chakaka* (❶) at the western (Murang'a) end, or *Central Star B&L* (❶), a bearable option for the desperate; ask for clean sheets if necessary. If you're **camping**, you can stay for free at *Savage Wilderness'* **river-rafting** base a few kilometres before Sagana (coming from Nairobi), signposted on the left. A day's river rafting here costs $95 (more details on p.143).

If you pass through the feverish commercial centre of **KARATINA** on a Tuesday, Wednesday, Thursday or Saturday, stop to have a look around the market; it's one of East Africa's biggest cattle and produce sales. There are several **lodgings** in town, including the reasonable *Karatina Tourist Lodge* (Private Bag, Karatina ☎0171/71522, ℱ72520; ❸) which has safe parking. Cheaper options include the clean *New Mugi Motherland Hotel 1995* (no phone; ❶), the *Elephant and Castle* (PO Box 370 ☎0171/72442; ❶), the more lively *Three-in-One Hotel* (PO Box 768 ☎0171/72316; ❷), and *Ibis Hotel* (PO Box 240 ☎0171/72777, ℱ72777; ❷) opposite Agip petrol station. **Camping** is possible at *Wajee Campsite* (PO Box 148 Nyeri ☎0171/60359) – turn off the main road 2km north of town onto the Gakonya road (it's about 20km). There's good, filling **food** at *Karatina Express Café* by the railway, with its shaded terrace and smooth service. The main **nightspot** in town is *Galaxy Club*, with soul on Friday and Saturday nights, and the obligatory Sunday jam session.

Karatina is also the base for **Mountain Lodge** (PO Box 123 Kiganjo ☎ & ℱ0171/30785; reservations through Serena, p.44; HB ❽–❾), the most accessible of Kenya's three highland tree-hotels (the other two being *Treetops* and *The Ark*), and the only one on the slopes of Mount Kenya. The lodge is set at an altitude of 2200m, about 30km from Karatina, mostly along good tarmac (the President's Sagana State Lodge is also up this way, so be discreet with your camera) – the signposted turning is just on the Nairobi side of town. Alternatively, if you're coming from the west, leave the Mount Kenya ring road at Nyeri Station (4km north of Kiganjo), and follow the signposted but badly pot-holed road up for about 20km. Or, a taxi from either Nyeri or Karatina shouldn't cost more than Ksh1500.

Mountain Lodge has consistently good **game-viewing**, and is less cramped than either of its competitors. All its rooms have private bathrooms and balconies which face the floodlit water hole. There's good food and service, and you can stay up all night if you choose, with continuous supplies of tea and coffee on hand. Or you can be picky about your animal-watching, tick off what you're interested in being woken to see, and then slumber through the herds of buffalo and antelope. They wake you at 6am in any case, and you have to be quick to see the shyer animals such as rhinos, as they vanish at the first click of a camera.

Towards Mount Kenya: Castle Forest Lodge

From Murang'a, a different kind of Mount Kenya accommodation is easily accessible. **Castle Forest Lodge**, nestling in the forest on the southern slopes of the mountain, is a private home, reputedly built for British royalty before World War I. Large, comfortable rooms and several cottages in the grounds can be reserved in advance (3rd floor, Arrow House, Koinange St, PO Box 29886, Nairobi ☎02/720290, ℱ719662, ℮campsite@thorntree.com, or via Let's Go Travel in Nairobi, see p.141; ❸ low, ❹ high), but it's not normally necessary. Meals are available to order and, in between sleeping and eating, you can walk in the woods, sit by the waterfalls of the Karute stream, or fish in it for trout. The only problem, if you don't have transport, is access. *Castle Forest* is about 50km from Murang'a, via Sagana and Kutus on the B6. From Kutus, head east on the B6 for just 400m, then turn left on the tarmac D458 and, after about 6km, at Rukenya, turn right onto a *murram* track. Fifteen kilometres up here (extremely slippery and slow-going when wet) you reach the Mount Kenya Forest boundary gate, *Thiba Fishing Camp*, and, 5km further, the house.

If you're keen to try an unusual approach to the summit of Mount Kenya, the seldom-used **Kamweti route** begins at the roadhead, eight steep kilometres north of *Castle Forest*. The managers at the house should be able to advise on guides and porters, though you'll most likely have to arrive fully equipped.

North to Naro Moru

Continuing up the A2 from Karatina, passing the turning to Nyeri (see p.214), and then going through Kiganjo, a second road turns left to Nyeri. The one to the right, which leads to *Mountain Lodge,* passes *Thego Fishing Camp* (❶), a dull but inoffensive government-run camp with basic cabins, a communal kitchen, bathrooms and toilet. As well as trout fishing, you can arrange for a guided trip (Ksh100 per person) to see caves once used as Mau Mau hideouts. Bring your own bedding. Heading on towards Naro Moru, you emerge from the folded landscape of Kikuyu cultivation onto a high, windswept plain. Here, you're crossing one of the great animal migration routes, severed by human population pressure over the last eighty years. Until 1948, when the two mountain parks were created, every few years used to see the mass migration of **elephants** from one side to the other. In 1903, a herd estimated at seven hundred animals was seen wending across the open country from Mount Kenya to the Aberdares. When the parks were opened, it was decided to keep the elephants away from the crowded farmlands in between, so an eight-kilometre ditch was dug across their route.

Naro Moru

The road climbs gently and steadily to **NARO MORU**, which stands on the watershed between the Tana and the Ewaso Nyiro river basins. The most straightforward **base** for climbing **Mount Kenya**, or simply exploring the mountain forests lower down, Naro Moru is nondescript, built around its now disused railway station. There's a post office (Mon–Fri 8am–1pm & 2–5pm) but no banks, the nearest is Nyeri or Nanyuki. There's not a lot in the food department either, though things are improving. If you plan to spend several days on the mountain, buy any special food you want in Nairobi. Naro Moru's offerings are strictly in the bread and milk, *karanga na chapati*, line.

There are several **cheap accommodation** options should you need a room at the end of the day. Besides the ominous-sounding *Silent Lodge* (❶), and the fresh and reasonable *Naro Moru Hotel '86* (❶), complete with *Kirinyaga*-viewing balcony, there's the much improved and recommended *'82 Lodge* (❶), with s/c rooms, and *Mountain View Hotel* (☎0176/62088; ❷) also with a balcony. Out of town, there's a clutch of alternatives. Cheapest and closest is the rather exposed **campsite** (Ksh200 per person), with its freezing showers and pretty expensive firewood, which is to be found at *Naro Moru River Lodge* (about 2km north of town and signposted). With the B&Ls in town, there's not really much point in paying over the odds for a hard bunk in one of the bunkhouses.

There are two more expensive options, too. **Naro Moru River Lodge** itself (PO Box 18 Naro Moru ☎0176/62622, ℱ62211; reservations through Alliance, p.42; HB from ❺ low, ❻ high; self-catering cottages ❹) is the only place where you can indulge yourself if you're feeling in need of creature comforts, and is very good value given its facilities. It has a welcoming log-fire atmosphere, pretty gardens, a trout stream with nature trail and good bird-watching. A blissful sauna, a heated pool facing the mountain, and horseback rides complete the picture. It tends to be full of upmarket mountain-climbing package clients and has an expensive but well-stocked equipment-rental shop.

Kids' rates are, for a change, substantially cheaper (20 percent of the adult rate). If it wasn't for everything being overpriced, a good alternative to Naro Moru as a west-side base would be *Mountain Rock Bantu Lodge*, about 8km north of Naro Moru (PO Box 333 Nanyuki ☎0176/62625, ℻62051, ℮mtnrock@form-net.com). The entrance can't be missed, as it's marked by two enormous Kikuyu figures carved out of tree trunks and flamboyantly painted, but the difference between "resident" and "non-resident" rates is unjustified. If money's no object, they have fairly decent **rooms** (B&B from ❺) with log fires, tented accommodation (from ❹), and a restaurant and bar. You can **camp** in the grounds ($6 per person; tent rental $13–22, or $23–39 with bedding, which is just daft), and there's a small water hole in the back garden that attracts elephants once in a blue moon. There's **horse riding**, too ($20–25 for 2hr), though the limited tack needs careful checking, and ask about fodder and water before galloping off. You can also do expensive escorted walks through the forest in the vicinity of the lodge.

The youth hostel and the road to the gate

The **youth hostel** site lies about 9km up the well-signposted track to Mount Kenya's Naro Moru Gate. You may get a lift up from the main road; otherwise break your walk with a *chai* at the *Kariaku Restaurant*. The hostel itself (PO Box 274 Naro Moru ☎0176/62414, ℻62078; ❶) is excellent and friendly, housed in a rebuilt farmhouse (the last incarnation burned down when a cooking cylinder exploded), and is a popular travellers' meeting place. The dorms are basic and comfortable, with hot showers and a well-equipped kitchen, and camping is welcomed in the grounds. They also have equipment for rent, at prices a good deal cheaper than the *Naro Moru River Lodge*.

If you're alone, and on a budget, the youth hostel is undoubtedly the best place to team up with others for the ascent (campers with their own vehicles tend to use the more expensive set-up at *Naro Moru River Lodge*). Three little *dukas* up the track, a kilometre or so beyond the youth hostel, sell one or two vital commodities, but they're very basic indeed.

Mount Kenya National Park

$10 per person daily, camping $2 per night. Entry allowed on foot; minimum group two people. Warden: PO Box 69 Naro Moru ☎0171/21575.

An extinct volcano, some three and a half million years old, with jagged peaks rising to 5200m, **Mount Kenya** is Africa's second-highest mountain. Its heart is actually the remains of a gigantic volcanic plug – the mountain stood at over 7200m above sea level about a million years ago – from which most of the outpourings of lava and ash have been eroded by glacial action to create the distinctive silhouette. These peaks are permanently iced with snow and glaciers, though the glaciers are retreating due to climate change. On the upper slopes, the combination of altitude and a position astride the equator results in forms of **vegetation** that exist only here and at a few other lofty points in East Africa. Seemingly designed by some 1950s science-fiction writer, it's hard to believe the "water-holding cabbage", "ostrich plume plant" or "giant groundsel" when you first see them.

Europe first heard about the mountain when the missionary Krapf saw it in 1849, but his stories of snow on the equator were not taken seriously. It was

MOUNT KENYA

▲ Maralal   ▲ Isiolo

▲ Nyahururu

N   0   10 km

Timau

Nanyuki   1   Meru

Embori   Kithaku

2   Nkubu

SIRIMON ROUTE   TIMAU ROUTE   3

BURGURET ROUTE   4   Kanyekine

Batian 5199 m   5

8   6   Lenana 4985 m   7

Vertical Bog   11 12   9   Bairunyi Clearing   Keria

10   see 'Peaks of Mount Kenya' map for detail   15 Chogoria

Naro Moru   14   13   CHOGORIA ROUTE

NARO MORU ROUTE   Mutindwa 16

Kariani

KAMWETI ROUTE   Chuka

17   Kamweti

18   19   Ena

21   20

Nyeri   Kagumo

Karatina   Kerugoya   Embu

Kutus

Sagana

Murang'a ▼   ▼ Thika   Mwea National Reserve ▼

ACCOMMODATION

Austrian Hut	**12**
Castle Forest Lodge	**19**
Chogoria Forest Station	**15**
Mackinder's Camp	**11**
Meru Mt Kenya Lodge	**7**
Met. Station Lodge	**13**
Minto's Hut	**6**
Mount Kenya Safari Club	**2**

ACCOMMODATION (continued)

Mountain Lodge	**17**	Thego Fishing Camp	**18**
Mountain Rock Bantu Lodge	**4**	Thiba Fishing Camp	**21**
Naro Moru River Lodge	**10**	Thuchi River Lodge	**20**
Old Moses' Camp	**3**	Transit Motel	**16**
Shipton's Camp	**5**	Urumandi Hut	**9**
Sirimon Bandas	**1**	Warden's Cottage	**8**
		Youth Hostel	**14**

only in 1883 that the young Scottish traveller, Joseph Thomson, confirmed its existence to the Western world. The Kikuyu, Maasai and other peoples living in the vicinity had venerated the mountain for centuries. Park rangers still occasionally report finding elderly Kikuyu high up on the moorlands, drawn by the presence of *Ngai*, whose dwelling place this is. It's not known, however, whether anyone had actually scaled the peaks before Sir Halford Mackinder reached the highest, Batian, in 1899. Another thirty years passed before Nelion (10m lower, but a tougher climb) was conquered. Both are named after nine-teenth-century Maasai *laibon* or ritual leaders.

Climbing Mount Kenya: practicalities

There are **four main routes** up Mount Kenya. The **Naro Moru trail** provides the shortest and steepest way to the top. The **Burguret** and **Sirimon trails** from the northwest are less well trodden; Sirimon has a reputation for lots of wildlife, while Burguret passes through a long stretch of dense forest. The fourth, the **Chogoria trail**, is a beautiful but much longer ascent up the eastern flank of the mountain.

Batian (5199m) and **Nelion** (5189m) are accessible only to experienced, fully equipped mountaineers – they look almost vertical – and the easiest route is Grade IV, making them a lot more testing than most of the routes up the Matterhorn. If you want to climb these peaks, you should join the Mountain Club of Kenya (PO Box 45741 Nairobi ☎02/501747; their clubhouse is at Wilson Airport, bus #34). They will not only put you in touch with the right people, but also give you reductions on hut fees.

On the question of **cost**, climbing Mount Kenya is an expensive business. A DIY four-day trek for two people, excluding guides or porters, costs anything between Ksh6000 and Ksh11,000 (including park fees, overnights, food, and transport to the roadhead, not including any additional equipment and tent rental). The cost of one porter/guide for this period would add anything between Ksh2000 and 4500 to the tally, whilst an organized trek easily costs over $100 a day. The park itself operates a sign-in/sign-out system, and you pay fees on entry for your anticipated stay. It's a bad idea to try to evade the exit gate on departure if you've stayed longer than intended: they will go looking for you and eventually organize an air search if you don't show up. Stories circulate of people being pursued to Nairobi and beyond for non-payment of huge rescue service bills.

If you need to **change money**, do so in Nairobi or in the big ring-road towns of Nyeri, Nanyuki, Meru, Embu or Karatina – Chogoria has no exchange facilities (Chuka town is the nearest), and neither has Naro Moru.

Location and climate

Anyone who is reasonably fit can have a crack at **Point Lenana** (4985m), but this climb has somehow acquired the reputation of being fairly easy, and lots of people set off up the mountain quite unprepared for high-altitude living – indeed, some 25 percent of attempts fail for this reason. If you try it, forget you're on the equator. Over about 4000m, the mountain is **freezing cold**, foggy and windy – wickedly so after dark; the air is thin, and it rains or snows, at least briefly, almost daily, though most precipitation comes at night. Mount Kenya's **weather** is notoriously unpredictable. Even during the rainy seasons, there are days when it's fairly clear, but driving up the muddy roads to the park gates may be nearly impossible, and if it's really bad, you probably won't be allowed in anyway. The most **reliable months** are February and August, although January and most of July can be fine, too.

Preparations

Above all, it's essential to have a **really warm sleeping bag**, four-season at the very least, ideally with an additional liner and/or Gore-tex bivouac bag. One **thick sweater** at the very least (better still, several thinner ones), and either a **windproof jacket** or a down- or fibre-filled one are absolutely necessary. A **change of footwear** is pretty much essential, too, as you're bound to have wet feet by the end of each day. **Gloves** and a **balaclava** or **woolly hat** are also handy. A light cagoule or anorak is good to have, as is a set or two of thermal underwear for the often shivering nights. Out of season (that is, most of the year), an **emergency foil blanket** is advisable and weighs and packs down to next to nothing. Another prerequisite is a **stove**, as you'll be miserable without regular hot fluids. Firewood is not available and cannot be collected once you enter the park. For **food**, dehydrated soup and chocolate are perhaps the most useful. Remember, excess baggage can be left for about Ksh60 a day at *Naro Moru River Lodge*, so take only what you'll need. Here you can also purchase a packaged mountain climb, all inclusive (PO Box 18 Naro Moru ☎0176/62212).

The Kikuyu and other tribes venerated Mount Kenya – *Kirinyaga* – as the dwelling place of the supreme God, *Ngai*. If you went beyond the peaks, some thought, you would find him. Medicine men and diviners routinely trekked up the mountain to seek his guidance, miraculous cures, or simply inspiration. Nowadays, it's mainly tourists who retread their steps: some 15,000 each year. Few of them, it seems, particularly respect, never mind venerate, the old mountain god, and several dozen tonnes of rubbish are left on its sides every year, only part of which is removed (mainly by boy scouts and other voluntary groups). Please take your trash down with you.

The *River Lodge* has a **rental** shop where you can get just about anything, at prices that may make you wish you'd simply bought it in Nairobi (see under "Camping equipment" in the Nairobi Listings, p.145); the youth hostel has a limited range of items for rent.

If you're travelling alone and don't meet a suitable companion (you must be in a group of two or more to make the climb), it's possible to hire a **guide or porter** at the *Naro Moru River Lodge* in Naro Moru, at *Mountain Rock Bantu Lodge*, 8km north of Naro Moru, at *Cousin Café* or *Nanyuki River Lodge* in Nanyuki, at the *Transit Motel* in Chogoria, or at the youth hostel up the Naro Moru route (the latter is the best place to find someone much more cheaply). Expect to pay up to Ksh850 per day for a guide, Ksh500 for a porter, Ksh600 for a cook (plus all their park fees – Ksh250 per day), but insist on a written agreement showing the wages, the number of days, who's providing the food – everything. If they ask for more (as they tend to do in Chogoria), they're trying to rip you off. You shouldn't pay the full fee until the trip is finished, nor should you entirely rely on your guide to make every necessary preparation. Incidentally, any guide now needs to possess an **official KWS guiding permit** – ask to see it, and don't be fobbed off with local guiding association cards – it isn't enough. Note that you're not likely to find a guide up at the park gates.

For a quick taste of the mountain, you can fix up a **day-hike** to *Mackinder's Camp*, inclusive of lifts up to the gate and back down again, for around $35 (plus park fees), through one of the caretakers of the youth hostel.

Mountain health

While good physical fitness certainly won't hinder your climb, the ascent itself is mostly just a steep hike, if rough underfoot in parts. It's the altitude rather than the climb itself that may prevent you from reaching the top. Much more germane than the training programmes that some people embark on is giving yourself enough time to acclimatize, so your body has a chance to produce extra oxygen-carrying red blood cells. Above 4000m, you are likely to notice the **effects of altitude**, and the speed of your climb is critical. Physical symptoms are unpredictable; they vary between individuals, and appear to be unrelated to how fit you are – indeed, fit young males often suffer the most acute symptoms. Breathlessness, nausea, disorientation and even slurred speech are all possible, and headaches are fairly normal at first, especially at night. All this can be largely avoided by taking your time over the trek, as minor symptoms gradually disappear. You may consider bringing a tent for this reason, to avoid the sometimes rapid climbs between huts. Do not attempt to climb from the base of the mountain (that is, from the ring road) to Point Lenana in less than 72 hours; if you've just arrived in Kenya, allow five days for the ascent. Giving yourself a week for the whole trip is a good idea. Keeping your **fluid intake** as high as possible will also help (three to five litres a day is recommended) and it's best to avoid alcohol. If someone in your group shows signs of being seriously tired and weak, stay at that altitude. Should the symptoms develop into unsteadiness on the feet and drowsiness, **descend immediately**, whatever the circumstances. The effects of altitude are remarkable – especially on bodies tuned only to sea level – and can quickly become very dangerous, even fatal. Every year, dozens of climbers are struck by pulmonary oedema (when water collects in the lungs), accounting for almost half the cases worldwide.

You may find Ibuprofen works against headaches and that Diamox is helpful against the general effects of altitude.

Accommodation on the mountain

Taking a **tent** is, outside the months of February or August, almost essential because the only other **accommodation** on the mountain is a handful of very basic cabins and mountain huts, which can become so cold at night as to threaten hypothermia and rob you of a night's much-needed sleep. For the Naro Moru route, bunks at the *Meteorological Station Lodge* and *Mackinder's Camp* (also known as *Teleki Valley Lodge*) are supposed to be reserved at *Naro Maru River Lodge*, though unless you want to be sure of a bed, in practice there's no problem simply turning up and paying there. If you have a tent, you can **camp** anywhere in the park, the only practical advantage of the campsites at the *Met Station* (3048m) and *Mackinder's* (4200m), and various other designated campsites on the mountain, being water pipes and "long drop" toilets. Most water on the mountain is reckoned to be safe to drink (exceptions are noted) and you're never far from it.

The *Meteorological Station bandas* ($8 per person) are good, but often burgled by monkeys. *Mackinder's Camp* ($11 per person for a bed in a concrete cell) has an informal alternative in the shape of the *Rangers' Cabin* nearby, with negotiable rates usually costing you about half the *Mackinder's Camp* price. Camping is allowed here and it's altogether a friendlier place to huddle than *Mackinder's*, with a fire burning most nights. Porters around *Mackinder's* will cook up a huge meal (given sufficient notice) for $4–5.

On the Chogoria and Sirimon routes there are several other basic **bunkhouses** and **cabins**, some permanently staffed (details follow under each route). *Warden's Cottage*, situated inside the park, near the main gate at Naro Moru is an ideal base camp for large groups. *Sirimon Bandas*, also in the park and off the A2, is situated close to the start of the Sirimon route. It, too, is self-catering, but has the added luxury of a caretaker. Bookings for both places can be made through KWS Tourism Department on ☎02/501081/2, 🖷501752, 🖂tourism@kws.org (see p.148). The best accommodation on the mountain is the *Meru Mount Kenya Lodge* self-service *bandas* on the Chogoria route.

Also available are the small, bare **huts** built by the Mountain Club of Kenya, which normally have four walls, a roof, bunks, and nothing else (free; the wardens at the gates used to collect fees but washed their hands of the affair given the deplorable state of the huts – details are given under the relevant routes). These are located near the peaks, thus making it possible to spend a day or two around the high tarns and glaciers before returning to the base of *Mackinder's Camp* (warmer and more oxygen). *Top Hut*, next to *Austrian Hut*, is reserved for MCK members. The huts have no facilities or staff – you must be entirely self-sufficient. Their foam mattresses disappeared long ago (presumably burned to warm the frost-bitten nights), and a closed-cell bedroll is essential.

The Naro Moru route

From the main A2 road to the *Meteorological Station*, where the driveable earth road ends, is a 26-kilometre haul; even from the youth hostel (p.178) it's at least a five-hour walk. *Naro Moru River Lodge* will taxi you up here – for an extortionate price – or you may be lucky and get a lift, but a completely free ride would be a miracle.

Some 9km from the youth hostel, you come to the airstrip, the **park gate and HQ,** and usually three or four gigantic buffalo chewing the cud on the lawn. Entry is the usual $10 national parks fee if you're going in for the day. Porters pay the residents' rate, and student card holders pay half-price. Don't overestimate; there are no refunds. From the gate, you leave the conifer plantations and occasional *shambas* behind as the road twists and climbs through shaggy forest into a zone of colossal **bamboo.** Look out for elephant and particularly **buffalo** if you walk this stretch, though you'll more often see their droppings and footprints. If you find buffalo on the path, you're supposed to lob stones at them – and they're supposed to move out of the way. Much safer is the tried and trusted retreat-steadily-without-taking-your-eyes-off-them-until-they've-gone approach: more people are killed by buffalo than by any other wild animal in Kenya.

The final 3km to the *Met Station* are a series of steep hairpins usually driveable only in a 4WD (and often not at all when wet). You start to get some magnificent views out over the plains from up here, while right under your nose you may find a three-horned **chameleon,** stalking cautiously through the foliage like a miniature dinosaur. The high forest is its favourite habitat. **Black panthers** – the melanistic form of the leopard found at high altitudes – can also be seen in this habitat, and the latest local denizen was a lion, who walked into a tent at the *Met Station* and made off with a duvet jacket.

With an early start, it's quite possible to reach *Mackinder's* (4200m) in one day, but unless you're already acclimatized, you'll probably feel well below par by

Guidebooks and maps

The **topographical map**, *Mount Kenya 1:50,000 Map and Guide* by Andrew Wielochowski and Mark Savage (available from Executive Wilderness Programmes, 32 Seamill Park Crescent, Worthing BN11 2PN, UK; also available in Kenya) covers just the mountain itself at 1cm:500m and includes a detailed rundown on the huts and technical information for scalers of Nelion and Batian.

If you're a **climbing** enthusiast, you'll want to get hold of the Mountain Club of Kenya's *Guide Book to Mount Kenya and Kilimanjaro* or the *East Africa International Mountain Guide* by Andrew Wielochowski (West Col Productions, 1 Meadow Close, Goring, Reading, Berks RG8 9AA, UK; also available in Kenya), which is adequate on the technical ascents.

Trekking in East Africa by David Else (Lonely Planet) is a usefully detailed, general companion.

As for **maps**, don't expect to find any in the Naro Moru area or at any of the park gates. The recent *Tourist Map of Mount Kenya National Park and Environs* (Ordnance Survey, through regular stockists) is an updated version of an excellent Survey of Kenya map. At 1cm:1.25km, it provides a very useful – and visually pleasing – overview of the whole district, showing all the routes, the region around the base and most of the ring road. It's frankly not much use for the final ascent, however.

There's also a quite user-friendly, small Survey of Kenya topographical map of the **peak area** at 1cm:250m that's worth getting hold of in Nairobi if you're intending to walk around the peaks.

the time you get there. It's far better to take it easy and get used to the *Met Station*'s 3050-metre altitude; perhaps stroll a little higher or, if you have a tent, climb an hour or so up to the tree line and camp there. Ready-erected tents can be rented at the *Met Station* if you can't afford the *bandas* (though, after the lion incident there was no camping for some months). The mountain's weather is another good reason to stop here. After midday, it often gets foul, and the infamous vertical bog is no fun at all in heavy drizzle and twenty-metre visibility.

Up the Teleki Valley

An early start from the *Met Station* the next morning should see you to *Mackinder's* by lunchtime, before the clouds start to thicken up. In fair weather, the **vertical bog** is not as daunting as it sounds: you keep to the left of the red-and-white marker posts where it isn't as wet. In wet conditions, however, it can be ghastly, as the rosette plants hold just enough freezing water to be able to reach certain parts in a bracing manner whenever you slip. As you reach the bog, you enter another vegetation zone, that of **giant heather**. Beyond and above the bog, the path follows a ridge high above the **Teleki Valley** with the peaks straight ahead, rising brilliantly over a landscape that seems to have nothing in common with the hazy plains below.

For **Mackinder's Camp**, you follow the contours across the valley side and jump, or cross by stepping stones, over the snowmelt Northern Naro Moru stream. The camp, virtually at the head of Teleki Valley, is a long stone and concrete bunkhouse with dishevelled tents tacked into the icy ground around it. Certainly no hotel, it does at least provide some warmth and the company of others: climbers, Kikuyu guides and porters. **Batian** and **Nelion** tower magnificently over the valley, with a third pinnacle, **Point John**, even closer. There's usually a fresh icing of snow every morning, but early sunlight melts most of it by midday.

Mount Kenya's high altitude flora

The mountain's **vegetation** is zoned by altitude. Above about 2000m, *shambas* and coniferous plantations cease and the original, dense cloud forest takes over, with the best and broadest on the mountain's southern and eastern, rain-facing slopes.

As you gain altitude (2400m), forest gives way to giant bamboo, with clumps up to 20m high. The bamboo, a member of the grass family, appears impenetrable, but dark-walled passages are kept open by elephants and buffalo. Again, the best bamboo areas are to the south, while on the dry, northern slopes, there's very little of it.

Above the bamboo (2800m) you come into more open country of scattered, twisted *Hagena* and St John's Wort trees (*Hypericum*), and then the tree line (3000m) and the start of the peculiar, Afro-Alpine moorlands. Above about 3300m, you reach the land of the giants – giant heather, giant groundsel, giant lobelia. Identities are confusing: the cabbages on stumps and the larger candelabra-like "trees" are the same species – giant groundsel or tree senecio – an intermediate stage of which has a sheaf of yellow flowers. They are slow growers and, for such weedy-looking vegetables, they may be extraordinarily old – up to two hundred years. The tall, fluffy, less abundant plants are a species of giant lobelia discovered by the explorer Teleki and found only on Mount Kenya. The name plaque below one of these (there's a little nature trail along the ridge above the Naro Moru stream) calls it an "Ostrich plume plant" (*Lobelia telekii*), and it's the only plant that could fairly be described as cuddly. The furriness, which gives it such an animal quality, acts as insulation for the delicate flowers.

Point Lenana

If you want to climb straight to **Point Lenana**, you're likely to find at least one group leaving early the following morning (say around 3am) with a guide, though it's not that difficult to find your own way up, especially if there's a moon. Leaving this early allows you to get to the top by dawn for a fabulous view (sometimes) from northern Kenya on one side to Kilimanjaro on the other. It's not advisable to rush into this final ascent, however. For most people, day three is better spent getting acclimatized in the Teleki Valley, making the climb to Point Lenana the next morning. And note, spending your third night on the mountain at *Austrian Hut*, just below Point Lenana, is a bad idea. Not only is *Austrian* in a disgusting state, but sleeping unacclimatized at high altitude is literally a nightmare.

Trekking around the peaks

Though most people head straight up to Point Lenana, trekking round **the peaks** is really a far more exhilarating experience, with the added chance to explore some of the tarns and glacial valleys on the north side. It's supposed to be easier to do this anti-clockwise in two or three days. If you want to do it in one, however, set off clockwise from *Mackinder's* via *Two Tarn Hut's* old site by **Hut Tarn**, set in a glorious and eerily silent col beneath the glaciers and scree. The walk from here round to Point Lenana is very much a switchback affair but, as long as the mists stay away, the scenery is fairy-tale. If you're fairly fit and acclimatized, it should take eight to ten hours. Both *Two Tarn* and *Kami Hut*, on the north side of the peaks, were demolished in 1999 by KWS, but you can still camp at both sites. *Austrian Hut* is the most suitable, though not most inviting, night stop, but again you may not get much sleep at this altitude.

Incidentally, your nights up in the mountain huts will normally be shared with large numbers of persistent **rodents** which you won't see until it's too late. Remember to isolate your food from them by suspending it from the roof. The familiar diurnal scavengers that you'll see are **rock hyraxes**, which are especially tame at *Mackinder's Camp*; the welfare service provided to them by tourists preserves elderly specimens long past their natural life span. Hyraxes are not rodents – the anatomy of their feet indicates they share a distant ancestry with elephants. You're likely to come across other animals at quite high altitudes, too, notably the **duiker antelope** on the moorlands.

The descent doesn't take long. You can do it in one day, right to Naro Moru or further, assuming you've left your vehicle at the *Met Station*, or else manage to find a lift. Rather than retrace your steps to Naro Moru, a more exhilarating and less frequently used alternative is to descend by one of the other routes: the Chogoria trail, for example. This would mean taking all your gear up with you, as well as extra food.

The Chogoria route

The **Chogoria trail** is scenically far superior to any of the others, and it's become more popular now that the road around the east side of the mountain has been paved. It's also the longest route, requiring good shoes and probably a plentiful supply of blister pads. A tent is preferable for the trek beyond the park gate. From the eastern side, the hike to the top can be done in three days, but it's easier to allow four or five if you're setting out from Nairobi.

Up to the park entrance

The hustly and not especially friendly village of **CHOGORIA** is your first target. Akamba, Kensilver and Sunbird Services have regular buses from

Met. Station (9km) & Naro Moru (about 35km) ◀

Burguret Route ◀

Naro Moru Route ◀

PEAKS OF MOUNT KENYA

▲ Sirimon Route to Park Gate (about 22km)

Terere
4714m ▲

Sendeo
4704m ▲

Shipton's
Cave

Liki Stream

Shipton's Camp
(4050m)

Polish Man's
Tarn

Nanyuki
North Stream

Hausberg Tarn

Hausberg
Col

(Old Kami
Hut site)
(4433m)

Lower
Simba Tarn

Oblong Tarn

Kami Tarn

Joseph
Glacier

Pt. Peter
4757m

Arthur's
Seat
4666m

Cesar
Glacier

Northey
Glacier

Krapf
Glacier

Gregory
Glacier

Harris
Tarn

Emerald
Tarn

Pt. Piggott
4957m

Batian
5199m

Nelion
5189m

Pt.
Thompson

Tyndall
Glacier

Pt. Slade

Darwin
Glacier

Lewis
Glacier

Lenana
4985m

Nanyuki Tarn

Hut Tarn

Tyndall Tarn

Tyndall Tarn

(Old Two Tarn Hut site)
(4490m)

Pt. John
4883m

Curling Pond

Austrian Hut
(4790m)

Lewis Tarn

Mackinders Camp
(4200m)

Ranger's Post

Northern Naro
Moru Stream

Teleki Tarn

Tilman
Peak

Grigg
Peak

Somerfelt
Peak

Castle
Hill

Lake
Hohnel

Hidden Tarn

▼ Kamweti Route to Castle Forest Lodge (about 25km)

▲ Timau Route

► Hinde Valley

Nithi North

N

The Hat (The Pillar)
▲
4639m

► Chogoria Route to roadhead (about 16km) & Chogoria village (about 46km)

🏠 Minto's Hut
(4190m)

Hall Tarns

Lake
Michaelson

Simba Tarn

Square or
Upper Simba Tarn

Hanging Tarn

Tooth Col

Delamere
Peak
▲

Macmillan
Peak
▲

Ruguti North Stream

Coryndon
Peak
▲

Gallery Tarn

Thomson Tarns

- - - Footpath
······· Walkable route
——— Stream
Col/ridge
Glacier

Enchanted
Lake

Carr Lakes

Rupingazi Stream
HOBLEY VALLEY

0   1 km

Nairobi – the journey takes 4–6 hours – which pass the Chogoria turn-off en route to Meru, leaving you with a three-kilometre walk. The *Transit Motel*, 3km south of Chogoria centre at Karaa Market (PO Box 190 Chogoria ☎0166/22096; B&B ❸) is by far the best of several **lodgings**, with reasonable self-contained rooms, most with a balcony but no nets, and a restaurant of sorts – alight at Kariani stage a few kilometres before the Chogoria turn-off, which leaves you with a 1.5-kilometre walk. *The Good Will* (❶) is in the village itself and considerably cheaper, but squalid and noisy. There are twin rooms (the toilet is not partitioned off from the sleeping area) but no running water, though you can order a bucket of hot water in the mornings. *Chogoria Guest House* (❶) is a marginally better option. *Lenana Restaurant*, in the Presbyterian Mission Hospital, has cheap snacks in a linoleum-lined hall. The branch of Barclays here doesn't change money (Chuka is the nearest place).

There are a number of **porter/guide** associations in Chogoria, most of whose members are extremely pushy. The most reliable association (but also the most expensive) is Mount Kenya Chogoria Guides & Porters based at the *Joywood Marima Hotel* (PO Box 107 Marima ☎0166/2226). Their usual (bargainable) rates are $10 a day for a guide, $60 for four-wheel drive transport to the park gate for three to five people. Remember, if you're alone you must have a guide to be allowed to stay in the park overnight, and he needs to possess an official KWS guiding permit.

From the hamlet of **Mutindwa**, 4km up the mountain, it's about 26km to the park gate. On weekends, you may stand a better-than-average chance of getting a lift, otherwise, you can **rent transport** at the *Transit Motel* or elsewhere in Chogoria. There are a number of options, with prices depending on the state of the track: halfway to the park gate (15km drive, 15km walk; up to Ksh1500); two-thirds (20km drive to Bairunyi Clearing, 10km walk; up to Ksh2000); to the park gate (30km; Ksh3000–4000); or to the roadhead, some 7km further (Ksh4000). It's a good idea not to pay (at least not everything) until reaching the destination – a feat that for most of the year is by no means guaranteed because of the weather. You may prefer to walk up in any case, because it gives you a chance to acclimatize. If you get a lift up early in the day, avoid climbing any higher before stopping for the night.

Walking up from Mutindwa, there's a good campsite after just a couple of kilometres at the **Chogoria Forest Station**, with firewood available. Exciting, dense rain forest follows, where you're likely to see colobus monkeys, spotted hyena, buffalo and numerous elephant droppings. Before, during and after the rains, though, you'll probably be more occupied with fending off swarms of hungry **tsetse** fly, which isn't much fun and runs the (slight) risk of sleeping sickness. The next available campsite is the only clearing in the forest, at a place called **Bairunyi Clearing**, 14km further up the track (no water). The national park's **Chogoria Gate** is 8km further up the increasingly steep and rough track (4WD vital, and not always enough), flanked by giant, creaking bamboo forest. If you arrive late in the day and are not going beyond the roadhead (7km on – the actual boundary of the national park), the rangers may waive park fees for that day, but be sure to keep receipts for the fees you pay to satisfy the rangers at whichever gate you exit from.

The park entrance and roadhead

The best **place to stay** is the very good and wonderfully sited *Meru Mount Kenya Lodge*, a group of self-service *bandas* just before the gate (no park fees payable), run by the district council (it may be worth booking in advance through Let's Go Travel in Nairobi, see p.141; Ksh1050 per person). They have a spartan shop that sells beer, and blissful wood fires in each *banda*. They're often visited by buffaloes, and you can sometimes see elephants at the nearby water holes, visible from the ridge of the hill behind the *bandas*.

Assuming you're not staying in the *bandas*, but it's time to stop for the day, you might as well stay put by the gate with your tent (if you have a tent), or go on to *Parklands Campsite*, twenty minutes' walk away, with toilets and, usually, water. To get there, stay on the main track for 500m then fork left – keep a look out, the turning is easily missed. Alternatively, follow the main track up from the park gate and you'll come to a "special campsite" with running water and toilet. This is a beautiful place to camp, but has special fees (reservable through the warden; $10 per person).

The nearest **mountain hut** is reached by branching left off the main track (it's well signposted) and continuing past *Parklands Campsite*. The uninviting *Urumandi Hut,* which is utterly run down, is an hour's walk up the track. It's long overdue for a refit, only retains three unbroken beds and, like all the MCK huts, has lost its complement of mattresses. There's water from the ravine nearby. The neighbouring *Urumandi Campsite* is equally unprepossessing – little more than an overgrown swamp and a derelict shed.

Both the main track and the side branch eventually meet up at the **road-head**, 6km further on. The side branch, via Urumandi, is the more interesting walk, but tougher on vehicles. The roadhead, with a small parking area, is on the north side of the Nithi stream and there's a very pleasant **campsite** here, with good stream water.

There are good walks round about, useful for acclimatizing to the three-thousand-metre-plus altitude. Short scrambles from the roadhead take you to the four sets of **Nithi Falls**, while longer walks (3–6hr round trip) take you north to **Mugi Hill**, **Lake Ellis** and the flat-topped peak Kilingo – the **Giant's Billiard Table**.

On the mountain

From the roadhead, all wheels are abandoned as you slog on foot up towards *Minto's Hut*, a six-hour (9hr from *Meru Mount Kenya Lodge*) stint away in the high moorlands. The route tracks along the axis of an ascending ridge, then flattens onto the rim of the spectacular **Gorges Valley**, carved deep by glaciation. There are unobstructed and encouraging views up to the peaks as you hug the contours of the valley wall.

Minto's Hut, like *Mackinder's* on the west side of the mountain, is three to five hours from Point Lenana. Situated by the four small "Hall Tarns", it's perched above the larger Lake Michaelson at the head of the valley below – a very beautiful place, inspiringly set off by giant groundsel, lobelia plants and weird volcanic formations inhabited by rock hyraxes. Unfortunately, you're better off camping here and leaving the hut and toilet to whatever types of rodents can survive its squalid conditions. Be aware that the available tarn water is not pure, and boiling it at this altitude will not kill the bugs, so you should use purifying tablets or iodine.

In the morning, assuming you didn't freeze to death, you have two options. The first is to head up to the ridge west of *Minto's* and follow it, through pretty scenery, to **Simba Tarn**, below Simba Col. From there, head due south around the peaks and past little **Square Tarn** before turning right to follow the contours for a tough kilometre to the so-called **Curling Pond** (matches have been held on the ice here) and *Austrian Hut*. Note, if you're thinking of a short cut straight up to Square Tarn, it's very steep.

Alternatively, from *Minto's* make for the base of the ridge extending east from Point Lenana, then tackle the cruel scree slope to the south for a ninety-minute scramble up to a saddle followed by a straight drop to the head of the **Hobley Valley** with its two tarns. From here, it's just an hour across to the base of Lenana Ridge, behind which, again, is *Austrian Hut*. Mercifully, whichever route you choose, this day's hike is a short one and at this altitude (over 4000m), you'll be glad to spend the rest of the day at one of the huts, recuperating for the final ascent. Considering the altitude, a safer and probably more comfortable option would be to spend a second night, acclimatizing at the base of Simba Tarn (tent only), followed by a pre-dawn assault on Point Lenana.

After the climb to Lenana, you have a ninety-minute **descent** from *Austrian Hut* along the edge of Lewis Glacier, tracking back and forth over miserable scree, to the Teleki Tarn at the head of the Naro Moru stream. *Mackinder's*, and the scent of civilization, is just an hour away down the valley. But if you can resist that lure, and it is still early in the day, *and* if you have enough food and water, you can continue around the west side of the peaks to Hut Tarn, then up and down over the ridges to the old site of *Kami Hut*, at the head of the Sirimon route on the north side. If you want to do it, and you feel acclimatized, there's no problem making it from *Minto's* to Point Lenana and on down to the *Met Station* in one day.

The Sirimon route

The **Sirimon route** leads up from the Mount Kenya ring road some 14km east of Nanyuki. It has certain advantages: it's the driest route, the scenery is more open, and it's renowned for wildlife. *Mountain Rock Bantu Lodge* specializes in inclusive three- or four-day **guided tours** up to Point Lenana using this route, and the *Naro Moru River Lodge* also offers trips up this way. Prices are around $450 per person (4 days) in a group of four, or $405 per person if there are two of you, including transport to and from the base of the trail, all food and equipment, and a last night at *Mountain Rock Bantu Lodge*. Park fees are an additional expense. Much cheaper, if you're just looking for a guide, is to enquire at the *Cousin Café* in Nanyuki (see p.191), or else at *Nanyuki River Lodge*.

Unpackaged walking on this route is fine if you're in a small group, but you're much less likely to find company up here than on the Chogoria or very busy Naro Moru routes, as there isn't any real "base town" to start from excepting a huddle of *dukas* on the ring road, 9km from the park gate. The route climbs over the northern moorlands, giving superb views on the way of the main peaks as well as the twin "lesser" peaks of Terere and Sendeyo (4714m and 4704m), which have small glaciers of their own.

Mountain accommodation on the way consists of *Old Moses Camp* (3300m, at the roadhead, 4WD access only; $10, students/children $8) and *Shipton's Camp* **bunkhouses** (4200m; $12, students/children $10). Both have recently been renovated with flush toilets adjoining the huts and can be booked through *Mountain Rock Bantu Lodge*, though you can also simply pay on arrival for a nominal mark-up.

The Burguret route

Mountain Rock Bantu Lodge's preferred route used to follow the **Burguret River** up from the hotel through thick bamboo forest and moorland, but this is now mostly overgrown and hard to follow without a guide (available at

Mountain Rock for Ksh1200 per day, excluding the guide's park fees). A 4WD vehicle can drive up to 3000m on this route and it terminates at *Two Tarn Hut's* old site, behind Teleki Valley. En route, it passes a clutch of caves described as a "Mau Mau conference centre". *Mountain Rock* still offers four-hour trips to the caves, including some waterfall hiking, for $6–7 per person, depending on group size, or the same on mountain bikes ($18–33 per person).

Other routes

The four trails described here represent only the most obvious and well-trodden of the mountain's hiking possibilities. All ground above 3200m is within the boundaries of the national park and, with time and sufficient food (and money to pay park fees), you could hike the moors and highland zone for weeks. On the north side, a very rarely used route leads up from Timau through dense forest, for which a guide, a good map and accurate orienteering skills are essential. The southern flanks of the mountain seem to have largely escaped the notice of hikers, but there are several forest stations in the vicinity of Embu and plenty of scope for exploration – the Kamweti route is a possibility (see p.176). Most of the southern slopes were a designated "Kikuyu reserve" during the colonial period, so few European climbers created routes up here. A **warning**: hiking in the forests, though feasible, is absolutely not advised unless you're with a guide; it's easy to get hopelessly lost, as a number of apocryphal tales circulating tell. Hyena and other hungry or bad-tempered beasts abound, and without serious jungle or rainforest experience, you're asking for trouble.

Over the equator: Nanyuki and Laikipia

North of Naro Moru, the El Niño-damaged A2 now rattles and lurches over fantastically deep potholes across the yellow-and-grey downs, scattered with stands of tall gum trees, roamed by cattle and overflown by brilliant blue roller birds, before dropping to the equator and Nanyuki. You might be forgiven for expecting something momentous to take place at **the equator**, but there's no "crossing of the line ceremony" here. Still, if you have any control over your transport, you'd have to be pretty cool just to breeze by.

There's a sprouting of several signs ("This sign is on the Equator") which, you can't help but notice if you are slightly cynical, are erected outside curio shops, whose salesmen will go to absurd lengths to entice you ("Hey guy! Want cocaine?"). What they actually offer is all the usual beadwork, carvings, soapstone and bangles at the sorts of prices you'd expect. There's even an "Equator Professor" who'll demonstrate the Coriolis effect of the earth's rotation using a bucket of water and a matchstick (aided by sleight of hand). In the northern hemisphere water gurgles through a plug hole in an anticlockwise direction, whereas in the southern hemisphere it flows clockwise. The demonstration is free, the "certificate" comes for a fee.

The town centre is just 1.5km down the road, so you could reasonably ask to be dropped at the equator and then walk in.

Nanyuki

NANYUKI has the dual distinction of being Kenya's air force town (a base which has had a lot of attention lavished on it in recent years) as well as playing host to the British Army's training and operations centre. For long an afflu-

▲ Isiolo & Meru (A2)

NANYUKI

Cathedral
Showground

ACCOMMODATION

High Life	
'Self-Contained Rooms'	**10**
Ibis	**7**
Jambo Hotel	**8**
Joskaki Hotel	**9**
Juba House Hotel	**11**
Nanyuki Guest House	**4**
Nanyuki River Lodge	**2**
Nanyuki Simbas Lodge	**1**
Nyakio B & L	**5**
Sirimon Hotel	**6**
Sportsman's Arms	**3**
Youth Hostel	**12**

RESTAURANTS

Maridadi Café	**A**
Marina Bar	**D**
Muneera's	**C**
Nanyuki Coffee House	**B**

Cloth & Hardware Market
Buttsons Supermarket Mobil Market
Covered Market Caltex Kenya Commercial Bank
Matatu Stage Standard Chartered Bank
Settlers Store
United Stores Clocktower Barclays Bank
Modern Sanitary Stores Nanyuki E Mail & Internet
BAZAAR ROAD
MARKET ROAD
Sikh Temple
Prison

River Nanyuki

0   200 m

▼ Mount Kenya Safari Club & Nyeri (A2)

ent place, the El Niño floods in the 1990s turned Nanyuki's once pristine streets into a series of potholes, and at the same time the town saw an influx of refugees fleeing the **ethnic violence** in Laikipia District between Kalenjin and Kikuyu. Most of them were housed in the slums to the west of town and have remained there ever since, despite the continuing decline in violence.

Nevertheless, Nanyuki remains in atmosphere very much a country town, and is oddly charming despite its increasing poverty. A wide, tree-lined main street and the mild climate lent by its altitude of 2000m bestow an unfamiliar, cool spaciousness that seems to reinforce its colonial character. Shops lining the main road include the Settlers Store (since 1938), the Modern Sanitary Stores (which sells camping gas), and United Stores with its pile of *Daily Telegraphs*.

The first party of settlers arrived in the district in 1907 to find "several old Maasai *manyattas*, a great deal of game and nothing else". Nanyuki is still something of a settlers' town and European locals are always around. The animals, sadly, are not. Although you may see a few grazers on the plains, the vast herds of zebra that once roamed the banks of the *Ngare Nanyuki* (Maasai – Red River) were decimated by hunters seeking hides, by others seeking meat (particularly during World War II, when 80,000 Italian prisoners of war were fed a pound each day), but most of all by ranchers protecting their pastures. As the zebra herds dwindled, so the lions became a greater threat to livestock; they retreated – under fire – to the mountain forests and moors. And the rhinos just disappeared, almost to the brink of extinction (see Solio Ranch on p.218).

Practicalities

If you're passing through Nanyuki, wholesome **food** is available at the *Maridadi Café*. Good snacks and, occasionally, great curries are to be had at *Muneera's*

Restaurant; *Mother's Choice Café*, next door, has sweet cakes and sausages. For a lively **drink**, try the *Marina Bar & Restaurant* opposite the post office, a popular hangout for tourists and soldiers. (Unfortunately you may meet with some verbal abuse while in Nanyuki, presumably on account of the British base and most likely if you are – or might be mistaken for – an off-duty serviceman.) *Nanyuki Coffee House* is a great old timers' place (serving both coffee and beer), wonderful in the low afternoon sun. Next door is *High Life Day and Night Club* which, not surprisingly, attracts all the low life. For **money-changing** in town, the best bet is the KCB (bureau de change open Mon–Fri 9am–3pm, Sat 9–11am). Standard Chartered has an ATM. If you're looking for a **guide** for the Sirimon route up Mount Kenya, try first the *Cousin Café* next to *Marina Bar & Restaurant*, or else the boys down at *Nanyuki River Lodge*. **Emails** can be sent from Nanyuki Email & Internet (Ksh60 per email).

If you have time before leaving, pay a visit to the **Nanyuki Spinners and Weavers** workshop (closed Sun), located about 1km down the Nyahururu road on the left, opposite the District Hospital. This women's group provides the Spinners' Web shop in Nairobi with rugs and other articles woven on hand looms, which you can buy here at reduced prices. There's also astonishingly ambrosial **wild honey** from the *dukas* a kilometre or so east of the last police barrier, on the road to Meru.

For **overnight stays**, you have a number of options, including **camping** at the *Sportsman's Arms*, or one of the places listed below.

Accommodation

High Life "Self-contained Rooms" (no phone). Basic, but tolerable, and very economical. **①**

Ibis Hotel PO Box 209 Nanyuki ☎0176/31536. On Bazaar Road, opposite the matatu stage. Clean, sparsely decorated rooms, but complete with slippers and Afro combs. **②**

Jambo Hotel PO Box 245 Nanyuki ☎0176/31894. Opposite *Joskaki Hotel*, reasonably clean and quiet, hot water, secure parking. **①**

Joskaki Hotel Bazaar St, PO Box 101 ☎0176/22820, ℱ32912. Good s/c rooms, and recommended for its generally excellent food and rooftop views of the town and Mount Kenya. Unfortunately, it's a vast, corridor-riddled warren and can be indescribably noisy when the bar is open all night, or there's a disco. **②**

Juba House Hotel PO Box 504 (no phone). A basic central stand-by, with a lively bar. **①**

Mount Kenya Safari Club 8km southeast of Nanyuki, accessible either from just north of the *New Silverbeck*, or from the north side of town; PO Box 58581 ☎0176/ 216940, ℱ216796; reservations through Lonrho, see p.43. Founded by Hollywood star William Holden, the heights of equatorial comfort are reached here – magnificent meals, slick service, and kinky round baths in the cottages. If you're mobile, it's fun to call in anyway (Ksh350 daily membership including use of the pool). A range of activities in and around the hotel – including tennis, riding, fishing, gyms, a bowling green, heated pool and an animal orphanage – all fill the day very pleasantly. And, if you ever dreamed of golf on the equator, what they term a "brutal" nine-hole course obliges. For all this, however, it's massively overpriced. **⑨**

Nanyuki Guest House PO Box 211 Meru ☎0176/22822. Ten minutes' walk out of town along the Nyahururu road. The prison-like exterior belies a good atmosphere, helpful manager and probably the cheapest self-contained rooms in the country. **①**

Nanyuki River Lodge PO Box 101 ☎0176/32523. Reasonable rooms and a pool, and would be good value if it wasn't for the hustly touts and curio pedlars at the entrance, and the uncertain security (its rowdy bar appears to be the mainstay these days). The guides have their own porters' association for Mount Kenya with reasonable rates (porter-guide Ksh600 per day) for tackling the Sirimon route, although their all-in package prices are as expensive as any ($405 per person for a four-day jaunt for two, $450 in a group of four). **②**

Nanyuki Simbas Lodge PO Box 211 ☎0176/22556. A peaceful place and actually quite pleasant despite the barrack-like motel rooms. Safe parking, and a reasonable restaurant. Currently much better, if more expensive, than *Nanyuki River Lodge*. **③**

Nyakio B&L Bazaar Rd, PO Box 179

℡0176/22505. Good s/c rooms, and a lively atmosphere thanks to the busy bar downstairs. **②**
Sirimon Hotel Biashara St, PO Box 326 ℡0176/32344. The tour drivers' favourite digs – sleazy but amiable, with clean rooms, excellent hot showers, and a video cinema (admission Ksh20). Slightly cheaper than the *Joskaki* and *Juba*. **①**
Sportsman's Arms PO Box 3 ℡0176/32347–8, ℱ22895. An old establishment, which used to be the base for visits to the *Secret Valley* (a *Treetops*-type establishment) until that burned down in 1981. Letters and photos smother the walls, reminders of the good old days. There's a wide choice of accommodation, from slightly dilapidated s/c wooden cottages, rooms in a new wing, and

even newer cottages. The rooms and newer cottages are better equipped, and there's a sauna, Jacuzzi and pool (Ksh100 for each for non-residents). The disco and jumping *nyama choma* joint at weekends might make sleeping difficult. B&B. Rooms and old cottages **④**; new cottages **⑤**
Youth Hostel Market Rd, near the post office, PO Box 1427 ℡0176/22112; not IYHA-affiliated. This used to be part of the Emmanuel Parish Centre, but is now just a friendly hostel with very cheap beds in single and double rooms. Accommodation is clean but cramped and very spartan, and makes no concessions to privacy – unless you're the only guest, of course, in which case it's not a problem. The toilets are a hazard. **①**

Moving on: Laikipia

Laikipia District is a vast plateau northwest of Mount Kenya, about the size of Wales, encompassing much of the transitional lands between the well-watered Central Highlands to the south and the semi-desert grazing steppe of the Samburu in the north. It also straddles the disputed division between the Kikuyu people in the east and the Kalenjin to the west.

On the face of it, Laikipia is not an obvious tourist destination: the land is generally flat (between 1800m and 2100m) and not terribly spectacular (unless the sky clears enough to give views of Mount Kenya to the southeast), and the few roads that do cross it are uniformly awful, often impassable in the rains. Laikipia also became notorious in the run-up to the 1997 general elections, when **ethnic violence** between Kalenjin and Kikuyus swept the district, leaving several hundred dead and tens of thousands homeless. The killings continued into early 1998, and though violence has since declined, there is still a degree of banditry, now usually carried out for short-term political gain rather than as a result of age-old inter-communal enmity.

For all this, however, Laikipia is also one of the most underrated places to see **wildlife** outside the confines of the national parks. Thanks mainly to its isolation, the district contains a wealth of endangered species. Some two thousand **elephants** still undertake a seasonal migration from Laikipia north into the Samburu rangelands during the long rains, and the district also supports an estimated 25 percent of the world's remaining population of **Grevy's zebra**, which is fast disappearing in its other habitats in Ethiopia and Somalia. Laikipia is the best place to see **black rhinos** (see also Solio Ranch on p.218), whose world population today is barely two thousand, five hundred of them in Kenya. They are grouped in five heavily-guarded sanctuaries, set-up by cattle farmers as part of an experiment in integrated ranching, and latterly also for tourism. As browsers, the rhinos don't interfere with cattle pasture, and do well in the same environment so long as the bush isn't cleared.

Getting there and around

If you're **heading to Nyahururu**, beware of the unpaved C76 road. Even in the dry season, and especially in periods of heavy rain, vehicles get stuck along it for days on end. Despite the setbacks, it's a good road for wildlife-spotting: you've every chance of seeing giraffes, gazelles and even elephants if you set off early. There's no public transport along this route, so your own 4WD is essential, though you might be lucky and catch a lift with a rancher in Nanyuki – ask at the *Sportsman's Arms*.

For **day-trips** (again, under your own steam), **Ol Pejeta Ranch** is the place to aim for, which contains one of Laikipia's biggest concentrations of wildlife, again including black rhinos. The ranch covers some 400 square kilometres, nearly a quarter of which is given over to a rhino sanctuary – **Sweetwaters Game Reserve** ($16 entry per person) – one inmate of which, "Morani", is tame enough to be approached very closely. There's also a **chimpanzee sanctuary** here, with animals from the Jane Goodall Institute in Burundi (chimps aren't otherwise found in Kenya). To get there, the easiest way is to take the fifteen-kilometre track, right (all-weather in theory), which starts south of Nakuru by the equator; otherwise, take the left (signposted) fork on the Nyahururu road 10km after Nanyuki, and continue along the abysmally muddy track (impassable during the rains) for 19km. For more information, contact The Sweetwaters Trust, c/o Ol Pejeta Ranching, PO Box 167 Nanyuki.

For the more adventurous, **luxury camel safaris** in the district are offered by Ewaso River Camel Hikes (p.143), and Northern Frontier Ventures (☎0367/3933, ℻02/447310) among others.

Ranches and accommodation

With few exceptions, **accommodation** in Laikipia is for the well-heeled only, and requires your own transport (there are no matatus or buses), although all places can arrange for you to be picked up from Nanyuki (at additional cost). Most guests fly in (contact Tropic Air Ltd, PO Box 161 Nanyuki ☎0176/32890–1, ℻32787, ✉tropicair@kenyaonline.com). Many **game ranches** have opened their doors to guests, and combine a quasi-colonial welcome and atmosphere with all-inclusive game drives and visits to the rhino sanctuaries. Other options, covered elsewhere in this book, are *Solio Game Ranch* near Nyeri (p.218) and *Colcheccio Lodge* north of Rumuruti (p.600). You can book most of the following at Let's Go Travel in Nairobi (p.141).

Borana Lodge between Mokogodo and Engare Ndare forests, reservations through Tandala Ltd, PO Box 24397 Nairobi ☏02/568804, ℱ564945, ⓔroyal.africasaf@commsol.sprint.com. Worth a mention only for being one of Kenya's costliest options. Surrounded by a private commercial "conservation" ranch, this has six cedar, thatch and stone cottages and offers day and night game drives, visits to a rhino reserve, entertainment at a nearby water hole and horse riding, all for a gigantic $580 per person per day. Booking via Let's Go Travel knocks it down to a mere $720 for a double (plus $30 per person admission to the ranch). ❾

El Karama Ranch 42km northwest of Nanyuki off the track to Maralal, PO Box 172 Nanyuki. From Nanyuki, fork right after 9km, continue for 23km, then turn left at the signboard "Ol Jogi – No Shooting" for 10km. Hats off to these guys – the guardian angels of budget travellers. An exceptionally nice set-up on the banks of the Ewaso Nyiro River, and highly recommended if you have a way to get to it. You're welcome to pitch your tent, and they provide a small amount of cheap farmhouse and self-service *banda* accommodation (bring food and drinking water), game rides on horseback (Ksh1500 per person) and escorted wildlife walks (Ksh300 per person). ❸

Il Polei Campsite ☏0176/31650, ℱ31744. Part of the Il Polei Group Ranch, an hour's drive from Nanyuki along the Doldol road, this campsite can only be rented out as a whole and can cater for three families. Elephants, leopards, greater kudu gerunuk and Grevy's zebra are some of the animals you may see in the 20 square kilometres put aside by the Mokogodo Masai in 1998 for wildlife conservation. ❹

Lewa Downs off the A2 Nanyuki to Isiolo road ⓦwww.lewa.org (see box opposite). A private, 220-square-kilometre wildlife sanctuary, and one of the country's most outstanding conservation

success stories. Options include the all-inclusive cottages attached to *Wilderness Trails* ranch house, *Lewa Tented Camp*, and exclusive access to the Samburu community-run *Il Ngwesi Lodge*.

Mogwooni Bandas 30km from Nanyuki, reservations through Cape Chestnut Ltd ☏0176/32526, ℱ32208. On a commercial cattle and sheep ranch on the bank of the Nanyuki River. Activities include horse riding, tennis and plenty of walking. ❸

Ol Pejeta Ranch House PO Box 763 Nanyuki ☏0176/23414; reservations also through Lonrho, p.43. Seven kilometres beyond (and more expensive than) *Sweetwaters*, this has long been a hideaway for the rich and famous, and is a genuinely classy option. There are only six bedrooms, lots of semi-tame giraffe poking around the gardens, two swimming pools, a resident naturalist, and the same activities as for *Sweetwaters*. FB ❾

Sweetwaters Tented Camp Ol Pejeta Ranch, PO Box 763 Nanyuki ☏ & ℱ0176/32409; reservations also through Lonrho, p.43. Upmarket but good value when compared with similar set-ups in the national parks and reserves, this is a well laid-out tented camp popular with Kenya residents, especially families, with high-quality food and service. The lower tents are probably preferable to the ones set on stilts. It specializes in night game drives, and there's also a pool, and camel- and walking-safaris are offered. FB ❻ low, ❼–❽ high, plus $58 per person for activities.

Tasia Lodge PO Box 137 Nanyuki. Owned by the Lekurruki Community Conservation Ranch, this place overlooks a small scenic valley where you have a good chance of spotting elephants. It has six self-contained rooms and a kid bunk house with a shower room, but the rates are steep given that it has neither the reputation nor the activities of the better-known places. ❾

Moving on: east to Meru

Leaving Nanyuki eastwards, the ring road skirts closer to the mountain than at any other point in its circumference. The land here is extremely fertile, but is block-owned for the most part by large commercial estates – you'll see ordinary *wananchi* (peasants) cultivating the verges between the road and the estate fences to eke out a living.

After 14km, you come to the village of **TIMAU**, unremarkable but for two outstanding – if expensive – stopover possibilities. Prices at both are per person, which makes for good value if you're on your own. If you'd like a barbecued rainbow trout lunch on the way, call in at *Kentrout Trout Farm*, 3km to the right down a rough, signposted track from the village (4WD in rainy weather; PO Box 14 Timau ☎ & ⓕ0177/41016; reservations can also be made through Deacons in Nairobi ☎02/228391; B&B ❹–❺, FB ❺–❻). Saturated with the permanent rush of the Teleswan River and shaded by African olive trees, it's a delightful and cool retreat if you're heading towards Samburu or further afield and need a break. As well as their delicious lunchtime alfresco buffets (Ksh800), whose ingredients are grown (or bred) on the farm; you can catch your own trout in the local fish ponds and have it prepared by the chef. They also have two wonderful, huge stone cottages for rent (all s/c), three rooms in a rambling old ranch house and a number of self-contained *bandas*. The gardens, river and indigenous forest teem with birdlife and the crashing of colobus monkeys in the trees. **Camping** is possible on request.

Lewa Wildlife Conservancy

A few kilometres down the Isiolo road, a signposted gate on the left takes you 8km along dirt track to the Lewa Wildlife Conservancy (ⓦwww.lewa.org), in the foothills of Mount Kenya. Formerly a cattle ranch, it includes the electric-fenced **Ngare Sergoi Rhino Sanctuary**, currently containing around forty rhinos, both black and white, and about six hundred Grevy's zebra which account for a tenth of the world's remaining wild population.

During the 1980s, elephants flooded into Lewa seeking safety from the heavy poaching further north, but as security in the north improved, they returned to their former range. However, there are always some on Lewa, and their numbers increase in the dry season, or whenever there is a fresh outbreak of poaching.

This is conservation as a business: there's a $35 per person entrance fee ($20 children), which goes to the local Il Ngwesi Samburu group ranch, and the original Lewa homestead is now a conservation centre and gift shop. There's exceedingly pricey all-inclusive **accommodation** available in eight cottages at **Wilderness Trails** (reservations through Bush Homes of East Africa, p.42; closed April, May & Nov; FB ❾) in an atmosphere reminiscent of a comfortable 1930s English country house. The welcome is congenial, the cooking excellent, and the price includes game drives in an antiquated Land Rover to Lewa Swamp to see the rare sitatunga water antelope.

The second accommodation option at Lewa Downs is **Lewa Tented Camp** (bookings through Bush Homes of East Africa, p.44; FB ❾), which is in the Ngare Sergoi Rhino Sanctuary itself. The main lodge building is a thatched cedarwood cottage, with a lounge overlooking a floodlit waterhole where rhino, elephant and other animals come to drink. Accommodation is in eleven well-spaced luxury tents raised on lava-rock platforms stilts, and there are optional horseback safaris ($15 per hour).

Accessed exclusively through the ranch is the much lauded **Il Ngwesi Lodge** (bookings through Let's Go Travel, p.141; ❾ for the entire lodge), a Samburu-owned and serviced eco-lodge, maintaining traditional use of land whilst encouraging the reintegration of wild animals. Profits go to Il Ngwesi Samburu group ranch members. There are four thatched *bandas* raised on stilts, water from a spring hauled by camel (even for filling the swimming pool), and solar power for lighting. A booking guarantees you'll get the place to yourself. It's self-catering, which means you provide food but it will be cooked for you. Camels are available for riding or walking trips, though visits to a nearby Samburu *manyatta* cost a mean $20 per person. Feedback from guests is mostly rapturous, though some find the whole set-up too tame. Most guests fly in to Nanyuki or Lewa and are picked up there.

The other great draw is *Timau River Lodge*, 2km east from Timau, and 1km off to the right (PO Box 212 Timau ☏ 0177/41230; B&B ❸–❹, FB ❹–❺). The dream of a charming Afghani couple, the "lodge" (actually a varied collection of s/c log, mud and "underground" houses) was planned and built supposedly to run on ecological principles, and though water is still heated by wood boilers and they've started a tree nursery to replace those used to build the houses, the idealistic but inefficient method of powering the lighting by sunlight and water-turbine, has since been replaced by a generator. There are semi-tamed colobus monkeys, an occasional visiting leopard, secluded waterfalls and river pools for bathing in, and a huge expanse of forest to get lost in. You can **camp** anywhere you like, or in a special campsite (Ksh300 per person which includes hot showers and other facilities; tent rental Ksh600). They also offer trout fishing, mountain climbing, camel riding and horse riding. The accommodation itself is wonderful: every *banda* has its own small kitchen and kids will adore the attic bedrooms in the largest *bandas*. There's also a communal cooking area with ancient Scottish cast-iron ovens for self-catering.

After Timau, the scenery acquires a real grandeur, passing through Lewa Downs (see p.197). The 70km from **Nanyuki to Meru** couldn't illustrate better the amazing variety of climate and landscape in Kenya. The road climbs steeply to almost 3000m, passing alternative routes to the peaks and giving unparalleled views of them in the early morning. But a spectacle you might not have guessed at is the panorama that spreads out to the north as the road drops once again – on a really clear day, after rain has settled the dust, this is devastatingly beautiful. Even on an average day, you can see as far as the dramatic mesa of **Ol Olokwe**, nearly 100km north in the desert. Isiolo (p.619) lies out there, too, first stop on the way to the northern wilderness.

Meru

Passing the Isiolo turn-off, the road to Meru suddenly plunges through verdant **jungle**, with glimpses through the trees of the **Nyambeni Hills** and the volcanic pimples dotting the plain. **Meru oak** is the commercial prize of this forested eastern side of the mountain, though judging by the number of active sawmills at the upper end of the town, supplies won't last much longer. The forest still comes almost to the town's edge, however, and paths lead off to cleared *shambas* where, for a year or two, just about anything will grow. The moist, jungly atmosphere around Meru, with wood smoke curling up against a background of dark forest, is very reminiscent of parts of West Africa (and the local Meru inhabitants are much darker-skinned than their neighbours) – a total change of mood after the dryish grasslands on the northwest side of the mountain.

Meru is, of course, the base for visits to Meru National Park (see p.433), and whilst concerns about security there have diminished (according to the Kenyan Wildlife Service), accommodation options are still limited for a park of this size.

Meru town

MERU town is strung out over 2–3km, the main road in from Nanyuki dropping steeply across the hillside to the town centre. It's an unusual place in an interesting location – there are great views from the upper (**Makutano**) half of town over the densely settled slopes – and well worth a stay.

Market

MAKUTANO

◄ 3, 4, 5 & Isiolo & Nanyu

MOI STADIUM ROAD

Hunter's
Makuti
Village

Prison
Industries
Showroom

Royal Paramount
Enterprises

Town
Hall

Meru
Museum

Consolidated
Bank

Barclays
Bank

Matatu &
Bus Stage

Market

Matatus to
Tharaka

KCB
Bank

Uhuru
Monument

Akamba
Office

Matatus
to Embu

Miraa
Trading
Area

Market

Standard
Chartered
Bank

MOI AVENUE

MERU   0 ──── 500 m

▼ Embu

ACCOMMODATION					RESTAURANTS & CAFÉS	
Brown Rock	9	Moran Hotel Meru	3	Rocky Hill Inn	4	African Restaurant	A
Hotel Castella	6	Nanyuki Guest House	1	Stansted Lodge	10	Ivory Springs Café	D
Continental Hotel & Bar	2	New Milimani	7	Hotel Three Steers	5	Julieta Restaurant	B
Meru County	8	Pig and Whistle	11			Keen Restaurant	C
						Springboard Café	E

Meru's municipal **market** is a large one and sells a wide range of goods – baskets, clothes, domestic utensils – as well as the agricultural produce of the district which is cheap and excellent. They grow the best **custard apples** in Kenya here, and if you like *miraa*, you won't find cheaper, bigger or better bunches anywhere (see box on p.200). There's a trading corner devoted to *miraa* in the town centre, which also has lip-smacking roast yams and sugar cane by the yard. The outdoor market in Makutano seems reserved largely for small traders offering more, wonderful, cheap *shamba* produce.

The tiny, but fascinating **Meru Museum** (PO Box 597 ☎0164/20482; Mon–Fri 9.30am–5.30pm, Sat 9.30am–2pm; Ksh200) is also a treat. It occupies the oldest stone building in town, a former District Commissioner's office, where you're likely to be the only visitor if it's not besieged by schoolchildren. Emphasis is on the traditional culture of the Meru people: small ethnographic exhibits, pick-up-and-feel blocks of fossilized wood, stone tools from the Lewa Downs prehistoric site and some woefully stuffed (and stinking) animals.

Outside, there's a particularly good **herbal pharmacopoeia** – a collection of traditional medicinal plants growing in the garden, where you can see what a *miraa* bush looks like, among others. Nearby, a pool contains a mean-looking crocodile, turtles and tortoises, and several psychotically aggressive monkeys try to get at you through their cage bars beside the museum's star attraction (for the schoolkids at least): "Three-legged Bull". The **Meru homestead** is well presented and feels authentic – you get the impression someone actually lives here on the museum grounds, a feeling accentuated by the escape route in the perimeter fence for fleeing from invaders, which seems to have the well-worn look of years of use. If you're really interested in the Meru people, ask at the museum about the **Njuri-Ncheke traditional courthouse**, approximately 9km north of Meru on the road to Maua, which was recently donated to the museum. The Njuri-Ncheke are a semi-secret society of elders sworn to preserve and uphold traditional cultural structures and religion, mainly through creating and enforcing traditional law and presiding over ceremonies and the

Miraa

Throughout Kenya, and especially in the Central Highlands and on the coast, you'll often see people selling and chewing what looks like a bunch of twigs wrapped in a banana leaf. This is in fact **miraa**, more commonly known abroad by its Somali name **qat**, a natural stimulant that is particularly popular among Somalians and Somali Kenyans. The shrub (*Catha edulis*) grows in the hills around Meru (the world centre for its production), and the red-green young bark from the shrub's new shoots is washed, stripped with the teeth and chewed, with the bitter result being something of an acquired taste (it's usually taken with bubble gum to sweeten it). *Miraa* contains an alkaloid called cathinone, a distant relative of amphetamine, with similar **effects**, though you have to chew it for some time before you'll feel them. When they do kick in, they include a feeling of alertness, ease of conversation and loss of appetite. Long-term daily use can lead to addiction, and it's also not always looked upon favourably, with signs prohibiting the chewing of it in many hotels and bars.

Miraa comes in bundles of a hundred sticks called "kilos" (not a reference to their weight) and various **qualities**, from long, twiggy *kangeta*, which is the ordinary, bog-standard version, to short, fat *gisa kolombo*, which is the strongest. As it loses its potency within 48 hours of picking, it's wrapped in banana leaves and transported at speed. Street stalls selling it often display the banana leaves to show that they have it, and the best place to buy *miraa* in many towns is where the express matatus arrive from Meru. The use of *miraa* by bus, truck and matatu drivers goes a long way towards explaining why they have so many accidents

There are no **legal restrictions** on the use of *miraa* in Kenya, although the Muslim imams have issued a *fatwa* (legal judgement) condemning it as an intoxicant, like alcohol, which means that it is forbidden to true believers. In fact, in many countries, including neighbouring Tanzania, as well as the US, Canada, Ireland and most EU countries (but not the UK), *miraa* is a controlled narcotic, the possession of which is a criminal offence. In the UAE, supplying any amount of it to anyone carries the death penalty, and several Kenyans are serving long sentences in Tanzanian prisons for carrying *miraa* across the border with intent to supply it.

administration of oaths. The museum may have a copy left of David Maitai Rimita's fascinating book on the Njuri-Ncheke (self-published, Meru 1988), which also covers Meru beliefs in supernatural spirits, witch-doctors, diviners and cosmology.

Practicalities

Meru is a hub for transport south, west and east. Numerous **bus** companies have their offices between the mosque and *miraa* trading area. The safest companies are Akamba (☎0164/20151), Kensilver (☎0164/30659), and KBS Stagecoach Express (☎0164/30186) for Nairobi, although chances are you'll end up on one of Sunbird Services' mangled wrecks; they have almost a dozen daily runs to the capital via Embu, and also run to Maua for Meru National Park (p.433). A helpful service is Arusha Express's twice-daily run to Malindi, and the daily Garissa Express (Garex) bus for Mombasa. As for **matatus**, most destinations are served from the main stage, with the exception of Embu (at the western end of Moi Avenue) and Tharaka, a little-visited district dominated by a series of dammed reservoirs on the Tana River, which is prone to bloody cattle raids.

Of the banks, Standard Chartered and Barclays both have ATMs. **Emails** can be sent from the Royal Paramount Enterprize, on the main road, by Meru Safari Club.

For **eating**, Meru will treat you well, at little expense. The most upmarket place, which isn't saying all that much, is the *Meru County Hotel*, with set lunches at Ksh500. *Ivory Springs Café* is the friendliest place, and its cookie-size samosas are satisfyingly tasty; the *Springboard Café*, opposite the KCB, does good snacks; and, opposite the cavernous *Continental Hotel* (a real drinkers' bar even for breakfast), is *African Restaurant*, a butchery and *nyama choma* joint. Also recommended for *nyama choma* is the zebra-striped *Keen Restaurant* on Moi Avenue, which is busier than most, whilst for chicken the place to head for is *Julieta*, next to Consolidated Bank. There's a fresh milk bar next to the KCB bank, and a supermarket – the Self-Choice – 2km up the Nanyuki road at the upper end of town.

If you fancy gyrating the night away, Makutano district is the centre for **nightlife**. Try the sweaty *Club Dimples* disco at the *New Milimani Hotel* (Wednesday ladies' night, Thursday studenty, Friday and Saturday hip-hop and soul, Sunday jams; food available); the barn-like *Hunter's Makuti Village* dance hall, nearly opposite, which sometimes also has live bands; and weekend nights at the classier *Three Steers* (see below). In town, try *Clouds* on Moi Avenue, with the usual Saturday night disco mayhem and a marathon Sunday dance which starts at 3pm.

In keeping with its market-town functions, Meru has no shortage of **accommodation**. If you have transport, there are a few places to consider even before you arrive.

Lodgings on the Nanyuki and Maua roads

Moran Hotel Meru 7km out of town on the Nanyuki road, PO Box 1200 ☎0164/244387. Another "country club" which has clearly seen better times – there's a haunted feel about the empty smoke-filled dining rooms. The pool's pump has been broken for years, and it's all rather damp, and overpriced. ❸

Nanyuki Guest House PO Box 211 ☎0164/20677. Some way out of town on the Maua road, but cheap, clean and very acceptable B&L. ❶

Rocky Hill Inn 8km out of town on the Nanyuki road ☎0164/41321. An ornate construction with chalets among pseudo-Japanese gardens. It has no proper water supply and is perhaps more a weekend *nyama choma* bar than anything else, but for all that, it's endearingly weird (beware the "soup trees") and astonishingly cheap. ❶

Lodgings in town

Brown Rock Hotel PO Box 247 ☎0164/20247. Overlooking Makutano stage and its market, this is a large establishment with cool rooms, though some are a little dark; the rooms up front or higher up are best. Hot water on request. ❶–❷

Hotel Castella PO Box 78 ☎0164/20873. Basic and noisy B&L. ❶

Continental Hotel & Bar PO Box 133 ☎0164/30755. This place would be marginally more inviting than the *Castella* thanks to its larger rooms, if it weren't for the shady drinkers it attracts. ❶

Meru County Hotel PO Box 1386 ☎0164/20432, ⓕ31264. The most modern of Meru's central options and fairly upmarket, with large, bright and breezy s/c balconied rooms (choice of bath or shower), a video lounge and reasonable restaurant. Well run and good value. B&B ❸

New Milimani Hotel Moi Stadium Rd, Makutano, PO Box 9 ☎0164/20224. 2km back up the hill, but better than the *Stansted*. Rooms here are decent and s/c, and the menu long (specialities are curries and *kinyeji*, the Meru version of *irio*: order well in advance). It's also the cheapest place with safe parking in town. Lively and noisy on Wednesday, and non-stop Friday–Sunday, when it hosts the *Club Dimples* disco – but deserted during the week. B&B ❷

Pig and Whistle PO Box 3160 ☎0164/31411. Without doubt the best place in town and well worth the price. Well-appointed individual cottages (concrete or wood, though the latter can get damp), all with telephones and baths, set in pleasant, shaded grounds. The hotel lounges and bar are wooden, with creaking floorboards, and there's an inescapable atmosphere of decaying colonial languor. Affordable menu, and *nyama choma* joint in gardens. ❸

Stansted Lodge PO Box 1337 ☎0164/20360. Just over 1km up the hill from the main matatu stage. Some decent enough rooms, some not;

some hot water, but generally overpriced, run down and not particularly friendly. ➋
Hotel Three Steers PO Box 155 ☎0164/30467, ℱ20634. Two kilometres along the Nanyuki road, this large motel-type complex has good clean rooms (s/c with hot water and telephones), a *nyama choma* joint, two bars and a cheap Indian-influenced restaurant. Loud disco (sometimes with guest bands) Friday and Saturday. Enclosed parking. Overpriced. B&B ➍

Embu and district

From **Meru to Embu**, the fast (and dangerous if going by matatu) road swoops around the eastern slopes of Mount Kenya through brilliant, vibrant scenery. Five kilometres south of Meru, you cross the **equator** once again. Hundreds of streams – run-off from luxuriant rainfall blown in by the south-east monsoon – cut deeply into the volcanic soil of this eastern flank. As a result, this side of the mountain has a much broader covering of jungle, which extends, *shambas* permitting, down to the level of the road and beyond. You plunge from one green and tan gorge to the next, and whether you enjoy the magnificent landscape or not depends on whether you dare take your eyes off the road. If you take an early-morning bus (slow, and considered safe), you can relax and admire. Sit on the right side for glimpses of snow-capped peaks, normally visible at this time of day.

Most public transport stops at **Chogoria**, a base for the eastern Mount Kenya ascent (see p.185), although if you're staying overnight you might consider continuing to the livelier (and friendlier) market town of **CHUKA**, which has a bank with exchange facilities and the *Kimwa Farmer's Hotel* (PO Box 794 ☎0166/30570; ➋), which has recently added the busy *Party Point* disco (mainly *ndombolo* Friday–Sunday, and *nyama choma*), as well as bizarrely decorating its car park with a life-size model of an elephant and a fibreglass replica of Mount Kenya, complete with cascading waterfall. In order to climb Mount Kenya from Embu, you'll need to get yourself over to *Castle Forest Lodge* and the Kamweti route (see p.176).

To Lamu: the cross-country route

Northeast Kenya has been plagued by well-armed bandits, displaced by the Somali civil war, since the 1990s, and the situation seems to be getting worse rather than better. From the Mount Kenya region therefore, the obvious and safest route to the coast is back to Nairobi, then down via Mombasa, from where most people catch a flight to Malindi and then take a bus to Lamu. At the time of writing, Garissa and environs, and the Garissa–Lamu cross-country route were out of bounds. Read Chapter Seven, "The North", and seek local advice if you do decide to go this way.

Thuchi River Lodge

If you have independent transport, or don't mind walking the 3km from the main road, there's **accommodation** on this side of the mountain in the shape of the once charming *Thuchi River Lodge* (PO Box 4 Runyenjes ☎0161/62101; B&B ➌), an establishment left over from the road-building exploits of the French company Kier, who constructed the road from Kangonde to Embu. A definite and uncanny feeling that this was once a thriving retreat, or a party which people abandoned in haste, prevails here. The owner will tell you that the lodge is open for business, but the scattered remnants of a bamboo fence which once separated the lodge from the workers' quarters, seem to tell a different tale. Apart from the occasional monkey in the trees, the place is peaceful and deserted. The accommodation is run down, there is an empty pool, a bar awaiting repairs, restaurant and even a squash court. Located a few hundred metres above the Thuchi River, it's exactly 27km south of Chogoria (29km north of Embu), then 3km east of the main road along the E652 track to nowhere.

Embu town

EMBU, like Meru, is situated at the bottom of a hill. At any rate, the town begins high and descends, with your expectations, to the centre. There's very little to get excited about here, and it's not obvious why it was chosen as the capital of Eastern Province. Certainly, without the apparatus of a provincial headquarters, Embu would amount to little. It does have a number of decent *hotelis*, though: *Morning Glory Hotel*, right opposite *Highway Court Hotel*, is reasonably maintained and serves cheap food (Ksh150 for chicken and chips); *Rehana's Café*, a little way up the hill near the post office, is a busy **eating place**, well known for excellent spicy samosas; and the spotlessly clean, Somali-run *Zamzam Hotel* serves sweetly spiced pilau and *mataha* (rice, maize, beans, vegetables and potatoes all mashed together and eaten with beef). At weekends, *King's Restaurant* on the B6 Nairobi road, 1km out of town beside the Shell station, has local **live music**. E–Touch, behind EMCO House and adjacent to a Catholic bookshop, is part of a chain of **internet cafés** you'll find all over Nairobi and increasingly in smaller towns. Beware though, as browsing can cost as much as Ksh80 per minute in these rural areas.

Accommodation

Should you need or want to spend the night here, there's plenty of choice in all ranges, though quality takes a nose-dive at the really cheap end.

Blueline Delphis PO Box 1576 ☎0161/20607. A friendly, relaxed and very clean new hotel with helpful and polite staff. It also serves gigantic portions of delicious *kienyenji*. Recommended. **❶**
Highway Court Hotel PO Box 354 ☎0161/20046, ℱ30659. By the BP station in the centre. Newish four-storey block with s/c rooms all with nets, good security and safe park-

ing, but not especially clean. It also has a rowdy first-floor disco and bar, so get a room at the top. B&B **❷**
Izaac Walton Inn PO Box 1 ☎0161/20128–9, ℱ30135. At the top end of town on the way in from Meru, this is by far the best option, with pleasant, shaded gardens and a welcoming, vaguely colonial atmosphere, though a little over-

▲ **❶**, **❷** & *Meru (B6)*

EMBU

Library

Kenya Cooperative Bank
Emco House
Exhibition Centre
Supermarket
BP
Bus & Matatu Stage
KCB
Nairobi-Embu Peugeot Service
Market
Mobil

N

0   200 m

▶ *Kitui & Siakago (B7)*

ACCOMMODATION

Blueline Delphis	7
Highway Court	3
Izaac Walton Inn	1
Kenya Scouts	2
Kubu Kubu	6
New Rembo	5
Prime Hotel Embu	4

RESTAURANTS & CAFÉS

King's Restaurant	D
Morning Glory Hotel	B
Rehana's Café	A
Zamzam Hotel	C

▼ **D** *(700 m) & Nairobi (B6)*

priced. Rooms have a choice of baths or showers, and there's a guarded car park. You can get a very satisfying buffet breakfast here for Ksh300 (lunches and dinner cost Ksh600). B&B ❹

Kenya Scouts Hotel PO Box 1859 ☎0161/30459. A few hundred metres further north from *Izaac Walton's*. A welcoming new place with rooms and dorms. ❶

Kubu Kubu PO Box 180 ☎0161/20191. Small, clean and comfortable rooms, 1km down the Kitui road, and a lively bar (*Jamaica*) playing blues and funk and serving good fried chicken. ❶

New Rembo PO Box 934 ☎0161/20647. Five hundred metres down the Kitui road, slightly run-down and unwelcoming, with singles only. ❶

Prime Hotel Embu PO Box 1241 ☎0161/30692. The best of the cheap options (in the town centre). Rooms (s/c) are fresh, with nets, there's hot water daily and it has safe parking. It also has a quiet bar (with pool table) and good *nyama choma* (try the goat). B&B ❷

West of Embu: the Mwea rice scheme

The two-hour trip straight **back to Nairobi** via Sagana is covered by dozens of buses and matatus daily. Sunbird Services buses are fast, but not particularly safe; Akamba's twice-daily run is slower but safer, as are Kensilver's 25-seaters.

Heading west, you begin to leave the red earth and lush vegetation of Mount Kenya behind as the land levels out into a series of intricately irrigated rice paddies, part of the **Mwea rice scheme**. Originally a resettlement area for landless farmers supported by Japanese NGOs and others, things turned sour in 1998–99, when the farmers began protesting against the National Irrigation Board which, being the only body authorized to buy their rice crop, was accused of exploitation in paying them less than the open market rate for their crop. After eight months of boycotts, demonstrations, and sometimes bloody confrontations between farmers and police, the government finally acted by sacking the entire Irrigation Board. The underlying problem, however, remains unchanged, in that the land belongs not to the farmers but the government, making the farmers little more than tenants obliged to grow a crop which they cannot sell freely. If you get stuck around here, most of the roadside villages have basic **accommodation**, the best being the *Makuti Remera* at Wanguru (PO Box 191 Wanguru ☎0163/40428; ❶), with some reasonable non-s/c cottages, and a *nyama choma* bar with occasional live music.

South of Embu: the Kiangombe Hills and Mwea National Reserve

A more leisurely alternative to the main Nairobi road is to head southeast along the tarmacked but rarely driven B7, skirting the intriguing Kiangombe Hills and their main town, Siakago, then past Mwea National Reserve and the huge Tana reservoirs, before reaching the crossroads at Kangonde, with roads west to Thika, east to Garissa (too dangerous to be a recommended route at the time of writing) or south along good *murram* to Kitui in Akambaland (p.371). Most **public transport** from Embu along this route goes to Thika, with only a few matatus bound for Kitui.

Siakago and the Kiangombe Hills

The main centre of the **Kiangombe Hills**, Siakago, can be reached from Embu by matatu five or six times daily, in all conditions except the worst rains. The relatively modest altitudes (Kiangombe peak is 1804m) aren't enough to lure climbers, even those willing to go off the beaten track, but the unspoilt hills, upstaged by Mount Kenya, and ignored by tourists and travellers, are worth a visit if you have an interest in the region's mysterious folklore.

The hills are the home of the **Mbere**, related to the Kikuyu, Embu and Meru. The Mbere have a reputation in Kenya as possessors of magical powers. Some villages have elderly sages, **Arogi**, credited with terrifying abilities, though others – the **Ago** – have more beneficent gifts like the ability to foretell the future or find missing goats. Information is hard to come by; local people either laugh or look blank when directly questioned about such "unprogressive" activities. Yet the *Ago* do make their existence known at critical times, as in 1987 when their bush fires are said to have brought on the delayed rains. And the forest rangers on the hills threaten poachers and illegal firewood-cutters with *Arogi* medicine to make their teeth fall out – witchcraft comes to the aid of conservation.

The identity of these "witches" – at best a hazy and mysterious one which people aren't in any hurry to talk about – is further confused by the supposed existence in the hills of a race of "**little red men**" whose diminutive size (estimated at 1.2m) and fleeting appearance and disappearance in the bush have led the odd, dreaming scientist to suppose that they might be australopithecine – ape-men hanging on into the twenty-first century in their remote forest tracts. They, and the *Ago-Arogi*, may be just part of the "old people" mytho-history of central Kenya, which is at least partially based on the real, ancient and probably Cushitic-speaking peoples of two thousand or more years ago. Such, anyway, are the stories that might draw you from Embu. If you've ever entertained thoughts of seeing a Bigfoot, or a Yeti, or the Loch Ness Monster – and if you kept an eye open for Nandi bears near Eldoret (see p.330) – it's an interesting trip.

Siakago

There are two roads to **SIAKAGO**, either the signposted *murram* road, 5km southeast of Embu on the B7 Kangonde road, which bumps along for some 23km, or along the better D467 *murram* road (11km) from Musonoke, further down the B7. Siakago is an unusually pleasant and relaxed one-street town, all deep-red earth, green vegetation and colourfully painted shop fronts. There's a scattering of *hotelis* (usually combined with butcheries), a petrol station, two B&Ls, a noisy little market (main days Tues & Fri), which mostly sells live stock at extortionate prices, and several mission churches set amid the huts and *shambas* on the outskirts. Siakago isn't a ki-Mbere word and its derivation is uncertain. It may well have derived from "Chicago", along with the group of American anthropologists who based themselves here in the 1930s and started the ape-men stories. The anthropologists were appalled at the **poverty** of the district, whose soil barely supports the population with corn and sorghum and sustains only the scrappiest *shambas* of cotton and tobacco as cash crops. Their plan was to relocate the Mbere to better land, a recommendation fortunately never acted upon. After the horrific famines and cholera outbreaks of the early 1980s, when the district's proximity to well-off Embu meant that they were largely overlooked, conditions began to improve but it did not last, and the Mbere still live a tenuous existence.

In **practical terms**, the very cheap *Check Inn Bar*, 300m down the Embu road (PO Box 157 Siakago; ❶) has basic accommodation and is a good base if you're going hiking. The bar is quite something, with every scrap of wall space covered with luridly imaginative religious murals ("No hiding place in this Wild World – Go to Jesus"), and they can provide food given enough notice. The other B&L is the *Felana Bar & Restaurant* (❶), 1km down the Embu road in a *shamba* with plenty of chickens. The rooms are s/c, and it promises to be "silent and clean".

The Kiangombe Hills

The Kiangombes rise behind Siakago town and look deceptively easy to **climb**. In fact, it's a stiff hike to the top. The main route approaches the summit area from the huts of the **forest rangers' station** beyond the village of Kune, 10km north of Siakago. You should pick up a **guide** at the forestry station, which usually has to be arranged the day before (or write or phone ahead to the Department of Environment and Natural Resources, Provincial Forest Officer, PO Box 2 Embu ☏0161/20683 or 20601). Escorted, you can make it up to the peaks and down again in five or six hours, but it's better as a two-day trip, with a self-contained overnight camp in the hills. Out of Siakago, *dukas* are few and poorly stocked, and there's no commercial accommodation.

There's no transport between Siakago and Kune, so you'll probably have to find your way on foot (unless you're driving), asking as you go. The walk should take about three hours. Once at the forestry station (thirty minutes' hike beyond Kune), ignore the vehicle track which winds into the hills; it's no longer used and soon becomes difficult to follow. Instead, use the **footpath** leading straight up from behind the huts. At any time but the end of the dry season, much of your way is likely to be impeded by thick vegetation. If you're alert to every photographic possibility, you'll find that concentrating on following the overgrown trail is tiresome – especially without a *panga* to trailblaze with. As you climb, human population quickly thins out; this is red-people territory and traditionally feared by the Mbere.

About four hours' hiking from the forest station, you reach the peaks area. From the **mountain meadows** just below the forested peaks, you can look back over the lower hills and down to the hut- and *shamba*-specked plains beyond. With luck, Mount Kenya and the Aberdares can be seen poking through their respective cloudy wreaths. But you may need help from an *Ago*, as well as luck, to see one of the little red people.

The Mwea National Reserve

Daily fees $15, students/children $5; $2 to camp.

Assuming you have your own vehicle (there is no public transport), the easiest way to get to **Mwea National Reserve** is via the B7 Embu–Kangonde road. At Machanga, 15km south of the D467 for Siakago, a signposted *murram* road heads off right for 11km, and is passable all year round. Further along the B7, on the south side of the hydro-electric Kamburu Dam, another signposted road heads in 23km via Masinga Dam from just before the village of Kaewa: the first 11km are tarmac, the remaining 12km *murram* which is liable to be impassable in wet weather. One kilometre to the left, at the end of the tarmac, is the hilltop *Masinga Dam Resort* (bookings through Tana and Athi Rivers Development Authority, PO Box 47309 Nairobi ☏02/535834–5; ❹), overlooking the reservoir and Mount Kenya, which has a choice of rooms (prefab or stone-and-tile with better views), and the benefit of a pool and the off-chance of lifts with workers at the hydro-electric dam. You can have lunch or dinner here for under Ksh500.

The reserve, fenced with electric wire, is well worth the effort if you're looking for solitude and want to avoid the touristy atmosphere in most other parks and reserves. It's a beautiful, peaceful area with a wealth of ornithological interest and wildlife – though hard to see – including giraffes, buffaloes, antelopes, crocs and elephants. With your own tent you can camp either by the main gate or on the sloping site near the shore of the reservoir itself, though swimming is at your own risk – the crocs have a mean reputation.

Around the Aberdares

The **Aberdare range**, which peaks at 4001m, is less well known than Mount Kenya. The lower, eastern slopes have long been farmed by the Kikuyu (more recently by European tea and coffee planters), and the dense mountain forests covering the middle reaches are the habitat of leopard, bongo, buffalo and some six thousand elephants. Above about 3500m, lions and other open-country animals roam the cloudy moorlands. Melanistic forms – especially of leopard, but also of serval cat and even bushbuck – are also present.

The Kikuyu called these mountains *Nyandarua* ("drying hide", for their silhouette) long before Thomson in 1884 named them after Lord Aberdare, president of the Royal Geographical Society. In their bamboo thickets and tangled forests, **Kikuyu guerrillas** hid out for years in the 1950s, living off the jungle and surviving thanks to techniques learned under British officers during the Burma campaign in World War II, in which many of them had fought. Despite the manhunts through the forests and the bombing of hideouts, little damage was done to the natural habitat, and Aberdares National Park remains one of Kenya's most pristine forest reserves.

On the western side, the range drops away steeply to the Rift. It was here, in the high **Wanjohi Valley**, that a concentration of settlers in the 1920s and 1930s created the myth of **Happy Valley** out of their obsessive – and unsettled – lives. There's not much to see (or hear) these days. The old wheat and pyrethrum farms were subdivided after Independence and the valley's new settlers are more concerned with making their market gardens pay. The memories live on only among veteran *wazungu*.

The Kinangop plateau (p.242) was settled by Europeans, too, but the high forest and moorland here was declared **Aberdares National Park** in 1950. The park, which stretches 60km along the length of the peaks, with the "Salient" on the lower slopes reaching out east (access to the Salient only if you're staying at *The Ark* or *Treetops*), includes, like Mount Kenya National Park, the worst of the weather. Rainfall up here is high, often closing the Aberdares to vehicles in the wet season, although the "tree-hotel" game lodges – *The Ark* and *Treetops* – stay open all year. Somewhat inaccessible, the park is nevertheless close enough to Nairobi to be well worth the effort of getting to **Naivasha** or **Nyeri**, the usual bases. You'll find less transport **travelling** in the lower Aberdares than around Mount Kenya, but it's still relatively easy to get around, with regular bus and matatu services between the villages. Heading over the mountains and **through the park**, however, **hitching** is the sole, very uncertain, option if you don't have a vehicle. Determination can pay dividends, but you could wait for days. If you're going to try, it's suggested you stop at the *Outspan Hotel* in Nyeri and try to arrange a lift. If you tire of this, matatu-hop your way towards **Ruhuruini Gate**, deep in the forest, and try waiting at the

△ Chania Falls, Aberdares

gate itself. This, like **Matubio Gate** on the Naivasha side (which you could also probably reach in a half-day of lifts and walking) is friendly and helpful and would certainly allow you to camp.

Nyahururu, the other important town in the region, has **Thomson's Falls** as a postcard attraction, and is also the setting-off point for a wild cross-country journey to Lake Bogoria in the Rift Valley, 1500m below (see Chapter Three). From here, too, begins one of the four routes into the northern deserts (see Chapter Seven), in this case to Maralal and Loiyangalani on the eastern shore of Lake Turkana. Though independent travel is still an option on this route, going up in the safety of a safari company's organized trip is recommended.

Aberdares National Park

Daily fees $27, children $10; $8 to camp, $15 in "special" campsites. Entry on foot with permission of the warden: PO Box 22 Nyeri ☎ 0171/55024 or Mweiga ☎ 24.

If you're **driving** into the park (which is the only really practicable way to do it, other than going by organized safari), you need four-wheel drive – it can rain at any time and the route across the mountains is sometimes closed during heavy rains. It's also a very sensible idea to have two spare wheels.

Once you're in, it's a beautiful drive, with waterfalls and sensational views more than compensating for comparatively scarce **wildlife**: buffalo, elephants (and colobus monkeys lower down) are most often seen. For animals in quantity, and for any real chance of seeing rhinos, giant forest hog, or the Aberdares' prize inhabitant, the bongo antelope, you really have to spend a night at one of the two **game-viewing lodges**, *The Ark* or *Treetops* – expensive perhaps, but not an experience you're likely to forget (see p.213).

There are several **accommodation** options in the high park, most easily accessed through the Kiandongoro Gate. The first, barely 2km inside the gate, is the self-help *Kiandongoro Fishing Lodge*, located on open moors above the Magura River. There are two stone-built, tin-roofed cottages, each with three separate bedrooms of two, four and six beds. You book as much space as you need through the warden (or take a chance and pay at the park gate), and share the central open-fire cooking and eating area with other guests. You need to take everything with you except water – food, warm sleeping bags, firewood. Wood-fired boiler tanks outside will produce hot water. Sadly, rumours abound of its possible closure – check at the park gates or with the authorities in Mweiga (PO Box 24). The other self-service option is *Sapper Hut* (reservations through Let's Go Travel in Nairobi, p.141; Ksh2000 for the hut; collect key from the *Fishing Lodge*), some 10km further west on a little tributary of the Chania River at around 3000m altitude. It consists of a wooden *banda* with a living room, double bedroom, fireplace, verandah and wood-fired boiler, but no shower, lamps, bedsheets or firewood, and only basic cooking facilities. Lower down (2300m), tucked into a glade surrounded by forest, there's the good *Tusk Camp*, 2km in from Ruhuruini Gate (reservations also through Let's Go). There are several wooden *bandas* here, an ill-equipped kitchen (bring pots, pans and cutlery), a pit latrine with one of Kenya's most regal views, and a caretaker to help you out. The catch is that you have to rent the entire place (Ksh5000) rather than just one *banda*. As for *Sapper Hut*, take bedding, towels, kerosene (for the lights), food and drinking water. Visits from here to the normally closed "Salient" sector of the park should be possible if you enquire first with the rangers at the gate; they used to levy a Ksh2000 fee for the admission key.

ABERDARES NATIONAL PARK

0   10 km

Nyahururu

Gilgil & Nyahururu

Shamata Gate

Rhino Gate

SOLIO GAME RANCH

Engore Ngobit River

KAREMENO TRIANGLE

SECTION IMPASSABLE

Satima (4001m)

Table Mountain

Maratini Hill

Hani River

Amboni River

Wanderis Gate

THE SALIENT

The Ark

Thaara River

Aberdare Country Club

Mweiga

Kiganjo

Kiganjo & Nanyuki

Tusk Camp

Treetops

Ruhuruini Gate

Chania Falls

Sapper Hut

Chania River

Tusha

Nyeri

Kiandongoro Gate

Naivasha

Reedbuck Campsite

Kiandongoro Fishing Lodge

Matubio Gate

Gura River

Kiganjo & Nanyuki

Nairobi (A2)

Othaya

Karuru River

Karura Falls

Gura Falls

Gura River

Kinangop (3906m)

Surfaced road
Track
Mountain grassland
Mountain rainforest

Murang'a

For **camping**, the basic *Reedbuck Campsite* near the *Fishing Lodge* is the only public site in the park. There are a number of "special campsites", but these are very expensive (Ksh5000 reservation fee, plus $15 per person per night), are equally bereft of facilities and were, in any case, closed until recently and, though open at the moment, may close again in future. Your last camping option is to be accompanied by an armed ranger.

The high moorlands have some exceptional **walking** and the three peaks – Satima (the highest) in the north, Kinangop in the south, and Kipipiri, an isolated cone outside the park above the Wanjohi Valley, in the west – can be climbed relatively easily, given good weather conditions: ask the Mountain Club of Kenya in Nairobi for details (see p.59). Hiking in the park is allowed only with the approval of the warden, so apply in good time. You may be offered, or required to take, a guide (whom you'll have to pay). If you drive, it's usually permissible to wander a short distance from your car. The situation changes from time to time – over the years there have been a number of near-misses with several, apparently human-hungry lions.

Road conditions vary considerably from one period of heavy rain to the next, and you really need to check this with the rangers at the park gates. Surfaces are mostly red *murram*, though there are a few, very steep, rocky sections.

Through the park

The park splits into two different environments – the **high moorland and peaks** which form the park's main body, and the lower **Salient** to the east where the vegetation is dense rain forest and there is considerably more wildlife. The Salient slopes (location of *Treetops* and *The Ark*) are closed to casual visitors; all the earth access roads have locked barriers. You can get keys to these, in theory, from the warden in Mweiga, or possibly from the rangers at the eastern gates (but not from Matubio Gate in the west).

In the mid-1990s, the government pledged to establish a wholly enclosed **wildlife sanctuary** in this area, partly to protect the park's sixty black rhino (the largest indigenous population left in Kenya), but mainly to arrest the conflict between wildlife and humans, which most visibly manifested itself in the trashing of crops and homes fringing the park by "rogue" or "rampaging" elephants. To this end, the rangers are currently busy clearing a path on which to erect some 380km of electrified fence (120km has already been erected). More information on the project can be obtained from Rhino Ark, PO Box 63410 Nairobi (℡02/749655, ℻748750 or 740721, ⓦ www.rhinoark.org.uk).

Unless you're planning several days of walking, fishing or camping, the most straightforward visit to the moorlands is to spend a day driving through from one side to the other between the main gates. There are two other eastern gates

Rhino Charge

Once a year, the exciting and potentially hair-raising **Rhino Charge motor race** takes place at different places around Kenya, attracting adventurers from across the globe. Since the first charge in 1989, the race, along with other fund-raising events, has raised over $1.3m (money contributed almost entirely by individual donors) for the Rhino Ark fencing project taking place in the Aberdares.

Anyone with a car can take part in this test of endurance, engineering and navigational skills across Kenya's rugged and beautiful terrain but, for environmental reasons, numbers are limited to a maximum of fifty vehicles and a strict policy of first-come first-allowed-to-drive is observed. The challenge is to reach ten control posts, set up in remote locations and whose whereabouts are only revealed to the entrants the night before the event. The teams of up to six people set off at dawn with ten arduous hours of driving ahead of them. Speed is not the objective, rather the contenders have to reach all ten checkpoints by the shortest route possible and the winner is the team that completes the course with the least distance recorded. For bookings and enquiries see Basics, p.58.

211

further from Nyeri (Wanderis and Kiandongoro) and two at the remote north end of the park (Shamata, accessible from Nyahururu, and Rhino Gate, from the B5 Nyeri–Nyahururu road), but there's no reliable route through the park from south to north, and the small circuit of tracks in the north is very rough. Driving via the park from Naivasha to Nyeri (or vice versa) is easy enough in good weather. If conditions are less than ideal, however, and you get stuck, you could be in for a long day – or a rather miserable night.

Naivasha to Matubio Gate

From Naivasha, follow the signs for the park via the Uplands road as if going to Nairobi, as far as the junction for Kinangop on the north side of town. From here, you climb about 14km, on reasonably intact tarmac, to another junction where the bad road begins. Go easy if you're driving – the cambered, rock-built surface is perfect for punctures. After another 5km or so, you reach Kipipiri junction and, seasonally, a strange egret nesting colony in eleven conifers along the roadside.

At **Ndunyu Njeru** centre, you pass the last chance of a puncture repair or petrol (fuel isn't always available) and the final stop of matatus up from Naivasha, before a few more kilometres of very bad surface. Finally, the road runs out of reasons to continue except to the National Park itself – becoming a narrow, quite acceptable, tarmac switchback that is apparently fifty years old – and climbs through the vegetation zones, with increasing evidence of elephants (dung everywhere), to pitch out finally through the highest extent of the forest to Matubio Gate, right on the threshold of the moorland. Along the last 7km there are some excellent views back over the climb and down to Lake Naivasha. Allow two to three hours to get this far.

Matubio Gate to Ruhuruini Gate

Allowing four hours from Matubio Gate to Ruhuruini Gate gives time enough, in good weather, for visits to the Chania Falls and the Karura Giant Falls.

Proper access to the top of the **Karura Falls** (there's no way down to the bottom) was only built in 1992, by the British Army's Royal Engineers, and they've created two superb, dizzy, timber viewpoints, one on each side, from which you can look across through dripping, Afro-Alpine vegetation, to the babbling, four-metre-wide Karuru stream as it plunges over the abyss, dropping nearly 300m in three stages. To the south, the distant veil of the **Gura Falls**, a kilometre or two across the yawning canyon, seems to make for a surfeit of dramatic beauty.

The much lower, sheer drop of the **Chania Falls** has old, rickety access walks and platforms (be very careful if they have not been replaced) and you can gaze from the top, or the bottom, and even contemplate a swim in the pool. It was in this vicinity, in 1984, that an American tourist was badly mauled by a lion, an incident that so unnerved the park's authorities that for many years there were tough rules on unaccompanied walking. This followed a controlled lion cull, aimed as much at public relations as at giving various herbivores (such as giant forest hog and bongo) a chance to rebuild their endangered populations. A cautionary sign by the path still warns about "wild animals", though there seems no reason to believe they favour this spot over any other.

Turning east, the 15km to **Ruhuruini Gate** descends in a breathtaking helter-skelter through the cloud forest, with stunning views across the jungle-cloaked valleys. Once out of the gate, the road down to Nyeri is in good condition and you soon reach tarmac.

The "tree-hotels"

For many visitors, a night in one of the two Aberdare "tree-hotels" is the stuff of dreams. Located in the park's otherwise inaccessible Salient area, the only visitors allowed in are guests of either *Treetops* or *The Ark* (on the lodge's own transport), which heightens the air of exclusivity since you cannot visit in advance to check them out. This multi-million-dollar industry is the closest you'll get on a package tour to "living bush", and the fact that both hotels are usually booked solid, and not just by safari-suited tour groups, affirms the attraction. Yet, having invested heavily for a night, both *Treetops* and *The Ark* can at first be a disappointment. After all the hype, you find yourself confined to the interior of a wooden building with a hundred or more fellow tourists, are shown to your tiny bedroom, and are then briefed on the animals you can hope to see and the things you're not allowed to do. It can all feel somewhat contrived.

But when the sun goes down and the floodlights come on, it's strange how quickly this is forgotten; the wildlife below draws everyone's attention and the cameras start clicking in earnest. Herds of heavyweights – elephant and buffalo especially – can be taken for granted, and the prospect of a night's sleepless vigil becomes magical, as even your cramped confines acquire a certain charm.

Treetops

Reservations through Block, p.42. Minimum age 7 years (no child rates), except on occasional "children's nights"; FB ❼ low, ❾ high, including lunch at the Outspan Hotel (see p.216). Aberdares National Park entry fees are extra ($27 each).

Perhaps Kenya's most famous hotel, **Treetops** was where Princess Elizabeth became Queen Elizabeth II, on the death of her father George VI, while she was staying in the original *Treetops* on the other side of the water hole. The original tree house was looted and burned down in 1955 by Mau Mau freedom-fighters; the present, much larger building is built on stilts among the trees. The lodge itself is tremendous fun, with growing branches of Cape chestnut twisting through the public rooms, and a dining room with trestle tables and polished benches. Intentionally like an officers' mess, it has something of the creaking atmosphere of a wooden ship. Last renovated in 1996, the bedrooms and shared facilities are nonetheless cramped. What you're paying for is the experience of *Treetops* – the opportunity to breathe the same air as the rich and famous. Photographs and letters framed on the varnished walls hark as far back as the 1930s and various royal and state visits.

During daylight hours, reality is never far below the surface. Through the forest, Kikuyu *shambas* and homesteads are visible in every direction and the main Nyeri road passes by just 3km away. The lodge is no longer *in* the forest, either. Down by the **water hole**, a large area is now virtually bare – red dust and dead wood – the result of foliage destruction by elephants. One patch has even been fenced in to protect new plant growth. The problem, as always, is balancing tourist receipts with the needs of wildlife – which themselves conflict with those of farmers on the slopes nearby. Many of the animals which come to *Treetops* are lured by the **salt** which is spread beneath the viewing platform every afternoon before the visitors arrive. This draws large herds of elephant and buffalo, but only very few rhino, and in the long term it would seem to ensure the ruination of the environment around the lodge. It certainly discourages those animals that need plenty of cover. The curious **giant forest hog** sometimes turns up, but **leopards** are rarely seen and the large **bongo**, that "shy and elusive forest antelope", hasn't put in an appearance for many years – understandably.

The Ark

Reservations through Lonrho, p.43. Minimum age 7 years (no child rates), except on occasional "children's nights"; FB ❼ low, ❾ high, including lunch at Aberdare Country Club (see p.216). Aberdares National Park entry fees are extra ($27 each).

For better game-viewing, **The Ark**, *Treetops'* upstart competitor, is set at a higher altitude, actually in the mountain forest. Here, they do on occasion see leopards (and, perhaps once a year, bongos), and there are almost guaranteed nightly sightings of elephant, rhino and buffalo. Transport from the *Aberdare Country Club* leaves daily at 2.30pm and 5pm, returning at 8am. You should try to get an afternoon nap as you'll be woken by buzzers through the night announcing the arrival of one of the "big five". The attraction for wildlife is the muddy pool and saltlick at the "prow" of the hotel, under the viewing terraces and next to a ground-level photographic hide. There's usually an animated scene here as the animals jostle for salt, and fights sometimes break out, especially when new-born calves are around. The accommodation has recently been comprehensively upgraded, but don't expect luxury; the rooms are still small, poky and dark.

Nyeri and around

Self-styled capital of Kikuyuland – a title the Kikuyu of Kiambu might dispute – **NYERI** is, more prosaically, the administrative headquarters of Central Province and one of the liveliest, most chaotic and friendly highland towns. Another former British military camp, it emerged as a market town for European coffee growers in the hills and for settlers on the ranching and wheat farms further north. Located beneath the Aberdares, it was on the front line – as much as there was one – during the war for Independence. Of more specialist interest, Nyeri was also the last home of Robert Lord **Baden-Powell**, founder of the worldwide scouting movement, whose cryptically named Paxtu cottage, now a small museum (Ksh250), stands in the grounds of the *Outspan Hotel* and whose grave and memorial are to be found on the north side of town.

An active, and attractive, trading centre despite its fantastically broken-up streets, Nyeri nestles in the green hills where the broad vale between Mount Kenya and the Aberdares drops towards Nairobi. Tumultuous markets, scores of *dukas*, and even a few street entertainers playing on soda bottles and bottle tops, lend it an air of irrepressible commercialism.

Recent history

The extraordinary density of **cultivation** in the tightly spaced *shambas* around Nyeri (maize, beans, potatoes, cassava, bananas, sugar cane, millet, squash and melons, tomatoes, citrus fruit, cabbages and carrots, as well as tea, coffee and macadamia nuts) is partly a hangover from white settlerdom, when a rapidly growing population was deprived of huge tracts of land and forced to cultivate intensively. Partly, too, it's the result of land consolidation: the "rationalization" of fragmented land holdings into unitary *shambas* that took place in the 1950s and turned people who had held traditional rights into deed-holding property owners. And partly, it's the simple consequence of an excellent climate and soil plus a birth rate reckoned (like Kisii's, see p.318) to be one of the highest in the world.

There's no doubt that the **changes** which have taken place in Nyeri District have been some of the most profound and rapid anywhere in the country. Even the villages of Kikuyuland are nearly all innovations of the last forty years, the irreversible effects of the Emergency. Until then, the Kikuyu had mostly lived in scattered homesteads among their crops and herds. British security forces, unable to contain open revolt in the countryside, began the systematic internment of the whole Kikuyu population into fenced and guarded villages, forcing the guerrillas into the high forests, and the villages of today have mostly grown from such places.

On Nyeri's main street, Kimathi Way, is a cenotaph, unusual in the frankness of its inscription: "To the Memory of the Members of the Kikuyu Tribe who Died in the Fight for Freedom 1951–1957".

Practicalities

The town has three **banks**, two branches of Barclays and a Standard Chartered, all with ATMs. **Email** facilities are available at Niblo Stationers on Kimathi Way.

Accommodation

Nyeri's role as rural business centre and major transport crossroads means there are plenty of **cheap places to stay** in town, as well as the historical and upmarket *Outspan Hotel* (see over).

April 27 Hotel off Kimathi Way, PO Box 316 ☎0171/2817. Very cheap, and with hot water, but get there early to be sure of a room. ❶

Bahati Restaurant & Lodging Kimathi Way, PO Box 148 ☎0171/71491. Basic, but clean, B&L (not s/c), with a popular restaurant. ❶

Central Hotel Kanisa Rd, PO Box 229 ☎0171/2235. Clean, secure and cheap, with s/c rooms (some with balconies). There's no better place to eat *kienyenji*, and breakfast is good too. It also has a new mini bar with a one-man guitar show every Friday and Saturday. Good value. B&B ❷

Crested Eagle Hotel PO Box 12465 ☎0171/4933. A good high-rise with standard s/c rooms and safe parking, but it's expensive and the *Zebra Bar* makes things noisy up until midnight. ❹

Greenhills Hotel Bishop Gatimu Rd, 1km south of town PO Box 313 ☎0171/30604, ℱ2199. The biggest hotel with the best facilities (*Outspan* excepted), close to the golf course with extensive gardens and lawns. There's a pool, restaurants and bar, and it can be noisy on Wednesday, Friday and Saturday nights due to its popular discos. ❹

Greenoak Restaurant PO Box 2169 ☎0171/2726. Friendly and safe, with fairly decent s/c rooms with 24hr hot water. The bar has great views over the street corner, and the restaurant is one of the best (see below). Recommended. ❶

Ibis Hotel Kanisa Rd ☎0171/4858 or 72777. Noisy at times, with dodgy security, but it's a good budget choice, with large, clean s/c rooms with nets. ❶

Kimathi Way Motel PO Box 2188 ☎0171/2799. A cheap lodging, with filling meals, but noisy (especially at weekends) and not terribly clean. ❶

Nyeri Inn 3.2km down the Kiganjo road, 1.5km from the Nyahururu junction, PO Box 159 ☎0171/31092. A gem if you don't mind staying outside town. Set in calm, tree-shaded gardens (ideal for kids), its offers several large, airy two-bed cottages for rent, each s/c with baths and hot water. Its restaurant serves mainly chicken. No security problems. Recommended. B&B ❷

Thingira Guest House off Kenyatta Rd, PO Box 221 ☎0171/4769. One of the nicest cheapies, close to the town centre, but with none of its bustle. The management are friendly, rooms (s/c) are clean, but there is no hot water. ❷–❸

White Rhino Hotel Kenyatta Rd, PO Box 30 ☎0171/4384. A laid-back atmosphere and *the* place for conscientious boozing. A shabby colonial hotel, reasonable rooms, nice gardens. ❸

The Outspan Hotel

Two kilometres west of the clocktower on Kanisa Road, off the Kiandongoro Gate Road, the *Outspan* (PO Box 24 Nyeri ☎0171/2424–26, ℱ2286; reservations through Block, p.42; B&B ❻ low, ❼ high), built in 1927, is the stately base for visits to *Treetops* (see p.213), where you check-in for lunch and are driven up in the afternoon. Set in beautiful gardens, with Mount Kenya rising behind, it offers more than enough reasons for staying here, too. The rooms vary in size, the larger ones being huge, with wonderful old baths, as well as more modern facilities (including satellite TV) in the new Chania Wing. There's a pool, and some good walks along the Chania riverbank down on the fringes of the lovely gardens, though you have to go with a guard from the hotel (Ksh150, or Ksh300 for a bird walk). With the right approach, though, you might find yourself a lift over the Aberdares – but ask early in the day, when people would be setting off, rather than later. Adjacent to the hotel is Nyeri Sports Club with its 3316-yard **nine-hole golf course**, the second oldest in Kenya, founded in 1910. It's also possible to arrange **day-trips** to the **Aberdares National Park** from here, which work out cheaper the more people you go with.

The Aberdare Country Club

Situated 11km out on the Nyahururu road near Mweiga, then 3km along a passable *murram* road (signposted), the luxuriously rural *Aberdare Country Club* (PO Box 449 Nyeri ☎0171/55620, ℱ55224, ℮ark@form-net.com; ❻ low, ❼ high) is the base for *The Ark* "tree-hotel" (see p.214). Like the *Outspan*, it's an exceptionally nice and atmospheric place, dating from 1938, with rooms in stone cottages (numbers 28 to 31 have the best views), and a wealth of things to do. For non-guests, the temporary membership fee (Mon–Thurs Ksh300, Fri–Sun Ksh500) includes use of the pool, nine-hole golf course (clubs and caddie extra; local rules award six inches grace if the ball lands on animal droppings or rolls into an aardvark's hole), tennis courts, and a visit (on foot) to their game sanctuary with its comical warthogs, reticulated giraffe, zebra, eland, waterbuck, impala et al. They also organize very reasonable Aberdares game drives (Ksh1300 plus park entry), horse riding (Ksh1600 per person for 1hr), and trips to Solio Game Ranch (Ksh7000 for a seven-seater vehicle, plus Ksh1600 per person entry fee; see p.218). Despite its popularity, it remains classy, and visitors are rarely disappointed.

Eating, drinking and nightlife

Nyeri has a number of interesting **eating** options. It also has a **cheese** factory – lots of its produce is available locally. There are also discos at the *Green Hills Hotel*, where Sunday afternoons feature traditional dances, and the *White Rhino Hotel* is a popular place for whiling away an afternoon with a bottle or five.

Bahati Restaurant & Lodging Kimathi Way. Known for its chicken cooked any way you want it, so long as it's fried or stewed.

Café de Ficus Kenyatta Rd. A bar with conspicuous booths, the only food available is *nyama choma*.

Greenoak Restaurant This is surprisingly good, dishing up great trout and *nyama choma*. If the weather's OK, the first-floor terrace-bar, overlooking the commotion below, is fun too.

Nyeri Cinema Beer garden and restaurant, *nyama*

choma, and an ice-cream parlour next to *Batian Tusker Bar*.

Outspan Hotel (see opposite). This atmospheric pile welcomes day-visitors for its excellent (if expensive) buffet lunches, or for tea on the lawn and a swim in the pool (Ksh200). The hotel's *Kirinyaga Bar* is pleasant enough for a beer in the evening in civilized surroundings, but it's not overly stimulating.

Zebra Bar at the *Crested Eagle Hotel*. A busy bar, open till midnight.

Routes out of Nyeri

A signposted route leads **west**, past the *Outspan*, up into the Aberdares and the park's Kiandongoro Gate in the high moorland. In the other direction, the road splits out of town, forking **south** to Murang'a via Othaya, or continuing **east** to the A2 Mount Kenya ring road and the quickest return route to Nairobi (also via Murang'a).

A fourth route takes you in a northwest direction heading out of town, splitting in two after 2km. Keep straight on if you want the A2 Mount Kenya ring road for Naro Moru and Nanyuki via Kiganjo. Fork left and the road (the B5) sweeps past the track for the Ruhuruini Gate in the forest of the Salient, then the unmarked tracks for *Treetops* and *The Ark* – with the turning for the *Aberdare Country Club* (see opposite) between them, just before the hilltop centre of **Mweiga**. The highway continues, in excellent condition, across lonely, forested ridges and wide savannah to Nyahururu (Thomson's Falls), on the northern fringes of the Highlands.

Sangare Ranch

Near Mweiga, you'll find Kenya's possibly most charming luxury tented camp, **Sangare Ranch** (reservations through *Savannah Camps & Lodges*, p.44; FB ❾). Access is via the *Aberdare Country Club*, either by matatu to the signboard near Mweiga (leaving you with a three-kilometre walk), or by car or taxi. The ranch will pick you up in their own 4WD from the club. Located some 5km north of the club, the landscape and atmosphere could hardly be more different: the track winds up and down precarious forested ravines before emerging onto a fresh high plateau of scrub and meadow with a good view of Mount Kenya when the air is clear. There are only six tents, each with wood-heated showers and solar-powered light, sited on the east side of a small freshwater lake. The **birdlife** is the main draw, with black-headed herons squawking loudly in the trees over the tents, some migratory pelican, and glimpses of crowned eagle, accompanied by a fantastic chorus of frogs and toads throughout the night. There are usually some elephants and buffalo in the vicinity, as well as zebra, gazelle, hyena, colobus and Sykes' monkeys, and the occasional leopard. The style is refreshingly informal, with superb farmhouse meals (cottage pie, treacle sponge pudding and the like) eaten in a small dining room with the manager and the camp's excellent botanical and wildlife guide. Horse riding is possible, as are guided walks to a nearby cave used by the Mau Mau in the 1950s, and night walks in search of bats, bushbabies, mongoose and the apparently beautiful maned rat. If you have the money, it's highly recommended.

Solio Game Ranch

Continuing westwards along the B5 from Mweiga, the **Solio Game Ranch** (PO Box 2 Naro Moru ☎02/249177 or locally ☎0171/55271–3, ℱ55235; single entry fee of Ksh1600, children under 12 free; open all year unless very wet) lies a few kilometres further on, off to the right. Privately run, Solio more or less single-handedly saved the Kenyan rhino population from extinction, by breeding them here for them to be subsequently translocated into the national parks and other Kenyan reserves. The figures speak for themselves. From an original population of 23 black rhino, there are now over 50; of the original 16 white rhino, imported from South Africa, the population now stands at over 70; and all of the relocated black rhinos, and most of the white, at Nakuru National Park's Rhino Sanctuary were bred here. Without 4WD, you can visit the ranch by hiring a vehicle and driver, or by joining a trip at the *Aberdare Country Club*. If you have your own wheels, the ranch provides maps, and a guide if there's one available (free). They have four basic campsites (water and firewood provided; Ksh400 per person). See also the section on Laikipia on p.194.

For a less conventional view of wildlife, the Gliding Club of Kenya operates from a field 2km south of Mweiga (contact Peter or Petra Allmendinger ☎ & ℱ0171/2748, ✉gliding@africaonline.co.ke; $50 for 10min), with two-seater aircraft and instructors available to introduce you to the sport.

Nyahururu (Thomson's Falls)

Like Nanyuki, **NYAHURURU** is almost on the equator, and it shares much of Nanyuki's character. It's high (at 2360m, Kenya's highest town), cool (in fact, very cold on January and February mornings), and set on open savannah lands with patches of indigenous forest and plenty of coniferous plantation. Since the fast, B5 road to Nyeri was completed, Nyahururu has been less cut off, but still there's an air of slightly wild isolation about it. It's something of a frontier town for routes heading north to Lake Turkana and the desert; a tarred road goes out as far as Rumuruti and then the fun begins (see p.600). Other roads join Nyahururu with Nanyuki (the C76, an extremely bad road, but good for game-viewing), Gilgil (p.247), and Nakuru and the remainder of the northern Rift Valley (p.251).

Joseph Thomson gave the town its original name when he named the nearby waterfall after his father in 1883. Many still call it "T Falls" – and not just the old settlers you might expect. Thomson's Falls was one of the last set-

Rumuruti & Maralal (C77)

NYAHURURU

Nakuru via Subukia (B5)

Nyeri (B5) & Nanyuki (C76)

The Falls

N

Manguo River

Catholic Church

Kenya Commercial Bank

Hospital

Co-op Bank

Mobil

Police Station

Barclays Bank

Railway Station (no passengers)

Town Hall

Nyahururu Stadium & A.S.K. Showground

Cinema

Heri General Merchants

Covered Market

HOSPITAL ROAD

Market

Total

Clocktower

BP

BP

KENOL

Maralal Bus & Matatu Stand

Muruthi Supermarket

Bus & Matatu Stage

Market

ACCOMMODATION

Baron	5
Cyrus Lodging	7
Equatorial	6
Good Shepherd B&L	2
Kawa Falls Hotel	8
Nyahururu Stadium	4
Nyaki Hotel	3
Thomson's Falls Lodge	1

RESTAURANTS

Double Visions	A
Gateway Restaurant	B
Muthengera Farmers Lodge	C

0   200 m

8 (200m), Gilgil (C77) & Ol Kalou

tler towns to be established. The first sign of urbanization was a hut built by the Narok Angling Club in the early 1920s to allow its members to fish for the newly introduced trout in the Ewaso Narok, Pesi and Equator rivers. In 1929, when the railway branch line arrived, the town began to take shape. The line has closed now, but the hotel built in 1931, *Thomson's Falls Lodge*, is still going strong, and Nyahururu remains an important market town – and not, in any sense, a tourist centre. Local people can react rather oddly to the presence of travellers in Nyahururu's lodging houses. If you're staying in town, be sensitive to the fact that some think you should stay in the lodge by the falls.

Thomson's Falls – and walks in the area

The falls themselves are pretty rather than spectacular – though they can be dramatic after heavy rain. They're a popular stop-off for tourists travelling between Samburu and Maasai Mara game reserves (fourteen minibuses at one time is nothing), and the lawns above the falls get crowded with picnickers from town at weekends. The souvenir-sellers on the cliff edge have learned to be less aggressive and, when the crowds leave, they're good company, if you want it. The town council's plan to evict them in order to make room for the tourist pavilion of a local political heavy, has so far seen no results.

The path leading down to the bottom of the 75-metre falls is somewhat dangerous, especially when wet. But certainly don't attempt to climb up again by any other route, because the cliffs are extremely unstable. With several hours to spare, you can search for a longer **walk** down into the forested valley, following the Ewaso Narok River. If you want to try this, cross the bridge first, then look for a way downstream. The spray-laden trees are shaken periodically by troops of colobus monkeys and, as on Mount Kenya, three-horned chameleons are always around if you look hard. This area is also fruitful for ornithologists – recent sightings include a crowned eagle with a colobus monkey in its claws.

A much shorter stroll also takes you over the bridge and past the electricity substation, beyond which the first trail you come to leads to the top of a hill with a communications tower and a skeletal lookout post. Excellent views from here stretch south towards Ol Kalou and the marshy trough of Lake Ol' Bolossat.

Another nearby stroll takes you in quest of the highest **hippos** in Kenya. Incredible as it seems, several hippos do live in the swampy area a kilometre or two back upriver above the falls. A kilometre from the turning off to the *Lodge* on the Nyeri road, you come to a small cluster of *dukas* on the right. Walk down towards the houses closest to town and, about 300m from the road, you emerge by Lake Ol' Bolossat. Immediately by the access path, the area is thick with reeds, but walk round the lake to the clump of trees and you can shin up one of these and select a natural observation platform. Sit and watch and you may see as many as six hippos. A remarkable sight, considering that immediately beyond them, on the other side of the lake, is a slum town, gradually encroaching on the natural habitat. The continual survival of these unique hippos will increasingly depend on the growth of the slum. Various organizations, including the management of *Thomson's Falls Lodge*, are pressing the local government to act before its too late, but the future of the animals remains bleak.

Thomson's Falls Lodge

For **accommodation**, most people do head out to the touristy lodge (PO Box 38 ℡0365/22006, 🖷32170; reservations in Nairobi on ℡02/340311, 🖷340311; B&B ③–④), which has recently had a facelift and is under new management. If you are content with nothing too fancy, it's good value, with its solid, Highlands-farmhouse atmosphere and log fires in the rooms. Some have big old-fashioned baths, others rather more basic showers – ask to see a selection. Service can be overbearing, the food is good, but avoid the coffee. Alternatively, you can **camp** in the grounds, still within earshot of the falls. The campsite (Ksh300 per person; no tents for rental) is popular with budget safari groups. The price includes showers and ample firewood; again, you need to specifically ask for them.

Accommodation in town

If the rooms at the lodge are out of your price range and you don't have a tent, the next place down is something of a drop. The *Kawa Falls Hotel*, 400m past the end of the market on the Ol Kalou road (PO Box 985 ℡0365/32295, 🖷32256; B&B ②), is a relaxed and friendly five-storey block with basic, if slightly damp and poky, s/c rooms, with safe parking, an airy first-floor bar, and it's away from the noise and hassling street kids in the centre. On the other side of town, an almost identical building houses the *Nyaki Hotel* (PO Box 214

T0365/22313; ❸), overpriced apart from its cheap singles (Ksh200), but it has recently been renovated and is in better condition than its rival. Cheaper is the *Baron Hotel*, a "tourist-class" establishment right in the centre at the start of the Ol Kalou road (PO Box 423 T0365/32056; ❷), but it suffers greatly from the loud *Equatorial Hotel* over the road and the matatu stage next door, the former jumping till 4am, the latter honking from 6am. Cheaper and much better if you don't mind the deeply religious atmosphere is the friendly and clean *Nyahururu Stadium Hotel* (PO Box 152 T0365/22608; ❶) by the ASK showground, above the Karabui Gospel Music Store; it also has good security. The *Good Shepherd B&L*, in a traditional compound by the *Nyaki Hotel*, has singles only (❶). *Equatorial Hotel*, also s/c and with a *nyama choma* joint and pool tables (and music most nights), and *Cyrus Lodging* (both ❶) are on the Ol Kalou road, opposite the matatu and market enclosure.

For **meals**, try *Gateway Restaurant*'s fried tilapia down the alley by the cinema, whilst *Muthengera Farmers Lodge* is recommended for chicken. There's more meat at *Double Visions*, a *nyama choma* joint next door to the *Nyaki Hotel*. Vegetarians should head for the *Cyrus*'s own restaurant, *Arafa*.

Whether eating out or not, the **market** is well worth a browse, especially on Saturdays. Find it anywhere west of the stadium – it sprawls out over most of the district, an indication of the town's rapid growth over the last decade or so.

For action after dark, check out the *Equatorial Hotel*'s **disco**, which has reggae and soukous (sometimes live) till midnight, and soul divas on tape later on. For more action in the dark, the **cinema** has showings twice every evening, with an extra matinée on Sundays for those escaping church. There is **email** access at Heri General Merchants, on Sharpe Road, half way between Barclays Bank and the clock tower.

Moving on from Nyahururu

There are several buses and matatus each day down to Nyeri, or you could hitch from outside the *Lodge*. The road was built, for most of its length, along a new route, so villages are few; for the most part it either bucks up and down across forested valleys or soars across immense plains of swaying grass. It's a fast road not much used by heavy transport and still in relatively good condition.

Nyahururu's other transport connections are mentioned below in the Travel Details. Remember, the unsurfaced road to Nanyuki can be treacherous in wet weather. For a spectacular change of scene, take the road down the **scarp** to Nakuru, via the Subukia Valley, following the route to Lake Bogoria described in Chapter Three.

Travel details

Buses and matatus

Around Mount Kenya

Unless you have a specific destination in mind, simply getting to the next town on the circuit is always easy, as there are frequent matatus from 6am to 6pm. Buses connect all the larger towns with each other, but run less frequently than matatus. Nyeri is something of an exception, where matatus all but monopolize the routes. Nanyuki–Nyahururu, Nanyuki–Isiolo and Nyahururu-Nakuru also have limited bus services. Eldoret Express runs helpful daily buses to Western Province, from Nyeri via Nyahururu, Nakuru and

Eldoret to Kitale. Nanyuki, Meru, Nyeri and Nyahururu all have at least one direct daily service to Nairobi, often more.

Around the Aberdares

From Nyahururu to Nyeri and vice versa, take the daily service between Nakuru and Nairobi, via the east side of the Aberdares.

To Rumuruti and Maralal (see Chapter Seven): two daily buses, but the last through bus leaves at 11am (5–6hr).

To Gilgil: frequent country bus and matatu runs; some go on to Nairobi.

To the coast: Mombasa is the only feasible destination, given the insecurity along the old route to Lamu. Arusha Express runs daily from Meru, bypassing Nairobi. Other services invariably call at the capital.

Trains

There is no longer a passenger service to any town in this chapter.

Flights

Forget about flying Nyeri–Nanyuki no matter what the circumstances: the airstrips are so close together and so far from the towns they serve that you could drive the sixty-kilometre journey faster.

Nanyuki to: Maasai Mara (daily; 1hr 30min); Nairobi (daily; 50min); Nyeri (daily; 10min); Samburu lodges (daily; 30min).

The Rift Valley

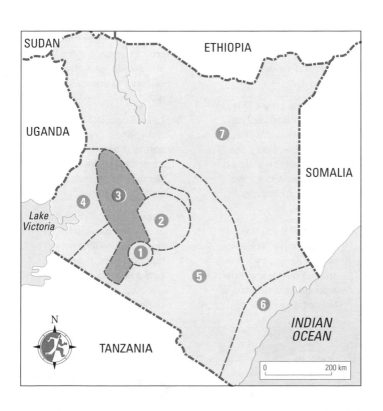

CHAPTER 3

Highlights

✳ **Olorgasailie prehistoric site** Stark site in the southern Rift Valley, with fossil evidence of one of our hunting ancestors preserved in situ. **See p.227**

✳ **Lake Naivasha & Hell's Gate National Park** Hauntingly atmospheric freshwater lake near Hell's Gate's sheer, red cliffs and winding gorge. **See p.234**

✳ **Menengai crater** This colossal crater outside Nakuru – the site of a nineteenth-century Maasai battle – makes a good hike, with superb views on a clear day. **See p.256**

✳ **Hyrax Hill** If you don't visit any other Stone-Age sites in Kenya, try to take an hour out for a wander around Hyrax Hill, east of Nakuru. **See p.258**

✳ **Lake Nakuru National Park** Woods, grasslands and lakeshore with the chance of seeing flamingos, black and white rhinos and leopards. **See p.260**

✳ **Kipkelion Monastery** This multinational Cistercian outpost is a fine retreat if you have time to prepare and write in advance, or a couple of hours to spare. **See p.267**

✳ **Lake Bogoria** Steaming hot springs, greater kudu antelope and remote campsites make this a highly recommended visit. **See p.269**

✳ **Lake Baringo** A beautiful freshwater oasis in the dry northern Rift, with hippos, crocs, over 400 bird species and several good accommodation options. **See p.275**

The Rift Valley

Kenya's **Rift Valley** is only part of a continental fault system that runs 6000km clean across Africa from Jordan to Mozambique. Perhaps Kenya's most important topographical feature, it is certainly one of the country's great distinguishing marks, acting as both a human and natural divide. As such, it has come to be seen as a monumental valley of teeming game and Maasai herders, a trough of grasslands older than humanity. This image is not entirely borne out by reality. The valley certainly is spectacular, a literal rift across the country, with all the stunning panoramas and gaunt escarpment backdrops you could wish for, and the plains animals are still abundant in places. Nevertheless, much of the game has been dispersed by human population pressure onto the higher plateaus to the southwest, and most of the Maasai nowadays live further south.

At least the Rift Valley's **historical influence** cannot be diluted. People have trekked down it, generation after generation, over perhaps the last two or three thousand years, from the wetlands of southern Sudan and the Ethiopian highlands. Some of these immigrants were the ancestors of the **Maasai**, who dominated much of the valley and its surroundings for several centuries before the Europeans arrived. Until the beginning of the twentieth century, they lived on both sides, and the northern **Ilaikipiak** group were a constant threat to caravans coming up from the coast. With European settlement, they were forced from their former grazing grounds in the valley's turbulent bottleneck and confined to the "Southern Reserve" for much of the colonial era. Although many have now returned to the valley, and many towns retain their ancient Maa names, the Maasai are at their most conservative and traditional in southern Kenya, so more background is included in Chapter Five.

In practical terms, the part of the Rift Valley covered in this chapter offers several exceptional **lakes**, a couple of excellent fast roads, lots of spectacular twisting tracks, and some of the wildest country in central Kenya. If you're at all interested in wildlife, especially birds, you'll find it a source of endless fascination, with wonderful **nature reserves** at **lakes Nakuru** and **Bogoria**, and freshwater ecosystems at **Naivasha** and **Baringo**.

Apart from **Naivasha**, **Nakuru** and the string of towns up the western escarpment – **Njoro**, **Elburgon** and **Molo** – the area covered in this chapter contains few places larger than a village; lodgings, strictly speaking, are scarce. Though there is usually somewhere to lay your head, this is a region where a **tent** will be worth its extra weight, and good walking shoes are a definite advantage. **Transport** in the higher, agricultural parts of the south is generally fine, but northwards, or off the main Nakuru–Baringo–Kabarnet axis, you can expect long waits, next-to-no buses and infrequent matatus. For **drivers**,

See map p.281

Lodwar & Lake Turkana

Sigor

CHERANGANI HILLS

Chesegon

Makutano

Tot

Chesengoch

Kapcherop

Chesoi

Kitale

Kapsowar

Cherangani

Moiben

Iten

ELGEYO ESCARPMENT

River Kerio

Eldoret

Tambach

Kabarnet

Loruk

Kampi ya Samaki

Lake Baringo

Marigat

Chebloch

Kimwarer

Loboi Gate

Kaptagat

Tenges

Maji Moto Gate

LAKE BOGORIA NATIONAL RESERVE

Lake Bogoria

See map p.270

Mugurin

Lake Solai

Bogoini

SUBUKIA VALLEY

Eldama Ravine

Kisanana

Nyahururu

EQUATOR (0°)

Makutano

Mogotio

Milton's Siding

Subukia

Monastery

Londiani

Kampi ya Moto

Solai Police Post

Kipkelion

Molo

MENENGAI CRATER

Mairu Kuni

Ol Kalou

ABERDARES NATIONAL PARK

Elburgon

Nakuru

Lanet

Kericho

Njoro

LAKE NAKURU NATIONAL PARK

Lake Nakuru

Mbaruk

Kariandusi

Lake Elementeita

Elmenteita

Gilgil

MAU ESCARPMENT

Mau Narok

Lake Naivasha

Naivasha

N. Kinangop

S. Kinangop

See map p.235

Bomet

HELL'S GATE NATIONAL PARK

Mt Longonot

Gatakaini

Narok

NAIROBI

MAASAI MARA NATIONAL RESERVE

NGONG HILLS

Kiserian

Olorgasailie

Kajiado

Magadi

Rumuruti

N

0   50 km

3

Uganda

Kisumu

Kericho & Kisumu

Kissi

Maralal

Nanyuki

Nyeri

Thika

Mombasa

Namanga

A1

B4

C77

B4

C51

C52

C48

C34

B1

A10

C35

A104

B4

C56

C69

A104

B3

C56

B3

D323

Namanga

the roads are steadily improving in this region, thanks in part to presidential favours earned: the B4 up to Baringo is superb. Note that the northern Rift is lower – and consequently hotter – than most up-country regions, so be prepared for some very **high temperatures** and don't underestimate your **water** requirements.

Olorgasailie and Lake Magadi

Before heading north and into the central Rift Valley, an interesting optional trip, and one which takes you instantly out of the commotion of Nairobi and down into a hot, sparsely inhabited part of the valley, is the journey south to the prehistoric site at **Olorgasailie** and the dramatic salt lake of **Magadi**. There should be two **matatus** from Nairobi leaving in the early afternoon; alternatively, the Akamba **bus** (1pm & 3pm; 3hr) is cheap, and the Maasai, who invade it *en masse* at Kiserian, are lovely company.

KISERIAN is your chance to buy last-minute provisions, as further south there's almost no food available. If you decide to stay in Kiserian, *Kituo Bar* is a basic **B&L** at the eastern end of the market square, with good *nyama choma* and a first-floor balcony overlooking the wonderful commotion of the market. Accommodation in a different class can be found at *Whistling Thorns*, 13km east of Kiserian on the newly tarmacked Isinya road (see p.105 for details). You should be able to catch a matatu from Kiserian. There is also a surprisingly good **restaurant** in the *Makena Village Inn*, a couple of kilometres back towards Nairobi on the main road. At the south end of Kiserian, *Tenco Hill Resort* offers odd live music weekends, including "Retired General" and his one-man band.

The scenery opens out dramatically as you skirt the southern flank of the Ngong Hills and descend steeply down the escarpment. Try to get a front seat, as giraffe and other animals are often seen. If you're travelling under your own steam, there's a pleasant picnic site at *Olepolos Country Club*, 12km after Kiserian. At Olepolos itself, there are a number of *nyama choma* joints, a good bar with chairs on the roadside under some trees, and entirely Maasai clientele.

Olorgasailie

Olorgasailie Prehistoric Site (1.5km from the main road; daily dawn to dusk; Ksh200) is signposted 3km after **Oltepesi**. You need to bring all requirements apart from water (ie food and bedding). The **accommodation** and **museum** are just above the excavations on a ridge overlooking what was once a wide, shallow lake. There are double *bandas*; you can make reservations in advance through the Public Relations Office at the National Museum in Nairobi (☎02/742131–4; ●) to be sure of beds, but it's rarely necessary – or you can camp. Do-it-yourself showers and free firewood are also available. Olorgasailie is a peaceful place to stay, while the **guided tour** around the excavations (included in the entrance charge) is not to be missed. A group from the Los Angeles County Museum and Smithsonian Institute refurbished the displays in 1994, and the site itself is endowed with numerous pathways, catwalks and informative signs.

The hand axe site

Between 400,000 and 500,000 years ago, the lakeshore was inhabited by "people", probably *Homo erectus*, of the **Acheulian culture** (after St Acheul in France, where it was first discovered). They made a range of identifiable stone tools: cleavers for skinning animals; round balls for crushing bones, perhaps for hurling or possibly tied to vines to be used, à la gaucho, as *bolas*; and heavy hand axes, for which the culture is best known, but for which, as Richard Leakey writes, "embarrassingly, no-one can think of a good use". The guides tell you they were used for chopping meat and digging. This seems reasonable, but some are very large, while hundreds of others (particularly at the so-called factory site) seem far too small, the theory being that they were made by children practising. The great thing about places like Olorgasailie is that the answers are not cut and dried, and there's plenty of room for the imagination to construct scenarios of how it might have been.

Mary and Louis Leakey's team did most of the unearthing here in the 1940s. Thousands of the stone tools they found have been left undisturbed, *in situ*, under protective roofs. Maybe the most impressive find is the fossilized leg bone of a gigantic, extinct elephant, dwarfing a similar bone from a modern elephant placed next to it. It was long hoped that human remains would also be uncovered at Olorgasailie, but despite extensive digging none have been found – more scope for speculation.

Staying on

Although you could conceivably look around the site before the next bus passes two hours later, and then ride down to Magadi, it's much better to give yourself a day and a night. Sitting in the shade of the open-sided picnic *bandas* with a pair of binoculars and looking out over what used to be the lake can yield some rewarding animal-watching, especially in the brief dusk. Go for a walk out past the excavations towards the gorge and you'll see more: gerenuk, duiker, giraffe, eland and baboons.

Contacts with Maasai are good here, too. If you'd like to take pictures, food is a more acceptable payment than money. There's usually also some jewellery for sale. And if you're enchanted with the peace and presence of Olorgasailie, and stay longer than you'd anticipated, you can cultivate further friendships – and collect some scant **provisions** – at the cluster of desolate *dukas* at Oltepesi, 3km back along the Nairobi road, where they also have warm beer and soft drinks.

Lake Magadi and west to the Nguruman escarpment

Heading south and descending, **Lake Magadi** is a vast shallow pool of soda, a sludge of alkaline water and crystal trona deposits lying in a Rift Valley depression, 1000m below Nairobi. This is one of the hottest places in the country. On a barren spit of land jutting out across the multicoloured soda, the Magadi Soda Company, until 1991 an ICI interest, has built the very model of a company town. Everything you see, apart from the homes of a few Maasai on the shore and a few *dukas* and places to eat in town, is owned and run by the corporation. You pass a company police barrier where you sign in and enter over a causeway, past surreal pink salt ponds. Now on company territory, a sign advises visitors that "it is dangerous to walk across the lake surface", just in case you were wondering. Note that some of the company police are touchy about you taking photos of the factory installations.

Despite this, the atmosphere here, somewhat surprisingly because of the nature of the work and harshness of the environment, is relaxed and welcoming. By comparison with the rest of Kenya, the company pays high wages; people tend to get drunk a lot, and accommodation and services are free.

Practicalities

Having arrived, you might wonder how you'll fill the time until the bus leaves for Nairobi the next morning. Behind the police station, which stands on the highest point of the peninsula, the lake glows unnaturally in the afternoon sun. Looking the other way (to the west), the road to the left leads to the "European" end of town, where a dozen or so managers live and where there's a strange, barren golf course; to your right, the town slopes gently down to a crusty shore where most of the Kenyan employees live. There's a Barclays Bank here with spectacularly unhelpful hours (Wed 11am–2pm – and you can't even count on that). There is also a thriving **daily market**, although choice is limited. *Oguts Hotel & Bakery* serves cheap and filling **meals**, and for a drink (you'll be refused entry at all three staff "clubs"), try the madhouse *Maasai Bar*, opposite the mosque.

The company has built blocks of apartments, a church, a mosque and schools and, with a touch of inspiration, a large, glittering **swimming pool**. The sign says "for residents only", but a beetroot face and rolling eyes should convince them otherwise. The poolside bar and *nyama choma* kiosk are popular in the evenings and, on weekends, there are even a few picnickers from Nairobi. Magadi has one **hotel** opposite the hospital, the *Lower Guesthouse* (PO Box 8 ☎0303/33000–8 ext 278 or 33278 out of hours; ➋) which officially isn't open to tourists, so a measure of tactful persistence might be needed. You can pitch a tent almost anywhere south of the township – though the utterly bizarre golf course (actually a rock- and thorn-strewn wasteland with not a blade of grass in sight) has two equally bizarre "Keep Off" signs. Anywhere here is baking hot during the day and a favourite haunt for baboons – but it's likely you'll be invited home by employees, anyway.

The lake

Many visitors come to Magadi specifically for its **birdlife**. There's a wealth of avifauna here including, usually, large numbers of flamingos at the southern end of the lake. At this end, there are also freshwater swamps which attract many species.

The **lake** itself is fascinating to walk across (on the causeways: in practice only the inlet between Magadi and the eastern shore). On the eastern side, where you first arrive, you can watch the sweepers in rubber boots shovelling the by-product, sodium chloride (common salt), into ridges on the technicolour "fields". Sodium chloride crystallizes on top of the sodium carbonate (the "soda") and is loaded on to tractor-drawn trailers and taken away to be purified for human and animal consumption.

But the company is primarily concerned with extracting the soda. Magadi is the second largest source of sodium carbonate in the world, after the Salton Sea in the USA, and the company's investment here is guaranteed – hot springs gush out of the earth's crust to provide an inexhaustible supply of briney water for evaporation. The dried soda is exported, first by rail to Mombasa via Kajiado and Konza, thence, much of it, to Japan. Magadi soda, used principally for glass-making, is Kenya's most valuable mineral resource. But, despite the "high" wages, you wonder how anyone can be persuaded to work in this lurid inferno: the first rains here are usually "phantom rain", the ground so hot that the raindrops evaporate before hitting the surface. It's important to wear sunglasses and a hat while out in the sun, and bring plenty of water.

Across from the town, on the western shore, Maasai will sell you *pombe* made from a base of roots and herbs, and fermented with honey. It's a lot cheaper than beer, and stronger, too. Asked if there was another name apart from the generic *pombe* they said, "We just call it Ups". Drinking it in the middle of the day is not advisable.

Moving on from Magadi

Returning to Nairobi from Magadi, the matatu leaves at 5am and the **buses** at 6am and 7am, or you could ask about hitching a ride on the soda **train** to Kajiado (on the main Kenya–Tanzania highway) or to Konza and Mombasa if you're headed that way. There's supposed to be a passenger service on Wednesday, usually leaving late afternoon – though you're advised to arrive early.

With your own vehicle (or Ksh800 to rent a company car if you meet a worker with a day to spare – it's the worker, not you, who can rent the car), you can drive on from the town, across the lake to the **hot springs** on the western side. Check the map in the police station first.

From the hot springs, you can drive to the Ewaso Ngiro River at the foot of the Ol Choroi plateau, also known as the **Nguruman Escarpment**. By the river there's a game warden's camp, near to which you may be able to pitch a tent. There is, however, no guarantee of this; the whole Ol Choroi area is private land, leased off the Elangata Enkutoko Group Ranch which is formed of the district's Maasai clans. The lessees have plans to encourage Maasai involvement in tourism initiatives, but some of the few travellers and overland trucks that have visited this spot in recent years have left rubbish, damaged the vegetation and lit fires in unsuitable places, causing resentment among local people. They get few visitors here and, in theory it's a good place to meet untouched Kenya, though you should be extremely sensitive to local feelings. Don't tamper with, or drive around, locked gates. And forget about trying to four-wheel-drive it up the rough track beyond the river, over the escarpment and on to the Mara. People have done that in the past, but the whole area is privately owned Maasai land and, for the moment at least, not accessible.

Into the central Rift Valley

Many travellers' first view of the Rift Valley is from the souvenir-draped **A104 Uplands road**. This barrels through the forests north of Nairobi, crosses a broad, bleak plateau, then flirts with the precipice before following the contours of the slopes above Naivasha and dropping into the Rift. They sell rhubarb up here, as well as plums, carrots and potatoes. In the wet season, you can find yourself driving over a thick, white carpet of hailstones between gloomy conifer plantations. All this contrasts dramatically with the endless, dusty plains below. With binoculars, you can pick out herds of gazelle, Maasai with their cattle and, bizarrely, a satellite-tracking station near the grey cone of Mount Longonot.

The Uplands road is a good one to hitch on, and buses and matatus often use it, although the latter, especially Nissans, have some of the most reckless drivers in the country, which is saying something; remember to sit on the left for the best views. If you have a car of your own, you can stop at some of the stands on the roadside: small sheepskins are often excellent value, but check they have been properly cured; the big woven grass baskets are also worthwhile and surprisingly cheap. Note that the last set of stands in the best location is also the most expensive. More seriously, if you are driving, treat this road as a continuous **black spot** – overtaking can be lethal.

The "**old road**", built by Italian POWs during World War II, runs parallel to and lower than the Uplands road; it's insanely bumpy and narrow and is only used by heavy goods vehicles which in theory are banned from the top road. Corresponding to its lower altitude, vegetation down here takes on a more Mediterranean aspect, candelabra euphorbia and spikey agave predominating. The little **chapel** before the Mai Mahiu junction for Narok, also Italian-built, seems fitting in this scene, though it's more often used as a pit-stop picnic site.

Whichever road you use, you pass Naivasha and continue on Kenya's contribution to the Trans-African Highway (a projected paved ribbon joining Lagos with Mombasa) into the central Rift Valley – and the area around lakes Elmenteita and Nakuru.

Lake Naivasha and around

Naivasha, like so many Kenyan place names, is a corruption of a local (Maasai) name *E-na-iposha* (heaving waters), a pronunciation still used by Maa speakers you'll meet in the vicinity. The grassy shores of the lake were traditional Maasai grazing land for centuries, prior to its "discovery" by Joseph Thomson in 1884. Before the nineteenth century was out, however, the "glimmering many-isled expanse" had seen the arrival, with the railway, of the first European settlers. Soon after, the Maasai *laibon* Ole Gilisho, whom the British had appointed chief of the Naivasha Maasai, was persuaded to sign an agreement ceding his people's grazing rights all around the lake – and the country houses and ranches went up. Today the Maasai are back, though very much as outsiders, either disputing grazing rights with the many European landowners still left here, or as workers on the vast horticultural farms, which export the bulk of fresh flowers sold in the UK.

The lake, a slightly forbidding but highly picturesque waterscape with its purple mountain backdrop and floating islands of papyrus and water hyacinth, has some curious physical characteristics. It is fresh water – Lake Baringo is the only other example in the Rift – and the water level has always been prone to mysterious fluctuations. It dropped massively in the 1980s (partly the unmysterious result of farmers to the north taking off some of the Thurusha River's inflow to irrigate their crops), though the shore has not receded enough to regain the areas that were cultivated in the 1950s when the lake was half its present size. Even though the lake level increased in 1998 following the El Niño floods, the outer edge of the fringing band of papyrus marks the shoreline the settlers knew and you can still see fence posts sticking up.

Perhaps of more immediate and visible interest is the lake's **wildlife**, especially its protected **hippo** population. The dull earth tremors you sometimes feel if you're camping add considerably to the already exciting African night. Despite their bulk, hippos seem to be remarkably sensitive creatures, and they must be able to see in the dark, too, for nary a guy-line is twanged. Both *Fisherman's Camp* and *Fish Eagle Inn* receive occasional nocturnal visits, especially now that the waters have risen to cover the ditches dug to keep them out

NAIVASHA

ACCOMMODATION
Heshima B&L	4
Ken-Vash	5
La Belle Inn	6
Lakeside Tourist Lodge	7
Mount Longonot Lodge	1
Naivasha Guest Inn	8
Naivasha Silver	2
Othaya Annexe	3

RESTAURANTS
Joe's Eating House	D
Jim's Corner Café	B
Centre Bakery	A
Kiwa Highway Motel	E
North Kinangop Hotel	C

Caltex
Total
North Lake Road Matatus
Nairobi, Nakuru Matatu Stand
Wholesale Market (outdoor)
Railway Club
Railway Station
Delamere Dairies
Barclays Bank
KCB
POSTA LANE
STATION LANE
Municipal Market (covered)
BIASHARA ROAD
North Kinangop Matatu Stand
KENYATTA AVENUE
Lakeside Matatu stand
Esso
Naivasha Ebony Curio Shop
Bus Stop (Nairobi, Nakuru)
Prison
See inset for detail
KARUKI
CHOTARA ROAD
MAMA NGINA ROAD
MORENDAT AVENUE

0   200m
0   2 km

▼ Nairobi (B3 Old Road) & Lake Naivasha road   ▼ Nairobi (A104 Uplands Road)

(apparently a drunken German tourist once went looking for hippos at 4am, and found them with tragic consequence). By day, you can occasionally see **giraffes**, floating blithely through the trees, taking barbed wire and gates in their stride. Naivasha has extraordinary **birdlife** too: all kinds, from the grotesque marabou storks to pet shop lovebirds in pairs (which are illegal to buy or sell), doves cooing in the woods and splendid fish eagles, whose mournful cries fill the air like seagulls. These, and the area's climate, with a light breeze always drifting through the acacias, make Naivasha a hard place to beat as a first stop out from Nairobi.

Naivasha town

All told, **NAIVASHA** town has little to offer as a place to stay. Unless you arrive late in the day, you may as well head straight on down to the lake. Coming from Nairobi on the **B3 old road** (recently resurfaced), you could ask to be dropped off at the lake road turning. If you're hitching or coming by bus or matatu, you may arrive on the **A104 Uplands road** and might be dropped inconveniently at the top junction, 1.5km uphill behind the town. It's possible to catch a matatu or bus straight down to the lake, but if you plan to spend any time in the area, you may want to go into the town of Naivasha first to stock up on essentials. Most travellers tend to do their own cooking, and the lakeside and town together offer a wide choice. For **food supplies**, the fruit stalls on the main road are good, though there is more choice at the covered market. The oddly named Naivasha Mattresses Supermarket, at the upper end of Biashara Road, is cheaper and has more variety than the Multiline Supermarket. There's good lake fish at the kiosk opposite *La Belle Inn* and, if you're driving, super-fresh milk and yoghurts at Delamere Dairies, 3km north on the Nakuru road. There's a **post office** on Moi Avenue (Mon–Fri 8am–1pm & 2–5pm, Sat 9am–noon) and two **banks**: Barclays (with an ATM) and KCB, both on Moi Avenue (both Mon–Fri 9am–3pm, Sat 9–11am).

Accommodation

If you do **stay in town**, there's one favourite old hotel, the *La Belle Inn*, and numerous lodgings ranging from the quite decent to the unspeakable.

Heshima B&L Kariuki Chotara Rd, PO Box 1141 ①0311/20631. Not as cheap as it was, though the rooms at the top are nice and the café is popular with Congolese music fans. They also run the *Waboko Hotel* on Moi Ave. ❷

Ken-Vash Hotel Posta Lane, PO Box 211 ①0311/30049, ⓕ30084. Naivasha's biggest hotel (61 rooms), with impersonal but efficient service, and reasonably quiet. Excellent rooms, safe parking. ❸

La Belle Inn Moi Ave, PO 532 ①0311/21007, ⓕ21119, ⓔnbc@africaonline.co.ke. A popular old staging post on the main street through town, with a variety of rooms recently rebuilt. Good customer service and restaurant, serving great fried breakfasts. They have one or two cheaper non-s/c rooms still available and an internet café, though connections can be very slow. B&B ❹

Lakeside Tourist Lodge Moi Ave, PO Box 894 ①0311/30267 or 20856, ⓕ30268. Spacious construction just off the Nairobi–Nakuru road. Good rooms and efficient service, but the food is sus-

pect (especially their "African buffet"), and there are no lakeside views. ❸

Mount Longonot Lodge Biashara St, PO Box 19 ①0311/21026. Next to Naivasha Mattresses, with an indifferent front restaurant, though the twenty s/c double rooms round the back are a pleasant surprise. All rooms have comfy wicker chairs. ❷

Naivasha Guest Inn Kenyatta Ave, PO Box 491 ①0311/21227. Two kilometres from the town centre, this is a well-kept joint to collapse into if you've just been dropped at the junction. Reasonable rooms (all s/c) with a nice terrace-bar-restaurant. Secure parking. ❷

Naivasha Silver Hotel Kenyatta Ave, PO Box 989 ①0311/22580. One step up from a regular B&L, with some quite nice rooms. ❷

Othaya Annexe B&L Kariuki Chotara Rd, PO Box 651 ①0311/20770. Cheap and cheerful, but not too clean; the s/c rooms have a large bed and a set price for a single or a couple. There's a good *hoteli* downstairs and a bakery on the premises. ❶

Eating and drinking

There's a whole clutch of cheap, local **places to eat** at on the western end of Moi Avenue around the Caltex and Total gas stations, the best of which is the delightful *Joe's Eating House*, with good *ugali*, meat stew and chapati, accompanied by singing in the kitchen and chickens pecking at your toes. Of the places listed below, don't miss *La Belle Inn* and, if you're driving, call in at the *Kiwa Highway Motel* above town on the Nakuru–Nairobi road.

Centre Bakery Kariuki Chotara Rd. Naivasha's main bread shop (though *La Belle Inn* caters for more esoteric tastes). Open till 8pm.

Jim's Corner Café Station Lane. A popular place,

formerly Brothers Café, but now under different management. Food is cheap and the portions are generous.

Kiwa Highway Motel A104 Highway, near the top

junction. A windblown *nyama choma* joint, fairly expensive except for beef at Ksh150 a kilo. There's also a bar and disco.

La Belle Inn Moi Ave (see "Accommodation", p.233). Recommended dishes include barbecued tilapia, spiced Louisiana crayfish and Naivasha bisque (lakefish soup). They have a wide choice for vegetarians (easily the best in town) and a nice line in pizzas and real croissants. They also sell choice picnic supplies (the "lunchbox" costs Ksh300), honey and capers.

North Kinangop Hotel Moi Ave. Inexpensive fish and chips and amazingly filling *mandaazi*.

Nightlife

Music is inescapable in Naivasha, as almost all the B&Ls double as café-bars which bounce along on the infectious rhythms of Congolese and South African sounds. Venues tend to have a short lifespan, though, so ask around for the latest. Among the established **clubs**, the *Salama Bar and Hotel* on Moi Avenue, opposite the station, is perhaps the liveliest; it also has cheap rooms, should the night's revelry prove too much. It might also be worth checking out the *A to Z Nightclub* on Kariuki Chotara Road. The *Railway Club* by the station (℡0311/20552) has live bands Thursday to Sunday evenings (closing time 3am). The *Scartman Disco* at the bottom of Station Lane, which plays African and soul music, also doubles up as a hotel. Otherwise, the *Golf Club* (north up Moi Avenue) is an almost exclusively white meat market, its "members only" rule applied only to locals.

Lake Naivasha

The fast new lakeside road has brought thousands of migrant workers to the **farming estates**, where they grow string beans, mangetout and flowers, all exported by air to European supermarkets. Great stretches of acacia scrub have been cleared since the late 1980s to make way for the expansion of the farms and the ugly lines of squalid field-hand housing that are still sprouting in the dust between the plantations. Passing through this scene of ragged-clothed backs stooping between the rows – with rambling country houses in the background – it's difficult to ignore the images of American slavery that repeatedly spring to mind. There are always people looking for work, of course (there seems to be little disapproval of the development), and there's a fair scattering of Europeans of very modest means eking out a living between the landowners. But the scale of the distinction between rich and poor is brutally apparent all the same. Happily, there are still patches of relatively undisturbed bush and the lakeshore remains a magnet for savannah game – zebra, giraffe and waterbuck congregate in certain areas, such as Crescent Island.

To **get to the lake** from Naivasha town, there's easily hitchable traffic, a regular shuttle of matatus, and a bus every hour or so (with regular 8am and 1pm return departures from *Fisherman's Camp*; see p.237).

Lakeshore accommodation

There's a wide variety of accommodation along **Moi South Lake Road** – everything from frugal *bandas* and camping to stately hotels and homestays. For these places, the number of kilometres (in brackets) refers to the distance from the lake road junction with the main Nairobi road (which is 3km from Naivasha town itself). Places to stay off **Moi North Lake Road** are generally more difficult to get to, as the road is unsurfaced – full directions are given in the listings where appropriate.

▲ Eburru & Gilgil

Gilgil & Nakuru ▲

LAKE NAIVASHA & HELL'S GATE

Maasai Gorge

Airstrip

3

MARULA

MANERA

MOI NORTH LAKE ROAD (UNPAVED) D323

EXTINCT VOLCANOES

NDABIBI ESCARPMENT

4

5

6

Rima Islands

Lake Naivasha

Naivasha

Picnic Site

Green Crater Lake

7

CRATER LAKE GAME SANCTUARY

Hippo Point

Crescent Island

8

9

10

11

Elmenteita Weavers

Kongoni

D331

Oloiden Lake

Police Post

13

Narok & Maiela

14

12 **A**

15

16

17

18

Sulmac dukas

Karagita

Airstrip

OSERIAN ESTATE

MOI SOUTH LAKE ROAD (PAVED)

A104 Nairobi (new road)

SULMAC ESTATE

Olkaria Gate

19 **20**

Elsa Gate

Fischer's Tower

Olkaria Geothermal Plant

see inset

21

NJORGA CIRCUIT

BUFFALO CIRCUIT

HELL'S GATE NATIONAL PARK

22

N

B3 Nairobi (old road)

Car Park (only place to park) & roadhead

Geothermal Plant

Checkpoint

Ol Basta

Very steep (4WD)

N

Longonot

Mount Longonot

0   5 km

▼ Narok road & Suswa

ACCOMMODATION

Burch's Marina	**8**	Fisherman's Camp	**16**	Longonot Ranch House	**22**	Ol Dubai Campsite	**21**
Crater Lake Camp	**7**	Kiangazi	**14**	Malewa River Lodge	**2**	Yelo Green Hotel	**10**
Crayfish Campsite	**17**	Kongoni Game Valley	**13**	Malu	**1**	YMCA	**18**
Eburru Guest Cottage	**3**	Lake Naivasha Country Club	**11**	Melili Cottage	**3**	
Elsamere	**12**	Lake Naivasha Lodge	**9**	Nairburta Campsite	**20**	**CLUBS**
Endachata Campsite	**19**	Lentolia House	**6**	Olerai House	**5**	Geothermal Club	**A**
Fish Eagle Inn	**15**	Loldia House	**4**		

235

The thorns of the rose

In 1995, when the Lake Naivasha Riparian Association (LNRA) and Earth Watch succeeded in getting Naivasha listed as a Ramsar Site – a wetland of internationally recognized ecological importance which, in theory, obliges both government and local inhabitants to preserve the lake – cynics among environmentalists remained unimpressed.

The ecological consequences of Naivasha's multimillion-dollar **horticultural industry**, which covers a large part of the land around the lake, was the primary cause for concern amongst the sceptics, who worried about the lake's fluctuating levels, and the farmers' continuing use of **pesticides** such as the highly toxic and ozone-layer-depleting methyl bromide, both of which adversely affect wildlife.

However, it's become increasingly apparent that the survival of the lake and its wildlife depends on a multitude of other factors ultimately linked to Kenya's **growing population**. Since 1977 the number of people living within five kilometres of the lake has risen from 50,000 to 250,000, and human waste has become a major problem. Naivasha's Municipal Sewage Treatment Plant has not worked properly for several years with the result that some partially treated effluent is finding its way into the lake, and people who have moved into new unplanned settlements, lured by jobs on the flower farms, are building pit latrines too close to the lake and causing the E.coli count in the lake water to go up.

The **lake's level** has always fluctuated and been very dependent on rainfall, but it is the human factors which have caused growing concern. There's no surface outflow, and the three small incoming **rivers** – one permanent and two seasonal – bring in large amounts of untreated waste from dairies upstream, including particularly toxic **cattle dip**, along with **phosphates** from people washing clothes. Water extraction from the farms and from the weir built on a tributary of the Malewa River, is placing additional strain on the lake's natural balance, already under pressure from papyrus clearance by small-scale farmers (papyrus helps diminish erosion and is a natural filter against siltation). More disturbing, however, is a plan to dam the Malewa to supply Nakuru town. The river is Lake Naivasha's lifeline, providing 90 per cent of surface water intake. Already deforestation in the mountains is reducing river flows, and if the dam goes ahead the harm done to Lake Naivasha would be devastating.

All these problems mean that the lake's wildlife has been seriously damaged, too. Until the exceptional 1997 rains raised the lake levels, thereby diluting the pollutants, the **fish eagle** had been especially badly affected and had not bred successfully at

Budget and mid-range accommodation and camping

Burch's Marina 2.3km; PO Box 40 ☎0311/21010. You can camp here (Ksh200), or stay in traditional *rondavels* (basic round houses with enclosed verandahs in a field), in square *bandas*, or in more expensive, if still basic, four-bed s/c cottages. The main attraction is the peaceful nature of the place: no noise after 9pm, you have to book in advance (allow two weeks for weekends), and you pay extra for bedding if you don't bring your own (gas stove, pots and pans are included if you rent bedding for the cottages). It's cheap, though. Hot showers are available and farm produce is for sale. *Rondavels/bandas/*camping ❶; four-bed cottage ❹ per person.

Crayfish Campsite 17km; PO Box 176 ☎0311/20239. Ten minutes from the lake, and cheap, but little more than a small field and bar, which can get noisy and is frequented by "better-paid locals", according to the manager. There's not much security, either, judging from the jolly and docile guard dogs, but it's inexpensive (Ksh150 per person, and you can rent a tent for Ksh200), there's hot water, and the usual eight-seat boat rides are offered (Ksh2000 per hour). If you order food, be prepared for a long wait

Fish Eagle Inn 19.3km, entrance beside *Fisherman's Camp*; PO Box 1554 ☎0311/30306, ⓕ21158. An unusual and pleasant if slightly over-priced restaurant/*banda*/campsite/health club complex. Calmer and more dignified than *Fisherman's Camp*, you can also camp here (Ksh150; no tent rental), kip in a dorm ($6 per per-the lake for some years. The birds were not getting enough to eat and **Louisiana crayfish**, introduced in the Seventies for commercial fishing, were largely to blame. By eating their way through the lake's flora (which as well as acting as a soak for excess nutrients and a sediment trap, is food and cover for some fish species and birds such as the coot), the crayfish caused the water to become murkier. This in turn meant that the fish eagle, unable to see its prey in the lake and unable to find any coots left in the area to feed on, became too undernourished to breed. Fish poachers dragging small mesh nets through the shallows exacerbated the situation. They not only helped to damage the vegetation, but seriously affected commercial fishing to the extent that a total ban was introduced in order to give the fish a chance to regenerate. Fortunately, since the ban, not only has the crayfish population crashed (a natural cyclical phenomenon), but fish numbers are growing, the coot have come back, the water is clearing, and the fish eagles are breeding again.

At the same time, some **companies** finally appear to be waking up to their responsibilities. Homegrown, which exports over 50 million flower stems to the UK each year, pays its workers a handsome $1200 annually, about five times the Kenyan average, whilst Oserian, the largest rose producer in Africa, has undertaken not to cultivate within 1km of the lake to avoid run-off (and possible future legal action), and has, in common with other producers, instituted extensive health checks on its workers who deal with pesticides. Lake Naivasha flower grower's group (LNFG) have got together and are experimenting with alternative methods of fumigation. Some farms have stopped using methyl bromide altogether and are encouraging environmentally friendly ideas such as using constructed wetlands which use sunlight and plants to cleanse waste water so that it can safely be reused or returned to the lake.

In spite of these optimistic signs, Lake Naivasha's **future** is still uncertain. Some of the areas 350 types of bird, hippopotamus and other wildlife are still threatened with extinction, and already the lilly-trotter, the great crested grebe and the crested helmet shrike have all but disappeared.

In 1999, the LNRA won the Ramsar Wetland Award and was commended as an inspiring example of community leadership, demonstrating that conservation and wise use of wetlands could be achieved in Africa. The long-term success of the environmentalists is not guaranteed, but the first steps have proved important in raising awareness and hopefully ensuring Lake Naivasha's continued regeneration.

son), or stay in a variety of dull if well-equipped *bandas* (with nets, hot water and spotless toilets); doubles are tiny, but the more expensive "suites" are cosier. The restaurant is good, and there's a gym (as well as sauna, steam room and outdoor pool; around Ksh600–700 extra per day for their use). Mountain bikes for rent. B&B ❹, HB ❺ **Fisherman's Camp** 19.3km; PO Box 79 ☎0311/30088; reservations through Let's Go Travel, p.141. This favourite budget hideaway consists of two areas. *Bottom Camp* has the best camping site in Naivasha, right by the water's edge, and is shaded by tall, beautiful fever trees. There's a choice of camping (Ksh200 per person; tent rental Ksh200 per person); four s/c, if rather dingy *bandas* (❸); and a "Youth Hostel" consisting of seven very basic dormitories, each with four narrow bunk beds, sometimes occupied by British soldiers on "jungle training" (Ksh300 per person). The *Top Camp* (☎0311/30276), now under a different management and known as *Candelabra Camp* (though if one is full they'll help get you a place in the other), has seven more *bandas* and one cottage (❸), overlooking the lake but high above the road. Five of its *bandas* offer basic shelter only (❷), with open cooking on charcoal *jikos* outside and bedding available (extra), while two also have hot water showers and toilets, suitable for small families (❷). The bar at *Bottom Camp* has limited food, as does nearby *Watalii Kiosk* (see "Shopping and services", p.240). Some people find the sometimes beery white Kenyan atmosphere at *Bottom Camp* off-putting; others love it. Rowing boats and bicycles (Ksh250–500) are for rent, and there's parascending (Ksh1500 for 15min) and water-skiing (Ksh800 for 15min). If you need fire wood, you can either buy it at the camp for Ksh100 or for Ksh60 at the nearby village. **Watalii Kiosk** see p.240.

Yelo Green Hotel 0.8km; PO Box 561 ☎ & ℻ 0311/30269. Far from the lake itself, and a little tatty, but with quite acceptable chalet-style *bandas* (all s/c with hot water), set in lovely bougainvillea-filled gardens. The owners are charming and help-ful, and there's a restaurant and bar (popular with locals at weekends). Great Rift Lakes Bikes and Tents is 1km down the road. However, room prices are a little over the odds. They also have a camp-site (Ksh200 per person). B&B ❸

YMCA 15.1km; PO Box 1006 ☎ 0311/30396. The idyllic, rural ambience the YMCA once had has been progressively nibbled away as the farms press in on all sides and the lake recedes – it's now a ten-minute walk away. The "Y" is still one of the lake's cheapest (and friendliest) places to stay – either camping in what's left of the acacia grove (Ksh150 per person; tents rented for Ksh200), staying in a dorm (for which you need bedding), or renting one of the spartan *bandas* – and certainly the easiest base if you're planning an early-morning hike into Hell's Gate National Park, as the Elsa Gate is just up the road. Firewood, eggs, lake fish and milk are sporadically available, but the shop has almost nothing. There's hot water, boat rental (Ksh2000 for an eight-seater) and food can be cooked to order. ❶

Hotels and lodges

Crater Lake Camp ☎ 0311/20613 ℮ crater@africaonline.co.ke; reservations through Southern Cross Safaris, p.142. Luxury tented camp (see "Green Crater Lake" on p.243). Superb views from the ten secluded, yellow-acacia-shaded *ban-das* (or from a specially built "raft" for bird-watch-ing), and nice touches like its china dinner service and silverware. You can also just drop in for lunch ($20). The price includes night game drives and escorted walks. No access for disabled visitors. FB ❾

Lake Naivasha Country Club 3.8km; PO Box 15 ☎ 0311/21004 or 21160, ℻ 21161; reservations through Block, p.42. The best hotel on the lake (still usually known as the *Lake Hotel*) and, despite the expense, still an excellent alternative base to Nairobi, with magnificent gardens and bird-watch-ing opportunities (and fish-eagle-eyed guides), good facilities (including a chilly swimming pool) and a lounge evocative of the old colonial days between 1937 and 1950, when flying-boats used to land on the lake en route between London and South Africa, and the passengers stayed here. It's suitable for children (small adventure playground and huge lawns) and visitors with disabilities (all ground-floor rooms; a few steps up to the dining room), but the generally old-fashioned rooms vary considerably from adequate to luxurious, so don't be afraid to ask. For casual visitors – usually attracted by the sumptuous lunchtime buffets in the garden (Ksh900) – there's an additional Ksh100 entry fee. There are bicycles for rent (Ksh200 per hour or Ksh800 per day), massages, bird walks (Ksh300), boat rides (Ksh3200 per hour for a seven-seat boat) and one-hour trips by Cessna aircraft (Ksh12,000). There's a money exchange facility, with the usual bad rates. No B&B. FB ❻ low, ❽ high.

Lake Naivasha Lodge, formerly *Lake Naivasha Holiday Villas* 3.5km; PO Box 685 ☎ 0311/20611, ℻ 21156; reservations in Nairobi at Arrow House, Koinange St; PO Box 70559 ☎ 02/224998, ℻ 212405, ℮ lake-nakuru@gatewayonline.co.ke. A lovely place in uncluttered, airy style with twelve spacious double rooms, s/c and spotless, some with private verandah overlooking the enormous gardens. Boat trips offered (Ksh2500 for an eight-seat boat for an hour; Ksh540 to Crescent Island). Ten-minute walk to the lakeshore through pleasant grounds. Secure parking. B&B is good value, half-board or full-board less so, though they're conven-ient. HB ❺ , B&B ❹

Ranches, cottages and homestays

For the ideal antidote to Nairobi, a number of extremely luxurious ranch and farmhouses lie dotted around the lake, as well as a couple of idyllically situat-ed cottages, these being well within the reach of even the lowliest budget. Reservations are handled by Let's Go Travel in Nairobi (see p.141) unless oth-erwise stated.

Eburru Guest Cottage Formerly known as *Mayers Soyet*, this is part of the as yet undevel-oped "Green Park Development", in beautiful walk-ing country (beware of buffalo). Two double bed-rooms in a basic but fully s/c cottage with gor-geous views over the lake and Mount Longonot.

Part of its charm is its inaccessibility – bring all your food (a kitchen/lounge is at your disposal). Water is provided. Matatus run twice daily (once on Sun) from Moi Ave in Naivasha, leaving you with a two-kilometre walk from Green Park Development gate; taxis Ksh700–1000. Hitching a ride on a *shamba* vehicle is also possible: ask at *La Belle Inn*. If you're making your own way here, see *Melili Cottage* below. ❸

Elsamere 22.1km; PO Box 1497 ☎0311/21055, ☏21074, ✉elsa@africaonline.co.ke). Joy Adamson's former home, open to the public as a conservation centre (see p.241), offers comfortable and very peaceful rooms in cottages, each with verandahs facing towards the lake. The grounds are beautiful, too, but they don't put up children under 7 years old unless by prior arrangement, and they can be snooty if you don't fit their picture of an ideal guest: they don't like the house to be treated as a hotel, and prefer a measure of enthusiasm for the lady and her works, or at least for natural history. Reservations advisable. FB only ❻

Klangazi 25.5km, PO Box 719 ☎0311/21052, ☏21059. A very personable homestay as guests of the family in a separate guest house, with a large verandah overlooking the valley. Three artificial pools (two for buffalo, zebra and antelope, the other for you to swim in) provide entertainment, and game drives (both day and night) are included in the price. The food is superb and served with excellent wines. FB ❾

Kongoni Game Valley 28.5km; PO Box 15026 Nairobi ☎02/890184, ☏890096. The plushest homestay in Naivasha, though not exactly the most tasteful – an enormous, overly modernized ranch house built by the Count and Countess de Perigny at the turn of the last century. FB ❾

Lentolia House Moi North Lake Rd; enquiries to Abigail Allison ☎0311/30277. Located 2km beyond Crater Lake Game Sanctuary, coming from Kongoni, then right for 2–3km. A delightful Edwardian house with an Italian-style central patio for rent in its entirety – it's very good value. Graceful and spacious, it comes with a large expanse of farmland. There are two double and four twin bedrooms. Kitchen staff are included in the price, but bring your own drinking water. Vegetables and dairy produce is usually available. Ask the staff to heat water for baths. Electricity 6pm–11pm only. ❻

Loldia House Moi North Lake Rd; Rick Hopcraft, PO Box 199 ☎0311/30024; reservations through Governor's Camps, p.42. Naivasha's oldest stone house, built in the 1940s by Italian POWs, with delightful period charm. Sweeping views of Mount Longonot over the grassy lawn, a grand piano in

the lounge and a claw-foot bathtub in the master bedroom. There's a small guest cottage nearby. Horse rides through herds of cattle and a flock of farmed ostriches can be arranged. For all that, way overpriced. FB ❾

Longonot Ranch House 10.5km, then left 8km up a rough track signposted "Kedong Ranch"; reservations at Safaris Unlimited, 328 Langata Rd, PO Box 24181 Nairobi; ☎02/891168 or 890435, ☏891113, ✉info@safarisunlimited.com. A traditional long ranch house (six double en-suite bedrooms), complete with full staff. Built by Martha Gellhorn, journalist and one-time wife of Ernest Hemingway, atop a hillock under the shadow of Mount Longonot, the attractions are manifold: stunning scenery, lots of wildlife (escorted game walks and night game drives available), stables and horse riding ($15 per hour). Reservations essential. FB ❽–❾

Malewa River Lodge (bookings through Let's Go, see p.141) This new place, run by and situated within the Kigio Wildlife Conservancy, stands on the banks of the Malewa, and has four buildings made of mud, timber and thatch, each consisting of a large sitting room with a pleasant open fire, a dining area and a spacious but cosy balcony overlooking the river. It can accommodate twelve people comfortably. Activities include trout fishing, horse riding, abseiling, canoeing and rafting. ❼

Malu PO Box 536 ☎0311/30181 or 21200, ☏20272, ✉malu@africaonline.co.ke. As you head towards Nakuru from Naivasha, Malu is off a terrible *murram* road on your right leading to Gilgil and Nyahururu. Getting here is a drag, but the end reward is exquisite. Nestled high up in an ancient cedar forest, the view you get of the Great Rift Valley, Lake Naivasha and Longonot is breathtaking, and the pristine air and tranquillity will leave you with second thoughts about returning home. Stay in one of the tastefully decorated private cottages or one of the large family villas; all of which have cedar-encased tubs in en-suite bathrooms, four-poster beds and a fire place. The homemade Italian food is excellent. Activities include fishing along the banks of the nearby Malewa River, horse and mountain bike riding. ❾

Melili Cottage Next to *Eburru Guest Cottage* and similarly delightful. Ideal for families (sleeps four) but bring your own food, sheets and towels. If you're driving to either cottage, turn left 13km north of Naivasha on to Moi North Lake Rd (unsurfaced and in places badly pitted). Turn right immediately, then left 3km further on, and then follow the road up through "Maasai Gorge". Ignore the turn-off to Gilgil and take the next right. Pass the barrier, go over the airstrip and turn left at a

reflective arrow, 100m past *Eburru Cottage*. ❹
Olerai House Four kilometres past the "Green Park" turn-off is the former home of Iain and Oria Douglas-Hamilton, who were involved in the struggle to ban the ivory trade (they still live on the estate). Six s/c double bedrooms in guest houses surrounding the main, flower-covered house; breakfast and lunch are served under fever trees from a long dug-out boat. Excursions, walks and boat rides are included in the price, which even so is hugely expensive at $640 a double. ❾

Eating and drinking

You can drop in for meals and drinks at *Fish Eagle Inn*, *Fisherman's Camp*, *Lake Naivasha Country Club*, *Lake Naivasha Lodge*, and the *Yelo Green Hotel*. *Crayfish Campsite* has a bar. *Geothermal Club* (21.8km along Moi South Lake Road) is a recommended gem of a place owned by *La Belle Inn* (see p.233), with some of the best views over the lake. Entrance is free, and a day's use of the pool costs Ksh100. They do excellent English breakfasts, gastronomic African dishes for lunch and dinner, and cheap drinks, all in a very relaxed atmosphere.

Shopping

There are a number of decent shopping options around the lake. The number of kilometres (in brackets) refers to the distance along Moi South Lake Road from the lake road junction with the main Nairobi road (which is 3km from Naivasha town itself).

Heidi Lange's at the junction of the Nairobi road and Moi South Lake Road – there's a small sign. This is where German-born artist Heidi Lange sells her batik seconds (very slight flaws). Prices range from Ksh100 to Ksh1000.

Shelabela House 2km, turn right at the signpost for Bee's Garden Farm; PO Box 108 ☎0311/20462, ℻21389. A swanky new hippyish gift shop, with supposedly antique tribal arts, a selection of textiles, and local medicinal and culinary herbs for sale. They also offer "Aura Soma Colour Therapy".

The Campbell Clause Gallery 3.3km ☎0311/20681. Galley/giftshop with a selection of crafts and artworks (the bronze Maasai warriors are rather good); well worth having a look if you're around that way.

Great Rift Lakes Bikes and Tents 3.5km; opposite the turning for *Lake Naivasha Lodge* ☎0311/20514, ℻21116. Two kiosks, one selling drinks and snacks at low prices, the other renting out bicycles (Ksh500 per day) and a variety of modern tents (Ksh500–800 for 24 hours). They also offer biking trips to Crescent Island, along a narrow causeway from private farmland.

Elmenteita Weavers & El Lorien 4.3km, and 800m along the signposted track. Two good browsing places. El Lorien (9am–5pm, closed Wed ☎0311/21062) sells fresh vegetables and Naivasha wine (Ksh200–400 a bottle), with singing women working in the back, but the main draw is Elmenteita Weavers (Mon–Sat 9am–5.30pm, Sun 9am–5pm; PO Box 85 ☎0311/30115, ℻740721),

a high-quality and very friendly weaving shop, with looms behind the showroom. Carpets and rugs, sweaters (some superb), *kangas* and *kikois* compete with various other bought-in crafts. Justifiably expensive. Credit cards accepted.

Karagita Village 4.5km. A little adobe and tin-plate village of flower-farm workers, immigrants and victims of ethnic strife elsewhere in the Rift, but very friendly if you take a genuine interest in the people and their way of life. This is not a tourist attraction, despite the roadside souvenir stalls, and intrusive photography will not be welcome. The black-and-white *Punda Bar*, at the start of the village, is a friendly place to hang out.

"Sulmac" dukas 17.6km. Sulmac (near *Fisherman's Camp*) is one of the biggest flower plantations in the area, employing over 4000 people. Near the main entrance, there's a small shopping centre where you can eat for next to nothing. Newspapers are on sale in the morning by the farm gate and, 500m further west, you'll usually find a gathering of ladies selling the produce from their small vegetable plots. If there was any land free, this would undoubtedly evolve into a small town. It's the main south lake transport focus, though a bus goes on as far as *Fisherman's Camp* and then back to Naivasha town around 8am and 1pm every day.

Watalii Kiosk 19.4km; PO Box 785 ☎0311/21327. Watalii Kiosk, on the road to Hell's Gate, is run by an energetic local councillor. Here you can rent bikes (Ksh420 a day, including a soft drink), stock up on supplies, or collapse in the speakeasy he set up for locals (pineapple wine Ksh10 a glass). There's also cheap food, but order early. The owner is a font of information and also organizes safaris, including speciality tours of tea, coffee, flower and barley (beer) cultivation processes. He also offers homestays (Ksh500) and a laundry service.

Getting around

It's possible to go **out in a boat** at most of the lakeshore establishments. *Burch's*, the *Lake Hotel* and *Fisherman's Camp* all have various vessels. *Fisherman's Camp* has a fast motorboat at about Ksh1750 per hour and a half-speed one for Ksh1000 (both take up to eight passengers). You need an hour in the fast boat to get over to the main concentration of hippos and back. Splashing along the papyrus-fringed shore just after the sun has come up, drifting among the pelicans and past other people's back gardens, is a rare pleasure – though large areas are now filled with a rank growth of weed and lilypads which makes it an exhausting one too. With luck (and a rod), you'll catch a tilapia.

Bicycles are a good way of exploring the lakeshore, and particularly for getting around Hell's Gate National Park: both *Fisherman's Camp* and Watalıı Kiosk (see above) rent out bikes, and both have good photocopied sketch maps of the lake and Hell's Gate. Other bike rental places include Great Rift Lakes Bikes and Tents, *Fish Eagle Lodge*, and *Lake Naivasha Country Club*. Incidentally, by all means give lifts if you're cycling – the locals, understandably, find it hilarious that foreigners should shed sweat for them, and it's a great way of making friends on equal terms. For Hell's Gate, you're better off entering by Olkaria Gate, which makes for an easier downhill ride to Elsa Gate.

Circumnavigating the lake **by road** is difficult unless you have wheels. With a vehicle, you soon reach the 30km mark and hit the dust and potholes which were the notorious condition of the whole lake road until a few years back; there's 35km of this (between an hour and two hours' worth) before you reach the Naivasha–Nakuru highway at a point 9km north of Naivasha. If you're hitching or using public transport, you'll find very few vehicles have reason to go beyond Kongoni Village and it's not really worth trying to go the whole way.

Exploring on foot can also be very pleasant. From *Fisherman's Camp*, it's worth walking up to the superb viewpoint, and visiting *Elsamere* (see below).

Lake dangers

Beware out on Naivasha. The possibility that underground springs may feed the lake, its location on the floor of the Rift Valley, and its shallowness, all combine to produce notoriously fast changes of mood and weather: grey and placid one minute, suddenly green and choppy with whitecaps the next. Naivasha shouldn't be underestimated, as boating mishaps are all too common. Watch out, too, for hippos, which can overturn a small boat easily enough if frightened or harassed. Although there's no bilharzia in Naivasha, the hippos, the dense weeds, and the reported recent sighting of a crocodile, combine to offset any enthusiasm you might have had for a swim.

Elsamere and the Environmental Education Centre

Twenty two kilometres down Moi South Lake Road, **Elsamere** (daily 3–6pm; Ksh350 ☎0311/21055, ⓦwww.elsatrust.org), former home of the naturalist and painter Joy Adamson, is now a conservation centre, open to the public in the afternoons: there's a video (which you don't have to watch), followed by a copious and civilized afternoon tea on the lawn (Ksh300). If you really like the place, you can take lunch (Ksh600) or dinner (Ksh1000) here, though you need to book ahead. It's unlicensed, but you can bring your own wine for dinner. There's also **accommodation** available, see p.239. If the house is somewhat shrine-like, the garden is a fine place to while away a couple of hours with a pair of binoculars: a troop of colobus monkeys (normally found only in moist forests) can be seen in the acacias around the grounds.

From Kinangop to Thika

If you're serious about hiking, mountain biking, or fairly adventurous expeditionary driving, a route from **North Kinangop to Thika** is a dramatic and attractive one to take to Thika. It cuts up from the Rift Valley and right over the southern flank of the Nyandarua (Aberdare) range – still, in large part, virgin mountain rainforest.

The approach **from Naivasha** is quite straightforward, as frequent matatus make the journey up to North Kinangop. Routine though it may be, this part of the journey is still spectacular. The road climbs constantly towards the **Kinangop Plateau**, with the Rift Valley and Lake Naivasha way below. The land hereabouts is Kikuyu farming country, once widely settled by Europeans, who were lured by the wide open moors, rocky outcrops and gushing streams. Sheep and cattle graze everywhere.

North Kinangop is nowadays a rather isolated rural community, a village of big rubber boots and raggy sweaters (it can freeze here at night), whose road becomes nearly impassable during the long rains. Transport onwards from here outside the rainy season though, is usually little problem – at least as far as South Kinangop. Tractors will pick you up and there are a few old lorries, too, trundling around. **South Kinangop** (also known as **Njabini**) is livelier than its northern counterpart, a small trading centre with a paved road straight to Naivasha (look out for the quaint, red-tiled colonial buildings which are now a Caltex station). You can also get matatus direct to South Kinangop from Naivasha. If you get stuck in South Kinangop, give the *Gimwa Rest Lodge* (❷) a try at the Thika end of town – clean, very inexpensive s/c rooms and good hot showers.

South Kinangop to Gatakaini is a thirty-kilometre stretch, taking seven to eight hours on foot or making a great mountain-bike trip. A *murram* road (the C67) does continue, but there's very little traffic as it switchbacks in descent, across a series of streams flowing south from the Aberdares to the Chania River. The road follows the river, with tremendous scenic variation, though almost always through forest – sometimes wild, sometimes conifer plantation. But after the turn-off (left) for **Kimakia forest station**, the occasional *shambas* and all signs of habitation stop completely. From here down, the forest is untouched mountain jungle – trees with huge dark green leaves, birds shrieking in alarm, the crashing of colobus monkeys, chameleons wobbling across the road and even tell-tale elephant dung. In the **wrong season**, the road becomes an appalling quagmire, really just for tractors (though you don't see many), but on foot, or even by mountain bike, there's no danger of getting stuck.

You reach tarmac and human population again at **Gatakaini** and, just before you do, there's the very pleasant *Kimakia Fishing Camp* (*bandas*, toilets and running water), unsupervised but a good place to spend the night with your own tent. The camp is run by the Fisheries Department (contact the Naivasha Senior Fisheries Officer on ☎0311/20505). At Gatakaini you can also find matatus and buses to get you down to the relative metropolis of Thika (see p.170). Irritatingly, towards evening public transport thins out and the country bus may leave you stranded at Gatura. If you have no luck hitching, give the excellent, but no longer appropriately named, *Tarmac End Inn* a try: a clean B&L with hot water, well inside the ❶ bracket.

Elsamere, and the neighbouring **Environmental Education Centre**, is the focus for the Naivasha region's environmental issues, with regular seminars and the involvement of scientists and researchers from overseas, plus local schools and universities.

Crescent Island Game Sanctuary

A very popular short trip is a visit to the **Crescent Island Game Sanctuary**. The "crescent" is the outer rim of a volcanic crater which forms a deep bay, the deepest part of the lake. The island is attached to the shore by a narrow causeway on the private land of Sanctuary Farm (about 6km from the lake road junction), but don't try to enter there; go instead to Lake Naivasha Country Club and ask at the reception desk about a **boat**. The fixed price is Ksh500 (plus Ksh300 entrance) and you have to state the time you wish to be picked up – if you miss the boat, you'll be charged for the cost of a search party. The boatmen are obliging, and will detour to show you the hippos and giant kingfisher. Once there, you're free to wander at will. At first you may think there's nothing there, but the island, barely two square kilometres, is home to hundreds of species of birds as well as gazelle, giraffe, waterbuck (caution – they can be dangerous) and some startlingly large, though harmless, pythons. **Horse riding** is available at Sanctuary Farm, at about Ksh800 per hour (☎0311/21324).

Green Crater Lake – Lake Songasoi

Now that people are visiting it, the once-mysterious (because rarely visited) **Green Crater Lake** is a straightforward target for a short trip – preferably with a vehicle, as it's 17km past *Fisherman's Camp* and 6km beyond the end of the tarmac and reliable transport. There is one matatu daily, leaving Crater Lake at 9am, returning towards 4pm (it leaves Naivasha at 3pm), which is really only of use if you're camping or staying at the *bandas* by the lake. A proper **game sanctuary** has been set up all round the crater, with entrance fees (currently just Ksh200, and Ksh50 extra if you bring a car), and there's an exclusive tented lodge in the crater itself (see p.238). In the sanctuary there are various tracks you can take, though the one to the crater rim is only for hikers or 4WD vehicles. You'll see a fair amount of plains game if you follow the perimeter fence; there are plenty of buffalo in the sanctuary, so exercise caution.

The brilliant, jade lake is quite breathtaking, in a small way: the Maasai consider its deep alkaline waters good for sick cattle, but it's also a favourite place for them, with sacred associations. From the main viewpoint on the west rim, it's possible to scramble up for ten minutes to the highest point. There are not many places where you can get down to the crater floor, but the easiest are on the south side.

Hell's Gate National Park

Daily dawn to dusk; $15, children $5; $8 to camp, $10 at "special" campsites. Warden: PO Box 234 Naivasha ☎0311/20510, ☎20577. Map: Survey of Kenya "Hell's Gate National Park" at 10cm:1.25km (1993). The road to the park at Olkaria Gate, 21.5km from the lake road junction, is tarred all the way (5km) through the geothermal area, but there's a very steep descent to the gorge and roadhead at the end.

The best expedition in the Naivasha area is the hike through the Njorowa gorge – **Hell's Gate**. This is a spectacular and exciting area, the gorge's red cliffs and undulating expanse of grassland providing one of the few remaining places in Kenya where you can walk among the **herds of plains game** without having to go a long way off the beaten track. Buffalo, zebra, eland, hartebeest, Thomson's gazelle and baboons are all usually seen; lions and leopards hardly ever, but you might just see a cheetah, and you'll certainly come across their footprints if you scan the trail. There are servals, one of the most delicate cats and, high on the cliffs, small numbers of klipspringer ("cliffjumper") antelope. Njorowa is a fairly small area and the quantity of wildlife varies seasonally. The gorge is occasionally rather empty of animals.

The main entrance road to Hell's Gate is just south of the YMCA, but the Elsa Gate is a further 1.5km along this track. If driving a small vehicle, be aware of the low clearance on some of the tracks. If you're wheel-less get there as early as possible in the day. It's about 25km to the roadhead and back and, while a fair number of vehicles visit at weekends, there are far fewer during the week, making your chances of a lift somewhat slim. The best time to arrive is dawn, when most animals are about. Try at any cost to avoid the midday hours, as the heat away from the cooling lake is intense. You'll need to carry plenty of water and some food (the only place to buy anything in the park is a simple staff kiosk in the Olkaria Geothermal Area).

There are also several **campsites** in the park if you want to stay overnight, with picnic benches, shower stands, taps and pit latrines. The nicest camping is at the shady and superbly sited *Ol Dubai* campsite on the clifftop south of Fischer's Tower. *Nairburta* and *Endachata* campsites (the latter a more expensive "special campsite") are across the gorge on the northern cliffs (see map "Lake Naivasha & Hell's Gate", p.235).

The upper gorge

From Elsa Gate, take a look first at the rock known as **Fischer's Tower**, after the German explorer who arrived at Lake Naivasha via Hell's Gate. The rock is a volcanic plug – the hard lava remaining from an ancient volcano after the cone itself has been eroded. It's now the home of a colony of very astute rock hyraxes ("dassies"), which look like large, shaggy guinea pigs and expect to be fed.

Continuing through the gorge along the main track, more and more animals are visible on the slopes leading up to the sheer cliffs. Ornithologists probably don't need reminding that at least one pair of rare **lammergeier eagles** used to nest on the cliffs. But they are rarely seen – report any sightings to a ranger. More obvious are the secretary birds: these you'll always see, mincing carefully through the grass at a safe distance.

If you're driving or on a mountain bike, you can take the longer Twiga and Buffalo Circuits. Twiga climbs up to the left from just inside Elsa Gate before you reach Fischer's Tower and then Buffalo Circuit ploughs through thick bush (don't go anywhere near the buffaloes, though, as they can be extremely unpredictable and dangerous). These tracks are insanely dusty but, when the dust clears, the views out over Hell's Gate and across to the Aberdares Range are magnificent.

Hell's Gate is somehow a very authentic-looking part of East Africa. Its colours and acoustics give it a distinct sense of place. It has been used several times as a film location, most recently for that stirring epic *Sheena – Queen of the Jungle* (a number of fibreglass rocks still litter the deep part of the gorge). Hell's Gate's more enduring significance is as the one-time outlet for the prehistoric freshwater lake that stretched from here to Nakuru and, it's believed, would have supported early human communities on its shores.

The lower gorge

At the southern end of the gorge (12km from the entrance), a second rock tower – **Ol Basta** – marks its transition into tangled ravine. Here, there's a car park where, if you're driving and want to get out, you'll have to continue on foot, as there's nowhere to park on the narrow, rocky track that follows the gorge to the south for a short distance. The nearby "Interpretation Centre" is now a **viewpoint**, a good place to picnic and to shelter from rain or sun. The best move you can make from this **roadhead** is to cross the gorge and follow the "Nature Trail" round the north side of Ol Basta. There's nothing nature trail about it, but it's easy enough to follow as far as the rock tower where most people turn back.

If you want to **hike in the ravine**, from Ol Basta the trail becomes more indistinct and it's quite easy to lose your way until you turn down into the head of the ravine itself. Beware of suggestions that there's a path around the south side of Ol Basta, directly above the eastern branch of the ravine: there is not, and trying to prove otherwise is dangerous. Equally dodgy is the very steep way down into the ravine just south of the gorge crossing, near the car park. You need tough walking shoes for this and shouldn't attempt it alone. Once down on the ravine floor, you've a one-hour walk or thereabouts southwards to the point where you can climb up to the road on the west side again. Watch out for unexpected slippery surfaces and seek advice if it's been raining, as flash floods sometimes rip through the ravine. It's a tough, exhilarating hike that most people should be able to do quite easily.

If you've come equipped for a night out, you can press on, to emerge after a further (and difficult) 12km at the end of the canyon – still 15km short of the Narok road. For orientation, aim for **Mount Suswa** – itself an area of great exploring interest, only properly documented in the last few years.

Otherwise, either turn back and retrace your path to Elsa Gate, or else climb up towards the noise and steam of Olkaria geothermal station. Here, on the cliff-top you can look out over the gorge and a Maasai *enkang* below, with your back to the first productive **geothermal installation** in Africa. The underground temperature of the super-heated, pressurized water is up to 304°C, one of the hottest sources in the world, and the station is eventually expected to supply half of Kenya's energy requirements. Surprisingly, although the whole complex is working at full tilt, the impact on the local environment appears to be small, and it certainly doesn't spoil the landscape until you're in the complex itself.

Heading for the main buildings through the scrub, and the maze of pipes and hissing steam jets, you meet a perfect new **tarmac road**. From here, you shouldn't have any problem getting a ride with plant workers down to the lake road at a point 2km past *Fisherman's Camp*. The road emerges near the Oserian farm where they produce carnations. If you hike it, allow about three hours to complete this section. There are fine views of Oloiden and Green Crater lakes.

Mount Longonot

Especially when the weather's right (most likely January–March and July–October), **Mount Longonot** (daily dawn to dusk; $15, children $5; $2 to camp) is worth climbing for the fabulous views in every direction as you circle the rim. Don't try to make the ascent from the lake road or Hell's Gate, however – it's further and steeper than it looks, and is covered in dense bush on its north slopes, frequented by buffalo. Moreover, it's a national park and you have to do things the right way. Head for Longonot village on the old Nairobi road.

If you're **driving**, there's a road that leads the 6–7km from just southeast of the level crossing by the main road to the base of the mountain, and you can leave your car there safely and get a drink. There's only one straightforward route up to the crater rim, and you may be escorted by Kenya Wildlife Service rangers. For **overnight stays** on the mountain, special permission may be needed from the warden and you need a tent; there are no official campsites. In the village, *Jogoo Bar B&L* is right by the train station – very cheap and basic, but friendly.

The Kalenjin peoples

In the central part of the Rift Valley, the **Kalenjin** form the majority of the population. Their name, actually a recent adoption by a number of peoples speaking dialects of Nandi, means "I tell you" in all of them. The principal Kalenjin are the Nandi, Terik, Tugen, Elgeyo, Elkony, Sabaot, Marakwet and Kipsigis, and more contentiously the Pokot. They were some of the earliest inhabitants of Kenya and probably absorbed the early bushmen or pygmy peoples who were here for hundreds of thousands of years before.

Primarily **farmers**, the Kalenjin have often adapted their economies to local circumstances. It is supposed that the first Kalenjin were herdsmen whose lifestyle has changed over the centuries. The pastoral **Pokot** group, who still spurn all kinds of cultivation and despise peoples who rely on anything but livestock, call the **Marakwet**, living against the western Rift escarpment, *Cheblong* (the Poor), for their lack of cattle.

The **Okiek** (Ndorobo) are another interesting clue to the past. These hunter-gatherers are a Nandi-speaking people, living in scattered groups in the forests of the high slopes flanking the Rift. Unlike most hunter-gatherers, they do very little gathering. Meat, and honey from their hives, are the traditional staples. They consider wild fruits and vegetables barely palatable, though cornmeal and gardening have been introduced, and they now keep some domestic animals too. They may be the descendants of Kalenjin forebears who lost (or ate) their herds. There are other groups in Kenya who live mostly by hunting – Ndorobo or Wanderoo – for whom such a background is very likely, and who are all gradually abandoning their old lifestyles and dislikes to the inexorable advance of "civilization".

Many of the mainstream Kalenjin played key roles in the founding of the Kenya African Democratic Union (KADU – now disbanded), but the most famous of their number in recent years was President Moi, a **Tugen** from Baringo District. Coming from a small ethnic group, his presidency for years avoided the accusations of tribalism levelled so bitterly against Kenyatta, and he still devotes time to touring the country, holding *Harambee* meetings and spurring development. In the run-up to the 1992 elections, however, what had long been muttered about became increasingly obvious: the country was not being run for the benefit of all. The president's firm grip on the reins of power was being exercised through the Kalenjin-dominated civil service, rather than the more ethnically mixed cabinet. This fact, coupled with the "ethnic cleansing" in the Rift Valley of non-Kalenjin by groups of surprisingly well-organized young men (widespread evictions from Rift Valley villages, the burning of compounds and several hundred people killed) fulfilled the president's own prophecy that multi-partyism would do nothing to harmonize tribal relations in the country. The same story repeated itself in the run-up to the 1997 elections, with Kikuyu the main victims. At the time of writing, with elections once more due in 2002, the country was bracing itself for more potential trouble. This time, however, a feeling of optimism was also in evidence, based on the belief that Kenyans had got wise to politicians' wily ways and were also keen to avoid the descent into anarchy which political violence had led to in neighbouring countries.

Up the mountain

Longonot's name comes from the Maasai *oloonong'ot*, "mountain of many spurs" or "steep ridges", and you soon find out why. The cone is composed of very soft volcanic deposits that have eroded into deep gulches and narrow ridges. The **hike to the rim** takes about an hour. At the top you can collapse (the last section is rather steep), and look back over the Rift Valley on one side and the enormous, silent crater on the other. Joseph Thomson, the first *mzungu* up here in 1884, was overcome:

The scene was of such an astounding character that I was completely fascinated, and felt under an almost irresistible impulse madly to plunge into the fearful chasm. So overpowering was this feeling that I had to withdraw myself from the side of the pit.

Avoiding the same urge, you can now walk, or scramble, down a steep **crater path**; you turn left from the gravelly landing on the rim and find the path after about ten minutes' walk. Exciting encounters with buffalo on the crater floor aren't uncommon: a 1937 guidebook observes that "any attempt to descend into the crater is accompanied by hazard".

The walk **around the crater rim** is what most climbers do. The anti-clockwise route is easier because the climb to the summit on the western side is quicker and steep sections more negotiable. It doesn't look far, but allow two to three hours. Much of the path is over crumbly volcanic tufa and has been worn, by a combination of walkers and rain, into a channel so deep and narrow that it's almost impossible to put one foot in front of the other.

Until recently, Longonot's crater was famous for its steam jets (the volcano is classed as "senile", not "extinct"). Although their vents, like pockmarks, are still visible in several places around the rim and on the crater walls, their emissions of steam have decreased since the Olkaria plant went on line, though the hot-air thermals are said to be still sufficient to deflect light aircraft. Another rumour is the existence of a tunnel running from the inside base of the crater on the south side and out onto the plain beyond.

Gilgil, Elmenteita and Kariandusi

GILGIL – pronounced "Girgir" by many Kenyans – is as dull a town as you could expect to find anywhere, with fragile-looking *dukas* and dusty streets with scavenging goats. On the outskirts lie the serried, pastel-coloured ranks of new housing for the hi-tech Gilgil Telecomms Industries workers, who assemble Zebra-brand computers among other things. If you're heading north towards Nyahururu and Maralal, you may well find yourself hitching or changing buses or matatus here. The pretty rooms and clean, threadbare beds at the cheap *Salama Lodge* (PO Box 721 ☎0367/5263; ❶) can be safely recommended as probably the best of the old lodges in town, which in Gilgil is not saying much. Otherwise, try the clean *Dakar Lodge,* opposite the bank (PO Box 452 ☎0367/5224; ❶), rebuilt after it burnt down in 1999, or *Ben Lisa Guest House* (no phone; ❶), also a new place, with hot water and safe parking. *Sakiwa Silent Lodge* (no phone; ❶) doesn't live up to its name and is pretty run down, while the *Mugoira B&L* (☎0367/5404; ❶) is cleaner, and slightly less raucous. A better option if you want to avoid the dusty town altogether is the very cheap *Haruma Base Complex* (no phone; ❶), situated twenty minutes north of

Gilgil on the Nairobi-Nakuru road, which has hot water and safe parking. Water supplies seem problematic, but in Gilgil maybe you should just count your blessings. The town has a supermarket, Gigil Mattresses, a bank next door, a post office (Mon–Fri 8am–1pm & 2–5pm) and several car mechanics and petrol stations, but not much else. For details of a wonderful cycling or driving route around the area, see the box on p.250.

Gilgil War Cemetery

En route to Nyahururu – "T Falls" if it slips off the tongue more easily – you'll pass **Gilgil Commonwealth War Cemetery**. If you've a couple of hours to spare, walk the 2–3km out of town into the quiet, breezy savannah and have a look. It's a good place to stop for a picnic and some moments of contemplation before flagging down a vehicle.

There are about two hundred graves here from the East African campaign of World War II and from the War for Independence – "the Emergency" – in the 1950s. Whether by accident (which doesn't seem credible) or design, the African graves are all at the bottom of the slope, and record no personal details apart from name and rank. The graves of British soldiers are higher up and the stones inscribed with family messages. Most are from World War II, but there are also poignant reminders of lives lost between 1959 and 1962, after the British government's futile attempt to prevent the inevitable (see p.643). The fact that not a single freedom fighter is buried here demonstrates the ambivalent attitude of Kenyans to their struggle for *Uhuru*. The Gilgil cemetery, one of over forty in Kenya tended by the Commonwealth War Graves Commission, is lovingly maintained, one of the most meticulously kept in the country.

The road climbs past *Gilgil Country Club* on through moorland and conifer plantations around the resettlement zone of Ol Kalou, where some of the most violent Mau Mau attacks took place, and over the equator to Nyahururu (see p.218), Kenya's highest town.

Lake Elmenteita

Beyond the turn for Gilgil, the fast road sweeps the eastern wall of the Rift Valley and pushes up high above **Lake Elmenteita**. It's a spectacular and primeval setting, framed by the broken caldera walls of several extinct volcanoes, which resemble a reclining human figure. The Maasai know these peaks as Elngiragata Olmorani (Sleeping Warrior) – a name which is ironically fitting, since the lake and its lands were expropriated from the Maasai at the start of the colonial period by Lord Delamere (the caldera is now also known as "Delamere's Nose"). You can get a good view from the big "parking lane" viewpoint – if you survive the rather desperate assaults from the curio sellers. This shallow soda lake, which has been known to shrivel to a huge white salt pond (the last time was in 1985), is a good site for flamingos when Lake Nakuru is out of favour, and always good for pelican: there are an estimated 300 bird species in all. Like Lake Nakuru, Elmenteita has no outflow, and so its accumulated alkaline salts make it uninhabitable for all but one species of fish, *tilapia grahami*. The lake once had a herd of hippos, but the droughts pushed them back to Lake Naivasha and they seem unlikely ever to return.

There are two top-notch establishments offering **accommodation** on the lakeshore. *Delamere's Camp* (reservations through Savannah Camps & Lodges, see p.44; FB ❾), a luxury tented camp within the private acacia-woodland **Soysambu Wildlife Sanctuary**, is highly recommended for enthusiastic amateur naturalists and bird-watchers alike. To get there, turn right off the Naivasha–Nakuru road at the signpost for Kasambara, take the right fork immediately, and the entrance is 1km further on, followed by 2km of rough track. The price includes day and night game drives which give you the opportunity to see the elusive bush babies, aardvark and other nocturnal wildlife, a possible poke around "Delamere's Nose" and as many, excellently guided, wildlife walks as you like (transport is also available). The setting is wonderful, with a lawn dropping down to the lakeshore (afternoon tea is taken there), and a spectacular view of the Sleeping Warrior and Mau Escarpment over the far side of the lake. Service is excellent, and there are even tame ostrich to feed. If you've really got money to burn, enquire about their treehouse accommodation, on the far side of the lake, which occasionally attracts leopards. The second Elmenteita option is *Lake Elmenteita Lodge* (PO Box 561 Nakuru; reservations through *Lake Nakuru Lodges*, 2nd floor, Arrow House, Koinange St, PO Box 70559 Nairobi ☏02/212405, ☏227062; HB ❺ low, ❻ high; FB ❻ low, ❼ high). This is one place it may be advisable to visit when it has been raining, to avoid the persistent breeze which is practically brown with dust in the dry season. Much more affordable and less fancy than *Delamere's Camp*, this ranch-style lodge, built around the 1930s brick homestead of the cattle farmer Lord Cole, has equally jaw-dropping views, but the disadvantage of being some distance above the lake (a track leads down to it). There's a resident naturalist, a pool, and a very good restaurant. A hundred metres down the driveway from the main road is the **Ostrich Park Farm** (Ksh250), which provides amusing entertainment for kids.

Whilst nearly all the land around the lake is part of the private (and fenced-in) Delamere Estate's Soysambu property, gaining access to most of it is easily achieved if you ask at the camp. Its southeastern corner, however, is public land, accessible through *Lake Elmenteita Lodge* (casual entry Ksh300), and apparently also via a track from the viewpoint lay-by; clear it with anyone you come across down there. Around the once-lush shores are a number of prehistoric sites. **Gambles cave**, 10km southwest of Elmenteita village at Eburru, is the most famous; if you're an enthusiast, you can visit it by making arrangements ahead of time – ask first at the National Museum in Nairobi (see p.113).

Digs and mines: Kariandusi

For an easier shot of prehistory, try a visit to **Kariandusi**, with a surprising sideshow in the shape of a neighbouring diatomite mine. Kariandusi (signposted off the main A104 highway, 1.5km to the right or twenty minutes' walk; daily 8am–6pm; Ksh200, children Ksh100) is an **Acheulian site** characterized, like Olorgasailie (p.227), by heavy hand-axes and cleavers. The site is very small, consisting of just two excavated areas cleared by Louis Leakey in 1928–31 and 1947, each displaying a scattered assortment of stone tools, many of them made of the black glassy volcanic rock, obsidian. The guide is knowledgeable, and there's a small **museum** too, which explains the formation of the Rift Valley, and has comparative skull specimens of our various distant ancestors.

Neither Kariandusi nor Olorgasailie have any signs of permanent habitation. This, and the fact that some 120,000 years ago Lake Elmenteita came right up to here, some 180m higher than its present level and contained fresh water, suggests that it attracted hunter gatherers who would wait by the water to catch animals coming to drink. Tools were made on the spot, and simply left for the next occasion, as the Acheulians had yet to invent receptacles to carry them in. As the lake levels fluctuated, many tools were covered by it, and as the waters

Between Gilgil and Nakuru, if you're hiking – or driving or cycling with a few hours to spare – give the fast (but by no means smooth and occasionally unnerving) main A104 a miss and follow the tarmac **former route** which mostly runs parallel to the new road a few hundred metres off on the right-hand side. The old road is potholed but quite negotiable and far from busy, serving as a rural footpath for people carrying firewood or cycling to the next hamlet.

You can join the old road at Gilgil by turning off the main highway at the junction 26.5km from Naivasha (Gilgil itself isn't signposted, though Gilgil Telecomms Industries and a host of schools and other places are). Go right through the quiet businesses and petrol stations of Gilgil and you arrive, 4km to the north of the town, at a fine viewpoint over Lake Elmenteita. Shortly after, on the right, you pass the obscure little **Church of Goodwill** – a settler's sentimental folly – still used on Sundays, in whose small graveyard rest the remains of a few old colonials and military men.

Shortly after the church, you pass Kariandusi prehistoric site and, rounding a bend, the diatomite mine (both left). Between the two, by the crash barriers to the right, a pale-coloured, rocky, 4WD track leads, after 3km, up over the railway line to a stream. Here you can leave your vehicle and climb (guided by the usual retinue of boys) to a crystal-clear, **warm-water source** in the woods – known, blandly enough, as *maji moto* (meaning "hot water"). You can swim in the natural swimming pool – there are usually people about, washing clothes or bathing. Beyond the Kariandusi junction, the old road dries up and you have to rejoin the highway. You can get onto the quiet road again at the turning to "Mbaruk", 3km further on, then follow the railway to Lanet, a suburb of Nakuru.

If you want to take further time out and see a remote part of the Central Province highlands, take a right turn off the old road, 4km after the "Mbaruk" turning and follow the steep dirt road under the railway bridge and steeply up to the **Mbaruk Valley**. This is a beautiful road, rugged in parts (again, you're best off with 4WD) but with splendid compensation in the lush, forested cliffs across its far side. There's even a little **waterfall** 3km along the way, though it's easy to miss unless it's in spate. At the Ngorika crossroads (tasty chapatis are provided at the *hoteli* on the corner) turn left and you hit the tarmac C69 after 6km, where, turning left again, you start to make a fine, looping descent to the Rift Valley floor, with distinctive flat-topped acacias between the sloping *shambas* and the glint of Lake Nakuru down in the distance.

To follow this route in the other direction, Nairobi-bound, take the left turning for the C69 immediately before the Lanet Esso petrol station, before you reach the railway bridge bend.

receded again, were then carried by streams to their present concentrated clusters (some of the tools have been "rolled" by abrasive action, which supports this theory). Nothing much is known about the tool-makers themselves, apart from the fact that they obviously had a formidable grip. The most likely candidate is *Homo erectus*, an early hominid whose remains have been found at Olduvai Gorge in Tanzania alongside Acheulian artefacts, but the puzzle is that the site bears no evidence of fire, nor of combination tools (for example stone axes with wooden handles), nor of carrying receptacles, which *Homo erectus* is generally known for. This would suggest that the tool-makers were a primitive form of *Homo erectus*.

The diatomite industry

Right next door, just 800m from the highway, is a **diatomite mine**

(Diatomite Industries, PO Box 32 Gilgil ℡0367/2097), which is a fascinating complement to the prehistoric site. Diatomite is a light, white, crumbly rock composed of the compressed silica skeletons of microscopic sea organisms (diatoms). The Kikuyu used it as body paint (*karia andus*), and a "clean" variety of it is still eaten by pregnant women and sick children (it's full of calcium). It also makes an excellent filter and absorbs water like silica gel. Brewers use it for filtration and it makes an effective insecticide in grain silos by dehydrating the weevils without poisoning the grain.

The manager will gladly tell you more about diatomite (they're happy to receive visitors), but the real excitement comes when you walk down into the mine itself: a track spirals down the inside of a giant bowl, scooped out of the ground by pick and shovel over the last fifty years. Before digging stopped, they reached a level, about 50m down, where high-grade, brilliant white diatomite is found. Here, a dozen or more **tunnels** dive into the cliffs to form a maze of ghostly subterranean passages, almost architectural in design and home to thousands of fluttering fruit **bats**. The tunnels are wonderfully cool and vents keep the air circulating. You'll be assured that the structure of diatomite makes rock falls extremely unlikely, but a number of shored-up passageways may leave you unconvinced and glad to have along an accounts clerk – or some other conscripted employee – to guide you. You need a torch even though the light goes in a surprisingly long way, but you can't really get lost.

Mining is still carried out on a small scale, using picks and shovels, though the principal source is now an open-cast pit nearer Lake Elmenteita. The whole place has a somewhat archaic air about it, but an ancient, rusting kiln is periodically fired up to dry the diatomite for packing.

Nakuru and nearby sites

As you approach **NAKURU** along the main highway from Nairobi, the *shamba*- and conifer-cloaked mound directly ahead is the southern flank of Menengai crater, while to the left are the scrub-covered eastern heights of the Nakuru National Park.

Were it not for the fact that Nakuru is a major transport hub and has a national park even closer to its centre than Nairobi's, there would be no special reason to visit. A noisy, dusty and hustly town, Nakuru is Kenya's fourth largest city (though it projects a noticeably busier and more energetic image than Kisumu, the third). It's also capital of the enormous, sprawling Rift Valley Province that stretches from the Sudanese border to the slopes of Kilimanjaro.

3

THE RIFT VALLEY | Nakuru and nearby sites

Roadside rip-offs

A word of **warning**: if you're driving, beware of anyone around Nakuru telling you there's anything wrong with your car – this is the con-mechanic capital of Kenya. **Tricksters** hang around along the roadside either between Lanet and the town centre or between the town centre and the national park main gate, and have recently also been seen along the road to Eldoret. They work in teams, pointing one after another at your wheels as you drive past or, if you stop anywhere, "discovering" oil dripping from your engine – anything to get you into their garage for a bogus repair job. Gangs have recently taken to placing large rocks across already badly potholed stretches of highway (especially between Nakuru and Eldoret), forcing you to slow right down: ignore their demands to stop.

Nakuru came into existence on the thrust of the Uganda railway and owed its early growth, at least in part, to **Lord Delamere**, the colony's most famous figure. In 1903, he acquired four hundred square kilometres of land on the lower slopes of the Mau escarpment, followed by two hundred more at Soysambu, on the other side of the lake. Eager to share the empty vistas with compatriots – though preferably with other Cheshire or Lancashire men – he promoted in England the mile-square plots being offered free by the Foreign Office. Eventually, some two hundred new settler families arrived and Nakuru – a name which as usual could mean various things, including "Place of the Waterbuck" (Swahili) and "Swirling Dust" or "Little Soda Lake" (Maasai) – became their country capital. It lies on the unprepossessing steppe between the lake and the flanks of Menengai crater. This desolate shelf has a nickname: "the place where the cows won't eat grass" (the pasture was found to be iron-deficient). Farmers near the town turned to the better prospects of pyrethrum, the plant used to make insecticide, as a cash crop.

Nakuru town

Still largely a workaday farmers' town, with unadorned old seed shops and veterinary paraphernalia much in evidence on the main street, Nakuru is a little Nairobi without the flashy veneer, its streets frequently undergoing ear-shattering repairs. Ongoing outbursts of ethnic violence in the Rift Valley have resulted in an influx of Kikuyu refugees from outlying parts of the province; it is, in many ways, more of a social barometer than Nairobi. The town can appear intimidating at first, especially if you arrive in the evening, and the beggars and street kids, many sniffing poppers and other solvents, are amongst the most pitiful you'll ever see. Since it's a stone's throw from **Nakuru National Park**, equally close to the prehistoric settlement site at **Hyrax Hill** and the vast bowl of the **Menengai crater**, and the jumping-off point for trips into the **northern Rift Valley**, you may find yourself passing through Nakuru more often than you'd like.

The town has some positive aspects, worth emphasizing if you're staying. The **market** is certainly animated and a pleasure to look around (though has its fair share of hassle), and there's a glimmer of charm still remaining in its colonnaded old streets and the **jacaranda**-lined avenues at the edge of town.

Accommodation

The **train** and **bus/matatu stations** are packed together at the east end of town with **lodgings** all around. Watch yourself at the bus and matatu enclosures, and if you need directions ask a driver or passenger. You're spoilt for choice for **cheap rooms**, with plenty of other places apart from the following found in the centre, though few of them stand out. A number of **mid-range hotels** are dotted about the western avenues, and are amazingly good value if you've just come from Nairobi. However, the sewers there can turn even the hardiest stomachs, and the distantly throbbing noise from the *Millennium Hotel* nightclub is also a nuisance. At the luxury end, there's nothing at all in Nakuru – most of the thousands of tourists on their way to the park stay in one of the two lodges there.

If you're **camping** go to the national park (see p.263) or use the campsite 17km back down the Nairobi road, a ten-minute walk off the road, and a similar distance from Lanet Gate, in the unlikely location of Greensteds School (☎037/210500; Ksh350). Turn off at the signs for the school and "The Battery Centre". There are good views, hot showers, a cheap bar filled with teachers on Fridays, and a bore hole which supplies drinking water.

Cheap to moderate

Amigo's B&L Gusii Rd, PO Box 1461
☏037/210170. This is one of the most popular cheapies, recently extended – a very basic secure lodging with a nice welcome, though rather dirty. The water, when there is any, is hot. ❶–❷

Amoodi's B&L Nehru Rd, PO Box 1731
☏037/41939. A no-frills B&L with excellent security, plenty of hot water, clean toilets and the cheapest twin beds in town, in shoe-box rooms. ❶

Carnation Hotel Mosque Rd, 1st floor, PO Box 1620 ☏037/43522. A branch of the *Manyatta Hotel*, which is opposite the *Pivot*, is a large but well-run and attentive establishment – the best in the town centre and very fair value, and with a good restaurant. The waiters are keen to persuade you to go on a park trip. ❸

Gitwamba Hotel Gusii Rd, PO Box 586
☏037/40754. One of the best joints in this quarter of town, with light, clean and spacious rooms (though only one s/c), good cheap breakfasts and a matatu stage opposite. Be aware it's raucous on disco nights – Wednesday and Friday–Sunday. ❶

Kerio Valley Lodge Gusii Rd, PO Box 234
☏037/41242. Simple non-s/c rooms in a quiet courtyard, and cheap. Sometimes there's hot water in the mornings. ❶

Lion Hill Bar & Lodgings PO Box 9556
☏037/850193. Right next to the park, by Lanet Gate, it mainly caters for local tour guides, but it has hot showers, mosquito nets and camping facilities (Ksh300 per person) The rooms are clean, very basic and the squeaking rodents hidden between the air vents reinforce your proximity to the wildlife. ❷

Mount Sinai Hotel Gusii Rd, PO Box 238
☏037/21779. Nakuru's best cheapie, opposite Stem Plaza Cosmetics. Great staff, good security and cool, functional rooms; restaurant down below. A tad overpriced. ❷

Mukoh Hotel Gusii Rd, PO Box 238
☏037/213516. Rather shambling place with 56 s/c and non-s/c rooms. Beds spotless, toilets less so, hot water. Overpriced. ❷

Pivot Hotel Lower Factory Rd, PO Box 1369
☏037/210226. Despite resembling a military hospital in every aspect, this is recommended: the rooms are shiny clean and have new mosquito nets. Go for rooms 1–15 to avoid the deafening disco din on some weekend nights. ❷

Seasons Hotel Government Ave, PO Box 3163
☏037/211986. Decent enough rooms – all self-contained – but dark and overpriced. ❷

Shik Parkview Hotel Kenyatta Ave, PO Box 614
☏037/212345 or 212346. Seventy-two rooms, clean and airy but on the small side. Separate bar and restaurant. The Nakuru Chess Club is resident upstairs (Wednesday and Friday 5pm, Sunday 2pm). ❶

Tropical Lodge Moi Rd, PO Box 4193
☏037/42608. A presentable, if rather gloomy, option with rooms big enough to swing several cats in and hot water morning and evening, but dirty bathrooms – wear the flip-flops they provide. ❶

Expensive

Kunste Hotel PO Box 1369 ☏037/212140; 2.5 km down the Nairobi road; see map p.261. A good hotel with sensibly priced rooms, but sometimes near deserted, which may explain (to the generous-minded) why staff customer service is so rusty. They sometimes allow camping. B&B ❸

Midland Hotel GK Kamau Highway, PO Box 908
☏037/212125, ℻44517. Long established and good value – basically a huge pub with rooms, all of which are s/c and comfy, if a tad gloomy. The old wing (no TVs), refurbished in 1997, is much more pleasant. Two bars, both open until midnight. Good disabled access. B&B ❸–❹

Stem Hotel PO Box 1076 ☏037/85391, ℻212332; Nairobi road, close to the Nakuru National Park Lanet Gate, 8km from the town centre; see map p.261. Pleasant (in a functional, motel manner), with a small pool, gym, steam room and sauna (Ksh80–200 per hour), acceptable s/c rooms, and good Indian Mughlai food (try the biriani). They also provide transport into the National Park (Ksh5000 per minibus), and normally allow camping. However, the bar gets busy (and noisy) at weekends, and as with all highway motels, it's advisable to lock your door at night. B&B ❹

Sundowner Lodge 1km down Kanu St off Lake Rd, in Langa Langa suburb; PO Box 561
☏037/214216, ℻211204. Run by the management of *Lake Nakuru Lodge* this would be a reasonable place if it were well maintained and not so overpriced. The rooms are dark and dingy; the food, which is served by inebriated-looking staff trying to avoid eye contact is tasty, but bring a torch at dinner times if seeing what you're eating is important to you. Saturday's "Africa Nite" is a disco with traditional dancers and acrobats. B&B ❹

Waterbuck Hotel West Rd, PO Box 3327
☏037/215672, ℻214163. As the town centre's most prominent hotel this seems to be the current "upmarket" choice, though at the moment it's undergoing long term renovations. It does a respectable and very reasonably priced buffet lunch, and the breakfasts are huge, but the accommodation itself is overrated, if cheap. It also has a new but rather dusty *nyama choma* joint round the back, and safe parking. ❸

Eating and drinking

Finding good **meals** is getting easier in Nakuru. As a guide, older, more down-at-heel establishments are bunched towards the east end of town near the railway station, while the west end, especially along Kenyatta Avenue, tends to be more upmarket.

Restaurants

The Courtyard Government Ave. Very relaxing place for a substantial feed – mainly grills, Indian, local and seafood – at around Ksh300; lunch curries Ksh240.

Nakuru Sweet Mart Gusii Rd. A long-established Indian eatery which does an excellent and massive vegetarian *thali*, good *bhajhias*, *masala tea* and a good range of breads. Very cheap, but avoid if you're on an oil-free diet.

Oyster Shell Club Rd/Kenyatta Ave, 1st floor. Magnificent dinners for under Ksh500, breakfast around Ksh200. Great service and atmosphere – real flowers and similar touches – although the dinner ambience can be marred by the *XTC Discotheque* upstairs.

Railway Station Restaurant An utterly time-warped retreat, though service is very slow. They used to silver-serve cornflakes and toast for breakfast, and still do immaculately served (though no

less gastronomically uncreative) colonial repasts at lunch and dinner. Around Ksh360.

Tipsy Restaurant Gusii Rd. Next door and similar to, but cheaper than, *Nakuru Sweet Mart*, and for the less hungry. The place looks clean, but there is no running water.

Snacks and bars

Café Lemon Tart Moi Rd. For snacks or breakfast this is hard to beat.

Jamia Hotel Mosque Rd, next to the mosque. Nothing outstanding, but open 24 hours.

Millennium Hotel Government Ave. Quite a pleasant beer garden and *nyama choma* joint – not a hotel – with thatched huts, wicker chairs and a wicked sound system.

Nakuru Coffee House Moi Rd. A reliable venue for real coffee and a bite to eat.

Waterbuck Hotel West Rd. A good snack menu all day, and a lively bar on Saturday nights.

Food shopping

If you're passing through in your own car, check the Sita Supermarket for **food supplies**, at the Sita shopping centre a few kilometres east of the town centre on the Nairobi road (the *Have More Restaurant* here is a good snack bar), or the shopping centre 4km west of town on the Kisumu road. The best supermarket in town is the main Uchumi on Kenyatta Lane, just off GK Kamau Highway (Mon–Sat 9.30am–8pm, Sun 9.30am–2pm). A smaller grocery is Gilani's on Club Road, while Gilani's Butchery on Moi Road has a good **cheese** counter where you can count on getting the cheap and excellent McLellan's Farmhouse brie-style rounds. Nakuru Patisserie on Club Lane has a wholesome selection of **bread** and baked bites. The main **produce market**, near the transport parks and railway station, has the full display of fruit and vegetables, but watch out for pickpockets and petty thieves.

Entertainment and nightlife

Nakuru is surprisingly jumping when it comes to **nightlife**. Try *Illusions Disco, Club Dimples*, or *Club Coco Savana* on Club Road, (the latter open nightly, with a jam session on Sundays and a good restaurant next door). Slightly less steamy are the famous weekend discos at the *Pivot Hotel* – their music is not at all bad – and the glitzy *XTC Discotheque*, above the *Oyster Shell Restaurant*. Also worth checking out for live bands are *Hotel Jams*, next to Afraha Stadium (especially Fridays).

If you're in town for more than a day, you may get the chance to see the Nakuru Players in action at their dour-looking **theatre** (☏037/40805) on Kipchoge Avenue. Of the two main **cinemas**, the Odeon and the Eros, both on GK Kamau Highway, the smaller Eros (screenings daily 6pm & 9pm, plus Saturday 3pm) is the more inviting.

Listings

Banks Scattered all over the town: there's a KCB with a "Bureau de Change" flagged on the western outskirts. All Mon–Fri 9am–3pm & Sat 9–11am. Both Standard Chartered at Moi Rd, and Barclays on Kenyatta Ave, have ATMs.

Books Ereto Bookshop, Kenyatta Lane, has a good range of African writers.

Car repairs If you really do have a problem, try and find out exactly what it is before approaching the myriad workshops at the western ends of Government and Kipchoge avenues. Get quotes from several places before bringing your vehicle down. Hertz recommend CMC Motors Group (☎037/211875–7) or D.T. Dobie (☎037/211775–7), both on George Morara Avenue.

Email DONA Communications, corner of Moi Rd and Kenyatta Ave (Mon–Sat 8am–6pm, Sun 10am–4pm; Ksh5 per min). Telephone and fax facilities available also.

Medical clinic Nakuru Medical Clinics, by Barclays on Kenyatta Ave (☎037/214655), has a range of specialists.

Music If you want to beef up your cassette collection, there are a number of cassette shops on Nehru Rd.

Parking This can be something of a problem, with a high chance of break-ins, dripping-oil scams and the like. Whether you're staying the night or not, the best plan is to park in a guarded hotel parking area – absolutely essential if all your luggage is inside. A small tip for the *askari* is normally expected.

Pharmacy A proficient one is Medika Chemists, 1st floor Equator House, Kenyatta Lane, next door to Uchimi (☎037/214847).

Post office Moi Rd/Kenyatta Ave (Mon–Fri 8am–5.30pm & Sat 9am–noon), with good telephone and fax facilities, and an EMS express mail counter round the back.

Travel agents Crater Travel, Inder Singh Building, just off Kenyatta Ave (PO Box 2631 ☎037/214896, ℱ215019), offers a full service for air ticketing, plus the usual range of (expensive) tour deals. Tayler's Travel, on Kenyatta Avenue itself (PO Box 527 ☎037/45806, ℱ212912) has a reputation for reliable hotel bookings, but doesn't accept Visa cards. For general local arrangements, especially Nakuru National Park visits and other safaris, Blackbird Tours (☎037/45383) is friendly and competent: fees are generally per vehicle, and so work out cheaper if you can form a group, but they're open to discussion. Current going rates are Ksh3000 for the use of a four-seater Suzuki, including the driver-guide but excluding park fees, for 5–6hr, and Ksh5000 for the use of a seven-seater Nissan minibus. They're happy to pick you up from your hotel.

Moving on from Nakuru

Travel options **from Nakuru** are wide open. You're less than two hours from Nairobi – a journey as easy to hitch as any in the country.

Heading the other way, the **bus** lines all run regular and frequent services to Eldoret, Kisumu, Kitale, Kisii and other points west (Akamba Bus is safest ☎037/213775–6). Alternatively, you can take the quieter road west, through the highland towns of Njoro, Elburgon and Molo, a route covered in this chapter on p.265. Southwards, you can get to Narok by **matatu** up the fantastic Mau escarpment (not a great distance, but allow a day to arrive). The most obvious destinations – in this chapter – are further north in the Rift Valley, around lakes Baringo and Bogoria especially, with at least two buses daily to Kampi ya Samaki at Lake Baringo, and matatus making the run to Kabarnet in the hills to the west. There's also a lavishly scenic route to Nyahururu through the Subukia Valley, an ascent of the Rift that, for sheer grandeur, comes close to the Naivasha escarpment (daily bus and matatu runs). If you're driving, the turn-off 2.5km down the Nairobi road is not signposted – turn left at the Shell petrol station opposite *Kunste Hotel*. A useful tip when entering Nakuru **bus station** from the railway station side is to go in via "Exit" to avoid the bevy of enthusiastic touts who hang around at "Entrance".

Menengai crater

Containing an enormous caldera, 12km across and nearly 500m deep in places, the extinct volcanic giant **Menengai** rises directly behind Nakuru, its sloping mass somehow not especially noticeable from the town. To reach it, head up

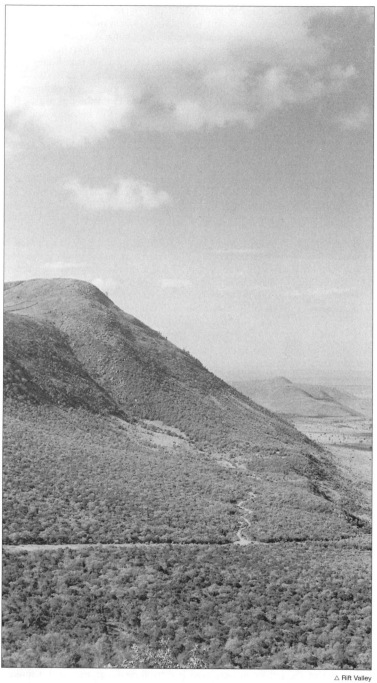

257

△ Rift Valley

Menengai Drive and take the fourth left turn (Crater Climb) through the modestly affluent suburbs above the town. Some 4.5km up the hill you come to a sign referring to a Campsite and Picnic Area, but no evidence of either. You could presumably camp by the trees here and get water from nearby houses, but you'd be ill-advised to leave your tent unattended and you should bring food. Half a kilometre away is a telecommunications tower: head for this then turn right, following the path through a fragrant forest of gum trees for twenty minutes, to a fire lookout tower on the bare cliff. From the top of this, the massive crater spreads out beneath you, a spectacular sea of bush-covered lava, its black waves frozen solid.

The crater was the site of a battle around 1854 in which the Ilpurko Maasai defeated the Ilaikipiak, whom they considered upstarts disrespectful to Batian, the *laibon* (paramount chief) of the time after whom the highest peak of Mount Kenya was named. At intervals throughout the nineteenth century, these **Maasai civil wars** flared up over the issue of true Maasai identity. In this case, it was not simply a matter of honour but also of grazing rights in the Rift Valley, especially around Lake Naivasha and on the scarp slopes. The Ilpurko were herders, while the Ilaikipiak from the north grew crops as well. Both had been preparing for battle for some time and it is said that hundreds of Ilaikipiak *morani* were hurled over the crater rim to their deaths. The place retains a sinister reputation – even the normally fearless Maasai traditionally have it as the dwelling place of devils and other evil – and local people prefer not to go near the edge.

A century later, on the highest point of this windy crest, the Rotary Club erected one of their familiar hyperbolic signposts, laden with multiple pointers. Apart from informing you that Nairobi is 140km away and Rome 5997km in the opposite direction, it also points out that the crater wall is 2272m above sea level and its area covers some 90 square kilometres – the whole dramatic extent of which you can see. You'll get fantastic views over Lake Nakuru if you walk down the dirt road along the south side of the gum-tree plantation.

From Nakuru town centre, it's about an eight-kilometre (three-hour) hike to the crater rim; on weekends, you might be lucky and get a lift, but there's no public transport. Taxis will take you, of course. If you walk, you're best advised to go up in company as muggings are a possibility.

Hyrax Hill

Hyrax Hill (daily 9.30am–6pm; Ksh200) is an easy target, 3.5km out of town, just to the left of the Nairobi road. Matatus bound for Lanet and Gilgil will drop you at the turn, then it's a two-kilometre walk to the small museum where you pay your fee. If you're driving, don't be misled by the sign next to the *Kunste Hotel* which appears to indicate a left turn here (the Subukia/Nyahururu road): it's about a kilometre further to the entrance track. The hill, named for the hyraxes which once scampered over it, has been a settlement site for at least three thousand years, and finds here date from the Neolithic period. It was discovered by Louis Leakey in 1926, excavated by Mary Leakey in 1937–38 and by others in 1965, 1973 and 1987. There's an excellent guide booklet (1983) on sale in the museum and a reprint of the paper in the journal *Azania* describing the most recent excavations. You can normally **camp** here, free or for a small fee (staff facilities only).

The Northeast Village

The path leading out to the right of the museum winds its way around the north side of the hill to an excavated pit dwelling, or at any rate a "sunken enclosure", with baulks left in place to show the depth of material that was removed during the digging. There are thirteen similar depressions in this "**Northeast Village**" (curiously named, as it is in the northwest), but it's uncertain exactly how they were used. They have yielded a tremendous quantity of pottery shards, tools made from flakes of obsidian and animal-bone fragments, but the absence of post-holes normally needed to support a roof suggests they may have been shelters for livestock rather than humans. Just as plausibly, a roof might have been added whenever needed, leaving no trace, and animals and people may have shared the shelters. The floor of the pit has been left exposed and is littered with stones and obsidian chips. Several reconstructed examples of the site's characteristic late-Iron-Age pottery (the Iron Age in Kenya essentially continued until the twentieth century) are displayed in the museum.

Excavations at Hollow F have discovered the floors of three oblong **houses**, facing onto the main pit, with rather frail foundations, suggesting a kind of lean-to or bender. This research, which included radiocarbon dating showing occupation of different hollows from something like 1100 to 1500 AD, led to the conjecture that the "village" had not all been occupied at the same time, but that pits and attached houses would be used for a number of seasons until uninhabitable, then abandoned for a newly built area nearby. Far from being a community, this could have been the home base of a single family, or even just an occasional encampment in the seasonal cycle.

It's believed the inhabitants would have been semi-nomadic Sirikwa- or Nandi-speaking (Kalenjin) herders. Today, the Kalenjin mostly live further west, but they're associated with so-called pit-dwellings elsewhere (see "In Search of the Sirikwa Holes", p.285) and, in the case of Hyrax Hill, they may have been forced to flee by an expanding Maasai population from the north.

The fort and burial sites

Following the path towards the top of the hill, you come to an exposed "**fort**" facing out towards Nakuru, which consists of a circle of hefty boulders enclosing a flattened area. Said to have been an Iron-Age lookout post, there's no way of being certain what this actually was, nor even how old it might be, since no artefacts have been found. From the fort, you can scramble over the volcanic boulders – the whole hill is a tongue of Menengai's lava – to the summit, where you get a good view of the southern part of the site and the lake. Now several kilometres away, the lake once extended, probably as fresh water, right to the base of the hill and across much of the Rift Valley, turning Hyrax Hill into a peninsula or even an island.

A hundred metres down the hillside you come to more Iron-Age pits and a **trench**. An extraordinary collection of bits and pieces was dug up here in 1974, including some eight thousand stone tools and six **Indian coins** between sixty and five hundred years old. Whether the oldest of these really implies the very early penetration of overseas foreigners into the interior, or whether the coins were simply buried or smothered, is unknown. Most likely they'd been handed down for generations and were either lost or hidden for safekeeping.

Nearby, in a fenced-in shelter, the massive stone slab which sealed a **Neolithic burial mound** has been removed to display part of a skull and some limb bones. The remains of a further nineteen Neolithic skeletons were discovered north of this, beneath a more recent Iron-Age occupation area marked by the two stone circles (which were hut foundations). Nineteen Iron-Age skeletons were also discovered, overlying the Neolithic graves, mostly of young men – possibly slain warriors – apparently buried unceremoniously or in a hurry, their skulls and limbs in tangled heaps.

These enigmatic graves have further, cultural implications: nine of the Neolithic skeletons are thought to be female and, unlike the male remains, they were found with accompanying **grave goods** in the form of domestic implements – dishes, pestles and flat mortars. The finds pose unanswerable questions. Certainly, many Kenyan peoples remember oral traditions of times when women were more socially and politically powerful than today; the female burials with grave goods might be evidence of this past. But the burials themselves are curious. The coincidence of nineteen skeletons at each level may be just that – coincidence. Or perhaps the Iron-Age survivors who buried their young men knew about the ancient Neolithic graves beneath.

Neolithic recreation

For a less dramatic, but more accessible, impression of life at Hyrax Hill, the **Bau game**, cut into the rock just before you get back to the museum, is a delightfully fresh record. *Bau* is the Bantu name for a game of skill and – depending on the set of rules used – amazing complexity that has been played all over Africa for a very long time. Two people play, moving pieces (cowries, seeds or pebbles) from one hole to another to win. There are a number of these "boards" around the hill; the one near the museum is a particularly good example.

Lake Nakuru National Park

Admission $27, children $10; $8 to camp, $15 in a "special" campsite. No entry on foot. Warden: PO Box 439 Nakuru ☏ 037/41605. Maps: Survey of Kenya Lake Nakuru National Park 1:30,000 (1994); Rowanya Enterprises Lake Nakuru National Park at 1cm: 500m (1990). You should be able to buy handy $2 colour maps, published by KWS, at the gate.

Though not large – some 10km by 25km – **Lake Nakuru** is a beautiful park, the terra firma mostly under light **acacia forest**, well provided with tracks to a variety of hides and lookouts. It's also one of the easiest parks to visit, with or without a vehicle of your own. Towards the end of the dry season in March, the lake is often much smaller than the maps suggest and, consequently, water birds are a greater distance from the park roads. The **northern side** of the park is commonly fairly busy with tour vehicles, but the **southern parts** are usually empty. A pleasure to drive around (it takes around three hours), its easy-to-follow topography means you really can't get lost or go far without arriving somewhere. And the contrast and apparent dislocation between the shallow soda lake with its primeval birds and the animated woodlands all around give it a very distinctive appeal.

Practicalities

The park has three gates. **Main Gate**, at the edge of Nakuru town, is also the park headquarters and has the main campsites nearby, plus a good, hand-painted map showing the most recent circuits, most of which are in fair condition. Entering through **Lanet Gate** gives the most direct access to the park's two **lodges** from Naivasha or Nairobi and avoids the congestion of Nakuru town. It's not properly signposted, however. Before you reach the edge of town, the 1.5-kilometre track to the gate starts opposite the *Stem Hotel*; if you've crossed the railway bridge you've overshot. **Nderit Gate**, down in the southeast corner, is only useful if you're coming cross-country from Lake Naivasha or over the Mau escarpment from Narok.

ACCOMMODATION

Backpacker's Campsite	5
Eldorado Lodge	9
Kampi ya Nyati	8
Kampi ya Nyuki	7
Kunste Hotel	1
Lake Nakuru Lodge	11
Lion Hill Bar & Lodging	4
Makalia Campsites	13
Naishi House	12
Njoro Campsite	6
Sarova Lion Hill Lodge	10
Stem Hotel	2
Wildlife Clubs of Kenya Hostel	3

LAKE NAKURU
NATIONAL PARK

Getting around

The most straightforward way to see the park if you don't have a vehicle is **by taxi**, especially as some of the taxi drivers around Nakuru town know the park well. The *Midland Hotel* is as good a place as any to track one down. This naturally works out cheaper for a group, but you'll probably want to reach an agreement with the driver before you're all present. Reckon on some stiff

The mystery of the vanishing flamingos

Despite their more or less continual absence since 1995, Lake Nakuru has always been considered a flamingo lake par excellence. At one time, it was believed that up to two million **lesser flamingos** (perhaps one third of the world's population) were massing in the warm alkaline water to feed on the abundant blue-green algae cultivated by their own droppings. In addition, the lake was also home to a small population of the much rarer **greater flamingo** (whose world population is estimated at a mere 50,000) which have less hooked beaks used to sift for small crustaceans and plankton with the birds' heads underwater.

Like Lake Elmenteita, Nakuru has no outlet, meaning that its level fluctuates wildly. In 1962, it dried up almost completely, and in the late 1970s, a combination of increased rainfall and decreased evaporation lowered the lake's salinity and raised the water level. The flamingos began to disperse, some to lakes Elmenteita, Magadi and Natron (the latter in Tanzania), some up to Turkana, but the majority to Lake Bogoria.

Since then, flamingos have been sporadically seen again in the surreal pink flocks that have become a photographic cliché, but the situation has become increasingly unpredictable of late, with the birds returning for two or three years then disappearing again. They were absent in late 1995, when the lake started drying up, and again almost completely in 1996. Water levels increased greatly due to the 1997–98 El Niño rains, with the result that the lake became too fresh for the flamingos. It took a while for the water to regain sufficient salinity to entice them back. From 2000 they began to return, but you'll still find a large part of the flock at Lake Bogoria, and a few others at Lake Elmenteita, Lake Magadi and at Lake Simbi on Lake Victoria.

A great debate rages in the press about the causes of their disappearance and its detrimental effect on the tourist trade. Over the last twenty years, land use in the lake's catchment area has changed dramatically, with large areas of forest being converted to small farms, and Nakuru town has undergone rapid growth and industrialization. Pollution from the town's sewer effluent and industries is believed to be a major factor (Kenya Wildlife Service and the World Wide Fund for Nature built nine new "refuse chambers" for the town in 1996), as are water diversion, soil erosion (leading to siltation) and even sand-harvesting along the Njoro River. The introduction in 1962 of a hardy species of fish, *Tilapia grahami* – partly to control mosquitoes – has encouraged large flocks of **white pelicans** in recent years and it's likely that their presence is another disruptive element (on Elmenteita a breeding colony of greater flamingos was forced off by the pelicans). The Nakuru Wildlife Trust has been studying the ecology of Rift Valley lakes since 1971 in an effort to find some of the answers, and the WWF now organizes educational trips to the park for local kids, as well as running a pilot scheme to monitor pollution from individual industries.

bargaining, then three hours at about $15 an hour, with park fees on top. Alternatively, contact Blackbird Tours at Caleb's Arcade in the *Carnation Hotel* (see Nakuru town "Accommodation", p.254).

An alternative – though admittedly not always a very practical one – is to **hitch** at the **Main Gate**, about an hour's walk from the town centre. The rangers are usually sympathetic to low-budget travellers. They may help by asking drivers on your behalf, you'll have no park fees to pay unless you get a lift, and if you don't you can camp at the backpackers' campsite. You should expect to spend the night in the park once you get a ride, so be prepared for this.

If you're on foot and don't have a tent either, things look more difficult, but you could always stay the night at the cheap and cheerful *Florida Day & Night Club B&L* (❶) right on the boundary between park and town. This won't give you a restful night, but you'll want to be up bright and early waiting for a lift in any case; there's the added bonus that you're bound to meet park staff here.

The best option has you **driving** around in your own vehicle and stopping where you choose. The park has a number of areas where you can walk and, of course, this gives you the option of staying, or eating, at the stylish **lodges** in the bush.

Accommodation

The park has two expensive lodges, a hostel and a few campsites, but most people simply go on day-visits, and stay in Nakuru town or elsewhere overnight.

Eldorado Lodge Bookings through Let's Go Travel in Nairobi; p.141. On the eastern side past the turning to Lanet Gate, this is popular with Nairobi weekenders, but is actually more of a *nyama choma* joint. Its breeze-block chalets aren't overly attractive, but it's a good place to fix up a lift into the park. ⑤

Lake Nakuru Lodge PO Box 561 Nakuru ☎037/85446, ⑨211204; Nairobi reservations through Lake Nakuru Lodges, 2nd floor, Arrow House, Koinange St, PO Box 70559 Nairobi ☎02/212405, ⑨227062. Established lodge based around an old Delamere Estate house in shady gardens, with a pool ($5 for visitors) and uninterrupted views of the lake, though several kilometres from it. The *banda*-style rooms are on the small side and rather dark, though the new and much more expensive chalet suites, down a viewing platform/walkway, are first-class. The food is nothing special. FB ⑤–⑦ low, ⑦–⑧ high.

Naishi House Bookings through KWS Tourism Department; p.148. This is a peaceful place, commanding a wonderful view of Nakuru Park, with a fully furnished kitchen and four bedrooms to suit a group of eight. There is a cleaner, and firewood is provided. Game drives in the company of a ranger can be arranged. ③

Sarova Lion Hill Lodge 12km from the city centre, PO Box 7094 Nakuru ☎037/850235, ⑨210836, reservations through Sarova, p.44. This is extremely comfortable, with a low-key atmosphere, helped along by friendly staff. There are good views from the very pleasant, chalet-style rooms stacked high above the main parts of the lodge, and the excellent meals are slightly cheaper than at *Lake Nakuru Lodge*. Pool and sauna (small fee for visitors); $90 per hour for game vehicle rental (up to nine people). FB ⑥ low, ⑦ high.

Wildlife Clubs of Kenya Hostel On the northern side of the park. Book through PO Box 33 Nakuru ☎037/850929. The only reasonably priced accommodation, but somewhat run-down. The dorm beds (Ksh600 per person) and do-it-yourself catering arrangements seem just about adequate – the kitchen is well equipped. You can also camp in the enclosed compound (same charge).

Camping

For accommodation under canvas, there's a specific **backpackers' campsite** (cold showers, high-level toilets, communal tap) on a pleasant grassy site under fine old yellow acacias, but beware the audacious vervet monkeys and baboons, who've taken to attacking campers and wrecking their tents. **Lion Hill Bar & Lodgings** just outside the park, by Lanet Gate has facilities for campers and there are two other regular campsites in the park: **Njoro Campsite**, a couple of kilometres down the west shore road and set back in the woods, and the somewhat elusive **Makalia campsites**, in a wonderful location at the southern tip of the park, on either side of the stream of the same name and close to the waterfall. Very few organized tours come down this way, but should you feel isolated, you may be reassured to know there's a ranger station fairly close by.

There are also a couple of "**special campsites**" in the northeast part of the park – **Kampi ya Nyati** (Buffalo Camp) and **Kampi ya Nyuki** (Bee Camp). They are both located in clearings among the trees between the road and the open shore, but the lighter and grassier *Nyuki* is the nicer of the two. Both have splendid "private" access to quiet vantage points on the shore through driveable tunnels of undergrowth. Bookings, as usual for special campsites, are supposed to be made in advance with the warden or through the National Parks headquarters at Nairobi National Park (see p.60).

Around the park

The **northern shores** of the lake are the most opened-up, with a busy route between the Main Gate and *Sarova Lion Hill Lodge*. The vegetation here is mostly lightly wooded acacia forest and, close to Nakuru town and its noise and pollution, this is the least interesting area for wildlife.

Lake Nakuru's wildlife

Fortunately, in view of the flamingos' here-today-gone-tomorrow caprice, there's a lot more to the lake's spectacle than the pink flocks. Its shores and surrounding woodlands are home to some four hundred other species of **birds** including, during the northern winter, many migratory European species.

There's a good number of **mammals** here as well. The lake isn't too briny for **hippos** – a herd of a dozen or more snort and splash by day and graze by night at the northern end. Nakuru has also become a popular venue for introduced species: there are **Rothschild's giraffe** from the wild herd near Kitale, and **lion** and secretive **leopard** from wherever they're causing a nuisance.

In the early 1990s, a number of **black rhinos** were relocated from Solio Game Ranch (p.218), and numbers are encouragingly increasing steadily year on year (present population 50, of which 28 were born in the park). In addition, ten **white rhinos** were donated by South Africa in 1994, and others were brought from Solio, bringing their number to 23. Electric fencing has been installed around the entire perimeter of the park – the only park in the country to be so enclosed – with the intention of maintaining a viable number of rhinos in one well-protected zone, secure from poachers. A huge investment, substantially from the World Wide Fund for Nature, has been expended on this major effort to save the rhino from extinction at a cost per beast – adding up to some £4000 per year – that is more than ten times the average income of the people on the other side of the fence.

You soon understand how Nakuru may have got its name (it is possibly Swahili for "place of the waterbuck"): the park is **waterbuck** heaven. With only a handful of lions and small numbers of leopards to check their population, the shaggy, red-deer-size beasts number several thousand, and the herds (either bachelor groups or a buck and his harem) are large and exceptionally tame. **Impala**, too, are very numerous, though their lack of fear means you rarely witness the graceful flight of a herd vaulting through the bush.

The two other most-often-seen mammals are **buffalo** – which you'll repeatedly mistake for rhinos until you get a look through binoculars – and **warthog**, scuttling nervously in singles and family parties everywhere you look.

Elephants are absent, but you're likely to see **zebra**, **dik-dik**, **ostrich** and **jackals** and, in the southern part of the park, **eland** and **Thomson's and Grant's gazelles**. More rarely you can encounter the odd **striped hyena** loping along the road in the eastern euphorbia forest at dawn, **reedbuck** down by the shore and **bushbuck** dashing briskly through the herbage. Along the eastern road, near *Lake Nakuru Lodge*, are several over-tame **baboon troops** to be wary of.

The park is also renowned for its very large **pythons** – the patches of dense **woodland** in the southwest, between the lakeshore and the steep cliffs, are a favourite habitat. One of these huge snakes dammed up the Makalia stream a few years back, when it died of internal injuries after swallowing a gazelle.

Lastly, if you tire of the living spectacle, go looking for the **Lion Cave**, beneath Lion Hill ridge in the northeast; it's an excavated prehistoric rock shelter and rarely contains lions.

Heading clockwise, the main track runs through the woods, past the lodge and into an exotic-looking forest of candelabra **euphorbia** – great cactus-like trees up to 15m high. At the southern end of this zone you come into a spell of more open country, past the turning (left) up to *Lake Nakuru Lodge*, and one or two side tracks down to the mud and the lakeshore (right), and then the road turns west into the southern park's dense acacia jungle. This is where you may see a **leopard** and, if they overcome their shyness, one of the park's thirty-odd **black rhino**. Several kilometres further, the road opens again onto wider horizons with plenty of buffalo, waterbuck, impala and eland all around. This is also the most likely area for seeing the park's introduced **Rothschild's giraffe** herd, which numbers some sixty or seventy, in several groups. In fact, their introduction has been so successful that some are now being moved elsewhere to ease pressure on the park.

Down in this **southern part of the park**, take a northerly side track and you can circle around the southern savannah; opt for a southerly side track and you plunge into deep scrub and thicket – perfect rhino country. Eventually, heading south, you reach the electric boundary fence and the perimeter patrol track, which you can follow, east or west, back to the main circuit route.

The **west shore**, especially "pelican point", has the best opportunities for seeing the **flamingos**, if they've returned, in their dense, rose-coloured photogenicity. In places, the road runs on what is virtually a causeway, past the lake's edge, with high cliffs rearing up behind. Photo conditions obviously depend on the time of day and the weather, but late afternoon usually produces the best results on this side of the lake; be careful not to over-expose – the most effective shots tend to be on the dark side.

Still heading clockwise, the main route leaves the shore and ploughs north, through **thick forest** with many high trees and dense undergrowth, back to the Main Gate.

Good **vantage points** around the lake include the northern **mud flats** (follow established tracks across the dry surface); the dead tree **watchtower** (northeast); *Kampi ya Nyuki* and *Kampi ya Nyati* campsites; *Lake Nakuru Lodge*, for a general view across unobstructed savannah; and the high "**baboon cliffs**" in the west.

West of Nakuru: out of the Rift Valley

West of Nakuru, the A104 is a fast, busy, single-lane road, along which long-distance lorries and buses thunder by at top speed. It's hair-raising if you're driving yourself, and even more wearing on the nerves if you're travelling by matatu. The surface varies but is generally good, the worst stretch running from Timboroa, some 90km west of Nakuru, for about twenty hilly, winding kilometres to Nabkoi. Beyond there it's mostly excellent.

If you're heading into western Kenya, there's a scenic and much quieter alternative to the main highway. This, the C56, climbs gently up to Njoro, Elburgon and Molo – in ascending order of altitude and size – before rejoining the Kisumu-bound fork of the main road (the B1).

Njoro

The turn-off (left) to Njoro and the Mau escarpment is 5km west of Nakuru, usually marked by the presence of a police roadblock. Along with Laikipia District north of Nanyuki and Nyahururu, the Njoro and Molo areas were those worst affected by the inter-tribal clashes that have rocked the Rift Valley since the advent of multi-party politics in 1991. Violence erupted again just before the 1997 elections and continued well into 1998, leading to the deaths of several hundred people and the displacement of tens of thousands. The number of clashes has declined since then, but there may be more around the December 2002 elections.

NJORO is the home town of **Egerton University** (main campus 5km out of town on the main road to Narok), whose other, equally remote, outpost is up the escarpment near Kinangop, north of Naivasha. The jacaranda-fringed main road runs straight past the "centre" of town – a great acreage of mud (or, at best, dust), backed by a humble row of *dukas* and *hotelis*. The only feature of note is the white and green mosque on the right, which broadcasts sermons and a noisy accompaniment from its congregation on Friday mornings – strange in this bleak Highlands town. There are one or two very basic B&Ls, but nothing notable.

Beyond the Narok junction, there's another and more soulful Njoro of wooden-colonnaded, tin-roofed, one-storey *dukas*. On this side of town are the post office and telephones (coin boxes only), a branch of the KCB bank and the Njoro Farmer's Petrol Station, a Shell garage. You emerge on the other side of town, past timber yards, into flat cereal country, with herds of dairy cattle and racehorses between the lines of gum trees and copses of acacia. Some 8km further along the C56 to Elburgon, past the junction for Menengai road, is the excellent **Kembu Campsite** (PO Box 23 Njoro ☎037/61413 or 61583, ⓔkembu@net2000ke.com; Ksh300 per person on the first night camping, then Ksh200 if staying for longer; two *bandas* ❸), signposted on the left. It has farm produce for sale and mountain bikes for rent, and the Nightingale family who run it also breed racehorses on their 900-acre farm.

Elburgon and Turi

ELBURGON is a good deal bigger than Njoro, and higher up. You're into seriously muddy, conifer country up here, the buildings, characteristically chalet-style, built of dark, weathered planks. In the centre, the town's second street branches off in a sea of mud (or dust) to the railway tracks and open-air market place. Down this street you'll find the post office, and several dirt-cheap B&Ls.

Elburgon is first and foremost a timber town, with logs and logging evident everywhere. It's wood money that gives Elburgon a degree of commercial prosperity and can be the only reason for the massive investment in the *Hotel Eel* (PO Box 36 Elburgon ☎0363/31271 or 31471, ⓕ31477; ❸). This oddly named **hotel** beats anything in Nakuru, although if you don't qualify as a Kenyan resident the rates are far higher than you'd expect in an up-country town. On offer are clean, comfortable rooms and cottages, secure parking, a disco at weekends and an adventure playground set in well-landscaped grounds. The **restaurant** serves good breakfasts and an imaginative choice of main meals (excellent steak with bacon and red wine). During the week, the place has all the atmosphere of an out-of-season holiday camp, but things liven up at weekends and holidays, when discos, video shows and traditional dancing are laid on.

En route to Molo, **St Andrew's School** at **Turi** has a locally renowned **teachers' club** on Thursday nights and sometimes at weekends. You can have a meal and a few drinks and pass an evening in as wide a range of company as you're likely to find anywhere.

Molo and the Mau Forest

West of Elburgon, the road winds and dips through the thick Mau Forest for several kilometres, with glimpses of railway viaducts across the valleys, until it emerges, still higher up, among the cereals and pyrethrum fields at **MOLO**.

Molo straggles for several kilometres down into a broad valley across the rail tracks and up the other side on to Mau Summit Road, where you find a post office, banks and several petrol stations with carefully tended floral forecourts. Head for the *Highlands Hotel* (PO Box 142 Molo ☎0363/21192; ➋), which is tremendous value for its huge, wood-floored rooms with log fires, and its lamb with baked potatoes speciality (Ksh200). Unfortunately, it's extremely quiet, but the misty gardens are pleasant, and they have riding stables. The bar and dining room only wake up a little in the evenings as various long-term guests return from a day's work on local civil engineering projects. *Green Garden Lodge* (☎0363/21080; ➋) is a plain but pleasant old place, decently kept up for no particular reason (there seem to be few, if any, guests). They offer 24-hour hot water and a cheap, tasty menu; sometimes they even have an old guitarist singing songs in the bar.

South of Molo, up into the **Mau Forest**, a newly graded road runs to **Keringet** (where the huge old estate, once owned by Italians, and exhibiting all the most ostentatious trappings of colonial wealth, is gradually crumbling) and on to **Olenguerone**. From here, the road tunnels eerily through a forest of huge gum trees, traipsed by elephant and even rhino, to Bomet (see p.416). There are several daily matatu runs along this route from Molo. The Kenya Wildlife Service has been trying for years to open up the mountain forest, like the Aberdares Park, but there is some stubborn resistance, not least from the forest's indigenous Okiek (Dorobo) hunter-gatherers, as well as from the loggers. There's more background on this area, and details of the Mau route to the Maasai Mara, on p.415.

If you have your own vehicle and are heading towards **Baringo**, you can avoid doubling back to Nakuru by heading north to the A104 from Molo and turning west towards Eldoret. After five kilometres, when you reach Makutano, take the surfaced road to the right, which goes through some wonderful mountain scenery via Eldama Ravine and Tenges, up to the C51 where you can turn right and join the B4 which takes you on to the lake.

Londiani and Kipkelion Monastery

West of Molo, there are two possible places to stay in the highlands, neither of them exactly routine receivers of visitors. The first, the *Kenya Forestry College Guest House* (➋), is near **Londiani**, a small town off the B1 highway, 12km west of the straggling row of huts and *dukas* that marks the railway's highest point – **Mau Summit** (2650m). Londiani is about 3km from the main road, with the odd matatu running there. For the *Guest House* you need to take the right turn a kilometre or so before the centre, signposted to "Ministry of Environment and Natural Resources . . .", and follow this narrower track, Forest Road, for 2km. Anyone around the new buildings should be able to direct you to the simply furnished bungalow guest house on the north side of the little campus – if in doubt ask to see the director. Although intended for the use of visiting academics and researchers, it's occasionally used by bird-watchers and passing hikers and is a peaceful, country retreat. The *Guest House* manager (reservations: PO Box 8 Londiani, or contact the District Forest Officer on ☎0361/64028 or 64005) is welcoming and flexible – you can self-cater or she can prepare meals. Camping is not normally permitted.

The Cistercian monastery

The second unusual target in the district is **Our Lady of Victoria Abbey**, a Cistercian monastery between Londiani and **Kipkelion**. The area was formerly known by the Maasai as "Lumbwa", but Kipkelion ("Kif-*kel*-ion") is the original and much-preferred Kipsigis name. Founded in 1956, this is the only Cistercian monastery in Africa and, deep in this rural hill country, the tall cement-block church is a remarkable sight – focal point of a small but impressive community of Kenyan, Ugandan, Tanzanian, Danish, Dutch, English and Irish monks. They make a living from their dairy herd and chickens, and run the only hospital in the area and an important school. Our Lady of Victoria began as a Trappist monastery, with the silence and strict rules the reformist order stipulates, but later reverted to the rather less stringent code of the older Cistercian order. The brothers still talk only when necessary, but they are happy to receive people (men and women) on retreat and ordinary lay visitors in their guest rooms and dining room. One of the brothers is responsible for visitors and you're likely to receive a very warm, and surprisingly loquacious, welcome. It's hardly necessary to say there's no phone, but if you like the idea of silence and contemplation in a harmonious rural setting, write to let them know you're coming (PO Box 40 Kipkelion). You should obviously leave an appropriate donation.

The monastery is sited rather remotely north of the C35 backroad which leads beyond Londiani towards Kisumu. A few **matatus** service this road, but to get up to the monastery without your own vehicle you need luck in scoring a lift or several hours to walk it. The monastery is 11km up a rough track – signposted "Monastery Hospital" – from the small centre of **Baisheli** on the C35 (15km west of Londiani), and the track is rough, narrow and steep in parts, winding through intensively cultivated Kipsigis *shambas*. If you're approaching from the west, the easiest route to the monastery is via **Kipkelion station**, signposted off the main B1 highway, 25km east of Kericho. The road to Kipkelion station, 10km of good tarmac, gives out at the valley-floor station itself; to continue to the monastery you have a rocky, three-kilometre climb then, turning right onto the C35, 6km to the track (left) up to the abbey. There's a "short cut" up to the monastery which is signposted ("Trappist", overwritten with "*Cistercian* Monastery 6km") just after you get onto the C35 – this track is often impassable. Note that none of the available maps of Kenya are any real guidance in this district; distances are significantly longer than they look.

The Northern Rift

North of Nakuru, the Rift Valley drops away gently and, as the road descends, so temperatures rise, the landscape dries and human population becomes sparser. Not far from Nakuru or Nairobi, and no longer necessarily, a difficult journey, this region has a bright, harsh beauty, quite different from the central Rift. Its **lakes**, Bogoria and Baringo, both make alluring targets.

It's worth remembering also that this region offers three possible routes up to Lake Turkana (Chapter Seven), two of them joining with the Kitale–Lodwar road west of the lake, the third curving up to Maralal for the east side. Although public transport is virtually nonexistent and the roads pretty rough, the **Kerio Valley** route (see p.279) deserves a special recommendation if you're visiting the west side of Turkana.

Lake Bogoria National Reserve and around

Daily 6am–7pm; daily fees: Ksh1000, children Ksh100, cars Ksh100, camping Ksh200 per person; access usually permitted on foot or bicycle. Warden: PO Box 64 Marigat ☎ 037/40746. See the map on p.270.

One of the least-visited lakes in the Rift Valley, **Lake Bogoria** is a sliver of saline water – unbelievably foul-tasting – entrenched beneath towering hills, 60km north of Nakuru. With the increasing pollution of Lake Nakuru, Lake Bogoria has, since the early 1990s, become the adopted feeding ground of tens (at times hundreds) of thousands of **lesser flamingos**, whose population has been stable since 1995. The lakeshore itself is one of the few places where **greater kudu** antelope can easily be seen. But the reserve is worth visiting as much for its physical spectacle as for the wildlife. It's largely a barren, baking wilderness of scrub and rocks, from which a series of furious **hot springs** erupts on the western shore, and the bleak walls of the Siracho range rise sheer from the east. Even in the far north of the country, there are few places so unremittingly severe.

Fortunately, the rigour of the landscape is relieved by three superb, shady **campsites**, one of which is nearly perfect. There are two **accommodation** options just outside the reserve's main Loboi Gate. The **warden** here (William Kimosop) is quite an authority on **birds** and, if he's free, will happily take you around, or accompany you in your vehicle (it's a good idea to try to arrange this in advance).

Further background information on the lake can be found in *A Guide to Lake Baringo and Lake Bogoria* by Marguerita North Lewis (Horizon Books, 1998), which is available in several of the Nairobi bookshops listed on p.145, priced Ksh600.

Main approaches and gates

The excellent B4 road running north from Nakuru to Baringo slices through a thinly populated region and carries little traffic – tortoises in the road present the greatest hazard to motorists speeding along the fast new tarmac. The road skirts to the west of Lake Bogoria by a margin of 20km and, whilst there's a track cutting across at Mogotio, it's extremely rough going even by 4WD. Much easier, and quicker, is to continue on up the B4 to the signposted junction a few kilometres before Marigat. From here, a fast tarmac road takes you straight to the **Loboi Gate**, some 20km further on. There are infrequent matatus from Marigat to Loboi Gate (most leave Marigat around 3–5pm), or you could simply wait for a lift at the junction – it's a safe bet something suitable will pass within the hour. Those staying at Lake Baringo often try to arrange lifts with fellow tourists from there. Returning to Marigat, matatus leave early at around 6–8am; one a day continues down to Nakuru.

Sixteen kilometres from the junction, 3km before the Loboi Gate, the best feature of the *Lake Bogoria Hotel* (PO Box 208 Menengal West ☎ 037/40225,

▲ The Kerio Valley & Turkana

LAKES BARINGO & BOGORIA

Tangulbei

▲ Maralal

Loruk

C77

Mukutan River

Lake Baringo

Hot Sulphur Springs

Kampi ya Samaki

Roberts' Campsite
Lake Baringo Club

Ol Kokwe Island

◄ Kabarnet & Eldoret

Parmalok Island

Island Camp

Ol Arabel River

C51

Molo River

Ol Arabel River

Marigat

E461

B4

Papyrus Inn

Lake Bogoria Hotel

Loboi Gate

Waseges River

S I R A C H O   E S C A R P M E N T

Maji Moto Gate

Bogoria River

Loburu hot springs

Lake Bogoria

N

Acacia Campsite
Riverside Campsite

Fig Tree Campsite

LAKE BOGORIA NATIONAL RESERVE

Emsos Gate

0   10 km

= = = = : 4WD roads

▼ Nakuru & Nairobi   ▼ Mogotio   ▼ Subukia & Nyahururu

ⓕ 40748, ⓦ www.bogoriasparesort.com; ❼) is a sanitized **thermal pool**; it also
has an ordinary, chlorinated "cold pool". A large stuffed lion dominates the
lobby, but even this does little to alleviate the blandness: it's really a town hotel
in the bush and quite out of keeping with the area. Rooms and cottages are
functional and taste-free, and way overpriced for non-Kenyans. The only alternative is the much more basic *Papyrus Inn* (PO Box 186 Marigat ☎037/43279;
❷), right by Loboi Gate. Toilets and showers are shared (hot water in buckets),
but it's friendly and there's a large garden bar and restaurant, and an area set
aside for **camping** (Ksh200). There's also the option of camping at the Loboi
Gate, just outside the reserve – there's usually water here but you'll need your
own stove or firewood and supplies – and there are three campsites at the
southern end of the lake, but difficult to get to unless you have 4WD. Of the
three, *Fig Tree* has the best location, while *Riverside* is the most basic, without
even a source of water. A rare treat for those without their own transport is that
you are allowed into the reserve on foot, so long as there are at least two of
you. In theory, this is only permitted as far as the Loburu hot springs, although
exceptions are made (and perhaps a ranger provided, for a fee) if you're heading for one of the three campsites further south.

Driving in from the south is shorter in terms of distance, but takes much
longer on the rough roads, and you'd need 4WD; most vehicles visiting
Bogoria come from Lake Baringo rather than directly from Nakuru. Using the
main southern approach, the reserve is signposted (right) off the B4, 36km
north of Nakuru at **Mogotio** (fill up on petrol here). Some 23km from this
junction, shortly after **Mugurin**, you fork left for the western **Maji Moto
Gate** (an incredibly rough 17km further, bringing you to the hot springs and
tarmacked lakeshore road), or right/straight ahead for the southern **Emsos
Gate** (an equally rough 13km, which brings you to the wooded part of the
reserve from where a further rough track leads to the springs, though a ranger
will probably be needed for this last section, see p.274). There's no public transport.

If you have a 4WD vehicle or are into hiking or mountain biking, you might
like to consider the **eastern cross-country approach** to Bogoria's Emsos
Gate, described below.

Subukia and the cross-country route to Lake Bogoria

An adventurous alternative to taking the main road north to Bogoria from
Nakuru is to approach the lake from the southeast, initially using the B5 tarmac route that ascends from the Rift Valley floor at Nakuru to the brim of the
eastern escarpment at Nyahururu. Along the way there are several turnings,
northwest, towards the lake. The tarmac portions of this trip can be made by
country bus or matatu (there are several daily runs between Nyahururu and
Nakuru via Subukia), but you should be prepared to **hike** the rest of the way
down to Bogoria if necessary – a good two days.

Aside from the pleasure of tackling roads used by very few tourists, this route
gives you a special feel for the Rift Valley's striking topography as it drops from
one monumental block of land to another, with dramatic changes of climate
and scenery. When you reach the plain at the bottom, you've an indelible
impression of the way the earth has split apart and sunk to form the Rift over
the last twenty million years.

From Nakuru, it's a short trip, 14km, past Menengai crater (left) to **Mairu
Kumi**, where the road divides. The left fork (unsignposted) leads, after 14km

of rough *murram*, to the police post at Solai (see "Down to Bogoria" opposite), while the right fork continues on tarmac to Subukia and Nyahururu. The Nakuru–Nyahururu road is busy with matatus and buses; a fertile, rural backwater has been opened up since the route was hard-surfaced in the late 1980s. Beyond the fork, you enter a steep, hilly landscape of Kikuyu *shambas*, increasingly interspersed with plots of tea bushes and pyrethrum. At **Kapai**, 29km from Nakuru, you begin the descent into the Rift, crossing the Equator after a further 2.5km.

From Nyahururu, the target is also the Solai police post. The early part of the route is particularly stimulating as it falls in a series of breathtaking steps over the fault lines until it reaches a high scarp above Subukia, where it hairpins its way steeply down to the valley. From the cool highlands around Nyahururu, you start to feel the heat building up. Fields of sugar cane and bananas seem to grow before your eyes in the hothouse atmosphere and the earth takes on a rich, redolent smell.

Using public transport, the police post at **Solai** is served rather infrequently by direct matatu from Nakuru, but a better bet for getting there from Nakuru (or indeed from Nyahururu or Subukia) is to take a matatu to Mairu Kumi and another one from there.

The Subukia Valley and Lake Solai

The **Subukia Valley** was the Maasai's "Beautiful Place" (*Ol Momoi Sidai*) and its lush pastures their insurance against the failure of the grass up on the Laikipia plateau. But they were evicted in 1911 to the "Maasai Reserve" and the way was clear for the **settler families**. It's easy to see why they chose this high valley because, despite its isolation (even greater in the 1920s), it has a soft, arcadian beauty far removed from the windy plateaus above or the austere furnace of the Rift Valley floor below.

The village of **SUBUKIA** has a scattering of *hotelis* and *dukas*, and a Fuelex filling station. Simple, but clean and friendly, lodgings are available at the *Malindi Hotel* at the southern end of the village (PO Box 15901 Nakuru ☎037/52223; ❶). Buses and matatus stop at the T-junction where the Subukia Valley road meets the B5, and there's regular transport to Nakuru and Nyahururu.

If you have transport of your own and two or three hours to spare, or a couple of days to walk it, you can take a major **diversion** up the Subukia Valley, then turn west and cut back south again, past small Lake Solai. To get started on this route, from the grubby junction at Subukia village where the main road passes, head north about 700m to an old T-junction, with roads to Nakuru (left) and Lower Subukia (right). Take the latter. The track, consisting of rough dirt and rocks, is easy to follow, but will clock up some 45km. Sources of food along the way are negligible, so you must be self-sufficient, and, although the road is being "improved" (made broader and more bone-shaking), transport is sparse except for one daily matatu between Subukia and Bogoini, departing Subukia at around 6pm, and returning around 3am. Matatus between Bogoini and Mairu Kumi via Solai are slightly more frequent, but you may still have to wait a fair few hours for one.

Lake Solai is a curiously isolated soda lake with a reedy shoreline grazed by cattle and a scattering of sisal plots. For many years it was a seasonal lake only, but has been a permanent feature since the early 1980s. South of Lake Solai, the road climbs through scattered euphorbia and acacias to the junction (hard right) at **Solai police post**. Lines of jacaranda streak the scenery at intervals all over this district, bordering old driveways – evidence of the erstwhile community of settlers, nearly all of whom have left.

Down to Bogoria

The most **direct route** from Subukia village to Bogoria begins by climbing 4km out of the valley on the tarmac to Nakuru. An unsignposted right turn (or left if you've just come from Nakuru) goes over the hill past the curious apparition of **St Peter's** – a quaint Anglican church that looks as if it just flew in from England – and then 15km down to the Solai police post.

From here, the 50km to Bogoria is rough in many places, though normally quite negotiable in a 4WD vehicle (allow 3hr). Hitching, however, varies from slow to impossible from this point on and there is no public transport. If you're on foot or bicycle and still want to do it, check your emergency water and food supplies, tighten your bootlaces – or check your brakes – and set off west.

The road descends steeply to the Solai Valley with its disused railway line, which you cross at a place called **Milton's Siding**. When you reach the tracks, follow the road, parallel, to the right which runs for a kilometre and then turn sharp left to cross them. The road descends in a series of steps to a broad, flat valley with a sharp, right-hand bend up the hill on the far side, which it crosses to reach **Kisanana** – life-saving *chai* and a place to stop for the night if necessary, though there's no formal accommodation.

From Kisanana, you turn left at the old signpost and follow decent *murram* tracks for some 5km to a fork around some buildings. Here you head left and are soon pitching up a diabolical slope – rarely used by motor vehicles and by all appearances dynamited out of solid bedrock – which winds up and over a scrub-covered **hog's back ridge** for some 7km, eventually twisting north and dropping to better red *murram*, interspersed, strata-wise, with white, rocky stretches. You come to a crossroads (turn left), then after a few hundred metres a T-junction at a place of a few huts called **Mugurin** (turn right), where you may find a solitary *hoteli* open with good tea and chapatis. From here, you're within the compass of the lake, some 25km away. The road descends steadily now as you travel north – there's only the odd signpost but no danger of taking a wrong turn: if in doubt, head right.

Emsos Gate: practicalities

Hidden in its deep bowl, **Lake Bogoria** – when approached from Mugurin – is only visible when you're almost on top of it. The final stretch of the track leading down to the Emsos Gate is steep and rocky as well as being savagely beautiful, the landscape transformed into a strident dazzle of red and blue and splashes of green. The lake itself, a glistening pool of soapy blue and white, has a mirage of pink flamingos tinting its shores. During the middle hours of the day, the heat is relentless, but the unparalleled **Fig Tree Campsite** is the incentive to make the trip. It's only forty minutes' walk from Emsos Gate and an absolute delight, unless your visit coincides with a fresh covering of vegetation after the rains, when squads of determined tsetse flies can ruin what is otherwise an unusually verdant and picturesque scene. Note, if you're driving, that the road around the southern shore is very rocky and slow-going, and that access to *Fig Tree Campsite* is difficult for trucks and large vehicles as certain stretches are narrow and rock-bound.

Enquire with the rangers about heading down further to the thickly wooded shore at the south end (they might provide an escort, for a fee), and also check with them about **food**; a few basics are usually available near Emsos Gate to eke out your rations. **Water** is not a problem – a permanent, miniature brook, clear and sweet, runs right through the campsite and provides a natural Jacuzzi. Less delightfully, the magnificent glade of giant fig trees which bathe the site in shade is a favourite haunt of baboons who gorge themselves day and night. In the fruiting season (December–February) you should be wary of camping directly beneath any concentrations of figs, for reasons which need no elaboration. Buffalo also graze near here and are not to be trifled with.

Getting around the lake

The **east shore road** has been quite impassable for years (a huge rock fall coupled with higher water levels), so there is no circuit round the lake. This also makes *Fig Tree Campsite* something of a dead end and, if you're down here and don't have your own vehicle, you may be in for a long wait before someone turns up to give you a lift out again. Your only option is to walk the 15km around to the Loburu hot springs on the western shore, passing *Riverside* and *Acacia Tree* campsites (accessible only by 4WD or on foot). If you're driving up this southern stretch, there's a river bed to negotiate before you reach the tarmac, for which 4WD is essential, and with the high lake level is not advisable unless you're with a ranger who knows the road. There are picnic sites near the hot springs and, although notices prohibit it, there seems little to prevent you from camping in the vicinity. The Bogoria Reserve **paved road** between the hot springs and the Loboi Gate is in excellent condition. By the hot springs is the junction for the dirt road out to the western, Maji Moto, gate, up a dreadfully steep, rocky incline (steely nerves and 4WD essential).

The Loburu hot springs

However you enter the reserve, you're bound to want to see the **hot springs**, a series of boiling water spouts on the shore. There's a drinks kiosk here, but no food. At present, the high lake level means that only one of the springs breaks the surface – the others signal their presence by the agitated green water above them, some steam and a strong smell. With normal water levels, they burst up from huge natural cauldrons of super-heated water not far below the surface and drain into steaming rivulets that cut through the crusty ground, continuously collapsing and reforming their courses down to the lake. Even at midday, when the sun glares like a furnace, clouds of steam drift across this infernal scene. Tufts of grass tempt you to sit down and reward you with vicious spines while, closer to the lakeshore, the macabre bleached skeletons of flamingos lie strewn in the sand and, in the background, the dull thundering of the springs fills the air. It's like some water garden in Hell. It's also **dangerous**. Picnickers sometimes think it's fun to boil eggs and heat tins of food in the pools, but the consequences of a fall can be messy and even fatal: over the years a number of people have slipped and died as a result. An *askari* has now been posted to watch out for visitors, but if you scald yourself, help might still be a long time coming.

None of which should keep you from going. Although they hardly touch Yellowstone or Rotorua standards, "hot springs" is a tame appellation for this very impressive, terrifying and photogenic phenomenon. And the **flamingos**, for some curious reason – possibly chemical – tend to flock in their greatest numbers to the shallows opposite the hot streams' debouchment (they appear immune to the heat). The Bogoria **fish eagles**, incidentally, have made a gruesome adjustment to their fierce, fishless environment: they prey on flamingos. Other birds to look out for include avocets, transitory pelicans and migratory steppe eagles.

Wildlife, with the exception of the flamingos, makes itself scarce, most animals preferring the remote and inaccessible eastern shore: buffalo, hyenas, klipspringer, impala, dik-dik, zebra, warthog and Grant's gazelle. The mild and nervous **greater kudu** formerly lived predominantly in the northeastern part of the reserve, but they have spread and multiplied significantly in recent years and are now frequently seen in the more exposed western parts of the reserve. The kudu is a splendidly unmistakable, striped antelope; the bulls have long, spiral horns, shaggy dewlaps and enormous, spoon-like ears. Once widespread, the great rinderpest epidemics of the last century, which took such a toll on cattle, wiped out much of the kudu population too, leaving pockets only in the least favourable cattle country. Today, Bogoria is the most southerly part of the greater kudu's range in Kenya.

Lake Baringo

Roadblock operates 7am–7pm; adults Ksh200, children Ksh50, vehicles Ksh100. Office: PO Box 79 Marigat ☎0328/51453. See the map on p.270.

At one time a barely accessible retreat favoured by just a few weekenders, **Lake Baringo** now has a fine road from Nakuru, and another from Eldoret. At present, it remains a peaceful oasis in the dry-thorn country, rich in birdlife and with a captivating character entirely its own.

The lake is freshwater (Naivasha is the only other Rift Valley lake that's not saline), so its fish support **birds** less often seen – fish eagles, pelicans, cormorants and herons, for example – as well as quite a sizeable **crocodile** population. **Hippos** are common, too. Though you rarely see much more than ears and snout by day, they come ashore after dark, and on a moonlit night their presence can be unnervingly obvious; even in pitch darkness, they're too noisy to be ignored. Although some reports claim Baringo crocodiles are too small to be a threat to swimmers, what constitutes a dangerous size in a Nile crocodile is debatable, and reliable sources suggest that some of the Baringo crocs are potentially dangerous (an alleged man-eater was shot in 1981). Swimming in the lake is inadvisable.

The **Il Chamus** (Njemps) people of the lakeshore villages live by an unusual mixture of fishing and livestock herding, breaking the taboo on the eating of fish which is the norm among pastoralists. Speaking a dialect of Maa – the Maasai language – these fishermen paddle out in half-submerged dinghies made from saplings of the fibrous *ambatch* tree that grows in profusion at the southern end of the lake.

The lake itself is heavily silted with the red topsoil of the region, and it runs through a whole range of colours every day from yellow to coral to purple, according to the sun's position and the state of the sky. Years of drought had reduced it so that a broad swathe of grass and reeds grew between the water's edge and the lakeshore properties. In recent years, there have been some heavy rains and lakeside acreage has been cut back once again by the advancing waters.

Baringo transport – and Marigat

Buses from Nakuru to **KAMPI YA SAMAKI**, the lake's only, and very small, town, run three times a day, but most Nakuru matatus come up only as far as **Marigat** (one direct vehicle a day leaves Nakuru around 1pm, and Kampi Ya Samaki for the return trip around 6am next morning). From Eldoret, you can catch a bus at 10am for Kabarnet, and go by matatu from there to Marigat. From Marigat you can hitch or get a local matatu to the lake. Kampi ya Samaki is 2km from the main road, beyond the council-run **roadblock** where you pay your admission fee (make sure you get a receipt). Motor boats to **Ol Kokwe Island** (Ksh600) leave on request from *Island Camp*'s jetty on the north side of Kampi ya Samaki, and Community Boats and Excursions, opposite *Roberts' Campsite* charges the same, though you may find it harder to organize the return trip. Otherwise, you'll have to bargain hard with the bevy of boat-trip touts. A Ksh200 landing fee is payable if you are neither staying nor eating at *Island Camp*.

Marigat

MARIGAT, by virtue of its location, ought to be the hub of the Baringo–Bogoria tourist circuit, but for now at least, it's a bland, dust-blown little place. Urban development here follows what seems to be an unusual course, as among the tin shacks stands an impressive bright green and white **mosque**. With two tiers of large windows, and a capacity that obviously exceeds the area's Muslim population, it dwarfs its humble wooden predecessor to the rear. Apparently funded by some wealthy Saudi-Arabian, Muslim Nubians from Eldama Ravine, working on the irrigation project south of Marigat, were the original congregation of this mosque. If you need **to stay** in Marigat, there are a couple of B&Ls on the main road near the junction with the B4, of which *Toyoy Timber Yard and Lodging* (PO Box 19 ☎0328/51268; ●) is clean and well kept. Alternatively, you can follow the sign at the junction to *Marigat Inn* (PO Box 62 Kabarnet ☎0328/21825; ●), 1.5km east of the junction, just beyond the end of the tarmac. The clean, s/c rooms with hot showers (and some non-s/c singles) are set in a small jungly garden, with a shop selling essentials, and a friendly restaurant where the food, while not exactly cordon bleu, is more than edible. The bar is located next door to avoid disturbing sleeping residents, but a more conducive drinking establishment is to be found opposite the *Toyoy*.

Lakeside accommodation

Inexpensive accommodation at Lake Baringo is headed by the *Roberts' Campsite* (PO Box 1051 Nakuru ☎0328/51403) in a large, acacia-shaded garden down on the lakeside beside *Lake Baringo Club*, with lots of space and great bird-watching, and a shop selling hand-printed *kangas*. Camping costs Ksh300 per person, firewood Ksh80. Alternatively, there are three good non-s/c *bandas* with electricity and bedding (Ksh800 per person; book ahead), and also a four- and a six-bed cottage (Ksh4000 for up to four people, Ksh500 for each additional person), and they have a very good, reasonably priced, restaurant. If you want to cook, or for some reason prefer to shower separately from the campers, there's an adjacent, private kitchen/shower block that can be rented for Ksh500 per night. There are no boats, but the Community Boats and Excursions office opposite the gate (a co-operative of boat operators, with fixed prices) can organize boat trips if you fancy one.

If you need somewhere cheaper, there are a number of basic B&Ls in **Kampi ya Samaki**. The best of them is the clean *Bahari Hotel Lodge*, on the left as you come in (PO Box 3 ☎0328/51408; ●), with a welcoming bar-restaurant. Ask for an upstairs room. Just before this, *Hippo Lodge* has reasonable rooms with mosquito nets (PO Box 24 ☎0328/51440; ●) – don't expect a quiet night here though, as it's a tour-drivers' hangout, but it does have excellent food (order early from Alice).

In a totally different league, you're faced with a difficult choice of three very attractive places to stay, all offering substantial residents' reductions. And if they're not in your budget, it's still worth splashing out for cold drinks and a swim on a casual visit.

Island Camp mobile ℡071/374069, ℱ037/850858; reservations through Let's Go Travel, p.141. Not as luxurious as some of Kenya's "tented camps", but who cares – the location is idyllic, on the southern tip of Ol Kokwe Island in the middle of the lake, dense with birdlife, as well as numerous varieties of lizard. There are 23 tents, each with expansive views over the lake, plus a small pool and bar. As well as boat trips, you can go water-skiing, and there are guided walks on the island. The stepped nature of the site makes disabled access to the island impossible. The price includes motor boat transfer from their jetty 2km north of Kampi ya Samaki. For casual visitors, the transfer costs Ksh600 return in the lodge's boats. FB ❾

Lake Baringo Club PO Box 23 Kampi ya Samaki ℡0328/51402, ℱ51401; reservations through Block, p.42. A sumptuous and unpretentious hotel, this is a regular stop on ornithological tours of Kenya: the lakeshore gardens are bursting with birds. Nurturing an interest in the natural environment is top of the agenda, with regular wildlife

films and nightly audio-visuals to introduce guests to the local bird species. Children are made very welcome and will be round-eyed at the experience of encountering lake hippos at close range, coming to graze the well-watered lawns after dark (guards keep a careful watch). Reasonable entry fees are charged to casual visitors (Ksh100 weekdays, Ksh150 weekends), and these are deducted from your bill if you eat – the meals are generally excellent (around Ksh1000 excluding drinks). For casual visitors, it's Ksh200 extra to use the small, but irresistible swimming pool, and kids have badminton and table tennis to keep them amused. FB ❼

Samatian Island mobile ℡0733/700015, reservations through African Explorations, PO Box 24513 Nairobi ℡02/577374–81, ℱ577851, ℯrusinga@africaonline.co.ke. Upmarket but rustic, a new place with staffed cottages – the staff include a cook, but you have to supply the food – on a small island in the lake, and a boat which can be hired (Ksh2500 per day) for trips around the lake or to the shore. ❻

Exploring the lake

Activities tend to centre around *Lake Baringo Club* or *Island Camp*, both of which are pricey, and include boat trips around the shores (Ksh3000 per hour for up to seven people), water-skiing (at *Island Camp*; Ksh1500 for 15min), camel rides (at *Lake Baringo Club*; Ksh350 for 30min), and visits to a nearby Il Chamus *enkang* (Ksh400). The headman here is paid a retainer and in return allows visitors to look around his compound and freely photograph his wives and children. The visit isn't a particularly comfortable one – you may feel obliged to buy some of the decorated gourds inscribed with planes and ostriches (among other motifs) which the women lay out – but your presence isn't resented.

There are, of course, cheaper ways of arranging excursions in the vicinity of the lake. There are at least four locally run boat-trip companies, each armed with a retinue of pushy young touts bad-mouthing the competition, who will all quote you the same starting price (currently Ksh3000 per hour for a boat which seats seven; if you are two or more, make sure you pay for the boat and not per person), which should be bargained down. Share this between a group and even the starting price becomes excellent value. The local boatmen may not all be trained wildlife experts, but most of them are practised at luring fish eagles by tossing them fresh fish; take your camera for spectacular close-ups as the birds swoop down for the bait.

Moving on from Baringo

Travelling **north of Baringo** is a hit-or-miss affair without your own wheels, so try to arrange something with mobile tourists. Otherwise, you'll have to hitch: there's no public transport either to Maralal or to Tot and Lodwar from

Bird-watching at Lake Baringo

Baringo's 448 species of **birds** are one of its biggest draws, and even if you don't know a superb starling from an ordinary one, the enthusiasm of others tends to be infectious, especially at *Lake Baringo Club*. The bird population rises and falls with the seasons (the dry season is the leanest time for bird-watching; many birds return with the rains), but the lakeshore resounds with birdsong (and frogs) at most times of year (try responding to some of the calls). It's surprisingly easy to get within close range of the birds – some species, such as the starlings and the white-bellied go-away bird, are positively brazen – so you'll find rapt amateur photographers lurking behind practically every bush.

Lake Baringo Club offers short, informal, morning or late-afternoon lecture **tours** with its resident ornithologist. Bird-watching by boat along the lake's reedy shore is best done in the morning, in combination with a visit to **Goliath Heronry** (known locally as Gibraltar), a rocky islet near Ol Kokwe Island where the birds breed, stop-ping over at the hot springs on Ol Kokwe itself. Afternoons can profitably be taken up on a trip out near the main road under some striking red cliffs, an utterly different habitat where, apart from hyraxes and baboons, you can see several species of hornbill, sometimes the massive nest of a hammerkop (wonderful-looking birds in flight, resembling miniature pterodactyls with their strange crests) and, with luck, the rare Verraux's eagle, a pair of which nest in the vicinity. Marabou storks are fed from the kitchens. You'll have a few dozen species pointed out to you in an hour. The world record "bird-watch" for 24 hours is 342 species – held by former Baringo ornithologist Terry Stevenson.

Of course, you can organize your own bird-watching. There's some interesting bush just beyond the *Club* to the south (accessible by walking back along the road), where you should see some unusual species such as the white phase of the para-dise flycatcher, grey-headed bush shrike, violet wood hoopoe and various kingfish-ers. Hippos commonly graze here, too, even in daylight hours.

here. If you're **driving**, there's the highly recommended and not too rough C77 from Lake Baringo towards Maralal (one day) or Samburu National Reserve (best done over two days). This route swings up from the lakeshore, leaving tarmac and tourism behind, and takes you into the rugged country of the Lerochi plateau, dotted with Tugen and Pokot settlements. With the right conditions, there are stunning views back over Baringo. You join the Rumuruti–Maralal *murram* road as far as Kisima, where you choose between a short journey to Maralal or some inspiring but wheel-shattering driving along the C78/79 to Samburu (see p.601). There's **fuel** at Marigat and at *Lake Baringo Club*, but none after that until Maralal or Archer's Post.

Returning to **Nakuru**, the first bus leaves Kampi ya Samaki at 6.30am, but Marigat is an easier departure point. You should find a local vehicle going there.

Kabarnet and the Kerio Valley

Many people make this trip in reverse order from Eldoret but, in either direc-tion, it mirrors the journey down the eastern side of the Rift from Nyahururu, covered in the "Lake Bogoria" section. If you're setting out from Marigat, fre-quent matatus climb the first stage to **Kabarnet**, the road soaring and plung-ing through at times almost alpine scenery. From Kabarnet, you should be able to matatu-hop all the way to **Eldoret**. Leave early, as services tend to fill up towards afternoon, and you'd be lucky indeed to catch a lift at night.

Kabarnet

KABARNET, for all its piney preamble and the zippy new road cutting up the escarpment, is a major letdown. Its setting is superb, perched on the **Kamasia massif** – the slab of Rift country, also known as the Tugen Hills, that remained upstanding on the brink of the Kerio Valley when the rest of the Rift sank – and the road up the escarpment offers breathtaking views over the Rift Valley floor to Lake Baringo. But the town itself could hardly be more dull. From a small nucleus of *dukas* on the hillside, it has been considerably expanded in every direction in accordance with its designated function as capital of Baringo District. The result is a motley scattering of offices and civil servants' housing interspersed with wasteland; the planners must hope this will rapidly fill with enterprising businesses and workshops. President Moi's home town (he was born in Sacho, 30km away), Kabarnet is clearly earmarked for development, but is expanding in area faster than it's growing in significance. Apart from its **post office**, **supermarket** and covered **market**, Kabarnet's only point of interest is a small **museum** (daily 9am–6pm; Ksh100) featuring exhibits on human evolution, headdresses from around the country, and artefacts and homesteads of the Tugen, Pokot and Il Chamus peoples who inhabit the region. A snake farm is also planned when funds allow.

Standing above the town, the faintly pompous *Kabarnet Hotel* (PO Box 109 Kabarnet ℡0328/22150; B&B ❹) is quiet and a bit tatty in places, but is worth a visit for its mountain views (Kerio Valley side offers better views) and above-average food (lunch costs Ksh450). There's also a swimming pool. Just across the road, *Lelian B Hotel* (PO Box 125 Kabarnet ℡0328/21458; ❶) offers clean but simple s/c rooms and the best value in town. *Lelian A*, opposite the market, is slightly cheaper but rather dingy, with shared washing facilities. *Hotel Sinkoro*, off the main road by the matatu stage (PO Box 256 ℡0328/21291; ❷), has safe parking and a passable restaurant, but it's not cheap for what you get.

Moving on from Kabarnet, you'll find buses in the morning only: three to Nakuru, and two to Eldoret, but none after 9am. Apart from those, there are matatus, which serve Nakuru and Eldoret, and also Iten, Marigat, Tenges and occasionally even Loruk.

Across the Kerio Valley: Kabarnet to Iten

The quickest and easiest route across the valley is the paved C51 (the alternative Kabarnet–Tenges–Kimwarer road is described at the end of this section). The excitement of this route builds only after you leave Kabarnet and plunge into the **Kerio Valley**, a drop of 1000m in not much more than the same distance. You'll find pretty constant matatu traffic across the valley (and two morning buses from Kabarnet to Eldoret), and the road has magnificent views as it rolls through **Chebloch**, with its old bridge over the Kerio River. A right here will take you along a very rough 4WD road (forget it during rains) to **Lake Kammarok National Reserve**, 25km to the north along the Kerio Gorge. Back on the main Kabarbet–Iten route, the road then turns sharply up the **Tambach escarpment** on the western side of the Kerio Valley, passing the hamlets of Biretwo, Tambach and Kessup. A turn right just before Biretwo is the start of the lonely trans-valley route north to Tot (see p.282). Also before Biretwo, look out for the **Torok Falls**, looming high above to your left at the top of the Tambach escarpment, which are worth a visit if you like waterfalls; count on a good half-day if you're hiking.

After a few more hairpins and a spectacular viewpoint (with obligatory curio and drinks stall), the road finally levels out at **ITEN**, a tiny grass-verged market town on the rim of the escarpment. Iten is the main centre this side of the Kerio Valley, with petrol, a KCB bank and a small market (handy for leather goods). Iten is also home to the remarkable **St. Patrick's High School**, which must be the world's top school for long-distance runners. Any tourists who fancy themselves as athletes would be welcome to train with the kids there – just ask (and prepare to be humiliated). The school is just after the main shops of Iten, on the road north to Kapsowar. It is possible to stay in town at the basic *Southern View Hotel* (PO Box 563; no phone; ❶), but a far better option lies 6km out on the Kabarnet road at **Kessup**. Here you'll find the *Lelin Overland Campsite* (PO Box 589 Iten; no phone), a friendly place with magnificent views and the choice of camping (Ksh300 per person) or *bandas* (❷), with wood-fired hot showers, and its own nature trail down to a waterfall with cave behind, or a longer (5hr) walk to a more spectacular waterfall, if desired. Food is available, though the menu is not large.

An **alternative** to the C51 heads south to Kimwarer. A turn-off from the C51 east of Kabarnet takes you to **Tenges** on a surfaced road that twists spectacularly along the spine of the Tugen Hills, with lovely views across the valley. You'll find some public transport to Tenges from Kabarnet, but very little when you turn right (west) for Kimwarer down in the valley over very bad *murram*. Kimwarer is more easily reached via a better road that meets the C51 just west of Chebloch at the bottom of the valley, which is plied about two or three times daily by matatu from Iten. Whichever way you're heading in this region, if you have a **tent**, use it. There are loads of potential camping spots in spectacular countryside, and the locals are a pretty trustworthy lot. As ever, ask permission from the village headman if you plan to stay near a settlement or on cultivated land.

Kimwarer is the largest community in the Kerio Valley, a company town for the **fluorspar mine** at the head of the Kerio River. As well as the approaches mentioned in the paragraph above, it can be reached by regular matatu from Eldoret via Kaptagat. With nothing but bush, Kalenjin herders and the occasional party of honey-hunters round about, Kimwarer's tidy managerial villas and staff quarters come as a surprise, and "Fluorspar Primary School" looks positively progressive with its brilliant paint job and playground trees all neatly labelled with their Latin names. The town has grown rapidly in the last few years as plans for the production of a thousand tonnes a day of fluorspar have been realized. Fluorspar (calcium fluoride) is used in the manufacture of steel, aluminium, cement – and CFCs. If you're interested, arrangements can be made to visit the "rock crusher".

North up the Kerio Valley

If you want to **explore the Kerio Valley** off the main Kabarnet–Iten C51 road, you'll notice a serious dearth of any kind of public transport. The route north from Chebloch along the east side of Lake Kamnarok National Reserve is passable only by 4WD. The road **north from Biretwo** on the west side of the reserve has, however, been upgraded recently as far as Chesengoch with a good *murram* surface passable in any ordinary car. In the past, this road has seen a fair amount of banditry, due to political strife between Pokot and Marakwet: at the time of writing, early 2002, it is safe to travel on, but it's worth keeping an ear to the ground and seeking local advice before using it.

Heading north on this road (there's an alternative route along the top of the Elgeyo Escarpment from Iten, described on pp.282–283), it's possible to

hitch the length of the Kerio Valley to Chesengoch. The problem lies between there and Tot, where the road has not yet been upgraded, though work is in progress. This section of the route has also in the past been prone to banditry and ethnic strife (see below). If you can get as far as Tot, you can continue on the B4, skirting the northeastern fringes of the Cherangani Hills to emerge onto the main Kitale–Lodwar road near Marich Pass (see p.341), where there's accommodation and public transport to both Lodwar and Kitale. Most of the time, however, you'll probably be "footing" or waiting by the side of the road; no matter (as long as you have several days), for this road, following one of the country's most beautiful valleys, is worth a few blisters. Note, however, that you'll have to be pretty well self-sufficient: the villages along the way have no facilities for travellers, and only limited supplies. Climatic conditions are best in the few months of vivid greenery after the long rains – and fiercest in February and March, just before they break. Densely wooded and not much cultivated in the south, for most of the year the valley resonates with dry heat and the rattle of cicadas and crickets. The first 40km skirt the western edge of the new **Lake Kammarok National Reserve**, with its distinctive alkaline lake, but for the time being you can still hike everywhere. The section from Tot to the Marich Pass is covered opposite.

The Elgeyo Escarpment and Cherangani Hills

Alternatively, you can head **north from Iten**, along a good *murram* road to Kapsowar, passing the villages of Singore and Bugar. Frequent matatus do the run from Eldoret. Some 4km after Bugar, the road branches right to continue north via Chebiemit, Chebara and Cheptongei, where bearing right will bring you to Kapsowar. From here, Chesoi is only 8km away as the crow flies, but 20km by road, a hike around the highland spurs which is much more easily accomplished in the other direction – from Chesoi to Kapsowar, a fine and easy walk mostly downhill.

From Chesoi, you can walk or hitch (but don't count on seeing a vehicle, much less on its having space) the 25 breathtaking kilometres down to **Tot**, turning left halfway at **Chesengoch**. This part of the road, from Kapsowar to Chesengoch and thence to Tot is still in pretty bad shape, but currently being upgraded. It has, however, been unsafe to travel in this area: see box opposite.

The Rift Valley is not short of astonishing vistas, but even here, few roads match the track down the **Elgeyo Escarpment** from Chesoi to Tot for precipitousness and sheer daring. The rocky, almost perpendicular slopes are dotted with **Marakwet** homesteads, the huts unusual in being built of stone (there's a limitless supply up here), which gives them an ancient-looking permanence rarely seen in Kenyan rural architecture. A thousand metres below, spreading like a grey-green carpet into the haze, are the scrubby, bush-covered plains of Pokot and south Turkana. Dozens of tiny wisps of smoke from charcoal burners combine to smudge out the distant peaks of Mount Kenya to the southeast. Places where the trees grow thicker mark the passage of temperamental seasonal streams which flood and dry up with the rains; Pokot goldpanners still find enough gold in them to trade with anyone passing through. To add to this distinctive sense of place, the escarpment itself is the location of an ancient **irrigation system**, feeding water from the hills down to the lush

Travelling in the Cheranganis – a warning

The northern reaches of the B4 along the foot of the Elgeyo Escarpment on the Trans-Nzoia/West Pokot border – especially around the village of Chesegon – were the scene of particularly brutal ethnic clashes in 1997 and 1998. As a result, this part of the road was infamous for armed hold-ups; as usual, the only advice is to give in to their demands (you run a real risk of getting shot otherwise). The road between Tot and Biretwo, especially the section north of Chesengoch, were also less than safe until recently. At the time of writing, things appear to have calmed down, but the Tot–Chesegon section is still inadvisable. If you are thinking of taking any of these roads, always check the current situation before travelling in this area.

Another factor to beware of if hiking in the Cheranganis is altitude sickness. From 1900m or so at Kitale, you may ascend to as much as 3300m in a couple of days and this can have a profound effect on the human body. For more details on symptoms and prevention, see Chaper 2, p.181. If you do start to feel ill, descend immediately and rest until the effects have passed before continuing your journey.

Water should be no problem to find, but you will need to purify it with chlorine or iodine. You should also take sunscreen, as the effects of UV are stronger at higher altitudes, and you can burn even on a cloudy day.

cultivation at the foot of the scarp. Most easily approached on the returning leg of a trip to Turkana (make sure you've enough petrol as there's no fuel along the way), the Elgeyo Escarpment road is – at any rate until it is upgraded – diabolical: too rocky for any kind of ordinary car and too steep for any but the most steel-nerved of drivers. It's a thrilling, gut-wrenching trip in a Land Rover – someone else's preferably – but think twice before driving *up* this road yourself. It is very, *very* steep and there's no fuel.

North of Tot, the B4 road continues through the villages of Chesegon, Lomut and Sigor to meet the A1 at the Marich Pass (see p.341). Between Tot and Sigor, there are very occasional matatus – one or two a day if you're lucky, but transport opportunities improve if you can coincide with weekly markets at Chesegon (Wednesdays), Lomut (Saturdays) and Sigor (Thursdays). The market at Lomut is particularly worth a visit. Matatus generally operate between these villages and Makutano near Kapenguria on the A1 (see p.341). From Sigor, they are relatively frequent. At the time of writing, the road from Tot to Sigor is safe to travel, but there has in the past been ethnic violence in this area – see the box.

The Marakwet canals and Chesoi

Whatever the truth about their origins, **the waterworks** (see the box p.284) are undeniably impressive in scope, if not especially in appearance, stretching north–south for over 40km to divert water from the Cherangani Hills' gushing streams into a branching layout of furrows and aqueducts. Instead of plummeting straight into the Kerio River, the water gets neatly distributed along the escarpment, with complex, unwritten laws to ensure that each Marakwet sub-clan is fairly provided for. It's a system without parallel anywhere else in the country and the results, as you'll see along the base of the scarp, are spectacular. Indeed, for a considerable distance up the Kerio Valley, there's a band of intensive, luxuriant gardening: tiny *shambas* slotted back-to-back between the spurs and down towards the main river. Magnificent, richly flavoured bananas are on sale everywhere. Many of the irrigation channels now pass under the road, but a few still flow over it and a great deal of ongoing repair work is obviously needed to keep the streams flowing in the right direction.

The Marakwet irrigation system

The Marakwet may have arrived on these slopes as far back as a thousand years ago. Part of the broadly related Kalenjin group of peoples, they claim to have taken over the **irrigation system** on the escarpment from its previous users. They say the channels were there long before their own forefathers arrived, and it is possible the original irrigators were a mysterious group called the **Sirikwa**. These people have disappeared, or more likely been absorbed, and the only reminders of them are their name and a lot of curious **holes**, earthworks and cairns (see p.285) noticed by archeologists around the Kerio Valley and in other parts of western Kenya.

Marakwet elders still remember stories of a small people called the **Terngeng**, who may have lived in pits in the ground something like those at Hyrax Hill and Moiben. Other stories refer to tall, long-haired, bearded men who roamed the Rift Valley. Either or both of these groups might have been responsible for the building of the irrigation system, but neither sounds very agricultural; perhaps the Marakwet's claim to have inherited the system but not built it is just a way of saying how old it really is.

The best place to see a good furrow is up near **Chesoi**, over the crest of the scarp. The land here buckles like a patchwork quilt, with the Cherangani Hills stretching west. "Chesoi canal" is a major water supply a couple of kilometres behind Chesoi centre, a metre-wide channel clinging to the hillside (ask someone to show you). In other places, the irrigation system has become almost a piped water supply, with hollow logs used as aqueducts, but this channel has been built with cement. Unfortunately, the water round about, diverted from the Arror River, tastes disgusting, even when boiled; it's a problem you encounter often in the Cheranganis.

There's nothing in Chesoi village itself – no water, no *hotelis* and certainly nowhere to stay – so stop down at the junction if you plan to overnight here. At least the people up here at the edge of the Cheranganis are delighted to meet strangers. As a start, go to the *Kosutany Hoteli* (a small *chai* shop), and ask if you can sleep on the floor. You could also **camp** easily, just about anywhere, if you can find a flat space – ask the landowner.

Moving on from Chesoi: walking in the Cheranganis

If you have the time and inclination, **walking in the Cheranganis** is exhilarating. The thickly forested hills are wild, hardly explored, and still home to bongo antelope. Higher up (Kamelogon peak on Mount Chemnirot is 3581m), they give onto mountain moorland and giant Afro-alpine vegetation, some superb hiking country where you're very unlikely to meet any others doing the same. A couple of days will see you over the southern ridges to Kapcherop, where you'll have no difficulty picking up transport west to Kitale.

For this route, you first climb through Chesoi village and past the mission for about ninety minutes through *shambas*; then there's an hour's walk through forest, mostly flat; ninety minutes of climbing through bamboo forest; and a further two hours though hilly pasturelands and woods before you reach **Kapiego**. Kapiego is a crossroads centre, a suitable stop for the night with a few *hotelis* and a morning and/or evening matatu run to Eldoret. From Kapiego, routes lead: northwest to Kalelaigelat summit (motorable to the base in a couple of hours, but with no matatus and no water); north to the main Cherangani peaks (again motorable in 2–3hr or a day's walk); and west on a little-used road to **Labot** and – 5km further – **Makutano** (*not* the Makutano near Kapenguria). Labot has some *hotelis*; Makutano has one, with no refreshments beyond *chai* and chapatis, though it is on another significant crossroads. Makutano does see some matatu traffic, though very sparse: one or two matatus pass through here most days on their way between Eldoret (which they leave at 6 or 7pm) and Kapsait (leaving there around 5am), plus the one to Kapiego, and there's usually one matatu a day between Labot (leaving there early evening) and Kitale (leaving there at lunchtime). South of Makutano, a quiet road leads down through grassland, then forest to **Kapcherop** (home of Kenya's international athletics champion Moses Kiptanui) – about a three-hour walk. Note if you're driving that the Kapiego–Chesoi part of this route is non-motorable and you can only drive to Kapiego from the south or west.

If your hiking plans are more ambitious, get hold of the relevant Survey of Kenya 1:50m-scale maps (see p.148) and set off, suitably equipped, over the high central districts of the massif. There are several, relatively easily scaled peaks up here. *Mountain Walking in Kenya* by David Else (Robertson McCarta, UK) provides detailed guidance on certain routes. The best base for exploring this area is *Sirikwa Guest House* (see p.339), with *Marich Field Studies Centre* (see p.342) as a lower-budget alternative. You'll be able to find local guides at both.

The Cherangani Highway circuit

The scenic D327 road from Makutano through **Kapsait** and **Kaibichbich** is known as the "Cherangani Highway", and the northern stretch forms part of a popular driving circuit if you have or can arrange your own transport. Starting at the junction on the A1 near Kapenguria, you can drive down through Kaibichbich to a junction north of Kapsait, where you take a left, passing through Kapsangar towards the peak of Kalelaigelat. Another left turn takes

---

In search of the Sirikwa Holes

To seek out the **Sirikwa Holes** near Moiben purely for their own sake would require a certain degree of scholarly dedication, but if you're approaching the Cherangani Hills from the Iten–Eldoret road, or following the route out of the northern Kerio Valley from Kapsowar (with a good map), a visit does make an interesting diversion. Needless to say, it's a lot easier with your own wheels. Matatus run daily from Eldoret or Iten to Moiben (continuing on to Chebororwa on the edge of the Cheranganis); you might have to change at the junction where the *murram* road to Moiben leaves the paved C51. Occasional farm vehicles pass this way, but you could be in for a long wait.

The Sirikwa Holes are some 6km west of Moiben. From the crossroads by the upper primary school and chief's office, follow the dirt track past another school on the left and out into farmland. You may need to ask directions, first for Rany Moi Farm and then for the holes themselves – known locally as "Maasai holes" or "Maasai homes". Don't ask for "Sirikwa Holes", as Moiben is the main location of Sirikwa District and you'd probably be directed to the district offices.

The holes are a collection of depressions, some circular, about 10m across and a few metres deep, others a longer oval shape, all ringed by large stones. Some holes are alone, others are joined by passages dug a metre or so into the ground. They closely resemble the pit dwellings at Hyrax Hill near Nakuru. So far, the site is relatively undisturbed, except for gaps in the stone rings where the odd stone has been removed for building. But, as the pressure from local farms increases, it seems likely that these enigmatic remains will eventually be demolished and ploughed over.

you northwest through **Sina** and back to meet the A1 at Chipkorniswa. The road does however suffer landfalls, and you should check on the current state of it before setting out. If staying at *Sirikwa Guest House*, you should have no trouble finding out about the state of the road.

The hills between Sina and the villages of Parua and Tamkal to its north are popular for hiking, with footpaths connecting the three villages, although you'll need a guide to follow them. All three villages are connected to the A1 by *murram* roads, and if you are going to Tamkal, its worth trying to coincide with market day, which is Tuesday.

Travel details

Nakuru is the whole region's travel hub. More local details are given in the appropriate sections. Peugeot taxis run from Nakuru to Nairobi constantly (90min).

Buses

Nakuru to: Eldoret (3 daily; 4hr); Kampi ya Samaki (2 daily; 3hr); Kisumu (7 daily; 4hr 30min); Nairobi (16 daily; 3hr); Nyahururu (2 daily; 2hr).

Matatus

Nakuru to: Kabarnet (in frequent; 3hr); Marigat (4 daily; 90min); Mau escarpment towns (frequent; 1hr); Nairobi (frequent; 2hr 30min); Narok (daily; 4–7hr); Nyahururu (frequent; 2hr); Subukia (infrequent; 90min); all over western Kenya.

Trains

There are currently no services to destinations in this chapter.

Western Kenya

CHAPTER 4

Highlights

✳ **Mfangano Island**
Vehicle-less, remote and rarely visited, Mfangano Island, in Lake Victoria, is famous among archeologists for its rock art.
See p.315

✳ **Tea country** Kericho, Kenya's tea capital and the most important centre for the bush in the whole of Africa, is surrounded by an endless rolling sea of brilliant green plantations.
See p.323

✳ **Kitale Museum**
Fascinating and well-displayed collection where you would not expect to find it. The nature trail, behind the buildings, runs through a forested valley, and teems with bird and insect life.
See p.336

✳ **Saiwa Swamp National Park** Home to the unusual sitatunga antelope, several species of monkey, and a variety of birds, Saiwa Swamp offers peaceful camping and the chance to explore on foot.
See p.339

✳ **Marich Pass Field Studies Centre**
Beautifully sited, much-praised centre, open to casual visitors, where you can easily fix up guided walks through the bush and visits to local Pokot communities.
See p.342

✳ **Kakamega Forest National Park** Unique patch of lowland rainforest, off the tourist trail, preserving a fauna that has more in common with central Africa than Kenya.
See p.354

Western Kenya

ike the tiers of a great amphitheatre, **western Kenya** slopes away from Nairobi, the major game parks and the coast, down to face the stage of Lake Victoria. Cut off by the high Rift wall of the **Mau and Elgeyo escarpments**, the western region of dense agriculture, rolling green valleys and pockets of thick jungle is one of the least-known parts of the country to travellers. Although more accessible than the far north, or even some of the big parks, it has been neglected by the safari operators – and that's all to the good. You can travel for days through lush landscapes from one busy market town to the next and rarely, if ever, meet other tourists or travellers.

It's not easy to see why it has been so ignored. Granted, the disastrous history of Uganda up until the late 1980s discouraged the through traffic that might otherwise have thrived. But there's a great deal more of intrinsic interest than the tourist literature's sparse coverage would suggest. What the west undeniably lacks are teeming herds of antelope and zebra, lions at the side of the road and narcissistic warriors in full regalia. What it does offer is a series of delightfully low-key, easily visited attractions. There are **national parks** at **Kakamega Forest**, a magnificent tract of equatorial rainforest bursting with species found nowhere else in Kenya; **Saiwa Swamp**, where pedestrians, for once, have the upper hand; and **Mount Elgon**, a volcano to rival Mount Kenya in everything but crowds. **Lake Victoria**, with the region's major town, **Kisumu**, on its shores, is a draw in its own right, dotted with out-of-the-way islands and populated by exceptionally friendly people.

Travel is generally easy. The region has a high population and many well-paved roads, so you'll rarely have long to wait for a bus or matatu, and driving is often a pleasure. If you're inclined to plan ahead, there *is* a vague circuit that begins in Kisumu (as this chapter does) and runs through **Kisii** (of Kisii-stone fame), Kericho, Eldoret, Kitale and Kakamega. You could easily do this in a couple of weeks – or a couple of months. But it's often more rewarding to let events dictate your next move: this area will repay your interest repeatedly if you take time to look around. Much of it, even the areas of intensive farming, is ravishingly beautiful: densely animated jungle near **Kakamega** and **Kitale**, regimented landscapes of tea bushes at **Kericho**, highland pastures and forests in the **Cherangani Hills**, and dank swamp and grasslands alive with birds by the lake.

There's almost no tourist infrastructure – the west has only a handful of hotels that could, by a long stretch of the imagination, be described as luxurious – but there's no lack of good, modest **lodgings**. **Food** is as cheap as anywhere and generally excellent; most of Kenya's tea and sugar comes from the west, and agricultural concerns are paramount.

▲ Lodwar

Marich Pass
Field Studies
Centre

UGANDA

Ortum

Sigor

Makutano

A1

Kapenguria

CHERANGANI HILLS

Mount Elgon

Suam

Endebess

CA8

SAIWA SWAMP
NATIONAL PARK

Mbale

A104

N

See Mt.Elgon
map p.343
for detail

Kitale

MOUNT ELGON
NATIONAL PARK

B2

CA6

C50

Kimilili

A1

Soy

Iten

Tororo

Malaba

A104

Webuye

C51

Bungoma

See Kakamega Forest
map p.355 for detail

Eldoret

Kaptagat

A109

Busia

Mumias

C40

KAKAMEGA
FOREST

Sega

Butere

Kakamega

Kapsabet

A104

B1

Shinyalu

C39

NANDI
HILLS

Siaya

Maragoli

EQUATOR (0°)

A1

Kisumu

Usenge

Chemelil

Asembo

Winam
Gulf

Ahero

A1

Lake
Victoria

Ndere
Island

Simbi
Lake

B1

B1

Rusinga
Island

Mbita

Huma
Lime

Kendu Bay

Sondu

Kericho

Sena

C26

Oyugis

Rioma

C23

Litein

Mfangano
Island

Homa
Bay

Marani

C24

Kamato
Gate

Rodi Kapany

Manga

Sotik

RUMA
NATIONAL
PARK

C19

Mirogi

Nyachenge

Kisii

C18

Miranga

C20

Tabaka

B3

Keroka

B3

Karungu

Rongo

Bomet

Thimlich
Ohinga

A1

Kilgoris

B3

Muhoro

C13

Migori

TANZANIA

C13

Isebania
(Sirare)

Lolgorien

B6

▼ Musoma

▼ Maasai Mara

▲ Soroti

▲ Lornuk

▲ Marigat

▲ Nakuru

▲ Nakuru

▲ Narok

0   50 km

Ethnically, the region is dominated by the **Luo** on the lakeshore lowlands, but other important groups speak dialects of Nandi (principally the **Nandi** around Eldoret and the **Kipsigis** in the Kericho District) and there are Bantu-speaking **Luhya** in the sugar lands north of Kisumu along with **Gusii** in the formidably fertile Kisii Hills.

Around Lake Victoria: Luoland

Lake Victoria is the obvious place to make for in the west, but frustratingly few main roads get close to its shores. Most travellers arrive in Kisumu, which has ferries linking up with the Kenyan ports of Kendu Bay, Homa Bay and Mbita. At one time, these also ran to Tanzania and Uganda, but international passenger services were suspended in 1997 after the lake became infested with water hyacinth (see the box on pp.294–5), and they have not been resumed.

Kisumu itself offers only incidental lakes views. In order to get a good look at the lake, take the short trip out of town to **Hippo Point** and the fishing village of **Dunga**, or ask around at the port for matatu-boat services to nearby fishing villages and islands. If you really must mess about in a boat, the best place to head for is **Mbita**, which has regular "matatu-boats" (called "engine boats" by locals) to Mfangano Island, one of the least-visited corners of Kenya, with the added attraction of some wonderful prehistoric **rock art**.

Kisumu

In the still, sultry atmosphere of **KISUMU**, the regional capital and Kenya's fourth largest town, a distinctive smell off the lake – not unpleasant – blows in on a vague breeze from central Africa, but the layout of the town turns its back on the water, focusing instead on its commercial centre and land links to the rest of Kenya. As a town with a sense of dignity, it has much more in common with Mombasa than with the hassle and grime of Nairobi or Nakuru. In the well-to-do residential district, guarded mansions are discreetly spaced along quiet, fragrant avenues and occasional expensive cars cruise the broad, colonnaded commercial streets. Even in the poorer quarters, it retains a great deal of tattered charm.

Kisumu's fortunes were founded on the lucrative lake shipping business, funnelling goods between Kenya, Uganda and Tanzania, and the town suffered badly as a result of the East African Community's break-up. During the 1980s and early 1990s, the port was practically dormant, with little or no merchandise passing through and signs of dereliction everywhere – empty warehouses,

▲ *Kiboso, Nakuru, Nairobi, Kisii & Homa Bay*

◀ *Kondele suburb, Kakamega, Kitale, Malaba &* **1**

◀ *Kisumu Airport & Busia*

▶ **22**, **23**, **24**, **25** ◀ *Hippo Point, Dunga & Impala Sanctuary*

KISUMU

ACCOMMODATION

Black & Black Guest House	4
East View Hotel	12
Imperial Hotel	16
Inca Hotel	14
Joy Guest House	24
Kimwa Grand Hotel	1
Lake View Hotel	15
Lodger's Palace Guest House	10
Milimani Resort Hotel	21
Miruka's Lodge	6
Mona Lisa	19
Museum View	17
Hotel/Café Natasha	18
New Rozy Lodge	7
New Victoria Hotel	5
Nyanza Club	25
Hotel Perch	2
Razbi's Guest House	11
River Sand Hotel	3
Hotel Royale & Riviera Casino	20
Saint Anna Guest House	22
Sunset Hotel	23
Tot Coffee House	8
Western Lodge	13
YWCA	9

RESTAURANTS & BARS

Expresso Coffee House	G
Gatiba Bar	D
Kenshop Bakery	E
Kimwa Annex	F
Mayfair Bakery	B
New Generation Cafe	H
Octopus Club	A
Señorita	C

BANKS

Barclays Bank	d
Central Bank	g
Co-op Bank	c
KCB	a
Kenya Commercial Bank	f
Postbank	e
Standard Chartered Bank	b

0 — 500 m

broken windows, deserted dockworkers' houses. The commercial shipping services to Tanzania and Uganda have now resumed on a modest scale and the port sporadically buzzes with activity, but it will take a long stretch of sustained growth to restore Kisumu to its former affluence.

Some history

The **railway line** from Mombasa had been stretched out as far as the lake by 1901 (pleasing and reassuring the British public who, after so many years, were beginning to have serious doubts about the project ever reaching completion), but the first train only chugged into the station at **Port Florence** (as Kisumu was originally known) in 1903 when the Mau Escarpment viaducts were completed. By that time, European transport had already arrived at the lake in the form of a steamship brought up from Mombasa piece by portered piece, having steamed out from Scotland in 1895. (There's an obscure subplot to this story of European incursion: many of the ship's parts were evidently seized en route from the coast and recycled into Nandi ornamentation and weaponry. It was five years before a complete vessel could be assembled and launched on its maiden voyage across the lake to Port Bell in Uganda.)

Kisumu was, by all accounts, a pretty disagreeable place in the early years. Apart from the endemic sleeping sickness, bilharzia, malaria and the nasty malarial complication known as "blackwater fever", the climate was sweltering and municipal hygiene primitive. But it quickly grew into an important administrative and military base and, with the consolidation of the colonies in the 1930s and 1940s, became a leading East African entrepôt and transport hub, attracting Asian investment on top of the businesses that had been set up at the railway terminus when the Indian labourers were laid off. Kisumu's rise seemed unstoppable until 1977, when the sudden **collapse of the East African Community**, more or less overnight, robbed the town of its *raison d'être*. The partial reformation of the community in 1996 has brightened prospects again, as have, ironically, the various wars and humanitarian catastrophies in central Africa. By 1999, the port was relatively busy, thanks largely to UN World Food Programme transit goods destined for Uganda, Burundi, Rwanda and Congo.

A general air of stagnation and decay is evident all around: the huge molasses refinery, which would have given a much needed boost to the region's economy (still heavily reliant on sugar cane), has never been finished, and there's no immediate prospect of any progress. The lamentable catalogue of stalled initiatives also includes the Rice Mill, the Lake Basin Development Authority headquarters, and the fourteen-storey Nyanza Provincial headquarters construction project. The town's **infrastructure** itself, already barely adequate, is rapidly collapsing: apart from the obvious disintegration of road surfaces, only forty percent of the population has piped water (there are occasional outbreaks of cholera), the council is able to collect only thirty percent of garbage created (which explains its fantastically insalubrious sidealleys), and none of the town's fire engines work (they have to rely on the ones at the airport). As the crisis has deepened, employment has become scarcer and scarcer, skilled manpower has migrated to other towns, and the population has dropped to under 200,000. Kisumu is now officially the **worst-fed town** in Kenya, as well as being the poorest, with some 45 percent of the population living on less than $150 a year.

But the picture isn't entirely bleak. Kisumu does have considerable charm, and it's no small advantage to be one of the few up-country towns with real character (though the slightly time-warped atmosphere of a place that's

Lake Victoria

The westward view from Kisumu gives you little sense of the vastness of **Victoria Nyanza** (**Lake Victoria**). The shores of the relatively narrow Winam Gulf curve gently to left and right, and it's difficult to grasp the fact that there's another 300km of water between the horizon and the opposite (Ugandan) shore, and an even greater distance south to Mwanza, the main Tanzanian port. Victoria, the second largest freshwater lake in the world (after Lake Superior), covers a total **area** of close on 70,000 square kilometres – almost the size of Scotland or Nebraska – of which only a fraction belongs to Kenya.

Outside knowledge of Lake Victoria is relatively recent. It was barely five centuries ago that the **Luo** first settled beside the vast equatorial lake they called **Ukerewe**, and the lake remained uncharted and virtually unknown outside Africa until well into the second half of the nineteenth century. Then, in the midst of the scramble to pinpoint the **source of the Nile**, the lake suddenly became a focus of attention.

To the nineteenth-century explorers, the search for the source of Africa's longest river was something of a crusade, and none was more obsessed with the pursuit of this geographical Holy Grail than the English adventurer **John Hanning Speke**. As soon as Speke set eyes upon Ukerewe in 1858, he was convinced that the long search was over, and he promptly renamed the lake in tribute to his sovereign, Queen Victoria. He returned to explore the area more comprehensively in 1860 and, in 1862, became the first European to sail the length of the Nile from Lake Victoria all the way to Cairo, famously confirming his discovery by cabling the Royal Geographical Society in London with the words "The Nile is settled". However, sceptics continued to counter that Lake Tanganyika was the true source, and it took a daring circumnavigation of Victoria, led by Stanley in 1875, to prove Speke right. Sadly, Speke did not live to glory in the vindication – he was killed in a shooting accident in 1874.

Lake Victoria was of great strategic significance to the explorers, but it was no paradise. **Bilharzia-carrying snails** flourished in the reeds around the lake's fringes, and the steamy shore was a fertile breeding ground for **malarial mosquitoes**. These hazards persist today. Though the Luo wash, swim and sail their vividly painted, dhow-like, mahogany canoes in and on Victoria Nyanza, the danger of bilharzia is all too real. Instances of the disease are rare after brief contact with infected water, but for the visitor it's not worth the risk: take care if you're going fishing or boating on the lake, and don't even think about going swimming. Newer health scares surface from time to time, and Western scientists have even speculated that the islands off the Ugandan shore may have served as hatcheries for HIV, the AIDS virus.

Lake ecology

Lake Victoria is the largest lake in Africa, filling a shallow depression (no deeper than 80m) between the Western and Eastern Rift valleys, yet is not part of the Rift system. Until the 1960s, it was home to around 320 different species of brilliantly coloured tropical **fish**, known as haplochromines or **cichlids** – all of them unique to the lake. Scientists, puzzling over how such a dazzling variety of species came to evolve in this largely uniform environment in the space of no more than a million years, have suggested that, at some stage in its history, the lake must have dried into a series of small lakes in which the fish evolved separately. Lake Victoria's cichlids are popular aquarium fish, and one of the commonest larger species, the tilapia, is a regional speciality, grilled or fried and eaten whole.

been treading water for over two decades may not be much comfort to its inhabitants). To anyone who's ever travelled in central Africa, Kisumu seems to have more in common with that region than with the rest of Kenya. It's a distinctly tranquil, easy-going town, the *manambas* in the bus station are

Over the last three decades, the cichlid population has dwindled to the extent that only eight species of fish now remain in the lake. Accusing fingers were pointed at the new-fish-on-the-block, the **Nile perch**, as the supposed cause of this mass extinction. Native to the Nile, but not to Lake Victoria, these carnivorous fish were introduced in the late 1950s to control mosquitoes, and established themselves extremely quickly. For the lake peoples they were a boon: they can grow to weigh as much as 250kg, and are both consumed locally and sold for export (in France, Nile perch steaks are sold as *capitaine*). But the voraciousness of these fish began to send shock waves through the lake ecosystem, and ecologists were thrown into a panic by the prospect of the perch eating their way through the entire cichlid population and ultimately starving to death themselves. The expert verdict was that the murderous perch should be fished to extinction in order to save the other species, but the perch received a stay of execution when it was suggested that over-fishing using fine-meshed nets was even more of a threat to the cichlids than predation. The result has been a booming trade in Nile perch (catches are five times as high as in the 1970s), but with unfortunate consequences on traditional fish mongering and processing as the big boys move in with modern vessels and factories, their products mainly destined for European tables.

Over-fishing is, in fact, just one of a series of factors responsible for the **deterioration** of Lake Victoria and its shoreline. Oxygen levels in the lake appear to be falling, with the result that algae are proliferating and the fish population is under threat. The link to human population growth is a direct one – recent studies have estimated that over three million litres of human waste drains into the lake every day. The Swedish development agency, SIDA, estimates that Kenya, which has the smallest share of the lake's shoreline, is in fact its main polluter. As well as human waste, sand harvesting, over-grazing and clearance of lakeshore vegetation and forest for cultivation, releasing excess nutrients and silt into the lake, have all disturbed the fine ecological balance of the shore area. The building of the causeway from Mbita to Rusinga Island turned the Winam Gulf into a pond with only one outlet, inhibiting currents, with serious consequences for the local lake environment.

A more sinister threat comes from the insidious **water hyacinth**, a native of Brazil which is believed to have arrived in the lake via Rwanda. This floating weed grows quickly around the lakeshore and spreads like a carpet across the surface, blocking out the light and slowly choking the lake to death, as well as snaring up vessels. In Uganda, troops were mobilized to collect any plants they came across and treat any new areas of growth with weed-killing chemicals (which was stopped after an outcry by ecologists). Tanzania has been experimenting with weed-eating weevils, but Kenya, which has yet to take any decisive action beyond an abortive beetle-experiment (they weren't all that hungry) and researching the side-effects of a fungus which is said to kill only the weed, has suffered most. Since 1997, the ports of Homa Bay and Kendu Bay, and even Kisumu, have been at times strangled by a mile-wide cordon of the weed, which has inhibited passage to all but the smallest canoes, with disastrous results for the local economy. Solutions have included the promotion of products (furniture, paper, even building materials) made from the hyacinth, and most recently, mechanical clearance which has enabled passenger ferries to start functioning again.

unusually laid-back, and any anticipation of claustrophobia is quickly soothed by the spacious, shady layout. On Sunday evenings, it seems the entire Asian community takes a constitutional along Oginga Odinga Road. The contrast with Nakuru, if you've just come from there, is striking.

The Luo

The **Luo** are the third largest ethnic group and one of the most cohesive "tribes" in Kenya. Their language, Dholuo, is distinctive and closely resembles the Nuer and Dinka languages of southern Sudan, from where their ancestors migrated south at the end of the fifteenth century. They found the shore and hinterland of Lake Victoria only sparsely populated by hunter-gatherers, scattered with occasional clearings where Bantu-speaking farmers had settled over the previous centuries. Otherwise, the region was wild: untouched grassland and tropical forest, dense with heavy concentrations of wildlife.

The Luo were swift invaders, driving their herds before them, always on the move, restless and acquisitive. They raided other groups' cattle incessantly and, within a few decades, had forced the Bantu-speakers away from the lakeshore. Nevertheless, over the generations, **intermarriage** (essentially the buying of wives) was common and the pastoral nomads were greatly influenced by their Bantu-speaking in-laws and neighbours, ancestors of the present-day Luhya and Gusii.

Early in the **colonial period**, the Luo benefited from some inspired, if dictatorial, leadership. They had inherited the institution of the *ruoth* (king or chief) from the original immigrants from Sudan. The *ruoth* of Gem, a location northwest of Kisumu, was Odera Akang'o, an ambitious and perceptive young man with an almost puritanical attitude to his duties. He had a private police force to inspect farms and report any idleness to him, and he regularly had his subjects beaten or fined for "unprogressive" behaviour. He introduced new crops and, under British protection, made himself quite a sizeable fortune. He was widely feared.

In 1915, the colonial government sent him, with two other chiefs, to Kampala. He returned full of admiration for the European education and health standards there, and ashamed of Gem and Luoland in general. Fired with enthusiasm, he applied his style of schooling and hygiene, bullying his subjects into sending their children to classes and keeping their shirts clean, while the British turned a blind eye. The results were rapid educational advances in Gem, which is still considered a progressive district today. Odera, unfortunately for him, was employed by the British to use his methods on the Teso people in Uganda, where they singularly failed. He was accused of corruption and sent into internal exile, where he died.

The Luo today are best known as fishermen, but they also cultivate widely and still keep livestock. Culturally, they have remained surprisingly independent, and are one of the few Kenyan peoples who don't practise circumcision. Traditionally, children had six teeth knocked out from the lower jaw to mark their initiation into adulthood, but the operation is rarely carried out these days. **Christianity** has made spectacular inroads among the Luo, with an estimated ninety percent being believers, but doesn't so far seem to have destroyed the traditional culture quite as thoroughly as it has elsewhere. Despite the ubiquity of Gospel, **traditional music**, especially the playing of the *nyatiti* lyre, is still very much alive and well worth seeking out.

Arrival and accommodation

Kisumu is a natural base, excellently located for exploring western Kenya; half a day's travelling should get you to any of the centres detailed in this chapter. The **bus** and **train stations** are on opposite sides of town: the first is sited by the big junction of the Nairobi and Kakamega roads, the second down the hill in the port area. It's a good idea to install yourself soon after arriving, before starting any energetic wanderings, as it gets tremendously hot here. Sundays are very quiet in Kisumu – more than most towns, on the "day of rest" the maority of places, including restaurants, shut down.

Accommodation

There's a wide choice of **places to stay**, with a good number of modest, mid-range hotels, though prices tend to be higher than usual. At the lower end, the B&Ls are mostly pretty basic, some verging on squalid. Temperature, humidity and mosquitoes will conspire to give you an uncomfortable night if you don't have a net or a fan (preferably both), so it's worth paying a little more for the few nights you may be in town. Unless you want to leave early, try not to stay near the mosque – the morning call to prayer is loud-speakered at 5.30am.

Boarding & lodgings

Joy Guest House Dunga, on the road to Hippo Point, PO Box 9105 ☎035/43406. A small (five rooms, all with nets), clean, family-run guest house, almost like a European *pension*, in Dunga village. ❷

Lodgers Palace Guest House Paul Mbuya Rd, PO Box 6234 ☎0733/761165. Good, breezy non-s/c rooms with nets, and friendly people. ❶

Miruka's Lodge Apindi St, PO Box 1717 ☎035/22131. Basic, dirt-cheap, grubby rooms. Avoid the unspeakable *Nasim's* next door. ❶

Mona Lisa Oginga Odinga Rd, PO Box 1435 ☎035/45058. Seedy at first glance, but really quite decent s/c rooms with nets behind the long established restaurant. ❶

New Rozy Lodge Ogada St, next to the *Octopus Club*, PO Box 548 ☎035/41990. Someone's lost their rozy-tinted specs: dingy and overpriced. ❶

Razbi's Guest House Oginga Odinga Rd, PO Box 1418 ☎035/41312. Formerly a well-thought-of stand-by which had become dirty and run down, but was under renovation at last check. One of the rooms has a lake view of sorts. ❶

Tot Coffee House Paul Mbuya Rd, PO Box 649 ☎035/44431. Big rooms but not exactly spotless, though s/c with bathtubs and hot water on request (and hopefully soon on tap), plus a restaurant downstairs. B&B ❷

YWCA off Ang'awa Ave, PO Box 1618 ☎035/43192. Offers rather bland good value but it's friendly and cheap, if erratically supplied with water. There's a canteen and it's also possible to camp here, though few people do. A few double rooms available (❷). Ksh250 per person in three- or four-bed dorms.

Cheap hotels

Black & Black Guest House Gor Mahia St ☎035/42571. Cheaper than the *New Victoria*, just up the hill, but rather tawdry in comparison, though it's friendly enough, and some of the rooms (all non-s/c) have nets. B&B ❷

East View Hotel Omolo Agar Rd, PO Box 857 ☎035/41871. Handy if you've just crawled off the bus, but antiseptically austere and about as lively as a morgue. Bizarrely, they don't allow you to see

your room before you pay for it (you should insist). No bar, safe parking. B&B ❷

Inca Hotel Ishmael Noo Ooro St, PO Box 112 ☎035/40158. Large clean rooms in a four-storey block, all s/c with hot water and fans, and colour TVs, and there are two suites at the same price. However, security is bad and theft from rooms has been reported. The first-floor bar is unusually quiet and laid-back. B&B ❸

Kimwa Grand Hotel Kondele suburb, 3km along the Kakamega road, PO Box 2226 ☎035/43928 or 21412, ℗21718. Sixty good s/c rooms with fans and nets, plus a good restaurant and safe parking. The main attraction is the music in the attached club (see p.301), but this makes it rather a noisy place. Catch a matatu from Oginga Odinga Rd. B&B ❸

Lake View Hotel Alego St, PO Box 1216 ☎035/45055. No exceptional views, though with its corner position, it does offer some breeze. Fairly comfortable, but overpriced. ❷

Hotel Natasha Otuona Rd ☎035/404380. Decent s/c rooms with hot water and mosquito nets, but there are better deals to be had elsewhere. ❷

New Victoria Hotel Gor Mahia St, PO Box 276 ☎035/21067 or 41007. Friendly and recently renovated, with clean s/c rooms with fans and warm showers. Rooms 206–9 have lake views. The best by far in its price range. B&B ❷

Hotel Perch corner of Mak'asembo Rd and Obote Rd, PO Box 1224 ☎035/45005. "Discover the new broom in the region," enthuses the bizarre blurb. One of the better town-centre options, opposite the car mechanics' area, with 200 s/c rooms, all with self-adjusting "air-cushioned" beds, all sound-proofed against the bar's "latest flavoured filtered music". B&B ❸

River Sand Hotel Accra Rd, PO Box 807 ☎035/22764. Gloomy corridors but bright, clean, airy s/c rooms, some with balcony access and lake views. B&B ❸

Western Lodge Kendu Lane, PO Box 1519 ☎035/42586. Relatively clean and secure (with a large locking cupboard in every room), it's a friendly place, and half the rooms have lake views. Unfortunately, there's no food and, when the near-by goods yard and port road are busy and the bar opposite turns the music up, it's noisy. ❷

Mid-range hotels

Imperial Hotel Jomo Kenyatta Ave, PO Box 1866 ☎035/22661–7, ⓕ22687, ⓔimperial@africanline.co.ke. The first choice for wealthy Kenyans, this seems determined to eclipse the opposition in terms of prices and flashiness. All rooms are AC, "deluxe" ones with satellite TV and mini-bars. The cocktail lounge has views over the lake, as do some rooms. Outdoor café and covered pool, and forex for guests. B&B ④–⑤.

Milimani Resort Hotel off Got Huma Rd, PO Box 2652 ☎035/23245, ⓕ23242, ⓔmilimani@swiftkisumu.com. A fairly new hotel in a secure compound in Kisumu's quiet residential district, with comfortable rooms (all with satellite TV). The staff are friendly and gracious, and there are good views from the upper floors. Downstairs is a restaurant and lounge (no alcohol served); planned additions of cottages and a pool have been stuck in the pipeline for years. B&B ④

Museum View Hotel near the museum, PO Box 544 ☎035/44248, ⓕ44666. A friendly place with large, bright s/c rooms, if a bit bare, with holey moquito nets, in a quiet location. B&B ③

Nyanza Club Aput Rd, PO Box 29 ☎22433 or 42705, ⓕ42703. You take out temporary membership of this old colonial club when you stay here, which entitles you to dine and make use of the facilities (golf, tennis, ping pong, snooker, squash and a swimming pool). The location is quiet, the rooms large and spotlessly clean with lake views and some with balconies, and the restaurant serves British, American, Indian and Chinese dishes, but not African. B&B ④

Hotel Royale Jomo Kenyatta Ave, PO Box 1690 ☎035/40924, ⓕ44644, ⓔtakawiri@net2000ke.com. Formerly a good place to meet people and still highly rated for its Wednesday evening Indian barbecue (Ksh350), it has now been overrun by a number of raffish bars and the *Riviera* casino and slot-machine parlour, which dominates the entrance. The rooms themselves aren't up to much considering the alternatives, though there is a swimming pool and some uncomfortable sunbeds, plus a disco Wed, Fri, Sat & Sun. B&B ④

Saint Anna Guest House 3km south at Milimani, PO Box 19100 ☎035/44617, ⓕ23585. In the posh residential area (follow the signposts from the Central Bank building on Jomo Kenyatta Ave), a modest Catholic-run two-storey hotel, with good large rooms and hot showers. Safe parking. B&B ③

Sunset Hotel Aput Lane, 2.5km out of town to the south, PO Box 215 ☎035/41100–4, ⓕ42445. Fronting on to the Impala Sanctuary (see below) and with a whiff of plasticky highlife, this five-storey complex wouldn't be out of place in Spain. Fraying around the edges, the main draws remain the views of beautiful sunsets from every room (all have balconies), and the baths – with enough hot water to fill them. Well-tended gardens complete with a green swimming pool, monkeys and parrots, and apparently the occasional nocturnal hippo. Ramps and lift access for disabled guests. A taxi from town costs around Ksh250. B&B ④–⑤

The town

The **market** by the bus station is the biggest and best in western Kenya, and an absorbing place to wander, crammed with fruit and vegetables (including some oddities like breadfruit) and all the usual household paraphernalia – pots and plates, reed brushes, wickerwork, and wooden spoons. The market is such a success that it has mushroomed out into the adjacent municipal park, much to the consternation of the local authorities. Three new market buildings were built in 1984 with a multi-million-shilling World Bank loan but, convinced that high rents on the new buildings coupled with unequal competition from squatters would slash their profits, the traders have steadfastly refused to move, and the buildings are still empty, concrete white elephants for which nobody can think of a use. For more on shopping in Kisumu, see "Souvenirs and artefacts" in the "Kisumu Listings" on p.302.

The prayer calls from Kisumu's pastel green-and-white **Jamia mosque**, not far away down Otieno Oyoo Street, sound odd in this town, but Islam is well established here, and Mumias (see p.361) an important regional influence dating from well back into the nineteenth century. The orthodox Shafi'ite mosque was built in 1919, though the women's section on the right was only finished in 1984. It currently has two imams, a Tanzanian and a Pakistani. Inside, the beautiful long mats are from Saudi Arabia.

Kisumu Museum

Foremost among the town's sights is **Kisumu Museum** (daily 8.30am–6pm; Ksh200). Engaging and ambitious, it is highly recommended, just a short walk east from the market. The single-roomed main gallery stands in a large garden with carefully labelled trees. Apart from the usual row of game heads around the walls, there are cases of "Mammals", "Primates", "Birds" (including two stray bats), "Amphibians and Reptiles", "Fish and Crustaceans from the Sea" and "Insects", all displayed with considerable flair and imagination. One of the prize exhibits is a 189-kilogram Nile perch, caught near Siaya in 1978, its grue-somely embalmed body now marooned on sturdy plywood supports. Heavier perch have been landed since, but at the time this mighty fish was a record-breaker. Particularly good use has been made of old and moth-eaten exhibits from Nairobi's National Museum. A free-swinging vulture, for example, spins like a model aircraft over your head while, best of all, centre stage, a lion is caught in full, savage pounce, leaping onto the back of a hysterical wildebeest in the most action-packed piece of taxidermy you're ever likely to see.

The **ethnographic** exhibits are uncommonly illuminating, too. The Maasai aren't the only people who take blood from their cattle for food: Kalenjin peo-ples like the Nandi and the Kipsigis once did the same, and even the Luo lived mostly on cow's blood mixed with milk before they arrived at Lake Victoria and began to cultivate and fish. There's a good selection of **musical instru-ments**, including a fine *nyatiti* (a Luo lyre, the East-African equivalent of the *kora*); it's the kind of thing crudely reproduced in a hundred curio shops and now occasionally heard at African concerts abroad. And look out for the dis-embodied hands pumping the bellows in the metal-working display.

Railway enthusiasts may be interested in the small display of early twentieth-century photographs showing the opening of the Port Florence terminus of the so-called Lunatic Line. The museum's other photographic display shows excavation work in progress at the remarkable Zimbabwe-like walled enclo-sures of the Thimlich Ohinga archeological site in South Nyanza (see p.311).

In separate halls from the main gallery are a disappointing **aquarium**, where you can see what your curried tilapia looked like before it left the lake, and a **snake house** with a fairly comprehensive collection of Kenyan species. Among them are venomous snakes from the Kakamega Forest and some unnervingly lethal-looking black mambas and forest cobras from the Kisumu area. Outside, a tortoise pen, a snake pit – one of the pythons was rescued from a hole beneath the tea counter at the bus station – and a croc pond are rather point-less extras. The crocodiles are fed on Mondays.

In the "**Traditional Luo Homestead**" you may come across the Kisumu Museum drama group rehearsing. An old Luo man used to live in the "First Wife's house", and would tell you in slow Swahili that this is how all the Luo used to live, and indeed how he himself was brought up. He seems to have gone to the ancestors, but the museum is good on guides and enthusiastic members of staff are often willing to show you around.

Walks around town: Dunga

For a pleasant walk out of town, you could head for Hippo Point and the Luo fishing village of **DUNGA**. From the vicinity of the *Sunset Hotel* you follow the main road – or the shoreline – south. Close by is the small **Impala Sanctuary** (daily 6am–6pm; free, but may introduce charges soon), which has a herd of 31 very tame impala and some vervet monkeys, plus a few distress-ingly small cages, due for an upgrade when funds allow – animal-loving donors sought – containing a couple of bored leopards, some baboons and a hyena (not laughing). It's more like a city park than a nature reserve, but worth a visit just for the chance to stretch your legs in the shade (accompanied by a warden, to protect not against wild beasts but "bad people").

The **Kisumu Yacht Club** along the lakeshore has seen far better days – to judge by the number of boats moored and the islands of floating water hyacinth – but it remains strictly members-only: the *askaris* will let you in and kindly turn you straight out again. Five hundred metres further on you come to **Hippo Point**, where you can watch often riotous sunsets from the rock-strewn shore while being bitten senseless by clouds of merciless mosquitoes. Hippos are still seen here, and boatmen will offer to take you out to view them. There's a strong, warm breeze at dusk, and it's a curiously stifling sensation to sit by this giant body of water without a whiff of ozone in the air. Around the lake, Luo fishermen cast their lines from the shallows. If you take kids, heed the playground warning – "Children Playing at Their Own Risk" – in front of the various indescribable pieces of machinery.

Dunga village itself is some 2km further, on the headland, a picturesque settlement with Dunga Fishermen's Co-operative Society the main feature on the shore. If you'd like to spend a night with the **fishermen** on their boats, the co-op is the first place to ask, though you should expect some good-natured negotiations first.

Eating and drinking

Kisumu has a number of reasonable **places to eat** – except on Sundays, when chips are about all that's on offer, and most places are closed anyway. Eat early, as many places tend to close shortly after dusk. Fish is the commonest dish, but there are some tasty curries around, too. There are **supermarkets** at Mega Plaza (Nakumatt; where the post office is on Oginga Odinga Road), and on Kenyatta Avenue (Yatin). Cheap and good *nyama choma* can be had in shack-type "**kiosks**" at the top of Olomo Agar Road, by the market, and fried tilapia at similar places on Alego Street, opposite the Akamba office and on the lakeside by the ferry dock – all served with a choice of *ugali* or chapatis. Good **bakeries** in town include Kenshop by the Mona Lisa in Oginga Odinga Road, Mon Patisserie up the street in Mega Plaza, and Mayfair on Ang'awa Avenue just off Kenyatta Avenue.

Bushmen Café Paul Mbuya Rd. In the same building as the *Lodgers Palace Guest House*, and run by the same management, this is an immaculate little diner with excellent *githeri* (Kikuyu bean and maize stew – the "special" version has meat in it) and other very Kenyan dishes.

Expresso Coffee House Otuona Rd. A volunteers' hangout with a long menu of fry-ups, juices and milk shakes. Despite the name, the espresso machine is defunct, although they'll make you a "cappuccino" of sorts with instant coffee. Closed evenings.

Imperial Hotel As well as a restaurant proper, there's a barbecue terrace with good *nyama choma*.

Kimwa Annex Restaurant Otuona Rd. A bright, clattery, self-catering canteen/bar open 24 hours with a reliable menu, popular with families and volunteers (especially for its pool tables). Good for cheap, filling plates of *kima* (mince) with rice or *githeri*.

Kimwa Garden Inn KNA House, Jomo Kenyatta Ave. Like the *Annex*, a good and filling self-service joint.

Mon Ami Mega Plaza, Oginga Odinga Rd. European and Indian dishes, cold beer, pub-like atmosphere, and CNN or English football on the TV. A favourite hangout with expats and Kenyans alike.

Mona Lisa Restaurant Oginga Odinga Rd. Highly rated for breakfast, but otherwise variable. Closes 6pm.

New Generation Café Oginga Odinga Rd. Reliable if unexciting chicken and chips.

Hotel Perch One of the few places for real African fare (try the *alia* dried meat), and filling Indian buffets Wednesday and Friday (Ksh400).

Señorita Oginga Odinga Rd. A long and varied

menu of Indian and African dishes, spaghetti even, but nothing Latin American or Spanish, despite the name. Bright and clean. Closes 6.30pm.

Somi Snacks Mega Plaza, Oginga Odinga Rd. South Indian vegetarian dishes including *masala dosa* and *idli sambar*, plus vegetarian pizzas,

falafel and, at weekends, vegetarian Mughlai dishes such as malai kofta. Open daily 8.30am–10pm.

Sunset Hotel The buffet lunches here, at about Ksh400, are a real blow-out, and there's a nice bar with snacks, overlooking the gardens.

Nightlife

If you make the effort, Kisumu more than rewards the enthusiastic, with ample opportunities for catching **live bands**, and sometimes even big-name stars. More run-of-the-mill **discos** are plentiful, too. At either kind of venue, you're now most likely to hear *ndombolo* – see the box below.

Apoc Complex Nyamasaria, 4km from town on the Nairobi road. Long synonymous with live *benga* – how long will it hold out against the tide from the other side of the lake? Beer hall and *nyama choma* too. Reached by matatu from the main stage.

Donna Club Kondele suburb, 4km out on the Kakamega road. Home of the old vanguard, with a huge dancefloor – guitarists, live *benga* and *Lingala*, as yet unconquered by *ndombolo*. Happy hour 7–8pm.

Gatiba Bar Kendu Lane. A pleasantly sleazy little bar with a loud jukebox, open daily till midnight.

Kimwa Grand Hotel Kondele suburb, 4km out on the Kakamega road. Excellent live music Friday–Sunday: Congolese *ndombolo* bands and resident group Extra Kimo. Family shows Sunday afternoons.

Lakers Country Club On the Kiboso road, 4km

from town – get a taxi. Big name Congolese bands and others, with Sunday family day and video shows.

Octopus/Bottoms Up Night Club Ogada St A pick-up joint of the first order – but for an enjoyable night out, this is relaxed enough if you just want to mingle over a beer or two. The restaurant is often empty, but the disco is always lively, and the *Pirate's Den* roof terrace (with barbecue and dartboard) is a popular, breezy rendezvous point, albeit with dire service.

Riviera Casino *Hotel Royale*. Just in case Kisumu's lodgings haven't extracted your last shillings, the casino here opens from 8pm to late, and there are slot machines from 10am on.

Show Breeze Club Mamboleo, near Kondele. Live *ndombolo*, some *benga*, in fierce under-the-belt competition with *Lakers* for the big stars.

Listings

Airlines Kenya Airways, Alpha House, Oginga Odinga Rd, PO Box 1427 ☎035/44055–6, ℱ43339; airport ☎035/40125 ext 06.

Banks Standard Chartered, Barclays and KCB all have ATMs. PEL Forex next to the British Council charges no commission for changing cash or

---

Ndombolo

Besides being known for bloody civil wars and dictators, the Congo (formerly Zaïre) has managed to establish and nurture an enviable reputation throughout Africa as the continent's dance music factory (one earful of any traditional stuff will tell you why). Whilst some Kenyans moan that the Congolese do little more than pinch and repackage their original ideas, the reverse seems very much the case. The most successful dance import is **ndombolo**, which has taken Kenya by storm and Kisumu in particular. Its chief exponents are Koffi Olomide and Le General Defao. Its invention is credited to Kinshasa street kids imitating the gait of chimpanzees, or, alternatively, to a parody of former President Laurent Kabila's limping walk. Latterly, the dance has taken on something of a controversial sexual flavour, which led to its being banned in Limuru, north of Nairobi, by the local chief, on the grounds of its "gyrations arousing the youth and forcing many to engage in unprotected sex".

traveller's cheques, with only slightly lower rates for the latter.

Boat trips Lake Victoria Safaris at the *Hotel Royale* (same phone, fax and email as the hotel) offers sightseeing trips on the lake for up to six people for Ksh3500 per hour, and fishing trips at Ksh25,000 a day or Ksh12,000 for half a day all in.

Books Sarl Bookshop, Oginga Odinga Rd next door to *Mona Lisa*; F.K. Shah, Oginga Odinga Rd by *Señorita* restaurant.

British Council Oginga Odinga Rd, PO Box 454 ☎035/45004, ✉bc-kisumu@africaonline.co.ke. The library is open Tues–Fri 10am–6pm, Sat 9.30am–1pm. British papers and magazines, and the BBC news channel on TV. You have to take out temporary membership (Ksh250 a day) to use their facilities, however. There are also occasional theatre productions here.

Car rental Try Kisumu Tours & Travel near Barclays Bank; PO Box 764 ☎035/41910, but check the car carefully.

Courier services DHL c/o Securicor, Bank St ☎035/22022 or 44024; Mon–Sat 6.30am–6pm.

Hospitals The main place is Nyanza Provincial General Hospital ☎035/44275 or 8; Aga Khan Hospital ☎035/43516, 43530 or 43713 is the best private hospital. You can call an ambulance on ☎035/42074.

Immigration The Immigration Department (PO Box 1178 ☎035/45002) on the first floor of a building behind Alpha House on Oginga Odinga Rd, opposite the British Council, is exceptionally helpful, stamping visa and visitor's pass extensions on the spot without objection. If you need a photo, there's a booth inside the entrance to the market.

Kisumu Show Held in the first week of August.

Library Off Gumbi Rd, behind the bus and matatu station; Mon–Thurs 9am–6.30pm, Fri 9am–4pm, Sat 9am–5pm.

Pharmacies Open late and on Sundays: Hillchem, New Station Rd near Oginga Odinga Rd (daily 8am–7pm) and at Kilimani Shopping Centre, Omolo Agar Rd (daily 7.30am–10pm; ☎035/44604); Miriu Chemists, Kondele suburb, opposite MTC (daily 7.30am–8pm; ☎035/44005); Dosefield, Alpha Centre, Oginga Odinga St (daily 9am–9pm); Winam, Ang'awa Ave, 100m from the clock tower (daily 8am–6.30pm).

Police Olmolo Agar Rd ☎035/44445.

Post office Mon–Fri 8am–5.30pm, Sat 9am–1pm. Poste restante available.

Souvenirs and artefacts The row of craft stalls opposite the *Hotel Royale* is one of the region's best hunting grounds for souvenirs. The things to buy here (if you have space) are the heavy, three-legged Luo stools. The best are intricately inlaid with beads, and dark brown from repeated oiling. Also on offer are bangles, wooden carvings and row upon row of soapstone knick-knacks. Soapstone (or Kisii-stone) is more expensive to buy in Kisumu than at source (Tabaka, near Kisii), but it's cheaper than in most places, and the craftsmen will carve designs to order. Pendeza Weavers (PO Box 1786 ☎035/44466, ✉pendeza-wp@yahoo.com) is a worthwhile visit, about 3km out of town past the museum on the Nairobi road, past the chief's camp (on the right in the large field) and indicated by a small white sign on the right. Handwoven *kikois* here are as cheap as you'll find; they turn up later at Spinner's Web in Nairobi.

Swimming pools A swim at the *Sunset Hotel* is always a pleasure – non-residents pay Ksh100. You might also take a dip in the *Royale*'s pool (Ksh100). The *Imperial* has a less enticing, semi-indoor pool, surrounded by a very plain concrete terrace (Ksh120).

Moving on

Kisumu is very well connected to the rest of the country by **bus** and **matatu**. There's a spanking new bus and matatu stage on Gumbi Road, behind the BP station at the intersection of Kenyatta Avenue and Otieno Oyoo Street, but it stands deserted as vehicles continue to use the BP station and the main road instead. They run to more or less anywhere in western Kenya, and to cities further afield like Nakuru and Mombasa. Eldoret Express buses stop here pretty much hourly on their way between Eldoret and Nairobi. Coast Bus has a daytime service to Nairobi at 9am and an overnight run to Mombasa at 6pm, taking 12hr. Akamba has its office on Alego Street (☎035/23554), with four buses daily to Nairobi (9am, 11am, 1pm & 8.30pm), and two for **Kampala** (both at noon). **Peugeots** for Nairobi leave from the BP station. If you're aiming for **Kakamega Forest**, buses and matatus run from the main stage to Kakamega town, from where it's possible to find transport to the forest (for details see p.352).

The **train** station (☎035/42338) is at the bottom of new station road. At last check, all passenger services had been suspended, but were due to resume in 2002 with a daily service to Nairobi, with second- and third-class seats available. The journey used to take thirteen hours. There was also a third-class-only service to Butere, which is expected to be running again when the Nairobi service resumes. Call the station for latest details.

The **ferry** service run by Kenya Railways on Lake Victoria is now back in action after a period of suspension caused by the water-hyacinth invasion. There are currently two boats a week departing Kisumu Tuesday and Thursday mornings at 9am for Kendu Bay, Kowuor, Homa Bay, Mbita and Asembo, each leg of the journey taking around an hour.

Kisumu **Airport** (☎035/40125), 5km up the Busia road, is served by Peugeots from Jomo Kenyatta Highway between the clocktower and Ang'ata Avenue. Kenya Airways runs three or four flights daily from here to Nairobi.

Siaya District and the road to Uganda

Heading northwest out of Kisumu, down a broad avenue of flame trees, you pass first the Sunni Muslim, Ismailia and Hindu cemeteries, then the golf club and emerge into the wide plains of **Siaya District**. Transport to the border town of Busia is fairly constant. The region is pleasantly rural but unremarkable. One possible place to stay, just off the road at **Siaya**, is the *Mwalimu Hotel* (❷) offering good-value rooms with breakfast.

USENGE (or Usengi), a short bus ride from Kisumu, is something of a diversion if you're en route to Uganda, and a useful target if you're planning an exploration of the district, but it's also a town of precolonial historical significance in its own right. The nearby hill, Got Ramogi, is by tradition the site where the first Luo arrived at the lake from further north. It's not a hard climb to the top for a satisfying view over the island-dotted lake, the lagoon below (Lake Saru), and the land which the Luo fought for and eventually won from the Bantu-speakers at the end of the fifteenth century. Usenge itself is a pretty town with a causeway over the lake that connects with the Uganda road. Lodgings there are cheap.

Busia

BUSIA, on the Uganda border, is a surprisingly nice little town and a better place to cross than Malaba, the busier frontier post on the railway line further north. The formalities are straightforward enough. Busia consists of a line of shacks and bars on the Kenya side, with a similar line in Uganda. If you're staying the night, the *Western End Lodge* (❶) is as cheap as they come, but has no sign and is not easy to find – it's south of the main drag, just off Bulanda Road by Jomo's Shop and the Jesus Praise Centre. Similar places on the Ugandan side cost more. Of much better standard is the *Farm View Hotel* on Hospital Road, a kilometre south of the main drag (PO Box 141 ☎0336/22470 or 22097; ❸), with good s/c rooms with nets, kids' play area, and "traditional" dancers and discos at weekends.

Whether you have a visa for Uganda or not (Irish passport holders don't currently need one, but British, American, Canadian, Australian, New Zealand and South African nationals do), you're normally allowed to **cross the border** to look around on the Ugandan side. Unless you're desperate for a bottle of cheap spirits, however, there's little point.

There are several daily **buses** from Busia to Nairobi (7hr) via Kisumu (3hr). Most companies run one morning and one evening service, but Akamba have one service only, departing at 7pm. **Matatus** serve Kisumu, Malaba and Bungoma, with morning departures to Kitale and Nairobi. On the Ugandan side, there are matatus to Jinja and Kampala. **Money changers** on both sides of the border will change Ugandan and Kenyan shillings, or give either for dollars or sterling, but check the current rates in advance. There is also a KCB bank on the Kenyan side.

From Kisumu to Kisii

If you want it to be, the ride **from Kisumu to Kisii** can be a rapid transition along the main A1 highway from dusty or flooded plain (depending on the season) up into the ample, fecund hills of the Gusii. But there are various ornithological diversions along the way, if you're independently mobile or enthusiastic enough to make the effort with public transport and your own feet.

There's also a fine **alternative route** from Kisumu to Kisii, using the first-class paved **lakeshore road** from Katito (south of Ahero) to Kendu Bay (see p.306), and then taking the road to Oyugis back on the A1, just a short journey from Kisii. Except when the Kendu Bay–Oyugis road is in very bad condition after heavy rain, the route takes barely longer than the direct approach.

Kisumu bird sanctuary

The swampland beyond Kisumu to the southeast is very rich in birdlife, and the first place worth investigating off the main A1 road is the **heronry** (Kisumu Bird Sanctuary; information from KWS District Warden, PO Box 1193 Kisumu ☎035/21105) on the way to **Ahero**. From April to May, especially, this is the nesting site of hundreds of pairs of not just herons, but ibises, cormorants, egrets and storks, the dark and curiously scruffy open-bill stork included. Ornithologically world famous, the sanctuary is a must if you're interested in birds.

To get there, take a right turn (south, towards the lake) around 7–8km from Kisumu (about 16km west of Ahero), to the school at **Orongo**, and from there branch left and follow the track for another 2–3km. Ask local people's advice, as the best vantage points and the easiest access to the colony move each year. The site is usually a good place to camp. This low-lying region between Kisumu and the Western Highlands is known as the **Kano plains** – disablingly hot, humid flatlands, swaying with sugar cane and rice fields, fertilized by occasional disastrous flooding.

There are a number of other breeding sites for herons and ibises beyond the sanctuary, some 20km from Kisumu, again to the right of the road in the marshy district southwest of Ahero.

Oyugis and the pelicanry

Climbing into Kisii District's round, picture-book hills, you arrive at the crossroads town of **OYUGIS**; like a number of other places, it was originally named after a local hero, and has a few reasonable B&Ls. The best is *Nyadendi Hotel*, a kilometre up the main road towards Kisumu (PO Box 33 ☎0384/31213; ❶), which is pleasant and friendly, if rather basic. *Oyugis Safe Lodge*, behind the matatu stage (PO Box 98 ☎0384/31085; ❶) is also friendly, and more central, though rooms are smaller and the hotel has the bizarre house rule that "our esteemed rooms occupants are expected in the rooms between 6.30pm to 8.30am daily", a curfew that may not be terribly convenient. Finally, a kilometre down the main road towards Kisii, *Hotel Ragama* (no phone; ❶) is quiet, rustic and even more basic than the other two. Apart from these and its matatu stage, Oyugis offers little but its pelican-breeding site.

The **pelicanry** is reached by turning east off the main road, 50m south of the Kendu Bay turn-off and a similar distance north of the matatu stand, and continuing (past *Safe Lodge*) up the *murram* in a three-kilometre arc, until you reach two huge fig trees, in a narrow stream-bed 200m from the road on the left, which is all it consists of. There is no office or signpost, nor anything apart from the pelicans to make you aware that it's a nature reserve. From August to March, you'll see the parent birds wheeling in the air from some distance and, when you get closer, there's the distinctive smell of pelican guano to guide you. With binoculars you can watch the shaggy **chicks** in their treetop nests ramming their heads down the parents' throats for fish; then, yakking desperately for more, attempting the same manoeuvre on each other. Sadly, the pelicanry now risks disappearing under pressure from the rapidly expanding human population around it. Much of the original fencing has been torn down, parts of the reserve have been built on, and elsewhere, nesting trees have been felled. Although there are plans to re-protect the site, this will in all probability be too little and far too late.

To Kisii

If you arrive at Oyugis early in the day and are feeling very fit, you can continue on the track past the pelicanry all the way to Kisii, along a route that becomes more and more beautiful as you climb up through dense *shambas* and forests, out onto **Manga ridge** above the town (see p.322). You might be lucky and get a lift some of the way – but don't count on it. If you have your own car, it's a pleasant half-hour drive.

South Nyanza

The territory south of Kisumu is interesting to explore – it's fairly easy to get around, if you're willing to go by matatu, and includes a number of small towns, the Lake Victoria islands, a national park and even an archeological site. This section covers the agreeable little town of **Kendu Bay**, the main town of **Homa Bay**, **Ruma National Park**, the intriguing ruins of **Thimlich Ohinga**, the islands of **Rusinga and Mfangano** (perch fishing for the rich; walking and hanging out for the poor) and, down near the Tanzanian border, the one-street town of **Migori**.

The **lakeshore** west of Migori is remote and, in parts, beautiful, with **Karungu Bay** a rewarding side trip. In the other direction, **Kihancha**, on the south bank of the Migori River, on another back-country route to Maasai Mara, is a pretty area.

South Nyanza is largely Luo country, but there are also scattered, rural communities of **Kuria** people down here. The Kuria have an interesting, quasi-matriarchal system found in various parts of Africa, which essentially allows women of means to "marry" younger women in order to have children without the need to live with a man. In practice, it's often a married woman who can't have children who invites a younger woman into her home. The young "bride", in turn, chooses a male partner, often in secret, to father (biologically speaking) her children, who are brought up by the two women without the involvement of the father or the older woman's husband. The older woman is sometimes a widow, sometimes simply a single woman. In any case, she lives like a male elder – attending to light business affairs but essentially waited upon hand and foot from dawn to dusk. It's a system with much to recommend it, especially when it takes care of unmarried mothers (who are barred from marrying men), who come into the family as "wives" – surrogate mothers – and whose children are automatically adopted. Ironically, despite these apparently female-controlled arrangements, it's male children that women-families want – and men who inherit land.

Kendu Bay

KENDU BAY's local fame comes from the curiosity of **Simbi Lake**, about 4km (45 minutes' walk) west of the village: head out of the village on the Homa Bay road and pass the left turn to Oyugis/Kisii. Just over 2km further on, over the river bridge, turn right down the path and walk for another fifteen minutes.

The lake, and the nearby Ondago Swamp, have been adopted as feeding grounds (in June and July) by a couple of thousand **flamingos**, refugees from Lake Nakuru (see p.262). With a steady trickle of naturalists and tourists now coming to Kendu Bay to bird-watch, the villagers are, inevitably, keen for a slice of the action. Among the suggestions that have been made are that the Homa Bay County Council should fence off Simbi Lake, impose admission charges, and make provision for local traders to set up stalls, but as yet they have not done so, and the lake remains a tranquil beauty spot where the only commerce is the odd local resident selling sugar cane.

Even without the flamingos, the lake is unquestionably weird: several bright green but changeable acres of opaque water sunk 20–30m below the surrounding land and only a few kilometres from Lake Victoria itself. It has no apparent source and its origins are somewhat mysterious. It looks like a huge meteorite crater with a footpath around the rim.

The **story** goes that an old wandering woman was refused hospitality one rainy night at the village that once occupied the site of the lake. A big beer party was going on and she was ignored. Only one woman would allow her to warm herself and the old woman insisted she and her family leave the village with her. The young woman tried to persuade her husband to come with them, fearing the old lady's revenge for her ill-treatment, but in vain. So the two women left alone. And later that night there was a tremendous cloudburst and the rain came down so hard that the village was swamped to become Simbi Lake. Further variations on the story (there are many) improve on the theme of drunkenness and debauchery to give a Sodom and Gomorrah ring to the tale. Other lakes in Kenya have similar tales of origin.

The little lake's shores are almost devoid of vegetation. Nobody goes out on it in boats and it doesn't look as if they fish there either. It's usually described with the catch-all term "volcanic" and is apparently extraordinarily deep. According to one local belief, visitors should throw money in to avoid bad luck. Whatever the natural explanation, it seems plausible that the area was inhabited when the lake was formed, the disaster accounting for the legends. Similar, though smaller, lakes can be seen east of Kendu Bay along the road to Kisumu.

If you're heading on to Homa Bay, you might like to see the **Oriang Pottery Centre** in the village of the same name, 2km past the Simbi Lake turning. It's a UNDEP-funded programme, relying on clay from the local river bed.

Practicalities and moving on

Kendu Bay has a good deal of intrinsic charm, though next to nothing to offer the casual visitor. The one-street old town is 500m off the Kisumu–Homa Bay main road, turning off just before the tarmac ends. The post office and petrol station are on the main road by its junction with the road to Oyugis. The ferry dock (a pier partly made of concrete-filled barges) is about a kilometre from the old town, with two boats a week each way between Kisumu and Homa Bay. One notable building in the old town is the gorgeous Masjid Tawakal mosque. You can look around it – though there's not much to see – and climb on the roof.

There's one **B&L** in the old town: *Milimani Bar & Restaurant* (PO Box 77; no phone; ❶) has eight very basic non-s/c singles and no showers. If you prefer somewhere really rustic, the *Kendu Country Hotel* (PO Box 184; no phone; ❶), hidden away a kilometre beyond the mosque, has no running water, but does have a well; it doesn't exactly advertise itself, but will rent you room if you can find the place. Much better than either of these is the *Hotel Big Five* at the Total station (PO Box 218 ☎0385/22416; ❶), a new place decorated with Disneyesque concrete trees and animals, whose rooms are set apart from its **restaurant** (which serves excellent fish) and a nightclub operating Friday, Saturday and Sunday nights. A few doors away, the *New Wedewo*, a shacky *hoteli* that's not much to look at, serves unbeatable *mandaazi*, and pretty good meals too.

The *murram* road up **to Oyugis** (on the main A1 highway between Kisii and Kisumu) is generally firm, but it sometimes takes a beating in wet weather and becomes, on occasions, impassable. Normally, though, you'll have no difficulty getting a matatu up to Oyugis or west to Homa Bay. The obvious alternative escape route is the tarred **lakeshore road** from Kendu Bay to Katito, where it meets the A1 on to Kisumu. This is an excellent, fast highway – another from an Israeli company – which swings beautifully for some 40km, the first 20km close to the lake. There's a wealth of interest in the surrounding Luo countryside, most of it so recently a rural backwater, with scenes of fishing boats and compounds of square, mud-brick-built, thatched houses (a fairly recent change; traditionally they were round). Now that this route has become a lakeside drive, the handful of modern houses – two-storey "villas", complete with tiles and wrought iron – barely look out of place and suggest a district that people are prepared to invest in.

Homa Bay

At first glance a scruffy and unremarkable place, the small port town of **HOMA BAY**, the region's main centre and also a good base for visits to Ruma National Park, Rusinga Island and Simbi Lake, is in fact one of the friendliest towns in Kenya.

The town itself admittedly has nothing much of interest, just a few dirty, pot-holed streets and an unusual straw-hat-shaped **Catholic cathedral** atop a low hill behind town, with an open-air central altar and great views. However, if you're into **traditional Luo music**, Homa Bay is the place to track down tapes of *nyatiti* (lyre), *orutu* (single-stringed bow fiddle) and *onand* (accordion) music, as well as the ubiquitous gospel pop. Most of the town is strung out along the main street, which starts at the jetty and runs uphill towards Rongo.

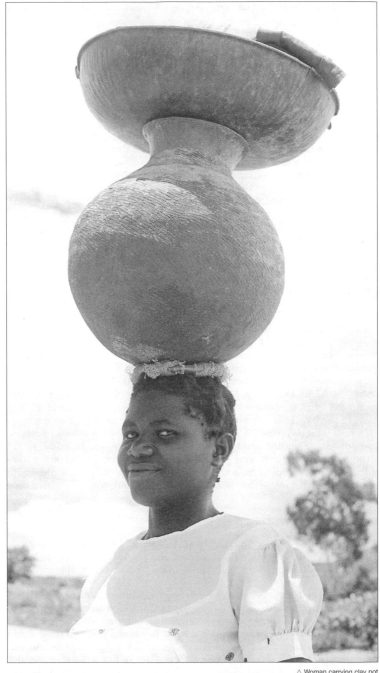

△ Woman carrying clay pot

On its way, it passes a turn-off for Kendu Bay (passing the Co-op Bank), a street that leads to Barclays Bank (with ATM), and another leading to the post office (where you'll find Postbank), then the matatu stage, with buses parked up in front. The market is between the street with Barclays Bank and the street with the post office.

Homa Bay used to have a busy port, which provided the focus for most of the town's activities (fishing, trade and a little tourism), but in June 1997 this, and much of the shoreline around, became completely hemmed in by over a kilometre of thick, vibrantly green **water hyacinth**. By all accounts, the weed infestation happened quite quickly, leading to some boats becoming trapped for several days. Six people actually walked for 4km over the weed to safety, and one woman gave birth to a baby boy – whom she named Victoria Junior – on a trapped boat. Boats to Kisumu and Mbita were suspended, and most of the local boats sold. The government has since had the dreaded hyacinth mechanically cleared, and fishermen keep the remainder at bay by hand, but the port is a shadow of its former self although passenger ferry services have been resumed. The shoreline of the lake is accessible by turning left just before the pier, by the *Homa Bay Hotel* (a cheap canteen, not a place to stay).

There's a handful of reasonable **accommodation** options, the most modern being the *Hippo Buck Hotel*, 2km out on the Rongo road (PO Box 274 ☎ & ℻0385/22032; B&B ❸), with clean s/c rooms including spotless bathrooms with hot water, a nice garden and good restaurant (especially fried fish). Look out for live *orutu* and *onand* music here on Friday and Saturday evenings. Opposite the *Hippo Buck* is the much more basic *Hill View Guest Lodge* (PO Box 829; no phone; B&B ❷), currently being renovated. In town itself, the best choices are the cheap, bright and breezy *Bay Lodge*, behind both the matatu stage and the post office (PO Box 96 ☎0385/21436; ❶), and the quiet, repectable *Summer Bay Hotel*, opposite Barclays Bank (PO Box 856; no phone; B&B ❶), which also offers safe parking. Above the matatu stand, *Doves Den Restaurant* offers large but basic rooms (❶) if you need something very cheap indeed, but the cheapest place in town, with very dingy though in fact self-contained rooms, is the *Snack Hotel* opposite the matatu stage (PO Box 402 ☎0385/22689; ❶). Finally, a recommended option with great views is the Swedish-NGO supported *Women's Centre*, on the hilltop, all the way through town (signposted; ❷).

As to **food**, there are lots of inexpensive *hotelis* almost everywhere. One of the best is the *Doves Den Restaurant* in the Salama Building above the matatu stage; from the pier, head up along the Rongo road, turn left after the market, then take the second right. Also worth trying are *Snack Hotel* opposite the stage by the Akamba bus office, and *Akiras Restaurant* in the same street as the post office.

Homa Bay is not especially hot on **nightlife**, but it does have a few bars worth checking out of an evening, including the *Cave Inn* on the main road, the *Lake View* on the same road as Barclays Bank, and the *Victoria Day and Night Club* opposite, which has live bands at weekends.

Got Asego

A **hike** up **Got Asego**, the impressive conical hill on the east side of town, is recommended. The hill is the highest of dozens of volcanic plugs (cores of old volcanoes) across the plain; from its table-sized summit, you'll have a 360-degree panorama of lakeshore and surrounding plains. It is remarkable how little of the land is not used – Luo thatched huts are interspersed with tin-roofed homesteads, a patchwork of small plots and agave hedges. Take binoculars and you can see more: clumps of papyrus drifting across the lake, and traffic along the road where it snakes east to Kendu Bay.

It takes about an hour to reach the top from the centre of town (actual ascent 30–45min), an easy climb but best tackled late in the afternoon (early morning ascents, though cooler, can be treacherous thanks to dew on the rocks). Head up the Rongo road, take the second left after the Total petrol station and turn right up the *murram* road after Homa Bay School. The hill itself is best approached up the northwest ridge, where there's a well-defined footpath. Beware of columns of ants.

Moving on

Matatus leave Homa Bay from the stage on the main road, serving Kendu Bay, Kisii, Kisumu, Mbita and Migori. If you don't find a direct vehicle to Kisii, the best way to head eastward is by taking a Migori matatu, which drops you at Rongo on the A1 highway, where you can soon find a Kisii-bound vehicle coming up from the south. Northbound, the road to Kendu Bay looks short on the map, but matatus take a good ninety minutes to bump along its rough surface. The road is then paved from Kendu Bay to Kisumu. Plenty of long-distance **buses** start their journeys in Homa Bay, making Nairobi an easy overnight (or daytime) ride. They park up on the main street in front of the matatu stage. Companies operating to Nairobi include Kenya Bus, Survival and Transafrica, all with offices in the row of shops in front of the matatu stage, Keroka Executive and Linear, who have no offices, and Akamba, whose office is 100m down, opposite the Elf petrol station (☎0385/22578). Akamba has only one night service, while Kenya Bus is the most frequent with four buses daily. All travel via Rongo, Kisii, Kericho and Nakuru, with the exception of Tawfiq (whose services we do not recommend), which travels via Kendu Bay and continues to Mombasa.

Ruma National Park

Daily 6am–6pm; $15, children $5, camping $2 per person. Warden: PO Box 420 Homa Bay; phone enquiries to Homa Bay on ☎ 0385/22544.

Ruma National Park (previously known as Lambwe Valley Nature Reserve) can be a little tricky to reach – the nearest matatu route (Homa Bay to Mbita) skirts the reserve by 11km – but if you're independently mobile and self-sufficient the effort of getting there is usually repaid by animal-watching undisturbed by the presence of other visitors; you're virtually guaranteed the place to yourself. Four-wheel drive is best for seeing the park, and in the rainy season – around April and October – essential.

The Lambwe Valley's 194 square kilometres of tsetse-fly-ridden bush is one of the few places in Kenya where you can see **Jackson's hartebeest** and two opposite extremes of antelope: the enormous, horse-like **roan** and the miniature **oribi**. There are about seventy of the beautiful **Rothschild's giraffe** and they're not hard to see above the tall grass. You'll have more difficulty spotting **leopard**.

Practicalities

To get there, head south out of Homa Bay along the main Rongo–Migori road, and turn off after 3km onto the Mbita road leading southwest. From this (signposted) turning, an eight-kilometre drive along the rough *murram* brings you to a signposted turning to the left, where another *murram* road runs for 11km to the gate and the reserve. If you're coming from Kisii or Kisumu, rather than Homa Bay, use the C18 road towards Karungu. A signposted murram road leads straight to the main entrance. You are likely to be greeted by surprised rangers – they get few visitors. There are two campsites in the park, but you'll need to bring your own equipment, food and water. There are plans to construct a forty-bed **eco-lodge** within the park, which have been shelved for lack of tenders, but may be revived given sufficient demand; details from the KWS facilities manager (p.148).

Work is in progress to make Ruma National Park more accessible to visitors, in order to safeguard its future, but for the present it isn't practical without your own transport. If you're dedicated, your best hope is to talk to the park warden in Homa Bay. You can find him through the manager of the BP petrol station and spare parts store.

Thimlich Ohinga

Thimlich Ohinga (daily 8.30am–6pm; Ksh200) is an archeological site of potentially huge significance – "the greatest stone enclosures in East Africa", as the Kisumu Museum bumper stickers declare. The site is the most striking example of an architecture whose remnants are scattered across South Nyanza. Similar to the drystone enclosures of Zimbabwe (of which Great Zimbabwe is the classic example), its main structure consists of a compound about 150m in diameter, inside which are five smaller enclosures – probably used as cattle pens – and at least six house pits, the sites of former dwellings. The walls range in height from 2.5m to 3.5m – higher than those of the seventeenth- and eighteenth-century stone ruins in the Inyanga Highlands in Zimbabwe. Outside the main compound wall on the southeast side, evidence of iron-working has been discovered.

Thimlich Ohinga in Luo means "thick bush with stone enclosures". It's estimated they were built around the fifteenth century by a people whose history has been forgotten. But successive generations of various communities have used stone enclosures and, in some places, modern Luo families have their homesteads inside such walls. It's certainly an unusual and worthwhile site. In up-country Kenya it rates as the equal of Hyrax Hill (see p.258) and is quite absorbing compared to Chetambe's Fort (p.350), but, as usual, if your interest in ruins is limited at best, pass on.

Arrival

You really need your own transport to get to Thimlich. **From Kisii** (105km) or **Homa Bay** (60km), head for Rodi Kopany on the C20 between Homa Bay and Rongo, where you take the C18 southwest, through Mirogi and Ndhiwa to Miranga. Just beyond Miranga's shops, a signpost shows the direction of Thimlich Ohinga down a rough *murram* track that can take an ordinary car when dry, but requires 4WD in the wet. After about 25km, on an area of flat land before the road begins its descent from the plateau, there's a crossroads, where a signpost formerly pointed the way east (left). Unfortunately, the signpost has now gone, as has the next one, 3km down the road, where you turn left again by the *Ohinga Hotel* (a basic café that will stretch to a tea and chapati if you're lucky) and neighbouring primary school, heading towards a small hill. A right turn after another kilometre or so will take you to the ruins. If you are very dedicated, and very intrepid, it is just about possible to do this **by public transport**, but there's nowhere to stay, barely anywhere to eat, and you won't get there and back in a day, so you'll need a tent and supplies. The way to do it is with a matatu from Homa Bay (via Rodi Kopany and Ndhiwa) that runs down the *murram* road to Mihoro. There are one or two matatus on this route most days, but some days there are none, and there's precious little other traffic. Assuming the matatu driver knows which crossroads is for Thimlich Ohinga, he will drop you there to walk the remaining 4km; it's a good idea to check when he's likely to do the return run.

If you're approaching **from Migori**, take the Isebania/Tanzania road, and after 4km turn off right onto rough *murram*, at the junction for Muhoro Bay, where there is a National Cereals and Produce Board depot. A couple of kilometres from the depot you reach another junction where you take a right and drive straight on through Suna and Macalder. The journey is about 55km from the Cereals Board Depot. All these roads necessitate 4WD in wet weather.

Rusinga Island

Far more practical than Ruma National Park or Thimlich Ohinga is a trip to **Rusinga Island**. The narrow channel between Mbita and the island was bridged by a **causeway** in 1984, whatever your map may show, so driving around Rusinga is quite feasible, as long as the rains aren't too heavy. The road from Homa Bay has recently been graded, but is still tough on suspensions and can get tricky in the rains. There is a steady stream of matatus (around Ksh100) from Homa Bay to Mbita throughout the day, but they're always packed, so make sure you get to the stage in plenty of time.

Mbita, straddled on either side of the causeway, is very unprepossessing indeed, but things improve once you get on to the island. The building of the causeway – partly over two dumper trucks which fell into the lake during the operation and couldn't be recovered – has had some unwanted side effects. Vervet monkeys now move onto the island to raid crops, and fish have become scarce on the Kisumu side of Rusinga because the causeway blocks the current, turning the water there into a stagnant pond. A bridge to replace the old chain ferry would have been the best solution to the island's access problem. As it is, the single bit of civil engineering represented by the causeway has ended Rusinga's slight isolation at what many local people feel is an unacceptable cost.

Mbita and around

Excepting some matatus which run around Rusinga Island, **MBITA** is as far as you can go by public road transport. The last matatu returns to Homa Bay around 3pm. There are, however, some wooden **engine boats** which connect Mbita daily with various ports on Mfangano Island, Takawiri Island, and Ranalo or Misori on the opposite side of Rusinga Channel, which provides road access northeast via Bondo to Kisumu. Note that these services dry up by mid-afternoon, so if you arrive late, you'll have to stay the night in Mbita (unless you've around Ksh2500 to spare to hire a boat).

Accommodation is limited to three, rather basic, choices. The best of these is *Patroba Ogweno Lodge* (PO Box 315 ☎0385/22184; ❶), down the alleyway by the *New Foxton hoteli*. Its better rooms are s/c with nets. More characterful, but perhaps not for lone women, is *Viking Lodge* (PO Box 12 ☎0385/22182; ❶), on the right side of the matatu stage, which has some dingy cells with nets but no s/c, off a lovely bougainvillaea-shaded courtyard which doubles as a bar, with music from 5pm to midnight. The only other option is the *Junction Inn*, just across the causeway on the left (PO Box 138; no phone; ❶). Down the road to Sido, the *Mara Victoria Beach Hotel*, currently just a bar with a pleasant lakeside location, plans to have rooms in the future. Plenty of cheap *hotelis* in town provide filling **meals**, the *New Foxton* being the best of them.

If you've an afternoon to while away, there's flourishing birdlife in the vicinity, and doubtless a lot more to be uncovered by adventurous travellers. **Sindo**, 10km south of Mbita, is reckoned a good place to go out in fishing boats, while from the top of **Gemba Hill**, just a few kilometres from the Mbita–Sindo road, there's a superb view across to Homa Bay and down towards Tanzania.

The island

RUSINGA is small and austerely pretty, high crags dominating the desolate, goat-grazed centre, and a single dirt road running around the circumference. Life here is difficult, drought commonplace, and high winds a frequent torment. The occasional heavy rain either washes away the soil or sinks into the porous rock, emerging lower down where it creates swamps. Ecologically, the island is in very dire straits: almost all its trees have been cut down for cooking fuel or to be converted into lucrative charcoal. These conditions make harvests highly unpredictable and most people do some fishing to make ends meet, either selling the catch on to refrigerated lorries or bartering directly for produce with traders from Kisii. And the causeway has forced them to make longer fishing trips. Yet the islanders, in common with their mainland cousins, remain an unfailingly friendly and cheerful bunch, who are more than happy to make contact with wayward travellers.

Aside from its friendliness, the island has two significant claims to fame. It is rich in **fossils**, and was the site of Mary Leakey's discovery of a skull of *Proconsul africanus* (a primitive anthropoid ape), which can be seen in the National Museum. And it was the birthplace of **Tom Mboya** (see Contexts, p.646), civil rights champion, trade unionist and charismatic young Luo politician who was gunned down in Nairobi in 1969, sparking off a crisis that led to over forty deaths in widespread rioting and demonstrations, and was a turning point for the worse in Kenya's independent history.

Tom Mboya's mausoleum lies on family land at **Kasawanga** on the north side of the island, about 7km by the dirt road from Mbita, or roughly 5km directly across the island. There's one matatu that does the round of the island most days, and the lorries that travel round the island collecting fish from local communities for sale inland will take paying passengers in the driver's cab if they have room, but otherwise you'll need to walk the whole way there and back if necessary (allow 4hr and take some water). Local residents will no doubt show you the way, but Rusinga is so small you're unlikely to get lost. Aim for the crags in the centre (if you're feeling energetic, you could climb the tallest to get a view of the whole island), skirt them to the right and then walk down to rejoin the road on the other side of the Tom Mboya Memorial Health Centre. There's a little *hoteli* here with cold sodas. From here, it's less than 2km to Mboya's mausoleum, the conical silver roof clearly visible just off the road. The mausoleum was built in the shape of a bullet to recall the manner of his death, and contains various mementoes and gifts Mboya received during his life, plus the briefcase he was carrying when murdered. The inscription on the grave reads:

THOMAS JOSEPH MBOYA
August 15th 1930 – July 5th 1969
Go and fight like this man
Who fought for mankind's cause
Who died because he fought
Whose battles are still unwon!

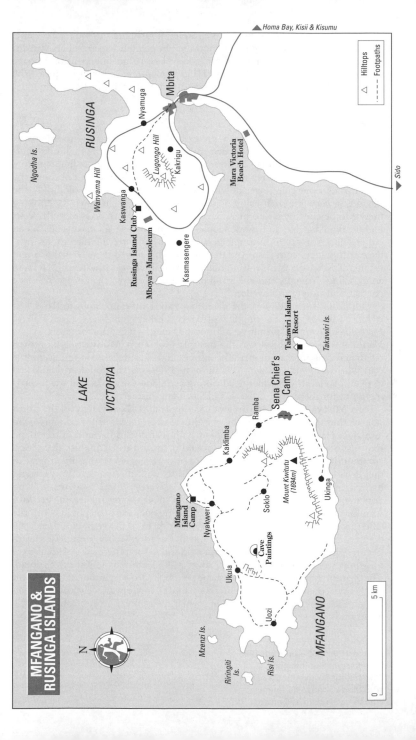

MFANGANO & RUSINGA ISLANDS

N

0   5 km

△ Hilltops
----- Footpaths

RUSINGA

Ngodha Is.

△ *Wanyama Hill*

Nyamuga ●

△

△

△

Mbita

△

Lugongo Hill
Kakrigu ●

△

Kaswanga
△

■ **Rusinga Island Club**
Mboya's Mausoleum

● Kasmasengere

△

Mara Victoria
Beach Hotel ■

▶ *Sido*

LAKE
VICTORIA

Takawiri Island
Resort ■

Takawiri Is.

Ramba ●

Sena Chief's
Camp

Kakiimba ●

△
▲ *Mount Kwitutu
(1694m)*

Mfangano
Island
Camp ■

● Nyakweri

● Soklo

● Ukinga

(Cave
Paintings

Ukula ●

Mzenzi Is.

*Riringiti
Is.*

Risi Is.

Uozi ●

MFANGANO

You don't have to know anything about the man to be impressed. In any other surroundings his memorial might seem relatively modest, but on this barren, windswept shore, it stands out like a beacon. Members of Mboya's family live right next door, and are usually on hand to open the gates. They are happy to see foreign visitors, who rarely come here, and they maintain the mausoleum themselves, so they always appreciate donations, though these are not obligatory.

Fifty metres past the Tom Mboya Secondary School, the path to the right takes you through *shambas* of millet and corn to a seasonally grassy lakeside called Hippo Bay. Here you can watch nesting fish eagles as well as, usually, hippos. If you're lucky, you may see the pretty and little-known spotted-necked otters that live around Lake Victoria and nowhere else in Kenya.

Also on this side of the island is the amazingly expensive ($350 per person) *Rusinga Island Club* (reservations through Mellifera, PO Box 29397 Nairobi ☎02/577374–9, ℱ564945, 🄴rusinga@africaonline.co.ke; ⑨), the sort of rustic-luxury retreat you would expect, with a high proportion of its clients flying in from a Maasai Mara safari to the nearby airstrip. Attractions here include sport fishing – Rusinga holds the record for the heaviest Nile perch ever landed – as well as water-skiing, windsurfing, bird-watching and guided sightseeing. There are excursions to islands inhabited only by birds, fossil walks including a short one to the cave where Mary Leakey discovered *Proconsul africanus*, and visits to see the cave paintings on Mafangano (see p.316). A lot of people fly in for a day-trip from Maasai Mara (bookable there through any lodge), which offers a chance to spot wildlife from the air, but it's possible (and a joy) to stay overnight – the club sleeps ten in thatched cottages. Boat excursions (watch the fish eagles for how to catch tilapia in style), activities, meals and drinks are all included in the price.

Mfangano Island

Said to have been inhabited for centuries, enigmatic **Mfangano Island** is out of range of the smallest fishing boats, and entirely without vehicles. The island is populated by a curious mixture of immigrants from all over Kenya, administered by a chief and three sub-chiefs with help from a trio of policemen. Monitor lizards swarm on the sandy shores and **hippos** are much in evidence out in the water.

Larger and more populous than Rusinga, with a similarly rugged landscape but better vegetation cover, Mfangano's greatest economic resource is still the lake itself. Traditional **fishing techniques** are unusual: the islanders fish with floating kerosene lamps hauled shorewards, or towards a boat, to draw in the schools to be netted. Of more immediate interest, however, are the island's **rock paintings**, certainly worth the trip if you're into such things, and a good excuse to get to know the island in any case. Because there are no vehicles, Mfangano's people rely on a network of temporary **footpaths** which are constantly changing course. If you arrive at Sena by boat, you can walk all over the island, though it's always easier if you have a guide – Ksh300–500 per day is a fair fee.

Practicalities

Unless you're rich enough to fly in, the only means of access to the island is on the large wooden boats with outboard motors ("engine boats") which run a matatu service, shuttling local people and their produce between Mbita and the surrounding islands and peninsulas. Most head around Mfangano in an anti-clockwise direction, calling at Sena, Nyakweri and Ukula, others head around clockwise, sometimes dropping in at Takawiri Island and Ukinga. **UKULA** (pronounced "Wakola"), is closest to the rock paintings (see below), and it makes sense to go there first, then work your way back, perhaps over a few days, to Sena. The first boat leaves Mbita around 10–11am, and the last no later than 4pm, and you won't be able to return the same day because boats back from Sena only run between 7am and 9am. The only way to do a day-trip is if you've enough money (around Ksh2500) to hire a boat plus skipper for the day.

It's a ninety-minute crossing to **SENA** – the chief's camp and also the capital of Mfangano. Sena has a small *duka*, a post office but no accommodation, as the island's only budget lodging – a rest house run by the chief in Sena – is no more. Unless you're well off, the only option is winging it with local residents. People have camped wild in the past, and at Ukula they've seen the odd traveller before and are more than happy to earn the cost of a B&L for putting you up overnight. Don't forget that Mfangano is desperately poor, without electricity or piped water, and you should bring anything you think you might need. Not surprisingly, the place sees few visitors of any kind and perhaps a handful of travellers each year.

It's another story if you've money to burn. With the success of the exclusive and expensive **Mfangano Island Camp**, a fishing lodge similar to Rusinga's, tourist numbers have increased slightly, but again most of the camp's visitors fly in from the Maasai Mara on a day-trip (fishing and bird-watching in the morning, lunching and lounging in the afternoon) and barely connect with the local people. The camp, a huddle of clay-and-thatch buildings laid out in the shape of a Luo homestead, but fitted out in deluxe style, overlooks a private bay and sleeps twelve (reservations through Governor's Camps, p.42; FB ❾, plus around $650 for a return flight from Maasai Mara for up to four people). There's a similar, though less expensive place on **Takawiri Island**, off Mfangano: the *Takawiri Island Resort*, which offers windsurfing, snorkelling and sailing, as well as fishing and bird-watching. Like *Mfangano Island Camp*, it faces west, for unforgettable sunsets. You can get there on a matatu-boat from Mbita, or else by light aircraft or on their own cruiser from Kisumu (reservations through Lake Victoria Game Safaris, PO Box 188 Kisumu ☎035/45088, ℻44644; FB ❼).

The rock paintings

From Ukula, an hour or two's walk into the interior (with a guide) brings you to a high, north-facing bluff on Itone Hill, with startling views out across the island's north coast. Here, in a gently scooped cave, are the **rock paintings**: reddish spirals and whorls, some with rays, up to 50cm across, that could come from any Von Daniken paperback. People will tell you they're very old, but nobody knows who painted them or why, or what they depict. Local people associate the site with supernatural powers and miraculous events, and in some measure fear them, too, which has so far helped prevent the vandalism which has afflicted other rock-art sites in Kenya.

The site is still used for traditional rain-making ceremonies, when elders pray to their ancestors to intercede on their behalf. As a result, locals believe that violating traditional practice may lead to something dangerous, so don't be surprised if you find people insisting that you stay put in Ukula for a day or two before setting out – the gods apparently need time to prepare for your arrival. If you're really into rock art, the Odengere Hills, also on Mfangano, are unique among Lake Victoria's prehistoric sites in that they have depictions of insects, some of them so fine that even the species can be identified. Experts are at a loss as to their significance. For site-by-site descriptions of Lake Victoria's rock art, see the 1994 (vol.9) issue of *Azania* (copies at the British Institute in Nairobi; see p.148).

Migori

MIGORI, down near the Tanzanian border, is basically an ever-expanding roadstead, spread out along 4km of the A1 highway. The main centre of activity seems to be the hospital, where the doctors are adept at treating arrow wounds inflicted during land skirmishes between Gusii, Maasai, Kipsigis and the new Kikuyu settlers. Market days are interesting for the variety of peoples and for traditional activities untainted by tourism. The Maasai people here are far less calculating and aloof than many of those further to the east whose lives have been invaded by cameras and minibuses, but you're likely to be the object of some curiosity. There are two good places to **stay**, but water supplies are sporadic, and even cold water may not be available on tap. Turn eastward just north of the bridge by Agip for *Gilly Hotel* (PO Box 831 Suna-Migori ☎0387/20523, Ⓕ20556; B&B ❷). Ignore the bland concrete exterior, as the welcome is warm, and rooms are very reasonable s/c with nets, the better ones with distant views of the river, and with good breakfasts, but try to get a room with an outside window, and don't believe tales of 24-hour hot water. *Girango Hotel*, at the south end of town (PO Box 1019 Suna-Migori ☎0387/20608; B&B ❷), is friendly, quiet and peaceful, with rooms in a number of outhouses scattered in pleasant gardens (guarded parking). There's a choice of different rooms, and the better ones are definitely worth the extra fifty bob they cost. Hot water is provided in buckets, and there are tubs rather than showers. There's a popular bar, and a licence for weekend discos has been applied for. If you need something cheaper, there are a few B&Ls around the matatu stand, and north of the bridge, such as the *Highway Lodge* opposite the post office (PO Box 79 Suna-Migori ☎0387/20387). For **food**, the *Exile Chis Palace* is the best of the *hotelis* just north of the post office, serving good, wholesome Kenyan staples. Also worth a mention for food, if only for its weirdness, is *Njiri's Bar & Restaurant*, a bizarre mock-Victorian castellated folly, 2km before Migori. Migori is not known for its **nightlife**, but the *Resort Club*, west of the main road just north of the bridge plays *ndombolo* music most nights.

If you've just arrived **from Tanzania**, there are "direct" (though not non-stop) **buses to Nairobi and Mombasa** leaving between 6am and 8am, or in the evening, going via Kisii, Kericho and Nakuru. Kenya Bus, Mombasa Liners, Linear and Universal have offices opposite the matatu stage. There are also direct buses to Eldoret in the morning only. Matatus serve Kisumu, Kisii and Homa Bay, with Peugeots to Karungu. Heading down **to Tanzania**, there are direct buses to Mwanza mornings and evenings, but otherwise you'll have to take a matatu to the border post at Isebania (also called Sirare), or at Kianja, cross on foot and take an onward vehicle from the other side. Lastly, if you're driving, you could consider taking the unsurfaced C13, 4km south of Migori, east into **Maasai Mara** (p.410), signposted Kehancha, but the road is in a pretty dreadful state, and especially prone to degradation caused by rains, so should only be attempted in 4WD, and then only in dry weather (the clay gets treacherous when wet).

The Western Highlands

The Western Highlands rise all around Lake Victoria in a great bowl. There's superb walking country throughout, in the **Nandi Hills**, for example, or in the little-known **Mau Massif**, east of Kericho. But the undoubted highlights are **Saiwa Swamp National Park** and the **Kakamega Forest**, recently accorded national park status of its own. For serious, sensibly equipped hikers, **Mount Elgon** must also be a major temptation, sharing much of Mount Kenya's flora and fauna, but none of its popularity. Also wonderful walking country are the high hills of the **Cheranganis**, though, like Elgon, they take some getting to. The highland towns are, on the whole, not arresting. **Kisii** is lively and perhaps worth a visit, but **Kericho** ("tea capital of Kenya"), **Eldoret** and **Kitale** are best thought of simply as bases for getting to the real attractions.

Kisii and around

Headquarters of the **Gusii** (or Kisii or Kosova) people, and district town of a region vying with Nyeri in having the fastest-growing population in the country, **KISII** is a bustling, muddy and rubbish-strewn trading centre in the hills, prosperous and hard-working with a muddy main street which has pretty much turned into a giant bus and matatu stage. For its small size, the town creates terrific noise and energy. It has more lodging houses per head than anywhere else in Kenya (albeit mostly terrible), and enjoys a profusion of excellent fruit and vegetables all year round, especially bananas and sugar cane. Lavishly fertile, the region gets rain all year, in remarkable contrast to the semi-arid lowlands of the lakeshore just a few kilometres away.

Kisii is also famous for its fine **soapstone**. Surprisingly, there's little of this to be seen in the town itself, though *Kwanji's Café* has a few pieces for sale. The best locality for watching the carvers and making on-the-spot purchases is Tabaka, some way south (see p.322). In Kisii iteslf, a large open-air **market** spreads itself along the main road north of the *Kisii Hotel* on Mondays and Thursdays.

Some Gusii history

The Bantu-speaking **Gusii** (after whom the town is named) were only awakened to the brutal realities of British conquest in 1905, when they rebelled – pitching themselves with spears against a machine gun. It was "not so much a battle as a massacre", one of the participants recalled, leaving "several hundred dead and wounded spearsmen heaped up outside the square of bayonets". In 1908, after the District Commissioner was speared in a personal attack, the same thing happened again, only this time the Gusii were trying to escape, not attacking. Crops were burned and whole villages razed to the ground. Churchill telegraphed from the Colonial Office: "Surely it cannot be necessary to go on killing these defenceless people on such an enormous scale."

The Gusii were totally demoralized. In a few brief years, the fabric of their communities had been torn apart, hut taxes imposed, and cattle confiscated to be returned only in exchange for labour. And then came World War I. Kisii was the site of the first Anglo-German engagements in East Africa, and thousands of men were recruited into the hated Carrier Corps by trickery or press gang.

It seems extraordinary that the exceptionally friendly people of Kisii are the grandchildren of the conscripts. The powerful, millennial religious movements which burst among them during the colonial period under the name **Mumboism** may partly account for the very strong ties of community they've maintained against all odds. Prophets and medicine men have always been important here, and even in today's superficially Christianized society, the Gusii have solidly kept their cultural identity. **Witchcraft** and **sorcery** still play important roles in the life of the town and its district. The practice of **trepanning**, for example, which involves tapping a small hole in the skull to relieve headache or mental illness, seems to be as old as the Gusii themselves. It has recently received the ironic laureate of medical journal credibility and the attentions of a German film crew. "Brain operations" are still performed, clandestinely, but apparently quite successfully. However, the rising influence of Christianity, as well as occasional abuses of power by witches, has led to spates of **lynchings** of suspected witches and sorcerers (the last in September 1998, when ten people were killed). Residents were reticent to divulge the names of the lynchers to the authorities, which prompted the local police chief to say: "We hope we can get them [the witches] and if possible charge them in court. This way we shall save their lives."

Accommodation

You'll find plenty of **places to stay**, although most of them are pretty awful and noisy, especially on Wednesdays and weekends when they have bars or discos, or else are situated near one (the *Storm* is the exception), and women travelling alone will definitely want to avoid most of the cheaper places (the

Whitestone is a possible exception). You should be prepared for power fluctuations during heavy rain – have some candles handy – and water supplies are uniformly erratic. It's worth staying the night, though, as, once you've settled in, there are several rewarding local **excursions**, and the town itself buzzes day and night with a slightly hassly energy.

Hotel Capital PO Box 966 ☎0381/20944. Unremarkable and overpriced for what you get, with a noisy bar. Rooms are s/c, but water is not guaranteed. Good views over the busy road. ❶

Highway Lodge PO Box 910 ☎0381/21213. Very basic, but dirt cheap and not outrageously filthy, with quite large non-s/c rooms. ❶

Kiango B&L PO Box 973 ☎0381/21190. This was a dingy place geared to short-term guests (soap, towel and condom provided), but undergoing renovation at last check. All rooms have balconies. ❶

Kisii Hotel PO Box 26 ☎0381/30134 or 20715. On the road out to Kisumu, this ramshackle but quiet place has an agreeable creaking colonial atmosphere and a half-decent restaurant. The large, s/c rooms have nets and furniture, and hot water round the clock, and there's guarded parking and a lovely, big, bird-filled garden. B&B ❷

Mwalimu Hotel PO Box 2427 ☎0381/31636. A charmless 1979 block, notable mainly for its staggering decrepitude, with most things broken, dirty, damp or caving in. The rooms have views, but the bar is rather male-dominated, with CNN at top volume on the TV, and pool tables upstairs. ❷

Njau Guest House PO Box 156 ☎0381/21375. The beds are clean if not much else, and the rooms are s/c though pretty basic, with no hot water. ❶

Sakawa Towers PO Box 541 ☎0381/21218. Overpriced, but a friendly and bright hotel in a block (until recently the tallest building in town) named after a Gusii medicine man and prophet. There are great town views from the roof and upper floors. All the rooms are s/c with nets and balconies, but some are cramped and terrifically noisy. Notable also for its one, kinky "suite", which comes complete with a bath (though you'd be unusually lucky to have enough hot water to fill it), two huge animal-skin drums doubling as tables, and a mirror affixed to the headboard of the king-size bed. Good restaurant and busy first-floor bar (with an *askari* at night on the gate leading up to the rooms). B&B ❷

Satellite Inn PO Box 973 ☎0381/31678 or 21190. A big, grubby boozer, with large, non-s/c rooms with nets, but otherwise basic. Get one with an external window. There's rooftop *nyama choma*, and a busy first-floor bar which gyrates to *ndombolo* on Friday and Saturday nights. ❶

Storm Hotel PO Box 973 ☎0381/30649 or 31820. Well-run middle-range choice, and the quietest in Kisii (no disco). There's a choice of adequate rooms, all s/c with nets, some more expensive suites, and an outside bar and *nyama choma* joint. Coming here at night, it's best to take a taxi (Ksh100) as there have been robberies on the approach road (which passes the police station). B&B ❷

Whitestone Delicious Hotel PO Box 401, no phone. Good-value cheapie, secure and clean with s/c rooms and hot water most of the time. ❶

Zonic Hotel PO Box 541 ☎ & ℻0381/30298. The top hotel in town, five storeys high with balconies for most rooms, and a restaurant, bar, underground disco (the location rather than the music), and a rooftop pool and terrace with a café and great views. On the minus side, the decor's a bit shoddy in places and the single rooms are rather poky considering the class of hotel, though the doubles are fine. ❺

Eating and drinking

Despite the noxious drain smells, the overflowing **market** is the first base for hungry travellers. The lodgings mostly have **dining rooms** or **restaurants** of their own, of which *Sakawa Towers*' is probably the most recommended (Ksh150 for lunch). Despite a dwindling menu, the *Kisii Hotel* is still considered the place where one dines out, especially at lunchtime when it's not raining, when the tables are spread out on the garden lawns. Reliable places for a shot of cholesterol include *Vienna Café*, opposite *Rangi Mbili*, which is open round the clock, and *The Tea Room*, just down the street. Slightly better are *Kwanji's Café*, with a pleasant atmosphere and wooden tables, and three places at the southern end of town, the *Masi Highbridge Café*, *Sun-Jua Hotel* and *Mashauri Café*, all offering the usual choice of stewed or fried meat with *ugali*, chips or rice, but in bright, clean surroundings. Of places to get a **drink**, the *Safe Lodge*'s beer-and-*nyama choma* joint is Kisii's answer to a Bavarian beer hall, loud and raucous; the meat is usually good. The atmosphere is almost Jamaican, in fact, complete with pool tables, rude boys and reggae music. *Pub Dot Com* opposite the *Zonic Hotel* is a bit more sophisticated, with loud music, mainly rap, and another favourite watering hole with music is the *Rainbow Bar*, near the hospital.

Listings

Banks Barclays has an ATM. Don't go near the KCB – they charge outrageous commission.

Earth tremors Kisii lies on a fault line and minor earthquakes are not uncommon – only a slight worry if you're asleep at the top of *Sakawa Towers* hotel at the time.

Football Kisii stadium is the home ground of Shabana FC, in Kenya's First Division.

Garage Rangi Mbili PO Box 532 ☎0381/30204. A very helpful parts store/workshop if your car is in trouble. Helpful anyway, for that matter – they're eager to meet travellers.

Hospital The main one is Kisii District Hospital,

Hopital Rd ☎0381/20471; a private option is Ram Hospital, Court Rd ☎0381/30236.

Kisii Show Held annually in July.

Police On the road to the *Storm Hotel* ☎0381/20223.

Post office Mon–Fri 8am–5pm, Sat 9am–noon. The entrance is round the side and the counters upstairs. Card- and coinphones outside.

Sports club Kisii Sports Club PO box 103 ☎0381/30169, with a swimming pool, golf, squash, darts, bingo and a bar. A friendly place with temporary membership available.

Moving on

Kisii is something of a route focus, with both regional and national bus and matatu services passing through. There are plenty of **matatus** leaving throughout the day for Homa Bay, Kericho, Kisumu and Migori, with others to Kakamega, Kilgoris, Oyugis, Rongo and Tabaka. Most leave from the main stage in front of the market. The exceptions are matatus for Nyachenge and Tabaka, which leave from the Shell station at the north end of town; and for Kericho and Kilgoris, which go from the bus park beside Rangi Mbili. There are also useful early-morning departures for Narok via the B3, passing the junctions for the C12 and C13 Maasai Mara access roads. **Bus services** are equally numerous: Akamba, with its office by the *Whitestone Hotel* (☎0381/30137) for Nairobi (9am & 9pm) and Homa Bay (7.30pm); Keroka Executive, with a shack just south of the *Whitestone Hotel*, for Homa Bay–Kisii–Keroka–Nairobi; Linear Coach (☎0381/31322), with an office opposite Akamba for Nairobi (pretty much hourly), Homa Bay, Kericho, Kisumu and Migori, and another office by *The Tea Room* for their Mombasa service; Stagecoach (☎0381/31673) for Eldoret, Homa Bay, Kericho, Kisumu, Malaba (on the Ugandan border), Migori, and Mumias; Transluxe for Migori, Sirare, Kisumu, Nairobi and Mombasa; and Tropex, with an office by the Tabaka matatu stage for the Migori–Kisii–Kisumu–Eldoret, Isebania–Kisii–Kisumu–Kakamega–Kitale, and Kilgoris–Kisii–Eldoret routes. All Nairobi buses call at Nakuru and Naivasha. The locations of the bus company ticket offices and matatu stages are marked on our map.

If you have your own wheels and are headed along the minor but increasingly popular route to **Maasai Mara** via Kilgoris and Lolgorien, note that beyond **Kilgoris**, the road to the Mara is difficult, even with 4WD, and the section down the Oloololo Escarpment can be impossible after rain. Heading for the east end of the reserve, the fastest route is via Sotik and the new road to Bomet and Amala River (see p.416).

Heading south, **Tanzania** is accessible by services to the **border crossing**, variously known as Isebania or Nyabikaye on the Kenyan side, and Serira, Sirare or Siria on the Tanzanian, as well as by daily, but not recommended, Tawfiq bus services to Mwanza (on Lake Victoria) and Dar es Salaam (on the coast).

Lastly, if you fancy **cycling**, you can buy an Indian three-speed roadster at the supermarkets in Kisii for under Ksh4000.

Tabaka

TABAKA is one of the most important centres in the world for **soapstone** (steatite) production. Most of the carvings are bought up by buyers from the curio shops in Nairobi and elsewhere, but shops selling the carvings now line the road through the town, and they are happy to sell direct to visitors.

The turn-off for Tabaka is at **Nyachenge**, 18km west of Kisii on the A1 Migori road. A sign to the left, if coming from Kisii, points to the St Amillus Tabaka Mission Hospital and Kisii Soapstone Carvers Co-operative Society. From here it's 5km into the village (6km to the Co-operative Society) on a rough *murram* road that's treacherous (and requires 4WD) in wet weather, though an ordinary car can traverse it if dry. Coming by matatu from Kisii, it's best to get one that goes direct, even if this means waiting. The alternative is hanging around just as long at the halfway point, or a long walk from Nyachenge. The last matatus from Tabaka back to Kisii leave around 5 or 6pm.

The soapstone quarries and carvers

Beyond Tabaka are the four **quarries**, with two main ones, the first on the left, and the other further down on the right. There must, however, be vast reserves of stone under the ground all over the district, which provides a large propor-tion of the world supply of soapstone. It emerges in a variety of colours and densities: white is easiest to work, shades of orange and pink harder, and rosy-red the hardest and heaviest. A number of families have become full-time carvers, but for most people it's simply a spare-time occupation after agricul-ture, a way of making a few shillings. You'll even see children walking home from school carving little animals from chips of stone. The professional carvers often specialize in a variety of designs from chess sets and traditional animals, to vases, cups and, more recently, human figures.

There's a number of recommended teams of carvers – ask for anyone from the Mogendi, Abuya or Obonyo families. They will usually be happy to show you around, sell you their work, and perhaps give you pieces of stone to try carving yourself: it's great therapy. The stone is dampened to bring up the colour and make it easier to work, then waxed to retain the lustre.

Manga Ridge

This dramatic escarpment **cliff** is two or three hours' walk north of Kisii, won-derful in the early morning – or the late afternoon, as long as you can arrange a ride back again.

Leaving Kisii on the Kericho road, turn left into Manga Road at the bottom of the hill, 500m after Barclays, and follow the road as it sweeps you towards and then alongside the ridge. After about 5km you can cut down one of the tracks across the lush valley to your left and continue straight up the escarp-ment (several hundred metres high). Beware of snakes lurking among the rocks and grass on the upward scramble. Alternatively, you can continue along the road for a further 5km to come up behind the ridge; from here it's a ten-minute hike up to the edge, where a path follows the cliff for a kilometre or two. Magnificent views out over Kisii and down to Lake Victoria are your reward. It's possible to get matatus to Manga from Kisii, but make it clear you want to get off at the ridge.

If you set off early enough, there should be time to walk the whole way around to **Oyugis** (see p.304), through the villages of Manga, Marani and Rioma, a total distance of about 40km. Down at Oyugis you arrive in the town past the pelican breeding site on the right. From Oyugis it's a quick matatu hop back to Kisii. A fine walk, this also makes for exuberant **cycling**, through the heart of Gusii-land, as the road loops and swerves in a landscape changing magically with every ridge and valley. Up here you'll find dusty lanes, avenues of cypress trees, grassy verges, old women smoking pipes, and self-contained, reserved, country hamlets, just a few kilometres from the mêlée of Kisii.

Kisii to Kericho

From Kisii to Kericho, the road first snakes up through banana gardens, fields of corn and sugar cane, and patches of tea. After 26km, you pass the largest town along the way, **Keroka**, an urgent and chaotic community strung out along the highway. Seventeen kilometres further, there's a rarity for the region: an excellent **lodging** in the form of the *Damside Hotel* (PO Box 340 Nyansiongo ☎0360/32256, ☏32275; ❶–❷), in a peaceful setting beside a small dammed stream and a pyrethrum field. There's a choice of s/c and non-s/c rooms in *bandas* and cottages, some very basic, dirty and without nets, though the better "Mzungu Cottages", which are individual round, thatched *bandas*, are comfortable, with clean beds and nets. Camping is also possible (Ksh300 per tent), and you can take meals in the pretty gardens. There are discos most nights.

Seven kilometres further (52km from Kericho), just off the road to the south, is **SOTIK**, on a high plateau at the start of the rolling swathe of **tea bushes** that stretches for hundreds of square kilometres up towards the crest of the Mau Escarpment. Sotik is quite a pretty little centre – despite the rutted side streets, you'd almost say well-kept – with its shrubs and borders. The village has a post office, a branch of Barclays (with 24hr cash machine), petrol and the usual cluster of shops, bars and restaurants. Coming from the main road, take a left just after Caltex for the best of the **lodgings**, the dubiously named *Hotwax Hotel* (PO Box 126 Sotik ☎0360/32313; ❶), a dirty, loud and decrepit three-storey block, whose only attraction is its jumping *ndombolo* sounds disco (Wednesday, Friday and Saturday nights). Slightly cheaper is the friendly *Al-Karim Hotel* (PO Box 615 ☎0360/32097; ❶), on the right past Caltex and the market if coming from the main road, with big, bare rooms, and a roof terrace offering views over the town and surrounding countryside. Neither hotel has running water, but hot water in buckets is available in the mornings.

Continuing along the route, the small *shambas* virtually cease on the approach to Kericho itself, especially on the eastern side of the road where the land shelves to the Kimugu Valley.

Kericho and the tea country

KERICHO, named after the early English tea planter John Kerich, is Kenya's **tea capital**, a fact that – with much hype from the tourism machine embellished by the presence of the *Tea Hotel* – is not likely to escape you. Its equable climate and famously reliable, year-round afternoon rain showers make it the most important tea-growing area in Africa. While many of the European estates have been divided and reallocated to small farmers since Independence, the area is still dominated by giant tea plantations. Compact and orderly, Kericho itself seems as neat as the serried rows of bushes that surround it. The central square has shady trees and flowering bushes – a bandstand would make it complete – and even the matatu park has lawns around it. It's a gentle, hassle-free place to wander, the people mild-mannered. Clipped, clean and functional, there's little of the shambolic appearance of most up-country towns. And, in many ways, it's an oddity. With so many people earning some sort of salary on the tea plantations or in connection with them, and so few acres under food or market crops, the patterns of small-town life are changed here. Most workers live out on the estates, their families often left behind in the home villages. Kericho is above all an administrative and shopping centre, and a relay point for the needs of the estates. The produce market is small and trading limited. Everything seems to close at 5pm.

In town, there's a substantial Asian population. Many of the streets have a strikingly oriental feel – single-storey *dukas* fronted by colonnaded walkways where the plantation "memsahibs" of forty or fifty years ago presumably did their shopping. This curious, composite picture is completed by the grey stone **Holy Trinity Church**, with its small assembly of deceased planters in a miniature cemetery. Straight out of the English shires and entwined with creepers, it tries so hard to be Norman that it's a pity to point out that it was only built in 1952.

Accommodation

Kericho has a decent number of **places to stay** and you should find something to suit, though prices seem high in comparison with hotels of similar standards elsewhere in the country. A couple of the best options are out along the Nairobi road, Moi Highway. You can **camp** at the *Tea Hotel* (Ksh200 per person) and at *Kericho Garden Lodge* (Ksh300 per person).

Fairview TAS Hotel Moi Rd, PO Box 1260 ☎0361/21507. The entrance, by a busy and characterful *hoteli*-cum-bar, is intimidating, but it should be safe enough (women steer clear though), with basic, none-too-clean rooms and yukky toilets, but it's quiet at night. ❶

Kericho Garden Lodge Moi Highway, PO Box 2002 ☎0361/20878. The non-s/c singles are rather poky, but the newer s/c singles and doubles are quite acceptable, clean with hot water, and some look out over the pleasant gardens, where you can camp (Ksh300 per person – the *Tea Hotel* is much better value). Unappetizing food, though, and women may find the atmosphere in the restaurant/bar/TV room off-putting. The price of a double room includes breakfast for one person only. ❷

Kimugu River Lodge (formerly *Kericho Fish Resort*) off Moi Highway, PO Box 25 ☎0361/20035, ✉kimuguriverlodge@yahoo.com. Take the signposted turning opposite the BP station, 700m northeast of the town centre, and follow this track for 600m to this rather downmarket alpine-chalet-like place, with a great location above a weir in the Kimugu River. The rooms are simple but very comfortable with hot water, but the concrete cottages are somewhat better than the newer wooden shacks. There's also a decent bar and restaurant. ❸

Mid West Hotel PO Box 1175 ☎0361/20611–4, ☏20615. A large, soulless place and popular conference venue. Nothing special to recommend it, but usually a safe bet if you want a proper hotel room. There's a health club with a gym, sauna and steam room (all Ksh150 per day), and a dartboard in the bar. ❸

Mwalimu Hotel Moi Rd, PO Box 834 ☎0361/21601. Adequate and relatively clean s/c rooms, kept separate from its bar-restaurant. Hot water only in the morning, and loos lack seats and toilet paper. Overpriced. ❷

New Sunshine Hotel Tengecha Rd, PO Box 1910 ☎0361/30037. Clean rooms with hot water, but small and overpriced. ❷

Rex Lodge Temple Rd, PO Box 579 ☎0361/31323. Basic, but respectable and friendly, with clean if sombre rooms – the best cheap deal in town. ❶

Safina Lodge John Kerich Rd, PO Box 1159 ☎0361/20509. Rather squalid, but dirt cheap. Singles only. ❶

Tea Hotel Moi Highway, PO Box 75 ☎0361/30004–5, ☏20576, ✉teahotel@chemtech.africaonline.co.ke (reservations made through Msafiri, p.43). Built, along with the nearby church, in 1952, for the tea corporation Brooke Bond, it fell on hard times with the collapse of subsequent owners Africa Tours and Hotels, but has improved of late. The rooms are large and comfortable, if rather worn around the edges, and the bungalows are even more spacious than the ordinary rooms, which cost the same (but both are overpriced). The gardens are beautiful and well kept, and you can still walk through them to the tea fields beyond. You can also camp (Ksh200 per person) and use the pool and attached washing facilities. The food is good, and the tea (as you might expect) is excellent – strong, fresh and well made – definitely the best cuppa you'll drink in Kenya. B&B ❺

Eating

Kericho has its fair share of cheap and fairly ungastronomic *hotelis*, heavy on the chips and *ugali*: busiest of the *hotelis* is the first-floor *Fairview TAS Hotel*, packed at lunchtimes with workers. The *Sunshine Hotel*, Kenyatta Road, is also popular, and slightly better. For altogether classier eating, venture out to the *Tea Hotel*, whose dignified colonial dining room has very reasonable set menus for lunch (Ksh400) and dinner (Ksh500), excellent service and a grand piano which you're free to play. Next door, the *Kimugu River Lodge* has an extensive menu of mainly Indian food – particularly Punjabi – including chicken *methi* and even crayfish *masala*. The *Mid West* is OK but uninspiring.

Those in need of a **bar** might try the *Sugetek Inn* on Tengecha Road, a typical rowdy tavern, mainly for men. For a nice cup of **tea** on the other hand, you can't beat the terrace of the *Tea Hotel*, overlooking the gardens and tea fields – worth sixty bob of anybody's money.

Listings

Banks Barclays, Standard Chartered, both with ATMs, plus the KCB are on Moi Highway at the Kisumu end of town.

Car repair Central Garage on Temple Road at the corner of Uhuru Road (☎0361/20061) has a solid reputation.

Internet access Chemtech, Temple Road, on the corner of Uhuru Road (upstairs).
Library By the *Mid West Hotel*. Not bad at all, though they go for quantity rather than diversity, with about ten copies of each title. Open Mon–Thurs 9am–6pm, Fri 9am–4p, Sat 8.30am–5pm.
Market Much better at weekends than weekdays, when there's a variety of fruit and vegetables, snacks and spices, at lower-than-expected prices.
Post office Mon–Fri 8am–5pm, Sat 9am–noon.
Swimming pool Clean but chilly, at the *Tea Hotel* (Ksh70).
Taxis A bit of a problem in Kericho: there are very few apart from matatus. After dark it's hard to get out much if you don't have your own vehicle or aren't prepared to walk.

Around Kericho

The area around Kericho is **tea country**. Kenya is the world's third largest producer after India and Sri Lanka, and the biggest exporter to Britain. As you gaze across the dark green hills, you might pause to consider that the land which you now see covered in vast regimented swathes of tea bush, was only a century ago virgin rainforest, only a tiny part of which – Kakamega Forest (p.354) – still survives. The estates were first set up after World War I with tea bushes imported from India and China. Big business as it is – and despite the relative prosperity of Kericho – you can't help feeling that the local population would be better served if this fertile land were given over instead to intensive cultivation of food.

Tea was almost the only sector of the Kenyan economy to benefit from the heavy 1997–98 El Niño rains, which led to a bumper harvest. However, strikes and unrest have afflicted a good part of the industry recently, caused by the usual volatile mixture of high-level mismanagement, suspected corruption, and belligerence lower down, specifically by the unregistered Kenya Union of Small-Scale Tea-Owners (KUSSTO). All this risks the possible disintegration of the para-statal Kenya Tea Development Authority, which would only make matters worse.

It is possible to **visit the tea estates** on a guided tour from the *Tea Hotel* (see p.325). The factories operate every day except Monday, the day after the pickers' day off. If you want to visit a tea factory and see the whole process, you can book a tour (usually about two hours) for two or more people, two weeks in advance (maybe one week at a pinch), costing Ksh200 per person plus Ksh500 for transport per group, unless you have your own. If you are alone, or if you cannot give the required notice, you may be able to tag along with a group that has already booked. Alternatively, you can just take a tour of the tea fields combined with a nature walk (Ksh200 per person). The hotel's guide, Peter Chirchir, is extremely well versed in the local birdlife (he has so far identified 166 species in the area), and can also be hired for **bird-watching** tours in the immediate vicinity, or at the Chagaik Dam and Aboretum (see below).

Kimugu Valley and Chagaik Dam

Down in the **Kimugu Valley**, behind the *Tea Hotel* and *Kimugu River Lodge*, you can get some idea of what the land was like before the settlers arrived. The valley is a deep, tangled channel of sprawling trees and undergrowth, with shafts of sunlight picking out clouds of butterflies. The cold brown waters of the Kimugu flow down from Chagaik Dam and allegedly harbour **trout**.

To get to **Chagaik Dam** and the graceful **arboretum** nearby, you'll need a lift in the Nairobi direction, past the KETEPA buildings to the turn marked "Chagaik", about 8km east of town. From there, turn right, then immediately

Tea (*Camelia sinensis*) is a psychoactive shrub originally native to China. Its effects are said to have been discovered by legendary third millennium BC Chinese emperor Shen Nung, who was apparently taking a cup of hot water in the shade of a shrub when one of the buds fell into it, making him an invigorating drink. For centuries the Chinese had a monopoly on tea, but with its rise in popularity at home, the British were keen for an independent source of supply, and eventually managed to smuggle some cuttings to India. The first tea was grown in Kenya in 1903, though it was nearly twenty years before commercial production got under way here. Kenyan teas are known for their strength and full flavour, and are a major component of most commercial blends sold in the UK and Ireland. Kenya's other main customers are Egypt, Pakistan and Afghanistan.

Tea production, though not complicated, is very labour-intensive. Picking continues throughout the year, and you'll see the pickers moving through the bushes in their brilliant yellow-and-green (KETEPA) plastic smocks, nipping off the top two leaves and bud of each bush (nothing more is taken) and tossing them into baskets. Working fast, a picker can collect up to seventy kilos in a day, though half that is a more typical figure; the piece-rate is set at less than three shillings per kilo picked. After withering, mashing, a couple of hours' fermentation and a final drying in hot air, the tea leaves are ready for packing and export. The whole process can take as little as 24 hours.

Tea can be harvested three years after planting, and in the first year of production it must be picked every eight days, then every fourteen days in the second year and every seventeen in the fourth, after which the bush must be pruned to keep it at the right height for picking, which can begin again after three months. Weeding is not necessary as the foliage is sufficiently dense to prevent other plants from growing under it.

The stimulating **effects** of tea are due to the presence of caffeine, and a cup of strong tea can contain as much caffeine as a cup of medium-strength coffee. The effect feels different because it is moderated by other alkaloids such as thebaine, which is a relaxant. Because the human body requires fluid to process caffeine and thebaine, tea depletes the body of water, even though it appears to quench a thirst. Like beer, therefore, tea should not be taken as a fluid against dehydration.

left; it's a five-minute walk to the arboretum – "Founded by Tom Grumbley, Tea Planter 1946–75". Acres of beautiful trees from all over the tropical and subtropical world lead steeply down through well-tended lawns to a lily-covered lake. There are magnificent stands of bamboo on the banks. Entry to this haven of landscaped tranquillity is unrestricted and you can picnic or rest up as long as you like, though there are gardeners around who would probably insist you didn't camp.

Across the lake, thick **jungle** drops to the water's edge. Mysterious splashes and rustles, prolific bird and insect life, and at least one troop of colobus monkeys, are a surprising testament to the tenacity of wildlife in an environment hemmed in on all sides by the alien ranks of the tea bushes.

Moving on

Kericho has hassle-free travel options in every direction: **southwest** to Kisii and Migori (near the Tanzanian border), **east** over the Mau Escarpment to Nakuru (route covered in Chapter 3, pp.265–268), or **northwest** to Kisumu on Lake Victoria and Kapsabet in the Nandi Hills. Heading **south to Maasai Mara** is more problematic, though the first part of the route, from Litein

(30km or so from Kericho) to Bomet, follows a fine new road through splendid farming country (see p.416). If you're going **east**, Nairobi and Nakuru buses generally originate in Kisii and pass through Kericho throughout the day (and night); you should have time for a leisurely morning.

Matatus leave for most destinations from the main stage, but for Kisumu, Migori and Kisii you'll find more departures on Moi Highway, opposite the Caltex garage, which is also the place to catch westbound **buses**. Kenya Bus has its ticket office here. The Akamba office (☎0361/20221) is on the Caltex forecourt, and that is where to board all Akamba services, and all Nairobi-bound buses.

The Nandi Hills

The journey **from Kericho to Kapsabet** is one of the most varied and spectacular in the west, through country often far wilder than you'd expect: bleak mountainous scrublands and jungle-packed ravines. Midway, you cross the Kano Plains and usually have to change transport at **Chemelil**, a major crossroads on the flat sugar lands. Beyond, the road zigzags into high tea country again, the homeland of the **Nandi**, the fiercest early opponents of the British, and the haunt of a crypto-zoological mystery known as the **Nandi bear** (see box on p.330).

Kapsabet

KAPSABET is the only town of any size before Eldoret but, even here, unless you arrive at the end of the day, there's little point in stopping. There are a couple of banks, a market, and a trio of reasonable **lodgings**. *Kapsabet Hotel* (PO Box 426 ☎0326/2041; ❷) is a fairly quiet place but a popular boozer, clean if scruffy, and boasting a restaurant that serves mountainous portions of chips. *Keben Hotel* (PO Box 240 ☎0326/2462; ❶), above a supermarket, contains three "lodges" on its three floors, *Tanzania, Kenya* and *Uganda*, with rooms named after towns accordingly. It also has a bar and quite a decent restaurant. The *Snack Hotel*, opposite the market (PO Box 129 ☎0326/2215; ❶), has very basic lodgings (amenities match the very low rates), but serves tasty and cheap **food** in its restaurant.

Eldoret

Although more bustling with trade than Kericho, and somewhat healthier and pleasanter than Nakuru, **ELDORET** has, in all honesty, hardly anything to do or see that couldn't be done or seen in dozens of other highland centres. At first glance, life here seems pleasantly humdrum, at least on the outside: ordinary occupations and careers are actively pursued; the **Uasin Gishu Plateau** all around is reliably fertile cereal, vegetable and stock-raising country; wattle plantations provide the tannin for the town's leather industry; the Raymond textile factory – one of the country's biggest – provides employment, as does a new armaments factory (with a ready market in neighbouring countries); and a centre of higher education, Moi University, has proved a shot in the arm for local schools. The town is also the terminus for the oil pipeline from Mombasa, which Uganda would like to extend to Kampala, and it also has one of the best

ELDORET

University Campus, Tambach, Iten & Kabarnet ▲

ACCOMMODATION				RESTAURANTS & NIGHTLIFE			
Aya Inn	9	Highlands Inn	2	Biharlal Catering	C	Opera House	I
Eldoret New Lincoln Hotel	8	Kabathayu Hotel & Lodging	6	Bismilahi Lengut	F	Otto Café	D
Eldoret Valley Hotel	4	Sirikwa Hotel	3	Cyclone Club	H	Places	A
Eldoret Wagon Hotel	1	Sosiana View Hotel	7	Elcove	K	Sizzlers Café	J
White Castle Motel	5			Kutana Club	L	Smiles	B
				New Tawfiq	E	Wood House	G

hospitals in Kenya. Eldoret's prosperity is shown clearly enough by the windows of the Eldoret Jewellers on the main road.

Another, darker face of Eldoret, however, is serious **ethnic strife**. In recent years, thousands of refugees from local fighting have flooded the town and its sprawling, poor suburbs. Eldoret – "the town where everyone thinks he is president", according to one disenchanted local – has repeatedly been the focus of conflict between the district's various Nandi-speaking Kalenjin (who have for many years been largely aligned with Moi and the KANU party) and Kikuyu- and Luo-speaking immigrants (who tend to favour a change of government). None of which is likely to impinge on a casual visit.

There's no real reason to stay in Eldoret very long, although you might find it a useful stop-over, and it's refreshingly unthreatening and friendly despite its size. The town's affluence is reflected by a wide variety of places to stay, eat and drink – and enough nightlife to see you through an evening or two.

Though places of interest are limited, you may wish to visit the **Kip Keino sports and book shop** in Oginga Odinga Street, set up by athlete and Christian philanthropist Kepchugi Keino. Keino's double gold at the 1964 Olympics blazed a trail that has since been followed by other Kenyan runners, mainly from this region of the country. Since retiring from sport, he has used his name and earnings to sponsor children's homes and other good causes.

Some history

Eldoret was a backwoods post office on Farm 64, later chosen in 1912 as an administrative centre because the farm's soil was poor and the deeds were never taken up by the owner. The name started as Eldare (a river), was then Nandi-ized to Eldaret, and finally misprinted in the *Official Gazette* as Eldoret. Pronunciation is fluid.

Before the town existed, the area was settled by **Afrikaners**. They gave it much of the dour worthiness that seems to have characterized its first half-century and which is perceptible even today, though most of the Boers trekked on after Independence. Modern inhabitants are mainly Kalenjin (Elgeyo and Nandi) but there's also a long-established and respected Asian community

The Nandi and the Nandi bear

At the end of the nineteenth century, the **Nandi** (dialects of whose language is spoken by all the Kalenjin peoples) were probably in the strongest position in their history. Their warriors had drummed up a reputation for such ferocity and daring that much of western Kenya lived in fear of them. Even the Maasai – at a low point in their own fortunes – suffered repeated losses of livestock to Nandi spearsmen, whose prestige accumulated with every herd of cattle driven back to their stockades. The Nandi even crossed the Rift Valley to raid Subukia and the Laikipia Plateau. They were intensely protective of their own territory, relentlessly xenophobic and fearful of any adulteration of their way of life. Foreigners of any kind were welcome only with express permission.

With the killing of a British traveller, Peter West, who tried to cross their country in 1895, the Nandi opened a decade of guerrilla warfare against the British. Above all, they repeatedly frustrated attempts to lay the railway line and keep communications open with Uganda. They dismantled the "iron snake", transformed the copper telegraph wires into jewellery, and took whatever livestock and provisions they could find. Despite increased security, the establishment of forts, and some efforts to reach agreements with Nandi elders, the raiding went on, often costing the lives of African soldiers and policemen under the British. In retaliation, **punitive expeditions** shot more than a thousand Nandi warriors (about one young man in ten), captured tens of thousands of head of livestock, and torched scores of villages. The war was ended by the killing of Koitalel, the *Orkoiyot* or spiritual head of the Nandi who, having agreed to a temporary truce, was then murdered at a meeting with the British. As expected, resistance collapsed (his people had believed Koitalel to be unassailable); the Nandi were hounded into a reserve and their lands opened to settlers.

Traditionally keepers of livestock, the Nandi have turned to agriculture with little enthusiasm and focus instead on their district's milk production: the highest in Kenya. *Shambas*, however, are widespread enough to make your chances of seeing a **Nandi bear** – the source of scores of Yeti-type rumours – remote. Variously said to resemble a bear, a big wild dog or a very large ape, the Nandi bear is believed to have been exterminated in most areas. But in the less accessible regions, on the way up to Kapsabet, many locals believe it still exists – they call it *chemoset*. Exactly what it is is another matter, but it doesn't seem to inspire quite the terror you might expect; the occasional savagely mutilated sheep and cattle reported in the press are probably attributable to leopards. As for the *chemoset*, a giant anthropoid ape, perhaps a gorilla, seems the most likely candidate, and the proximity of the Kakamega Forest may account for the stories. This is a surviving tract of the rainforest that once stretched in a continuous belt across equatorial Africa and is still home to many western and central African species of wildlife (though not, as far as is known, giant apes). The *chemoset* possibly survived up until the early twentieth century in isolated valleys, even if it is extinct today. Whatever the truth, if you camp out in the Nandi Hills, you won't need reminding to zip your fly sheet.

(Juma Hajee's supermarket, now a shopping arcade, was the oldest business in the town); in addition there are Somali-speakers, the remnants of a European community, and immigrants from the rest of Kenya.

Eldoret's status as capital of the Kalenjin homelands probably has a great deal to do with its choice as the location for Kenya's newest "international" **airport**, which admittedly only receives occasional French charters and a couple of flights a day from Nairobi. The original projected cost of Eldoret International Airport ran to over $83.3m, but the Kenyan government was forced to scale down the project under tough proposals from the IMF and the World Bank. Sparks flew when Kenya requested a $50m loan for repairs to the Nairobi–Mombasa road (currently in a worse state than ever) – international donors jettisoned the request, arguing that if Kenya could afford a new international airport in an up-country town (not to mention a new presidential jet), it could afford to cover the cost of routine repairs to its principal highway as a matter of priority.

Accommodation

Eldoret has no shortage of **accommodation**. Cheap places tend to be grubby or clearly intended for "short-term guests". You may have to explain to the management the innocent way you intend to spend the night. There are also one or two quaint old haunts from way back. The Reformed Church Centre should allow **camping** in the field.

Cheap hotels and lodgings

Aya Inn Oginga Odinga St, PO Box 401 ☎0321/62259. A spotless, friendly place with a couple of rowdy but good-natured and fun bars and a *nyama choma* restaurant. ❶

Eldoret Valley Hotel Uganda Rd, PO Box 734 ☎0321/32314. Slightly threadbare but scrupulously clean with smallish s/c rooms, hot water most of the day and serving decent Kenyan fare. ❶

Kabathayu Hotel & Lodging Arap Moi St, PO Box 832 ☎0321/31073. A simple, clean B&L in a Somalian area, situated over a very male-dominated bar: not one for lone women. Good views from the roof terrace and good food to be had nearby. ❶

Reformed Church of East Africa Conference and Training Centre 2km out of town on the Kapsabet road, PO Box 746 ☎0321/62749, ℻62870. Secure accommodation with a minimum of stimulation. Take a matatu from the junction of Nandi Rd with Oginga Odinga Street, and ask for "Conference". ❶

Sosiana View Hotel Arap Moi St, PO Box 840 ☎321/33215. Situated by the transport terminus, this five-storey block has good views – the best from the fifth floor, which is also the quietest, though more of a climb. ❶

Moderate to expensive hotels

Eldoret New Lincoln Hotel Oloo Rd, PO Box 551 ☎0321/22093. With original fixtures and fittings, and a creaking charm that seems to augur imminent collapse, this is Eldoret's most interesting hotel. It's close to the transport park and top-volume nightclubs, and it can be noisy but not excessively so. It's slightly overpriced, and beware of leaving valuables in rooms, but there's a pleasant bar and decent food. B&B ❷

Eldoret Wagon Hotel Elgeyo Rd, PO Box 2408 ☎0321/62270–2, ℻62400. Sunny, and with quiet, comfortable rooms, *nyama choma* bar and safe parking, this gets quite lively at weekends. Much more intimate than the *Sirikwa* opposite. B&B ❸

Highlands Inn Elgeyo Rd, PO Box 2189 ☎0321/31165. Spacious, presentable and normally quiet, with safe parking, and baths in all rooms, but no nets. Outside there's a small kids' playground and an alfresco bar/restaurant serving *nyama choma* and other standards, and another bar and restaurant inside. Very good value. B&B ❷

Sirikwa Hotel Elgeyo Rd, PO Box 3361 ☎0321/63433, ℻61018 (reservations through *Magret International*, Phoenix House, 3rd floor, Kenyatta Ave, PO Box 67440 Nairobi ☎02/224273 or 6 ℻223245). The town's "premier" hotel, this is a monolithic and faintly pompous pile, that would be more at home in Spain than western Kenya, but comfortable if you can ignore the insidious antiseptic smell. Rooms are very good, with real baths, the "superior suites" bizarrely have two bathrooms, and it has a large pool (Ksh100 for day visitors). B&B ❺

White Castle Motel Uganda Rd, PO Box 566
☏ 0321/33095 or 62773, ℉ 62209. Although first impressions are very unpromising – a bland modern building on a noisy road – the rooms turn out to be far better than average, and there's a lift after the initial two steps. Overpriced, though. B&B ③

Eating and drinking

Eldoret has plenty of good places to grab a bite, with a clutch of established snackbars, several options for dinner, and one or two evening haunts. For your own supplies, head for the markets west of Oloo Road, or a supermarket: Uchumi behind the Tota station, or Eldo Supermarket at Juma Hajee's Arcade. Also worth a visit is the **Dorinyo Lessos Cheese Factory** at the end of the track south of Kenyatta Street, where you can buy various European-style cheeses (quarter kilo minimum purchase), or yoghurt or ice-cream (smaller quantities available).

Baker's Yard Juma Hajee's Arcade, Elijah Cheruiyot Rd. Excellent place with biscuits, pies, cakes and pastries as well as bread, and also good for a quick filter coffee.

Biharlal Catering Kago St. An excellent place for vegetarian Indian meals, snacks and sweets; good for lunch but closes at 6.30pm.

Bismilahi Lengut Hotel Oloo Rd. A large, bright and cheap eating place near the market.

Elcove Soko House, Oloo Rd ☏ 0321/31253. The decor is Indian and the menu expansive and imaginative – subtly spiced curries, authentic Chinese, and good shots at Italian – all mostly available. Drinks (including a good house red) are priced to "keep out the riff-raff", according to the owner. Well worth a splurge.

New Tawfiq Hotel Arap Moi St. Standard, cheap Kenyan fare; mainly of interest because it's open 24/7.

Otto Café Uganda Rd. Popular *hoteli* with a long and well-priced menu and excellent *mandaazi*. Lives up to its reputation, and the downstairs seating area is one of the few up-country places with real atmosphere, but closes at 6.30pm, so you'll have to make your evening meal tea rather than supper if you want to eat it here.

Sirikwa Hotel Huge barbecue buffet lunches at weekends for Ksh500 – worth it if you've just spent three days in the Kakamega Forest or up Mount Elgon.

Sizzlers Café Kenyatta St. A popular American-style joint, offering speedy, high-quality burgers plus ice-cream and other desserts.

White Castle Motel Café Uganda Rd. Traditional Kenyan food such as fried or stewed chicken with chips or *ugali*. Again.

Nightlife

Most of these places charge a small entry fee at weekends but, with the exception of Sam's and the Opera House, are free midweek.

Cyclone Club Kenyatta St. A sweaty, run-down disco, but loud and enjoyable, and packed out at weekends.

Kutana Club Oloo Rd, next to the *New Lincoln*. Rustic African atmosphere and beery bonhomie, with a live visiting band at weekends. Music is mostly African, especially Congolese.

Opera House (Club Santa Cruz) Oloo Rd. Very firmly established nightspot, with some live acts, and jam sessions Tuesdays until dawn. Pronounced "O-pair-a" rather than "Oprah" if you're asking people about it. Reggae is usually the dominant sound.

Places Uganda Rd. Sophisticated decor, a sunken dance floor, and a well-mannered clientele, with snacks available and good DJs. Music is dominat-ed by Swahili rap and African dance.

Sam's Discotheque Uganda Rd, under the *White Castle Motel*. Middle-of-the-road nightspot with a mixed clientele, always busy. Wednesday is ladies night, Friday soul, 6pm Saturday–6am Sunday all-nighter, with a jam session 3–7pm on Sundays if schools are out.

Smiles Uganda Rd. A sweaty den of iniquity and outrageous pick-up joint, but fun in a sleazy kind of way. Music is mostly Congolese or reggae.

Wood House Kenyatta St. A mix of music, with the emphasis mostly on reggae, guest DJs from as far afield as South Africa, and occasional sound clashes, but Friday is soul night and Saturday jam night. A bit dead midweek, however.

Listings

Banks Barclays, Standard Chartered and KCB (two branches) all have ATMs. ABC Forex (banking hours), Zul Arcade, Oginga Odinga St, has slightly better exchange rates for cash, but charges a whopping $10 each to change traveller's cheques. Wall Street Forex in Barng'etuny Plaza on Uganda St has slightly lower rates for cash but the same rates for traveller's cheques and charges no commission on either.

Books Eldoret Emporium on the corner of Elijah Cheruiyot St and Oginga Odinga St has a good selection of Kenyan books, as does Student's Choice on Oginga Odinga St, which is easier to browse and also carries foreign titles plus magazines such as *Time* and *Newsweek*. Uchumi supermarket stocks quite a lot of American pulps, and a huge range of British, American and Indian magazines, as well as UK tabloids. The library on Utalii St has a good African history section.

Eldoret Show Held in the first week of March.

Hospitals Eldoret Hospital, Makasembo Rd ☏ 0321/62000–1; Eldoret District Hospital ☏ 0321/33011.

Internet access Numerous places include Sosiana.com in Uganda Rd by the *Eldoret Valley Hotel*; Into Computers in the Eldo Centre; D2D in Dharma Rd just off Uganda Rd; and Barhani Cybercafé in Oginga Odinga St opposite the *Aya Inn*.

Pharmacies Several on Kenyatta and Oginga Odinga streets; out of hours try Asisco Pharmacy, Bandaptai House, off Nandi Rd east of Nyala Rd (☏ 0321/62496; daily 7am–midnight).

Police Uganda Rd, opposite Caltex ☏ 0321/32222–3.

Post office Mon–Fri 8am–5.30pm, Sat 9am–noon. Cardphones outside.

Swimming pool The *Sirikwa Hotel* has a pool (non-residents Ksh100) in its large, dull, grassy gardens. At weekends it's overrun with Kenyans in holiday mood.

Moving on

The main **matatu** enclosure is at the east end of Arap Moi Street, and has services for Kabarnet and Kakamega, as well as main road services for Kisumu, Kitale and further afield. Eldoret Express buses (for Kitale and Nairobi) also stop there, as do Linear Buses (for Kisumu and Kericho) and the one daily bus (10am) for Kabarnet. Matatus for Iten leave from the stage opposite the library in Oginga Odinga Street, whilst services for Kapsabet and some for Kisumu go from the corner of Oginga Odinga Street and Nandi Road. For Kaptagat they leave a block east on the corner of Nyala Road. The Akamba bus office (☏ 0321/61047) is on Arap Moi Street, opposite *New Tawfiq Hotel*. There are no more passenger trains from Eldoret.

Eldoret International **Airport** (☏ 0321/63377) is 16km out of town on the Kapsabet road. Matatus bound for Kapsabet or Kisumu will drop you there. There are two daily Kenya Airways flights (morning and evening) to Nairobi, except on Sunday when the morning flight goes to Kisumu instead.

Heading directly towards the **Ugandan border**, there's little to delay your progress to Malaba, two or three hours away. Bungoma and Webuye, en route, are covered on pp.350–351.

Eastbound on the busy A104 road from Eldoret to Nakuru, uphill and then down again, the sombre scenery is dotted with moors and conifers, and the road itself is a fast one.

For **Kakamega Forest** (see p.354), if you don't want to go all the way round to the other side and approach it from Kakamega town, you can take a bus or matatu going to Kisumu via Kapsabet, and get off at the D267 turning about 20km after Kapsabet (signposted "Kisieni 12km"), from where it's a walk of about three hours to the *Rest House* (see p.358).

Kaptagat and the Tambach Escarpment

If you arrived in Eldoret early enough in the day, there are two worthwhile bases outside town to head to for a night or longer.

Near **Kaptagat**, 20km from Eldoret on the well-surfaced C54/C55 road, en route to the Kerio Valley, has two very pleasant places to stay. **Naiberi River Campsite**, (PO Box 142 Eldoret ☎0321/33029, Ⓕ62916, Ⓔcampsite @africaonline.co.ke) offers excellent camping by the Naiberi River (Ksh200 per person), some rustic, but cosy, and fully equipped s/c *bandas* (❷), and dorm accommodation (Ksh500). They also have a restaurant with *hoteli*-style basics at reasonable prices and more expensive Indian specialities, but you may not be too keen on the almost exclusive company of Brits and Aussies (it's popular with overland groups) if you're looking for "the real Kenya". It's 1.5km off the main road, a couple of kilometres before the Kaptagat village turn-off, and matatus will happily drop you off at the junction. Alternatively, call the owner (Mon–Fri 10am–5pm; ☎0321/32644–5) or email him (Ⓔfactory@kenknit .com) to arrange a free lift from Eldoret.

For somewhere a bit more special, the **Kaptagat Hotel**, 500m off the main road a couple of kilometres further on (PO Box 2900 Eldoret ☎0321/62992), was a colonial hangout in days gone by, which had rather gone to seed, but has now been renovated. Set in extensive and beautifully kept grounds, including lawns, woodland and a river, it offers a choice of cottages with s/c single rooms off a common lounge (❸), or double rooms with a slightly higher standard of comfort (❹), and also allows camping. Alternatively, you can just pop in for a meal or a drink, or picnic in the grounds (Ksh100 per person to enter).

If you intend to cross the Rift Valley to Lake Baringo, you'll find a fair number of matatus bound for Kabarnet, and two daily buses, using the tarmacked **Tambach Escarpment** route. This is a spectacular journey: from the high pastures and wheat fields of the plateau, the valley suddenly yawns out beneath, some 1500m below. However, the route down to the fluorspar mine at Kimwarer, which passes through Kaptagat and used to be the main way across the valley, no longer sees much traffic. Still worth the effort if you have time, or a solid vehicle of your own, it's an incredible hairpin descent that seems to go on forever. Kerio Valley route details continue on p.278.

Soy

In the other direction (west) out of Eldoret, there's transport towards Kitale by bus, minibus or Peugeot throughout the day, but the **Soy Country Club**, a third of the way there, is nice enough to break your journey for (PO Box 457 Eldoret ☎0733/781841; B&B ❷). A very pukka country retreat, this is a peaceful place to stay, with single-storey wings laid out in classic colonial style, complete with wood-tiled roofs, brick chimneys and a formal garden. It had become rather run-down, but is now under new management and improvements are promised. The rooms at any rate are comfortable, and there's a swimming pool (non-residents Ksh75), restaurant and bar. You can camp here cheaply, too. Guests are rare except at weekends.

In the **SOY** area, look out for the famous herd of **Rothschild's giraffe**, now very rare. Most often seen as specks in the distance – barely distinguishable from dead trees – on the dry plain near the junction between the B2 (to Soy) and the A104 (from Eldoret), they occasionally appear near the road, especially around dawn and dusk. They stand their ground and, for giraffe close-ups, the only place you'll do better is at the Langata Sanctuary near Nairobi, where a number of the Soy animals have been relocated in recent years. Be warned, however, that it's definitely not a good idea to be seen taking photographs in the area due to the proximity of the military barracks to the south of Soy. Unfortunately, the herd has been declining in numbers due to the demise of the acacia trees on which they feed, and the KWS is now looking to relocate all of them.

Kitale and northward

KITALE is smaller than Eldoret, and not much more exciting, but it has more going for it from a traveller's point of view, primarily because it is the base for visits to **Mount Elgon** and the superb, very underrated, hiking country around Kenya's second giant volcanic cone. It's also an obvious base for the **Cherangani Hills**, and a straightforward departure point for trips to the west side of **Lake Turkana**. There's a **national park** nearby – the little-known but easily accessible **Saiwa Swamp**, where for once the tables are turned on drivers: you can explore on foot only. The town itself boasts a good **regional museum**, one excellent restaurant, and a host of great nightlife possibilities.

The majority of travellers only pass through here on the way to Lake Turkana, which is a shame. Unless you're on a tight schedule, the museum, Mount Elgon and Saiwa Swamp, as well Kitale's friendly people (even the streetkids, once you get to know them) add up to a good reason to delay a day or three. The town itself is calm and unprepossessing, with smooth tarmac streets planted with trees, and a lively northern district around and beyond the market, almost a slum in parts, where visitors rarely wander, but shouldn't encounter serious problems if they do.

Some history

Originally Quitale, a relay station on the old slave route between Uganda and Bagamoyo in Tanzania, the modern town was founded only in 1920, as the capital of Trans-Nzoia District. When the first settlers arrived (mostly after World War I), this vale of rich grasslands between Mount Elgon and the Cherangani Hills was apparently almost uninhabited. But just a few years earlier it had been a Maasai grazing area, and a group who refer to themselves as "Maasai" still live on the eastern slopes of Elgon. With the arrival of the railway in 1925, the town and the region around it began to flourish, with a fantastic array of fruit, cereals, vegetables and livestock, and all the attendant settler paraphernalia of agricultural and flower shows, church fêtes and gymkhanas. This heady era lasted barely forty years, but the region's **agriculture** is still famous; almost anything, including such exotic fruit as apples and pears, can be grown here. The Kitale Show happens each year at the end of October or beginning of November.

The town's present population is a mix of several tribes, including Nandi, Pokot, Marakwet, Sabaot and Sengwer, as well as a few Luhya, Kisii, Kikuyu and Asians. As a result, it has ironically become a focus for these same people fleeing ethnic violence and bloody cattle-rustling raids in the surrounding region, especially along the Trans-Nzoia/West Pokot border area, to the northeast of Kitale, and was the venue for **peace talks** held during 1998–99, since when the ethnic violence has declined markedly.

Kitale Museum and the VI Agroforestry Project

Given its location, **Kitale Museum** (daily 8am–6pm; Ksh200) is remarkably successful. Originally the "Stoneham Museum", a collection opened to the public by a lieutenant colonel on his Cherangani farm in 1927, it was transferred here in 1972. For the most part, Stoneham's curious collections are just that: collected curiosities in striking contrast to the recent, more educationally motivated, Kenyan additions.

The **ethnographic displays** on Pokot, Elkony (Elgon), Luhya, Maasai, Turkana and Luo are interesting, though perhaps more so if you've seen the stuff in real life and now have a chance to return and see it again. Among the artefacts are Kamba carvings – skin-covered animals and smooth polished abstracts; a Pokot goat bell made from a tortoise shell; Pokot bowls used for collecting blood from cattle; and intricate Turkana belts and beadwork. In the small room to the right of the entrance in the main building is a collection of traditional musical instruments (as well as an old piano), which really are becoming museum pieces as younger generations embrace more cosmopolitan musical genres like pop and gospel (though you can buy cassettes of traditional Luhya music in town).

The motley wildlife collection on the walls and downstairs is perhaps best ignored, but the entomology is more interesting – a very fine collection of butterflies and bugs collected in the region in recent years, sadly mostly unlabelled. Incidentally, if you're fed up with the diet of KTN and KBC TV, the museum occasionally screens real celluloid **wildlife documentaries**. They prefer larger groups, though they'd be happy to oblige if you have a special request, are especially keen, or if your visit coincides with one by schoolchildren.

Outside, there are a few display cases containing **snakes**, a **chameleon pit** and the inevitable **tortoise pen**, with its hinged- and leopard-tortoise inmates. Unless it's the mating season, though, it's as boring for you as it must be for them. The recreations of Nandi and Luhya homesteads make an interesting point of comparison with the realities of present-day villages.

Next to the main entrance, the octagonal **Museum Hall** has some bold murals of Turkana, Maasai, Nandi and Luo domestic life, commissioned by the National Museum and painted by Maggie Kukler. There's occasionally live music or a disco here. The museum also has a craft shop, laboratories and a surprising **nature trail**, which transports you, in a few steps, from suburban Kitale to a chattering, dripping, riverine rainforest with abundant insect and birdlife; look out for Ross's turaco, a large, deep purple bird with a square red crest, commoner here than in other forests. If you're lucky, you might also spot colobus and vervet monkeys. The trail follows a stream with a muddy path and rickety footbridges (unsuitable for anyone with mobility problems), but the forest itself is natural and some of the trees stately. The picnic site, near the end of the trail, is a wonderful place if you can cope with the bugs.

Next door to the museum, the Swedish-backed **VI Agroforestry Project** (PO Box 2006 ℡0325/20139; daily 8am–5pm; free) was set up to educate cultivators in Trans–Nzoia and West Pokot about the basics of tree planting. This accomplished, it has now progressed to concerning itself with the problems of soil erosion and over-grazing, and offers practical advice to farmers on the selection of plant and tree species best adapted to local conditions. There's a small gallery here with well-captioned photographs explaining their work and, outside, a "demonstration *shamba*" which showcases environmentally sound techniques to increase crop yield.

Practicalities

Barclays and SCB both have ATMs, and will change cash and traveller's cheques. Soy Supermarket in Kenyatta Street sells weekly editions of some UK newspapers, but for provisions, you're better off at the Suam Supermarket across the street. Nowhere in town offered internet access at last check (though that should change very soon), but you can send emails from the Computer Services shop on Kenyatta Street, diagonally opposite the *Rock Hotel*.

Accommodation

If you're heading north out of town anyway, you may want to stay at **Sirikwa Guest House** (*Barnley's House*; p.339). If you don't have your own vehicle, allow at least an hour to get there. In Kitale itself, there are a number of **cheap lodgings**, down to the usual standard, the most economical found at the grubby north end of town, past the market. As to **mid-range hotels**, you're spoilt for choice. Note that Kitale suffers from sporadic cuts in its water supply, which affect even the better hotels. If you're **camping**, it's usually OK to use the grounds of the Kitale Museum, but ask the curator first (around Ksh200).

Alakara Hotel Kenyatta St, PO Box 1984 ℡0325/20395, ℻30298. A large, clean, bright place with surprisingly good beds, baths in most rooms (cheaper non-s/c rooms available) and 24-hour hot water. The restaurant is good too. B&B ❷

Bismilahi B&L PO Box 1191; no phone. 100m up from the market, this place is adequate and dirt cheap. ❶

Bongo Hotel Moi Ave, PO Box 530 ℡0325/20593. Decent, properly furnished s/c rooms, but since the rise of the *Alakara* and *Lantern*, no longer the first choice. Serves up excellent buffet breakfasts. B&B ❷

Executive Lodge Kenyatta St, PO Box 2275 ℡0325/31698. Secure, but off-puttingly dark, with small and tatty rooms, some s/c. There's a TV room and a reasonable restaurant attached, but at the same price you'd be much better off at the *Alakara* opposite. B&B ❷

Highview Hotel Moi Ave, PO Box 2925 ℡0325/31570. A friendly highrise with good, breezy and relatively clean s/c rooms with nets, but sporadic hot water (mornings only), and its two bars can make things noisy at night. ❷

Kahuroko Lodge Moi Ave, behind the Shell garage, PO Box 2290; no phone. Basic lodgings fronted by a bar-restaurant, rather noisy and not for lone women. ❶

Kitale Club PO Box 30 ℡0325/31330 or 8, ℻30924. One kilometre out on the road towards Eldoret, and on the site of the old slave quarters (the circle of stones in the car park is said to have surrounded a ring to which they were chained at night), this old colonial club (Ksh500 daily membership on top of any other charges) now comes complete with a golf course (Ksh800) and pool (Ksh100). ❹

The Lantern Kenyatta St, PO Box 484 ℡0325/31138. Behind its uninviting entrance are the best lodgings in town: calm, clean and welcoming, with parquet floors and proper baths and nets in all rooms. The more expensive "deluxe" doubles are huge and have balconies fronting onto the street. B&B ❷

Mount Loima Lodge PO Box 1517 ℡0325/31929. A little further on from the *Bismilahi* and on the same side, similarly basic and cheap. ❶

New Kitale Villa Moi Ave, PO Box 4240 ℡0325/30695. Above *Club Villa*, with grotty non-s/c rooms, but it's very friendly and good for a night out – the club plays upbeat sounds day and night. Women on their own might prefer to look elsewhere. ❶

New Mbuni Lodge Moi Ave, PO Box 951 ☎0325/31736. Cheap and noisy, with a bar and disco upstairs. Non-s/c singles only. ❶

Eating and drinking

The best **food** in Kitale is to be found at *The Lantern* on Kenyatta Street, which has a vast, mouth-watering menu, including excellent Chinese and Indian dishes suitable for vegetarians, as well as meats and French-style cuisine, red wine and Irish coffees too. Service is professional and unobtrusive, the surroundings pleasant, and the food exquisite, especially if you've been living on a miserable diet of *ugali* and *irio* for a few weeks; recommended for a splurge (around Ksh500–600 for a meal). Other dependable options include the *Alakara Hotel*, with a good lunchtime buffet for Ksh350, and the *Kitale Club*, if you don't mind paying the admission fee. *Executive Lodge* is cheaper and has good Kenyan fare – chips, rice or *ugali* with everything – including samosas. The *Bongo Bar and Restaurant*, next door to the hotel, is similar. Cheaper still are *Villa Coffee House* (*New Kitale Villa*) on Moi Avenue, a clean and bright little place with a good menu, and *Iroko Roots Café*, opposite. As elsewhere, many restaurants are closed on Sundays.

After dark, there are a number of places providing drink and lively conversation. Currently in with the crowds are the *Bongo*, either of the *Highview*'s bars, and the more sedate *Alakara*, which is an enduring meeting place but closes at midnight. All three are generally suitable for women, though you should use your judgement at the *Highview* (some nights are calmer than others). Of the more energetic nightspots (women should go accompanied to these), try *Max* at the *Theatre Club*, opposite the *Kitale Club* (Friday and Saturday nights); the sweaty *Mombaleo* opposite *New Kitale Villa*; or the popular *Rock Hotel* disco, at the north end of Kenyatta Street. On Moi Avenue at *New Kitale Villa*, *Club Villa* is a cheerful and friendly dive with upbeat music and videos day and night, and resident DJs Friday and Saturday nights. The *Railway Hotel* near the station is, in fact, a bar and open 24/7.

Moving on

As well as the main matatu and bus park near the municipal market, there's a smaller gathering opposite Kitale Museum on the corner of the Lodwar road. Matatus from here go to Eldoret, Kimilili, Kiminini, Kakamega and Kisumu. But, if in doubt, go to the main matatu stage.

Heading west, if you're interested in exploring **Mount Elgon** (full details start on p.342), access is a doddle, with two or three matatus daily to *Mount Elgon Lodge* near the park's Chorlim Gate. If you miss these, the next closest destination is Endebess, reached quickly enough by regular matatus (which continue to the Ugandan border at **Suam**), or you could catch one to Kimilili if you plan to hike outside the confines (and restrictions) of the national park; you should arrive early in the day if you want to make significant progress up the mountain before dark (Chorlim Gate is a twelve-kilometre walk away). **Southwards**, Kakamega and Kisumu are, with luck, no more than two or three hours away down the A1, a very busy road. As ever, Akamba **buses** (☎0325/31732) are the best bet for long hauls back to Nakuru and Nairobi, though with only two buses daily (9am & 9pm), you may find Eldoret Express's frequent departures more useful: they leave when full, which is approximately hourly. It may be worth enquiring at the railway station whether **passenger train services** have resumed along the Kitale–Eldoret–Nairobi line.

Most people setting off from Kitale are **heading north** (route details in Chapter Seven, pp.591–592). The road to Lodwar and Kalokol near Lake Turkana is mostly in pretty good condition, although the eighty-kilometre stretch north of Marich Pass has broken up almost completely, making for a very bumpy ride. It's still OK in 2WD so long as you go slowly over the broken sections, and the only cause for concern is flash floods which bar the way for a few hours, occasionally washing away a short stretch. There are several matatus a day (no buses) – best caught early, from around 8am – and enough traffic to make hitching a practical option. Remember to take water, and also to stock up on provisions, as you'll only find more basic stuff on sale further north (fresh fruit and veg is expensive and of low quality in Lodwar). If you're driving yourself, note that there is nowhere to get fuel between Mukatano and Lodwar. With a tent, it may be more fun to spend the night before at **Saiwa Swamp National Park** rather than in Kitale itself. And you could further delay your progress north by stopping over at the Marich Pass Field Studies Centre.

Sirikwa Guesthouse – Barnley's House

You could also stop off for a day – or quite happily for a week – at the homely **Sirikwa Guesthouse and Campsite** (PO Box 332 Kitale ☎072/767055 or 783530; or c/o Soy Supermarket in Kitale ☎ & ⓕ0325/20061), signposted off to the right precisely 23.6km north of Kitale on the A1. Situated on a tree-covered hill, there are superb gardens to camp in (Ksh360 per person including firewood, use of a bathroom, *banda* and barbecue facilities), three furnished tents with electricity (❸; may be replaced by *bandas* in future) and the Barnley family's fine old house (B&B ❹, FB lower end of ❺), which provides excellent meals, taken with the family, to order. Laundry can be arranged most days. Another great draw here are the **guides** (Ksh600/day; Ksh300/day for a porter; Ksh1200/day for the ornithologist), who can take you on some exceptional walking and bird-watching trips into the Cherangani Hills, from day-walks to week-long hikes. Three- to four-day trips to Marich Pass (p.342) are recommended, or you can visit Kongolai Escarpment (more bird-watching), or Tata Falls (local beauty spot). This is also an excellent base for visiting Saiwa Swamp and Mount Elgon.

Saiwa Swamp National Park

Open daily; $15, children $5, Ksh200 for vehicle; car park; entry on foot. Warden: PO Box 753 Kitale ☎0325/55022.

Specially created for the protection of the **sitatunga**, a rare and vulnerable semi-aquatic antelope, **Saiwa Swamp National Park** is the country's smallest park. Despite its accessibility – no distance from *Barnley's House* – it is rarely visited, which is a pity. The requirement that you walk (rather than drive) around the two square kilometres of jungle and swamp, plus the chance of seeing the antelope as well as various monkeys and birds, make it an exciting and interesting goal for a day. If you're staying at *Barnley's*, think about hiring a guide there for the trip – not at all expensive, and really worthwhile.

Game-watching

The **sitatunga** (pronounced "statunga") is an unusual antelope with strange splayed and elongated hooves, which you probably won't see because the animal lives most of its life partly submerged in water and weed. It's hard to see quite how the hooves help it "to move freely on the surface of boggy swamps": the theory makes sense, but the design needs more work – the warden may be able to show you a sitatunga hoof if you are interested. Otherwise, the sitatunga is reddish-brown with a moth-eaten look, very large ears and, on the males, horns. Due to poaching, numbers in the park were down from over 70 when it opened to 27 at the last count and, unfortunately, the park is inadequately fenced and protected.

Sitatunga can be found in scattered locations throughout western and central Africa, but only at Saiwa Swamp have they grown really used to humans. They can be watched from the **observation platforms** which have been built in the trees at the side of the swamp – one on the east side, three on the west. The best times are early morning and late afternoon, and the furthest platform is less than a kilometre from the campsites (see below). These lookouts are unmaintained, Tarzan-esque structures enabling you to spy down on the life among the reeds. The park also shelters plenty of **bushbuck**, easily distinguished from the sitatunga by their terrified, crashing escape through the undergrowth as you approach. The sitatunga evidently have steadier nerves, as they pick their way through the morass of waterweed regardless of human attention.

A delightful, simple to follow, **early-morning walk** takes you across the rickety duckboards over the swamp and down a jungle path on the eastern shore. Here you're almost bound to see the park's four species of **monkey**: colobus, vervet, blue, and the distinctively white-bearded de Brazza monkey.

Saiwa Swamp is also a great draw for ornithologists, with a number of untypical Kenyan **bird species**, including several turacos (though the great blue is apparently no longer among them), many kingfishers, and the splendid black-and-white casqued hornbill. Most conspicuous of all are the **crowned cranes**, whose lurching flight is almost as risible as their ghastly honking call.

Practicalities

The park – known locally as *Swam'* – lies to the right of the main Kitale–Lodwar road, near the village of **Kipsain** (also known as Kipsoen). Matatus call at the village, which is some 18km from Kitale and off the main road. From here, if you fail to get a lift, it's a poorly signposted five-kilometre walk to the park gates. If you have a tent, you can camp in the park (Ksh200), where there are three good sites grouped together, but nothing at all in the way of facilities, apart from a clean, piped water supply at the staff village, plenty of firewood, and a small *duka*, open sporadically. You'll need to make a fire, as the swamp mist makes it very chilly up here at night. Otherwise, the best base is at Sirikwa, just up the road (see p.339), where the Barnleys are a mine of information about the park, and also keep maps of it.

Kapenguria, Ortum and the Marich Pass

KAPENGURIA – off the highway north, is surprisingly small given its status as the capital of West Pokot, and notable only for its role of minor notoriety in colonial history (see the background on Kenyatta's trial in Contexts, p.643). If you turn off the main road to visit, you'll find an immaculately tarred main street leading incongruously up through the hovels of "old Kapenguria" to the smarter new town on higher ground, with its hospital, large police station, huge-red-octagonal Catholic church (stained-glass windows and a spire), and the West Pokot District headquarters.

Also here is the excellent **Kapenguria Museum** (PO Box 383 ☏0324/2050; daily 8am–6pm; Ksh200), occupying the prison where Kenyatta and his colleagues were detained during their parody of a trial. Their individually named cells have been "restored", and contain copies of contemporary press reports, photographs, depositions and the charges laid against each of the men (some almost laughably nebulous). Largely inaccessible during the colonial period, the town was deliberately chosen to hinder the work of the defence lawyers – "a maze of rascalities", one of them called it. All six defendants were found guilty of belonging to Mau Mau and sentenced to seven years in jail with hard labour. Much more visually interesting are the ethnographic displays of Pokot and Cherangani cultures, including well-described photographs of traditional ceremonies (circumcision dances and initiatory groups), musical instruments, and a telling series on the changes wrought by "modern" life. Look out for the chisel for removing teeth, and the small Cherangani horn "for sucking after making incisions on both sides of the head if one has a headache" – both are in the Cherangani Gallery, showcase #3. In the museum grounds are three reconstructed Pokot and Cherangani family compounds, which the museum caretaker will be happy to explain to you. Oddly prescient, given the recent flare-up of ethnic violence and cattle-raiding in West Pokot, is the pastoralist Pokot compound, featuring solid mud roofs which were designed to deflect firebrands flung by raiders.

Matatus from Kitale will drop you on the main road (A1) at **Makutano**, the service town for the western Cherangani Hills, from where you'll have to hire a taxi, squeeze into a shared one, or take a *boda-boda* for the last few kilometres to Kapenguria town itself (the turn-off is just north of Makutano). Makutano is also where you'll find **accommodation** and **food**. The *Salama Hotel* by the matatu stage offers the usual staples in copious portions, and also has very basic rooms (no phone; ❶). Better is the *Elgonnia Springs Hotel* (PO Box 132 ☏0324/2284; ❶), which can be found by heading north from the matatu stage and turning right after 100m, just before the Caltex station. It has small but decent s/c rooms with water most of the time, and a bucket of hot water on request. It also has a bar with food, and is due to open a second branch called *Ista Plaza*, of a slightly higher standard, a little further north, opposite the Esso station.

North of Makutano, the road enters the truly spectacular countryside of West Pokot proper, winding up the western ridge of Lenan Forest, then plunging steeply to the Marun (or Moruny) River. After some 45km you reach **ORTUM**, beautifully positioned beneath the heights of the Cheranganis, close to the **Marich Pass**, and a good locale to start hiking in the hills. There are at least two cheap **B&Ls** here – *Somtowo Hotel* just off the main square (PO Box 218; no phone; ❶), and *New Savannah Inn* just beyond the post office (no phone; ❶) – and people are pleasantly uninterested in your presence. Of a large number of *hotelis*, the winner is *Rafikis' Hotel* on the main square, which serves tasty meals and manages cold sodas despite the absence of electricity. You can do a short **hike to a waterfall**, three hours' walk up from Ortum. From the post office, head past the *New Savannah Inn*, cross the main road, and the first dirt track takes you straight there.

Matatus plying between Kitale and Lodwar will drop you off anywhere on the main road. Otherwise, you can take a matatu from Kitale to Makutano, and pick up an onward vehicle there. Heading into the Kerio Valley (p.278) on the other side of the Cheranganis, you'll find plenty of matatus between Makutano and Sigor, especially on Sigor's market day (Thursday), with fewer onward to Tot, unless you can coincide with weekly markets at Lomut (Saturdays) and Chesegon (Wednesdays).

An excellent base to make for in this district is the **Marich Pass Field Studies Centre** (PO Box 564 Kapenguria; no phone), beautifully sited on the banks of the Marun River, just north of the small shopping centre of **Marich**, at the junction of the A1 Lodwar and B4 Kerio Valley roads: the centre (sign-posted) is 1km off the Lodwar road. There is a short-cut on foot from just north of the B4 turn-off, by a signpost that reads "Marich Mixed Boarding Primary School", but the path (at twenty rather than ninety degrees to the right) is not easy to follow, and it's worth enlisting local help. The centre has a lovely shaded campsite (Ksh250 per person; one tent available for rent at Ksh100), some good *bandas* with mosquito nets (s/c ❸, non s/c ❷), including one s/c *banda* adapted for wheelchair use, and a dorm block (Ksh300 per person). Firewood, stoves and lamps are available for a small fee. The food is basic but impressively plentiful – order well in advance – and drinking water comes pure from the well. Even if you're not staying, it's well worth dropping in for a picnic (daily admission Ksh70), as the centre is surrounded by dense bush, quivering with bird and animal life, and there are guides to help you on excursions around the hills, to Pokot villages and local markets if you have the energy (fixed rates: Ksh250 for 6hr, Ksh400 for 12hr). **Mount Sekerr** (Mtelo) is the peak that looms to the northwest – it's a three-day hike to the top (3354m) and back. Nearer Marich, 3206-metre **Mount Koh** to the southeast is a one-day hike if you've got 4WD to get half way up; two full days otherwise.

Mount Elgon

Straddling the Kenya-Uganda border, **Mount Elgon** is hidden in clouds most of the time, its precise outline hard to discern. The name comes from the Maasai **Ol Doinyo Ilgoon**, meaning "Breast Mountain", and like Mount Kenya, it's an extinct volcano, around whose jagged and much eroded crater rim the flat-topped peaks crop up like stumpy fingers of an upturned hand. The two mountains are comparable in bulk, but Elgon is lower (below the snow-line) and less precipitous – an encouragement, perhaps, if the thought of tackling the "loneliest park in Kenya" was putting you off.

Part of the east side of the mountain is enclosed within the confines of **Mount Elgon National Park**. Outside this zone, however, you're as free to hike and camp as anywhere in Kenya, subject always to the mountain's potentially restricting location on what has in the past been a sensitive border (see p.344). With better security nowadays, moves are afoot to enable tourists to visit the national parks on both sides of the border together, which would entail arranging to take a Kenyan ranger as far as the hot springs on the border, where you would be handed over to the care of a Ugandan ranger, or vice-versa if coming the other way. You would also then have to visit Suam to complete border formalities, though ways may be found around this in future. If you are interested in doing this, you should contact KWS headquarters in Nairobi (p.148) to see if it is possible and obtain clearance to do it. You will also need to hire the services of a ranger (see p.345), and to stay on the mountain overnight, which means bringing enough food and shelter for all of you.

If you do manage to cobble things together, there's invigorating walking country up near the peaks, and the smoothing effects of erosion make hiking

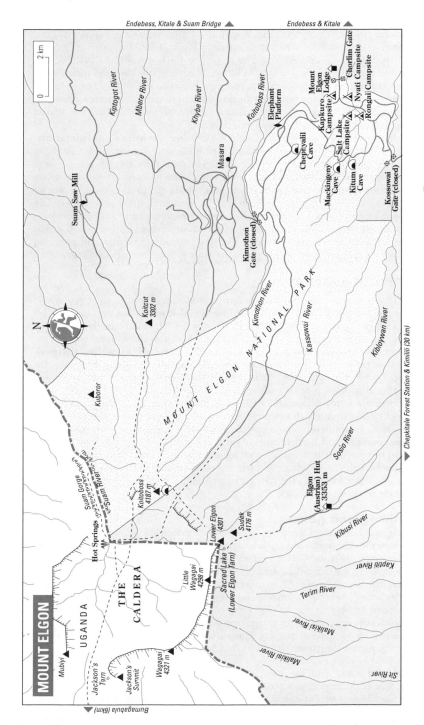

MOUNT ELGON

Chorlim Gate
Mount Elgon Lodge
Nyati Campsite
Kapkuro Campsite
Salt Lake Campsite
Rongai Campsite

Elephant Platform

Koitobboss River

Khybe River

Mbere River

Kiptogot River

Chepnyalil Cave

Mackingeny Cave
Kitum Cave

Kossowai Gate (closed)

Masara

Suam Saw Mill

Kimothon Gate (closed)

Kimothon River

Kassowai River

Kibloywan River

MOUNT ELGON NATIONAL PARK

Koitcut 3302 m

N

0   2 km

Kuboror

Sosio River

Elgon (Austrian) Hut 3353 m

Chepkitale Forest Station & Kimilili (30 km) ▼

Koitobboss 4187 m

Suam Gorge
Suam River

Hot Springs

Lower Elgon 4301

Sudek 4176 m

Kibusi River

Kaptii River

Terim River

UGANDA

THE CALDERA

Little Wagagai 4298 m

Sacred Lake (Lower Elgon Tarn)

Malikisi River

Malikisi River

Sit River

Mubiyi

Jackson's Tarn
Jackson's Summit

Wagagai 4321 m

Bumagabula (5km) ▼

relatively easy. The highest peak, **Wagagai** (4321m; there's also another Wagagai nearby, at 4298m), is across the caldera in Uganda, but the most evocatively shaped peaks (Sudek, 4176m; Lower Elgon, 4301m; Koitoboss, 4187m; and Endebess Bluff, 2563m) belong to Kenya. The mountain has good rock-climbing but you must be properly equipped; the best is on the cliffs of Lower Elgon, Sudek and the nearby pinnacles. Again, you'll need clearance from someone in authority. Actually up in the caldera (technically in Uganda), the **warm springs** by the Suam River provide a tempting bath.

In the 1980s, Elgon was the scene of a number of **violent confrontations** between elephant poachers and armed park rangers. The last serious outbreak was in 1988 and resulted in several deaths. For some time, Kenyan officials were turning back non-4WD vehicles, even outside the park, and preventing hikers on foot from climbing. In 1992, **ethnic strife** swept the communities of Elgon's eastern slopes as the democracy movement gained momentum. The people of Kimilili, Endebess and Kolongolo towns were victims of arson, sporadic violence and furious bouts of intimidation directed against non-Kalenjin by gangs of youths of uncertain identity. Fortunately, violence and poaching have since abated, and should not affect your visit to the park as a tourist.

Practicalities

In most respects, you should treat a trip up Mount Elgon much as you would one to Mount Kenya (see p.178). However, **altitude** is less of a problem on Elgon and, given several days to climb it, few people will be badly affected by the ascent, except perhaps near the summits. Access to the national park is easy, with two or three matatus most days from Kitale, and **hiking within the park** is now permitted if you take a **ranger** as a chaperone/guide (Ksh600 per day, or Ksh300 for half a day). It is possible to reach the peak from within the national park on foot or with a vehicle, but the vehicle would have to be an extremely sturdy, high-slung 4WD, and you'd need steely nerves, as it's a steep, rocky and extremely muddy ride up to the start of the trail to Koitoboss Peak. Indeed, the route is often completely impassable (January and February are the best months), and at other times of the year even the area west of Chorlim Gate can be extremely treacherous, with plenty of mud, slippery tyre-ruts and ample opportunities to bog down or even roll your vehicle. Without a car, you would need to bring supplies for your party, including ranger, for all the time you are likely to spend in the park.

Timing and guides

Elgon is best from December to March and rather less good in June and July, with the heaviest rains falling during the April to May and August to September periods. This is a lonely mountain, and while there are no specific permanent restrictions on hiking outside the park boundaries (which enclose less than a quarter of the Kenyan slopes), it's probably better not to go up alone. You aren't likely to see anyone else for a day or two, and if something were to happen to you on the heights you can forget about rescue. Finding **guide-porters** is easy enough in villages around the base. Just ask around, and expect to pay up to Ksh500 per day, plus park entrance fees if necessary. As usual, women travelling alone should try and hitch along with a group.

Maps

If you plan more than a look into the park by vehicle, it's useful to have the *Mount Elgon Map & Guide* by Andrew Wielochowski, obtainable from Executive

Wilderness Programmes, Haulfryn, Cilycwm, Llandovery SA20 0SP
(℡01550/721319, 🖷720053; £6.50 including postage within the UK, $13 from
elsewhere), and sometimes available at bookshops such as Prestige and Primrose
Sundries in Nairobi or in the UK. Survey of Kenya maps are also available, and
the 1:125,000 map can be obtained without clearance, though border sensitivity means some other sheets may be restricted at times (see "maps" p.148).

Equipment

Take a **compass** and supplies for at least two to three days of self-sufficiency.
Suggestions on clothing and equipment can be found in the Mount Kenya section (p.178). A **tent** will enable you to stay up in the peaks area, and a **torch**
is required if you fancy poking about the caves. If you have a vehicle (4WD
essential in the rainy season), you can adjust these requirements. The park
rangers are often willing to accompany drivers for a fee (Ksh600 per day, or
Ksh300 for half a day).

Accommodation

Inside the park itself, and on the slopes of the mountain, **camping** is the most
obvious way to stay ($2 per person per night), and for hiking deep within the
park, it's your only choice. You should try, if at all possible, to **camp** at one of the
sites in the lower half of the park – they're highly recommended as some of the
most beautiful in the country – and visit the caves. There are four campsites within a kilometre of the Chorlim Gate, of which *Kapkuro* (or *Kuro*), the nearest to
the gate, has a couple of brand new *bandas* available (❸), with water and showers.

   Mount Elgon Lodge (PO Box 7 Endebess; no phone, but the park gate can
take messages on ℡0325/30319; reservations through *Msafiri Inns*, p.43; B&B
❹, FB ❺), is located 1km outside the park on the track leading to Chorlim
Gate (no park fees payable). It has been run at a loss for many years but still
manages to stay open, which is good news if you've money for a splash, and are
partial to faded remnants of the British empire. It's an atmospheric retreat,
despite the emptiness, if rather run-down. The manorial reception rooms have
lovingly polished wood-block floors and quintessentially English garden views,
and the bedrooms are comfortable enough (no nets, but the few mosquitoes
here aren't malarial). You can choose between one of three original rooms up
a creaking flight of stairs ("Cherangani" is the best), or a modern room in the
block overlooking the lawns. The water supply is erratic. **Camping** in the
grounds is an accepted, and very acceptable, alternative to taking a room
(Ksh350 per person, including use of bathroom and showers).

   An alternative base is **Delta Cresent Farm**, on the way to Chorlim Gate
from Endebess (4km from the former, 2km from the latter; PO Box 126
Endebess ℡0325/31462, 🖷30067, 🌐www.dcfelgonsafaris.com), where you
can camp in your own tent (Ksh200 per person), borrow a small tent (Ksh500),
or sleep on a bed in a large tent or *banda* (Ksh1500). The campsite is beautifully kept, on a farm with geese and giraffes, as well as horses and camels
(which are available for riding), and there are cooking facilities, a lounge, and
food and drinks available. Although the farm is accessible from Endebess by
boda-boda, however, it's a four kilometre hike from the park.

The routes

There are three **routes** up the Kenyan side of Elgon: one directly into the park
and two hikes around either side, both passing through fine scenery and neither very severe (the northerly one is currently out of bounds).

Direct to the park

Daily fees $15, children $5; camping $2 per person; vehicle carrying up to five people Ksh200, six or more people Ksh500. Warden: PO Box 753 Kitale ☎ 0325/31456–7.

The only currently allowed entrance into the **national park** (unless you have permissioin to enter from the Ugandan side) is through **Chorlim Gate**, which lies some 12km beyond Endebess. Kimothon and Kossowai gates have been closed and unstaffed for some time – using them risks landing you in a lot of trouble, as you will be assumed to be evading park fees. To reach Chorlim Gate, stock up on petrol at Kitale, and head northwest towards Endebess along the tarmac road. There's a brown Kenya Wildlife Service signpost marking the left-hand turning to the national park, 500m after the Kenya Seed Company and ADC compounds. From here, a mostly decent *murram* road heads straight to *Mount Elgon Lodge* and Chorlim Gate (passable with 2WD in dry seasons). If you miss the turning, there's another left turn signposted at Endebess, leading to the same *murram* road (this route is boggier and not for 2WD). Matatus usually run three times a day to *Mount Elgon Lodge* from Kitale (leaving at around noon, 2pm and 5pm, depending on custom), and there are frequent services to Endebess, leaving you with a pleasant two-hour walk, of which you can take a *boda-boda* for the first couple of kilometres. Hoping to find a spare seat in a tourist vehicle isn't really an option: with barely a handful of visitors per month you might be in for a long wait.

Once inside the park, the fine (signposted) campsites a few kilometres from the gate are a good target. If you're exceptionally lucky, a night vigil at **Kitum Cave** may be repaid by a visit from the elephants; the bats and the forest are compensation if you're not. You'll need permission from the rangers and a good torch, and be warned that this is a potentially dangerous exercise: plan your

Kitum Cave and the Ebola virus

Kitum Cave earned a certain notoriety when it featured as the opening and closing location of *The Hot Zone*, a "true-life thriller" about **Ebola** written in 1994 by an American journalist, Richard Preston. Ebola is a virus so deadly it is scientifically classed as a Level 4 pathogen (HIV is only Level 2). Mercifully, it's rare: the only serious outbreaks in the last twenty years occurred in Zaïre (now Congo) and Sudan in 1976, and then again in April 1995 in Zaïre. In the more recent plague, around 250 people in the Congolese town of Kikwit died after contracting the virus. The manner of death by Ebola is so gruesome that hysterical global media coverage surrounded the outbreak – effectively, the virus liquefies the vital organs of the living victim, and death occurs within days. Scientists have yet to gather any solid data about the origins and means of transmission of the virus, or the identity of its natural host. The link to Kitum Cave is a tenuous, probably meaningless one. Isolated incidences of Ebola infection are reported every few years and, in two such cases (described in gut-churning detail by Richard Preston in his book), the victims had visited Kitum Cave shortly before they became ill. In an attempt to discover whether the cave harbours the virus in some form, the US Army's Infectious Diseases Unit, in conjunction with the Kenya Medical Research Unit, mounted a research operation in Kitum Cave in 1988. The team made *Mount Elgon Lodge* their base, donned spaceman-type anti-virus bio-safety suits, and set about making a comprehensive examination of the cave, testing thousands of resident insects, birds, hyraxes, bats, monkeys, baboons, and samples of guano and dung, for Ebola. They found absolutely nothing. Preston's book, going all out for sensationalism, hangs a question mark over the conclusiveness of these findings, but those who know the Elgon area well unanimously write the theory off as irresponsible scaremongering.

escape route well. For **Koitoboss Peak** (4187m), follow the driveable track into the moorlands to the trailhead outside the park (allow 3–4hr to cover the 30km; a ranger should accompany you in your vehicle; 4WD only, and then only safely January–February: ask the rangers whether it's been improved, as there were plans to regrade it). From here it's a three-hour hike to the pass at the southern base of the peak, where there are flat (but cold and windy) places where you can camp. You can then make the one-hour scramble to the top, or take a two- to three-hour diversion to the Suam Springs in the crater.

Crossing into Uganda

If you want to **cross the mountain into Uganda**, check with the rangers or with KWS in Nairobi (p.148) whether this is possible. Arrangements would have to be made with the Ugandan parks authorities on the west side of the mountain, but such arrangements are likely to become easier in the future.

Failing that, the border post at **Suam** is now open, and a lot more easy-going than those further south at Malaba and Busia, which are used by commercial traffic. Suam is easily accessible by matatu from Kitale and Endebess. On the other side, there are matatus to Kapchorwa and thence to Mbale, where you'll find onward transport to the rest of Uganda.

Kimilili and the Western Trail

The **second route** up the mountain is a popular one with **hikers**. It begins in **KIMILILI**, a village on the way to Bungoma from Kitale (heading south from Kitale towards Webuye, turn right off the A1 after about 30km; there are frequent matatus from Kitale and Bungoma), from where it's a long but invigorating trek up to the moorlands (lifts are scarce). In Kimilili, *Jasho Lodging* (℡0338/21020; ❶) is recommended for cheap but decent **rooms**, the *Mount Crest Hotel* (PO Box 870 ℡0338/21037; ❷) for something slightly better, and also for **meals**. Kimilili is a lively place on a Thursday, when the **market** attracts rural dwellers from a wide radius. You may be allowed to **pitch a tent** at Kimilili Catholic Secondary School, just outside the town.

The next day, by allowing yourself a good eight to ten hours to cover the 40km, you should be able to reach the Elgon Hut (or Austrian Hut); the hut is disused, but it's usually possible to camp near here. The first step **up the mountain** is to take a ride by matatu, which is only possible early in the morning, from Kimilili to **Kapsakwony**, 7km away (top up with water here if you forgot in Kimilili). At the fork above the village, bear left, then after 2km, turn right at the "Forest Station 25km" signpost. You may get a lift from here, past the Forest Reserve Gate (small fee) to the last village, **Kaberua**, 2.5km further up (see the sign there, "Chepkitale Forest Stn 21km"), but from Kaberua on, you'll almost certainly have to walk. Eight kilometres above Kaberua, the trail gets noticeably worse as it plunges into the cathedral gloom of tsetse-fly-infested bamboo forest. An hour of this and you break into open stands of moss-enveloped giant podocarpus trees ("podos") with spiralling trunks. The trail rolls upwards, you crest a hill, and the entire southern Elgon Ridge system is spread out before you.

The **Chepkitale Forest Station** has plenty of abandoned buildings for shelter, but uncertain water supplies, so it's worth struggling on the last two hours (7km) to the **Elgon Hut**. There's a stream near the hut but little firewood, so remember to collect some on the way. A rough jeep track continues past the hut, but you're unlikely to meet anyone up here.

The **trail** from the hut is well marked with occasional cairns and white blazes: a brisk three to four hours the following morning should see you to

Elija Masinde's Dini: the cult of the ancestors

In the 1940s and 1950s, there was a resurgence of **Bukusu resistance** and nation-alism in the *Dini ya Msambwa* (Cult of the Ancestors) movement, spearheaded by the charismatic prophet-rebel, **Elija Masinde**. The heart of the movement was in the Elgon foothills between Kimilili and the Ugandan border. It called for the eviction of all *wazungu* and the transfer of their property to Africans. As the *Dini* spread, there were violent confrontations with colonial forces, and a number of deaths. Masinde was sent into internal exile but, by now a folk hero, his followers kept the sparks of resistance alive throughout the more organized uprising of Mau Mau in the Central Highlands, until Independence was finally obtained. The movement collapsed in the early years of *uhuru*, when Masinde was allowed home to Kimilili and his continued denouncements of all authority and claims to divine inspiration began to lose their coherence. Until his death in the 1990s, he could still be seen on the streets of Kimilili – a rather terrifying figure shouting at the wind.

Lower Elgon Tarn, a good place to camp, from where it's another hour to the top of Lower Elgon itself, the highest peak on the Kenya side. Starting out from the hut, a two-hour hike will bring you up to the ridge that leads up to the peak of Lower Elgon (just beyond this, there is a high valley which has the southeast caldera rim, seen from the rear, as its head.) There are duiker ante-lope to be seen bouncing away through the scrub everywhere. Next, you climb a false summit, then dip down, paralleling the series of tabular peaks on your right which form the southern crater lip. From the **tarn**, the trail swerves cru-elly up through a gap in the rock wall to put you on the summit of Lower Elgon.

Alternatively, you could make the five-hour trek from the hut to **Koitoboss Peak** and the **Suam hot springs**. To get down to the springs from the Elgon Hut, take a two-hour hike towards Lower Elgon as described above, but then, instead of following the ridge, leave the trail and cut across the valley, follow-ing the rim to Koitoboss Peak, inside the national park. Down in the crater, to the left, are the springs. Depending on your supplies and the state of security, you can either turn back to the hut for a second night there or continue around the crater rim to drop down off the mountain on the northeast side, traversing the upper part of the national park and, ideally, allowing a night camped on the mountain. Note that if you're found inside the park, or if you exit through Chorlim Gate, you may have some explaining to do and you'll have to pay park fees at least.

Kimothon route (currently closed)

There's a **third route**, on the north side of the park, which obviates some of the lengthy foot-slogging of the trail from Kimilili, but it is currently out of action. It would involve entering the park at the Kimothon Gate, which has been closed for some years now, and is still illegal, partly because of Ugandan cattle rustlers who used to operate here, and partly because of the parlous state of the approach road. Word is, however, that the gate may reopen in the future, so it might be worth checking with KWS to see if this has happened. The route starts in Endebess and leads west about 12km up to the village of **Masara** and thence to **Kimothon Forest Station**. After spending the night in the station, continue the next day across the park on the well-marked trail to Koitoboss and the Elgon (Austrian) Hut. Downhill from here, you can follow the Kimilili trail (about 40km, as described above) in reverse. Once you reach Kapsakwony there are matatus for the last 7km to Kimilili; it's a ten-hour knee-wobbler of a hike if you want to walk the whole way.

Wildlife

Vegetation on Mount Elgon is similar to Mount Kenya's, and equally impressive, with bamboo and podocarpus forests (the latter more accessible than Mount Kenya's) giving way to open moorland inhabited by the strange statues of giant groundsel and lobelia. **Wildlife** isn't easily seen until you get onto the moors, but some elephant and a fair few buffalo do roam the woods (be extremely wary of both). The best place to see **elephant** used to be the Elephant Platform – herds would congregate here to feed on the acacias – but large numbers were wiped out by Ugandan poachers in the turbulent 1980s, and the remainder became somewhat more reclusive. While the Kenya Wildlife Service is confident that poaching is now under control, and estimates that the elephant population in the park is approaching 200 (in two groups, with more on the Uganda side), it remains to be seen how long they will remain under effective protection. The lions have long gone and, though there are still leopards and servals, you're not likely to see one. The primates are more conspicuous: blue monkeys (found only in western Kenya) and shaggy colobus crash through the forested areas, troops of olive baboons patrol the scrub, and along the Kimothon River there's a scattering of rare de Brazza's monkeys.

The Elkony Caves

Elgon's most captivating attraction is the honeycomb of caves on the lower slopes, inside the national park boundaries. Some of these were long inhabited by one of the loosely related Kalenjin groups, the **Elkony** (whose name, in corrupted form, was given to the mountain), and used both as living quarters and as stock pens at night. There is evidence that the caves may have had a ritual function as well – **Chepnyalil Cave** contains a structure that might have served as an altar or shrine, and its walls are painted with a red-and-white frieze of cattle. To find the cave from the park gate, head north for 2km to the signposted junction for the Caves (south), Park Gate (east) and Koitoboss Peak (north), and turn right 2.5km towards Endebess Bluff, taking the narrow and overgrown track on the left just before the waterfall. Male circumcision ceremonies among the Luhya people are also linked with the caves (as well as others in the region), where boys spent their month-long initiation period, before returning home as men, covered head-to-toe in the white diatomite powder found nearby (especially visible at Kitum). The Elkony were officially evicted from the caves by the colonial government, who insisted that they live in the open "where they could be counted for tax", but caves with ceilings as high as two-storey buildings were still occupied by extended families within living memory.

Some of the caves are so large and labyrinthine that deep exploration is only possible with navigational aids and breathing apparatus. It is rumoured that there is a route that leads far into the mountain and emerges in Uganda, a secret passage known only to coffee smugglers. The largest and most spectacular cave is **Makingeny**, marked by a cascade falling over the entrance.

Early explorers believed that some of the caves were man-made, and one report referred to "thousands of chisel and axe marks on the walls". If you actually visit the caves, you'll realize very quickly (from the stench and football-sized droppings, among other clues) that generations of elephants were responsible: the well-signposted **Kitum Cave** achieved TV fame as the salt fix of local elephants, which still walk into the caves at night to gouge the salty rock from the walls with their tusks. The elephants, though no longer free to migrate back and forth between Elgon and the Cheranganis as they once did, are still occasional troglodytes. There have been cases of them falling into crevasses or dying under rock falls caused by their over-eager salt-mining.

The Uganda road: Webuye, Bungoma and Malaba

This is perhaps the least interesting part of western Kenya to look at: largely monotonous undulating grasslands and sugar fields, dotted here and there with gigantic granite boulders. But it is still the route by which the majority of Africa overland travellers come into the country (when central African security issues permit them to do so), and the most obvious one for those planning to head **out to Uganda**.

If you're making your way to the south from this district down towards Kakamega and Kisumu, the busy A1 will take you through some fine strands of forest and tropical woodland, heralding the Kakamega Forest zone (see p.354) to the southeast.

Webuye and around

WEBUYE certainly offers very little to attract visitors. It's the site of the giant Panafrican (abbreviated as "Pan") Paper Mills, which dominate the countryside around – with its strong, noxious odour as much as anything else. The explanation for the factory's siting is **Webuye Falls**, gushing through rock clefts behind and above the mills, about 5km from the main road. Formerly known as Broderick Falls, Webuye is a nice spot for a picnic, as long as you have a car for access, but the falls are hardly spectacular. To reach them, turn off the main road at the factory and climb northwards between housing developments and mills, passing a school. From there, the plant (the largest paper factory in Africa) belches smoke across the hot plains.

Webuye has the usual assortment of banks, shops and petrol stations, and if you find yourself in need of a **room**, there are two main options: the *Webuye Motel* on the southeast side of town nearest the factory (PO Box 553 ☎0337/41328; bed only ❷), has an unexciting selection of rooms, some s/c, some nets, but mostly pretty dingy, all within sniffing distance of the factory and its sirens; and the superior *Park Villa Hotel* on the Kitale road, west of town (PO Box 1000 ☎0337/41290, ☎0337/41216; B&B ❹), a well-kept and welcoming roadside stop with busy bars and a small pool (Ksh165 for visitors), all rooms s/c with nets, and there's even a sauna (Ksh330 per hour).

Chetambe's Fort
A few kilometres away, on top of the steep scarp that rears up beyond the Kitale road, lies a different kind of monument, the remains of **Chetambe's Fort**. This was the site, in 1895, of a last-ditch stand by the Bukusu group of the Luhya tribe against the motley line-up of a British punitive expedition, which had enrolled Ugandan, Sudanese, Maasai and even other Luhya troops. A predictable – Hotchkiss gun – massacre took place, with negligible losses on the attackers' side. How they managed to storm the scarp in the first place, however, is a mystery: presumably the Bukusu were all inside their walled fort at the top.

With Kenya's historical sites being so few, it's worth the effort to scramble up the steep slope if you're interested. Not surprisingly, perhaps, the "Fort" itself is quite unimpressive. All that remains these days is an overgrown, semicircular ditch, perhaps 100m from end to end. A more convincing reason for going there is to talk to the people who live nearby, some of whom can show you the site, and will tell you stories of finding bones in the compound area, of women coming here to weep in the evenings, and even of animal sacrifices to the dead warriors.

If you have your own transport, a roundabout alternative to the slog up the cliffs is to continue following the road which leads past Webuye Falls. The *Nabyole Lodge* up here is quite a good **B&L**, with cold drinks and a restaurant. They'll direct you on to Chetambe's, about 8km further on reasonable *murram*.

Bungoma and into Uganda

The main road to Uganda continues west. The smooth tarmac and monotonous scenery encourage fast driving, and number-plate spotters will be able to tick off vehicles from all over eastern and central Africa on this one well-pounded stretch.

Sizeable as it is, **BUNGOMA** manages to be unremittingly dull, built around a lower street which is its main drag, and a parallel upper street, with a covered market, banks (of which Barclays has an ATM) and a post office. There's no reason to visit, as it's 2km off the main A104 road, but if you do find yourself here, there are unexpected "sugar-belt style" comforts at the *Bungoma Tourist Hotel* on the lower street, at the southern end of town, (PO Box 972 ☏0337/30009 or 30801; ❶). *Wings Hotel*, on the lower street at the north end of town by the Total station (PO Box 1982 ☏0337/30967; ❶), is less of a drain on the resources and provides clean, quiet rooms. *Hotel Simba* (PO Box 663 ☏0337/30312; ❶) is louder and livelier, but a good place to drink, with music most nights. For **eating**, your best bets are *Bobby's Restaurant* and the *Coast Hotel*, both on the upper street.

Two kilometres south of town at **KANDUYI**, where Bungoma's main drag meets the A104, *Grandma's Hotel* (PO Box 225 ☏0337/30549; ❶), is spartan but very friendly, and handy for transport along the main road.

Malaba: the Ugandan border

MALABA lies at the end of both the road and the (presently defunct) railway line. While there are usually endless lines of lorries waiting on both sides of the border with **Uganda**, pedestrians have been crossing for some years now without difficulty. Formalities are relatively simple, and Irish citizens do not currently need a Ugandan visa, although Brits, North Americans and Australians and New Zealanders do. Money changers are on hand both sides of the border. Try to find out the current rates in advance (around Ksh1800: $1 in early 2002) and watch out for scams (such as trying to pass off Ush105,000 as Ush150,000): count the currency you're buying carefully before handing yours over.

Arriving in Kenya, note that there are currently no passenger train services, but several bus companies do the run to Nairobi, of which Akamba (☏0337/54232) has the safest reputation. Matatus serve Bungoma, Kisumu, Kitale and Eldoret; on the Ugandan side, they run to Tororo, Jinja and Kampala. Few people hang around here, but if you do need to stay, there's no shortage of unappetizing **B&Ls** along the kilometre of lorry-choked road which constitutes Malaba. While near the border, especially if distracted by the formalities of crossing, don't make the mistake of relaxing your security routines – many people are robbed soon after arrival here.

Kakamega and Kakamega Forest

KAKAMEGA is the headquarters of the **Luhya**, a loosely defined group of peoples whose only clear common denominator is a **Bantu language**, spoken in more than a score of vernaculars, that distinguishes them from the Luo to the south and the Kalenjin to the east. Numerically, the Luhya (Abaluhya/Luyia) are Kenya's second largest ethnic group, and most are settled farmers.

The town itself was founded as a buying station on the ox trail known as Sclater's Road, which reached here from the coast in 1896. Historically, its only fame came in the 1930s, when gold was discovered nearby and more than a thousand prospectors came to the region. Very few fortunes were made. Today, it's a lively town, but with little to detain casual visitors.

Conversely, the nearby **Kakamega Forest** is one of western Kenya's star attractions; if you have any interest at all in the natural world, it's worth going far out of your way to see. Fortunately, it's fairly easy to get to from Kisumu or, if you've been in the Mount Elgon region, from Webuye along a very scenic stretch of the A1.

Moving on, Akamba buses (☎0331/20743) run daily to Nairobi, via Kapsabet and Nandi Hills at 7.30am, and via Kisumu and Kericho at 7.30pm. Coast Buses has a service to Nairobi and Mombasa at 5.30pm, and to Mumias and Bungoma at 8.30am. There are matatus to Kericho, Kisumu, Webuye and sometimes Bungoma.

Practicalities

If you arrive late in the day (or after around 2.30pm in 2WD, when the rain starts to fall), you may want to **stay in town** rather than arrive in the forest after dark. There are several decent lodgings and one or two pleasant places to eat.

Accommodation

Bendera Hotel PO Box 423 ☎0331/20777. Unexpectedly good B&L – clean and welcoming, with decent-sized s/c rooms. Happily the music from the downstairs bar-restaurant doesn't really filter upstairs. ❶
Franka Hotel PO Box 621 ☎0331/20086. Plenty of clean s/c rooms, some with good views, and there's hot water in the mornings plus food and beer in the bar downstairs. ❶
Golf Hotel Khasakhala Rd, PO Box 118 ☎0331/30150–4, ☏30155 (reservations via Msafiri Inns, p.43). A relatively luxurious hotel with its pretensions comically clipped by the vultures hopping over the lawns. All guests become temporary members of the adjacent Sports Club (golf, squash courts) and there's a pool and gift shop. However, non-Kenya resident rates are high. B&B ❺
Premier Hotel Cannon Awori St, PO Box 1961

☎0331/30134. Kakamega's newest option (parts of it still not completely finished at the time of writing), with attentive staff and large, comfortable s/c rooms, some with balconies, and a choice of baths or showers. Its bar features Congolese and Luhya *isukuti* music (so those in need of quiet should ask for a room as far as possible away from it, especially on a Friday or Saturday). B&B ❸
Salama Hotel Cannon Awori St, PO Box 70 ☎0331/20013. Cheap and friendly Somali-run B&L, but extremely basic, with tiny slummy rooms off a courtyard at the back of a fly-blown eating place, and worse toilets. ❶
Vike Guest House PO Box 1649 ☎0331/30314. The best cheapie, with good balconied rooms, all s/c with spotless squat loos, nets, and hot water in the morning. It can get loud at night, though, thanks to its ground-floor bar and echoing acoustics. Excellent value. ❶

KAKAMEGA

N

Mumias (C40)

RESTAURANTS & BARS
Deep Fry Ltd	E
JB Café	D
Lawino 2000	F
Merry Eating House	A
Musera Bar & Restaurant	B
Pizza Hut Café	G
Umoja Bar	I
Uncle Dave's Club	C
Wayside	J
Western Hotel	K
Western Region Bar	H

ACCOMMODATION
Bendera Hotel	4
Franka Hotel	2
Golf Hotel	6
Premier Hotel	3
Salama Hotel	5
Vike Guest House	1

MUMIAS ROAD

Mumias Matatus ★

Mobil

Library

Vaghela Bookshop ★

Akamba Buses

Deep Supermarket

Coastline Buses

Hindu Temple

Mama Watoto Supermarket

Shell

Standard Chartered Bank

KCB (bank)

Muliro Garden

Town Hall

KENYATTA AVENUE

SUDI ROAD

BP

Shell

Taxis

CANNON AWORI STREET

Kenol

Market

Matatu & Bus Park

Total

Barclays Bank

Caltex

KHASAKHALA ROAD

Kakamega Sports Club

100 m

0

ASK Saowground, Kakamega Forest National Reserve & Webuye (A1)

Kisumu & Kakamega Forest National Reserve (A1)

Eating and drinking

In addition to the hotel restaurants, there are some great cheap **eats** in Kakamega, and plenty of places to drink and listen to music, too. One good cheap eatery is the *Merry Eating House* – don't be put off by its dingy exterior or tumbledown interior: the fried tilapia is excellent. Other places worth trying include: *Lawino 2000* and the adjacent *JB Café*, both dirt cheap (under Ksh100) and friendly; *Deep Fry Ltd* (no prizes for guessing what it serves); the long list of Kenyan standards at the *Western Hotel*; and *Pizza Hut Café*, a bright little place that only actually has one variety of pizza on the menu, and fairly awful at that, but offers plenty of other choices. For **drinking places** with character, you're spoilt for choice: *Musera Bar and Restaurant* is very mellow; *Uncle Dave's Club* and *Umoja Bar* are for more hardened boozers, as is *Western Region*, which has pool tables; while *Bendera Hotel* and the *Wayside* both have good local jukebox sounds.

Listings

Books Vaghela Bookshop by the Akamba bus office has a reasonable selection of Kenyan and other English-language fiction. The library is open Mon–Thurs 9am–6pm, Fri 9am–4pm, Sat 9am–1pm; it should have some background on the Kakamega Forest.

Initiation ceremonies In August every year, Kakamega hosts a mass circumcision and initiation ceremony for boys from all the Luhya-speaking communities in the district. It's not certain how much you can get involved, but the party atmosphere should be unmistakeable. Ask locally.

Internet access A few places in the complex opposite the Total station offer internet access, and it's also available at the KCB bank. You can send email from Tina Taws opposite the *Franka Hotel*.

Kakamega Show End of November for three days at the ASK Showground.

Kenya Wildlife Service To reach the KWS office, go past the *Golf Hotel*, turn right at the roundabout, follow the road past the District Commisioner's office (which it's behind) to the next junction, where you turn left and it's on the left after 50m (☏ 0331/30603).

Market There's a very lively one next to the bus station. Among the local produce on offer you'll find natural remedies and medicines made from forest plants. Main market days are Wednesday and Saturday.

Supermarkets Mama Watoto near *Musera Bar*, and Deep Supermarket next to Agip.

Swimming pool A small one at the *Golf Hotel*.

The Kakamega Forest

Kenya Wildlife Service District Warden, PO Box 879 Kakamega ☏ 0331/30603; free entry.

Some four hundred years ago, the tract of rainforest now called **Kakamega Forest** would have been at the eastern end of a broad expanse of forest stretching west, clear across the continent, virtually unbroken as far as the Atlantic. Three hundred years later, after the advent of the human population explosion and widescale cultivation, the forests everywhere had receded, and had reduced Kakamega to an island of some 2,400 square kilometres, cut off from the rest of the Guineo-Congolan rainforest. Today, with an area not surpassing 230 square kilometres, it's a tiny patch of relict equatorial jungle, famous among zoologists and botanists around the world as an example of how an isolated environment can survive cut off from its larger body. The Kakamega Forest is a haven of shadowy gloom for over 300 species of birds, 45 percent of all recorded butterflies in Kenya, seven species of primates and other mammals, as well as snakes, various other reptiles and untold varieties of insects. Many of these animals are found nowhere else in East Africa because similar habitats no longer exist. The very real fear among environmentalists now is that even this tiny surviving remnant of rainforest, unique in Kenya, is itself in grave danger of complete elimination.

Although there's talk of building national-park-style gates "one day", nothing has yet been done: it is indicative of the forest's current plight. Despite a laudable scheme aiming to educate the local population about the forest (see the box p.359), the lack of any coherent backing or action from the authorities means that the long-term future of the forest isn't looking bright. Pressure from the local people who need grazing for their livestock, land to cultivate, and firewood, amounts to a significant threat. The present area is less than a tenth of what it was in 1900, and its closed canopy cover (which indicates the forest's health and maturity) has dropped from ninety to fifty percent. This has led to the inevitable degradation of the local natural habitat, which in turn has led to some species being threatened, and some – like leopard, which was last seen in 1992 – becoming extinct (the year coincided with an attack by Nandi villagers on the forest cats which, they claimed, had been killing their live-stock). Much of the wardens' time is spent patrolling the forest or observing it from lookout points on nearby hilltops, although some newspaper reports in 1998 accused the wardens themselves of adding to the forest's destruction by illegally selling off plots for cultivation. The way things stand, the survival of this unique habitat depends to a considerable degree on the continued support and concern of visitors to the region.

The forest is fragmented, interspersed with open fields of grassland, cultivated stream margins, small settlements and even tea plantations, though the latter have in part been planted by the government in order to provide a natural protective barrier, as well as to give the locals an alternative source of income to plundering the forest. **Two main areas** can be visited. The first, which has been accessible for many years, is the central **Kakamega Forest Reserve**, lying to the southeast of Kakamega town and somewhat off the beaten track. It is to a part of one of the densest stands in this area that most visitors come, to the **Forest Rest House** in the glade at its edge. The second section, the recently opened-up **Kakamega Forest National Reserve**, is northeast of the town and very easy to get to.

The central district: Kakamega Forest Reserve

On arriving at *Forest Rest House* (see below), visitors are greeted by an official guide (a member of Kakamega Biodiversity Tour Conservations Operators), whose name should be on the board outside the hut on the path up to the house. You will be given a brief introduction to the region and the conservation work being done by KEEP (see box on p.359; all guides should have a KEEP identity card), which is attempting to educate villagers and schoolchildren on the outskirts of the forest on the importance of preserving it. You may be asked to make a contribution to the effort (Ksh100 minimum), though this is optional – until KWS install their long-talked-about gates, you are not obliged to pay anything for entering or walking in the forest.

It's best to take up the offer of a **guide**, especially if you're a woman on your own (there are five female guides here; otherwise, ask for Wilberforce, Moses or Ben, who are all reliable). Exceptionally for a profession that usually attracts hustlers out for easy money, this lot are professional and knowledgeable (they have to pass an exam before becoming guides). Some are nothing short of encyclopedic and will rattle off the Latin name of any plant or creature you care to enquire about. Their walks are tremendously enjoyable, and they are happy to tailor walks to your particular interests. The fee is Ksh100 per person, plus any tip you care to add (about Ksh200–300 for three hours is about right). Expect a wander along the labyrinthine jungle paths, with birds, monkeys, chameleons and other animals pointed out to you, most of which you would miss on your own. A pair of **binoculars** is more or less indispensable if you're out to watch birds. You'll also find members of the guiding association at *Rivendell Gardens* and *Rondo Retreat Centre*.

Among the most common **birds** are the noisy and gregarious black-and-white-casqued hornbill and the very striking, deep violet Ross' turaco. You may also see familiar-looking African grey parrots and, circling above the canopy on the lookout for unwary monkeys, the huge crowned hawk eagle. But Kakamega's avian stars are the **great blue turacos**, glossy, turkey-sized birds looking like dowagers in evening gowns. They're easily located by their raucous calls; a favourite spot at dusk is the grove of very tall trees down by the pumphouse. They arrive each evening to crash and lurch among the branches as they select roosting sites.

The forest draws mammal-watchers as well, particularly for the **monkeys**. Troops are often seen at dusk, foraging through the trees directly opposite the *Rest House* verandah. Apart from the ubiquitous colobus, you can see blue monkeys and the much slimmer black-cheeked white-nosed monkey (most easily recognized by its red tail). They're often seen milling around with the hornbills. You may also see pairs of giant forest squirrels capering in the tree-tops; the deep booming call you sometimes hear in the morning is theirs.

At **night**, armed with a powerful torch, you might catch a glimpse of bush-babies, palm civets, genets or a potto, a slow-moving, lemur-like animal whose name aptly conveys its appearance and demeanour. The forest is also home to several species of fruit bat, of which the hammer-headed fruit bat (*Hypsignathus monstrosus*) is the largest in Africa, with a wingspan of a metre and an enormous head. Other nocturnal Kakamega specialities are the otter shrew, which lives in some of the forest streams, the tree pangolin (a kind of arboreal scaly anteater) and the flying squirrel.

The forest's **reptile life** is legendary, but few people seem to actually see any **snakes** (you're much more likely to come across **chameleons**). Reptiles spend a good deal of time motionless, especially when frightened, and to see any in the dense foliage you have to be well tuned in. Visible or not, however, snakes are abundant and you certainly shouldn't walk in the forest in bare feet or sandals: the gaboon viper, growing to a metre or more in length, and fatter than your arm, is a dangerous denizen of the forest floor. To avoid an encounter, simply walk heavily – they're highly sensitive to vibration and will flee at your seismic approach.

If you have time for more than one daylight walk, you could ask a guide to show you the way to **Lirhanda Hill**, via a trail rich in medicinal plants. You will be shown which leaves, berries and saps the forest dwellers chew, swallow or anoint themselves with to treat various ailments. Lirhanda Hill itself is a lookout point, offering fine views over the whole expanse of forest, with the sombre bulk of Mount Elgon glowering in the distance. Cutting into the hill-side near the top is a gold-mining shaft, long disused and now home to a large colony of bats. With a powerful torch and a steely nerve you can grope your way along the tunnel to meet them at close quarters.

Arrival

There are several ways of **getting to** the *Forest Rest House* – beware that maps of Kenya invariably locate the forest incorrectly. If you're **driving**, the easiest road is from **Khayega**, some 10km south of Kakamega on the A1. From here, an earth road leads 7km to Shinyalu. The junction is marked by signposts for the Arap Moi Girls' School and the Office of the President. Keep right at Shinyalu and continue for another 5km, and turn left just after the barrier and a signposted arrow. From here, it's less than a kilometre up the trail to the *Rest House*. An alternative route from Kakamega turns off to the left at the southern edge of Kakamega town, past the KWS offices, up to Shinyalu, whilst there's a more direct route from Eldoret and Kapsabet starting at Chepsonoi on the C39 (signposted "Kisieni 12km D267"). Both these routes are in worse condition than the Khayega road. Note that whichever approach you're taking, the surfaces get treacherously slippery in wet weather (especially for low clearance 2WDs). Given the relatively metronomic afternoon rains, this limits you to getting there between 10am and 2pm, when the road is at its driest. Even so, 4WD is advisable.

If you're using **public transport**, the best way is to catch a matatu from Kakamega to **SHINYALU**, from where it's a lovely two-hour walk to Isecheno, along the road heading left. If you don't want to walk, you'll have to hitch a lift with a passing vehicle, or else hire a *boda-boda* bicycle taxi (baggage permitting; Ksh50). Shinyalu itself often has a cattle auction and a major market on Saturdays, when it's worth pausing an hour to soak up the atmosphere of cowboys and corrals in the jungle. It's perfectly possible, of course, to hire a private **taxi** for the trip from Kakamega to the *Rest House* (Ksh600–800), but beware that both taxi drivers and matatu touts sometimes overcharge tourists for the run to the forest (especially if it's raining). **From Eldoret**, any bus or matatu heading towards Kisumu via Kapsabet, Chavakali and Maragoli will pass the turning for Isecheno at **Chepsonoi**, signposted "Kisieni 12km D267". From the junction it takes about three hours to walk through the gorgeous forest scenery to the *Rest House*.

Accommodation

If you're not fussed about luxury, the wooden **Forest Rest House** is a delight. Someone writing in the visitor's book calls it a "budget *Treetops*", a description that scarcely does it justice. Ringed by forest, the *Rest House* has just four first-floor two-bed rooms, with a long verandah facing onto the wall of tropical greenery a few metres away. There are blankets and pillows but no sheets, and you might bring an extra blanket or sleeping bag as it can get decidedly chilly early in the morning. Water supplies are somewhat erratic. When the pump is working, each room has a functioning bathroom and toilet, otherwise you have to fetch water from the pumphouse. There's no electricity and the closest reliable *dukas* are about 3km away on the road to Shinyalu, so it's best to bring your own supplies. For candles and simple staples – bananas, chai, mineral water, biscuits, sodas and occasional beers – there's a small *duka*/canteen on the way to the pumphouse, which is open daily. Here hot meals are cooked to order (given a few hours' notice); apart from breakfast, the food is generous, reliable and very fresh, and a much better bet than struggling to build your own cooking fire in the campsite or underneath the *Rest House* itself (during the wet season it can rain for days on end).

To be sure of a room – especially at weekends – you can **reserve in advance** (write to: The Forester, PO Box 2731 Kakamega, Western Province; rates are very economical, at around Ksh200). Alternatively, you can **camp** at the site next to the *Rest House*, or even underneath it (Ksh127 per person), but don't leave tents unattended. In dire straits, other arrangements can be made locally (ask Susie in the canteen about her *bandas*): Kakamega Forest is becoming popular.

There are two alternatives to the *Rest House*. The upmarket option is the **Rondo Retreat Centre**, a fine old 1928 sawmiller's house (location for much of the filming of Harry Hook's *The Kitchen Toto*) about 4km east of the *Rest House* turning (reservations c/o Trinity Fellowship, PO Box 2153 Kakamega ℡0331/30268, ℻20145, ✉T-FRONDO@maf.org; no phone at the centre; FB ➐). This is a comfortable base: very fresh and elegant, furnished like an English country house with just enough clutter to make it feel homely, and wonderful bright four-poster bedrooms. Crowned cranes strut about on the cool lawns. The dining room is open to non-residents when the hotel is not fully booked,

"Keep our forest"

Building on groundwork laid by the Kenya Indigenous Forest Conservation Project, the **Kakamega Environmental Education Programme** (KEEP) was set up by the guides at *Forest Rest House* to co-ordinate environmental educational programmes to primary and secondary school children from the local area. This combines lessons with visits to the forest, and it is hoped that by convincing the children of the importance of protecting and preserving the forest, the message will be passed to their parents and other family members. They've started a tree nursery to demonstrate to the children some basic tree-planting techniques, as well as giving information on how to recycle waste paper, tins and so on. If enough sponsorship is raised, there are plans to build an office and hall for educational purposes, and to establish a reference library.

They're especially keen to involve environmentalists and other experts in their effort: "to give us ideas, material and mental assistance for our project". You can also become a "Friend of KEEP" for a subscription of Ksh1500 per year. If you're interested in joining, or can offer any other help, contact Wilberforce Okeka, c/o Kakamega Forest Station, PO Box 88 Kakamega, or meet up with him at *Forest Rest House*.

but the Christian management does not serve alcohol. Arrangements can be made to collect guests from Kakamega town or even Kisumu. Again, the way to get here without your own transport is by matatu to Shinyalu and *boda-boda* or on foot from there. Much less formal, and a deal cheaper, but a few kilometres out of the forest, is the delightful Swedish-run **Rivendell Gardens**, 1.5km south of Shinyalu, 500m off the track to Khayega (reservations advisable: PO Box 1136 Kakamega ☎0331/41316, ℗02/724900, Ⓔlwanga @wananchi.com; ❷). Run by Gunilla Fagerholm and Bertil Lindström, *Rivendell* is a welcoming and relaxed retreat, with an old-looking but actually brand-new wooden ranch house (where you're free to use the living room with the family), a few guest *bandas* (not yet s/c; there will be six eventually) in the gardens, and heaps of things to keep you entertained: Scrabble, videos, and rabbits for the children; a trip around the heavens on a telescope; another telescope for bird-watching (at least forty species from the verandah); guides to Kakamega Forest; and fascinating trips to nearby villages. Their food is excellent, too, with vegetarians well catered for (try the banana flour burgers), though you need to book a day ahead if you just want to drop in for lunch (Ksh500). There's no electricity in the *bandas*, just hurricane lamps and candles. Wonderfully romantic, even if the occasional "moonshine concerts" on the balcony (Vivaldi, Mozart and Streisand belting from the stereo) are a bit cheesy. Camping is allowed (Ksh200 per tent), and they can pick you up from Kakamega or Kayega.

Kakamega Forest National Reserve

Some 20km north of Kakamega town, there are two turnings off to the right: one is signposted to the Kakamega Forest National Reserve; the other, 50m further on, is signposted "Kenya Wildlife Service Kisere Nature Reserve 6km" and "Kambiri 7km D267". It's the first track you want. The Kakamega Forest National Reserve Forest Station is 2–3km along the way and you can pick up a guide (belonging to the Kakamega Biodiversity Tour Conservations Operators) to help you orientate yourself if you wish, though they have in the past been prone to overcharging (see over). Women on their own might prefer to take a guide from the *Forest Rest House* anyway.

For visitors with their own vehicles, it's easier to get around this part of Kakamega Forest than the central zone. The forest proper is, in fact, a fair walk from the base of the KWS-run *Udo's Bandas and Campsite* (❷), named after the ornithologist Udo Savalli. Here there are seven thatched *rondavels* (soon to be upgraded), sleeping one or two people each, and a stream for fresh water, but no food (book through the Kenya Wildlife Service District Warden, PO Box 879 Kakamega ☎0331/20425 or 30603). You can also camp ($2). As in the central district, all visitors, whether staying or just there for the day, are asked to make a contribution to the forest conservation programme, although this is optional – a recent scam involved charging visitors an "entrance fee" of Ksh100 for every walk they made, guided or not. At present, there is no official fee for entrance to the reserve, though you will of course be charged for a guide, and you can demand an official KWS receipt if you think you're being conned.

A number of driveable – and walkable – tracks through the coolness of the forest begin just beyond the forest station. The main trail is well signposted and there are numerous branches and "exit" trails that allow for a relatively quick return when you've had enough of the deep forest. It's not a place you're likely to get lost in, despite its remoteness.

The significant difference between the reserve here and the forest further south is the age of the growth in the reserve. Many of the **trees** are colossal (indeed some have plaques inviting you to guess the girth – answers round the back). The climate is generally drier and there's a greater diversity of habitat, including areas of scrub, young forest and ancient forest. It's an impressive area and, as in the southern forest, there's a huge variety of birdlife and many monkeys.

An easy excursion from the forest station is to the **Isiukhu Falls**, a rather feeble waterfall 1.5km away along a rocky path. **Buyangu Hill viewpoint**, a four-kilometre drive or walk from the forest station, is much more worthwhile – a precipice with a spectacular vista east across the forest to the Nandi Escarpment.

The **Kisere Forest Reserve** (as signposted at the turn-off) is a separate area, a small outlying part of the main reserve and home to de Brazza's monkeys among others, with some superb examples of the prized timber tree, the Elgon olive.

Onwards from Kakamega

The obvious routes out of the area lie along the A1 to Kitale or Kisumu. The road **down to Kisumu** is a real roller-coaster, though in relatively good condition (occasional patches of pot-holes), with a final eight-kilometre descent over the picturesque, boulder-strewn Nyando Escarpment, which brings Lake Victoria into view. In clear weather, it allows fantastic panoramas across the sugar fields of the Kano plains towards the massif of the Mau and the Kisii hills. Look out for the florid **church** on the left, the headquarters of a local denomination that models itself on the Coptic church, founded in Egypt in the early years of Christianity.

Alternatively, there's a beautiful road **east to Kapsabet** in the Nandi Hills, starting at the bustling rural centre of Maragoli/Chavakali (also spelled Chyvakali and Kyavakali), along the Kisumu road. Note that Maragoli is the "shopping centre" on the A1, while Chavakali, effectively part of the same community, is a kilometre or so off to the east.

Lastly, if you have time and inclination for a diversion far off any beaten track, you could visit the small town of **Mumias**, the sugar belt's biggest processing centre and also one of western Kenya's Muslim strongholds. The road from Kakamega is paved and there's regular transport.

Mumias

MUMIAS was originally *Mumia's*, one of the more important up-country centres, capital of the Luhya-speaking mini-state of **Wanga**, and well established by the middle of the nineteenth century at the head of an important caravan route to the coast. **King Mumia**, who came to power in 1880, was the last King of Wanga. He inherited an army of 10,000 soldiers, half of whom were dispossessed Maasai from the Uasin Gishu Plateau known as the Kwavi. It was this army that was largely responsible for the smashing of Bukusu resistance at Chetambe's Fort fifteen years later (see p.350).

Even at the beginning of Mumia's reign, Europeans were beginning to arrive in the wake of Arab and Swahili slave-traders, who in turn had been settling in since the 1850s with the full accord of the Wanga royal family. The first was Joseph Thomson in 1883, and by 1894 there was a permanent British sub-commissioner or collector of taxes posted here. Mumia had always welcomed strangers, and he allowed the slavers to continue their work on other groups of the Luhya (notably the Bukusu), but he was unprepared for the swift usurpation of his authority by the British, whom he'd assumed were also there to trade. He was appointed "Paramount Chief" of a gradually diminishing state and then, as an old man, was retired without his real knowledge. He died in 1949, aged 100, and with him expired Kenya's first (and only) indigenous, up-country state, almost without notice.

The town's present **mosque** was built in King Mumia's honour and its Koran school is just one of about 25 around the town. Mumias has long been a centre of Islam, famous for its coastal ways, but today women in *buibuis* – the long, black coverall of the coast – are rarely seen. According to the chairman of the Mumias Koran Schools Committee, Islam is losing ground to Catholicism because of sectarian quarrelling between Muslim leaders and because, while mission and government education have an equal standing, the *madrassas* must take second place after school hours. If you're interested, Mumias Mission has published a slim pamphlet outlining their side of the story, and the Catholic church is quite an impressive old building.

The Butere–Kisumu train

Leaving Mumias, a paved road leads directly to Kisumu. There was an alternative in the form of a daily **train from Butere**, 12km down the road. This branch line was intended to reach Mumias, but never did. The train service was suspended at last check, along with the train between Kisumu and Nairobi which connected with it, but Kenya Railways does intend to reinstate it, so it might be worth checking if you are interested. Though not steam-hauled since 1988, the train was nearly as slow when diesel-hauled, taking more than three hours to cover barely 60km, but it was a boon to rural dwellers with more time than money, as a ticket (third-class only) cost a mere Ksh38.

Travel details

Kisumu is the west's transport centre. Buses and matatus run from there to most major centres in this chapter within half a day.

Buses

Bungoma to: Nairobi (several daily; 6hr); Kisumu (several daily; 2hr); Mombasa (1 daily; 12hr).

Eldoret to: Nairobi (approximately hourly; 5hr); Kampala (2 daily; 6hr); Kabernet (1 daily; 2hr); Kericho (4 daily; 5hr); Kisumu (4 daily; 3hr); Kitale (approximately hourly; 1hr 30min); Malaba (2 daily; 3hr); Nakuru (approximately hourly; 2hr 30min).

Kakamega to: Nairobi (5 daily; 7–9hr) via Kisumu and Kericho, or via Kapsabet and Nandi Hills; Bungoma (1 daily; 2hr) via Mumias (1hr); Mombasa (1 daily; 14hr).

Kericho to: Nairobi (frequent; 6hr); Kisumu (sever-al daily; 2hr); Kisii (frequent; 3hr).

Kisii to: Kisumu numerous daily runs (2hr); Mombasa (2 daily; 14hr); Migori (several daily; 2hr); Homa Bay (several daily; 2hr); Nairobi (sever-al daily; 7–9hr) via Kericho.

Kisumu to: Eldoret (4 daily; 2hr) via Kapsabet (1hr 15min); Kakamega (2 daily; 2hr); Mombasa (1 daily; 12hr); Nairobi (frequent; 8hr) via Kericho (2hr) and Nakuru (4–5hr).

Kitale to: Nairobi (several services daily and overnight; 8–11hr) via Eldoret (1hr 30min) and Nakuru (4hr).

Matatus

With nearly half the population of Kenya living in this region, matatus are widespread and most minor roads have services. Many also run on bus routes at approximately the same fare, but to even less predictable schedules. As usual, Peugeots move faster than Nissan minibuses, which are faster than vans. Slower vehicles are safer.

Bungoma to: Nairobi (6hr); Busia (45min); Eldoret (2hr); Kimili (30min); Malaba (30min); Nakuru (5hr); Wembuye (30min).

Eldoret to: Nairobi (4–6hr); Iten (30min); Kabarnet (1hr 30min); Kakamega (2hr); Kaptagat (20min); Kericho (2hr); Kisumu (2hr); Kitale (1hr); Lodwar (6hr); Malaba (2hr 30min); Mumias (2hr 30min); Nakuru (3hr); Soy (20min).

Homa Bay to: Rongo (30min); Kendu Bay (1hr 30min); Kisii (1hr); Mbita (2hr); Migori (1hr 30min).

Kisii to: Homa Bay (1hr); Kericho (2hr 30min); Kisumu (2hr); Migori (1hr 30min); Rongo (30min).

Kisumu to: Nairobi (5–6 hr); Eldoret (2hr); Kakamega (1hr); Kendu Bay (1hr 30min); Kericho (1hr 30min); Kisii (2hr); Kitale (3hr); Nakuru (3hr).

Kitale to: Nairobi (5–7hr); Busia (3hr); Eldoret (1hr); Endebess (30min); Kakamega (3hr); Kimilili (45min); Kiminini (20min); Kisumu (3hr); Lodwar (4–5hr); Lokichokio (6hr); Makutano (for Kapenguria) (30min); Malaba (2hr 30min); Suam (45min).

Trains

Passenger services from Kisumu to Nairobi are expected to resume in 2002. For information if the situation changes, contact Kenya Railways in Kisumu on ☏035/42211, or in Nakuru on ☏037/212211.

Ferries

Kisumu to: Asembo (2 weekly; 8hr) via Kendu Bay (2hr), Kuwuor (3hr), Homa Bay (4hr) and Mbita (6hr). There are currently no ferries to Uganda or Tanzania. There are however matatu-style engine-boat services from Mbita to various ports on Mfangano Island (see p.315).

Flights

Eldoret to: Nairobi (13 weekly; 1hr); Kisumu (1 weekly; 20min).

Kisumu to: Nairobi (25 weekly; 1hr).

Onward connections nationwide from Nairobi (total journey time Eldoret or Kisumu to Mombasa 3hr 30min).

5

The Mombasa Road and major game parks

CHAPTER 5

Highlights

✳ **The Taita Hills** Steep and densely cultivated, the untouristy Taita Hills are like an outcrop of up-country highland Kenya, peaking out of the dry plains. Visit the skull caves, rock niches where the heads of Taita ancestors are interred. See p.379

✳ **Mzima Springs** A remarkable oasis, bubbling with crystal-clear water and inhabited by hippos, crocodiles and a diversity of smaller species. Check out the walkways and underwater viewing chamber. See p.394

✳ **Tsavo East National Park** Vast and empty park, except for the plentiful elephants, offering spectacular vistas and relatively easy access. See p.396

✳ **Maasai Mara National Reserve** At any time of the year, Kenya's most famous park yields an extraordinary diversity of wildlife, but a visit during the annual wildebeest migration can be truly awesome. See p.410

✳ **Meru National Park** After years in the tour planners' wilderness, this remote and beautiful park has recently been rehabilitated. It offers exceptional landscapes and great lodge options. See p.433

5

The Mombasa Road and major game parks

T his chapter can't really be said to deal with a region. It covers the well-travelled **route** from **Nairobi to Mombasa** and a number of detours off it, along with six of the country's **major game parks**, most within reasonably easy reach of the capital: Amboseli, Maasai Mara, Meru, Samburu-Buffalo Springs-Shaba, and Tsavo East and West.

The **Mombasa Highway** is Kenya's most important thoroughfare, yet was in amazingly bad condition even before El Niño threw a tantrum (rehabilitation work is set to continue until 2003), and with scenic interest marginal for much of the journey, the temptation is to head straight for the coast, stopping only at the **Amboseli** or **Tsavo game parks**. If you have time enough, however, and the inclination to get off the main road (a rental car is helpful), there are some rewarding diversions: east into **Akamba country** and the towns of **Machakos** and **Kitui**, or south towards the base of **Kilimanjaro** (the mass of the mountain lies across the border in Tanzania) and the **Taita Hills**. Despite the trail of safari vans towards the parks and coast, these are side roads that are not greatly explored.

The **game parks** in this chapter are, together with the coast, the most visited parts of Kenya – and the archetypal image. This is not to take anything away from their appeal. If you travel around Kenya, it would be absurd not to visit at least one of the parks, for the experience is genuinely fabulous. In the 24,000 square kilometres (10,000 square miles) covered by the six parks, animals, not humans, hold sway. Their seasonal movements, most spectacularly in **Maasai Mara**'s wildebeest migration, are the dominant plots in the drama going on all around. It's not difficult to see the wildlife, but it does require patience and an element of luck that makes it exciting – and addictive.

Summaries of the game parks' individual attractions are given in the introduction on p.386. **To visit**, most people will either already be on a safari, or will book one once in Kenya – either from the coast or from Nairobi. The increasingly popular alternative is to **rent a vehicle**, a sensible if quite expensive option if you want to have more than a few days of wildlife-viewing, and the freedom of choosing your own route. With a limited budget, a no-frills camping safari is still about the only practical way; there are more details on the ins and outs in Basics, pp.45–46, and plenty of operators listed at the end of the Nairobi and Mombasa sections (pp.140–143). It remains possible, though by no means easy, to explore the parks by **hitching around** with whoever you meet and **camping** at designated sites. More specific details are included in the sections on each park.

Between Nairobi and the coast

If you take one of the **express buses** for your journey down from Nairobi to Mombasa, you might well end up believing that there's nothing worth stopping for along the way and, if you take the **train**, you won't see anything anyway as it travels in both directions at night. On the other hand, with a little touch of imagination and, ideally, the luxury of a hired vehicle of some kind for covering the parks, this stretch of the country has a great deal to offer. And any detour into the less well-known parts of **Kamba territory** or down to

Taveta and the foothills of **Kilimanjaro** should prove a worthwhile antidote to the more purple-rinse excesses of safari-land.

Machakos and Kitui – "Ukambani"

One very good way to start a trip heading towards the coast, if you're in no particular hurry, is to take an excursion right into the heart of **Ukambani**, the

The Akamba

The largely dry stretch of central Kenya from Nairobi to Tsavo park and north as far as Embu has been the traditional homeland of the Akamba people for at least the last five centuries. They moved here from the regions to the south in a series of vague migrations, in search, according to legend, of the life-saving **baobab** tree whose fruit staved off the worst famines, and whose trunks held vast quantities of water.

With a diverse economy in better years, including mixed farming and herding as well as hunting and gathering, the Akamba slowly coalesced into a distinct tribe with one Bantu language. As they settled in the hilly parts, the population increased. But drier areas at lower altitudes couldn't sustain the expansion, so **trade** for food with the Kikuyu peoples in the fatter highlands region became a solution to the vagaries of their generally implacable environment.

In return for farm produce, the Akamba **bartered** their own manufactured goods: medicinal charms, extra-strong beer, honey, iron tools, arrowheads and a lethal and much sought-after hunting poison. In the eighteenth and nineteenth centuries, as the Swahili on the coast strengthened their ties inland, **ivory** became the most important commodity in the trade network. With it, the Akamba obtained goods from overseas to exchange for food stocks with the highlands tribes.

Long the **intermediaries** between coast and up-country, acting as guides to Swahili and Arab caravans, leading their own expeditions and settling in small numbers in many parts of what is now Kenya, the Akamba were naturally enlisted by early European arrivals in East Africa. Their broad cultural base and lack of provincialism made them confident travellers and employees, and willing **soldiers and porters**. Even today, the Kenyan army has a disproportionately high Akamba contingent, while many others work as policemen and private *askaris*.

In the early years of **colonialism**, the Akamba were involved in occasional bloody incidents, but these seem to have been more often the result of misunderstandings than anything concerted. The most famous of these blew up after an ignorant official at Machakos cut down a sacred *ithembo* tree to use as a flagpole. On the whole, the Akamba's old trade links helped to ease their relations with the British. Living – and dying – with British soldiers during **World War I** gave them insights into the ways of the Europeans who now ruled them. Together with the Luo and Kikuyu, the Akamba suffered tens of thousands of casualties in white men's wars.

Akamba **resistance to colonialism** was widespread but mostly non-violent. As early as 1911, however, a movement of total European rejection had emerged. Led by a widow named Siotune wa Kathake, it channelled opposition to colonialism into frenetic dancing, during which teenage girls became "possessed" by an anti-European spirit and preached radical messages of non-compliance with the government. Later, in the 1930s, the Ukamba Members Association (one of whose leaders was **Muindi Mbingu**) was formed in order to pre-empt efforts to settle Europeans in Ukambani and reduce Akamba cattle herds by compulsory purchase. Five thousand Akamba marched in peaceful protest to Kariokor Market in Nairobi – a show of collective political will that succeeded in getting their cattle returned.

land of the Akamba people (adjective and language: Kamba). Buses, matatus and Peugeot taxis leave from Nairobi's Country Bus Station (aka "Machakos Airport") for Machakos all the time, although what used to be a journey of a little over thirty minutes is more likely to take ninety minutes, thanks to vastly increased traffic along the two-lane Mombasa Road. In addition, there's also at least one company that runs a daily Nairobi–Mombasa service by way of the town. From Machakos, frequent buses and matatus continue to Kitui, from where you could catch transport to Kibwezi, back on the Mombasa Road.

Machakos

The Imperial British East African Company's first up-country post, established in 1889, **MACHAKOS** is ten years older than Nairobi (and therefore the first capital of Kenya according to some Akamba people) and is, in comparison, a striking indication of the capital's rapid growth. "Machakos" is really a corruption of Masaku's, after the headquarters of an Akamba chief of the time. The name is still seen all over town.

Distinctly friendly, and overwhelmingly Kamba, the town has a backdrop of green hills and a tree-shaded, relaxed atmosphere to its old buildings that is quickly endearing, despite the evident poverty in the fringing slums and the rubbish piled up around seemingly every street corner – a sight common to most Kenyan towns. The surrounding Mua Hills have lent their name to a brand of jam from the orchards which thrive on their slopes. The weaving of **sisal baskets** (*vyondo*) is a more visible industry, though, and a major occupation for many women, either full-time or behind the vegetable stand. Machakos effervesces and it's a great place to stay for a day or two, especially on Monday and Friday, market days, and above all if you are into buying some *vyondo* (baskets). Look for (though you can scarcely miss) the truly splendid and quite venerable **mosque**.

Practicalities

Apart from the many produce markets scattered about town, there are two **supermarkets**: Nafuu and Nova (both open Mon–Sat 8am–8pm & Sun 9am–6pm). The Barclays and Standard Chartered **banks** have ATMs. **Emails** can be sent from Creative Edge (PO Box 2319 ☎0145/21139), no browsing (Ksh50 per email sent & Ksh20 per email received). For **buses and matatus** to Nairobi and Mombasa, head for the main stage in the centre of town. For services to Kitui (with connections there for Embu), the stage is just up on the Embu road, beside the noisy *jua kali* metal workers' area.

The town is rarely visited by tourists, but accommodation and meals are easy. Machakos has the usual range of **eating places**, few of them gastronomically enticing. Two of the best are the enjoyable *Kenny's Boiling Pot*, in the same building as *Masaku Lodge*, with its balcony overlooking the street; and the *T. Tot Hotel*, popular with expats and serving good samosas, *chai* and passion-fruit juice. *The Place* is new and cheap (Ksh300 for a large roast chicken), but its bar, crowded with Tusker beer posters and tables draped in glistening plastic covers, is off putting. *Classic Café*, near *Kenny's*, is more inviting and serves a variety of African dishes. Worth trying is their *bahazi*. As for **hotels**, the *Masaku Lodge* (PO Box 274 ☎0145/21745; singles only; ❶), *T. Ten* (PO Box 841 ☎0145/20157; ❶) and *Lalla Salama* by the mosque (PO Box 66 ☎0145/21198; ❶) are utterly basic B&Ls, the last with rooms ranging from rank to airy and comfortable (ask to see a selection). There are loads of other budget choices scattered throughout town. The more upmarket options are:

Garden Hotel PO Box 223 ☏0145/20037, ☏21515. Ten minutes from the town centre and overlooking the Iveti Hills, this is something of an aberration, a totally plush, muzak-piped, "international-class" hotel with a health club, sauna and steam bath. Compared to its Nairobi counterparts, a bargain. Resident Tanzanian band Everest Kings are another bonus (playing Friday and Saturday

nights, and Sunday afternoons), almost reason enough in itself to visit Machakos. D&B ❹
Ikuni Hotel PO Box 1069 ☏0145/21080. A large place with a wide range of rooms, mostly grotty and overpriced singles, but its busy restaurant makes up for it a little. They have discos Wednesday, Friday and Saturday nights, and comedians and a one-man guitar show on Sunday

afternoons. Ask for a mosquito net. B&B s/c **3**, non s/c **2**

Kafoca Club (Kenya Armed Forces Old Comrades Association) PO Box 595 ☎ 0145/21933. Despite the uninspiring name, this businessmen's hangout is well run, and fairly wholesome, with a bar and

TV-video lounge and a good restaurant with plenty of meat and fish dishes which, according to the manager, are gout proof. S/c rooms are way overpriced, but non-s/c are more reasonable. Safe parking. Bed only: s/c **3**, non-s/c **2**

Crafts

For **vyondo**, visit the outdoor **market**, or ask for the Machakos District Co-op Union, in Ngei Road, opposite the Co-op Bank. The finished articles are much cheaper without the strap (buy lengths of sisal braid and fit your own), and there are reductions if you buy several: the choice of colours is second to none. If you like the genre, it's worth buying several and posting home a parcel. In connection, the Machakos branch of the women's Maendeleo ya Wanawake organization can be contacted at PO Box 904 (☎ 0145/21600).

The Machakos miracle

The whole of Ukambani is prone to **drought** and, according to conventional environmental wisdom, its farms and plots should have blown to dust long ago, especially under ever-increasing population pressure. In the 1930s, when the population was five times less than now, a British Colonial soil inspector condemned the Ukambani Hills as "an appalling example" of environmental degradation in which "the inhabitants are rapidly shifting to a state of hopelessness and miserable poverty and their land to a parched desert of rocks, stones and sand."

Seventy years later, it would be unfair to paint the same picture. Instead of relying on cattle herding, as they did in the past, many Akamba have shifted into small-scale agriculture as a means of survival, with surprising results. You even find apples offered for sale by the roadside, an "exotic" fruit otherwise confined to the perennially rain-soaked orchards of Kisii near Lake Victoria. The trick has been the clever use of the little rain which does fall, through small-scale **terracing** and **irrigation techniques** (such as using roads for catchments) learned by Akamba soldiers while serving in India during World War II. So much for the hopelessness of the 1930s; the situation has been turned around so successfully that some have begun calling this "The Machakos Miracle".

On to Kitui

Frequent buses and matatus ply this route: the tarmac road passes through some attractive scenery, particularly as you wind down the hill out of Machakos, where high cliffs and chunky, maize-covered hills rise everywhere. **Wamunyu**, en route, was the birthplace of the modern **Kamba carving** industry, evidenced by numerous self-help and co-operative carvers' societies and their shops. Akamba men who served in World War I were introduced to the techniques of wood sculpture by the Makonde ebony carvers on the Tanganyikan coast. Today, the vast majority of carvings in Kenya are produced by Akamba artists, often in workshops far from Ukambani. In Wamunyu, some three thousand people, many of them children, eke out a living with wood carving. The main problem appears to be the middlemen, who take much of the profits: if you're after wood carvings, try to buy them direct from the people who make them. Cutting out the middlemen means they're cheaper here, and you can, with a touch of persistence, come up with your own ideas for a carving – if you have time to return at a later date to pick it up. Still, it's a disappointment that the serried ranks of identical antelopes and rhinos don't do justice to the tradition, even if it is a short one. If you want to stay here, there are a number of basic **B&Ls**, the best of which are *Manisani Guest House* in Elimu Building (PO Box 171 ☎0141/63291; ➊) and *Highway Inn Bar* (➊).

Kitui town

KITUI, like Machakos 58km to the west, lies in an impoverished area and, from time to time, is badly hit by drought, with attendant malnutrition and occasional outbreaks of cholera. Despite its proximity to Nairobi, this region at the very edge of the Highlands is one of Kenya's least developed. The town is small and hasn't any outstanding features of interest, but there's a sizeable Swahili population, descendants of the traders and travellers who crisscrossed Ukambani in the nineteenth century. The town's mango trees were planted then, and the abundance of lodging houses is a reminder of the trading tradition. Kitui was the home village of **Kivoi**, the most celebrated Akamba trader. He commanded a large following which included slaves, and it was he who met the German missionary **Ludwig Krapf** in Mombasa and guided him up to Kitui in 1849, where the European was the first to set eyes on Mount Kenya.

Despite the lack of sights (excepting perhaps Kauma Glass Mart, *the* place for drums and plastic religious icons), the town's atmosphere is the main draw, both a busy market and trading centre with streets lined with arcaded shops, yet also calm, relaxed and unhustly, and an ideal place to get away from more mundane hassles for a few days. The inhabitants are generally very friendly, and making genuine friends here seems easier than elsewhere.

Practicalities

There's nowhere to **stay** in Kitui above the budget category, and nothing much to choose between them, either. Hot water is invariably supplied in buckets. In the town centre, try: *Umau Guest House* (PO Box 202; no phone; ➊), which is friendly and has six large s/c rooms with nets and cold showers; the cleaner *Ark House* (PO Box 230 ☎0141/22461; ➊), with seven s/c rooms around a courtyard; *Kithomboani Hotel* (➊), under the same management, with thirteen cleanish s/c singles only, with nets; and *Walimu Guest House* (PO Box 3911; no phone; ➊), also s/c, nets and window screens, with the novelty of breakfast thrown in. The best location is offered by the friendly if none-too-

RESTAURANTS & CAFÉS
Parkside Hotel — C
Riverside Motel — A
Travellers Café — B
Yokozuna Café — D

ACCOMMODATION
Ark House — 2
Kithomboani Hotel — 4
Mumoni Guest House — 5
Umau Guest House — 3
Walimu Guest House — 1

Nairobi, Machakos, Embu & ➊

Shell
Total
National Bank

Matatu & Bus stage
Mwingi Express
Takrim/ Takwa Bus
Akamba Bus
KCB Bank

Clothes Market
Open Air Market
Kauma Glass Mart
Supermarket

SWAHILI QUARTER

0   100 m

➎ (2km) & Kibwezi road (B7)

clean *Mumoni Hill Lodge* (PO Box 411; no phone; ❶), 2km from the centre down the Kibwezi road just before the end of the tarmac. It's a peaceful retreat with four simple rooms with attached toilets (no showers), a relaxed and somnolent bar, and a lovely setting in large grounds planted with mango trees and plots of maize. They cook food to order, and you can **camp** here, too.

For **food**, you'll find a row of cheap eateries backing on to the Swahili quarter. Other places to try include the *Parkside Hotel*; *Travellers Café*, which has good snacks and is frequented by NGO staff; the popular *Yokozuna Café*; and the *Riverside Motel*, 1500m out of town on the Machakos road in Kalundu Market, serving especially good chicken and fish. Kitui's nightspot of the moment is *Reflections*.

If you're heading towards the coast from Kitui, apart from baobabs which sprout up sporadically on both sides of the route, the Kitui–Kibwezi road (which is nearly all *murram*) is uneventful and isolated. You're better off going back to Machakos and down the Mombasa Highway.

Akamba **buses** (☎0141/22052) have daily departures to Nairobi (8.30am) and Mombasa (7pm), both via Machakos. Takrim/Takwa Bus (☎0141/22599) has some cheap fares (Mombasa at 5pm & 6pm; Nairobi twice a day), with connections to Dar es Salaam in Tanzania. Some morning matatus leave for Embu (p.203), but catch them early unless you're happy to spend the day matatu-hopping. The road to Embu is only partially tarred to Kangonde (work recently resumed on completing this stretch), with fast tarmac and more public transport continuing from Kangonde (on the Thika–Garissa road) via Mwea National Reserve (p.204) to Embu. Scenically dreary in this direction, the road is best travelled coming south towards Kitui, where the town appears as a miraculous oasis of lush greenery after the endless miles of red dust.

The Mombasa Highway

If you travel down by **bus**, sit on the right of the vehicle for the best of the scenery, from which vantage you may, in exceptionally clear conditions, see **Kilimanjaro** (best in the morning or late afternoon), either on the stretch between the small settlements of Sultan Hamud and Kiboko, or to the west of Tsavo train station. Occasionally you'll pass troops of Baboons waiting on both sides of the road for a lull in the traffic. If you **drive** this route yourself, **be careful** – seeing large trucks with slogans such as "Don't Hunt What You Can't Kill", constantly overtaking each other, can be an unnerving experience. Well before the infamous El Niño rains made their mark, many sections of the road were badly broken up, with the result that some car rental companies now insist you take 4WD. Work by a Chinese company to resurface the road will continue until around 2003, with the Mombasa–Voi section already surfaced, though it's unlikely the new version will last much longer than its past incarnations. More seriously, the road for the most part is pot-holed, narrow and still receding at the edges, and consequently dangerous: road-users frequently encounter each other with deadly impact. **Driving at night** is ill-advised, as dipped headlights are still something of a novelty, and the highway itself has a reputation for nocturnal hold-ups and car hijacking. Though incidents seem to be few and far between, if you have to travel after dark, make sure you have a spare tyre and keep your eyes on the road for reflecting objects which may be small nail-ridden planks left by potential robbers. Also be sure to drive with a full fuel tank. **Petrol stations** appear fairly regularly at the settlements between Nairobi and

Map labels (The Nairobi–Mombasa Highway):

THE NAIROBI-MOMBASA HIGHWAY

0   100 km

N

Naivasha   Mount Kenya   Garissa

Thika   Kangundo   Mwingi

NAIROBI

Athi River   Wamunyu   Kitui

Machakos

Isinya

Magadi

Simba   Nzaui

Kajiado   Sultan Hamud

Emali   Kiboko

Makindu

AMBOSELI NATIONAL PARK   Makutano   Kibwezi

Namanga

See 'Amboseli National Park' map for detail

KIMANA WILDLIFE SANCTUARY   Mtito Andei   Tsavo Safari Camp

TSAVO EAST NATIONAL PARK

Mount Kilimanjaro   Oloitokitok   C103   Rombo   See 'Developed Area' map for detail   Tsavo   Galana River   C103

Arusha   Moshi   Lake Chala   Maktau   TAITA HILLS   Wundanyi   Voi   See 'Tsavo East' map for detail   Malindi

Taveta   Mwatate   Maungu

Lake Jipe   TAITA HILLS GAME SANCTUARY

See 'Chala & Jipe' map for detail

TANZANIA   TSAVO WEST NATIONAL PARK   TAITA/RUKINGA RANCH   Mackinnon Road   Samburu   Mariakani

Mombasa

Dar es Salaam

A104   A109   B7   C103

Voi, but supplies thereafter are not guaranteed until Mariakani, 120km further on and just 32km inland from Mombasa. The current state of the road means you should count on two days to cover Nairobi–Mombasa comfortably, though it is possible in one, exhausting, eight- to ten-hour drive. Note: there are no longer any banks or ATMs in any town along the highway.

> This section does not cover the **Amboseli** or **Tsavo national parks** – see p.402 and p.391.

Around Emali: Kibiki and Nzaui

Heading southeast from Nairobi, the road runs along the east side of Nairobi National Park, passing at its end the junction for the A104 to Athi River, Namanga, Amboseli and Tanzania, before skirting the Kapiti Plains on your right. Five kilometres after the Athi River junction, there's reasonable **accommodation** at the *Small World Country Club* (PO Box 78 Athi River ☎0150/22006; ❷), a motel–restaurant with basic self-contained *bandas*, secure parking, unexciting snacks (and painfully slow service), and a bar with a disco at weekends. Unfortunately, it smells rather strongly due to the Kenya Meat Commission's giant abattoir in the area.

The train stations

If you're desperate for water or a place to stay the night, the lonely little **train stations** dotted every 15km or so along the line are usually amenable. Station masters are often helpful and glad of a break in routine – the two trains don't exactly fill their days. If you're doing something uncommon like walking or cycling down to the coast (people have done so), the stations are oases.

After here, there's a long drive along smooth tarmac to the truckers' stopover of **Salama**, the first of many one-horse towns on the way to Mombasa, providing lodging, food and beers for truckers and lost-looking Maasai. With a few exceptions, the **B&Ls** in these places (all ❶) are very basic, far from clean and, given their clientele, not for lone women. Many double as beer-soaked 24-hour day-and-night clubs, which goes some way towards explaining the atrocious driving along the highway. The next settlement, **Sultan Hamud**, has the marginally more salubrious *Savannah House* (☎52027) and the new *Park Guest House* (☎52209; ❸), which has self-contained rooms and hot water. Further on, **Simba** has its squalid *Simba Lodge*. Before Simba, the first centre of any real significance is **EMALI**, which lies on the boundary of Maasai and Akamba territory. There's good accommodation here at the *Kindu Mall Bar* (PO Box 147 Emali ☎22 Emali; ❶), which also has an unthreatening 24-hour bar and restaurant serving tasty *nyama choma*. The *Emali New Paris Hotel* (PO Box 187; no phone; ❷) has a disco every night which ends at 1am, a large tented bar, some self-contained rooms, and communal bathrooms and toilets which are rancid. Three kilometres beyond Emali, just after the railway flyover, a sharp turn to the right marks the start of the rough mud and *murram* C102, which heads off south to Amboseli's eastern gates. Just beyond here, the small centre of **Kibiki** is the regular Friday venue for a major **cattle market** which attracts hundreds of Maasai herders, as well as Akamba people and Kenya Meat Commission buyers. It's an animated scene and worth a pause if you coincide.

A north turn from Emali leads up into the Machakos Hills with the dramatic **peak of Nzaui**. Enthusiastic reports have been received from hikers who have climbed this steep pinnacle. Without transport, you'll need a matatu ride from the Emali crossroads to Matiliku, some 15km from the main road. Nzaui rears up ahead. With luck, you'll find some schoolchildren to guide you up – it's a popular local trip. From the top of the 500-metre precipices on the south face there are sweeping views across the Kamba and Maasai plains to Mount Kilimanjaro. If you have a vehicle, there's also a lazy way up Nzaui from the north, approached near the village of Nziu, further along the same road.

Kiboko and Makindu

There's good **accommodation** at the petrol station oasis of **KIBOKO**, 160km from Nairobi, in the shape of **Hunter's Lodge** (PO Box 77 Makindu; reservations through Mada Holdings, Kimathi House, Kimathi St, PO Box 40683 Nairobi ☎02/221439, ☎332170; B&B ❹). Named after the J.A. Hunter of rhino-potting notoriety (p.401), this promises a lot as a place to stay, with its acacia-backed garden on the banks of the dammed Kiboko (Hippo) River, a tranquil birdlife haven over on the other side. The "old rooms" are nothing special for the money, service is sluggish, and the food can be quite ordinary; however, the "new rooms" have verandahs overlooking the small reservoir, which more or less makes up for everything. Ask nicely and they'll probably allow you to camp. It's also a good place to hitch lifts. In town there's *Wamu Bar* (PO Box 144 Kiboko ☎030/22381; ❶), very clean basic lodgings, with toilets outside the compound (you have to get the keys to use them). The bar is dull, but you can bring your own tapes and the large selection of beers provides entertainment.

Back on the main highway, twenty minutes east of *Hunter's Lodge*, you pass the ostentatious Sikh temple at **MAKINDU**, sometimes strung with what look like Christmas lights, and prettily unmistakable. They give a warm welcome here to travellers who want to stay, on the usual understanding (leave a donation). Of the B&Ls, *Villa Park Lodge* is a reasonable choice.

Thirteen kilometres further on is the **Makindu Handicrafts Co-operative**, which has blossomed in recent years to provide work for almost fifty active members. Fifteen percent of the takings go to run the place and buy wood; the remainder is divided equally among the carvers. You can watch and photograph members at work, though it has to be said many of their carvings are fairly obnoxious, with "Maasai maidens" and similar panderings more and more prominent. Still, they know their market and the set-up obviously suits the co-op members. There are some nice pieces among the tour-bus fodder, but for a more personal souvenir, the rejects heaped up outside the shop are better value and have more character than the polished creations within.

The road from here on to Mtito Andei is unusually scenic, with grand, sweeping views south over the Chyulu Hills and glimpses of lava flows and strange rock outcrops just to the north. Large, fantastic **baobabs** dot this stretch of the highway, some, it is said, over a thousand years old. In the past, they were credited with all manner of spiritual powers and associations, and oral history has it that they attracted the Akamba to this area by the sponge-like centres of their trunks, which can hold huge amounts of water and are a vital source of liquid during droughts. As to their strange, ungainly appearance, some legends tell that the baobabs used to be in the habit of walking around the countryside on their roots, until one day God got fed up with their peregrinations and resolved to keep them forever rooted to the soil, by replanting them upside down. In the low evening sunlight, the baobabs, and the colourfully dressed Akamba women working the tiny plots of maize nestled between them, are one of the highway's most beautiful sights.

Kibwezi

KIBWEZI is a small Akamba trading centre off the main road at the B7 Kitui junction. The best **accommodation** here is the *MSIP Guest House* (also called the *Danida Guest House*, PO Box 65 Kibwezi ☎98 Kibwezi; bed only ❷), in a pleasantly shaded, tranquil location: follow the signposts from town for 2km. Formerly the headquarters of a Danish irrigation project, it's a friendly stopover, with clean, carpeted s/c rooms with nets, hurricane lamps (electricity only arrived in town in 1998) and cheap food to order. In town, the *New Face Hoteli* offers good food and fantastic murals. Kibwezi also boasts a small **market** where you can occasionally buy spiky green **soursops** – one of those fruits you either love or loathe. The town is also known for its **honey**, which you'll be offered by countless sellers along the road. When it's good, it's delicious, but try it before buying as some is adulterated with sugar syrup. The art of beekeeping is a Kamba speciality but local custom varies – the honey often has a smokey taste after the bees have been smoked out when the keepers collect it. Bottom price is about Ksh120 for a wine-bottleful. In and around **Kinyambu**, 16km from Kibwezi, you'll see thirty or so grass and brick huts, distinguishable from human dwellings by their lack of windows. Each hut contains up to ten hives, owned and tended by a number of local women's co-operatives, together called "The Kibwezi Honey Project". Along this stretch of the main highway you might also see Maasai cattle herders, here at the northernmost limits of their territory, a strange pastoral contrast with the trucks and buses thundering by.

Mtito Andei to Tsavo

A big sprawl of service stations and snackeries rises out of the dry country at the start of **Tsavo National Park**; it marks **MTITO ANDEI** (which means "Vulture Forest", sometimes softened to "Eagle Forest"). The *Tsavo Inn* (PO Box 20 ☎0147/30342), by the Caltex garage, is a pleasant enough retreat if you don't mind the odd missing bath plug, with a tempting pool (Ksh120 for casual guests), but is overpriced for non-residents: *Rough Guide* readers get resident's rates – just show your copy. **Rooms** in the bungalow rows are large if a little frayed, but have nets and baths (B&B ❹ residents, ❺ non-residents). Don't miss the fascinating 1963 Michelin map in the lobby (there was no tarmac at all to Mombasa in those days). **Camping** should be possible at the gate to Tsavo West National Park (see p.391), 500m away, which is also the best place to try **hitching a lift** around the park. If you're driving, there's a beautiful **campsite** *(Kamunyu Camp)* an hour's drive – 27km – east of Mtito Andei on the banks of the Athi River, but you'll need to get directions from the Total station in town. If you want a cheap lodging in town, try the *Okay Safari Lodge* (PO Box 34 ☎0147/30120; ❶), clean and basic but loud, and OK for a cold beer or three.

The road between Mtito Andei and Voi has only been partially resurfaced, and the diversion is incredibly dusty – roll up your windows. The only place to get anything to **eat** along here is at **Manyani**, 2km past Manyani Gate for Tsavo East National Park. It has a number of very basic *dukas* and *hotelis* serving *githeri* and *ugali* to weary travellers. There's no guarantee of fuel here or at the almost derelict *Maneaters' Motel* (no rooms), by the gulch of the Tsavo River just after Tsavo Gate for Tsavo West National Park (*tsavo* is Kamba for "slaughter"). On the opposite, north bank, there's the *Riverside* **campsite**, 500m from the gate – you should be extremely wary of the baboons here as someone who was foolish enough to feed them died after he was savagely mauled. The campsite and motel are in the vicinity of the famous **man-eating lions** that played havoc with the building of the railway in 1898. The two lions seem to have been preternaturally lucky, since they eluded Colonel Patterson's various weapons for nearly a year and ate 28 Indian labourers in that time, as well as the unfortunate Superintendent C. H. Ryall who was dragged off a train carriage by the man-eaters during the hunt. The Field Museum in Chicago has the two stuffed man-eaters on display, and in 1998 organized an absurd research project to some nearby caves, where they had hoped to obtain the remains of Ryall himself: they found nothing. You won't see lions either, but along this section of the road through Tsavo park you may well come across **elephants**. Always a brick-red colour from the soil, they used to be one of the commonest animals on the road, but increased traffic and the gradual erosion of their habitat (by herders, agriculture and the elephants themselves) means you have to be a little lucky to see them.

Voi

The sight of so many school children in **VOI**, as opposed to street kids, is refreshing if you have just been travelling through the Central Highlands and the Rift

Valley. It's 5km outside the main gate to Tsavo East National Park, at the junction for the Taita Hills and Taveta, and is the only sizeable town between Machakos and Mombasa. With new roads being built and lodgings and shops springing up everywhere, the place is fast becoming the best town to stop off for tourists on their way to the coast, parks or Nairobi. If you have time to kill, check out the **sisal factory**. You can watch the whole simple process from the crushing of the sisal spikes, through drying and combing, to the final twisting into rope. The town's **market days** are Tuesday and Friday. There are plenty of petrol stations (but Barclay's Bank has closed and there's no ATM in town), a small supermarket and pharmacy (both in the shopping complex under the *Tsavo Park Hotel*), and plenty of cheap *hotelis*. There are several excellent **cheap lodgings**.

Ghana Guest House PO Box 492 ☏0147/30291. A basic little place, 500m from the centre on the northside slip road, but friendly and run by women, clean and peaceful (no bar), with some s/c rooms (hot showers), all with nets. ❶

Jumbo Guest House PO Box 579 ☏0147/2503. Next to the market square and bus park. Can be noisy, but cheap enough considering it offers s/c rooms. ❷

Lady Diana Lodge PO Box 368 ☏0147/2534. A red building stuck in the middle of a sisal field, 2.5km out on the Mtito Andei road, this has cheap, breezy rooms with good views and nets (but only one s/c, with hot water in buckets), food to order (including *nyama choma*), and a disco Friday and Saturday. A taxi out here costs around Ksh150. The *Ikanga Travellers Lodge* on the main road nearby is squalid, but plays good reggae in its bar. ❶

Silent Guest Resort PO Box 143 Voi ☏0147/30112, ☏2727. A well-run hotel in a modern complex opposite the bus park and Mobil petrol station, with s/c and non s/c singles, doubles and triples. Very clean with TV, satellite, fans and nets in every room. A wide variety of continental and Indian meals, including theme buffets. Recommended. ❹

Tsavo Park Hotel PO Box 244 ☏0147/30050, ☏30285. Right by the bus stop beside the GPO, new and utterly anomalous, this is a surprisingly plush international-standard hotel, with very well-appointed and spotless rooms, all with balconies, nets, fans and phones, and satellite TVs planned. There's a gift shop and forex, safe parking, and a (soundproofed) disco underneath. Very swish restaurant (mainly European fare), and cheapish buffet lunches (Ksh450 per person). B&B ❹

Vuria Lodging PO Box 29 ☏0147/2269. 600m from the bus station, with fans, mosquito nets and real toilets, and a bar downstairs. ❶

The Sagala Hills

An unusual day-trip from Voi – with some lovely walking country largely unvisited by tourists – is the **Sagala Hills**, which rise just south of Voi. Five matatus run daily from town to **Sagala village**, 20km away, a small rural centre with little more than a store, a small *hoteli* serving nice *chai* and chicken, and a bar opposite the football field. From Sagala, you'll need a local to guide you around – children will be happy to oblige. A 45-minute walk takes you past a small bridge to the even smaller settlement of **Talio**, which has wonderful views of the Taita Hills, Mount Kasigau and the savannah below. There's a small store selling toilet paper, chewing gum and sodas. From here, small paths lead off through the green fields to the base of the hills (1–2hr) where there are other little villages. Apart from some steep rocks which are used by climbers from time to time, and occasional sightings of baboon or mongoose, the main attraction here is the impression of a timeless rural existence yet to be tainted by modernity. Visitors are rare, so please be tactful, especially with a camera, and be generous with your time. In Talio itself, you can either **stay** locally (someone should be happy to earn a few bob by putting you up), or you can pitch a tent somewhere – ask at the school.

Moving on

Leaving Voi, the **train** to Mombasa (1st class Ksh1410, 2nd Ksh1130, 3rd Ksh95) departs at 4.11am; in the other direction, the Nairobi-bound train (1st class Ksh2100, 2nd Ksh1475, 3rd Ksh210) passes through town at 11pm. The station (☏0147/30435) is five minutes' walk south of the market. The four-times-weekly train to Taveta is suspended, with little likelihood of a resumption of service. **Buses** come in all day for both Nairobi and Mombasa, with some (Malindi Bus) continuing on to Malindi. There are at least two daily buses to Taveta, with additional overnight services coinciding with Taveta's market days on Wednesday and Saturday, as well as some matatus. Wundanyi in the Taita Hills is served by several matatus a day, the last leaving around 5pm. For descriptions of Taveta and the Taita Hills, see pp.379–386.

To the coast

After Voi, the road veers across the relentless **Maungu Plains**, also known as the Taru Desert, a plateau of "wait-a-bit" thorn and occasional baobabs which forms the migratory corridor for wildlife passing from Tsavo East to the foothills of Kilimanjaro. Dull and scenically dreary for much of the year, after heavy rains the plains come alive with colour, and during May and June can be carpeted in white-and-blue convolvulus flowers. Before you get away from the Voi area completely, look out for Kenya's weirdest roadsign, some 14km to the south on the left, erected by the local Round Table association: "The world 24 hours pram pushing record was set here 10th January 1972 – Distance 249.7

Taita and Rukinga wildlife conservancy

Twenty-five kilometres east of Maungu, a right turn opposite Tsavo East's Buchuma Gate (signposted "Taita Ranch HQ") heads off a dusty 16km to **Galla Camp** (PO Box 630 Voi; no phone; reservations through Savannah Camps & Lodges, p.44), gorgeously sited on an exposed *kopje* (eroded rock promontory) scampered over by rock hyrax fearful of the eagles circling overhead. The views are spectacular, with a 360-degree panorama over Taita and Rukinga ranches, the Taita Hills and the distant foothills of Kilimanjaro. Whilst intended primarily for pre-booked visitors on expensive all-inclusive packages (❾, including game drives), it's also possible simply to drop in unannounced and pay much cheaper rates for self-catering bed space in the permanent tents (❺). Though rather basic by usual "luxury tented camp" standards, it's comfortable enough, and the views, informal atmosphere, as well as the silence, make for a very relaxing stop-over between Mombasa and Nairobi. If you're not driving, ring Savannah to arrange transport; they can even pick you up from the night train at Voi.

The ranches are part of a privately run venture which aims to protect wildlife by involving tourists and researchers. The combined area of 680 square kilometres is strategically placed on the migration route of plains game, elephant and lion from the Galana River in Tsavo East to the foothills of Kilimanjaro in Tsavo West. Despite the thickness of the bush, spotting elephants is usually easy (especially from the vantage of the *kopje*), and the nearby water hole – intended primarily for the cattle corral nearby – also attracts baboon, buffalo, gazelle and occasional cheetah and lion. The staff are happy to guide you on walks.

The main purpose of the camp, however, is as a base for visiting the new **Taita Discovery Centre**, 16km west in the neighbouring Rukinga Ranch (access also along 16km of dirt track from Maungu, signposted "Rukinga Ranch") – which is a hands-on educational project with a visitor centre comprising a butterfly farm, live animal house, museum and library, and lab facilities for research students. You can stay there in the bunk-bedded *bandas* (self-catering ❹), or can **camp** in your own tent. There are showers and a bar. Information on the **field courses** (which seem very well thought out, with plenty of variety) from Savannah Camps & Lodges.

miles from start." A kilometre further on, a signposted track on the right takes you to *Maungu Safari Lodge* (PO Box 3 Voi ☎0147/30264; B&B ❸), a pleasingly decrepit colonial-style place (electricity evenings only, if you're lucky), with seventeen s/c **cottages** with nets, and virtually no guests. Some rooms are tatty, others have huge beds, and there's a swimming pool.

The roadstead of **Maungu** itself, roughly 25km from Voi, has two B&Ls, the better one being the *Susana Lodge* (PO Box 225 Voi ☎0147/30260; ❶), with some very basic s/c rooms, usually with clean beds if not much else, and no electricity or nets. It prides itself, bizarrely, on its hot beers. Ten kilometres down a rough signposted track from Maungu is the ostensibly much posher *Westermann's Safari Camp* (PO Box 88552 Mombasa ☎011/472155; HB ❺), which unfortunately is not very appealing, with tiny, dark chalets, no power and little atmosphere. Its guests are almost exclusively German package tourists. Much better is *Galla Camp*: see the box opposite.

After Maungu, the next place with food (but not much, and no petrol) is **Mackinnon Road**, distinguished by its Sayyid Baghali Shah Pir Padree Mosque, right by the railway track. Past **Samburu** ("butterfly" in Maa; again no fuel supplies), the country is peopled mostly by members of the large **Mijikenda** ethnic group, though their distinctive, droopy, thatched cottages are often replaced nowadays by more formal square ones, increasingly also whitewashed and tin-roofed in the coastal manner. The **Duruma** Mijikenda of this district herd cattle, make charcoal and grow a little sisal – there's little else they can do in such a dry region. The small centres of **Maji ya Chumvi** ("salt water"), **Mariakani** ("place of the *mariaka*": the Kamba arrows used in nineteenth-century wars against the Maasai), and Mazeras bring you closer into the coastal domain.

Mazeras is a largely Duruma village and here **the coast** really takes over. The landscape has a quite different cast with its mango trees, lush cultivation of bananas and cassava, and (encouragement for weary travellers) the sublime sight of endless stands of **coconut palms**. For details about Mazeras and the route along the ridge to the north of Mazeras, see p.488. Ahead, the main road plunges with a certain abandon and lacking much of its tarmac down the steep scarp to the Indian Ocean and Mombasa (p.446).

The Taita Hills

A good option, if you have your own car and a spare day or two – or if efforts to hitch into Tsavo proved fruitless – is to head off west from **Voi to Taveta**, a very accessible, but largely unvisited region. Apart from being a route into Tanzania, the **Taveta road** has some interesting possibilities to the north and south, while for much of the time the magnificent mass of Kilimanjaro looms on the horizon.

Wundanyi

To get a glimpse of the local culture of this region, go up into the **Taita Hills**. Several matatus pitch through the fertile chasms on a switchback road to the little district capital of **WUNDANYI**. After the sultry, dry plains, you're transported into another world. From the junction at Mwatate, the road twists up 14km into amazingly precipitous and beautiful hills, striped with cliffs, waterfalls and dense cultivation, and highly populated; near the peaks are patches of thick forest. There's notable prosperity up here, and a strong sense of community. Most of

Thrush under threat

Keen ornithologists head for the Taita Hills in search of *Turdus helleri*, the **Taita olive thrush**. This robin-like bird, the size of a European thrush, has a close relative in the ordinary olive thrush of the Highlands: olive brown on top, red-breasted and red-billed. The Taita *Turdus* is distinguished by its much darker head and the fact that it appears to live only in the Taita Hills above 1600m – which gives it all of four square kilometres (1000 acres) of potential habitat. As it depends on virgin forest for its survival, the Taita olive thrush is a very rare bird indeed, and may even be extinct. Two or three were seen at Mbololo in 1953, and eight in the Ngangao Forest in 1965; it may also survive on Mount Ngangai. The bird has a bold, liquid warbling song. Good luck with the binoculars.

the people speak the Taita language, a member of the coastal Bantu family related to Swahili and Mijikenda.

The **Taita people** are welcoming, and Wundanyi is an attractive and enjoyable centre. The conifer trees and a babbling brook running past the football field reinforce the feeling of departure from the thornbush and scrub below. This sense of suspended reality is accentuated by the **cave of skulls**, 1.5km outside the town, one of many ancestor shrines in the hills (there's one for each clan). Ask someone to show you the way: it's 500m before the *Mwasungia Scenery Guest House*, hidden in a banana grove just below the road, or ask at the guest house itself. In the niche rest the skulls of nineteen Taita ancestors, exhumed from their graves. Traditionally, the shrine was an advice centre where life's perplexities were resolved by consultation with the dead, and was also where sacrifices were made in times of drought to ask the ancestors to intercede for rain. Beside the niche is a sacred *mvumo* tree, which always grows near water – a good omen. Christianity has eroded some of the reverence that the Taita once had for these shrines – and traditional dances and rituals have almost completely disappeared – but the niches are left undisturbed nonetheless.

Practicalities

There are two **accommodation** possibilities, the only central one being the basic *Msangachi B&L* (❶) near the market. The other option, recommended for its helpful owners and lovely location rather than for its facilities, is the cheap, family-run *Mwasungia Scenery Guest House* (PO Box 1026 ☏ c/o Cecilia Mwachala, Wundanyi Prison 0148/2790; ❶), 2km from town along a dirt track signposted at the junction at the entrance to town (though you'll have to ask for the building). Rooms are basic, with no electricity or running water, but the welcome is friendly, they can rustle up some food, and this is the best place to settle into if you're interested in finding out more about the Taita: the owner is knowledgeable, and can also take you on walks around the hills to see waterfalls, skull caves (see above), and a cliff-top tree from which villains were once hurled to their fate. There's a choice of good **places to eat**. At the top end of town, near the matatu stage, the *New Wundanyi Motel* is recommended for tasty meals and a lively atmosphere – especially emanating from the bar – whilst *Tsavo Hill Café*, overlooking the market, has great service, wicked pizza and good curries. Next to it, the *Dairy Co-op Milk Bar* offers fresh milk, yoghurt, coffee, cakes, "sconze" and *mandaazi*. Downhill, just up from the post office and KCB bank, *Bistro 35 Cafeteria* is bright and cheerful. The big **market days** in Wundanyi are Tuesday and Friday. **Moving on** from Wundanyi, matatus to Voi leave in the morning and early afternoon, some continuing on to Mombasa (leave early if headed for Taveta; you'll have to wait at Mwatate).

Taveta and lakes Chala and Jipe

West of the Wundanyi turning at Mwatate, the **road to Taveta** jumps off the tarmac and you follow the railway line through the southern arm of Tsavo West, mostly in a cloud of brilliant red dust. The road was set to be tarmacked a few years back, but the money strangely disappeared – a lamentable state of affairs, especially in contrast to the fast smooth tarmac on the Tanzanian continuation of the road. A number of maps mark a *Murka Lodge* along here, but it has been closed for years and Taveta is the first, and only, place worth stopping at. You're almost certain to see some game on these plains, especially in the rainy season.

Taita Hills Wildlife Sanctuary

One place attracting much tourist traffic in this district is the 110-square kilometre **Taita Hills Wildlife Sanctuary** (entry $21), which isn't in the Taita Hills at all, but in the hillocky lowlands 15km beyond Mwatate. It's run by the Hilton chain, with two of their lodges and a tented camp acting as bait (all ❾; reservations ☎0147/30243 or 30270, ℱ30007). The setting of the lodges can't compete with Tsavo or even Amboseli (and they're much more expensive, too), though you can do early-morning **balloon safaris** here (around $400 for 90min). The 24-tent *Safari Hilton Camp* is the least tacky of the three and has a more immediate "bush" feel, with no electricity but a good atmosphere; however, children under 5 aren't welcome here or at *Salt Lick Hilton Safari Lodge*. Most of the visitors here are on fleeting air safaris from coast-hotel holidays. If you're managing without your own transport, there is virtually no chance of getting a lift into the sanctuary itself, though you could walk the half-kilometre from the road to the first hotel, *Taita Hills Hilton Safari Lodge*, just outside the reserve, if you feel like indulging in a *Hilton* meal. Having used the lodge facilities (which include a large pool and water-hole game-viewing terraces), you're entitled to free entry to the sanctuary. The lodge itself is a graceless concrete block that could be anywhere.

The sanctuary is well managed and, for most of the year, full of wildlife. Its small size means the rangers always have a good idea of where the animals are hiding out and it's not uncommon to see two dozen species of mammals – among them large numbers of lions, elephants and grazers – in a morning game drive (included in the rates if you're lodging there). During the drier parts of the year, when the animals are not dispersed, *Salt Lick Lodge* on the southern side of the sanctuary provides water-hole game-viewing to rival the "tree hotels" of the Central Highlands. But it's for its bizarre **architecture** that *Salt Lick* is most famous: from a distance it looks like a clump of mushrooms sprouting from the swamp. Each of its rooms is a kind of turret on stilts, all of them linked by mock-suspension bridges – there's even a drawbridge at the lobby. This camp ensemble is supposedly in keeping with the area's **World War I** battle history – most of the important Anglo-German engagements in East Africa were fought on these plains.

Taveta

Somewhat off the beaten track, **TAVETA** is situated on the Tanzania border at the end of the rural corridor running between the northern and southern

| Taveta and lakes Chala & Jipe

sections of Tsavo West National Park. Taveta has a mixed population of Taveta, Taita, Maasai, Akamba, Kikuyu and Luo, and even some Makonde (originally from Mozambique, they were brought in the 1930s to work the sisal estates). There's a KCB bank (Mon–Fri 8.30am–1pm, Sat 8.30–11am) and a petrol station, and the town is gradually joining metropolitan Kenya. With the recent improvement in East African relations amid talks of resurrecting the East African Union, things look set to change still further. If you're leaving Kenya at Taveta, note that there is a longer walk than you might expect to the Tanzanian side of the frontier – allow at least an hour. For a few moment's reflection, there's a **World War I cemetery** at the entrance to town.

The main **accommodation** options are at the end of the main street, which runs to the right (north) on the other side of the railway level crossing as you enter the town. The best option is the nonetheless rather run-down *Chala Hotel* (PO Box 16 ☎0149/2245 or 2212; ❸), which has small rooms around an internal courtyard, some with hot water, some with fans, others with nets, but is vastly overpriced for tourists. They serve good, basic food, and have a relaxed TV bar, and the chance to organize local excursions. In the cheap lodgings bracket (make sure you get a mosquito net), the not-very-salubrious *Livingstone Guest House* (❶) is nearby, on the road behind the *Taveta Hotel*; cleaner and brighter, 50m further up the road from *Chala Hotel*, is *Kuwoka Lodging House* (PO Box 51; no phone; ❶), which features magnificent, gaudy murals in its front restaurant.

The best places to **eat** in town are the *Taveta Hotel*, on the square between the *Chala Hotel* and the bus station, and a couple of restaurants either side of the KCB bank on the street leading to the border post: the *Taveta Border Hotel* (good samosas and chips) and *Golden Fish Hotel*. The local banana stew is also popular, though you might balk at eating eight bananas in one sitting – even if they are smothered with gravy. For something completely different, try the *Taveta Prison Canteen* at the entrance to town, which has sodas and roast meat.

Daily **buses** to Voi, continuing to Mombasa, leave at 8am from outside the Garex office at the main bus and matatu stage by the market facing the rail line, with additional 10am services on Wednesdays and Saturdays. The less reliable Tukutendereza Bus (Mombasa daily 8.15am & 10am) leaves from by the level crossing. There are plenty of matatus, too.

To explore the **Taveta region** without your own wheels, you'll have to rely on infrequent local matatus (better on market days: Wednesday and Saturday in Taveta; Tuesday & Friday at Chumvini) and the occasional private vehicle. Early morning matatus continue to Oloitokitok (p.409), near Amboseli National Park, to coincide with its market days on Tuesday and Saturday. If you're driving, note that the **road to Oloitokitok** can be pretty rough going, and is often impassable in the rains.

Lake Chala

Transport isn't such a problem to **Lake Chala**; you could, if necessary, walk most of the twenty-kilometre round trip, and there are **buses** to Chumvini (beyond Chala) on Tuesday, Wednesday, Friday and Saturday. A four-square-kilometre crater lake north of Taveta, Chala has one shore in Kenya and the other in Tanzania. It's right by the road to Amboseli, 8km from the junction outside Taveta and just a ten-minute walk up the slope. Hidden in its crater, it would be easily missed were it not for the signposted turning to **Lake Challa Safari Lodge**, 4km before Chala village (bookings: PO Box 16 Taveta ☎0149/2245 or 2212; or in Mombasa ☎011/313207, ☏311789; HB ❺, FB

⑥). Perched on the crater rim, this friendly place sees few visitors, but has some of the most spectacular room views in Kenya – straight over the lake, with Kilimanjaro looming behind.

Lake Chala is very deep and remarkably blue. Bilharzia-free, it was also believed to have no crocodile population and has always been considered a pleasant place to bathe. However, the death while swimming of a young British traveller in March, 2002, and the discovery of her body, missing an arm, points strongly to the presence of crocodiles, or at least a crocodile, in the lake. Until further evidence suggests otherwise, you are strongly advised not to swim here – as signs and local people are likely to emphasise from now on. The lake, which is still paddled over by a few friendly fishermen in their dugouts, is spiritually significant and lake monster stories are part of the folklore. There are no **camping** facilities, but you can camp for free in a number of places away from the lodge on the crater rim (the best views are to the north of the lodge), eat and drink at the lodge, use their pool and, if you don't want to scramble down the vertiginous crater wall, take their flight of steps to the lakeshore (there are fees for the pool and steps).

Crocs and monsters aside, keep a lookout for the pinkish snake that a number of readers have independently reported seeing inside the crater wall – possibly a red-phase spitting cobra. You may also see green mambas, monitor lizards, large skinks, monkeys and baboons (be especially wary of the latter if you're camping).

Lake Jipe

Equally interesting, and totally different, is **Lake Jipe**, 35km south of Taveta. It's fed by Kilimanjaro's snowmelt at its northern end, passing via Lake Chala's underground outlet, as well as by streams flowing to the south from the Pare Mountains, across the border in Tanzania. The Kenyan shore is flat and thickly carpeted in reed beds. Several villages at the northern end make a living from fishing, while Jipe's southeastern shore lies inside Tsavo West National Park.

Grogan's Castle

Seven kilometres from the Voi–Taveta road, **Grogan's Castle**, a white mansion on an isolated hill rising from the plain along the track to Lake Jipe, deserves a little detour. This extraordinary residence was built in the 1930s by Ewart Grogan, one of the most influential early colonists. His reputation was founded on a walk from the Cape to Cairo which he undertook in 1898, on a notorious public flogging he carried out on three of his servants (nearly killing one of them), and on his wealth: his gilt-edged reputation was such that Grogan was able to dictate terms to the governor before he even arrived in Kenya. At the peak of his prosperity, he owned over 2,500 square kilometres of land.

The "castle" was evidently built as a kind of hacienda for the **sisal estates**. It is totally run down these days – the only residents of the house are a large colony of bats – but it can be visited if you tip the *askari* (ask for him at the settlement of "Grigan" at the foot of the hill, a one-kilometre walk). It's an enigmatic building, much of it stuck together with aircraft aluminium and tin roofs. There are two enormous circular living rooms with spectacular 360-degree views out towards Kilimanjaro and Lake Jipe. The huge bedrooms have mosquito-screened bed niches, whose steel mesh make them look more like animal cages. On one of the landings an ostentatious cash cupboard is suitably positioned, presumably for the casual display of wealth to passing guests. It will probably end up one day as an expensive lodge, and there are rumours of its having been "grabbed" by the local MP (it seems Grogan left no heirs, at least not in Kenya).

Oloitokitok ▲   Kitani Bandas ▲

Mkuu

Mount Kilimanjaro

44

Ziwani

45

Ziwani

Sisal

Estates

44A   45A   49

46   T S A V O

Chala

Campsites
Lake Chala
Safari Lodge

Lake
Chala

T A N Z A N I A

A23

47   A23

Old Mbuyuni
Gate

63

Taveta

Grigan

Grogan's
Castle

Jipe

Sisal

Estates

Fishing
villages

N O R T H   P A R E

Vilima
Viwili

62E

M O U N T A I N S

Lake Jipe

Jipe
Gate

62

Public
Campsite

Lake Jipe
Safari Lodge

62A

62D

Bobby's
Camp

62B

62C

Kasigau Gate ▼

There is no public transport to the lake, indeed very little transport at all. Short of finding a driver in Taveta to take you there, your only option, and by no means an unpleasant one, is to walk. The flat land between the Voi road and the lake is heavily planted under sisal, cotton fields and even coconuts. There are also wide areas of low bush. It's an unusual part of Kenya, rustling with bird and animal life. The Macmillan map, *Tsavo East and West National Parks*,

Kitani Bandas

51A

SERENGETI
PLAINS

51

WEST NATIONAL PARK

50
48
Murka

Maktau

Maktau Gates
64

A23

Wundanyi and Voi

57

SERENGETI
PLAINS

N

TSAVO WEST NATIONAL PARK

SOUTHERN SECTOR

56

62 Road junction number

0   10 km

LAKES CHALA AND JIPE

Kasigau Gate

is a useful aid in the area. Driving or walking, head east from Taveta along the Voi road, turning right after 7.5km at the signpost for "Lake Jipe Safari Lodge", 1km beyond the turning for Ziwani Sisal Estate. From here, the track heads straight through the Jipe Sisal Estate to the lakeshore villages, 27km from the junction, passing the unmistakable Grogan's Castle on your right (see box on p.383).

The lakeshore and national park

At **Mukwajoni**, the fishing village 2km before the park gate, you'll find only the most basic provisions (apart from fish), so bring supplies from Taveta. There's nowhere to stay, though someone may be happy to put you up in their hut for a small fee. When exploring the bush around the lakeshore early in the morning, beware of **hippos**; you should keep a sharp eye out, especially between the park gate and the village. A feasible target for a couple of hours' **walk** are the two hills, Vilima Viwili, just outside the park boundary and about 2km east of the track. Once at the lake, the track becomes confused as it heads south towards Tsavo West's **Jipe Gate** (for details of park fees and regulations, see p.391) – keep as close to the lake as you can, as the gate is right on the shore. The rangers here are friendly and have little to do; they also have a **boat** ($5 per person) for a spot of crocodile and hippo-spotting, or for just messing about in. There's a **campsite** just inside the gate ($8 per person), with toilets and showers. Despite the vicious attentions of mosquitoes, this is a peaceful and rewarding spot, and a paradise for ornithologists. For something more substantial, the Swiss-run *Bobby's Camp*, 1km from the lake and 500m from the gate, has nine large, simply but comfortably furnished tents under thatched roofs, and meals and drinks available to casual guests (reservations: Royale Tours & Safaris, PO Box 99034 Mombasa ☎011/475255; HB ❺, FB ❼ including a game drive). If you're not staying, you might still be able to do a game drive with them around the park to see its unusually angry **elephants** (a probable indication of poaching over the border in Tanzania). *Lake Jipe Safari Lodge*, 5km from the gate on the Maktau track (also inside the park), is a larger and less intimate setup, with rooms in small and not terribly attractive pink *bandas*, but it's been closed for years and is still looking for a buyer.

Leaving the park, you've only really one option, which is a fifty-kilometre drive northeast to the gate at **Maktau**, a small settlement with another gate to Tsavo West's northern sector on the opposite side of the road (you won't need to buy another ticket unless staying another day), a war cemetery, a few *dukas* and nothing else.

The parks

In these animal-rich national parks, the first realization of where you are – among real, uncaptured wildlife – is truly arresting. Which parks to visit can seem at first a pin-in-the-map decision: any of them can provide a store of amazing sight and sound impressions.

Amboseli and **Tsavo** are the two most accessible, with ever-busy game lodges, well-worn trails, large numbers of tourists in the high seasons, and large, if brutally diminished, herds of elephant. Amboseli, with its picture-postcard backdrop of Mount Kilimanjaro and guaranteed **elephants**, is an instant draw, but the flat topography and lack of vegetation cover means you'll be sharing the stunning vistas with dozens of other safari vehicles. Tsavo, in contrast, is huge enough to escape company completely, except at **Mzima Springs**, for which it's worth being part of the crowd if necessary.

Maasai Mara has the most fabled reputation, with horizons of wildlife on every side. Somewhat isolated in the west, it requires a specific, usually there-

△ Hot air balloon trip, Maasai Mara

and-back visit, but it's well worth the effort (and perhaps the cost), especially during the yearly **wildebeest migration** that takes place sometime between July and November (at its most spectacular in August). The Mara is also *the* place to see **lions** – lots of them. The downside is its popularity: you'll find safari vehicles around almost every corner.

The **Samburu/Buffalo Springs/Shaba** complex and **Meru**, on the north side of Mount Kenya, have different varieties of animals, such as northern races and species of giraffe, zebra, antelope and ostrich. Samburu – dry, thorny and split by the Ewaso Nyiro River – is increasingly popular and noted for its **crocodiles** and **leopards**, albeit baited ones. Meru, however, is perhaps the most beautiful Kenyan park – isolated, verdant and surprisingly unvisited.

Practical considerations

Conditions can change rapidly in the parks. The effects of **climate** have led to several temporary closures over recent years and impressions one season may be quite different the next. **Security** is also a consideration, especially in the northern parks and reserves of Meru, Samburu, Shaba and Buffalo Springs, where banditry from the northeast (see Chapter Seven) and Somalia occasionally spills over. We've detailed the current situation under each, but you'd be advised to check up on the latest with a reputable travel agent in Mombasa or Nairobi.

It's important, if you want to get as much as possible out of your visit, to have detailed **maps** of the parks. These are often available in the park lodges or on the gates, but not always, and prices are higher than you'll pay in Nairobi. The best map for each park is mentioned in the brief details at the start of each park section, although the Kenya Wildlife Service is currently in the process of putting together its own colour maps and information sheets (available at park gates for $2) which, going by the ones already published (Amboseli, Tsavo and Nairobi National Park) are as accurate and detailed as you'll need. However, bear in mind that information on campsites and lodgings in any of the maps isn't always up to date. Accommodation options change regularly in most of the parks.

The latest **entry fees** for non-residents are also given at the beginning of each park section. The most popular, Amboseli and Maasai Mara, are also the most expensive, followed in price by Tsavo East and West, then Meru, and then the Samburu, Buffalo Springs and Shaba group. You have to pay separately for each of these or obtain a Smartcard which covers the main KWS parks you may want to visit – for more information see Basics, p.60.

For some idea of their current **animal-viewing potential**, the order of enthusiasm in recent travellers' accounts places Samburu and Maasai Mara way out in front in terms of variety and numbers to be seen, then Amboseli and Tsavo East, followed some way behind by Tsavo West, with Meru last of all. If you're interested in **birds**, you'll find favourable places to watch with your binoculars in all the parks, but it's worth pointing out that Maasai Mara (mostly open plains) is not, on the whole, good for birds, while by contrast Samburu (with its riverine environment) can be exceptionally rewarding.

When to visit

The parks usually get two **rainy seasons** – brief in November or December, more earnest in April and May – but these can vary widely. In Maasai Mara, they can merge together in one season from November to May. Meru also gets heavy rainfall, but it's more scattered. As a general rule, you'll see more animals during the **dry season** when they are concentrated near water and the grasses are low. After the rains break and fill the seasonal watering places, the game tends to disperse deep into the bush. Moreover, if your visit coincides with the rains, you may have to put up with some frustrating game drives, with mud and stranded vehicles. By way of compensation, if your plans include luxury accommodation, you'll save a fortune at lodges and tented camps in the low season (April 1–June 30 and, to a lesser extent, July 1–November 30). Most places reduce their **tariffs** by anything from a third to a half between April and June, with savings particularly spectacular for singles.

Driving

The parks in this chapter are open all year round. If you're **driving** during the rains, remember that none of the park roads are paved and unless you'd be content to keep to the main graded tracks, you will need a 4WD vehicle to

Environmental concerns

Off-road driving

Be sensitive to the great damage that can be done to delicate ecosystems by driving off marked roads. Despite the lush, tropical growth after the rains, there's nothing tough about the very seasonal vegetation. Even apparently innocent diversions off the main tracks can scour fragile, root-connected grasslands for years, spreading dust, destroying the integrity of the lowest levels of vegetation, and hindering the life cycles and movements of insects and smaller animals, with consequent disruption to the lives of their predators. Thus a destructive chain reaction is triggered which is difficult to halt. The effects of this are especially visible in Amboseli and Maasai Mara, both of which are now ecologically at risk.

So, use only **signposted roads** and tracks, or ones marked on official maps, though in some areas it can be hard to judge whether you're following an agreed route, or the tracks of others who broke the rule . . . If this means being denied the opportunity to see one of the "Big Five", consider the fact that cheetahs, for example, are very sensitive to noise and interference by vehicles, and hunt only by day – when surrounded by minibuses, they may offer great photo-ops (as any brochure shows), but are unable to hunt. Don't be encouraged by those safari minibuses which do go off-road: these are operating illegally and should be reported to the rangers at the gates. If you're with a safari group, agree not to encourage off-track driving for the sake of getting closer to the animals. And don't be afraid to ask the driver to keep to the main route: most are only doing what they perceive their clients want. The scenery and habitats are as important as the animals.

Speed limit

Stick to the official maximum speed limit posted at the gates, usually 30kph or 50kph. This avoids accidents and prevents too much dust being kicked up.

Animal rights

Animals have right of way, and are not to be disturbed (even if sitting across the track). This means keeping a minimum distance of 20m, having no more than five vehicles viewing an animal at any one time (wait your turn if there are already five there), no loud noises or flashed headlights, and not following the animals if they start to move away.

Driving at night

Night driving (usually 7pm–6am) is illegal in all Kenyan parks and reserves without express permission from the warden.

Litter

Take only photographs and memories, leave nothing behind. Collecting firewood (for camping) is strictly prohibited, as is picking wild flowers.

venture down the smaller ones. A night spent stuck in the mud in Maasai Mara (a likely enough occurrence if you only have 2WD) isn't recommended, nor is trying to reverse down a boulder-strewn slope in Tsavo West. In any case, a normal saloon will be shaken to bits on the average park road, and most car-rental companies will insist you have 4WD.

Accommodation in the parks

If you're visiting independently, with or without a vehicle, it may well be worth bringing a **tent** (consider renting or buying one in Nairobi – see p.145). Without one, Amboseli, Maasai Mara and Samburu are very limiting if you are watching your budget, as there is no cheap *banda* accommodation at any of these. In any case, camping out adds to the adventure. If you're visiting the parks on a more comfortable basis and staying in **lodges** or **tented camps**, it would be wise to make **advance reservations** as there's heavy pressure on beds during the peak seasons. Note that if you book via a travel agent, you may be given **discounts** on official "rack rates", sometimes up to ten percent off. Obviously, if you reserve rooms or tents at places in the same hotel group (see pp.42–44), making changes to bookings is easier.

Animal-watching

Game-viewing soon loses its more self-conscious aspects. Our wildlife colour section will help you identify the larger mammals you're likely to encounter, and the "Wildlife" account on pp.667–685 provides further background reading (see also the "Books" section on pp.688–689). **Rangers** can usually be hired for the day (official KWS rates are Ksh500 per day, or Ksh300 for four hours, though an additional tip is usually expected) and, if you have room, someone with intimate local knowledge and a trained eye is a good companion (knowing some Swahili animal names is a help – see pp.745–746). Most of the lodges and tented camps have their own 4WD vehicles and run regular "game drives". These can be very worthwhile because the drivers usually know the animals and the area. Expect to pay $30–50 per person for scheduled departures and $120–150 for exclusive use of the vehicle for two to three hours.

The usual pattern is two (or sometimes three) game drives a day: at dawn, mid-morning and late afternoon (though if you keep this up for more than a day or two you'll be exhausted). In the middle of the day, the parks are usually left to the animals; you'll be told it's because they are all hiding. A more likely reason is that the midday hours are a lousy time to take pictures. The animals are around, if sleepy, and if you can put up with the heat while most people are safely in the lodges, it can be a tranquil and satisfying time.

To see as much as possible, stop frequently to scan with **binoculars**, watch what the herds of antelope and other grazers are doing (a predator will usually be watched intently by them all), and talk to anyone you meet on your way. The best time of day is sunrise, when nocturnal animals are often still out and about and you might see that weird dictionary leader, the aardvark.

Baboons: a warning

More serious than the occasional robbery in the parks is the continued, unstoppable damage done by those loutish hooligans, **baboons**. A locked vehicle might be safe; an unwatched tent certainly isn't. Insurance companies don't cover such contingencies.

The Tsavo national parks – East and West

Daily 6am–6.30pm; each park $23 per day/overnight, children $8; private vehicle Ksh200, camping $8 per person. Warden of Tsavo West: PO Box 71 Mtito Andei ☏0302/22480, 22483 or 22455; warden of Tsavo East: PO Box 14 Voi ☏0147/30049. No driving after 7pm. Speed limit 30kph Tsavo West, 40kph Tsavo East. Maps: Macmillan Tsavo East & West National Parks Map at 1cm:4.2km (1988); Survey of Kenya Tsavo West SK78 (1994) and Tsavo East SK82 (1985; out of date for accommodation) at 1cm:2.5km; the KWS colour A3 flyer available at the gate (1998; $2) lacks topographical detail, but is the most up-to-date for accommodation and roads.

Biggest by far of the Kenyan national parks, and together one of the largest in the world, the combined areas of **Tsavo West** and **Tsavo East** sprawl across 21,000 square kilometres of dry bush country, an area the size of Wales or Massachusetts. **Tsavo East** is the larger portion, though all of it north of the Galana River has been closed to the general public for years (poaching there appears to be prevalent). South of the river, the great triangle of flat wilderness with Aruba Dam in the middle has become popular with coastal safari departures, since you can be sure of seeing plenty of animals in a very open environment. The traditionally popular part of Tsavo is a mere 1000 square kilometres, the tall grass-and-woodland **"developed area"** of **Tsavo West**, located between the Tsavo River and the Mombasa Highway. Here, the combination of good access, excellent facilities and magnificent landscapes attracts tourists in large numbers, while the well-watered, volcanic soils support wooded grasslands and a great quantity and diversity of animal life – though it's not always easily observed.

With their numbered junctions and clearly defined *murram* roads and tracks, the Tsavo parks are easy to get around, so long as you have a map. If you're in one part of the park, make sure you are officially exited by going through one of the main gates before trying to enter the other, or else you will be sent back. Don't forget the distances involved, however: if you set off somewhere, be sure you have time to get back to base by nightfall – both parks close their gates at 7pm, and it's illegal to drive around after then.

Tsavo West: access and accommodation

If you're looking for a visit outside an organized safari tour and don't have your own car, **Tsavo West** is probably the easiest as well as the cheapest of the big parks to explore. From Nairobi or Mombasa, take a bus to **Mtito Andei** (park headquarters and a service town for the lodges; see p.376). The gate here is one of the busiest in the country and your chances of getting a ride are good. *Kilaguni Lodge* should be able to arrange transport if you're coming by public transport, as they have regular evening staff transports from the gate. If you get stuck, the rangers are usually helpful and may allow you to camp just inside, though there's plenty of budget accommodation in Mtito Andei itself, barely 500m away. The easiest option, of course, is just to **fly in**: contact East African Air Charters in Nairobi (p.144), which runs flights to the main lodges when there are enough passengers (around $150 return).

The lack of low-budget **accommodation** – a problem that affects all the main parks to some degree – is less of an obstacle in Tsavo West. There are four **campsites** dotted around: one just inside Chyulu Gate, with shower and toi-

5

let, and conveniently close to *Kilaguni Lodge*; another, again with basic showers and toilets, a twenty-minute drive from the Mtito Andei Gate near the park headquarters at Kamboyo Hill; a third just inside Tsavo Gate; the fourth at Lake Jipe in the far south (p.383). In addition, there are two recommended and well-equipped self-service **banda camps**, *Kitani* and *Ngulia*, which have a number of simple but comfortable chalets, and are miles cheaper – as well as more charming – than the lodges. You have to bring and cook your own food here, an attractive proposition if you're sick of *ugali* and chips, or obsequious lodge service for that matter. Details for both are given below.

Finch Hattons Tented Lodge Kampi Ya Simba, 15km northwest of junction 38, 65km from Mtito Andei Gate, PO Box 71 Mtito Andei ☎0302/22468, ℱ22473; reservations PO Box 24423 Nairobi ☎02/60432–2, ℱ604323, ℮finchhattons@icon-nect.co.ke. Named after the aristocrat who introduced royalty to the bush, *Finch Hattons* must be the suavest and most accomplished of numerous luxury tented camps springing up around Kenya: fine bone china, cut crystal glasses and chandeliers, piped Mozart, impeccable service and food. The camp is sited around the springs and pools of a source of the Loolturesh River, where crocodile and great pink-and-grey hippo splash. The 35 tents are, of course, totally luxurious, with antique commodes, brass lamps and Afghan rugs (rooms 1–7 are best). Not the best place for children as the site and the pools are unfenced, and you may feel rather constricted by the formality of it all. FB ❾

Kilaguni Lodge Off junction 8, about 30km from Mtito Andei Gate, PO Box 2 Mtito Andei ☎02/340000 or 0302/22471, ℱ22470; reservations through Serena Hotels in Nairobi, p.44. The oldest park lodge in Kenya (1962), and still one of the better ones, as much as anything for its prime site by a large (floodlit) water hole and terrific wildlife ambience. There's a busy atmosphere and it's very often full – this is not a quiet place – but it keeps up impeccable service. Good-sized rooms (most facing the wildlife action, with stunning views towards the Chyulu Hills and Kilimanjaro), lush gardens, small pool, petrol. Game drives available (Ksh3500 for a nine-seater Nissan for half a day). Casual visitors welcome (see p.394). Recommended. FB ❼ low, ❽ high.

Kitani Bandas (*Kitani Safari Camp* on maps) Off junction 36, 12km south of *Kilaguni Lodge*, 8km from Mzima Springs, PO Box 3 Voi; bookings through Let's Go Travel in Nairobi, p.141. In an exposed red-earth site with some shade, the twelve three-bed *bandas* are pleasingly simple and down-to-earth, bliss after the studied excesses of the lodges. Each has a kitchen (with gas cooker), a bathroom and mosquito nets. Frequent sightings of buffalo and plains game. Bring all you need, including food and drinks. **④**

Ngulia Safari Camp 18km west of *Ngulia Lodge* between junctions 17 and 18 (bookings through Let's Go Travel in Nairobi, p.141. This would be a delightful place to stay, if it were not for the flee-infested mattresses and dodgy toilets. However, if you do find yourself having to stay, it's a friendly place and you might get a lift around the park for some animal-spotting. Its location, nestled up the heavily vegetated north slopes of Ngulia Hill, gives great views and it even has its own water hole. The six three-bed *bandas* have bathrooms, showers and kitchens, but no hot water. As with *Kitani*, bring your own food. They have drinking water, but you might feel safer using iodine or chlorine tablets. **④**

Ngulia Safari Lodge 48km west from Tsavo Gate, off junction 18, PO Box 42 Mtito Andei ☎0147/30091, ℱ30006; reservations through Kenya Safari Lodges & Hotels, p.43. Somewhat isolated in the more mountainous eastern side of the park close to the rhino sanctuary, this is open-plan and offers tremendous views over the plains far below, but has less immediate wildlife appeal than *Kilaguni*. Still popular and well maintained despite its age (1969), this is less swish, but friendly and more than adequate. There are two water holes by a terrace, but they rarely attract anything except buffalo who like to sleep there at night during the dry season. Leopards occasionally show up at dusk for a meal of meat tied to a tree by two nervous young men. There's a swimming pool and a pair of high-powered binoculars for scanning the plains. There are no game drives, but casual visitors are welcome and they also have petrol. FB **⑥** low, **⑦** high.

Voyager Safari Camp (formerly *Ziwani Tented Camp*); reservations through Heritage Hotels, p.43. On the park's western boundary by junction 44, about 40km south of the "developed area", but most easily reached from the Taveta–Taita Hills road. On a glorious site by a small hippo and croc-odile pool, beside a dam in the Sante River, with twenty full-size, permanent tents overlooking the Tsavo River and excellent food. It's quite a dis-tance from the park's main attractions, however, but early-morning guided walks in the bush around the lodge more than compensate. Game drives $21. Less formal and under half the price of its rival, *Finch Hattons*. FB **⑤** low, **⑥** high.

Exploring the "developed area" of Tsavo West

If you are eager to see particular species, Kilaguni's **information centre** (usu-ally open during the high season) should have up-to-date locations of **lion prides** and **cheetahs**, and possibly **leopard sightings**, too. But touring around the rest of Tsavo West is, for the most part, a question of following your inclinations.

The "developed area" is the hilliest sector of any of the parks covered in this chapter, and there's an unending succession of fantastic views across the plains, dotted with volcanic cones and streaked with forest at the water margins. When the animals are abundant – and their numbers fluctuate tremendously, being most visible in the dry seasons – every turn in the track seems to bring you face to face with zebra, giraffe, huge herds of buffalo, casual prides of lions, or methodical, strolling elephants, almost orange from the dust. Among the more unusual animals to look for are the beautiful and shy **lesser kudu** ante-lope (always, it seems, running away).

In the 1960s, Tsavo had the biggest population of **black rhinos** in Africa – between 6000 and 9000 – and they were a common sight. By 1981, they had been poached to barely 100 individuals (the story is enlarged in the box on p.400–401). The situation today has improved a little, though most rhinos have been removed to the safety of the **Ngulia Rhino Sanctuary** (4–6pm daily; free, but if a ranger accompanies you, he'll expect a tip) where, if you drive around for long enough, you're almost bound to see one (you can always visit the holding pen in the middle of the sanctuary and inspect the latest arrivals).

For information on the **southern** part of **Tsavo West**, read the sections on Lakes Chala and Jipe on pp.381–386.

The trip further on, that takes you around the foot of **Rhodesian Hill**, is recommended too, and **Poacher's Lookout** (also called Ranger's Lookout), near *Kitani Bandas*, is a very promising place for a quiet scan with binoculars. There's a thatched shelter here where you can sit in the breeze.

Mzima Springs

The biggest attraction in Tsavo West is **Mzima Springs**, 48km from Mtito Andei and close to both *Kilaguni Lodge* and *Kitani Bandas*. This stream of crystal-clear water was made famous by Alan Root's film *Mzima: Portrait of a Spring*, which followed crocodiles and hippos in their underwater lives. Go very early to avoid the tour-bus atmosphere and you won't be disappointed. The luxuriant growth around the water reverberates noisily with birds and monkeys and, with luck, some of the night's animal visitors may still be around.

There are **two large pools**, connected by a rush of rapids and shaded by stands of date and raffia palms. The upper (or long) pool is the favoured **hippo** wallow, while the **crocodiles** have retreated to the broader expanse of water lower down. It's worth walking around this lower pool to the right where, if you're stealthy, you have a good chance of seeing them. Just make sure there's not one on the bank behind you. This word of caution applies equally to hippos, but they seem settled in their routine, content to snort and flounder at an irritating point just a little too far from the path for visitors' satisfaction. At the side of the top pool, a circular underwater **viewing chamber** has been built at the end of a short pier. Unless you are exceptionally lucky, all you'll see is a blue swirl of perpetually revolving fish.

Mzima's two **nature trails** (really tree trails) aren't of great interest unless you happen to be a botanist, but it is easy nevertheless to spend a couple of hours in the area. Try to sit for a while completely alone on the bank and you'll begin to piece together the ecological miracle of the place, as the animals and birds forget about your presence. This is where those khaki safari outfits are actually practical.

Mzima Springs has a direct pipeline to Mombasa, completed in 1966, and is the source of most of the city's **drinking water**. Two hundred and fifty million litres of water per day gush out here, filtered to aquarium transparency by the lava of the **Chyulu range** to the north. This dark, largely unexplored, forested ridge creates its own rainfall: the porous rock absorbs the water like a sponge and gravity squeezes it into Mzima.

Plans were mooted in 1952 to build a weir in order to raise the lower pool's level. This would have destroyed the river terrace, however, and by ruining the hippos' "nursery" would probably have caused them to stop breeding. The National Parks trustees stepped in and effectively stalled development, summoning independent engineers to devise a way of taking water from beneath the lava, *above* the spring. There are one or two signs of the pipeline in the area but most are unobtrusive. Mzima has been left whole.

Kilaguni Lodge

While *Kilaguni* is an expensive place to stay, sooner or later you're bound to turn up, and rightly so: a visit (free) is rewarding enough just for the pleasure of sitting on the terrace with a cold beer and watching the enthralling circus going on a few yards away at the **water holes** (neither *Finch Hatton's* nor

Voyager Safari Camp encourages day-trippers). Lunches here cost around $18 per person. In the high seasons, casual visitors tend to be herded into a separate "visitors' centre", which has its own bar, restaurant and information desks, but not as much wildlife interest, so try to infiltrate the main reception area anyway, which is open to the panorama of the savannah and Chyulu Hills. Dazzling **birds** hop everywhere, **hyrax** scamper between the tables, and **agama lizards** skim along the walls (the miniature orange and blue dragons are the males in mating drag). In the grass below the terrace lives a colony of **dwarf mongooses**, while pompous **marabou storks** pace slowly up and down awaiting jettisoned bread from the dining room. Out by the water hole, **baboon troops**, **antelope**, **buffalo**, **zebra**, **giraffe** and **elephant** provide constant spectacle, with the occasional kill adding tension. At dusk, hundreds of **swallows** swoop back and forth over the human drinkers to their nests in the roof and, later, **bats** swoop while **genets**, **jackals** and **hyenas** come for the meat scattered under the floodlights. You may get exceptional permission from the warden to drive here at night for this, most likely if you're camping or staying at *Kitani Bandas*.

Ngulia Lodge

The autumn **bird enthusiasts** at *Ngulia Lodge* are a more earnest crowd than *Kilaguni's* guests. The lodge is a stop-over on the annual southern migration of hundreds of thousands of European birds. It seems to be situated on a narrow migration "corridor", but the reasons for its attraction for the birds – apart from its isolated lights – aren't really known. Ornithologists gather in November and early December to band the birds that are trapped in mist nets, and their occasional recapture in places as far afield as Malawi, Iran and Germany slowly helps to build a picture of where the birds are moving to. Perhaps not altogether surprisingly, few are ever caught at *Ngulia* again. Again, admission is free, and you can take lunch or have a dip in the pool (Ksh400).

Lava flows

The **lava** that purifies Mzima's water can be seen in black outcrops all around this part of Tsavo. The **Shetani lava flow** is a spectacular example. Only 200 years old (the Chyulu Hills themselves are less than 500 years old), the eruption that spewed it out must have been a cataclysmic event for local people, and is still the focus of stories about fire and evil spirits (*shetani* means "devil" in Swahili, deriving from the same Arabic linguistic root as "Satan"). Legend has it that many people were buried by the hot lava flow, and their plaintive cries can be heard on certain nights. The local people appease the ghosts by leaving them offerings of food which, of course, are gone by daybreak. There are **caves** here that, despite one or two warnings, are worthy of investigation (you'll need a torch). One of them even has a ladder and a trail of identification plaques by the bones of luckless animal victims who stumbled down.

Chaimu crater is fun to walk over, but also dodgy. The lava is brittle, honeycombed and unstable, and very few plants have taken hold yet. It is possible to climb up to the volcano's crater rim, but this can be surprisingly hard work on the scree and shouldn't be attempted in the heat of the day. And beware: when poking around Tsavo's caves and lava zones, you should be alert to the possibility of disturbing large **sleeping animals** as well as **snakes**. Remember, too, that Tsavo's lions have a reputation for ferocity. In the park, you should leave your vehicle at designated nature trails only, or where there's an obvious parking area. And beyond the national park boundaries you should stay on your guard – the animals aren't fenced in.

Tsavo East National Park

Across the highway, the railway, and the apparent natural divide that separates Kenya's northern and southern environments, lies **Tsavo East**. Apart from some tumbled crags and scarps near Voi, this is an uninterrupted plain of flat bush, vast and empty, dotted with the crazed shapes of monstrous baobab trees. It's a forbiddingly enormous reserve and at times over the last couple of decades it has seemed an odd folly, especially since the whole of the sector north of the Galana River – almost two-thirds of the park's area – has been closed to the public due to the long years of war against elephant and rhino poachers (see the box on pp.400–401). Since 1991, however, the situation has changed dramatically: the poaching has been more or less stamped out; the elephants, if not the rhinos, are once again on the increase; and Tsavo East, just a few hours' drive from the charter arrivals hall at Mombasa airport, finds itself very much the centre of tourist attention, especially for budget camping safaris. The **northern sector** is still not routinely open to that kind of tourism due to small-scale poaching; the warden is restricting access to upmarket, low-profile camping and walking parties. Private visits to the northern sector are only possible with express permission from the Rangers' HQ near *Voi Safari Lodge*, and even so you'll probably have to take (and pay for) a ranger for the duration.

Access and getting around

There are presently no scheduled **flights** to the park. Tsavo East has five **gates**, including **Mtito Andei Gate** in the northern sector which only offers access to *Tsavo Safari Camp* (see opposite). **Buchuma Gate** at the southeastern end is the one most used by safari vans from Mombasa, handy for Aruba Dam but far from the Galana River. Remote **Sala Gate** is the one used if you're coming from Malindi; it's 110km due west of Malindi along a seemingly endless dirt road, but there's no public transport further west than Kakoneni, 80km short of the gate, and safari vans are unlikely to offer you a lift without some form of payment. On the western side, **Manyani Gate**, near Mudanda Rock, is little used, but offers a choice of routes into the park. The main gate, and the one you should aim for if hitching, is at **Voi**, about 4km from the town (p.376). The rangers here seem a helpful crowd, with sensible attitudes to lifts and hitching: you can go with them to *Voi Safari Lodge* on their 8pm staff bus. At the gate itself, there's a small educational centre (though the insects in the glass cases look as if they flew in and perished there), and a short **nature trail**, plus a small **staff canteen** with the usual warm beers, sodas, bread and dusty vegetables.

Campsites

There are four public **campsites** in the park, two of them outstanding. The most popular is **Voi Campsite**, just 500m inside **Voi Gate**, which plays host to a fair number of organized tours. There are basic toilets, showers and running water, and some unfurnished *bandas* which give additional protection against baboons. You can usually get permission to camp here without a vehicle (it probably depends on how recently a lion was spotted). Apart from its convenience, it provides considerable excitement in the shape of Eleanor, one of Daphne Sheldrick's **elephant orphans**, and her young, male consorts. The elephants, now fending for themselves and completely unafraid of humans, visit the small artificial water hole in front of the cottages every evening. They can, and regularly do, steal food and anything else that appears to be edible. Take care, there's an accident waiting to happen here. There's another site nearby –

Ndolo Campsite – for which you'll need wheels, at the western edge of Kanderi Swamp, off junction 173. The other public campsite is way out on the eastern side of the park, 10km west of junction 176. At Sala Gate, your only option is to camp inside the rangers' compound (for a fee – bargain hard).

Lodges and luxury tented camps

Crocodile Camp 9km outside Sala Gate, PO Box 81443 Mombasa ☏0147/30124, ⓕ30123. One of the few African Safari Club places to admit drop-in visitors, this – like *Tsavo Buffalo Camp* – is right on the river, but larger (fifty beds), and has a more formal, lodge-like feel, with landscaped gardens and imposing public areas. Lunch Ksh700. No game drives unless pre-booked. FB way overpriced at ➒

Epiya Chapeyu 5km east of junction 163, on south bank of the Galana River; reservations through Alphatauri Ltd, PO Box 14653 Nairobi ☏02/749796 or 750000, ⓕ750990, ⓔbigi@wananchi.com. Unstuffy, Italian-run camp in a lovely location, with apparently frequent visits by a group of immature male elephants, and hippo at night. The twenty tents have bathrooms but no furniture and are closely spaced, the better ones in the front row facing the river. The food is Italian, and they're happy with unannounced guests, even for lunch, so long as they have room. Rates are per person, which makes it good value if you're on your own. Game drives and guided walks in the northern sector possible. Prices are poised to rocket here after its complete renovation. Recommended. FB ➏

Galdessa Camp 4km west of junction 111, south bank of the Galana River, reservations Mellifera Bookings, PO Box 24397 Nairobi ☏02/574689, ⓕ564945, ⓦwww.galdessa.com. This Swiss-run luxury tented camp organizes walking and fishing safaris along the river, plus camel safaris and, like *Epiya Chapeyu*, is in one of the few areas in Tsavo East where you have a chance of spotting a black rhino. However, with the surrounding bush vegetation, there's little chance of seeing much wildlife at the camp itself, and the rates are extortionate: $650 for a double. FB ➒

Patterson's Safari Camp 8km east of Mombasa Highway and Tsavo West's Maneaters Gate, PO Box 49265 Nairobi ☏02/43389, ⓕ47159, ⓔpattersons@iconnect.co.ke. Situated on the banks of the Athi River, this is an ideal location if you want to visit both parks from one base. Not as flashy as its counterparts, the eco-friendly architecture,

white sand and spacious self-contained tents, together with a friendly and helpful bunch of staff, give it the wild and yet intimate feel of a tropical island. As well as hippos, crocs and a resident elephant, there's also plenty of birdlife thanks to its proximity to the Yatta Plateau. FB ➏

Satao Camp (Mukwajuni Camp) PO Box 90653 Mombasa ☏011/475074, ⓕ471257; bookings through Southern Cross Safaris, Ratna Square, Nyali. East of *Aruba Lodge*, off junction 144, this is a fairly new forty-bed luxury tented lodge. Well run, with a good atmosphere, and a water hole which attracts elephants, occasional lions and plains game. FB ➏

Tsavo Buffalo Camp 2km outside Sala Gate, PO Box 556 Malindi ☏0147/2549, ⓕ0123/30715, ⓔcoralkey@africaonline.co.ke. Eight round *bandas* nicely sited on the Galana River, a breezy dining area under a thatch roof, but otherwise not much shade and no game drives. Elephants and hippos are frequently sighted, and it's the cheapest option short of camping. Walk-in lunches Ksh650. Rates are per person (so good-value singles). B&B ➍ or FB ➎

Tsavo Safari Camp ☏0302/22459–1; reservations through Kilimanjaro Safari Club, p.43; closed mid-April to end June; access through Mtito Andei Gate, then 16km along a dirt track. This tented camp, for pre-booked visitors only, is located on the east bank of the hippo- and croc-filled Athi River, accessed by pulley-powered dinghies. It's a remote and peaceful place, with enthralling birdlife and escorted game-viewing trips. There's a swimming pool, too, and porcupines and hyena come up to the dining area. Accommodation is in 27 "luxury" tents and 9 s/c cottages. FB ➎ low, ➐ high.

Voi Safari Lodge PO Box 565 Voi ☏0147/30019, ⓕ30080; reservations through Kenya Safari Lodges & Hotels, p.43. This lodge, near Voi Gate, is almost as busy as its Tsavo West counterparts, with a magnificent savannah-scape plunging to the horizon and almost guaranteed game-viewing from the terrace. The style is agreeable 1970s glam-kitsch: look out for the photo of Miss World 1972. FB ➏ low, ➐ high.

Tracking through the park

With minibus safaris increasingly taking in Tsavo East, the emptiness of the park is no longer as overwhelming as it was, but its vast size means you will

Patterson's Camp
Maneaters Gate

Tsavo West

Tsavo

Y A T T A   P L

Galdessa Camp

Lugard's Falls
Crocodile Point

170

150

110

169

111

160

161

Epiya Chapeyu

172

Airstrip

108

171

168

Manyani Gate

167

112

159

164

Manyani

Mudanda Rock

166

107

Mbololo River (seasonal)

A109

148

147

Airstrip

Aruba Lodge

138

Voi Safari Lodge

Park HQ

102

Ndolo Campsite

136

104

137

151

105

174

152

Voi

Voi Gate

Voi River (seasonal)

Aruba Dam

Voi Gate Campsite & Bandas

153

142

154

141

139

196

N D A R A

Taveta

Ndara

195

PLAINS

156

155

S A G A L A   H I L L S

A109

Maungu

M A U N G U

102   Road junction number

TSAVO EAST NATIONAL PARK (SOUTH)

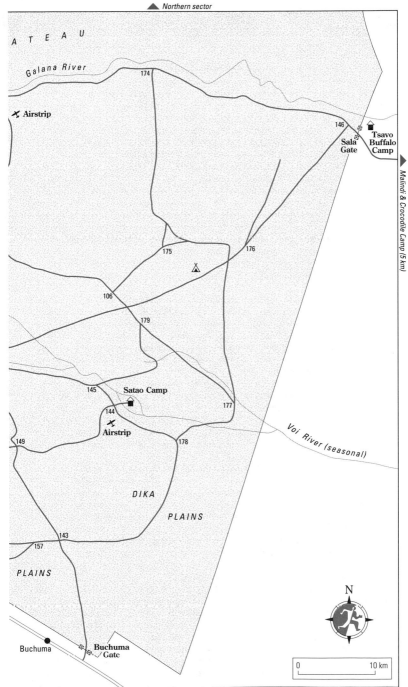

Saving the elephants . . .

Tsavo East was for a long time the contentious focus for conservation issues. The question of how to manage the elephants – or whether to manage them at all – is still the paramount one, in theory. The policy for years has been to hunt the ivory poachers and allow the elephants to reach a natural balance by starving themselves to a population their habitat could sustain. But the cycles of overpopulation and drought were too long for anyone to know if this was working out or not, and concerns are now being raised about the destruction of Tsavo East's remaining woodland by the pachyderms. Elephants, which are intelligent animals with complex kinship patterns, soon migrate to the increased security of national parks, often assembling in huge herds out of protective instinct.

Such questions have been submerged for many years by the overbearing problem of poaching. In 1972, Tsavo's elephant population was over 17,000. Today it is 8700. The social structure of the herds in many districts has been badly distorted, with many elders wiped out and too many inexperienced younger elephants unable to fend for themselves or to act in a properly mature and sophisticated, elephantine way. Taking account of only natural factors, orphaned infant calves are automatically doomed, while young elephants under ten years have only a fifty–fifty chance of surviving to maturity; nearly half the present population consists of juveniles under ten years old.

There was a lull in the poaching in the early 1980s, but by the end of the decade any complacency was brutally shattered by an unprecedented slaughter of elephants in their thousands – mostly mature animals with large tusks, but including many with little ivory to offer. The poachers were no longer marginalized Akamba killing an occasional elephant with an old gun or poisoned arrows, but a new breed of ivory-hunters, equipped with automatic weapons, going in and wiping out a whole family group in a single attack.

In 1988, it emerged that the Somalian government (as it then was) was mounting a concerted assault on Tsavo's ivory – perhaps in collusion with Kenyan Somalis and park-rangers-turned-poachers – aiming to profit from the tenfold increase in the value of ivory on the world market over the previous three years. Somalia announced it would be exporting 8000 tusks of what it called "confiscated ivory", an incredible figure equivalent to Somalia's own entire elephant herd.

The then Kenya Ministry of Tourism and Wildlife, concerned for the country's tourist image and allegedly covering up for some people on its own payroll, reacted in a curiously defensive way, admitting to poaching tallies far less than the reliable estimates available. President Moi was said to be furious. He personally ordered park rangers to shoot poachers on sight, then beefed up manpower and equipment in the Anti-Poaching Unit and deployed the paramilitary General Service Unit (or GSU, a force more commonly seen on university campuses) into the bush. Ethnic Somalis living near the boundaries of Tsavo East were summarily rounded up and trucked north to Wajir and Mandera, rekindling a bitter resentment which goes back a long way and has nothing to do with poaching.

As the news made the headlines in Kenya, some people started counting the casualties among the defending park staff, a number of whom were also killed. The spectacle unfolding – of a dirty war being fought on the plains amongst mutilated and unmovable elephant corpses, while the tourist minibuses followed each other in search of the perfect picture – was not a glamorous one.

The 1989 international agreement on a five-year ivory trade moratorium (renewed in 1994) had a remarkable effect on the numbers of new elephant corpses being logged in Tsavo. Equally dramatic was the unprecedented aggression with which the

Kenyan parks authorities started carrying out their duties under the auspices of the bluntly pragmatic new Director of Wildlife and Conservation Management (which became the Kenya Wildlife Service), Dr Richard Leakey. Leakey obtained huge injections of cash and military equipment for the war: armed men caught in the parks without authority were liable to be shot on sight, which deterred even the most reckless poachers and raised another human rights cloud over the country. Before the 1989 ban, three elephants a day were being killed by poachers; in 1990 fifteen were lost; in 1991 and 1992, almost none. The problem, however, has not disappeared completely – in 1993, 75 were poached, 35 were lost in 1995, 29 the next year, 43 in 1997, and 60 in 1998. Given the parallel rise in the Kenyan elephant population, from 19,000 in 1989 to around 27,000 in 1997, these figures are considered acceptable by KWS. What poaching there is currently seems to centre around the closed northern sector of Tsavo East. Official figures and comment are notable by their absence, fuelling speculation that powerful figures may be involved. More worrying is the pressure from some countries to open up the ivory trade again, which succeeded in 1999 in allowing Zimbabwe, Botswana and Namibia to resume trading in ivory, leading to concerns that this may reopen the floodgates to poachers. Fortunately, this has not been the case and the elephant population continues to grow.

...and the rhinos

The black rhinos, of course, are even further down this vicious path to near-annihilation. Their estimated number in Kenya is about 500 (up from 330 in 1989, at the height of the poaching) – that is, somewhere around a quarter of the total population of the species, which remains under a serious threat of total extinction. More than 95 percent of Kenya's rhino population (most of them in Tsavo) was destroyed in the 1970s. The poaching business suddenly and dramatically escalated when the hunters began buying automatic weapons to slaughter what are essentially quite vulnerable animals.

This escalation wasn't just the result of land pressure and human hardship in the countryside. More significant was a radical expansion of the market for rhino horns – not, as is popularly supposed, in China (where minute quantities of powdered rhino horn are used for tonics and aphrodisiacs – it's hoped that Viagra may stifle this trade), but in Yemen. Oil money made the rhino-horn dagger-handle – traditionally the prerogative of the rich – suddenly within reach of thousands of Yemeni men. Many tons of horns were smuggled out of Mombasa in dhows.

Yet the savage groundwork was laid long before. After World War II, the Makueni area southeast of Machakos was designated as an Akamba resettlement area. The colonial Kenya Game Department sent in one J.A. Hunter to clear it of unwelcoming rhinos: he lived up to his name, shooting 1088 black rhinos from 50,000 acres. The Akamba didn't take to the scheme and it fizzled out. Today, your chances of seeing black rhinos in the wild in Tsavo are slim. They still hang on in the wilderness sector north of the Galana, where the war between the poachers and the Kenya Wildlife Service has never quite died out.

At the brink of disaster, there are now concentrations of breeding black rhinos in a number of ranches and sanctuaries – notably at Ngulia in Tsavo West (50 animals), Nakuru (54), Solio (53), Lewa Downs (30), and in Laikipia District to the northwest of Mount Kenya (15). White rhinos have also been brought up from South Africa and there are an estimated 150 or so now in Kenya, most of them located in conservation projects in Solio, Lewa and Nakuru. Saving the rhino has become a national cause.

still have the uninterrupted pleasure of exploring the wilderness, much of the time, completely alone. It's easy to get away off the two or three beaten tracks, and you may find something special – a **serval** perhaps, or a **striped hyena**. Until 1990, you were likely to get unforgettable glimpses of the mountainous carcasses of elephants. The elephants of Tsavo, attuned to the potential dangers they face in the bush, have taken to spending much of their time near the lodges and park roads where, shot by cameras, they are relatively safe. Large herds are not uncommon but, when you see them, you'll notice the scarcity of really mature adults.

The Voi River's wooded margins often hide a profusion of wildlife: try the **Kanderi Swamp/Ndolo Campsite** at junction 173 and the pretty lookout point at junction 174. Keep the windows up when driving through the tall grass and undergrowth, not only for security against large animals, but as a defence against the tsetse flies that may mistake your vehicle for a large animal. **Mudanda Rock** is particularly recommended at certain times of the year. Like a scaled-down version of Ayers Rock in Australia, it towers above a natural dam which, during the dry season, draws elephants in their hundreds. **Yatta Plateau** which stretches from Mtito Andei towards the Galana River, along the eastern banks of the Athi River, is amongst the earth's largest lava flow and has become one of the ornithological wonders of the world, with birds migrating from Malawi, Oman, Iran, and even as far away as Germany and Russia.

For many years, the obvious focus in Tsavo East was the beautiful **Aruba Dam**, with its now-defunct *Aruba Lodge* (a *banda* and camping set-up on the north bank of the seasonally meandering Voi River, off junction 105). The dam lake is visited by thousands of animals and remains an excellent spot for animal-watching. From Aruba, most people head up towards the **Galana River**, unmistakable with its fringing cordon of branching doum palms. If you've got permission to visit the northern sector of the park, it's possible to cross the Galana at junction 160 in the dry season, but beware the smoothness of the rock bed, which belies the fact that many unwitting drivers all too easily get stuck in the attempt (note that Suzuki 4WD jeeps are notoriously underpowered, which makes judging your line all the more important). Just to the east of here are the spectacular **Lugard's Falls**, where you can park and clamber around the bizarrely eroded rocks. Even in relatively dry seasons, the force of the falls, which progress from foaming rapids to narrow cascades gouged deep into the bedrock, is quite something. Some safari companies use the falls as a picnic site – apparently with KWS sanction – as evidenced by a litter of plastic wrappers and cigarette butts: please take your rubbish with you.

A kilometre east of the falls, another short diversion takes you to **Crocodile Point**, something of a let-down as the crocs are extraordinarily hard to see until you get up close, which you're no longer allowed to do. Hippos are easier to spot though.

Amboseli National Park

Daily 6am–6.30pm; $27 per day/overnight, children $10; private vehicle Ksh200, no camping. Warden: PO Box 18 Namanga ☎ 0302/22250–1. No driving after 7pm. Speed limit 40kph. Maps: the most up-to-date is the A3-size KWS Amboseli National Park flyer (1998; $2) available at the gates, which has a useful sketch map of all the tracks, sights and accommodation. More topographical detail is provided on both

Macmillan Amboseli National Park Map at 1cm:750m (1988), and Survey of Kenya SK87 at 1cm:500m (1990), but both are dated and many roads have changed.

Amboseli is a small and very touristy park. It has suffered badly from off-road driving and its climate makes it a bleak, shimmering plain most of the year. Scenically, however, it is totally redeemed by the stunning spectacle of **Kilimanjaro**, towering over it and (as in those clichéd safari photographs taken with telephoto lenses) appearing almost to fill the sky. Sunrise and sunset are the best times to see the mountain, especially during the rainy season when the air is much clearer, but for the most part it remains tantalizingly shrouded in a thick shawl of cloud. In the right light, the snowy massif, washed coral and orange, is devastatingly beautiful.

On the animal side, Amboseli, like Tsavo, is **elephant** country *par excellence*. You will see large herds, some with big tusks. Predators, apart from hyenas and jackals, are relatively scarce (lions are almost absent, thanks to the revenge wrought by the Maasai upon their expulsion from the park), but good numbers of herbivores are present. In the dry season, most of the animals crowd into the impenetrable marshy areas and patches of acacia woodland where food plants are available. But during and shortly after the rains the picture is different, the animals more dispersed and the landscape greener.

The **erosion** of the grasslands by circling minibuses did much to destroy the park's purpose in the 1980s, turning it into a vehicle-clogged dustbowl that appealed little to animals or tourists. A concerted programme of environmental conservation, road-building and ditch-making was initiated, and this, combined with the toughest approach of any park to off-road driving (including fines and ejections), has improved the situation enormously. In 1992–93 heavy rains caused major floods, turning Amboseli into a swamp. The Kenya Wildlife Service responded with a $2 million rehabilitation plan to rebuild park roads and culverts that had been destroyed, but the same thing happened again in 1997–98; these cycles of flood and subsequent drought were amplified by the recurring El Niño effect, and seem to have become nature's way of culling the weakest and least adaptable animals. Unfortunately, this cycle also leaves the park more open to damage by vehicles: even at 10kph, the amount of dust thrown up is astounding.

Also troubling the park is relations with the local Maasai, who were evicted from the land they had grazed for centuries when the park was created, in 1973. As a result, some replied by spearing and poisoning animals that strayed outside the park, including rhino and lion, and others became poachers. Things have since settled down, and the Maasai are now entitled to a cut of the KWS revenue from tourists. They have also recently started benefiting from a number of upmarket tented camps built on their land outside the park, from which they extract daily entry fees and rent.

The route from Nairobi

The road is tarmac all the way to Namanga on the Tanzanian border, from where it's a very bumpy 76km along rutted *murram* to the park's centre: about four hours non-stop from Nairobi. Public transport will only take you as far as Namanga (there are a few buses from Nairobi's County Bus Station), from where you'll have to hitch. As usual, the best chances are with Kenyan weekenders. If you've got the money, it's easier to **fly in**, on the daily 7.30am Airkenya flight from Nairobi's Wilson Airport ($135 return; p.154).

Driving from Nairobi, turn right off the Mombasa Highway on to the A104 for Namanga after 23km, just after the dusty Bamburi Cement clinker grind-

Emali, Chyulu Hills & Tsavo West

Eremito (Lemboti) Gate

Namaga
(Meshanani)
Gate

Namanga

C103

Lake Amboseli
(seasonal)

Lake Conch

Lake
Kioko

Lake Simek

Airstrip

Ol Tukai Olokenya
Lodge

Olokenya
Swamp

Amboseli
Lodge

Enkongo
Narok
Swamp

Observation Hill

Public Campsite

Tortilis Camp

Kitirua
Gate

Kimana
(Olkelunyiet)
Gate

Park HQ

Amboseli
Serena Lodge

Tsavo West, Oloitokitok, Kimana Wildlife Sanctuary & Kilimanjaro Buffalo Lodge

23 Road junction number

0   5 km

Namanga (dry season only)

ing plant, at the southeastern extremity of Nairobi National Park (p.155). If you're hitching or going by public transport, your first destination is the small town of Athi River, 5km down the Namanga road, reached by bus/matatu #110 from Nairobi's KBS bus station. **ATHI RIVER** (also called **Kitengela**) isn't particularly interesting in itself, boasting an export processing zone, cement factory and plenty of dust. There's a colonnaded colonial post office and a Standard Chartered bank and, if you get stuck here, a few **places to stay**. The *Prince View Motel* (PO Box 97 ☎0150/22321; ❷) is the local hot spot and offers good self-contained rooms; couples can share a single, which seems to be the norm around here. There's also a **campsite**, *Hippo Valley Inn* (signposted behind the cement factory), with *bandas* available (❷).

Isinya and Kajiado

The road onwards from Athi River through the Kapiti Plains is unfortunately pretty dull, broken only by the **Maasai Ostrich Farm** (☎0150/22505–6; Ksh100 including tour), signposted 7km off on the right 15km south of Athi River. Primarily a commercial farm providing meat to local butchers, they also have guided tours of the farm, a swimming pool, limited food and large picnic grounds. There's also the comical attraction of ostrich races, usually on Sundays.

At **Isinya**, which is now connected with tarmac to the Magadi road (p.227), there's a **Maasai Leatherworking and Handicrafts Centre**. It's touristy, but you can find some unusual work among the beaded key-rings and "marriage necklaces". Check out the handmade shoes and massive, heavy leather bags. If your stomach is strong, you can visit the tannery, and they're happy to see you in the workshops, too. Donations from a church in Folkestone, England, of all places, help Isinya's community.

Further south, in the gentle hills where Maasai country really begins, is the district capital **KAJIADO**, which lies on the Magadi soda railway line. Set among sisal spikes and acacia, it's a friendly market town with a relaxed provincial feel, that provides an ideal stop-over after the hassle of Nairobi. Maasai in all their gear mix with other Kenyans in its busy streets and bars, and the daily **market**, part of which shelters in a modern breeze-block and corrugated-iron building near the mosque, is fascinating. The *Kajiado Inn* (**❶**), opposite the train station, has the best **cheap rooms** in town, plus a *nyama choma banda* and a bar-restaurant downstairs. Supposedly more upmarket, but overpriced for its small tatty rooms, is *Embeut Resort* (PO Box 262 Kajiado ☎0301/21217; B&B **❹**), 1km back along the Nairobi road, with round s/c *bandas* with nets. There's a *nyama choma* bar, too, which has live music on the last Friday and Saturday of each month (*ndombolo* and other dance). Basic lodgings include *Thayu B&L* (**❶**), at the junction with the Nairobi–Namanga road, which isn't terribly welcoming and tends to be full of drunks, and the weird Maasai *1811–1971 Day and Night Club* (**❶**) which has scrubby rooms but bags of atmosphere. For **cheap eats**, try *Impala Restaurant* opposite the KCB bank, or the bright and breezy *Naitiil Restaurant* (signposted), unfussy but cheap and hygienic. If you're after **nightlife**, there are a number of busy bars and day-and-night clubs: expect inquisitive stares, but a friendly if slurred response.

Namanga

The scenic interest picks up after Kajiado, as the road snakes into the hills, giving views of the conical Mount Meru in Tanzania (4565m), and your first glimpses of Kilimanjaro if the sky's clear. **NAMANGA** town sits square on the border, only 130km from Arusha in Tanzania. The petrol station, from where the *murram* road leads off east towards Amboseli, is probably the best place to start if you're trying for a lift into the park.

Namanga River Lodge is the grandest **accommodation** option (PO Box 4 Namanga ☎67 Namanga; **❹**). A colonial oddity composed of wooden cabins set amid pretty gardens, it was the halfway house on the old safari trail between

Amboseli's history

The park has been getting smaller and smaller ever since it was created. It began as part of the Southern Maasai Reserve at the turn of the last century. Tourism arrived in the 1940s and Amboseli Reserve was formed as a wildlife sanctuary. Unlike Nairobi and Tsavo national parks, created at the same time and sparsely inhabited, Amboseli's swamps were used by the Maasai to water their herds and they saw no reason not to continue sharing the area with the wildlife and – if necessary – with the tourists. In 1961, the Maasai District Council at Kajiado was given control of the area. But the combined destructive capacities of cattle and tourists began to tell in the 1960s; a rising water table in the following decade brought poisonous alkali to the surface and decimated huge tracts of acacia woodland. Kenyatta declared the 400-square-kilometre zone around the swamps (the present-day Amboseli) a national park, a status that utterly excluded the Maasai and their cattle. Infuriated, they all but exterminated the park's magnificent long-horned black rhinos over the next few years, seizing on Amboseli's tourist emblem with a vengeance (the survivors were moved out by the authorities). They also obliterated a good part of the lion population, which has still not recovered. Not until a piped water supply was set up for the cattle did the Maasai finally give up the portion of land within Amboseli's boundaries. They still, however, periodically pursue lion (which, of course, kill their cattle), although compromise appears to be the order of the day: in the dry seasons, you'll see numerous herds of cattle and their herders encroaching well into the park unhindered, as they always did.

Nairobi and Arusha. The place has a likeable, slightly cranky atmosphere, and has clearly seen better days – the era of baggy trousers and printed frocks seems just around the corner, but it's overpriced for non-Kenyans. Good snacks are served, and you can also happily camp in the garden (Ksh300 per person). Much better value are the s/c rooms (hot water in buckets) at the *Namanga Safari Lodge* next door (PO Box 5 Namanga ☏29 Namanga; ❶), with its pleasantly kitsch garden and bar, reasonable food, and cheaper camping, too (Ksh150 per person). Best of the two basic B&Ls is *Orock County B&L* (❷), at the start of the track to the *River Lodge*.

On the main road from Nairobi are several large **tourist emporiums**, including one not far north of Namanga and the other in the town itself, at the big petrol station. Both are packed to overflowing with Maasai bead- and leather-work, as well as Makonde ebony carvings from southern Tanzania and, of course, Kamba animals and Kisii soapstone. They're not especially cheap but, depending on the volume of business, you can strike reasonable bargains and the choice is huge. The glass beads used in the beadwork are not African; they come from the Czech Republic, which exports them to Peru and the Native American reservations as well as East Africa. And don't be misled by the expensive black-and-white marriage necklaces, which are not traditional Maasai ware; nor are the carved animal pendants. As with any art, styles change and innovations are emulated. Amongst all the trinketry are genuine used articles which tend to attract high prices. For these, you might do better by making offers to people you meet on the road. Bartering clothes or food often works to the benefit of both parties.

Park accommodation

From Namanga, a long, corrugated road – comfortable only at cowboyish high speed, and very slippery when wet – takes you to the park gate. Only one road connects the gate with "Ol Tukai" park centre; a second, which cuts right across Lake Amboseli on many maps, is rarely passable, and even in dry weather risks getting you bogged down in a treacherous version of quicksand – take care. **Arriving**, as most people do, around midday in the dry seasons, Amboseli seems a parched, unattractive place, with Kilimanjaro disappointingly hazed into oblivion. And heading straight for Ol Tukai, with its lodges, workers, filling station, fences and barriers, doesn't improve first impressions. During the rains, however, it all looks far more impressive, with the lake partially filled, and a number of other seasonal lakes and ponds flanking either side of the road, the occasional home of small flocks of flamingos, pelicans, and other migratory species.

Lodges and bandas

If you want to spend the night in Amboseli, you need money: the only budget option is staying at the single **campsite** outside the park (see opposite), and even then you'll probably need wheels. Otherwise, the closest **rooms** are at the B&L in Kimana (p.408), and in the Kimana Community Wildlife Sanctuary (p.409). Wherever you stay, be wary of semi-tame baboons and vervet monkeys, who will grab anything not tied down if it looks tempting, and can give a nasty bite if irritated.

Amboseli Lodge Ol Tukai area ☏ & ℻0302/22421–2; reservations through Kilimanjaro Safari Club, p.43. Staff at this, the main package destination, are helpful and friendly, food is good, and the cute chalet accommodation is comfortable. But the main draw is the fantastic full-on view of Kilimanjaro from all public areas and some of the rooms. Maasai dancers evenings, and optional cultural talks. Murky green pool, showers and meals (Ksh880 per person) available to casual visitors, as are game drives $35 per person. FB ❻ low, ❼ high.

Amboseli Serena Lodge Southern park area ☎0302/22622, ℱ22430; reservations through Serena, p.44. Favoured for its location by the Enkongo Narok Swamps which attract plenty of wildlife, this is beginning to need a revamp, with slightly tatty rooms and public areas. Thankfully, the pink sugarcube architecture is well hidden behind a jungle of tropical plants and creepers (you can plant trees, if you like, to save future visitors the sight), which encourages a kind of intimate, pseudo-bush feeling accentuated by touches like a stream running through the dining room. You can drop in for lunch (Ksh870), but the pool is for overnight guests only. Game drives $35 per person. Petrol. FB ❼ low, ❽ high.

"Drivers' bandas" Ol Tukai area. If you haven't got a vehicle and get dropped off at Ol Tukai, this is the sneaky cheapie, but needs a lot of tact and persuasion before you get admitted, and even then if the management suspect you have money, you'll be obliged to stay in a lodge. Tour drivers pay dirt-cheap B&L-type rates, and once in, you can eat cheaply in the drivers' canteen, and make friends in their bar – a more enlivening experience than the luxury lodges – and you may even be able to arrange a reasonably priced game drive. ❶

Ol Tukai Lodge Ol Tukai area ☎0302/22623 or 22253, ℱ22280; reservations through Block Hotels, p.42. The most expensive of Amboseli's three lodges, and deservedly so: built in 1996, with stylish "rustic-safari" architecture, friendly staff (not too formal), and good wooden cottages looking out beyond the fence towards the Amboseli Plains (but not Kilimanjaro). Two cottages are designed for disabled visitors, and there's good access throughout. Nice pool, and educational videos and Maasai dancers most evenings. The headquarters of Cynthia Moss's Amboseli Elephant Research project are nearby. Game drives $35 per person. FB ❻ low, ❽ high.

Tortilis Camp Outside the southern park boundary at Kitirua; reservations through Cheli & Peacock Safaris, p.143. This luxury camp has seventeen double "tents" (ie double beds on concrete floors under wicker roofs with en-suite bathroom), with all the amenities you'd expect in a five-star city hotel. Set atop a low hill, it gives stunning views of Kilimanjaro and northern Tanzania as far as Mount Meru. The pool at sunset is quite something, and there's a feeling of intimacy with the wildlife. The camp is managed as a conservation project, which includes paying a proportion of your fee to local Maasai, and the possibility of (unduly expensive) visits to a Maasai *enkang*. Laudable aims, but makes you wonder where the rest of the money ($326 double in high season) is going. Game drives $110 per person/day. FB ❽ low, ❾ high.

Camping

There are no **campsites** within the park, and only one outside it (Ksh600 per person), accessed from the signposted tracks leading west from *Amboseli Serena Lodge* or south from Observation Hill. It's a fine, wooded site, though no longer overrun with wildlife since it was partially fenced. Apart from warm sodas, a couple of toilets are the only facilities, and even water supplies are unreliable. You're also likely to be hassled by Maasai looking to pose for pictures, offering trinkets or visits to their *enkangs*, or simply demanding cash.

Exploring the park

Small enough to cover easily in two or three game drives in a single day, most of Amboseli is open country with good visibility. Because of this, you escape the nagging feeling you may get in other parks, that you may be in the wrong place and *that's* why you're not seeing any animals – here, you can look everywhere.

A good first stop is **Observation Hill**. Early in the morning, with Kilimanjaro a pervasive sky-filler to the south, the swamps of **Enkongo Narok**, replenished underground from the mountain top, are looped out in a brilliant emerald sash beneath. You can get out and walk around up here, and chat with the heavily armed wardens posted there supposedly to keep a watch on poachers.

There's always a concentration of animals along the swamps and the driveable tracks which closely follow their fringes. The swamps are permanent enough to keep **hippo** here all year and there are hundreds of **elephant** and

buffalo plus, predictably, a raucous profusion of **birdlife**. **Lake Kioko**, between Lake Amboseli and Ol Tukai – most easily seen along the track between junctions 21 and 26, is a special oasis, and **Olokenya Swamp** with its seasonal lakes north and east of Ol Tukai, is always worth slow exploration.

Lions are very rare, but **cheetahs** are seen fairly frequently in the woods a little further south, and there must be thousands of **giraffe** among the acacias. Look out, too, for the beautifully formed, rapier-horned **fringe-eared oryx** antelope, and **gerenuk** stretching up to forage in the trees.

The open plains are scoured by **zebra** and haphazard, solitary **wildebeest**. The two species are often seen together – a good deal from the zebras' point of view because in a surprise attack the predator usually ends up with the less fleet-footed wildebeest. There are tail-flicking **gazelle** out here, too: the open country provides good protection against lion or cheetah ambushes.

Lastly, if you need a fix of local culture, opinions vary widely about the **Maasai cultural bomas** which are set up just outside the park west of *Amboseli Serena Lodge* (between junctions 33 and 34). After paying a fee (which varies greatly with your perceived ability to pay, from between Ksh300 and $30 per person), you get the right to take as many pictures as you want, and may be treated to a display of traditional dancing, whilst the Maasai get the right to pitch their curios at you with practised persistence. Incidentally, much of the jewellery offered is neither made nor worn by Maasai – only the leather-and-beadwork necklaces and pendants are.

Kimana, Oloitokitok and points onwards

Once in the park, you shouldn't have too much difficulty lining up lifts onwards. If you're **driving**, there are two routes **east out of Amboseli**. One heads through **Eremito Gate** (Iremito, or Lemboti) towards the **Chyulu Hills**, then winds south to Tsavo West along the spine of the lava ridge – definitely 4WD unless you're feeling reckless. The Chyulus are favourite caving country with long, safe explorations possible. The Cave Exploration Group of East Africa found **Leviathan Cave** here, the longest and deepest lava tube in the world. Before reaching the Chyulus, this route crosses the main C102 *murram* road from Emali (p.374) on the Mombasa Highway to Oloitokitok (p.409) at **Makutano**, a tiny featureless Maasai trading centre. There's no problem with the Emali–Oloitokitok road in dry weather, but take care in the wet (4WD only), as it acquires some extremely tricky mud patches, and gets very slippery towards Oloitokitok. There's daily but not frequent **public transport** along this road in both directions.

The second, and more travelled, road (the C103) is in a terrible condition, even with a four-wheel drive. It leaves Amboseli in the southeast through **Kimana Gate** (also called Olkelunyiet), passing the roadstead of **KIMANA** at the junction with the C102 Emali–Oloitokitok road. *Romunja B&L* here has basic rooms (❶). As a result of concerns about **security**, you still supposedly have to travel in convoy with an official vehicle or armed guard to Tsavo West, although there hasn't been an incident since the early 1990s. The latest schedule is thrice-daily departures in either direction (8.30am, 10.30am & 2.30pm from Ol Tukai and Tsavo's Chyulu Gate; 2–4hr). Otherwise, you can pick up an escort at Ol Tukai, but he'll expect payment. It's possible to circumvent this arrangement if you're headed for Oloitokitok and Taveta, or up the C102 to Emali.

Turning left at Kimana, a ten-kilometre drive down the C102 takes you to the signposted turning to the **Kimana Community Wildlife Sanctuary**

(PO Box 362 Oloitokitok; daily 6.30am–7pm; $10). This is one of a growing number of Maasai group-ranch ventures setting aside land for wildlife conservation and tourism; self-imposed restrictions prohibit any livestock grazing or settlement except in times of severe drought. The 41 square kilometre site was demarcated in 1994 and opened in 1996, helped along by a £10,000 grant from Kuoni Travel, and is advised by the environmental group Friends of Conservation (p.65). The habitat includes plains, acacia woodland, and a wetland area watered by springs whose water holes are frequented by lion, leopard, cheetah and hyena as well as antelope. There are three **campsites** in the sanctuary, the best signposted "Kimana Leopard Camp" from the main road. Two kilometres further up the C102 (1km short of Isinet roadstead), outside the sanctuary but still on ranch land, is the large 112-bed **Kimana Lodge** (☏0302/22258–60; reservations through Kilimanjaro Safari Club, p.43; ❺ low, ❼ high; game drives $28 per person), with accommodation in two-room wooden cottages, and the attractions of a hippo pool and a nearby natural spring, which sees the occasional leopard turning up for the meat-bait laid out at night (there are spotlights). The price includes nature walks to the Sinnet Springs.

Oloitokitok and the road to Taveta

Branching off the C103 between the parks at Kimana, you can climb south 15km up the slippery C102 to the Maasai country town of **OLOITOKITOK** right on the border with Tanzania, with Kilimanjaro's jagged satellite peak Mawenzi dead ahead. Oloitokitok (pronounced "Loytoktok") should be nothing to get excited about – just an interesting, bustling little town by the Amboseli–Tsavo circuit. But it is ignored by 99 percent of the tourist minibuses, and it's in a fabulous position, closer to Kilimanjaro than anywhere else in Kenya and high above the plains (altitude 1700m). It is a relaxed and recommended place to settle into if you're interested in finding out more about the Maasai, as this is their easternmost major centre. Oloitokitok is also a border crossing for the Tanzanian town of Moshi a couple of hours away, nestled behind the mountain. And it's close to Kilimanjaro's Kibo Peak, 25km as the crow flies: you can arrange climbing tours up the mountain at *Kibo Slopes Cottages*, and there are enough willing guides and porters in the village, but don't get caught in Kilimanjaro National Park without having paid the fee. The Tanzanians take the offence extremely seriously.

On Tuesdays and Saturdays, when many Maasai are in Oloitokitok centre for the **weekly markets**, there's a fair amount of matatu traffic between here and Emali, as well as a service to Taveta (some leave the day before to get to Oloitokitok). At other times, you will have to take potluck with transport – start early. Oloitokitok has a petrol station, a post office and KCB bank (which takes ages to change money), as well as a few **B&Ls** at the top of the hill near the market. Best of these is the Christian-run *Safari's Lodge* (PO Box 291 ☏0302/22088; ❶). Otherwise, *Hilltop Lodge* (PO Box 59 ☏0302/22303; ❶) and *Mawenzi Safari Inn* (PO Box 365 ☏0302/22306; ❶), are both reasonable. *Mwalimu Lodge* in the lower part of town is a serious watering hole. Superior to all is the modern *Kibo Slopes Cottages* (PO Box 218 ☏0302/22091, ℱ 22427; B&B ❹), 1km down a track to the left of the customs post, with good s/c rooms (hot running water morning and evening), some with good views, but overpriced unless you're in a larger group, when the four-bed cottages (❹) make sense.

On market days, you can catch a matatu-bus to the town of Taveta (p.381), almost 100km away near the southwestern tip of Tsavo West National Park.

The route, which skirts the border with Tanzania and the flanks of Kilimanjaro, is far off the beaten track, but scenically rewarding, as well as the shortest and fastest way to get from Amboseli to Voi on the Mombasa Road. Even faster, and kinder to your vehicle if you're driving, is the tarmac road on the Tanzanian side, but it's expensive if you haven't got multiple-entry visas for both Tanzania and Kenya. On the Kenyan side, the road is unsurfaced except for the first 9km of soothing tarmac to Illasit (where the tarmac veers off right towards Tanzania: keep going straight), and often becomes impassable in the rains when the fine dust turns to mud. Leaving Oloitokitok, the landscape changes from scrubby cattle pasture to neat – if dusty – plots of sisal and maize plantations, marking the end of Maasai territory. There are only a few settlements, acting as market centres for Maasai and Taveta agriculturers, but the next accommodation is 58km away at **Chumvini** (Njukini), where the dogged *Gatanga Guest House* (PO Box 53 Taveta ☎0149/2639; ❶) has some basic non-s/c rooms, a down-at-heel bar with funny murals, a butchery and *nyama choma*. From here, you'll find more frequent transport on to Taveta (daily matatus, and buses on Tues, Wed, Fri & Sun). Further on, 10km short of Taveta, is the wonderful aberration of **Lake Chala** – see p.382.

Maasai Mara National Reserve

Daily 6.30am–7pm; $27 per day/overnight, children $10; private vehicle Ksh200, camping Ksh480 per person. Senior warden: PO Box 60 Narok ☎0305/22068 or 22268. No driving after 7pm. Speed limit 40kph. Maps: Survey of Kenya SK86 at 1cm:1km (1987) is preferable to Macmillan's Maasai Mara at 1cm:1.25km (1988), but both are out of date and omit newer accommodation; the sketch map you get at the park gate is useless.

For a long list of reasons, **Maasai Mara** is the best animal reserve in Kenya. The panorama sometimes resembles one of those wild animal wall charts, where groups of unlikely looking animal companions are forced into the artist's frame. You can see a dozen different species – or more – at one time: gazelle, zebra, giraffe, buffalo, topi, kongoni, wildebeest, eland, elephant, hyena, jackal, ostrich, and a pride of lions waiting for a chance.

The reserve is a great wedge of undulating **grassland** nearly 2000m above sea level, watered by one of Kenya's bigger rivers, the Mara. It is in the remote, sparsely inhabited southwest part of the country, snuggled up against the border and, indeed, an extension of the even bigger **Serengeti Plains** in Tanzania. This is a land of short grasses, where the wind plays with the thick, green mantle after the rains and, nine months later, whips up dust devils from the baked surface.

But Maasai Mara's climate is predictable, with ample rain, and the new grass supports an annual **wildebeest migration** of up to one and a half million animals from the dry plains of Tanzania. To travel through the reserve in August or September, while the wildebeest are in possession, is a staggering experience, like being caught up in the momentum of a phenomenal historic event. Whether you're watching this or a pride of lions hunting, a herd of elephants grazing in the marsh, or hyenas squabbling with vultures over the carcass of a buffalo, you are conscious all the time of being in a realm apart. There are few places on earth where animals hold such dazzling sway – it's as if you had found yourself in the New York of the natural world.

With its plentiful vegetation and wildlife, and heavy rainfall, the reserve's **ecology** appears at first sight to be relatively resilient to the effect of the huge

MAASAI MARA
NATIONAL RESERVE

ACCOMMODATION

Mpata Safari Club	1
Mara River Camp	2
Kichwa Tembo	3
Little Governor's Camp	4
Mara Intrepids Club	5
Fig Tree Camp	6
Mara Simba Lodge	7

▲ Molo

Olenguerone

*M A R A
F O R E S T*

▲ Kericho

Kapkoros

◀ Sotik & Kisii

B3

Bomet

Longisa

Kapkimowa

C12

▲ B3 & Kisii

Sigor

Amala River

Ngorengore

C13

Ewaso Ngiro

▶ Narok, Naivasha & Nairobi

PO

C12

▶ Mara Sopa Lodge

Kaboson

Gorgor

Mara Safari Club

Lemek

*L O I T A
P L A I N S*

Mara River

Kioleleo

Paradise Mara Lodge

Aitong

N

See 'Maasai Mara
- North West Area'
map for detail

① ②

Mara Bridge

Musiara
Gate

*Musiara
Swamp*

Talek River

Siana
Springs
Camp

Olololo Gate ③ ④

Governor's
Camp

RHINO RIDGE

⑥ Talek

⑦

Sekenani
Gate

Sekenani
Camp

▶ Narok

Olkurruk
Mara Lodge

Mara Serena
Lodge

⑤

Talek
Gate

Mara River

Sarova
Mara
Camp

Mara
Sopa
Lodge

Ololaimutiek
Gate

◀ Kilgoris

✈ Airstrip

Keekorok Lodge

OLOLOLO ESCARPMENT

Hippo Pools

Sand River

New Bridge

Sand River Gate

TANZANIA

0   10 km

5

number of tourists who visit it every year. However, one glance at the clouds of dust rising behind vehicles in the dry season shows up the real fragility of the place. The Mara is the most visited park in Kenya (over 2000 beds in and around the reserve, plus their vehicles), and there are signs that the balance between tourist numbers and wildlife can't be maintained much longer. In parts, erosion gullies started by off-road driving (which turns soil into dust by killing the protective cover of vegetation) has created dust bowls, which themselves begin to spread through the effects of natural wind and water erosion. Similarly, during the rains, many roads become impassable, causing a welter of parallel tracks to appear, many of them knee-deep in mud by the time the rains move on, and which take years to heal.

On entering the reserve, you'll be handed a copy of the relevant **bye-laws** and rules, which should be strictly adhered to, but which sadly in practice rarely are. The Maasai Mara is a beautiful and sensitive environment which can survive only if properly respected, but the first step should really be taken by the reserve authorities in actually bothering to enforce their regulations (at present, a lamentable *laissez faire* prevails).

Getting to the Mara

Part of the reason for the Mara's fantastic spell is its isolation: a trip here is an expedition, and you might as well plan it as such. The vast majority of visitors come on pre-booked safari packages, which invariably work out cheaper than going under your own steam.

If you're organizing it yourself, access is most straightforward, and most expensive (currently $165 return), by the scheduled daily **air services** from Nairobi (see p.154). By all accounts, the twelve-seater flights are thoroughly enjoyable, with plenty of wildlife and the pilot announcing the lodges he would like to land at in his preferred order. Most of the lodges have their own *murram* airstrips, except *Keekorok* and *Mara Intrepids Club* which have tarmac. **Airstrip transfers** to your lodge by jeep cost around $25 per person, with a minimum of four people usually required.

By **road**, however, the rewards are more intimate, including the long **drive** across the Rift Valley from Nairobi, sweeping across dry, stupendous vistas of range lands – the heart of the Maasai country. Cattle are the economic mainstay, but extensive wheat fields are pushing south. While the land often looks empty, if you stop for five minutes, chances are that someone will appear – to request something or to offer a photo pose, or just to pass the time of day.

Whilst the rest of the country's roads took a severe beating in the 1997–98 El Niño rains, the newly resurfaced B3 from Mai Mahiu junction on the old Nairobi–Naivasha road to Narok and Ewaso Ngiro (17km beyond) survived unscathed, with not a pothole in sight. Construction work is currently underway to tarmac the extension of the B3 from Kapkimowa on the Amala River, which should finally provide year-round 2WD access from Narok to western Kenya, and make access easier to Maasai Mara's western gates. The C12 which goes from Ewaso Ngiro to the reserve's Sekenani Gate is also being surfaced – at the time of writing, the first 40km were paved, with the remaining 40km being passable by 4WD, and by 2WD in dry weather – allow about two hours to the gate. Note, however, that the C88 from Naivasha which joins the B3 at Mai Mahiu is in a terrible state: more potholes than tarmac. There's one **accommodation** option at Mai Mahiu, should you get stuck hitching or matatu-hopping: *Mount Longonot Transit Hotel* (PO Box 9 Mahiu; no phone; B&B ❷), 500m down the Narok road, has some unexceptional s/c *bandas*, plus a bar and a bad restaurant.

If you're in a low-clearance, **2WD** car, your only route in and out of the park is via Sekenani Gate, and that only in dry weather. Once in the reserve, only the eastern section (between Sekenani Gate, *Keekorok Lodge*, *Mara Serena Lodge* and *Fig Tree Camp*) is practicable. Don't even dream of trying another route – you're guaranteed to get stuck.

In a **4WD**, your options are wider, but you still have to be an experienced rough-road driver to get much further than usual 2WD territory. Access routes via Talek, Musiara and Oloololo gates are all possible in dry weather (avoid them in wet), but even then can be exceedingly treacherous, with the main problem being frequent watery **mud pits** across the track. If at all possible, try driving around these, avoiding all areas of mud, whose smooth and apparently firm surface often disguises deep traps from which you can only hope to get towed out. A covering of vegetation usually means a relatively solid surface. If avoiding the pools isn't possible, the most common advice is to aim straight through the centre. There are two ways of tackling them, depending on their appearance. If the pool is large, first kick off your shoes and wade through the entire length of the pool to check its depth and subsurface (better getting muddy than bogged down) – if the water's less than a foot deep, and the subsurface relatively firm (ie your feet only sink in a few inches), you should be able to drive across: engage 4WD, slip into first gear, and drive slowly (but without decelerating) straight through the middle (not at the sides, as you risk getting trapped there in deep mud). Alternatively, if there's a sufficiently hard shoulder on one side, you could try driving across at speed with one wheel on it (beware of toppling over in a Suzuki) – you need good control for this. For smaller pools, gathering up speed on the approach and then barrelling across in second gear usually works, but at the risk of clogging up the carburettor.

On a **swampy black cotton soil** surface, especially during or after rain (which in practice means the land west of *Mara Serena* and *Fig Tree Camp*, and north of *Mara Serena* to Oloololo Gate), you'll need all your wits about you, as even the sturdiest 4WDs have little or no grip on this. The usual way involves a mixture of high-rev driving and luck, which leaves you open to hair-raising spins and sudden, crunching jolts, as well as the possibility of getting bogged down when you lose control. Much better might be to keep in second gear as much as possible, and keep your speed down. Try to keep at least one wheel within a well-defined rut or on more solid ground, as this makes spinning and sideways sliding less likely. Approaching deep mud is really touch and go – drive as fast as you dare (keeping control over the car), never over-steer when skidding (it'll send you into a spin and may get you bogged down), keep the accelerator pressed, and pray.

If you do **get stuck**, stop immediately (spinning the wheels will only get you even more stuck): try reversing once (rev the engine as far as it will go before engaging the gear). If this doesn't work and you don't have sand ladders, you'll just have to wait for another vehicle to pull you out.

If you do decide to drive to the Mara, give yourself plenty of time – a good six to seven hours non-stop from Nairobi or Naivasha to the eastern end of the reserve, or all day (9–10hr non-stop) with an early start to the western end. And if you intend to do more than a tank's worth of driving, remember to stock up with cans of **petrol** at the last town you pass through (usually Narok). Although you may be able to buy petrol at one of the lodges (at a price), don't depend on it. Many only keep enough fuel for their own vehicles; others only keep diesel.

Narok

NAROK is the funnel through which almost all road transport enters the Mara. It's the last place to get fuel, a cold drink or almost anything for over 100km before you enter the reserve. First impressions aren't encouraging. *Afrikano*, on the left as you enter from the east, is a tourist trap of the first order, charging exorbitant prices for curios, food and drinks. In the same vein, over the road, a brassy atmosphere pervades the Kobil service station and snack bar which, being the first petrol station on the way into town, waylays most of the minibuses with its big-game cut-outs, reticulated sunshades and cluster of souvenir shops selling very expensive Maasai paraphernalia (the same stuff is half the price in Nairobi). If you need petrol, the Total station on the far side of town is cheaper and less hassly. When buying petrol, watch the pump counter carefully. If you're **hitching**, the Kobil station is probably the best point to wait and ask. If the direct approach doesn't appeal (there'll be plenty of refusals), try the bridge over the Engare Narok River on the west side of town.

Petrol rip-offs, tourist bazaars and touts aside, Narok is actually quite a lively little place, full of Maasai out shopping or doing business at the market. There's also the small but perfectly formed **Narok Maa Cultural Museum** (daily 9am–6pm; PO Box 868 Narok; provisional ℡0305/22095; Ksh200), on the right as you come in, which is an excellent introduction to the Maasai (and Samburu) way of life. The walls have a fascinating collection of photographs taken by Maasai women, using disposable cameras given to them for the project, depicting important parts of their daily lives, such as water carrying, milking cattle, and raising children. Considering that it was the first time that any of the women had ever held a camera, the compositions are extraordinarily well judged. The captions, too, are great: "This photo is showing a bad thing. The women have to carry the heavy water containers all the way. They have to walk for 30km to get water from the wells, because there is no dam in the neighbourhood of their *enkang*" and "This man is milking a cow that has just given birth. Normally I should have done that. It is uncommon for men to milk – they only do it when there are no women around." There are also black-and-white portraits of Maasai taken by Joy Adamson in 1951, as well as helpfully labelled everyday and magical artefacts (look out for the ovine chastity belt, used when there's not much grazing, which puts a solid leather barrier between the ram and his desire). For researchers, there's a storage room containing many more artefacts, though it isn't officially open to the public. There are advanced plans to move the museum to a purpose-built site over on the west side of the river, which may include a campsite.

Practicalities

If you're headed for the reserve but arrive in Narok after 4pm, you'll end up having to stay the night here, as you won't have time to get to the reserve by nightfall (gates close at 6.30pm). **Accommodation** is no problem as regards quantity, but quality and cost are another matter. You get reasonable value at the *Transit Hotel* (PO Box 384 ℡0305/22288; ❸), opposite the Kobil station, with safe parking but so-so food. A little further up on the same side, also with parking, is the four-storey *Nenkai Plaza Lodging & Restaurant* and a fast-food bar (no phone; ❷), with s/c but rather grubby rooms. *Chambai Hotel* (PO Box 783 Narok ℡0305/22591; ❷–❸),a tall building with a satellite dish near the mosque and opposite the market is a better option. The spacious clean self-contained rooms with powerful hot showers (without curtains) are wonderful after a long bone-rattling drive to Narok from Nairobi. Not all rooms have TV and satellite, so ask for one that does. The best rooms are on the top two floors.

Also decent is *Kanga Lodge* (❷) at the west end of town (turn right at the Agip station and matatu stage), with simple but acceptable rooms. Another cheap and basic option is the *Rainbow Café B&L* (PO Box 82 ☎0305/22373; ❷), beside the mosque. You can **camp** at the *Members Club* (PO Box 4 Narok ☎0305/22383; Ksh200), 1km west of the Agip petrol station, which also has a few cheap and basic non-s/c *bandas* in a muddy site (❶). Security is uncertain, as there's a rather rough bar here.

For **food and drink**, *Kenol Restaurant* (6.45am–10.30pm), part of Kenol petrol station & supermarket, is on the left-hand side of the main road, heading towards the Mara. Catering as it does for reputable safari groups, the food is good, making it the best place to stock up before you enter the reserve. Worth trying is the marinated and deep-fried tilapia with rice, or the *masala* chicken. They also do fresh cold mango and passion-fruit juice. *Hillside Cave Day & Night Club* does good chicken and *kienjeji*, and at night features a bizarre mix of traditionally-garbed Maasai and westernized Kenyans drinking and listening to reggae. *Fun Rose Fast Food* opposite *Hillside*, is open 24hours and serves an array of cheap snacks such as *samosas*, as well as chicken and chips. The *Three In One Bar & Restaurant* on the main road features live music at weekends. National Bank of Kenya (Mon–Fri 9am–3pm, Sat 9 11am) and the **post office** are both on the main road. **Emails** can be sent from Sky Apple Enterprises (Ksh150 per hour; Mon-Sat 8am-7pm) in Maa Towers, a building opposite the Commercial Bank of Kenya. If you want cheap **beer** in the Mara, stock up now (you'll have to truck back the empties to reclaim the deposit). Note: there is no ATM in Narok.

Alternative routes to Narok: over the Mau Escarpment

From Lake Naivasha (at the end of the lake road tarmac by Kongoni police station), and **from Nakuru via Njoro**, steep roads twist up over the **Mau Escarpment**. If you're starting out **from further west** you can also get to Narok by the gradually improving Molo–Olenguerone road (see p.267). But this latter route also allows the option of a more direct approach to the west end of the reserve (see overleaf). All these routes are for 4WD only.

The **Mau Range**, not as high but just as massive as the Aberdares, is little known and rarely visited. In the thin, clear air, Maasai and Nandi graze their cattle on luxuriant pastures, and large but steadily shrinking domains of thick, dark forest are still the home to **Okiek hunter–gatherers**. Called Dorobo by the Maasai, the government is currently trying to open up some 600 square kilometres to planters and settlers, despite the fact that it's protected under Kenya's Forest Act. For the moment, it's enrapturing country and highly recommended for **hiking** if you have the time. As a preliminary to Maasai Mara, the Mau is a compelling alternative to the long rolling switchback of the main Mai Mahiu–Narok road. By **matatu**, the Nakuru–Narok route is a little easier than the other two; the village of East Mau, near the peaks, is your first destination.

There's little **accommodation** in the Mau range. **Enangiperi**, for example, roughly the halfway point, has one, very basic "lodging" (more a bed in a barn) and you may find yourself asking, or being invited, to stay with people. This can arouse suspicions in the local authorities, who are very unused to travellers in these parts and are sensitive to the arrival of strangers because of ongoing friction between local people and immigrant farmers and landlords from other parts of Kenya. The region saw some of the bloodiest **ethnic feuding** in the run-up to the 1997 elections, which displaced thousands of families. This shouldn't put you off visiting the region, however – it's wonderful countryside and there have been no incidents in the last couple of years, though it might be worth asking Kenyans about the current situation in advance of any trip.

Into the reserve from Narok

Once through Narok, you have a choice of routes after 17km. You could branch left for the **C12** road (new tarmac for 30km and then dirt track for 37km: it should all be surfaced within a few years if the authorities are to be believed), which makes its way south towards the Sekenani Gate and the eastern section of the reserve, where *Keekorok Lodge* and the reserve headquarters are the main human focuses. Or turn right, along the **B3** road to **Ngorengore**, for the western end of the reserve, the Mara River, and most of the other lodges and camps. Although the B3 itself (to Amala River) is easily driveable in 2WD in dry weather, this route can be treacherous and uncomfortable during or after rains, and isn't to be contemplated without a 4WD vehicle. In the wet, you're looking at five to six hours' driving and sliding from Narok to the Musiara or Oloololo gates. However, work started (and is continuing sporadically) on tarmacking this road to meet up with the older tarmac at Amala River – check the situation with the matatu drivers in Narok. See below for route descriptions from Ngorengore to the reserve.

Into the reserve from the north and west via Bomet and Ngorengore

From Kericho, due north of the reserve, leaving the C23 Kericho–Kisii just before **Sotik**, the route goes via the fast new B3 tarmac highway to Bomet (40km). There's a fair number of matatus making this run, but nothing much at **BOMET** when you get there. The overblown village consists of just three streets running round the back of the Mobil station, containing a small market, a few meagre *hotelis* and *dukas*, a KCB bank (Mon–Fri 9am–3pm, Sat 9–11am), post office, and three very basic and dirt cheap **lodgings**: *New Paradise Lodge* (❶) is over a bar and so is loud; *Kwa-Sisi Lodge* (❶) is more secure, and claims to have hot water; *Farmers House* (❶), at the end of Bomet on the left just after the Mobil station, is more modern in appearance, but otherwise undistinguished.

Past Bomet, the B3, direction Narok, heads southeast; the tarmac goes just beyond the Amala River (which becomes the Mara River further downstream). During the day, most matatus only run as far as the Amala River, although there are some early-morning matatus from Kisii and one mid-afternoon one from Kericho for Narok. Note that there's no public transport south to the reserve from Ngorengore, and no accommodation at all until the campsites at the reserve gates, so a tent would be handy if you get stuck.

If you're driving, you can follow the unsurfaced B3 past Amala River for about 19km, then turn right at the cluster of *dukas* at **Ngorengore** onto the C13 (4WD only) for Oloololo and Musiara gates at the western side of the reserve. Unless you're an extremely experienced driver, the C13 is for dry weather only, and even then has some very dodgy patches of deep mud along the way (see the box on p.413). Alternatively, you can continue for another 44km from Ngorengore to Ewaso Ngiro and the turning onto the much easier C12 (partly tarmacked, and okay for 2WD in dry weather) for the eastern side via Sekenani Gate. Note, however, that if it's been raining, even 4WD vehicles find the normally easy B3 hard going, as the wet clay makes escaping from ruts more or less impossible.

It's also possible to head straight for the western side of the Mara from Bomet by turning right off the B3 onto the (unpaved) C14 for Sigor and Kaboson, but this route, though shorter, is very rough and difficult to navigate (don't even think about it if you haven't got 4WD). You should stop regularly along the way to check with local people that you're on the right track. The first important (and *unmarked*) turning, is about 5km south of Bomet. At Kaboson the C14 continues northwest towards Kilgoris and Kisii; you need to turn off left in order to cross the Mara River and join the C13.

Into the reserve from the west via Kilgoris

From Kisii and South Nyanza, you have two options if you're driving: either going via the new Sotik–Bomet road (see p.416), or alternatively heading south to **Kilgoris** and **Lolgorien** and thence over the extremely rough Oloololo Escarpment to the gate of the same name at the far west of the reserve. Be warned, however, that this route is the worst of the lot, 4WD only, and then only scarcely passable in dry weather.

Into the reserve from Tanzania

On this last route, you're almost certain to be in a private vehicle; there's a twelve-kilometre gap between the Tanzanian formalities and the Kenya Police post at the Sand River Gate, where they'll sign you in and tell you where to go to complete formalities when you reach Nairobi. If you need to change money, there's *Keekorok Lodge*, 10km away, which will do so for you (full details on p.421), but the exchange clerks there have been known to limit this to an unhelpfully small amount like $20, unless you're going to stay at the lodge.

If you're driving out of Kenya to Tanzania in your own vehicle (not a rented car, which is only permitted with certain car rental operators and explicitly stated at the time of booking), you should, if possible, check the formalities in advance at Nyayo House in Nairobi, or at a provincial headquarters like Nakuru or Kisumu. As there are no facilities at Sand River, the police there seem to like photocopies of everything to be left with them, including your log book. As they have no photocopy machine, get these done well in advance.

Group Ranch entrance fees

Understandably unhappy at having been forced off the reserve lands, a number of Maasai Group Ranches adjacent to the reserve decided to create their own **wildlife trusts**, partially supported by KWS and other bodies, primarily to milk their own share of the tourist megabucks which hitherto flowed only into the local Transmara County Council's coffers. On paper, the aims are laudable: to promote the sustainable use of the natural and cultural resources found in the region; to ensure that environmental impacts from tourism are kept at a minimum; and to ensure a more equitable distribution of benefits derived from tourism. In practice, of course, corruption and local power-politics have already come into play, but perhaps it's too early to judge how the schemes are faring.

Although there are no official gates where you can buy the tickets, all of the more upmarket tented camps and lodges situated outside the reserve now insist you buy them, whether you intend to enter the reserve proper or not. In time, it seems likely that even the budget campsites outside the gates will have a person assigned to collect the fees. At least the tickets, which should have a silver hologram set across the central tear, are also valid for the reserve itself, whilst normal reserve tickets bought at the gates are equally valid in the adjacent Group Ranch lands. The Group Ranch tickets cost the same as the reserve tickets: $27 for adults, $10 for children.

Camping on a budget

Travellers on a budget aren't well catered for in Maasai Mara. If you can't afford the more expensive lodges and luxury tented camps, there are very few alternatives to do-it-yourself **camping**. Although there are about half a dozen campsites within the reserve itself, access to these is virtually impossible with-

Ngorengore ▲

MAASAI MARA-NORTHWEST AREA

N

Mara River

OLOOLOLO ESCARPMENT

Mpata Safari Club

Public Campsites

Mara River Camp

Airstrip

C13

WARNING: Except for the all-season Mara Serena Lodge to Keekorok route, the tracks on this map are not suitable for non-4-wheel drive vehicles & are often impassable in rain.
READ OUR ROUTE ADVICE CAREFULLY!

Mara Bridge

Leopard Gorge

Leopard Luga

Miti Mbili Luga

◄ Kilgoris

Airstrip

Kichwa Tembo Camp

Wildebeest River Crossings

Miti Mbili Plain

Oloololo Gate

Musiara Gate

Musiara Swamp

Murram Pits

Two Trees

Little Governors' Camp

TOPI PLAIN

Murram Pits

RESERVE BOUNDARY

◄ Mara Serena Lodge (main route)

Governors' Camp

Airstrip

Governors' Paradise Camp

Mara River

Euphorbia Luga

Fig Tree Camp, Keekorok Lodge & Talek Gate Campsite

◄ Oloololo Gate

PARADISE PLAIN

TWO HILLS

RHINO RIDGE

Wildebeest River Crossings

Dry season crossings only

◄ Keekorok Lodge (all-seasons)

Mara Serena Lodge

Hippo Pools

Airstrip

OL DOINYO OSEYIA

Dry season crossings only

Mara Intrepids Club

0   5 km

Talek River

▼ Mara New Bridge & Keekorok Lodge (Dry weather route)

out a guide and your own, very sturdy 4WD transport (they're marked on the *SK86 Survey of Kenya* map). However, the Mara extends far beyond the limits of the reserve, and game is usually in plentiful supply north of the boundaries, where most of the campsites are found.

You should remember to be particularly wary of snatch-and-run **baboon raids** at the Mara campsites – baboons are prone to grab anything inviting-looking, whether edible or not, and dash off with it to examine it later. And avoid irritating these loveable simians, as they have been known to attack humans when provoked. Apparently, they have a particular fondness for tooth-paste, but your camera bag is just as likely a target, if left within reach. You would be asking for trouble if you left your tent unguarded, either from rob-bery or wreckage by baboons (and probably both). Either pack up each morn-ing or leave someone behind – perhaps a ranger if you can agree about his fee.

Campsites outside the main gates are found at, clockwise from west to east: Oloololo, Musiara, Talek, Sekenani, Ololaimutiek and Sand River, and gener-ally charge around Ksh200–400 per person per night (exceptions are noted below). Most lack even basic facilities, though drinking water may be available, and you can expect some good-natured pestering by the rangers, who will try to extract money by taking you on game drives in your vehicle – sometimes with success, other times not. With tact, you can sometimes camp in the vicin-ity of lodges and tented camps located outside the reserve boundaries: a low-key approach (and stressing your self-sufficiency) helps. Be careful, though, as the reserve isn't fenced, and its denizens might get curious (or hungry). The best and some of the rest are as follows.

Musiara Gate has one of the most popular sites. You can camp by a little stream and, while you're safe enough, you're almost guaranteed to hear at close quarters the spine-tingling grunting roars of the Musiara lion prides. The rangers are quite happy to have campers and, if you have your own vehicle, will often be prepared to accompany you after dark for a meal at *Governors' Camp*.
Oloololo Gate's campsite has wonderful views of the escarpment and is also very welcoming. There are three further sites (no facilities) on the east bank of the Mara River, just outside the reserve. These can be booked through the warden in Narok, but in practice you can turn up and camp without making prior arrangements. They're hard to locate but better than most of Talek River's, with deep shade from the trees and fewer flies. You're likely to have to pay Group Ranch fees here. There's another recognized site just downstream of *Mara River Camp* on the river bank, reached by turning sharp left before entering the camp. Some lively hippos are found here and the site has the advan-tage of being close to the road and near the camp. You can also pitch at a spectacular vantage point near *Olkurruk Mara Lodge*, high above the reserve an hour's drive from the Oloololo Gate. This is a good site if you're arriving late from the west.
Sand River's campsite is perhaps the best, with toilets and fresh water from a stream, and it's nicely located in a spot where animals come to

drink at night. The attraction is its isolation: per-haps too isolated, as, again, there have been rob-beries, and the site acquired an unsavoury reputa-tion after the murder here of Julie Ward. The site is within the reserve, so you'll have to pay park fees.
Sekenani Gate has a number of campsites: *Sekenani Gate Campsite* itself is pretty basic. Just down the track to the east of the gate, *Olperr Elongo Campsite* is much better, as well as cheap-er (Ksh250 per person), with toilets, showers and security, tents and equipment for rent, and the option of full-board camping for Ksh1400 per per-son. It might also have bicycles for rent (for use outside the reserve) at Ksh1000 for a half day. Also here, 2km from the gate, is the fenced-in *Mara Springs Safari Camp* (reservations through Mountain Rock, 2nd floor, Jubilee Insurance House, PO Box 40270 Nairobi ☎ & ☏ 02/210051, ✉ mtnrock@form-net.com; $5 per person to camp, $15 per person in their tents; *bandas* ❹), a little more comfortable, with hot showers, spring water, kitchen and 24hr security, and the attraction of escorted "ecological and herbal medicine" hikes into the Naunaree Hills ($7–15 per person).
Talek Gate has a large number of campsites along the north bank of the Talek River, east of the gate. Several are the more-or-less permanent ter-ritories of camping safari operators – fetch up when a group is in and you may be able to avail yourself of facilities, water and drinks, for a small

Considering the vast numbers of tourists who pass through Maasai Mara every year, the isolated incidents which are occasionally splashed across the tabloids world-wide – the most notorious being the murder of Julie Ward at Sand River in 1988 – are thankfully just that: isolated and extremely rare. That said, be aware that the late 1990s saw a number of armed robberies from tented camps as well as from basic campsites in and around the Mara, in which at least one guard was shot dead. Security at all camps has since been stepped up but, in the unlikely event of finding an intruder in your tent at night, the advice is simply not to resist, or else pretend to be asleep, as one tourist did. You might also consider leaving any unnecessary valu-ables in a Nairobi hotel safe, and conceal any you might have with you (passport, traveller's cheques etc) in a plastic bag under the tent as you sleep.

charge. There have been a number of robberies here (read the Security box overleaf). *Riverside Campsite* is a public site with basic facilities five minutes' walk west of Talek Gate and the bridge, and has a kitchen, hot showers and flushing toi-lets. Nearby, the small centre of Talek has a few *dukas* and *hotelis* (*Pilot's Inn* is apparently the best) but no petrol.

Lodges and tented camps

If you're considering treating yourself, either in a safari package or independ-ently, it's worth choosing where you stay carefully, although competition, and demanding clients, keep standards high in every price range. Pressure on the two thousand-odd beds in and around the Mara can be intense, so booking ahead is essential if you want to be sure of your camp or lodge.

With the exception of the very expensive *Mpata Safari Club* and, at the other end of the spectrum, the cheaper *Voyager Safari Lodge*, the **lodges** and **mid-range tented camps** are all about the same price, and offer pretty much the same level of service. There's nothing intrinsically cheaper about sleeping under canvas: private bathrooms in brick, wood or concrete tent-annexes, hot show-ers and some remarkably good food in the middle of the wilds naturally hoist prices sky-high. Incidentally, you'll rarely find baths, even in the most expen-sive places – water is scarce, despite what the state of the roads might tell you, so showers are the order of the day. In the truly astronomic league, there are about half a dozen **luxury tented camps**, which are really little different from their mid-range cousins, with the exception of more pampering service and fewer guests, but even so you'll rarely have the place to yourself despite pre-tensions of exclusivity. Most of the guests arrive by air, so transfers from the nearest airstrip are also included.

One common **additional cost** is **game drives** in the lodge or camp vehi-cles, which come to around $35 per drive (or $70–100 for two or three). The most luxurious of the tented camps have two or three game drives worked into their full-board price. If you fancy **game drives at night** (with spotlights), you'll usually have to stay in one of the places outside the reserve, as driving inside is forbidden between 7pm and 6.30am without special permits. If you're **driving yourself**, it obviously makes most sense to go to a lodge or tented camp with optional game drives. If you have poor luck with animals in your own vehicle, you can always go out on an organized game drive. These are the camps that tend to be favoured by Kenya residents.

Note that **low-season rates**, although an attractive fifty–sixty percent off the normal high-season rates, usually apply only to the long rains from mid-April to the end of June, when the grass is high and animals difficult to spot. You'll also have problems driving into and around the reserve (courtesy of slippery clay and bogging black cotton soil), which makes getting a flight there and back the only dependable option, especially for places on the western side of the reserve (currently $165 return from Nairobi's Wilson Airport, see p.154).

Lodges: game drives not included

Keekorok Lodge ☎ 0305/22525–6, ℗ 22412; reservations through Block, p.42. A large and perennially busy hotel, *Keekorok* is situated in a rather open location, but a good hour closer to Nairobi by road than *Mara Serena*, its main competitor, and handy during the rainy season for access to the plains. The longest-running accommodation in the reserve, it still has high standards, but rooms vary in size and style, and though comfortable, some could do with a refit. There's a pleasant walkway round the back to a bar overlooking a small lake, where there are hippos and monkeys. Balloon flights ($385) lift off daily at 6am, and they can provide game scouts if you have your own vehicle (Ksh500 for two hours). A walk-in African buffet lunch costs $16. ⑥ low, ⑧ high.

Mara Serena Lodge ☎ 0305/22252, 22059 or 22137; reservations through Serena, p.44. Although the largest hotel in the reserve, this has, perhaps, fewer tour groups and is a touch less streamlined than *Keekorok*. It's located in a quieter area of the reserve and its architecture is more integrated into the surroundings. The design of the lodge is based on a re-creation of two Maasai *enkangs* with smallish but appealing cave-like rooms, up on a ridge with excellent views but little immediate wildlife appeal. Balloons again, and a pool. Reasonable value for money. Incidentally, access to Oloololo Gate is atrocious, whatever your map might say; Sekenani Gate via *Keekorok Lodge* is the easiest option. ⑥ low, ⑧ high.

Mara Simba Lodge ☎ 0305/222590 or 22051; reservations PO Box 66601 Nairobi ☎ 02/444401–2, ℗ 444403; or PO Box 84334 Mombasa ☎ 011/311093 or 316474. Located 5km south of Sekenani Gate, then 7km west, on the east bank of the Talek River. The lodge that is closest in style to a coastal resort hotel with its steep *makuti* roofs and wood-framed buildings. The rooms, in six two-storey wood and stone *bandas*, are large, AC, have great showers and views from verandahs over the river. The pool is clean but cool, and there's excellent buffet-style food (and an impressive vegetarian menu by Kenyan standards). A resident naturalist conducts walking safaris (and night-time game drives) outside the reserve, and there's a floodlight across the river. Downside: they have an overbooking policy, which

means that singles may have to share – a bit rich given the price. Petrol. Recommended for the river views. ⑥ low, ⑧ high.

Mara Sopa Lodge ☎ 0305/22196–7; reservations through Kenya Holidays, PO Box 72630 Nairobi ☎ 02/336088 or 336724, ℗ 223843, ⓔ sopa@africaonline.co.ke. By Ololaimutiek Gate on the east side, outside the boundary, with good management. Beautiful, large *banda*-style rooms with huge bathrooms. Pool. Good location for the wildebeest migration. Most guests arrive by air. ⑧ low, ⑨ high.

Mpata Safari Club ☎ & ℗ 0305/22538; reservations through Mpata Investments Inc, 20th floor, Anniversary Towers, PO Box 58402 Nairobi ☎ 02/217017, ℗ 217016. Up on the northern spur of Oloololo Escarpment overlooking *Mara River Camp*, about 25km from the Mara River Bridge along a pretty dreadful track, and thus most easily accessible by plane. Twenty stone-built *bandas*, including twelve suites, designed by the architects of the *Safari Park Hotel* in Nairobi and totally out of keeping with the area. Each *banda* has, among other comforts, a private verandah and a Jacuzzi from which to watch the sunset. The restaurant serves French cuisine and there's a twenty-metre pool. Obvious disadvantages are difficult access, its distance from the reserve proper, and its very high prices. ⑨

Olkurruk Mara Lodge ☎ 0305/22493–4 or 22496, ℗ 22495; reservations through Express Travel Group, Bruce House, Standard St, PO Box 40433 Nairobi ☎ 02/334722–7, ℗ 334825. One of the smallest lodges (small enough to be really friendly), with extraordinary views over the western half of the reserve. Very isolated on Oloololo Escarpment and, if you're coming by road, not for the faint-hearted – it's a good hour up from the Mara Bridge and the two western gates, which also means that game trips down to the reserve proper are once-a-day-only or all-day affairs. Thatched, luxury *bandas*, each divided into two twin rooms (rooms no. 1 and no. 4 have the finest outlooks). ⑥ low, ⑦ high.

Voyager Safari Lodge ☎ 0305/22546; reservations through Heritage, p.43. Upstream on the Mara, and miles from the reserve, near *Mara Safari Club*. Good game-viewing in the vicinity, but the hippos seen from the bar don't quite compensate for few elephants, or predators (cattle are widely grazed here). Rooms are adequate, but small, and there's a pool. The price, though, is almost half that of its competitors. **⑤** low, **⑥** high.

Mid-range tented camps: game drives not included

The following **tented camps** ("mid-range" is purely a relative description, nearly all are luxurious) offer optional game drives and airstrip transfers above their basic, full-board rates. A "package" including three game drives a day adds $60–100 per person per day to the bill. The less accessible western-end places can arrange road transfers from *Keekorok Lodge* or Sekenani Gates for around $25 per person, usually for four people minimum.

Fig Tree Camp ☎ 0305/22131 or 22161, ℱ 22131; reservations through Mada Holdings, 1st floor, Kimathi House, Kimathi St, PO Box 40683 Nairobi ☎ 02/221439 or 218321, ℱ 332170, ℮ madahold@kenyaweb.com. Close to Talek Gate and just outside the boundary (but subject to park fees), usually accessible by 2WD in dry seasons. The location is lovely, overlooking a bend in the Talek River (tents 1–25 occasionally see animals coming to water), and it's unpretentious, which makes a welcome change from the bigger lodges. Though the food's nothing special, the whole camp has recently been renovated and the bathrooms are among the best in the Mara. There are solid-built rooms as well as comfortable tents (the former in fragrant gardens, the latter overlooking the river), all rather closely spaced, and a small pool and fun treetop bar. Balloon flights ($385), horseback safaris ($30) and game walks ($17) are also available. The friendly, on-site balloon team can always advise on the whereabouts of local wildlife. **⑥** low, **⑦** high.

Kichwa Tembo Camp ☎ 0305/22465, ℱ 22501. A very highly thought-of Abercrombie & Kent operation and rival to nearby *Governors' Camp* with many loyal repeat guests. Deep in the trees at the foot of the Oloololo Escarpment just outside the reserve, with excellent food and a pleasant pool, and famous for its black-tie dinners. Meryl Streep and Robert Redford stayed here while filming *Out of Africa*. Still, there's something strangely artificial about the place. Due to the liveliness of the local fauna, *Kichwa Tembo* (which means "elephant's head") is fenced in. **⑦** low, **⑧** high.

Mara River Camp ☎ 0305/22186 or 22188; reservations through Savannah Camps and Lodges, p.44. Just outside the reserve 3–4km north of the Mara Bridge on the rough Oloololo Gate–Ngorengore road, on the south bank of the river. With more rustic facilities than most tented camps – plain but wholesome food, water heated over log fires – *Mara River Camp* is rated by enthusiastic naturalists and serious photographers

and film-makers (and there's a resident ornithologist who conducts walks). There are sixteen rather closely spaced tents, all with river views. Wandering hippos and occasional elephant rule out the possibility of manicured gardens or a pool. Great riverside breakfasts. **⑥** low, **⑧** high.

Rekero Camp Reservations through Bush Homes of East Africa, p.42. Although outside the reserve, this place has comfortable thatched, s/c cottages, which can accommodate up to ten guests. On request, the Beatons who run the place can mobilize a traditional tented camp for three nights for four to ten people. As well as night and day game-viewing, activities include bush walks, picnics, and cultural visits to Maasai and Dorobo communities. **⑨**

Sarova Mara Camp ☎ 0305/22386 or 22194, ℱ 22371; reservations through Sarova, p.44. The most accessible of all the Mara camps and lodges on the main C12 entrance road, just inside the Sekenani Gate. Over seventy well-furnished tents in attractive, jungly gardens, with lily ponds full of fish, and families of mongoose populating the shrubberies. Very popular, especially with locals and Indians, as they have a vegetarian menu every day for every meal. There's also a pool. A little too touristy for some, but good value so long as you don't have kids (no reductions). FB **⑥** low, **⑧** high.

Sekenani Camp ☎ 0305/22454, ℱ 22458; reservations through Chartered Expeditions Kenya, 3rd floor, Campus Towers, University Way, PO Box 61542 Nairobi ☎ 02/333285, ℱ 228875. On the reserve boundary 6km southeast of Sekenani Gate (which you have to pass through). Small and select, with fifteen large, very private tents on stilts snuggled up to trees, with baths as well as showers, excellent food and a personal approach. The lack of a pool – and the no electricity policy – dismay some visitors. There's no perimeter fence, so you get escorted to and from the dining area across a plank bridge by a spear-wielding Maasai. The camp is run in collaboration with 26 Maasai families, and the policy is to cause as little disrup-

tion to wildlife as possible. ⑥ low, ⑨ high.
Siana Springs Intrepids Camp ⓣ0305/22553,
ⓕ22429; reservations through Heritage Hotels,
p.43. On the site of the former *Cottar's Camp* (an
old Kenya residents' favourite), this complete refit
(a lovely pool and sultan-esque tents with every
conceivable comfort) is a determined effort to
reproduce an old-style mood and manners. The

main advantages here – apart from the convenient
location, off the main Narok entry road – are the
long-established site outside the reserve, shaded
by mature trees, with elephant and leopard hides,
and a good programme of walking trips in the
vicinity, accompanied by a first-rate naturalist.
Night game drives by spotlight outside the reserve.
Don't forget to zip-up your tent. ⑦ low, ⑧ high.

Luxury tented camps: game drives included

Governors' Camp ⓣ & ⓕ0305/22273; reservations through Governors' Camps, p.42–43. Located
in the woods on a bend in the Mara River on the
site of an old hunting camp and close to the fantastic game-viewing of the Musiara marsh (more
or less impassable during the rains, as is the track
up to Oloololo Gate), *Governors'* has retained its
exclusive "bush" atmosphere despite the large
number of tents (38), with no expense spared
Elephants trundle through at night; guards keep
watch for more dangerous visitors and escort
guests between their tents and the (excellent)
restaurant. No pool. Tents 1–3 have no river views,
and 25–30 can be noisy. Road access is difficult at
the best of times, so guests tend to fly in.
Extremely high rates (currently $440 double), and
derisory children's reductions. ⑨
Little Governors' Camp ⓣ & ⓕ0305/22040;
same reservations details as main camp. Reached
by a two-kilometre drive and then a rope-pulled
boat across the Mara, this is the annexe from
which the *Governors'* balloons fly. Hidden in the
trees by its own water hole, with wonderful bird-
watching, it's one of the reserve's smallest and
most intimate set-ups, always fully booked in
advance of the main camp. It has 27 beds, 3 of
them double. No pool, and difficult disabled access
(steep steps). There's also an annual encampment
called Governors' Paradise Camp – which is set up
between *Governors'* and *Little Governors'* in May
or June after the long rains. Same rates as

Governors' Camp. ⑨
Mara Intrepids Club ⓣ0305/22321; reservations
through Heritage Hotels, p.43. Thirty tents parked
on a bluff overlooking the Talek River, just about
accessible by road in the rains. Four-poster beds
in the "tented suites". Baited leopards come daily,
and there's a watchtower and swimming pool. It's
also the base for the innovative Night Sight
Safaris, an Israeli-run hi-tech outfit which uses ex-
army infra-red video cameras and scopes to view
game at night ($100 per person, $50 kids, $20 for
a video tape of the night's viewing). A stylish way
to dispose of your savings. ⑦ low, ⑨ high.
Mara Safari Club ⓣ0305/22172, ⓕ22105;
reservations through Lonrho, p.43. Very modish
tented camp, spaced out in a garden high up on a
calm oxbow loop of the Mara River, but over 40km
outside the reserve's Oloololo Gate along the terrible Ngorengore road. There are fifty "tents", all the
last word in luxury, with four-poster beds, huge
marble bathrooms, and verandahs with private
views of the river. Hippos wallow and yawn in the
chocolatey water below the camp (kept out of the
camp by electric fences), while monkeys rampage
through the trees on the opposite bank. Facilities
include a heated swimming pool – at nearly
2000m not such a bad idea. Balloon flights and
visits to Maasai villages are available, but facilities
are way overpriced (currently $430 in high season)
considering the camp's size and location. ⑨

Around the reserve

Wherever you go there are **animals**. This is the one part of Kenya where the
concentrations of game that existed in the nineteenth century can still be seen.
The most interesting areas, scenically and zoologically, are **westwards**, signalled by the long ridge of the Oloololo Escarpment. If you only have a day
or two, you should spend most of your time here, near the **Mara River**.

It sometimes seems that wherever there are animals there are **people** – in
minibuses, in land cruisers, in rented Suzukis, often parked in ravenous, zoom-
lensed packs around understandably irritable lions, leopards and cheetahs (the
official limit is five vehicles around an animal at any one time, although up to
sixteen vehicles (over a hundred people) have been reported around three

Vicarious pleasures

As usual, if you're not staying in luxury accommodation, a taste of the high life can be had if you drop into a **lodge** for a drink or something to eat (generally expensive – establish the price first). Some of the lodges and camps, *Keekorok* especially, get heavily invaded during the high seasons, and casual visitors have been known to abuse the lodges' hospitality, so these lodges may turn away non-residents. Changing into decent clothes probably won't help – staff know exactly who's who – but discretion and some words of Swahili might. Swimming pools are usually out of bounds. The only shops are lobby gift boutiques. If you're lucky you might find a lodge willing to sell you some fuel, though at high prices. If you don't see pumps or anticipate a refusal, go direct to the oiliest part of the staff compound and ask.

cheetahs. This popularity is highly seasonal – it can be overbearing around Christmas – but it needn't spoil your visit. If you aren't driving yourself, encourage your tour driver to explore new areas (but not off-road) and perhaps stress you'd rather experience the reserve in its totality than tick off animal species. The reserve is crisscrossed with **tracks** but the level plains tend to encourage off-track driving. So far this hasn't had quite the damaging effect it has in Amboseli – the Mara's ecosystem is less fragile and there's more of it – but there are signs that a balance won't be maintained much longer: look at the stretch along the edge of the forest to the north of *Governors' Camp*, and read the box on "Environmental Concerns" on p.389.

Fast **roads**, with improved, hard-core surfaces and theoretically uncrossable banks and ditches alongside, have been laid in various parts of the reserve, especially the east, and there is now a good all-weather route from Talek Gate to Sekenani Gate, inside the reserve. During the rains, however, and for some weeks after, the western parts of the reserve can be very wet and treacherous. The bolder tracks on our maps should be passable all year round, but the smaller tracks, especially in the northwest, are often waterlogged. Here too, the crossings over the tributaries of the Talek are often impassable. If you're trying to cross the reserve at this time of year, the downstream one, 6km north from the *Mara Intrepids Club*, is the one to aim for, as the camp's Land Rovers may be able to tow you across if the water is high – an experience in a Suzuki that's slightly more exciting than most people want. It's worth noting that the only permanent **east–west route** across the Mara is the long haul via Mara New Bridge on the southern boundary to *Mara Serena*. Heading up from *Mara Serena* to Oloololo Gate, however, the main road skirts the western edge of Olpunyata Swamp, which is completely impassable in wet weather. Similarly dreadful is the shorter but ill-defined jumble of tracks known as the New Mara Serena Road, on the eastern edge of the swamp, for which you'd definitely need a guide in wet weather, and plenty of time in dry.

Visiting Maasai villages

One diversion which you are likely to be offered, especially if you are travelling on an organized safari, is a visit to a **Maasai** *enkang*, usually called, incorrectly, a *manyatta* (see box p.426). Forget about the authenticity of tribal life: this is the real world. Many children are sick, many of the young men have fled to the fleshpots, and everyone wants your money. Unprepared and uncomfortable, most visitors find the experience a deeply depressing rip-off – $15–20 each in a group from a lodge or tented camp, or around Ksh400 per person if you arrange it yourself (note that unless you hand the money over to your

Maasai hosts yourself, a large percentage of what you pay will remain in the hands of your lodge, or your driver). If you can forget any TV-documentary illusions, and actually sit down and talk to people, the experience can be transformed and full of laughter, as it will be if you have your own children with you (see, for comparison, the accounts of similar meetings with Njemps, Samburu and Elmolo people – p.608 and p.615).

The animals

Big, brunette **lions** are the best-known denizens of the reserve and there are usually several prides living around the **Musiara Swamps**, which are dry much of the year. It is sometimes possible to watch them hunt, as they take very little notice of vehicles. While lions seem to be lounging under every other bush, finding a **cheetah** is much harder (they can often be seen on the *murram* mounds alongside the Talek–Sekenani road). These are solitary cats – slender, unobtrusive and somewhat shy. When they move, their speed and agility are marvellous. If you are lucky enough to witness a kill (cynicism about such voyeurism is quickly dispelled when you find yourself on the spot), it's likely to take place in a cloud of dust, a kilometre from where the chase began. But cheetahs are vulnerable to too much harassment. Traditionally, they hunt at dawn and dusk (at the same times as tourists are hunting for photographs), but there is evidence that they are turning to a midday hunting pattern when the humans are shaded in the lodges – not a good time of day for the cheetah, which expends terrific energy in each chase and may have to give up if it goes on for more than thirty or forty seconds.

Leopards are rarely seen by visitors, though there are plenty of them. You can give yourself a serious case of risen hair when you come across their footprints down on the sandbanks at the edge of the Mara River outside the reserve boundary. But they are largely nocturnal and prefer to remain well out of sight. You would have to crane your neck at a lot of trees to have much chance of seeing one. Their deep, grating roar at night – a grunt, repeated – is a sound which, once heard, you carry around with you.

If you have a ranger with you, he's certain to know the current news about the **black rhinos** – every calf born is a victory – though finding them is often surprisingly difficult. Check out Rhino Ridge, where a handful of the reserve's surviving *faru* are sometimes obligingly positioned. There are also now some **white rhinos** in the reserve, brought up from South Africa and closely guarded. They are thought to be doing well, though only one of them has been spotted recently.

Maasai Mara's other heavyweights are about in abundance. The Mara River surges with **hippo**, while big families of **elephant** traipse along the forest margins and spread out into the Musiara marshes when the herbage is thick and juicy. The park is home to an estimated thousand or so elephants, with another five hundred living in the districts beyond its boundaries. **Buffalo** are seen all over and can be menacing when they surround a small Jeep in a thundering herd of several hundred tons. It is the solitary old bulls that you need to watch out for – their reputation (and that of old rhinos) is not exaggerated. Tourists' vehicles get stoved in quite often, so always back off.

Among all these outstanding characters, the herds of humble grazers fade quickly into the background. It's easy to become blasé when one of the much-hyped "big five" (elephant, rhino, buffalo, lion, leopard) isn't eyeballing you at arm's length – but those are the hunter's trophies, not the photographer's. **Warthog** families like rows of dismantled Russian dolls, **zebra** and **gazelle**, odd-looking **hartebeest** and slick, purple-flanked **topi** are all scattered with

After deep reflection on my people and culture, I have painfully come to accept that the Maasai must change to protect themselves, if not their culture. They must adapt to the realities of the modern world for the sake of their own survival. It is better to meet an enemy out in the open and to be prepared for him than for him to come upon you at home unawares.

Tepilit Ole Saitoti, Maasai (Elm Tree Books).

When the first European hunting safaris made the Mara world-famous in the early years of last century, they were ransacking a region recently deserted by the Maasai. Smallpox had ravaged the Maasai communities and rinderpest had torn through their cattle herds. As a consequence, the wild animals had the region virtually to themselves. Traditionally, the Maasai hunted only lion and, in times of famine, eland and buffalo, the "wild cattle". Only the Okiek people (the "Dorobo in Maa", meaning "people without cattle") hunted for a living. The Maasai themselves had always lived in some harmony with the wildlife.

By 1961, after half a century of sport, the white hunters had succeeded in bringing the Mara's lion population down to nine and, to a chorus of alarm, the Maasai Mara Game Reserve was created, to be administered by the Maasai District Council at Narok, exclusively as a game sanctuary – and a tourist attraction. By then, improved medicine and veterinary facilities had eased the old hardships of the traditional Maasai way of life. They were expanding again, and now land was becoming the biggest issue.

Of all Kenya's peoples, the Maasai have received the most attention. Often strikingly tall and slender, dressed in brilliant red cloth, with beads and metal jewellery, and the young men with long, ochred hairstyles, they have a reputation for ferocity, pampered by an arch superiority complex. Traditionally, they lived off milk and blood (extracted, by a close shot with a stumpy arrow, from the jugular veins of their live cattle), and they loved their herds more than anything else, rarely slaughtering a beast. They maintained rotating armies of spartan warriors – the *morani* – who killed lions as a test of manhood. And they opposed all interference and invasion with swift, implacable violence. Their scorn of foreigners was absolute: they called the Europeans, who came swaddled in clothing, *iloridaa enjekat* or "those who confine their farts". They also derided African peoples who cultivated by digging the earth – the Maasai even left their dead unburied – while those who kept cattle were given grudging respect so long as they conceded that all the world's cattle were a gift from God to the Maasai, whose incessant cattle-raiding was thus righteous reclamation of stolen property.

Some of this noble savagery was undoubtedly exaggerated by slave- and ivory-traders, anxious to protect their routes from the Europeans. That said, the Maasai have on the whole been stubbornly conservative, with a disinclination to change their traditional ways which has tended to mark them out as the whipping boys of Kenyan development. At the same time, something close to a cult of the Maasai has been around ever since Thomson walked *Through Maasailand* in 1883. In the early years of the colony, Delamere's obsession with the people and all things Maasai spawned a new term, "Maasai-itis", and with it a motley crop of romantic notions about their ancestors alluding to ancient Romans, Egyptians and even the lost tribes of Israel.

abandon across the scene. The topi are peculiarly characteristic of Maasai Mara, and there are always one or two in every herd standing sentry on a tussock or an old termite mound. Topi and **giraffe** – whose dream-like, slow–

These days, the tourist industry gives the Maasai a major spot in its repertoire. Maasai dancing is *the* entertainment, while necklaces, gourds, spears, shields, *rungus* (knobkerries), busts (carved by Akamba carvers) and even life-sized wooden *morani* (to be shipped home in a packing case) are the stock-in-trade of the curio and souvenir shops. For the Maasai themselves, the rewards are fairly scant. Cattle are still at the heart of their society; there are dozens of names for different colours and patterns, and each animal among their three million is individually cherished. But they are assailed on all sides: by uplands farmers expanding from the north; by eviction from the tourist/conservation areas within the reserve boundaries to the south; and by a climate of opposition to the old lifestyle from all around. Sporadically urged to grow crops, go to school, build permanent houses, and generally settle down and stop being a nuisance, they face an additional dilemma in squaring these edicts with the fickle demands of the tourist industry for traditional authenticity. Few make much of a living selling souvenirs, but enterprising *morani* can do well by just posing for photos, and even better if they hawk themselves in Nairobi or down on the coast.

Many men persevere with the status of warriorhood, though modern Kenya makes few concessions to it. Arrested for hunting lions, and prevented from building *enkangs* for the *eunoto* transition in which they pass into elderhood, the *morani* have kept most of the superficial marks of the warrior without being able to live the life fully. The ensemble of a cloth tied over one shoulder, together with spear, sword, club and braided hair, is still widely seen, and after circumcision, in their early days as warriors, you can meet young men out in the bush, hunting for birds to add to their elaborate, taxidermic headdresses. But there is considerable local frustration. When the pasture is poor, the *morani* have little compunction about driving their herds into the reserve to compete with the wildlife. All but a few of the Mara's black rhinos have been slaughtered for their horns in the last few decades (though a few more have now been brought in from elsewhere). And there have even been isolated attacks on tourist camps in and around the reserve.

Land is the great issue today. The Maasai have still not fully come to terms with the idea of individual ownership of it, although a promising development for them has been the recent introduction of wildlife reserves run by Maasai Group Ranches (see the box on p.417), which seems at last to be providing a steady source of income from tourism. "Range schemes" – plans for growing wheat or rearing cattle – are also common now, though they are just as likely to benefit newcomers from other parts of Kenya as the local Maasai. The lifestyle is changing: education, MPs and elections, new laws and new projects, jobs and cash, all impinge on the Maasai's lives – with mixed results. The traditional Maasai staple diet of curdled milk and cow's blood is rapidly being replaced by cornmeal *ugali*. Many Maasai have taken work in the lodges and tented camps, while others end up as security guards in Nairobi. For the majority, who continue to live semi-nomadic lives among a welter of constraints, the future would seem to hold little promise. But that stubborn cultural pride – the kind of hauteur that keeps a cattle-owner thoroughly impoverished in cash terms, while he counts his 220 beasts – may yet insulate the Maasai against the social upheavals that seem certain to rock the lives of many Kenyans in the twenty-first century.

motion canter is one of the reserve's most beautiful and underrated sights – are often good pointers for predators in the vicinity. And the reserve has rare herds of **roan antelope** – swaggering, horse-sized animals with sweeping, curved horns, that you'll see elsewhere only in Ruma National Park near Kisii.

The wildebeest migration

It is the annual **wildebeest migration**, however, that plants Maasai Mara in the imagination. With a lemming-like instinct, finally gelled into mass movement, the herds gather in their hundreds of thousands on the withering plains of Serengeti to begin the long, streaming journey northward following the scent of moisture and green grass in the Mara. They arrive in July and August, pouring over the Sand River and into the eastern side of the reserve around *Keekorok*, gradually munching their way westwards in a milling, unsettled mass and turning south again in October. Never the most graceful of animals, wildebeest play up to their appearance with frolicsome, unpredictable behaviour, bucking like wild horses, springing like jack-in-the-boxes, or suddenly sprinting off through the herd for no apparent reason.

The **Mara River** is the biggest obstacle they come up against. Heavy rains falling up on the Mau Range where the river rises can produce a sudden brown flood which claims thousands of animals as they try to cross. Like huge sheep (they are, in fact, most closely related to goats), the brainless masses swarm desperately to the banks and plunge in. Many are fatally injured on rocks and fallen branches; others are skewered by flailing legs and horns. With every surge, more bodies bob to the surface and float downstream. Heaps of bloated carcasses line the banks, injured and dying animals struggle mournfully in the mud, while vultures and marabou storks squat in glazed, post-prandial stupor.

The migration's full, cacophonous impact is awesomely melodramatic – both on the plains where the multitudes graze and cavort, and at the deadly river crossings. This superabundance of meat accounts for the Mara's big lion population. Through it all, the **spotted hyenas** scamper and loiter like psychopathic sheep dogs. Half a million wildebeest **calves** are born in January and February before the migration; two out of three perish without returning to the Serengeti.

Balloon flights

From the ground, the migration of the wildebeest is a compelling phenomenon, bewildering and strangely disturbing, as you witness individual struggles and events – in particular if you have a chance to watch near one of the river crossings. From the air, in a **hot-air balloon**, it resembles an ant's nest. At $360–400 per person for the sixty- to ninety-minute flight plus breakfast with *vin mousseux* (or a Bloody Mary, depending on how you feel) **balloon "safaris"** are the ultimate in bush chic. Just watching the inflation and lift-off at dawn is a spectacular sight, especially at *Little Governors' Camp*, deep in the woods. Trips are run by several of the larger camps and lodges, including *Keekorok*, *Serena*, *Siana Springs* and *Fig Tree*. In order to avoid frightening the animals unduly, however, there is now a minimum height below which the balloons are not permitted to fly.

You don't have to be staying at the lodge they fly from: they'll come and pick you up at 5.30am. Operators include:

Adventures Aloft for flights from *Fig Tree Camp*; reservations through Mada Holdings, 1st floor, Kimathi House, Kimathi St, PO Box 40683 Nairobi ☎02/221439 or 218321, ⓕ332170, ⓔmadahold @form-net.com. Great staff. Until a few years

back, *Fig Tree* also offered flights in a microlight, whose great advantage over hot-air ballooning was that you were free to take a trip at any time of day – not just at the crack of dawn. Currently suspended, it's worth contacting Mada Holdings in

case flights have been resumed.
Balloon Safaris for flights from *Keekorok Lodge* and *Siana Springs Intrepids*; reservations through Balloon Safaris Ltd, Wilson Airport, PO Box 43747 Nairobi ☎ 02/502850–1, ⓕ 501424. From *Keekorok*, the prevailing winds tend to carry the montgolfiers westwards and higher: fine for a grand view, but less satisfactory for animal-watching.
Mara Balloon Safaris Ltd for flights from *Little*

Governors' Camp; reservations through Governors' Camps, p.42. The most spectacular take-off site, and the only people to cook your breakfast on the balloon's burners after you land.
Transworld Kenya Ltd for flights from *Serena Lodge*; reservations through Transworld Kenya Ltd, 5th floor, Corner House, Mama Ngina St/Kimathi St, PO Box 44690 Nairobi ☎ 02/33312, ⓕ 333488, ⓔ transworld@form-net.com.

The Samburu/Buffalo Springs/Shaba national reserves

Daily 6.30am–6.30pm; each reserve $15 per day/overnight, children $5; private vehicle Ksh200, camping $8 ($10 in a "special" campsite). District Warden (Samburu): PO Box 53 Maralal ☎ 0368/2053 or 2412. No driving after 7pm. Speed limit 30kph. Map: Survey of Kenya SK114 Shaba, Samburu and Buffalo Springs at 1cm:500m (1990).

Up in the north of the country, in the hot, arid lowlands beneath Mount Kenya, **Samburu National Reserve** was set up in the late 1960s, a tract of country around the richest stretch of the Ewaso Ngiro (or Uaso Ngiro) River. In this region, the permanent water and the forest shade on the banks draw plentiful wildlife in the dry season and maintain many of the less peripatetic species year-round. While the wildlife spectacle doesn't always match that of the southern parks, the peace and scenic beauty of Samburu is unquestionable and, in the kind of mood swing which only an equatorial region can produce, the contrast with the fertile farming country of the Highlands just a few kilometres to the south couldn't be more striking. In the background, the sharp hill of **Koitogor** rises in the middle of Samburu Reserve, making a useful reference point. And on the horizon, 30km to the north, looms the gaunt red block of **Ol Olokwe** mountain. Head up into the scratchy bush in the south of **Buffalo Springs Reserve** and the whole region is spread out before you.

Of the popular game parks, Samburu is usually reckoned the most remote and inaccessible. This has more to do with its location than with present practicalities. On the fringes of what is still called the "NFD" (Northern Frontier District), the combined Samburu/Buffalo Springs/Shaba national reserves were closed for many years after their creation, because of the war against Somali irredentists that flared over northern Kenya in the 1960s and early 1970s. Isolated incidents of banditry have recurred ever since, with major **security concerns** being raised during 1997–98, which saw a number of armed hold-ups of tourist vehicles as well as attacks on locals, some using guns that had apparently been rented out by home guards. Security has since been beefed up within the reserves, but the **road up from Isiolo** is still prone to occasional **banditry** – check the situation with a reputable travel agent in Nairobi, or with the police at the checkpoint just north of Isiolo. Although your chances of running into serious trouble are extremely slim, should you be unlucky enough to get on the wrong end of an AK-47, the usual rule applies: don't resist (though you might consider concealing valuables in the vehicle before leaving Isiolo).

Practicalities

In practical terms, **access** isn't difficult. If you're circling Mount Kenya, Samburu Reserve is close at hand, a couple of hours north of Nanyuki (see p.191). Buses and matatus run down onto the hazy plain as far as Isiolo (p.619), as does the tarmac and, if you don't have wheels, this is normally as far as you can go without hitching, although there are one or two matatus which daily venture across the jolting dirt track to Archer's Post. But waiting at the Isiolo police barrier usually gets you a lift into the reserve itself in a few hours. If you're driving independently, Isiolo is a straightforward target. You may be required to wait at the police checkpoint for a convoy to form for the short continuation to the reserve; you won't wait long, as there are plenty of safari vans which cover the stretch every day.

Note that the **daily/overnight fees** chargeable in each reserve apply even if you're only in transit to the other: if you enter, you pay.

Lodges and tented camps

There are five lodges/camps in Samburu/Buffalo Springs, and one in Shaba. They mostly offer very good low-season rates (April to July, except Easter) at fifty–sixty percent of high-season rates for doubles, dropping right down to thirty percent for singles. All prices are for full board.

Buffalo Springs Lodge Reservations through African Tours and Hotel Limited, PO Box 30471 Nairobi ☎02/336858, ⓕ218109). On the south side of the river in the more arid Buffalo Springs Reserve, this place has fallen on hard times and when not busy it can feel a rather desolate sort of place. Things aren't helped by its increasingly tatty accommodation: the cottages are OK, but avoid the tents (same price) which are barely adequate. On the plus side, there's good game-viewing across the swamp from the bar (floodlit at night):

they bait a crocodile for the cameras, just as other lodges bait leopards. Casual visitors are welcome to use the pool (Ksh200), showers, and bar. Lunch is expensive at $18 per person, but there's Samburu dancing daily at 2.30pm (Ksh200). You can also cash traveller's cheques, at a bad rate. No game drives. ⑥ low, ⑦ high.
Larsens Tented Camp ☎0164/31373–4, ⓕ31375; reservations through Block, p.42. East of *Samburu Lodge*, this is Samburu's smallest camp, very upmarket and highly recommended if you

don't mind the vaguely snooty atmosphere common to all such places, with seventeen en-suite tents facing the river. Game drives are part of the deal, and the food is excellent. No children under 7 or children's rates, and no pool (you can use the one at *Samburu Lodge*). ⑦ low, ⑨ high.

Samburu Intrepids Club ☎0164/30811, ⑥20022; reservations through Heritage Hotels, p.43. Upstream of the other lodges and camps on the north bank, an impressive and very luxurious development, and a good deal cheaper than *Larsens*. All 25 tents are on stilts, furnished with unecological mahogany furniture, four-poster beds, fans and electricity. Also offers game drives, camel safaris and bird walks. Good value out of season. ⑤ low, ⑧ high.

Samburu Lodge ☎0164/30762 or 30778, ⑥30781; reservations through Block, p.42. On the north bank, beautifully located on a heavily wooded broad bend of the river as it passes near the Samburu Reserve headquarters, this is the oldest lodge in the reserves – with rooms of various standards and a pool. Despite a frenetically busy atmosphere around the riverside terraces and

crocodile-viewing bars, the glorious setting is hard to fault. Excellent food. Good mechanics and fuel available. ⑥ low, ⑧ high.

Samburu Serena Lodge ☎3900 Radiocall Nairobi; reservations through Serena, p.44. On the south bank, just outside Buffalo Springs Reserve. Well managed, with a good pool and great food, but not one of Serena's best. ⑥ low, ⑦ high.

Sarova Shaba Lodge ☎0164/30638 or 0161/2467; reservations through Sarova, p.44. Downstream on Ewaso Ngiro River in the otherwise empty Shaba Reserve. Immaculate and very attractively landscaped, with a superb swimming pool (Ksh345 for casual visitors) and streams running through public areas (the thick vegetation obscures views of big animals), but the fact that the crystal-clear spring which feeds them was expropriated from the local population (a concrete well was dug for them instead) jars a little. Mosquito-netted rooms with fans, and Samburu ceremonial marriages for those tying the knot around Christmas. Excellent naturalist. Petrol. ⑥ low, ⑦ high.

Campsites

There are four public **campsites** in Buffalo Springs Reserve, not far from the main gate, Ngare Mara. This Champagne Ridge camping area used to have a nasty reputation for robberies, but security has been boosted and there have been no attacks in the last few years. As usual, you face the hassle of having to pack your tent each day before setting off on the animal trail. If you don't have a vehicle, being dropped off at Champagne Ridge could prove painful if nobody turned up to give you a ride out again. Still, it's a pretty area among the acacias, and it abounds with giraffe and other animals. There's also one "special" campsite in Buffalo Springs – *Kubi Panya*, on the Maji ya Chumvi stream.

Three other sites lie on the north bank of the Ewaso Ngiro River in Samburu, a few kilometres to the west of the bridge and park HQ. Except for the farthest of these – *Buffalo Special* campsite, which has toilets and showers – there are no facilities.

Initially, the best move for the wheel-less is to get to the area of *Samburu Lodge* and **camp** near the park headquarters: not a wonderful site, with no toilets or running water (and the lodge may even make you pay for that commodity), but convenient and legal, if somewhat unhygienic. You can walk to the lodge's riverside bars and restaurant (though if after 6.30pm, get an escort – there are animals everywhere), sometimes flop in the pool (depending on circumstances and numbers – it's occasionally restricted to guests), gloat over the crocodiles in the river below, and peer darkly through binoculars at the regular but brief evening cabaret of leopards retrieving bait from a tree on the far bank. If your finances stretch, you can shell out $45 or so for a two-hour morning or evening game run in one of the lodge's land cruisers, or around $125 for the whole vehicle. Most people camping here without their own vehicles seem to manage to find the occasional ride around the reserve, if only because the opportunities exist to meet travellers with their own transport over a drink.

Note that the **baboons** at the campsite here are beyond being an amusement. Leave your tent and its contents only under guard. The fact that baboons sometimes fall shrill victims to crocs at the water's edge seems less distressing after a day or two spent in the area.

Exploring the reserves

Except during and immediately after the rains, scrubby bush country takes up most of the reserve district, but there are some large acacia thickets, especially in the eastern part of **Buffalo Springs**. Here, the **springs** themselves are a welcome target; these are pools of clear if weedy water, one of which has been sanitized with concrete for the benefit of swimmers and (most of the time) the exclusion of crocodiles. If you have any doubts at all, do not swim. *Buffalo Springs Lodge*, a few kilometres away, is low-key and always welcoming for a drink. There's a fine jungly marsh reaching nearly to the terrace, where you'll often see animals.

If Samburu's **wildlife** is occasionally disappointing, it may be fairer to say that the dry country ecosystems are prone to large variations in animal populations as they move in search of water and pasture. Some visitors have tremendous luck and it can provide consistently excellent animal-watching. The best areas are along the south side of the river in Buffalo Springs Reserve, close to *Samburu Lodge*. Poaching has wiped out the rhino here, but lions are often seen – again, most often in Buffalo Springs.

Meanwhile, the locally burgeoning **elephant herds** have ruined some sections of the riverine forest. The range of rarer, and localized, races and species compensates, though. Common and conspicuous among these are the **reticulated giraffe** with its beautiful jigsaw marking; **Grevy's zebra**, the large, finely striped species that has a bushy mane and outsize ears; the **Somali ostrich**, which has blue rather than pink legs; and the **gerenuk** ("camel head" in Somali), the antelope species that stands on its hind legs to reach the foliage

Leopards at Samburu

Samburu's **leopards** are a regular sight – at least from the terraces at *Samburu* and *Samburu Serena* lodges, both of which have taken to baiting the trees on the opposite banks with haunches of meat. Between drinks and dinner, guests get a floodlit view of the stealthy predator reduced to a giant pussycat. The stampede for cameras doesn't encourage the leopards to stay long, so efforts are made to attach the meat firmly to the tree. It's all pathetically contrived (and you can forget worthwhile pictures or videos at that distance without expensive equipment), but only with luck or dogged persistence will you see a wild leopard other than in such circumstances, and it's hard to blame the hotels for making the most of the local attractions. You should beware, at *Samburu Lodge*, of occasional excursions by the leopards across the river to the human zoo, hence the signs warning "Do not stray beyond the lit path".

Recent research has shown how little is really known about these cats. For the most part, they live off any small animals that come their way. The popular notion that they consume many baboons is apparently misled. Baboon troops will turn on an attacking leopard instantly and, unless surprised, usually manage to fend it off. Less organized monkeys of all kinds, however, are often caught, and in Samburu (for those leopards not on the lodge gravy train), the favourite hunting grounds are the stands of forest and clumps of strange, branching doum palms by the river which sometimes shake with monkeys. Black-faced vervet and blue monkeys are the commonest inhabitants.

which it feeds upon. Samburu's **birdlife** is diverse and prolific and includes the marshal eagle, pygmy falcons, hornbills and Egyptian geese.

Shaba

Across the rutted surface of the Marsabit road lies the **Shaba National Reserve** (more fees to pay), the third of the Samburu district reserves. Unfortunately, if *Sarova's* grandiose lodge is not within your budget, you'll need a tent to be able to stay the night, as there's no other accommodation. There are theoretically two campsites, though they can be closed if there's been much banditry or cattle raiding; the better one is on the banks of the Ewaso Ngiro, some 9km from Natorbe Gate. Neither have any facilities. Unusually, you are permitted to walk in places (certainly from the airstrip to *Sarova Lodge*); ask the ranger at the gate to point out where. If you've got wheels, you might consider venturing out of the reserve to the east to visit Chanler's Falls, 30km beyond Chanler's Falls Gate on the Ewaso Ngiro River, but double check the security situation first with the rangers – there's no one here except for Samburu herders and, if you're unlucky, heavily-armed raiders.

For **animals**, Shaba is rated the equal of its two neighbours and its **springs** mean that it is better watered. If you can put up with the intense heat, the scenery provides spectacular compensation and the animal-watching is good, with lots of elephants, jackals and a few lions, and plains game including beautifully marked Grevy's zebra, reticulated giraffe and the gerenuk, which rarely if ever drinks, extracting water from morning dew on leaves.

This was also the area where Joy Adamson experimented with the release of hand-reared **leopards**. So, if you're mobile and have a day to spare, Shaba is highly recommended and it's certainly much less visited than Samburu or Buffalo Springs.

Meru National Park

Daily 6am–6.30pm; $20 per day/overnight, children $5; private vehicle Ksh200, camping $8 ($10 in a "special" campsite). Warden: PO Box 11 Maua ☎0164/20613. No driving after 7pm. Speed limit 40kph. Map: Survey of Kenya SK65 at 1cm:1km (1988) has the junctions and is the most recent but campsites and accommodation are out of date. It's not easily available in Kenya (try Prestige Bookshop in Nairobi), so try to order from abroad (see "Information, websites and maps" on p.21).

You don't see **Meru National Park** on many safari itineraries. Of the main parks covered in this chapter, it is the least visited – unspoiled and pristine. Abundantly traversed by **streams** flowing into the Tana River on its southern boundary, and luxuriantly rained upon, the rolling **jungle** of tall grass, riverine forest and swamp is lent a hypnotic, other-worldly quality by wonderful stands of prehistoric-looking **doum palms**; and with the high cover they provide, you can never be certain of what's going to be around the next corner.

True, the **animals** aren't always as much in evidence here as they can be in some other Kenyan wildlife parks, but the even more noticeable absence of minibuses and land cruisers more than compensates. After visiting some of the less bushy parks, where the animals can be spotted from miles away, Meru's intimate, unusual landscape is quickly entrancing. Most of the time you really are alone in this surreal wilderness.

Meru is the area where the Adamsons released their most famous lioness **Elsa** back into the wild, and where their later series of experiments with orphaned

SHABA NATIONAL RESERVE

Chanler's Falls (Losesia)

Chanler's Falls (Losesia)

N

E810

E810

Laga Loko

Ewaso Ngiro River

Shaba
Gate

Isiolo

1524 m

Ewaso Ng'iro River

0   5 km

Airstrip

Sarova
Shaba
Lodge

Chanler's
Falls
Gate

Natorbe Gate

E810

Archer's Post (1 km)

Archer's Post

cheetahs was cut short by the murder of Joy Adamson. Until 1988, you could always guarantee a close encounter with **white rhinos** – close enough to see how they got the name, from the Afrikaans *weit* (meaning wide), a reference to their lugubrious grass-cropping mouths. Unlike black rhinos, they are remarkably good-natured animals. The head keeper of the Meru herd used to encourage visitors to pet them and even sit on them when they were lying down. Morning and evening, the five docile beasts were gently prodded out to graze around the park headquarters and campsites, then brought back at midday to the dust-wallow of their pen to snooze through the heat. The thousands of pounds' worth of horn that they carried on their noses ensured they could never be left unguarded, which required the full-time attention of a team of rangers.

All of this simply wasn't enough to keep them alive. A gang of about thirty **poachers**, armed with automatic rifles, stormed the rhinos' night-time paddock, killing all five, injuring several rangers and escaping with the booty of hacked-off horns.

Despite the recent Adamson's Falls bridge, which connects Meru to Kora, and a dozen or so new signposts, it's worth having a mobile phone here as the park is still not very accessible, especially to the independent traveller. With few KWS posts and accommodation options, it's extremely easy to get lost in the dense vegetation. And be under no illusion: even now, Meru's location is potentially dangerous. Lying in the open plains beyond the relative security of the Mount Kenya region, it's an easy target – as well as escape route – for the bandits and cattle rustlers who have blighted northeastern Kenya over the past two decades (see Chapter Seven). Things were especially bad in 1988 and 1989, when Somali poachers virtually ruled the park and were mainly responsible for the carnage that tore through their eastern parks and reserves. During their bloody tenure, two French tourists were shot dead when they unwittingly drove into a poachers' hideout. Such was the international outcry that followed their murder, and that of George Adamson in the adjoining Kora National Park a few months later, that the Kenyan government made a huge and successful effort to rout them. Since security was beefed up considerably in the mid-1990s (at a cost of some 12 million shillings), there have been no incidents involving tourists.

Practicalities

Most visitors driving to Meru National Park come via Meru town (see p.198) towards the New Murera Gate. If you're **driving** during the rainy season, however, the alternative route, offering direct access from the town of Embu (see p.203) through Ura Gate, can be hazardous, so check with locals before setting off.

Coming the conventional route from Meru, the last fuel and supplies (there's no fuel in the park) are in Maua, one hour into the **Nyambeni Hills** on a pretty, paved road, with steep tea terraces and plantations of *miraa*. The park's **New Murera Gate** is about 30km east of Maua, down a red *murram* road – the condition of which is sometimes diabolical – with magnificent scenery over your shoulder as you go: the Nyambenis towering above exotic *shambas* of bananas, sugar and corn, and the sky, as often as not, a gaudy cloud-mural of gathering storms. Gradually, as you descend, the scene gives way to the lank grass, termite cathedrals and the scattered trees and streams that characterize the park's savannah. If you fancy an organized tour, both Kimbla Safaris (PO Box 40098 Nairobi ☎02/891288, ☏891592, ✉kimbla@form-net.com) and

MERU NATIONAL PARK

0   10 km

N

Mwiera Bundas
New Murera Gate
Bisanadi Gate
Park HQ
Leopard Rock Lodge
Meru Mulika Lodge
Kiendani Special Campsite
Bwatherongi Campsite/Bundas
Old Park HQ
R. Bwatherongi
R. Rojewero
Developed Area (Many tracks)
Elsa's Kopje Tented Campsite
Adamson's Falls
R. Rojewero
Elsa's Special Campsite
Adamson's Falls Bridge
Bisandukui Special Campsite
Ura Gate
Tana River
Adamson's Bridge
Mwingi
Maua & Meru

Africa Expeditions (PO Box 24598 Nairobi ☎ & ℻02/561054) sometimes include Meru in their overland truck itineraries.

Without your own vehicle, getting to the park isn't easy. From Meru town there are frequent buses and matatus to **MAUA**, from where other matatus run as far as Kiutini – a third of the way between Maua and the park gate. From there, however, you'll have to hitch the remaining 20km and, even once there, you'll have to rely on the warden taking pity on you and giving you a guided tour, so you might just as well try for a lift with tourists in Maua, or rather about 3km up the hill before it at the junction, but you could stand for literally days without any luck. There's a friendly **hotel** at the junction, the *Kiringo Hill Tourist Lodge* (PO Box 300 Maua ☎0167/21081; B&B ❶–❷), which has reasonable s/c rooms, better ones in cottages, but little hot water. In **Maua** itself, the best option is the calm *Maua Basin Hotel*, signposted 100m off to the left as you come in (PO Box 452 ☎0167/21519; ❷), with a choice of s/c and non-s/c. The *Maua Lodge*, opposite *Kenol* where the matatus and buses drop you, is rather more basic (PO Box 343 ☎0167/21117; ❶). There's a branch of Barclays with an ATM, and the *El Niño Memo Pub* is notable for its name, as well as for good, simple food.

At first sight, Maua is an attractively bustling little market town, despite the smouldering piles of rubbish and the glue-sniffing streetkids, unusual in such a remote place. Gorgeously sited at the lower end of a verdant valley planted with maize and *miraa*, sometimes foggy in the morning, it gives way to stunning vistas over the national park and the deserts beyond. Yet there's also a discernible undercurrent of tension in the air, thanks to bitter rivalry between Meru and Somali **miraa traders** which boiled over in January 1999 following the mysterious death in London of the local MP, who also doubled as a *miraa* trader. Locals were quick to blame Somali drug barons for his death, and promptly set about a series of violent protests and revenge attacks, in which several people were killed. Though the aftermath of this explosion may simmer for years, the average visitor is unlikely to become aware of these problems.

Lodges

There are two places currently in operation. The expensive and very beautiful *Elsa's Kopje Tented Camp*, on the former site of Mgwango (or Mughwongo) Camp by junction 19, has recently opened, and is the most exclusive unit in the park, with only 32 beds. The price includes guided walks and day and night game drives (bookings through Cheli & Peacock Safaris, p.143; ❾). More affordable, though still way out of budget range, is the relatively new thirty-bed *Leopard Rock Lodge,* along the Murera River, (reservations through Meru Park Adventure Ltd, PO Box 208 Maua; or PO Box 56032 Nairobi ☏02/34464, ☞862527, ✉leomi-col@bushmail.net; ❻ low, ❽ high). However, the place is already being renovated to compete with *Elsa's Kopje* and its prices are likely to rise. There's a swimming pool, and a footpath running along the river (hippos and crocs) and up to the top of Leopard Rock, which used to be visited by lions, not leopards. Activities include game drives, guided bush walks, boat-trips on the Tana River, and visits to Meru farms, *miraa* plantations and a Boran village.

Nearby, 6km from the gate and also in the northern "developed area", will be the new incarnation of *Meru Mulika Lodge* (which may open within this edition's lifetime). Its new owners have not yet been announced and it remains to be seen whether the paradisal charm of the old version will be retained: apart from a pool, it had a wonderful terrace fronting onto the verdant **Mulika Swamp**, where you could watch elephants, oryxes, ostriches and others.

Bandas and campsites

Thankfully, given the upmarket lurch of the lodges, there is still one remaining *banda* site offering reasonably priced **accommodation**. Right by the entrance to the park is *Murera Bandas* (❹), four units, each with two-bedrooms, a double and a single, plus a shared barbecue area. Large groups can also be accommodated in a nearby dormitory, which has bunk beds and a central kitchen. The **public campsite** is 18km from the gate near the old park headquarters, on a stretch of open ground running down to a wooded stream. There are toilet and shower blocks, and firewood is plentiful, but bring your own bedding. The other option is to pick one of the "special" campsites dotted throughout the park (ask the rangers or the warden which are available, as they tend to open, close and move about fairly regularly), none of which have any facilities except supplies of firewood. There are usually rivers nearby for water. Bookings for the *bandas*, public and "special" campsites can be made through KWS Tourism Department (see Basics, pp.60–61).

Exploring the park

Meru's many tracks are mostly sandy and firm; some of the junctions have signposts which are useful as long as you have the Survey of Kenya map, and the baboons haven't ripped them off again. The whole park is uncontaminated by tourism and it's easy to get lost in the vast wilderness. Drivers have been known to find themselves in Tsavo East after a night of relentless searching for a lodge or a main gate and though you're no longer required to take a ranger with you, it's eminently advisable if you intend exploring south of the "developed area", more to provide radio back-up in case of breakdown or getting lost than to combat bandits.

Without going too far, there are still plenty of enticing areas to investigate. The **Rojewero River**, the park's largest stream, is an interesting watercourse: densely overgrown banks flash with birds and monkeys and dark waters ripple with turtles. Large and very visible herds of **elephant**, **buffalo** and **reticulated giraffe** are common, as are, in the more open areas, **gerenuk**, **Grevy's zebra** and **ostrich**. A few **white rhinos** have been reintroduced and more will follow – a definite sign that the park is becoming a safer place. Predators seem scarce, though they may simply be hidden in the long grass – the smaller grazers must have a nerve-wracking time of it here. Large numbers of **leopards** captured in the stock-raising lands of Laikipia (pp.194–196) have been released in the park in recent years, but as usual you have little chance of seeing them.

Onwards to the Tana River

The adjoining **Kora National Park** was the home of George Adamson (of *Born Free* fame), murdered by poachers or cattle-rustlers in August 1989 when he drove through their barricade. The reserve was promptly upgraded to national park status, but Adamson's grave was subsequently desecrated. Kora, and the three national reserves south and east of Meru – **Bisanadi**, **North Kitui** and **Rahole** – are all in the Land Rover expedition category, a total of 4500 square kilometres of scrub and semi-desert, and the Tana's dense forest where they fringe the river.

Regrettably, with the history of **bad security** in the area, trips to the region are extremely ill-advised at present. Check out the situation very carefully before entering the area.

Travel details

Road details for the main Nairobi–Mombasa route are given in chapters 1 and 6.

Buses

Kitui to: Machakos (4 daily; 1hr); Mombasa (daily; 9hr); Nairobi (3 daily; 2hr 30min).
Machakos to: Kitui (4 daily; 1hr); Mombasa (daily; 8hr); Nairobi (frequent; 1hr–1hr 30min); Voi (daily; 5hr).
Maua to: Embu (3 daily; 3hr); Meru (3 daily; 1hr); Nairobi (3 daily; 7hr).

Namanga to: Nairobi (daily; 4hr).
Narok to: Nairobi (2 daily; 4hr).
Taveta to: Mombasa (2 daily; 5hr); Voi (4 daily; 3hr).
Voi to: Malindi (daily; 4hr); Mombasa (frequent; 2hr); Nairobi (frequent; 4–5hr); Taveta (4 daily; 3hr).

Matatus

Kitui to: Embu (infrequent; 3–4hr); Machakos (8 daily; 45min).
Machakos to: Kitui (8 daily; 45min).
Namanga to: Nairobi (daily; 3hr 30min).
Narok to: Nairobi (daily; 3–4hr).
Oloitokitok to: Emali (infrequent; 2–3hr); Taveta

(market days; 2hr 30min).
Taveta to: Oloitokitok (market days; 2hr 30min); Voi (2–3 daily; 3hr).
Voi to: Taveta (2–3 daily; 3hr); Wundanyi (4–5 daily; 1hr 30min).

Trains

Voi to: Mombasa (4.11am daily; 4hr); Nairobi (11pm daily; 9hr).

The coast

CHAPTER 6

Highlights

✳ **Fort Jesus** Seven centuries of coastal history are on show in this fascinating museum in Mombasa. See p.460

✳ **Recoda** Wonderful restaurant in the old town of Mombasa serving a huge range of traditional Swahili food. See p.463

✳ **Mwaluganje Elephant Sanctuary** Bordering Shimba Hills National Park, this has almost guaranteed elephant-watching and a fine new tented camp. See p.497

✳ **Tiwi Beach** Quieter and less expensive than Diani Beach, with the reef close to shore, and some excellent low-key cottage developments. See p.497

✳ **Wasini** Tiny, undeveloped island community, a beachcomber's paradise with wonderful diving and snorkelling. See p.515

✳ **Arabuko-Sokoke Forest** East Africa's largest tract of indigenous coastal forest, with excellent guided walks possible, and the chance to see a range of monkeys, birds and butterflies. See p.523

✳ **Gedi** Try to visit this former town first thing in the morning or as the sun goes down, when the ruins are at their most atmospheric. See p.526

✳ **Watamu** Stunning bays, islets and casuarina-shaded beaches, with glorious coral gardens and good diving opportunities. See p.529

✳ **Lamu** Compelling, history-soaked city-state, the most distinctive town on the coast, with no roads or vehicles. See p.554

6

The coast

Nearly everyone arrives on the coast at **Mombasa**, a much more enjoyable place to spend time than Nairobi. Kenya's second city is a tropical centre *par excellence*: steamy, lazy, at times unbelievably dilapidated, but genial. To the north and south there are superb **beaches** and a number of pockets of tourist development – of which the resort strip to the immediate north of the city is the busiest – but the coast is not yet highly developed in the Florida or Spanish *costa* sense. For many visitors (and this is one area where inexpensive package tourism has really taken off), the resort areas represent little more than sun, sea, sand and, even in the AIDS era, sex. You can, of course, have a wonderful time on the beaches doing nothing very much, but there's a lot more to this part of Kenya than some travel brochures might have you believe – and plenty to do if total lassitude drives you nuts after a few days.

Most obviously, the beaches are the launch pad for one of the most beautiful **coral reefs** in the world, rated in the top three by experienced divers, along with Australia's Barrier Reef and the Red Sea. With breathing apparatus you can do some spectacular dives, including night and wreck dives, but with even the most limited equipment – a snorkel and mask (or "goggles"), easily obtained almost anywhere – you can still enter what really is another world, either taking a boat or swimming out to discover sections of reef for yourself. The three most spectacular zones, enclosed in **marine national parks**, are far to the south off Wasini island, the area between Watamu and Malindi, and in the extreme north, off Kiwaiyu island.

The string of **islands** that runs up the coast – the main ones being Wasini, Funzi, Chale, Mombasa itself, Lamu, Manda, Pate, Kiwaiyu – are all worth visiting. Apart from their beach and ocean attractions, most of them have some archeological interest, which is also a constant theme on the mainland: the whole coast is littered with the **ruins** of forts, mosques, tombs and even whole towns. Some of these – including **Fort Jesus**, **Lamu** and the ruined town of **Gedi** – are already on the tourist circuit, but there are dozens that have hardly been cleared or investigated and they make for compelling exploration. Fort Jesus Museum in Mombasa has a map of locations.

The **far northeastern coastal region** of Kenya is effectively out of bounds for casual visitors. Roaming Somali guerillas and other desperados, armed to the teeth, make the area extremely dangerous, with attacks on vehicles and even local villages far from unknown.

Islam has long been a major influence on the coast, and the annual month of fasting – Ramadan (see p.54 for dates) – is widely observed. Visiting the coast during **Ramadan** might leave a slightly strange impression of a region where everyone is on night shift, but in practical terms it usually makes little difference.

Nature and wildlife

The hundreds of kilometres of sandy beach that fringe the low-lying coastal strip are backed by dunes and coconut palms, traversed by scores of streams and rivers. Flowing off the plateaus through tumbling jungle, these waterways meander across a narrow, fertile plain to the sea. In sheltered creeks, forests of **mangrove** trees cover vast areas and create a distinctive ecological zone of tidal mud flats.

Wildlife on the coast is in keeping with the region's lush, intimate feel. The big game of up-country Kenya is more or less absent (though Shimba Hills National Park near Mombasa is an exception), but smaller creatures are

Responsible snorkelling, diving and fishing

Kenya's coral reefs are among the world's most beautiful, and fragile, ecosystems. A reef is a living entity: every branch or cluster of coral consists of thousands if not millions of individual living organisms called polyps, growing ever outwards as the older ones die and become covered in new growth. Coral grows extremely slowly, some species taking over a decade to expand a couple of centimetres.

Solid though it seems, coral is extremely sensitive, and even something as seemingly insignificant as a small change in sea temperature – such as happened in the 1997–98 El Niño event – can have disastrous effects. Even now, many sections of Kenya's reefs have barely begun to recover, and large sections appear grey and dead. Equally disastrous are human pressures, whether through accidental pollution or more deliberate activities. The damage caused by careless trawling and anchoring is obvious. Less obvious are the potentially damaging results of snorkelling and diving, so a few rules are worth bearing in mind.

If you haven't dived for a while, take a refresher course at one of the PADI schools at the beach hotels, and practise your buoyancy control in the safety of a swimming pool. Read the box on "Diving" on p.506.

When mooring a boat, ensure that you use established mooring points to avoid damaging the coral with anchors and chains. If there are no buoys, drop your anchor well away from the reef, and swim in.

Dive and swim carefully, never touching the corals, no matter how solid they appear. Even gentle abrasions can kill some polyps and all coral suffocates if covered with silt or sand thrown up by a careless swipe of fins (flippers) close to the sea floor. For this reason, some companies don't provide fins for snorkellers. If you do wear them, always be aware of where your feet are, and use only your hands to swim when you're close to anything. If you're an inexperienced diver, keep a good distance from the coral to avoid crashing into it.

Don't touch or feed anything, as your actions may cause stress to the animal, and interrupt behaviour. Although several companies encourage it, it's best not to feed fish. In some species, it encourages dependency, can change their behaviour (just like baboons on land, some fish can become aggressive), and it destabilizes the food chain.

Don't collect marine souvenirs. Souvenir collecting of shells, coral and starfish disrupts the ecosystem and is illegal in Kenya, and in most countries, as is all trade in sea- turtle products. Getting caught – whether in Kenya or at your airport of arrival – can land you in serious trouble. Similarly, although they are widely for sale, you shouldn't buy any of these items. With no market, people will stop collecting them. Note that the shellfish will have been killed to provide the shells you're offered.

Big game fishing takes a direct toll on the marine environment by reducing the population of natural predators, kicking off a potentially destructive chain reaction by increasing the populations of their prey, in turn increasing pressure on organisms further down the food chain. Among the game-fishing fraternity, steadily falling catch rates have spurred talk of introducing quotas. It seems likely that regulations will be imposed by law before the boat operators get around to it themselves. If you do go game fishing, you may prefer to tag and release your catch rather than killing and landing it.

6

THE COAST

abundant. **Monkeys** are especially common, with troops of baboons regularly seen by the road, and vervet and Sykes' monkeys frequently at home in hotel gardens. **Birdlife** is prolific – if you harbour even a mild interest you should make a point of bringing binoculars. On the **reptile** front, snakes – brilliant disguise artists – are rarely seen, but lizards skitter everywhere, including upside down on the ceiling at night, and bug-eyed chameleons waver across the road, sometimes making it to the other side. So do giant millipedes, up to thirty centimetres long, harmless scavengers and known as Mombasa Expresses after the well-known slow train. **Insects**, including some fierce mosquitoes, are here in full force. But most, including the glorious butterflies of the Jadini and Arabuko-Sokoke forests, are attractive participants in the coast's gaudy show.

Transport to the coast

The **train journey** between Nairobi and Mombasa is, for many people, a highlight of Kenyan travel. While its poor safety record makes it difficult to recommend unreservedly (there have been two serious derailments, with fatalities, in recent years), all the research trips for this book have made frequent use of it For more details see pp.34–35 and pp.152–153. **Buses** from Nairobi to Mombasa go by day as well as night, but most of the road is dull. For coverage of the route, see Chapter Five, pp.366–379.

You can also **fly** to Mombasa, Malindi, Lamu, Kiwaiyu and even Ukunda (for Diani Beach) from Nairobi. Flying to Lamu from Nairobi makes sense if you have the cash (Ksh9350 one way, Ksh13,750 return; see "Moving on from Nairobi" on pp.153–154) and not much time, as you avoid retracing your steps between Lamu and Mombasa, but it's not an interesting flight. If you'd like to fly for the fun of it, the Malindi–Lamu hop (see "Travel details" on p.583) costs Ksh3661 one way, Ksh6160 return and gives stunning views over jungle and reef. For details on flying into Mombasa's Moi International Airport, see p.454.

Coast practicalities

There are four main **resort** areas – three to the north and one to the south. The suburban district north of Mombasa, consisting of **Nyali**, **Bamburi**, **Mtwapa** and almost merging into **Kikambala** on the north side of Mtwapa Creek, is the first, often known as "North Coast"; further north comes **Watamu**, about two hours from Mombasa; and lastly **Malindi**, twenty minutes beyond Watamu. Along the "South Coast", south of Mombasa, **Diani Beach**, forty minutes' drive from the city, is the principal focus, with the lower key **Tiwi Beach** to the north of it. However, most of these places have little that is recognizably Kenyan about them and, if you stay at an "all-inclusive" hotel, you won't see much of "real" Kenya. Apart from the odd small development, however, the rest of the coast is virtually untouched.

This part of Kenya is the most affected by the **seasons**. April, May and June are much less busy, and much cheaper, than the rest of the year. While the beaches tend to be damp and the weather muggy and overcast, you can make large savings on package holidays or, if you're travelling independently, reduce your hotel costs by as much as fifty percent.

As an alternative to hotels, you can stay in **self-catering villas**, **apartments** and **cottages**. There are various options along the beaches north of Mombasa, at Malindi and at Tiwi and Diani beaches, and it's a very sound financial proposition for families or groups. Kenya Villas, Westminster House, Kenyatta Avenue, Nairobi (PO Box 57046 ☎02/338072), acts as an agent for many holiday-home owners.

One word of warning: tempting as it can be, **sleeping out**, except on the most deserted of beaches, is very unwise. Although the reputation of some areas for daylight theft and more grievous assaults is unfairly exaggerated, to sleep out anywhere near Mombasa or Malindi is asking for trouble – you'll have to find a room or pitch up at one of the handful of recognized campsites.

Mombasa and around

Arriving in **Mombasa** by plane or train in the morning, there's ample time, if the heat doesn't fell you, to head straight out to the beaches. But you should consider spending a day or two in Mombasa itself, tuning in to the coast (and to Kenya if you've just jetted in), catching the cadences of "Kiswahili *safi*" (pure Swahili) and looking around Kenya's most historic city. If you have time, there are two worthwhile trips you can make inland to areas that are much less known: **Shimba Hills National Park** to the southwest and, well off the beaten path to the northwest, the **Mijikenda country** between Mazeras and Kaloleni. If you would rather take this latter detour before reaching the coast proper – and it's a pleasant introduction to the region – buses from Nairobi can drop you at **Mazeras** (see p.488), a simple hitchhike or bus ride away from Mombasa.

Mombasa island has no proper beaches of its own. The nearest are **Shelly Beach**, covered in more detail on p.493, and **Nyali Beach**, covered on pp.473–477. Shelly Beach is relatively uninteresting and narrow, with the reef close to the shore, but fairly peaceful. Nyali is pretty good, crowded at weekends and holidays, and the reef here is much further out. There are several public points of access to Nyali Beach, but the easiest is right by the entrance to the *Nyali Beach Hotel*. Most of the time, hotels don't mind if you use their own beaches, bars and restaurants. If it's simply a swim you're after, see "Swimming pools" on p.472.

Mombasa

Kenya's second city can come as a revelation. There's a depth of history here, and a sense of community which Nairobi lacks. And, whereas Nairobi has very clear boundaries between rich and poor districts, things are less clearly defined in Mombasa. Sleazy, hot – you're always thirsty – and physically tropical in a way that could hardly be more different from the capital, **MOMBASA** is the slightly indolent hub of the coast – a faded, flaking, occasionally charming city that still feels, despite its gentle sprawl, like a small town that was once great.

Mombasa is actually an island, connected to the mainland by two causeways to the west, and by a bridge to the north, but still linked only by ferry to the south. The city is intricate and its streets wriggle deceptively. At its appealing heart is the **Old Town**, a lattice of lanes, mosques and cramped, old houses sloping gently down to the once-busy dhow harbour. **Fort Jesus**, an impressive reminder of Mombasa's complicated, bloody past, still overlooks the Old Town from where it once guarded the harbour entrance. It's now a national monument and museum.

Clustered all around you, within easy walking distance, is the whole expanse of downtown, modern Mombasa, with its wide streets and refreshing lack of high-rise buildings (though their number is steadily growing). While you won't doubt it's a chaotic city – there are no traffic lights left in working order for example – the atmosphere, even in the commercial centre of one of Africa's busiest ports, is invariably relaxed and congenial. Rush hours, urgency and paranoia seem to be Nairobi's problems (as everyone here will tell you), not Mombasa's. And the gaping, marginal slums that one expects to find outside African cities hardly exist here. True, Likoni and especially Changamwe, on the mainland, are burgeoning suburbs that the municipality has more or less abandoned, but the brutalizing conditions of the Mathare Valley, Kibera and Korogocho shantytowns in Nairobi are absent.

Despite the palms, the sunshine and the happy languor, all is not bliss and perfection. **Street crime**, though it hardly approaches Nairobi's level, is still a problem, and you should be wary of displaying your valuables or accepting invitations to walk down dark alleys. Likoni ferry and the area around the junction of Jomo Kenyatta Avenue with Mwembe Tayeri Road are two hotspots for pickpocketing and bag snatching, so be particularly wary in those places. But, as a general rule, Mombasa is a far less neurotic city than Nairobi and, in stark contrast to the capital, there's nowhere in the centre that could be considered a no-go area. One indication of this is that the city stays awake much later. Climatic considerations may partly explain it but, at an hour when central Nairobi is empty but for taxis and *askaris*, Mombasans are to be seen strolling in the warm night, old men conversing on the benches in Digo Road, and many shops are still open. The small-town freedoms remain healthy here and it all adds up to a city that is richly satisfying and rewarding to stay in.

Ethnically, Mombasa is perhaps even more diverse than Nairobi. Asian and Arab influence is particularly pervasive, with fifty mosques and dozens of Hindu and Sikh temples lending a strongly Oriental flavour. Still, the largest contingent speaks Swahili as a first language and it is the **Swahili civilization** that, more than any other, accounts for Mombasa's distinctive character. You'll see women wearing head-to-foot *buibuis* or brilliant *kanga* outfits, men decked out in *kanzu* gowns and hip-slung *kikoi* wraps. The smaller community of settlers and European expatriates figures less prominently here than in Nairobi, but it continues to wield disproportionate economic and social clout.

As a tourist town, Mombasa doesn't go out of its way to please. Indeed, one of its best qualities is its utter lack of pretension. It is principally a port: **Kilindini** harbour takes up most of the western side of the island. Increasingly, too, Mombasa is an industrial city, boasting one of East Africa's major oil refineries (on your right as you arrive by train). In short, Mombasa is not a resort. Visiting sailors are as important to its tourist economy as bona fide tourists, and (a grievous shortcoming) the island has no real beaches. The vast majority of the obvious tourists that you'll see around the place are here only for the purpose of a shopping trip from their North or South Coast beach hotels. You may not be able to resist the lure of the beaches for too long, but Mombasa deserves a little of your time unless you are in a big hurry; there are few places in the country with such a strong sense of identity.

Some history

Mombasa is one of East Africa's oldest settlements and, so long as you aren't anticipating spectacular historical sites, it's a fascinating place to wander. The island has had a town on it, located somewhere between the present Old Town and Nyali Bridge, for at least 700 years, and there are enough documentary snippets from earlier times to guess that some kind of settlement has existed here for at least 2000 years. Mombasa's own optimistic claim (frequently repeated in the tourist literature) to be 2500 years old, comes from Roman and Egyptian adventure stories.

Early tales

Precisely what was going on before the Portuguese arrived is still barely discernible. An armchair traveller, Al-Idrisi, wrote the following in the early twelfth century about a place called *Manfasa* that was in roughly the right location: "This is a small place and a dependency of the Zanj (coastal people). Its inhabitants work in the iron mines and hunt tigers. They have red-coloured dogs which fight every kind of wild beast and even lions." This sounds most unlikely, but then the history of Mombasa is a series of unlikely episodes. **Ibn Battuta**, the roving fourteenth-century Moroccan, spent a relatively quiet night here in 1332 and declared the people of the town "devout, chaste and virtuous . . . their mosques . . . strongly constructed of wood . . . the greater part of their diet . . . bananas and fish". But another Arab writer of a hundred years later found a less ordered society:

Monkeys have become the rulers of Mombasa since about 800 AH (1400 AD). They even come and take the food from the dishes, attack men in their own homes and take away what they can find. The master of the house chases the thieving monkey and does not cease cajoling him until the animal, having eaten the food, gives back the dish or vessel. When the monkeys enter a house and find a woman they hold congress with her. The monkeys divide into bands each with its own chief and march behind him in an orderly manner. The people have much to put up with.

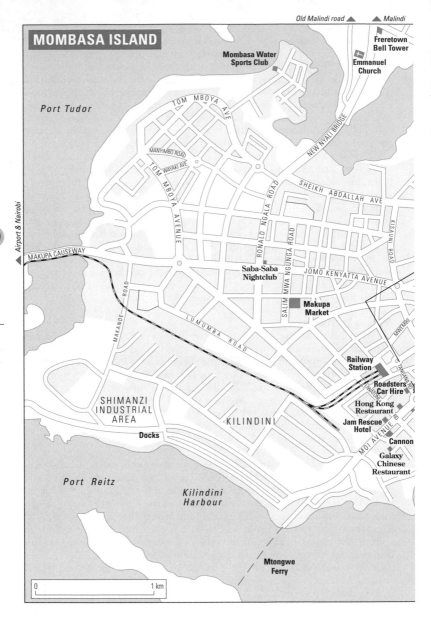

Early Portuguese visitors

Mombasa had considerably worse depredations to put up with after **Vasco da Gama's** expedition, full of mercenary zeal, dropped anchor on Easter Saturday 1498. After courtesy gifts had been exchanged, relations suddenly soured and the fleet was prevented from entering the port. A few days later, richer by only one sheep and "large quantities of oranges, lemons and sugar cane", da Gama went off to try his primitive diplomacy at Malindi, and found his first and last ing ally on the coast.

Mombasa was visited again in 1505 by a fourteen-strong fleet. This time, the king of Mombasa had enlisted 1500 archers from the mainland and stored arsenals of stone missiles on the rooftops in preparation for the expected **invasion** through the town's narrow alleys. The attack, pitching firearms against spears, poisoned arrows and stones, was decisive and brutal. The town was squeezed on all sides and the king's palace (of which no trace remains) was seized. The king and most of the survivors slipped out of town into the palm groves which then covered most of Mombasa island, but 1513 Mombasans had been killed – as against five Portuguese.

The king attempted to save Mombasa by offering to become a vassal of Portugal, but the request was turned down, the Portuguese unwilling to lose the chance to **loot** the abandoned town, picking over the bodies in the court-yards and breaking down the strongroom doors until the ships at anchor were almost overladen. Then, as a parting shot, they fired the town. The narrow streets and the cattle stalls between the thatched houses produced a conflagra-tion that must have razed Mombasa to the ground.

Portuguese occupation

In 1528, the Portuguese returned once again to wreck and plunder the new city that had grown on the ashes of the old. In the 1580s, it happened twice more; on the last occasion, in 1589, there was a frenzied **massacre** at the hands of the Portuguese and – coincidentally – a marauding tribe of nomads from the interior called the Zimba (about whom little is known except their canni-balistic notoriety). The Zimba's unholy alliance with the Europeans came to a treacherous end at Malindi shortly afterwards, when the Portuguese, together with the townsfolk and 3000 Segeju archers, wiped them out.

Remarkably, only two years after this last catastrophe, Mombasa launched a major land expedition of its own against its old enemy, Malindi. It had finally met a decisive match. The party was ambushed on the way by Malindi's Segeju allies, who themselves stormed and took Mombasa, later handing over the town (in which they had little interest) to the Portuguese at Malindi. The Malindi corps transferred to Mombasa, the Malindi sheikh was grandly installed as sultan of the whole region, and the Portuguese set to work on **Fort Jesus**, dedicated in 1593.

Once completed, the fort became the focus of everything that mattered in Mombasa, changing hands a total of nine times between the early seventeenth century and 1875. The first takeover happened in 1631, in a **popular revolt** that resulted in the killing of every last Portuguese. But the Sultan, lacking sup-port from any of the other towns under Portuguese domination, eventually had to desert the fort and the Portuguese, waiting in Zanzibar, reoccupied it. For the rest of the seventeenth century they continued to hold Mombasa, at first consolidating their control of the Indian Ocean trade.

Omani rule

Meanwhile, however, the **Omani Arabs** were becoming increasingly powerful. And as Dutch, English and French ships started to appear on the horizon, time was clearly running out for the Portuguese trading monopoly. Efforts to bring settlers to their East African possessions failed, and they retreated more and more behind the massive walls of Fort Jesus. Portugal's East African "empire" was under siege, and in 1696–98 Fort Jesus itself was isolated and besieged into submission by the Omanis who, with support from Pate and Lamu, had already taken the rest of the town. After 33 months almost all the defenders – the Portuguese corps and some 1500 Swahili loyalists – had died of starvation or plague.

Rapid disenchantment with the new Arab rulers spilled over in 1728 into a mutiny among the fort's African soldiers. The Portuguese were invited back –

for a year. Then the fort was again besieged, and this time the Portuguese gave up quickly. They were allowed their freedom, and a number were said to have married and stayed in the town. But Portuguese power on the coast was shattered for ever.

The new Omani rulers were the **Mazrui** family. Soon after the return of some kind of normality in Mombasa, they declared themselves independent of Oman, a direct challenge to the **Busaidi** family who had just seized power in the Arabian homeland. Civil war in Oman prevented the Busaidis from doing much about their wayward overseas agents; with the **Nabahani** family in Pate no longer paying much allegiance either, control of what were fast reverting to independent states was increasingly difficult. As usual, though, the lack of unity on the coast prevented any lasting independence.

The British take over

Intrigue in the Lamu Archipelago led to the Battle of Shela (p.555) and Lamu's unwittingly disastrous invitation to the **Sultan of Oman**, Seyyid Said, to occupy its own fort. From here, and by now with **British** backing, the Busaidis went on to attack Mazrui Mombasa repeatedly in the 1820s.

There was a hiccup in 1824 when a British officer, **Captain Owen**, fired with enthusiasm for defeating the slave trade, extended British protection to Mombasa on his own account, despite official British support for the slave-trading Busaidis. Owen's "Protectorate" was a diplomatic embarrassment and – not surprisingly – did not last long. The Busaidi government was only installed when the Swahili "twelve tribes" of Mombasa, the traditional inhabitants of the immediate hinterland, fell into a dispute over the Mazrui succession and called in Seyyid Said, the Busaidi leader. In 1840, he moved his capital from Oman to Zanzibar and, with Mombasa firmly garrisoned, most of the coast was soon in his domain.

Surviving members of the Mazrui family went to Takaungu near Malindi and Gazi, south of Mombasa. British influence was sharpened after their guns quelled the mutiny in 1875 of al-Akida, "an ambitious, unbalanced and not over-clever" commandant of the Fort. Once British hegemony was established, they leased the **coastal strip** from the Sultan of Zanzibar and Fort Jesus became Mombasa's prison, which it remained until 1958.

Since independence, Mombasa has seen a gradual decline, as air has taken over from sea for much freight transport, while the rise as a port of Dar es Salaam in Tanzania has provided Mombasa with competition. The New Nyali Bridge has been the city's only major construction project, with a bridge at Likoni much mooted but never built. 1993 saw violence on the streets between supporters and opponents of the fundamentalist Islamic Party of Kenya, led by charismatic preacher Sheikh Khalid Balala, and while the IPK does have a number of sympathizers in the city, its level of support is difficult to gauge as it has never been afforded legal status nor allowed to contest elections.

Arrival, city transport and information

Most people arrive in Mombasa by **plane** from Europe or Nairobi, or on the overnight **train**, a rather more civilized mode of transport, and one which leaves you pretty much in the middle of town. Alternatives are by **bus** and **matatu**, which will drop you off even more slap-bang in the centre of things.

If you've never been to Africa before, flying into Mombasa and merely driving through the suburbs to your hotel throws you into the place more quickly than arriving in Nairobi's cosmopolitan embrace. You may even experience some level of **culture shock** from the poverty, the noise and the up-frontness of everything, but it's not a shock that will last long.

Getting around Mombasa is best, and easily done, on foot. With no bus services, **city transport** consists of matatus, which run from the GPO to Nyali Bridge, Tudor Docks and Likoni ferry, or taxis, a ride in which to anywhere in town shouldn't cost more than Ksh100–200.

The city's **tourist information** office, operated by the Mombasa and Coast Tourist Association, is on Moi Avenue, near the Tusks (Mon–Fri 8am–noon & 2–4.30pm, Sat 8am–noon; ☏011/225428, Ⓕ228208). Although offering little in material terms (apart from brochures and an averagely useful map of Mombasa for Ksh200), the staff are helpful, and can advise you on a range of transport and accommodation matters.

Coastal culture: Swahili

The coast is where East Africa meets the Classical World, and the influence of that world over many centuries is reflected in the local culture. One result is that **Islam** has long been the dominant religion here, and one thing you'll notice if coming from upcountry is the profusion of mosques and the correspondingly lower number of churches. Five times a day, towns and villages up and down the coast resound to the cry of the *muezzin*, Muslim festivals are big here, and during Ramadan you'll find many restaurants and cafés closed up, at least in the daytime (see the box on p.54). Nonetheless, Islam here takes rather a relaxed form, and you'll certainly have no difficulty finding a beer, for example, or a bar to drink it in.

Partly through the intermediary of Islam, with its direct and simple tenets, foreign ideas have shaped the society, language, literature and architecture of the coastal region. More than the pragmatic Portuguese, whose interests seem to have been entirely mercenary, immigrants and traders from Arabia, Iran and India – once or twice even China – have been a subtle and gradual influence on the coast. They would arrive each year in March or April on the northeast monsoon, the dry *kaskazi* wind, and return in September on the southerly monsoon or *kuzi*.

Some, by choice or mishap, would be left behind. Through intermarriage from the earliest times (even before Islam appeared on the scene in the seventh century), a distinct ancient civilization called **Swahili** emerged. Swahili, which is thought to derive from the same Arabic root as *sahel*, meaning edge or coast, is also a language, known to its speakers as **Kiswahili**. It is one of the more mainstream of the Bantu languages, which are spoken throughout much of Africa south of the equator. Like all old languages used by trading peoples, Swahili contains strong clues about who the people mixed with. Despite popular misconception, Swahili isn't based on Arabic any more than English is based on Latin, but it is full of words derived from Arabic and peppered with others of Indian, Portuguese and English origin.

The Swahili are not a "tribe" in any definable sense; no less than, say, Americans, they are the result of the mixed heritage reflected in their language. Questions of family background and status in the community have traditionally loomed large: families that trace their roots – not always very plausibly – to foreign shores in the distant past tend to claim superior social status. Nor, predictably, was skin colour ignored. Essentially Muslim, the Swahili interpretation of the religion varies from place to place and according to circumstance. Rigidity of form is an alien concept in Swahili culture. Essentially coastal, not all Swahili trade, nor do they all fish – some Swahili groups even avoid eating fish. Coconuts, mixed farming, cattle and goats are all vitally important.

By train

Though the previously daily service was recently reduced to four a week, arriving on the night **train** from Nairobi is still the best way of getting to Mombasa. It loops down the steep scarp to the ocean as you wake up to the rustle of starched waiters and the clatter of buckled teapots and, though the carriages need refurbishment, the quality of service on board is generally high and the trip is still a reminder of the era of leisurely rail travel. For full details see pp.34–35 & 153–154. When you walk out of the station into the glare of the morning sun, **Haile Selassie Road** is directly ahead, leading in one straight kilometre to the city's main north–south thoroughfare, **Digo Road**. The **Old Town** begins on the far side of Digo Road. To the left of Haile Selassie are markets and bus stations; to the right, a concentration of hotels; then, parallel to it, **Moi Avenue**

The towns

Like the language, it was long thought that the towns of the coast began as implants, that is, as Arab, or even Persian, trading forts. It is now known that most were already in existence before any of the great post-Islamic wars and migrations took place in the Middle East. Mombasa, Malindi, Lamu and a host of lesser-known settlements are essentially ancient African towns that have always tolerated and even encouraged peaceful immigration from overseas. The Swahili style has always been to welcome the new and the sophisticated.

With few exceptions, however, any attempt to compromise the independence of these towns was met with violent resistance. The Portuguese were the least successful. When they arrived at the end of the fifteenth century, cultural memories of the Moorish occupation of their own country were still fresh. Accommodation to Islam was not on their agenda and, despite a long acquaintance with the coast, they never established an enduring colonial presence, as they did in Goa on the southwestern Indian coast, further along the same trading route.

The slave inheritance

Slavery on the coast was originally less a black-and-white moral issue than is commonly assumed. In the past, it was not unusual for people in need to "lend" a member of the family to others in exchange for goods or services. The Mijikenda peoples (see p.490 for more background), for example, maintained close links with the coastal towns, trading their produce, providing armed forces when the towns were under threat, and being supplied in return with overseas trade goods, especially cloth and tools. As traders, the Swahili sometimes accumulated surpluses of grain on the coast at times of severe drought inland. In exchange for food supplies, Mijikenda children would be taken to the towns by their relatives and fostered with Swahili families with whom they had links – to become, in effect, slaves. Later, the children intermarried, or paid off the debt and returned, though a small number were probably sold overseas. But when slavery itself became a major aspect of commerce, and the available foreign goods irresistible (cloth, firearms and liquor from Holland, France, England and America), then any trace of trust in the old arrangement vanished. The weak and defenceless were captured and sold to slavers from the coast (or, in the case of the Akamba who live further inland, beyond the Mijikenda, they sold their own prisoners and insane), often to end up on Dutch or French plantations around the Indian Ocean or in Arabian households. And, with the domination of the Sultan of Oman on the coast in the early nineteenth century, and the large-scale emigration of Arabs to East Africa, slaves from the far interior were increasingly set to work on their colonial coastal farms and plantations. When the British formally freed the slaves in 1907, they became part of Swahili society.

– the tourist strip. If you pick a taxi out of the swarm awaiting the train's arrival, Ksh100–150 should be the going rate to be taken to any town-centre hotel, no more than a five-minute ride, though you should have no security problems walking.

By road

Arriving by **bus** or **car** from Nairobi, first impressions can be dismal. You come over the Makupa Causeway with the railway, then diverge from it on the island to head 4km straight down **Jomo Kenyatta Avenue**. Although Mayor Balala had begun to clean things up since taking office (he resigned early in 1999), "shabby" is still the adjective that comes irresistibly to mind as you bump down this erstwhile showcase avenue: a scene of broken windows, crumbling facades and out-of-date hoardings smothers the street from its inception, via the triumphalist Independence Roundabout to its final disintegration in the diesel-laden environment of the Mwembe Tayari bus parks. If you get out at Mwembe Tayari, walk on down Kenyatta to Digo Road and your mood should lift a little. If you're driving, there's rarely any problem **parking**, with lots of parking bays, some with meters (charges nominal), around the intersection of Digo Road and Moi Avenue. Don't, of course, leave anything valuable unattended in the car.

Arriving by road from **Dar es Salaam**, you first reach the swarming suburb of Likoni, where you take the ferry to Mombasa island (5min; every 15min; hourly 1am–4am; passengers free, cars Ksh30, motorbikes Ksh15). Be **warned**: in recent years there have been increasingly frequent incidents of muggings and sneak-theft around the ferry, usually at dusk. Keep an eye on your vehicle windows while waiting in line: there's evidence to suggest that one or two gangs are targeting people just as the ferry is about to depart.

By air

By air, you arrive some 10km from the city centre at **Moi International Airport** on the mainland near Port Reitz. Try to change into cool clothes before arrival – essential if you're being picked up from the airport and going straight on safari – as there's really nowhere to do it at the airport. Although the arrivals hall routinely swarms with the newly arrived and the soon-to-depart, the staff stay admirably cool and formalities are carried out with a minimum of fuss: passport checks take seconds. If you haven't got a **visa**, they are usually issued on the spot without delay ($50 or equivalent per passport). The luggage carousels seem to work more often than not and reports of items going missing are rare, though pilfering from luggage does occur – take valuables in hand baggage. There are **bank booths** for exchanging money just outside the customs area, and a forex bureau that's open round the clock. Note that if you're flying directly on to Nairobi, you'll be clearing customs in Mombasa. And if you're going straight on safari, you won't touch Mombasa island at all. Vehicles pass through the back of Changamwe, a poor suburb, on their way out to the highway.

There is no airline bus service from the airport into town, nor currently any public bus, and the nearest matatu service is a kilometre away. Several of the **taxi** firms (Airport Taxis, for example) have fixed rates which are posted, or which they will show you on request, and the hassle is generally not severe. The price to the centre of Mombasa is Ksh610, sometimes bargainable, depending on the day's business. Fares are also fixed for the beach resorts, depending on which hotel you're headed for (Diani Beach around Ksh2640; Nyali Beach Ksh890; Tiwi Beach Ksh2250; Shanzu Beach Ksh1510). You'll make a small saving but pay in lack of comfort by taking an unlicensed cab. You can call Airport Taxi Services on ☏011/433211–20.

You can also arrange to have a rented **car** waiting for you at the airport. Most rental companies that have offices or outlets in Mombasa will do this for you, though you'll usually need to go to their office in town to complete the paper-work and pay the deposit.

If you really want to get into town the cheapest way possible, walk just under a kilometre from the airport to the first row of shack-like shops at the road junction for Magongo, where you can pick up a matatu to the GPO for Ksh15. You could even walk the 4km to the main road, where there are even more matatus. On the way, on the left, is an enormous Akamba woodcarvers' "vil-lage", where the art of woodcarving has been reduced to not much more than a human conveyor belt. It isn't a place you're likely to bother visiting unless you are out here anyway and there are no special reductions should you want to buy; it's just a good education in a lowly sector of the tourist industry and, that said, quite entertaining.

Accommodation

None of the well-known resort hotels is located on Mombasa island, and tour operators almost never offer city hotels, for obvious reasons: there's nothing that could be described as luxury. If real comfort is what you want, the closest option, the *Nyali Beach Hotel*, is a short drive or taxi ride from the centre, on the mainland to the north. This, and subsequent hotels along the North Coast, are covered in the section "North of Mombasa", p.473. At the other end of the scale, the city has a fair scattering of cheap lodgings, but none that really stands out as the obvious focus for budget travellers. There's a YWCA – good for long stays for men as well as women – but no youth hostel and no campsite. Note that **water supplies** in Mombasa are fairly erratic (you'll see the water carri-ers with their jingling hand carts around the city) and many cheap places fea-ture the tell-tale buckets and plastic basins in bathrooms that indicate water often has to be carried up. The tap water – when there is any – is usually safe to drink except in the rainy seasons, when it mixes with sewage. If in doubt, get bottled water.

Basic lodgings

You might reasonably expect to find a concentration of cheap **lodgings** in the Old Town. Curiously enough, this isn't the case, though most of them cluster in the streets just to the west. All are on the Central Mombasa map on pp.456–7, unless stated. None of these cheap places has running hot water, but the lukewarm "cold water" is fine for showers in Mombasa's sticky climate.

Balgis Lodge Digo Rd, PO Box 1506 ☏011/316126. Across from the junction with Old Kilindini Rd, this is a respectable though basic place, but water is sporadic, not all rooms have fans and some lack windows. **❶**

Berachah Lodge Haile Selassie Rd, at the corner of Digo Rd, PO Box 82192 ☏011/224106. A choice of s/c or non-s/c singles and doubles, not the best value in town, but central and clean enough, though there's rather a loud jam session here on Friday evenings. **❷**

Daba City Guest House Mwembe Tayari Rd by Coast Bus, PO Box 1688 ☏011/316041. New and

very clean and respectable cheapie with self-con-tained rooms and nets. **❷**

Eias B&L Corner Digo Rd and Bungoma St, PO Box 82577; no phone. Friendly basic lodging with shared showers and toilets. Clean and cheap, and in a good position on the edge of the Old Town. **❶**

Hydro Hotel Corner of Digo and Langoni roads, PO Box 85360 ☏011/223784. Once a friendly old stand-by, this is now really just a doss-house and knocking shop, but dirt cheap, especially the dorm beds (Ksh100). Women would not want to stay here. **❶**

Leejim Hotel Duruma Rd, PO Box 80094

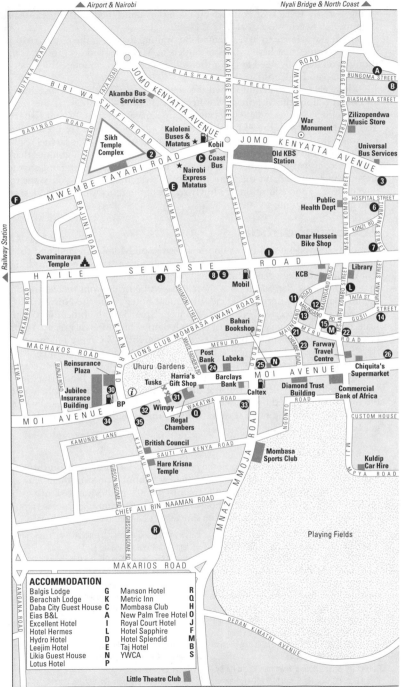

6

THE COAST | Mombasa

ACCOMMODATION

Balgis Lodge	**G**
Berachah Lodge	**K**
Daba City Guest House	**C**
Eias B&L	**A**
Excellent Hotel	**I**
Hotel Hermes	**L**
Hydro Hotel	**D**
Leejim Hotel	**E**
Likia Guest House	**N**
Lotus Hotel	**P**

Manson Hotel	**R**
Metric Inn	**Q**
Mombasa Club	**H**
New Palm Tree Hotel	**O**
Royal Court Hotel	**J**
Hotel Sapphire	**F**
Hotel Splendid	**M**
Taj Hotel	**B**
YWCA	**S**

Little Theatre Club

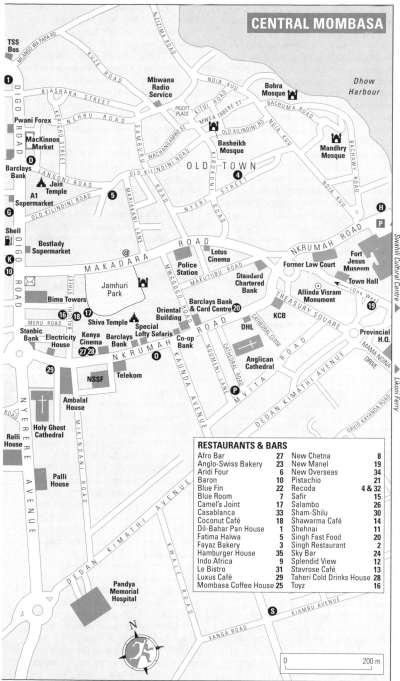

CENTRAL MOMBASA

TSS Bus

Dhow Harbour

Mbwana Radio Service

Bohra Mosque

Pwani Forex

MacKinnon Market

Basheikh Mosque

Mandhry Mosque

Barclays Bank

Jain Temple

OLD TOWN

A1 Supermarket

Shell

Bestlady Supermarket

Fort Jesus Museum

Lotus Cinema

Police Station

Former Law Court

Town Hall

Bima Towers

Jamhuri Park

Standard Chartered Bank

Allinda Visram Monument

Barclays Bank & Card Centre

Stanbic Bank

Shiva Temple

Oriental Building

KCB

DHL

Electricity House

Kenya Cinema

Barclays Bank

Special Lofty Safaris

Co-op Bank

Provincial H.Q.

NSSF

Telekom

Anglican Cathedral

Ambalal House

Holy Ghost Cathedral

Ralli House

Palli House

Swahili Cultural Centre ▶

Likoni Ferry ▶

RESTAURANTS & BARS

Afro Bar	27	New Chetna	8
Anglo-Swiss Bakery	23	New Manel	19
Aridi Four	6	New Overseas	34
Baron	10	Pistachio	21
Blue Fin	22	Recoda	4 & 32
Blue Room	7	Safir	15
Camel's Joint	17	Salambo	26
Casablanca	33	Sham-Shilu	30
Coconut Café	18	Shawarma Café	14
Dil-Bahar Pan House	1	Shehnai	11
Fatima Halwa	5	Singh Fast Food	20
Fayaz Bakery	3	Singh Restaurant	2
Hamburger House	35	Sky Bar	24
Indo Africa	9	Splendid View	12
Le Bistro	31	Stavrose Café	13
Luxus Café	29	Taheri Cold Drinks House	28
Mombasa Coffee House	25	Toyz	16

Pandya Memorial Hospital

N

0   200 m

▼ Likoni Ferry & South Coast

☎011/222867–8. A sizeable place, with reasonable facilities and very friendly, though somewhat lacking in atmosphere. B&B ❷

Likia Guest House Off Chembe Rd, behind Moi Ave, PO Box 85345 ☎011/223460. Down an unprepossessing back alley, this is a cheap, friendly little place. Fairly hygienic, with clean sheets and fans in most rooms. No mosquito nets though, and the water problems are a pain. ❶

Metric Inn Wakatwa Rd, off Moi Ave, on the south side of the Tusks behind *Wimpy*, PO Box 98658 ☎011/222155. B&L with small but acceptable rooms, the more expensive s/c. There's a laid-back bar and restaurant at the front. ❶–❷

New People's Hotel (Mombasa Island map, pp.448–9), Abdel Nasser Rd, by the main bus and matatu offices, PO Box 16639 ☎011/229715. Big, undistinguished and noisy block – the established place to stay if you're taking a bus up to Lamu, Garissa or Malindi in the morning, as they leave from right outside. Past the rough-looking reception, things brighten up upstairs. Singles tend to be dingy and cube-like, but better s/c doubles are quite acceptable, and those facing the street have real baths (though no hot water to fill them). ❶

Ramadhan Guest House (Mombasa Island map, pp.448–9) Abdel Nasser Rd, between Malindi and Mombasa/Coast Express bus offices, PO Box 3248 ☎011/229965. A good-value cheapie with airy, reasonably clean rooms with fans and nets, but shared bathroom facilities. ❶

Taj Hotel Digo Rd, entrance on Bungoma St, PO Box 82021 ☎011/313545. A friendly welcome but becoming run down, with a very mixed bag of rooms, not all s/c or with nets. The best ones are the doubles on the roof, with a huge shared balcony overlooking the street. ❷

YWCA Corner of Kaunda and Kiambu avenues, PO Box 90214 ☎011/312846. Pleasant ambience with good security, open to men as well as women. Popular with East Africans working or studying in Mombasa, so book ahead (Ksh200 fee). Upstairs rooms are breezier and better, with fans and nets, and sometimes hot water in showers. Cleanish, if dilapidated toilets. Funds generated assist local women's projects. For long stays, on HB basis during the week and FB at weekends, they charge just over Ksh10,000 per person per month, including laundry. No guests in rooms, no curfew (taxi back from towns costs around Ksh100–200). Prices are per bed in double rooms; travelling alone, you have the choice of sharing a double room with a stranger, or paying for both beds yourself. ❷

Moderate hotels

Head to any of these for basic hotel services, with breakfast included and self-contained rooms, some with air-conditioning. You might care to check your AC unit before choosing the room. Some generate so much water that your windowsill can become a veritable bird bath, attracting all the pigeons in Mombasa. Occasional reports are received of a group of Mombasa hotels in this price range which mistreat their guests and in which theft and prostitution are common and intimidating. They are not listed here.

Excellent Hotel Haile Selassie Rd, PO Box 90228 ☎011/227683. Big, clean s/c rooms with real baths (but no hot water), nets and fans. A reliable first base if you're arriving on the train, but noisy on the one night a week (currently Thursday) when there's a band on the roof. Slightly overpriced. B&B ❸

Hotel Hermes Msanifu Kombo St, PO Box 98419 ☎011/313599. Not a great choice and becoming run-down and boozy (the downstairs bar is open until 11pm). Mostly large rooms, all with fans and nets (rooms are also sprayed nightly), but rather overpriced. B&B ❸

Manson Hotel Kisumu Rd, PO Box 83565 ☎011/222419–21, ✆222422. Newish hotel with large, clean rooms with balconies, some with fans, others AC. TV lounge and bar-restaurant on the ground floor. The welcome isn't warm, but good value overall. B&B ❸

New Palm Tree Hotel Nkrumah Rd, PO Box 90013 ☎011/315272 ext 17. This must have been quite a grand place once upon a time, and it still has bags of charm, despite getting frayed around the edges. Rooms are spacious and clean, all s/c with fans but no nets. There's also a sunny first-floor courtyard with, bizarrely enough, sunbeds. Altogether much better than similarly priced competitors. B&B ❸

Oceanic Hotel (Mombasa Island map), Mbuyuni Rd, five minutes' walk from the Likoni ferry, PO Box 90371 ☎011/223496, ✆229022. Tired 1960s hulk that has seen better days, and is in need of a good lick of paint, but good value if you're not too fussy, with sea views from all rooms, but no beach – catch the ferry for Shelly Beach on the opposite side of the Creek. Murky green pool and scrubby gardens. The adjoining *Swagat* Indian restaurant is quite reasonable. B&B ❸

Hotel Splendid Msanifu Kombo St, PO Box 90482 ⊤011/220967, ⊕312769. No longer as splendid as it was: rooms vary a lot (avoid the small, windowless, interior ones), and the AC can be noisy, so check it along with the bathroom before taking a room. On the positive side, there's a lift and the better rooms have balconies and fans, but nets have to be asked for. Popular for its fourth-floor roof garden bar/restaurant. ❸

Expensive hotels

Remember that the **resort hotels** are out of town. Compared with Nairobi, the following city hotels tend to be very good value.

Lotus Hotel corner of Mvita and Cathedral roads, PO Box 90193 ⊤011/313207, ⊕311789, ⊜lotushotel@supercopier.com). Overflowing with greenery, with plain but very neat and clean rooms, and located on a quiet corner not far from Fort Jesus, the *Lotus* is the best bet in Mombasa and often full. Every room has AC and a phone. Credit cards accepted. B&B ❹

Mombasa Club Bachawy Rd, opposite Fort Jesus, PO Box 90270 ⊤011/312449, ⊕311810. Temporary membership (Ksh2478 a week, Ksh8673 a month), or an invitation from a member, allows you to use the facilities at this rather posh old colonial club, including accommodation, with a range of rooms available at different prices. ❹–❺

Royal Court Hotel Haile Selassie Ave, PO Box 41247 ⊤011/223379, ⊕312398, ⊜royalcourt@swiftmombasa.com. A six-storey block, with lift access, close to the railway station, that has two giant Arabic coffee pots in the stylish reception and faint touches of Swahili decor elsewhere. Twin rooms are a good size and face out over town, but singles are small and lack the views. All have spotless modern tiled bathrooms (with baths and hot water). Good rooftop terrace bar (see "Bars", p.466), which can be loud on Fridays. Good value. B&B ❹

Hotel Sapphire Mwembe Tayari Rd, PO Box 1254 ⊤011/491657, ⊕495280, ⊜sapphire@ikenya.com. Near the train station, a modern interconnecting five- and ten-storey block. The 110 rooms are all AC, with satellite TV and phones, and the benefit of the only hotel pool in central Mombasa (8am–8pm; day guests pay Ksh200 adults, Ksh150 children). More expensive suites have kitchens. There's also a health club with gym, massage, Jacuzzi, steam bath and sauna. Three restaurants (including Chinese and Indian). Annoying piped music throughout. Good value. B&B ❹

The City

Mombasa is not a city with a huge number of sights, but most visitors will want to check out its main one, Fort Jesus, in the shadow of which lies Mombasa's Old Town, still a charming hive of narrow lanes, mosques and carved Swahili doorways. In the modern town centre, the tusks that feature on so many postcards are not wildly exciting, though fans of 1930s architecture might appreciate one or two of the buildings from that era on Digo Road. Further afield, there's a baobab forest and a seventeenth-century pillar tomb which are worth a visit.

Fort Jesus

For all its turbulent past (see pp.450–451), today **Fort Jesus** (daily 8.30am–6pm; Ksh200, children Ksh100; ⊤011/312839) is a quietly studious museum-monument, surprisingly spacious and tree-shaded inside its giant walls, and retaining most of its original (over the centuries much repaired) character. The curious angular construction was the design of an Italian architect and ensured that assailants trying to scale the walls would always be under crossfire from one of the bastions. It is a classic European fortress of its age.

The best time to visit is probably first thing in the morning; the guidebook on sale is an interesting source of information. Look out especially for the restored **Omani House**, in the far right corner as you enter the fort. Avoiding head contact with the lintel, climb up to the flat roof for a wonderful view over

Mombasa. Interesting in their own way, too, are the uncomfortable-looking, wall-mounted **latrines**, overhanging the ditch just south of the Omani House, which would presumably have been closed in with mats. It is immediately obvious that Fort Jesus was not so much a building as a small, resolutely fortified town in its own right. The ruins of a church, storerooms, and possibly even shops are up at this end and, to judge by some accounts, the main courtyard was at times a warren of simple dwellings. Captain Owen described it in 1824 as being: "... a mass of indiscriminate ruins, huts and hovels, many of them built wherever space could be found but generally formed from parts of the ruins, matted over for roofs."

Most of the archeological interest is at the seaward end of the fort, where you'll find the **Hall of the Mazrui** with its beautiful stone benches and eighteenth-century inscription – and a sad quantity of more modern graffiti as well. A nearby room has been dedicated entirely to the display of a huge plaster panel of **wall paintings**, made with carbon and ochre by bored Portuguese sentries. Their subjects are fascinating: ships, figures in armour (including the captain of the fort wielding his baton), fish, and what seems to be a chameleon. Illiteracy precluded much writing but, oddly enough, there's nothing obscene either. The small **café** above the room with the wall paintings has been serving first-class lime juice for years (or, if you want something to eat, the museum **restaurant**, behind the ticket office, has a lunch dish each day and various snacks).

A **sound and light show** takes place daily except Tuesdays and Sundays at 7.30pm. This is organized by Jahazi Marine (☎011/472213 or 471895, ✉jahazi@africaonline.co.ke), as part of a dinner package including a hotel pick-up and dhow cruise for $70, or just the dinner and show at Fort Jesus for $40.

Fort Jesus Museum

The **museum**, on the eastern side of the fort where the main soldiers' barracks block used to be, is small, but still manages to convey a good idea of the age and breadth of Swahili civilization, and also has a decent display of Mijikenda ethnography (see p.490). Most of the displays are of pottery, indigenous or imported, some from as far afield as China and some of it over a thousand years old. A number of private collections have contributed pieces and there's probably still a wealth of material in private hands. Look out for the big carved door taken from the Mazrui house in Gazi (p.512) and also the extraordinary whale vertebra used as a stool. The museum has a good exhibit on the long-term project to recover as much as possible from the wreck of the *Santo Antonio de Tanna*, which sank in 1697 while trying to break the prolonged siege of the fort. Some 7000 objects have already been brought to the surface, but the bulk of the ship itself remains nine fathoms deep in the harbour.

The Swahili Cultural Centre

The name is promising, but at present the **Swahili Cultural Centre** (free; PO Box 42042; ☎011/222947, ✉scc@swiftmombasa.com) offers nothing likely to impress the casual visitor. Located on the quiet east side of Mombasa island, off Mama Ngina Drive, near Fort Jesus and next to Mombasa Hospital, the centre is part of a United Nations Development Programme project on the coast, created to alleviate youth unemployment and foster traditional skills. Crafts courses operate in joinery and woodcarving, textile manufacture and embroidery, with associated classes in Swahili design and business management running alongside. It's possible to visit, informally, at any time during the week, though you should go in the morning or late afternoon if you want to find any students there. Let them know in advance if you're coming with a large group. The variety of buildings that make up the centre are set among trees on ancient coral cliffs above Mombasa Harbour, and could become a popular attraction if there was a bit more to do. Meanwhile, embroidery (including some very fine *kofia* skull caps) and a limited selection of carvings are available for sale, at more or less fixed prices.

The Old Town

From Fort Jesus, the **Old Town** is an easy objective. If you've got the time and the inclination for in-depth exploration, pick up a copy of the guidebook *The Old Town Mombasa*, published by the Friends of Fort Jesus and available there as well as in some bookshops (see "Listings", p.470). It has a good map, and loads of information on architecture, history and distinguished past residents.

First impressions – of a quarter entirely devoted to gift and **curio shops** – are none too encouraging. But this turns out to be purely the result of Fort Jesus' adjacent car park and tourist appeal, and the shops don't extend far into the Old Town. They are especially ostentatious down at the end of Ndia Kuu Road, where several emporiums are overwhelmingly luxuriant in their displays and multilingual enticements; one or two of them even provide free coffee. Many sell a lot of worthless junk and some deal in shells, including shell lamp stands, ornaments and the like, a trade which operates on the fringes of the law in Kenya, and threatens marine wildlife. Further west, away from the fort, the stores are smaller, and correspondingly cheaper and less pretentious, with a couple of mouldering genuine antique shops along Kibokini Road. For more about buying crafts, see p.467.

Mosques and other architecture

The Old Town is not, in fact, that old. Most buildings date from the nineteenth century, and though there may be foundations and even walls that go back many centuries, you'll get a clearer guide to the age of the town from its twenty or so **mosques**.

The **Mandhry Mosque** on Bachawy Road, founded in 1570, is officially the oldest; rarely open to visitors, it has a striking minaret. The **Basheikh Mosque** on Old Kilindini Road, painted in cream and white, is also acknowledged to be very old – "about 1300", they'll tell you, though this may be exaggerated. Entering the mosques – as long as they aren't locked – is usually all right for men who arrive properly covered and barefoot. Sometimes you may be expected to wash hands and feet as well. Women, however modestly dressed, will as often as not be politely refused.

Much of the other **architecture** in the Old Town is profoundly influenced by the Indian-style Zanzibari tastes of the Busaidi occupiers of the nineteenth century. This is particularly noticeable in the elegant fretwork balconies and shutters still maintained on a few houses, notably on Ndia Kuu. For older relics, you'll have to look further. There are a number of quite ancient tombs along the seafront, especially towards the northern end of the Old Town, some of which have pillars; this is the part of Mombasa considered to be "medieval", or in other words pre-Portuguese.

Returning south along the twisting **seafront road** ("seafront", although the harbour can only be glimpsed), you come to the gigantic mosque of the Bohra Muslims: "Burhani Masjid for Dawoodi Bohra Community", says the sign. In the unassuming setting of the Old Town, it is an imposingly massive edifice.

The dhow harbour

The **dhow harbour** is wildly overrated. There are usually a few boats in port but you can no longer expect to see dozens, let alone hundreds, of dhows, even at the end of the northeast monsoon in April, traditionally the peak time for arrivals. Seasonal variations are less important now that the big *jahazis* have engines. Nor are you likely to have the opportunity to go aboard one of these exotic vessels – a tourist tradition, with coffee and souvenirs, that has died out. Instead, try to imagine how it must once have looked, chat to the many policemen standing around, and check with them before raising your camera (the harbour is sometimes considered a strategically sensitive subject). In fact, you might consider concealing it: muggings and other hassles have become common. Attempting to travel by dhow from Mombasa is, regrettably, an equally discouraging story. Lamu holds more promise (see "Travel details", p.584).

The Jain temple

Heading up towards Digo Road, you might enjoy stopping by at the **Jain temple**, whose entrance is in Langoni Road (daily 10am–12.30pm; free; remove shoes and anything made of leather, and women are requested not to enter during their monthly period). This sublime creation – intricate icing sugar outside, scrupulously clean and scented within and decorated in dozens of pastel shades – was only built in 1963. Jainism is an Indian religion contemporary with Buddhism and commonest in Gujarat (home of the majority of Kenyan Asians), which holds all life to be sacred. The Jain faith prohibits the eating of any kind of animal – in its extreme form, even root vegetables are taboo – and aspires to release adherents from the physical universe and its eternal cycle of death and rebirth. The temple interior is ornamentally magnificent: the painted figurines of deities in their niches are each provided with a drain so they can be easily showered down, while around the ceiling, exquisitely stylized pictures portray scenes from a human life, including a familiar snake temptation in a garden.

Walks around Mombasa

For the most part, the rest of Mombasa's pleasures are simple. Strolling, with plenty of cold-drink stops, is a time-honoured Mombasan diversion. You will probably want to see that immortal pair of **elephant tusks** on Moi Avenue. To get to them, you have to run the gauntlet of curio booths that have almost hidden the cool hideaway of Uhuru Gardens on the right, with its Africa-shaped fountain. And when you get there, you may regret your determination to view the tusks close up: they are revealed as grubby aluminium.

More rewarding, if you have the time and inclination for a **long walk**, is the circuit that takes off around the breezy, seaward side of the island down **Mama Ngina Drive**: a fine morning's or evening's walk, when it seems to become the meeting place for half of Mombasa's Indian population. You can get back to town on a matatu from the market by Likoni ferry. There are lots of places to sit and watch the waves pounding the coral cliffs through the break in the reef. On the clifftop, protruding from the far side of the golf course (Mombasa Golf Club ☎011/225531; KGU affiliates Ksh1416, others Ksh1770), are the stumpy, insignificant remains of Fort St Joseph, built in 1826 to defend Mazrui Mombasa against the attacks of the Busaidi Omanis. Come down this clifftop promenade at weekends or in the early evening and you'll find plenty of other people doing the same – there are even food stalls in several places. At the end of Mama Ngina is an extensive and surprising forest of enormous **baobab trees**, frequently associated with ancient settlements on the coast.

Finally, to the west of the Likoni ferry roundabout is a huge pillar tomb, the **Mbaraki Pillar**. Supposedly the burial place of a seventeenth-century mainland sheikh, chief of one of the "twelve tribes", its eight-metre height is impressive enough, but it is nevertheless dwarfed by the towers of the nearby molasses refinery.

Eating

The city is full of places to eat, and **street food** is much better – and more available – than in Nairobi. During the day, you can get green coconuts (drink the coconut water, then scrape out and eat the jelly-like flesh); sugar cane juice, freshly wrung from the cane; and cuplets of *kahawa thungu* (thick bitter coffee, usually flavoured with ginger).

By the bus stalls up Abdel Nasser Road and along Jomo Kenyatta Avenue and Mwembe Tayeri Road, you'll also find *miraa*. Street stalls farther afield, along Nyerere Avenue for example, sell freshly fried potato crisps and cassava. Many stalls (mostly open at night) offer what amount to full meals for under Ksh100, including *nyama choma* (roast meat), *muhogo wa nazi*, *samaki wa kupaka*, *chapati*, *marondo*, and pilau. Try the spicy little kebabs (sometimes chicken, and called "chicken tikka" anyway). Some also sell cigarettes, sodas, and *miraa*. As well as around the bus termini on Abdel Nasser Road and along Jomo Kenyatta Avenue, you'll find them outside *Casablanca Day & Night Club*, nearby on Mnazi Moja Road, at the junction of Nkrumah, Digo and Moi Avenue at *Salambo Disco*, and further north on Digo Road outside the market.

Restaurants

Mombasa is well supplied with good, **cheap restaurants**. Especially if you're newly arrived from up-country, they are one of the city's chief delights, as a discernible cuisine involving coconut, fish, chicken, rice and beans, incorporating spicy Asian flavours, begins to make an impression on your palate. Unfortunately, many Swahili restaurants have closed down, but you'll still find some excellent places stretched out along the north coast, and easily accessible by 24-hour matatus from outside the GPO: the best of these have been listed on p.477 (Nyali) and p.481 (Bamburi to Shanzu). The best seafood restaurant by a long way is *Tamarind* on the mainland side of Nyali Bridge, see p.477. Phone numbers are given in the reviews when it's usually a good idea to book.

Swahili food

Recoda Nyeri St, Old Town. Mombasa's best restaurant for Swahili food and one of its oldest (opened in 1942, partly to record old Mombasa – hence the name and the photos on the walls at the Moi Ave branch). Open evenings only, it's a good excuse to throw off any misgivings and plunge into the Old Town after dark. Choose from a limited but very cheap selection of fish, creamed beans, cassava, banana, *mahamri* and *mushkaki* with salad. If you're not prepared to pick your portion, they'll bring you a never-ending selection. Go early, as by 8pm they're running out of favourites. Ksh200–300 sees most people incapacitated, though you can eat pretty well for half that. Closed Ramadan. There's also a branch at the Moi Ave Tusks, open all day, which leans towards roast meal.

Fast food and hotelis

Afro Bar Nkrumah Rd. Breakfasts, stews and curries, and good *nyama choma*, especially in the evenings, with a choice of beef, goat or chicken, washed down with a cold beer, all for around Ksh200–350.

Aridi Four Hospital St. Bright and breezy cafeteria serving basic meals, snacks, all-day breakfast and excellent passion-fruit juice.

Baron Digo Rd. Really more of a beer hall than a restaurant, though their beer isn't the cheapest in town, but they do have decent food at moderate prices, with pizzas, grills and fish dishes (around Ksh200–300 a meal), and their lobster thermidor – if they ever really have it – has got to be a bargain at Ksh450 with chips or rice.

Blue Fin Meru Rd. Fish or chicken and chips, and other dollar-a-meal fry-ups, plus juices, but portions are small. Closed Sundays.

Blue Room Haile Selassie Rd. Self-service with lots of spotless aluminium tables, fans and a cool court-yard. Very Western, and you pay the price for things like pizzas, though basics are not too expensive, and they have excellent vegetarian choices.

Coconut Café Behind the GPO, across from *Toyz* nightclub. Cheap but filling fare: curry and rice, sausage or chicken and chips.

Café Havillah Ground floor, NSSF Building, Nkrumah Rd. Stews, curries and other staples, though rather pricey (Ksh200–300) for what it is.

Lotus Hotel Corner of Mvita and Cathedral roads. Clean and efficient, with steaks, grills and curries; the food is generally well cooked (though the goat can be a plateful of bones) and the chef is willing to do anything not already on the menu given a day's notice. Expect to pay around Ksh300 for a meal.

New Manel Off Treasury Square. Very cheap Kikuyu dishes such as *githeri*, plus biriani, pilau and spaghetti, but they could do with some lessons from the locals on how to make tea.

Shawarma Café Gusii St. Spit-roast chicken, pitta bread, sandwiches and curries, and shawarma kebab of course. Open daily till 11pm.

Singh Fast Food Nkrumah Rd. A pleasant, cheer-ful little diner with low-priced curries, pilaus, chicken dishes, snacks and breakfasts as well as good fruit juice.

Splendid Hotel Moi Ave. The rooftop *nyama choma* is fun, and the location itself is delightfully airy, but ordering from the general menu can be unpredictable, and often slow.

Indian cooking

Indo Africa Haile Selassie Ave ☏072/713022. Much more expensive than the almost adjacent *New Chetna*, and with less choice, but North Indian rather than Gujarati. Decor notable for being absent, though the food is reliably good (and less abdominally challenging than *New Chetna*'s). Try the prawn or fish masala, or *muttar paneer* (cooked, homemade cheese with peas) for vege-tarians. Easily Ksh500 and up. Open daily.

New Chetna Haile Selassie Ave ☏011/224477. A long-time favourite for cheap and tasty vegetarian Gujarati dishes at low prices. The eat-all-you-can vegetarian *thali* (Ksh210) is superb. The food can be very hot, so not for the uninitiated. Recommended. Daily 8am–9pm.

Safir Maungano Rd, behind the *Splendid Hotel*. Indian and Swahili food in a small dining room or at one or two pavement tables. Curries, biriani and pilau for lunch; chicken tikka and tandooris for dinner. Good eating for under Ksh200.

Sham-Shilu Moi Ave, behind BP service station by the Tusks ☏011/316278. Mughlai dishes, fish and prawn curries, and some vegetarian dishes, at around Ksh500 a meal.

Shehnai Restaurant Fatemi House, Maungano St ☏011/312492. Mughlai specialities with a good reputation, in a spacious and light interior with somewhat regal furniture. You're spoilt for choice (100 dishes): try *Achar Gosht* (tender mutton cooked in spices and flavoured with pickles), or *Machi Tandoorwalli* – rock cod marinated in spices and grilled in a clay oven. Vegetarian around Ksh450, non-veg Ksh650. Noon–2pm & 7–10.30pm, closed Mon.

Singh Restaurant Mwembe Tayari Rd ☏011/493283. A bit of a walk from the centre of town, but very tasty Punjabi curries when you get there. Noon–2.30pm & 7–10.30pm, closed Mon.

Splendid View Restaurant (tucked behind the *Splendid Hotel*, with a view of it). Try the *Faluda* for an extraordinary gastronomic experience. Mon–Sat 10am–2pm & 6–11pm, Sun 5–11pm.

Stavrose Café Sheikh Jundani Rd/Maungano Rd. A small place that's been serving Indian snacks, tikka dishes and kebabs for years. Lunches around Ksh150–200. Mon–Fri 9am–7.30pm, Sat 9am–3pm.

Foreign cuisines

Galaxy Chinese Archbishop Makarios Rd, off the far end of Moi Ave (see map, pp.448–449) ☏011/226132. Good Chinese food – they also have branches on Diani Beach and Bamburi Beach. Daily 11.45am–2.30pm & 5.45–11pm.

Hamburger House Kisumu Rd, just past the Tusks off Moi Ave. Well above average, with an extensive menu.

Hong Kong Moi Ave, 350m west of the Tusks ☏011/226707. Cantonese, with pleasant service and good food: try the chicken cashew, prawn piripiri or sate beef. Around Ksh400. Open daily 11am–2.30pm (3pm Sat & Sun) & 6–11pm.

Hunter's Steak Bar Mezzanine floor, Ambalal House (South Tower), Nkrumah Rd ☏011/311156. A very German *kneipe* (pub), with waiters in silly pith helmets and bandoliers, grilled steaks and seafood to the fore. No music, cold AC. Around Ksh1000 a head. Closed 3–6.30pm, Saturday evenings and Sundays.

Le Bistro Moi Ave. Modern and stylish, with very reasonable charcoal-grilled offerings, and econom-ical lunchtime set menus (Ksh200). Around Ksh500. Daily 9.30am–10.30pm.

New Overseas Moi Ave, 200m west of the Tusks ☏011/230729–30. Excellent-value Cantonese cooking, focusing on seafood, with some more expensive specialities including raw tuna fish *sashi-mi* Ksh400–700. Daily 11am–3pm & 5.30–11pm.

Snacks and juice bars

For **snacking**, and the **drinks** you'll probably want to consume ceaselessly, there are corner cafés, hole-in-the-wall juice bars, and confectionery shops all over town.

Anglo-Swiss Bakery Chembe Rd. A good place to buy something to eat with your coffee at the Mombasa Coffee House.

Camel's Joint Behind the GPO, next to Jamhuri Park. An outdoor place, with ice-cream (including "scud", blended mixed fruit topped with ice-cream), juices and snacks.

Dil-Bahar Pan House Digo Rd, at the corner of Bungoma Street. Indian snacks, *pan* (see below), excellent *chai* and an extensive selection of juices including melon, watermelon and custard apple. A lovely calm refuge for a few hours, or a place to read the paper.

Fayaz Bakery Jomo Kenyatta Ave. An excellent place for cakes and biscuits. Their chocolate tart is definitely worth a try if you fancy something sweet.

Luxus Café Nkrumah Rd, facing Holy Ghost Cathedral. Excellent passion-fruit juice and a wonderful shady terrace. Good for simple orders such as sodas, and with a pleasant view of the Holy Ghost Cathedral.

Mombasa Coffee House Moi Ave. The Kenya Coffee Board's elderly establishment does a good pineapple pie.

Pistachio Chembe Rd. It's hard to beat this snack bar for the quality of its ice-cream and various kinds of coffee, but it isn't cheap. Breakfast is good value, however, and they also do lunch dishes.

Taheri Cold Drinks House Nkrumah Rd. Excellent juices, plus samosas, sausages, meat pies and kebabs. Closed weekends.

Pan shops

Highly characteristic of Mombasa are the Indian **pan shops**, often doubling as tobacconists and corner shops. Worth trying at least once, *pan* is a natural stimulant and digestive, chewed and sucked but not swallowed. Its main ingredient is a chopped or shredded nut, called betel nut (though in fact it comes from the areca palm), which is flavoured with your choice of sweet spices, chopped nuts and vegetable matter, syrup, and white lime, from a display of dishes, all wrapped in a hot-sweet, dark green leaf, which really does come from the betel vine. Tobacco is optional, but best avoided by novices. Pop the triangular parcel in your mouth and munch – it tastes as exotic and unlikely as it sounds – spitting out juice as you go. Two of the best *pan* counters in town are at the *Dil-Bahar* café (see above) and the *New Chetna* restaurant (see p.464).

Drinking and nightlife

Despite the city's overwhelmingly Muslim population, you won't go thirsty. There are several **nightclubs** too, though you might not guess as much during the day. Always check bills carefully as mistakes are increasingly common.

If you don't fancy joining the clubbing throng, then a stroll around the generally safe Old Town will uncover one or two **coffee-sellers** serving black *kahawa* from traditional high-spouted jugs. A perfect accompaniment to the coffee is perfumed almond *halwa* (which in Kenya means the gelatinous Indian variety, not the sesame sweet of the Middle East); of the best places to buy it is *Fatma Halwa Shop* at the corner of Langoni and Old Kilindini roads, which is open till 1am daily except Sunday.

Bars

Casablanca Mnazi Moja Rd, just off Moi Ave. This draws a big mixed crowd to a lively terrace, and the prostitutes gather here in force, especially upstairs. They can be a pain – or a laugh – depending on your mood. Cold beers, some (usually good) food, rooms by the hour, or even for the

whole night. Food and drinks expensive by local standards.

Excellent Hotel Next door to the hotel, a large and cool old-timers' place. Unhustly, and no prostitutes. There's a live band upstairs on the roof one night a week (currently Thursday; free entry).

Le Bistro Moi Ave. This grillroom is also good for a calm beer (cheaper Tues–Fri 4–8pm), and is generally free of prostitutes. Snooker table. Open daily till midnight.

Lotus Hotel One of the nicest places in town for a civilized beer, with a comfortable open-air bar as well as an air-conditioned one.

New Palm Tree A calm and cool, if somewhat dull, bar, where you can drink at about the lowest prices in the town centre.

Royal Court Hotel Forget the unexceptional ground-floor bar, and head up by lift to the fifth floor, where a flight of steps leads you to a breezy rooftop terrace, great for idle drinks while watching the sunset over town.

Sky Bar Moi Ave. Not exactly the place for a quiet drink: there's lots of action, gay as well as straight. You can't avoid company, as the prostitutes are out in force.

Nightclubs and live music

The major tourist hotels are situated outside town and, consequently, so are the flashiest **discos**, though the hotel discos themselves are generally pretty dull: for details of the best of the rest, read the "Nightlife" sections on p.509 (Diani), and p.481 (Bamburi and Shanzu). This, unfortunately, leaves Mombasa itself depleted of high-tech action, and few bands find it worthwhile to play on the island when the resorts pay more. Most of Mombasa's older-style nightclubs at the more disreputable, dock end of Moi Avenue have passed away. The recommendations given below are established and enjoyable. On busy nights (Wed, Fri & Sat), men are charged up to Ksh200 entry, while women are admitted half-price or free.

Jam Rescue Hotel Moi Ave 400m west of the Tusks, at the corner with Liwatoni Rd (see Mombasa Island map). Traditional Kikuyu and Swahili music Wednesday to Saturday nights.

New Florida Nightclub & Casino Mama Ngina Drive, overlooking the ocean (see Mombasa Island map). Attempts a slick scene, with a choreographed floor show (currently ex-Bolshoi dancers escaping the collapsed rouble) and lots of glitter, but everyone knows what it's really for. While in the essentials it doesn't seem to differ noticeably from its Nairobi namesake – thumping disco, grinding hookers – it does benefit from the terrace by the sea, a pleasant little gaming room (free entry until 7.30pm; open from 6pm) and keg beer. It's 2km from the centre, so take a taxi here, or at least back.

Saba-Saba Corner of Jomo Kenyatta Ave and Ronald Ngala Rd (see Mombasa Island map). Often has live music, even in the day, and always provides a sweaty, local atmosphere.

Salambo Moi Ave. Open during the day as a dozy bar with very limited snacks, this comes to life at night as the city's only really local disco, with no panderings to tourists or to glitzy style (wonky hallway mirrors excepted). Monday to Saturday there's a mix of *ndombolo*, Congolese sounds, funk and reggae, with midnight shows, acrobats, dancing and beauty contests; Sunday features a day-long jam session. Open 24 hours.

Splendid Hotel Live *benga* in the roof bar on Wednesday nights, with resident Pioneer Band playing mainly traditional Swahili music on Friday, Saturday and Sunday nights.

Toyz Baluchi St, behind the post office. Mixed feedback on this, central Mombasa's main club with professional DJs, plastic palm trees and air-conditioning, plus drinks that become more expensive as the night wears on, and a good mix of sounds. Wednesday, Friday and Saturday nights are packed, but other nights can be deserted. Live music Sunday afternoons; Sunday evenings are good for dancing without being hassled.

Shopping

Mombasa is a good city for **shopping**, with a generally wide choice, and fewer hassles as you window-shop than in Nairobi. Once you know where to go for crafts, the business of buying souvenirs improves markedly. For cloth, Mombasa is blessed with Biashara Street.

The main tourist street, as you'll soon discover, is the stretch of Moi Avenue between the Tusks and Digo Road – a number of the retail businesses here are housed in premises going back to the early twentieth century. However, it's hard to take in the architecture when the pavement is lined with souvenir stalls. Sisal baskets, soapstone, beadwork and fake ebony carvings make up eighty percent of the wares. Those at the Digo Road end of Moi Avenue tend to be the most aggressive at touting their wares, and getting past without stopping is not easy while, if you do halt, making cool decisions can be fraught. The line of stalls on **Chembe Road** seems to be in something of a backwater, and they're more fun to deal with.

If you're **buying crafts** in Mombasa, whatever else you do, first go and have a look at Haria's Gift Shop on Moi Avenue, near the Tusks (Mon–Sat 9am–6pm; credit cards accepted). They consistently offer good deals and you may even be able to get things here more cheaply than on the street. Labeka, also on Moi Avenue (Mon–Sat 8.30am–5.30pm), is another good store for browsing, with sensible prices and a pleasant, hassle-free environment.

The usual rules apply when **bargaining** – don't start the ball rolling if you're not in the mood and never offer a price you're not prepared to pay. If you want quite a few items, it's worth browsing for a well-stocked stall and then, as you reach one near-agreement after another with the stallholder, add a new item to your collection. This way you should be able to buy well-finished *vyondo* (sisal baskets) in the range of Ksh300–400, small soapstone items for Ksh50–100, and bracelets and necklaces for a similar price. It's impossible to estimate what you'll pay for carvings as the price depends as much on the workmanship as on the size of the piece. If you expressly *don't* want to purchase ebony (the wood is increasingly rare), you'll run into some amusing conversational one-way streets with stallholders who are a dab hand at "proving" their lumps of dyed acacia wood are ebony.

Markets

For a return to earth, visit Mombasa's municipal market, **Mackinnon Market**, which has a splendid abundance of tropical fruit, including such exotics as jackfruit (too big for most people at around 10 kilos) and soursops (a taste you'll either love or hate). Behind the market is a row of stores devoted to spices, coffee and tea and several good sweet shops. Apart from the Mackinnon and the big street market off Mwembe Tayari, there's **Makupa Market** in the heart of Majengo, the island's low-income housing district. A colourful, multipurpose market with a busy, rural atmosphere, it's well worth a visit. Go 1.5km up Jomo Kenyatta Avenue, then turn left at Salim Mwa Ngunga Road.

Cloth and hardware

Mombasa is also a cheap place to buy the **fabrics** the coast is famous for. Check out the latest *kanga* designs in **Biashara Street** (especially the section between George Morura Street and Digo Road), where they are usually available before anywhere else in Kenya. *Kangas* are distinguished from *kitenges* in that they also carry a printed message, whether "Jambo from Kenya" for the tourists, or more subtle proverbs and sayings in Swahili, still used as a means of communicating messages, either from a husband buying the cloth for his wife or mother-in-law, or by a wife to her husband. Some of the home-produced patterns (usually by "Rivatex") are so good – unusual combinations of brilliant fast colours used to startling effect – they are beginning to make an impact abroad, though prices are usually higher than for imports (Ksh750 for a pair of cotton *kitenge*, for example, as opposed to Ksh350 for an Indian or Indonesian version). Synthetic (nylon) cloth is much cheaper, around Ksh200–300 for *kangas*, Ksh250 for *kikois*, and Ksh450 for Maasai-style checkered wraps. You can also have clothes made to measure (Ksh800 for a dress, for example). It's worth checking prices in several shops before buying, and perhaps going with company so you can bargain for several lots at once: they are always sold in pairs.

In the high season, Biashara Street swarms with other tourists looking for "the real Mombasa", so you'll need all your haggling skills; it's actually quite difficult to budge prices more than a token Ksh40–50 for the sake of politeness, as business is just too good.

Beyond Mackawi Road, Biashara Street shifts from textiles to a less gaudy section of **household goods**, such as winnowing trays, coconut graters, palm bags, mats, spoons and furniture. It's more mundane, but just as interesting to browse. For genuine Indian **sarongs**, have a rummage through the Old Town.

Music

If you harbour even a passing interest in African **music**, Mombasa is as good a place as any to stock up on a few tapes. Prices are low: expect to pay between Ksh150 and Ksh180 for an original cassette, slightly less for dubbed tapes (for imported big names these are invariably low-quality pirates, but the copies of Taarab and traditional music are perfectly legit).

The best place for finding traditional Mijikenda music and Mombasan Taarab, as well as traditional songs from the Wa-Bajuni of Lamu District, is Mbwana Radio Service (☎011/221550), just off Pigott Place in the Old Town. You'll find popular African dance tunes (*soukous*, *ndombolo*) as well as reggae and US soul divas in the street stalls all around town, especially in the streets between Biashara Street and Haile Selassie Road towards Digo Road – just follow your ears. Kikuyu and Kenyan pop, as well as ubiquitous gospel pop (the cause of the disappearance of traditional music in many parts of the country is available from the more permanent stuctures: try Zilizopendwa Music Store, a blue shack on George Morura Street.

Safari operators

Mombasa is increasingly important as a **safari hub**, though for safaris further out, it's easier and cheaper to organize a trip from Nairobi (pp.139–143). **Renting a car** for an independent safari, prices tend to be a little cheaper in Mombasa than in Nairobi if you deal with a local company (Ksh3400–4500 per day for a small saloon rented over a week, including insurance and waivers), but the big multinationals remain expensive (Ksh4000–5000). See "Listings"p.470 for details of companies.

There are a number of **safari** possibilities from Mombasa apart from an overnight at the Shimba Hills National Park (see p.495). Expect to pay $150 and upwards for a one-day safari (5am pick-up from your hotel) to Tsavo East, including lunch at *Voi Safari Lodge*. Air safaris, even to the Mara, are also quite feasible, though much more expensive (upwards of $500 for two days and one night), although only spending one night you run a higher risk of disappointing game drives. If you're going to **Lamu**, don't bother with inclusive arrangements: just take a flight there and sort out accommodation when you arrive. Many of the companies listed below also offer half-day **city tours** of Mombasa ($25–35), and day-trips to places like Malindi and Gedi ($100 combined) and Arabuko-Sokoke Forest. Things are much cheaper if you take public transport – full details are given throughout this chapter. The same applies to the much-touted overnight stays in Zanzibar: compare the $350 asking price with the regular $226 return airfare (including departure taxes).

Abercrombie & Kent 3rd floor, Palli House, Nyerere Ave, PO Box 90747 ☎011/316549, ☎314734, ◉www.abercrombiekent.com. Impeccable reputation for luxurious tailor-made

lodge tours. Expensive. KATO (Kenya Association of Tour Operators).

African Quest Safaris Palli House, Nyerere Ave, PO Box 99265 ☎011/227052, ☎316501,

@taradamji@africanquest.co.ke. Large operator doing both camping and lodge safaris, from around $100 per day. KATO.

Big Five Ground floor, Ambalal House, Mikindani Rd, PO Box 86922 ☎011/311426, ✆311498, @www.bigfiveafrica.com. Specializing in expensive lodge air safaris (two nights from $740), and lodge safaris by road (two nights at Tsavo and Amboseli $540). They're also agents for various dhow trips ($50–100 per person) and day-trips ($60–120 per person), with an overnight at Shimba Hills costing $160 per person. KATO.

Farways Safaricentre Msanifu Kombo St, PO Box 87815 ☎011/223307, ✆227239, @farways@africaonline.co.ke. Good value and personal service from a small, long-established company with an excellent network of operator contacts, including car rental, Zanzibar trips, accommodation bookings and safaris.

Hatfield & Holleman ☎ 0733/607442, @hatfield@form-net.com. Knowledgeable, exclusive and expensive tailor-made safaris. The general aim is to provide a more complete safari experience than just seeing animals – and includes educational two-way discussions with locals, rangers and conservationists about local issues. From $300–500 per person per day.

Pollman's Tours and Safaris Corner of Taveta Rd and Shimanzi Rd, PO Box 84198 ☎011/316732, ✆314502. One of the biggest (you'll see their vehicles everywhere): reliable package-tour safaris. Lodge safaris from $200 per day. KATO.

Rhino Safaris Rhino Building, Nyerere Ave, PO Box 83050 ☎011/311141, ✆315743, @rhinomsa@africaonline.co.ke. Branch of the respected Nairobi company, but not as immediately impressive. Three-night lodge and luxury tented camp tour in Tsavo and Amboseli for $610. Half-day Mombasa city tour for $26. KATO.

Somak Holidays Somak House,

Mombasa–Malindi Highway, Bamburi, PO Box 90730 ☎011/487358–9 or 486197, ✆487324, @stlmsa@africaonline.co.ke. Dependable upmarket operation. KATO.

Southern Cross Safaris Kanstan Centre, Nyali Bridge, PO Box 90653 ☎011/475074–6 or 474951–2, ✆471257, @sales@southerncrossafaris.com. Branch of the well-respected Nairobi company (p.142), also agents for *Satao Camp* in Tsavo East. Lodge safaris from around $170, and overnights at Shimba ($140–150 depending on the season). KATO.

Special Lofty Safaris 1st floor, Hassanali Building, Nkrumah Rd, PO Box 81933 ☎011/220241 or 315789, ✆314397, @slofty@ikenya.com. Conscientious operator running its own safaris. They prefer you taking the more expensive but still well-priced "made to order" trips, though they can run camping safaris from about $120 per day. The main draw is their experience and their land cruisers (a more personal way of travelling than by Nissan minibus, though they have these too). KATO.

Tour Africa Safaris Ground floor, Social Security House (NSSF), Nkrumah Rd, PO Box 87336 ☎011/316172, ✆316197, @flights@tasmba.co.ke. Travel agency selling lodge safaris organized by its parent office in Nairobi (see p.142), and camping safaris arranged through other companies. A five-day jaunt in high-class lodges costs $600–800. They also arrange safaris in Tanzania, including the lesser-known national parks, from $90–120 per day camping, or $150–180 in lodges. KATO.

UTC Moi Ave, PO Box 84782 ☎011/316333-4, ✆314549, @www.unitedtour.com. This "ground operator" makes the bulk of its business in providing transport and drivers for other companies, but also offers a selection of reasonably priced, tried and tested itineraries. KATO.

Listings

Airline companies Airkenya ☎011/229777, airport ☎011/433982; Air Tanzania ☎011/224462; Coast Air ☎ 011/433320; Condor ☎011/312737; Kenya Airways ☎011/221251–9; Mombasa Air Safari ☎011/433061 or 434264–5.

American Express c/o Express Travel Group, Makena House, Nkrumah Rd, PO Box 314408 ☎011/311805, ✆314408.

Banks The best rates are at any of the numerous foreign exchange bureaux springing up around the city, but you need your purchase receipt when changing traveller's cheques and few accept Visa cards. Pwani Forex, Digo Rd opposite Mackinnon

Market, is efficient and seems to give the best rates for traveller's cheques (Mon–Sat 8.30am–5pm). Of the banks, the speediest is the Commercial Bank of Africa, Moi Ave (Mon–Fri 8.30am–2.30pm). Otherwise, you'll find branches of Barclays, most with ATM machines for Visa cards, throughout the city (Mon–Fri 9am–3pm, first and last Sat of the month 9–11am). Standard Chartered bank also has ATMs at its Maritime House (Moi Ave) and Treasury Square branches. Co-op Bank is on Nkrumah Rd; Postbank is east of the Tusks on Moi Ave. On Sundays you'll have to go to the airport to find a forex bureau open, unless you fancy your chances with the black market money changers hanging around the corner of Moi Avenue and Digo Road (usual rules apply: don't let them take you down a dark alley, in a shop is best, never hand over your bucks until you have the shillings in your hand and have counted them, and don't be put off checking by the old "quick, quick, the police are coming" ploy).

Bicycles Mombasa has no bike rental, but buying one is cheap enough: Omar Hussein (Mon–Sat 8.30am–1pm & 2–6pm; ☎011/225899) on Haile Selassie Ave near Maungano Rd has a good selection. A three-speed Indian roadster costs Ksh3200, with mountain bikes upwards of Ksh7000.

Bookshops Mombasa has few compared with Nairobi, and most only stock schoolbooks and stationery. Bahari Bookshop, and Kant Stationers on Moi Ave, or Citizen's Bookshop at the corner of Jomo Kenyatta Ave and Joe Kadenge St are the best. There are also quite a few stalls around town selling used books. For maps, the best place is Harria's Gift Shop on Moi Ave.

Bus company booking offices/stages Akamba Bus, Jomo Kenyatta Ave ☎011/490269 or 492696; Busscar, Abdel Nasser Rd ☎011/222854; Busstar, Abdel Nasser Rd ☎011/224739; Cat Bus (Hood), Jomo Kenyatta Ave ☎011/311075; Coast Bus, Mwembe Tayari Rd ☎011/220158; Falcon, Abdel Nasser Rd, opposite *New People's Hotel* ☎011/311060; Gantaal, Abdel Nasser Rd ☎072/700360; Interstate 2000, Jomo Kenyatta Ave ☎011490776; Linear Jomo Kenyatta Ave ☎011/311033; Mombasa Liners (Mombasa Raha), Abdel Nasser Rd ☎011/314823; Ocean Liners, Abdel Nasser Rd ☎011/229721; Safeways, Jomo Kenyatta Ave, opposite *Fayaz* bakery (no phone); Sunbird, Jomo Kenyatta Ave ☎011/491705; Takrim, Jomo Kenyatta Ave ☎011/495946; Tausi, Jomo Kenyatta Ave ☎072/787538; Tawfiq, Jomo Kenyatta Ave ☎011/432066; Tawakal, Abdel Nasser Rd ☎0733/821218; TSS, Digo Rd, opposite *Elias B&L* ☎011/221839; Universal Liners, Jomo Kenyatta Ave, opposite *Fayaz* bakery ☎011/342696.

Car rental Avenue Motors, Moi Ave, ☎011/225126, ✉avenue@africaonline.co.ke. Avis, Moi Ave, PO Box 45456 ☎011/223048 or 220465, also at Moi Airport ☎011/434021–3 and *Serena Beach Hotel* ☎011/485721; Budget, Saroya House, Moi Ave ☎011/221281, ☏221282; Galu Safaris/Southern Cross Safaris, Kanstan Centre, Nyali Bridge ☎475074–6, ☏471257, ✉saes@southerncrosssafaris.com; Glory Car Hire, Moi Ave ☎011/313561, ☏221159, ✉glorycarhire@net2000ke.com; Hertz/UTC, Moi

Ave ☎011/316333–4, ☏314549, ✉utcmba@africaonline.co.ke, also at Moi Airport ☎011/433211; Kedev Car Hire, Off Links Rd, Nyali ☎011/487356, ☏486378, ✉kedev@africaonline.co.ke; Kuldip's Car Hire, Mji Mpya Rd ☎011/223780, ☏313347, ✉Kuldipstr@form-net.com; Leisure Car Hire, Fisherman's Inn, Mwamba Drive, Nyali ☎011/471274, ☏474278; National Car Rental, Pearl's Arcade, Nyerere Ave ☎011/228318, ☏222139, ✉natcarma@africaonline.co.ke; Special Lofty Safaris, 1st floor, Hassanali Building, Nkrumah Rd ☎011/220241 or 315789, ☏314397, ✉slofty@ikenya.com; Unik Car Hire and Safaris Fatemi Building, Maungano Rd, PO Box 89200 ☎011/314864, ☏311384.

Cinemas The Kenya, Nkrumah Rd, is the most promising. Otherwise, try the Lotus on Makadara Rd. Both survive on a diet of Indian epics and love stories, with a few American films thrown in.

Consulates Austria Mr T. Gaal, 3rd floor, Ralli House, Nyerere Ave ☎011/313386; Belgium Mr F. van Burkom ☎011/2202319 or 314531, ✉fvanburkom@ke.safmarine.com; Canada Mr N. Tejpar (Canadian warden), Farways Safaris, Msanifu Kombo St ☎011/223307 or 9, ✉farways@africaonline.co.ke; Denmark & Finland Mr J.H. Nielsen, c/o Comarco, Liwatoni Rd ☎011/316243; France Mr M. Smewing ☎011/4352612, ✉smewing@transami.co.ke; Germany 4th floor, Palli House, Nyerere Ave ☎011/314732 or 228781; Greece Mr P. Ch. Lagoussis ☎011/224482, ✉mtv@africaonline.co.ke; Hungary Mr M. Kirkland, Southern Cross Safaris, Nyali ☎011/4750746, ✉mike@southerncrosssafaris.com; India Bank of India Building, Nkrumah Rd ☎011/224433, ✉cimsa@swiftmombasa.com; Italy Capt. M. Esposito ☎011/227325 or 313033, ✉esposito@alphakenya.com; Netherlands Mrs B.R. Patalia, ABN-AMBRO Bank, Nkrumah Rd ☎011/3110435, ✉bhanu.patalia@ke.abnamro.com; Norway Mrs A. Sondhi, c/o *Reef Hotel*, Nyali ☎011/4717712, ✉reefmsa@swiftmombasa.com; Poland Mr R. Noor ☎011/312056 or 226974, ✉reshadi@interocean2000.com; Portugal Mr F. Pereira ☎011/2236914, ✉ffkmsa@africaonline.co.ke; Seychelles Mrs M. Sonon ☎011/224923, ✉mason@wasahlan.africaonline.co.ke; Spain Mr S. Lieman ☎011/220724, ✉neffauto@africaonline.co.ke; Switzerland Mrs H. Saad-Bisig ☎011/474121, ✉safarisp@africaonline.co.ke; Tanzania 3rd floor, Palli House, Nyerere Ave ☎011/228596, ✉tancon@africaonline.co.ke; UK

Mr James Knight, Seaforth Shipping, Cotts House, 2nd floor, Moi Ave ☎ 3137767 or 311528, ✉ jknight@africaonline.co.ke; USA Mr N.K. Mudukitsa, Moi Airport ☎ 011/433943, ✉ nmudukit@africaonline.co.ke.

Contraceptives Condoms can be bought in any supermarket or pharmacy. The Family Planning Association, which can supply oral contraceptives, is in Mali House, Kenyatta Ave, off Digo Rd ☎ 011/316937.

Courier services DHL, Ukumbusho House, Treasury Square, Nkrumah Rd ☎ 011/223933, 🖷 227837; FedEx, Diamond Trust Arcade, Moi Ave ☎ 011/227775; TNT Express Worldwide, Oriental Building, Nkrumah Rd ☎ 011/313881; UPS, Fedha Towers, Kaunda St ☎ 011/252200.

Dhow cruises Jahazi Marine Ltd (PO Box 89357 ☎ 011/472213 or 471895, ✉ jahazi @africaonline.co.ke) does "cultural trips", sailing around Mombasa in the morning, lunch at their otherwise expensive *Jahazi Restaurant* overlooking Tudor Creek, and afternoons spent at the floating market, visiting a traditional herbalist and dhow builder. They also offer "Mombasa by Night" dhow cruises (around $70 per person), including a son-et-lumière performance at Fort Jesus, and a French-style lobster dinner inside served by waiters dressed up as Portuguese, supposedly to remind you of the good old days when the only tourists were heavily armed raiders.

Hospitals Pandya Memorial Hospital, Dedan Kimathi Ave (☎ 011/314140–1 or 314262–3), is hygienic and efficient, and has an ambulance service, as does St John's Ambulance Service (☎ 011/490625). If you're planning to be out in the wilds a lot, Africa Air Rescue (AAR), Harbour House, Moi Ave (☎ 011/311009 to join, 312405–6 in an emergency) offers short-term membership of its "flying doctors" scheme (see p.30).

Immigration You can get visitor's pass extensions at the Provincial Headquarters on Mama Ngina Drive (☎ 011/311745), but leave enough time, as you always have to wait. If heading for Tanzania, visa issuing from the consulate is available Mon–Fri 9am–2pm and takes about an hour – you need two passport photos plus the fee ($20 for Americans, $30 for Australians and New Zealanders, $50 for Brits, and South Africans, free for Irish).

Internet access Many places around town at generally low rates (Ksh1 per minute or less – much the same as Nairobi), including Cyber Garden 77 on Makadara Rd, *Blue Fin*, *Mombasa Coffee House*, and a couple of places in the Jubilee Insurance Building. Plenty of others.

Libraries Kenya National Library, Msanifu Kombo Rd (Mon–Thurs 9am–6pm, Fri 9am–4pm, Sat 9am–5pm); Fort Jesus Museum (archeology; Mon–Fri 8am–12.30pm & 2–4.30pm); British Council, Kisumu Rd, off Moi Ave (Tues–Fri 9am–5pm, Sat 10am–1pm; ☎ 011/223076) – has a small air-conditioned library with recent editions of British papers and temporary membership available (Ksh200 per day).

Luggage storage Apart from hotels, the only place to leave bags is the railway station, and their rates (Ksh80 per piece per day) seem excessive.

Maps The Survey of Kenya town plan *Mombasa Island and Environs* is useful, but it predates the new Nyali Bridge and many street name changes. More up-to-date but not hot on detail is *The Streets of Mombasa Island* map (1998; Ksh200–250). The street-plan book *Mombasa A to Z* (Kenway 1996) is best of all, but out of print: it's worth enquiring in case they do a new edition. If you want to get Survey of Kenya maps of the coast, it's the same story as in Nairobi (see p.148), but authorization is unlikely to be given to tourists. The relevant addresses are the Provincial Surveyor's office, 12th floor, Bima House, Digo Rd (Mon–Fri 9am–12.30pm & 2–4pm), and the DC's office, Room 19, Provincial Headquarters, Mama Ngina Drive, which you must visit if you think it's worth trying to get "the letter of authorization". If you fail, as you probably will, return to Bima House and see if there's anything they can do to help.

Motorbike rental Gabwanja, Ocean View Plaza, Bamburi ☎ 072/411137; Pedo Bikes, Kongoni Rd, near Mamba Village roundabout on mainland north of Nyali Bridge ☎ 011/471193.

Pharmacies The staff at Diamond Arcade Pharmacy, Diamond Arcade, Diamond Trust Building, Moi Ave (Mon–Fri 8am–6pm, Sat 9am–4pm; ☎ 011/316351), are pleasant and helpful. Yudah Pharmaceuticals, by *Leejim Hotel* in Duruma Rd, is open late (Mon–Fri 9am–9.30pm, Sat 9am–8pm; ☎ 0773/619808). Eden Pharmacy opposite the *Blue Room* in Haile Selassie Rd is open late and on Sundays (Mon–Sat 8.30am–9pm, Sun 2–9pm; ☎ 011/226947). There's no longer any 24hr cover in Mombasa: hospital dispensaries can supply necessary drugs and medicaments out of hours.

Post office and telephones (see also "Courier services"). The post office for free *poste restante* and main services is the General Post Office (GPO) in Digo Rd (Mon–Fri 8am–6pm, Sat 9am–noon). There are cardphones here.

Supermarkets A1 Supermarket, corner of Hospital St and Digo Rd (Mon–Sat 8.45am–6.30pm, Sun 9am–1pm); Chiquitas, Moi Ave (Mon–Sat 9am–6.30pm); Bestlady, Digo Rd, opposite Haile Selassie Rd (Mon–Sat 7.30am–8.30pm, Sun 10am–5pm).

Swimming pools The only one in town is at *Hotel Sapphire* (8am–8pm; Ksh200 adults, Ksh150 children). Further out, you could try the Mombasa Women's Association, Nyerere Ave, halfway to the Likoni ferry (schooldays 5–7pm; Sat, Sun & school holidays 10am–noon & 2.30–6pm; adults Ksh130, children Ksh110).

Taxis Kenatco (Ambalal House, Nkrumah Rd ☎011/227503) runs reliable 24hr taxis with fixed prices to the beach hotels. Another 24hr firm is Voda Taxis in Maungano St (☎011/222798). Unlicensed taxis hailed in the street are cheaper if you bargain well.

Theatre The Little Theatre Club (PO Box 81143 ☎011/229258) on Mnazi Moja Rd is the occasional venue for the Shangari Players, who put on works by African playwrights. LTC Players occasionally put on African productions, but on the whole they're an outlet for amateur dramatics in the expat/settler community. Seats are about Ksh400 for non-members.

Vaccinations The Public Health Department in Msanifu Kombo St, opposite the end of Hospital Rd, gives yellow fever, typhoid and cholera jabs Mon–Fri 8am–12.30pm & –4.30pm.

Worship The Catholic Holy Ghost Cathedral is on Nyerere Ave. The Anglican Memorial Cathedral is off Nkrumah Rd, down on the right near Fort Jesus. The main Hindu temple is the new Shiva Temple by Jamhuri Park; there is also a Swaminarayan temple on Haile Selassie Rd at the corner of Bajuni Rd. The main Sikh temple is on Mwembe Tayari Rd. There are mosques all over town.

Moving on from Mombasa

Matatus to most destinations north and west of Mombasa, including Bamburi and Shanzu beaches and Mtwapa Creek, leave from near the GPO on Digo Road. Matatus to Malindi congregate at the south end of Abdel Nasser Road, near the junction with Mackawi Road by the mosque. For destinations further afield, its better to catch a bus: details are given on p.473. The overnight **train** for Nairobi leaves four times a week (Tues, Wed, Fri & Sun – but may return to a daily service in the future) at 7pm, arriving at 8.55am, and costs Ksh3000 in 1st class, Ksh2100 in 2nd, and Ksh300 in 3rd. Dinner, breakfast and a bed are included in 1st and 2nd class.

Flights

There are no direct scheduled flights from Mombasa to Europe, or to African destinations outside Kenya and Tanzania. However, there are a number of

Airport departures

When you're due to leave, before setting off for **Mombasa airport**, check and double-check the departure time with the airport or the ground agent. Note that if you're coming from a South Coast hotel, it can take a surprisingly long time to cross on the Likoni ferry, get through the city and out the other side to the airport. A taxi from town currently costs Ksh610 with Airport Taxis (☎011/433211–20), who have fixed rates. There are no buses or matatus to the airport, but a matatu from Jomo Kenyatta Avenue to Magongo will drop you less than a kilometre short. Once in the terminal, if you're travelling independently, or suspect you may be in the wrong queue, repeat your destination airport to everyone you deal with. Don't forget that, if it isn't already included in your fare, you'll have to pay a **departure tax** (cash only, but also payable in sterling or in shillings) of $20 on international flights, including Zanzibar, plus Ksh400 compulsory insurance (around $5). For internal flights, the tax is Ksh300 plus Ksh200 compulsory insurance. If flying out of the country, avoid having any quantity of Kenya shillings left to re-exchange as the rates are poor and the commission swingeing, though you are allowed back to the forecourt bank booths from the departure lounge. On a further downbeat note, the duty-free shop has nothing Kenyan that isn't cheaper in town, and it does not accept shillings.

direct, non-stop **charter flights**, which you might be able to get a seat on. Airline bookings can either be made direct (see Listings, p.469), or – often more cheaply – through a travel agent. Vogue Tours & Travel, opposite the Anglican Cathedral on Nkrumah Road (℡ 011/223592, ℻ 223613, ℮ vogue@millygroup.com) is reliable, and can advise on cheap flights back to Europe (with various airlines out of Nairobi, or by Condor charter weekly from Mombasa to Frankfurt, currently $329 one-way, $434 with onward connection to London). Don't forget the departure tax (see box). Note also that if you're headed for Tanzania, including Zanzibar, you'll need to have had a yellow fever jab (and the yellow passport that comes with it). For details see "Travel details" on p.583.

Buses

There are services to **Lamu**, **via Malindi and Kilifi** with TSS, Tawakal, Mombasa Liners and **Malindi via Bamburi**, **Kikambala and Kilifi** with Busscar and others, from Abdel Nasser Rd.

Heading for **Nairobi and the west**, competition is fierce, with reputations tarnished all round and accidents not uncommon. The safest bus company is Akamba. Most companies run at least one day bus (7–8hr) and one at night (9hr), and the usual fare is Ksh400. The night journey can be cold: take warm clothes. Busscar runs frequent services through the day. Tawfiq's buses go on to Malaba, but have a terrible safety record; Akamba connects with its services to western Kenya and Uganda. Coast Bus can be hair-raising but goes through to Bungoma, Kisumu and Kakamega. Linear runs through to Homa Bay on Lake Victoria.

Be aware that tourists on coastal bus services, especially Mombasa to Malindi or Nairobi, have been targeted by thieves using drugged food and drink to render their victims unconscious.

International services to Tanzania are run by Tawfiq, Takrim and Interstate 2000, if you're prepared to use them, running to Dar es Salaam from the corner of Mwembe Tayari Rd with Jomo Kenyatta Ave, via Tanga. Cat Bus runs four services a week. Universal Liners runs a bus to the western border crossing at Isebania (Sirare). For **Uganda**, Tawfiq runs a daily bus to the border at Malaba, and Tausi runs one to Busia, but your safest bet is with Akamba through to Kampala, twice daily changing at Nairobi.

See "Travel details" p.583 and "Listings" p.470 for further information.

North of Mombasa

It's easy to get out of Mombasa for the day to explore the nearby **North Coast**. If it's busier, brasher, and generally less pastoral than the **South Coast** (see p.491), there are also more targets for a day-trip up here, with correspondingly less appeal if you simply want to stretch out on the beach. The resorts start just ten minutes' drive from the city centre. Alternatively, without your own vehicle, there is ample transport from the Abdel Nasser Road bus and matatu area near the *New People's Hotel*. Or simply walk over to the other side of Nyali Bridge and flag down transport. You won't wait long.

Nyali and Nyali Beach

Nyali, the comfortable suburb of Mombasa closest to the town, has a few minor items of interest of its own – apart from three of the North Coast's main

MOMBASA: NORTH COAST

MTWAPA

Mtwapa Creek

Shanzu Transitional Workshop

Ngomongo Villages

Prison

Old Bus Park

School

Shops

Shanzu Beach

Diamond Shopping Centre & Shanzu Bazaar

North Quarry Nature Trails

Bamburi Beach

Barclays Bank

Ocean View Plaza

Total

Bamburi Cement Factory

Kenyatta Beach

Bamburi Nature Park

Planet Centre

Links Road

Caltex

Bombolulu Cultural Centre

BEACH ROAD

KISAUNI

Horse Riding Centre

Nyali Golf Club

Mamba Village Crocodile Farm

KONGOWEA

Shiva Cave

see 'Mombasa Island' map

Ratna Square Shopping Centre

Port Tudor

NYALI

Police Station

Nyali Beach

NYALI ROAD

MOMBASA ISLAND

Hindu Temple

NYALI BRIDGE

0   2 km

N

ACCOMMODATION

Bahari Beach	19
Baharini Chalets	4
Bamburi Beach	9
Bamburi Beach Villa	13
Bamburi Chalets	4
Cowrie Shell Beach Apartments	4
Fishermen's Leisure Inn	15
Fontana	7
Giriama	14
Kenya Beach	8
Kigotho's Hotel	17
Moffat Court Apartments	21
Mombasa Beach	18
Mombasa Safari Inn	1
Mombasa Serena Beach Hotel	2
Neptune Beach	5
Nyali Beach Holiday Resort	22
Nyali Beach Hotel	24
Nyali Luxury Beach Apartments	23
Ocean View Beach	12
Petuscha Hotel	3
Plaza Beach	6
Rami's Beach Cottages	13
Reef	16
Severin Sea Lodge	6
Sonia Apartments and Beer Garden	1
Tamarind Village	25
Travellers Beach	10
Voyager Beach Resort	20
Whitesands	11

RESTAURANTS & BARS

Biene Bar and Restaurant	B	Pirates	C
Bora Bora Club	B	Prime Time Bar & Restaurant	G
Hong Kong	F	Splendid View Café	E
Jungle Village	B	Tamarind	H
Maharajah	A	Tembo Disco	D
New Bamburi Water Sports	B		

hotels. It was the site of **Johan Ludwig Krapf**'s first missionary toehold on the east coast, four years before Livingstone arrived in Africa. Krapf reached Nyali with his wife and baby daughter in May 1844. His wife died of malaria on July 13, their baby the next day. The pathetic graves – still carefully tended by parishioners of St Peter's Church, Nyali – are to be found at the end of the road leading past the *Tamarind Restaurant* (see p.477) and a couple of cement silos. Opposite, on a small knoll, is the stone **Krapf Memorial**.

There's another reminder of Mombasa's history in the site of the **Freetown Bell**, at the Nyali Road junction. The bell was erected by the Society of Freed Slaves in the 1880s to warn the people of Freetown (named after Sir Bartle Frere, who founded the freed slave community here) of any impending attack by Arab slavers. The district still has inhabitants who trace the roots of their freed-slave ancestors back to Malawi and Zambia. The bell hung silently under its small stone arch until the 1920s when it was removed for safekeeping to the nearby Emmanuel Church (Freetown's parish church, erected in 1889), where it is still in use. The bell you see at the Nyali Road junction is a plastic replica.

Behind Nyali Beach and the hotels, you can't miss **Mamba Village** on Links Road (daily 8am–6.30pm; Ksh450, children Ksh250). Nothing to do with poisonous snakes, this is the biggest crocodile (*mamba*) farm in Kenya, with hefty entry fees to the "crocodile trail" and film show. A series of semi-natural pools, created in a disused quarry, houses many thousands of crocodiles at all stages of growth (and a special freaks sideshow of congenitally deformed croc-lets – not a pleasant sight). The over-all effect – with "croco-burgers" in the snack bar, the 5pm Pavlovian bell-ring feedings, and unlimited saurian souvenirs – is tacky in the extreme, and the crocodile trail sits uneasily with the skin-farming half of the "village", which is not on show. Also part of the empire is the adjacent **Botanical Garden and Aquarium** (daily 9am–6pm; Ksh150, children Ksh70), which includes a thir-ty-minute guided walk around its snake park and gardens, specializing, no great surprise, in the weirdest things they could find, including carnivorous plants and "fishes which blow up for not being eaten" (ie puffer fish). Also here is the *Mamba International Nightclub* (see p.477). Further down Links Road, the Mamba outfit now also offers **horse riding** (daily 8–11am & 3- 6pm; 1hr beach trips Ksh950; better-value lessons at Ksh2900 for ten 30min stints, or Ksh3900 for ten hour-long rides).

Across the road from *Mamba Village* is **Nyali Golf and Country Club** (PO Box 95678 ℡011/471589), a stuffy sort of place that doesn't go out of its way to welcome non-members. They maintain a dress code for men (shirts with collars, socks) in return for which they offer an ordinary swimming pool, squash, tennis (Ksh11,600 for a week's membership) and, of course, golf (free for members, Ksh2400–2600 for non-members, or Ksh1200–1300 if playing with a Nyali Club member; caddy Ksh130 for nine holes). A restaurant of the reliable Minar group has opened next door, specializing in Mughlai cuisine (daily; complimentary hotel shuttle service; ℡011/471220).

The main public access to the **beach** at Nyali is right by the entrance to *Nyali Beach Hotel*. It gets pretty busy at weekends. One oddity a little way south is a cave containing a natural *lingam* (phallic representation of the Hindu god Shiva) in the form of a stalacmite, plus a natural rock formation resembling Shiva's son, the elephant-headed Hindu god Ganesh. The area is maintained as a temple by the local Hindu Union, but visitors are welcome (remove shoes when entering the temple cave) and the site includes a pleasant ledge over-looking the ocean and a roofless cave containing two more Shiva *lingam* sta-lacmites. The story attached to the cave tells of a certain cow who was in the habit of rubbing her udders on the stalacmite to exude milk (pouring milk on the *lingam* is a way of worshipping Shiva). Her herder, afraid that the cow would damage her udders, hit her to get her to stop, upon which he was attacked by a swarm of bees. Admitted to hospital, he was treated by an Indian doctor who, hearing the story, decided to investigate, and was amazed to dis-cover the Ganesh rock and the Shiva *lingam*.

Accommodation

All the larger hotels can arrange dhow trips, scuba and snorkelling, and trips to Nyali Golf Club, and in the evenings put on cheesy bands and other enter-tainment. Beaches here are generally narrow, often covered at high tide, and prone to pestering by beach boys. Taxis from Mombasa cost around Ksh600.

Bahari Beach Hotel PO Box 86693 ℡011/472822, ℱ472021, ℮bahariho@africaon-line.co.ke. Formerly an African Safari Club place (still attracting mainly German clients), built in 1971 and refurbished in 1997, but lacks the char-acter of more modern places, and can feel a little stuffy. In common with most Nyali hotels, rooms lack sea views (they overlook the manicured gar-

dens instead) and the beach – at the bottom of a small cliff – is just a narrow strip of sand uncov-ered at low tide. Accommodation is in several two-storey blocks, and rooms are spacious and have balconies. Facilities include a gym, kid's pool and tennis courts HB ❺

Fisherman's Leisure Inn Mwamba Drive, PO Box 84902 ℡ & ℱ011/471278, ℻fishermans.visit-kenya.com. Next to the *Reef Hotel*. Not by the beach, no views and not an obvious choice in its scruffy grounds, this Indian-run place is actually outstanding value, offering a choice of spotless standard rooms (all AC, with nets, TV, phone and minibar) and some huge two-bedroom (four-person) apartments, complete with fully equipped kitchenettes and fridges. There's also a pool and Jacuzzi, and the *Lobster Pot* restaurant (see opposite). Recommended. B&B ❹

Kigotho's Hotel (formerly *Roy's Pride Rock*), Links Rd, PO Box 86178 ☎011/472538 or 472855. Another relatively cheap option set back from the coast (no view), this offers fourteen slightly tatty apartments (one-bedroom with double bed, two-bedroom with a double and two single beds) in separate blocks in the garden, all with fans, equipped with kitchenettes with fridges, and real baths as well as showers. There's also a small pool and a cheap bar-cum-*nyama choma* joint. ❸ low, ❹ high.

Moffat Court Apartments Mt Kenya Rd, PO Box 34126 ☎011/473351 or 472407, ⓦwww.africaonline.co.ke/moffatcourt. Turn right after Mamba Village. A dull modern three-storey block, but cheap, offering sixteen s/c suites, one- or two-bedroom (each bedroom with a double bed), and safe parking. Prices bargainable in low season. ❹

Mombasa Beach Hotel PO Box 90414 ☎011/471861–5, Ⓕ472970, ⓦmombasabeach-hotel.kenya-safari.co.ke; reservations through Kenya Safari Lodges & Hotels, p.43. Despite the clumsy 1970s architecture, there's a good atmosphere here – largely the result of its shady, clifftop location and the fact that it attracts many more African guests than its competitors. Facilities include a safari booking office, tennis courts, and two pools (one huge, the other down at the beach), plus the usual watersports. Lift access, but no specially designed disabled rooms. HB ❺

Nyali Beach Holiday Resort PO Box 1874 ☎011/472325, Ⓕ472402. Terracotta-roofed Mediterranean-style development right on the beach, with two pools (one for children; Ksh300/Ksh150 for non-guests). Most of the sixteen rooms face both the pool and the beach, as do the self-catering apartments or "cottages" (four or six people; Ksh5000–8000) equipped with kitchens. All rooms are large, s/c and clean, with AC, nets and TVs. Much better views than *Nyali Beach* at a fraction of the price. Restaurant and games room, safe parking. Recommended. B&B ❹

Nyali Beach Hotel PO Box 90581 ☎011/471551–2, Ⓕ471987,

Ⓔnyalibh@africaonline.co.ke; reservations through Block, p.42. Pleasant, bustling and well maintained, this is one of the coast's oldest (1946) and most reputable hotels. There are two good pools, a Jacuzzi and extensive gardens. Good disabled access (lifts and specially designed rooms), kids' paddling pool, PADI diving school, and wind surfing and mini-sailing offered for free. Standard rooms are very comfortable, but the only sea views are from the more expensive Palm Wing. Unreasonable phone charges, and overpriced in high season. Discos Wednesday, Friday and Saturday. B&B ❼

Nyali Luxury Beach Apartments PO Box 82843 ☎011/474125, Ⓕ223268. Next to *Holiday Resort*. Three-bedroom (six-person) self-catering apartments with a pool but no views. Bargaining essential. ❼

Reef Hotel Mwamba Drive, PO Box 82234 ☎011/471771–2, Ⓕ471349, Ⓔreef@africaonline.co.ke. One of Nyali's best, a large and friendly 1972 resort (renovated in 1994), and very much family oriented, with baby sitters, day-long supervized kid's activities, and a playground and paddling pool to keep them busy. The Garden Wing is a little glum, but there are sea views from the Sea View wing (same price). Facilities include a disco, three pools (and pool games), massage, Jacuzzi, tennis courts, a PADI diving school and the usual watersports. Courtesy bus to Mombasa. HB ❻

Tamarind Village Cement Silo Rd, PO Box 95805 ☎011/474600–2, Ⓕ473073, Ⓔvillage@tamarindmsa.co.ke. Next to the celebrated *Tamarind Restaurant*, this is a luxurious self-service apartment complex with classy touches of Lamu architectural style. Rooms – all en suite with kitchens and AC – overlook Mombasa harbour, and there's a gym and two pools. No beach. ❻

Voyager Beach Resort ☎011/475114–5, Ⓕ472544, Ⓔinfo@VoyagerResorts.co.ke; reservations through Heritage Hotels, p.43. Impressive communal areas, all meshwork *makuti* ceilings and marble floors, but the beach is a let-down: small and narrow, bounded by unsightly rubble and concrete defences, and covered at mid- and high-tides. Facilities include two tennis courts, three pools (and paddling pool, but nothing much else for children), sea tricycles, a gym and disco (the *Starion*), and a PADI diving school. The *Voyager* is probably the only hotel on the coast to offer "aqua jogging", where you're provided with a buoyancy belt and then run on the spot in the pool. All-inclusive ❻

Eating and drinking

Kigotho's Hotel. Unfussy *nyama choma* (barbecued meat) and beer.

Lobster Pot, Mwamba Drive, at *Fisherman's Leisure Inn*. The Sunday curry lunch buffet here is famous.

Mamba International Nightclub at Mamba Village (℡011/475180). Huge and popular *makuti*-roofed club, with an expensive sound system and laser light shows (Friday & Saturday at midnight). There's a mixture of sounds (including jazz, bhangra, *ndombolo*, reggae and cheesy disco), depending on the crowd, though Friday tends to be soul night; Saturdays tend to attract a large Indian and *wazungu* crowd. On Sunday afternoons during holiday periods (April, August and December, 3–10pm) there are family shows, acrobats and jugglers.

Maxim's Bar at *Mombasa Beach Hotel*. French-style pretensions, with all the usual overpriced favourites (lobster thermidor and so on); the bouillabaisse Marseillaise (seafood soup) is worth trying.

Tamarind Cement Silo Rd ℡011/474600–2, ℱ474630, ⓦwww.tamarind.co.ke; reservations advisable. From Nyali Bridge, go right at the traffic lights by Freetown Bell Tower, then follow the signs. In a stupendous position, with Mombasa spread out across the creek, the *Tamarind* is one of the best eating houses in Kenya. Go for the seafood platter – excellent value at Ksh3800 for two; otherwise, the set menu is Ksh1750 per person. At the jetty below, the same people run the *Nawalilkher* (aka *The Tamarind Dhow*; ℡011/471948, ℱ471257, ⓦtamarinddhow.com), a *jahazi* sailing dhow which has been converted into Kenya's most expensive dining experience: the two-hour lunch session ($20) sails at 1pm, the four-hour evening bash, including a dance band, departs at 6.30pm ($70; closed Sun). If you've still got cash left over, the *Golden Key Casino* (℡011/471071) on the Tamarind's roof will relieve you of it.

> For details of **dhow**-trip operators, read the box on p.507. Information on **scuba diving** is in the box on p.506.

From Nyali Bridge to Kenyatta Beach

Beyond the Freretown Bell and the junction for Nyali – always jostling with people trying to get transport to their shifts at the hotels – the main coast road ploughs through an area of burgeoning suburban growth. Ignored by the resort developers because it's too far from the sea, the primitive living conditions and milling activity here can come as a shock if you're fresh off the plane. Utange Camp (a Somali "intellectuals" refugee camp, full of writers, performers, musicians and their families) is not far away and its inhabitants have imposed an additional burden on the district. This is the Kenya coast that doesn't appear in the brochures. Matatus from Mombasa GPO or Abdel Nasser Road to "Mtwapa" or "Serena" come along this way, as far as Mtwapa town on the other side of Mtwapa Creek. Before you get back to the shore again, there are two very worthwhile objectives to be visited – **Bombolulu** and **Bamburi Quarry Nature Park** – both of them recommended outings whether you're travelling independently or on a package.

Bombolulu

Workshops Mon–Fri 8am–12.45pm & 2–5pm (free); showroom Mon–Sat 8am–6pm (free); Cultural Centre Mon–Sat 8am–5pm (visitors Ksh320, including free transport from north coast hotels); PO Box 83988 Mombasa ℡011/473571, ℱ475325, ⓦwww.africaonline.co.ke/bambolulu.

Just off the main road 3km north of Nyali Bridge (matatu from Abdel Nasser Road or GPO in Mombasa), **Bombolulu** (founded 1969) is a crafts training school and manufacturing centre that employs over 260 disabled people, mostly polio victims, in its five handicraft workshops (which you can visit). The

jewellery workshop is the programme's biggest money-spinner, with hundreds of original designs in metal and local materials (old coins, seeds) now being exported to the USA and Europe – you'll come across them in charity gift catalogues. A more recent development is the opening of a **cultural centre**, incorporating six traditional homesteads from several of Kenya's peoples, around a central restaurant and dance floor, where traditional crafts, cooking and farming are demonstrated while visitors can join in the dances of various tribes (lunchtimes).

Bamburi Quarry Nature Park

Daily 9am–5pm; feeding time 4pm; Ksh450, children Ksh225.

Five kilometres beyond Bombolulu, the **Bamburi Quarry Nature Park** (also called Haller Park) is the result of an unusual attempt to rehabilitate a giant quarry. The Bamburi Cement Factory (whose giant kilns are visible from miles around) has been scouring the land for limestone here since 1954, at the rate of 35 hectares each year. In 1971, they began a concentrated programme of tree-planting in an effort to rescue the disfigured landscape, to put the small-is-beautiful principle into conservation practice: a modest contribution in a land of vast wildlife parks, but a terrific success. Later, as the project gained momentum, fish-breeding was established, and large numbers of animals and birds introduced, including several **hippos**. There are plenty of **crocodiles** in a setting devoid of Mamba Village's landscaped excesses and quite a comprehensive collection of snakes, including some dangerously unprotected poisonous ones. You'll have the opportunity to get close to a number of other, harmless, creatures, including pelicans, crowned cranes, various antelopes and some splendid giant tortoises.

The walking paths wind through dense groves of casuarina, a tree known for its ability to withstand a harsh environment, across ground which is mostly below sea level, permanently moist with salty water percolating through the coral limestone bedrock. The fish-farming side of the operation experiments with different types of **tilapia**, a freshwater fish highly tolerant of brackish conditions, many tons of which now reach shops and restaurants every year, including the park's own *Whistling Pines Restaurant* (Mon–Wed & Sun 12.30–3pm, Thurs–Sat 12.30–3pm & 7.30–10pm; ☎011/487464 or 485340), which unsurprisingly also dishes up croc meat. There are two entrances: one on the main road opposite *Tembo* nightclub, and the main entrance opposite the cement factory itself. Mtwapa or Serena matatus from the GPO or Abdel Nasser Road will drop you at Bamburi Nature Trail bus stop by the first of these, but the main entrance is nearer the restaurant.

Other wildlife sites

On a similar theme and run by the same people as the Quarry Park, though not as impressive, are the newer **North Quarry Nature Trails** (daily 6.15am–6.30pm; Ksh200, children Ksh100), 4km further north (same buses and matatus: ask for "Bamburi Beach"), opposite the turning for *Bamburi Beach Hotel*. Intended mainly for joggers and cyclists (there are several looping tracks, and bicycles can be rented for use on the trails (Ksh120–350per hour), there's also a live Butterfly Exhibition Centre. Lastly, if the concept hasn't yet bored you, **Nguuni Wildlife Sanctuary** is the third of Bamburi Cement's sites (pre-booked visits only, through Baobab Farm, PO Box 81995 Mombasa ☎011/485901–4, ⒻLINE486459–60, ⓌLINEwww.baobabadventures.com), good for bird-spotting and for its herds of farmed **eland** and **oryx antelope** (ever wondered where the game meat on your plate came from?). There's also an ostrich farm (ditto).

Kenyatta and Bamburi beaches

These two contiguous stretches of beach, together with Shanzu just to the north (see p.481), are the heart of the "North Coast". If you're out for the day, there should, in most cases, be little difficulty in visiting a hotel and using its beachfront, especially if you buy some drinks or take a meal there. The exceptions are the "all-inclusive" places, which charge steep daily admission (anything up to Ksh3000). The beach itself is entirely public; it's the access to it which has been progressively restricted by the hotel developers. Either way, *Whitesands* and *Mombasa Serena Beach* are the nicest hotels along this stretch.

One beach that is unquestionably public is **Kenyatta Municipal Beach**, almost the only beach in the country where you'll see droves of ordinary Kenyans by the seaside. There's a great family atmosphere here – and consequently little or no hassle. The beach goes far out at low tide, exposing plenty of coral pools and miles of sand for undisturbed walks. There are sailing boats for hire and trips offered, and at the fringes under the low coconut trees, pedlars sell ice-creams and sodas, snacks and drinking coconuts, while others rent out inflated car inner tubes. For many though, the main attraction is *Pirates* (daily except Tues, pools 10am–5pm, restaurant and bar 10am midnight; ☎011/486020), a combination of waterslides, restaurant and breezy bar, with a similarly relaxed feel. The slides are a required outing for kids: they're as good as you'll find anywhere, certainly in Africa, consisting of one long, steep and fast one, with a big jump, and one curling and gentle. The slides cost Ksh300 per day, or Ksh100 for just the children's pools. The restaurant serves good if not amazingly cheap Mediterranean food. It's also the venue for popular discos (Wednesday, Friday and Saturday), with a mixed crowd and music.

Practicalities

The three shopping centres each have adequate, if expensive, supermarkets and pharmacies. The first is a development called The Planet Centre, on the corner of Links Road and the main highway. Ocean View Shopping Plaza, next to the hotel of the same name, has a branch of the efficient Commercial Bank of Africa (Mon–Fri 9.30am–2.30pm). And the shops just north of *Whitesands* include a branch of Barclays **bank** (Mon–Fri 9am–1pm & 3–5pm, Sat 9–11am) and a small **post and telephone office** (Mon–Fri 8am–12.30pm & 2–5pm).

Accommodation

Nearly thirty **beach hotels** throng the six-kilometre shoreline that makes up Bamburi Beach. If you're travelling on a tight budget, you'll find there's nowhere cheap to stay in the vicinity and – unless you're returning to Mombasa – you should forge on to the other side of Mtwapa Creek for some cheap hotels, or continue to the altogether more appealing beach and budget accommodation at Kikambala (see p.486).

Baharini Chalets Bamburi Beach, PO Box 90371 Mombasa ☎011/487382, ☎223496. The cheapest of three adjacent apartment/chalet complexes tucked in behind a coral rag-rock headland, with a variety of large rooms, with nets, fans and verandahs. Some have sea views, others have cooking facilities. There's also a pool, and a beach restaurant and bar popular with prostitutes. If you're coming by public transport, get off at the *Severin Sea Lodge*. The off-note is the sometimes dodgy clientele. Prices negotiable. ❷

Bamburi Beach Hotel Bamburi Beach, PO Box 83966 Mombasa ☎011/485611–8, ☎485900, ☎saleom@africaonline.co.ke. Unexceptional mid-sized resort hotel with a nice pool, but slow service and dated style. On the plus side, most rooms have sea views, and it's a bargain if you're not too fussy. Facilties include PADI diving school, glass-bottomed boats, snorkelling and squash courts. HB ⑤

Bamburi Beach Villa Kenyatta Beach next to *Pirates*, PO Box 82623 Mombasa ☎011/486161–2. Mediterranean-style terracotta-roofed self-catering development, with modern two-bedroom "cottages" (sleeping five, let out by the day) with verandahs on the beach, and apartments in a three-storey block set further back (with views, let out by the month). All have kitchens. ⑥

Bamburi Chalets next to *Cowrie Shell*, PO Box 84114 ☎011/485706 or 485594. By far the best of the self-catering places, with nine large two-floor cottages (sleeping six people) with fun 1970s styling, plenty of furniture, and well-equipped kitchens, though only five have sea views. Fully serviced. Pool, no food. AC, fans, verandahs and some nets – all currently let out on a long-term basis (two years) to English teachers. ⑤

Cowrie Shell Beach Apartments next to *Baharini Chalets*, PO Box 10003 Bamburi ☎011/485971, ☎486580. Pleasantly weather-beaten two-bedroom apartments sleeping four, with kitchens, verandahs and views of the sea through the coconut trees, better equipped than *Baharini*, somewhat more respectable, and run by a very friendly Greek lady. There's a pool and laundry, but no food (nearest supplies at Shanzu shops), and the beach is partially fenced to discourage beach boys. Discounts for longer stays. Four-person apartment ④

Fontana Hotel PO Box 86291 Mombasa ☎011/487554 or 6. Sixteen pleasant rooms with balconies overlooking a pool behind a restaurant on the main road with a very impressive *makuti* roof. Quiet, but no beach. B&B ③

Giriama Hotel Kenyatta Beach, 100m south of the turn-off for *Pirates*, PO Box 86693 Mombasa ☎011/486720 or 6, ☎486366, ✉giriama@africaonline.co.ke. A quiet, friendly and unpretentious little place, popular with Danish holidaymakers, with cool rooms, two pools and a beach bar. ④

Kenya Beach Hotel Bamburi Beach, PO Box 95748 Mombasa ☎011/485821–2, ☎485574. One of the old generation, circa end-1960s, with the usual *makuti*-roofed reception resembling so many others. It's simpler and smaller than most, but friendly and attracts a mixture of nationalities. Watersports limited to windsurfing, snorkelling and glass-bottomed boats. HB ⑤ low, ⑥ high.

Neptune Beach Hotel Bamburi Beach, PO Box 83125 Mombasa ☎011/485701–3, ☎485705, ✉neptune@africaonline.co.ke. Slightly downmarket, but refreshingly lacking in pretension, this is a

fun package destination with good staff and cheerful atmosphere. Currently a bargain. B&B ④ low, ⑤ high; FB ④ low, ⑤ high.

Ocean View Beach Hotel Bamburi Beach, PO Box 81127 Mombasa ☎ & ☎011/485953. An ageing hotel right on the beach, with an informal, if slightly downmarket, atmosphere. Rooms are OK, with AC and nets, but getting tatty. Small but pleasant shaded gardens, and suitable for children (there's a playground, and the pool is equipped with springboard and slide), despite the prostitutes in the bar. There are also some small, long-stay self-catering apartments. HB ④ low, ⑤ high.

Plaza Beach Hotel PO Box 88299 Mombasa ☎011/485321–4, ☎485325. Spotless with white tiles, cool AC rooms and minimalist decor. Narrow plot and limited watersports; but well-priced overall. B&B ④

Rami's Beach Cottages Kenyatta Beach, next to *Bamburi Beach Villa*, PO Box 90223 ☎011/486575, ☎227221. Older and more characterful than its neighbour, but more expensive, slightly run-down and there's no pool. It has three four-bed family cottages. ⑥

Severin Sea Lodge Bamburi Beach, PO Box 82169 Mombasa ☎011/485001–5, ☎485212, ✇www.severin-sea-lodge.com. Large, well-run but expensive resort hotel, with excellent sports and watersports, but no beach at high tide. Noted also for its *Imani Dhow* restaurant, which is a converted Zanzibari *jahazi* dhow, rather oddly placed in the gardens when really it should be in the water. "Comfort Class" rooms overpriced in high season, but low season (April–June) prices are pretty reasonable. B&B ⑥

Travellers Beach Hotel Bamburi Beach, PO Box 87649 Mombasa ☎011/485121–6, ☎485678, ✇travellershtl@swiftmombasa.com. Big, fun, package-tour set-up with lots of shops and activities. You can swim into the lobby then slide out again, but you can't go on the beach at high tide, when it's submerged: four pools make up for that. Facilities include floodlit tennis and AC squash courts, night-club, children's playground, windsurfing, and a health club with sauna, Jacuzzi and steam bath. Dull gardens, and somewhat tenement-like blocks, though spacious and well-appointed rooms with AC and TVs. Good Indian restaurant (*Sher-e-Punjab*, see opposite). Good value. HB ⑥

Whitesands Hotel Bamburi Beach, PO Box 90173 Mombasa ☎011/485926–9, ☎485652, ✉whitesands@form-net.com, reservations through Sarova, p.44. A very impressive, self-confident operation, with not a *makuti* roof in sight. Enormous public areas, with four interconnecting freeform pools (complete with fake beach and island) and busy restaurants. Standard rooms have sea views of sorts; larger executive rooms have satellite TV but no sea view. The hotel has the longest seafront on the Mombasa North Coast,

offering jet skiing, scuba diving, windsurfing, pedalos, kayaks, and trips by "banana boat" and catamaran. However, the atmosphere may be too formal for some. HB ⓿

Eating, drinking and nightlife

Apart from the multifarious attractions of *Pirates* on Kenyatta Beach (see p.479) and the expensive hotel restaurants, there are a good number of other **eating places**, most of which line the unpretty Mombasa–Malindi road. Matatus from Mombasa GPO or Abdel Nasser Road for Mtwapa or "Serena" run past most of the following, both day and night (fares around Ksh20); without haggling, taxis from town cost around Ksh1000, depending on how far north you're going.

Beach Corner *Baharini Chalets*. The only bar/restaurant on the beach barring those in the big hotels, so very popular, as well as a pick-up joint.

Biene Bar and Restaurant ☎011/486439, off Ocean View Shopping Plaza by *New Bamburi Water Sports*. Genuine German cooking (but only Tusker beer), goulash, pork and sausages. Daily specials at Ksh320–340 for a main course. Open 9am–midnight, closed Tues.

Bora Bora Club Ocean View Shopping Plaza (nightly from 9pm) Some say it's the best disco on the coast – it's certainly one of the glitziest, with floor shows after midnight and a bevy of prostitutes waiting to way-lay sozzled punters. Busiest Thursday and Saturday; Ksh300.

Breakers *Bamburi Beach Hotel*, Bamburi. Disco and club, nightly from 11.30am, better than the usual hotel fare, with acrobatic shows. Currently closed for renovation.

Hong Kong Just north of the Planet shopping centre ☎011/4854422 or 486137. Average Cantonese specializing in seafood, in an uninspiring circular dining room. Ksh500–700. Daily 11am–2.30pm (3pm Sat & Sun) & 6–11pm.

Jungle Village Ocean View Shopping Plaza. An upmarket German-run boozer and *nyama choma* joint with a pool. Mon–Fri from 5pm, Sat & Sun from noon.

Maharajah In the *Indiana Beach Hotel*, Bamburi ☎011/485895–6. North Indian Tandoori. Free transport from North Coast hotels. Open from 7.30pm daily except Tues, also open Sat & Sun 12.30–3pm, with buffet lunches on Sunday.

New Bamburi Water Sports 100m from *Bora Bora* ☎011/485315. On the beach and popular for a Sunday afternoon booze-up, with fresh fish and *nyama choma*, and "African hair stylists" who will

plait your hair. The main draw is live weekend music (Friday from 8pm, Saturday 2.30–6pm & 9pm–2am, Sunday from 3pm), with discos other evenings (jazz and blues on Tuesday, African on Thursday, karaoke night on Wednesday). Bar open daily 8am–midnight; Ksh100 after 8pm Saturdays and 3pm Sundays, free other times, happy hour 6pm–midnight.

Prime Time Bar & Restaurant Bombolulu. A very local dive (bring only money for drinks and the ride back), featuring resident Kamba dance band *Katito*.

Sher-e-Punjab *Travellers Beach Hotel*. Unusual among hotel restaurants in that this one has acquired quite a reputation for style and quality. There's a Ksh861 lunchtime buffet.

Splendid View Café 100m north of the *Hong Kong* ☎011/314763 or 487270. This Indian Mughlai is fibbing about the view, unless you count pink chairs and splendidly tacky fantasy paintings on the wall. The food's good though, with unusual daily specials like Baluchistani mutton *sajji* (whole roast leg of lamb), lots of chicken and seafood, and a daily tandoori BBQ. Shaded seating outside, and free transport from North Coast hotels. Under Ksh500 per person. Noon–2pm & 7–10pm, closed Mon.

Tembo Disco 100m north of the *Splendid View*, opposite Bamburi Quarry Nature Park ☎011/485078, ⓦwww.tembo.net. Garden bar and restaurant open 24hr, with an underground disco (Mon–Sat 9pm–6am, Sun 3pm–6am; women Ksh80, men Ksh150) playing mixed music (currently world beat on Wednesdays, *ndombolo* on Fridays, and soul night including even some Motown on Sundays), with occasional shows and body-building. Taxis wait outside.

Shanzu

At the northern end of the piece of coast between Mombasa Harbour and Mtwapa Creek, Shanzu is dominated by exclusive holiday clubs, and is really too far from Mombasa to be a worthwhile day-trip for the beach, although it does have a couple of other attractions that may appeal to some.

The most unusual of these, 1km east of the Mombasa–Malindi road and copiously signosted, are the **Ngomongo Villages** (daily 9am–5pm; Ksh500, children Ksh250; ☎011/486480; ⓦwww.ngomongo.com). Like Bamburi Nature Park, this is a reclaimed quarry, but one with a twist: as well as trees, it's been planted with a collection of eleven mock rural homesteads, complete with permanent inhabitants in matching dress, representing the "most colourful tribes of Kenya". Don't expect authenticity, but do expect a fun half-day out in Kenya's only theme park. There are Akamba wood carvers, musicians, herbalists, and the unavoidable crocodile pit, with less common attractions of hands-on activities like archery, Luo-style hook fishing, Turkana-style harpoon fishing, grain pounding, and tree planting. There's also the *Kienyeji Bar & Restaurant*, whose lunchtime African buffet costs Ksh550.

Also worth a visit is the Shanzu Transitional Workshop for Disabled Young Women, 350m east of Ngomongo, run by the Mombasa Girl Guides (Mon–Fri 8am–12.30pm & 2–4.30pm; c/o Mrs D.P. Shah, PO Box 80890 Mombasa ☎011/223078). Here, fourteen young women between 18 and 20 years old are currently being trained or employed in practical handicraft skills, turning out a small selection of well-made clothes (great Bermuda shorts), jewellery and leatherwork which is for sale. The idea is to graduate them with enough vocational training to enable them to become self-sufficient in the community. They don't get many visitors, so go and support the project if you can.

You'll find a large cluster of shops at Shanzu, by *Sonia Apartments*, with everything including the good Kelele Record Shop which sells African music CDs, and email, internet and telephone services in the same enclosure. At Shanzu Bazaar, nearby, there's a clinic (Dr A.S. Buran ☎011/485238), and an aromatherapy centre (Body-Line Institute ☎011/486350).

Accommodation

There is precious little budget accommodation in Shanzu, and even among the beach hotels, seven are run by the Swiss-based African Safari Club company as resorts exclusively for their clients, and can only be booked through that company in Europe. Those listed here can be booked in the usual way.

Mombasa Safari Inn PO Box 87458 Mombasa ☎011/485094. One of the few cheapies in Shanzu, friendly with modern s/c rooms, and a popular outdoor bar and restaurant (see p.483). ❷

Mombasa Serena Beach Hotel Shanzu Beach, PO Box 90352 Mombasa ☎011/485721–4, ⓕ485453, ⓔmombasa@serena.co.ke, reservations through Serena Hotels, p.44. Beautifully put together in "high-Swahili" style, and very stylishly maintained, this is the most attractive proposition on this stretch of coast, even if the rooms are on the small side. There are loads of activities, most of them free: floodlit tennis and AC squash courts, minigolf, windsurfing, PADI diving school, snorkelling, canoeing, and sailing, and they even take proper care of children. Great food (Ksh1200 for a drop-in evening meal). The beach front is popular with beach boys as well as the sea turtles. "Village" HB ❽ low, ❾ high.

Petuscha Hotel Shanzu, PO Box 88548 Mombasa ☎011/485860. Kenyan-German run, with five spotless, modern and comfortable rooms with AC or fans, two with real baths (others with showers), fronting onto a small pool and gardens. Use of split-level sitting room with plenty of books. Room only ❸

Sonia Apartments and Beer Garden Diamond Shopping Centre, Shanzu, PO Box 84963 Mombasa ☎011/485196, ⓕ313196. Spacious double rooms arrranged around the courtyard restaurant and lively 24hr bar. All have their own cooking facilities and AC. Fairly basic, but clean enough. Good value, so long as you don't mind the rather sleazy atmosphere. ❸

Turtles

Several parts of Shanzu Beach, notably at *Mombasa Serena* hotel, are popular with **sea turtles** out for a spot of egg-laying. There are educational talks about this endangered species at *Serena* (Monday 7pm), where loud water sports are banned.

Eating, drinking and nightlife

Shanzu is pretty tacky when it comes to eating places and watering holes, with most places catering purely for a captive market of package tourists. Don't expect to find any ordinary Kenyan eateries. One of the most laid-back places is the *Mombasa Safari Inn*, a cheery bar and restaurant with good grills, which is relatively cheap (main courses around Ksh300, and a full splash for around Ksh500). The bar attracts prostitutes, but the outdoor atmosphere is mellow, and it's open daily from 8am until the last customer leaves. Another place worth trying is the *Cha Cha Bar*, next to the *Petuscha Hotel*, a pleasant and laid-back outdoor bar-restaurant under an octagonal *makuti* roof, where you'll pay around Ksh400 for a meal, Ksh900 for seafood (food daily until 11pm, bar open later). The prostitutes are less of a hassle here than at other Shanzu venues, and there's occasional live music in the evenings.

Mtwapa Creek and north

Mtwapa Creek marks the edge of Greater Mombasa, and tropical suburbia – with its scattered villas, supermarkets, clubs and restaurants (and poverty) – is more or less left behind. From here on, the road heads more determinedly, with fewer distractions, up to Kilifi, Watamu and Malindi. Note: if you're **continuing north**, beyond Kikambala, skip to p.517.

Mtwapa

MTWAPA itself is in many ways the most pleasant of the main-road settlements, with a more established feel than Bombolulu, and a more ordinary Kenyan atmosphere. There are several fairly rudimentary **hotels** (see Kikambala map, overleaf), which are cheaper if you check in after 4pm and leave by 10am (you pay for the night only, as opposed to the day and night). The best is *Sweet Heart Lodge*, east of the main road, just north of the market (PO Box 82716 Mombasa ☏011/485456; ❷). Also clean and well-kept is the *Kamanjiro Super Guest House*, on the east side of the main road about 600m north of the bridge (PO Box 2021 Mombasa ☏0733/824633; ❷). If you need something cheaper, the rather down-at-heel *Glasther Guest House* (☏011/485853; ❶) lies down a turning on the west side of the main road, directly opposite the one that leads to the *Sweet Heart*.

The main reasons to pause in Mtwapa are **boats** and **big fish**: the creek is fast becoming a focus for yachties and game fishermen. Day-long **dhow trips** (with snorkelling opportunities, and the $60 fee includes a trip up Mtwapa Creek and lunch at their *Aquamarine Restaurant*) are run most days (except Sun) by Kenya Marineland (PO Box 70 Mtwapa ☏011/485248 or 485866, ℻485265, ⓦwww.kenyamarineland.com), leaving their jetty at around 9.30am; turn right at the signboard in Mtwapa 550m north of the bridge, and head along the dirt track for 1.5km, or ring ahead to get picked up from your hotel (free). There's also a 350,000-litre **aquarium** here (Ksh200, including entry to the obligatory reptile and snake park), and a "Maasai Village" for die-hard tourists.

KIKAMBALA & MTWAPA

0   2 km

ACCOMMODATION

Club Sun 'n' Sand	1
Continental Beach Cottages	7
Glasther Guest House	11
Kamanjiro Super Guest House	12
Kanamai Holiday Centre	9
Le Soleil Beach Club	6
NK Villa Palm Garden	3
Palm Tree Cottages	5
Pombo Cottages	4
Sea-Top Club & Lodging	2
Sweet Heart Lodge	10
Whispering Palms Hotel	8

RESTAURANTS & BARS

Animo Bush Village	B
Casuarina Nomad	G
Chicken Banda	E
Claudio's Italian	F
Fayaz	D
Moorings	H
Muscat Dishes	C
Porini Le Coco-de-Mer	A

Kilifi

Majengo Market

Jumba La Mtwana

Caltex

Mtwapa

Kenya Marineland

Mtwapa Creek

N

Shanzu Beach

Mombasa

For **food**, the pleasant *makuti*-roofed *Casuarina Nomad*, 300m north of the bridge on the right, has delicious chargrilled meat and seafood. Also good are *Chicken Banda* further up on the east side of the main road, and *Fayaz* across the street a little further. *Muscat Dishes*, at the northern end of the village, serves tasty Swahili dishes, *nyama choma* and curries. For upmarket eats, the floating *Moorings Restaurant* is in a fine, breezy location on the north side of the creek, accessible down a track left 300m after the bridge, and has a mainly seafood menu (Tues–Sun 10am–11pm; ☎072/411812; main courses Ksh300–600) and reasonably priced drinks. It's a good place for talk and tales – and to hook up with others, either in person or via the notice board. Similarly stylish, but on dry land, is the excellent *Claudio's Italian Restaurant*, 600m beyond Kenya Marineland, which has wonderful views of the creek as it meets the ocean (dinner daily, lunch Wed–Sun; ☎011/485368; around Ksh1000). *Aquamarine* at Kenya Marineland itself is overpriced, at getting on for Ksh2000 a meal. For **nightlife**, there's a large number of ever-changing disco and live music venues, which rise and fall according to the fashion of the day: just ask around. More dependable are the discos at *Casuarina Nomad* (daily 5pm–6am), which usually feature "cocktails" of traditional dancers at weekends, and the more clubbish *Workshop*, overlooking *Moorings Restaurant* on the creekside (Wednesday, Friday and Saturday) that switches on when *Moorings* switches off, around 11pm.

Jumba la Mtwana

A totally different site worth pausing for (and worth a day out of town in its own right) is **Jumba La Mtwana** (daily 8am–6pm; Ksh200, children Ksh100). This national monument, one of three between Mombasa and Malindi, is the ruined centre of a wealthy fourteenth- or fifteenth-century Swahili community. The sign for the three-kilometre access road is 2km north of Mtwapa Creek bridge; if you're travelling by public transport and are dropped off at the junction, you have a good chance of getting a lift.

Jumba la Mtwana means "mansion of the slave", but it has been deserted for some 500 years and probably had a different name in the past. It's a small site in an enchanting setting among baobabs and lawns above the beach. This seems a strange place for a town, right on an open shore with no harbour, and it's possible the inhabitants were pushed here by raiding parties from inland groups, and relied on Mtwapa Creek as a safe anchorage for the overseas traders who visited yearly. Jumba is fortunate in having good water, but why it was deserted, and by whom, remains a mystery. A helpful little guidebook which costs Ksh20 is sometimes available at the ticket office – much of this account has been culled from it.

Compared with Gedi, further north (see p.526), Jumba's layout is simple. Though it lacks the eerie splendour of that much larger town, it must once have been a sizeable settlement; there were three mosques within the site and a fourth just outside. Most of the population would have lived in mud-and-thatch houses, which have long since disintegrated. In Swahili culture, building in stone (in fact, coral "rag" of different densities) has traditionally been the preserve of certain privileged people, principally the long-settled inhabitants of a town; newcomers would almost always build in less durable materials appropriate to their shorter-term stake in the community. It is believed that building in stone required legal sanction, as it was the material used for mosques.

The best of Jumba's mosques is the **Mosque by the Sea**, which shows evidence of there having been a separate room for women, something which is only nowadays becoming acceptable again in modern mosques. The cistern where worshippers washed is still intact, with coral foot-scrapers set nearby and a jumble of tombs behind the north wall facing Mecca. One of these has a Koranic inscription carved in coral on a panel facing the sea and must have been the grave of an important person:

Every soul shall taste death. You will simply be paid your wages in full on the Day of Resurrection. He who is removed from the fire and made to enter heaven, it is he who has won the victory. The earthly life is only delusion.

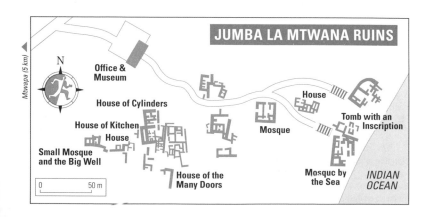

The **people of Jumba** seem to have been very religious and hygienic – virtues that are closely associated in Islam. Cisterns and water jars, or at least the remains of them, are found everywhere among the ruined houses, and in most cases there are coral blocks nearby which would have been used to squat on while washing. Latrines are all stone-lined with long-drops. Of course, it is possible that the poorer people of Jumba lived in squalor in their mud huts, yet even the **House of Many Doors**, which seems to have been a fifteenth-century "boarding and lodging", provided guests with private washing and toilet facilities.

Look out for the two **smaller mosques**, each with its well-preserved, carved coral *mihrab* (the arched niche that indicates the direction of Mecca), and for the strange chinks in several walls (in the House of the Cylinders and the Small Mosque), the purpose of which is unknown.

Jumba Beach is a good place to while away an afternoon – in fact, late afternoon, when the atmosphere hangs among the ruins like cobwebs, is probably the best time to come. Strange but attractive screw pines grow, aerial-rooted like mangroves, in the sand. You can take a **picnic** here, too; there are toilets and showers by the ticket office.

Kikambala

For a day-trip out of Mombasa without your own transport, **KIKAMBALA**, a few kilometres further up the coast, is about as far as you'd want to come (Kilifi-bound matatus and Malindi-bound matatus and buses from Abdel Nasser Road in Mombasa pass here regularly). Note that the topography here is very flat. The sea goes out for nearly a kilometre and it's largely impractical for bathing except at high tide, so if you're just coming for the day, consult a tide table before setting off (daily newspapers print this). Much of the coastal strip here is still thickly forested and the beach itself is a glorious white expanse, though it's 2–3km from the highway and there are no matatus. The only official **campsite** in the area is at the Kanamai Conference & Holiday Centre, or "Kanamai Youth Hostel". The first low-budget beach spot north of Mombasa, it makes a good stop-over, and if you plan to stay more than a night you're not utterly marooned – there's usually someone with a vehicle at the site who'll be going to the *dukas* on the main road most mornings and, once or twice a week, if you help with petrol, into Mombasa.

You could also splurge on a day pass at the all-inclusive *Club Sun'n'Sand* (10am–5pm Ksh1300; 5pm–midnight Ksh1700), which is another thirty minutes' walk further north. Unless you happen to be staying at them, the other Kikambala addresses are not worth a special visit.

Accommodation

The Kikambala **hotels** are virtually the last on the coast north of Mombasa until you reach Kilifi. One downside of being this far out of town, if you haven't got a car, is that taxis into Mombasa cost over Ksh1800 each way. Vehicles normally approach the beach properties from the northern access road (other roads can get tricky in bad weather), 7.4km north of Mtwapa Bridge (signposted for "Sun 'n' Sand"). Coming from the south, it's often quicker to cut in 5.3km north of Mtwapa Bridge, which heads straight to *Kanamai*.

Club Sun 'n' Sand 2.1km along northern access road, PO Box 2 Kikambala ☎0125/32407–8, ⓕ32133, ⓦwww.sunnsand.com). One of the oldest hotels on the Kenya coast, originally built in 1932 and recently reopened as an all-inclusive club – it's among the biggest in the country, with nearly 300 bright, functional rooms, furnished with some style. Three large pools, with diving boards, an extended "river" and slides. Lots of activities, including a kids' club. Efficient, pleasant staff make this one of the most popular and regularly recommended club-hotels on the coast. There are several small shops and *dukas* near the gate if the club atmosphere begins to get claustrophobic. FB ❼ low, ❽ high.

Continental Beach Cottages 3.6km along northern access road, PO Box 124 Kikambala ☎ & ⒡ 32190. Not a great deal of atmosphere, but quiet and friendly, with a reasonable, slightly green pool, all set amid lots of tall, established coconut trees. The cottages ("singles" with one double bed, "doubles" with two twin-bed rooms) have AC and nets, some with TV. Choice of self-catering or eating in the restaurant. Self-catering cottages for two with one double bed. ❸

Kanamai Holiday Centre 5.3km north of Mtwapa Bridge, then 3km along *murram*, PO Box 46 Matwapa ☎0125/32101, ⒡ 32048. Big, sprawling but pretty place under the coconuts, run by the National Christian Council of Kenya. Apart from double-room accommodation (roomy and well furnished, with good fans and nets), there are beds in dormitories (very basic, but spotlessly clean; Ksh100–150), or camping pretty much wherever you like (Ksh200 per person). *Kanamai* offers basic cheap meals in the dining room and has a shop with a few provisions, but there's no bar and, for a stay of several days, you should bring supplies. A half-hour stroll north along the sandy lane through the woods brings you to the *Whispering Palms Hotel*, where you can join in all the usual holiday pursuits. ❸

Le Soleil Beach Club 3.2km along northern access road, PO Box 84737 Mombasa ☎0125/32195–6, ⒡32164, ⒠lesoleil@africaonline.co.ke. More like a tropical office block than a hotel, this is as tacky as it is popular, with a cos-

mopolitan variety of budget package tourists and tons of activities (and unlimited food and booze) covered in the all-inclusive price. No daily visits. FB ❺

NK Villa Palm Garden Hotel 1.8km along northern access road, PO Box 115 Kikambala ☎0125/32229. Quite an attractive, shady establishment, but plays on its reputation with low-budget German package tourists. Modest pool. Studio apartments with kitchen and living room, or double rooms. ❸

Palm Tree Cottages 2.6km along northern access road, PO Box 82448 Mombasa ☎0125/26436. Four-bed houses with room for two more in each. Not especially good value and a very uninspiring plot. ❹

Pombo Cottages 2.3km along northern access road, PO Box 351 Kikambala ☎011/829650. Slightly run-down but nonetheless pleasant two-bedroom cottages (one room with a double bed, the other with twin beds), self-catering but with food available at the restaurant. ❹

Sea-Top Club & Lodging 1.7km along northern access road, PO Box 226 Kikambala ☎0125/32184. Substantial *nyama choma* bar and nightspot with nightly discos featuring Congolese sounds, soul, Caribbean and funk. Simple s/c rooms for weary clients. Fans, but no nets. ❷

Whispering Palms Hotel 3.9km along northern access road, PO Box 5 Kikambala ☎0125/32087 or 32159, ⒡32029, ⒠whispers @africaonline.co.ke. Peaceful, isolated hideaway for a mix of package tourists from Britain and Europe, but old-fashioned and would benefit from an overhaul. The grounds are shaded by, at times, quite noisy palm trees, and there's a colony of Wahlberg's epauletted fruit bats. Slightly cheaper than its equivalents closer to Mombasa. ❹

Eating and drinking

Outside of the hotels, there aren't many **restaurants** and **nightlife** options, though there are a couple of places along the main Mombasa–Malindi road. *Porini Le Coco-de-Mer*, 6.5km north of Mtwapa Bridge (daily 10am–11.30pm; ☎0125/32117) is a long-established restaurant set in jungly gardens, and is friendly and laid-back, specializing in Seychelloise cuisine (lots of seafood and chicken, coconut milk and cassava), where a splurge will set you back Ksh600–900. *Animo Bush Village*, 3.3km from Mtwapa Bridge and then 1km (signposted) left, is a former rural nightclub fallen on hard times, which is now for the most part a somnolent bar and *nyama choma* joint, with traditional bands and dancers (Saturday and Sunday afternoons 3–5pm), and mixed dance music – reggae and *ndombolo* especially – on Friday, Saturday and Sunday nights (5pm–3am). They also provide cleanish s/c rooms with fans (Ksh500).

Inland from Mombasa

MAZERAS is just a short hop from Mombasa or, if you're coming from Nairobi, marks the end of the long vistas of scrub; it's perched right on the edge of the steep scarp, amid bananas and coconuts. If you're travelling by road, it isn't a bad idea to break your journey here and savour the new atmosphere. The *hotelis* serve good, flavourful, coastal *chai* and, for the travel-weary, Mazeras has a delightful **botanical garden** (daily 6am–6pm; free) – bamboo, ponds and green lawns for a snooze in the shade – just a couple of hundred metres back towards Mombasa. Across the road and up the hill a little way is a **mission** and its century-old church, signs of an evangelical presence in the hills behind Mombasa that goes back, remarkably, over 150 years.

For historians of Methodism and the Church Missionary Society or (more likely) connoisseurs of palm wine, the **road to Kaloleni**, 22km north of Mazeras is a required sidetrack; see the map on p.445. It's a beautiful trip in its own right: wonderfully scenic, looping through lush vales with a wide panorama down to the coast on the right and masses of **coconut trees** all around. There are frequent buses and matatus from Mombasa (the Kobil station at the junction of Jomo Kenyatta Avenue with Mwembe Tayari Road) to Kaloleni via Rabai, which makes this an easy day-trip away from the coast, especially appealing in the high season if your sense of adventure has become numbed by the influx of tropical paradise-seekers. If a round trip appeals, arrive in Kaloleni before mid-afternoon and you'll be able to catch a matatu further north to Kilifi, and from there back to Mombasa. If you're driving, note that there's no petrol at Mazeras, and only irregular supplies at Kaloleni, so fill up in Mombasa or Mariakani.

Rabai

RABAI, capital of the **Wa-Rabai** Mijikenda and site of the first Christian mission to be established in East Africa, is the first village you come to, 5km from Mazeras. It's also one of only two Mijikenda villages still occupying its original *kaya* (see p.490). A German pastor, the Reverend **Johan Ludwig Krapf**, came here in 1846 after losing his family at Nyali (see p.473), and left his mark on the community when, 41 years later, the imposing **St Paul's church**, now blue and white, was erected. The centre of the village and the church, surrounded by school rooms and sports fields, lie half a kilometre off the main road on the right as you come into Rabai from Mazeras. For the church and museum, fork left after 200m. Opposite the entrance to St Paul's, the first church to have been built (1846–48) now houses the modest **Krapf Memorial Museum** (daily 9.30am–6pm; adults Ksh200, children Ksh100). Signs all along the road from Mombasa point the way to it, but strangely, the building itself bears no sign whatsoever to tell you what it is. Not the most exciting place in Kenya, it contains a few well-presented photographs but little else. The ticket, however, includes a guided tour and explanation, with visits to a full-scale replica of the *kaya* (tourists are not allowed to wander through the real one), and the village's nearby viewpoint over the countryside. Next door to the museum is the house where Krapf used to live, and the adjacent cottage of Johann Rebmann, Krapf's proselytizing partner, is used as a school room. Between them, the two missionaries managed to explore a great deal of what is now Kenya without the demonstrations of firepower so many of their successors thought necessary. Krapf worked out the grammar of Swahili and produced a translation of the Bible. For all its significance, though, Rabai "centre" has, in all truth, hardly anything to offer, and there's nowhere in the village to stay, the nearest accommodation being *Sammy's Rendezvous* (see below).

Ribe

RIBE (the Wa-Ribe village) is more substantial than Rabai, but harder to get to. Seven kilometres from Rabai, an unmarked track snakes up to the right from a deep valley floor: the village is 1.5km along it. Buses stop by the track. If you're driving, continue to a sign (on the right) for a lead mine. There are two bars and *hotelis* and a factory at the junction, which spews its dust over the neighbouring coconut and banana groves. Ribe itself is the second village along the track, about 4km from the main road. It consists of a few small shops and a shady **bar-restaurant** with a courtyard and rooms (❶). Another option, just before the turning on the main road (5km north of Rabai), is *Sammy's Rendezvous B&L* (❶).

Fifteen minutes' walk away from Ribe, through the *shambas* and dense undergrowth, is a tiny **cemetery**, regularly cleared of weeds and creepers, near the site of Ribe's Methodist mission, itself crumbled to its foundations and now completely overgrown. It isn't hard to find, and it's worth visiting if only to take a look at the pathetic graves of those few missionaries who struggled all the way here before succumbing in what must have been nearly impossible conditions. They were often very young: the Reverend Butterworth, whose carpentry skills ensured him a welcome arrival, died aged 23, just two months after getting there; they used his new tools to make the coffin. It isn't surprising that the cemetery faces out to sea, towards Mombasa, supplies, the mail and new settlers.

Kaloleni

The paved road comes to its end at **KALOLENI**. On the way, you pass through dense coconut groves where many of the trees have been initialled to avoid ownership disputes. The tapping of **palm wine** (*mnazi*), banned by the government, is still widely practised here, with the **Giriama** section of the Mijikenda leading the field. They call palm wine "the mother of the coconut", since tapping the trees for juice hinders formation of the nuts.

Tapping is done by cutting off the flower stem, binding it tightly and allowing the sap that would have produced new coconuts to collect in a container – usually a baobab pod – tied to the end. Here it ferments rapidly and has to be regularly collected. Variations in the local demand for *mnazi*, which is most often drunk at community gatherings like weddings and funerals, and in the coastal market for *copra* (the dried coconut flesh used in soap and oil manufacture), tend to influence the owners of trees in their decision whether to tap or to grow *copra*. You will see trees with the stepnotches that enable the tappers to reach the top ending several metres below the crown, indicating that a tree has been left a number of years to develop coconuts.

Palm wine is locally available up and down the coast. Because it is illegal, you won't find it openly on sale, but you should be able to locate a supply easily enough with a few discreet inquiries. It usually comes in plastic mineral-water bottles, and costs a lot less than beer – about Ksh30–50 a litre. It is best when

The Mijikenda peoples

The principal people of the coastal hinterland region are the **Mijikenda** ("Nine Tribes"), a loose grouping whose Bantu languages are to a large extent mutually intelligible, and closely related to Swahili. They are believed to have arrived in their present homelands in the sixteenth or seventeenth century from a quasi-historical state called Shungwaya, which had undergone a period of intense civil chaos. This centre was probably located somewhere in the Lamu hinterland or in the southwest corner of present-day Somalia. According to oral tradition, the people who left it were the Giriama, the Digo, the Rabai, the Ribe, the Duruma, the Chonyi, the Jibana, the Kauma and the Kambe (not to be confused with the Kamba of the interior).

All these "tribes" now live in the coastal hinterland, with the **Giriama** to the north of Mombasa and **Digo** to the south – the largest and best-known groups. They share a degree of common cultural heritage. Each tribe has a traditional **kaya** central settlement, a fortified village in the forest, usually built on raised ground some kilometres from the coast, but sometimes right by the shore. Some Mijikenda peoples built only one *kaya*; others spawned secondary *kayas* or even whole clusters. The *kayas* still exist, although they are now sacred glades rather than fortified villages, and the dwelling place of ancestral spirits. In theory, they each contain a *fingo* – a charm said to derive from the ancestral home of Shungwaya – but these have nearly all been destroyed or, like the grave posts made from the *brachylinum* tree called *kigango* (*vigango* in the plural) that were also formerly a feature of each *kaya*, stolen for private collections of "primitive art" or loft-converters' ideas of interesting objets d'art.

Today, most *kayas* are run-down, but they are still remembered and visited by one or two elders. While their sacred aspect has ceased to have much relevance for most Mijikenda, their true significance comes out under pressure: when a German hotel developer took a fancy to Chale island (the whole of which is a gazetted *kaya*), he had to "buy" two Digo medicine men to appease the spirits – not best pleased with having their groves smothered in concrete. Nor is their human value the only reason to care about the *kayas*. Along with belief in their sacred qualities comes a local conservation tradition. In these forest tracts of between five hectares and three square kilometres nothing has ever been cultivated or disturbed. They represent a biological storehouse of immense diversity, unique along the East African coast. A WWF-backed botanical research programme run by the National Museums of Kenya has been under way for several years to map out the *kaya* ecosystems and to encourage the elders to reassert their authority over each one, something of an urgent matter as many are current-

cold, but rarely is, and you drink it (discreetly) through a reed straw with a coconut-fibre filter. As well as *mnazi*, tapped from the coconut palm, there is another variety of palm wine called *mukoma*, which comes from the doum palm, and is generally considered an inferior brew.

The only places to **stay** in Kaloleni are two basic guest houses, the tin-roofed *Bububu Guest House* near the bus and matatu stand (❶), and the slightly better *makuti*-roofed *Kaloleni Guest House*, 700m up the old Kilifi road behind the post office and near St Luke's hospital (❶), which has the advantage of mosquito nets. Neither has running water, and washing is with buckets.

Moving on, there are frequent buses and matatus back to Mombasa via Rabai and Mazeras, and less frequent matatus up to Kilifi, 40km away (catch these at the bottom of the hill by the Kilifi junction).

ly under threat from "land-grabbing" developers, usually well-connected and unscrupulous individuals or local politicians. More than twenty *kayas* have so far been gazetted in Kwale District, south of Mombasa, and the process has now started in the Kilifi area. There may be more than fifty altogether, though some could be so small they will disappear under the hoe or the caterpillar tractor before anyone remembers them. It may be possible to visit a *kaya*, but they are by no means tourist attractions. If you're genuinely interested, contact the Coastal Forest Conservation Unit (CFCU), PO Box 86 Ukunda ☏0127/2518, ℮cfcu.kwale@swiftmombasa.com – the office is 3km south of Ukunda on the Lungalunga road, signposted to the right. The possibility that one or two of the old sacred groves might be opened to tourists to generate income still seems some way off. *The Kaya Complex* (Thomas T. Spear, Kenya Literature Bureau, Nairobi 1978) provides interesting reading on the subject.

Like so many other Kenyan peoples, the Mijikenda had age-set systems that helped cut across the divisive groupings of clan and subclan to bind communities together. Much of this tradition was lost during the last century; the installation of a new ruling elders' age-set, for example, required the killing and castration of a stranger.

Economically, the Mijikenda were, and still are, diverse. They were cultivators, herders (especially the Duruma and, at one time, the Giriama), long-distance traders with the interior, makers of palm wine (a Digo speciality now diffused all over Mijikenda-land), hunters and fishermen. They have local market cycles – four-day weeks in the case of the Giriama (days one and two for labour, day three for preparation, and day four, called *chipolata*, for market). They have successfully maintained their cultural identity, warring with the British in 1914 over the imposition of taxes and the demand for porters for World War I, and preserving a vigorous conservative tradition of adherence to their old beliefs in spirits and the power of their ancestors. This is most apparent in the relative ease with which you can pick up cassettes of **traditional music**, especially in Mombasa: wonderful rhythms and some very delicate *chivoti* flute melodies, with only a slight discernable Islamic influence, if at all. If you're really interested and have time to spare, even casual enquiries inland will elicit invitations to weddings or, less likely, funerals, where the old traditions – and music – are still very much centrepieces, despite the Christian veneer. Many Mijikenda, however, have found conversion to Islam a helpful religious switch in their dealings with coastal merchants and businessmen. This conversion seems to be the latest development in the growth of Swahili society.

The South Coast

A continuous strip of beach runs between Likoni and Msambweni, backed by palms and broken once or twice by small rivers. Along the whole coast south from Mombasa to the Tanzanian border, there's just one highly developed resort area, **Diani Beach**. South of Diani, the coast is little known and, in most tour operators' minds at least, nobody stops again until they reach **Shimoni**. This is great news if you have the time to go searching out untrodden beaches by car, bicycle or motorbike (all available to rent), or using the good local public trans-

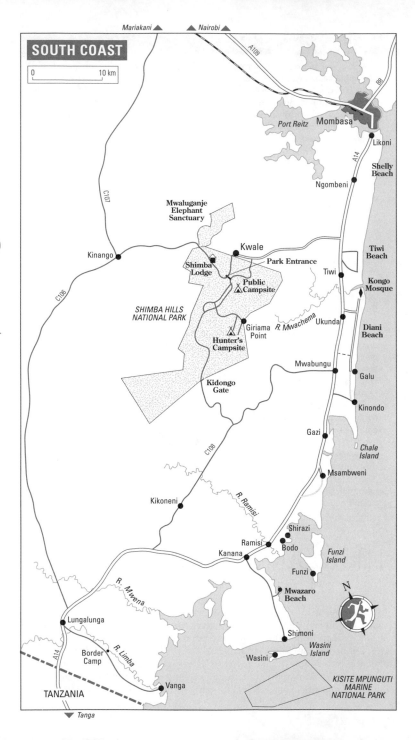

port. With your own transport, or with a safari company, you can also visit the **Shimba Hills National Park** and the neighbouring Mwaluganje Elephant Sanctuary, either overnight or on an easy day-trip excursion.

Most of the people who live along the coastal strip here are **Digo**, and their neat rectangular houses, made of dried mud and coral on a framework of wood, are a distinctive part of the lush roadside scene. Although they belong to the Mijikenda group of peoples, the Digo are unusual in being matrilineal: they traditionally traced descent through the female line, so that a man would, on his death, pass his property on to his sister's sons rather than his own. It is an unusual system with interesting implications for the state of the family and the position of women. However, the joint assault of Islamic and Western values over the last century has shifted the emphasis back towards the male line, and in many ways, women in modern Digo society have less freedom and autonomy than they had a hundred years ago.

Likoni and Shelly Beach

Taking the Likoni ferry (matatus from the post office on Digo Road) makes the sense of separation from Mombasa more immediate than crossing the

Likoni and the 1997 violence

The run-up to the chaotic December 1997 Kenyan general elections was fraught with violence, both in the Rift Valley (which had suffered similarly before the 1992 elections, when some 1000 lives were lost) and – disastrously for Kenya's tourist industry – on the coast. The flashpoint was **Likoni**. For many years the focus for "up-country" immigrants, who had arrived in vast numbers to cash in on the tourist boom, Likoni had also attracted the ire of the government when the – traditionally anti-government voting – immigrants returned an opposition MP to the Likoni seat in 1992.

Over the following years, political and inter-tribal tension between immigrants and the indigenous Digo and Muslim inhabitants worsened, coming to a head in July 1997 when an unauthorized rally calling for constitutional change ended in violence. Shortly afterwards, gangs of thugs armed with guns and machetes started attacking homes, shops and bars. At first, the government blamed a group of "marauding drug addicts and drunks".

Then in August, a raid on Likoni police station by a "mysterious militia" resulted in the deaths of seven policemen and the theft of 44 automatic weapons. In the following hours, seven other people were also found dead. In Likoni, graffiti on the walls of the suddenly almost-deserted town appeared, reading: "Three days to go or you die". Almost a thousand people took refuge in the Catholic Church at Likoni, which itself was attacked two weeks later, resulting in two deaths. The subsequent and unusually well-orchestrated violence – including the murder of several members of a band playing at *Shelly Beach Hotel* – claimed the lives of seventy people, and caused an exodus of immigrants, with around 100,000 people displaced.

Conspiracy theorists were quick to blame KANU ethnic-cleansing and gerrymandering in the run-up to the elections, a claim subsequently given credence first by a police swoop involving the arrests of several high-ranking KANU officials, and then by the findings of the 1998–99 **Akiwumi Clashes Inquiry** which showed that much of the violence had been premeditated by politicians who had paid the thugs, arranged their transport and supplied them with weapons.

Fortunately, since 1999 things have been calmer, and similar violence is not expected in the elections scheduled for 2002.

bridges heading out of the city to the north. More pragmatically, the lack of a bridge has deterred developers and contributed to the South Coast's fairly late arrival in the tour brochures (though Diani is certainly making up for lost time). The ferries (free for foot passengers, Ksh35 for cars) operate around the clock (every 15min, 4am–1am; every hour, 1am–4am). Beware of **pickpockets** here: keep your hands free, don't shake hands, and ensure money belts are secure and can't be cut off from behind.

LIKONI itself is a busy creekside suburb of Mombasa, straggling down the southbound road for a good 3km. A coast road runs off around the headland to the east (see Mombasa island map, pp.448–9), served by infrequent matatus, but Shelly Beach – named after its shells – is narrow and has large patches of exposed coral rag rock (bring rubber- or plastic-soled sandals), and tends to be strewn with seaweed, while the sea here is only feasible for swimming at high tide. Unless you're booked into a hotel already, hop on a bus or matatu and make for Tiwi or Diani. Apart from a host of very local (if rough-looking) eateries and good streetfood at Likoni ferry, the only real **restaurant** is the excellent *Island Paradise Bar & Restaurant*, next to *ACK Guest House*, whose tilapia, oddly enough (it's from Lake Victoria, not the Indian Ocean), is very good. For **nightlife**, there are two clubs: *Jack City*, to the right as you get off the ferry and *The Office* at the start of the road to Shelly Beach. Be warned, however, that both of these places can be pretty rough after nightfall, with thefts common and stabbings not unknown.

Accommodation

The following addresses are all Mombasa PO boxes; distances are from the Likoni junction. Matatus from the junction run to just short of *Sea Breeze*. See Mombasa island map, pp.448–9.

ACK Guest House (formerly *CPK Guest House*) 300m, PO Box 96170 ☎011/451982. Even on a low budget, the Anglican Church of Kenya's coastal retreat might seem an odd choice. But it's well run, the better rooms are fine (showers and fans) and good value and, while it's not on the beach, it's handy for Mombasa and South Coast transport. There's a good swimming pool (and one for kids), and basic food in the attractive patio dining room overlooking the road, which is a popular meeting place for locals. B&B ❸

Childrens' Holiday Resort 3.5km, PO Box 96048 ☎011/451417. A low-budget bungalow establishment from another age, the *Resort* is a non-profit trust that goes way back, occupying a peaceful, flat sandy site under the coconut palms, right on the beach. Families are preferred, but couples and singles aren't excluded. Self-catering only (utensils provided, but cooker and fridge only in the larger s/c cottages), all with electricity, some s/c but most with outside showers and toilets. Nets on request. Bring your own bed linen. Basic, but good value. Cottages for two-plus. ❸

Kwetu Beach Resort 4km ☎072/866401, reservations through PO Box 42947 Nairobi ☎02/343828. A quiet, family-run place just

beyond the *Sea Breeze*, with clean, jolly s/c rooms and a homely atmosphere despite the attached bar/restaurant. B&B ❹

Reliable Beach Apartments 1.5km, PO Box 82630 ☎011/451595, reservations ☎011/491954. Good-sized apartments on a plot of general ugliness, with no facilities apart from a small pool. On a positive note, it's next to the beach. Two-bedroom apartments (up to four people). ❹

Sea Breeze Beach Cottages 4km, PO Box 90228 ☎011/227683. Not on the beach and overpriced, with somewhat run-down s/c rooms (no nets) and linoleum everywhere. Sleepy bar and murky green pool. The *Children's Holiday Resort* is a better alternative. ❸

Shelly Beach Club Hotel 2.8km, PO Box 96030 ☎011/451001–4, ⓕ451349, ⓔsbh@wananchi.com. An affordable all-inclusive resort (including unlimited booze, until the bar closes at midnight), populated entirely by British package tourists. By no means the most beautiful hotel on the coast and there's refreshingly little pretence to class (starting with the curio stalls outside reception), but it's well run. Rooms are AC; no day visitors. Rates negotiable. FB ❻

Shimba Hills National Park

Entry $20, children $5. Warden: PO Box 30 Kwale ℡0127/4159 or 4166. Map: Survey of Kenya SK93 at 1:40,000 (1980), or Sapra Safari's The Kenya Coast.

Probably Kenya's most underrated wildlife refuge, **Shimba Hills National Park** is under an hour from Mombasa, even less from Likoni and, at 500m above sea level, wonderfully refreshing after the humidity down below. The hilly park of scattered jungle and grassland is comparatively little visited, which is all to the good, and has a quite wonderful game-viewing lodge and one of the best-situated camping and *banda* sites anywhere.

Kwale and access to the park

The most straightforward option for visiting Shimba is on a **safari from Mombasa** or from the coast. Trips from most coast hotels and travel agents cost about $80–100 for a day-trip, $155–180 for an overnight at *Shimba Lodge*, and include park entrance fees but not game drives or nature walks.

If you're **driving**, you'll probably need high-clearance 4WD in all but the driest weather and, even so, the southern access road via Kindango Gate is atrocious and often impassable. Note also that Kwale doesn't always have petrol. There are fairly frequent **matatus** to **KWALE** from Likoni ferry bus park. The park's **main gate** is inside the park, some 5km beyond Kwale along an elephant-dunged *murram* road. Buses and matatus from Kwale will drop you here – in theory it's illegal to walk, although there is no sign to tell you this. At the gate, you can try for **a lift** around the park. Since your best bet is with Mombasans, Sundays and public holidays are the easiest times. The last bus back to Mombasa from Kwale is at 8pm. In case of need, there are two **lodgings** in town. *Golden Guest House* (PO Box 272 ℡0127/4112; ❶) is the best, with pretty clean, s/c rooms and nets. Kwale has one of the world's biggest deposits of **titanium ore**, which Canadian company Tiomin Resources was set to mine, until the government unexpectedly shelved the project in September 2000 following a campaign by environmentalists and local residents.

Moving on from Kwale, a rarely used route away from the coast heads northwest to Mariakani on the Nairobi highway, which is served by a few daily matatus. The first and only major town on the way is **Kinango**, where you might have to change vehicle. If you get stuck here, the only **hotel** is the basic *Kinango Silent Rest House* (❶). There are matatus from here to Mariakani and Likoni.

Shimba Lodge

Shimba Lodge (℡0127/4077; reservations through the *Nyali Beach* in Nyali see p.476 or Block Hotels, see p.42; no children under 7; HB ❸) is a "tree hotel", a kind of coastal *Treetops*, though actually superior in all respects to the original. Check-in is from 3pm, but if you're driving and give advance notice, you can arrive early at the lodge for lunch (Ksh850). It's all intensely atmospheric, as the building, apparently constructed entirely of pitch-dark timber (though it's actually mainly just cladding over the concrete), rises up through the trees and creepers, with aerial plantlife, birds, butterflies and humans all sharing the deep forest glade. The staff are instructed to speak in whispers, and remind guests to do so.

Given the rates, the standard rooms, with shared showers and toilets, might seem a disappointment at first, but when there are bushbabies on the branch outside, the possibility of a leopard, and a sweeping view of the dam and perhaps a fish eagle in the trees opposite, you don't spare too much thought for luxuries. From nearly all the rooms, on three floors, and from several bars and observation platforms, you have views across the small, dammed lake to thick forest. The best feature is the tree-level **walkway**, which runs for 100m or so from one end of the lodge to a platform high above the ground near a small clearing. Here you can watch elephants, warthogs, forest antelope and monkeys galore – if you're lucky. After dark, spotlights illuminate bushbabies, hundreds of bats and a whirling hailstorm of jungle insects. It's a memorable evening – and the food is good.

The early-evening "sundowner" **nature walk** (5pm; $15) is always enjoyable. The next morning there's the option of a proper **game drive** in the park (6am; $15), with the opportunity to see the sable antelope for which Shimba is famous.

Around the park

Predators are rare in Shimba Hills, but you may well see **elephant**, especially from the vantage of Elephant Hill or at the nearby **Sheldrick Falls**, particularly if you go early in the day. There are armed guards at Elephant Hill who will escort you to the falls; it's a very pretty walk down a steep hillside, atmospheric and partly wooded to the falls, but a long hike back up again – take water, and swimming gear if you want to splash in the pool, directly under the waterfall. Allow about three hours for the excursion. The elephant population in Shimba is estimated at between 500 and 600, up from 300 in 1977. The poaching which decimated Tsavo's herds was thankfully absent here, and the Mwaluganje Elephant Sanctuary (see p.497) has been a great success.

Look out also for the park's three **Maasai giraffe**, the product of a tentative experiment. Although Shimba had never had giraffe naturally, a small nucleus was introduced a decade ago after having been rescued from smugglers attempting to take them abroad. Unfortunately, one died in transit, another female died shortly after arrival, and the two males just disappeared, leaving only two females and distraught rangers. Two breeding males were then brought in, one more of the females died, but the other finally gave birth in December 1996, to the delight of everyone, though unfortunately she died soon after, and the group now consists of just three males, although there are plans to bring in some females to keep them company. Spurred on by this modest success, **zebra** and **ostrich** have also been introduced. Shimba is best known, however, for its indigenous herds of **sable antelope**, magnificent-looking animals as big as horses, with great, sweeping horns. The park is their only habitat in Kenya (the similar but even bigger roan antelopes, which were relocated from western Kenya, died out, it's thought, through lack of necessary minerals). You may well see groups of chestnut-coloured sable females but the territorial, jet-black males are more solitary and harder to find. If you have a guide he'll know where to look, but they're most commonly seen in the area overlooking the ocean, between the public campsite and Giriama Point. Another good place to head for is **Makadara picnic site**: there are bats in the toilet and it's supposed to be a good place to see buffalo.

Camping in Shimba Hills

What Shimba Hills may lack in wildlife it more than makes up for with enchanting views in every direction, especially seawards. Haze tends to blot out

Mombasa itself but the fringe of Diani Beach is usually visible. **Camping** is possible at two sites ($8 per person). The **public campsite** is located at one of the best vantage points in the park, about 3km from the main gate. The four *bandas* here (❸) are adequate (though the bedding, lamps, shower and nearby toilet can't be relied on, and the water needs purification), but the setting is sublime: a thickly forested bluff hundreds of metres above the coconut-crowded coastal plain. It's well worth spending the night up here just for the sunrise. If you do, you'll probably have the place to yourself. *Hunter's Camp* is preferred by Kenyans, but has no facilities whatsoever (book with the rangers).

Mwaluganje Elephant Sanctuary

To the northwest of Shimba and the area where the "sundowner walks" normally take place, just outside the national park, lies the **Mwaluganje Elephant Sanctuary** ($10). Situated on the slopes of the privately owned Goloni Escarpment, it's a remarkable success story of a compromise solution. It was created in 1995 to defuse conflict between the local Duruma farmers and elephants, who had made a habit of trashing their crops and killing farmers attempting to defend their livelihoods. After consultation between the local people, Kenya Wildlife Service, and the Eden Wildlife Trust, 240 square kilometres were set aside for the sanctuary, separated along a third of its boundary from farmland with electric fencing, but left open elsewhere to keep the elephants' migration routes open.

The low-lying areas around the Manolo River are dominated by baobab, while thick brachystegia forest covers the escarpment's flanks, and harbours a surprising wealth of wildlife. You are "guaranteed" to see elephants here and, in time, it's hoped that threatened species can be relocated here from other parts of Kenya. Apart from the prolific birdlife, you might also see zebra, bushbuck, warthog, monkeys and (rarely) leopard.

The main gate is beyond the Shimba Hills park entrance, 14km west of Kwale, then 2km along a signposted track to the right (4WD only in the rains). There is another gate (Golini) along a track 5km northwest of Kwale. The only **accommodation** in the sanctuary is *Travellers Mwaluganje Elephant Camp* (PO Box 87649 Mombasa ☎011/485121–6, ☎485678, ✉travellershtl@swiftmombasa.com; ❽). Most guests come on overnight packages from the coast ($158–172 per person), though day excursions are also available ($78–$92 per person including lunch, transport, park fee & game drive). Set along the shoulder of a low hill facing a well-established elephant trail, there are twenty twin-bedded tents under thatch roofs, each with verandah (watch the elephants walking past), bathrooms and electricity. You can also go on an escorted game drive through the sanctuary ($26 per person). The place still feels new and a little raw, but the setting along a water hole is delightful, and the staff extremely pleasant.

Tiwi Beach

Back on the coast, and south of Likoni, the first real magnet is **TIWI BEACH**. Popular among budget travellers having a bit of a splurge, Tiwi rates as genuine tropical paradise material and attracts lots of Anglo-Kenyan families down from Nairobi. The reef lies just offshore, and there are good snorkelling opportunities at high tide, especially at the northern end. Beach hustlers and all the attendant hassles have mostly yet to arrive, especially in the northern section (fronted by

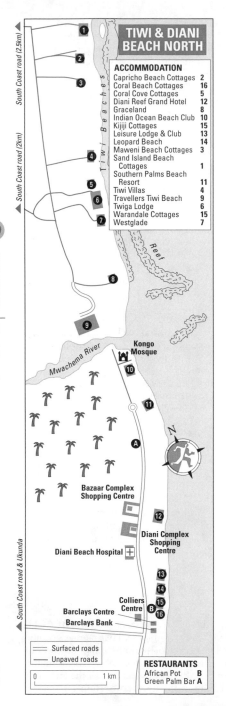

TIWI & DIANI BEACH NORTH

Kongo Mosque

Mwachema River

Bazaar Complex Shopping Centre

Diani Complex Shopping Centre

Diani Beach Hospital

Colliers Centre

Barclays Centre
Barclays Bank

South Coast road (2.5km)

South Coast road (2km)

South Coast road & Ukunda

=== Surfaced roads
— Unpaved roads

0   1 km

Sand Island, Capricho and *Maweni*). With the exception of the large new *Travellers Tiwi Beach Hotel* at its southern end, Tiwi is still cottage territory, with nearly a dozen plots vying with each other for business. The only restaurants as yet are at *Travellers Tiwi Beach Hotel*, *Tiwi Villas* and *Twiga Lodge*, the latter with the best bar. The main drawbacks (some might say its advantages) are the lack of bars, restaurants and nightlife, and its isolation from the rest of the coast. More serious are nagging concerns about security if you're walking anywhere: don't take any valuables.

There are two roads down to the beach from the main South Coast highway. The first, signposted for *Sand Island, Capricho* and *Maweni*, is a narrow sandy track some 17km from the Likoni ferry; the second, about 1.5km further south, has a bigger clump of signboards and is much wider, and more reliable for driving in rain. Using either road, you're strongly advised not to walk, certainly if you've got all your luggage with you: these access roads through the cashews have seen many *panga* (machete)-point robberies. Waiting for a ride won't be a huge problem as there's a fairly frequent taxi service (it should cost Ksh200–300), and most places will happily pick you up for free from the main road if you call ahead. Taxis from Mombasa cost about Ksh1600.

In the dry season, you can walk to the end of Tiwi Beach and wade across the Mwachema River to Diani Beach and the strange Kongo Mosque, right next to the *Indian Ocean Beach Club*. But again, there have been incidents of robbery down here, and you are not advised to go alone, certainly not with any valuables.

Accommodation

The seasons on Tiwi, as regards prices and availability, are slightly different from other parts of the coast in that they reflect the school holidays of their regular clients. At Christmas, Easter, and in July and August, it's hard to get in anywhere – advance booking is a very good idea. Price codes refer to the cost for two people sharing a one-bedroom cottage, where available; there are always big savings for groups in larger cottages. There isn't much in the real budget range unless you're camping (although *Coral Cove* has budget rooms), but the extra expense is well worth it if you choose carefully.

Capricho Beach Cottages PO Box 5177 Diani ☏0127/51231, ℉51010, ⓌＷwww.dianibeach.com /cottages/capricho; office hours 8–11am & 4–5pm; closed May. Where *Sand Island* has the advantage in its beach and ambience, *Capricho* has better-designed vault-roofed cottages with plenty of cool space, and a pool (Ksh200 per person per day, including guests), and no dogs (*Sand Island* loves dogs). Bed linen and mosquito nets can be rented with advance notice, and you can hire a cook/housekeeper for Ksh200 per day if you don't bring your own (which is what most White Kenyan guests apparently do). Marginally cheaper than *Sand Island*, but more expensive than *Maweni*. ❹

Coral Cove Cottages PO Box 96455 Likoni ☏ & ℉0127/51062, Ⓦwww.aussiemike.com /coralcove. From the makers of Nairobi's infamous *Buffalo Bill's*, something rather different: excellent, large, stand-alone cottages with fine new bathrooms and an attractive, palm-shaded beach, all bathed in a laid-back atmosphere provided by low-key but consistently helpful management. Loads of dogs and cats, an aviary and a silly parrot. The sea here is shallow (good for children), and favoured by turtles for laying eggs, so be careful where you step. Fruit, veg and fish vendors call daily. You can hire a cook/housekeeper for Ksh350 per day. The price itself is a bargain. Double rooms ❷, cottages ❹

Graceland (Tiwi Sea Castles) PO Box 96599 Likoni ☏0127/51048, ℉2147, Ⓦwww.tiwibeach.com/graceland. One of Tiwi's most luxurious developments, with comfortable rooms, and three-bedroom cottages housing up to eight people, and the choice of B&B, half-board or full-board. B&B ❹

Maweni Beach Cottages PO Box 96024 Likoni ☏0127/51008, ℉51225, ℮julianestephan @kenyasouthcoast.com. A variety of relatively simple self-catering cottages. Slightly cheaper than either of its northerly neighbours, but actually more genteel, conscientiously managed, and very well kept, in beautiful gardens with absolutely stunning sea views, wild dik-diks, and an *askari* on the beach to keep an eye on your things while you swim. You can also hire the services of a cook for Ksh250 per day. ❸

Sand Island Beach Cottages PO Box 5516 Diani ☏0127/51233, ℮sandisland@africaonline.co.ke. Long established and well maintained, with fully equipped self-catering rustic cottages – all sea-facing – with new kitchen equipment and decent bathrooms. The old Kenya atmosphere is refreshingly informal, with charming family management, and the site is very attractive, with a shifting sand isle exposed with the tides just metres across the water, and safe swimming possible at all times. There's a coral garden nearby, and use of snorkelling equipment is free. The products of a working citrus orchard are available, and there are the ruins of old slave quarters in the grounds. Various cottages sleeping two to six people. Recommended. ❹

Tiwi Villas PO Box 86775 Mombasa ☏072/774669; can also be booked in the UK ☏01304/202077, ℉210272. Cottages, but not self-catering (fridges and cookers were removed, but there is a restaurant). The seven two-bedroom front cottages house four, with superb sea views, but are cramped, dark and rather basic. There are also thirteen one-bedroom (two-person) cottages at the back of the site. There's no beach, as the site is perched on a coral rock promontory, and the small pool hardly compensates, though you can use the beach next door. ❸

Travellers Tiwi Beach Hotel PO Box 87649 Mombasa ☏0127/51202, ℉51207, ℮travtiwi@wananchi.com. The beach's only tourist hotel, a large and somewhat impersonal package affair. The main attraction is arguably the longest swimming pool in Kenya, actually a series of pools connected by canals and slides. The public areas are on one side, and rows of three-storey apartment blocks on the other. There's also a nightclub (*Diamonds*, from 9pm nightly), and a good Indian restaurant (*Shor-e-Punjab*; closed Mon lunch). Watersports include waterskiing, windsurfing, snorkelling and scuba diving. Free entry for day visitors. Wheelchair friendly. FB ❺

Twiga Lodge PO Box 96005 Mombasa ☎0127/51267. Basic hostel and campsite trading on a reputation established in the 1970s, and still popular with overlanders and budget travellers despite much better competition. The draw of its lively bar aside, it's now just the place you end up if you don't know about the alternatives. Apart from a variety of dismal cell- or barrack-like rooms (no self-catering facilities, and some lack toilets), you can camp (Ksh150 per person). There's an adequately stocked provisions store and the bar-restaurant does reasonable food. ❸

Westglade (formerly *Minilets*). Currently closed, this was a place for which reports were invariably positive, with relaxed and friendly management, helpful staff, and neat chalets prettily scattered down a sloping old coral garden hillside, featuring a swimming pool at the bottom. Due to reopen under new management, so may be worth checking out.

Dhow trips and diving

For details of **dhow-trip operators**, read the box on p.507. Information on scuba diving is in the box on p.506.

Diani Beach and around

DIANI BEACH ought to fulfil most dreams about the archetypal palm-fringed beach. The sand is soft and brilliantly white, the sea is crystal-clear turquoise, the reef is a safe thirty-minute swim or ten-minute boat ride away and, arching overhead, the coconut palms keep up a perpetual slow sway as the breeze rustles through the fronds. Competition for space, however, has begun to seriously mar Diani's paradisiacal qualities, but the main drawback is the droves of hustlers – the "beach boys" – who had become such a threatening presence a few years back that the vast majority of hotel guests virtually never ventured across the boundary from their guarded hotel gardens onto the public sands. Now that the hotels have posted security guards (*askaris*), the beach boys have become more astute and formed themselves into cartels (some worryingly connected to local politicians), and tourists do, once again, dig sandcastles and walk along the strand. Another (minor) drawback is that the beach tends to get covered at high tide, or leaves only a narrow strip of sand. As elsewhere in Kenya, all the beach is open to the public; it's only the access routes that are restricted by some hotels.

If you're coming by public transport **from Mombasa**, first catch a matatu from Abdel Nasser Road, Jomo Kenyatta Avenue, or outside the GPO on Digo Road, to Likoni ferry (Ksh5) to make the crossing (free for foot passengers; Ksh35 for small cars). Once in Likoni, walk up with the crowd to the well-marked matatu stages on the left side, and catch one for "Diani" or "Beach" (Ksh30). If there are no direct ones, get one to Ukunda (Ksh30), and then make a connection down to the beach road (Ksh20) – you'll find plenty of transport both day and night. Don't walk, especially if you're burdened with luggage or valuables: the three-kilometre link road has a bad reputation – hard to tell how well founded – for muggings. Taxis from Mombasa cost around Ksh2000–2500. You can in theory fly from Mombasa to Ukunda airstrip, a couple of kilometres west of Diani post office, though it would be quicker and cheaper to take a taxi. Coming direct from Nairobi, however, you might consider the plane trip worthwhile – Airkenya flies three times a week (Ksh6500 each way).

There's an increasingly heavy scattering of proper shops along the strip, as well as a new post office. The main **shopping areas** on the north side are the

Bazaar Complex Shopping Centre (1.6km north of the junction) and Diani Complex Shopping Centre (1.4km). On the south side, the commerce kicks off with the Agip petrol station (900m) and Diani Beach Shopping Centre (1km), where vervet monkeys scamper across the designer *makuti*. There are more shops and businesses outside *Diani Sea Resort* and opposite *Diani Sea Lodge*.

Accommodation

Running 300m behind the beach, the Diani Beach road feels like Kenya's number-one strip in the high season. Fortunately, thick forest separates the road from the shore, though more of the **Jadini Forest** disappears every year as one new plot after another is cleared, usually not entirely legally. The **tourist hotels** that fill the plots are expensive by Kenyan standards and, if you've been travelling on a budget, the prices will come as a shock. If you're coming from abroad they seem more reasonably priced, and you'll find standards generally high. Most offer low-season reductions, which are generally good value.

The distances in the following listings are from the Ukunda junction on the Diani Beach road, by Barclays Bank.

Camping and budget rooms

Budget accommodation along the beach is sparse and none of the big hotels will entertain campers in their gardens. If you're a family or in a large group, renting a cottage (see overleaf) is invariably better value than taking a room, and gives you the chance to cook up some local food in your own style. In addition to places listed here, *Diani Beachalets* (under "Cottages and apartments" below) has cheap two-person *bandas*.

Chale Sea Villas 11km south of the junction, just before *Pinewood*, PO Box 1766 Ukunda ☎072/842121, ✉wildroveraf@hotmail.com. A range of accommodation including dorm beds (Ksh500), double rooms, and one- or two-bedroom *bandas*, as well as camping (Ksh250 per person) way down on Galu Beach past the *Neptune*. There's a restaurant serving breakfast and basic meals, and the *bandas* are equipped with kitchens. Pick-ups from Mombasa for a fee. ❸

Dan's Camping 1.4km south of the junction, next to the defunct *Trade Winds*, PO Box 5019 Diani Beach ☎0127/3136. The former home of Dan Trench who died in 1990, the son of the family which once owned much of the land down here, this was once something of an institution. Unfortunately, it has since sunk into a pretty sad state: the garden is a clutter of luxuriant foliage, and the *bandas* are now unusable. Bad security in the past, but no reports of incidents lately. There are fish-sellers on the beach early morning and afternoons – give fish to the manager, who's a dab hand at cooking. Camping Ksh300 per person.

Glory Palace Hotel 500m west of the junction on the way to Ukunda, PO Box 85527 Ukunda ☎0127/3392. More than adequate unit in this mini-chain of hotels, with a pool. Security appears sound, but caution would nonetheless be advised. B&B ❷

South Fork 1.4km south, then 800m from the road, PO Box 231 Ukunda ☎0127/3053. Low-budget accommodation and campsite, set back in pleasant grounds, but a good fifteen-minute walk from the beach at *Trade Winds*. Several large s/c rooms and a number of smaller and cheaper B&L-style non-s/c rooms. Bicycle rental can be arranged, and camping costs Ksh150 per person. ❷

Tandoori Guest House 3.5km south of the junction, behind *Tandoori Bay Restaurant* ☎0127/2020. The cheapest rooms in Diani (as opposed to Ukunda), and very reasonable for the price: clean, some of them pretty large, all with nets, three s/c, three not. The big disadvantage of this place is that it's off the beach, though you can walk to it easily enough. ❶

Cottages and apartments

As in the Tiwi Beach cottage listings, price codes refer to the cost of the whole cottage if double rooms are not available. As always, the larger cottages offer big savings for groups. Prices for most of these are negotiable, especially for poverty-stricken backpackers out of season. See maps on pp.498 and 501 for locations.

Coral Beach Cottages 300m north, PO Box 168 Ukunda ☎0127/2005, ⊕3138. On a parched, run-down site, this isn't an obvious first choice, especially as only two of its seventeen cottages are up for short-term rent. On the plus side, they face out over the sea, and prices are reasonable. ❸

Diani Beachalets 6.5km south, PO Box 26 Ukunda ☎0127/2180. By far the best value on Diani, welcoming and homely, visited by duiker antelopes, bushbabies and colobus monkeys, this peaceful refuge is bang on the beach, with a variety of abodes, from simple two-bed *bandas* with fridge, electric light, communal showers and cooking area, to nice, s/c cottages with kitchen, sitting room and verandah. Fresh fish, fruit and veg from pedlars. There is also a library and tennis courts, and the beach is pretty well deserted. *Bandas* ❶, cottages ❸

Kijiji Cottages 600m north, PO Box 5542 Diani Beach ☎ & ⊕0127/2187, ✉forbes@dianibeach.com. Formerly part of *Warandale*, these are the nicest cottages in Diani, extremely well kept, with a choice of different shapes and sizes, all spacious, comfortable and secluded. Sea-facing cottages cost slightly more (*Bonde* is the finest of the lot, with a superb terrace) but *Carudi*, away from the sea, is the most spacious. There's a pool, and regular visits by vervet, colobus and Sykes' monkeys as well as bushbabies. The staff clean for you, and you can hire a cook (Ksh250 per day). ❺

Vindigo Cottages 700m south, PO Box 77 Ukunda ☎0127/2192, ✉vindigocottages@hotgossip.co.ke. Seven vaguely down-at-heel self-catering cottages in woodland, with a pleasing rustic feel. The kitchens are fully equipped and the rooms are very private, with fans, electricity, running water in the showers and high-level toilets. Some have lovely views over the beach through the trees. The services of a cook can be hired for Ksh250 per day, fishermen and fruitsellers call daily and there are three night *askaris*. ❹

Warandale Cottages 600m north, PO Box 11 Ukunda ☎0127/2186, ℮warandalecottages@yahoo.com. In the same group of cottages as *Kijiji*, and sharing the same grounds and pool, these are very similar, not quite as well kept, but still very clean, pleasant and spacious, some sea-facing, others (cheaper) set back among the trees, with the advantage of more likely bushbaby and monkey sightings. ➍

Wayside Beach Apartments 1.4km south, follow signs to *Trade Winds*, PO Box 83451 Mombasa ☎0127/3119, ℱ011/487214. Stylish two- to six-bed self-catering apartments in a building around a good pool, set between the main road and defunct *Trade Winds* hotel, but not located on the beach and getting tatty. Sauna and Jacuzzi both out of commission. ➍

Hotels north of the junction

Generally, the more interesting abodes worthy of major expenditure are to the south of the Ukunda junction – an area which also retains some flicker of pre-hotel times. To the north, the scene is brasher and more despoiled, and there's no forest either. Most hotels provide some sort of nightly entertainment, including uniformly cheesy bands at dinner time. For locations of the hotels see Tiwi & Diani Beach North map, p.498.

Diani Reef Grand Hotel 1.6km, PO Box 35 Ukunda ☎0127/2723, ℱ2196, ℮dianireef@kenyaweb.com. A 1970s construction with over 300 centrally air-conditioned rooms (with minibar, but no fans or nets), this is one of the largest hotels on the coast, with an international accent – fussy public areas, seven restaurants and numerous bars. Regular and deluxe rooms in different wings, all cool and comfortable, with not much to distinguish them but the size of their balconies. Facilities include windsurfing, scuba-diving school, pedalos and inflatable canoes, the *Regent* casino and *Disco Ngoma* (nightly 9pm–2am), and there's a babysitting service. Wheelchair accessible. HB ➑ low, ➒ high.

Indian Ocean Beach Club 3.6km, PO Box 73 Ukunda ☎0127/3730, ℱ3557, ℮iobc @africaonline.co.ke; reservations through Block, p.42. Opened in 1992, this is one of the best hotels on the coast. State-of-the-art rooms, wonderful Lamu-style architecture and attentive management, with most watersports free and swimming possible at all tides in the creek. Fine groves of baobabs in the gardens, and ocean-front rooms don't cost much more. Very grown-up, not ideal for kids, but a great place for a honeymoon. Casual guests welcome (free), but you need permission to use the pool. Wheelchair friendly. HB ➐

Leisure Lodge & Club 1.2km, PO Box 84383 Mombasa ☎0127/2011–14, ℱ2046, ℮leisure@africaonline.co.ke. One of the earlier Diani hotels (1971) but recently revamped, and in a striking location on low cliffs hollowed by bat-filled caves. The fine, tree-shaded beach is tucked beneath. There are several pools, an eighteen-hole par 72 golf course opposite the entrance, and a casino in the grounds (which explains the heavier than usual security presence; open daily 9pm–3am, or later if there are still punters playing). There is a choice of standard rooms lacking sea views, but with AC, nets on request and satellite TV; club rooms which are slightly more spacious, with two extra swimming pools for their exclusive use, and "Golf Villas", which are even more luxurious, with a private pool shared between each four villas. There's also a PADI diving school, windsurfing school and tennis courts, but no ocean-swimming at low tide. Popular with German and Swiss package tourists. FB ➏

Leopard Beach Hotel 800m, PO Box 34 Ukunda ☎0127/2721 or 2110–2, ℱ3424, ℮leopardb@africaonline.co.ke). Mid-range and a touch dated in feel (it was built in the 1970s), but with good facilities. Set in lush gardens with ponds and waterfalls populated by lizards. Friendly staff, a good atmosphere and decent food. Steps down to the beach. Some standard rooms (all AC with minibars) and most cottages have sea views. Facilities include tennis, volleyball, canoeing, windsurfing, snorkelling, glass-bottomed boats and PADI diving school. Good value. HB ➏ low, ➐ high.

Southern Palms Beach Resort 2.9km, PO Box 363 Ukunda ☎0127/3721, ℱ3381. Opened in 1992, this is a spacious and well-appointed package hotel with rooms in four-storey blocks with thatched roofs, two fabulous pools (one with Jacuzzi and mock desert island, both with water-level bars) that children as well as adults adore, friendly management and staff. PADI diving school, windsurfing, floodlit tennis courts, squash, gym. And for all this, it's a bargain. Recommended. HB ➏

Beach boys and the tourist police

If you're staying in a hotel, spending some peaceful time on the beach can appear virtually impossible. Frustration can set in as the days slip by and you still haven't really been for a swim, or a wander by the shore, because of the hordes of **hustlers** plying their wares, or their camel rides, or their boat trips, or just themselves. Always acknowledge them: ignoring their greetings really is considered very rude. The least painful solution is quickly to strike up a friendship of sorts with one beach boy, to buy at least something, or to go on a boat trip. Once you have a friend, and have done some business, you have some rights, and you'll find you can then stroll on the beach with far fewer hassles from the others. It's not so easy for single women, but the principle for most situations still applies – don't fight it. There is no need, incidentally, to feel physically threatened on the beach. Every hotel has its *askaris* (security guards) posted along the boundary between the plot and the beach, and they usually stay alert to the slightest sign of trouble – which is rare indeed. The beach boys and hawkers have in fact been cleared off the beaches at Malindi and Watamu, and Diani should be next, but as one hotelier put it, "These initiatives always start off in Malindi, but they tend to get as far as Watamu and then fizzle out before they reach us down here." One piece of practical advice: if you're bargaining, don't complicate matters by trying to swap clothes for crafts. You'll still be expected to pay some cash, and will end up feeling more ripped off than ever.

Hotels south of the junction

Apart from the most popular hotels covered in the following listings, there are several others, and more look set to appear for years to come – to the depreciation, at least in aesthetic terms, of the whole area. Rough tarmac now continues another 4km beyond the end (6.5km south) of the good road, as far as the *Pinewood* on Galu Beach. Distances given are south from the junction.

Africana Sea Lodge 4.2km, PO Box 84616 Mombasa ☎0127/2624, ℻2145; reservations through Alliance, p.42. On the same plot as *Jadini Beach*, and jointly owned with that and the *Safari Beach*, whose facilities guests can use, the *Africana* is sold as an all-inclusive fun hotel for couples, and is one of the few places which pulls off the balancing act between package tourism and personal service, with accommodation in comfortable but unembellished *bandas* (no sea views). FB ➒ low, ➑ high.

Baobab Beach Resort 5.9km, PO Box 32 Ukunda ☎0127/2623, ℻3032, ℮r.baobab@africaonline .co.ke. An elegant and well-kept all-inclusive club (formerly *Robinson Club Baobab*, built in the 1970s), part of the German TUI chain, located at the end of Diani Beach proper on a coral rock promontory. Unfortunately, only the first row of bungalows have sea views. Day visits Ksh1700 half-day, Ksh2200 full-day. ➏

Diani Sea Lodge 3.5km, PO Box 37 Ukunda ☎0127/2060, ℻3439, ℮dianisea@africaonline .co.ke. A large, slightly downmarket, Mediterranean-style all-inclusive version of the jointly owned *Resort*. The 145 AC rooms are a let down: despite the good-sized double beds and

frame-fitted nets, most are small, in bungalows set back in the gardens, and only ten are sea-facing. Pool and childrens' pool, gym, tennis court, crazy golf, windsurfing and PADI diving school. Mainly German clientele. Daily admission Ksh1650. Not the best all-inclusive, but cheap. Wheelchair accessible. FB ➎

Diani Sea Resort 2km, PO Box 37 Ukunda ☎0127/3081–3, ℻3439, ℮dianisea @africaonline.co.ke. Built in 1991 and much more cheerful than its all-inclusive sister hotel, with consistently good service, nice staff and plenty of things to do. It lacks local style, though: the 170 satellite-TV-equipped rooms are in the same style as *Diani Sea Lodge* and are due for a refit. Most guests are German, many on long stays. Great pool (Ksh300 for casual visitors), gym, tennis and squash courts, crazy golf, windsurfing and PADI diving school. HB ➎

Jadini Beach Hotel 4.2km, PO Box 84616 Mombasa ☎0127/2622, ℻2269; reservations through Alliance, p.42. Diani's longest-established resort hotel (1960s) with high standards and good atmosphere, refurbished in 1991. Busy and cosmopolitan, and good for kids, with its daytime creche and activities. Besides the usual watersports, facilities include a PADI-accredited diving school, three tennis courts, the atmospheric *Jambo Village* restaurant, a petrol station with regular prices, and St Stephen's Chapel for Sunday morning repentance. Rooms are big and bright, most with sea views. Guests can also use the facilities at *Africana Sea Lodge* and *Safari Beach Hotel*. HB ⑤ low, ⑦ high.

LTI-Kaskazi Beach Hotel 300m, PO Box 135 Ukunda ⊕0127/3170–9, ⓕ2233, ⓔkaskazi@africaonline.co.ke. Well run and competitively priced, successfully balancing classy atmosphere with package-tour popularity. Heavy on the Arabic styling, with white-tiled floors, tinkling fountains and soaring *makuti* roofs. One of the few all-inclusive hotels to welcome day visitors (Ksh800 without lunch, Ksh950 with), and the only place in Diani with drinking water in the taps. There's the sad little ruined seventeenth-century "Diani mosque" in the garden, basically just an old wall. FB ⑥

Neptune Paradise Village 8.5km, on Galu Beach, PO Box 696 Ukunda ⊕0127/3620, ⓕ3019, ⓔnep_sc@africaonline.co.ke. Decent rooms with pink cane furniture in tightly packed regular rows of two-storey *bandas* (no sea views), and a plot that requires lengthy, shadeless walks and has been extended seawards to the point where there is no beach left at high tide. Facilities include two full-size pools, two kids' pools, tennis courts, minigolf, a bowling green, a scuba-diving school, windsurfing, and catamaran trips. All-inclusive, with mostly German clientele. Reasonably priced, but still overrated. Day visits Ksh1800. FB ⑤

Nomad Hotel 4.8km, PO Box 1 Ukunda ⊕0127/2155, ⓕ2391, ⓔsales@nomads.net. Not only the cheapest and least formal of the Diani hotels, with positive and helpful management, but with the best views, too. Each of the seventeen twin-bed *bandas* and three cottages (with fans, not AC) has a terrace fronting onto the beach – barely 20m away – the view framed by leaning coconut palms, the odd baobab and the bobbing heads of

beach boys. The thatch-and-straw *bandas*, though not luxurious, are cosy, and perched nicely between the palms, some with additional rooms at the back for children, and there are larger and more expensive cottages. There's a good seafood restaurant, too. No pool but a dive school. Rates negotiable; recommended. B&B ⑤ low, ⑧ high.

Papillon Hotel 5.5km, PO Box 5292 ⊕0127/2613–5, ⓕ2152, ⓔonearth@africaonline.co.ke. Next door and superior to the snooty *Ocean Village Club*, and one of the few all-inclusives, with a really cheerful holiday atmosphere. Staff are helpful and friendly, and there's loads for kids to do, with a playground, children's swimming pool and busy daily club. Most of the cool, pleasant rooms have sea views, too. Other activities include scuba diving, catamarans, pedalos and windsurfing, as well as glass-bottomed boats and snorkelling. Very good value. Day visits Ksh1500 till 6pm, Ksh1800 till midnight. Recommended. FB ⑤

Pinewood Village 11km, on Galu Beach, PO Box 190 Ukunda ⊕0127/3128, ⓕ3131, ⓦwww.pinewood-village.com. An extremely stylish condominium on a nearly deserted stretch of beach far to the south of the main Diani strip. Well-thought-out four- or six-bed staffed houses, with direct dial phones, free sporting facilities and laundry, and (unusually) water from their own wells. They aim to avoid nasty hidden extras. Self-cater or use the restaurant. Good value. HB ⑤

Safari Beach Hotel 5.1km, PO Box 90690 Mombasa ⊕0127/2311–9, ⓕ2357; reservations through Alliance, p.42. The best of the Alliance hotels, with good sports and watersports facilities (and PADI diving school), excellent food, a disco, and a daily children's programme with full-time staff. The rooms are comfortable and spacious, set in two-storey *bandas* ranged up a gentle, wooded slope at the rear of the hotel. Guests can also use the facilities at *Africana Sea Lodge* and *Jadini Beach Hotel*. HB ⑧

Around the resort

Enjoying yourself on Diani isn't difficult. You can rent snorkelling gear (about Ksh250) from just about anywhere, and float out across the lagoon to the **reef**. Remember how fiercely the sun is likely to burn and wear a T-shirt unless you're very brown. You need to be a confident swimmer: there are no strong currents nor any real danger, but the reef is 600–1000m away and swimming back on the ebb tide can be tiring. Alternatively, a trip to the reef at low tide on one of the outrigger **canoes** is highly recommended. The crews know all the good (or at least the more reasonable) spots for snorkelling and it shouldn't cost you more than Ksh1000 for an hour or three. One of the best areas is directly opposite *Baobab Beach Resort*, about 300m out towards the reef, where there is a cluster of coral heads. The sheltered lagoon behind the reef is also ideal for **windsurfing** (Ksh500 per hr).

When you tire of the beach and the sea, or of just lying under the palm trees, you could **rent a bicycle** and go off exploring – from about Ksh600 per day. By matatu, Mombasa with its Old Town and shopping possibilities is an easy enough target for a day out. There's also the eighteen-hole par 72 **golf course** opposite the *Leisure Lodge* (which runs it) on the north side of the junction. For details of **dhow-trip** operators, see the box opposite.

Kongo Mosque

For a short excursion with a goal, you could aim for the **Kongo Mosque** at the far north end of the beach, at the mouth of the Mwachema River, but it's not a place to visit on your own, and certainly not if carrying anything valuable, as the spot is known for muggings. It's most easily reached through the grounds of the *Indian Ocean Beach Club* – which gives you the opportunity to visit one of Diani's best-looking hotels. Beyond the boundary fence and inevitable *askari*, the Kongo Mosque is surrounded by venerable baobabs. Also known as Diani Persian Mosque, the building is enigmatic and disconcerting, with its five heavy wooden doors. There's an electric atmosphere here, the barrel-vaulted mosque brooding like a huge tomb under the trees. It is too complete to be considered a ruin, and has recently been fenced in by local Islamic leaders who have encouraged the community to start using it again, mainly in response to repeated attempts by local politicians to appropriate the mosque and communal land for "development".

Although a sign suggests otherwise, you will, suitably attired and accompanied, be allowed to have a look around. Named after a forest, the mosque is

---

Diving on the South Coast

Many South Coast hotels, and a good number along the North Coast, have **dive centres**, where you can do everything from a basic beginner lesson plus assisted dive (around $80) to a full course giving you an internationally recognized (usually PADI) qualification ($300 to "Open Water"; an additional $280 to "Advanced Open Water"). If you already have scuba certification, single dives cost $25–30. You can nearly always take a free dip in the pool wearing diving equipment, to test your affinity – most people find breathing underwater curiously addictive.

Before choosing a centre, take time to compare the equipment of several companies, and ask them about their environmenal policy, safety procedures and general experience. They should at the very least have up-to-date PADI ("Professional Association of Diving Instructors") or BSAC ("British Sub-Aqua Association") accreditation, and ideally be affiliated to Scuba Schools International (SSI). One of the oldest and best-established outfits, with an excellent reputation and good equipment, is Diving the Crab, on the beach between *Jadini* and *Africana* hotels on Diani (Blue Wave, PO Box 5011 Diani Beach ☏0127/3400 or 2369–70, ℻2372, ⓦwww.divingthecrab.com), the only company offering state-of-the-art "Nitrox" technology, which mixes nitrogen and oxygen to reduce decompression complications and enable longer dives. If you need more information, contact PADI directly in the United States at 30151 Tomas St, Rancho Santa Margarita, CA 92688–2125 ☏1-800/729 7234 or 949/858 7234, ℻949/858 7264, ⓦwww.padi.com.

The Dive Sites of Kenya and Tanzania (see Contexts, p.698) is highly recommended reading for divers as well as snorkellers. See also the box on "Responsible snorkelling, diving and fishing" on p.443.

thought to be either fourteenth or fifteenth century and the one remaining building – maybe the only stone one – of a Wa-shirazi settlement here (see p.513). The river mouth was the first safe anchorage south of Mombasa.

Dhow and snorkelling trips ·

The following is a list of the main **dhow-trip operators**, all of which operate out of the South Coast. Unless stated, all will pick you up from your hotel (South Coast, and North Coast as far as Kikambala), either for free or for a nominal extra charge. For the most part, the dhows are not under sail but are powered by on-board or out-board motors. All can be booked direct, or though your hotel. If you're going to combine a dhow trip with snorkelling, see the box on p.443.

Dolphin Dhow Barclays Centre, Diani Beach (Blue Horizons Adventures, PO Box 85636 Mombasa ☎ & ⓕ0127/2094, ⓦwww.dolphindhow.com). Day-long dolphin-spotting trips combined with snorkelling (no flippers provided; bring your own). Early-morning pick-ups from North and South Coast hotels. Lunch on board. Dolphin sightings obviously not guaranteed. $90–95.

Funzi Island Club near Barclays, Diani Beach, PO Box 1108 Ukunda ☎0127/2044, ⓔfunzicamp@africaonline.co.ke). This expensive hotel also offers dolphin-spotting trips by dhow combined with crocodile spotting on the Ramisi River estuary. No snorkelling. Early-morning pick-ups from North and South Coast hotels. $80–90.

Kinazini Funzi Dhow Safaris Glory Car Hire office, Diani Beach Shopping Centre, ☎0127/3182. Trips with a more cultural bent, with a cruise through Funzi creek and the mangroves, a visit to the ruins on Funzi island, and visits to a local school, a private house and a market place, with lunch on the uninhabited island of Kinazini. $75–80.

Paradise Lost/Shirazi Bay Diego House, opposite Barclays Centre, Diani Beach (Exotic Destinations, PO Box 5050 Diani ☎0127/3514, ⓕ3389). Day-trips combining a morning mangrove cruise and snorkelling, lunch in Shirazi Bay and an afternoon village trip, for $75–85.

Pilli-Pipa Dhow Safaris Colliers Centre, PO Box 5185 Diani Beach ☎ & ⓕ0127/2401; office ☎0127/3559 or 0127/52286). Hugely enjoyable dhow day-trips to Kisiti Marine National Park for outstanding snorkelling (field guides, masks, snorkels and fins provided), with a late lunch of crab claws, fine wine and Swahili food at a private house on Wasini Island. Departures most days at 8.30am from Shimoni jetty (collection can be arranged from both South and North Coast hotels). $95–100.

SSI East Africa (Blue Wave) By *Nomad Hotel*, PO Box 5011 Diani Beach ☎0127/2369–70, ⓕ2372, ⓔssi@africaonline.co.ke. Offers mangrove trips (by motorboat; 3–4hr) from *Jadini Beach Hotel* in Diani south to mangrove channels in front of Chale Island, where you might see grey herons, fish eagles, cormorants and kingfishers.

Wasini Island Restaurant & Kisite Dhow Tours *Jadini Beach Hotel*, Diani Beach, PO Box 281 Ukunda ☎0127/2331 or 3055, ⓕ3154, ⓦwww.wasini-island.com. Established over twenty years ago and environmentally aware, offering day-long dhow and snorkelling trips at Kisiti, with a seemingly endless seafood lunch at their restaurant on the north side of Wasini Island upon your hungry return. Costs $60 from Shimoni jetty, or $80–85 including early-morning transport from your hotel. Equipment and field guides are available on board. Scuba diving, if you've already got accreditation, costs an additional $50 for two dives, or $30 per dive for beginners. Dolphin spotting also possible.

THE COAST | Diani Beach and around

Jadini Forest

For a walk, or a jog, it's more interesting to head south along Diani Road. Here there are more hotels, of course, but also, approaching the end of the paving, some wonderful patches of jungly forest comprising the dwindling **Jadini Forest** ("Jadini", disappointingly, turns out to be an embellished acronym of the Trench family initials, including Dan's, see p.502). There's the almost obligatory snake park, but if you'd like to search for some animals in the wild rather than support this venture, then any of the tracks leading off to the right will take you straight into magnificent stands of hardwood trees, alive with birds and butterflies, and rocking with vervet and **Angolan colobus monkeys**. The latter, whose population is estimated at around 1500, have come in for some special attention lately, as concern has mounted over land encroachment and deaths from speeding cars. The resultant campaign, spearheaded by the Wakuluzu Colobus Trust (at Colobus Cottage, 3.7km south; PO Box 5380 Diani Beach ☎0127/3519, ✉colobus@africaonline.co.ke), has put up warning signs and speedbumps, and – most inventively – the wire, rope and wood "colobobridges" at known danger spots over the road, which the monkeys quickly learned to use. You can pick up more information at Colobus Cottage, which also has a **forest nature trail** in its grounds (a guided half-hour walk costs Ksh300). Of the other monkeys, **baboons** are most common, and are nasty-tempered pests: their nutritious diet of hotel leftovers means they've multiplied greatly, and are not afraid of humans. Keep your distance, as there have been many incidents of unwary tourists getting scratched and bitten. Overly tame **Sykes' monkeys** are also becoming a pest.

Snakes you are unlikely to come across. You'll be told the forest is the haunt of leopards, which is extremely unlikely. Come down here at night and you will see eyes in the dark, probably those of **bushbabies** – it's hard to believe that even leopards would put up with so violent a destruction of their habitat.

Eating, drinking and nightlife

Most of the hotels have snack menus, salad bars and all the rest. If you're on a budget, choose carefully and avoid the dubious temptation of Ksh200 fruit-juice cocktails, and you can still depart satisfied. The following listings, in north-to-south order (distances from the junction), include some of the best, and some of the best-value, places to eat and drink apart from the hotels.

Finding food for **self-catering** is straightforward enough, with ambulant fish and fruit sellers on the beach, various stalls along the beach road, and many supermarkets (see "Listings" p.510).

Restaurants

Galaxy Bazaar Complex Shopping Centre, 1.5km north ☎0127/2529. Classy Chinese restaurant with main dishes at around Ksh350–600. Free pick-up from hotels. Open daily 9.30am–midnight.
Shan-e-Punjab Diani Complex Shopping Centre, 1.4km north ☎0127/3092. Indian restaurant and snack bar with an open-air garden, serving veg and non-veg Punjabi dishes. Around Ksh800 for a meal, Ksh1200 with seafood. Open daily 10am–midnight.
L'Incontro Colliers Centre, 300m north. Italian restaurant serving very decent pizzas and calzoni (Ksh350–500) as well as espresso coffee to a

mainly Italian clientele (which is a telling sign of its authenticity).
Globe Diani Beach Shopping Centre, 1km south. Good and moderately priced home-style English cooking, with main courses at around Ksh350–450, and proper puddings for afters.
Legend 2km south. Monstrous Italian construction, originally intended to be a casino, now operating as a totally over-the-top restaurant and bar with nice espresso – half-acre swimming pool with lifesize elephant models (free use of pool if you buy drinks), *boriti* poles painted pink and an elderly crooner on white piano accompanied by

drum machine. Daily 8pm–3am.

Ali Barbour's Cave 3km south ☎0127/2033. Bizarrely built inside a deep coral cave: you enter at ground level and descend. The lavish French and seafood menu runs to around Ksh4000 for two (with wine) – good food, well presented. Even if you're not eating, it's worth dropping in just to have a look. Don't wear shorts. Open daily from 6pm.

Nomad Restaurant 4.8km south. Attached to the hotel, a quality seafood menu in the "formal"

makuti-roofed restaurant by the entrance, with soup served in a large breadroll. More popular is its beach bar (see below). Open evenings only from 7.30pm.

Boko Boko 200m past *Club Neptune Village*, 9.3km ☎0127/2344. Long-established Seychellois restaurant (slightly spicy, Creole cooking) set in a lush garden. Large *makuti*-cone hall with a few tables. Recommended, and surprisingly reasonable, with main dishes from around Ksh400.

Cheaper food and bars

Green Palm Bar 2.7km north. Opposite the closed *Golden Beach Hotel*, a popular upmarket place with cocktails under a *makuti* roof. The drinks are pricey but the food is reasonable, with set meals at Ksh350–400.

Leopard Beach Hotel Staff Canteen 800m north. In the entrance to the hotel, then first left. It may seem strange, but the canteen is open to all, and serves decent Kenyan food at very low prices, although the choice of dishes is not great (it's meat stew, greens and *ugali*, basically). They will probably be surprised to see a tourist eating there, but they won't have any objection.

African Pot 300m north. By *Coral Beach Cottages*, a pleasant bar serving the usual Kenyan fare (tilapia, stew, pilau) at reasonable prices (Ksh200–300), with cold beer. Most of the food is good, but they're a bit heavy-handed with the salt on their *nyama choma* (you can tell them you want it without).

Riziki Kwa Munga Cafeteria 700m south. A small shack in amongst the curio stalls just north of the Agip station, serving cheap and basic, but very good, Kenyan food. Great for breakfast (omelette and chapati with tea) or lunch (beans in coconut sauce and pilau), and extremely cheap.

Red Lion Bar & Restaurant 2km south. *Makuti*-meets-Cotswolds, and the closest you'll get on the coast to an English country pub. There's a pleasant beer garden, grill room, and Italian food and ice-cream. Closed Mondays.

Forty Thieves Beach Bar & Restaurant 3km south. This budget beachside hangout is a good place for a daytime drink – a bit of a local watering hole – and perfect in the evening when their beach front is floodlit. Discos on Wednesday,

Friday and Saturday (and plenty of barefoot racing around the beach); live band and curry buffet on Sunday, and English premiership football matches live on TV.

Tandoori Bay Opposite *Diani Sea Lodge*, 3.5km south. Down-to-earth Kenyan food at moderate prices, but no tandoori dishes despite the name.

Pavillion Beach Bar 3.8km south. A pleasantly laid-back drinking venue on lawns by the beach, reached through the disused buildings of the now-defunct *Two Fishes Lodge* hotel, and popular with residents and tourists alike. There's moderately priced food, and a live band (though somewhat middle-of-the-road) on Saturday and Sunday afternoons from 1pm. Open daily except Monday 10am–7pm.

Nomad Beach Bar 4.8km south. At times wildly popular beach bar down at the water's edge, open 9am–6.30pm or later, with snacks, seafood, plenty of booze, a Friday night "locals' night", and famous Sunday lunch curry buffet (Ksh500) – a real family affair, with regular live jazz or a one-man-band.

Sundowner Beside Galu Kinondo supermarket (7km south). A very cheap restaurant and bar, completely unpretentious and not a hustler in sight, serving brilliant African food, seafood (crab, octopus or tuna and rice) plus some German dishes, all freshly prepared, with a laid-back, relaxed atmosphere.

Mr T Roof Garden Bar & Restaurant 9.2km south). A little overpriced for the standard menu of tourist and African food (main dishes Ksh300–500) but it's the breeze and the company that attract the clientele.

Nightlife

To get around Diani Beach at night without your own vehicle, you'll have to rely on getting rides or walking. Hitching up and down the Diani road is generally safe and not too difficult and, while hotels issue warnings about walking on the beach at night (and there are *askaris* in number to underline them), under a full moon it's a pleasure that's hard to resist. In a group, minus your valuables, and not passing long stretches of bush, you're unlikely to have any problems.

Giriama dancing is one often touted entertainment – probably not something to go out of your way to find (though the group "Drums of Africa" is exceptionally good), but fun if you happen upon it. A couple of professional troupes work the hotels, performing acrobatically to the accompaniment of superb drumming. You're also likely to happen across **Maasai dancers**, of varying degrees of authenticity. The guttural polyphonic singing is fascinating, though the performances usually end with a "Maasai market" where they flog you overpriced and not necessarily Maasai trinkets. Rarest of all are the **Taarab bands** (see p.717), who sometimes play in hotel dining rooms on special occasions or public holidays. Such entertainment is very seasonal and you won't find much going on when the crowds aren't in occupation. There are several **discos** along the road, each with its own idiosyncrasies. None of them even starts to warm up before 11pm. Drinks are priced at hotel rates or a little less.

Tropicana Behind Agip petrol station (900m south), the oldest disco on Diani is an open-air affair, with *makuti* roofs and a basic cement dance floor. Reggae or Lingala (Congolese music) most evenings. Ksh100–150.

Shakatak 3.5km south. Wooden dance floor and air-conditioning, but a bit of a dive. Tends to play the heaviest mix on the strip. Ksh100. Open from 9pm.

Bushbaby 3.8km south. Open-air club opposite the defunct *Two Fishes Lodge*, which attracts hotel staff as well as intrepid hotel guests in search of local colour. Slightly sleazy, but fun for a bop, with Lingala on Wednesdays, soul on Thursdays and reggae on Fridays. Open from 9pm.

Listings

Bakery The Austrian *Bungoma Bakery*, by Agip petrol station, has a good range of fresh European breads and cakes.

Banks Barclays (Mon–Fri 9am–3pm, Sat 9am–11am), with ATM; the very efficient Commercial Bank of Africa at Diani Beach Shopping Centre (Mon–Fri 8.30am–2pm); Diani Forex opposite Galu Kinondo supermarket at the southern end of the strip (Mon–Fri 9am–1pm & 2–5pm, Sat 9am–1pm).

Bicycle and motor bike rental Unfortunately, the collapse in tourism has also seen off most of the bike-rental places: try either South Fork (p.502), or arrange an informal deal with the guys at the curio kiosks. Bargain hard (you shouldn't pay more than Ksh600 a day, much less if over a week).

Car rental Glory Car Hire, Diani Beach Shopping Centre ☏0127/3392; Hertz has offices at the *Jadini Beach Hotel* (☏0127/2149), *Safari Beach Hotel* (☏0127/2726) and *Indian Ocean Beach Club* (☏0127/3730).

Doctors Dr Rekhi, Diani Beach Hospital, recommended (☏0127/2435–6); Dr Philip Varghese, outside *Diani Sea Resort* (☏0127/2588 or ☏011/227189; Mon–Fri 9am–12.30pm & 2.30–6pm, Sat 9am–1pm); Dr Lalit D. Kotak, opposite *Diani Sea Lodge* (Mon–Fri 8.30am–12.30pm & 2.30–6pm, Sat 8.30am–12.30pm).

Hospital Diani Beach Hospital (☏0127/2435–6),

next to Leisure Lodge Golf Club and Diani Complex, is small and modern.

Internet access Relatively expensive compared to Mombasa or even Ukunda, but available at several places including Hot Gossip by *Legend* (just north of the post office), Diani Link at Diani Beach Shopping Centre, Tourist Information and Services Centre behind *Tandoori Bay*, and Top Africa Safaris at the Colliers Centre.

Notice boards Onjiko's Supermarket, behind Agip petrol station, has a reasonable board for buying and selling.

Pharmacy South End Pharmacy, at Diani Beach Shopping Centre.

Post office opposite the junction for *Trade Winds* hotel, 1.4km south of the junction. Mon–Fri 8am–12.30pm & 2–5pm, Sat 9am–noon.

Supermarkets Muthaiga Mini Market, Diani Beach Shopping Centre (expensive; Mon–Sat 9am–6.30pm); Onjiko's, behind Agip (much cheaper, but limited range); KFI, just up from *Diani Beachalets* with a good range; and Shan-e-Punjab, Diani Complex (Mon–Sat 8.30am–7pm), which has the best range of wines and spirits on the South Coast. Cabin at Colliers Centre (daily 9am–6pm) is small but has the advantage of being open Sundays. Galu Kinondo supermarket, at the south end of the beach, is only a basic provision store.

Taxis Most hotels have taxis in their forecourts,

and there's also a stand opposite Barclays Bank. Otherwise try Call On Taxis by *Tandoori Bay* restaurant (☎ 0127/3163 or 3459), or Malibu Taxis at Diani Beach Shopping Centre (☎ 0733/857458 or 700306).

Telephones There are cardphones at the post office, and many of the internet offices also have international phone services.

Travel agents There are various safari agents by the Agip garage and in the shopping centres along the strip, which open and close frequently enough. The less reputable ones will hustle any passing tourist for business, but don't be taken in by the first one you visit: shop around.

Ukunda

Until a few years ago just a village on the highway, **UKUNDA** is now a scruffily burgeoning town and the main service centre for the resort hotels, strung out along the Likoni–Lungalunga road, with a post office (Mon–Fri 8am–12.30pm & 2–5pm), Total petrol station, a couple of places with internet access (BTS near *Casino Pub*, for example), which is cheaper than at Diani Beach, branches of KCB and Postbank (both opposite Total) and hundreds of *dukas*. Only marginally touched by tourism, Ukunda has a life of its own, not all of it pleasant: the sprawl is an increasingly deprived area, and along with Likoni (p.493) was a major centre of the ethnic violence that swept the region prior to the 1997 elections, in which some 100,000 "upcountry" people were forced to flee. Still, if your holiday isn't otherwise adventurous, it's worth a visit to see something of Kenya a little less unreal than the strip.

If you need accommodation in Ukunda (and if you're on a budget, you could consider staying here and simply catching matatus down to the part of the beach you want), there are several cheap **B&Ls**, the best of which is *Corner Guest House* (PO Box 855; no phone; ❶), just north of the junction for the beach road. Quieter is the family-run *Combatto Lodge*, 1.5km north (PO Box 16 Ukunda ☎ 0127/2571; ❶), with reasonable B&L-standard rooms, awful mattresses, fans and a dozy bar. Located 400m back towards the junction, a more expensive option and the only one with a pool is *Hotel Rock Paradise* (PO Box 1266 Ukunda ☎ 0127/3492; all s/c ❸), though at the price you should be able to find a cottage in Diani itself.

For **nightlife**, almost anything here comes as a shock after Diani's more urbane delights. All the bars can seem (and sometimes are) pretty rough places, so go with a Kenyan friend if you can. Currently, the best are *Jambo Nightclub*, which has a DJ and a lively crowd; the more mellow *Juhudi Club*, set back from the main road, 600m south of the beach road junction, just before Total; and *Casino Pub*, just south of that.

South to Shimoni

The Diani Beach road returns to gravel south of the *Pinewood*, although it continues in a driveable condition, through the little village of Kinondo, right down to Chale Point. 300m offshore, **Chale island**, until recently an uninhabited beauty spot, has sadly been acquired by a German developer, with the help of two local MPs, despite its being a gazetted Mijikenda *kaya* (see p.490) and not the property of anyone. The resulting, ill-conceived *Chale Paradise Island* (PO Box 4 ☎ 0127/3535–6, ℻ 3319, ✉ islands@africaonline.co.ke; FB ❽) has totally disrupted local relations and wiped out acres of natural vegetation. If the ancestors are to be allowed their say, its days are numbered, yet the new owners claim the development has been sensitive, that "only" a third of the island has been built upon and that the other part is a "nature reserve". If you want to see for yourself, you can't avoid bumping into adverts and hoardings for the place all over the South Coast.

Gazi

Down the main coastal highway south of Ukunda, **GAZI** is next, a sleepy little village just off the road. It was once headquarters of the Mazrui leader **Sheikh Mbaruk ("Baruku") bin Rashid**, who acquired a reputation for torturing prisoners after half-suffocating them in the fumes of burning chillies. The story was perhaps intended to discredit him, as he was the principal figure behind the Mazrui Rebellion in 1895, an uprising against British authority that saw Mbaruk flying a German flag at his house and supplying his men with arms donated by the Germans. The British had to send for troops from India; even so, fighting continued for nine months before an Omani puppet regime was re-established and the rebels crushed. Mbaruk died in exile in German Tanganyika.

His mansion is now a primary school, which you can look around out of school hours. More than 150 years old, it was obviously a very grand place – the heavy ceiling timbers show that it once had an upper storey – but it is now sadly neglected. Fort Jesus Museum has plundered its fine front door and unfortunately left an ugly scar. To know where to stop for Gazi, you'll have to ask, as there isn't a sign on the highway. The village itself is on a deep, mangrove-filled bay and has no beach to speak of. "Gazi Beach", about 2km south of the village, is more promising.

Msambweni

Continuing down the road, **MSAMBWENI** is a sizeable village with a famous leprosarium. The road to the beach (there's often a police checkpoint at the junction) goes through the village, following the coast for several kilometres before turning back to the highway. The beach is lovely – low cliffs and less uniformity than Diani – and there are no beach hassles down here, but the tide goes out for miles, with lots of rock pools.

The only **accommodation** remaining at Msambweni Beach is *Salima Club* (PO Box 9 Msambweni ☎ & ⓕ0127/52032; ❺), a kilometre from the village. The architect did some original and beguiling work here on half a dozen self-catering beachfront cottages, now looking a bit weatherbeaten, but still charming and all with terraces overlooking the beach. There's also a beautiful pool beneath a baobab tree, but no restaurant. Accessibility can be a problem if you don't have your own transport – it's a kilometre from the village and a good half hour's walk from the main road, although the village is served by regular matatus from Likoni and Lungalunga.

Funzi island

If, instead of returning to the main road from Msambweni, you follow the coastline (either on the rough track or the beach), you will eventually reach **Funzi island**, separated from the mainland by a narrow channel that you can walk across at low tide. You can easily camp on the island if equipped for a fair amount of self-sufficiency. Funzi village is at the southern end, about 6km from the mainland, and there are beaches and sections of reef scattered close to the forested shore on both sides of the island. The exclusive *Funzi Island Club* – a tented camp in a grove of mango trees (PO Box 90246 Mombasa ☎0127/2044, ⓔfunzicamp@africaonline.co.ke; all-inclusive ❾; closed May & June) – is a place to dream about.

Shirazi (Kifunzi)

The coast highway meanwhile passes through verdant regions of parkland, with borassus, doum and coconut palms (borassus are the ones with a bulge in the trunk) interspersed with swampy dells, before the landscape is firmly established as rolling fields of sugar cane, culminating in **Ramisi**, the coast's main sugar-producing area until the closure of its factory.

On the shore, just before you reach Ramisi, is the tiny and very old settlement of **SHIRAZI**, also known as Kifunzi (which means "little Funzi"). Any of the tracks through the sugar fields on the left of the road will take you to the hamlet – a scattering of houses in the jungle and a small harbour among mangroves. The people of Shirazi call themselves **Wa-shirazi** and are the descendants of a once-important group of the Swahili-speaking people. During the fifteenth and sixteenth centuries, they ruled the coast from Tiwi to Tanga (Tanzania) from their eight settlements on the shore. Around 1620, these towns were captured by the Wa-vumba, another Swahili group. The Wa-shirazi, now scattered in pockets along the coast, speak a distinctive dialect of Swahili. Historians used to think they originally emigrated from Shiraz, in Persia, but it now seems likely that very few of them have Persian ancestry and that the name was adopted for political reasons. Shirazi/Kifunzi, which may be one of the original eight villages, is an important Wa-shirazi centre.

Shirazi, like many villages on the coast, is a backwater in every sense. The people cut a small quantity of *boriti* (mangrove poles) – much less than they used to; they also fish and grow some produce in their garden plots, which are continually being raided by monkeys. But the setting is memorably exotic and worth the three-kilometre walk from the main road. They don't have sodas at Shirazi, but they do have coconuts and tranquillity.

The people who run Funzi Island Fishing Club have a camp on the shore at **Bodo**, just to the southwest of Shirazi. Bodo is a small cargo port, where you can sometimes pick up a ride to Pemba, Tanzania, a seven-hour voyage. See "Travel details", p.584. This is also from where Kinazini Funzi Dhow Safaris run their **dhow day-trips** (see box on p.507).

There are some unspectacular ruins of walls and a disused well amid tangled foliage just a 100m or so to the south of the village. On the north side is the more interesting hulk of a Friday mosque, its *mihrab* still standing. Elders here describe how earlier inhabitants were routed by the Maasai and fled to the Comoros Islands. They remember when the mosque was still intact, though by the beginning of the twentieth century it had already been abandoned.

Shimoni

There are several matatus each day from Likoni to **SHIMONI**, but they tend only to run early in the morning and after lunch. Vehicles for Lungalunga will drop you at the turn-off where you could wait for a lift, or a matatu, though through matatus will be packed to the gunwhales by the time they reach here. A few years back, when Reagan's America enjoyed cosy relations with Kenya, the United States had its eye on getting a naval base on Wasini. This would be a far worse calamity for this remarkable area than the reach of another tentacle of tourism, but thankfully, for the moment, it seems to be on the back burner. For the present, Shimoni and the rocky sliver of Wasini island, just offshore, remain both idyllic and fascinating – a rare combination.

The Shimoni Slave Caves

While you're in Shimoni, you should visit the **caves** (daily 8.30–10.30am & 1.30–6.30pm; Ksh100) after which it was named (*shimo* in Swahili). Shimoni's

Shimoni

ACCOMMODATION		RESTAURANTS	
Camp Eden	1	Wasini Island	A
Mpunguti Lodge	4	Restaurant	
Pemba Lodge	2		
Shimoni Reef Lodge	3		

N

KWS

Immigration Office Jetty Slave Caves Customs Office

W A S I N I   C H A N N E L

A

Wasini

W A S I N I   I S L A N D   Mkwiro

I N D I A N   O C E A N

SHIMONI & WASINI

0   1 Km

caves have achieved fame in Kenya, if not much further afield, through Kenyan-born singer Roger Whittaker's melodramatic warblings. A place of refuge from Maasai and other raiders, the caves are thought to have been used for storing slaves prior to shipment to Zanzibar. The evidence takes the form of metal rings attached to the rocks, to which it is supposed slaves were attached, and a now silted-up passage would have led them to boats waiting on the shore. National Museums of Kenya has agreed to investigate the caves for further evidence, and there are 5km of silted-up caves to excavate. Meanwhile, they have been opened to the public with an explanatory tour included in the price (proceeds to fund local development projects). Shafts of sunlight pierce through holes in the forest floor to illuminate the stalactites and dangling lianas quite beautifully. Six species of bat nest in the caves, of which you can see members of two on the tour (the insect-eating bats fly out en masse at dusk).

The tour will also eventually include the ruined two-storey building opposite the cave, formerly the headquarters of the Imperial British East African Company, which was for a time based here. Nearby, the fish auction house by the jetty is also interesting – there's an auction every morning – though exciting exhibits like marlin and shark are rarely on the slab.

Accommodation

Although Shimoni is small, the demand for **accommodation** by big-spending game-fishermen has brought two hotels. The Pemba Channel (the Tanzanian island of Pemba lies 50km offshore) is considered one of the world's very best stretches of sea for hunting big fish; it is impressive to think that marlin weighing a quarter of a ton and tiger sharks of close on half a ton race through these waters.

Since Wasini Island is an alluring ten-minute boat ride away, there's no reason to spend the night in town, but Mwazaro Beach is a very pleasant rustic alternative, down a turning halfway along the *murram* road between the highway and Shimoni village.

Camp Eden Bandas 300m to the right (west) of the village centre behind KWS (reservations through KWS, PO Box 55 Ukunda ☎0127/52027). Wonderful for naturalists, a group of *makuti*-roofed *bandas* in the forest, run by the Kenya Wildlife Service. ❸

Mwazaro Beach 7.5km from the main road junction (Shimoni Lobster Company, PO Box 14 Shimoni; no phone; reservations through Holiday Homes, p.45). "Where God makes holidays" is how the German owner describes his very low-key development on the east coast of the Shimoni peninsula, halfway between the highway and Shimoni close to the delta of the Ramisi River, and somewhere rather special. Naturally air-conditioned *makuti bandas* with good fitted nets, no electricity as this is a sacred Digo *kaya*, but excellent Zanzibari cooking, a lovely private beach, with mangrove swamps (eight of the nine species of mangrove native to Africa can be found there), excellent snorkelling at the nearby reef, plus creek and sea trips. It's very idyllic, but not easily accessible – a kilometre off the Shimoni road, on which transport is pretty sparse, but well worth the effort if you really want to get away from it all. Camping is Ksh150 per tent plus Ksh100 per person without meals (but you'll also want to take those, though tea, coffee and drinking water are free). FB ❺.

Pemba Lodge 800m to the right from village centre, PO Box 84851 Mombasa ☎0127/52016–7, ℱ52416, ✉marlin.pemba@net2000ke.com. For anglers, divers, snorkellers or anyone else, the lodge's speciality is big game and fly-fishing, but it also has a diving school and offers eight-day diving trips aboard the twenty-metre *M.Y. Kisiwani* ($1120), plus Ramisi River trips, nice rooms and a pool. FB ❽

Shimoni Reef Lodge 300m to the left (east) of village centre, PO Box 82234 Mombasa ☎012/52015 or 011/471771, ℱ471349. Part of the Reef group of hotels, open all year, and aimed less at sport fishermen than at divers. Excellent accommodation in ten bungalows, rather average food. Sea-water swimming pool. Well priced. ❺

Wasini island and offshore

WASINI is easily reached. *Wasini Island Restaurant* (PO Box 281 Ukunda ☎0127/2331 or 3055) will speed lunchers across the channel in their boat, but otherwise you'll have to hire a dhow (Ksh600–2000 depending on your bargaining skills). Local people use *jahazi*, sailing boat "matatus" which – notwithstanding the resentment of the diesel men – you should be able to use, too (Ksh200–300 each way in theory). This is certainly more fun, but you'll need to haggle determinedly.

Only 5km long and 1km across, Wasini has just a thousand inhabitants, and is totally adrift from the mainstream of coastal life, although the recent introduction of telephone wires signals change. There are no cars, nor any need of them: you can walk all the way around the island in a couple of hours on the narrow footpaths through the bush, though few people do. With something of Lamu's cast about it, the island is completely undeveloped, and **Wasini village**, an old Wa-vumba settlement, is built in and around its own ruins. It's a fascinating place to wander and there's even a small pillar tomb which still has its complement of inset Chinese porcelain. The **beach** in front of the village is littered with shells, but don't assume anything: a lot of them have been collected from the reef and dumped here, and people will try to sell them to you, so it wouldn't be wise to treat them as legitimate beachcombings – and, strictly speaking, trade in seashells is illegal in Kenya. Nevertheless, the wealth of interesting items on the shores of Wasini – not just shells, but shards of pottery, pieces of glass, scrap metal – add up to a beachcomber's paradise you could explore for hours. Incidentally, residents are getting frustrated by seeing little if any of the tourist bucks rolling into their pockets. If you have a choice, try to buy souvenirs from local hawkers rather than the established gift shops.

Behind the village is a bizarre village green, an area of long-dead **coral gardens** now raised out of the sea but still periodically flooded at spring tides. It's covered in a short swathe of "sea grass" – a tasty vegetable called simply *mboga pwani* (sea vegetable). Walking through the coral grottoes with birds and butterflies in the air leaves a surreal impression of snorkelling on dry land.

Exploring the rest of the island is highly recommended – look out for monkeys in the mangroves and parrots in the palms.

Accommodation in Wasini is very limited (more by the island's total reliance on rainwater than by anything else), but there are usually houses for rent for under Ksh500 per day in either the ancient village of Wasini itself or the newer settlement at the other end of the island, **Mkwiro**. There's also a **banda** and **camping site** known as *Mpunguti Lodge* or *Masood's* (PO Box 19 Shimoni ☎0127/52288; HB ❸). It's very simple – no electricity, though flush toilets and showers have been installed and two rainwater tanks mean that there is sufficient water for most of the year. The owner has quite an impressive collection of old pottery and ceramics; he's trying to persuade the Fort Jesus people to help him set up a museum. All beds are traditional Swahili. There's magnificent Swahili cooking and you can also **camp** here for Ksh200 per person. The owner can also arrange trips to the Marine National Park.

Rather more luxurious, but no less relaxing, is the house used by Pilli-Pipa dhow safaris (p.507) for lunching its day-tripping guests (on succulent crab claws, fried seaweed and other delights). If you contact them in advance, they can pick you up. Full-board costs $50 per person (not s/c), and there's the opportunity of snorkelling trips and scuba diving (PO Box 5185 Diani Beach ☎ & ☏0127/2401,🖳www.pillipipa.com).

Kisite-Mpunguti Marine National Park

Open 6am–6pm daily; $5, children $2. Warden: PO Box 55 Ukunda Shimoni
☎0127/52027.

Wasini has ideal conditions for **snorkelling**, with limpid water all around. Both Pilli-Pipa and *Wasini Island Restaurant* (details for both above), a few minutes to the west of the village, run full-day trips in large dhows to the reefs around Kisite island, part of **Kisite-Mpunguti Marine National Park**, which usually has some of the best snorkelling in Kenya. Similar trips, on a more informal, ad hoc basis are run from *Mpunguti Lodge*.

The boats normally go out of the Wasini channel to the east, then turn south to pass the islets of **Mpunguti Ya Chini** and **Mpunguti Ya Juu** ("little" and "great") on the port side. Kisite islet, a coral-encircled rock about 100m long, 5km to the southwest, is the routine destination. The best parts of the Kisite anchoring area are towards the outer edge of the main "coral garden". There are fish and sea animals in abundance, including angel fish, moray eel, octopuses, rock cod and some spectacularly large (sixty-centimetre) sea cucumbers. At certain times of the year, however, the water is less clear, and it looks as if repeated anchorings have destroyed much of the coral in at least one small area, where the shallow sea bed is littered with broken ends and grey debris. Ask the crew if you'd like to try to find a better area: **Mako Koke Reef**, the other main part of the park, is about 4km to the west.

Vanga

Kenya's southernmost town, **VANGA** is also the largest of the coastal settlements to have been left alone by the tourist industry. Getting here involves travelling down one of the country's most beautiful, and usually deserted, roads, from the Shimoni junction to Lungalunga, on the Tanzanian border. The seventeen-kilometre *murram* road to Vanga begins, curiously, midway through the Kenyan border post at Lungalunga, where you have to explain your purpose to the officials. There arc a couple of lodgings here – *Muthangini Border Lodge* (❶) and *Thomas Bar* (❶) – but nothing of interest. Turning left, the track skims the Tanzanian border through *shambas* and, as it nears the sea, tunnels through tall forest in deep shade. Vanga itself is in the **mangroves**, approached through the swamp down a causeway which is regularly flooded by spring tides.

The largish village has a main street and a number of stores and *hotelis*, where men come in the evening to chew *miraa* and reflect on the community's isolation. "We have no employment", is a common complaint; the fishing co-operative is the only local provider of a cash income, but it isn't always able to buy the entire catch and members are not supposed to sell to anyone else. Many people sell garden produce in Mombasa, which explains the matatu departures through the night to ensure early arrival at the markets.

Most people are unlikely to come to Vanga as there isn't anywhere to stay in the town or anything much to do. The big old house on the seafront is a nineteenth-century British customs house, cared for, in theory, by the National Museums of Kenya but in practice falling down. For the less fastidious, dugout canoes can be rented very cheaply for wobbly punting trips through the mangroves. Vanga is a sure antidote to a surfeit of Diani and Malindi: local residents are more than willing to accommodate visitors and you may be plied with excellent palm wine.

Onward to Tanzania

Lungalunga is the Kenyan border post if you're heading south to Tanzania, and easily reached by matatu from Likoni, or occasionally direct from Mombasa (Jomo Kenyatta Avenue at Mwembe Tayari Road). After completing border formalities on the Kenyan side, you can take a matatu or a taxi, or walk the 6km to Horohoro on the Tanzanian side. There are money changers at both border posts, who will change Kenyan shillings for Tanzanian shillings, or cash dollars, and no doubt euros, into either. Try to ascertain the current rate before entering into negotiations, and always check your change carefully. If buying Tanzanian shillings, you usually get the best rate on the Tanzanian side, and in fact you'll get a better rate for Kenya shillings here than you will in Dar es Salaam or Tanga. Heading on, you can get a through bus to Dar es Salaam (try to get to Lungalunga by 9am to be sure of getting one), or take a *dala dala* (the Tanzanian expression for a matatu) to Tanga, and get onward transport from there. The journey to Tanga takes about two and a half hours, and a further five hours to Dar.

The coast from Kilifi to Malindi

From Mtwapa Creek up to **Malindi**, the landscape is a diverse collage, from rolling baobab country and sisal plantations as you near **Kilifi** to groves of cashew trees after it; thick, jungly forest and swamp characterizes Mida Creek, and there's a more compact, populated zone of *shambas* and thicket as you

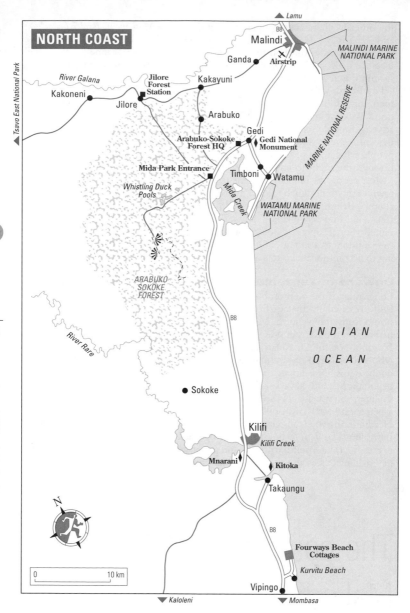

NORTH COAST

Lamu

Malindi

MALINDI MARINE NATIONAL PARK

Ganda

Airstrip

River Galana

Jilore Forest Station

Kakayuni

Kakoneni

Jilore

Arabuko

Gedi

Arabuko-Sokoke Forest HQ

Gedi National Monument

Mida Park Entrance

Timboni

Watamu

Whistling Duck Pools

Mida Creek

WATAMU MARINE NATIONAL PARK

ARABUKO SOKOKE FOREST

River Rare

INDIAN

OCEAN

MARINE NATIONAL RESERVE

Tsavo East National Park

Sokoke

Kilifi

Kilifi Creek

Mnarani

Kitoka

Takaungu

B8

Fourways Beach Cottages

Kurvitu Beach

N

0   10 km

Vipingo

Kaloleni

Mombasa

approach Malindi. **Kilifi** and **Takaungu creeks** are stunning – the clash of blue water and green cliffs almost unnatural.

There is wide scope for **beach hunting** along this part of the coast. Malindi and, to some extent, Watamu have been developed, but Kilifi functions largely as a Giriama market-centre and district capital, while Takaungu seems virtually unknown, a throwback to pre-colonial days. There's also superb **snorkelling** at **Watamu** and **Malindi marine national parks**. And the ruined town of **Gedi**, deep in the forest near Watamu, is one of the most impressive archeological sites in East Africa.

Kilifi and around

Between Kikambala and Kilifi lies a major **sisal-growing** area, focused around the small town of **Vipingo** (one or two *dukas* and *hotelis*, but not much else). Across thousands of acres, plumb-straight rows of fleshy-leafed, cactus-like sisal plants stretch in every direction, the surviving **baobab trees** standing out bizarrely (see box below). Towards Kilifi, the road bucks through a hilly area and the baobabs grow more profusely amid the scrub.

If you want **to stay** cheaply on this relatively undeveloped coastline, *Fourways Beach Cottages* is a good target (reservations: 3rd floor, Canon Tower New Wing, PO Box 83365 Mombasa ☎011/229405, ⓕ315060; ❹). An attractive modern complex of spacious self-catering tiled cottages and apartments, most with ocean views, there's also a restaurant and minimarket (both sometimes closed, so bring your own supplies), and a little pool next to an idyllic stretch of beach. Significantly, the reef is much closer to the shore in this area (Kurvitu Beach) than further south – a plus point for snorkellers. If you're travelling by public transport, ask the bus or matatu driver to drop you 1.6km north of Vipingo (18km north of Mtwapa), where you'll see a gravel track off to the right and a small rash of signboards including one for *Fourways* – it's about 3km along. **Be warned**, however, that this track has in the past been the scene of attacks and robberies on tourists – ring beforehand to check the situation.

6

THE COAST | Kilifi and around

Baobab stories

The **baobab**'s strange appearance has a number of explanations in mythology. The most common one relates how the first baobab planted by God was an ordinary-looking tree, but it refused to stay in one place and wandered round the countryside. As a punishment, God planted it back again – upside down – and immobilized it. Baobabs may live well over 2000 years, making them among the longest-living organisms. During a severe drought, their large green pods can be cracked open and the nuts made into a kind of flour. The resulting "hungry bread" is part of the common culture of the region. The tangy white pith of the baobab fruit is boiled with sugar to make a popular bright red sweet that you will see on sale at street stalls.

Takaungu

Ten kilometres before you reach Kilifi, there's a turn-off to the right to **TAKAUNGU**. Although there are a couple of matatus most days from Mombasa to Takaungu, the chances of a lift are relatively slim if you get dropped off at the turning, but the walk (5km) is not too long. Takaungu is enchanting – a quiet, composed village of whitewashed Swahili houses situated on a high bluff above **Takaungu Creek**. There are three mosques and one or two small shops and *hotelis*, but no formal lodgings except for the exceedingly expensive *Takaungu House* (☎0125/22479; ❾; with deep pool; bookings through Bush Homes of East Africa, p.42). If you want to stay in the village and you speak a little Swahili, people will put you up for a very reasonable

▲ Malindi

KILIFI & MNARANI

Kobil — Masjid ul Noor Mosque

Kayas Office
Microlight Office

@ — A — Barclays Bank
Postbank — B — KCB
Bus & Matatu Park — Market — C
— 3 — Kilifi
— 4 —

Swynford's Boatyard

Mnarani Ruins — 5 — 6

— 7 — 8
Mnarani

RESTAURANTS & BARS
Arcade Café — A
Kilifi Café — B
New Kilifi Hotel — C

Kilifi Creek

N

ACCOMMODATION
Al Ponte Pizzeria & Trattoria — 4
Bandari Beach Fishing Club — 5
Baobab Lodge — 2
Dhow's Inn — 8
Kilifi Bay Beach Resort — 1
Mnarani Club — 6
Tushauriane Lodge — 3
Giriama Guest House — 7

0 — 1 km

▼ Mombasa

price. Food supplies are variable; women will prepare food if you ask, and especially if you supply the ingredients. There's no produce market, but a small fish market by the creek – be there when the catch arrives to get the tasty ones. Takaungu is a place that repays time spent getting to know it. If you just want to sit back and relax, pass it by and head on to Lamu.

There's a small seaside **beach**, 1km east, through the secondary school. **Takaungu Creek** is startlingly beautiful, the colour of blue Curaçao, and absolutely transparent; the small swimming beach on the stream is covered at high tide, but you can still dive from the rocks. Upstream, the creek disappears between flanks of dense jungle. When you're ready to move on, the tiny, council-operated rowing boat provides a slow and almost free service across the creek to the Kilifi side; from there, it's a five-kilometre (ninety-minute) walk through the sisal fields to Kilifi bridge.

Kilifi, Mnarani and the creek

Kenya's coastline was submerged in the recent geological past, resulting in the creation of the islands and drowned river valleys – the creeks – of today. **KIL-IFI**, a small but animated place, is on such a creek. When the Portuguese knew it, Kilifi's centre was on the south side of the creek and called **Mnarani** (still the name of the village on that side). Together with Kitoka on the north side of Takaungu Creek, and a settlement on the site of the present town of Kilifi, these three constituted the "state" of Kilifi.

Kilifi town

With the building of the **bridge** in the 1980s, Kilifi's economy was dealt a hard blow. All the creek-side trade made possible by the ferry's endless delays and breakdowns ceased (the ferry itself is now a half-submerged wreck), and many bars and *hotelis*, and half the town's lodgings, closed.

The town is draped along the north side of the creek to the east of the bridge. If you're driving you'll probably pass it by; even most public transport travellers only see it from the inside of a bus while more fares are being picked up. But staying the night is not an unpleasant prospect, and while there's not a lot of choice it's certainly a better plan than arriving late in Malindi.

There are three **banks** in town (Barclays with an ATM, Postbank with Western Union facilities, and KCB), and a **post and telephone office** (Mon–Fri 8am–12.30pm & 2–5pm) down near the market. **Moving on**, note that buses to Lamu (for route details, read the "Moving on" section on p.548) and Garissa pass by around 8am. There's lots of transport to Mombasa or Malindi.

Accommodation

Hotels are thin on the ground, especially if you want to stay in town. For beach accommodation, see the section under Kilifi Beach.

Al Ponte Pizzeria & Trattoria 1km from the centre, PO Box 1214. On the north side of the creek by the bridge, this pizzeria has six large s/c rooms with fans and nets and murals, the better ones with views over the creek. Safe parking. B&B ❸

Bandari Beach Fishing Club Mnarani, on the south shore of the creek, 300m off the road from *Dhows Inn* to the Mnarani ruins, PO Box 508 ☎ & ℱ0125/22151, ℮ bandariclub@africaonline.co.ke. Small, friendly German-run guest house that hosts parties of game fishermen, but is happy to put up travellers, with airy, clean rooms with hot water and fans, a small, cooled pool, European food and excellent coffee. Low-cost boat and fishing trips, and safaris to Tsavo East are all possible. HB ❹

Dhows Inn Mnarani, at the south side of the bridge, PO Box 431 ☎ & ℱ0125/22028. Big, clean, good-value s/c rooms with hot water at this popular upmarket boozer and restaurant with a penchant for country music. B&B ❷

Giriama Guest House Mnarani, on the road between *Dhows Inn* and Mnarani ruins, PO Box 487 Mtwapa ☎0125/25414. Cheap and basic singles. ❶

Mnarani Club South side of the creek, entrance near the bridge, PO Box 1008 Kilifi ☎0125/22318–20, ℱ22200, ℗ www.mnarani.com. An all-inclusive resort with good food and service, and two categories of rooms (it's worth paying a bit extra for the more spacious Creek View rooms with bathtubs and parquet rather than lino-tile floors). The views over the creek from the hotel's pool are classic, and there's a private beach. The establishment also boasts a cat restaurant and what they claim is the world's biggest ashtray, but it doesn't admit children under 16. FB ❽ low, ❾ high.

Tushauriane Lodge By the bus and matatu station, PO Box 259 ☎0125/22521. Ask at the hardware shop on its right side for the owner. The tallest and only option in the town centre. Basic and not terribly clean non-s/c rooms with mosquito nets but no fans – dingy, but very cheap. Unsafe parking. ❶

Eating

As for **eating** options, the **Oloitipitip Market** has a wide range of fruit and vegetables. The *New Kilifi Hotel* (closes 8pm) is a very busy local joint near the bus station, serving good cheap meals and snacks, whilst a good stand-by for snacks and fry-ups is the long established *Kilifi Café*. *Arcade Café* does tasty meals in fresh, clean surroundings in the small arcade it shares with Postbank. More upmarket, try the superb wood-oven-baked pizzas at *Al Ponte Pizzeria & Trattoria* (see accommodation above), in a great creekside location beside a gigantic gnarled baobab. **Nightlife** is concentrated on the main junction in Mnarani, south of the creek, where *makuti*-thatched *Creek Garden* bar and restaurant concentrates on *hango* and African beats, while the almost adjacent *Dhows Inn* has softer music.

Mnarani ruins

There's little of **sightseeing interest** in Kilifi itself. Its two main **mosques** – one a stumpy shed in the town centre, the other a new and attractively minareted blue, green and white temple, the Masjid ul Noor, at the north junction – more or less sum it up, but across the creek are the more interesting **Mnarani ruins**, which sit under the trees high above the water. To get to them, take the road west from the junction with the main highway at *Dhows Inn* and the *Creek Garden*, turn right at the end down towards the creek, and the site is signposted on your left near the old ferry landing – "follow the green posts" and then up a rather steep flight of stairs (7am–6pm; Ksh100, children Ksh50). The site is archeologically famous mainly for the large number of inscriptions found on its masonry, all in a difficult, and so far untranslated, form of monumental Arabic. They can be seen in several places, in particular in the well-preserved mihrab of the main mosque. Just behind this is a very tall octagonal white pillar tomb, which dominates the remains. In front of the mosque, a precipitous well plummets right down to creek level. A little way removed from the main mosque (signposted in front of the office), a smaller one is hidden away among the baobabs. As a whole, the site, though small, is pretty and photogenic, though for the non-buff its most memorable aspect is a superlative position and, after the visit, the opportunity to cool down in the creek along with the local kids.

Kilifi Creek

Kilifi's seaside-settler/yachtie community tends to hover around the informal bar-restaurant at **Swynford's Boatyard** (℡0125/25067), which is *the* place for making contacts if you have any ideas of Indian Ocean crewing in mind, and also a possible place to make contacts for sea-fishing excursions. There's no public transport here: if you don't have your own car you'll have to walk, unless you can get a lift. It's a little further up the south side of the creek from the old ferry landing, accessible via a dirt road from the old main road, 1km inland, then right 2km down a steep track to the waterfront. Easier access on foot is along the shore of the creek, but this is only easy at low tide. *Swynford's* is a friendly place, with fine views of the creek and the dramatic new bridge. They turn out fresh and simple seafood dishes, including fish and chips, crab samosas and weekend lunch buffets (Ksh400), and there's a notice board for yachties and fishermen to exchange news and trade kit.

The Giriama and the Kilifi kayas project

In recent decades, as the **Giriama** section of the Mijikenda (see p.490) has expanded, Kilifi has become one of their most important towns. Giriama women are quickly noticed by everyone for their unusual **dress**, although it's gradually disappearing. Traditionally a kind of kilt of grass or leaves, it is now made of *kanga* cloth with hips and buttocks accentuated by a bustle of coir fibre stuffed underneath. Older women still occasionally go topless but younger women usually cover up, at least in town. The Mijikenda peoples, and the Giriama especially, are known as great sorcerers and practitioners of witchcraft, and Kilifi is still the frequent scene of accusations that sometimes reach the press. Kilifi is also now the site of an office of the coastal project working to conserve the Mijikenda's sacred groves, or *kayas* (the other office is at Ukunda – see p.511). The main work at present is to identify and gazette the *kayas* of the district but, in time, it's hoped that tourist visits will be feasible. If you're interested in finding out more about the project, call at the office near the *Mkwajuni Hotel*, or contact them in advance (PO Box 596 Kilifi ℡0125/22140, ℅cfcu.kilifi @swiftmombasa.com).

Kilifi Beach

The real **beaches** around Kilifi are mostly accessible only through private property, and the best are up on the open coast to the northeast of the town. Along this ten-kilometre tarred road, however, there are several fairly recent developments. Distances for the following are given from the main Mombasa–Malindi road.

Baobab Lodge 3.2km, PO Box 537 ☎0125/22570, ⓕ22566; reservations through Mada Holdings, Kimathi House, Kimathi St, PO Box 40683 Nairobi ☎02/221439, ⓕ332170, ⓔmadahold@form-net.com. Attractively sited amid densely planted gardens and baobabs, in a pleasant position on a bluff above the shore. Tennis courts and a good pool with lots of shade (Ksh200 for non-residents), but little beach to speak of and no sea-swimming at low tide. The rooms, though, are spacious and well furnished, with AC and fans, but lack sea views. Next door is the *Kilifi Beach Club* for drinks and average

food. Closed May and June. B&B ❹
Kilifi Bay Beach Resort 6.5km, PO Box 537 ☎0125/22264 or 22511, ⓕ22258, ⓔkilifibay@kenyaweb.com; reservations as for *Baobab Lodge*. The best of Kilifi's hotels, with a stunning location right on the beach (the best rooms have stupendous sea views; all have balconies), mature tropical gardens with coconut palms, a freeform pool for when the tide is out, great four-poster beds, spacious *makuti*-roofed communal areas, good service and decent breakfasts. Water sports can be arranged. HB ❻

Arabuko-Sokoke Forest, Gedi and Kipepeo Butterfly Farm

Heading north from Kilifi to Watamu and Malindi, a number of interesting diversions en route provide a possible break from beach-related activities. Most of these centre around the **Arabuko-Sokoke Forest**, where you can walk, cycle or drive in search of the "small six" – the main stars in the forest's array of wildlife, in contrast to the "big five" of the savannah parks. Nearby, the ruins at **Gedi** provide by far the largest and most interesting of the coast's ancient stone ruins. If you're in a hurry, you can visit both forest and ruins together in a day, or alternatively, you can make excursions to either or both using Malindi, Watamu or even Kilifi as a base.

The Arabuko-Sokoke Forest

Forest Visitor Centre near Gedi 8am–4pm; PO Box 1 Gedi ☎0122/32462, ⓔsokoke@africaonline.co.ke.

The cashew trees lining both sides of the road north of Kilifi soon give way to tracts of jungle where monkeys scatter across the road and hornbills plunge into the cover of the trees as you approach. This is the **Arabuko-Sokoke Forest**, the largest patch of indigenous coastal forest left in East Africa. At one time it would have covered most of the coastal hinterland behind the shoreline settlements, part of an ancient forest belt which stretched from Mozambique to Somalia. If you have a car or a few days for some walking, there are some 400 square kilometres to explore, a tiny part of which in the far north (six square kilometres) was declared a national park in 1991.

The ban on cutting timber in the forest (often ignored), and on clearance of land for agriculture, has not endeared it to **local residents**, who have seen it as a useless waste of land, and are particularly not amused when elephants from the forest come out and decimate their crops. To combat this ill feeling, Kenya Wildlife Service, National Museums of Kenya and a forest support group, the Friends of Arabuko-Sokoke have pioneered a number of projects to make conservation of the forest useful to the local community. Among **initiatives** up and running are the Kipepeo Butterfly Project (see p.529), and a bee-keeping scheme in which people living around the forest are given beehives at low cost to produce honey from forest flowers; if you want to try some, it's sold at the Forest Visitor Centre and other outlets. Licences are also issued for the gathering of deadwood for fuel, and the harvesting of medicinal herbs, and an initiative is under way to contribute towards school fees for local children out of income generated from visits to the forest by tourists. The problem of incursions by elephants onto cultivated land is by no means confined to Arabuko-Sokoke, but electric fences are planned along parts of the forest boundary to prevent greedy pachyderms from having a jumbo munch-out on neighbouring *shambas*. If you would like to get involved in forest conservation projects, you can join the **Friends of Arabuko-Sokoke Forest** (Ksh1000 per year) at the Visitor Centre (PO Box 383 Watamu), or via their website at Ⓦwww .watamu.net/foasf.htm.

Beside elephants (usually evidenced by their dung), Sykes' monkeys and yellow baboons, the forest shelters two rare mammal species: the 35-centimetre-high **Aders' (or Zanzibar) duiker** is a tiny, shy antelope, usually living in pairs, but which you're more likely to see around Gedi, where tourists no longer disturb them as much, and the extraordinary **golden-rumped elephant shrew**, which has been adopted as the symbol for the forest. The size of a small cat, this bizarre animal resembles a giant mouse with an elongated nose, running on stilts. In one of those mystifyingly evolved animal relationships, it consorts with a small bird, the **red-capped robin chat**, which warns it of danger and picks up insects disturbed by the shrew's snufflings. Your best chance of seeing a shrew is to look for its fluttering companion among the tangle of branches: the shrew will be close by. It can usually be seen (but not for long – it's very speedy) on the walk along the Nature Trail close to the Visitor Centre, or along the sandy tracks further inside the forest. You may also spot it darting across forest trails ahead of you. The exceedingly rare **Sokoke bush-tailed mongoose** is unlikely to put in an appearance – there have been no sightings since the mid-1980s. El Niño, which wreaked havoc over most of Kenya in 1997–98, was a boon for Arabuko, seeing an explosion in insect and frog populations, in turn providing a feast for their predators. The rains even attracted hippos into the park, though these have now gone, and the forest remains second in Africa only to the Okavango Delta in Botswana for the diversity of its frog population, a fact very much in evidence after a good rainfall. Those with a specific interest in amphibians can find photos and sound-clips of the forest's frogs and toads on the Frogs of Arabuko-Sokoke Forest website at Ⓦwww.calacademy.org/research/herpetology/frogs/kfrogs.html.

The forest is also home to a glorious variety of butterflies (see Kipepeo Butterfly Farm, p.529) and six globally threatened **bird species**, including the small **Sokoke scops owl**, which is found only in the red-soiled *cynometra* section of the forest, and the **Sokoke pipit** – both very hard to spot, although guides are on hand to help locate them. The other endangered birds are the Amani sunbird, Clark's weaver, East Coast akalat and spotted ground thrush.

Practicalities

Whether driving or walking, head first for the **Forest Visitor Centre**, 1.5km south of Gedi and the Watamu junction on the Malindi–Mombasa road, which provides an information pack of maps and fact sheets (Ksh50), a Visitor's Guide detailing routes through the forest (Ksh120), and an excellent colour booklet (Ksh350) with bird lists and advice for visitors. Entry to the forest is free, though Kenya Wildlife Service plans to introduce fees to support the school bursary scheme mentioned above. The visitor centre is also the place to pick up a **guide** (see below). If you've got a tent, use it. **Camping** is permitted (Ksh200 per person per night), but apart from the main site beside the Visitor Centre, you must be self-sufficient, and there are restrictions on the lighting of fires.

Walking is best done in the morning or late afternoon, and although this isn't the Amazon, a degree of preparation is wise if you plan on venturing far down any of the tracks leading off the main road. Survey of Kenya maps would be useful (the *Kenya Coast* tourist map at the very least), though the Visitor Centre maps are more than adequate for the main trails. A **compass** is also helpful. Official **ASF guides** are provided at the Visitor Centre, and cost Ksh400 (per guide for up to six people) for three hours, Ksh500 for up to six hours, Ksh900 for up to ten hours, and Ksh400 in the evening or at night. All are professional and well versed in forest ecology. You can also use them for fantastic **night walks** (the chorus of frog calls is awesome), which would otherwise be impossible on your own. A specialist guide to locate birds costs Ksh100 more on the day walks.

An organized early-morning **birdwalk** (Ksh100) leaves the Visitor Centre on the first Saturday of every month at 6.30am. For the masochistic, a cheery group of beer-swilling joggers boards vehicles at *Ocean Sports* in Watamu at 5pm most Mondays, Wednesdays and Fridays, for anything between 3km and 10km of self-inflicted suffering, followed by a booze-up back in Watamu.

Routes

A **nature trail** takes you from the Visitor Centre around the first part of the forest which, after rain, is spectacularly adorned with the nests of foam-nest tree frogs. It takes most of a morning, but is an easy walk and excellent introduction to the forest and its (medicinal) uses. Bring water and insect repellent. Another easy walk is to the **tree house**, a viewing platform atop a tree by a former sand quarry, from which you get superb vistas over the forest.

If you're short of time, there are several **driving routes**, more if you have 4WD, which are also suitable for bikes (see "Listings" on p.547 for details on bike rental in Malindi). The main route starts at the Mida entrance, 2km south of the Visitor Centre on the main Mombasa–Malindi road, and goes up to the View Point through brachystegia forest – look out for the rare Amani sunbird on the way. From the View Point, which looks east over the forest to Mida Creek and the Indian Ocean, a walking track continues for another 2km to a second viewing point which looks west onto cynometra forest and a large exposed escarpment. There are other paths along the western edge of the Whistling Duck Pools (at the junction between the brachystegia and cynometra forest on the main driving track between the Mida entrance and the viewpoints), which are a favourite haunt for white-faced whistling duck, little grebe and open-billed storks, as well as the odd elephant. Little used, but apparently excellent, is the "elephant track" (14km), which passes through both mixed and brachystegia forest; it starts at Gedi Forest Station, heading west for 8km before joining the driveable track to Jilore Forest Station. A left turn here takes you 5km down to the Mida entrance on the Mombasa–Malindi road. If you're going by taxi, haggle well, and before starting, drop in at the Visitor Centre, which has details of the routes.

Another approach to the forest from Malindi heads west on the road to Tsavo East, passing through Kikayuni and Jilore villages. Roads that can be driven or cycled – even walked if you can reach them early enough by matatu from Malindi – lead from both places down to the Mombasa–Malindi highway. **Kakayuni** is the larger of the two villages, and offers a forest road of 10km or so, leading via the small centre of **Arabuko** to the highway. Mostly, however, this path goes through marginal forest lands. A better bet is to continue to **Jilore**, whose location, high on a ridge overlooking a bend in the Sabaki/Galana River, contrasts impressively with the deep forest all around.

The turning for Jilore Forest Station is to the left, just before you reach Jilore village, and the station about 3km down the track. At the first crossroads after the forest station's three huts, turn left: a good trail leads for 16km in a southerly direction to the Kilifi–Malindi highway. If you're doing this trip by car, the track is driveable (though 4WD helps over the deep sand), and it's also clear enough for walkers to follow without getting lost. The track is seldom used by motorists and you're not likely to see other people. Around its halfway mark, the soil changes from red *murram* to a light grey, soft coral sand, signalling the transition back to the coast proper. If you've been pootling along gently on a rented cycle from Malindi, this is pretty well the end of the relaxing bit, and you'll have to start getting off to push. Your eventual emergence onto the main highway, 5–6km south of Gedi, is sudden. Here, you could wait for a short time for a matatu straight back to Malindi or, if the day is still young and your energy not completely sapped, turn inland again a couple of kilometres north up the road, where the other track (described above) leads to Arabuko and Kakayuni.

Gedi

Ruins open daily 7am–6pm; Ksh200, children Ksh100. Warden: PO Box 5067 Malindi ☎ 0122/32065, ✉ gedimuseum@swiftmalindi.com. Two paths signposted near Gedi village at the junction of the Malindi and Watamu roads – it's a ten-minute walk.

The Arabuko-Sokoke Forest may partly explain the enigma of **GEDI** (sometimes spelt Gede). This large, thirteenth- to seventeenth-century Swahili town was apparently unknown to the Portuguese, despite the fact that, for nearly a hundred years, they maintained a strong presence only 15km away in Malindi, at a time when Gedi is judged to have been at the peak of its prosperity. It is not mentioned (at least by the name of Gedi) in any Arabic or Swahili writings either and, bafflingly, it has to be assumed that, set back from the sea and deep in the forest, it was never noticed.

The **ruins** are confusing, eerie and, in the late afternoon, hauntingly beautiful. Even if you are resolutely uninterested in seeing any of the other sites on the coast, don't miss this one. Forest has invaded the town over the three centuries since it was deserted, and baobabs and magnificent buttress-rooted trees tower over the dimly lit walls and arches. Gedi has a sinister reputation and local people have always been uneasy about it; it has collected an unhealthy share of ghost stories and tales of inexplicable happenings since 1948, when it was opened as a national park and tourists started to visit. Some of this cultural memory may derive from the supposed occupation of the ruins in the eighteenth century by **Oromo**-speaking people (probably ancestors of the Orma, whose present-day territory starts just north of Malindi), a tribe of irrepressible expansionists whose violent and unsettled lifestyle was long a major threat to the coastal communities. This part explains how they got to be known, until recently, as *Galla*, an offensive term which was applied to them by the native Amhara and Mijikenda. The Oromo, it's believed, were the original cause of Gedi's desertion by its inhabitants.

The longer you stay here, the further you seem from an answer to Gedi's anomalies. The display of pottery shards from all over the world in the small **museum** shows that the town must have been actively trading with overseas merchants, yet it is 5km from the sea and 2km from Mida Creek; the coastline has probably moved inland over the centuries, so it might previously have been further away still. Then, at times of supposed Oromo aggression, sailing into Mida Creek would have been like entering a lobster pot. The reasons for Gedi's location remain thoroughly obscure and its absence from historical records grows more inexplicable the more you think about it.

Gedi tingles spines easily, even today, particularly if you are on your own. James Kirkman, the archeologist who first worked at the site, remembers: "when I first started to work at Gedi I had the feeling that something or somebody was looking out from behind the walls, neither hostile nor friendly but waiting for what he knew was going to happen." Kirkman's booklet, usually available at the entrance gate (Ksh50), has a lot of interesting details as well as a plan of the site, which we've reproduced here. Its directions, however, tend to lead you in circles; it's better just to follow your nose.

Any bus or matatu travelling between Malindi and Watamu or Kilifi can drop you off at Gedi junction, where the B8 Malindi–Mombasa road meets the turn-off for Watamu. The junction is a ten-minute walk from the site, which is clearly signposted.

The site
The town seems fairly typical of medieval Swahili settlements. It was walled, and originally covered about a quarter of a square kilometre – some 45 acres. The majority of its estimated 2500 citizens, or at least inhabitants, probably lived in mud-and-thatch huts, long overwhelmed and dissolved by jungle, on the southern, poorer side of town, the side away from Mecca. The palace and the "Stone Town" were in the north. When the site was reoccupied at the end of the sixteenth century, after a hiatus of fifty or so years, a new inner wall was built, enclosing just this prestigious zone.

Mombasa-Malindi-Watamu Junction (1 km)

Museum
Car Park
Office
House of the Sunken Court
Dated Tomb
Pillar Tomb
House
Palace
Fluted Pillar Tomb
Well
Great Mosque
Pillar Tomb
House of the Dhow
Mosque
Mosque
Mosque
Large House
Mosque
East Gate of Inner Wall
Mosque
South Gate of Inner Wall
Alignment of the Inner Wall
Alignment of the Outer Wall
Mosque

0   100 m

GEDI RUINS

The **Palace**, with its striking entrance porch, sunken courts and honeycomb of little rooms, is the most impressive single building. The concentration of **houses** to its right is where most of Gedi's interesting finds were made and they are named accordingly: House of the Scissors, House of the Ivory Box, House of the Dhow (with a picture of a dhow on the wall). If you have already been to Lamu, the tight layout of buildings and streets will be familiar, although in Gedi all the houses were single storey. As usual, sanitary arrangements are much in evidence. Gedi's toilets are all of identical design, and superior to the long-drops you find in Kenya today. While many of the houses have been modified over the centuries, these bathrooms seem original, almost as if the town was purpose-built, like a housing estate. Look out for the **House of the Sunken Court**, one of the most elaborate, with its self-conscious emulation of the Palace's courtyards.

Gedi's **Great Mosque**, one of seven on the site, was its Friday mosque, the mosque of the whole town. Compared with other ruined mosques on the coast, this one is very large and had a *minbar*, or pulpit, of three steps in stone, rather than the usual wooden construction. Perhaps an inkling of the kind of people who worshipped here – and they were both men and women – and their form of Islam, comes from the carving of a broad-bladed **spearhead** above the arch of the mosque's northeast doorway. Whoever they were, they were clearly not the "colonial Arabs" long believed by European classical scholars to have been the people of Gedi: it's hard to believe that Arabs would have made use of the spear symbol of East African pastoralists.

Nearby is a good example of a **pillar tomb**. These are found all along the coast and are associated with men of importance – chiefs, sheikhs and senior community elders. The fact that this kind of grave is utterly alien to the rest of the Islamic world is further indication that coastal Islam was distinctly African for a long time. Such tombs aren't constructed any more, though there's a nineteenth-century one in Malindi. It looks as if the more recent waves of Arab immigration to the coast have tended to discourage what must have seemed to them an eccentric, even barbaric, style. The **Dated Tomb** next door to the office gives an idea of Gedi's age. Its epitaph reads 802 AH – or AD 1399. Also by the office, the new **museum** exhibits finds from the site including imported artefacts such as Chinese Ming vases and Spanish scissors, evidence of trade with lands very far afield. There are also exhibits of Swahili cultural artefacts, and temporary exhibitions in the adjoining salon.

Gedi wildlife

It's easy to spend hours here, and rewarding to walk down some of the well-swept paths through the thick jungle away from the main ruins. In the undergrowth, you catch spooky glimpses of other buildings still unexcavated. And with patience you'll see a **golden-rumped elephant shrew** (see p.524). Gedi also has monkeys, bushbabies, tiny duiker antelope and, according to local belief, a huge, mournful, sheep-like animal that follows you like a shadow down the paths.

Watch out, incidentally, for the *siafu* **ants** that have colonized many of the ruins. They form thick brown columns massing from one hole to another and sometimes gather in enormous clumps. Be careful where you put your feet when stepping over walls. And try not to stand on the walls themselves: they are fragile, and the freedom to walk around Kenya's ruins without restriction isn't likely to continue if they suffer as a result. Incidentally, the **snake farm** near the entrance isn't the best of its kind; just a guide/tout who takes you to a *shamba* (farm) in the forest where a couple of snakes are produced and paraded around the guide's neck.

Kipepeo Project Butterfly Farm

Daily 8.30am–5pm; Ksh100, children Ksh50. PO Box 58 Gedi ☎ & ℱ 0122/ 32380, Ⓦ www.watamu.net/kipepeo.html.

Close by the entrance to Gedi ruins is Kenya's first working butterfly farm, **Kipepeo** ("butterfly" in Swahili). This is the base for a project which helps local residents benefit from the proximity of the forest by exploiting the overseas market for exotic butterflies – for preserved collections and walk-through butterfly "farms". People catch adult butterflies with a net, and place the females on plants of the species eaten by their caterpillars, encouraging them to lay eggs. When hatched, the caterpillars are looked after and kept in food until they pupate, at which point the chrysalises are taken to the butterfly farm, where they are shipped to foreign customers and the breeders paid for their trouble. Some pupae are also kept for the farm itself, while those which are not sold simply return to the wild. Vistors to the farm can see the butterflies at various stages of development, from larva (caterpillar) through pupa (chrysalis) to adult (butterfly). The project's visitor centre provides information on the project and Arabuko-Sokoke Forest in general, and also has local handicrafts on display, as well as locally produced honey. Morning is the best time to visit, when the butterflies are most active and you have a chance of seeing them emerging from their pupae.

Watamu

After Gedi, **WATAMU** seems fairly superficial. It consists simply of a small agglomeration of hotels, a strip of beachfront private homes, a compact coconut village of *hotelis* and curio stands, and the **beach**. It tends to cater for package holidaymakers staying in the large hotels along it, but there's still plenty for the backpacker – beautiful beaches, a superb marine park and lively young nightlife. Watamu is well used to tourists: making friends is easy, and you can look around the village without being too badly pestered. As the beach is part of the marine park, KWS regulations have recently been enforced to clear beach boys and hawkers off the beach.

Although one or two of the hotels are very pleasant, the beach and the coral offshore are the main justification for visiting Watamu. Fortunately, they are justification enough. This is an exceptional shoreline, with three stunning **bays** – Watamu Bay, the Blue Lagoon and Turtle Bay – separated by raised coral cliffs and dotted with tiny, sculpted coral islets scuttled over by crabs. If you like beach walks, bring a pair of rubber or plastic-soled sandals – the coral rock is sharp. Out in the **Watamu Marine National Park**, the submerged crags of living coral gardens are – despite all the visits in glass-bottom boats – as vivid and magically perfect as they must have been for millennia. And, despite the high profile of tourism here, there's an easier-going atmosphere than at, say, Diani or Malindi, with fewer security problems than at Malindi and the coastline north and south of Mombasa. Watamu is a good place to go **diving** – or to learn the skill, with at least three diving schools offering one-off dives or approved courses at standard rates (p.535). It's worth knowing, however, that from June to October **seaweed** is often swept onto the beach and the sea can be murky, while in July it's often too rough to snorkel or dive anyway.

Among environmental intiatives, one that many hotels participate in, and individual tourists can contribute to, is **Watamu Turtle Watch** (PO Box 125 ☎ 0122/32118, ℱ 32280, Ⓔ wtwkenya@swiftmalindi.com), a project to protect the eggs of threatened marine turtles from poaching (in both senses) by pay-

▲ Gedi, Malindi & Mombasa

0   250 m

Watamu Mosque

Curio Stalls

Curio Stalls

Mama Lucy's

Beach

SDA Camp

Bio Ken Reptile Park

Watamu Bay

see inset for detail

Watamu

Supermarket

Blue Lagoon

Gate

Turtle Bay

WATAMU MARINE NATIONAL PARK

Kilepwa Island

Mida Creek

ACCOMMODATION

Aquarius Beach Hotel	10
Ascot Residence Hotel	7
Barracuda Inn	11
Beach Veiw Guest House	3
Blue Bay Village	13
Bustani ya Eden	18
Hemingway's	15
Hotel Dante	9
Malob Guest House	4
Marijani Holiday Resort	1
Mt. Nyambene Meru Lodge	5
Ocean Sports	14
Plot 28 – Mrs Simpson's	19
SDA Youth Camp	12
Tiki House	6
Turtle Bay Beach Club	16
Villa Veronika Mwikali	8
Villas Watamu Resort	17
Watamu Beach	2

RESTAURANTS & BARS

Come Back Club	C
Happy Nightclub	D
Ujamaa	A
Watamu Stockists	B

Watamu Marine Park Office

WATAMU MARINE N.P.

Marine Park Beach

WATAMU

0   1 km

ing local people to guard nests. The same group also pays fishermen to hand in turtles that have become ensnared in fishing nets for rerelease into the sea, and individuals can sponsor a nest for guarding or a turtle for release. Turtle Watch is informed when nests they are gaurding hatch, so if you contact them, you may be able to go and see the baby turtles scuttling down the sand from their nest into the sea.

Getting to Watamu is easy, with frequent matatus making the run from Malindi. Buses and matatus between Mombasa or Kilifi and Malindi will drop you at the Gedi junction, leaving you to walk, hitch, wait for a matatu, or take a taxi for the last 6km. The road from Gedi and the junction is dead straight. Just before Watamu, it passes the settlement of **Timboni**, with three speed humps; just down an alley to the left (east) of the road by the third hump, the Women's Health Centre sells excellent handmade neem soap, using coconut oil and extracts derived from the neem tree. Introduced into this part of Kenya from India, the neem has numerous medicinal properties and its leaves are used as a natural mosquito repellent.

Coming into Watamu itself, the road from Gedi passes the **post office** (Mon–Fri 8am–12.30pm & 2–5pm) before it hits the beach road, which matatus scud up and down all the time. Just north of the junction, behind the post office is a **supermarket** with, next door, a very pricey internet office. If you continue up the beach road a little way past the turning for the supermarket, a road off to the right takes you into **Watamu village**. Just under a kilometre beyond that, on the left, a superb little **reptile park**, Bio-Ken (daily 9am–noon & 2–5pm; Ksh300), breeds green and black mambas for anti-venom, and houses a large collection of snakes, plus a few tortoises and a token croc, and you'll be guided round by someone who actually knows a bit about the scaly slitherers.

A right turn at the beach road junction brings you to four main resort hotels – *Blue Bay Village*, *Ocean Sports*, *Hemingways* and *Turtle Bay* – twenty or thirty private homes and, at the end of the narrow bar along which the road runs, the marine park ticket office. And that's Watamu.

Watamu village

Watamu village is a weird mixture of unhurried fishing community and frenzied Germanophile souvenir centre. The traditional rubs elbows with the pseudo-hip; Samburu and Maasai *morani* in full ochred splendour stand around waiting for photographers (and potential female customers); the Jamia Mosque has a notice which reads "All Muslims are Well Come for Prayers. No Trespass. By Management."

The centre of the village is a small **square** at the end of the tarmac road, with a couple of curio shops. The square's main purpose seems to be to allow the curio-stand owners to size up the latest punters as they arrive (German and Swiss tourists on their way to the *Watamu Beach Hotel* pass this way). But the pressure to buy is relatively subdued and after a couple of visits down here your face, and dress, become known and you can go about your business with a nod and a smile. Not that there's anything much to be done; apart from a few bars and restaurants, there's little to keep you from the beach. There's also no longer a bank in town – if you need to change money, the safari operators will usually oblige. Mama Lucy's supermarket sells, among other things, honey from Arabuko-Sokoke Forest (see p.523).

There are a couple of good **restaurants** on the road into the village. *Ascot Hotel* caters mainly to Italians, and has a superb wood-fired pizza oven, and wine at moderate prices; the *Dante* is usually very enjoyable, reasonably priced, and has cheap beer. For **bars and nightlife**, try the *Happy Night Club* and the *Come Back Club*, both popular and open till late. More dubious are *Watamu Stockists* and *Ujamaa Bar & Restaurant*, essentially pick-up joints posing as a *hoteli* and a pub; the former is very lively, sometimes bordering on rough, shows dodgy kung fu and B-movies and serves lightly spiced Swahili food.

Bicycle rental is offered by a number of outlets, especially in high season when it gets quite competitive (Ksh300–600 per day, depending on season and number of days). Bikes are a great way of getting to know Watamu, with the Gedi ruins and anywhere on the beach road easily reachable in thirty minutes or so.

Village accommodation

There's a wide variety of **accommodation** in the village itself – everything from humble and uninviting B&Ls to a pleasant holiday hotel. Bear in mind that some establishments either close or just tick over out of season, remaining open with a skeleton staff. As ever, the tour places are much cheaper if you book them as part of a package. The very central places risk being loud at night, thanks to nearby nightclubs.

Ascot Residence Hotel PO Box 348 ☎0122/32326, ℱ32239, ⓦwww.ascotresidence.com. Seems to occupy most of the middle of what you feel should be Watamu village. Looks like a very expensive hotel but is very good value, catering mainly for Italians: well-designed rooms with massive beds, fans and patios, and a large dolphin-shaped pool. Good breakfasts. It can become fairly lively in high season. ❸

Beachview Guest House PO Box 483 ☎ & ℱ0122/32383. A new place, clean and friendly, with a nice pool, a roof terrace with views of the beach, and spotless s/c rooms, each with a kitchen. ❷

Hotel Dante PO Box 183 ☎0122/32243. The one to go for if you're counting the pennies, though it doesn't have the *Veronika*'s shady garden or breakfasts. The pool is out of commission. Small, but clean and homely s/c rooms with fan. ❷

Malob Guest House PO Box 105 ☎0122/32260. A quiet B&L, a cheap but decent alternative to the *Dante* or *Villa Veronika*. ❷

Marijani Holiday Resort PO Box 282 Watam ☎ & ℱ0122/32448, ⓦwww.muenchen-info.com/kenia/watamu. A very pleasant surprise: friendly, welcoming, and informal Kenyan–German-run place, with superb rooms in two stylish houses. The rooms are very comfortable and exceptionally good value, with huge four-poster beds and spacious nets, fans, and spotless bathrooms (showers). All have fridges, some have kitchens or (oddly) sunbeds, and separate kitchens are available. There's even a three-bedroom family house in case you have a big enough family to fill it. Safe parking; bicycle rental (Ksh100 per hour); surfboards (Ksh300 per hour). Not on the beach, nonetheless highly recommended. ❸

Mt Nyambene Meru Lodge PO Box 23; no phone. Gloomy rooms, rather grubby (use a sheet sleeping bag if you have one), but dirt cheap. ❶

Tiki House PO Box 227 ☎0122/32444. A small place hidden away inside the village (the entrance is painted in zebra stripes), with three different-sized s/c rooms, and use of shared kitchen facilities. ❷

Villa Veronika Mwikali PO Box 57 ☎0122/32083. More or less a B&L, run by a Kikamba–Swiss couple, with fairly ordinary, rather pricey s/c rooms with fans, nets and fridges around a courtyard. Little touches, however, like the potted plants and table cloths, and the overall shady, intimate, almost Mediterranean feel of the place help to make it a favourite. ❷

Beach hotels and other accommodation

Several of these establishments focus on watersports, with diving and game fishing on offer. The big fishing competition in the first or second week of March can make accommodation scarce. But in May and June the hotels usually have excellent low-season rates, sometimes available only in packages of seven nights. The following listings are arranged from north to south. Matatus from Watamu, and some from Malindi, only go as far as *Turtle Bay Beach Club*, though they'll usually drop you further south if you ask.

Barracuda Inn PO Box 1085 ☎0122/32522, ℱ32296, ⓦwww.barracudainn.com. Unusual hotel with impressive *makuti*-vaulted reception on the shore of the Blue Lagoon, populated mainly by Italians, and well worth considering for an excellent-value getaway break (though note that the

THE COAST | Watamu

6

second-floor open-air dining terrace is inaccessible to wheelchairs). The beach outlook is only matched by the *Watamu Beach* and here the scene is more intimate. Ground-floor rooms are more spacious – all have telephones and AC. Nightclub, tennis and pool offered. **❻**

SDA Youth Camp PO Box 222 ☎ 0122/52265. Run by the Seventh Day Adventists mainly as a lecture place for schoolkids. For those on a really low budget, three simple if very run-down rooms in the main building and a *banda* with a hole in the roof (no nets or fans in any), and a basic but well-equipped kitchen. Dubious water and toilet facilities, but lots of camping space, all set in the dunes under coconuts and casuarinas with a view of the Blue Lagoon you could die for. **❶**

Aquarius Beach Hotel PO Box 96 ☎ 0122/32411, ☎ 32512, ⓦ www.aquariuswatamu.com; closed off season). Very pleasant if misleadingly named hotel, far from the beach. Comfy if slightly sombre rooms have AC plus ceiling fans. HB **❺** low, **❻** high.

Blue Bay Village PO Box 162 ☎ 0122/32626, ☎ 32422, ⓔ bluebay@africaonline.co.ke. Well-established, again mostly Italian-patronized all-inclusive holiday complex, with beautiful, palmy gardens and a good pool, marred by dire Europop muzak on tap. If you're going to stay, don't compromise – only the deluxe suites (twice the price) are worth the money (standard rooms lack AC). FB **❻**

Ocean Sports PO Box 100 ☎ 0122/32008, ☎ 32266, ⓦ www.oceansports.net. Slightly macho, impersonal place, whose reputation ("Open Shorts") has sailed before it for years. During holiday times it swarms with young "Kenya Cowboys" (White Kenyans) doing very much their own thing, and everything is priced in pounds sterling, but it's right on the beach, and allows camping. Blue marlin trophies gawp from the walls, rooms (fans and AC) are getting run down, and food is variable: chips with everything. Fine if you like a laddish atmosphere, but not particularly welcoming otherwise. HB **❻**

Hemingway's PO Box 267 ☎ 0122/32624, ☎ 32256, ⓦ www.hemingways.co.ke; reservations through Express Travel Group, PO Box 40433 Nairobi ☎ 02/334722–7, ☎ 334825. Sharing a plot with *Ocean Sports*, the contrast is great. From October to April, landing sharks and marlin is still high on the agenda, but this is a really top-class hotel where the atmosphere tends towards formal and there's nothing much for children. Rooms in the new wing are wonderful, with huge beds, direct-line telephones, fans and AC; all rooms have sea views. Lovely beach with a number of coral outcrops within swimming distance. Food is variable. Snorkelling, dhow cruises, creek fishing and day-trips. HB **❾**

Turtle Bay Beach Club PO Box 457 Malindi ☎ 0122/32003, ☎ 32268, ⓦ www.turtlebay.co.ke. Expertly run, all-inclusive holiday club, full of happy holidaymakers (mainly British, some German). Lots to do, lots to eat, and plenty to drink. Cramped gardens. Facilities include PADI diving and windsurfing schools, tennis, and a giant chessboard. Participates in community and environmental initiatives. You can have a one-day sample of club life for Ksh2000. **❻** low, **❼** high.

Bustani ya Eden PO Box 276 ☎ 0122/32262. Plain, comfortable chalet-style rooms, all s/c (hot and cold water) with fans, attached to a locally renowned (not to say notorious) bar-restaurant, with reasonably priced seafood and African dishes. No beach. B&B **❸**

Villas Watamu Resort PO Box 150 ☎ & ☎ 0122/32321. Some 400m from the road, a German-run Mediterranean-style self-catering villa development (not a *makuti* roof in sight) with a dramatic line in verandahs and a huge pool, as well as a restaurant. Not overly exciting, and no beach (15min walk), but security is good and the rates, for spacious AC accommodation with fully equipped kitchens, are very reasonable. Clean and proper. **❺**

Plot 28 – Mrs Simpson's PO Box 33 ☎ 0122/32023, ⓦ www.watamu.net. Barbara Simpson has been hosting word-of-mouth guests at her house near the shore for years, though she has now passed the management over to friends. She has eight rooms for rent, all s/c with hot water, fans and nets, some with solar-powered electricity. The beach here is deserted, with no beach boys for miles. Exceptional snorkelling trips can be arranged, although you can simply swim out 300m to the nearest reefs, as well as bird-watching trips to Arabuko-Sokoke Forest, the Galana (Sabaki) River and Mida Creek, and even turtle-watching expeditions. Meals are taken family-style, all together, and there's afternoon tea at at 4.30pm daily. Participates in community and environmental initiatives. The guest book contains comments like: "much better than home" and "I should have come here years ago". FB **❺**

Watamu Marine National Park and other excursions

The **Watamu Marine National Park** (daily 6am–6pm; $5, children $2; Warden PO Box 333 Watamu ☎0122/32393) stretches along the coast from the Blue Lagoon to Mida Creek. Its **total exclusion zone** for fishermen has not been greeted with rhapsody all round. On the other hand, tourists come in larger numbers every year and Watamu evidently hasn't gone far wrong in identifying their needs. This is prime **snorkelling** and **diving** territory, highly rated even by professionals, as the reef is in excellent condition and the water usually totally clear. Harmless **whale sharks** visit the area regularly, a highlight for any diver.

If you've never taken a swim before in a shoal of coral fish, the spectacle can be breathtaking: every conceivable combination of colour and shape – and a few inconceivable ones – is represented. It seems impossible that fish should take such forms. The ostentatious dazzle of some of them, especially the absurd parrot fish, can be simply hilarious. The most common destination is the "**coral gardens**", a kilometre or two offshore, where the boat drifts, suspended in 5–6m of scintillatingly clear water. Here, over a group of giant coral heads, where fish naturally congregate and where offerings of bread have obviously further encouraged them, you enter the unusual park. A booklet called *The Watamu Snorkeller's Guide* by Richard Bennett is available at *Hemingway's* Fishing Centre (Ksh350), with a map of the coral off Watamu, articles on the main types of fish, and suggested snorkelling routes. Alternatively, you can get a laminated colour chart of the most common coral fish to take along to identify them (Ksh200).

If you can **dive to the sea floor**, you'll get an intense experience of sharing the undersea world with the fish and the coral. Watch out for the small, harmless octopuses that stay motionless until disturbed and then jet themselves across the sea bed – they're brilliant masters of disguise, altering their form, texture and colour to fit their surroundings. Above, the boat's hull creates a deep shadow which, associated with food from the passengers, attracts thousands of fish. As you return to the surface, they move out of the way in mysterious unison, each one avoiding all the others in a kind of natural light show of fantastic beauty. If such adventures aren't your forte, the glass bottoms of the boats provide an alternative view – but it's often a rather obscure and narrow one.

For **visits to the park**, *Ocean Sports* and *Hemingway's* both run glass-bottom boat snorkelling trips (Ksh800, including park fee). Otherwise, you'll have to haggle with the boatmen along the beach, or outside the park headquarters and ticket office down at the south end of the Watamu road at Temple Point. Expect to pay Ksh600–800 per person (including park fees) for a two-hour trip in a glass-bottomed boat combining the coral gardens with a trip along Mida Creek. Masks, snorkels and sometimes fins are provided, but remember to take plenty of sun cream and a T-shirt. Boats wait until everyone has had enough of swimming, so will stay as long as you want to. A four-hour snorkelling trip for two should cost under Ksh2000, including park fees. From the park HQ, a track leads 500m or so to a pretty little beach at Temple Point, with some sunshades and small boats, by the entrance to Mida Creek.

Grouper and dolphin spotting – and Sudi island

At the entrance to Mida Creek is a famous group of caves. Known as the "**Big Three Caves**", these are the meeting place of a school of **giant groupers**, or rock cod, that once numbered only three but are now many more. Up to 2m long and weighing over 300 kilos, these are placid, stationary monsters – thankfully for anyone intrepid enough to dive down 3–4m for a closer look. The site is a good kilometre offshore and there are some moderate currents; boat trips normally only take place at the turn of neap high tides, when visibility, depth and currents give the optimum conditions. You need a permit from the park warden to visit the Big Three Caves – this is usually given freely.

Less predictable sea excursions are also arranged in quest of **dolphins**. These are fairly frequently seen offshore, but it's become accepted practice to pay only a nominal charge for the trip if you're unsuccessful. Check it out before committing yourself. A new excursion, offered by most hotels, is to **Sudi island** in Mida Creek, where a boardwalk takes you right through the mangrove swamps.

Diving and game fishing

From September to April, the **diving** possibilities are extensive at Watamu and you don't need to go far; most of the best dive sites are within thirty minutes of the beach. There are three dive centres, and if you're an experienced diver the best plan is probably to visit all of them and make your own assessment of their competence and suitability. Scuba Diving Kenya offers the lowest prices, but Aqua Ventures caters better for absolute beginners.

The sort of **money** involved, if you're a qualified diver, is something around $30 per dive including equipment, less (around $20 per dive) with your own equipment (excluding tanks and weights). There are reductions if you book a series of dives, and small supplements for night- and wreck-dives. If you haven't dived for a while, you should be asked to do a check-out dive (usually free) or a one-day refresher. Lastly, if you're a beginner, you can do either a one-day, one-dive course (around $70), or opt for the proper PADI course of four dives over five days – leading to certification and your log book – for around $250 inclusive (to "Open Water" level).

Aqua Ventures *Ocean Sports* PO Box 275 ☎ & ⓕ 0122/32420, ⓦ www.diveinkenya.com.
Scuba Diving Kenya Next to *Blue Bay Village*, PO Box 160 ☎ 0122/32099, ⓕ 32430, ⓦ www.scuba-diving-kenya.com.
Turtle Bay Beach Club PO Box 457 Malindi ☎ 0122/32003, ⓕ 32268.

Hemingway's Fishing Centre organizes sea-fishing trips (shark, marlin, sailfish and swordfish are among the game) at £225–300 (Ksh24,750–33,000/$315–420) a day for two or £350–500 (Ksh38,500–55,000/$490–700) for up to four people depending on season – individuals may be able to tag along with a group.

Malindi and around

When Vasco da Gama's fleet arrived at **MALINDI** in 1498, it met an unexpectedly warm welcome. The king of Malindi had presumably heard of Mombasa's attempts to sabotage the fleet a few days earlier and, no friend of Mombasa himself, he was swift to ally himself with the powerful – and dangerous – Portuguese. Until they finally subdued Mombasa nearly one hundred years later, Malindi was centre of operations for the Portuguese on the East African coast. Once Fort Jesus was built, Malindi's ruling family was invited to transfer their power base there, which they did, and for many years Malindi was virtually a ghost town as its aristocrats lived it up in Mombasa under Portuguese protection.

Malindi's reputation for hospitality to strangers has stuck, and so has the suggestion of sell-out. As a steadily growing development area for the cultivation of, deutschmarks and lire – and now euros – the town is slipping towards cultural anonymity: it can't seem to make up its mind whether it wants to be a Mombasa

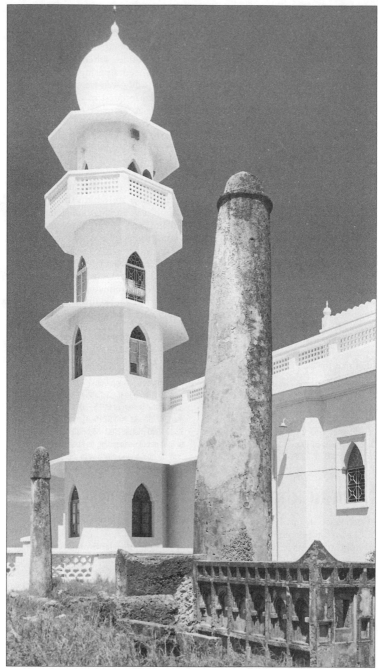

△ Pillar tombs, Malindi

or a Lamu. While retaining a Swahili atmosphere, which Mombasa has partly lost in urban development, it utterly lacks Lamu's self-contained tranquillity. Heavily dependent on tourism, the town has gone into decline economically as holiday-makers have turned their sights elsewhere. It's now making great efforts to reverse that trend, starting with a clear-out of the beach boys and hawkers that were such a nuisance to tourists in the past, and aiming to abandon its former dependence on the Italian package-tour market. Nonetheless, although Malindi makes an excellent base for visits to places like Gedi ruins and Arabuko-Sokoke Forest, it remains a town unashamedly geared towards beach tourism.

Consequently, whether you enjoy Malindi or not depends, at least in part, on how highly you rate the unsophisticated parts of Kenya, and whether you appreciate a fully fledged resort town for its facilities or loathe it for its tackiness. And of course it depends on when you're here. During the summer-holiday season (Malindi's best month, sea- and weather-wise, is August), as well as in December and January, the town can sometimes be a bit nightmarish. In a busy high season (and it's a while since Malindi has seen one) everything African seems to recede behind the swarms of window-shopping tourists and Suzuki jeeps. Even so, Malindi at its worst is still relatively placid compared with, say, Spain or the Greek islands, and off season (reduced here to the long rains only – April to June) can seem positively subdued, as if exhausted. At this time of year, when it is often damp and grey, with piles of seaweed washed ashore, Malindi has the air of a south of England beach resort: the faded muddle of an ageing seaside town – garnished with tropical plants. It was opened as a settlers' coastal escape in the 1930s, which in Kenyan terms is a very long time ago, and the last of the sun-wrinkled generation of a bygone era can still be seen walking on Lamu road.

Fortunately, Malindi has some important saving graces. Number one is the **coral reef**. The combined Malindi/Watamu Marine National Park and Reserve encloses some of the best stretches on the coast. Kisite-Mpunguti, on the south coast, and Kiunga, further north, are reckoned by some connoisseurs to be even better, but the Malindi fish have seen many more strange faces in masks and have become so used to humans that they swarm in front of you like a kaleidoscopic snowstorm. Malindi is also a **game-fishing** centre with regular competitions, and a bit of a **surfing** resort, too. Good-sized rollers steam into the bay through the long break in the reef during July and August and in early September, whipped up by the southerly monsoon winds which are likely to get you sand-blasted on the beach.

Despite the heavy reliance on tourism, Malindi still has some interest as a Kenyan town with an ancient history and a few places of interest other than its beach and reef. An interesting old Swahili quarter, one or two "ruins", a busy market, shops, *hotelis* and plenty of lodgings all compensate for the tourist boutiques, beauty salons and real estate agencies. The fact that Malindi has a broad range of places to stay within walking distance of the beach – and a broad range of places to eat and spend money within walking distance of the hotels – gives it a clear advantage over Watamu, Diani or the places more immediately north of Mombasa. As for the Italian package tourists, they have left the town with something that nowhere else in Kenya can boast: some of the best pizzas, pasta and ice-cream in the whole of Africa.

The best way to get around Malindi and its environs is **by bicycle** (several places rent bikes – see "Listings"). The flat countryside around Malindi is ideal and Gedi (90min) or Watamu (2hr) are easy objectives, with the guarantee that you'll be blown either there or back by the wind, depending on the time of year. The northern reaches of the wonderful Arabuko-Sokoke Forest are within easy reach too (see p.523).

Arrival, orientation and information

As far as practicalities go, Malindi is uncomplicated. Arriving from the south, the main **bus station** and matatu area is about ten minutes' walk south of town along the Mombasa road, from where you can walk, or take a taxi; a cab to the centre shouldn't cost more than Ksh100, or Ksh200–300 to the beach

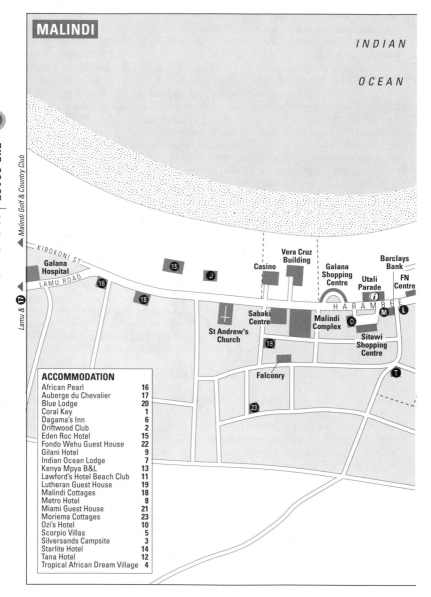

MALINDI

INDIAN

OCEAN

Malindi Golf & Country Club ◀

KIBOKONI ST

Galana Hospital

LAMU ROAD

Lamu & ⑰ ◀

Vera Cruz Building

Casino

Galana Shopping Centre

Utali Parade ⓘ

Barclays Bank

FN Centre

H A R A M B E E

Ⓜ Ⓛ

Sabaki Centre

Malindi Complex Ⓞ

Sitawi Shopping Centre

St Andrew's Church

⑲

Ⓣ

Falconry

㉓

ACCOMMODATION

African Pearl	16
Auberge du Chevalier	17
Blue Lodge	20
Coral Key	1
Dagama's Inn	6
Driftwood Club	2
Eden Roc Hotel	15
Fondo Wehu Guest House	22
Gilani Hotel	9
Indian Ocean Lodge	7
Kenya Mpya B&L	13
Lawford's Hotel Beach Club	11
Lutheran Guest House	19
Malindi Cottages	18
Metro Hotel	8
Miami Guest House	21
Moriema Cottages	23
Ozi's Hotel	10
Scorpio Villas	5
Silversands Campsite	3
Starlite Hotel	14
Tana Hotel	12
Tropical African Dream Village	4

hotels. Coming from Lamu or Garissa, you'll be dropped by the companies' booking offices in the town centre between the market and the messy, noisy high street where the cheapest of the B&Ls are found. The main focus of town is from here up to the misleadingly named Uhuru Gardens (a dusty patch of shade) and then north along the commercial Harambee Road. Malindi **airport** is barely 3km south of the town centre and you can walk into Malindi

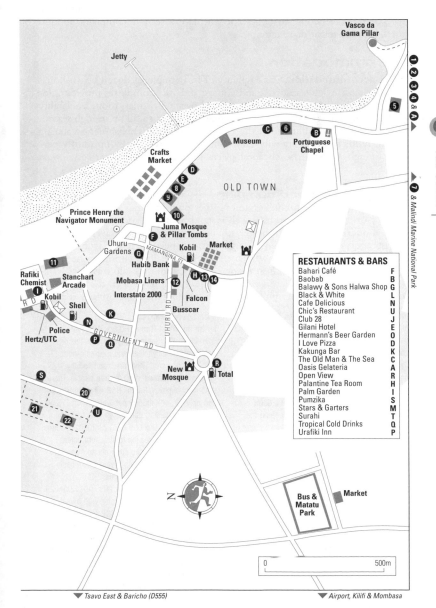

RESTAURANTS & BARS

Bahari Café	F
Baobab	B
Balawy & Sons Halwa Shop	G
Black & White	L
Cafe Delicious	N
Chic's Restaurant	U
Club 28	J
Gilani Hotel	E
Hermann's Beer Garden	O
I Love Pizza	D
Kakunga Bar	K
The Old Man & The Sea	C
Oasis Gelateria	A
Open View	R
Palantine Tea Room	H
Palm Garden	I
Pumzika	S
Stars & Garters	M
Surahi	T
Tropical Cold Drinks	Q
Urafiki Inn	P

Tsavo East & Baricho (D555)

Airport, Kilifi & Mombasa

in half an hour. Matatus heading to the main stage (which is about halfway between the airport and the town centre) will pick you up on the main road just outside the airport; otherwise, taxis charge around Ksh500 to beach hotels, or Ksh300 into town. The **tourist office** is on the first floor of the Malindi complex on Harambee Road (Mon–Fri 8am–4.30pm; ☎0123/20747, ℱ30429), and whilst it doesn't have any hand-outs, they're good for general advice, have a pretty exhaustive collection of brochures to leaf through, and keep records of hotel prices for Malindi, Kilifi, Tana River District and Lamu. They're also the people to contact if you have a serious complaint about a hotel, safari operator or restaurant.

Accommodation

As for **accommodation**, there's plenty of it: a couple of dozen beach hotels and all-inclusive "club resorts", and cottage and villa complexes providing for the crowds of high-season visitors, though over Christmas, room availability may be restricted. The cheap town lodgings, too, tend to fill up in high season, and also during Maulidi and at the end of Ramadan. Establishments catering essentially for tourists generally vary their prices seasonally, by up to fifty per cent, though as usual the cheapest places keep the same low prices all year round.

Budget rooms and camping

There are lots of cheap choices among the town lodgings, with some good traveller-oriented guest houses as well as standard **B&Ls**, and one or two more unusual offerings. The youth hostel, still much referred to in travel guides and tourist information, and even on signposts, has been well and truly defunct since the early 1990s. If you want to stay for some time, consider one of the bungalows at the *Lutheran Guest House*. Lastly, beware that solo travellers walking between town and the *Silversands Campsite* area have been the victims of muggings in the past, so it's probably worth avoiding that road on foot at night.

Blue Lodge PO Box 209; no phone. The tall blue building near *Fondu Wehu* is a standard B&L popular with locals, and the best of the ultra-cheap options. Most rooms with nets, some s/c. ❶
Dagama's Inn PO Box 5073 ☎0123/31942. Not bad if you can get one of the two front rooms with fans (both doubles), but somewhat overpriced, though they also have cheap beds in a dorm (Ksh300 per person), and you can sleep on the roof if they're full. B&B ❷
Fondo Wehu Guest House PO Box 5805; no phone. Charming family-run guest house, far from the beach but popular with *wazungu*. Seven good rooms with nets and fans, but not s/c. Very laid-back and always popular. B&B ❷
Gilani Hotel PO Box 380 ☎0123/20307. Above the restaurant, entirely overhauled and refreshed, but insufficiently to justify the prices. The four upstairs rooms at the front with balconies are the best and only reasons to stay here. B&B ❷
Kenya Mpya B&L Mama Ngina St, PO Box 209 ☎0123/30461. Big enough rooms in a four-storey block, not all s/c or with fans, with cleanish

sheets. Very cheap. ❶
Lutheran Guest House PO Box 409 ☎0123/21098. Set in a large garden, this has double rooms only (clean and mosquito-netted with fans, two s/c). There are also two fully equipped bungalows, each for four people. There's a no-alcohol policy. Rooms B&B ❷, bungalows bed-only ❸, or Ksh5500 per week or Ksh17,250 per month, including utilities.
Metro Hotel PO Box 609 ☎0123/20902. No fans, no nets – no good reason to stay here unless you're flat broke and the other cheap places are full. Beers are as cheap as they come. A basic sleaze-house, and not for women. ❶
Miami Guest House PO Box 998 ☎0123/31029. Spacious and very clean and airy, with a vast *makuti* roof – a posh kind of B&L with ten s/c and non-s/c rooms, but poor breakfasts. Use of kitchen if required. ❷
Ozi's Hotel PO Box 60 ☎0123/20218, ℱ30421. Very secure and friendly, popular with travellers, but none of the rooms are s/c, though all have ceiling fans. Next to mosque. Free laundry (five

items a day). B&B **❷**

Silversands Campsite 2km from the town centre, PO Box 422 ☎0733/802926. If you're prepared to forego a little comfort in order to camp on the beach then this is the only place (Ksh150 per person). Various *bandas* are also on offer, with great views over the ocean (far surpassing anything offered by the big hotels), but most are ancient, not s/c, and exceedingly grotty. They range from dingy huts with mosquito nets to more reasonable, small s/c chalets, and there are discounts if you pay for two or more days at once. There's a callbox and a snack and cold drinks store on the site, which is guarded and supervised, though there have nonetheless been reports of thefts from the *bandas* (not helped by sometimes unhelpful management), and the road from town is dangerous after dark. Many people pay a small fee

(Ksh200) to spend the day in the neighbouring *Driftwood Club*. **❷**

Starlite Hotel Mama Ngina St, opposite the market, PO Box 194 ☎0123/30424, ℗21225. A good choice if you've just arrived, with helpful staff and large s/c rooms with nets, wonky fans and balconies. Usually clean bar the odd sheet (which they'll replace), with a guarded car park. Surprisingly quiet given the central location. **❶**

Tana Hotel PO Box 766 ☎0123/20234, ℗31447. While still quite basic, it's clean and well-kept, with nets as well as fans, and very handy for buses to Lamu, Garissa or Mombasa. Rooms in the main block can be stuffy and hot, but there are slightly dearer s/c rooms around a quiet courtyard at the back. Good, busy restaurant with plenty of choice. **❶**

Hotels in the town centre and north

One of Malindi's main package-tour **hotels** (the *Blue Marlin*, where Ernest Hemingway once stayed) has gone under, leaving *Lawford's* and the *Eden Roc* as the main package hotels in town, with newer establishments scattered to the north, and behind the town centre to the west. All have pools, but watersports are very limited (you're usually picked up to be taken south of the centre). With no reef offshore, there's no snorkelling, and the current makes windsurfing only practicable for the experienced. Distances given are from the Uhuru Gardens in the town centre.

Hotel African Pearl 1.7km, PO Box 5835 ☎ & ℗0123/31612. Personable hotel run by an English–Kenyan couple, with cool, spacious rooms, plus two self-catering cottages (with kitchens, but no fridges) and a fully equipped gym. The best rooms are characterful and comfortable and have large verandahs. Hot water, nice grounds and a pool. Bar and restaurant (with *nyama choma*) at the front near the road. Safe parking. Prices negotiable; choose and bargain well and it's good value. B&B **❹**

Auberge du Chevalier (Kibokoni Riding Centre) 4km, PO Box 857 ☎0123/21273, ℗21030. An ideal retreat for horsey honeymooners, offering excellent rooms with remarkably robust beds constructed from solid tree trunks. There's a riding school attached to the hotel. B&B **❹**

Eden Roc Hotel 1.5km, PO Box 350 ☎0123/20480–1, ℗20333, ℮edenroc@africaonline.co.ke. Large old package-tour place, with a calm atmosphere a world away from the clutter of *Lawford's*, with huge and largely untended gardens stretching several hundred metres down to the dunes and the beach. Friendly if somewhat disorganized management. Good for children, with

a great playground, a kids' pool, and someone to look after them by day. No watersports on site (you're collected in the morning). Cheaper rooms with fans, and some suites. B&B **❹**

Lawford's Hotel Beach Club 300m, PO Box 20 ☎0123/20440–1, ℗20459. Very uninspiring package hotel, though with an ideal location if you want to stay in Malindi town centre, and the service is usually good. "Standard" rooms are mediocre; the "superior" ones are much nicer than the superficial surcharge would suggest. Dive centre. B&B **❺**

Malindi Cottages Harambee Rd, 1.5km, PO Box 992 ☎ & ℗0123/21071. Unexceptional cottages in gardens with a murky pool. The one-bedroom (two-person) cottages are rather basic but large enough, with gale-force fans and clean bathrooms, whilst the two-bedroom (four- to five-person) ones are self-catering with kitchens, small verandahs and huge sitting rooms.

Moriema Cottages 1.5km, PO Box 235 ☎0123/30816. Worth considering if you want to self-cater for a short time – each cottage has gas rings, sink and fridge – but it seems expensive. Cottages come equipped with fans, nets and carpet. B&B **❸**

Suitably protected by reefs, this is where the greatest development has taken place in the last few years, with one **resort hotel** after another reaching almost down to Casuarina Point. Taxis are cheap, and shouldn't cost more than Ksh300 to Casuarina Point, or Ksh200 to the *Driftwood*.

Coral Key Just before *Silversands Campsite*, 2km, PO Box 556 ☎0123/30717–8, ℻30715, ⓦwww.coralkeymalindi.com. Lively and sporty Italian-run resort, with rooms in 38 two-storey brick buildings, some designed for the disabled, but not all AC. Five pools, children's pools, and a fine Italian restaurant and pizzeria. Trendy Friday disco, plus gym, watersports, glass-bottomed boat, volleyball, horse riding, tennis, and a rock-climbing wall. They also run *Tsavo Buffalo Camp*, just outside Tsavo East (p.397). B&B ❺

Driftwood Club 2.2km, PO Box 63 ☎0123/30569, ℻30712, ⓦwww.driftwoodclub.com. Trading on its good food and established reputation among the Anglo–Kenyan community, this is an informal set-up, friendly and excellent value. Facilities include squash courts and a diving centre attached to the hotel. As well as the AC rooms in *bandas* around the grounds, there are "B Class" non-s/c but still very comfortable *bandas* for travellers on a lower budget who might feel like a semi-splurge but not want to go the whole hog. Also, three two-bedroom AC self-catering villas, and two beautiful but expensive luxury two-bedroom AC cottages with their own private pool but far from the beach and pretty isolated. Cheap day membership (Ksh200) entitles you to use the pool, bar and sunloungers. Half board is good value. B&B ❻

Indian Ocean Lodge 4km, PO Box 171 ☎0123/20394; reservations through Savannah Tours & Lodges, p.44. Near Casuarina Point, 300m down the turning from the main road to the marine park, on the left as you hit the bend, with no sign but a baobab tree by the black metal gates. Set in a small garden on a coral promontory overlooking the bay and a few ancient baobabs, this is a wonderful aberration, definitely a place for a honeymoon, and as expensive as it is exclusive. The lodge consists of just two two-storey Arabic-styled houses, containing five en-suite rooms. Each is huge and extremely luxurious, with magnificent balconies. Service is effortlessly classy, and the common dining room, lounge and terraces are delightfully fitted with antiques. On top of this, the management are refined and friendly. Small pool. Free snorkelling trips, and scuba diving and other excursions can be arranged. No seasonal rates. FB ❾

Scorpio Villas 1km, PO Box 368 ☎0123/20194, ℻21250, ⓦwww.scorpiovillas.com. An exceptionally well-conceived "village", dense with tropical vegetation. Each villa has a kitchen and dedicated staff and is divided into large rooms, each with its own bathroom and private patio. Eat "at home" or in the restaurant. Great for families and very cosmopolitan. Excellent value and bargaining is possible. B&B ❹

Tropical African Dream Village 2.7km, PO Box 939 ☎0123/20444, ℻31872, ✉tropical@swift-malindi.com. The result of a merger of two adjacent hotels, this is a huge all-inclusive *makuti* and tropical garden complex – an Italian-slanted holiday resort with a wide range of watersports available. Rooms are classed as "African", "British colonial" and "Swahili–Lamu", and are all spacious and pretty deluxe, with a nod to the styles suggested by the names. Maasai security guards, in traditional garb, keep out anyone with no specific business at the hotel. Wheelchair friendly with specially designed rooms for guests with disabilities. FB ❼

The Town

Other than the beach and the sea, strolling around town is the occupation of most of Malindi's temporary residents, and is not without its idiosyncratic rewards. The old part of Malindi is a half-hour diversion: interesting enough, even though there's nothing specific to see and few of the buildings date from before the second half of the nineteenth century. But the juxtaposition of the earnest and ordinary business of the old town with the near-hysterical *mzungu*-mania only a couple of minutes' walk away on Lamu Road produces a bizarre, schizophrenic atmosphere that epitomizes Malindi.

The town has an amazingly salacious reputation which is not entirely home-grown. Some European tour operators have in the past been quite inventive in their every-comfort-provided marketing strategies. In the immediate aftermath of the first AIDS-awareness crisis in the late 1980s, there was a massive slump in German tourism to Malindi, but memories are short, it seems; a quick glance at some of the town's bars at night is enough to convince you that the sex safari is back in full swing. Though Germans still come, in recent years Italians have dominated.

Archeologically, Malindi's offerings are scant. The two **pillar tombs** in front of the Juma (Friday) Mosque on the waterfront are fine upstanding examples of the genre, though the shorter one is only nineteenth century. This being Malindi, its appearance is usually described as "circumcised", though Islamic scholars on the coast tend to dispute the automatic phallic label applied by foreigners.

Malindi's other monuments are Portuguese. **Vasco da Gama Pillar** (1499), down on the point of the same name, makes a good target for a stroll. The **Portuguese Chapel** is a tiny whitewashed cube of a church now covered with *makuti*, whose foundations were laid in the sixteenth century on the site of a Portuguese burial. The most recent Portuguese bequest is the ugly 1959 **Monument to Prince Henry the Navigator** on the seaward side of Uhuru Gardens. These monuments however contrast uncomfortably with the "Vasco da Gama = Killer" and "Da Gama traitor" graffiti which appeared around town in 1998, on the 500th anniversary of da Gama's arrival in Malindi and which are still visible in some places.

Malindi also has a little zoo called the **Falconry** (daily 9am–5.30pm; Ksh300), with various birds, snakes, crocodiles and a giant tortoise. The former customs and excise building on the waterfront has been set aside for use as a town **museum**.

Crafts and shopping

There are two main outdoor areas to head for when you're in the buying mood. Most obvious is the **crafts market** on the seashore below the old town. Naturally, if you stray down here you'll be pounced upon, and leaving without buying anything isn't easy. On the other hand, you can also leave with all sorts of little free gifts if you strike the right bargain. The other area is the **Malindi Handicraft Co-operative**, 2.5km north of the new market and matatu stage (daily 8am–6.30pm), where you can see and freely photograph the wood-carvers at work. Note there's no bargaining at all in their shop, but you can discuss prices direct with the carvers and place specific orders.

Alternatively, for more expensive crafts and the possibility of browsing unhurriedly, try one of the **upmarket shops** along Harambee Road, just to the north of Uhuru Gardens. Prices are naturally very high, but visits are useful for checking comparative values and gauging top prices. At Rasani's Arcade, for example, they have lots of top-quality crafts and objets d'art, including old Lamu silver and jewellery as well as more familiar items available on the street. Al-Nur nearby has pricier but even finer pieces.

Snorkelling and watersports

Not unexpectedly, **snorkelling** ("goggling") and other **watersports** are Malindi's touristic *raison d'être*. Windsurfing, water-skiing, diving and deep-sea game fishing are all cheaper here than at the resorts around Mombasa. Malindi Bay is the main wave-surfing stretch and surfboards are available from all the tourist hotels in town. Unfortunately, all watery activities are marred somewhat by the Galana (Sabaki) River's annual outpouring of thousands of tons of prime red topsoil from the up-country plateaus. The cloudy water prevents the growth of coral north of Vasco da Gama Point and, ironically, Malindi Bay and the tour-group hotels dotted along it face out across dun-coloured sands to a muddy-brown seascape from November to January when the up-country short rains that carry the mud (exacerbated by deforestation along the river-banks) coincide with the southerly currents of the *kaskazi* monsoon. Murky as it is, this water is not unpleasant to swim in. Note that the shore can get very windy around September, and in June–July and November the beach becomes covered in seaweed – many hotels clear their beachfronts daily, though the sea-weed is clean and perfectly harmless, and in fact prevents erosion of the beach (clearing it is prohibited within the limits of the marine park).

Beach **access** is not a big problem, though the easiest place – and closest to the road – is on the south side of town at *Silversands* beach. The beach at the town centre and to the north is a good five to ten minutes' walk from the road. There are several public access points (see our map), and some hotels will allow use of their beach access for a small fee, which means you can use their pool and leave your towel and clothes on their guarded premises. *Driftwood*, for example, allows use of their pool and premises for Ksh200 per day (and it's also a good place to eat). The all-inclusive hotels charge much more (*African Dream* levies $25), but this does include lunch and free drinks.

Malindi Marine National Park

Trips out to the **marine park** (daily 7am–7pm; $5, children $2) can be arranged with the boat-trip salesmen who make their rounds of *Silversands Campsite* (and elsewhere) most mornings. Alternatively, make your own way down to the park office and very pretty beach at **Casuarina Point**, 5km from town, where you can choose your boat, captain and all. You should find a little room for discussion but won't be able to knock down prices much below the current going rate of Ksh1000 (excluding park fees) for two hours, especially at peak seasons. Note that your outing may be curtailed if you bargain too ruthlessly. Try to check out the condition of masks and snorkels, and insist on a set for each member of the party. Flippers aren't likely to be up to much (assuming they fit you). The six square kilometres of the national park take in the loveliest areas of coral garden, a couple of kilometres offshore, and the trip is worth every shilling you finally agree on. Unless you have a mortal fear of snorkelling or getting wet, don't bother with the **glass-bottomed boats** (about Ksh2500 for two hours), which generally have saucepan-sized windows. The **snorkelling** itself is sublime and, especially if you've never done it before, an experience which will stay with you forever. It's possible to **camp** (Ksh50 per person) at a site by the park office (PO Box 109 ☎0123/20845), where there are also a couple of *bandas* for those without tents (❷).

With your own or rented gear, of course, you could swim to the reef outside the boundaries of the marine park. All the beachfront hotels from Vasco da Gama Point south as far as *White Elephant Sea Lodge* (3.6km from the town centre) are to the north of the marine park, but the reef is anything from 300–800m offshore.

There are two **dive centres**, both also diving schools: Scubadiving Malindi, based at the *Driftwood* (☎0123/20155, ⓦwww.scubamalindi.tullfan.com), which is the cheaper of the two, and promises "special rates for backpackers"; and Blue-Fin, based at *Tropical African Dream Village* (☎0123/83449, ⓔblue-fin@libero.it). Both offer one-day introduction courses and five-day PADI Open Water qualification courses. Good diving zones to ask about include Shark Point, Tewa, Barracuda Point and Fargialla. Diving isn't generally possible during the rains, as they roughen up the sea beyond the reefs. For general advice and information about diving, see the Watamu account (p.534) and the boxes on p.506 and p.443.

The Marafa Depression: Hell's Kitchen

Northwest of Malindi, the **Marafa Depression** is the remains of a large sandstone ridge, now reduced by wind, rain and floodwater to a series of gorges, where steep gullies and narrow arêtes alternately eat into or jut from the main ridge wall. The colours of the exposed sandstone range from off-white through pale pinks and oranges to deep crimson, all capped by the rich tawny topsoil. It's particularly dramatic at sunset.

"Hell's Kitchen" is the common nickname for this pretty spectacle, though the locals call it *Nyari* – "the place broken by itself" – and tell numerous moralizing **stories** about its dark origins. The village that once stood here was favoured with the news of a forthcoming miracle, and the villagers were commanded to move on. All did so, except one old woman who refused to believe such nonsense. The village (and the old lady) disappeared soon after, leaving *Nyari*. Whether that was the miracle is not reported, but it's interesting to note how the story varies according to the teller – in Islamic circles "God talked through an angel" to deliver the message, while among traditionalists, "the gods informed a wise woman".

To get there, fork right at the end of Marafa village, and the canyon is about 500m along on the left, invisible until you're right at its edge. At the lip of the gorge, the first signs of commercialism – a small car park and a couple of seasonal souvenir stands – don't detract much from the site. It's easy to descend the steep path to the bottom and you can count on spending an hour or two exploring the natural architecture of what looks like an early *Star Trek* set. There's a scattering of *dukas* and *hotelis* among Marafa village's whitewashed, thatched houses, and one basic but very welcoming **hotel**, *Marafa Hell's Kitchen Guest House* (PO Box 6 Madina via Malindi; B&B ❷), at the end of the village, on the right facing the depression, with clean rooms, beds with mosquito nets, shared toilet and shower, and a pleasant garden. They can also arrange guided walks to Hell's Kitchen, and provide food given some notice. A **campsite** is also being set up in Marafa, and should be up and running by mid-2002.

With a vehicle, you might sensibly combine a visit to the Marafa Depression with the Arabuko-Sokoke Forest (see p.523) by crossing the Galana/Sabaki River – if the bridge across the river at Jilore (marked on some maps) actually existed. In its absence, take the road out of Malindi heading north (which involves a left turn on the other side of the Sabaki bridge) and from there go via **Marikebuni** and **Magarini**. You're looking at a round trip of about 80km, one which – given the vagaries of **public transport** – only drivers could manage in a day. Daily **buses from Malindi** to Marafa leave at 10am, 11.30am, 2.30pm, 3.30pm and 6.30pm.

Eating, drinking and nightlife

You're presented with two basic options for **eating** in Malindi. The first is ordinary *hoteli* fare supplemented by a scattering of seriously cheap Indian-style juice and samosa bars in the ramshackle eateries dotted about the market by the Lamu and Garissa bus company offices. The second is a much higher-price bracket that includes the big hotels and a small number of more lavish restaurants catering mainly for tourists. It's worth remembering that the main package market here is Italian, and some of the Italian-run places do make very fine Italian food, which can be a nice change if you've been living on a diet of *nyama choma* and pilau for weeks.

If you're buying your own food, **Malindi Market** is celebrated for fruit and vegetables – second, on the coast, only to Mombasa's. In the way of **delicatessen**, Malindi's speciality is smoked sailfish, absolutely delicious and available as a starter at several restaurants, including the *Driftwood* and *The Old Man and the Sea*. It can also be bought in packets from Baharini Ventures behind *I Love Pizza*, but they only sell it frozen in packets of a half or quarter kilo. They also sell honey from Arabuko–Sokoke Forest (see p.523). Cheese is available from the Dairyline Ventures cheese shop in Utali Parade on Harambee Road.

Basic eateries and bar-restaurants

Bahari Café Town centre near Juma Mosque. Good, tasty, cheap food, but often rather slow in coming.

Bawaly and Sons Halwa Shop Town centre near Uhuru Gardens. Highly deserving of a mention, a long-established spot famous for its excellent fragrant version of the gooey jelly (of which "Turkish Delight" is a dull relation), sold as far afield as Australia and the UK. The minimum order is half a kilo, but you can eat a small amount on the spot and have the rest wrapped up to take away. Tiny cups of spiced *kahawa* come free.

Café Delicious Government Rd. A small diner serving breakfasts, snacks and basic cheap meals.

Oasis Gelateria South side of Malindi, on the beach before *Silversands*. This big snack bar is very good – as much for the metropolitan touches like cheap soda water on tap, inexpensive home-made bread, delicious omelettes and espresso – as for the forty flavours of ice-cream. Sadly, it's part of a huge and hideous time-share complex which has occupied what remained of Silversands public beach. Open daily 9am–11pm in high season, 3–11pm in low.

Open View By Total roundabout on the outskirts of town. Good Kikuyu food including meat stews and *githeri*.

Palantine Tea Room Mama Ngina St, next to *Kenya Mpya B&L*. Large and busy local eatery; *ugali* or chips with everything. Cheap, and open round the clock.

Palm Garden Harambee Rd. Primarily a bar rendezvous for the sex trade, which also serves inexpensive if very variable curries and seafood. To avoid the prostitutes and rather hustly scene on the front patio, eat in the garden at the back. The pizzas are also worth avoiding. A good place to hit on Fridays and Mondays, when there's live music from the Seawaves band.

Stars and Garters Harambee Rd, next to Barclays Bank. Brash and busy *makuti*-roofed complex, especially popular for the English football screened on its satellite TVs in the bars. Good range of snacks, and fuller meals too, including Indian dishes, pasta, seafood and grills.

Tropical Cold Drinks Government Rd. The best place in town for fruit juices, with the *Al-Harani* across the street also good in case *Tropical Drinks* is closed.

Upmarket restaurants

Baobab, next to the Portuguese Chapel on the seafront. Morerately priced seafood (Ksh450–700), curries, Italian and African dishes (Ksh200–300), worth patronizing for cheap, cold beer and its sweeping views over the beach and fishing boats. Open daily 8am–11pm.

Bar Bar Sabaki Centre, Harambee Rd. A little piece of Italy in Kenya, with authentic and wonderful pizzas and pasta (Ksh250–350), and excellent espresso coffee, as well as pricier meat and seafood dishes. Minus points are the wall-to-wall Italian package tourists, Italian TV on at top volume most of the time, and live Italian music on Friday nights.

Bistrot Pizzeria Galana Shopping Centre, Harambee Rd. Italian-style tourist trap, with pleasant tables under shade outside.

Driftwood Club South of *Silversands* beach ☎0123/30569. Always a good place to eat, but the Ksh500 Sunday curry buffet is worth planning your day around, and prices in general are far from unreasonable. Starters include smoked sailfish and oyster bisque, and the salads and chocolate cake are good, too.

Gilani Hotel Smart, laid-back and very colourfully decorated eating-house, with a nice terrace on the street. Reasonably priced pasta, curries and seafood.

I Love Pizza ☎0123/20672. Very swish indeed, this is Malindi's classiest restaurant, and the pizzas and pasta dishes (Ksh250–500) are really not bad. They push their seafood, though, which is also good. Recommended. Open daily 11am–3pm & 6.30–11pm.

Surahi ☎0123/30452. A fancy Indian restaurant (rated one of Malindi's best) with a limited range of fairly expensive dishes and an uncluttered, cool dining room. Worth a try but not unmissable. Tues–Sun noon–3pm & 7–11pm.

The Old Man & The Sea ☎0123/31106. High-class, slightly quirky restaurant with an international menu (starters include smoked sailfish, sashimi and gazpacho), specializing in seafood and steaks, with some vegetarian dishes.

Drinking

After dark, especially in high season, Malindi throbs with action. For **live music** try *Mgandini* and *Come Back*, both off the airport/Mombasa road, on the left if coming from town. Out here too, you'll find the *Market Village* club, inside the Malindi Showground, where international African music stars some-times perform. The entrance price for all these places is nominal – except, of course, when they are hosting someone like Samba Mapangala. Drinks are also cheap and you can usually feast on a half kilo of *nyama choma*. It's always more fun to go with someone from Malindi – though you should have no worries at all about taking a taxi and going on your own.

Black and White Harambee Rd. A bar popular with (mainly black) local residents and (mainly white) tourists, which tries to have a different event or promotion (such as a free game of pool with every beer) each night of the week, and live music on Saturdays.

Chic's Restaurant Little food despite the name. A popular beer garden, at its liveliest on Saturday nights with local bands playing 7pm–midnight.

Hermann's Beer Garden Harambee Rd, next to *Stars and Garters*. Very German – come for a beer

and snacks such as bratwurst to start the evening. Fish soup, steaks and seafood available too. Open daily from 9am till the last customer leaves.

Kakunga Bar A very local dive with cheap beer, a juke box (almost extinct in Kenya) and a warm welcome.

Pumzika Cheap and friendly local hangout, open 24hr and currently playing mainly hip-hop.

Urafiki Inn Opposite *Palm Garden*, past Agip and the police station. Cheerful and unthreatening.

Nightclubs

Club 28 Harambee Rd, adjacent to *Eden Roc Hotel*. Originally exclusively for under-28s, this small nightclub has its ups and downs.

Fermenta Disco Bar Galana Shopping Centre from 8pm. Expensive Italian "piano bar" which plays Euro-trash when not inflicting karaoke.

Hotel discos A speciality of the south side of Malindi, usually in a different hotel each night

through the week, but rather insipid affairs out of season and the music's rarely anything to rave about. When you're weary of bopping, the Casino Malindi has free entry to anyone playing (daily 9am–3.45am; Ksh500 if not playing). It's almost worth playing a few hands or spins just to watch the grim-looking Italian bosses tending their novice Kenyan croupiers.

Listings

Airlines Cheapest flights to Lamu are Kenya Airways (Utali Parade, PO Box 634 ☎0123/20237 or 20574; airport ☎0123/20192 or 20971), with daily flights costing Ksh3661 one way. They also run between one and three flights daily to Nairobi. Much more expensive are the daily Airkenya flights (office at Galana Shopping Centre, PO Box 548 ☎0123/30808; $70 to Lamu, Ksh5385 to Nairobi as quoted by the airline), which also flies daily to Mombasa (Ksh2000). You can book flights at their offices, or at any travel agency, though the less reputable of these will charge you more.

Banks Barclays bureau de change (Mon–Fri 9am–4.30pm, Sat 9–11am), KCB and Standard Chartered (both Mon–Fri 9am–3pm, Sat 9–11am). Standard Chartered and Barclays have 24hr ATMs for Visa cards. Postbank is in the Malindi Complex on Harambee Rd. The casino changes money at any time, but at bad rates. Dollar forex bureau should be open in the FN Center on Harambee Rd by the time you read this.

Bicycle rental Available everywhere. *Silversands Campsite* is an old hand and its bikes cost a very reasonable Ksh200 per day or Ksh1200 per week.

Other places may have better bikes, but prices are higher.

Books Nimmy's Books at Sitawi Shopping Centre on Harambee Rd has a few new and used imported titles.

Car rental Galu/Southern Cross Safaris, Malindi Complex (℡ 0123/20493, ℱ 30032); Henson's Tours, Vera Cruz Building, Harambee Rd (℡ 0123/30581, ℱ 31943, ℮ info@hensonsafaris.com); Hertz/UTC, Tana Building, Harambee Ave (℡ 0123/30443).

Horse riding Try the Kibokoni Riding Centre north of town (see p.541). You'll pay around Ksh800 an hour, including a guide, for short bush rides in the vicinity. Beginners can go on a leading rein.

Hospitals The Galana Hospital on Lamu Rd (at the north end of town on the road to Lamu, just past *Sultan Villas*; ℡ 0123/ 30575) is the best in an emergency. Alternatively, Malindi District Hospital in Hospital Rd (℡ 0123/20490–1) is pretty decent.

Immigration A decrepit-looking office on the waterfront road by the Juma Mosque (℡ 0123/20149).

Internet access Africa on Line, Galana Centre; Malindi Connections, Malindi Complex; Swift Global, Stanchart Arcade; *Palantine Tea Room*, Mama Ngina St.

Pharmacy Malindi Chemists, Sitawi Shopping Centre; Rafiki Chemist, Noorani Arcade, Harambee Rd, next to *Palm Garden*.

Post and telephone office The main post office is just off Harambee Rd opposite the police station (Mon–Fri 8am–5pm, Sat 9am–noon), and has a good *poste-restante* service. The adjacent telephone office is open Mon–Fri 7am–12.30pm & 2–6pm. They sell phone cards for the cardphone, which is cheaper to use than placing a call through the operator. There's also a fax machine.

Supermarkets There are several small places in the shopping arcades up Harambee Road in the town centre, the best – with the widest range – being Sona at Galana Shopping Centre. Try also the Italian Supermarket at the Sabaki Centre.

Taxis Now designated with a yellow stripe to show that they are licensed; you'll be offered their services everywhere, or you can call one (Baobab Taxis ℡ 0123/30499), who promise "negotiable rates" (though you'll find their fixed rates posted opposite the Portuguese Chapel on the baobab tree that serves as their HQ).

Travel agents A good scattering along Lamu Road and the seafront all offer similar services, including train bookings. As well as the companies listed under "Car rental" above, try North Coast Travel on Harambee Rd near Barclays Bank (℡ 0123/30312), or Scorpio Enterprises at *Scorpio Villas* (℡ 0123/31390).

Moving on from Malindi

The main **bus and matatu park** is a ten-minute walk south of town along the Mombasa road, with frequent services to Gedi, Watamu, Kilifi and Mombasa, and infrequent local matatus and buses for points inland. Details of these services are given throughout the text. In addition, some matatus for Watamu leave from the centre of town by the market in Mama Ngina Road.

Flying to **Lamu** (cheapest on Kenya Airways from Malindi; Ksh3611 one way, Ksh6160 return) is an experience not to be missed, but bus services are the much cheaper alternative. Services start off from Mombasa, and pass by their Malindi booking offices in the centre of town by the market (marked on our map) at around 8.30am each day. The companies serving Lamu are TSS (no office), Mombasa Liners (℡ 0123/31502) and Interstate 2000 (℡ 0123/30850). It's advisable to buy your ticket for Lamu the day before – otherwise you have an exceedingly uncomfortable standing-up experience to look forward to. On a number of occasions throughout the 1990s, buses were subject to **bandit raids** and in February 1999, one bus was randomly sprayed with bullets in a failed attempt to get it to stop, injuring two passengers and its armed escort. Security has now been stepped up, with armed soldiers on board, and banditry along the road has eased off. At any rate, always check out the current situation before deciding whether to travel by bus.

If you're **driving** your own vehicle, you'll definitely need an armed escort from Minjila junction just south of Garsen to Mokowe, the port for Lamu (the bargainable starting price for two soldiers is Ksh1000), if not from a roadblock north of Malindi at Gongoni. Note that you have to leave your vehicle at Mokowe, in any case, and catch a boat to Lamu (Ksh40 per person).

Malindi to Lamu

Installed by a window on the bus, you can fully appreciate the flat, gentle, dull landscape, sometimes brown and arid, but more usually grey-green and swampy with plenty of large birdlife, which opens out as Malindi's low hills are left behind.

When the scenery palls, the bus trip is enlivened by the other passengers and by stops at the Tana River Delta area towns of **Witu** (see p.552), Mkunumbi and sometimes Mpeketoni for *chai* and a bite to eat. Occasional flashes of colour – the sky-blue cloaks of **Orma** herders or the red, black and white of shawled **Somali** women – break up the journey, along with wonderful **birdlife** and **wild animals** too: giraffe and antelope, notably waterbuck, even the odd elephant if you look hard enough. If you're driving yourself, you could also make a diversion to the **Tana River Primate National Park**.

The new Chinese-built road is fast tarmac from Malindi to Garsen. Beyond Minjila – 7km south of Garsen at the junction for the Garissa and Lamu roads (the old road to Lamu from Garsen itself, marked on all maps, was washed away by El Niño) – the tarmac is rough and continues for only 20km, before trundling along the mud-and-*murram* New Garsen Causeway, hurriedly rebuilt in the aftermath of the 1997–8 floods. This was scheduled to be surfaced, too (which would vastly reduce the risk of hold-ups), but the Chinese pulled out, complaining of inadequate security provided for them after a spate of *shifta* attacks.

Garsen itself isn't anyone's favourite place, and something of a dead-end now that the Lamu road bypasses it. There's no electricity or bank, but there is petrol, a post office and police station. There are a couple of lodgings and no shortage of *hotelis*. In season, incidentally, Garsen's mangoes are reckoned to be some of the best and cheapest in Kenya.

Tana River Primate National Park

No charges at present.

Inland, north of Garsen, is the **Tana River Primate National Park** – main refuge of two of Kenya's rarest and most beautiful monkeys. It isn't easy to get to without your own vehicle, but buses heading for Garissa occasionally stop in Mnazini village, otherwise it's a six-kilometre walk from the main road (so long as the area isn't flooded). If the district is flooded, you'll almost certainly find yourself being taken by poled canoe from just down the Mnazini track all the way to the village itself; it takes about an hour. Regarding **security**, the reserve itself appears relatively secure, and is guarded by a special team of armed KWS rangers. However, the village of **Wenje**, just to the north, has acquired local notoriety as the base for a gang of bandits which operates in the area – take local advice if you're driving.

Mnazini is a fine, coastal-style village beneath mango trees. There are no lodgings but *hotelis* will take you in for the night once you've cleared it with the sub-chief and the headman. One of the village shops also has most of what you're likely to need for a few days' stay in the reserve. Beyond Mnazini, there's nothing in the way of food but occasional fruit and garden vegetables.

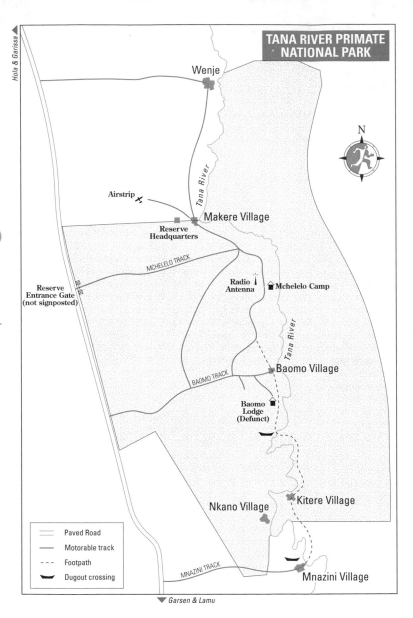

TANA RIVER PRIMATE
NATIONAL PARK

N

Hola & Garissa

Wenje

Tana River

Airstrip

Makere Village

Reserve
Headquarters

MCHELELO TRACK

Radio
Antenna

Mchelelo Camp

Reserve
Entrance Gate
(not signposted)

B8

Tana River

BAOMO TRACK

Baomo Village

Baomo
Lodge
(Defunct)

Nkano Village

Kitere Village

Paved Road
Motorable track
Footpath
Dugout crossing

MNAZINI TRACK

Mnazini Village

Garsen & Lamu

Nobody in the area knows Tana River Primate National Park by that name.
Locals all refer to **Mchelelo**, the site of the primate research headquarters.
The twelve-kilometre walk to get there involves two river crossings over the
Tana's meanders, and there's no way you'd find the route through the **bush**
and **gallery forest** unguided. Pokomo **guides** are happy to help and not
hustling.

Depending on water levels, you may find you can wade across. If you need a boat, it shouldn't normally cost anything. You enter the forest at Kitere and walking thereafter becomes much more pleasant in the cool shade.

Reserve practicalities

Mchelelo Campsite is small, secluded, and ravishingly pretty, with a shower and long-drop. It's the site of a National Museums of Kenya research camp and the primatologists here are not used to visitors. If you don't have a letter from the NMK (and preferably an introduction and advance warning sent ahead) you may not be able to stay here. In that case, they are likely to direct you on to the park headquarters at **Makere**.

If you're **driving**, the Baomo or Mchelelo tracks to the river are the ones to use, though the latter doesn't seem to be signposted from the road. The track to Baomo is indicated on the road, but *Baomo Lodge* itself, while it still appears on some maps, is abandoned.

If you're lucky, you'll be made reasonably welcome at Makere, or at least allowed to camp. It has to be reiterated, however, that they don't have organized facilities for visitors – and you may even be given a section of fully armed rangers on the anti-poaching force to accompany you, in military fashion, as you walk the paths looking for monkeys and watching the area's superb birdlife. One or two young guides from Makere village will also help to locate the primates, as will the KWS rangers.

Wildlife

The reserve's protected inhabitants include **Tana River red colobus** and **Tana River crested mangabey** monkeys, both extremely rare and vulnerable. These species occur more commonly in the rainforests of western Uganda and Congo, and are indicative of the time, centuries ago, when these great forests covered the whole of Africa – west to east. In the meantime, continued encroachment on the forest threatens both species of monkey; the colobus very rarely leaves the trees.

Your chances of seeing groups of both monkeys are good. The forest areas are fairly restricted, even within the reserve, and it's not difficult to find them in a day or two. Other wildlife in the area includes blue monkeys, baboons, Grevy's and Burchell's zebra, oryx, lesser kudu, various squirrels and even lions, giraffe and buffalo. On the east side of the park you can see elephants, and there's also a small seasonal population of the endangered Hunter's hartebeest, or hirola, here. At one time it was possible to make raft and boat trips on the sluggish river, dodging large numbers of hippos and crocodiles, but such adventures haven't operated as commercial safaris for years (see overleaf for details about something like this further downstream). You're likely to find local people willing to take you.

Around the Tana Delta

If you have a 4WD vehicle or a little patience, the trip north to Lamu can be stretched over several days, with time to explore the fascinating region around the **Tana Delta**: on the west side, the Pokomo village of **Ngao** and other villages on the river itself; on the east, a dune-shrouded coast and **Kipini**, with the Swahili ruins of **Ungwana**, **Shaka** and **Mwana** all within 12km. Do, however, make careful enquiries about any recent bandit attacks in the region before going. If you're genuinely interested, try to see the warden of the museum at Fort Jesus for further information.

As yet almost wholly untouched by tourism, the region to the north of the Tana River Delta – centred around the little fishing village of **Kipini** at the mouth of the Tana and the larger market centre of **Witu**, 21km inland – more than repays the slight hassle of finding a room. Though it's hard to believe, with its lack of electricity, tap water or telephones, **Kipini** was once the headquarters of Tana River District, before it was shifted to Hola at Independence. Nowadays, its erstwhile role is evident only in a mixed population of Orma, Pokomo, Bajuni, Somali and Swahili, who get by on fishing, small-scale farming and some herding. Unfortunately, things look set to change – somebody is selling off communal land to developers, and prime beach front is going cheap. Big-time investors are moving in, and have also tried vast agricultural schemes, most failing, but displacing many pastoral people in the process. The villagers have been examining proposals to protect the Tana's ecosystem by putting it under the Ramsar Treaty (which obliges governments and others to protect wetlands of ecological importance), as well as to combat illegal trawlers off the coast, which damage corals, kill turtles and have already caused the disappearance of swordfish. To get a closer look, you can organize local boat rides up the Tana from Kipini – passing crocodiles, and hundreds of birds, such as malachite and pied kingfishers, African fish eagles, and goliath herons. Further upstream is the Ozi Forest.

To get to Kipini, leave the Lamu bus at Witu, where there's a connecting matatu to the village. There are no formal **lodgings**, but you should be able to stay with a local family for the price of a B&L; plenty of cheap, wholesome Swahili *hotelis* serve delicious *dalasini* cinnamon tea. Alternatively, you could stay in **Witu** (again, no formal lodgings, though the German NGO, GASP, has an excellent guest house which it may let you use), and rent a **bicycle** locally for getting around. From Witu, **buses** for Malindi pass through at around 10am, with Lamu-bound services arriving a little earlier. There are few if any vehicles along the road after 2pm.

You can **stay** neart the delta mouth at the expensive *Tana Delta Camp* in the dunes near the ocean (reservations also through Bush Homes of East Africa, p.42; closed April–June ❾), with six "luxury" double tents and one *banda*. The place comes highly recommended: there are boat trips and excellent guided walks available (including mud baths if you're in the mood), as well as canoes and water-skiing, but the price ($285 per person per night) is high.

The Lamu Archipelago

A cluster of hot, low-lying desert islands tucked into the coast near the Somalian border, **Lamu** and its neighbours have a special appeal that many find irresistible. While each town or village has its own distinct character, together they epitomize a separate spectrum of Swahili culture. For although the whole coast is – broadly – "Swahili", there's a world of difference between these islands and the coconut beaches of Mombasa and Malindi.

To a great extent the islands are anachronisms. Electricity arrived here only a few decades ago, there are still almost no motor vehicles, and life moves at the

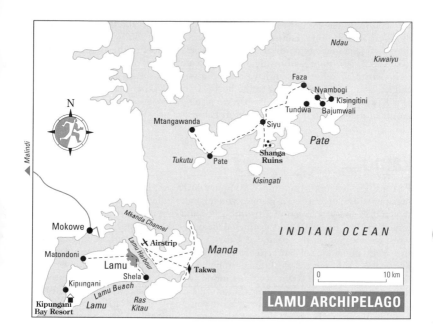

pace of a donkey or a dhow. Yet there have been considerable internal changes over the centuries and Lamu itself is now changing faster than ever. Because of its special position in the Islamic world as a much-respected Islamic teaching centre, Saudi Arabian direct aid has poured into the island: the hospital, schools and religious centres are all supported by it. At the same time, there have been efforts to open up Lamu beyond its present tourist market, which so far has encompassed only low-budget travellers and short-stay air safaris. Rich foreign sponsors are eagerly sought and several lodging houses have been set up with what is bluntly called "white-girl money". Islanders are ambivalent about the future. A string of hotels along the beach, a bridge to the mainland – all seems possible, and all would contribute to the destruction of Lamu's timeless character. Some up-country officials working here might not disapprove – with only two bars, the town is not a popular posting.

But the damage that would be done goes further than spoiling the tranquillity. The Lamu Archipelago is one of the most important sources for knowledge about pre-colonial Africa. **Archeological sites** indicate that towns have existed on these islands for at least 1200 years. The dunes behind Lamu Beach, for example, are said to conceal the remains of long-deserted settlements. And somewhere close by on the mainland, perhaps just over the border in Somalia, archeologists expect one day to uncover the ruins of Shungwaya, the town which the nine tribes that comprise the Mijikenda people claim as their ancestral home. The whole region is an academic's delight, a source of endless confusion and controversy, and a place where there is still real continuity between history and modern life.

At least for the present, the islands survive. **Lamu island** itself, most people's single destination, still has plenty to recommend it, despite a serious fire in 1993 and the inevitable sprouting of TV satellite dishes. **Manda**, directly opposite, is little visited except for the lifeline it provides with the outside world – the local airstrip. **Pate island** (see p.576), accessible by dhow or motorboat, makes a fascinating excursion if you have a week or more in the area. **Kiwaiyu** (see p.582), not quite within the archipelago, but exotic and alluring enough to be worth the effort if you have time, is a wisp of a beach island 9km long and less than 1km across, lying to the northeast of the other islands. Those who visit Kiwaiyu normally arrive by private plane, but you can easily reach it by grouping together to charter a dhow in Lamu.

Lamu

Perhaps best left until the end of your stay in Kenya, **LAMU** may otherwise precipitate a change in your plans as you're gently lulled into a slow rhythm in which days and weeks can pass by unheeded and other objectives can easily be forgotten. For many people, Lamu's deliciously lazy atmosphere is the best worst-kept secret on the coast. Eyes, ears, tongue and nose get a comprehensive work-out here, so that actually *doing* anything is sometimes a problem – like walking through treacle. Hours can be blissfully spent on a roof or a verandah just watching the town go by, its mood swinging effortlessly from one of the day's five prayer calls to the next, from tide to tide, and from dawn to dusk.

If this doesn't hit the right note for you, you may actually rather hate Lamu. Hot, dirty and boring are adjectives that have been applied by perfectly sane, pleasant people, and you can certainly improve your chances of liking the place by not coming here at the tail end of the dry season, when the town's gutters are blocked with dried refuse, the gardens in the houses wilt under the sun and the heat is sapping.

Lamu is something of a **myth** factory. Conventionally labelled "an old Arab trading town", it is actually one of the last viable remnants of the **Swahili civilization** that was the dominant cultural force all along the coast until the arrival of the British. In the late 1960s and early 1970s, Lamu's unique blend of beaches, gentle Islamic ambience, funky old town, and host population well used to strangers, was a recipe which took over where Marrakesh left off. It acquired a reputation as Kenya's Kathmandu: the end of the (African) hippie trail and a stop-over on the way to India. Shaggy foreigners were only allowed to visit on condition they stayed in lodgings and didn't camp on the beach.

Not many people want to camp out these days. The proliferation of good, reasonably priced lodgings in the heart of the town encourages an ethos more interactive than hippie-escapist. Every other traveller you've met along the way seems to end up here, in an ever-recycling community. Happily, travellers and locals cross paths enough to avoid any tedium – though for women travelling without men, this can itself become tedious (see p.569). Having said that, there can hardly be another town in the world as utterly unthreatening as Lamu. Leave your room at midnight for a breath of air and you can stroll up a hushed Harambee Avenue, or tread up the darkest of alleys, where you need fear absolutely nothing. This is an exhilarating experience.

Some history

The undeniably **Arab** flavour of Lamu is not nearly as old as the town itself. It derives from the later nineteenth century when the **Omanis**, and to some extent the **Hadhramis** from what is now Yemen, held political and cultural sway in the town. The first British representatives in Lamu found themselves among pale-skinned slave-owning Arab rulers. The cultural and racial stereo-types that were subsequently propagated have never completely disappeared.

Lamu was established on its present site by the fourteenth century, but there have been people living on the island for much longer than that. The fresh-water supplies beneath Shela made the island very attractive to **refugees from the mainland** and people have been escaping here for 2000 years or more – most recently in the 1960s, when Somali secessionists and cattle-raiders caused havoc. It was also one of the earliest places on the coast to attract settlers from the Persian Gulf; there were probably people from Arabia and southwest Asia living and intermarrying here even before the foundation of Islam.

In 1505, Lamu was visited by a heavily armed **Portuguese** man-of-war and the king of the town quickly agreed to pay the first of many cash tributes as protection money. The alternative was the sacking of the town. For the next 180 years Lamu was nominally under Portuguese rule, though the Portuguese favoured Pate as a place to live. In the 1580s, the **Turkish** fleet of Amir Ali Bey temporarily threatened Portuguese dominance, but superior firepower and relentless savagery kept them out, and Lamu, with little in the way of an arse-nal, had no choice but to bend with the wind – losing a king now and then to the Portuguese executioners – until the Omanis arrived on the scene with fast ships and a serious bid for lasting control.

By the end of the seventeenth century, Lamu's Portuguese predators were vanquished and for nearly a century and a half it had a revitalizing breathing space. This was its **Golden Age**. Lamu became a republic ruled over by the *Yumbe*, a council of elders who deliberated in the palace (now a ruined plot in the centre of town), with only the loosest control imposed by their Omani overlords. This was the period when most of the big houses were built and when Lamu's classic architectural style found its greatest expression. Arts and crafts flourished and business along the waterfront made the town a magnet throughout the Indian Ocean. Huge ocean-going dhows rested half the year in the harbour, taking on ivory, rhino horn, mangrove poles and cereals. There was time to compose long poems and argue about language, the Koran and local politics. Lamu became the northern coast's **literary and scholastic focus**, a distinction inherited from Pate. Women achieved a higher status than in the past, though ironically the best-known Lamu woman of the time, the poet **Mwana Kupona**, is famous for her "Advice on the Wifely Duty" given to her daughter. The house where she lived for a while is up behind the fort.

For a brief time, Lamu's star was in the ascendant in all fields. There was even a famous victory at the **Battle of Shela** in 1812. A combined Pate–Mazrui force landed at Shela with the simple plan of capturing Lamu – not known for its resolve in battle – and finishing the construction of **the fort** which the Nabahanis from Pate had begun a few years earlier. To everyone's surprise, par-ticularly the Lamu defenders, the tide had gone out and the invaders were mas-sacred as they tried to push their boats off the beach. Appalled at the overkill and expecting a swift response from the Mazruis in Mombasa, Lamu sent to Oman itself for **Busaidi** protection and threw away independence forever. Had the eventual outcome of this panicky request been foreseen, the Lamu *Yumbe* might have reconsidered. Seyyid Said, Sultan of Oman, was more than happy to send a garrison to complete and occupy Lamu's fort – and from this toehold in Africa, he went on to smash the Mazrui rebels in Mombasa (see p.451), tak-ing the entire coast and moving his own sultanate to Zanzibar.

A stepping stone in the plans of the mighty, Lamu gradually sank into eco-nomic collapse towards the end of the nineteenth century as Zanzibar and Mombasa grew in importance. In a sense, it has been stagnating ever since. The building of the Uganda railway from Mombasa, and the banning of slavery, did nothing to improve matters for Lamu in economic terms, and it seems that decline has kept up with the shrinking population. However, the new **resettlement programme** on the mainland at Lake Kenyatta (Mpeketoni) is already spinning off new faces to Lamu, and a revived commercialism from up-country has taken root around the market square.

Arrival, orientation and information

The **bus trip** ends at **Mokowe** on the mainland, where a chugging *mtaboti* (motorboat bus; Ksh40) takes you out around the creek for the thirty-minute ride to the town. They're timed to coincide with the buses, though there are other less frequent services throughout the day. Grab your luggage, ignore the chaotic boat touts pulling you every which way, and jump on the boat which seems fullest – they all go to Lamu. If you **drive** to Lamu yourself, you'll have to leave your vehicle in the car park where it will, by all accounts, be safe; tipping the *askari* beforehand may improve security further. Don't be misled by boys who try to sell you a *mtaboti* charter, just wait for the next public *mtaboti* with everyone else. **Flying** in, planes land on Manda island, across the harbour directly opposite the town. The short boat trip from here (Ksh100 to Lamu Town on boats run by the airlines, or to Shela on boats run by *Peponi Hotel*, in principle for customers only) gives a wonderful panorama of Lamu's nineteenth-century waterfront.

Whichever way you arrive, you'll inevitably be met by a bevy of **beach boy hustlers** offering to take your baggage and guide you to a hotel. Be advised that if you go with them, they'll claim at least a third of your room rent from the hotelier, which will mean a fifty percent mark-up on your bill. Some hotels refuse to co-operate with these beach boys, and we recommend staying in them (specified in our accommodation listings). Unfortunately, however, it's very difficult to avoid the "services" of these characters. They'll certainly not allow you to stand around on the quayside looking at your map and working out which hotel you want to go to and how to get there. You may therefore find it easier just to let one of them guide you to a hotel (you can always change places the following day, when the hustlers are not around). If you ask to be taken to a hotel that refuses to co-operate with the beach boys, they will try all sorts of lies to avoid taking you there – telling you that it's closed, or taking you to an unmarked hotel and trying to persuade you that it's the one you want. If you're determined, however, you can avoid the beach boys by knowing in advance how to get to your preferred hotel from the jetty, by telling them firmly but politely that you do not want their help (they will probably follow you anyway), and by announcing to the receptionist on arrival that they have followed you against your wishes and that you will not stay if the hotel intends to pay them commission and add it to your bill. The beach boys also sell *bangi* – though you'd be very ill-advised to buy it from them (set-ups are common) – and they will be keen to offer their services as **guides**. If for some reason you feel that you need a guide in Lamu, your best bet is to ask other travellers to recommend one, or visit the **Lamu Tour Guides Association**, whose members carry small white laminated ID cards. You'll need to tell any guide you engage which places you would like to visit and agree a fee: Ksh200–300 per day would be an acceptable wage.

When discovering Lamu for yourself, you shouldn't get lost too easily if you remember that **Harambee Avenue** – the Usita wa Mui or Njia Kuu – runs parallel to and 50m behind the waterfront, and that streets leading into town all climb slightly uphill, but getting lost is rather wonderful anyway. In the listings that follow, the terms Mkomani and Langoni are quite often used. These are the two main parts of Lamu town – Mkomani the northern end and Langoni the southern.

Lamu's **Tourist Information Centre** (℡0121/33449 or 33324, ℻33251, ⓔlamupoly@africaonline.co.ke; Mon–Fri 8.30am–noon & 2–4.30pm, Sat 8.30am–1pm), run by a local couple near the German Post Office Museum, is really a business offering various services (hotel booking, dhow trips, guided tours, excursions), but also giving information and advice, and an email service is planned. If you need a **map** to supplement ours, they sell one for Ksh300, as do the shops at the Lamu Museum and the Swahili Cultural Centre.

Accommodation in Lamu town

The better **lodgings** in Lamu town are generally those on the waterfront or those with a height advantage; places on Harambee Avenue tend to be suffocatingly hot. There's also a small number of relatively pricey lodgings and private houses in **Shela** – which has become an alternative, upmarket base to Lamu town, with a quieter, more refined atmosphere. Shela acccommodation is covered on p.570.

In December, January, July and August, and particularly during Maulidi (see the box on p.567), **room availability** can be tight, so book ahead if you can (though several places don't have phones). Out of season, you may find some places closed. There are no fixed **room prices** in Lamu: it all depends on the season, as well as your bargaining skills. A trend in recent years has been the "gentrification" of a number of erstwhile hippie hangouts – with attendant price increases that outstrip those in the rest of the country. If you like the place, aim to agree a rate for the duration of your stay and pay daily. You may find, at peak times, that some lodge owners insist their prices are fixed – simply a rather unfair bargaining position when rooms are scarce. The price codes given refer to the standard price, without bartering, for a double in high season.

Water in Lamu

Before you settle in, try to ascertain the quality of the lodging's **water supply**. You'll soon appreciate the critical problem here; a handful of lodgings seem to have overcome it and advertise 24-hour water as a feature. Lamu is one place where it's quite common to catch hepatitis – an unpleasant and lasting souvenir usually associated with drinking infected water. You should check where the water comes from. If the house or lodging has a long-drop toilet and an open drinking-water cistern in the same bathroom, move on. It only takes one cockroach falling in the water to contaminate it.

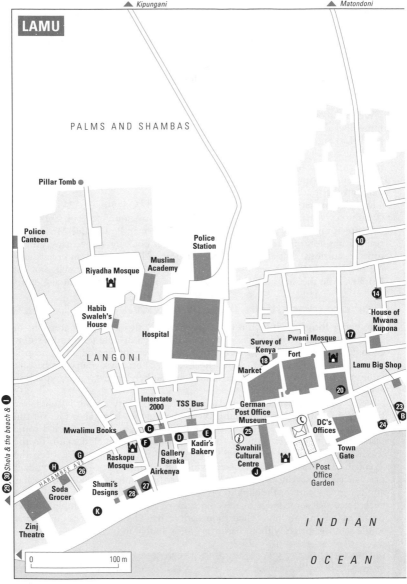

Kipungani ▲   Matondoni ▲

LAMU

PALMS AND SHAMBAS

Pillar Tomb ●

Police
Canteen

Police
Station

Muslim
Academy

Riyadha Mosque

Habib
Swaleh's
House

Hospital

Survey of
Kenya

Pwani Mosque

House of
Mwana
Kupona

LANGONI

Fort

Market

Lamu Big Shop

Interstate
2000

TSS Bus

German
Post Office
Museum

Mwalimu Books

Kadir's
Bakery

Swahili
Cultural
Centre

DC's
Offices

Raskopu
Mosque

Gallery
Baraka

Town
Gate

Airkenya

Post
Office
Garden

Soda
Grocer

Shumi's
Designs

INDIAN

Zinj
Theatre

OCEAN

0   100 m

For **camping**, your choices are all a little way out of town, at *Peace Villas*,
Talking Trees or *Dodo Villas*.

Budget guest houses

These are the lodgings where you really have the opportunity to haggle. How
many people you are, how long you intend to stay and when you will actual-

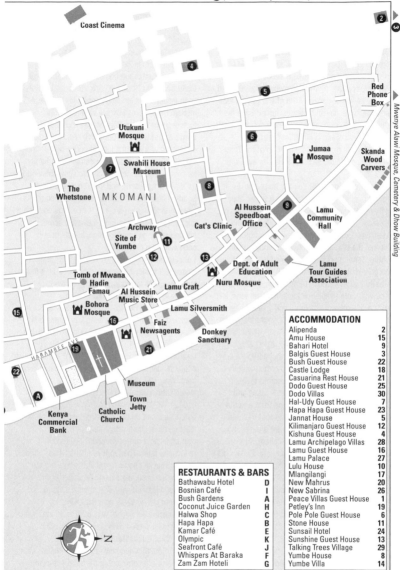

Coast Cinema

Red Phone Box

Utukuni Mosque

Swahili House Museum

Jumaa Mosque

Skanda Wood Carvers

The Whetstone   M K O M A N I

Al Hussein Speedboat Office

Lamu Community Hall

Archway

Cat's Clinic

Site of Yumbe

Dept. of Adult Education

Lamu Tour Guides Association

Tomb of Mwana Hadie Famau

Nuru Mosque

Al Hussein Music Store

Lamu Craft

Lamu Silversmith

Bohora Mosque

Faiz Newsagents

Donkey Sanctuary

HARAMBEE AVE

Museum

Town Jetty

Kenya Commercial Bank

Catholic Church

Mwenye Alawi Mosque, Cemetery & Dhow Building

N

ACCOMMODATION

Alipenda	2
Amu House	15
Bahari Hotel	9
Balgis Guest House	3
Bush Guest House	22
Castle Lodge	18
Casuarina Rest House	21
Dodo Guest House	25
Dodo Villas	30
Hal-Udy Guest House	7
Hapa Hapa Guest House	23
Jannat House	5
Kilimanjaro Guest House	12
Kishuna Guest House	4
Lamu Archipelago Villas	28
Lamu Guest House	16
Lamu Palace	27
Lulu House	10
Mlangilangi	17
New Mahrus	20
New Sabrina	26
Peace Villas Guest House	1
Petley's Inn	19
Pole Pole Guest House	6
Stone House	11
Sunsail Hotel	24
Sunshine Guest House	13
Talking Trees Village	29
Yumbe House	8
Yumbe Villa	14

RESTAURANTS & BARS

Bathawabu Hotel	D
Bosnian Café	I
Bush Gardens	A
Coconut Juice Garden	H
Halwa Shop	C
Hapa Hapa	B
Kamar Café	E
Olympic	K
Seafront Café	J
Whispers At Baraka	F
Zam Zam Hoteli	G

ly pay are all useful chips and, unless the town is heaving with travellers, you shouldn't have any problem getting some kind of discount. "No touts" in the review means you won't be guided here by a hustler – because the establishment in question does not pay commission.

Alipenda PO Box 115 ☎ 0121/33241 or 32002; no touts. Behind *Balgis Guest House* and to the left

– no sign but it's an unmistakable whitewashed building with battlements and a turret. Though some distance from the town centre, this is an exceptionally friendly family house, with a good kitchen and five huge guest rooms (all s/c with nets and fans). ❷

Balgis Guest House Signposted 100m north of the red phone box, PO Box 02 ☏0121/33171. Heading north from town, turn left at the signpost, which is opposite a green and white mosque, and it's the tall white building 50m ahead of you, with no sign on the building itself except a "Save the Dugong" sticker on the door. Eleven s/c rooms (all with verandahs and ceiling fans) with some Swahili furniture, the best higher up at the front with the benefit of sea breeze. Has its own well. B&B ❸

Bush Guest House PO Box 22; no phone. Eight rooms in a tall building accessed from an alley between Harambee Ave and the sea, only two of them s/c, but clean, secure and with nets and fans. Small kitchen and communal lounge overlooking the sea, and a roof where you can sunbathe. Starting price is over the odds, but can be bargained down in low season. B&B ❸

Castle Lodge PO Box 10; no phone. Beside the fort, with eight simple rooms, some with fans, all with nets, none s/c. Rooms 1 and 2 are the best, overlooking the market; 8 and 9 on the roof have good views. ❷

Casuarina Rest House PO Box 10 ☏ & ℻0121/33123; no touts. Over the old police station (now Kenya Airways), with a whole variety of rooms from very basic to quite comfortable, in an admirably dreamlike welter of staircases and floors (the best are the two at the front and the two on top). You can sleep on the roof if all the rooms are full. Only two rooms are s/c, but most have fans. Kitchen available. Excellent waterfront roof terrace. Bargain hard. Room only ❷ low, ❸ high.

Dodo Guest House Harambee Ave, PO Box 210 ☏0121/33408. Three rooms, one s/c, in a small house, no sign but just round the corner from the Tourist Information Centre, which runs it, and where enquiries can be made. Another *Dodo* house, near the Swahili House Museum, has more rooms, the best of which is on the roof. Both ❷

Hapa Hapa Guest House PO Box 213 ☏0121/33145. Behind the popular eatery of the same name. Two big double rooms at the front and two less appealing non-s/c singles at the back. Solid walls, but only one room has a fan – top-floor rooms are open to the *makuti* roof, which keeps a breeze blowing. ❷

Kilimanjaro Guest House PO Box 17 ☏0121/33179. Darkly atmospheric staircase with heavy stone arches and coral rag walls, almost church-like. The six rooms themselves are unexceptional but perfectly acceptable, all clean and tidy and with nets. The best ones are under the roof, airy and with good views. Use of kitchen, but the "rooftop restaurant" is now just a verandah. Keep your room locked at all times, however, as this place has a reputation for petty pilfering. ❶

Kishuna Guest House PO Box 25 ☏0121/33001. In an inconvenient location near *Jannat House*, a modern three-storey building with a *makuti*-thatched roof terrace. Reasonable, if unexciting. ❸

Lamu Guest House PO Box 240 ☏0121/33338; no touts. A well-maintained old house right in the heart of things, owned by the same Indian family for seven generations (175 children saw the world for the first time here, and it's also where Omar Sharif filmed *The Young Indiana Jones*). Four of its seventeen rooms are s/c, but the ceilings are high and there are nets and fans. Inevitably somewhat hot and stuffy given its location, but clean and good value. No kitchen. ❷

Lulu House PO Box 142 ☏ & ℻0121/33539. A pleasant, if somewhat soulless, purpose-built lodging house, with ten rooms (all s/c bar two). Breakfast on the roof. B&B ❸

Mlangilangi PO Box 260 ☏ & ℻0121/33285. A large old Swahili house, nothing fancy and could do with a fair bit of renovation (long promised, but nothing done as yet). There are two doubles (the best on top with views and a balcony), and an entire six-bed apartment. The doubles need heavy bargaining. B&B ❸

New Mahrus Hotel PO Box 25 ☏ & ℻0121/33001. Rambling old place in a good location, though not on the waterfront, and one of the least Lamu-esque hotels, though it does have its own creaking if run-down charm. Wide variety of rooms and rates. The top floor is "first-class" and nothing special (rooms 1 and 2, overlooking the fort, are the best), the second floor is "second-class" and just ordinary B&L standard. Its rooftop restaurant closed years ago. B&B ❶

New Sabrina No phone. Very basic and unappealing B&L with shared bathrooms. Cheap. ❶

Peace Villa Guest House PO Box 160 ☏0121/33020. A good ten- or fifteen-minute walk from the town centre, out in the sand and palm trees (follow the phone lines behind the *Kishuna* until you reach a clearing and it's over to your right painted white, red and black), this is the only place to camp in Lamu town – if you really want to. Most people use the dorms or double rooms (s/c, with fans), but management is slack, and there are reports of swindles regarding dhow trips. ❶

Pole Pole Guest House PO Box 195 ☏0121/33344. Getting a bit run down, but still

THE COAST | Lamu

pleasant, especially if you're used to B&Ls, with a bird's-eye view from the roof – the highest in Lamu. The helpful staff should let you use the kitchen. Nets and fans in most rooms. ❷

Sunshine Guest House PO Box 224 ☎0121/33087. A pleasant, slightly mouldering place with a good terrace and competitive rates. Use of kitchen (with cooker and fridge) is a bonus. Five of the ten rooms are s/c, all have fans and nets over the beds (try and get one without window screens). Bathrooms are a bit grubby, but it remains good value. ❷

Talking Trees Village Halfway between Lamu and Shela along the main footpath, 100m from the beach beside Lamu Ginners, PO Box 260 ☎0121/32257. Run by *Bush Gardens* restaurant (see p.569); talk with them before going. A peaceful and beautiful site (putting aside the barbed-wire fence), but a twenty-minute trudge from either Lamu or Shela. Small *banda* and room in a house, and camping (Ksh500 per person). Food available, and use of kitchen. ❷

Lodgings and hotels

Some of these are gems and in most cases worth the extra outlay if you can afford it. Breakfast is usually included.

Amu House PO Box 230 ☎ & ⑨0121/33420. Restored, American-owned stone house with additional rooms on top, built in the same style. Extremely attractive and welcoming. Good value. B&B ❹

Bahari Hotel PO Box 298 ☎0121/33172, ⑨33231. A big lodging on several floors paying token tribute to local styles, with coral-rock cladding on the walls. Twenty basic but spacious s/c rooms, with amusing four-poster beds, nets and fans, some with fridges. Always a crowd of travellers. Haggle hard for a good deal. B&B ❸

Dodo Villas PO Box 210 ☎0121/33408. Behind *Talking Trees*, halfway between Lamu town and Shela, this new place has a lot of potential and large s/c rooms, but is not really finished yet, though up and running. Allows camping in the grounds (Ksh300 per tent), and has good views from the roof terrace. Will eventually have a pool. B&B ❹

Hal-Udy Guest House PO Box 25 ☎0121/33354. Hidden away at the back of town, a lovely and charming place with a friendly family feel. The six large rooms, accessed up a creaky wooden staircase, all s/c with nets and fans, contain lots of old furniture and four-poster beds. Roof terrace. Use of kitchen. B&B ❸

Jannat House PO Box 195 ☎0121/33414. Hugely atmospheric place, owned by a Swedish family and arranged around a jungly courtyard with much of its original decoration (stuccowork niches and furniture) still intact. Nice rooftop verandah with comfy chairs. All rooms are s/c with nets and fans, but no hot water. Rather overpriced for what you get. B&B ❹

Lamu Archipelago Villas PO Box 339 ☎0121/33247, ⑨33111. The s/c rooms aren't that great but the position, right on the waterfront, is a plus. Don't take a back room, though. B&B ❸

Lamu Palace Hotel PO Box 421 ☎0121/33272, ⑨33104; reservations through Romantic Hotels, PO Box 12396 Mombasa ☎011/222502, ⓔislands@africaonline.co.ke. The biggest thing to hit Lamu's waterfront in years, a three-storey construction incorporating a restaurant terrace and bar. Has 23 AC s/c rooms, but only four face the sea (no balconies). The seamless tourist class style appeals to many, but puts off those looking for something more real; look elsewhere and you'll get a better deal for half the price. B&B ❻

Petley's Inn PO Box 4 ☎ & ⑨0121/33107. Under the same ownership as *Lamu Palace Hotel*, for which it seems to function as a kind of annexe, periodically closed dependng on business. The eleven rooms have fans and nets (the best two face the sea), but only some are AC, and have been done up in "upmarket-rustic" style – not to everyone's taste. There's a small roof-level swimming pool. The rooftop bar is a lively evening hangout. Overpriced, but they take credit cards. B&B ❺

Stone House Hotel PO Box 193 ☎0121/33544, ⑨33149; reservations through Kisiwani Ltd, PO Box 70940 Nairobi ☎ & ⑨02/446384, ⓔkisiwani@swiftkenya.com. An overly modified eighteenth-century house with orange coral rag-rock stuck on most walls, the rooms furnished in a mixture of Swahili and up-country styles. The thirteen rooms (three not s/c) have phones, but none are as classy as the brochures suggest. Rooftop restaurant. B&B ❹

Sunsail Hotel PO Box 400 ☎0121/32065–6, ⑨32666. Brand new conversion in the old stone "Mackenzie" trader's house on the waterfront. Modern intrusion has been kept to a minimum, keeping much of the building's charm. The eighteen rooms have high ceilings and smart tiled bathrooms, but only the two at the front have sea views. Italian food planned. B&B ❸

Yumbe House PO Box 81 ☎ & ⑨0121/33101. A

THE COAST | Lamu

lovely conversion, professionally managed, and a positive alternative to *Petley's* if you want some real comfort and style. Every room has a fridge, but the top room is definitely the best. Singles are good value. *Yumbe Villa* is an annexe a few minutes' walk away. B&B ❹

House rentals

It's often possible to rent **private houses** by the week or month. Some of these are occupied part of the year by their owners (often *wazungu* Lamuphiles) and rented out the rest of the year in part or in whole, while others are second homes belonging to local families who make a few extra bob by renting them out to tourists. There's always a kitchen, usually a houseman (though for his services you'll pay an extra negotiated rate), and varying quantities and standards of furnishings. If you persist in putting word around that you want to rent a place you shouldn't have to wait more than a few days. Good places to start are at the Tourist Information Centre or at *Alipenda* guest house.

Lamu town

Perhaps surprisingly for so laid-back a corner of Kenya, there's no shortage of things to do in Lamu. The **town** itself is unendingly fascinating to stroll through, with few monuments but hundreds of ancient houses, arresting street scenes and cool corners to sit and rest. And the **museum** outshines all others in Kenya bar the National Museum in Nairobi.

Initially confusing, Lamu is not the random clutter of houses and alleys it appears. Very few towns in sub-Saharan Africa have kept their original **town plan** so intact (Timbuktu in West Africa is another), and Lamu's history is sufficiently documented, and its architecture well enough preserved, to give you a good idea of how the town developed. The main division is between the **waterfront** buildings and the town behind, separated by **Usita wa Mui**, now Harambee Avenue (actually a narrow alley for the most part). Until around 1830, this was the waterfront, but the pile of accumulated rubbish in the harbour had become large enough by the time the fort was finished to consider reclaiming it; gradually, those who could afford to, built on it. The **fort** lost its pre-eminent position and Lamu, from the sea, took on a different aspect, which included Indian styles such as arches, verandahs and shuttered windows.

Behind the waterfront, the **old town** retained a second division between **Mkomani** district, to the north of the fort, and **Langoni** to the south. These locations are important as they distinguish the town's long-established quarter (Mkomani) from the still-expanding district (Langoni) where, traditionally, newcomers have built their houses of mud and thatch rather than stone or modern materials. This north–south division is found in most Swahili towns and reflects the importance of Mecca, which is due north.

Lamu is divided further into over forty *mitaa* or "**wards**", corresponding to blocks. The names of these suggest a great deal about how the town once looked and they're all listed in *Lamu Town: A Guide* by James Allen (out of print; copies in Lamu Fort Library). *Kinooni* ward ("whetstone corner") boasts to this day a heavy block of stone on the corner for sharpening swords, reputedly imported from Oman. And *Utakuni* ward ("main market") still has a row of shops, even though most of this north side of town is now purely residential.

It is difficult to construct a guided tour of Lamu – serendipity comes to everyone here, and in any event, you're better off exploring in snatches, wandering around whenever you have a spare hour or two – but the following things are worth pursuing whenever you lack the energy for the beach.

Stone architecture

Lamu's **stone houses** are unique, perfect examples of architecture appropriate to its setting. The basic design is an open, topless box enclosing a large courtyard, around which are set inward-facing rooms on two or three floors. These rooms are thus long and narrow, their ceilings supported by close-set timbers or mangrove poles (*boriti*). Most had exquisite carved doors at one time, though in all but a few dozen homes these have been sold off to pay for upkeep. Many also had *zidaka*, plaster-work niches in the walls to give an illusion of extended space, which are now just as rare. Bathroom arrangements are ingenious, with fish kept in the large water storage cisterns to eat the mosquito larvae. On the top floor, a *makuti* roof shades one side. In parts of Lamu these old houses are built so close together you could step across the street from one roof to another.

The private space inside Lamu's houses is inseparable and barely distinguishable from the public space outside. The noises of the town percolate into the interiors, encouraged by the constant flow of air created by the narrow coolness of the dark streets and the heat which accumulates on upper surfaces exposed to the sun. You can find out more in Usam Ghaidan's book *Lamu: A Study in Conservation*, which has reams of architectural and technical information; unfortunately, it is out of print, but can be consulted in the town library (see "Listings" p.573).

Lamu Museum

The one place you should definitely count on devoting an hour or so to is **Lamu Museum** (daily 8am–6pm; Ksh200, children Ksh100), built in 1891 on the ocean front, and serving as the residence of the British colonial governors before Independence. Of Kenya's regional museums, this is the one that best lives up to its name. There's no need to fill spare rooms here with game trophies and trivia, the region's history provides more than enough material.

As you enter, there's a large aerial photo of the town for a fascinating bird's-eye insight. Elsewhere, exhibitions of **Swahili culture** – architecture, boats and boat-building, domestic life – are displayed. There are also rooms devoted to the non-Swahili peoples of the mainland: farmers like the **Pokomo**, **Orma** cattle herdsmen and **Boni** hunters. Two magnificent ceremonial **siwa horns**, one in ivory from Pate, the other from Lamu itself in brass, are the prize exhibits – probably the oldest surviving musical instruments in black Africa. The Pate *siwa*, slightly more ancient, dates from between 1690 and 1700. Wooden imitations are on sale all around town.

Lamu Fort Environment Museum

The **fort** (daily 7.30am–6pm; Ksh200, children Ksh100), which was begun in 1809 and completed in 1821, seems oddly stranded in its modern-day position, deprived of its role as defender of the waterfront. At least you need no longer worry about accidentally getting it in your camera viewfinder, as was the case until 1984, when it served as a prison. It's now a national monument and open as a museum. The "temporary exhibition" first installed in 1993, however, is still there, unrefreshed. It's an enthusiastic display of information about the environment and evolution, incorporating local sea life in tanks, but it looks more like an elaborate school project than anything you would expect to find in a public building.

It's fun to walk round the ramparts of the fort, getting bird's-eye views of the town. Look out for the very interesting set of colour photos of archeological sites in the Lamu Archipelago. The town's library is here, too, see "Listings" on p.573.

Other museums

In the least-spoiled part of Lamu, the regional museum has restored an eighteenth-century house to an approximation of its original appearance – the **House Museum** (daily 7.30am–6pm; Ksh200, children Ksh100). Unfortunately, the house is very small and the guided tour included in the entrance fee is extremely brief. Since the house consists only of a small courtyard, two sleeping galleries, two toilets and an upstairs kitchen and roof, this is very poor value. Indeed, there are plenty of private houses, and even a number of guest houses, with superior architectural interest. There's talk of a combined ticket for all Lamu's museums to encourage visits, though that wouldn't make the House Museum any more worthwhile. The old **German Post Office** (same hours and cost as the House Museum) of the short-lived "Witu-land Protectorate", for long a mouldering wreck, was spruced up with money from the German Embassy and reopened in December 1996 as a museum. Unfortunately, even an ardent philatelist would have difficulty in extracting much interest from its two rooms – just a few old posters, photocopies of German stamps, weighing scales and a sorting rack.

Tradition and morality in Lamu

A number of **old photographs** on display in the museum belie pronouncements about "unchanging Lamu". The women's cover-all black **buibui**, for example, turns out to be a fashion innovation introduced comparatively recently from southern Arabia. It wasn't worn in Lamu much before the 1930s when, ironically, a degree of emancipation encouraged women of all classes to adopt the high-status styles of **purdah**. In earlier times, high-born women would appear in public entirely hidden inside a tent-like canopy called a *shiraa*, which had to be supported by slaves; the abolition of slavery at the beginning of the twentieth century marked the demise of this odd fashion.

Outsiders have tended to get the wrong end of the stick about Swahili seclusion. While women are undoubtedly heavily restricted in their public lives, in private they have considerable freedom. The notion of **romantic love** runs deep in Swahili culture. Love affairs, divorces and remarriage are the norm, and the *buibui* is perhaps as useful to women in disguising their liaisons as it is to their husbands in preventing them. Which gives a slightly different timbre to the attentions shown by Lamu men to unattached *wazungu* women. Frustration isn't always the reason, money usually is.

All this comes into focus a little when walking the backstreets. You may even bump into some of Lamu's **transvestite** community – cross-dressing men whose community is accepted and long established and derives from Oman. In fact, the more you explore, the more you realize that the town's conventional image is like the walls of its houses – a severe facade concealing an unrestrained interior.

Mosques

When you start checking out some of Lamu's 23 **mosques**, you'll find that any tone of rigid conformity you might expect is lacking. Most are simple, spacious buildings, as much refuge/men's clubs as places of prayer. There's no special reason to enter them; their doors are always open and there's little to see. Male visitors, covered up and suitably humble, are normally allowed inside; women are generally excluded. Unfortunately, the **Mwenye Alawi Mosque** at the north end of town, once Lamu's only exclusively female mosque, has been taken over by the men, leaving the women to pray at home.

The oldest-known mosque is the **Pwani Mosque**, by the fort, parts of which date back to the fourteenth century. At one time it would have been the place of worship on a Friday for the whole of Mkomani quarter. Lamu's present Friday mosque is the **Jumaa Mosque**, the big one in *Pangahari* ward ("sword-sharpening place").

The star of Lamu's mosques, as well as being one of the youngest, is the sumptuous **Riyadha Mosque** down in Langoni, well to the back of town. It was built at the beginning of the twentieth century and has brought about a

Dhow trips

Where the hotel hustlers left off after you settled in, the dhow-ride men take up the challenge. You'll be persistently hassled until you agree to go on a trip and then, as if the word's gone out, you'll be left alone. The truth is that your face quickly becomes familiar to anyone whose livelihood depends upon tourists.

In fact, the **dhow trips** are usually a lot of fun and, all things considered, very good value. The simplicity of Swahili sailing is delightful, using a single lateen sail that can be set in virtually any position and never seems to obstruct the view. Sloping past the **mangroves**, with their primeval-looking tangle of roots now at eye level, hearing any number of squeaks and splashes from the small animals and birds that live among them, is quite a serene pleasure.

Basically, the **price** you pay will depend on where you want to go, for how long, and how much hard work it's going to be for the crew. Agree on the price beforehand (a full day with lunch for less than Ksh500 per person is unlikely, but out of season, you might get a couple of hours for Ksh100), then gather as large a group as is practicable and pay up afterwards. Try also to agree on who's supplying food and drink apart from any fish you might catch (funny, but the guests rarely catch fish; it's the crew who keep hauling them up). Whatever you pay, chances are it'll be much cheaper than any equivalent trip taken in Malindi or Watamu.

A couple of pertinent **practical points**: cameras of the more expensive kind are easily damaged on dhow trips; wrap them up well in a plastic bag. And take the clothes and drinks you'd need for a 24hr spell in the Sahara – you'll burn up and dry out otherwise. Dhow crews think it's all very amusing.

Dhow destinations

There are limitless possibilities for dhow trips, though only a short "menu" is usually offered. One variation which is not especially recommended is a dhow trip to Matondoni – these tend to end up being over-organized when you get there. The cheapest trip is a slow sail across Lamu harbour and up Takwa "river", fishing as you go, followed by a barbecue on the beach at **Manda island**, then back to town. This might commence with some squelching around in the mud under the mangroves, digging for huge bait-worms. If the trip is timed properly against the tides, you can include a visit to **Takwa ruins** or, for rather more money, you can stay the night on the beach behind the ruins and come back the next day. This is usually done around full moon. Few sailors are prepared to venture out into the ocean, so Takwa has to be approached from the landward side up the creek, and this can only be done at high tide – and if misjudged can mean a long wait at Takwa before you can set off again.

A further variation has you sailing south down Lamu harbour, past the headland at Shela and out towards the ocean for some **snorkelling** over the reefs on the southwest corner of Manda around **Kinyika rock**. Snorkel and mask are normally provided, but bringing your own is obviously much better; note that the snorkelling here, though excellent, is difficult for beginners, as there are strong currents at all but neap tides, and the sudden swells can make keeping your position virtually impossible.

6

THE COAST | Lamu

565

radical shift in Lamu's style of Islam, and indeed in the status of Lamu in the Islamic world. It was founded by a descendant of the prophet, or sharif, called **Habib Swaleh**, who came from the Hadramaut (Yemen) to settle in Lamu in the mid-nineteenth century (his house is close by the mosque, acknowledged with a plaque, but still a more or less empty wattle-and-daub structure, containing a caretaker's bed and a few old papers). Habib Swaleh and his group introduced a new freedom to the five-times-daily prayers with singing, tambourines and spontaneous readings from the Koran. They attracted a large following, particularly from the slave and ex-slave community, but gradually from all social spheres, even the aristocratic families with long Lamu pedigrees. Some of the other mosques adopted the style but the Riyadha, apart from being Lamu's largest, is still the one most closely associated with this kind of inspirational worship. Non-Muslim men who visit while worship is in session are likely to be invited in and encouraged to sit cross-legged with the rest of the assembly. Any sense of stale ritual is far removed: the atmosphere is light, the music infectious, and more than one *mzungu* has converted to Islam here. The Riyadha is also famous as the spiritual home of Lamu's annual **Maulidi** celebration (see box opposite).

Next to the Riyadha is the big, square **Muslim Academy** – like the Riyadha itself, and so much else in Lamu, heavily under Saudi patronage. Both men and women are allowed to have a look around, but there's very little to see. More interesting is the chance to talk to some of the foreign students.

Other sights

After the fort, the only other national monument in Lamu (though you may not believe it when you see it) is the fluted **pillar tomb** behind Riyadha Mosque. This may date from as far back as the fourteenth century, and the occasional visit by a tourist might persuade the families in the neighbourhood that it's worth preserving; it can only be a matter of time before it leans too far and collapses on a passing *mtoto*. In the middle of town, by a betel plot, is another tomb, that of **Mwana Hadie Famau**, a local woman of the fifteenth or sixteenth century. This has been walled up and lost the porcelain-embedded pillars which would have stood at each corner.

Up along the waterfront you won't miss the **donkey sanctuary**, founded in 1987. Lamu District has over 3000 donkeys and the International Donkey Protection Trust, a Devon-based charity, has put energy and resources into setting up and maintaining this rest home for old and lame beasts that would otherwise perish of exhaustion or end up in a stew. It's not a tourist attraction, but it does rely heavily on donations from visitors and the staff are welcoming (visits daily 9am–1pm). If you call in, don't forget to shut the gate behind you. In February 1999, thirty donkeys were "arrested for straying and loitering in the town", and were promptly locked up at the donkey cells.

On a similar theme, but much less agreeable to visit, is the **Lamu Cat Clinic** (Mon–Fri 8am–noon & 2–4pm), a block behind Harambee Avenue near the *Bahari Hotel*. The island's cats, which number several tens of thousands, are thought to have originated in Egypt, and were then transported down the coast with early sailors. Some people say that they can talk (possibly if you're on *bangi*), but beware of deliberately insulting them, as many believe that they may be evil *majini* spirits, or else carry the souls of deceased ancestors come to spy on their descendants; the population were understandably suspicious when they found out that the clinic's main aim was to neuter stray cats (akin to castrating your ancestors, in a manner of speaking). However, as the centre's founder relates, one cat's just like another, and he's seen nothing strange, as yet.

Lamu's annual **Maulidi**, a week-long celebration of Muhammad's birth, sees the entire town involved in processions and dances, and draws in pilgrims from all over East Africa and the Indian Ocean. For faithful participants, the Lamu Maulidi is so laden with *baraka* (blessings) that some say two trips to Lamu are worth one to Mecca in the eyes of God. If you can possibly arrange it, this occasion is the time to be in Lamu, but unless you make bookings, you'll need to arrive at least a week in advance to have any hope of getting a room. Starting dates are roughly 24 May 2002, 13 May 2003, 1 May 2004 and 20 April 2005.

Unfortunately, the centre itself is in a sorry state: there's cat urine everywhere, the cages are small and their mewing inmates – some have evidently gone mad – are pitiful and underfed. Not one for the kids. Donations desperately needed.

Heading north out of town, through *Tundani* ward ("fruit-picking place") and *Weyoni* ward ("donkey racetrack"), you reach the **cemetery**, goal of many religious processions and an interesting short walk. Past suburbs, you come out by the slaughterhouse and rubbish dumps, populated by marabou storks. In the inlet behind them, several large **dhows** and smaller boats are moored. Many are rotting, but one or two are quite new, even unfitted. Tradition notwithstanding, Lamu, rather than Matondoni (see p.571), seems to be the island's main boat-building centre. If you have dreams of owning a dhow (they make great houseboats), a representative price for a forty-foot hull is £4000/$6500. The price depends entirely on the time the *fundis* take to build it – two years isn't unusual.

Eating

There are enough **restaurants** and passable *hotelis* in Lamu to enable you to eat out twice a day for a week without going back to your first port of call. And, nowhere else in Kenya is there such a concentration of eating places with an overwhelmingly budget-traveller clientele. Unfortunately, the rock-bottom prices of only a few years ago are rising fast and some places are already expensive by Kenyan standards. It's still possible to eat fully for as little as Ksh100 for the basics, but you can easily pay ten times as much in some of the waterfront eating houses. Again, prices really rocket in the peak seasons.

A fine balance has been achieved between what is demanded and what can be supplied: yoghurt, fruit salad, pancakes, muesli, milkshakes and puréed fruit juices have become Lamu specialities. Superb lobster (actually crawfish, so no claws) and crab dishes, oysters, snapper and delicious steaks of swordfish, barracuda and shark are also on many menus – it's a nice change to find a fishing town where you can actually eat seafood relatively cheaply. A number of ordinary **hotelis** serving the up-country staples – beans, curries, pilau, steak, chicken, chips, eggs, even *ugali* and *karanga* – crowd along Harambee Avenue, particularly down in Langoni. Meat is notoriously stringy; several of the tourist-oriented places receive regular supplies from Malindi by plane.

If you spend any time in Lamu, you'll probably run into someone offering you a "genuine" Swahili **dinner at home**. At its best, this is a great way of seeing how the majority of Lamu's inhabitants live, and the food can be delicious. On the other hand, it can also feel a little contrived, and the price demanded at the end (which, like everything in Lamu, depends mainly on your perceived ability to pay) might not necessarily be any cheaper than having eaten in a decent restaurant. One local character in particular, known as Ali Hippy, seems

6

THE COAST | Lamu

In the old days, when *Petley's* restricted its roof to guests, and casual drinkers in the downstairs bar were sneered at, they often used to "run out" of **beer**; people would buy it direct from the Kenya Breweries depot, or go to the police canteen. Nowadays, although you can always get a drink (bottles of rot-gut Safari "whisky", totally colourless, as well as expensive bottles of wine, appear out of nowhere if you spread the word), only *Petley's* (5pm–midnight daily) or the *Lamu Palace* (all day) have alcohol licences. At other places, you can sometimes order "ice-cold tea". The police canteen does, however, still offer the cheapest beer in town.

More common is **bangi** (marijuana), but be aware that it's illegal in Kenya, and if caught in possession, you risk up to eight years in jail (recently reduced from fifteen) and no sympathy from your embassy. There have been reports of beach boys working in tandem with the police.

to have cornered the market in this, and his whole family joins in providing entertainment – not everybody feels it's a bargain, however, usually depending on how much they've agreed to pay. As in a restaurant, you should pay after your meal, not before.

If you enjoy doing your own **cooking** (several lodgings have kitchens you can use), a whole new world starts to open up. Try, for example, cooking fish in coconut: any restaurant will show you how to grate out the flesh and strain off the cream from the coconut to use it as a basis for sauces, using a conical coconut basket. Tamarind is another good complement to fish. The rebuilt **produce market** in front of the fort – run for the most part by up-country women – has everything you'll need, with separate sections for meat, fish, and fruit and veg; for fresh fish or shellfish, get there very early. By 9am all the interesting ones have been sold. Check out also the "**crab and lobster market**", little more than a pair of weighing scales over a ditch in an alley, south along the shore just in from the last building ("Hodi Hodi"). Lamu has wonderful **fruit** and is famous for its enormous, aromatic **mangoes**, but you should also try the unusually sweet and juicy **grapefruit**. While you're here, you might also find one of Lamu's traditional exports, **betel**, the green vine you see trailing out of all the empty plots in town. The sweet hot-tasting leaves are wrapped around other ingredients, including white lime and betel nut, which stains the teeth red, to make *pan*. Rather sweeter, the *halwa* shop is on Harambee Avenue in Langoni, and there's a good bakery facing the right side of the fort.

Lastly, try the tiny mutton kebabs (wrapped in a chapati) and cakes which are sold along Harambee Avenue at night, around the corner from the *Casuarina* – they cost next to nothing and are usually delicious.

Hotelis and snacks

Bathawabu Hotel Harambee Ave, Langoni. Dead cheap, busy local *hoteli*.

Bosnian Café Harambee Ave, Langoni. Cheap hole-in-the-wall *hoteli* for snacks and the cheapest juices in town.

Halwa shop Harambee Ave, Langoni. Lamu's main outlet for the sticky confection, just Ksh250 per kilo. Nameless and unidentified except for its blue door (there's a wooden plaque for Al-Hussein boat charters next to it), but once you've been you'll never forget the hot kitchen and the huge copper vat.

Kamar Café (formerly called *New Star*), Harambee Ave, Langoni. Unchanged for two decades (apart from the name), in a large and tatty *makuti*-roofed shelter. One of the few restaurants catering even-handedly to travellers and locals, and one of the cheapest in town. Especially good for breakfast before an early-morning walk to the beach. Daily 5.30am–10.30pm.

Seafront Café Next to the Swahili Cultural Centre, and open till midnight, this travellers' restaurant offers coconut fish or beans, rice, pilau and

karanga, to variable standards.
Zam Zam Hoteli Harambee Ave, Langoni. Cheap *hoteli* with rarely a *mzungu* to be seen.

Cafés and restaurants

Bush Gardens On the waterfront, competing for the same business as *Hapa Hapa* but more upmarket. A seafood and kebab place with a popular following and a charming proprietor, though food quality varies from very average to first-rate. Not as costly as you might expect. Worth patronizing for the garlic bread alone. Daily 7am–10pm.

Coconut Juice Garden Harambee Ave. Good juices and shakes; you can order any combination you want such as orgasmic coconut and banana, or wonderful passion fruit and pawpaw. They also do food.

Hapa Hapa Popular and friendly, very central rendezvous – the food is generally good, occasionally excellent, and there are its famous pint jugs of freshly pressed juices and milkshakes (Ksh50) too. More down-to-earth than *Bush Gardens*, and a good place to while away the hours at any time of day.

Lamu Palace Restaurant This impressive restaurant is quite reliable and often does realistically priced all-you-can eat seafood buffets as well as the more expensive crab and lobster staples. However, it can feel rather uncomfortable spending all this money just yards away from the more impoverished waterfront.

Olympic Popular for juices, snacks and meals.

Petley's Inn The rooftop bar and restaurant does genuinely good food at prices that are not grossly inflated, but it's loud – if only they wouldn't play the same few tapes night after night.

Stone House Rooftop Restaurant Upmarket eats, mainly seafood and pasta, sometimes very good.

Whispers at Baraka Harambee Ave, Langoni ☎0121/33355. Pretentious it may be (it comes with a *parfumerie*, "Baraka Gallery" gift shop and invitation-only "artistes' colony"), but it's not easy to resist real espresso and wonderful cakes and pastries, unless you're really counting the pennies. Expensive. Daily 9am–8.30pm, closed 2–4pm low season; closed May–June.

Around the island

The one place everyone goes on Lamu is, of course, the **beach**, which more than repays the slight effort of getting there. The walk is enlivened by the village of Shela, at the start of the beach 3km south of Lamu town, one of three villages on the island. Don't take any valuables if you walk here – there have been muggings in the past. Fewer people see the **interior** of Lamu island itself, which is a pity, as it's a pretty, if rather inhospitable, reminder of how remarkable it is that a town exists here at all. Much of it is patched into *shambas* with the herds of cattle, coconut palms, mango and citrus trees that still provide the bulk of Lamu's wealth. The two villages you might head for are Matondoni and Kipungani.

Dhow trips with a beach barbecue are the stock-in-trade of the waterfront hustlers, and as such are hard to avoid even if you wanted to; always fun, they also give you the chance to see the ruins of Takwa on Manda island (see p.575).

The beach

A usually deserted twelve-kilometre sickle of white sand, splashed by bath-warm sea and backed by empty **sand dunes**, Lamu's **beach** is the real thing; you half expect Robinson Crusoe to come striding out of the heat haze. Unprotected by a reef, the sea here has some motion to it for once, and it is one of the few places on the coast where, at certain times of the year, you can body-surf (August is probably best). Beyond *Peponi Hotel*, it's also a beach where formerly, on your private square kilometre, you could sometimes dispense with a swimming costume. Not any more. There were two rapes a few years ago, muggings are no longer unheard of, and there is now a two-man Kenya Navy security post in the dunes. Women may also find that wanderers along the beach can be a nuisance. Stay in shouting distance of other sun bathers and preferably go to the beach in company.

Beware of the **sun**, a more likely assailant. There's absolutely no cover and you'll find that the cooling breeze is too strong for erecting a sunshade. You'll need to take a drink or a bag of grapefruit and some skin protection. Coconut oil, sold in town, is used by some to avoid drying out, but you need a deep tan to begin with, otherwise it fries your skin. Ordinary sunscreen cream is available in town. Lastly, and perhaps obviously, bear in mind that if you walk for miles along the beach in the early morning, you'll have to do it back again in the heat of the day.

Getting to the beach, you can either walk the pleasant shoreline from Lamu's harbour down to Shela village (30min at low tide; 40min at high tide, when you take the track that veers inland after the last of the dhows) and then head as far down the sands as you like, or you can get a dhow to take you (price negotiable, between Ksh200 and Ksh500), or try to find a motorboat taking a bunch of local people down (Ksh50 per person). The third option you might be tempted to try – striking out across the *shambas* behind town and heading direct for the middle of the beach, is actually a time-consuming and exhausting short cut that involves wading through deep sand. On arrival at Shela, if you've walked along the shore, you can reward your limited exertions at the *Bahari Restaurant* with a drink or a bite to eat, or head straight for the cold beers at *Peponi*.

Shela

SHELA, once a thriving settlement, is now in limbo, midway between rural decline and upmarket tourist boom. Its people, who trace their ancestry back to Manda island and speak a dialect of Swahili quite distinct from Lamu town's, are gradually leaving the village, many of them going to Malindi. A number of fine old houses have been bought by foreigners and converted into ravishing holiday homes, decked in bougainvillea and empty most of the year (some can be rented; see opposite). While it's an utterly hedonistic place to lounge away a few days, you won't have the thrill of staying among the mosques and street life of Lamu town itself.

Shela's only sight is the strange, much-photographed **Friday Mosque**, built in 1829, which stands out for its rocket-shaped minaret, unusual in East Africa. If you're suitably dressed and bare-footed, ask politely to go up to the top.

The gaggle of beach boys playing football at low tide, or loafing around the hotel terrace sizing up the latest speedboat tourist arrivals from Manda airstrip, are part of the limited **gay scene**. The atmosphere of an embryonic Key West is beginning to pervade Lamu, and *Peponi* ("Heaven"), its only international-class hotel, is the natural venue.

If you seriously want to spend all your time on the beach, **staying** in Shela seems the obvious solution, and there are several quite stylish possibilities, although, unlike Lamu town, there's almost nowhere in the really cheap price categories. Equally restrictive, there are virtually no **restaurants** aside from those in the hotels, though there are one or two samosa vendors on the beach.

Hotels

Bahari Guest House 100m north of *Peponi*, PO Box 59 ℡0121/32046; no touts. You pay for the location here, which, above the sea-lapped restaurant of the same name, is immaculate. The five rooms (all s/c), are simple but nicely done and just about give good value in low season. High season rates however are overpriced, so bargain hard. Kitchen. B&B ❸

Bongo House PO Box 284 ℡0121/33479. A small but good-value place near the Friday Mosque, with four large s/c rooms. ❸

Island Hotel PO Box 179 ℡0121/33290, ℮33568; reservations through Kisiwani Ltd, PO Box 70940 Nairobi ℡ & ℮02/446384, ⓔkisiwani@swiftkenya.com; sometimes closed May to mid-June. Fifteen spacious, attractively furnished rooms, and a restful atmosphere. Rustic luxury just about sums it up, and the penthouse is especially appealing – almost open-air, like sleeping on the roof but in privacy and comfort. Fans in all rooms and nets on frames. Good, reasonably priced rooftop restaurant – the *Barracuda* – candelit at night, with mild but tasty Swahili curries, grilled fish, and vegetarian dishes, plus juices and snacks all day, but no alcohol licence. B&B ❺ including boat transfer from airport.

Kijani House PO Box 266 ☏ 0121/33235–7, ⓕ 33374, ⓦ www.kijani-house.com; closed May and June. Pretty and comfortable French-owned hotel, well run but not as luxurious as you might imagine from their brochure – and their high prices. The superior rooms are excellent (1, 3, 4 and 5 are best), but the standard ones are over-priced. Two small pools. Non-seasonal rates. B&B ❻

Peponi Hotel PO Box 24 ☏ 0121/33422–3, ⓕ 33029, ⓔ peponi@africaonline.co.ke; closed May and June. Shela's main beachfront focus, where everyone stops in for a cold drink (or a good single malt). It's fabulously situated, and offers superb food and service. The best rooms have the high numbers, from 21 upwards, but the standard rooms (in the four undistinguished block-like structures across from the main building), are just that – if you can afford to stay, then pay the extra

for rooms in the main house. Non-seasonal rates. B&B ❽

Pwani Guest House PO Box 59 ☏ 0121/33540. Stylish, roomy house, co-owned with the *Bahari*, overlooking *Peponi*. The five rooms here (all s/c) offer various options, but all, by Shela standards, are a good deal, with their old furniture, antique stuccowork (room 3 especially) and soft light. The top rooms are brilliant. B&B ❹

Shela Rest House PO Box 305 ☏ 0121/33091, ⓕ 33542, ⓔ shela@africaonline.co.ke. Up past *Island Hotel*, turn first right and then left (it's easier with someone to show the way). Eight rooms, only two s/c, all very different, including a funny one on a converted balcony with only curtains for privacy (and security). Even without haggling, these are the cheapest rooms in Shela. ❸

Shela Royal House PO Box 305 ☏ 0121/33091, ⓕ 33542, ⓔ shela@africaonline.co.ke. From the same firm that runs *Shella Rest House*, a new, bright and breezy place, away from the beach, but friendly and with a nice roof terrace. ❹

Shela White House At the top of the alley leading past *Shela Pwani*, PO Box 305 ☏ 0121/33091, ⓕ 33542, ⓔ shela@africaonline.co.ke. Five s/c rooms in a stand-alone three-storey house, of which two are sea-facing, and three are s/c. They can cook food to order, or you can use the kitchen. Roof terrace. B&B ❹

House rental

If you're looking to **rent a house**, there are a dozen or more private houses available from time to time, most of which will cost you a fortune unless you're in a big group and can share the cost. Ask for *Jasmin House* (good for kids as it has a large garden), *White Rock*, or *Nyumba ya Giovanna* (Giovanna's House, opposite *Shela Rest House*). Much cheaper houses (Ksh3000–5000) are available if you ask around. The following are upmarket options and mostly renovated townhouses:

Beach House, Shela House and Palm House (reservations PO Box 39486 Nairobi ☏ 02/442171, ⓕ 445010 ⓔ shela@africaonline.co.ke; UK bookings through Scott Dunn World ☏ 020/8672 1234, ⓕ 8767 2026). Three luxury houses near the Friday Mosque, with *Beach House* right on the waterfront, sleeping twelve, and costing from $7000 per week, while *Shela House* sleeps ten from $4200, and *Palm House* eight from $2800. All come complete with house staff. *Beach House* was purpose built, the other two converted, and none of the interiors owe much to traditional Swahili style.

Bustani Square (Going Places, PO Box 14776

Nairobi ☏ 02/442312–3, ⓕ 446402, ⓔ going-places@swiftkenya.com). At the north end of the village about 100m from the sea, in its own gardens. Sleeps four, terrace with views, services of a cook and houseman included.

Kisimani House (reservations in Nairobi on ☏ 02/882409). Ostensibly the oldest house in Lamu, with beautiful décor (downstairs mostly original) and terraces; sleeps eight and has house staff. From $1050 per week. *Jihari House*, next door, is linked by a communicating walkway, so by renting both you can even accommodate a group of sixteen.

Matondoni and Kipungani

MATONDONI is the most talked-about destination on Lamu apart from Shela and the beach. It's a fine walk if you start early, with a hot return made

The Swahili are renowned for the imagery, rhythm and complexity of their **proverbs**. *Kangas* always have some kind of adage printed on one side and these are often traditionally Swahili. The first of these few – an admonishment to be patient – is the one you will most often hear. There's a nice website at ⓦwww.glcom.com/hassan/Kanga.html.

Haraka, haraka: haina baraka – Haste, haste: there's no blessing in it.

Nyumba njema si mlango – A good house isn't (judged by) its door [ie, don't judge by appearances].

Mahaba ni haba, akili ni mali – Love counts for little, intelligence is wealth.

Faida yako ni hasara yangu – Your gain is my loss.

Haba na haba kujaza kibaba – Little by little fills the jug.

Kuku anakula sawa na mdomo wake – A chicken eats according to her beak [interpretations invited].

Mungu alitolandika, haliwezi kufutika – What God has written cannot be erased.

Heri shuka isiyo kitushi, kama shali njema ya mauwa – Better an honest loincloth than a fancy cloak (of shame).

Mke ni nguo, mgomba kupalilia – A wife means clothes (like) a banana plant means weeding.

more bearable by the prospect of a cold drink at the end – the soft sand track isn't fun in blazing sunshine. A sane, enjoyable alternative is to go by **donkey**: fix up a beast through your guest-house reception, or you can take one of the sand dhows on its trip from Lamu jetty to Matondoni, get some lunch and walk back along the line of the telephone wires. In truth, Matondoni itself is not wildly exciting and its fame as the district's principal dhow-building centre seems misplaced.

If you really want to look **around the whole island**, proceed from Matondoni to **KIPUNGANI**, one hour's walk from the end of the beach (4hr from Shela village). This is the halfway mark on the round-the-island walk; the whole trip takes eight or nine hours at least. It is useful to know the state of the tides for the stretch from Matondoni to Kipungani, as you can take a direct route through the mangroves at low tide (but don't get caught out). Kipungani has an upmarket **hotel**, 1.5km before the village, in the shape of *Kipungani Explorer* (Lamu office under *Lamu Archipeligo Villas*, PO Box 63 ⓣ & ⓕ0121/33432; reservations through Heritage Hotels, p.43; closed after Easter to early July), a delightful "desert island" complex of fourteen simple mat-and-*makuti* thatch *bandas* up on the beach, with bar and restaurant decorated with driftwood and the products of beachcombings. It's expensive (FB ⓭), but with justification; the food is superb and the welcome, service, and sense of blissful isolation are everything you could ask for. The views over the sands and channel are exceptional, and there's a pool, too. Excursions, windsurfing and snorkelling trips are all on offer. You can get there direct from Lamu town by speedboat (30min), or more slowly by dhow. Check first with the office in Lamu if you want to go for lunch (Ksh1000).

Listings

Bank KCB is the only bank in Lamu (Mon–Fri 9am–3pm, Sat 9–11am), is reasonably efficient, and charges Ksh50 commission per traveller's cheque, and one percent on cash, in both cases plus two percent or Ksh200 (whichever is greater), and it's worth checking your receipt before signing. You can also get cash advances on Visa cards, but the commission (4.5 percent) is swingeing, and we've received reports in the past of them charging up to fifteen percent, so ask first.

Books (see also "Library") Try the museum for a small selection of new souvenir books, and the Mwalimu Bookshop for a small and rather dusty selection of African novels.

Cinemas The Zinj Theatre on Harambee Ave in Langoni screens American or Indian films (9pm nightly, plus women-only showings on Wed & Sun at 2.30pm; Ksh20). It also occasionally screens live English Premiership or European Champions League football matches. Coast Cinema shows videos.

Clothes and tailors A number of shops along Harambee Ave will run up clothes very cheaply in a day or so. The easiest way to end up with something that fits is to provide a model garment. Shumi's Design, on the waterfront in Langoni, is recommended. Langoni is the place to hunt out *kangas* and *kikois*.

Crafts and souvenirs Woodcarving shops are mostly found along Harambee Ave in Mkomani. Model dhows, chests, furniture and *siwa* horns are all attractive but bulky. Beautifully hand-carved safari chairs are also a hassle to carry, but worth the effort for the prices. Some of the shops selling jewellery and trinkets have genuinely old and interesting pieces. Look out for tiny lime caskets in silver, earlobe plugs in buffalo horn or silver, and old coins. A recommended silversmith is Lamu (Slim) Silversmith on Harambee Ave just up from the donkey sanctuary. They'll make jewellery for you; bargain hard. There are also expensive but unusual jewellery pieces at Gallery Baraka at the southern end of Harambee Ave (Mon–Sat 9am–1pm & 3.30–7.30pm). The Swahili Cultural Centre (daily 9am–12.30pm & 2–4pm) has a small selection of not terribly inspiring dresses and bags made by trainee girls working above the German Post Office, and a few other curios.

Discos There's usually a disco on Fridays at the *Civil Servants' Club*, about 1km south of the GPO, entrance on the waterfront, and Saturdays at the *Police Canteen* (ask at the police station). The *Full Moon Party* (where you go to Manda Island for a beach barbecue) is "fun but used by dhow boat captains as an excuse to smoke pot and seduce white girls", says one visitor.

Fax Several guest houses now have fax machines. The going rate for an international fax is about Ksh500 per page.

Film Camera film and processing (Ksh500 for negatives and prints of 36 exposures in three days) are available from Faiz Newsagents at the northern end of Harambee Ave.

Health Be more than ordinarily careful about the water you drink. Malaria can also be a problem: if

you get a fever go straight to the hospital. For your teeth, you can buy toothbrush sticks (*msuake*) from the market.

Henna painting A number of women around town offer this attractive dye-painting for hands and feet. The best have portfolios of designs to choose from. Expect to pay around Ksh200 for both hands or both feet. If done properly, your hands or feet will be bound in cloth for twelve hours and the design should stay for up to six months. Try "Hodi Hodi" at the south end of the port by the lobster and crab market.

Hospital The new hospital (℡0121/33012) attracts patients from a huge part of northeastern Kenya, but it's better to seek treatment elsewhere (Malindi, for example) if possible. There are also several private clinics – ask around.

Immigration In the District Commissioner's (DC's) offices on the waterfront. Go there before your pass expires. It shouldn't cost anything unless your total stay in the country will exceed ninety days, in which case it will cost Ksh2400 to extend beyond that.

Internet access The high cost of trunk calls to the nearest server has put out of business all the companies in Lamu town that were offering internet and email services, but the Tourist Information Centre has plans to run one in the future. Meanwhile, Royal Office in Shela will let you send an email for Ksh150.

Library The town library is on the top floor of the fort (Mon–Fri 8am–12.30pm & 2–5.30pm, Sat 10–12pm; ℡0121/33201; five-visit pass Ksh100). It's a surprisingly good collection, with lots on Lamu, as well as a sixteenth-century Koranic manuscript.

Music cassettes Al-Hussein Hand Craft, on Harambee Ave, has tapes of Taarab, traditional Wa-Bajuni and Mijikenda music.

Newspapers and magazines Arrive about 11am, and are available from Faiz Newsagents, at the northern end of Harambee Ave. They also sell tide tables. Newspapers get snapped up quickly in Lamu and the supply is limited.

Photocopying Faiz Newsagents on Harambee Ave, and the shop opposite, both have machines (Ksh4 for A4).

Police The days of hassle are long gone. Don't fail to stand still, however, if you're on the waterfront whenever the national flag is lowered, or you'll find yourself "in discussion" with them. Lamu is also a favourite place to trap tourists who have failed to extend their visitor's permit (see "Immigration").

Post and telephone office Open Mon–Fri 8am–5pm, Sat 8–11.30am. *Poste restante* available. There are cardphones outside but they don't always have phone cards for sale.

Speedboat charter Not exactly in keeping with the spirit of Lamu's lifestyle, it certainly gets you from A to B effectively, but drinks diesel fuel at an unbelievable rate, which makes it expensive. Al Hussein, which comfortably seats four, plus captain and "small captain", can be chartered at their office on Harambee Ave in Mkomani (PO Box 156 ☎0121/33509) or try Al-Hussein Hand Craft. Rates are currently around Ksh5000 for Pate, Ksh12,000 to Kiwaiyu, and Ksh8000 to Faza. In Shela, *Peponi Hotel* offers a similar service, at similar prices.

Spices and herbs There's a good little shop opposite Raskopu Mosque in Langoni.

Supermarkets Lamu Big Shop (daily 9am–12.30pm & 5–10pm in theory, but often shuts earlier), and Soda Grocer (Mon–Sat 8.15am–12.30pm & 4–10pm, Sun 8.15am–12.30pm), both on Harambee Avenue.

Swahili lessons Being suffused in Swahili culture, Lamu is a good place to learn – the Tourist Information Centre can put you in touch with a teacher, and also offer a 21-day course including accommodation at *Dodo Villas* for $1500. Alternatively, ask at the Department of Adult Education on Harambee Ave or at Lamu Museum.

Travel agents Tawasal Tours (PO Box 248 ☎ & ℻0121/33584, ℮ tawasal@africaonline.co.ke), at *Milimani Guest House*, a ten-minute walk inland from the fort (ask), specializes in ecological and educational trips for college groups. As ever, prices depend on how much they think they can squeeze out of you.

Windsurfing Satan at *Talking Trees* charges Ksh500 an hour; Baka Windsurfing at *Peponi* in Shela charges Ksh650 per hour, Ksh1200 per hour with lessons.

Moving on from Lamu

Most visitors come and leave by plane, not so much for convenience as for safety: the road to Minjila junction on the way to Malindi and Mombasa has always been prone to bandit attack. Incidents are far fewer now, and at time of writing (early 2002), it's over two years since the last bus was actually held up, but bandits are still active along the road, and most tourists prefer to play it safe.

Nonetheless, four **bus companies** currently run daily to Mombasa via Malindi and Kilifi: Mombasa Liners, TSS, Interstate 2000 and Tawakal Minibuses. All leave Mokowe jetty on the mainland between 7am and 7.30am; the ferries leave Lamu Town at 6–6.30am to connect. The buses are supposed to travel in convoy but rarely do unless there's been a recent incident, and bandits have traditionally targetted the first or last buses on the convoy (usually Tawakal and Mombasa Liners respectively). Buy tickets (Ksh400 to Mombasa) the day before or earlier to be sure of a seat. The booking offices are all at the south end of Harambee Avenue near *Kamar Café* (daily 8.30am–12.30pm, 2.30–4.30pm & 7–8.30pm). Tawakal ("We fly, others run") is the fastest, and costs Ksh50 more then the others; it also fills up quickly so should be booked as far in advance as possible.

Travelling by air, Kenya Airways, under *Casuarina Guest House* (Mon–Fri 8am–12.15pm & 2–5pm, Sat morning only; ☎0121/32040–1) has daily **flights** to Nairobi (Ksh9350) via Malindi (Ksh3661). Airkenya, on Harambee Avenue between Gallery Baraka and *Whispers* (daily 8am–12.30pm & 1.30–6pm; ☎0121/33445) has daily flights to Mombasa at 3.45pm ($85 each way) via Malindi ($65). They also fly daily to Kiwaiyu ($65), and to Nairobi ($135). **Tickets** should be booked or reconfirmed as early as possible. Cancelling tickets you've already got from Mombasa, Malindi or Nairobi is a big pain, as refunds are usually only available from the issuing agent. The connecting boats to the airport on Manda cost Ksh100.

Manda island

Practically within shouting distance of Lamu town, **Manda** – with next to no fresh water – is almost uninhabited and, apart from being the site of the main airstrip on the islands, and the location of the old ruined town of **Takwa** (favourite destination of the dhow-trip operators) is not much visited either. Significant archeologically for the ruins of Takwa and Manda, the north side of the island is also the location of the very exclusive *Blue Safari Club*, a more or less private establishment catering for heads of state and similar clients (it charges over $1000 in high season). Altogether different is the *Manda Beach Club*, run by the same people as Chale Island (p.511), which has already managed to offend Shela's inhabitants with its loud disco music, floodlights at night, and by the purchase of a plot of land at Shela for the sole purpose of piping water over to Manda. The former hotel at Ras Kitau, facing Lamu island, is abandoned.

The island is crisscrossed with paths through the jungle, should you be taken by the urge to spend a day there. But go soon. Rumours have been flying around the archipelago that either an American naval facility, or a new seaport for northeast Kenya, or a gas terminal for the finds around Garissa, is going to be built on Manda. The hoteliers and farmers were given notice to leave a few years back and the dredgers started clearing the channels. For the moment it's all quietened down again, although the US dredger crews have returned and are hunkered down in Lamu. **Motorboats** run by the airlines make the crossing from Lamu town to the Manda **airstrip jetty** – where they sell "duty-free mangoes" in the "departure lounge" – and you can use them if you want to visit the island, though airline passengers get priority.

Takwa ruins

Whether you make a flying visit to **Takwa** (daily 8am–6pm; Ksh200), a thirty-minute boat ride from Lamu, or sleep out on the beach behind it (there are some shelters), the site is well worth seeing. A flourishing town in the sixteenth and seventeenth centuries, it was deserted, as usual, for no one knows what reason, and is in many respects reminiscent of Gedi. As at other sites, toilets and bathrooms figure prominently in the architecture. In Islam, cleanliness is so close to godliness as to almost signify it – the Takwans must have been a devout community. The doors of all the houses face north towards Mecca, as does the main street with the **mosque** at the end of it. The mosque is interesting for the pillar at one end which suggests it was built on a tomb site (that of a founder of the town perhaps), and for the simple lines of its *mihrab*, so different from the ornate curlicues of later designs. Another impressive **pillar tomb** stands alone, just outside the town walls, its date translating to about 1683, and it still occasionally attracts pilgrims from Shela (some of whom claim descent from Takwa), who come to pray for rain.

Takwa has been thoroughly cleared but, in order to preserve it for the future, hardly excavated at all. What has been found, however, suggests an industrious and healthy community, living in an easily defensible position with a wall all around the town, the ocean on one side behind the dunes and mangroves on the other. Despite this, they appear to have left in a panic and, as usual, there's ample room for conjecture about why. Part of the great appeal of Kenya's ruined towns lies in the open debate that still continues about who, precisely, their builders and citizens were, and why they so often left in such evident haste. And there's always the fascinating possibility that old Swahili manuscripts will turn up to explain it all.

If you'd like to stay overnight at Takwa, there's a simple dormitory-style *banda* available at the ruins, where you can stay for around Ksh1000 per person. Facilities are minimal, but the setting is magnificent. You need to take all food and water requirements.

> ## Elephants ahoy!
>
> One of the strangest wildlife spectacles in Kenya – which you're most unlikely to see unless you organize an expedition especially and have plenty of time to wait – is the sight of **elephants swimming** between the mainland and Manda Island, with only their trunks and flapping ears above the water. Some forty to fifty members of the much larger mainland Dodora herd have a traditional migratory route which takes them, just before the onset of the long rains (usually one day in March), across the narrow Mkanda Channel to Manda island. The mangrove leaves amply supply their food and salt requirements, and though there's no water, amazingly, the elephants have somehow learned that by rolling in the ground, they can make troughs which then catch the rain. Despite the herd's proximity to Somalia and that country's rampant elephant poaching, their unusual migration perhaps explains how they continue to survive – even from the air, the elephants are almost impossible to see, thanks to the luxuriant cover of the mangroves – and on the ground, you could be within yards of one without seeing it, its presence signalled only by steaming dung.

Pate island

Only two hours by ferryboat from Lamu, totally unaffected by tourism and rarely visited, **Pate island** has some of the most impressive ruins anywhere on the coast and a clutch of old Swahili settlements which, at different times, have been as important as Lamu or more so. There are few places on the coast as memorable.

Pate is mostly low-lying and almost surrounded by mangrove swamps; no two maps of it ever agree (ours on p.553 shows only the permanent dry land, not the ever-changing mangrove forests that surround it in the shallow sea), so getting on and off the island requires deft awareness of the tides. This apparent remoteness coupled with a lack of information deters travellers but, in truth, Pate is not a difficult destination, and, in purely physical terms, it's an easier island to walk around than Lamu, with none of the exhausting soft sand.

A matatu **motorboat** (one of three plying the route; Ksh70 to Mtangawanda, Ksh100 to Faza, Ksh150 to Kisingitini) leaves daily except Friday, about one hour before high tide (which can be very early in the morning), from the municipal jetty at Lamu. On reaching the **Mkanda Channel**, you pass the ferry making the return trip; the Mkanda is navigable only at high tide, and even then it can be a close call when the boat is overloaded, as it usually is. The boat, sometimes accompanied by dolphins, then calls at a deserted spot called **Mtangawanda** (the dock for Pate town, which takes 2–3hr from Lamu), followed by **Faza** at the northern end of the island, which is up to four hours away from Lamu, finally docking at Kijinitini (Kisingitini), thirty minutes further on.

The obvious plan, having walked to Pate town from Mtangawanda dock (1hr, though you'll need directions after 45min for the minor side track; it gets slippery in the rains, so watch out), is to walk through **Siyu** to Faza, returning to Lamu by ferry from there. You could also do this in reverse, of course, but there is a major drawback in that the boat might not pick you up at Mtangawanda on its return if, as often happens, it's full. The walk itself can be done in a day if the tides force an early start, but you may well find yourself wanting to stay longer and breaking for at least a night in Siyu.

Two other possibilities include catching a dhow from Mtangawanda to Pate town instead of walking, though arriving at low tide means you'll have to wade through shallow waters which are favoured by stingrays – or you can catch a connecting *mtaboti* ferry at Mtangawanda for Siyu (1hr).

Some history

According to its own **history**, the *Pate Chronicle*, the town was founded in the early years of Islam with the arrival of Arabian immigrants. This statelet is supposed to have lasted until the thirteenth century, when another group of dispossessed Arab rulers – the **Nabahani** – arrived to inject new blood into Pate. The story may have been embellished by time but archeological evidence does support the existence of a flourishing port on the present site of Pate as early as the ninth century; probably by the fifteenth century the town exerted a considerable influence on most of the quasi-autonomous settlements along the coast, including Lamu. As usual, the claims of the royal line to be of overseas extraction were by now more political than biological in nature.

The first **Portuguese** visitors were friendly, trading with the Pateans for the multicoloured silk cloth for which the town had become famous, and they also introduced gunpowder, which enabled wells to be easily excavated, a fact which must have played a part in Pate's rising fortunes. During the sixteenth century, a number of Portuguese merchants settled and married in the town, but as Portugal tightened its grip and imposed taxes, relations quickly deteriorated. There were repeated uprisings and reprisals until, by the mid-seventeenth century, the Portuguese had withdrawn to the security of Fort Jesus in Mombasa. Even today, though, several families in Pate are said to be *Wa-reno* (from the Portuguese *reino*: kingdom), meaning of Portuguese or part-Portuguese descent.

During the late seventeenth and eighteenth centuries, having thrown out the old rulers and avoided domination by new invaders like the Omani Arabs, Pate underwent a **cultural rebirth** and experienced a flood of creative activity similar to Lamu's. The two towns had a lively relationship, and were frequently in a state of war. At some time during the Portuguese period, Pate's harbour had started to silt up and the town began to use Lamu's, which must have caused great difficulties. In addition, Pate was ruled by a Nabahani king who considered Lamu part of his realm. The disastrous Battle of Shela of 1812 (see p.555) marked the end of Lamu's political allegiance to Pate and the end of Pate as a city-state.

Practicalities

Apart from the motorboat (see above), you can, of course, choose to take a dhow to Pate, and even up to Kiwaiyu. If you have the time, and some companions, it's a fine trip, for which you should allow a good four to five days in all. Alternatively, if you have less time but can afford to spend a lot more, you might look into taking a speedboat (see "Listings", p.574) which would enable you to reach Pate town direct, from the south, at high tide, in less than half an hour. But you'd have to wait until the next high tide to get out of Pate creek, unless the speedboat went round to Mtangawanda or Siyu, leaving you to walk. There are many possible permutations.

Accommodation on Pate island is rarely a problem but, with no proper lodgings, a **tent** is a useful back-up. Normally, you'll be invited to stay by someone almost as soon as you arrive in a village. It's wise to take **water** with you (five litres if possible) as Pate's supplies are unpredictable and it's often very briny. As for **food**, most islanders live on home-produced food and staples brought from Lamu and, although there are a few small shops on the island, it's a good idea to have some emergency provisions. These make useful gifts as well. **Mosquitoes** and flies (especially in May and June) are a serious menace on Pate. The shops sell mosquito coils but, during the day, you may be glad to have some repellent.

If you plan on spending several days on Pate, and you're interested in the archeology of the region, you should ask for **advice** and **contact names** from Lamu Museum and Lamu Fort, and don't forget to have a good look at the photo display at the latter.

Pate town

From the dock at Mtangawanda (which has the only **beach** in the vicinity – watch out for sharks), a narrow **footpath** leads to Pate through thick bush; ask for the *ndia ya Pate*, the "path to Pate". Once on the trail it's easy to follow. You cross a broad, tidal "desert", pockmarked with fiddler crab holes, then climb a slight rise to drop through thicker bush, and arrive after an hour on the edge of town.

Despite its small size, you would hardly describe **PATE** as a village. Yet, reduced to the status of sub-location, its only link with government an assistant chief, its sole provision a primary school, the town is today a mere shadow of its former self. But at least its inhabitants are said to remain the richest on the island, thanks to their cash crop, **tobacco**, possibly introduced by the Portuguese and certainly grown here longer than anywhere else on the coast.

There's no electricity, no alcohol and obviously no cars. After Lamu it comes as a series of surprises. The town plan is pretty much the same – a maze of narrow streets and high-walled houses – but here the streets are made of earth, and the houses are built of coral and dried mud, unplastered and somehow forbidding. The overall layout is confusing, with little slope, as in Lamu, to help direction. Pateans do, in fact, refer to the "upper" and "lower" parts of town – Kitokwe and Mitaaguu respectively. The lower part is down near the town dock, which is only briefly underwater at high tide. There's a house which sometimes lets out rooms in this quarter: ask for the *nyumba ya Abala Hassan* or *nyumba ya Abdullah* (Abala Hassan's house, or Abdullah's house). There are no fixed prices (but it shouldn't be much over Ksh1000, including food), and Abdullah himself is very friendly and welcoming. The house is clean, has great views from the top rooms, and the food is filling. He can also arrange a guide for looking round the island.

If you arrive from Mtangawanda in the "upper" part of town – reputedly poorer and less friendly – you're likely to be struck immediately by the *Wapate* – the **people**, and notably the women. Brilliant, determined ladies, with short, bushy hair and rows of gold earrings, stare out directly, unhidden by *buibuis*. Some wear nineteenth-century American gold dollars or half-dollars, though these reminders of the great Yankee trading expeditions have become so valuable that many have been sold. Big **earlobe plugs** made of silver, gold or buffalo horn can also be seen, as well as nose-rings. If you speak any Swahili, you're likely to find the dialect here unrecognizable. *Wazungu* are rare and, after Lamu's studied repose, Pate is arrestingly upfront in its dealings with foreigners.

At night, the town resounds with the chimes of dozens of big old **wall clocks**, further reminders of American trade here in the nineteenth century, which, juxtaposed with the muezzins' calls to prayer, sound thoroughly bizarre.

The Nabahani ruins

More layers are peeled off Pate's enigmatic exterior when you start to explore the ruins of the **Nabahani** town just outside the modern one. The acres of walls, roofless buildings, tombs, mosques and unidentifiable structures are fascinating, the more so perhaps because this isn't an "archeological site" in the commonly expected mould. Tobacco farmers work in the stony fields between the walls.

Boys will guide you around the ruins for a small payment, but don't expect anyone to take you at night; although it's very beautiful in a full moon, you'll have to go alone because the locals are afraid of the *djinn* and ghosts living there. Most impressive are the **Mosque with Two Mihrabs**, a nearby house that still has a facing of beautiful *zidaka* (niches) on one wall, and the remains of a sizeable mansion. This last building, you'll be told, is a **Portuguese house**. Certainly, the worn-down stumps of bottle glass projecting from the top of one of its walls do lend it a curiously European flavour, and in the plaster on another wall are scratched two very obvious galleons. Its ceiling slots are square for timbers rather than round for *boriti*, as elsewhere in the ruins.

Shards of pottery and household objects lie in the rubble everywhere, but many of the interiors of the buildings are so clogged with tangled roots and vegetation that getting in is almost impossible. It is worth persevering, however: the sense of personal discovery is exciting and immensely satisfying if you can ignore the mosquitoes that silently home in on bare skin when you walk through the weeds.

Many of the walls and buildings have already been demolished to obtain lime for tobacco cultivation. Without weighty financial backing, it's hard to see how the National Museums of Kenya (NMK) could ever preserve the remains of old Pate as well as compensate the farmers. Gradually, tragically, it is all returning to the soil. In the meantime, see it – and photograph it – while you still can.

Siyu

The **path from Pate to Siyu** is a slightly tricky eight kilometres. Having set off in the right direction, the first half-hour is fairly straightforward; if in doubt, bear right. You come to a crossroads (easily missed unless you look backwards) and turn right. This narrow red dirt path soon broadens into a track known as the *barabara ya gari* (the "motor highway" – there was once a car); it takes you to a normally dry tidal inlet where you veer left a little before continuing straight on through thick bush for another hour to reach Siyu.

Wherever the bush on either side is high enough you may come across gigantic **spiders' webs** strung across the path. The matching spiders are brightly coloured, non-hairy, and merely waiting for insects, but they are nevertheless intimidating. Fortunately, they have the sense to build their webs high up and well out of the way.

Siyu town

SIYU is even less well documented than Pate. Still less accessible by sea, the town was a flourishing and unsuspected centre of Islamic scholarship from the seventeenth to the nineteenth century and apparently something of a **sanctuary** for Muslim intellectuals and craftsmen. While Lamu, Pate and other trading towns were engaged in political rivalry and physical skirmishing, Siyu never had its heart in commerce or maritime activities, and never attracted much Portuguese attention. Instead, there was enormous devotion to **Koran-copying**, **book-making**, **text illumination**, and cottage industries like the **woodcarving** and **leatherwork** for which it's still famous locally. Siyu **sandals** are said to be absolutely the best, though plastic flip-flops have forced almost all the makers out of business. Siyu **carved doors** are among the most beautiful of all Swahili doors, with distinctive guilloche patterns and inlays of ground shell.

The sources of wealth and stability for Siyu's florescence are a little mysterious, but the town's agricultural base obviously supported it well and it was probably the largest settlement on the island in the early nineteenth century, with up to 30,000 inhabitants. In 1873, the British vice consul in Zanzibar could still describe it as "the pulse of the whole district".

These days you wouldn't know it. Less than 4000 people live here, and signs of the old brilliance are hard to find. Siyu lost its independence and presumably much of its artistic flair when the sultan of Zanzibar's Omani troops first occupied the fort in 1847 – though it was twenty years before the Omanis were able to hold it for more than a brief spell. Built in the early nineteenth century (no one knows for sure by whom), **Siyu Fort** is the town's most striking building and indeed, in purely monumental terms, the most imposing building on the whole island. Substantially renovated, it is one of the few surviving traces of the glory days. It's freely accessible, though watch out for dangers like the well and the unstable walls. Around the outskirts of Siyu on the south side are a number of quite impressive **tombs**. The big domed tomb with porcelain niches dates from 1853.

Most of Siyu's houses today conform to the "open-box" plan typical of the Kenyan coast: yellowish mud with a ridged *makuti* roof, open at each end. These houses stand, each on its own, with no real streets to connect them so, although it's larger than Pate, Siyu feels far more like a village. The cultural isolation of these communities from each other, a separateness which continues to this day, is easily appreciated after arriving in Siyu from Pate. There are still few *buibuis* here, but there's much less jewellery in evidence and the atmosphere is altogether less severe.

For **accommodation**, it helps if you've had a word with the museum people in Lamu.

Shanga ruins

You'll need the help of a qualified guide if you hope to visit the ruins of **SHANGA**, a large Swahili town at least 1000 years old, which would be almost impossible to find unaided. Expect to pay around a couple of hundred shillings for a guide. Shanga is on the south coast of the island, about an hour's walk from Siyu. You have to fight your way, literally, through the undergrowth when you arrive at the site. The most impressive sight is the white pillar tomb, eminently phallic, which you come to first. The very large Friday mosque nearby and a second mosque nearer the sea are only the most obvious of innumerable other remains in every direction.

In 1980, Shanga was largely cleared, and partly excavated, by a team from the NMK, with Cambridge University archeologists and Operation Drake participating. More recently, London University excavated the site. What they found is a walled site of thirteen acres, with five access gates and a cemetery outside the walls containing 340 stone tombs. There was even a sea wall. Inside the town, 130 houses were surveyed, together with what looks to have been a palace similar in some respects to the one at Gedi. Shanga is believed to have been occupied from the ninth to the fourteenth centuries and, like Gedi, no very convincing reasons have been found for why it should have been abandoned, nor why it was never mentioned by travellers and traders of the time.

Limited work has been done here to restore some of the plaster in a set of wall niches and on the fluted pillar tomb, but on the whole the clearing and excavating only seems to have encouraged the jungle. Getting from one ruin to the next isn't easy. Dangerously camouflaged **wells** and **snakes**, both common, add further to the Shanga experience. If you walk on down to the sea – and assuming you have a certain capacity for hardship in paradise – there's a beautiful **beach** and some ideal camping spots.

Faza

Siyu to **FAZA** is a shorter walk than from Pate to Siyu and more interesting, through waist-high grass, fertile *shambas* and sections of bush. It takes about two hours, but you'll need guidance, at least as far as the airstrip inherited from a 1980s oil-prospecting venture. From there it's straightforward. An hour or so out of Siyu, you reach the first *shambas*. There are usually people on the path; if you catch up with someone from behind, announce your presence before trying to pass. Strangers are rare and you could give someone quite a fright.

On a coast of islands, it's not surprising that Faza itself is almost an island, surrounded by tidal flats and mangroves. A secondary school, health centre, police station (with nothing to do) and even a post office and telephone exchange have made Faza the most important settlement on Pate island. There's even a Land Rover ambulance donated by Saudi Arabia, the only vehicle on the island. Every few years a lodging house opens, but the lack of visitors forces them to close sooner or later. There's a very unprepossessing council guest house which is available in theory. **Private accommodation**, though, is easy to find. Fishing is the commonest occupation, with much of the catch going to a cold room at Kisingitini, from where it's shipped to Mombasa. Faza suffered a serious fire in 1990, which razed many houses to the ground and caused devastation. Today, you would hardly know.

As a contemporary Kenyan rural centre, Faza makes an interesting place to walk around and you're almost certain to have plenty of time to fill before the boat leaves. One part of the village is devoted exclusively to cattle stalls, but goats run everywhere, ruining the efforts of the primary school headmaster to prevent soil erosion on the badly rutted and sloping football field. A fine evening stroll takes you across the mud on a new concrete causeway to the thickets on the "mainland", where the island's expanding secondary school is located. From Faza you could, if you wanted, walk on to the **other villages** on the island, all fairly modern and bunched together within forty minutes of Faza: Kisingitini, Bajumwali, Tundwa (Chundwa), and the closest, Nyambogi.

Faza's history and archeology

Archeologically Faza has less to offer than its neighbours. It was one of the most defiant Swahili towns over any attempts to usurp its independence. It was razed by the Pate army after a dispute over water rights in the fifteenth century, and again by the Portuguese in 1586 after collaborating with the Turkish fleet of Amir Ali Bey. On this occasion, the entire population was massacred and the head of Faza's king was taken to Goa in a barrel of salt to be paraded triumphantly in the streets. Faza's unfortunate history may partly account for its relative lack of ruins, but one success is commemorated in the **tomb** of Seyyid Hamed bin Ahmed al-Busaidy (also known as Amir Hamad), commander-in-chief of the sultan of Zanzibar's forces, who met his death in 1844 under a hail of arrows. He was on an expedition against Siyu and Pate, and retreating to the relative safety of Faza when he was ambushed by a party of Siyu bowmen. His grave (*kaburi*), with a long epitaph, lies just outside Faza.

There are several ruined mosques around Faza, including the very crumbled Kunjanja Mosque. The ruins of the eighteenth-century **Mbwarashally Mosque** (also known as the Shala Fatani Mosque) merit a visit, however. Now theoretically protected by the National Museums of Kenya, the mosque – barring its *mihrab* – is just a pile of rubble; the *mihrab*, however, turns out to incorporate exquisite and unusual heart motifs, including the *shahada* (the Islamic creed) inscribed within an inverted heart shape.

Kiwaiyu

From Faza you're within striking distance of the desert island retreat of **Kiwaiyu**, about an hour by *mtaboti*, if you can find one. It is likely, however, that a group dhow charter in Lamu would be a cheaper way to visit. For Ksh3000–4000 a day all-in, you can charter a small dhow for four or five days, including breakfast and dinner, snorkelling and fishing gear, and plenty of fresh water. Split this price among five or six people and it becomes very cheap. The best advice is to form an enthusiastic group around the lodgings in Lamu, then start direct negotiations, as soon as possible, with whoever is going to be running the show. Too often, arrangements are made with dhow hustlers that owners and crew can't or won't honour.

You can expect to spend 24 to 36 hours on the journey in each direction, depending on wind, tides and the skill of the crew – though with the wind behind you it's possible to get up to Kiwaiyu in under eight hours. The snorkelling around the **Kiunga Marine National Reserve** is nice enough, though not as consistently good as Malindi/Watamu, but the experience of sailing, the nights under the stars, and the acquaintance of the Swahili crew are altogether highly recommended.

If a dhow trip does not appeal, you can **fly** to Kiwayu with Airkenya daily from Nairobi ($156 each way), Mombasa ($150), Malindi ($130) or Lamu ($65).

On Kiwaiyu, **budget travellers** stay at the reasonable *Kasim's* camping and *banda* site, near the beach on the inshore coast of the island just a few hundred metres north of **Kiwaiyu village**. *Kasim's* consists of several palm-mat *bandas*, plus a couple of unusual tree houses (❶; camping Ksh200). Most people just drag one of the cane beds down onto the beach and sleep under the stars. The village has limited provisions in a couple of shops, but most people eat what is prepared each day and served in the little "dining room".

Five minutes south of *Kasim's* is the village, a quiet, rural place but friendly enough. A further ten minutes south, you come to the "Italian cold store" – a stalled shellfish export project with attached accommodation, which looks like a long-term investment that's being ignored. Ten minutes' walk further still, you reach a house on the high southern tip of the island. This is a fishing camp (the plane you may have seen parked near the village belongs to the owner), but it's strictly private and does not provide accommodation to walk-in visitors. From here, the superb, ocean-facing beach, with the reef close offshore, is just a scramble down the sandy hillside. There are one or two first-class **snorkelling** spots off this southern tip of the island, with huge coral heads and a multitude of fish. Ask for precise directions as it's possible to spend hours looking and still miss them. You'll need good footwear to survive the dead coral reef.

Luxury lodges

There are two **luxury lodges** at Kiwaiyu. The one on the island itself is *Munira Island Camp*, about 2km north of Kiwaiyu village, a group of *bandas* planted on the crest of the island to catch the breeze (bookings through PO Box 40088 Nairobi ⓣ02/512213, ⓕ512543, Ⓦwww.kiwaiyuisland.com; FB ❾). "Mike's Bandas", as the establishment is also known, is very laid-back and civilized, and there's plentiful birdlife in the vicinity. It's a favourite with Anglo-Kenyans and those who find even *Peponi* too busy. Return transfers are around $150 by speedboat from *Peponi*, $80 by dhow, or free from *Kiwaiyu Safari Village*, the other lodge, on the mainland a little further north.

Kiwaiyu Safari Village (bookings in Nairobi on ⓣ02/503030, ⓕ503149; all-inclusive ❾) is nestled on a pristine, palm-shaded beach across the channel from the northern end of Kiwaiyu, within the Kiunga National Marine Reserve. The combination of exclusive, palm- and grass-thatch cottages (all s/c) and excellent food and watersports makes for a romantic getaway at a very high price (from around $600/day for two).

Travel details

❻

More detailed information on various transport companies, prices and schedules are included in the "Moving on" sections throughout this chapter.

Buses

Buses operate in both directions with the same frequency.

Mombasa to: Busia (1 daily; 15hr); Dar es Salaam (3 daily; 14–16hr), via Tanga (7hr); Garissa via Kilifi, Malindi, Garsen and Hola (2–3 daily; 8–10hr); Kisumu (1 daily; 12hr); Lamu via Kilifi and Malindi (4 daily; 7–8hr); Malaba (1 daily; 15hr); Malindi via Kilifi (aproximately hourly; 90min); Nairobi (frequent, but especially around 7am and 7pm; 7–9hr).

Matatus

Likoni to: Kinango via Kwale (1hr); Kwale (30min); Lungalunga (2hr); Msambweni (1hr); Shelly Beach (15min); Shimoni (1hr 30min); Ukunda (30min). Sometimes direct to Diani Beach (45min) – otherwise change vehicles at Ukunda.

Mombasa to: Bamburi (15min); Kaloleni (1hr 30min); Malindi (1hr 30min); Mariakani (1hr); Mtwapa (30min); Nairobi (6hr); Nyali ("Reef") (15min). Occasional services to Kinango via Mazeras (1hr 30min).

Trains

For booking details, see "Moving on from Mombasa" (p.472).

Mombasa to: Nairobi (Tues, Wed, Fri & Sun at 7pm; 13hr 55min).

Flights

Kiwayu to: Mombasa (Airkenya daily; 1hr 55min) via Lamu (15min) and Malindi (1hr 20min); Nairobi (Airkenya daily; 1hr 45min).
Lamu to: Kiwayu (Airkenya daily; 15min); Malindi (Kenya Airways and Airkenya both daily; 30–35min); Mombasa (Airkenya daily; 1hr 10min); Nairobi (Airkenya and Kenya Airways both daily; 1hr 20min–2hr 5min.
Malindi to: Kiwayu (Airkenya daily; 4hr 50min–6hr 5min); Lamu (Kenya Airways and Airkenya both daily; 30–35min); Nairobi (Airkenya daily, Kenya

Airways 1–2 daily; 1hr 15min).
Mombasa to: Dar es Salaam (Air Tanzania 6 weekly; 1hr 30min) via Zanzibar (50min); Kiwayu (Airkenya daily; 5hr 25min–6hr 40min) via Malindi (25min) and Lamu (1hr 10min); Nairobi Wilson Airport (Kenya Airways 6–7 daily, Airkenya 2–3 daily; 1hr–1hr 15min); Nairobi Kenyatta Airport (Regional Air Services/British Airways daily; 1hr); Ukunda Airkenya 2 weekly; 15min).
Ukunda to: Mombasa (Airkenya 2 weekly; 15min); Nairobi (Airkenya 3 weekly; 1hr 15min–2hr).

Sea travel

Dhows from Lamu to Mombasa are relatively straightforward (though the other direction is virtually impossible). Once you've found an agreeable captain and assuming it's the right time of year (roughly once a week from December–March). The procedure starts with a visit to the District Commissioner's secretary's office (see p.573) for a form absolving the captain and the government of all responsibility in the case of mishap. Then take one copy to the captain, which he'll present to customs, on the first floor across the courtyard, when he files his crew and passenger manifest. They'll tell you it's a 36-hour trip to Mombasa, but count on some doldrums and allow up to three or even four days. Bring fruit and anything else you anticipate needing to break the monotony of unvarying fish and *ugali* meals. You should get a passage for less than Ksh2000.

Bodo (small village near Shirazi) to Pemba (Tanzania); frequent cargo dhow; 7hr; around Ksh1000–2000.

Shimoni frequent cargo dhows to Pemba (around Ksh1000–2000) and Zanzibar (around Ksh2000–3000). Customs and immigration have offices in Shimoni. The journey is much more difficult the other way, however, as many boats are smuggling goods from Tanzania into Kenya and do not want to complicate matters by carrying foreign passengers.

The North

CHAPTER 7

Highlights

✳ **Central Island National Park** Totally untouched volcanic sanctuary in the middle of Lake Turkana, where Nile crocodiles breed. A memorable boat trip from the lake's western shore. See p.597

✳ **Maralal** Remote supply town with a wild atmosphere. Try the exuberant *Buffalo Hotel* or Yare Safaris' base where annual camel races take place. See p.601

✳ **South Horr** Lush oasis hemmed in by mountains, with fine camping and great opportunities to meet Samburu people. See p.609

✳ **Loiyangalani** End-of-the-world kind of place on the eastern shore of shimmering Lake Turkana, home of the fishing and croc- and hippo-hunting Elmolo people. See p.611

✳ **Marsabit** Remotely located in the northern deserts, a highland oasis with a fascinating cultural mix. Visit Marsabit National Park with superb crater lakes, elephants and amazing birdlife. See p.624

7

The North

There is one half of Kenya about which the other half knows nothing and seems to care even less.

Negley Farson, *Last Chance in Africa*

Kenya is rarely thought of in terms of desert, but **the North** – over half the country in area – is exclusively arid land, burned out for more than ten months of the year. Unfortunately, it's also renowned as the most **dangerous** area in Kenya, with cattle-rustling, tribal feuding and armed banditry making a large swathe of the north, east of the Isiolo–Marsabit–Moyale road, too risky to visit. See the box on p.618 for fur-

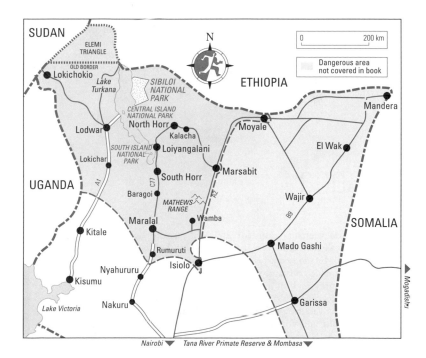

Nairobi ▼   Tana River Primate Reserve & Mombasa ▼

ther advice and precautions. Apart from these trouble spots, the old Northern Frontier District (still called NFD by many) remains one of the most exciting and adventurous parts of Africa for travel: a vast tract of territory, crisscrossed by ancient migration routes, and still tramped by the nomadic Samburu, Boran, Rendille, Gabbra, Turkana, and Somali herders.

The target for most travellers is the wonderful jade splash of **Lake Turkana**, very remote in feel and highly unpredictable in nature (when British sailors first ventured out on it, they reckoned it could turn "rougher than the North Sea"). To get there, you have the option of organized camping safaris, as well as *matatus* and lorries up from the hub of highlands Kenya. Elsewhere in the north, travelling can be harder going, usually by gut-shaking lorries, with heat and dust constant, the water often briny and useless for washing. But the **desert towns** have their own rewards, not least in the bewilderment of arriving and finding places so little known yet so important to an enormous compass of countryside and population.

Because of the layout of the **roads** and **tracks** that radiate north from the Central Highlands, you'll need to make a decision about which "spokes" to cover; there are few east–west routes. Don't be over-ambitious. Bus and *matatu* services are patchy at best, whilst lorries and hitching can work out, but are exhausting. If you're driving, water, enough fuel and mechanical know-how should be your priorities since you'll need to be almost self-sufficient. Most people on business, and relief workers, now fly to the North, and cannot conceive why a tourist would even want to go there, let alone by land transport. In practical terms, the current situation limits you to the two main routes up to Lake Turkana, the Mathews Range and, with caution, the route to Marsabit, which then doubles back to Turkana via North Horr.

Though the landscape is parched for most of the year, when the **rains** do come (usually around May) they can have dramatic effect, bringing torrents of water along the ravines, tearing away fords and bridges, and sweeping over the plains to leave an ooze of mud and new shoots. In these conditions, you can easily be stranded – even along the paved road up to Lodwar. However, if your plans are flexible, it's an exciting time to explore. Driving your own vehicle during the rainy season is not recommended unless you've got 4WD and experience.

Turkana

Lake Turkana stretches south for 250km from the Ethiopian border, down through Kenya's arid lands, bisecting the rocky deserts like a turquoise sickle. It's hemmed in by sandy wastes and black-and-brown volcanic ranges, and the lake scene changes constantly. The water, glassy, milky blue one minute, can become slate-grey and choppy or a glaring emerald green, sometimes even jade, the next.

The lake was discovered for the rest of the world only in 1888 by the Austrians **Teleki** and **von Hohnel**, who named it "Rudolf" after their archduke and patron. Later, it became eulogized as the "Jade Sea" in John Hillaby's

ELEMI
TRIANGLE

ETHIOPIA

OLD BORDER

Lokichokio & Sudan

Lokitaung

Ileret

North
Island

SIBILOI
NATIONAL
PARK

Koobi
Fora

Lake
Turkana

Alla Bay

Camp Turkana

Gajos

Moiti
Hill

Kalokol

Fishing
Lodge

Namoratunga
(Prehistoric Site)

Hurran Hurra

CENTRAL
ISLAND
NATIONAL
PARK

North Horr

Eliye
Springs

Gas

Marsabit & Chalbi Desert

Lodwar

N

SOUTH
ISLAND
NATIONAL
PARK

MOUNT KULAL

Oasis
Lodge

Loiyangalani

Peak
2293 m

Gametrackers
Campsite

OL DOINYO MARA

Lokichar

NYIRU RANGE

0   50 km

SUGATA VALLEY

South Horr

Kurungu
Camp

Kitale

Maralal

book about his camel trek. The name "Turkana" only came into being during the wholesale Kenyanization of place names in the 1970s. By then, it had also been dubbed the "Cradle of Mankind", the site of revelatory fossil discoveries in the field of human evolution. And it was becoming something of a spiritual mecca for atavists, an excuse for a week of riotous assembly in a safari lorry or a dignified weekend in a Cessna and a lakeshore lodge.

But to depict Lake Turkana as "Kenya's latest touristic discovery", as one or two glossies would have you believe is, thankfully, a monstrous piece of hype: there are two lodges, one on each shore, catering for perhaps a dozen people between them at any one time. Otherwise, there are a few B&Ls, one or two windy campsites and that's it. As yet, the only **asphalt** – that certain sign of imminent change – is the crooked finger that reaches north from **Kitale** to **Lodwar** and on to **Kalokol** on the western shore.

Ecology and climate

Lake Turkana is the biggest permanent desert lake in the world, with a shoreline longer than the whole of Kenya's sea coast. Yet today it has been reduced to a mere sliver of its former expanse. Like some gigantic sump, with rivers flowing in but no outlet available, a staggering three metres of water depth **evaporates** from its surface each year (nearly a centimetre a day). As a result, it is alkaline, though not inimical to some aquatic life.

In common with other lakes with no outflow, the **water level** is subject to sometimes wild fluctuations. From the mid-1980s to 1997, the level receded steadily, leaving parts of the 1980s shoreline over 8km from the lake. But the 1997–98 El Niño rains, combined with completion of both the Turkwel Dam hydroelectric scheme in Kenya and River Omo irrigation projects in Ethiopia, led to a six-metre rise in the lake level in the space of less than a year. By 2001 the lake was slowly receding once more as the effects of these rains diminished. The result of this has been relief all round, as fish stocks have recovered from years of drought and former fishing villages rediscover their vocation. Yet less than 10,000 years ago the lake surface was 150m higher, and spread south as far as the now desolate Suguta Valley.

This mammoth inland sea fed the headwaters of the Nile, which accounts for the presence of enormous **Nile perch** (sometimes weighing over 100kg) and Africa's biggest population of **Nile crocodiles** – between 10,000 and 22,000 of them. Turkana is one of the few places where you can still see great stacks of them basking on sand banks. There is a profusion of **birdlife**, too, including European migrants seen most spectacularly on their way home between March and May. And **hippos**, widely hunted and starved from many of their former lakeshore haunts through lack of grazing, still manage to hang on in fairly large numbers, though you won't see many unless you go out of your way.

Climatically, Turkana is devastatingly hot and dry for ten months of the year, and unpleasantly muggy during the rains. It is notorious for its strong easterly **winds** which, while not incessant, puff and gust energetically most of the time and occasionally become demonic. The winds, more than hippos or crocodiles, are the cause of most accidental deaths of local people on the lake.

The **people** you are most likely to meet are **Turkana** (p.593) on the western and southern shores of the lake round to Loiyangalani, **Samburu** (p.608) south of Loiyangalani, **Elmolo** (p.615) to the north of Loiyangalani, and **Gabbra** (p.623) to the east. The Turkana and Samburu are pastoral people with great reverence for their cattle, the Gabbra herd camels, while the Elmolo are traditionally property-less hunters and fishers.

Getting there

There are **three road routes** to Turkana: one to the western shore from Kitale and two to the east shore from Maralal and Marsabit (the latter very remote). There is no route connecting the east and west shores – the volcanic **Suguta Valley** forms a blazing hot barrier.

The **western approach** from **Kitale to Lodwar** is the one used by most independent travellers without their own vehicles. There's no bus, but a number of crammed **matatus** leave Kitale for Lodwar every morning from around 6am (see Chapter 4, p.339).

On the east, the **Maralal–Loiyangalani route** is the one used by nearly all of the Turkana **camping safari** lorries (the main operators are Gametrackers and Safari Camp Services, see pp.140 & 141). If you can afford $400–500 or so for a week-long trip, it has definite advantages: magnificent scenery and a great sense of adventure.

The third route, from **Isiolo to Loiyangalani** via **Marsabit** and **North Horr**, is feasible if you are prepared to wait around for days for lifts, first from Isiolo to Marsabit, and then on to North Horr. But it's not much used and you should be prepared to give up the idea after a day or two if nothing is going your way. The safari company Gametrackers uses this route for their longer Turkana Bus trips via the Chalbi Desert, and may give you a lift (route details are given on p.628).

A last option is **flying**. As there are no scheduled flights, the price is variable but always expensive, costing around $1500 for hiring a small plane, so obviously it works out much cheaper in a group. Ask around at Nairobi's Wilson Airport, or try one of the companies listed on p.140-143, or an air charter company (p.144). Although flying here destroys much of the sense of the lake's isolation, and the usual brief visit doesn't give enough time to explore, the flight itself – low down between the Aberdares and Mount Kenya – is sublime.

North to Lodwar and the western lakeshore

From Kitale, a number of **matatus** leave for Lodwar in the early morning (the first at around 6am), with the last stragglers leaving just after midday, taking about seven hours. Check the going rate with other passengers, as tourists are sometimes ripped off on this route. Alternatively, you might try **hitching** – there are plenty of trucks and jeeps bound for the aid centre at Lokichokio, northwest of Lodwar near the Sudanese border, and stopping a vehicle is not too difficult, though you'll have to bargain hard for the price. Make sure you take plenty of water for this trip, as unexplained delays, breakdowns and the like are all too common.

The best part of the journey is the beginning – covered in Chapter Four – as you pass **Saiwa Swamp National Park** (p.339) then go through the green valleys of **Trans-Nzoia** and **West Pokot** towards **Kapenguria** (p.340), site of the trial of Kenyatta and five colleagues in 1953. Kapenguria, or rather the turn-off for it at Makutano, is reputedly a good place for lining up lifts, with a relief supply lorry passing through daily at around 3pm. The ride costs around Ksh300 for a place in the back, not the fastest way, but with great views. The last **petrol station** and bank before Lodwar are at Makutano. Beyond here, the road scales a neck of the Cherangani Hills (pp.282–286), then plunges headily along their northern slopes, following a tributary of the Turkwel River before slipping through the defiles of the **Marich Pass** (p.342) with its excellent *banda* and campsite, and down onto the scorching South Turkana Plains.

From the thorny wilderness of the **Turkana Plains** beyond, it's hard to extract much of scenic interest unless you're a desert aficionado, though the regular stops to pick up increasingly wild-looking passengers maintain gently heightening expectations about the far north you're heading into.

Once down on the plains, the tarmac begins to break up, but not so badly as to necessitate 4WD. There is a possible detour to the **Nasalot National Reserve** ($15, children/students $5; access by car only – Ksh200 extra – unless you arrange a walking escort with the rangers at the gate), which bounds the northern slopes of the mountains and the southern fringes of the south Turkana plains. From the gate, 6km off the Lodwar road (signposted on the left), the winding paved route drops several hundred metres into the heat, with plunging precipices and spectacular views all round, to the **Turkwel Gorge** and **hydroelectric dam**.

As the reserve is mostly covered with thick bush, **spotting animals** isn't all that easy: the elephants here, though larger than their southern cousins, hide themselves pretty well, and your best chance of seeing them is on the paved road at dawn or dusk. You'd be unusually fortunate to see any of the reserve's lions and leopards. Otherwise, the diminutive dik-dik antelopes are plentiful, if shy – you'll see them bounding into the bushes ahead of you, and there are also buffalo and warthogs. Camping is not allowed, but there are some extremely good value **bandas** by the dam (Ksh300 per three bed-room).

Beyond Nasalot back on the main A1 Lodwar road, another detour to the right takes you to the **South Turkana National Reserve** (free entry, though there are plans to extract charges as for Nasalot), which lacks Nasalot's scenic grandeur, but is where the elephants migrate to between March and July.

Lodwar

For most Kenyans, mention of **LODWAR** conjures up remote and outlandish images of the badlands, an aberrant place where anything could befall you. And the Turkana District capital is, to put it mildly, a wild town – unformed, loud, and somehow incongruous in this searing wilderness. During the 1980s it became Kenya's desert boom town, the lake's fishing, the possibility of oil dis-coveries and the new road from Kitale all encouraging inward migration. While **Turkana people** have always predominated, **Luo** and **Luhya** also arrived in search of opportunities. With the exhaustion of farming country in the south, Lodwar and the area around it became increasingly attractive to pio-neers and cowboys of all sorts. But this expansion has now fizzled out and the harsher realities of economics have asserted themselves: children plead for "shillingi" wherever you go, and the wannabe "guides" and hustlers are more persistent than elsewhere. Newspapers arrive with the first *matatu* each after-noon, hours after the rest of the country have received theirs, and men sit read-ing them, discussing the daily stories, trying to reduce the **isolation** felt here. When news of the August 1982 "coup" came through, the police in Lodwar immediately freed all the prisoners and relaxed with beer for the rest of the day. It's that sort of town.

Whispers about **oil** in the north have long since ceased; most of the NGOs pulled out as the famine receded in the late 1980s (though the war in Sudan seems to be gradually drawing them in again), and the only dream left lies in tourists' pockets, where cheap trinkets suddenly become worth a week's wage. From the shrivelled overpriced fruit and vegetables (trucked up from Kitale) and all the small signs of affluence – radios, bicycles, stereos, factory furniture – that still draw in the people from the sticks, Lodwar's lasting impression is of a sad, desolate place.

Until very recently, **the Turkana**, the main people of the western shore of the lake, had very little contact with the outside world, or even with the Republic of Kenya. You'll still see older people in more remote parts wearing very few clothes or, in some cases, animal skins; and some of the head-loads carried by Turkana women seem little short of miraculous. Linguistically, the Turkana are related to the Maa-speaking Samburu and Maasai. Indeed, along the northwest shore of the lake, the people are probably an old mixture of Turkana and Samburu, although, like the Luo (also distantly related by language), the Turkana did not traditionally practise circumcision. They moved east from their old homeland around the present-day borders of Sudan and Uganda in the seventeenth century. The desolate region between the lake and the Ugandan border which they now occupy is barely habitable land, and their daily struggle for existence has profoundly influenced the shape of their society and, inevitably, helped create the funnel into modern Kenya which Lodwar, with its road, has become.

The Turkana are more individualistic than most Kenyan peoples and they show a disregard for the ties of clan and family that must have emerged through repeated famines and wars. Some anthropologists have begun to suggest that loyalty to particular **cattle brands** is a more important indicator of identity than blood or lineage. Although essentially **pastoralists**, always on the move to the next spot of grazing, they do grow crops when they can get seed and when the rains are sufficient. Often the rains fail, notably during the prolonged drought of the early 1980s, which took a terrible toll on children. The situation has eased since then, but life is still very much a matter of day-to-day survival, aided here and there by hand-outs from the UN and other agencies. With characteristic pragmatism, the Turkana have scorned the taboo against fish so prevalent among herders, and **fishing** is a viable option that is increasingly popular.

Turkana **bellicosity** is infamous in Kenya (Turkana migrants to the towns of the south are frequently employed as *askaris*). Relations with their neighbours – especially the Merille to the north of the lake, the Samburu to the south, and the Pokot to the southwest – have often been openly aggressive. British forces were engaged in the gradual conquest of the Turkana – the usual killings, livestock raids and property destruction – and they succeeded, at some cost, in eventually disarming them of their guns in the 1920s. But the Merille, meanwhile, were obtaining arms from Abyssinia's imperial government, and they took advantage of the Turkana's defenceless position. When war was declared by Italian-held Abyssinia in 1940, the British rearmed the Turkana, who swiftly exacted their savage revenge on the Merille. They were later disarmed again. Now, it is the Turkana who are the victims once again: in the far north, heavily armed Toposa raiders from Sudan are thought to have killed almost ten thousand Turkana in recent years.

Violence is no longer in the air down at **Ferguson's Gulf** – though you might see older Turkana men with scars on their arms and chests to indicate who they've killed: females on the left upper arm and chest, males on the right. Turkana directness is unmistakable in all their dealings with *wazungu*. They are, for example, resolute and stubborn bargainers, while offers of relatively large sums for photos often leave them stone cold – not necessarily from any mystical fear of the camera, but because of a shrewd estimation of what the market will stand, and hence, presumably, of their own reputation. Unlike the Maa-speaking warriors, the Turkana rarely pose for photos for a living, although the exceptions are increasing in number.

Practicalities

Lodwar is an incredibly hot, dusty town most of the year, but for a day or two you may find the rough, frontier atmosphere exhilarating, especially after the faintly parochial air of the Highlands. There's a KCB **bank** (which changes traveller's cheques, though you might have to wait for hours), a **post office** (Mon–Fri 8am–1pm & 3–5pm, Sat 9am–noon; international calls are theoretically possible) and a number of places to stay.

Most presentable of the town centre **lodgings** is the *Turkwel Lodge* (PO Box 14 ☎0393/20166 or Lodwar 900; bed only ❶, B&B in cottages ❷), a fairly clean place with the very definite luxury of fans in each room, nets in most, a good restaurant and a bar popular with expats, with a disco Fridays and Saturdays (free before 9pm). This is where officials and aid workers stay. A sign in the rooms says: "We hope your stay with us will be quite nice". It's certainly quite noisy, with Congolese tunes thumping out until the early hours. The *Nature Hotel* opposite (PO Box 123 ☎0393/21254) is worth checking out; it has s/c *bandas*, a half-decent restaurant and a bar. Considerably cheaper and less salubrious are: *Africana Lodge* (PO Box 99 ☎0393/21254; ❶), with some s/c rooms; and *Air Fan Lodge* (PO Box 433; no phone; ❶), non-s/c rooms only but all have fans (dependent on the dodgy electricity) and some nets in a basic, secure compound. At a rock-bottom price is the *Beer Garden* (PO Box 19 ☎0393/21218; ❶), a relaxed sort of place to collapse into after a heavy session.

There are two **lodgings outside town**. Perched on a slight hill, and shaded by acacias, *Nawoitorong Guest House* (PO Box 192 ☎0393/21208, ⓕ21572, ⓔedfrhp@imul.com; rooms B&B ❶; cottages B&B ❸; camping Ksh100 per person), is the best, signposted 1km south over the Turkwel bridge, then 1.5km east. This is part of the Turkana Women's Conference Centre, a co-operative which rehabilitates and cares for widows, single mothers and drought victims. Starting with four women in 1984 who began baking bread, it currently employs over 35 and uses the money generated to educate Turkana women about basic issues such as health and hygiene. Solar-powered lighting is supplemented by kerosene lamps, there are good showers, they still bake their own bread, and serve occasionally excellent food. The non-s/c rooms in the main compound are spotless and have great mosquito nets, but lack privacy and can be noisy; better but more expensive are the three stand-alone s/c cottages. Male tourists can stay as well as women

On the left along the track to *Nawoitorong* is the *Lodwar Club* (PO Box 123 ☎0393/21252; ❸), with five s/c rooms with some nets and ceiling fans, in a modern but already mouldering block, and optional use of kitchen facilities. There's also an under-used *nyama choma* bar.

There are a few reasonable *hotelis* in town for **food**. *Hotel Salama* is good all round; the *Africana* has good chapatis (and tourists); *Mombasa Hotel* has hot, spicy food as well as omelettes and pasta and is open 24hr, as is the Somali-run *Rafiki Hotel* which has pilau and some pasta; *New Safari Hotel* also serves pilau, fried meat and *mboga*; *New Lodwar Tourist Hotel* has chicken and *kienyeji*; the *Beer Garden* has *nyama choma*; and *Delicious Café* is the only place to eat *irio*. All are fast and cheap. More upmarket are the *Nature Hotel* and *Turkwel Lodge*, which both do pepper steaks, various kinds of grilled meat and the usual rubbery chicken. **Drinking** can be done virtually anywhere, and the range of bottled beers available, often cold, beats that of most Highlands towns; *Nature Hotel* and *Turkwel Lodge* are the most refined. For more characterful drinking try: the *Beer Garden* and *DM's Corner Bar* (both relaxed and mellow); the *New Chamunga B&L* (lurid seats and clientele); *Lodwar Rest House Bar* (*ndombolo* music till late); *Bahati Bar* (drink till you drop); and the *Salama*, where you can also chew *miraa*.

Apart from just hanging around and taking in the scene, there's not a lot to do in Lodwar. If you have the time and some spare energy, you can **hike** up one of the hills behind the town (the guides from *Nawoitorong Guest House* are best). Lodwar's canopy of acacias makes it surprisingly invisible below, but the view stretches for miles. For **handicrafts**, you'll find good woven baskets on sale at *Nawoitorong*, as well as in the town's streets, where boys will also offer you Turkana trinkets. If you plan any walking, you might want to pick up a pair of **5000-mile shoes** (flip-flops made from old truck tyres), which are comfortable and virtually unbreakable – they're made by the old men outside *DM's Corner Bar*.

Note, when heading **back to Kitale** by *matatu*, you will have to book your seat – and almost certainly pay for it – the evening before. Most leave in the early hours, connecting nicely with buses returning to Nairobi, though you may be lucky and find some during the day if you want a more civilized trip.

Kalokol

Though Ferguson's Gulf (see p.596) is the only easily accessible place to head for on the lakeshore, the village you want initially is called **KALOKOL** (formerly known as Lokwar Kangole). There are several *matatus* making the trip daily from Lodwar; if you're hitching, try the Kobil station or wait further up along the road.

There's little point in visiting Kalokol for its own sake. It has a surprising amount of hassle for such a small place (600 or so permanent inhabitants), and only one basic **lodging**, *Kalokol Tours Lodge & Hotel* (PO Box 3 ☎18 Kalokol; ❶), which is overrun by irritating wannabe guides. It does, however, have space to pitch a tent (Ksh50) and also offers **camel safaris** (the catch being that you have to buy the camel, only to resell it later at half the price). Unless you're a seasoned bargainer, you can forget their offers of boat trips, as the prices are ridiculously high – far better to enquire with the fishermen on the lakeshore proper, 4km to the east.

The dancing stones of Namoratunga

During the one- to two-hour journey to Kalokol, look out for the **standing stones of Namoratunga**, 15km before Kalokol on the right, some fifty metres off the road. They're easy to miss, being only a small cluster of metre-high cylindrical stones similar to the sacks of foraging sold by the Turkana, with the curious oddity that the Turkana have the habit of balancing small rocks on top of the large stones. Like a miniature Stonehenge, the pillars are a spiritual focus and, usually in December, they're the scene of a major gathering of Turkana clans. The stones pre-date the arrival of the Turkana, but little is known about them, even by the Turkana (the name "namoratunga" is used by them to describe any standing stone site). One theory, that the stones were aligned with the positions of important stars in Eastern Cushitic astronomy and were therefore used to determine the dates of ritual ceremonies, appears to have been discounted. Some people call them "dancing stones", following a legend which had a small tribe of people dancing on the site. When strangers arrived (possibly the Turkana), the dancers pleaded with the visitors not to laugh at them, a plea which they ignored, with the result that the dancers were turned to stone. More plausible reasons for their existence might be the concentration of haematite and copper ore around the site, the smelting of which (for making weapons) may have acquired ritual significance in the past. Uphill from the stones you'll find several raised rock cairns covering ancient graves, some perfectly delineated with larger regular stones. It's fascinating, and all rather mysterious.

A fishy story

In the late 1970s, **Kalokol** acquired a big Norwegian-aided fish-filleting and freezing plant and many Turkana came to the co-operative there looking for a livelihood. Altogether, around 20,000 had homed in on the lake's fishing opportunities by the early 1980s. Many were persuaded to give up their herds, but thousands of animals were driven down to the lakeshore while their owners looked for work, bringing ecological disaster to the area around Kalokol and Lodwar. Firewood gathering and over-grazing were the main causes, coupled with the prolonged drought that afflicted much of sub-Saharan Africa at that time. The fish project was a failure almost from the beginning. The plant's electricity requirements could not possibly be met by the local supply; it ran the cold rooms for just two days. Then the trawler sank. And as these major setbacks were being contemplated, the diversion for irrigation of water from the Omo River in Ethiopia, and the construction of the Turkwel Dam in south Turkana, began to decrease the lake's supply, leaving the Norwegian jetty high and dry several kilometres from the shore. Compounded by plummeting fish stocks, the project was finally abandoned amidst bitter recriminations and accusations of corruption and mismanagement. The joke, if there is one – and a lesson to all NGOs – is that the Norwegians had only considered freezing the fish: as soon as the project was jettisoned, the locals moved in, broke the factory's windows, and embarked on the glaringly obvious solution that had eluded the Europeans – inside the shaded, breezy hulk of the factory, they simply laid out their fish to dry.

While **food** supplies have improved a little with the opening of a few *dukas*, Kalokol doesn't have a lot in this line and it's not a bad idea to bring at least some fruit with you from Kitale or Lodwar. Water supplies, too, are erratic, and iodine or purifying tablets are essential. *Skyways Hotel* serves good meals and has the edge over *Kalokol Tours Lodge & Hotel*, whose menu is mostly wishful thinking.

The village is especially good for buying **Turkana crafts** and souvenirs: wonderful (and far too big) baskets, sharp wrist knives and finger knives, rich-smelling, oiled head stools, ostrich shell necklaces, and a whole array of snuff and tobacco horns made of cowhorn (traditionally) or pieces of plastic piping. When you've had enough, transport of one sort or another usually leaves at midnight for Kitale, and a number of *matatus* leave throughout the day for Lodwar.

Ferguson's Gulf

To visit the lake, you might want to pay one of the children in Kalokol to be your guide, though it's easy to find your own way there (just follow the road east for 4km). Having been dry for much of a decade, the El Niño rains of 1997–98 once again filled **Ferguson's Gulf** though the years since have again seen a decline in the lake's level.

Simply being by the lake fills the time here, with the constantly mutating background of the western shore across the bay, as well as the closer prospect of Turkana fishermen, hundreds of species of birds, and the occasional glimpse of crocodile or hippo on the water surface. From a distance, the activity at the water's edge seems silent since the wind whips the sound away westwards, lending the whole scene a bizarre, dream-like quality. Down on the shore you can talk with the children who follow you everywhere, and who often speak good English. If you make friends, you can be taken looking for snakes (be careful), to see *tembo* brewing (always by women) or, if you're lucky, to a dance.

Ordinary teenagers' and children's dances happen several times a week, but are best when there's a full moon: the boys tie cans of stones to their ankles and pretend to ignore the girls' flirting.

Although guests often **swim** in the lake, which is pleasantly warm, the threat of a crocodile attack, while remote, is ever-present and you are advised to stay out of the water. Hippos are certainly much more to be feared, as are the lake's peculiarities of climate. The tales surrounding the two human skulls that lay (and may still lie) in the sand below the lodge are varied, but they are probably the result of drowning accidents on the remote eastern coastline. One of them was certainly far from ancient. They're a very effective reminder of the precariousness of life here.

The lodge and Longech

It's about 6km through scrub and palm groves from Kalokol to the *Lake Turkana Fishing Lodge* (⑤); after 4km, turn left at the (defunct) Italian fishing project sign and continue for another 2km. From the jetty at the end, you have to get a boat to the lodge ($8 return). If, as seems likely, the lake waters begin once again to recede, the crossing should become fordable by foot (ignore the children screaming "Crocodile! Crocodile!" and trying to get you in their boats – unless you want a short boat trip and a new friend).

The lodge has been opening and closing sporadically for many years now, and has had several different owners – check out the current situation at the Kobil station in Lodwar, the owner of which is currently the lodge's proprietor. The lodge itself is perched at the end of a sandy spit, offering shade, shelter from the fan-heater wind and a beautiful view across the lake. It caters mostly to weekend visitors who arrive by air, and midweek it's invariably empty. Its **campsite** has moved down to the mainland by the former Italian fishing project (a rotten Ksh500 per person), though with the amount of hassle you can expect from local kids this isn't likely to appeal for very long in any case. Alternatively, people may give you bed space in **LONGECH**, the village that stretches a couple of kilometres down the former shoreline, for a small fee or for a trade of some of your belongings. Fresh or dried fish is usually available, but the only other food is the lodge's expensive set menu.

When you're tired of wandering around Longech, being mobbed by toddlers, watching the fishermen paddling out on their waterlogged rafts, and the pied kingfishers hovering and plunging over the shallows, there are a few active things to do. If you're feeling rich and macho, you can rent **fishing** rods and the lodge's boat and, with luck, land several hundred pounds of Nile perch. By all accounts, though, the perch don't play properly and almost line up to be landed. Fishermen rate the tiger fish as more of a fighter. The lodge will cook your catch for you and you can add your mark to the fishermen's tales on the walls of the bar.

Central Island National Park

A trip to **Central Island National Park** is highly recommended. This is one of two island national parks in the lake (the other is the less accessible South Island). Central Island is a unique triple volcano poking gauntly out of the water. The island covers just five square kilometres, most of which is taken up by two crater lakes (a third has dried up) hidden behind its rocky shores. One of the lakes is the only known habitat of an ancient species of tilapia, a reminder of the time when Lake Turkana was connected to the Nile. The island is the nesting ground for big colonies of water birds but, like some African Galapagos, it really belongs to the reptiles. Crocodiles breed here in the largest concentration in Africa, and at the right time of year (usually April–May) you can witness the newly hatched croc-lets breaking out of the nests and sprinting with loud squeaks down to the crater lake where they'll pass their first season. The vegetation is scant, but some of the sheltered lees are overgrown with thick grass and bushes for a short period each year, and the nests are dug beneath this foliage.

Boat trips are expensive: from the lodge they cost around $130 for a ninepassenger vessel and $60 for a boat that takes up to four only. Alternatively, *Kalokol Tours Lodge & Hotel* can arrange a trip, but expect to pay extra for "guiding fees" and transport from and back to Kalokol. Forget their astronomical starting price (Ksh10,000), you should aim to bargain down to around Ksh3000. A national parks' entry fee of $15, children $5) will be demanded by the park warden or his rangers – one of whom normally accompanies each trip – which, in view of the activities of some of the parks staff in the area (croc hunting), leaves a bitter taste. If you find a boat, the best plan is to go immediately rather than make arrangements in advance. Do be sure, however, that it is thoroughly lake-worthy and that the crew know what they are doing; vicious squalls can blow up fast and it's at least 10km to the island. Taking your own compass might be a good idea.

Boats across the lake

Also worth enquiring about, both in Lodwar and Kalokol, is whether the Fisheries Commission boat to **Loiyangalani** on the eastern side of the lake has been reinstated. This used to leave at the end of each month to collect taxes and fees, taking upwards of eight hours and charging a small fortune for a lift. You may also be able to **rent a boat** with a helmsman at Ferguson's Gulf or Eliye Springs (see below) for the same trip, but unless you offer a more than substantial sum (something over $200) the fishermen may not consider the risk as being worthwhile. Also just about accessible from here are the remote archeological sites of **Koobi Fora** and **Sibiloi National Park** (see p.616), 48km across the lake. Enquire at *Kalokol Tours Lodge & Hotel* for the boats (starting price Ksh15,000, which should be bargained hard), and check the state of the boat before you go. Alternatively, enquire about the National Museums' boat, which supposedly leaves once a month.

Eliye Springs

Eliye Springs, 66km south of Lodwar, used to be *the* place for travellers on the lakeshore and still attracts the occasional overland truck and self-sufficient 4WD weekenders. **Getting there** and back is the main problem. Failing a lift in Lodwar (where you might wait for days), you might **rent a vehicle** (4WD advisable) with driver at around Ksh2000 for the round trip. However, if you'll be staying overnight or longer at Eliye Springs, don't count on the vehicle returning to pick you up, and it's a long walk back.

Alternatively, you could **walk** from Ferguson's Gulf or Kalokol: just follow the coast for 55 or so sweltering kilometres, and take plenty of drinking water. There are crocodiles along the shore for much of the way, which makes a night walk ill-advised. Another possible route from Kalokol is a little shorter (45–50km); it cuts across the desert inland and this *is* really only feasible overnight, preferably by moonlight, due to the heat. A guide will cost around Ksh1200, and it's quite an adventure – bring plenty of water. The only other possibility is to **rent a boat** from Ferguson's Gulf for up to Ksh500 per hour; the boat seats four, and the trip takes four to six hours. If you're only going one way, you will still have to pay for the return leg regardless.

Eliye Springs itself readily compensates for the hassles of the journey – a paradisal place with rustling doum palms watered by hot springs, with gorgeous views, and nothing to do except lounge about and swat flies. The *bandas* (❸; camping Ksh200), although run down, are adequate and have comfortable beds. There is also a pool fed by the springs and a bar; meals can be prepared if ordered in advance.

Onwards from Lodwar: Lokichokio

It's possible, but by no means easy, to explore the region of Turkana **north of Ferguson's Gulf** and **Lodwar**. A paved road (in bad condition) turns left across the river outside town and goes up to **Lokitaung**, branching left after about 60km for **Lokichokio** (Lokichoggio, often called just **Loki**) and the Sudanese border. Travel here is strictly in convoy but even this does not guarantee safety: 1996 saw an upsurge in shootings and armed banditry on this road, with several fatalities, one just 7km from Lodwar. The current wisdom is that you should get to where you're going before 3pm, as bandit attacks after then are more likely. If you do get held up, give them what they want. Clearly, travel here is not advisable. If you want go anyway, *matatus* leave Lodwar early in the morning and foreign relief vehicles may also consider giving you a lift. Alternatively, you might try approaching airlines at Wilson Airport in Nairobi (p.144), from where there are daily NGO flights to Lokichokio.

Loki itself, an unremittingly dry and rocky place with steel freight containers lining the road, is even more of a cowboy town than Lodwar, with an eclectic mix of rough international types, businessmen, tribal Turkana, haggard relief workers, doctors, pilots, nurses, missionaries and shady arms-dealers. And beer. Loki is the major UN aid centre for southern Sudanese fleeing the civil war in Sudan (there's a big refugee hospital), and the main supply centre for NGOs within Sudan, with hundreds of personnel, Kenya's busiest airfield, and numerous bars for tired and frustrated relief workers. Ironically enough, Loki is also the centre for arms-running into Sudan: poke around some of the *dukas*, and you'll find AK-47s, ammunition and even bombs openly for sale. There's no accommodation for travellers, so you have to arrange matters with the aid workers (which can be expensive). The refugee centre itself is at **Kakuma**, 108km south of Loki on the Lodwar road.

Maralal, the Mathews and East Turkana

The journey up to **Loiyangalani** is the most exciting route to Lake Turkana – anyone who's been there will talk your ear off telling you about the adventures they had on the way. From Nairobi, the distance is a good deal shorter than to the west coast, but even full tilt on the rough roads it's a full two-day **drive**. Saloon cars can make it as often as not (though vicious bedrock greets many a sump, and the car-rental companies aren't enthusiastic), but to be sure of arriving you'll need 4WD (a long-wheel-base Suzuki jeep is ideal) and spare petrol. Even then, if you go during the rainy season, you could be held up for 24 hours or more at several points.

The obvious solution is a **camping safari**, though, as with any group travel, this has its limitations. Still, a week isn't long enough for irritations to detract from the experience and most people thoroughly enjoy these trips, coming back loaded with amazing souvenirs and photographs, and stories of weird and wonderful encounters. A major drawback is the brevity of organized trips and the fact that they therefore run to a rough timetable. The oldest, and many think the best, outfit is Safari Camp Services' **Turkana Bus**, which runs every other Saturday throughout the year with ancient Bedford lorries. They have loads of experience. Gametrackers also uses Bedfords (or land cruisers if the group size is small), and have renewed their fleet of vehicles. Their fortnightly round trips (departing Fridays) via the Chalbi Desert are unique and highly recommended. Unlike Turkana Bus their way to the lake is different from their route back to Nairobi and their lakeside campsite, 7km south of Loiyangalani, is pretty close to paradise (Safari Camp Services uses a site at Loiyangalani itself, away from the lake).

If your budget is tight, but you have time and a flexible attitude and don't want a spoon-fed adventure, the maximum exposure to Turkana and the north comes from travelling completely independently. This may require some patience, especially at **Baragoi**, the terminus for **public transport**, where you'll find any traffic few and far between due to cattle-rustling which has displaced a lot of the inhabitants.

The routes to Maralal

Three roads lead to **Maralal**, the Samburu District town at the end of the first stage of the trip north.

Nyahururu to Maralal: C77

The easiest route, the **C77**, rolls up from Nyahururu via Rumuruti: tarmac to Rumuriti, decent *murram* but dull scenically to Maralal. Each morning at least one **bus** and three or four *matatus* leave Nyahururu. The C77 bounds over the ranching and cereal country of **Laikipia**, settled after World War I by British soldiers, but once a Maasai stronghold. Most of the settlers have left, and it's a bleak, somewhat forlorn region, racked by inter-tribal violence in the early 1990s, after the change-over to multi-party democracy. Cattle-rustling is also prevalent, which only complicates matters. All this is extremely unlikely to affect tourists, as most of the incidents have taken place in remote villages.

Rumuruti (onomatopoeic Maa for "mosquito") is hardly noticeable any more, it merely marks the end of the paved road. The road to Rumuruti was built in the early 1980s for a government minister who lives there and needed to be able to get to and from Nairobi without using a tractor. Maralal was connected with electricity at the same time, because, say the cynics, it would have been too obvious if the lines had only gone to his house. There's some very good game country in the vicinity, and for **night stops** in Rumuruti you might check out the *Tumaini Country Restaurant* which has rooms and claims, "We are famous for making people happy", or try *Mama Kanyi Guest House* with cheap s/c rooms (both ➋). Equally inviting is the dilapidated *Laikipia Club* with its improbable efforts to preserve the old values. The best place, however, is the self-service cottage accommodation at *Kifuko Bandas* (c/o Cape Chestnut Ltd, ℗0176/32208; ➌), 10km southeast of Rumuriti along a rough dirt track; check first in Rumuruti, or at Let's Go Travel in Nairobi (p.141), whether they're still open.

The road follows the **Ewaso Ng'iro River** (see the Laikipia map on p.194) for some way beyond Rumuruti into Samburu-land proper, where the two other routes described below join it. Passing *Bobong Campsite* on a bluff to the left, then the turn-off (after 27km) for the luxurious but extraordinarily expensive *Colcheccio Lodge* – it costs $560–610 for a double – sited on its bank (reservations through Tandala Ltd, PO Box 24397 Nairobi ℡02/568804, ℗564945,

@royal.africasaf@commsol.sprint.com; or through Let's Go Travel in Nairobi, ⑨), the road climbs, broad and stony, towards Maralal's plateau. At **Suguta Marmar** (the boundary between Central Province and the Rift Valley), 20km south of Maralal, there's little more than a livestock auction yard, and a basic checkpoint, not authorized to check tourist credentials, plus a few cheap *hotelis* and the basic *Checkpoint B&L* (①).

Lake Baringo to Maralal: C77

The second route is the lonely but well-constructed *murram* road from the **Rift Valley**, which in its earlier stages has breathtaking views back over Lake Baringo and some fascinating Pokot villages on the way. It's only a D road, but don't be discouraged for that reason from driving it (though there have been occasional hold-ups at gunpoint along the way). There are no buses, and you'd be lucky to find a *matatu*. For the best chances of **hitching** success, ask at *Lake Baringo Club* or wait at the Kampi ya Samaki junction (see p.275).

Isiolo to Maralal: A2 and C79/C78

The maddeningly corrugated **A2** comes up from **Isiolo** past Archer's Post (p.622), then heads off left as the **C79** past the turn for Wamba, where it becomes the **C78**. Despite a continuation of the A2's washboard surface, the C79/78 has everything to recommend it scenically, including some magnificent desert buttes and sweeping views over the valley of the Ewaso Ngiro River, which flows on through Samburu. The isolated incidents of **banditry** in the early 1990s appear to have ceased. The garishly decorated "Babie Coach" runs this route (Isiolo–Maralal), leaving one or the other town every other day, usually packed full of Samburu warriors. *Matatus* run daily in both directions. Your best chances of **hitching** a ride are at the Samburu lodges inside the national reserve (see pp.430–431), or at the Isiolo police barrier.

Maralal

Some of the Laikipia settlers would have dearly liked to set themselves up around the cool, conifer-draped highlands of **MARALAL**. But even before British administrators made this the district capital, Maralal had been a spiritual focus for the **Samburu people** and, despite some dithering, the colonial administrators didn't accede to the settlers' demands.

Maralal is a peculiar town, spread with exaggerated spaciousness around a depression in the hills. Samburu people crowd its dusty streets, with a brilliant collage of skins, blankets, beads, brass, and iron, and a special smell, too – of sour milk, fat, and cattle. The main hotel is called *Buffalo Hotel*. The place sets itself up for Wild West comparisons and the climate is appropriate – unbelievably dusty, almost always windy and, at 2220m, sharp enough at night for log fires and braziers. All it needs is wolves – and even there hyenas fill the role.

Of course, the regular arrival of safari lorries means that Maralal has plenty of persistent souvenir salesmen. Yet despite this, it's a good place to get to know the Samburu and especially worthwhile on Christian holidays. Many Samburu around the town have become Catholics and the colourful procession on Palm Sunday – mostly thousands of women, waving branches and leaves – is riveting.

A notable resident of Maralal until 1994 was the travel writer and Arabist **Wilfred Thesiger**, who had made the town his home and had adopted a number of orphaned boys. Thesiger made his name with his accounts of the Shiite Arabs of the southern Iraqi marshes and the Bedu of the Arabian peninsula,

▲ *Kirisia Forest (4km) & Opiroi (35km)*

Slaughter House

▶ *(4km), Kisima, Wamba & Isiolo*

MARALAL

RESTAURANTS & BARS

Club 26	A
Jamaica Complex Hotel	B
Maralal Safari Hotel	E
Nanyuki Hotel	D
Pop-Inn Hotel	C

ACCOMMODATION

Buffalo Hotel	2
Green Bar	7
Jamaru Hotel	4
Kariara Hotel	6
Kimaniki Hotel	5
Kinyangu Paradise B&L	1
Maralal Safari Lodge	8
Midpoint Hotel	3
Yare Safari Club & Campsite	9

Sakhu Video Theatre

Old Market (Miraa)

Jovenna

Total

Matatu Stand

Stadium

Police Line

Pharmacy

Maendeleo Ya Wanawake (womens group)

KCB Bank

Market

Plastic Boys Shop

D.C. HQ

Samburu County Council

BP

Police

Kenyatta House

N

▼ *Nyahururu & Wamba*

▼ *Baragoi (2km) & National Sanctuary* ⑧

100 m

0

and followed up these achievements with several books on Kenya, notably *My Kenya Days*. Among the Samburu he found equally congenial companions for his old age.

If you forget to visit the liberally signposted **Kenyatta House**, don't fret. The fact that Kenyatta was detained here in 1961 before his final release doesn't really improve the interest of this unexceptional and empty bungalow. It seems a pity it's a national monument and not some family's home.

Guides and crafts

On arriving in Maralal, you'll invariably attract a flock of persistent and annoying "guides" offering evening excursions to see **traditional dancing** in nearby *manyattas*, or else visits to local **Samburu witch doctors** and **blacksmiths** and a nearby **Turkana village**. Use your judgement before accepting, making it absolutely clear how much you are prepared to pay, and bringing plenty of chewing tobacco and *miraa* for the old men. The reason behind this unwelcome attention is the town's high unemployment, caused by a massive influx of previously nomadic herders following the drought of 1982–85 and the subsequent explosion in cattle-rustling, which led many Turkana and Samburu to lose their livestock.

An attempt to tame the guides by organizing them into disciplined groups is the **Plastic Boys' Co-operative Self-Help Group**, so named after the street children who used to make dolls and trinkets using plastic bags and cartons. They have now progressed, under the guidance of the Kenya Wildlife Service and various NGOs, to carving and selling woodcrafts, spears and other touristy items. Their shop is in the market, and they should be able to sort you out with some of the more reliable guides, should you need one. For more "authentic" souvenirs, the women's group Maendeleo Ya Wanawake has a shop selling distinctly used calabashes, headrests and dolls. They can also point you in the right direction should you want Samburu beadwork.

Maralal National Sanctuary and Safari Lodge

Maralal Safari Lodge (PO Box 70 ☎0368/2060; bookings 2nd floor, Windsor House, Muindi Mbingu St, PO Box 15020 Nairobi ☎02/211124, ℱ211125), signposted 2–3km out of town on the Lake Turkana road, is comfortable, under-subscribed and very attractive with its huge wooden chalet-style rooms (B&B ❼). Your patronage is welcome in the bar and restaurant, and you can sit on the terrace to watch the animals from the surrounding **Maralal National Sanctuary** and Yamo Forest (zebra, baboon, impala, eland, warthog, buffalo and hyena) filing up the hill to the concrete water hole a few metres away.

Accommodation

Setting aside the excellent lodge, Maralal has a large number of **cheap lodgings**, the more acceptable of which are listed here; the mid-range *Yare Safari Club* also has **camping** facilities.

Buffalo Hotel PO Box 28 ☎0368/2028. The main travellers' haunt, decent, but more expensive than usual and not for light sleepers. No s/c. ❶
Green Bar PO Box 7. Friendly with a decent restaurant. Singles only. ❶
Jamaru Hotel PO Box 245 ☎0368/2215. Maralal's largest; rather spartan but with a good, busy restaurant, and some s/c rooms too. ❶–❷

Kariara Hotel PO Box 68. The cheapest and best in town, this is also Maralal's only two-storey hotel. It has basic but clean rooms, festooned with bougainvillea, all with mosquito nets; bring your own padlock. Get a room on top – on a good morning you can see Mount Kenya. ❶
Kimaniki Hotel PO Box 117 ☎0368/2444. Rooms behind a noisy bar-disco to suit night owls. ❶

Kinyangu Paradise B&L PO Box 193
⊕0368/2297. Another local joint, its bar is open
till midnight and frequented by Samburu and
Turkana tribesmen. Cheap and reasonable. ➊
Midpoint Hotel PO Box 93 ⊕0368/2221.
Acceptable if not overly clean, with hot water (not
s/c) and food available. Singles only. ➊
Yare Safari Club and Campsite PO Box 281
Maralal ⊕0368/2295; in Nairobi ⊕ & fax
02/214099, ©yare@africaonline.co.ke. Just over
4km down the Isiolo road, beyond Wilfred

Thesiger's old home, *Yare* is Maralal's main tourist
centre, with some beautiful thatched *bandas*, a
good restaurant, well-stocked bar and pleasant
campsite next to a camel pen (Ksh200 per person;
under Ksh100 for tent rental). There's a resident
Samburu blacksmith who plays superb Samburu
guitar, camels available for hire ($3 per hour
including handler), and walks can be arranged
($20 per day), as can mountain-biking treks to
Lake Turkana or other parts of Samburu District.
Telephone, fax and email is also available. B&B ➌

Eating, drinking and entertainment

Maralal boasts a surprising number of good **restaurants** as well as the usual
run of cheap and filling eating houses. The popular Somali-run *Pop-Inn Hotel*
is easily the best, with a great atmosphere, breakfasts, pilau and *dengo* (a deli-
cately spiced stew of root vegetables and small beans). *Maralal Safari Hotel* serves
githeri to Samburu warriors with lolloping reggae in the background. *Jamaica
Complex Hotel* is big on *nyama choma*, whilst the *Nanyuki Hotel*, by the *matatu*
stand, has huge portions of Swahili food (*mchele* stew a speciality) at criminal-
ly low prices. The *Midpoint Hotel* and *Kinyangu Paradise B&L* are also recommended.

A night spent in Maralal's numerous **bars** can be exhilarating, infuriating,
dangerous or just plain daft. *Buffalo Hotel* used to be the best of the lot, but most
of the colourful ex-pats in the area have gone, and you are now more likely to
encounter wheedling con merchants and a host of bizarre local nutcases.
There's a **cinema** opposite the *Starlight Bar* which usually gets in some genuine celluloid on Saturdays. The bar itself is a straightforward drinking den full
of broken stools and fallen pride. Predictably enough, *Jamaica Complex* resounds
to baseline slow jam and rootsy reggae, while *Kimaniki* hosts the dancey *Club
24* from Friday to Sunday. The similar *Club 26* is almost opposite *Kinyangu
Paradise B&L*.

Maralal International Camel Derby

The Maralal International **Camel Derby** provides for a strange weekend (second
week) in August. Anyone may enter, or just spectate, as dozens of competitors from
East Africa, Europe, China, Australia and South Africa battle it out over 11-kilometre
amateur and 42-kilometre professional stages. Entry fees are very reasonable: amateur class, including camel and handler, is Ksh2500; professional Ksh2000. There's
also a locally-run funfair, marathon, and javelin and *rungu* (club) throwing contests,
as well as a possible tie-in with a Kenya Mountain Bike series race. The event is
based at the *Yare* site. For more details, contact *Yare Safari Club* or the Organizing
Committee, Maralal Festival and Camel Derby, PO Box 281 Maralal ⊕02/214099,
⊕32709, ©yare@africaonline.co.ke.

Other practicalities and moving on

If you're **continuing north**, note that Maralal is the last place where you can
rely on supplies of **petrol**, and **change money** – at the smart KCB bank
(Mon–Fri 8.30–2.30am, Sat 8.30–10.30am), at *Yare Safari Club* (also the representative for Kato and KTF for the area and able to offer up-to-date information on security), or at the *Maralal Safari Lodge* (where they don't have much

7

cash). If **beer** is important to you (and it can assume great importance up in the desert), then stock up on that too before heading off.

If you don't have your own vehicle, you may find a source of **rides onward** at *Yare* or the lodge, but you're more likely to catch vehicles by staying in town and spreading the word at the petrol stations. Let it be known you are willing to travel in the back of a lorry – many people will assume you're not. Supply lorries do go up to Loiyangalani and your chances of scoring a lift – eventually, even if it takes you a week – are good. Irregular rides, again with transport vehicles, is the way to get to Baragoi (the northernmost limit of public transport), and to Nyahururu and Isiolo. Nakuru is served daily by Nyayo Bus. There are early morning *matatus* for Nairobi, otherwise catch one to Rumuruti or Nyahururu, and change there. Goldline Bus for Nairobi leaves nightly at 2am.

Wamba and the Mathews Range (Lenkiyio Hills)

In terms of the vastness of the north, the **Mathews Range** is virtually on Maralal's doorstep. The range, most of which is a forest reserve, is impressively wild hill country, with Mathew Peak (Ol Doinyo Lenkiyio) rising to 2375m. Lower down, the mountains are heavily cloaked in forest and thick bush; unusual vegetation includes "living fossil" cycad plants, giant cedars and podocarpus. Among the animal life, you can look out for (but shouldn't expect to meet) small numbers of black rhinos – every one of them known and tracked, for its own safety, by forest guards and their Samburu staff – and really outstanding butterflies. This is first-rate walking and exploring country for hardy travellers, but you need to be fully self-sufficient, which includes having all your food requirements.

First target is **WAMBA**, a one-street town 5km off the C78/79 highway, roughly midway between Maralal and Isiolo. You can get the odd *matatu* here from Maralal, or use the Babie Coach which passes by the Wamba turning just after midday (heading out from Maralal one day, coming back from Isiolo the next). Wamba's main focus is its large, modern Catholic hospital outside town. *Saudia Lodge* (❶), in town, is pretty well the only **B&L**, with clean, pleasant and very cheap rooms. There are a few *dukas*, though they have no fuel and little in the way of fresh food, only basic fruit or veg. You might try *Imani Bar & Restaurant* which serves the usual limited range of stews and a reasonable *githeri*.

The big mountain you can see outside town (9km to the peak as the crow flies) is **Warges**. Guides from Wamba will take you up there, though they'll stress how full of wild animals it is and how much their lives (not yours of course) are at risk. If you have a serious interest in witchcraft, one of Kenya's most respected **witch doctors** lives in the shadow of the mountain. Forget the town guide – he is resolutely *not* a tourist attraction. Instead, make discreet enquiries with the Kenya Wildlife Service rangers who regularly pass through Wamba, or else, if your Maa is good enough, with one of the young Samburu *morani*, but make sure you are accompanied by someone who really knows the place.

Kitich Camp and campsite

The main route from Wamba is towards the expensive bush-luxury *Kitich Camp* and the nearby KWS station campsite. If you're four-wheel-driving, you basically set off towards Barsaloi (Parsaloi) along a rough road that commences just half a kilometre along the Wamba access road. From here you drive 15km, then turn right and do a further 17km to **Ngilai** (follow the yellow stones). Some 6km further, you fork left to ford the **Ngeng River**. With the mountains looming all around, this is the way into the heart of the Mathews; the campsite is a couple of kilometres up the track on the other side, and *Kitich Camp* some 4km further north. Note that there's no fuel along the way and normally none for sale at Kitich.

If you're on foot, find a guide in Wamba and set off cross-country, direct to Ngilai, crossing several *luggas*, and seeing almost nobody on the way. The distance is about 30km and an exhausting day's walk; double-check in Wamba whether the site is still open. Ngilai has a Lutheran mission (2km out of the centre to the north) and a single shop, which may put you up for the night if you can't make the final 8km to the campsite before nightfall.

Once there, the **KWS campsite** is pleasant and shady, with showers and toilet, and water available from the nearby pools. Note that there is no food available at the campsite and, while you can go angling in the river, there's a limit to how much catfish a person can stand. Unfortunately, **Kitich Camp** (bookings through Bush Homes of East Africa; p.42), nestled unobtrusively on the river bank beneath towering giant figs, doesn't go out of its way to welcome travellers, and a night here – at $650 – is exceptionally expensive.

If you want to walk any distance, you're strongly advised to take a guide, either from the camp or from the campsite (where they'll seek you out if you're camping). There are some fine **excursions**, including short walks up the valley to wonderful, deep, rock pools where you can swim. The area around the Ngeng Valley is thick with wildlife. There are elephants everywhere, buffaloes, hyenas, leopards and plenty of more innocuous game. You really have to watch yourself, especially if you go down near the river. It's a lot of fun, but take care.

North from Maralal: into Samburu-land

The first stretch of the road **north from Maralal** climbs higher into the **podocarpus forests** of the national sanctuary, before dropping down across the Lopet Plateau to the Elbarta Plains, 15km east of the scorching Suguta Valley. The northern boundary of the sanctuary has been scarred by climatic changes and the wholesale burning of much of its valley sides, presumably to make way for cattle pasture. Other theories posit the local administration police ("Home Guard"), or Kenya Police Reserves (heavily armed Samburu herders) as responsible, suggesting that they remove the natural cover which facilitates the **cattle-rustling** raids that have become endemic between the Samburu and their northern Turkana neighbours. The raids come to a head at the end of the year and during the dry months of January and February, as Samburu herders take their livestock up north towards Baragoi on the Samburu–Turkana border. Once in the Suguta Valley, stolen cattle are difficult to retrieve due to the valley's exceptionally high temperatures (up to 60°C), lack of water and the rough terrain.

Twenty kilometres from Maralal, a detour to the left takes you through the village of **Poror**, past a large wheat-farming project and, after 6km, to the dramatic scimitar edge of the **Losiolo Escarpment**. There is a charge of Ksh100 per person to enter the area; Ksh200–400, depending on your bargaining skills, to camp. The Rift Valley is, by its nature, bordered from end to end by vertiginous escarpments and each one seems more impressive than the last. But Losiolo is not just an escarpment, it's a colossal amphitheatre dropping down to Suguta Valley, 2000m below. Try to get here very early in the morning. From Poror, the road north is increasingly rough and hot as it drops down through the Samburu Hills on to the Lopet Plateau. Settlements from here on are few but evenly scattered. The first is **Morijo**, which has some basic *chai* kiosks, one or two Somali-run *dukas*, a mission and a police station. **Marti**, 20km further north, is much the same.

Baragoi

Sitting 37km north of Marti is **BARAGOI**, in the heart of the barren Elbarta Plains, watered only occasionally by run-off from the Samburu Hills and Ndoto Mountains. The river which skirts the town is dry for much of the year, and in times of drought the pits which are dug into it by women fetching water can reach depths of over 6m. It's a blistering, dusty and unforgiving land, dotted here and there with sun-bleached bones and populated only by red-robed semi-nomadic herders armed with spears or bows and arrows to protect their cattle, goats and camels against the endemic rustlers (*ngorokos*).

First settled in the 1930s, Baragoi retains its original function as the region's major livestock market, attracting both Samburu and Turkana for whom the town also marks the invisible boundary between their respective grazing lands. Yet, things have changed a lot over the last few years. A construction boom has spawned dozens of one-storey cinder-block buildings in which half a dozen new hotels, numerous bars and restaurants have taken root. A clue to this sudden expansion lies in the name of a bar at the north end of the village – *Bosnia Wines & Spirits*. Shortly after the UN resolved to send peace-keepers to former Yugoslavia, a 900-strong Kenyan battalion was despatched to help patrol a ceasefire line around the self-proclaimed (now defunct) Serbian Republic of Krajina. News of the detachment spread quickly, particularly of the astronomical sums to be made serving in UNPROFOR (soldiers were paid up to $1200 a month, compared with the average Kenyan monthly wage of around $70). Samburu warriors from around Baragoi and Lesriken, 25km east, were quick to enlist for the second and third missions to Bosnia, the last of which returned in 1994.

The rewards were indeed beyond belief for the veterans, and for men who in the past had been expected to kill a lion in order to prove their manhood, the ferocity of the fighting left them unfazed. What did shock them, however, were the atrocities they witnessed, committed against ordinary civilians and now the subject of war crimes tribunals.

The Bosnian experience has not been without its problems. For some, sudden wealth has led to alcoholism as hard spirits have become affordable, and even cocaine abuse, and on arriving in Baragoi you'll be assailed by the usual band of desperate types, madmen and "guides" who missed out on their brothers' good fortunes. Unpleasant though the reception is, weather the storm (the locals will help you out of any serious trouble) and you'll find that Baragoi is a fascinating place, well worth a day or two of anyone's time.

The livestock market

Despite the UN money, life for the majority remains a hard and restless search for water and pasturage, often violently conflicting with other herders grazing the same territory. Down off Bosnia Street to the northwest of town is the **livestock market**. It's a gentle, unhurried affair where old men with gnarled hands and ostrich plumes in their hair play *ngiles* (*mbau*) with stones and seeds on "boards" carved out of the bone-dry earth as they wait for business to

The Samburu

The **Samburu** are historically close to the Maasai. Their languages are nearly the same (both Maa) and culturally they are virtually indistinguishable to an outsider. Both came from the region around present-day northwest Turkana in the seventeenth century. The Samburu turned east, establishing themselves in the mountain pastures and spreading across to the plains; the Maasai continued south.

Improvements in health and in veterinary care over the last century have swelled the Samburu population and the size of their herds. Many in the driest areas of their range in the northeast have turned to camel herding as a better insurance against drought than cattle. Since livestock is the basis of relations between in-laws (through the giving of "bridewealth" from the husband to his wife's family), having camel herds has disrupted patterns of marriage and initiation into new generations because camel herds increase more slowly than cattle herds. And the reality on the ground is all about twice as confusing as it sounds on paper. Memories, recording every transaction over successive generations, are phenomenal (the Samburu have only just begun to acquire writing).

The Samburu age-set system, like many others in Africa, is a complicated arrangement to which a number of anthropologists have devoted lifetimes of investigation. Essentially it's a gerontocracy (rule by old men) and the elders are assured, by the system they manipulate, of having the first choice of young women to marry. The promiscuous and jingoistic – but, by Samburu reckoning, still juvenile – warriors are forced to wait, usually until their thirties, before initiation into elderhood. Marriage and children brings them a measure of real respect. In turn, they perpetuate the system on their own sons, who have everything to gain by falling in line and much to lose if they withdraw their stake in the tradition, perhaps by going to Nairobi or the coast to look for work.

For women the situation is very different. They are married at fifteen or sixteen, immediately after their clitoridectomy and before they have much chance to rebel. But they may continue affairs with their *morani* boyfriends, the unmarried juniors of their new, much older husbands. This polygamy in itself seems to be an important motivating force for the whole generation system. For the warriors and their girlfriends, there's a special young people's language – a vocabulary of conspiratorial songs and idioms – which has to be modified with the initiation of every age-set, so that it's kept secret from the elders.

This highly intricate system is now beginning to collapse in many areas, with a widespread disruption of pre-colonial ways; even the circumcision initiation of boys to warriorhood is less of a mass ceremony. While herds are still the principal criterion of wealth, people in some areas are turning to agriculture. After the rains you can see planting holes at the roadside in certain places, with corn the main crop. There are enormous problems for such initiatives, especially when there's no aid or government support, but they do show that the standard stereotypes don't always fit. As for the *morani* warriors, opportunities for cattle-raiding and lion-killing have diminished with more efficient policing of their territories, although there are still annual clashes with the Turkana in the north of Samburu-land. For some, tourist hunting has taken over. You can even see *morani* in full rig striding past the hotels on the Indian Ocean beaches.

---

arrive. Here, Samburu deal with Rendille and Turkana, some of whom may have spent up to seven days walking their livestock south from the lake. In turn the Samburu, and sometimes Turkana, trek southeastward for five or six days to reach Isiolo where, with luck, they resell their animals at a profit.

If the herder is of **courting** age (Samburu *moran*; Turkana *lmoli*), Isiolo is also where he buys the beads, necklaces and bangles with which to woo his bride.

Once back home, he will not only present her with these gifts, but mime and sing the attributes of the animals which will provide him and his family with their means of survival. For these semi-nomads, animals are the source of all wealth, and the young herder must represent them favourably to attract the attention and confidence of a bride. To this end, he selects a single castrated bull, camel or goat which he then mimics, indicating with his hands and gestures its size, colour, the shape of its horns, even its temperament. There's a comical side to all this, too, for even the poorest herder, whose beast may only be a goat with lopsided horns, must dance to attract a spouse and does this by raising a few smiles with a self-deprecating parody of his goat. Dances are held almost nightly in the *manyattas* on the outskirts of town, wild and hugely enjoyable events at which you are bound to be made welcome. Cameras, of course, are generally not acceptable. Ask around at the market or else try one of the *manyattas* behind the primary school.

Practicalities

The best **accommodation** in town is the basic, but clean, *Morning Star Guest House* (PO Box 37; singles only, ❶) with a decent restaurant and bar. *Bosnia Wines & Spirits* (❶), also singles only, is spartan but clean and cheap; the beds are narrow but have the benefit of nets. *Mount Ngiro B&L* (❷) distinguishes itself in having the only doubles in Baragoi; it's full-board only and comparatively expensive, though bargaining is possible.

The best **bar and restaurant** is *Zaire Hotel* on Nachola Road, a colourful and cheerful place, open till 11pm, with Baragoi's only really cold drinks, Congolese music and the weird sight of Samburu and Turkana herders in full rig supping tea and nibbling scones. For simple and filling staples like *githeri*, *Flora Hotel*, *Al-Mukaram* and *Wid-Wid Hotel* are all cheap.

There are no official **money-changing** facilities, but there is a **post office** (Mon–Fri 8am–5pm) and decent **car mechanic** (Dalfer Welders, opposite the post office). Emergency **petrol supplies** can be had, at a price, from Mount Ngiro Supplies. There's been talk for years of a new Bosnia-financed petrol station at the head of Bosnia Street, but nothing substantial as yet.

Moving on from Baragoi

Baragoi is the last stop for **northbound** public transport, which means you have to line up a lift with supply lorries, mission jeeps and the like. The police station on the north side of town is helpful, but be prepared to wait for several days. You might also find a Turkana Bus safari lorry to take you to Loiyangalani – a generous tip for the driver and cook(s) is in order. Going **south to Maralal** is easy if uncomfortable: two Land Rover *matatus* leave daily from outside the post office (7am & 9am).

South Horr and Kurungu Camp

Baragoi marks the end of the forbidding Elbarta plains, as the road now climbs into ravine and mountain country, fantastically green if there's been rain. Some 30km from Baragoi, a track to the left towards Nyiru, signed by a red gas cylinder, leads to Desert Rose Camel Safaris (p.142), which organizes luxury camel treks of six days or more in the surrounding *luggas* and hills and up to Lake Turkana, with vehicle back-up and two nights at their *Desert Rose Lodge* (FB ❾).

There's a positive jungle all year round at the oasis village of **SOUTH HORR** (*horr* means "flowing water"), wedged tightly between the Nyiru and Ol Doinyo Mara mountains. With its pleasantly somnolent atmosphere, ample shade and relaxed herders lounging under the trees, it's a great place to bunk down for a night or three, and making friends is easy despite the language barrier. There are a few cheap *hotelis* and cold drinks at *Nhiro Serima Bar*, but only rarely beer. If you stay the night, you've a choice of half a dozen basic **B&Ls** (all ❶). There's good, dirt-cheap **camping** at the *Forest Department Campsite*, located up a rough trail to the left of the road a kilometre before South Horr. Facilities consist of long-drops, an *askari*, and a river for drinking water, bathing and washing the dust out of your clothes. This site, a short walk from South Horr village where most vehicles stop, is a good base for meeting up with supply or mission vehicles in hopes of a lift north.

Well worth a visit in the village itself is SALTLICK (Semi-Arid Lands Training and Livestock Improvement Centres Kenya), which concerns itself with supporting the local pastoralist Samburu communities via honey-production projects and cash-crop experiments involving the Senegalese acacia gum tree; it's a mine of information on Samburu culture. For a more intimate experience, you might try asking about the **camel market** which is held on occasions a few kilometres south of the village at a roadside well.

Kurungu Camp

For a place to bump into motorized tourists, the delightful **Kurungu Camp**, 6km past the village along the sandy, vegetation-festooned track, is preferable to Loiyangalani. This is a well-kept **campsite** operated by Safari Camp Services (p.141), surrounded by flowering bushes and shaded by distinguished old trees. The *bandas* are derelict and supplies of cold drinks can't be relied on. Camping out here (about Ksh100 per person) is fabulous.

It's worth spending a couple of nights at Kurungu and exploring the **mountain forest** around you – it hides lots of wildlife and bursts with birds and butterflies. Unfortunately, nearly all athe elephants and buffaloes have been poached. You can be guided by Samburu *morani* up the lower slopes or, more ambitiously, on the stiff hike up to **Nyiru peak**, which has stunning views over Lake Turkana. If you entertain thoughts of any more daring expeditions in the region, **camel hire** should cost in the region of Ksh600–1000 per beast per day. Be careful if you're embarking on anything way off the beaten track. Many men who will sell themselves as **guides** have led surprisingly sheltered lives; they don't know the desert like the backs of their hands any more than you do. Real knowledge and experience are sought after and more expensive.

At Kurungu, you are also likely to have the (mixed) pleasure of **Samburu dancing**, especially if on an organized safari. For about Ksh300–500, you are allowed into the arena to take as many pictures of the dancers as you want, although they do not mask their displeasure. Scepticism is briefly swamped by the hour-long jamboree that follows. A troupe of *morani* goes through an informal dance programme, flirtatiously threatening the audience with whoops and pounces. Young women and girls join in – sometimes with the evident disapproval of older Samburu onlookers – to be propositioned with whisks of the men's ochred hair-dos. Meanwhile, there's the constant offering of necklaces, trinkets, spears, pouches and more photo poses, to be negotiated individually with those who are too old or too young to dance.

Down to the lake

After South Horr, the track winds down between the Nyiru Range to your left and the Ol Doinyo Mara mountains to the right, before opening onto featureless plains of black lava with the massif of Kulal dominating the northern horizon. The lava is hard and jagged – a vicious test for tyres – and the track itself, pummelled to a fine dust, can become a quagmire after a rainstorm. This is Turkana territory. The numerous **stone circles** and **cairns** around here are the remains of settlements and burial sites, which, with a keen eye, you'll learn to recognize all over the region. Most distinctive are the low semicircular constructions, which you'll see in use as you approach the lake: these serve as shelters against the viciously hot wind that blows almost incessantly off the flanks of Kulal. The burial cairns are by no means as ancient as they appear, as traditionally neither the Turkana nor Samburu (who migrated from this area a few hundred years ago) buried their dead, but instead simply left the bodies out in the open for wild animals to eat. The more important members of the community, such as blacksmiths and respected elders, were sometimes buried under cairns, or were left in a hut whose door would be walled up. The site would be abandoned and thereafter never again be used for human habitation. Since Independence and the rise in the power of Christian missions, however, both Turkana and Samburu are now obliged to bury their dead.

Just when you were beginning to wonder, **Lake Turkana** appears as the road drops away in front: a stunning vista of shot blues and greens, with the black, castellate silhouette of South Island hanging as if suspended between lake and sky. Descending a little further along a viciously rocky stretch of road known to drivers as The Staircase, you come to several bays where people have swum in the past (beware of crocs), a few tiny temporary fishing settlements and, an hour or so later, Loiyangalani.

Loiyangalani and around

LOIYANGALANI – "the place of the trees" – is a vague agglomeration of grass huts, mud huts, tin shacks, a police station, a school, a pair of campsites, "the mission" and "the lodge". It's a small community far from metropolitan Kenya, without newspapers and often without beer (a real measure of its isolation). The land around is mostly barren and stony, scattered with the carcasses of livestock, with palm trees and acacias clustered around the settlement's life source, a **hot spring** of fresh water. This empties into two pools near the police station, one for men, the other for women.

The village came into being in the early 1960s with the *Oasis Lodge* and its airstrip, and the Italian mission to the **Elmolo** people, a small group who live by hunting and fishing on the southeastern lakeshore. Somali raiders ransacked both establishments in 1965, but since then the two institutions have been left alone. The mission is now starting to thrive and its net of influence has reached most of Loiyangalani's more permanent inhabitants, especially the children who come to the school.

For all its apparent drabness, the village isn't dull. When you've had enough of haggling for artefacts and fantastic quartz, onyx, amethyst, and other semi-precious stones collected from Kulal – as well as the odd fossil – you can wander over to the springs and the school. You'll inevitably pick up a cluster of teenagers – Turkana, Elmolo, Samburu, Rendille – eager to practise their English. Swahili has never made much impact up here and English is the usual teaching medium. Education is perhaps the most positive of the major influences – which otherwise include state interference, Christianity and tourist money – bringing pressure to bear on local customs and traditions.

The **mission**, while changing the structure of traditional society (through conversions to Catholicism, which have been particularly effective among the Elmolo), is at the same time helping to make local people sufficiently independent to resist unwanted change and to make choices about their future, by

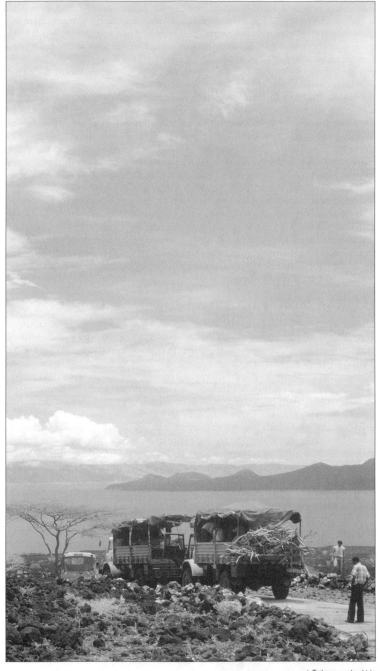

△ Turkana overland trip

helping to set up income-generating schemes such as the shops, some of the boats and a new service station. Some of the Italian missionaries are extremely open and informative and, although you can't be assured they'll have any time to meet you, the chance to talk to them about Loiyangalani may well arise if you're around for a few days. For non-Christians, however, the whole concept of missionaries and their work can be difficult to swallow. For all their schools and clinics, it's difficult to escape the feeling that these people – for so long "untouched" by the outside world – managed very well with their original beliefs and traditions, which formed the basis of their society, cosmology and human relations. With Christianity now ascendant, the old structures are breaking down fast and some risk being lost completely (the Elmolo lost their language in March 1998 following the death of its last speaker, for example). By preferring to convert children, rather than their more obstinate parents, the deeper morality of the well-meaning missionaries is questionable at best. More positively, there's a small library at the mission, which you're free to use.

Loiyangalani's **"beach"** is a grubby strip a couple of kilometres down the road. Many of the loose stones on the shore shelter scorpions (not serious) and carpet vipers (very serious). In the evenings, **dances** often take place around Loiyangalani – informal, energetic, pogo-ing performances for fun, always worth checking out. Track them down by the booming sound of collective larynxes. It's the girls who ask the boys to dance, and you're welcome to join in (no cameras or torches unless permission is expressly given and paid for, usually Ksh300 per person).

Practicalities

The German-run *Oasis Lodge* (PO Box 14829 Nairobi ☎2 Loiyangalani; FB ❼; closed mid-May to mid-July) tries to be exclusive, and certainly charges as though it was. There's a Ksh300 daily entrance fee to casual visitors to discourage them from drinking the entire stock of beer; the fee at least entitles you to swim in its two, jealously guarded pools. The **accommodation**, however, in windblown and rather basic "chalets", is certainly not worth the expense. More useful is the lodge's **car-rental service**, ideal for visiting Sibiloi National Park (see p.616), but the prices are very high (upwards of $200 per day including driver). Similarly expensive are its hiking trips up Kulal and around (around $100 per person per day). Fishing boats can be rented for Ksh2500 per hour, with fishing licences an additional Ksh500. You're advised to bargain hard for all the lodge's services, and to double-check on any price before taking anything on.

Much more down to earth is the **B&L** run by "Mama Changa" (the charming "Mrs Bead", who doesn't speak English), who, apart from supplying much of the Turkana's beadwork necklaces and bracelets, has eighteen cleanish but perfectly adequate rooms round the back of the misnamed *Cold Drink Hotel* (its fridge broke down in 1984), each with a kerosene lamp and free drinking water (❶). This is the place to meet up with other travellers and drivers, should there be any. Totally different in style, but equally pleasant and recommended, is *Mosaretu Camp*, adjacent to *Oasis Lodge*, which is run by the local branch of the women's Maendeleo Ya Wanawake movement. Apart from camping (Ksh150–200 per tent; watch out for snakes and scorpions), they have five traditional *bandas* (❶) under the palm trees, with mosquito nets, mattresses and food-aid sacks used for roofing ("USA CORN: Not to be Sold"). There are toilets and showers, and a kitchen is being built. Near the head of the airstrip, the *Sunset Strip* **campsite** is used by *Safari Camp Services'* "Turkana Bus". The palm trees here are mainly useful for giving shelter from the wind lashing down from the fortress bulk of Kulal, but the campsite is marred by the high wire perimeter fence – built to allow you to leave your gear with some confidence. There are toilets and excellent showers. Last, but not least, 7km to the south of Loiyangalani on the lakeshore (a long hot walk) is probably Lake Turkana's most perfect campsite, operated by Gametrackers for their Turkana safaris, with thatched *bandas* facing out over the lake. There's no shade, but the *bandas* are a delight and the views unparalleled. They use it for only two or three days a week, so you may be able to do a deal with the caretaker.

Food is more difficult. The *Cold Drink Hotel* is nothing special, and has a propensity to charge tourist rates. Food is cheaper and drinks colder from the modestly named *Hilton Hotel* opposite and *South Island Hotel* a little further down. If there are beers in town, you'll find them at *Cold Drinks Shop* at the south end of the village.

South Island National Park

If you want to visit **South Island National Park** ($15, children $5), you should ask about a trip at the lodge first, but spread the word and you may find a much cheaper means of getting there. It's a thirty-kilometre round trip, so the weather needs to be fair. By all accounts, it's one of the weirdest places to stay a night, in the unlikely event of the warden allowing you to do so; its volcanic vents, rising some 300m above sea level, give out a ghostly luminous glow that has long put off local fishermen from venturing there.

Mount Kulal

On dry land, you could make a stab at climbing **Mount Kulal**, if you have the energy. There are two summits, joined by a narrow and dicey ridge. The climb itself, once you're on the right track, is straightforward enough, but talk to some gem-hunters who may guide you up. And note that, although Kulal seems to tower over Loiyangalani, two days is barely enough to walk to the base and back; you really will need transport unless you're very determined and suitably equipped. The views from the top are fabulous, with the lake on one side and the searing Chalbi Desert on the other, and bird-watchers have the added incentive of a rare species of **white-eye** peculiar to the mountain. Bring all the **water** you will need, as there are no supplies on the mountain.

Elmolo Bay

At **Elmolo Bay**, 8km north of Loiyangalani, lives the last viable community of **Elmolo people**. To visit them, you pay a fixed fee per person, depending on the size of your party (around Ksh300–400), to the headman, to be given the freedom of the village, including the right to take photos and a trip to the island opposite the bay to look for crocodiles. During the week, the children are nearly all at school in Loiyangalani; they come home at the weekend, which is the best time to visit. Impromptu dances start, little hands are slipped engagingly into yours for a walk around the low, grass huts. Older people stare rather blankly from the entrances. The ground is a litter of fishbones, string, shreds of cloth. Someone sets up a stall of beadwork and gourds – apparently identical to what you could find up and down the Rift Valley. It's a novel, disturbing experience which contrives to be stage-managed and voyeuristic at the same time. Because of their friendliness, their small number and the increased interest shown in them, the Elmolo risk being taken advantage of by tourists. However, the usual rules apply: ask before you take pictures and be generous with your time and your wallet.

The Elmolo

The people of Loiyangalani with the best claim to be the original inhabitants are the **Elmolo**. In Kenya, they're famous for being famous. Dubbed "the smallest tribe in the world" (in number, not size, and even smaller after a rival tribe, the Boran, raided the community, killing men of fighting age). The Elmolo call themselves *el-Des*, but their usual name comes from the Samburu *loo molo onsikirri*, "the people who eat fish". They once inhabited South Island, but now occupy a couple of islands in Elmolo Bay, and a few gatherings of grass huts on the torrid shores 8km north of Loiyangalani. Most of the 600-strong community live here, partly by **fishing** and the occasional heroic crocodile or hippo hunt (officially banned), partly by **cash receipts** from tourist visitors (see p.614).

The Elmolo are enigmatic. At the time of Teleki's discovery of the lake, they spoke a **Cushitic** language, the family of languages to which Somali and Rendille belong. Recent linguistic research on historical migrations points to their having arrived on the shores of Lake Turkana at a very early time – perhaps over 2000 years ago. They seem to have no tradition of livestock-herding, which might have been kept up if they had turned, like the Turkana, to fishing as a supplement. Today they speak **Samburu** (the last Elmolo-speaker died in March 1998) and have started to intermarry with them. This, as well as the mission's influence, has been quite significant in raising their numbers (from less than 200 twenty years ago) and also in diluting their cultural identity. Once strictly monogamous, polygamy isn't uncommon now and they also send some children to the school in Loiyangalani as weekly boarders. On the slope, right behind the village, a new Catholic church looms.

All this signals the final curtain for a culture and history that has been largely ignored or denied. The conventional wisdom about hunter-gatherers in Kenya is that they are often the descendants of pastoralists who lost their herds. But if the Elmolo are, as some say, pastoral Rendille who took to fishing in order to survive, then it's strange that they have never tried to replace their herds. For without herds, they could never hope to pay bridewealth for wives from their non-fishing neighbours in the traditional way. A better explanation, and one favoured by the Elmolo themselves, is that their people have always been fishermen and hunters and, until very recently, pressures from other tribes, particularly the Turkana, had pushed them almost to the point of annihilation.

By the the end of the twentieth century, the Elmolo fishing culture was beginning to rub off on other ethnic groups and even the Samburu have started to eat fish. As long as thirty years ago, Peter Matthiessen wrote in *The Tree Where Man was Born*:

The Samburu and Turkana may linger for weeks at a time as guests of the Llo-molo, who have plenty of fish and cannot bear to eat with all these strangers hanging around looking so hungry. Other tribes, the Llo-molo say, know how to eat fish better than they know how to catch them . . . "We have to feed them," one Llo-molo says, "so that they will feel strong enough to go away."

The Elmolo are a charming and hospitable people, and how they survive in their chosen environment is almost beyond belief. Outwardly similar in dress and appearance to the other people of the area, they are slightly smaller, but the bowed legs which are supposed to be the characteristic result of their diet seem to be confined to the older people – you might have thought all that fish would give them strong bones.

Incidentally, don't get worried when a mother hands you her child, then asks for money (anything up to Ksh5000); she's not selling her offspring, but simply wants you to sponsor the child's education with a large wad of cash.

Over on the island – which, because of Lake Turkana's lowering, you can now reach by a causeway – you should see **crocodiles** if you walk softly and approach the far shore cautiously. On the island's stern, rocky beaches, the remains of Elmolo fish picnics and old camps can be found everywhere; one find was a nearly fossilized hippo tusk from some long-ago feast. Today, a hippo hunt has to be organized discreetly (strictly speaking, hunting hippos is illegal) and usually takes place further north on the marshier shores below Moiti Hill. Hippos have gone from Loiyangalani.

Sibiloi National Park

Sibiloi National Park (daily fee $15, children $10) provides a powerful temptation to go further north – even for jumping ship if you came up to Turkana by safari tour. **Access** is the main problem, as vehicles heading there from Loiyangalani are extremely rare (a two-week wait might be considered lucky). If you have enough money (upwards of $200 per day), the easiest way is to hire one of *Oasis Lodge*'s battered Land Rovers (with driver). With your own vehicle (high clearance 4WD essential for the first section along the northern flanks of Mount Kulal), a full day's drive might get you there, but be sure to get precise directions from as many people as you can beforehand in Loiyangalani, as most maps are useless. From the Loiyangalani–North Horr road, turn left after some 45km, after the road begins to drop down from Mount Kulal's rocky shoulder. From here, a completely desolate track heads due north for 40km to the settlement of Hurran Hurra, where a left should get you to the camel watering-point and settlement of Gajos, another 40km northwest. Another left here (heading west, then northwest) begins to drop down towards the lake and the national park itself. **Camp Turkana**, near the shore just south of Alia Bay, marks the park's southern boundary, with the National Museums' base of Koobi Fora another 10km further up. Getting back down without your own transport is a matter of waiting (a potentially long time) for any southbound transport: the museums people are obviously the best bet for this.

Apart from **flying in** (around $1000 return from Nairobi's Wilson Airport – you have to negotiate with the pilots), an alternative way of getting there is by boat from Ferguson's Gulf on the lake's western shore, near Kalokol (p.595). Prices vary according to your bargaining skills and perceived ability to pay, though around $200–300 for a return crossing is probably normal (you may have to pay more, however, to convince your boatman to wait longer than one night for the return leg if you're into an extended stay, and he'll expect you to arrange all his food and accommodation requirements, too). There's also an infrequent National Museums supply boat from here.

Discoveries in human prehistory

Sibiloi was created to protect the sites of numerous remarkable **hominid fossil** finds that have been made since 1968 by Richard Leakey's, and latterly Kamoya Kimeu's, team from the University of Nairobi. The park, more than 1600 square kilometres of rock desert and arid bush, is an exceptional source because many of the fossils are found on the surface, blown clean by the never-ending wind. The finds set back the dates of intelligent, co-operative, tool-making behaviour among hominids further and further all the time, but most of the species concerned are assumed to have died out. The crucial discoveries that will link humankind to our prehuman ancestors have yet to be made. One striking find made at Sibiloi in 1972 was "1470", the skull of a *Homo habilis* over two million years old, believed to be a direct ancestor of modern *Homo sapiens*. Sibiloi was declared a national park a year later. As more and more discoveries are made here (currently nearing 200), on the other side of the lake (where excavations have yielded the earliest *australopithecine* known, *Australopithecus anamensis*, dated between 4.2 and 3.9 million years), in southern Ethiopia and at Olduvai in northern Tanzania, evolutionary theories are beginning to flesh out.

The so-called **museum** at the "expedition" headquarters in Alia Bay, where some of the fossils (including part of a one-and-a-half-million-year-old elephant) are supposedly displayed *in situ*, isn't easily traced; all that was found on a last attempt were empty ranger buildings and unhelpful staff. There are no real facilities for visitors and, apart from water supplies, you need to be self-sufficient. In Nairobi, you might try contacting Safari Camp Services (see p.141) which organizes occasional specialist tours to Sibiloi for visiting US paleontologists, archeologists and anthropologists, guided by experts in the field.

Animal life

At times, Sibiloi has a surprising wealth of **wildlife**. Indeed, until the 1930s, there were large numbers of elephant living here. Rainless years, ivory hunters, and especially the increase in the herds of livestock, contributed to their demise. But lion, cheetah, hyena, both kinds of zebra (the ordinary Grant's and the finer-striped, taller Grevy's), giraffe, ostrich, Grant's gazelle, topi, kudu and gerenuk all occur here, though there's no guarantee you'll see much. Because of the protection from hunters, hippos and crocodiles are numerous. The tree cover is minimal. The closest you're likely to come to finding trees is the petrified forest of stone trunks, reminders of the lush vegetation of the lakeshore in prehistoric times.

The northeast

Northeastern Kenya has a single and limited travel circuit: up through **Isiolo** to **Marsabit Mountain and National Park**. It's well worth doing, especially as it's the only route in the northeast currently considered relatively safe. Beyond, or east of Marsabit, the remote administrative outposts of, Mandera, Wajir and Garissa are too dangerous to visit (see box, overleaf).

Travel in the northeast – a warning

The **northeast** of Kenya has long been known for lawlessness, but what was sometimes dismissed as only the exaggerated fear and ignorance of "down-country" Kenyans, acquired a more brutal reality in the 1990s which continues today.

Since the flight of Somali dictator Siad Barre in 1991, and that country's anarchic disintegration into warring fiefdoms, northeastern Kenya has borne the full brunt of Somalia's desperate refugee crisis. Recurring armed clashes have caused Somali families in central and southern regions to flee their homes. One of the largest recent population flows occurred in March 2000 when up to 10,000 fled into northeast Kenya. Because the border is largely an uncontrolled one, the war itself occasionally spills over too, with the situation further complicated by Somali clans such as the Degodia acquiring automatic weapons and using the confusion to settle old scores with neighbouring clans, which occassionally escalates into fully fledged massacres of whole villages. There's also the largely unknown quantity of the "Oromo Liberation Front", which claims parts of Kenya and Ethiopia as the Oromo-speaking peoples' homeland, and which has been blamed for a number of civilian massacres, and increasingly cold-blooded bandits, who primarily target commercial vehicles, foreign aid workers and refugee camps.

All this has been made more volatile by the prolonged drought, which has affected most of the region since 1996. The El Niño floods of 1997 only led to several more seasons of below-normal rainfall, claiming thirty to fifty percent of the region's livestock and its first human lives in 1999. The dryness continued and culminated in a further severe drought in March–June 2000 (the worst in sixty years), at a time when long-term economic decline had already left 48 percent of Kenya's rural population in absolute poverty. Whatever the complicated situation on the ground, you can be sure of one thing, there are more people than before with guns, ammunition and little else. Armed attacks on remote villages and convoys have become commonplace. And with no sign of improvement on the economic front, ruthless opportunists are on the increase and there can be no easier pickings for them than tourists. Given the low volume of traffic, it's not advisable to visit this region as any form of land travel poses a serious risk.

The military presence in the northeast is pervasive: roadblocks, vehicle searches and armed escorts are part of everyday life, yet for all this the military presence is also almost entirely ineffective. Very seldom do incidents reported result in arrests. Indeed, some accuse the police of being complicit in the crimes.

We've endeavoured to note the current security situation for all parts of this chapter, but you're strongly advised to seek advice on the ground before travelling anywhere covered in the following pages as the situation can change quickly. For example, the area between Isiolo and Archer's Post, including Samburu and Buffalo Springs National Reserves, was considered safe for several years before 1997, after which it suffered repeated attacks on villages and tourists. Though the situation in the parks is now controlled by the KWS, things could easily change again.

In summary, the main no-go area at the time of writing is the entire region east of the A2, meaning everything east of the Isiolo–Marsabit–Moyale road, including Wajir, Habeswein, El Wak, and Mandera. Areas where extreme caution are advised are the roads from Mwingi to Garissa, Garsen to Garissa, and the last 30km of the road up to Moyale. Areas currently regarded as relatively safe, but better visited with organized safari groups, include the Isiolo–Marsabit–Moyale road itself, Archer's Post to Maralal, and the road from Malindi to Garsen and Lamu. It's no longer recommended to spend more then a few hours in Isiolo, but travel logistics may make a night in the town unavoidable. Travellers passing through the town are advised to aim to get to their destination well before dark. If visiting the regions mentioned, use your judgement, and ask advice everywhere you go, but bear in mind that the region has never been declared a safe zone by the government, even since before Independence. Driving at night, incidentally, is not only the height of folly, but is also illegal.

Travel throughout the northeast has a special quality. The normal stimuli of passing scenery, animals, people and events fleetingly witnessed is replaced with a massive open sky, shimmering greenish-brown earth, and just occasionally a speck of movement – some camels, a pair of ostriches, a family moving on with their donkeys. It's a sparse, absorbingly simple landscape. And not the least of its attractions is the restful absence of hassle and shove, and a solitude hardly found anywhere else.

A visit to **Moyale** offers the possibility of a brief trip to **Ethiopia**, and is the only recognized crossing into that country and beyond. Incidentally, the road up from Moyale to Addis Ababa is entirely surfaced. There are generally no special conditions attached to crossing for a few hours to wander around.

Isiolo

ISIOLO is the northeast's most important town and the hub for travel to Marsabit and Moyale, though not a particularly safe place to spend a great amount of time.

Southernmost of the "Northern Frontier" towns, Isiolo is on the border between two different worlds – the fertile highlands and the desert. A measure of the untamed badlands beyond is given by the three military training schools based here: Infantry, Combat Engineering and Artillery, as well as a tank regiment. Isiolo is a frontier in every respect. The **Somali influence**

▲ Samburu, Marsabit & Wajir

ISIOLO

N

0   200 m

Livestock
Market

BP

Akamba
Bus

Matatus
(for east)

Total

KANISANI ROAD

Jamia
Mosque

District Commissioner (D.C.)

Covered Market

Produce
Market

SHANTY
TOWN

Utamaduni

Matatu Stand
(for south)

Matatu
Stand

Caltex

Playing
Field

Catholic Church

ACCOMMODATION	
Bomen Hotel	5
Hotel Classica	10
Jamhuri Lodging	3
Jeddah Hotel	4
Mashallah Hotel	2
Mocharo Lodge	8
Nanyuki Guest house	6
Pasoda Lodge	9
Silver Bells Hotel	7
Talent Lodge	1
RESTAURANTS & CAFÉS	
Al-Hilal Café	E
Bomen Hotel	C
Coffee Tree Hotel	F
Frontier Green Café	D
Salama Restaurant	B
Talent Lodge	A

▼ Meru & Nanyuki

here is something noticeable everywhere in the northeast, and Isiolo is one of their most important towns in Kenya because it was here that many veteran Somali soldiers from World War I were settled. Recruited in Aden and Kismayu, they gave up their nomadic lifestyle to become livestock and retail traders.

But **the town** is really a cultural kaleidoscope, with Boran, Meru, Samburu and some Turkana inhabitants as well as the Somalis. To someone newly arrived from Nanyuki or Meru, the upland towns seem ordinary in comparison. Women from the irrigated *shambas* around Isiolo sell cabbages, tomatoes and carrots in the busy market. Cattle owners, nomadic camel traders and merchants exchange greetings and the latest news from Nairobi and Moyale. In the livestock market, goats scamper through the alleys. Hawkers stroll along the road raising their Somali swords and strings of bangles to the minibuses heading up to Samburu National Reserve (see p.429). And, in the shade, energetic *miraa*-chewing and hanging around are the major occupations. *Miraa* has a long history in Somali culture, and the Nyambeni Hills, where most of the Kenyan crop is grown, are just 30km away (p.435).

Practicalities

If you get a late **bus** from Nairobi you'll arrive in the middle of the night, and the town can be seen glittering out on the plain far below for an hour or more beforehand. During Ramadan, lanterns glow along the pavements for the *miraa* sellers and most of the shops are still open. You can find a B&L or sleep on the bus until dawn – probably a safer bet. There is no longer a bank in Isiolo, but there is a **post office** (Mon–Fri 8am–1pm & 2–5pm).

Accommodation

If circumstances necessitate an overnight stay then Isiolo boasts one reasonable, mid-range **hotel**. Of the more humble **lodgings**, all are cheap, and several surprisingly good value. There's also a good place 10km south of town in the form of the shaded *Rangeland Hotel* (☎0165/2340; ❷), which also has a small playground for children.

Bomen Hotel PO Box 67 Isiolo ☎0165/2389, ⓕ2225. The best and most expensive in town: clean, polite and serving good breakfasts. Rooms lack fans, but are s/c and have nets, and hot water mornings and evenings. ❸

Hotel Classica PO box 334 ☎0165/2098. On the south side of town, opposite the gargantuan Catholic church, this place has comfortable beds in s/c rooms (hot water), but already showing signs of old age. Safe parking. ❶

Jamhuri Lodging PO Box 88 ☎0165/2065. Newly renovated, clean, courteous and mellow – currently the most popular cheap place. Laundry facilities. Not s/c. ❶

Jeddah Hotel PO Box 335 ☎0165/2264. The newest in town, on the same street and similar to the *Jamhuri*, also clean and secure. ❶

Mashallah Hotel PO Box 378 ☎0165/2142. Clean, functional, Somali-run apartment block with

both s/c and cheaper non-s/c. Not terribly welcoming. Doubles and singles. ❶

Mocharo Lodge PO Box 106 ☎0165/2385. Good value and safe parking. Recommended. ❶

Nanyuki Guest House PO Box 451 ☎0165/2168. Reasonable and dirt cheap, with spartan rooms, nets, fresh cold milk, dry-cleaning facilities and safe parking. ❶

Pasoda Lodge PO Box 62 ☎0165/2162. Quiet and clean, with inexpensive meals. All rooms s/c with nets. Safe parking. ❷

Silver Bells Hotel Between the *Bomen* and *Pasoda*, PO Box 247 ☎0165/2251. Clean, quiet and mid-priced, with a grubby cocktail bar which sells only beer and soda. ❶

Talent Lodge PO Box 174 ☎0165/2262. Basically a boozer with cheap rooms, pleasant but sometimes dirty. ❶

Eating and drinking

Somali *hotelis* provide excellent **food**, day and night. Now that you're in the northeast, you'll see pasta (usually spaghetti) appearing quite prominently on menus – one of the better Italian bequests to the Somalis.

Al-Hilal Café Pretty good – especially noted for its samosas – and it has some ultra-cheap accommodation.

Bomen Hotel The *nyama choma* at the patio bar is worthwhile for meat-eaters.

Coffee Tree Hotel Down-to-earth eats.

Frontier Green Café A brilliant, tree-filled garden-restaurant with disco (Wednesday, Friday and Saturday), fluorescent spider's webs and UV tubes

– in outlandish contrast with the rest of the town. Long popular for its good spiced *chai* for next to nothing a glass. The bar is open 24hr.

Salama Restaurant The best in town – especially for an early breakfast or their very good spaghetti.

Talent Lodge A worthwhile move on a hot afternoon for a cold beer on their rooftop terrace, though the broken bottles and legless chairs somewhat mar the atmosphere.

Shopping and guides

Isiolo is one of the best places to buy **bracelets** of copper, brass and aluminium. Prices are generally around Ksh50 for the simple ones, up to Ksh200 for the heavier, more complicated designs, if you can bargain effectively (starting prices are much higher). Short "Somali swords" in red leather scabbards are also much in evidence. The "sharp boys" who mob you near the markets will invariably offer to guide you to one of the few blacksmiths in town to watch the fascinating process of twisting the wires for the bangles. Profits come from buying rough bangles, then polishing and selling them. If you go, you're generally expected to make a purchase and tip a few shillings to the boys. While the bangle and knife salesmen throng as soon as you sit down for a *chai*, their approach is rarely aggressive (though see the note about tyre-spiking below). Women offer small wooden dolls with woven hair, which in the past were given to young girls as both toys and fertility charms. Some of the former "sharp boys" have recently teamed up to start the **Utamaduni Self-Help Group** (PO Box 16; office in the market opens Mon–Fri 3–5.30pm), which aims to organize and rehabilitate homeless and orphaned youth in community-based projects (for example, by building small bridges over sewage ditches). Though some of their members are still a little rough around the edges, it's a laudable venture, and the best place to get a **guide** for visiting local *manyattas* (they must have an ID card; you should pay between Ksh500–800 for a full day). For trips further afield, test the guide first on a one-day trip in the environs of Isiolo before trusting him on a longer journey.

Moving on from Isiolo

When heading north, waiting in Isiolo is a predictable part of the trip. The only public transport onwards from Isiolo is to Wamba (see p.605) and Maralal via Archer's Post, details for which are given overleaf. Otherwise, there are no buses and only limited *matatu* services north or east from Isiolo, so your only options for travel to Marsabit and Moyale are either **self-drive**, which is ill-advised for all but the most experienced, well-equipped and mechanically skilled driver, or **hitching a ride** with a truck in convoy. If you're lucky, you might get a lift with one of the mission or aid vehicles. Note if you're driving that Isiolo is the last **fuel** stop until Maralal or Marsabit, and beware also that tyre spikers were until recently at work at Isiolo police barrier; while you stamp about, change your wheel and arrange for your puncture to be repaired, an army of souvenir pedlars pitch their gear at you.

To Nairobi via the Central Highlands

If you're travelling by **bus**, Akamba has two daily services to Nairobi via Nanyuki, Kiganjo, Nyeri and Karatina, departing at 7.30am and 8pm, arriving in Nairobi at 1pm and 2am respectively. Their office is in the *Maendeleo Hotel* building. The cheaper Eastern Express has one daily departure at 7.30am, which doesn't stop in Nyeri, and has a reputation for insane drivers. For *matatus* you have to be at the market stage before sunrise – last departures at 6am are not unheard of.

North to Marsabit and Moyale

For many years this route has been considered highly dangerous due to attacks by **bandits**. Though the situation changes from year to year, the main trouble spots at the time of writing were the first 40-odd kilometres to Archer's Post (sporadic highway-style hold-ups of tourist vehicles bound for the Samburu national reserves, so don't dawdle), and the approach to Moyale, which is subject to more frequent raids from neighbouring Ethiopia. **Matatus** go as far as Archer's Post, which is only helpful if you're visiting Samburu or Shaba national reserves (see pp.429 & 433). Otherwise, try for trucks at the **police road-block** 3km north of Isiolo at the **end of the tarmac**, by the junction for Wajir, where drivers sign their vehicles out of town. There are usually a few heading up to Moyale daily, and most take passengers (for a fee). You'll have to stand on top of the load along with the other, usually male, passengers, although given the state of the roads, this is actually more comfortable than sitting down. Alternatively, Gametrackers' Turkana Bus passes through Archer's Post early in the morning every other Sunday, which – if the driver's amenable – can take you as far as Marsabit, probably for a fee. If you do get a lift, the 262km to Marsabit takes seven to ten hours, with the next leg to Moyale (245km) anything from ten hours to two days, depending on the state of the road and the frequency of hold-ups, natural or otherwise. Trucks charge upwards of Ksh1000.

West to Maralal

The **Isiolo–Archer's Post–Maralal** run is served by the wacky Babie Coach, a converted Bedford lorry which makes the journey every day between Isiolo and Maralal (or vice versa), leaving one town at around 9am to reach the other five to six hours later – though you could stop off in Wamba (p.605) to explore the grandly mysterious Mathews Range. On the days that Babie Coach is on its homebound run to Isiolo, you may find the odd *matatu* going to Maralal. If you're **driving** the route yourself, bring enough fuel for the whole journey – there are no supplies at Wamba.

To Marsabit and North Horr

No matter the speed, this is a fantastically uncomfortable trip, with rocks, ruts and corrugations that shake smaller vehicles to breaking point. Somewhat unbelievably, the road is said to have been surfaced at least three times in the past, all the way to Moyale – not a trace of which remains.

Passing over the occasionally dry Ewaso Nyiro River and a police barrier, you hit the agglomeration of shiny-roofed shacks and rows of *dukas* which is **ARCHER'S POST**. This is as far north as you'll get by *matatu*, although lifts into Samburu and Shaba national reserves (see pp.429 & 433) may be forthcoming

Peoples of the northeast

Identities in the northeast can be confusing. The largest group are the **Boran**, part of the **Oromo peoples** (formerly called Galla, an Amhara term of abuse), whose homeland was near the Bale Mountains in Ethiopia, from where they suddenly exploded out, in all directions, in the sixteenth century. The pastoral Boran developed and flourished in what is now southern Ethiopia, but Menelik's conquest of the area and the oppressive Amhara regime caused some of them to move down to the lowlands (much less suitable for their cattle) of northern Kenya; the first Boran arrived in Marsabit only in 1921. Similarly recent Ethiopian immigrants to the region between Marsabit and Moyale are the **Burji**, an agricultural people who were called down by colonial administrators in the 1930s who wanted crops grown to feed themselves. The Burji took quickly to Western education and trade, and as a result dominated Marsabit politically in the first decade after Independence. There's little love lost between the nomadic Boran and the settled Burji.

At around the time of the Oromo expansion, another group of people - the forefathers of the Gabbra - arrived in northern Kenya, causing havoc in the region, only to be themselves pressured by the ensuing expansion of **Muslim Somalis** from the east. The ancestors of the **Gabbra** became "Boranized" to the extent that they changed their language and adopted Boran customs. Although most Boran and Gabbra, especially those who adopted a more sedentary life, have adopted Somali styles in dress and culture, they eschew Islam, in preference for their own religions. The **Rendille**, to the northwest of Marsabit, look and act like Samburu, with whom they are frequently allied; they speak a language close to Somali but have non-Muslim religious beliefs. They normally herd camels rather than cattle and, to a great extent, continue to roam the deserts, facing the prospect of settling down without any enthusiasm at all and visiting Marsabit only for vital needs or a brief holiday.

In Marsabit itself, distinctions other than superficial ones are increasingly hard to apply as people intermarry, more children are sent to school, and down-country ideas – and Christian missionaries – percolate up the road. Still, language and religious beliefs remain significant in deciding who does what and with whom, and outside the town, individual tribal identities are as strong – and potentially bloody – as they have ever been.

---

from Kenya Wildlife Service personnel, who frequent a number of particularly good bars. There are some **rooms** here, too, should you fail: try *Accacia Shade Inns*, which also has a **campsite** (with no guarantee of security). There's no **petrol** available; the nearest is an expensive trip to either *Samburu Lodge* or *Sarova Shaba Lodge* in the reserves (see p.431). Finally, advertising "hard and pertinent facts about the Samburu people", **Samburu Cultural Centre** (daily 10am–4pm; PO Box 548 Isiolo), half a kilometre from Archer's Post market along the Samburu National Reserve road, has a small **ethnographic museum** and *manyatta*, complete with ironmongery, woodwork and beadwork for sale, displays of dancing, and more.

North of Archer's Post, the road veers northwest and for thirty minutes the great mesa – over 2000m – of **Ol Olokwe Mountain** (or Ol Doinyo Sabache) spreads massively across the horizon in front of you. If you're travelling independently with a vehicle, it can be climbed. If you fancy something more organized and worthy, **Namunyak Wildlife Conservation Trust** (PO Box 88 Wamba; information and bookings from Let's Go Travel in Nairobi, p.141) is a community-wildlife venture set up in 1995 to preserve some 300 square kilometres of land around the mountain for the benefit of local Samburu. They offer walking safaris up the mountain led by Samburu *morani*, rich ground for bird-spotters with frequent sightings of Gambaga flycatcher, shining sunbird, the tiny cisticola, stone partridge, and Kenya's largest nesting colony of Ruppell's vultures. You might also see dik-dik, klipspringer, Chandler's mountain reedbuck, rock hyrax, vervet monkey, olive baboon, and (very rarely) leopard and elephant.

For several hours beyond Ol Olokwe you roar across the flat **Kaisut Desert**. **Laisamis** isn't much of a break – a low windblown cluster of tin-roofed huts and Samburu, offering sodas and toothbrush sticks to passers-by – and the Losai National Reserve isn't any different from the rest of the scenery. The **approach to Marsabit**, though, is unmistakable. The road begins to climb and suddenly you're on a hilly island in the desert, a region of volcanic craters, lush meadows and forest. The branches of the trees on the steep slopes are disguised by swathes of Spanish moss, looking at first glance like algae-covered rocks in shades of grey and green.

Marsabit town

MARSABIT is a surprise. It's hard to prepare yourself, after the flat dustlands, for this fascinating hill oasis, in the desert but not of it. Rising a thousand metres above the surrounding plains, *Saku*, as the mountain is known by locals, is permanently green, well watered by the clouds which form and disperse over it in a daily cycle. The high forest is usually mist-covered until late morning, the trees a characteristic tangle of foliage and lianas.

The town is capital of the largest administrative district in the country, as well as a major meat- and livestock-trading centre. Small and intimate in feel, the lively cultural mix in the main market area is the biggest buzz: transient **Gabbra** herdsmen and **Boran** with their prized short-horn cattle, women in the printed shawls and chiffon wraps of **Somali** costume rubbing elbows with ochred **Rendille** wearing skins, high stacks of beads and wire, and fantastic braided hairstyles. There are government workers here, too, from other parts of Kenya, and a scattering of **Ethiopian immigrants** (mainly Burji) and refugees. For some Marsabit background, try Mude Dae Mude's novel *The Hills are Falling* (Transafrica, Nairobi 1979), now out of print but you might still find a copy in Nairobi. If you're interested in **traditional music**, ask for George's Music Store in Marsabit – George is happy to answer queries, and has a great selection of cassettes.

MARSABIT TOWN

Police Barrier

0   200 m

Esso

N

Shell

George's Music Store

Market Area

KCB

ACCOMMODATION
Al-Jazeera	5
Badassa Hotel	1
Safari Garden Hotel	4
Marsabit Highway Hotel	2
Marsabit Hotel	3

Police Station

RESTAURANTS & BARS
Chalbi Bar	A
Mountain Bar & Restaurant	B

Isiolo

Moyale, North Horr & Loiyangalani

Marsabit National Park

Practicalities

For **changing money**, the KCB is open Monday to Friday 9am–1pm and Saturday morning 9–11am. There's also a **post office** (Mon–Fri 8am–5pm), and several reasonable places to **eat and drink**. The *Al-Jazeera* serves decent meals, and there's very cheap food in a lively atmosphere at any time of day from the *hotelis*: hefty pancakes, *githeri*, *mandaazi* and *nyama choma*. The *hotelis* double as butchers so you can select your own slab for roasting from the carcasses hanging up. There's a well-stocked grocery next to the *Kenya Lodging*. If you're thirsty, the *Mountain Bar & Restaurant* (PO Box 20 ☏0183/1342) is the die-hards' drinking den, with a mix of characters and the occasional dispute over prostitutes – or try the *Chalbi Bar B&L*, opposite the *Marsabit Highway Hotel*.

Accommodation

Safari Garden Hotel (PO Box 176 ☏0183/2221; ❶) used to be an outstanding **place to stay**, but has been getting decidedly run down since its Ethiopian owners left: no longer clean, but still relatively modern and cosy, and cheap. Other places include the large but rather miserable *Marsabit Highway Hotel* (PO Box 110 ☏0183/2236; ❶), with a bakery below (fresh bread every afternoon), and some self-contained rooms with double beds; the *Badassa Hotel*, an unexceptional B&L with a decent *hoteli* (❶); the *Al-Jazeera*, which offers extremely cheap and peaceful accommodation and very safe parking (❶); and a little further out, by the market, is the cheaper *Marsabit Hotel* (❶). Whichever you choose, ask about **hot water** before moving in as at night temperatures can drop very low (by some accounts, *Marsabit* means "place of cold") and lukewarm showers are no fun. New boreholes mean that the town is currently well supplied with water, and electricity is generally reliable (unless the diesel-powered generator breaks down). If you want **to camp**, head for the national park's main gate (see p.626).

Walks out of town

There are a number of trips you can make on foot from Marsabit in a few hours or less – particularly good restoratives if you haven't got your own vehicle and failed to get into the national park (see p.626). The easiest, with rewarding views, is the short walk up to the big wind-powered **generator** on a hill just west of the town. Turn left just before the police barrier and simply follow the path.

A longer excursion takes you up to the **VOK transmitter** behind the town, an excellent morning or afternoon hike through lush forest with magnificent panoramas of the whole district from the top. There are wells up here, too (see below). During the rainy season, everything is tremendously green and you walk over flowering meadows through clouds of butterflies.

From there, you should be able to see the closest sizeable crater, **Gof Redo**, about 5km north of the town in the fork of the roads to Moyale and North Horr. Follow either road from the fork for about 3km, then turn left or right accordingly for a one-kilometre cross-country walk. The crater is quite a favoured hideout for greater kudu, and there's a population of cheetah around here too, not infrequently seen from a vehicle (but likely to flee if you're on foot). You can scramble down the crater wall. Gof Redo can't really be missed, but a friend from town would be reassuring.

Even easier is a walk to the "**singing wells**" at Ulanula (called Hulahula by some). These are less exotic than they sound, but they're still a good excuse to explore. Ulanula is a conical peak to the right of the Isiolo road, about 6km from town. Leaving Marsabit, you cross two bridges, then turn left and climb 200–300m up a narrow, tangled ravine. A concrete holding-tank, visible from the road, gives the place away. Behind it are two natural wells, the first with a wooden trough in front, the second longer and apparently deeper, containing a fluctuating depth of brown, frog-filled water. A silent pumphouse stands by.

The **singing** is done not by the wells but by the Boran herders who use them. When the water is low, human chains are formed to get it out with luxuriantly leaking leather buckets; singing helps the work. At the driest times of the year you may be lucky and witness this, but try to get here early. Animals are usually driven to the wells after dawn, and it's a brisk 75-minute walk from town. Go out there in the late afternoon, though, and you should get a lift back with one of the day's vehicles up from Isiolo.

Onward from Marsabit

One or two trucks do occasionally spend the night in Marsabit, to or from Moyale or Isiolo. Otherwise, the convoy to Moyale usually passes in the afternoon, and that towards Isiolo anytime between 5pm and 11pm. The best place to wait is at the **police checkpoint**, 300m from the Esso garage on the Isiolo road. Ask around the petrol stations if you're trying to hitch a lift to Loiyangalani; with your own tent, your first target is Kalacha, otherwise aim for North Horr. If you are **driving**, supplies of petrol are usually available.

Marsabit National Park

Daily fees: $15, children $5. Map: Survey of Kenya Marsabit National Reserve SK 84 at 1cm:1km.

Having made the long journey to Marsabit, you'll certainly want to get into the **park**. The forest is wild and dense, its two crater lakes idyllically beautiful. Except during the long rains (March–June), there's a good chance you'll see some of the long-tusked Marsabit **elephants**, relatives of the famous Ahmed – a big tusker to whom Kenyatta gave "presidential protection", with elephant guards tracking him day and night (now replicated in fibreglass in the National Museum in Nairobi). His replacement, Mohammed, whose tusks were estimated at a cool 45kg each side, has also gone to the elephant's graveyard. The park is also renowned for its **greater kudu** antelope and there's a very wide range of other wildlife. Between the nearly impenetrable forests of the peaks and the stony scrub desert at the base of the mountain, however, you'll need a little luck for sightings. This is a rewarding park, but one where you have to look hard.

Practicalities

The park's **main gate** is at the edge of town, past the bank and the District Commissioner's office. It's not often visited and you may be in for a long wait if you want a lift around its forest tracks. In addition, government officers and soldiers garrisoned in town drive up to the **lodge** (see below) fairly frequently. This short trip, with the view over the first lake – Gof Sokorte Dika – and its forested rim, is a lot better than nothing. You might also be able to convince an armed ranger to escort you to the first lake (say Ksh500) – it's a wonderful walk through the forest, with clouds of butterflies and the occasional mouth-drying encounter with buffalo or elephant.

If you **drive in the park** without 4WD, make sure you can get back out. Some of the tracks in the forest are steep and tend to be muddy.

There's a **campsite** near the main gate (100m down the hairpin to the left of the ranger's house) which is free in theory, although the rangers may request a small fee, especially if you wish to use the new toilet and shower block. It's a wonderfully shaded place overrun with baboons swinging on the lianas.

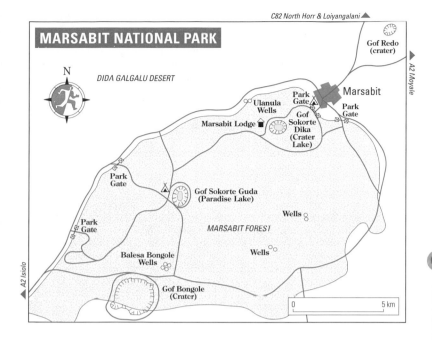

MARSABIT NATIONAL PARK

Gof Redo
(crater)

DIDA GALGALU DESERT

N

Ulanula
Wells

Park
Gate

Marsabit

Marsabit Lodge

Gof
Sokorte
Dika
(Crater
Lake)

Park
Gate

Park
Gate

Gof Sokorte Guda
(Paradise Lake)

Wells

MARSABIT FOREST

Park
Gate

Wells

Balesa Bongole
Wells

Gof Bongole
(Crater)

0   5 km

A2 Isiolo ▲

A2 Moyale ▶

There are several other places to camp in the park. Gof Sokorte Guda (Lake Paradise), a stunning, dark pool a kilometre across for much of the year, has wonderful sites on its crater rim, where a night would be chilly and thrillingly spent – lion, leopard and the rare and shaggy striped hyena are all seen and heard from time to time. This *Lake Paradise Special Campsite* costs $10 per person (plus park entry fee), but does not include the Ksh500 or so "guiding fee" for the obligatory accompanying ranger.

Marsabit Lodge (PO Box 488 ☏0183/2411, ℱ2416; FB ❼) has recently reopened and has been somewhat renovated, which is wonderful news, given the exquisite beauty of its location on the shore of Gof Sokorte Dika and the outstanding views from all its rooms. Elephants are no longer common visitors, since the salt that lured them is no longer laid out.

Marsabit's fauna

Your animal count in the park will very much depend on the season of your visit. Good rains can encourage the grazers off the mountain and out into the temporarily lush desert, and the predators (always far fewer) will follow. **Elephants** especially are tremendous wanderers, sometimes strolling into town, causing pandemonium. More problematically, the people of Marsabit have been encouraged to cultivate around the base of the mountain, at the same time creating a barrier to the elephants' free movement and unintentionally providing them with free lunches.

The **birdlife** in the park is amazing: almost 400 species have been recorded, including 52 different birds of prey. Very rare **lammergeiers** (bearded vultures) are thought to nest on the sheer cliffs of Gof Bongole, the largest crater, which has a drivable track around its ten-kilometre rim. Marsabit is also something of a **snake** sanctuary, with some very large cobras – this isn't a place to go barefoot or in sandals.

To Kalacha and North Horr

Reaching North Horr from Marsabit is getting easier, though continuing the logical next step down to Lake Turkana and Loiyangalani is still somewhat difficult. There is a more or less regular passenger lorry which leaves Marsabit "often", as well as mission, Education Department, commercial and aid vehicles.

En route, **MAIKONA** is a friendly Gabbra settlement on the fringes of the **Chalbi Desert**, with a thriving daily market for goats and cattle (the camels which become ubiquitous from here on tend to be traded at Isiolo). As with all the villages up here, keep your camera out of sight, and ask permission if you want to take **photographs**: belief in the camera's evil eye is prevalent. *Kamkunji Hotel* may have one or two rooms. Some 5km north is a small, seemingly miraculous oasis pond of blue water with a sweet green grass fringe. It's the last fresh water until **KALACHA**, a regular night stop for some of the longer Turkana expeditions (Gametrackers stays here). Kalacha is the neatest village in all Africa, with its "streets" defined by rows of carefully placed stones, and litter, if there were any, is quickly blown away by the furnace wind. There's a church designed by a German architect, two very basic *dukas*, a bar that sells very hot beer, and the humble but friendly *Bismillahi Hotel* which has rooms. But the real treat is the remarkably good mission-run **campsite** – dusty and barren yet with decent showers and even a rather inventive swimming pool/water tank, that subsequently feeds an irrigation system. The water, pumped up by a windmill, is sporadically chlorinated. Local Gabbra cluster to sell their wares and to pick up what useful items they can.

From Kalacha to North Horr, the track streaks out over blinding white salt pans and shifting quicksands, ducks behind straggly oasis clusters of half-dead palm trees, and finally loses itself in a vast orange expanse rimmed only by the floating hulks of very distant mountains. The exact path of the road varies annually, and in April is often impassable when the rains bring with them a circus of flamingoes. **NORTH HORR**, when you finally reach it, is a welcome haven, with a handful of *dukas*, the Somali *Al-Rachid Hotel*, opposite the mosque, for traditional fare, rooms at the *Mandera Central Hotel*, and even a red phone box that works. From here on down to Loiyangalani, the terrain becomes even tougher as the road painfully climbs the volcanic foothills of Mount Kulal, but the view from the top, looking down over the lake far away, can be spellbinding.

To Moyale and beyond

From Marsabit, the **journey to Moyale** takes between five and nine hours depending on the vehicle. For the first three of these you descend from the mountain's greenery past spectacular craters – Gof Choba is the whopper on the left – to the forbidding black moonscape of the **Dida Galgalu Desert**. Dida Galgalu means "plains of darkness", according to one Boran story. Another account derives it from Galgalu, a woman buried here after she died of thirst trying to cross it. The road arrows north for endless miles, then cuts east across watercourses and through bushier country beneath high crags on the Ethiopian frontier. En route, you pass a new refugee centre at Lugga Walde (or Walda), 80km before Moyale (a UN and American IRC charity camp), and the turning to the small village of **Sololo** on the Ethiopian border, arrestingly sited between soaring peaks, which can be climbed for stunning views over the northern plains and Ethiopian highlands. Sololo has a mission, which may let you camp in their grounds, and a single lodging/brothel (the *Treetop*). Note that the road to Sololo, and the last stretch into Moyale, sees occasional **armed hold-ups**, though nothing as vicious as those further south and east. Again, the usual rule applies – travel in convoy, and don't resist.

There are some magnificent, towering **termite mounds** along the northern part of the route. They're a sight that seems quintessentially African, yet one which can be quickly taken for granted as the 250km from Marsabit to Moyale roll by with a few slight bends, a couple of scenery changes and the occasional lone herder with his livestock. Over distances that would take days to cover on foot you can see where you have been and where you are going – as if the pastoralists' conservatism were reflected in the landscape.

The road doubles north again and winds up through the settlements of Burji farmers – an agricultural people who emigrated from Ethiopia early in the twentieth century – past their beautifully sculpted houses and sparse fields, to Moyale.

Moyale

Straddling the Ethiopian border, **MOYALE** makes Marsabit look like a metropolis. Though the town is growing rapidly, and was recently supplied with electricity, the centre is small enough to walk around in fifteen minutes. You'll find several sandy streets, a pretty mosque, a few *dukas*, a bar, a camel-tethering ground, two petrol stations (one of which occasionally belies its defunct appearance), a big police station, a fairly large market area, a new KCB bank and an incredibly slow post office – five weeks to Europe. Moyale is not much to write home about in fact, and there's not a lot to do except wander around, perhaps try some camel milk (very rich and creamy) and pass the time of day with everyone else, with or without the aid of *miraa*. Note that there is the odd shooting in town involving "Ethiopian bandits", with the local population as victims. It's a regular enough occurrence, it seems, judging by the practised haste of the shopkeepers in sealing up their businesses on hearing even distant gunfire.

The most interesting aspect of Moyale is its **architecture** – at least, the good number of traditionally built houses which are still standing (the rest were bombed and shelled during World War II, after which the good citizens of Moyale clubbed together for "less fortunate people", contributing £80 to the colony's "Food for Britain Fund"). The Boran build in several styles, including circular mud-and-thatch huts, but in town the houses are rectangular, of mud and dung on a wood frame, with a flat or slightly tilted roof projecting 1–2m to form a porch, supported by sturdy posts and tree trunks. The roof is up to 50cm thick, a fantastic accretion of dried mud, sticks, scrap, and vegetation. Chickens and goats get up there, improving the roof's fertility, and every time it rains another layer of insulating herbage springs up. As a result, the houses are cool while the outside temperature hovers above 30°C for most of the year (July and August are cooler).

Practicalities

Accommodation is very limited and all firmly in the budget category. The most established B&L is *Barissah Hotel* (❶), which shares frontage with the bar. It has a dozen dark cubes around an earth compound, and, while it's hardly clean, it's friendly enough. The **restaurant** has *karanga* and chapatis every evening, 24-hour *malayas*, and a permanent supply of warm tea. You need to bring a padlock, and "showers" (a basin of water) have to be ordered.

A second lodging, where family and guests share the same roof, is *Bismillahi B&L* (❶), across the way from the *Barissah* behind the Esso pumps. It's slightly more expensive, and facilities here don't match the *Barissah*'s, but the food is good. *Silent Lodge* (❶), just outside town near the police barrier, has clean, three-bedded rooms and is perhaps the most promising place. There are other B&Ls on the main street, past the mosque.

The water in Moyale can be briny at times and it's worth bringing a few litres of drinking water up from Marsabit. You can obtain **clean water** in Moyale from the Ministry of Water.

Into Ethiopia

The most interesting prospect in Moyale is to cross the valley into **Ethiopia** and spend a few hours, or even a night, there. For Kenyans and Ethiopians, the border is an open one. For foreigners there are just a few formalities on the Kenyan side, none on the Ethiopian side, and crossing is easy. Doubtless the situation depends much on the latest directives from Nairobi and Addis, and on relations between the two governments, which have generally been good, although local tensions are currently high between competing clans in the district, exacerbated by Ethiopian pastoralists who have encroached on the Kenyan side.

You can increase your chances by ensuring your Kenyan visa (if you have one) is a multiple-entry type, thus allowing you back in again. Naturally, an Ethiopian visa wouldn't hinder your progress either, though the embassy in Nairobi is not likely to concede that entry through Moyale would be permitted (by the rule book, tourists go into Ethiopia only by air through Addis Ababa). As temptation, however, the Ethiopians have trumped the Kenyans and have built a smooth tarmac road from the border all the way to Addis.

Ethiopian Moyale is larger than its Kenyan counterpart and noticeably more prosperous with some piped water, and a long-established electricity supply. There are several bars, a hotel that wouldn't look out of place in a small town in Greece, lots of simple stores, and plenty of eating places. You can pay for everything in Kenyan shillings. The market buzzes colourfully with camels and goats, piles of spices, flour and vegetables. Otherwise, life here seems much the same as over the border, but easier. As a back-door view of Ethiopia, however, it may be no more representative than the other side of town is of Kenya.

Travel details

Because of their importance, particulars about road transport are given throughout the chapter. On the main axes – Kitale–Lodwar, Nyahururu–Baragoi and Isiolo–Moyale – you will rarely be stuck for a ride too long. Least frequented is the route up to Loiyangalani and this, together with Isiolo–Moyale, has no bus service.

Buses

This indicates the minimum service you can expect in the north. The reverse service applies on each route with the same frequency. Arrival times are not guaranteed.

Isiolo to: Maralal (every 2 days).
Nyahururu to: Maralal (daily; 90min).

Flights

Flights to Lake Turkana are usually part of all-inclusive weekend packages at around $500–700 per person at either Ferguson's Gulf (*Fishing Lodge*) or Loiyangalani (*Oasis Lodge*). Otherwise, contact one of the plane charter companies listed on p.144.

contexts

contexts

History

The picture of Kenya's past that the first Europeans formed – a multitude of primitive peoples with no appreciable history – has been brushed aside in the last fifty years. Techniques have been found for tracing past events and migrations by combining oral traditions and comparing languages. Nevertheless, Kenya's precolonial past is still the subject of endless conjecture and, up-country, it's difficult for the traveller to keep much sense of it – especially since the physical record in ancient architecture is virtually nonexistent. On the coast, settlement ruins, old documents and the Islamic tradition help considerably to retain the feeling of a long past. What follows, up to the colonial period, is a much condensed overview, intended to pull together the historical accounts of individual peoples that are given throughout the guide. More emphasis here is given to the firmer history of the last hundred years or so.

The cradle of humankind

Kenya seems to be the place where human beings first evolved. The oldest remains belonging indisputably to **ancestral hominids** have been found on the shores of Lake Turkana, and more recently in the Tugen Hills. Even so, concrete evidence of the origins of humanity remains scant, and new finds could easily turn the latest theories upside down.

The East African **Rift Valley** is ideal territory for the search for human origins: volcanic eruptions have repeatedly showered thick layers of ash and cinders over fossil beds, building up strata that can be reliably used to compare ages. The **Leakey** family has been instrumental in much of the work that has been done. Olduvai Gorge in Tanzania, was the first major site to disclose evidence of human prehistory, and Louis Leakey and his wife, Mary, worked there from the 1930s. Their son, Richard, went on to explore the Turkana region and found even older fossils, putting Kenya in the spotlight of scientific attention. A suggestion in support of the "cradle of humankind" idea is that the Rift Valley's very formation – a major event on the earth's crust, which began some twenty million years ago – may have been the environmental spark that was the catalyst for human evolution.

At any rate, while current research pushes the dates back further and further, it hasn't answered the biggest question: if this is the cradle, who were the parents? The search for an **evolutionary line** linking humans directly with more primitive primates is still the number-one priority. Theories change so fast that books published in the 1960s and early 1970s contain ideas that today have been completely overturned. The "**ape-men**" australopithecines are no longer regarded as ancestors of *Homo sapiens* and it is now known that our own ancestors shared evolutionary time with them in East Africa. The fossil skull 1470 (its catalogue number), discovered by **Bernard Ngeneo** in 1972 and now in the National Museum in Nairobi, is evidence of this. Between two and three million years old, it's an example of *Homo habilis*, "handy man", a direct human ancestor.

Until Ngeneo's discovery, it was thought that while the massive, plant-munching *Australopithecus boisei* did eventually die out, its slighter, higher-brow neighbour *A. africanus* survived, adapting and evolving into the *Homo* line. Now it's believed all three species lived on the savannah and forest margins at the same time. A recent flood of discoveries of *Homo* fossils shows that the evolutionary line that eventually led to human beings was already established as long as five million years ago. In 2000, new finds in the Tugen Hills from a hitherto unknown species named *Orrorin tugenensis* seem to be the remains of a creature from around six million years ago that was still an ape but an ape that, crucially, walked upright on two legs, making it almost certainly the first hominid. Almost as important was the 1984 discovery of the nearly complete 1.6-million-year-old skeleton of twelve-year-old "Turkana Boy," a member of the species *Homo erectus*, our immediate ancestor. It was *erectus* ("upright" man – though in fact the australopithecines probably spent most of their time upright, too) who developed **speech**, discovered how to make **fire** and improved enormously on the **tool-making** efforts of *Homo habilis*. **Olorgasailie** and **Kariandusi** are two "hand axe" sites, probably belonging to *Homo erectus*, which have been used within the last five hundred thousand years. And it was *erectus* who, if the "cradle" theory is right, spread the humanoid gene pool to Asia, Europe and the rest of Africa, where, over the next few hundred thousand years, *Homo sapiens* emerged on the scene.

Early inhabitants

Real history begins with the **hunter-gatherers**. Numbering probably fewer than a hundred thousand, living in small units of several families, and either staying in one place for generations or moving through the country according to the dictates of the seasons, these earliest human inhabitants may have been related to the ancestors of present-day Pygmy and Bushman peoples, and probably spoke "click" languages similar to those spoken by the Bushmen today (Khoi and San). Remnant hunter-gatherer groups still live in remote parts of Kenya – the **Boni** on the mainland north of Lamu, the **Sanye** along the Tana River and the **Okiek** and **Dorobo** in parts of the highlands – but their languages have mostly been adopted from neighbouring peoples. The hunting and gathering way of life is one that has persisted in the cultural memories of most Kenyan peoples, and some of the groups who still practise it may have veered away from farming or herding societies in times of hardship.

The earliest distinct migration to Kenya was of **Cushitic**-speaking people from the Ethiopian Highlands. Occasional hunters and gatherers themselves, they were also livestock herders and farmers; over the centuries, they filled the areas that were too dry for a purely subsistence way of life. They also absorbed many of the previous inhabitants through intermarriage. Having herds and cultivating land brought up questions of ownership, inheritance and water rights, and an elaboration of social institutions and customs to deal with them. The Cushites left evidence of their settlements in burial cairns and living sites at places like Hyrax Hill, near Nakuru. Stone cairns and hollow depressions in the ground are found all over the Kenya Highlands and in the Rift Valley, especially out in the dry areas towards Lake Turkana. The same people may have built the irrigation works still used today along the Elgeyo Escarpment, west of Lake Baringo. They had a strong material culture, using stone, particularly obsidian, to produce beautiful arrowheads, knives and axes, and they made a whole range of pottery utensils.

The **Somali** and **Rendille** of the northeast are the main groups still speaking Cushitic languages, though their arrival in Kenya was more recent. Today, only the Boni speak a language related to the Southern Cushitic of the first farmers and herders, although the Boni themselves are hunter-gatherers. For the most part, the earliest Cushites were absorbed by peoples who came later and they adopted new languages and customs. The changes were not all one-sided, however: **circumcision** and **clitoridectomy**, practised by the early Cushites, became important cultural rituals for many of the peoples who succeeded and absorbed them.

For present-day Kenya, the most important arrivals began to reach the country in the first few centuries AD. From the northwest and the headwaters of the Nile came the **Nilotic**-speaking ancestors of the so-called **Kalenjin** peoples; from the west and south came speakers of **Bantu** languages, forebears of today's **Kikuyu**, **Gusii**, **Akamba** and **Mijikenda**, among others. (Bantu, a word coined by twentieth-century linguists, derives from the common stem for "person" – *ntu* – and the plural prefix *ba*. The word is not found in any of the six hundred contemporary Bantu languages, spread across the continent, but it may have been the one used for "people" in the original proto-language before it diversified.)

Along with their languages, the new arrivals also brought new technologies, including iron-working. **Iron** had enabled the Bantu to spread from the Nigeria/Cameroon area across central Africa, clearing the virgin forests and hoeing the ground for their crops. Eastwards, they encountered new Asian food crops – bananas, yams and rice – which had arrived in East Africa by way of the Indonesian colonization of Madagascar. This new diversity of foods helped people to settle permanently in chosen regions. The Kalenjin peoples consolidated in the Western Highlands. The Bantu were particularly successful and, as their broad economic base took hold across the southern half of Kenya, their languages quickly spread. Herding, hunting, fishing and gathering were important supplements to the agricultural mainstay, while trade conducted with their exclusively pastoral or hunter-gatherer neighbours, especially in iron tools, carried their influence further.

By about 1000 AD, Kenya's Stone-Age technology had been largely replaced by an Iron-Age one and, as human domination of the country increased, the beginnings of real specialization in agriculture and herding set in among the peoples.

Down on **the coast**, Bantu immigrants mixed, over several hundred years, with the longer-established Cushitic-speaking inhabitants and with a continuous trickle of settlers from Arabia and the Persian Gulf. With the advent of Islam, this melange gradually gave rise to a distinct culture and civilization – **Swahili** – speaking a Bantu language laced with foreign vocabulary. The Swahili were Kenya's link with the rest of the world, trading animal skins, ivory, agricultural produce and slaves for cloth, metals, ceramics, grain, ghee and sugar, with ships from the Middle East, India and even China. The Swahili were the first Kenyans to acquire firearms. They were also the first to write their language (in the Arabic script) and the first to develop complex, stratified communities based on town and countryside. Swahili history is covered in more depth in Chapter Six.

Later arrivals

New **American crops** – corn, cassava and tobacco – spread through Kenya after the Portuguese arrived in the early sixteenth century. They undoubtedly increased the country's population capacity, while enabling a greater degree of permanent settlement and providing new trade goods.

At about this time, a pastoral **Nilotic**-speaking people, distantly related to the earlier Kalenjin arrivals, began a migration from the northwest. These were the first **Luo**-speakers who, some generations earlier, had left their homeland (around Wau in southern Sudan) for reasons that were probably largely economic. In the alternately flooded and parched flatlands around the Nile, unusual conditions could be catastrophic. The Luo ancestors were always on the move, herding, planting, hunting or fishing. Politically, they had a fairly complex organization as, for months on end, while the Nile flooded, communities would be stranded in concentration along the low ridges. Several good years might be followed by drought, and population pressure then forced less dominant groups to go off in search of water and pasture. The overall trend was southwards. Groups of migrants picked up other, non-Luo-speakers on the way, gradually assimilating them through intermarriage and language change, always drawing attention with the impressive regalia and social standing of their *ruoth* – the Luo kings.

On the shores of Lake Victoria, where they finally settled, sleeping sickness is thought to have wiped out many of the Luo herds. But they were pragmatic, resourceful people, whose background of mixed farming and herding during the era of migration supported them. They turned to agriculture and, increasingly, to fishing.

Towards the end of the seventeenth century, another Nilotic, pastoral people, the **Turkana**, appeared in Kenya. Linguistically closer to the Maasai Nilotes, they seem to have shared the Luo resilience to economic hardship and they, too, have (recently) turned to fishing. Also like the Luo, and almost unique among Kenyan peoples, they have never practised circumcision.

The Maa-speakers – **Maasai** and **Samburu** – were the last group to arrive in Kenya, and their rise and fall had far-reaching effects on neighbouring peoples. Moving southwards from the beginning of the seventeenth century, their nomadic pastoral lifestyle enabled them to expand swiftly and, in a few generations, they were transformed from an obscure group into a dominant force in the region. Culturally, they borrowed extensively from their neighbours, especially the **Kalenjin** peoples, who spoke Nandi. Nandi words and Kalenjin cultural values were adopted, including circumcision, the age-set system and some ancient (originally probably Cushitic) taboos against eating fish and certain wild animals. It's likely that much of the "traditional" Maasai appearance also owes something to these contacts. The Maasai migration was no slow spread. Their cattle were periodically herded south and other peoples were raided en route to enlarge the herds; by 1800, they were widely established in the Rift Valley and on the plains, everywhere between Lake Turkana and Kilimanjaro. In response to Maasai dominance, many of the Bantu peoples adopted their styles and customs. Initiation by genital mutilation, probably already practised by most Bantu-speakers, was imbued with a new significance – especially for the Kikuyu – by intermarriage and close, if not always peaceable, relations with the Maasai.

Severe **droughts** in the nineteenth century pushed the Maasai further and further afield in search of new pastures, bringing them into conflict, and trade, with other peoples. Drought, disease and rinderpest epidemics (which killed off their cattle) were also responsible for a series of civil wars between different Maasai sections in the second half of the nineteenth century.

These **Maasai civil wars** disrupted the **trading networks** which had been set up between the coast and the interior, mainly by Swahili, Mijikenda,

Akamba and Kikuyu. Dutch, English and French goods were finding their way up-country, and American interests were already being served nearly two centuries ago, as white calico cloth (still called *amerikani* today) became a major item of profit. From western Kenya and Uganda, **slaves** were being exported in exchange for foreign commerce in the last throes of the slave trade's existence. Largely in response to slavery and widespread fighting, the first **missionaries** installed themselves up-country (the earliest went inland from Mombasa in 1846). Throughout this period, the Maasai disrupted movements through their territories and attacked Swahili slavers, Bantu traders and explorer-missionaries alike. The Maasai *morani* were specifically trained for raiding – a kind of guerrilla warfare – but, while their reputation lived on, they were bitterly divided among themselves and not organized on anything like a tribal scale.

By the time Europe had partitioned the map of Africa, the Maasai, who could have been the imperialists' most intractable enemies, were unable to retaliate effectively. The **Nandi** of the Western Highlands, the main people of the Kalenjin group, who had begun to take the Maasai's place as Kenya's most feared adversaries, put up the stiffest resistance. They were organized to the extent of having a single spiritual leader, the *orkoiyot*, who ruled what was in effect a theocracy. Their war of attrition against the British delayed advances for a number of years. But the Nandi did not have the territorial advantage that would have helped the Maasai, and the murder of their *orkoiyot*, **Koitalel**, by the British, destroyed their military organization.

The scramble for Africa

All Kenya's peoples resisted colonial domination to some degree. In the first twenty years of British attempts to rule, tens of thousands were killed in ugly massacres and manhunts, and many more were made homeless. Administrators – whose memoirs (see "Books", p.689) are the most revealing background for that period – all differed in their ideas of the ultimate purpose of their work and the best means of imposing British authority.

British interests in East Africa at the close of the nineteenth century had sprung from the European power struggle and the "scramble for Africa". The 1885 Berlin Conference chopped the continent into arbitrary spheres of influence. Germany was awarded what was to become Tanganyika; Britain got Kenya and Uganda. In 1886, formal agreements were drawn up and Kilimanjaro was ceded to Victoria's grandson, the Kaiser, giving each monarch a snowcapped equatorial mountain.

But rivalry wasn't far beneath the seemingly amicable surface and Germany clearly had Uganda earmarked. Sir William Mackinnon, who for a decade had been pressing for a licence to start trading, was now given permission to start commercial operations with his Imperial British East Africa Company (IBEAC) in 1888. The company officers – mostly young and totally inexperienced English clerks – established a series of trading forts at fifty-mile intervals in a line connected by a rough ox-track leading from Mombasa into Uganda. Machakos, Murang'a and Mumias all began as IBEAC stations. **Uganda** was the focus of interest, since Kenya – decimated by drought, locusts, rinderpest and civil war – seemed largely a deserted wasteland. And Uganda was strategically important for **control of the Nile** – which had long been a British preoccupation. Conspiring foreign powers were mentioned darkly in the House of Lords. Britain's claim was in danger of lapsing if Uganda could not be properly garrisoned and supplied. It was also a centre for the **slave trade** that Britain, in need not of slaves but of new markets, was committed to wiping out. And in the back of many minds was the kind of sentiment expressed by the London *Times* in 1873:

There seems no reason not to believe that one of the finest parts of the world's surface is going to waste under the shroud of malaria which surrounds it, and under the barbarous anarchy with which it is cursed. The idea dawns upon some of us that some better destiny is yet in store for a region so blessed by nature, and the development of Africa is a step yet to come in the development of the world.

In the end, the practicability of developing "some better destiny" for Uganda proved out of reach.

With the bankruptcy of the IBEAC and its failure to establish any kind of administration, the British government formally stepped into the breach in 1885 and declared a **protectorate** over Uganda and Kenya. Having acquired the region in a haphazard lottery, the government was now forced to do something with it. A useful gesture was required and Her Majesty's government decided to build a **railway**. This classic, valedictory piece of Victorian engineering took six years to complete and cost the lives of hundreds of Indian labourers. Financially, it was a commitment which grew out of all proportion to the likely returns and continued to grow long after the last rail was laid. But its completion transformed the future of East Africa. From now on, the supply lines were secure and the interior only a month's journey from Europe by ship and rail. Suddenly, the prospects for developing the cool, fertile Kenya highlands looked much more attractive than the distant unknowns of Uganda and its powerful kingdoms.

More immediately, the railway physically divided the **Maasai** at a time when they were already disunified and moving into alliances with the British. Their grazing lands, together with the regions of the **Kalenjin** peoples and the **Kikuyu** on the lower slopes of the highlands, were to become the heartland of white settlerdom.

The Kenya colony

While the government, typically, dragged its feet, the story circulated that Kenya might be a land of opportunity: a new New Zealand, or even a Jewish homeland. A party of Zionists was in fact escorted around Kenya but declined the offer. It was Sir Charles Eliot, the Protectorate's second governor, who was the main mover behind the **settlement scheme**. While there was an undercurrent of consideration for "the rights of natives" which shouldn't be forgotten, the growing clamour of voices claiming the support of British taxpayers – who had met the bill for the railway – outweighed any altruism. Eliot's extravagant reports on the potential of BEA (British East Africa) were published and government policy was directed towards getting the settlers in and making the railway pay. Landless aristocrats, middle-class adventurers, big-game hunters, ex-servicemen and Afrikaners (the farming land was also advertised in South

Africa) began to trickle up the line. Using ox-wagons to get to the tracts of bush they had leased, they started their farms from scratch. Lord Delamere, governor himself for a time, was their biggest champion. In the years leading up to World War I, the trickle of settlers became a flood and by 1916 the area "alienated" to **Europeans** had risen to 15,000 square kilometres of the best land. Imported livestock was hybridized with hardy, local breeds; coffee, tea, sisal and pineapples were introduced and thrived; European crops flourished in super-abundance and cereals soon covered vast areas.

Nearly half the land worth farming was now in the hands of **settlers**, but it had rapidly become clear that it was far from empty of local inhabitants. Colonial invasion had occurred at a low point in the fortunes of Kenya's peoples and, unprepared for the scale of the incursion, they were swiftly pushed aside into "native reserves" or became squatters without rights. As populations recovered, serious land shortages set in. The British appointment of "chiefs" – whose main task was to collect a tax on every hut – had the effect of diverting grievances against colonial policy onto these early collaborators and laying the foundations of a class structure in Kenyan society. Without a money economy, employment was the only means available to pay taxes and, effectively, a system of forced labour had been created. The whole apparatus quickly became entrenched in a series of **land and labour laws**. A poll tax was added to the hut tax; all African men were compelled to register to facilitate labour recruitment; squatters on alienated land were required to pay rent, through labour; and cash cropping on African plots was discouraged or banned (coffee licences, for example, were restricted to white farmers). The highlands were strictly reserved for white settlement, while land not owned by Europeans became Crown Land, its African occupants "tenants at will" of the Crown and liable to summary eviction.

Asians, too, were excluded from the highlands. While the leader of Kenya's Indians, **A.M. Jeevanjee**, had called for the transformation of Kenya into the "America of the Hindu", the proposal never came near consideration by the British. Barred from farming on any scale – except in the far west, where they developed sugar cane as an important crop – Indians concentrated on the middle ground, setting up general stores (*dukas*) across the country, investing in small industries and handling services.

World War I

World War I had a number of profound effects, although there were comparatively few battles in Kenya itself. Some 200,000 African porters and soldiers were conscripted and sent to Tanganyika (German East Africa), where one in four of them died. Those who returned were deeply influenced by the experience. They had seen European tribes at war with each other, they had experienced European fallibility, and witnessed the kind of organization used to overcome it.

General von Lettow Vorbeck, the German commander, waged a dogged campaign against British forces despite the fact that his own were vastly outnumbered, with the aim of engaging as much manpower as possible and taking the heat off German forces in Europe. Nevertheless, the Germans lost the war – and Tanganyika – to the British, and the Crown's commitments in East Africa were suddenly multiplied.

Sir Edward Northey, governor of Kenya at the time of armistice, pushed his **Soldier Settlement Scheme** through without difficulty. Its aim, to double the settler population in Kenya to nine thousand and increase revenue, seemed promising enough to a government sapped by war. But the Soldier Settlement Scheme was bitterly resented by Africans, particularly those who had fought beside the soldiers and were now excluded from their gains.

Early nationalism and reaction

Political associations sprang up among those with a mission education and ex-servicemen: the Kikuyu Association, the Young Kikuyu Association and the Young Kavirondo Association. **Harry Thuku,** secretary of the Young Kikuyu Association, realized its potential and re-formed it as the East Africa Association in order to recruit on a nationwide basis. The hated registration law by which every African was obliged to carry a pass – the *kipande* – was a prime grievance, but tax reduction, introduction of land title deeds and wage increases were demanded as well. Alliances were built up with embittered Indian associations and 1921 saw a year of **protests** and rallies. These culminated in Thuku's detention, **violent suppression** and the shooting by police of 25 demonstrators at a mass rally calling for Thuku's release. He remained in detention for eleven years.

The Indian constituency eventually secured two nominated seats (not elected) on the Legislative Council. Africans, meanwhile, remained voiceless, landless, disenfranchised and segregated by the colour bar.

As the settlers became established, they began to contribute appreciably to the income of **the colony** (which Kenya had officially become in 1920). Most of them seem to have believed that they were in at the beginning of a long and glorious pageant of white dominion. Indeed, settler self-government, along Canadian or South African lines, was a declared aim. African demands were hardly heeded by the authorities, but the Colonial Office was in a difficult position over the **Indians**, who were already British subjects and whose demands for equal rights they had trouble in refuting. Tentative proposals to give them voting rights, allow unrestricted immigration from India and abolish segregation caused alarm and indignation among the settlers. Their **Convention of Associations**, already arguing the case for white home rule, formed a "Vigilance Committee", which worked out detailed military plans for rebellion, including the kidnapping of the governor and the deportation of the Indians. Sensing a crisis, the Colonial Office drew up a white paper and a grudging settlement was reached that allowed five Indians and one Arab to be elected to the Legislative Council (the colony's local government), as opposed to eleven Europeans.

The primacy of African "interests", admirably reiterated yet again in the Devonshire Declaration, was still denied any real expression, least of all by Africans themselves. A system of de facto **apartheid** was being practised. It was in this climate in the 1920s and 1930s that, floating above their economic troubles, the settlers had their heyday – the **Happy Valley life** so appallingly and fascinatingly depicted in *White Mischief* and other books.

Education, Kenyatta and the Kikuyu

The opportunities available to Africans came almost entirely through **mission schools** at first. Again, there was conflict between government and settlers on the question of **education**. The Colonial Office was committed, on paper at least, to the general development of the country for all its inhabitants, while the white farmers were on the whole adamant that raising educational standards could only lead to trouble. A crude form of Swahili had become the language of communication between Africans and Europeans. But the teaching of English was a controversial issue that hard-liners foresaw eventually rebounding on government and settlers alike. In frustration, self-help **Kikuyu independent schools** were set up in the 1930s, primarily in order to teach their own children English.

Whether barring access to English education would ultimately have made any difference is debatable, but by the late 1930s there were already enough educated Africans to pose the beginnings of a serious challenge to white supremacy. One of these was **Jomo Kenyatta**. Born in the late 1890s, Kenyatta, went to a mission school and was baptized a Christian. He was also circumcised, and initiated into Kikuyu adulthood. His name was adopted from the shop he ran in Nairobi, Kenyatta Stores, which in turn was named after the traditional beaded belt (kenyatta) he always wore.

After Thuku's imprisonment and the subsequent bloodshed at Nairobi in 1921, the East African Association was dissolved. It was succeeded by the **Kikuyu Central Association (KCA)**, which Kenyatta joined in 1928. The KCA was the spearhead of **nationalism** and lobbied hard for a return of alienated land, the lowering of taxes and for elected African representatives on the Legislative Council. It also protested against missionary efforts to outlaw **"female circumcision"**, on the grounds that the church was attempting to undermine Kikuyu culture. This last conflict led to a leadership crisis in the KCA and for a number of years threatened to swamp other issues. But Kenyatta spent most of the period between 1931 and 1946 in Britain, campaigning for the KCA, studying anthropology under Malinowski at the London School of Economics and writing his homage to the Kikuyu people, *Facing Mount Kenya*.

Kenya survived the 1929 stock market crash and the resulting world **trade slump** as the colonial government became increasingly committed to the struggling settlers it was now bailing out. Exports fell catastrophically; coffee-planting by non-whites was still prohibited and the tax burden continued to be placed squarely on Africans. Faced with this crisis, even some of the settlers began to accept that large-scale changes were in order. Just as awareness was growing that the economy could not survive indefinitely unless Africans were given more of a chance to participate in it, Kenya was thrown into World War II.

World War II – and Mau Mau

Perhaps not surprisingly, soldiers were easily recruited into the **King's African Rifles** when Italian-held Ethiopia (then Abyssinia) declared war on Kenya. Volunteers wanted money, education and a chance to see the world; conscripts, filling the quotas assigned to their chiefs, faced a life at home or on the reserve that was no better. Propaganda immediately succeeded in casting Hitler's image as the embodiment of all racist evil. Some Africans thought the war, once won, would improve their position in Kenya. They were partly right. Military campaigns in Ethiopia and Burma owed much of their success to African troops and during the war their efforts were glowingly praised by Allied commanders.

On the soldiers' return, a new awareness, more profound than that felt by those returning from World War I, came upon them. The white tribes of Europe had fought the war on the issue of self-determination; the message wasn't lost on Africans. Yet still, in almost every other sphere of life, they were demeaned and humiliated. The KCA had been banned at the outbreak of war, allegedly for supporting the Italian fascists, and African political life was subdued. Real change, for 99 percent of the population, was still a dream.

Kenya's food-exporting economy had done well out of the war and it was clear the colony could make a major contribution to Britain's recovery. The post-war Labour government encouraged economic expansion without going far enough to include Africans among the beneficiaries of the investment. Industrialization gathered momentum and there was a rapid growth of towns. There was also further promotion of **white immigration** – a new influx of European settlers arrived soon after the war – and greater power was given to the settlers on the Legislative and Executive Councils. Population growth and intense **pressure on land** in the rural areas were leading to severe disruptions of traditional community life as people were shunted into the reserves or else left their villages to search for work in the towns. On the political front, militant **trade unionism**, dominated by ex-servicemen, gradually usurped the positions of those African leaders who had been prepared to work with the government.

Postwar African politics

A single African member, Eliud Mathu, was appointed to the Legislative Council in 1944. More significant, however, was the formation of the **Kenya African Union** (**KAU**), a consultative group of leaders and spokesmen set up with the governor's approval to liaise with Mathu. The KAU's first president was Harry Thuku, but it was **Kenyatta's return** from England in 1946, to an unexpectedly tumultuous hero's welcome, that signalled a real departure for African political rights and the birth of a new current of nationalism. KAU was transformed into an active political party – and ran straight into conflict with itself. The **radicals** within the party wanted sweeping changes in land ownership, equal voting rights and abolition of the pass law. The **moderates** were for negotiation, educational improvement, multiracial progress and a gradual shift of power. Nor were the moderates convinced that their own best interests lay in confronting the British head on; they had all achieved considerable ambitions within the settler economy. Kenyatta was ambitious himself, but the Europeans mistrusted his intentions and rumour-mongered about his communist connections, his visit to Russia during his time abroad and his personal life.

Despite Kenyatta's efforts to steer a middle course, KAU became increasingly radical and Kikuyu-dominated. While he angled to give the party a multi-tribal profile to appease the settlers, he also managed to sacrifice some moderates in the leadership for the sake of party unity. But there were defections as well. Several radicals, including **Dedan Kimathi**, joined an underground movement and took **oaths** of allegiance against the British. Betrayal of the movement was punished by execution and collaborators with the government faced the same threat. Oath-taking groups emerged secretly all around the Central Highlands and, by 1952, a central committee was organized to co-ordinate activities.

The Mau Mau Rebellion

The question of how much the KAU leadership was involved in what came to be known as **Mau Mau** (from *muma*, a traditional Kikuyu oath) is one that reappeared time after time in the years leading to and after Independence. Certainly Mau Mau attracted large numbers of young men from the rural periphery of towns like Nyeri, Fort Hall (Murang'a) and Nairobi, and they used Kenyatta's name in their propaganda. Many members had taken part in strikes in the late 1940s. They were mobilized into violent action by the shortage of land on the reserves and the contrast with the new-found success of the settlers. There was a burning desire to oust the Europeans from the "White Highlands". The Mau Mau oath-takers called themselves the **Land and Freedom Army. Ex-soldiers** who had fought for the British, many of whom had learned guerrilla warfare in Burma, were crucial to their military effort.

Kenyatta played a delicate political game, condemning strikes and even oath-taking but ready to seize on any chance to exploit the situation. In 1952, incensed by simmering African nationalism and random outbursts of violence on white farms, the settlers pressured the government into declaring a **state of emergency**. Mau Mau was banned and all African nationalist organizations were proscribed. Kenyatta and other KAU leaders were arrested, convicted of founding and managing Mau Mau – on the flimsiest evidence – and sent into internal exile. For the next four years, while "**The Emergency**" blazed and African political life was brought, once again, to a virtual standstill, the full weight of British military muscle was brought to bear against the revolt.

Thousands of **British troops** were sent to Kenya. To them, every African was a potential terrorist, every homestead a Mau Mau hide-out. As the troops moved in, the hard-core guerrillas fled into the forest and lived off the jungle for months on end, launching surprise attacks at night. They relied on considerable support from the Kikuyu homesteads for supplies, intelligence reports and stolen weapons. Under emergency powers, a policy of "villagization" was enforced and tens of thousands of Kikuyu were relocated to "secure villages" or detained in barbed-wire concentration camps. At one point, one-third of the entire male Kikuyu population was being held in detention. It was during this period that the cluster of closely related small tribes known today as the Kalenjin, acquired their name, which means "I tell you" in their common language, Nandi. Forging together the Nandi, Pokot, Elgeyo, Marakwet, Tugen and others under a single umbrella, it was largely the creation of the colonial authorities, seeking to recruit and reinforce support against the Kikuyu-dominated Mau Mau.

The **end of the revolt** came with the British capture and execution of Dedan Kimathi, the Land and Freedom Army's commander-in-chief. Helicopters and defoliant were brought in to flush out the last pockets of resistance, but in any case morale was low. The Western press made much of Mau Mau atrocities, though a total of just 32 European civilians and about 50 troops were killed in the struggle. For Africans, the figure was around 13,000 men, women and children, mainly Kikuyu. Many of these, uncommitted to Mau Mau, yet living in key locations as far as the British were concerned, were caught, sometimes literally, in the crossfire.

The authorities described Mau Mau as a tribal uprising, a meaningless explosion of tension. Paranoid settlers perceived an external communist threat in the revolt. Some observers went so far as to call it a Kikuyu civil war between those established on the reserves and others – the guerrillas – newly displaced from European farms. And while Akamba, Maasai, Luo, Meru and Embu did join the Land and Freedom Army, its membership was overwhelmingly Kikuyu-speaking. As a focus for nationalism, the revolt served as a political barometer: the tension between the loyalists and the rebels and their sympathizers was the fulcrum on which Kenyan politics was to swing in the years leading up to and after Independence. Jomo Kenyatta was in many ways lucky to have been forced to sit out the period in detention.

Independence – *uhuru*

With the emergency over, the KAU leaders still at liberty set about exploiting the European fear of a repeat episode. Anything that now delayed the fulfilment of African nationalist aspirations could be seen as fuel for another revolt. There was no longer any question of a Rhodesia-style, white-dominated Independence. Settlers, mindful of the **preparations for independence** taking place in other African countries, began rallying to the cry of multi-racialism in a vain attempt to secure what looked like a very shaky future.

At the 1960 Lancaster House Conference in London, African representatives won a convincing victory by pushing through measures to give them majorities in the Legislative Council and the Council of Ministers. Members, all nominated by the colonial authorities, included **Tom Mboya**, the prominent and charismatic Luo trade unionist, and the radical politician **Oginga Odinga** (another Luo), as well as **Daniel Arap Moi** and the Mijikenda leader **Ronald Ngala**. A new constitution was drawn up and eventual access to the White Highlands was accepted. The declaration promised that "Kenya was to be an African country": the path to Independence was guaranteed. **Macmillan** was saying as much in his "Wind of Change" speech given to the South African parliament at the time the Lancaster House Conference was meeting.

The settlers perceived a "calamitous betrayal", with universal franchise and African-dominated independence expected within ten years. (In fact, it happened earlier than anticipated.) Minority tribal associations, meanwhile, foresaw troubles ahead if the **Kikuyu-Luo elite** achieved independence for Kenya at the cost of the smaller constituencies. In 1960, the Kenya African National Union (**KANU**) was formed. Soon after, a second, more moderate party, the Kenya African Democratic Union (**KADU**), was created, with Britain's help, to federate the minority, largely rural-based, political associations in a broad defensive alliance against Kikuyu-Luo domination. One of KADU's leading members was Daniel Arap Moi.

Elections were held in 1961 and KANU emerged with nineteen seats against KADU's eleven. But KANU refused to form a government until Kenyatta was released. Settlers began to leave the country, selling their farms and evacuating before the predicted collapse of European privilege – or even holocaust – that some feared if the "leader unto darkness and death" were set free.

A temporary coalition government was formed, composed of KADU, European and Asian members. Kenyatta was duly released and, six months later, a member resigned his seat, making room for him on the Legislative Council. In 1962, Kenyatta became Minister for Constitutional Affairs and Economic Planning – a wide portfolio – in a new coalition government formed out of the KADU alliance and KANU. Despite a second London conference to try to reach an agreement about the federal constitution demanded by KADU, the question was left in the air. Independence elections the following year (though the Somalis of the northeast, who had no wish to be in Kenya, boycotted them) seemed to answer the constitutional question. KANU emerged with an even greater lead and a mandate for a non-federal structure. On June 1 – **Madaraka Day** – Kenyatta became Kenya's first prime minister. And on December 12, 1963, control of foreign affairs was handed over and Kenya became formally **independent**.

The Kenyatta years – *harambee*

It was barely sixty years since the pioneer settlers had arrived. Many of them – those who hadn't panicked and sold out – were now determined to stay and risk the future under an **African government**. Despite his unjust seven years in detention, Kenyatta turned out to have more consideration for their interests than could have been foreseen. He held successful meetings with settlers in his home village; his bearded, genial image and conciliatory speeches assuring them of their rights and security quickly earned him the respected title *Mzee* (Elder) and wide international support. Many Europeans retained important positions in administration and the judiciary.

Milton Obote and Julius Nyerere, leaders of newly independent Uganda and Tanzania, held talks with Kenyatta on setting up an **East African Community** to share railways, aviation, postal services and telecommunications, and customs and excise. This was formally inaugurated in 1967. There was a mood of optimism: it looked very much as if Kenya had succeeded against all the odds.

But there were urgent issues to contend with. **Land reform** and the rehabilitation of freedom fighters and detainees were the most pressing. Large tracts of European land were bought up and a programme to provide small plots to landless peasants was rapidly instigated. Political questions loomed large as well. On December 12, 1964, Kenya became a republic, its head of state no longer the Queen, but rather President Kenyatta. KADU was dissolved "in the interests of national unity", its leaders absorbed into the ruling KANU party. There was, it seemed, no longer any need for an opposition: everyone was on the same side and Kenya was henceforth a de facto one-party state. For the sake of "national security", British troops were kept on, initially to quell a revolt of ethnic Somalis in the northeast and an army mutiny in Nairobi. A defence treaty has kept a British force at Nanyuki ever since.

There was heavy emphasis on co-operation and unity. The spirit of *harambee* (pulling together) was endorsed by Kenyatta at all his public appearances. *Harambee* meetings became a unique national institution, fund-raising events at which – in a not untraditional way – donations were made by local notables and politicians towards self-help health-care and educational programmes. During the 1960s and 1970s, hundreds of *harambee* schools were built and equipped in this way. But the ostentatious gifts, and particularly the guaranteed press coverage the next day with donors listed in order of value, sometimes reduced the *harambee* vision of community development to an exercise in patronage and competitive status-seeking.

On the **economic front**, the first decade of Independence saw remarkable changes and rapid growth. Although only a quarter of the country gets enough rainfall to make it agriculturally reliable, the settlers' fairly broad-based crop-exporting economy was a powerful springboard for development; one, moreover, that wasn't difficult to transfer to predominantly African control. While many large landholdings were sold *en bloc* to African investors, smaller farmers did begin to contribute significantly to export earnings through coffee, tea, pyrethrum and fruit.

Industrialization proceeded at a slower pace. Kenya's mineral resources are very limited and the country relies heavily on oil imports. **Foreign investment** wasn't especially beneficial, as investors were given wide freedoms to import equipment and technical skills and to re-export much of the profit.

Growth, rather than a radical redistribution of wealth, was the government's main concern. Although by 1970 more than two-thirds of the European mixed farming lands were occupied by some 50,000 Africans, and the overall standard of living had improved considerably, income disparities were greater than ever. And 16,000 square kilometres of ranch lands and plantations remained largely in foreign hands.

From the outset, it was clear that the fruits of Independence were not going to be shared fairly. Kikuyu-Luo domination – but particularly Kikuyu – was irksome and strongly resented by other groups. It was perhaps inevitable that the people who had lost most and suffered most under British rule should expect to receive the most benefits from Independence. However, many Kikuyu had also been able to take advantage, as far as it was possible, of the settler economy by earning wages, setting up businesses and sending their children to school.

The resettlement programme was abandoned in 1966, its objectives "largely attained". But many peasants, having been squatters on European farms, were now "illegal squatters" on private African land. Thousands migrated to the towns where unemployment was already a serious problem. Kenya was becoming a class-divided society.

Political opposition

It was in this climate that KANU's leadership split. **Oginga Odinga**, the party vice-president, resigned in 1966 to form the socialist **Kenya People's Union** (**KPU**) and 29 MPs joined him. The ex-guerrilla Bildad Kaggia became deputy head of the KPU and a vocal agitator for poorer Kikuyu. Kenyatta and Mboya closed ranks in KANU and prepared for political conflict. KPU was anti-capitalist and claimed to speak on behalf of the masses, who it maintained had been betrayed by *uhuru*. On foreign affairs it was firmly non-aligned. Denouncing the opposition, KANU – led in this respect by Tom Mboya – stressed the need for close ties with the West, for commercial enterprise and foreign investment, and for economic conditions that would attract foreign aid. Ideologically, KANU talked of "African socialism". KPU's stand was claimed to be divisive: the country should be pulling together to fight the triple evils of poverty, ignorance and disease. KPU was barely tolerated for three years, its members harassed and detained by the security forces, its activities obstructed by new legislation and constitutional amendments.

In KANU, Odinga was succeeded (briefly) in the post of vice-president by Joseph Murumbi and then, with behind-the-scenes encouragement from the British government's Foreign and Commonwealth Office in London (which wanted to avoid a radical in the job), by Daniel Arap Moi.

Odinga had strong, grassroots support in the Luo and Gusii districts of western Kenya. But **Tom Mboya**'s supporters came from an even broader base, including many poor Kikuyu. By the end of the 1960s, speculation was mounting about whether he would be able to take over the presidency on Kenyatta's death. As the *Mzee's* right-hand man he was widely tipped to succeed – a possibility that alarmed Kenyatta's Kikuyu supporters. The republic's second political **assassination** (the first was that of Pia Gama Pinto, an outspoken Goan communist politician who was killed in 1965) decided the matter: Mboya was gunned down by a Kikuyu assassin in central Nairobi on July 5, 1969. No high-level complicity in the murder was ever brought to light, but Mboya's death was a devastating blow to Kenya's fragile stability, setting off shock waves along both class and tribal divisions. There was widespread fighting and rioting between Kikuyu and Luo, fuelled by years of rivalry and growing feelings of

Luo exclusion from government. During a visit by Kenyatta to Kisumu – where he attended a public meeting at which Odinga and his supporters were present – hostility against his entourage was so great that police opened fire, killing at least ten demonstrators.

The KPU was immediately banned and Odinga detained without trial. Although the constitution continued to guarantee the right to form opposition parties, non-KANU nominations to parliament were, in practice, forbidden. There was a resurgence of oath-taking among Kikuyu, Meru and Embu, pledging to maintain the Kikuyu hold on power. The Kikuyu contingent in the army was strengthened and a new force of shock troops, the General Service Unit (GSU), was recruited under Kikuyu officers; independent of police and army, it was to act as an internal security force. In the early 1970s, Kikuyu control – of the government, the administration, business interests and land – gripped tighter and tighter.

Internationally, however, Kenya was seen as one of the safest African investments – a model of stability and democracy only too happy to allow the multinational corporations access to its resources and markets. The development of the tourist industry helped give the country a bright and positive profile. And, in comparison with most other African countries, some still fighting for independence and others beset by civil war or paralysed by drought, Kenya's future looked healthy enough.

But in achieving record economic growth, foreign interests often seemed to crush indigenous ones. An elite of rich profiteers – nicknamed the **Wabenzi** after the Mercedes Benz they favoured – extracted enormous private gains out of transactions with foreign companies. Nepotism was blatant and Kenyatta himself was rumoured to be one of the richest men in the world. For the mass of Kenyan people, life was hardly any better than before Independence. Graduates poured out of the secondary schools with few prospects of using their qualifications; population increase was (and remains) the highest in the world; and, most damaging of all, land distribution was still grossly unfair in a society where land was the basic means of making a living for nearly all.

In 1975, in the first ever explicit public attack on the Kikuyu monopoly of power, the radical populist MP **J.M. Kariuki** warned that Kenya could become a country of "ten millionaires and ten million beggars". He was arrested for his pains then, some weeks later, was found murdered in the Ngong Hills. Reaction was stunned and a massive turnout at his funeral was followed by angry **student demonstrations**. Kariuki's appeal had derived from unimpeachable honesty and forthrightness and a stubborn perseverance in addressing the issues of economic and social justice. He riled his opponents by his sincerity and his refusal to espouse any easily shot-down ideology. Although a Kikuyu himself, from a non-ruling northern clan, a former Mau Mau detainee and at one time a close associate of Kenyatta, he was unquestionably a threat to the Kikuyu power base. A parliamentary report on his death had two prominent names deleted at Kenyatta's demand. "Kariuki's death", wrote the then outspoken *Weekly Review*, "instils in the minds of the public the fear of dissidence, the fear to criticize, the fear to stand out and take an unconventional public stance." Kenyatta and the Kikuyu clique meant business. In the following years, a number of other MPs were detained. The burning issue of landlessness was no longer one many people were prepared to shout about.

As criticism at home was suffocated, foreign criticism of the direction Kenya was taking began to grow. Early in 1975, a series of bomb explosions in Nairobi – attributed to a "poor people's" liberation group – drew attention to the country: the foreign press carried reports of entrenched **corruption** from the president and his family down. Kariuki's murder and, later, a parliamentary row over ivory smuggling in which Kenyatta was heavily implicated, refocused attention on Kenya. But the government was far from inviting serious condemnation from the West. Kenya was seen, despite its formal non-alignment, as a staunchly anti-communist ally of Britain and America, and a recipient of massive grants and loans (for which, in return, foreign investors were allowed to reap handsome profits). And, as was rightly pointed out, there was no clear successor to the president nor any effective opposition worth cultivating.

Kenyatta had retreated into dictatorial seclusion, propped up by close Kikuyu cronies, among them Chief Koinange and Charles Njonjo, who ten years later was to cause a political storm. As parliament, and even the cabinet, took an increasingly passive role in decision-making, the pronouncements from the *Mzee*'s "court" began to be accompanied by vague suggestions of threats to his government from unspecified foreign powers. By 1977, the **East African Community** had ceased to function. Its structure had always favoured Kenya as the strongest member, and it was wracked by mistrust between Kenya and Tanzania, then further torn by Idi Amin's 1971 coup in Uganda. Kenya finally seized the lion's share of community assets, mostly ships and rolling stock in the territory at the time. Hostility towards socialist policies in Tanzania, delayed elections, further detentions and growing allegations of corruption formed the sullen backdrop to **Kenyatta's death**, in bed, on August 28, 1978.

Kenya in the 1980s – *nyayo*

The passing of the *Mzee* took Kenya by surprise. There was a nationwide outpouring of grief and shock. Mourners filed past the coffin for days. For many, however, there was also a profound sense of relief, and anticipation that an era was over and the future might better reflect the ideals of twenty years earlier.

Fears about the succession proved unfounded as vice-president **Daniel Arap Moi** smoothly assumed power with the help of Mwai Kibaki and Charles Njonjo. He quickly gathered popular support with moves against corruption in the civil service (where the mass of Kenyans felt it most), his stand against tribal nepotism (he himself comes from a minority language group, the Nandi-speaking Kalenjin), and the release of all Kenyatta's political prisoners. The press, too, traditionally circumspect and conservative, relaxed a little. Moi assured Kenya and the world that, while he would not be making radical departures from Kenyatta's policies, the more blatant iniquities of the old guard's paternalistic system would be ironed out.

But the honeymoon was short. Odinga and other ex-KPU MPs were prevented from standing in the general elections of 1979. **Student protests**, focusing on the anniversary of Kariuki's murder, began again; the closing of the university became an annual event. On the international scene, the whole Indian Ocean region became strategically important with the fall of the Shah of Iran and the Soviet invasion of Afghanistan. Kenya developed significantly closer ties with the **United States**, extending military facilities to American vessels in exchange for gifts of grain after a failure of the harvest in 1983. Ironically, the country's own surplus had been exported the previous year.

In the first year or two of his presidency, Moi's **Nyayo** (footsteps) philosophy of "peace, love and unity" in the wake of Kenyatta found wide appeal, and his apparent honesty and outspoken attacks against tribalism impressed many, making him friends abroad. But the failure to make any adjustments in economic policy in favour of the rural and urban poor soon resulted in strong, if muted, criticism at home.

The coup attempt

Two major events rocked the government in the 1980s. On Sunday August 1, 1982 – three months after constitutional amendments were pushed through by Njonjo to make Kenya officially a one-party state (to prevent Oginga Odinga registering a new political party, the Kenya Socialist Alliance) – sections of the Kenya Air Force attempted a **military coup**. Kenyans woke to the sound of continuous Bob Marley on the radio, a repeated coup broadcast and, in Nairobi at least, sporadic gunfire. There was widespread confusion for several hours. The People's Redemption Council, who had taken the radio station, were unknown: there had been no lead-up. Most of the army was on military exercise in the north, and at first the Air Force rebels were in control. During the course of the day, hundreds of shops, especially in Nairobi, were looted, mostly by civilians. Asians, particularly, suffered huge losses: Asian women were raped and many Asian homes ransacked.

By the end of the day, the "coup" had disintegrated into a free-for-all. But as it became clear that there was no prearranged support among other armed forces, the army and the GSU consolidated against the KAF, shooting hundreds of men, raping and killing women and patrolling the streets on the lookout for rebels. Dozens of students were killed. The government announced 159 deaths, but witnesses claim to have seen more bodies on a single street.

In the immediate aftermath of the coup attempt, thousands of airmen were arrested and the service itself was disbanded. The university, believed to be a "breeding ground for subversion", was dissolved. Fourteen airmen were sentenced to death though only two, who had fled to asylum in Tanzania, were eventually executed when handed back to Kenya. There had been considerable Luo involvement in the attempt to seize power and Oginga Odinga was once again placed under house arrest.

The Njonjo affair and after

Foreign investors held their breath and tourist bookings slumped, but post-mortems of the uprising faded as the country was distracted by a new political drama – the "**Njonjo affair**". In May 1983, Moi announced to parliament that he had evidence that a foreign power was grooming a senior colleague to take over as president. The charges were unspecific but the Attorney General **Charles Njonjo**'s name was mentioned and he rapidly fell from grace. A member of the Kikuyu elite who had shored up Kenyatta, Njonjo was a skilled politician with a wide circle of influence outside Kenya. His name was often linked with apartheid South Africa and Israel and, during the judicial inquiry into his activities, it was alleged that he had embezzled KANU money, and that he was privy to the coup attempt and also to another in the Seychelles. More crucially, there was intense rivalry between Njonjo and **Mwai Kibaki**, the sober and respected vice-president, over the question of succession.

The case, which filled the papers for over a year, was brought to a close with the purge from KANU of Njonjo's associates. He himself was ordered to pay back misappropriated funds, but was eventually granted a pardon by the president on Independence Day 1984, with the understanding that his political life was terminated.

Whatever lay behind it – most likely Njonjo's designs on the presidency – the Njonjo affair succeeded in distracting the public and easing away the volatility engendered by the coup attempt. Oginga Odinga and a number of other political detainees were released. More broadly, provincial administration was increasingly "de-tribalized", with officials working away from their home areas. And, on another front, a complete restructuring of the educational curriculum put new emphasis on technical and vocational studies.

For university candidates, a new quasi-military **National Youth Service** programme was launched, with students engaged in public works across the country. Student unrest continued, however. Twelve students were killed in February 1985 when the GSU broke up a meeting on the campus, ostensibly about canteen food, but considered subversive by the authorities. And on the other side of the political fence, KANU "youth wingers" began taking the law into their own hands, forming vigilante groups to attack criminal suspects and those suspected of "causing disunity".

Kenya today

Economically, Kenya has come a long way since Independence. But, with the population today standing at nearly four times what it was forty years ago (8 million then; around 30 million today), the rate of increase in the standard of living is levelling off, and by some indexes has actually declined in the last two decades. Politically, any improvement in Kenya's position is more open to question. While the last decade has seen a dramatic shift from the formal one-party state to a multi-party system, this has not been accompanied by great improvements in government accountability or rule of law. On the contrary, the international reputation the country enjoyed in the 1960s and 1970s has been steadily eroded by countless examples of human rights abuses during the latter part of Daniel Arap Moi's presidency, and appears to have bottomed out with the second multi-party elections of 1997.

Some of Kenya's outstanding shortcomings include: a **corrupt judicial system**, as reported by the organization African Rights; some of the worst prisons in the world, (more than 800 prisoners died in detention in 1995 according to the Kenya Human Rights Commission); systematic **torture** of criminals and political prisoners (Amnesty International); massive **corruption** throughout the economy, from the small bribes needed to obtain routine forms to backhanders and fraud on a gigantic scale (several ongoing financial investigations); criminal **under-investment** in infrastructure, including Kenya Railways, which resulted in a major, fatal train derailment in March 1999; and **anti-intellectualism** in the KANU government that seriously jeopardizes the viability of all higher education – colleges and universities frequently close for long periods as a result of student unrest.

Development and tourism

Kenya is largely agricultural, and heavily reliant on the fortunes of **coffee** and **tea** on the world markets. It is the world's biggest tea exporter after Sri Lanka, and together the crops account for just over half the country's export earnings. **Horticulture** – especially cut flowers, soft fruit and vegetables air-freighted to European supermarkets – accounts for around twenty percent of hard currency earnings.

Kenya has no oil reserves and, despite the building of alternative **energy** providers like the Turkwel Dam scheme and the geo-thermal power station at Lake Naivasha, still has to import three-quarters of its energy requirements.

While the country's imports continue to outstrip its exports, servicing the national debt – around $7 billion – costs Kenya a far smaller proportion of export earnings than many poor countries have to surrender. **Development** is, however, deeply dependent on foreign aid grants and loans. When they are not under suspension for non-compliance with IMF and World Bank conditions, few African countries receive as much. In society, there are persistent spectres: a fresh half-million **school leavers** each year competing for only 70,000 new jobs in the swelling towns; an unwieldy, obstructive **bureaucracy**; minimum wage rises that trail behind inflation; parastatal organizations that are notoriously corrupt and resistant to change; and repeated chronic failures

Although now internationally renowned as a wildlife conservationist, **Richard Leakey** rose to prominence as a **paleontogist** from the shadows of his eminent parents Mary and Louis Leakey. They had made the first really significant finds in the history of early human evolution, at Olduvai Gorge in Tanzania, but Richard went on to make even more remarkable discoveries at Koobi Fora near Lake Turkana. He published several books and eventually became head of the National Museums of Kenya in Nairobi.

In 1989, facing an international outcry over the poaching of elephants and the serious impact that was already having on the tourist industry, President Moi hired Leakey to take charge of the **Kenya Wildlife Service**. Leakey's first move was a characteristically bold one: he invited the world's press to watch Moi ignite Kenya's US$3-million stockpile of confiscated ivory – producing the most memorable photo opportunity of the Moi presidency. With Moi's solid support, Leakey created anti-poaching units, briefed to shoot to kill any poachers apprehended in the parks, and transformed the KWS from a demoralized sector of the civil service into what one senior member of staff called "the most radical institution in Africa". The World Bank and other donors were so impressed they gave over US$140 million in grants. The poaching stopped, the elephants and rhinos were saved from the brink of extinction, and Kenya's international image was partially restored.

But Leakey's success went too far for some local politicians, particularly in Maasai-land. His confrontational approach to the balance of human and animal needs in the parks – all humans out – infuriated many. And he seemed incorruptible: the KWS had dried up completely as a source of patronage.

In June 1993, on a routine flight at the controls of his Cessna plane, Leakey crashed, losing both legs in the accident. Foul play was suspected, but not proven (at the time, he'd been bitterly opposed to the grabbing of a 200-square-kilometre chunk of the Tana River Delta initially earmarked for the world's largest wetlands reserve, the Tana River Delta Wetlands Reserve). Within months he was walking on artificial limbs, anxious to get back to work. But there had been a mood change in his employers. The Minister of Tourism, Noah Katana Ngala, announced that a secret probe had found evidence of corruption and serious mismanagement at the KWS. No more bitter irony could be imagined. In January 1994, Leakey called a press conference and publicly announced his **resignation**.

The KWS had become a ruthless organization to work for, in which failure to come up to Leakey's standards could mean lack of prospects and poor financial rewards. However, it was the intense campaign of vilification by certain Maasai politicians that was the crucial factor in engineering his downfall.

of the government to respond positively to instances of ethnic strife and crime that hinder foreign investment and disrupt tourism. The average yearly income of around £180 ($300) is currently dropping at a rate of around seven percent each year, and it's officially acknowledged that nearly half of all Kenyans are underfed.

Natural factors, too, have been important in trimming economic growth. The savage **drought** of 1984, poor rains in 1992, and El Niño **flooding** in 1997 and 1998 all resulted in near-famine conditions in many parts of the north and east. In January 1999, the government started buying emergency food stocks from maize farmers in the Rift Valley, which was the only region to have done well out of the El Niño weather. While the bad years tend to be balanced by bumper harvests in the good years, there's a continuing chronic shortage of storage facilities to help smooth the troughs, and therefore little confidence that similar disasters won't recur.

Leakey's replacement was **David Western**, a milder, less charismatic figure who was able to find a modus operandi that seemed to be producing results acceptable both to local people and to conservationists. His park fee reforms were widely praised.

Leakey, meanwhile, entered politics. In May 1995 he joined a group of opposition intellectuals and applied to register a new party, **Safina**, announcing that Kenya needed a solution to its manifold failures: "If KANU and Mr Moi will do something about the deterioration of public life, corruption and mismanagement, I'd be happy to fight alongside them. If they won't, I want somebody else to do it". The party's application was turned down and it was only registered days before the 1997 elections, too late to put forward a presidential candidate. Leakey was denounced by Moi, accused of being a racist colonial, bent on destabilizing Kenya with foreign backers. There is no doubt that Leakey commands support and respect overseas, earned by his thick-skinned energy rather than diplomatic skills. But, equally undoubtedly, Leakey is a patriotic Kenyan, and accusations of collaboration with foreigners to undermine Kenya smack of the most shameless hypocrisy. Remarkably, after Leakey's political ambitions were curtailed in such an underhand way, he accepted the KWS role for a second time, after David Western was sacked in 1998.

Western has always disagreed with Leakey's view that parks were self-contained ecosystems, which would eventually need fencing. He talked instead of a "strategy of decentralization, addressing problems of human–wildlife conflict". He received widespread support and the reasons for his dismissal are not entirely clear, though it's widely presumed that he fell out with the KANU hierarchy by failing to attract the international limelight that comes so easily to Leakey. KWS's finances went from surplus to debt within Western's first year, growing steadily worse each year. Poaching, too, began to reappear, and the Samburu game parks became a haven for bandits. KWS suffered a partial pull-out of international donor support, and Leakey's reappointment was quite possibly the only solution. Another controversial figure, the Kikuyu business tycoon **Charles Njonjo**, was made KWS chairman.

In May 1999, at the insistence of the IMF and World Bank, Moi appointed Leakey **Cabinet Secretary** and head of the civil service, with particular responsibility for fighting corruption, but less than two years later, he was forced to resign, and officials he had appointed were dismissed by his successor in favour of those more loyal to Moi and his inner circle of Kalenjin politicians. The IMF was dismayed, and suspended all loans. Leakey, meanwhile, is likely to remain a thorn in KANU's side for some time to come.

In the **tourist industry** – now the biggest earner of foreign exchange – the first sign of serious disquiet among foreign tour operators was the attention given to Kenya's **AIDS** problem in the late 1980s. Highlighted by the British Army's ban on some coastal resorts for soldiers on leave, and the rumour that the virus could be spread by mosquitoes, the scare caused bookings, particularly from Germany, to crash.

Further adverse publicity damaged the industry in Britain as the case of **Julie Ward**, whose murder in the Maasai Mara was at first clumsily covered up, unfolded for month after month. It still remains unresolved. In isolated but widely reported incidents, several other tourists were murdered in the 1990s.

In the run-up to the 1992 election, **political violence** and ethnic cleansing caused a slump in tourism. Worse was to come in 1997, with massive disruption to the coastal economy, first by pre-election violence and the forced expulsion of tens of thousands of up-country workers from south of Mombasa, and then by the actual closure of many hotels as tourists stayed away.

Two serious **train crashes** on the chronically underfunded Nairobi–Mombasa line (one attributed to flood damage, the other, in March 1999, to poor maintenance) resulted in dozens of casualties, including a number of tourists). Added to this catalogue of calamity, the imposition of expensive **visas** for British travellers damaged Kenya's standing still further.

Elephant poaching, too, has seriously damaged Kenya's tourist industry. While the ivory scandals which smeared Kenyatta's family have not been repeated under Moi's presidency, the scale of the slaughter from the mid-1980s on far exceeded anything during Kenyatta's rule. In 1989, Kenya announced a major offensive on **ivory smuggling** and succeeded in persuading most importing countries, including the USA, Britain, Hong Kong and Japan, to place a blanket ban on any further consignments. The Wildlife Service, under the new directorship of **Richard Leakey**, took brutal control of the situation, hunting down poachers and protecting the herds, thus salvaging at least a fragment of Kenya's reputation in conservation and tourism circles.

The political climate

Back in 1987, an **Amnesty International** report roundly condemned Kenya's human rights record; an American congressional delegation was "stunned" by the mistreatment of political detainees and the fears expressed by Kenyans – as well as by its own abrupt treatment at the hands of the Kenyan Special Branch. The USA's strategic geopolitical relationship with Kenya was no longer so special, nor so strategic, as to prevent it from openly criticizing the country, and the 1990s saw a dramatic chill in relations between Washington and Nairobi, largely as a result of the outspokenness on human rights of the former American ambassador **Smith Hempstone**.

During the **one-party era**, however, Moi always appeared firmly in control and it was never clear why opposition of any kind was dealt with so harshly. Despite efforts to throttle all dissent, the groundswell of resentment continued to grow. An opposition group, **Mwakenya** (a Swahili acronym for Union of Nationalists to Liberate Kenya), one of several murky organizations mounting anti-government campaigns, attracted attention through its pamphlets, calling for the replacement of the Moi government, new democratic freedoms and an end to corruption and Western influence. While Mwakenya barely identified itself and didn't appear to pose any serious threat to the government, hundreds of people were arrested in the late 1980s. Their defence lawyers tended, in turn, to get arrested themselves. As reported by Amnesty, a number of detainees died in custody and prisoners were routinely tortured and kept in waterlogged cells beneath Nyayo House in Nairobi.

The development of an **underground opposition** in Kenya wasn't surprising. For years, public meetings of more than five people were only permitted with police approval (rarely granted). Dissent, even within the sole party, KANU, was crushed, and further illiberal measures were adopted by the government, including the change from secret balloting at elections to a public beseen-and-counted **queue-voting** system, in which voters lined up behind the candidate of their choice. The government also passed a law empowering it to dismiss judges.

As power became increasingly concentrated in fewer and fewer hands – and whose hands became a topic for rumour – only the **church** and a few powerfully connected politicians dared to question the government. President Moi, a regular churchgoer, has always sought to avoid confrontations with senior clergy – though the suspicious death of one clergyman in a head-on collision on the A104 (see below) was partly instrumental in pushing the government into conceding to the demands for a multi-party system.

The path to multi-party democracy

It was the grisly murder in February 1990 of **Robert Ouko**, the Luo foreign minister, at his farm near Kisumu, that sparked off the first explosion of **civil unrest** in a rolling crisis that has beset the government ever since. Ouko, a stout Moi supporter who enjoyed excellent personal relations with governments in both Britain and the USA, was widely viewed as a potential successor to the presidency, and was backed by Britain for the vice-presidency in 1988.

When Ouko's death was reported, a week of **rioting** shook the country, although it was most violent in Kisumu, Ouko's home town. It is widely believed that his murder was the work of government bullies exceeding their briefs to threaten him (a parallel has been drawn with the murder of J.M. Kariuki in 1975). Ouko's popularity with the foreign press and the suave and articulate contrast he made with the president – combined with his threat to expose corruption – were the likely motivating factors.

Although the riots of February 1990 dismayed the government, July of that year saw Central Highlands towns in **violent tumult** as public opposition to the government mounted in the wake of demands for a multi-party system by three heavyweight public figures. The former cabinet minister **Kenneth Matiba**, together with the then radical **Raila Odinga** (son of the much-respected veteran of the political scene, Luo leader Oginga Odinga) and the ex-mayor of Nairobi, **Charles Rubia**, declared themselves for a multi-party system and denounced the violent mass evictions that had recently taken place in the Nairobi slum of Muoroto: the three were subsequently detained without charge for over a year. Several human rights and pro-democracy lawyers were also arrested, while one who escaped arrest, **Gibson Kamau Kuria**, was given refuge in the US embassy. A Nairobi **pro-democracy rally** on July 7 (banned by the government) degenerated into attacks on buildings and security forces. There were dozens of deaths in street battles with armed police. President Moi blamed "hooligans and drug addicts" for the explosion.

Ouko's murder and the July 7 Saba Saba (Swahili for the seventh day of the seventh month) riots were followed by the gravely embarrassing death in a road accident of the outspoken **Bishop Alexander Muge** on his return from a visit to western Kenya. Muge's car collided head-on with a lorry which veered onto the wrong side of the road. The Archbishop, who had spoken out forcefully against the Muoroto evictions, had been warned against his visit to Luo-land in the most menacing terms by the Minister for Labour, who subsequently resigned from the cabinet.

In this hostile, nervous climate, the government came down hard on **journalists**, virtually stifling local newspapers and accusing the foreign press, and

Ethnic violence

At least 3000 people were killed in violence between different **language groups** in the Rift Valley, western Kenya and on the coast during the 1990s. And at least 300,000 people were displaced, nearly all of them non-Kalenjin, in ethnic cleansing.

For years, any reference to multi-party politics by KANU leaders was accompanied by dire warnings of the bloody consequences for tribal harmony of such a system. Once the government was forced into a corner on the issue by foreign aid donors, the prophecy was quickly realized. Ethnic allegiance swamped the new political order before it had even consolidated, so that the opposition parties were unable to formulate policies and election strategies that were free of ethnic considerations. Every move involved calculations of ethnic voting. FORD-Kenya tried the hardest to be ethnic-free, but KANU still seemed to be pulling the strings.

The **Kikuyu**, **Luo** and **Luhya** have been emigrating from their densely populated parts of Kenya for decades, buying marginal farmlands in the **Rift Valley** and other normally unproductive areas, trying to apply their farming techniques among the local Kalenjin and Maa-speakers and benefiting from local aid and subsistence initiatives. In most towns, at least until recently, it has been Kikuyu traders who ran many of the shops and small businesses.

The victims of the early attacks in various parts of Rift Valley Province described organized gangs of youths terrorizing non-Kalenjin homesteads and villages while local police arrived too late to do anything or just stood by. As KANU politicians warned that the Kalenjin should watch their backs for attacks by "outsiders", so their predictions were soon coming true. The KANU "policy", if such it was, began to work, as Kikuyu vigilante groups began to retaliate and, in turn, provided spurious justification for Kalenjin fears. In electioneering terms, however, it proved totally counterproductive, as the government lost more votes from disgust with their inaction than it gained from forcing opposition voters out of marginal KANU constituencies. Probably the aim was simply to demonstrate to the world at large, through the media, that multi-partyism in Africa leads to tribal violence. In this – to the Moi government's lasting shame, and despite all the evidence of its fabrication – it succeeded.

In 1992, although the opposition had feared that an early election date would defeat it in its disorganized infancy, as the delays on setting the date continued against the background of ethnic violence (while Moi declared he was waiting for everything to be "all right in the country"), it began to look like the government agenda was to *allow* tribal divides to set in firmly in advance of the election. Accusations of **majimboism** – the creation of ethnic blocks – began to fly.

The violence in 1992 and 1997/8 was not so much the "clashes" or "fighting" (certainly not "tribal war") of newspaper headlines, as unprovoked attacks, muggings and vandalism. The perpetrators, who carried spears, *pangas*, bows and arrows and clubs – but rarely guns – looted property, stole livestock, burned houses, and beat up or killed anyone who got in their way. Their message was, "Get off our land", and thousands of victims moved to refugee camps outside Eldoret and other big towns. Whether the 2002 elections produce similar upheavals remains to be seen, but most observers are quietly optimistic that they won't.

particularly the **BBC** in Nairobi, of mischief-making. The corporation was just the latest in a notorious line-up of divergent – and diversionary – "enemies" of Kenya, including the Ku Klux Klan and Colonel Gaddafi.

Relations with the international community plummeted. Against all the prevailing trends in Africa, Moi's stubborn resistance to adopting a multi-party system riled his overseas backers. He seemed barely aware of the end of the Cold War and the hard reassessment of aid distribution taking place among the rich countries.

In 1991, the steady build-up of an opposition lobby became so powerful it could not be dismantled and jailed, member by member. For the first time ever, the threat to the government looked substantial and set to endure. The Luo leader **Oginga Odinga** – effectively Kenya's elder statesman – set up the **Forum for the Restoration of Democracy** (**FORD**) in association with his son Raila Odinga and a committed group of lawyers, chief among whom was the influential chairman of the Law Society, **Paul Muite**. FORD quickly attracted government opponents from all quarters and was soon established as a mass movement for change, far removed from the shadowy, ideology-laden opposition movements of the previous decade, such as Mwakenya. Kenneth Matiba and Charles Rubia, recently released from detention, both joined FORD, and the long-time government critic **Martin Shikuku**, dissatisfied with KANU and sensing a sea-change in Kenyan politics, also joined, having defected from the ruling party.

The response to FORD, at home and overseas, was mixed. President Moi, in typically charming, uncompromising mood, referred to the movement as "rats" that would be "crushed", and blamed the energetic Nairobi diplomatic corps – and in particular the American ambassador of the time – for supporting anti-government forces. But this foreign support was not unanimous: the British High Commission kept their heads down and, in London, the Foreign Office quietly – but unconstructively – opined that multi-party democracy might bring about tribal clashes.

By the end of 1991, however, Kenya's immediate future was increasingly out of Moi's control. John Troon, the ex-Scotland Yard man hired by Moi to investigate Ouko's murder, revealed that the greatest suspicion fell on the president's closest advisor **Nicholas Biwott**, and his internal security chief, **Hezekiah Oyugi**. Biwott and Oyugi were both sacked and then arrested (they were later released "for lack of evidence", but not reinstated).

In the wake of this damaging news, the **Paris group** of donor nations suspended balance-of-payment support to Kenya for six months, pending economic and political reforms. Moi got the message. Within days he announced there would be multi-party elections for the next parliament and a free vote for the presidency, though he made it clear that multi-partyism had been foisted upon him and he saw no good could come of it. The constitutional amendment that had legalized the one-party state in 1982 was repealed and the stage was set for the registration of opposition parties and the first, legal, mass rallies.

The 1992 elections

There were convulsions in KANU, with many, if not all, ministers facing the loss of their seats in a free election. Among those who quickly resigned was former vice-president **Mwai Kibaki**, who formed the **Democratic Party** (DP) which soon found support in parts of eastern and northeastern Kenya, and especially among the Kikuyu, notably in Nyeri.

The government, however, had dealt itself a good hand before the elections were announced. Kenya's first-past-the-post electoral system and KANU's popularity in underpopulated districts (leading to huge overrepresentation for the areas of KANU support) were both very helpful. As, too, was the overwhelming (if more or less obligatory) support for KANU from the media, particularly the radio. But the party in power had some aces up its sleeve that were only revealed weeks before polling day.

Corruption is so widespread in Kenya that it infects every strand of society, and is accepted by the majority of people as the way things are. That, however, is not the view of Kenya's bankers, led by the IMF.

In 1996, some US$730 million worth of aid was released to Kenya, following the willingness of the Minister of Finance, **Musalia Mudavadi**, to toe the IMF line. Though not warmly approved of by Moi, it gave Kenya's parlous finances some much needed breathing space. Mudavadi ultimately fell out with the IMF and lost his job after the 1997 election: his replacement, **Simeon Nyachae**, was more hawkish and less appeasing. Nyachae, however, also lost his job, in 1999, ostensibly because he refused to stand up against the IMF, but allegedly because he was getting too close to those near the top who owed billions of shillings to the banks.

The collapse of the IMF talks with Mudavadi, during the run-up to the elections in 1997 (with the fund demanding action on rampant **corruption**, and the government offering to do very little) led to the suspension of $220 million worth of aid. Moi had balked at the austerity measures demanded – cutting education and health care, laying off public employees, removing food subsidies – but finally implemented them.

In October 1997, a presidential advisor, **Joshua Kulei**, was accused by *Finance* magazine of having amassed a fortune of £100 million. Allegations in the follow-up issue, along with details about Moi's son Gideon, didn't make the newsstands. The Kulei allegations had first appeared in the *Rift Valley Times*, whose publisher and writer were promptly locked up.

However, the most sensational scandal concerned **Goldenberg International**, which, between November 1990 and December 1992 and already with a monopoly on exports of gold and diamonds from Kenya, was granted a 35 percent export bonus by the government. The company claimed to have exported over £49 million worth of gold and diamonds, thus claiming £17m from the treasury in export bonuses. Kenya, of course, has no gold or diamonds. The fraud undermined the value of the Kenya shilling and an early political casualty of the affair was finance minister George Saitoti, who must have given his approval and consequently lost his job (though he held the vice-presidency until 1997, and remains a senior KANU figure).

When Kenya was hit by drought and famine in early 2000, President Moi called for international aid, and the IMF, World Bank and various donors stumped up, only for the World Bank in September of that year, to withdraw its support on the grounds that funds had gone astray. Germany, meanwhile, announced that it would channel aid through NGOs only, and not give funds to organizations in the hands of politicians.

At the insistence of the IMF and World Bank, a Kenya Anti-Corruption Authority (KACA) was set up in 1997 to look into the problems and bring cases against perpetrators. Unfortunately, when it tried to bring four cases involving close allies of President Moi in December 2000, the High Court ruled that only the Attorney-General could prosecute corruption cases, and KACA was thus unconstitutional. When an Economic Crimes Bill was introduced into parliament to reverse this ruling, Attorney-General Amos Wako added an amendment excluding all cases dating from before 1997, thus conveniently preventing KACA from looking into the funding of KANU's last two election campaigns. That Bill was then thrown out having failed to obtain the necessary two-thirds majority for a constitutional measure in parliament. The IMF has now refused any loans to Kenya until an effective anti-corruption law is passed.

To begin with there was the **voter registration scandal**. Since the previous election, in 1988, between three and four million young people had turned 18. Few of them had received national identity cards, a prerequisite of voter registration, and there were unexplained delays in issuing the cards in time for the elections, at least in many non-KANU-voting areas. Then, parliament quietly passed a law that almost guaranteed Moi's continued presidency whatever the outcome of the general elections. To win the presidency, the candidate had to have at least 25 percent of the vote in five out of the eight provinces. Barring unexpected, huge reversals, only one man would achieve that.

Another new law came into force shortly before the election specifying the president had to form a government entirely from his own party (an anti-coalition law). Having split the opposition, this was nice timing.

FORD was finding the transformation from opposition lobby group to **political party** very hard to manage. As a party it was promiscuous in the welcome it extended to every ex-KANU minister who made the leap. Within weeks, the contest for the leadership of FORD and the nomination for a presidential candidate was in full swing.

Less than six months old, the FORD party began to disintegrate. There had always been a division between the established opposition, fronted by Oginga Odinga and led by Paul Muite and his lawyers' circle, and the newer opposition of displaced KANU people and establishment and business figures out of favour with the ruling party. Three months before the election, FORD split into FORD-Kenya (FORD-K; presidential candidate Odinga) and FORD-Asili (FORD-A; candidate Kenneth Matiba).

In parts of Kikuyu-land, **FORD-K** earned the nickname FORD-Kihii (*kihii* means an uncircumcized boy), an ethnic jibe against FORD-Kenya's Luo supporters. With the split, the ethnic divisions of multi-party politics were revealed. It became impossible to enter the political arena without constant reference to the language groups of the politicians and their supporters. Of all the parties, FORD-K was the most ardent in its rejection of tribally based politics. With Odinga, a Luo, as presidential candidate and Muite, a Kikuyu, as his running mate, the country's two largest ethnic groups were well represented. FORD-K was intellectually the strongest party, too, with a radical programme, but pragmatic economic policies, drawn up by an impressive group of economists, including expat businesspeople.

FORD-A was the big, centrist, Kikuyu party, with major support from business, its leader Matiba a serious threat to KANU. During Matiba's year of incarceration he had suffered two strokes and been refused permission to travel abroad for treatment. There was thus a well-founded fear in KANU about his personal animosity towards key figures in the ruling party.

The **Democratic Party**, despite support from a range of backgrounds, never looked, in the 1992 elections, like a serious contender to win the presidency or a majority in parliament, as its opposition credentials were suspect, leader Mwai Kibaki having only recently resigned from KANU. This was to change dramatically in the following five years.

There were opposition efforts until the last minute to forge tactical alliances in order to oust Moi and KANU. But, in the climate of mutual suspicion and risk-assessment, none materialized. KANU, meanwhile, having started 1992 in disarray, was looking stronger again by the end of the year. By **printing billions of shillings**, the government was able to buy support for KANU on a massive scale. Encouraged by the largesse, there were a number of significant returns to the KANU fold as the divisions among the opposition became clearer and a KANU victory less unthinkable. Many had no deepseated opposition to KANU, just a deep-rooted fear of being on the losing side.

On the coast, the banned fundamentalist **Islamic Party of Kenya** was something of a wild card. Khalid Salim Ahmed **Balala**, the IPK leader, spent much of the run-up to, and aftermath of, the election in detention, held on the trumped-up charge of "imagining" the death of President Moi.

At the last minute, the election date was switched from December 7 to **December 29**, the worst possible date for a good voter turnout. It was sure to favour the rural rather than the urban, the unemployed rather than those in work (who had registered to vote at their places of work rather than in their home villages, where many would be over Christmas) and, on balance, KANU over the opposition.

And so it turned out. Voting was low and, when the boxes were finally counted after several days, KANU had 100 seats out of the total of 188. Seventeen of these were returned "unopposed" as the opposition candidates had been physically prevented from presenting their nomination papers. There was, undoubtedly, widespread ballot-stuffing and fraud but, with only 200 local and foreign election monitors to check 7000 ballot boxes, little to prevent it. In the presidential race, Moi received 1.9 million votes to the opposition candidates' combined 3.2 million.

The first session of Kenya's new multi-party parliament was suspended for two months, a slap in the face for opposition MPs whose disgust with the outcome of the election had at first led to a call to boycott their seats. The two months gave KANU a chance to buy back a number of MPs into the party (as a result there were a number of by-elections in western Kenya, usually accompanied by violence) and to try to come up with some sort of strategy for dealing with the superior intellectual and rhetorical strengths of the opposition.

KANU had lost all but one of its cabinet ministers to opposition candidates and, with a total lack of people of ministerial calibre on the government back benches, Moi was put in the extraordinary position of having to offer defeated cabinet ministers their posts back as nominated MPs (the Kenyan parliament at the time had 200 seats – 188 of which were elected seats and 12 of which were nominated, the latter in the president's gift). KANU has almost no MPs from the Kikuyu or Luo communities.

The aftermath of the elections

Despite the bad taste left by the elections, the international community was little better impressed with the divided opposition parties who, acting together, could easily have defeated KANU. The **IMF** and **World Bank** decided that there had, in the end, been much support for the incumbents and, after a false start – with a row in which Moi called their economic demands "suicidal and dictatorial" – agreement was reached with foreign donors to pick up the aid programme, two years after it had ceased.

In November 1993, donor nations finally agreed around US$500 million in new aid, although this did little to refill the badly depleted coffers pilfered since the end of the 1980s. The aid was contingent on stringent conditions, foremost among them a dramatic raft of privatizations of nationalized industries, including post and telecommunications, the railways and the national produce and cereals board. Privatization was demanded partly out of obedience to economic theory, partly in an effort to reduce the cash available for siphoning off for political patronage.

In the **FORD-K party**, the activities of its elderly leader alarmed some of the membership. Oginga Odinga's agreement with Moi in 1993 to seek a partnership with the government to improve the economy and infrastructure in western Kenya, rather than going all-out to topple KANU, was judged a sellout, and when it was further revealed that the old man had received at least

Ksh2 million from the director of the scandal-ridden financial institution **Goldenberg International** (see box on p.658), the FORD-K party was torn apart. As a result, the hard-line younger FORD-K activists, including Oginga's son Raila Odinga, quit FORD-K and formed the National Development Party. Oginga Odinga died in January 1994, his departure hailed by KANU as a sad day for Kenya. State TV and President Moi paid him moving tributes and KANU offered to help meet funeral and other expenses.

FORD-A, meanwhile, steadily declined in confidence and credibility while its own ageing leader, Kenneth Matiba (today its sole MP) made increasingly wild accusations and pronouncements, including a bluntly racist attack on Kenyan Asians whom he accused of plundering the country.

Early in 1995, the ex-Kenya Wildlife Service chief, **Richard Leakey** (recently sacked from his conservation post by Moi), joined lawyer Paul Muite to form a new political party, **Safina** ("The Ark"), with the intention of binding together the fragmented opposition. Moi's reaction was unsubtle: "What do I say to Leakey? I say no, no and no to any white man who wants to lead Kenya". Safina's application to register as a legal party was turned down and, at a meeting in Nakuru, Leakey and party leaders were beaten up.

The 1997 elections

Two years of economic slowdown followed, with strikes by teachers and nurses, mass demonstrations for constitutional reform, the breakdown of relations with the IMF (which led to a run on the Kenya shilling), IMF and World Bank insistence on reforms and good governance, KANU in-fighting for succession with Moi manoeuvring for control, and the many-headed opposition repeatedly splitting and reforming in a variety of brief experimental alliances. Senior figures in the three main parties (Martin Shikuku, now the leader of FORD-A; DP leader Mwai Kibaki; and Michael Wamalwa of FORD-K) finally agreed to work together as an **alliance**, which would put forward a single presidential candidate. Richard Leakey co-ordinated the alliance and raised funds. But Kenneth Matiba's ambitions for the presidency, not to mention those of Martin Shikuku, should the alliance not work out, were clear signals that the opposition would be in no better a state of united readiness than in 1992. When Moi finally unbanned Safina it was too late for the party to organize a presidential candidate.

But at the same time as the opposition was left awry, the run-up to the 1997 elections saw internal divisions in Moi's KANU beginning to show. A rift began to appear between the vehemently anti-Kikuyu **KANU A** – dominated by Maasai strong-man William Ntimama and Simeon Nyachae, a politician from the Kisii region widely seen in his camp as a possible successor to Moi – and the more wily **KANU B**, led by George Saitoti and Nicholas Biwott, who foresaw little future for the party, post-Moi (1997–2002 is his last term in office), without the involvement of the Kikuyu. Moi leans towards KANU B and appears to place great trust in Biwott, his former personal assistant from the Keiyo Kalenjin sub-group, who styles himself "Total Man".

For most of 1997, Kenyan politics polarized between KANU hardliners and the National Convention Executive Committee (NCEC) – a coalition of religious leaders, unionists and student activists – and the country was kept guessing as Moi swung between conciliation and hardline, man-the-barricades rhetoric.

By June 1997, the opposition, and particularly students, were howling for reforms in advance of the elections. Rallies were called for July 7, a date commemorating the 1990 "Saba Saba" pro-democracy rally. The police response, including the **storming of the university**, left more than a dozen dead after protests around the country, and included the beating up of elderly churchmen and the savage cudgelling of women with babies, witnessed by millions of TV viewers.

There were protests from all Kenya's big aid donors and outraged depositions from Nairobi's diplomatic community. Moi panicked. Although he refused to talk to the NCEC, he agreed to meet with the parliamentary opposition in a grouping that came to be known as the **Inter-Party Parliamentary Group**. Reforms to the law and the unbanning of most opposition parties were suddenly on the agenda, and Moi regained the initiative.

Repression alternated with promises of reform through the rest of year, accompanied by a series of national strikes until, in November 1997, the Constitutional (Amendment) Bill passed its final reading in parliament. The **reforms** saw the long overdue removal of the archaic sedition laws – the Chief's Act and the Public Order Act, two pieces of legislation that were designed to restrict basic freedoms of movement and speech. In the context of the Moi government, these laws, along with the Societies Act, were effectively exploited to emasculate and cower the opposition, restricting its operations, especially in areas considered to be KANU zones. Reforms, forced upon Moi, like multi-partyism five years earlier, had been brought about by mass action,

Wangari Maathai and the Green Belt Movement

One of the government's most outspoken and consistently credible critics is the former chairwoman of the National Council of Women of Kenya, Professor **Wangari Maathai**. A founding member of FORD, she was also the instigator, in 1977, of the **Green Belt Movement**, Kenya's remarkable grassroots environmental lobby. The Green Belt Movement has planted more than 12 million tree saplings around the country (planting more trees every year than the government has in a decade) and is responsible for a transformation in environmental awareness, especially among the rural poor, and particularly among women, who have done most of the planting. Unlike Maendeleo Ya Wanawake, which, over the years, has come to be seen as essentially a tool of KANU, the Green Belt Movement is not aligned with any political party.

In March 1992, Maathai, on hunger strike in Uhuru Park with the wives and mothers of political prisoners, demanding their release, was clubbed unconscious by police, and she later became involved in the commission of inquiry over ethnic violence in the Rift Valley.

Articulate and trenchant, Maathai has clashed directly with President Moi over his plans for a high-rise development in Uhuru Park, and most recently has spearheaded the demonstrations against the destruction of Nairobi's Karura Forest. She has often accused the government of corruption and the misappropriation of aid funds. After her colleague John Makanga was violently arrested in 1993, and she received death threats, Maathai went into hiding. She came out to receive the 1993 Edinburgh Medal, awarded for an outstanding contribution to humanity through science. Most recently she and her movement have been spearheading the campaign against the degazetting, and inevitable subsequent destruction, of over 10 percent of Kenya's forest (see p.65).

Wangari Maathai claims to have no political ambitions, but her charisma, her fame and her impeccably nationalist and internationalist views must make her a leading candidate for Kenya's – and Africa's – first woman president or prime minister.

the falling out with the IMF, increasing international isolation, and the fear in Moi's camp that the youth in particular would take Mobutu's downfall in Zaire as encouragement to pull down their own president (the two leaders have often been compared). The new laws also provide for equal access to state media by the opposition – in theory. But people can still only associate with institutions that are registered: the Societies Act bans true freedom of association.

Despite the impending reforms, Mombasa erupted in violence in August 1997, when two police stations were attacked, six policemen killed, weapons stolen and dozens of up-country people later killed and thousands more expelled by armed gangs who terrorized the district of **Likoni**. Notices circulated "reclaiming" the coast for its indigenous inhabitants, and demanding the largely Kikuyu newcomers – who tend to support the opposition – return to their home districts. For once, the police acted on the side of the victims of what was widely presumed to be a resumption of government-inspired ethnic cleansing, and arrested two local KANU party chiefs.

The elections were held, once again, on December 29, though this time they were beset from start to finish by **organizational chaos** and **severe weather**: two returning officers, and their ballot boxes, were swept away in a flooded river. Many polling stations opened late, or not at all; ballot papers were delivered to the wrong constituency, or were insufficient for the number of queuing voters; electoral commission staff walked out of polling stations in protests over pay; and boxes remained uncollected.

The **vote**, predictably, split along ethnic lines, with the Kalenjin constituencies of the Rift Valley, along with the Maasai and Samburu, the Somali, Turkana, coastal and many Luhya and Kisii constituencies, largely voting for Moi and KANU. Mwai Kibaki's Democratic Party performed extremely well in the Kikuyu areas, even better than expected given it was five years since he had left KANU. In the Kikuyu heartland, not even Jomo Kenyatta's son, Uhuru Kenyatta, (a Moi family business associate), could win a seat for KANU in his Gatundu South constituency. In the presidential race, Moi polled 2.4 million votes against Kibaki's 1.9 million.

Charity Ngilu, the daughter of a minister in the Ebenezer Gospel Church, who had been expected to do well with her Social Democratic Party, put over a feisty, honest and hard-working image: "Ngilu beats up official" headlined one newspaper, about a hapless official she suspected of tampering with voter forms. But her support was largely limited to her Kamba ethnic base. **Raila Odinga**, too, with his **National Development Party** (NDP), was well supported, but only locally, in Luo-land.

Mwai Kibaki and Raila Odinga both called for a rerun of the presidential election, and Kibaki challenged the election results through the courts. Paul Muite and Richard Leakey's Safina party accepted the results, however, and Leakey quit politics soon afterwards (see box on p.652).

A postscript to the elections was (and continues to be) the **succession question**, and the wooing by KANU of Michael Wamalwa's FORD-K and Raila Odinga's NDP, both with their grassroots support in the west. This **Luo-Luhya alliance with KANU**, with the patronage flowing from Nairobi, was the latest twist in Moi's continued determination to control the country.

In April 1998, a consultative forum was set up as a preliminary to the formation of a **commission on constitutional reform**. In May 1999, however, Moi announced that the review of Kenya's constitution would be conducted by parliament where, of course, KANU and the NDP commanded a majority. In December, parliament duly voted to appoint a select committee on constitutional reform under Raila Odinga, prompting opposition politicians and religious leaders to set up a rival, independent commission called Ufungamano. The parliamentary select committee eventually proposed a 15-member commission to reform the constitution, and Professor Yash Pal Ghani, an academic in the field, was brought in to head it. He, however, refused to take office until Ufungamano was brought in, and amazingly he managed to achieve a merger between Ufungamano and the parliamentary commission, though nominations to the new, 27-member Constitutional Review Commission thus created were still subject to vetting by Moi, and its recommendations to a vote by parliament.

The turn of the millennium

The horrific August 1998 **bombing** of the American Embassy, apparently by Osama bin Laden's Al-Qaida organization, in which more than 250 people were killed and 5000 injured, led to a suspension of ordinary faction fighting and a genuine mood of public reconciliation. Charles Njonjo, a figure in the political wasteland for fifteen years, took up the chair of the disaster fund. But the lull was short-lived. As the dust settled, business as usual was quickly resumed. The judicial inquiry into ethnic clashes resumed its grindingly slow process, while there were more than 100 further killings, mostly of Kikuyu, in Laikipia and Nakuru districts, in January 1999. The police made no arrests.

Ethnicity is dangerously to the fore. Questions of prior **rights over land** are being brought up across the country, in every sphere of life, even when there is little history of dispute, in order to raise the political temperature and increase KANU's leverage. **Majimboism** (see box) is widely debated.

Majimboism

The infamous **majimboism** (federalism) debate that is related to the constitutional reform exercise has become vigorous in recent years. Coastal legislators, who have long pioneered the crusade, now claim to have released a blueprint for a federal government system. In July 1998, a number of MPs from Central Province – Kenya's most prosperous region – uncharacteristically plunged into the fray with a call for their own *jimbo* (federal state) called Kirinyaga. The MPs not only advocated the creation of a region that would bring the economically powerful "Gema" (Kikuyu, Embu and Meru) communities together, but also suggested Nairobi as their *jimbo* headquarters.

The possibility of the country's capital city becoming the headquarters of Kenya's most developed *jimbo* shook majimboists into a serious rethink. Three coastal MPs – Mathias Keah (KANU), Emmanuel Karisa Maitha (DP) and Suleiman Shakombo (Shirikisho Party) – advocated a system that would address "all socio-economic and political issues". "What we want is *jimbo* for political, economic and social development which will ensure that all the people residing in the region benefit from the resources and improve their standards of living".

The **Shirikisho Party**, founded on the eve of the 1997 elections, is an exclusively coastal outfit whose main agenda is to fight for *majimbo* (plural) and the rights of the coastal peoples. The party was at one time threatened with deregistration for allegedly promoting violence, notably the Likoni killings and ethnic cleansing.

A religious link to the *majimbo* quest in both the Coast and North-Eastern provinces is already being floated by opponents of the system. Church leaders in particular are wary of the campaign, pointing out that a large majority of the legislators calling for majimboism in the two regions are Muslims.

Kenya's ethnic rifts are mirrored by long-existing **economic disparities** that need to be addressed. The supporters of KANU (mostly Kalenjin, Maasai, Samburu, people of the northeast, and some small coastal ethnic groups) include many of Kenya's marginalized communities, who have benefited the most from the KANU government's limited hand-outs and subsistence support. Because of their poor, often pastoral, economies, they tend to lag behind in educational opportunities. In contrast, the opposition – ethnically dominated by the Kikuyu and Luo – is based in the most economically developed regions and communities, where ambitions constantly outstrip the limited rewards that Kenya can offer to educated and business-minded people.

In the field of **international relations**, 1999 ended with an agreement between Kenya, Uganda and Tanzania to revive the old East African Community, leading eventually to a single market and single currency. The September 11, 2001 attacks on US targets gave Moi the opportunity to pose as America's number one ally in the region, offering a strategic base in East Africa to US forces in the hope of financial aid in return.

Kenya today is, in many respects, a harsh and bitter country below the surface. Very little makes sense, socially and politically, beyond calculations of **personal interest** for those powerful figures whose voices are heard. The reality of civic life in Kenya is one of interminably drawn-out court cases, pointless public enquiries, corruption on a scarcely believable scale and flagrant police brutality every day, in every town. Kenyans, rich and poor, have been badly let down.

Perhaps Kenya will hold together if the country can remain a political patchwork – with the KANU-supporting marginal districts separated from each other by fertile opposition regions of high population density. But the drawing-in by KANU of Raila Odinga's mainly Luo NDP from the west of Kenya, and bordering Moi's Rift Valley heartland – may shift Kenya's political centre of gravity away from Nairobi altogether. And the possibility that an east African regional power base is being constructed in **Eldoret** is the disturbing conclusion that may have to be drawn from the reopening of its international airport and bullet factory. There's an interesting flaw in the Kalenjin armour with which Moi shields himself in the town: the Nandi. Increasing numbers of Nandi in Eldoret, their main home, are refusing to have any truck with KANU. They don't accept the Kalenjin label foisted on them – they are the largest group among the "Kalenjin" peoples, all of whom speak Nandi.

With the December **2002 election** looming, a merger between KANU and Raila Odinga's NDP may be on the cards, to create a new party that Moi and Odinga hope will guarantee electoral success – a development with unforeseeable consequences for the opposition parties and their followers, particularly the Kikuyu. Some Kiambu Kikuyu might be expected to support a broader-based KANU party (Uhuru Kenyatta is a leading light in KANU), but most Nyeri Kikuyu would not.

Moi is keeping everybody guessing about his declared intention to retire and hand over power. His problem is that, out of office, he will be open to prosecution on corruption and human rights charges arising from his activities as president. One possible solution to this dilemma is that the constitutional review commission will propose a ceremonial head of state, above politics and above the law, with Moi the most likely candidate for the position. Either way, as head of government or ceremonial head of state, Moi and his inner circle are unlikely to relinquish any more power than they have to, and even if 2002 does see the election of new blood to positions of power, Moi and his friends hope to ensure that these will be people loyal to them.

Kenya finds itself in a disastrous predicament, and any sense of stability is

In March 1999, the veteran KANU politician and Minister of Home Affairs, **Shariff Nassir**, twice publicly threatened the press with "problems" if they persisted in "printing lies" and "criticizing the government". The press duly responded by reporting his threats verbatim, together with essays pointing out that Kenya had progressed, however shakily, from dictatorship to an era of democracy, and that the threats were those of a man clearly out of step with the times. The infamous **sedition laws** which had previously gagged the media were repealed in 1997, and Nassir's threats were shrugged off.

However, after so many decades of dictatorship and press control, Kenya's newfound freedoms are far from guaranteed. Although established high-circulation dailies like the **Nation** and **Standard** seem able to criticize with relative impunity, the government is still a dab hand at more sinister forms of censorship. In March 1998, the newly appointed Information and Broadcasting Minister Joseph Nyagah accused an unnamed section of the press of "taking advantage" of the lax laws to conduct a "vicious campaign" to undermine presidential authority and national stability. At the end of the month, Moi himself ordered the closure of the *Star* newspaper, for having reported on the armed forces. At the same time, the *Nation* group's radio and TV licence was cancelled, allegedly due to a dispute with a local businessman, but the *Nation* claimed the decision demonstrated "a deep-seated fear of truth in public life and the values of free expression". The *Nation* was sanctioned early in 1999, for publishing a leaked document from the Akiwumi tribal clashes inquiry, for which it was banned from reporting for a month. Other papers are treated less kindly: the editors and owners of the magazines **Finance** and **Law Monthly**, both of which favour scandalous headlines accusing one politician or another of corruption, repeatedly face arrest and the impounding of their presses or files, as does the long-suffering editor of **Kenya Confidential**, who seems to spend more time in jail than out.

Despite this far from perfect environment, the advances in press freedom over the last few years are remarkable, and have played an instrumental part in pushing Kenya from dictatorship towards democracy. With donor pressure still very much on Kenya to comply with their conditions of more democracy and accountability, these press freedoms seem likely to continue – at least as long as the donors keep up the pressure. However, the government's control over the executive and judiciary remains tight and threats from the likes of Nassir, at present taken lightly by the press, may still be realized.

Whatever the climate for local journalists, there is no doubt that Kenya is one of the best places in Africa in which to work as a **foreign correspondent**. Based mostly at Chester House in Nairobi (and largely unimpeded if not greatly encouraged), foreign reporters put Kenya, more than most other African countries, under intense international scrutiny. Responding to their reports in a robust, credible fashion, however, has never been the government's strong point.

illusory. More than ever before, resolving the problems of landlessness, unemployment and poverty – the root causes of Kenya's internal conflicts – must remain the priority. It would be refreshing if the KANU government were to initiate pragmatic reforms to its practices, by actively prosecuting the embezzlers of Kenya's precious public funds, and by putting humanity plainly at the top of its agenda, signalling a genuine concern for the country's people. The brute realities of the international economic order make these tasks difficult for the best-intentioned governments. But, after nearly four decades in power, it's clear that the KANU government is incapable of addressing these issues independently. Perhaps the best that can realistically be hoped for is that it avoids completely alienating the opposition parties and the international community. Without their involvement, Kenya's future, on current form, is not bright.

Wildlife and environment

Despite the tremendous losses of the twentieth century, Kenya teems with wildlife. In one place or another, not just inside the protective boundaries of the forty-odd parks and reserves, it's possible to see almost all of the country's big animals. Even outside the parks, if you travel fairly widely, you're almost certain to note various gazelles and antelopes, zebra and giraffe – even hippo, buffalo, crocodile and elephant. Monkeys and baboons can be seen almost anywhere and are a regular menace.

If this impression of abundant wild animals slightly alarms you, rest assured that any danger is minimal. Outside the park boundaries the big cats are hardly ever seen, and man-eating lions and enraged elephants are no more a realistic cause for concern than the few remaining rhinos, which live entirely within the parks; buffalos, though plentiful, are only really dangerous when solitary. Perhaps the one animal to be a little wary of is the hippo, especially on land. For lonely hikes – on Mount Kenya, Mount Elgon and the Aberdares, for example – hiring a guide is sometimes a good idea. Statistically, however, your chances of being attacked by a wild animal in Kenya are very small.

The country's **birdlife** is even more noticeable than its mammals, and astonishingly diverse, attracting ornithologists from all over the world and converting many others as well. There are over a thousand species in all, ranging from the thumb-sized red-cheeked cordon bleu to the ostrich.

This introduction to Kenya's habitats, mammals, birds, reptiles and amphibians complements our colour guide at the front of the book, which will prove useful in identifying the main species of mammals likely to be seen on safari. For more detailed coverage, a good full-length field guide is very valuable – some recommended **books** are listed on p.688.

Forest and woodland habitats

Several forest types are present in Kenya, including mountain, coastal and lowland dry forests.

Highland forests

The highlands support rich forests, which give way to agricultural lands as you approach Nairobi. The characteristic landscape in the highlands is patches of evergreen trees separated by vast meadows of grasses – often wire grass and Kikuyu grass.

The highland forest is quite limited in extent in Kenya; it's typically found above 1500m, and also on isolated massifs. It bears some resemblance to lowland forest, but contains different tree species and does not normally grow as tall or dense. Typical trees of this forest include **camphor**, **Juniperus procera** (the "cedar" tree of East Africa) and **podocarpus**. The better-developed forests are found on the wetter, western slopes of the massifs. Above the forest line, stands of giant bamboo are found at altitudes of over 2500m. Along the lower, drier edge of the highlands, trees grow less high and are dotted in fields of tall grass; various species of olive tree are commonly found here.

The **main highland forest areas** are to be found on Mount Kenya, Mount Elgon, the Mau Escarpment, the Aberdares and Mount Marsabit. **Mount Kenya** displays a mountain summit plant community (known as **Afro-Alpine**), which bears a strong similarity to that found on other high East

African mountains (there's more on Mount Kenya's high-altitude flora on p.184). The highest part of the montane forest belt, at altitudes over 2900m, is characterized by a giant form of St John's wort. Above this, giant heather and *Proteus* trees form a heather belt, whilst at even higher altitudes, open marshy moorland is found, dominated by tussock grasses, giant groundsel and giant lobelia. Higher still, the tree groundsel comes into its own (this has an upper limit of 4460m).

Several species of **near-endemic birds** are associated with the highland forest habitat. These are Jackson's francolin (a game bird of high-altitude forest undergrowth), the dazzling golden-winged sunbird (golden-yellow wings and long, yellow tail streamers) and Hartlaub's turaco. Other typical birds of these forests and streams include African black duck, mountain buzzard, bar-tailed trogon, white-starred robin, mountain warbler and mountain wagtail.

The Kakamega Forest

West of the Rift Valley, the 240 square kilometres of Kakamega Forest, and a few adjacent outliers, are examples of the Guineo-Congolian **equatorial forest**, which is more typically a feature of central and west Africa and is now very restricted within Kenya. For this reason, many bird and plant species not encountered elsewhere in Kenya are found here – it's a memorable experience to be in the forest at first light when the shafts of morning sun spear their way through the tallest boughs of the semi-evergreen trees.

Lowland and coastal forest and woodlands

Very few areas of **lowland rainforest** are left in Kenya, mainly restricted to the coastal strip, and the banks of the lower Athi and Tana rivers. The soils of these forests quickly lose their fertility when cleared for agriculture, and many of the areas that remain are degraded.

Lowland woodland areas are found inland of the coastal forest strip and away from the rivers. Woodlands are defined as more open forest areas with the ground flora dominated by grasses and the forest canopy covering as little as twenty percent of the area. Trees in such woodlands may average only 4–5m high.

The rainforests, all threatened by human incursions, include **Witu Forest** near Lamu, the **Mida-Gedi Forest**, the **Sabaki River Forest** near Malindi, forest fragments in the **Shimba Hills** and the **Ramisi River Forest** on the southern coast.

The most important area of natural forest is the **Arabuko–Sokoke Forest**, which lies slightly inland along the western side of the main coast road, south of Malindi and north of Kilifi. Arabuko-Sokoke is unique in that it comprises a largely unbroken block of 420 square kilometres of coastal forest, consisting of brachystegia woodland (containing a huge variety of birdlife), dense cynometra forest, and zones of mixed lowland rainforest that are very rich in plants, mammals and insects.

Large areas of the coastal plain are covered in moist, tree-scattered grasslands. On the beach itself, tall **coconut palms** and the rather weedy-looking **casuarina** (known as whistling pine) dominate the high-tide line.

Grassland

Grassland with scattered trees (wooded savannah) covers vast areas in Kenya, both in the **Lake Victoria basin** (which includes the Mara), and **south and east of Mount Kenya** at elevations of 1000–1800m. This type of ecosystem prevails because of regular fires. Many of the trees that persist are broad-leaved and deciduous, protected from fire damage by their corky bark. In areas with a similar altitude, but with more erratic rainfall, a thin scattering of tall, flat-topped acacia trees, along with shorter acacias, occurs amongst the grassland, producing the archetypal imagery of the East African landscape.

Desert and semi-desert

Typical desert and semi-desert flora comprises **thornbush and thicket**. Thirty kilometres inland from the Indian Ocean, beyond the fringes of the Arabuko-Sokoke Forest and others, is the eastern edge of the **Nyika wilderness**, which stretches west to the edge of the highlands. Nyika is characterized by an often impenetrably thick growth of stunted, thorny trees, which are grey for most of the year, but become green during the rainy season. Scaly-barked species such as acacia and euphorbia species occur in this plant community.

Desert grass-bush and the drier **desert scrub** communities cover nearly seventy percent of the land area of Kenya, mainly in the east, north and north-east. These areas are at low altitude (below 600m) and have unreliable rainfall, suffering long droughts, a lack of regular flowing water and strong wind exposure. Vegetation is sparse and scrubby, with bushes and occasional, widely scattered tall trees, mainly baobab, *mwangi* and *mgunga* (acacia) trees. Much of the ground free of bushes is covered by dispersed bunches of grass and other low shrubs. However, much of the soil surface here is bare.

The true desert habitat is drier still and plant life is very limited in some areas. Many of the trees and bushes (if present at all) are dwarf. Large areas are bare, stony desert with a thin and patchy growth of desert grasses and perhaps a few bushes along dry river margins or dry water courses.

Wet habitats

The Kenyan coast is dominated by two major habitat types, sandy beach and mangrove forest. There are also some offshore rocky islands and coral reefs along the coast, which provide refuge for birds, but there are no breeding sites of pelagic seabirds (birds of the open ocean) in the country. Many species of shore birds (waders) are found in tidal creeks and estuaries, for example at Mida Creek, on the Sabaki estuary, and also on the Lamu Archipelago. One unique wader species, the **crab plover** – a pied wader which runs to catch crabs for food – overwinters at Mida Creek.

Lakes

The savannah of the **Great Rift Valley** is dotted with bird-rich lakes, ranging from the two freshwater lakes – Naivasha and Baringo – to intensely saline ones like Magadi and Bogoria. The Rift Valley acts as a magnet to passage and wintering birds.

The vast expanse of **Lake Victoria** is an example of an oligotrophic lake – fed mainly by rainwater falling on to the lake's surface, rather than being fed by rivers and streams. As a result, it has a relatively low nutrient concentration. A feature of the lake is its papyrus beds and marshlands which harbour birds not found elsewhere in Kenya.

Rivers

There are very few permanent riverine habitats in Kenya, because the country is so dry, but those river systems which exist are extremely attractive to birds and mammals. The best examples of such rivers are the **Tana** and **Athi-Galana–Sabaki** systems.

Mangrove forest

Marine mangrove swamps are found in many parts of the coast. The largest tracts, and the areas from which most mangrove poles (*boriti*) are cut for the building trade, are in the Lamu Archipelago, but all the coastal creeks are more or less bordered by mangroves (*mkoko* in Swahili). There are also areas of saline grassland on the landward side of some of the mangrove thickets. Although fun to travel through by boat, mangrove forests are not noted for their faunal diversity. One unusual animal you're bound to see is the **mudskipper**, a fish on the evolutionary road to becoming an amphibian.

Mammals

Kenya has more than a hundred species of large native mammals. The majority of species are vegetarian grazers, browsers and foragers at the lower end of the food chain – animals such as monkeys, rodents and antelopes. The big predators are fewer in species and tend to be the dominant topic of conversation at game lodges. Everyone remembers seeing lions for the first time or cheetahs. To see a leopard is often a personal goal, and a highlight. Once you get the bug, you'll be looking out for a lone striped hyena, rather than the common and gregarious spotted version, or for a serval cat rather than a cheetah. But don't ignore the less glamorous animals. There can be just as much satisfaction in spotting a shy, uncommon antelope, or in noting rarely observed behaviour, as in ticking off one of the more obvious predatory status symbols.

> The **cross-references** given below lead to pages in our colour guide at the back of the book.

Primates

There are twelve species of primates in Kenya, excluding *Homo sapiens*. They range from the pint-sized, slow-motion, lemur-like potto, found in Kakamega Forest, to the baboon. Kenya no longer has any great apes (the family to which the gorilla and the chimpanzee belong), although they probably only became extinct in the western forests, of which Kakamega is a relic, in the last five hundred years, during which time the region was widely settled by humans. The legend of the Nandi Bear (see p.330) is probably connected with those passed-down memories. A new **chimpanzee sanctuary** has recently been established at Sweetwaters in Laikipia, "stocked" with chimps from Jane Goodall's famous Gombe Stream reserve in Tanzania.

Today, the primate you are certain to see almost anywhere in Kenya, given a few trees, is the **vervet** (p.xviii), a small, lightweight monkey that has no difficulty adjusting to the presence of humans and, if possible, their food. The vervet is one of the guenons – typical African monkeys, with distinctive facial markings and hairstyles, all wonderfully adapted to a life on the prowl for fruits, leaves, insects and just about anything else small and tasty. Almost as common in certain areas, notably on the coast, is **Sykes' monkey** (p.xix). At Diani Beach, a number of Sykes' troops have become notoriously accustomed to stealing food from hotel dining tables, and large males will even raid bedrooms. Up-country populations of Sykes' (or blue) monkey appear to be more timid.

It's up-country where you are most likely to see the beautiful, leaf-eating **black and white colobus monkeys** (p.xviii) – although they can also be spotted in the Diani forest. They are usually found high in the tree canopy; look out for the pure white young. The related Tana River red colobus is only found in the remote Tana River Park, which also shelters the dwindling population of Tana River crested mangabeys, a partly ground-dwelling monkey with a characteristic Mohican-style crest of hair. Other rare or more localized monkeys include: the red-tailed guenon of the far west; the stocky but distinguished looking De Brazza's monkey, with its white goatee, found almost exclusively in Saiwa Swamp National Park; and the **Patas monkey** (p.xviii), a moustachioed plains runner of the dry northwest and Laikipia.

If you stay in a game lodge, you are quite likely to see **bushbabies** at night, as they frequently visit dining rooms and verandahs. There's a large, cat-sized species (the greater galago) and a small bushbaby not much bigger than a kitten (the lesser galago). Both are engaging animals, with sensitive, inquisitive fingers and large eyes and ears to aid them in their hunt for insects and other small animals.

On safari, you'll have plenty of opportunities to watch **baboon troops** (p.xviii) up close. Large males can be somewhat intimidating in size and manner, disconcertingly so towards women. Troops average forty to fifty individuals, who spend their lives, like all monkeys, in clear, but mutable social relationships. Rank and precedence, physical strength and kin ties all determine an individual's position in this mini-society led by a dominant male. The days revolve around the need to forage and hunt for food (baboons will consume almost anything, from a fig tree's entire crop to a baby antelope found in the grass). Grooming is a fundamental part of the social glue during times of relaxation. When baboons and other monkeys perform this massage-like activity on each other, the specks which they pop into their mouths are sometimes parasites – notably ticks – and sometimes flakes of skin.

Rodents and hyraxes

Rodents aren't likely to make a strong impression on safari, unless you're lucky enough to do some night game drives – or preferably walks. In that case you may see the bristling back end of a **crested porcupine** (p.xix) or the frenzied leaps of a **spring hare** (p.xix), dazzled by headlights or a torch. In rural areas off the beaten track you may occasionally see hunters taking home **giant rats** or **cane rats** – shy, vegetarian animals, which make good eating. Kenya has several species of **squirrel**, the most spectacular of which is the giant forest squirrel, with its splendid bush of a tail, and the nocturnal flying squirrel – which actually glides, rather than flies, from tree to tree, on membranes between its outstretched limbs. Both are most likely to be seen in Kakamega Forest. Very widespread, however, are the two species of **ground squirrel** – striped and unstriped – which are often seen, dashing along the track in front of the vehicle, in Tsavo National Park and the Samburu reserves.

Rock hyraxes (p.xxiii), which you are certain to see at Hell's Gate National Park and on Mount Kenya, look like they should be rodents. In fact the rock hyrax and closely related tree hyrax are technically ungulates (hoofed mammals) and form a classificatory level entirely their own. Their closest living relatives are elephants, with which they share distant common ancestry. Present-day hyraxes are pygmies compared with some of their prehistoric ancestors, which were as big as a bear in some cases. Rock hyraxes live in busy, vocal colonies of twenty or thirty females and young, plus a male. In a few places they are extremely tame and wait to be fed by passing hikers. Usually, however, they are timid in the extreme – not surprising in view of the wide range of predators that will eat them.

Carnivores

Kenya's carnivores are some of the most exciting and easily recognizable animals you'll see. Although often portrayed as fearsome hunters, pulling down plains game after a chase, many species do a fair bit of scavenging and all are content to eat smaller fry when conditions dictate or the opportunity arises.

Of the large cats, **lions** (p.xxii) are the easiest species to find. Lazy, gregarious and physically large – up to 1.8m in length, not counting the tail, and up to a metre high at the shoulder – they rarely make much effort to hide or to move away, except on occasions when a large number of tourist vehicles intrude. They can be seen in nearly all the parks and reserves, and their presence is generally the main consideration in determining whether you're allowed out of your vehicle or not. Popular parks where lions are normally absent are Hell's Gate and Lake Bogoria (you can hike in both); parks which are inhabited by lions, but in which you can generally hike, include the Aberdares and Mount Kenya. "Man-eating" lions appear from time to time but seem to be one-off feline misfits. Normally, lions hunt co-operatively, preferring to kill very young, old or sick animals, and making a kill roughly once in every two attacks. When they don't kill their own prey, they will steal the kills of cheetahs or hyenas.

Leopards (p.xxii) may be the most feared animals in Kenya. Intensely secretive, alert and wary, they live all across the country except in the most treeless zones. Their unmistakable call, likened to a big saw being pulled back and forth, is unforgettable. Although often diurnal in the parks, they are strictly nocturnal wherever human pressures impinge, and sometimes survive on the outskirts of towns and villages, carefully preying on different domestic animals to avoid a routine. They tolerate nearby human habitation and rarely kill people unprovoked. Accidents do occur, however, and disturbed individuals occasionally take to human-hunting – or are forced to become "man-eaters" through infirmity. For the most part, leopards live off any small animals that come their way, pouncing from an ambush and dragging the prey up into a tree where it may be consumed over several days. Monkeys, especially the relatively less organized species such as colobus and vervet, are frequent prey. Baboons, unless very unlucky, are usually able to mob a leopard to defend the troop. The spots on a leopard vary from individual to individual, but they always appear in the form of rosettes. Melanistic (black) leopards are known as panthers or black panthers, and seem to be more common in some areas (Mount Kenya and the Aberdares, for example) than others.

In the flesh, the **cheetah** (p.xxii) is so

Lioness

different from the leopard, it's hard to see how there could ever be any confusion. Cheetahs are lightly built, finely spotted, with small heads and very long legs. Unlike leopards, which are highly arboreal, cheetahs never climb trees. They live alone, or sometimes briefly form a pair during mating, and hunting too is normally a solitary activity, down to eyesight and an incredible burst of speed that can take the animal up to 100kph (70mph) for a few seconds. Cheetahs can be seen in any of the large, up-country parks, though Nairobi National Park is as easy a place to find them as any.

Other large, Kenyan cats include the beautiful part-spotted, part-striped **serval** (p.xxiii), found in most of the parks, though somewhat uncommon; and the aggressive, tuft-eared **caracal** (p.xxii), a kind of lynx, which is seen even less often than the serval, favouring drier zones like Tsavo East and the Samburu complex.

The biggest carnivore after the lion is the **spotted hyena** (p.xxi); it is also, apart from the lion, the meat-eater you will most often see. Although considered a scavenger *par excellence*, the spotted hyena is a formidable hunter, most often found where antelopes and zebras are present. Exceptionally efficient consumers, with immensely strong teeth and jaws, spotted hyenas eat virtually every part of their prey, including bones and hide and, where habituated to humans, often steal shoes, unwashed pans and refuse from tents and villages. Although they can be seen by day, they are most often active at night – when they issue their unnerving, whooping cries. Clans of twenty or so animals are dominated by females, which are larger than the males and compete with each other for rank. Curiously, female hyenas' genitalia are hard to distinguish from males', leading to a popular misconception that they are hermaphroditic. Not surprisingly, in view of all their attributes, the hyena is a key figure in local mythology and folklore.

In comparison with the spotted hyena, you are not very likely to see a **striped hyena**. A usually solitary animal, it's slighter and much rarer than its spotted relative, though occasionally glimpsed very early in the morning.

The commonest members of the dog family in Kenya are the **jackals**. The black-backed or silver-backed jackal (p.xx) and the similar side-striped jackal, can be seen just about anywhere, both species usually in pairs. The golden jackal is most likely to be seen in the Mara. **Bat-eared foxes** (p.xx) are also not uncommon, and unmistakable in appearance. However, the unusual and rather magnificent **hunting dog** (p.xx) is now more or less extinct in Kenya, having been present in reasonable numbers thirty years ago. Canine distemper has played a big role in their decline, as have human predation and habitat disruption.

Among smaller predators, the unusual **honey badger** or **ratel** (p.xx) is related to the European badger and has a reputation for defending itself extremely fiercely. Primarily an omnivorous forager, it will tear open bees' nests (to which it is led by a small bird, the honey guide), its thick, loose hide rendering it impervious to their stings. **Genets** (p.xxi) are reminiscent of slender, elongated cats (they were once domesticated around the Mediterranean, but cats proved better mouse-hunters). In fact they are viverrids, related to mongooses. and are frequently seen after dark around national park lodges, where they live a semi-domesticated existence.

Most species of **mongoose** (p.xxi) are also tolerant of humans and, even when disturbed out in the bush, can usually be observed for some time before disappearing. Their snake-fighting reputation is greatly overplayed: in practice they are mostly social foragers, fanning out through the bush like beaters on a shoot, rooting for anything edible – mostly invertebrates, eggs, lizards and frogs.

The **civet** (p.xxi) is a stocky animal, resembling a large, terrestrial genet. It was formerly kept in captivity for its musk (once a part of the raw material for perfume), which is secreted from glands near the tail. Civets aren't often seen, but they are predictable creatures that can be seen wending their way along the same paths at the same time night after night.

Elephants

Elephants (p.xxiii) are found throughout Kenya. Almost all the big plains and mountain parks have their populations. These are the most engaging of animals to watch, perhaps because their interactions, behaviour patterns and personality have so many human parallels. Like people, they lead complex, interdependent social lives, growing from helpless infancy, through self-conscious adolescence, to adulthood. Babies are born with other cows in close attendance, after a 22-month gestation. The calves suckle for two to three years, from the mother's two breasts between her front legs.

Elephants' basic **family units** are composed of a group of related females, tightly protecting their babies and young and led by a venerable matriarch. It's the matriarch that's most likely to bluff a charge – though occasionally she may get carried away and tusk a vehicle or person. Bush mythology has it that elephants become embarrassed and ashamed after killing a human, covering the body with sticks and grass. They certainly pay much attention to the disposal of their own dead relatives, often dispersing the bones and spending time near the remains. Old animals die in their seventies or eighties, when their last set of teeth wears out and they can no longer feed.

Seen in the flesh, elephants seem even bigger than you would imagine – you'll need little persuasion from those flapping, warning ears to back off if you're too close – but they are at the same time surprisingly graceful, silent animals on their padded, carefully placed feet. In a matter of moments, a large herd can merge into the trees and disappear, their presence betrayed only by the noisy cracking of branches as they strip trees and uproot saplings.

Managing the elephant population (see the "Poaching Wars" box on p.400–401) leads to arcane ecological puzzles in which new factors keep emerging; current wisdom suggests that elephants are in a way "architects" of their environment. Overpopulation is usually the result of old migration routes being cut off, forcing the animals into unnatural reserves – like the Mara – where their massive appetites can appear to be destructive. Adults may consume up to 170kg of plant material daily – that works out at well over a hundred tons of foliage through the Mara's collective elephant gut every day. However, this foliage destruction by crowded herds also puts new life into the soil. Acacia seeds sprout much better after being eaten and dunged by elephants than if they simply fall to the ground. Dung beetles gratefully tackle the football-sized elephant droppings, break them into pellets and pull them into their burrows where the seeds germinate. Elephants also dig up dried-out water holes with their tusks (they're either right- or left-tusked, in the same way as humans favour one hand or the other), providing moisture for other animals.

Rhinos

There are two species of **rhinoceros** (p.xxiv) found in Africa – the hook-lipped or black rhino, and the much heavier wide-lipped or white rhino. Both are on the brink of extinction in the wild. The shape of their lips is far more significant than any alleged colour difference, as it indicates their respective diets (browsing for the black rhino, grazing for the white) and favoured habitats (thick bush and open grassland respectively).

Rhinos give birth to a single calf, after a gestation period of fifteen to eighteen months, and then the baby is not weaned until it is at least a year, sometimes two years, old. Their population growth rate is slow compared with most animals – another factor contributing to their predicament.

White rhinos have been extinct for several hundred years in Kenya, but reintroduced animals (principally from South Africa) have always done well – when allowed the chance to do so out of the sights of poachers.

The smaller black rhinos were, until the mid-1970s, a fairly common sight in most of the parks. In the 1960s, Amboseli, for example, had hundreds of magnificent black rhinos, some with graceful, long upper horns over a metre in length. The facts behind their rapid and depressing decimation are given in some detail on p.401.

Today, there are fewer than 500 black rhinos in Kenya, and just a few dozen white rhinos. You can see black rhinos in Maasai Mara, Lake Nakuru, Nairobi, Aberdares and Mount Kenya national parks and Ngulia Rhino Sanctuary in Tsavo West. White rhinos can be seen in Maasai Mara and Lake Nakuru. Small numbers of both species can also be encountered at private ranches in northern Kenya, especially in Laikipia, north of Mount Kenya. Such is the threat to their survival, the exact location of rhino groups is not always made widely known.

Hippos

Hippopotamuses (p.xxv) are highly adaptable, and found throughout Kenya wherever rivers or freshwater lakes are deep enough for them to submerge in and have a surrounding of suitable grazing grass. By day, they need to spend most of their time in water to protect their thin, hairless skin from dehydration.

Hippos can be found everywhere from the humid estuary of the Tana River to the chilly mountain district of Nyahururu, including the briny Lake Nakuru in the central Rift Valley and Lake Turkana in the semi-desert of the northwest. After dark, hippos leave the water to spend the whole night grazing, often walking up to 10km in one session. In the Maasai Mara, they wander across the savannah; at Lake Naivasha they plod through farms and gardens; and everywhere they are rightly feared.

Hippos are reckoned to be responsible for more human deaths in Africa than any other animal. These occur mostly on the water, when boats accidentally steer into hippo pods, but they can be aggressive on dry land, too, charging and slashing with their fearsomely long incisors. They can run at 30kph if necessary and have a small turning circle. Although uncertain on land (hence their aggression when cornered), they are supremely adapted to long periods in water. Their nostrils, eyes and ears are in exactly the right places and their clumsy feet become supple paddles – as can be seen from the underwater observatory at Mzima Springs in Tsavo West National Park, for example.

Zebras

Zebras (p.xxiv) are closely related to horses and, together with wild asses, form the equid family. Of the three species of zebra, two live in Kenya. Burchell's has thick stripes and small ears and is found in suitable habitats in most parts of the country, while Grevy's is a large animal with very fine stripes and big, saucer-like ears, restricted to Tsavo East and the northern parks and reserves.

Burchell's zebras found in Kenya are mostly the *granti* subspecies and often called Grant's zebras. In the far north, they tend to have a very short mane, or even none at all. In Tsavo West and other parts of southern Kenya, they tend to exhibit the "shadow striping" typical of the species in southern Africa (fawn stripes between the black ones). In Amboseli and the Mara, Burchell's zebras gather in migrating herds up to several thousand strong, along with wildebeest and other grazers. In contrast, Grevy's zebras live in small territorial herds.

Pigs

The commonest wild pig in Kenya is the **warthog** (p.xxv), regularly sighted throughout Kenya up to altitudes of over 2000m. Quick of movement and nervous, warthogs are notoriously hard to photograph as they're generally on the run through the bush, often with the young in single file,

Burchell's zebra

tails erect. They shelter in holes in the ground, usually old aardvark burrows, and live in family groups, usually a mother and her litter of two to four piglets, or occasionally two or three females and their young. Boars join the group only to mate, and are distinguishable from sows by their prominent face warts, which are thought to be defensive pads protecting their heads during often violent fights. Although a favourite prey animal of large cats – and humans – the warthog's survival doesn't appear to be threatened, although its rooting and wallowing behaviour brings it into conflict with farmers.

Two other much rarer pigs, both nocturnal, live in Kenya: the huge, dark-coloured **giant forest hog**, a bristly, big-tusked pig which lives in the highlands and is most likely to be seen from a tree hotel on Mount Kenya or in the Aberdares; and the **red river hog** or **bush pig** which is very rarely seen, though not uncommon in dense forest, close to agriculture and river margins.

Giraffes

The tallest mammals on earth, **giraffes** (p.xxv) are common and unmistakable. Non-territorial, they gather in loose leaderless herds and spend the day browsing on the leaves of trees too high for other species (acacias and combretums are favourites), while at night they lie down and ruminate. Bulls test their strength while in bachelor herds. When a female is in heat, which can happen at any time of year, the dominant male mates with her. She will give birth after a gestation of approximately fourteen months. Over half of all young, however, fall prey to lions or hyenas in their early years.

Kenya has three types of giraffe, differentiated from each other by their pattern and the configuration of their short horns. Most often seen is the **Maasai giraffe**, with two horns and a very broken pattern of dark blotches on a buff or fawn background. This is the giraffe you'll see in Maasai Mara, Amboseli and Tsavo West. Roughly north of the Nairobi–Mombasa road (a natural dividing line) lives the dramatically patterned **reticulated giraffe**, which normally has three or five horns and boldly defined chestnut patches on a very pale background. The more solidly built **Rothschild's giraffe**, which has a pattern more like crazy paving (also with well-defined blotches) and usually two horns, is found only in parts of western Kenya (and over the border in Uganda). There's disagreement among zoologists over whether any of the giraffe's subspecies should be accorded the status of separate species – particularly concerning the reticulated giraffe – but they all interbreed.

Hollow-horned ruminants

This category of mammals includes buffalo and all the antelopes – exemplified by the 28 two-toed cud-chewers illustrated on pp.xxvi–xxxii of our colour wildlife guide. The **buffalo** itself (p.xxvi) is a very common and much-photographed safari animal, closely related to the domestic cow. Buffalos live in herds of 100 to 300 and rarely make much effort to move when vehicles approach. Indeed, they aren't troubled by close contact with humans, and you don't have to read the papers in Kenya long before finding an example of buffalos trampling crops or goring a farmer.

The rather ungainly **hartebeest** family (p.xxvi) includes one of the rarest antelopes in Kenya, Hunter's hartebeest of the lower Tana River. The Coke's hartebeest or kongoni, however, is found widely in southern Kenya, and **topi** (p.xxvi) are practically emblematic of the Maasai Mara, their main habitat. The white-bearded **wildebeest** (p.xxvi) is also particularly associated with the Mara. Their spectacular annual migration through the reserve is described on p.428.

Of the **gazelles**, the most obvious are **Thomson's** and **Grant's** (both p.xxvii), easily seen at the roadside in many parts of southern Kenya. The range of Grant's gazelle extends further north to encompass the northern parks (Samburu, Meru) where "Thommies" are absent. The **gerenuk** (p.xxvii) is an unusual browsing gazelle able to nibble from bushes standing on its hind legs (its name is Somali for "giraffe-necked"). Although considered an arid land specialist, its range encompasses most of Kenya east of the Rift Valley. The **impala** (p.xxviii), although not a gazelle, is closely related and very common throughout much of Kenya.

The **reedbuck** and **waterbuck** (p.xxviii) are related to each other, both spending much time in or near water. The common or Bohor reedbuck has a patchy distribution in southern Kenya, whereas the waterbuck is common in many central and southern areas.

Some of the smallest antelopes in the world are quite easily seen in Kenya. **Kirk's dik-dik** (p.xxix) is a common miniature antelope found all over the country, measuring no more than 40cm in height, which usually pairs for life. The **suni**, which is uncommon, but can be encountered almost anywhere in forest cover, is even smaller (32cm). Other small Kenyan antelopes – all fairly widespread, but nowhere common – include the surprisingly aggressive **steenbok** (p.xxxii) which, despite a height of only 50cm, defends itself furiously against attackers; the **oribi** (p.xxxii), with its rather charming foreplay (when the female is in heat, the male pushes his head under her hindquarters and pushes her along on her forelegs like a wheelbarrow race); and the **klipspringer** (p.xxxii), which has hooves wonderfully adapted for scaling near-vertical cliffs.

The duikers (from the Dutch for "diver", referring to their plunging into the bush) are larger – the **common duiker** (p.xxix) is around 60cm high – though they appear smaller because of their hunched posture. The common duiker is found throughout the country in many habitats, but most duikers are more choosy and prefer plenty of dense cover and thicket. These include the tiny Zanzibar duiker (whose range in Kenya is restricted to the Arabuko-Sokoke Forest), the widespread red duiker and blue duiker, and the more localized black-fronted duiker (Mount Kenya and Mount Elgon) and yellow-backed duiker (Mau Forest).

Kenya's big antelopes are the *Tragelaphinae* – twisted-horn bushbuck types – and the *Hippotraginae* – horse-like antelopes. The **bushbuck** itself (p.xxx) is notoriously shy – a loud crashing through the undergrowth and a flash of a chestnut rump are all most people witness. The **bongo** is a particularly impressive member of this group, now confined to the highlands of Mount Kenya, the Aberdares (where it's sometimes seen at tree hotels), and possibly the Cheranganis and Mau Escarpment. The **sitatunga** (p.xxix) is a smaller relative, semi-aquatic by nature, found in Kenya only in remote corners of the Lake Victoria shoreline and at the very accessible Saiwa Swamp National Park, where they are easy to see. Also easily spotted, almost anywhere in the country, is the huge, cow-like **eland** (p.xxx), with its distinctive dewlap. The two species of kudu are not uncommon where they exist at all, but they are very localized. Both are browsers. You're most likely to see **greater kudu** (p.xxx) at Lake Bogoria or Marsabit and **lesser kudu** (p.xxx) in Tsavo West or East, but neither species in the Mara.

The horse-like antelopes include the very fine **fringe-eared oryx** (p.xxxi), which is found almost everywhere except the Mara; the massive **roan antelope** (p.xxxi), restricted to the Mara and the Lambwe Valley in western Kenya (after an abortive relocation attempt to Shimba Hills, southwest of Mombasa); and the handsome **sable antelope** (p.xxxi) which lives, and thrives, only in the Shimba Hills.

Other mammals

Dugong

Of Kenya's other mammals, you're not likely to see more than a glimpse. Rarest of all is the **dugong**, the marine mermaid-prototype, of which there are believed to be seven or eight individuals remaining, drifting in the shallows around the Lamu Archipelago.

The insectivorous **elephant shrews** are worth looking out for, simply because they are so weird. Your best chance of a sighting is of the golden-rumped elephant shrew, at Gedi on the coast (see p.524).

The **aardvark** (p.xix) is one of Africa's – indeed the world's – strangest mammals, a solitary termite-eater weighing up to 70kg. Its name, Afrikaans for "earth pig", is an apt description, as it holes up during the day in large burrows – excavated with remarkable speed and energy – and emerges at night to visit termite mounds within a radius of up to 5km, to dig for its main diet. It is most likely to be common in bush country well scattered with tall termite spires.

Pangolins are equally unusual – nocturnal, scale-covered mammals, resembling armadillos and feeding on ants and termites. Under attack, they roll themselves into a ball. The ground pangolin, the only species found in Kenya (most pangolins are arboreal), lives mainly in savannah districts.

Kenya's many **bats** will usually be a mere flicker over a water hole at twilight, or sometimes a flash across the headlights at night. The only bats you can normally observe in any meaningful way are fruit bats hanging from their roosting sites by day. The hammer-headed fruit bat, sometimes seen in Kakamega Forest, has a huge head and a wing span of over a metre.

Birds

Kenya boasts the second-highest country bird list – after the Congo – in Africa, at over 1070 species (this compares with no more than 300 for Britain and around 600 for North America). Nearly eighty percent of Kenya's birds are thought to breed in the country, with the remainder breeding during the northern summer in the Palaearctic region (Europe, north Africa and Asia north of the Himalayas) but wintering in tropical Africa. Many of these are familiar British summer visitors, such as swallows, nightingales and whitethroats, which have to negotiate or skirt the inhospitable Sahara on their migration. In winter, the migrant terns and waders can seem to dominate Kenya's shorelines, and the Palaearctic swallows and warblers may comprise a large proportion of the birds in bushland habitats.

If you're a novice **bird-watcher**, Kenya is an excellent place to start. No amount of wildlife documentaries can do justice to the thrill of glimpsing your first colourful bee-eaters overhead (twelve species have been recorded in Kenya, three or four of which you might expect to encounter), watching rollers and shrikes swoop from perches to hunt insects, or seeing groups of vultures wheeling and dipping in the skies overhead as they prepare to arrive at a kill. The wide variety and accessibility of habitats makes bird-watching in Kenya highly rewarding. The keenest independent bird-watchers might expect to encounter over 600 species in a four-week period, whereas some of the organized bird-watching tour groups, living and breathing birds for a three-week period, might record over 700 species in that time; one tour group holds the African record of 797 species in 25 days. However, even for those just dipping into the hobby or with limited time and choice of itineraries, Kenya offers some wonderful surprises.

Interesting bird records from the country can be submitted to the **Bird Committee** at Nature Kenya, PO Box 44486, Nairobi (℡02/749957 or 741049). Another useful contact is the **African Bird Club** (c/o BirdLife International, Wellbrook Court, Girton Rd, Cambridge CB3 0NA, UK), which produces an excellent regular bulletin and occasional monographs and itineraries. See also "Bird-watching in Nairobi" on p.117.

Distribution

Only a few species of birds are found throughout Kenya. Three which will become familiar to sharp-eyed visitors are the **laughing dove**, the **African drongo** (an all-black crow-like bird with a forked tail) and the **grey-headed sparrow**. Most other species have well-defined distributions dependent on habitat type, itself a reflection of altitude and rainfall patterns.

Part of Kenya's bird diversity can be explained by the large numbers of species reaching the edge of their known ranges inside its borders. These include birds originating in the Horn of Africa but having their western or southwestern limits in Kenya (for example, the Somali bee-eater), species widespread in southern Africa which reach their northern limits here (such as the rufous-bellied heron), coastal species which are confined to the east (for example, the mangrove kingfisher), species from west African equatorial forests whose ranges just overlap the forest patches in west Kenya (for example, the grey parrot), and species occurring along the southern edge of the Sahel which reach the extreme southeast of their range in Kenya (for example, the Abyssinian roller).

Many Kenyan birds display two more or less separate populations, one on the coast, the other in the highlands. This is determined by habitat: the coastal areas tend to have much less rain than the highlands, and are much hotter with a more severe dry season. In some species, such as the widespread speckled mousebird, two distinct races are evolving.

Endemic and near-endemic species

Of over a thousand species of bird found in Kenya, there are only six **endemic species** (that is, species found only in Kenya). Although these species are unlikely to be encountered by the novice and can be difficult to identify, their existence serves to emphasize Kenya's remarkable birdlife. They comprise two species of cisticola (small, skulking species, found in dense vegetation), a species of lark found only in the Marsabit and Isiolo areas, Sharpe's pipit (found in high grasslands in western and central Kenya), Clarke's weaver (found only in and around the Arabuko-Sokoke Forest), and Hinde's pied babbler (found in the vicinity of Kianyaga near Embu).

Many bird-watchers are attracted to Kenya by the large number of **near-endemic species**, confined to northeast Africa, for which Kenya offers a reasonably accessible chance of a sighting. These include Heuglin's bustard, the Somali bee-eater (a very pale, open-country bee-eater found in the north and often noted at Samburu), Hartlaub's turaco (a green species of turaco, only found in highland forests in East Africa), and the small Sokoke Scops owl found most easily around the Arabuko-Sokoke Forest.

Large walking birds

Several species of large, terrestrial (or partly terrestrial) birds are regularly seen on safari. Their size and common form of locomotion (though the secretary bird and marabou stork can both fly perfectly well, and the ground hornbill is not flightless) makes them the birds most frequently spotted by non-ornithologists.

The locally common, distinctive **ostrich** is found in dry, open plains and semi-desert. The world's biggest bird, at up to 2.5m high, it is virtually absent from the coastal strip, but can readily be seen in Nairobi National Park and most others.

The **secretary bird** is a large, long-tailed, long-legged bird, grey-white in colour with a scraggy crest (the quills of which gave it its name), black on the wings and black "stockings". A bird of dry, open bush and wooded country, often seen in pairs, it is most commonly noticed stalking prey items which it has disturbed from grassland. Prey includes beetles, grasshoppers, reptiles and rodents, sometimes up to the size of a hare. Secretary birds are scarce in west Kenya and at the coast, but can be seen easily in Nairobi National Park.

Secretary bird

The **marabou** is a large, ugly stork, up to 1.2m in height, with a bald head and a dangling, pink throat pouch. Most specimens look as if they're in an advanced state of decomposition. The marabou flies with its head and neck retracted (unlike other storks) and is often seen in dry areas, including towns, where it feeds on small animals, carrion and refuse.

Another reasonably common walking bird is the **ground hornbill**. This impressive creature lives in open country and is the largest hornbill by far, black with red face and wattles, bearing a distinct resemblance to a turkey. It's not uncommon to come across pairs, or sometimes groups, of ground hornbills, especially in the Mara, trailing through the scrub on the lookout for small animals. They nest among rocks or in tree stumps.

CONTEXTS | Wildlife and environment

Flamingos and ibises

Many visitors to Kenya are astounded by their first sight of **flamingos** – a sea of pink on a soda-encrusted lake which, together with the salt-rich smell of the lake and the stench of the birds' guano, powerfully evokes East Africa. Two species are found in Kenya, the greater flamingo and the lesser flamingo. Both are birds of the Rift Valley lakes and adjacent areas, and both are colonial nesters.

Much the commoner of the two is the **lesser flamingo**, smaller, pinker and with a darker bill than its greater relative. The Rift Valley population of lesser flamingos, with over a million birds gathering at one time at lakes Bogoria and Nakuru, is one of only three populations in Africa. This species is nomadic, moving in relation to fluctuating food supplies, water levels and alkalinity, and flocks can leave or arrive at an area in a very short period of time – an estimated 400,000 birds have been recorded leaving Lake Bogoria over a seven-day period. Lesser flamingos feed by filtering suspended aquatic food, mainly blue-green algae that occurs in huge concentrations on the shallow, soda lakes of the Rift.

Greater flamingos may occur in their thousands, but are considerably fewer in number than the lessers. They are bottom feeders, filtering small invertebrates as well as algae. Although greaters tend to be less frequently nomadic than their relatives, they are more likely to move away from the Rift Valley lakes to smaller water bodies and even the coast.

The most widely distributed **ibis** species (stork-like birds with downcurved bills) is the **sacred ibis**, which is found near water and human settlements. It has a white body with black head and neck, and black tips to the wings. Also frequently encountered is the **Hadada ibis**, a brown bird with a green-bronze sheen to the wings and noisy call in flight, found near wooded streams, cultivated areas and parks in southern Kenya.

Water birds

Most large water bodies, apart from the extremely saline lakes, support several species of **ducks and geese**, many of which breed in Europe, but overwinter in Africa.

Several species of **herons, storks and egrets** occur in areas with water, or can be observed overflying on migration. The commonest large heron is the black-headed heron, which can sometimes be found far from water. Mainly grey with a black head and legs, the black heron can be seen "umbrella-fishing" along coastal creeks and marsh shores: it cloaks its head with its wings whilst fishing, which is thought to cut down surface reflection from the water, allowing the bird to see its prey more easily.

The **hamerkop** is a brown, heron-like bird with a sturdy bill and mane of brown feathers, which gives it a top-heavy, slightly prehistoric appearance in flight, like a miniature pterodactyl. Hamerkops are widespread near water and build large, conspicuous nests that are often taken over by other animals, including owls, geese, ducks, monitor lizards or snakes.

Guineafowl

Four species of these large, grey game birds are found in Kenya. The **vulturine guineafowl** is a bird of very arid areas, recognized by the long tapered feathers hanging from the base of the neck over a royal-blue chest. The well-known **helmeted guineafowl**, a bird of moister areas, has a bony yellow skull protrusion (hence its name). The crested and the Kenya crested guineafowl are both birds of thickets.

Birds of prey

Kenya abounds with birds of prey – kites, vultures, eagles, harriers, hawks and falcons. Altogether, over 75 species have been recorded in the country, several of which are difficult to miss.

Six species of **vulture** range over the plains and bushlands of Kenya and are often seen soaring in search of a carcass. All the species can occur together, and birds may travel vast distances to feed. The main differences are in feeding behaviour: the lappet-faced vulture, for example, pulls open carcasses; the African white-backed feeds mainly on internal organs; the hooded vulture mainly picks from bones.

Two other birds of prey that are firmly associated with East Africa are the **bateleur**, an eagle that is readily identified by its silver wings, black body, chestnut red tail, stumpy body shape and wedge-shaped tail; and the **fish eagle**, whose haunting calls render a sense of emptiness and space to many a wildlife television documentary. Fish eagles are generally found in pairs near water, often along lake shores.

Cranes and bustards

Kenya's national bird, the **crowned crane**, is found in the south and west of the country. It is a distinctive, elegant bird, the head crowned with an array of yellow plumes. Crowned cranes are often seen feeding on cultivated fields or in marshy areas.

Crowned crane

Some nine species of **bustard** occur in the plains and grasslands of Kenya. These large, open-country species are long-legged and long-necked and are very well camouflaged among the browns and yellows of their African backdrop. The heaviest flying bird in the world, the Kori bustard, is commonest in the Rift Valley highlands. Bustards are affected by intensive, small-scale agricultural and human presence, and several species have undergone a decline in Kenya.

Parrots and lovebirds

Eight species of *Psittacidae* have been recorded in Kenya, three of which are introduced. The parrot species that you're most likely to see is the **brown parrot**, which occurs in wooded areas in the west of the country. Lovebirds are small, green, hole-nesting birds (like small parrots) and are readily seen in the acacias around Lake Naivasha, where a feral breeding population of **yellow-collared lovebirds** has become established. This species has been introduced to Kenya from Tanzania, and hybridizes with the introduced and very similar **Fischer's lovebird**.

Go-away birds and turacos

These distinctive, related families are found only in Africa. Medium-sized and with long tails, most **go-away birds** and **turacos** have short rounded wings. They are not excellent fliers, but are very agile in their movements along branches and through vegetation. Many species are colourful and display a crest. The largest, the magnificent **great blue turaco** (blue above, and green and brown below) is found only in the western forests in Kenya – notably at Kakamega, where it is one of the largest species in the forest. Other turacos are generally green or violet in colour, and all are confined to thickly wooded and forest areas. Open-country species, such as the widely distributed and common

white-bellied go-away bird (go-aways are named after their call), are white or grey in colour.

Mousebirds

Three species of mousebird are found in Kenya. Their name derives from their rapid scampering through thick tangles of branches using unusually adapted claws. They can be identified by their slight crests and their long, tapering tails. Generally grey or brown in colour, they're noisy and feed actively in quite open vegetation. The **speckled mousebird** is a very common species throughout southern Kenya, often found in small groups at forest margins and in suburban gardens.

Rollers, shrikes and kingfishers

A family of very colourful and noticeable birds of the African bush, **rollers** perch on exposed bushes and telegraph wires and hawk flying insects. They take their name from their impressive courtship flights – a fast dive with a rolling and rocking motion, accompanied by raucous calls. Many have a sky blue underbody and sandy-coloured back; long tail streamers are a distinctive feature of several Kenyan species. The **lilac-breasted roller** is a common and conspicuous species.

Shrikes are found throughout Kenya. Fierce hunters with sharply hooked bills, they habitually sit on prominent perches, and eat insects, reptiles and small birds.

Kingfishers are some of Kenya's most colourful and noticeable birds, with eleven species found here. They range in size from the tiny **pygmy kingfisher**, which feeds on insects and is generally found near water, to the **giant kingfisher**, a shy fish-eating species of wooded streams in the west of the country. Several kingfishers eat insects rather than fish and they can often be seen perched high in trees or on open posts in the bush where they wait to pounce on passing prey. A common and widespread insectivorous species is the **chestnut-bellied kingfisher**.

Hornbills

Named for their long, heavy bills, surmounted by a casque or bony helmet, hornbills generally have black and white plumage. Their flight consists of a series of alternate flaps and glides. When in flight, hornbills may be heard before they are seen, the beaten wings making a "whooshing" noise as air rushes through the flight feathers. Many species have bare areas of skin on the face and throat and around the eyes, with the bill and the casque often brightly coloured, their colours changing with the age of the bird. Thirteen species have been recorded in Kenya, most of them omnivorous, but tending largely to eat fruit. Several species are common open-country birds; **silvery-cheeked hornbills** are sometimes seen in Nairobi. Hornbills have interesting breeding habits: the male generally incarcerates the female in a hollow tree, leaving a hole through which he feeds her while she incubates the eggs and rears the young.

Woodpeckers

The abundance of trees within such a variety of habitats in Kenya means that many species of woodpecker (up to fourteen) are present. One species you're almost certain to encounter is the sparrow-sized **cardinal woodpecker**.

Sunbirds

Sunbirds are bright, active birds, feeding on nectar from flowering plants, and distributed throughout Kenya, wherever there are flowers, flowering trees and bushes. Over 35 species have been recorded in the country, with many confined to discrete types of habitat. Common species in the Nairobi area are **variable** and **scarlet-chested sunbirds**. Males are brightly coloured and usually identifiable, but many of the drabber females require very careful observation to identify them.

Starlings

The glorious orange and blue starlings which are a common feature of bushland habitats – usually seen feeding on the ground – belong to one of three species. The **superb starling** is the most widespread of these, found everywhere from remote national parks to gardens in Nairobi. It can be identified by the white band above its orange breast. Similar starlings are the larger **golden-breasted**, often seen in Tsavo National Park, and **Hildebrand's** (also orange-breasted), which is commonest around Machakos but can be encountered all over southern Kenya.

Weavers and whydahs

These small birds are some of the commonest and most widespread of all Kenyan birds. Most male **weavers** have some yellow in the plumage, whereas the females are rather dull and sparrow-like. In fact, many species appear superficially very similar; distinctions are based on their range and preferred type of habitat. Weavers nest in colonies and weave their nests into elongated shapes, which can be used to help in the identification of the species. Many nests are situated close to water or human habitation and sometimes hang suspended. The **golden palm weaver** is the species you'll commonly see on the coast, often in hotel gardens.

Whydahs are also known as widow birds. The **paradise whydah** has extremely ornate tail feathers, with the central pair of tail feathers flattened and twisted into the vertical. Male paradise whydahs are mainly black in colour, and perform a strange bouncing display flight to attract females.

Reptiles and amphibians

There is only one species of crocodile in Kenya – the big **Nile crocodile** which, left to grow, can reach 6m or more in length and is considered a cunning and dangerous animal. You'll see them in the Mara River, in the Tana, at Mzima Springs in Tsavo West, in great numbers in Lake Turkana and, if you take the trouble to look, in many other rivers and large bodies of water.

Kenya has many species of **snakes**, some of them quite common, but your chances of seeing a wild specimen here are more remote than in Australia or the USA, or even certain parts of Europe. In Kenya, as all over Africa, snakes are both revered and reviled and, while they frequently have symbolic significance for local people, that is quite often forgotten in the rush to hack them to bits with a *panga* upon their discovery. All in all, snakes have a very hard time surviving in Kenya.

Common **non-poisonous species** of snakes include the rock python (a constrictor growing up to 5m or more in length), the egg-eating snake and the sand boa. Common **poisonous species** include the green and black mambas (fast, agile, arboreal snakes), the boomslang, the spitting cobra and the dangerous puff adder, which is probably responsible for more bites than any other, on account of its sluggish disposition. Most snakes flee on detecting the vibrations of human footsteps.

Jackson's chameleon

Tortoises are quite frequently encountered on park roads in the morning or late afternoon. Some, like the leopard tortoise, can be quite large, up to 50cm in length, while the hinged tortoise (which not only retreats inside its shell but shuts the door, too) is much smaller – up to 30cm. In rocky areas, look out for the unusual pancake tortoise, a flexible-shelled species that can put on quite a turn of speed but, when cornered in its fissure in the rocks, will inflate to wedge itself inextricably, to avoid capture. Terrapins or turtles of several species are common in ponds and slow-flowing streams. On the coast, sea turtles breed and it's not unusual to see them from boats during snorkelling trips.

Lizards are common everywhere, harmless and often colourful. The commonest are **rock agamas**, the males often seen in courting "plumage", with brilliant orange heads and blue bodies, ducking and bobbing at each other. They live in loose colonies often near human habitation; one hotel may have hundreds, its neighbours none. The biggest lizards, **Nile monitors**, grow to nearly 2m in length and are often seen near water. From a distance, as they race off, they look like speeding baby crocodiles. The other common monitor, the smaller savannah monitor, is less handsomely marked.

A large, docile lizard you may come across is the **plated lizard**. This intelligent, mild-mannered reptile is often found around coastal hotels, looking for scraps from the kitchen or pool terrace. At night on the coast, the translucent little aliens on the ceiling are **geckoes**, catching moths and other insects, and worth encouraging. By day, their minuscule relatives, the day geckoes (velvet grey and yellow), patrol coastal walls. In the highlands you may come across prehistoric-looking three-horned **Jackson's chameleons** creeping through the foliage – and there are several other species, living in most parts of the country, which you are most likely to see squashed flat on the road.

In the **amphibian** world, you'll probably only come across the odd toad, sitting under a footpath light, waiting for insects to drop on to the ground. There are, however, dozens of species of frogs and tree frogs, ranging from the common squeaker to the red and black rubber frog.

Books

There is a substantial volume of reading matter on Kenya, though much of the European output has been fairly lightweight and the more scholarly works tend to be indigestible. You might want to subscribe to *The Journal of African Travel Writing*, a twice-yearly, 100-page publication ($10 yearly in the US, $14 abroad; PO Box 346, Chapel Hill, NC 27514, USA ⓦwww.unc.edu/~ottotwo) which always contains a wide-ranging selection, from poetry and anecdotes to literary criticism.

For pre-departure reading, the growing body of **Kenyan literature** provides a good foretaste. Some of the following titles may be most easily available in Kenya (for imports in the UK, try the Africa Book Centre, 38 King St, London WC2E 8JT ☎020/7240 6649, ⓕ7497 0309; ⓔafricabooks@dial.pipex.com). **Publishers** are given in brackets after the title, unless the book is out of print (o/p). Very useful are the internet bookstores, such as amazon.com, amazon.co.uk and bol.com, which will try to get just about anything, and are cheap and convenient if you know exactly what you want. You can also buy Kenyan books on line from Nairobi's Legacy Bookshop at ⓦwww.Legacybookshop.com.

Although a number of authors have written in the older languages of Kenya, **English** still predominates as the medium for artistic expression, a situation which creates dilemmas for writers struggling both to reach a readership at home and to find viable channels for publication. Most Kenyan fiction is more cheaply available in Kenya than abroad.

Titles marked ▣ are particularly recommended.

Travel and general accounts

Bartle Bull *Safari: A Chronicle of Adventure* (Penguin, UK/US). A great, macho slab of a book, jammed with photos. It's grotesque but utterly compelling – even if the cruelty and foolish waste of the hunting era, so recently past, is emotionally wearing.

Negley Farson *Behind God's Back* (o/p). An American journalist's account of his long overland journey across Africa on the eve of World War II. A lively book if you can stomach the alarming shifts between criticism of the colonial world and participation in its worst prejudices.

Dick Hedges *Tilda's Angel* (Book Guild, UK). If you want to know all about the man behind Safari Camp Services and the Turkana Bus, this is

for you. Good on what makes Anglo-Kenyans tick.

John Hillaby *Journey to the Jade Sea* (o/p). An obvious one to read before a trip to Lake Turkana. Hillaby's account of his walk in the early 1960s is dated and not always informative – an adventure, as he writes, "for the hell of it", with sprinklings of tall stories and descriptions of loony incompetence.

J. Ludwig Krapf *Travel and Missionary Labors in Africa* (o/p). The account of the first missionary at Mombasa, and the first European to set eyes on Mount Kenya.

David Lamb *The Africans* (Vintage, US). There's really no contest between Lamb, a *Los Angeles Times* hack, and Marnham (see below) for a contemporary view of the continent. *The Africans* has been something of a best seller, but Lamb's fly-in, fly-out technique is a muddled, statistical rant, couched in Cold War rhetoric; even when ostensibly uncovering a pearl of wisdom, he can be unpleasantly offensive.

Patrick Marnham *Fantastic Invasion: Dispatches from Africa* (o/p). Although written in the 1970s, nothing since has matched this withering and devastatingly sharp collection, which includes several essays on Kenya. An excellent book, which tunnels beneath the mountain of dross written about Africa.

★ **Peter Matthiessen** *The Tree Where Man Was Born* (Harvill, UK/Petersmith, US). Wanderings and musings of the Zen-thinking polymath in Kenya and northern Tanzania, first published in 1972. Enthralling for its detail on nature, society, culture and prehistory, and beautifully written, this is a gentle, appetizing introduction to the land and its people.

George Monbiot *No Man's Land* (o/p). A journey through Kenya and Tanzania, providing a shocking exposé of Maasai dispossession and a major criticism of the wildlife conservation movement.

Dervla Murphy *The Ukimwi Road* (Flamingo, UK/Overlook, US). Murphy's bike ride from Kenya to Zimbabwe becomes – for her – a trip through lands lost to AIDS and neo-colonialism.

★ **Shiva Naipaul** *North of South* (Penguin Twentieth Century Classics, UK/Penguin, US). A fine but caustic account of the late Naipaul's life and travels in Kenya, Tanganyika and Zambia in the 1970s. Always readable and sometimes hilarious, the insights make up

for the occasionally angst-ridden social commentary and some passages that widely miss the mark.

Craig Packer *Into Africa* (Chicago University Press, UK/US). A professor of ecology, evolution and behaviour, Packer puts it all to good use in day-by-day reflections during an eight-week field trip.

Joyce Poole *Coming of Age with Elephants* (Hodder & Stoughton, UK/Hyperion, US). Deeply sympathetic account of studying the social and sexual behaviour of elephants in Amboseli.

Keith B. Richburg *Out of America; a Black Man Confronts Africa* (Basic Books, UK/Harcourt Brace, US). Nairobi bureau chief for the Washington Times from 1991–94, Richburg discovered that he was American, not African, and preferred it that way. A rather depressing read – and partial by the nature of its author. Journalists need stories, and that usually means bad news – this is unfortunately likely to stoke the flames of moral relativism.

Rick Ridgeway *The Shadow of Kilimanjaro* (Bloomsbury UK/Henry Holt & Co, US). The American adventurer and filmmaker took a walk in 1997 through the bush from Kilimanjaro to Mombasa – mostly through Tsavo West and East, along the Tsavo-Galana River. Robust, readable and full of passionate enthusiasm for the wild country and the wildlife.

Oona Strathern (editor) *Traveller's Literary Companion: Africa* (o/p). Brief selections of literature from or about virtually every African country, including a good raft of Kenyan pieces.

Louis Taussig *Resource Guide to Travel in Sub-Saharan Africa: Vol 1*

East and West Africa (Hans Zell, UK/KG-Saur, US). Extraordinarily detailed country-by-country coverage of every published source of interest to travellers or expatriates, as well as bookstores, libraries, mapping institutes, children's resources and conservation societies, to list just a few.

Wilfred Thesiger *My Kenya Days* (o/p). The account of thirty-odd years in northern Kenya by a very strange man indeed – an old Etonian noble savage with no interest in modern Africa, wedded to his own ego and a reactionary, glamour-laden view of his tribal companions.

Joseph Thomson *Through Maasailand: To the central African Lakes and Back* (Frank Cass, UK/International Specialized Book Services, US). First published 1885, these two volumes detail Thomson's African journeys of exploration.

Daisy Waugh *A Small Town in Africa* (Mandarin, UK). A year in the life of Isiolo.

Evelyn Waugh *A Tourist in Africa* (o/p). First published in 1960, Waugh's diary of a short trip to Kenya, Tanganyika and Rhodesia is determinedly arrogant and uninformed, but funny, too – and brief enough to consume at a single sitting.

Essays

Wahome Mutahi *How to be a Kenyan* (Kenway Pubications, Kenya) A satirical view of Kenyan life by one of the country's most popular newspaper columnists. Painfully funny, and rather close to the bone, the book takes a humorous look at Kenya's very worst side – it won't put you off the country, but it will certainly give you a chuckle at Kenya's expense. Mutahi followed it up with a sideswipe at Kenyan

women entitled *How to be a Kenyan Lady*.

Renato Kizito Sesana *Father Kizito's Notebook* (Koinonia Media Centre, Kenya) Kenyan life from the Catholic perspective of Fr Kizitos weekly columns in the Sunday Nation. Full of insights into the struggle to survive that most people here call life, infused with humour and compassion.

Wildlife

Having a field guide makes a huge difference to travelling on safari. Many of the following not published in the US, but are easily found in Kenya itself.

Mohamed Amin, Duncan Willets and Brian Tetley *The Beautiful Animals of Kenya* (Text Book Centre, Kenya). Lavish photos but sparing text, an easy, lightweight book, but more a tourist souvenir than a serious guide to Kenyan wildlife.

Michael Blundell *Wild Flowers of East Africa* (o/p). Botanical companion in the series.

★ **Jean Dorst and Pierre Dandelot** *Larger Mammals of Africa* (HarperCollins, UK). Readable and accessible with lively illustrations, though it tends to favour classifying many races as separate species.

Richard E. Estes *The Safari Companion* (Chelsea Green, UK) This book aims to explain not only what animals you're looking at, but also what they're doing, and its illustrated explanations make fascinating reading.

T. Haltenorth and H. Diller *Mammals of Africa* (HarperCollins, UK). A rival for Dorst and Dandelot, which tends to find fewer species in the variety of mammals out there. With its superabundance of detail, this might look like first choice, but the somewhat stylized paintings are less meaningful than Dorst and Dandelot's when you're thumping through the bush, and much of the text is superfluous for all but the professional zoologist.

John Karmali *The Beautiful Birds of Kenya* (Text Book Centre, Kenya). Like its companion volume, *Beautiful Animals*, a tourist souvenir of Kenyan birds with lots of colour photos.

Jonathan Kingdon *The Kingdon Field Guide to African Mammals* (Natural World, UK) A detailed and comprehensive catalogue of African land mammals, illustrated with photographs and distribution maps for each species.

Ray Moore *Where to Watch Birds in Kenya* (Transafrica Press, Kenya). Invaluable tips and background for the devoted bird-watcher.

Ber van Perlo *Birds of Eastern Africa* (HarperCollins, UK). An essential pocket guide, providing clear colour illustrations and distribution maps

for every species known to occur in East Africa, though little by way of descriptive text.

Dave Richards *Photographic Guide to the Birds of East Africa* (New Holland, UK). Over three hundred colour photos.

Chris Stuart and Tilde Stuart *Field Guide to the Larger Mammals of Africa* (New Holland, UK/Ralph Curtis, US). Good field guide published in the late 1990s.

Nigel Wheatley *Where to Watch Birds in Africa* (Christopher Helm, UK/Princeton University Press, US). Tight structure and plenty of useful detail make this a must-have for serious bird-watchers in Africa; 25 pages on Kenya.

John Williams *Birds of East Africa*; *Field Guide to the Butterflies of Africa*; *National Parks of East Africa* (all HarperCollins, UK). *Birds* is the standard spotter's tome. *Butterflies* is exotic and useful – if you can get hold of a copy. *National Parks* covers parks, reserves, mammals and birds, but there's too much space devoted to long lists of fauna, and the practical details for the parks are too dated to be of any use.

Zimmerman, Turner and Pearson *A Field Guide to the Birds of Kenya and Northern Tanzania* (Adlard Coles Nautical, UK). Comprehensive coverage in a brand new paperback edition.

Colonial writers

★ **Isak Dinesen (Karen Blixen)** *Out of Africa* (Penguin, UK/Vintage, US). This has become something of a cult book, particularly in the wake of the movie. First published in 1937, it describes Blixen's life (Dinesen was a nom de plume)

on her Ngong Hills coffee farm between the wars. Read today, it seems to hover uncertainly between contemporary literature and historical document. It's an intense read – lyrical, introspective, sometimes obnoxiously and intricately racist, but worth pursuing and never superficial, unlike the film. Karen Blixen's own *Letters from Africa 1914–1931* (trans. Anne Born, Chicago UP, US) gives posthumous insights.

Harry Hook *The Kitchen Toto* (o/p). By way of an antidote to a surfeit of settlers' yarns, this screenplay tells the story of Mwangi, a Kikuyu house-boy caught up in the early stages of the Mau Mau rebellion. Writer-director Hook's movie is as keen as a country *panga* and draws masterful performances from a largely unknown cast.

Elspeth Huxley *The Flame Trees of Thika* (o/p); *The Mottled Lizard* (o/p). Based on her own childhood, from a prolific author who also wrote numerous works on colonial history and society, including *White Man's Country*, a biography of the settlers' doyen, *Lord Delamere*, and *Out in the Midday Sun: My Kenya*, both as readable, if also predictable, as any. Her last book, *Nine Faces of Kenya* (Harvill, UK) is a somewhat dewy-eyed anthology of colonial East African ephemera. More interesting is the collection of her mother's letters, *Nellie's Story*, which includes some compelling coverage of the Mau Mau years from the pen of a likeably eccentric settler.

Beryl Markham *West with the Night* (Penguin, UK/Northpoint, US).

Markham made the first east–west solo flight across the Atlantic. This is her only book about her life in the interwar Kenya colony, drawing together adventures, landscapes and contemporary figures. Not great literature, but highly evocative.

Richard Meinertzhagen *Kenya Diary 1902–1906* (o/p). The haunting day-to-day narrative of a young British officer in the protectorate. Meinertzhagen's brutal descriptions of "punitive expeditions" are chillingly matter-of-fact and make the endless tally of his wildlife slaughter pale inoffensively in comparison. As a reminder of the savagery that accompanied the British intrusion, and a stark insight into the complex mind of one of its perpetrators, this is disturbing, highly recommended reading. Good photos, too.

Judith Thurman *Isak Dinesen: The Life of a Story Teller* (Penguin, UK/Picador, US). A biography that sets the record straighter and was the source of much of the material for the *Out of Africa* film.

Errol Trzebinski *The Lives of Beryl Markham* (Mandarin, UK/Norton, US). In which, among much else, it is suggested that Markham did not, and could not, have written *West with the Night*.

Kenyan fiction in English

Chinua Achebe and C.L. Innes (editors) *African Short Stories* (Heinemann, UK/US). A collection which treats its material geographically, including Kenyan stories from Jomo Kenyatta, Grace Ogot, Ngugi and a spooky offering (*The Spider's Web*) from Leonard Kibera, brother

of Sam Kahiga (a short story by whom appears on p.707).

Thomas Akare *The Slums* (o/p). A bleaker read than Mwangi, but also more humane. Without quotation marks, the dialogue melds seamlessly into the narrative; no doubts about the authentic rhythms of Kenyan English here. But much is assumed to be understood and there's much that won't be, unless you're sitting under a 25-watt light bulb in a River Road B&L.

Lalage Bown (editor) *Two Centuries of African English* (o/p). Includes non-fiction extracts from the work of J. M. Kariuki (*Mau Mau Detainee* – see p.696), Ali Mazrui on intellectuals and revolution, Githende Mockerie and R. Mugo Gatheru recounting their childhoods, and Tom Mboya on Julius Nyerere, first president of Tanzania.

Charlotte H. Bruner (editor) *Unwinding Threads: Writing by Women in Africa* (Heinemann, UK/US). Also geographical, with succinct introductions to each region. East Africa features Kenyan writers Charity Waciuma and the excellent Grace Ogot, whose *The Rain Came* is a bewitching mystery myth, combining traditional Luo tales with her own fiction in a perplexingly "Western" form. There's a new Heinemann collection edited by Bruner, entitled *African Women's Writing*.

Sam Kahiga *Flight to Juba – Short Stories* (Longman, Kenya); *The Girl from Abroad* (o/p). Vital, exasperating, obnoxious and plain crazy – a writer to love to hate (see excerpted story, p.707).

John Kiriamiti *My Life in Crime* (Spear, Kenya) This racy autobiographical account, penned in prison by a professional robber, was so successful that the author went on to write two novels (*Son of Fate* and *The Sinister Trophy*) plus an account of his time as a villain told from his fiancée's point of view (*My Life with a Criminal: Millie's Story*).

J. Roger Kurtz *Urban Obsessions, Urban Fears: the postcolonial Kenyan*

novel (James Currey, UK/Africa World Press, US). Explores the relationship between Kenyan fiction in English and the city of Nairobi. Includes a comprehensive bibliography of all the Kenyan novels in English since Ngugi's *Weep Not, Child* was first published in 1964.

Bramwell Lusweti *The Way to the Town Hall* (Macmillan, Kenya). Enjoyable satire aimed at small-town politicians and businessmen. A Swahili dictionary (to translate the characters' names) is a help.

Marjorie Oludhe Macgoye *Victoria* and *Murder in Majengo* (Macmillan, UK). Two novels – available in one volume – putting a Luo woman's view on life in Kenya from one of the country's few published women writers.

Charles Mangua *Son of Woman* (Spear, Kenya) Less down and out, but a lot more "street" than Meja Mwangi, Mangua tells the tale of a son of a prostitute and his misadventures: hard-bitten and cynical, but engaging nonetheless. In a very different style, his second novel, *A Tail in the Mouth*, looks at the Mau Mau rebellion through the eyes of a young man caught up in it and swept along by events.

Ali Mazrui *The Trial of Christopher Okigbo* (o/p). A clever "novel of ideas" from the US-based political scientist, who always succeeds in infuriating both critics of Kenya and its supporters. His book, *Cultural Forces in World Politics* (James Currey, UK/Heinemann, US) is a survey of cultural and political ideas which also addresses the issues surrounding Salman Rushdie's *Satanic Verses*.

David Mulwa *Master and Servant* (o/p). Growing up in colonial Kenya: a funny and affecting string of episodes.

Ngugi wa Thiong'o

Ngugi wa Thiong'o, the dominant figure of modern Kenyan literature, currently lives in the USA: although his books in English are not banned in Kenya, his political sympathies are not welcome.

Ngugi's work is art serving the revolution – didactic, brusque, graphic and unsentimental. His novels, especially the later ones, are unforgiving: the touch of humour that would leaven the polemic rarely comes to the rescue. Powerful themes – exploitation, betrayal, cultural oppression, the imposition of Christianity, loss of and search for identity – drive the stories along urgently. Characters deal with real events and the changes of their time, struggling to come to terms with the influences at work on their lives.

Ngugi's style is heady, idealistic and undaunted, never teasing or capricious. Disillusioned with English, his first work in Kikuyu, in collaboration with Ngugi wa Mirii, was the play *Ngahiika Ndeenda* (*I will Marry When I Want*), and its public performance by illiterate peasants at the Kamiriithu Cultural Centre in Limuru got him detained for a year. Ngugi's work in the Kikuyu language is now banned, or rarely available, in Kenya.

Most of Ngugi's writings in English are published in the paperback Heinemann African Writers series. Try *Secret Lives* (Heinemann, UK) for short stories, *Weep not, child* (Heinemann, UK) for a brief but glowing early novel or, for the mature Ngugi, *Petals of Blood* (Heinemann, UK/EP Dutton, US) – a richly satisfying detective story that is at the same time a saga of wretchedness and struggle (see p.703 for an excerpt). Others include *The River Between* (Heinemann, UK), on the old Kikuyu society and the coming of the Europeans; *A Grain of Wheat* (Heinemann, UK), about the eve of Independence; *Devil on the Cross* (Heinemann, UK, written in detention on scraps of toilet paper); and *Matigari* (The Patriots). *Matigari*, first published in Kikuyu by Heinemann in 1986 (published in the US by Africa World Press), had a remarkable effect in the Central Highlands. Rumours circulated that a man, Matigari, was spreading militant propaganda against the government. The police even tried to track him down, before realizing their mistake and confiscating all copies of the book.

Apart from *I will Marry When I Want*, Ngugi has written two other plays, *The Black Hermit* and *The Trial of Dedon Kimathi* (with Micere Mugo). Academic works include *Moving the Centre* (o/p), a collection of essays. Ngugi's contribution to Kenyan literature is enormous, and delving in is rewarding, if not always easy.

Mude Dae Mude *The Hills are Falling* (Kenya Literature Bureau, Nairobi). Life from Marsabit to Nairobi.

★ **Meja Mwangi** *Going Down River Road*; *Carcase for Hounds*; *Kill Me Quick* (all in Heinemann's African Writers series, UK/US, the latter two titles now o/p). Mwangi is lighter and more accessible than Ngugi, his fiction infused with the absurdities of urban Nairobi slum life. *Going Down River Road* is the best known: convincing scenes, chaotic action and sharp dialogue (though it's never clear whether the English/American street cool is meant to be real, or an effort to render the Swahili-Kikuyu "Sheng" slang of the slums). Great in situ reading. Mwangi was shortlisted for the Commonwealth Writers' Prize, with *Striving for the Wind* (1992), set in a rural rather than urban location.

★ **Ngugi wa Thiong'o** *Decolonising the Mind: The Politics of Language in African Literature* (Heinemann, UK/US). Ngugi has long been closely associated with attempts to move Kenyan literature and African literature in general towards expression in the readers' mother tongues (see box opposite).

Kenneth Watene *Sunset on the Manyatta* (East African Publishing House, Kenya). A Maasai man in Germany.

Kenyan poetry

The oldest form of written poetry in Kenya is from the coast. **Swahili poetry** reads beautifully even if you don't understand the words. Written for at least 300 years, and sung for a good deal longer, it's one of Kenya's most enduring art forms. An *Anthology of Swahili Poetry* has been compiled and rather wood-enly translated by **Ali A Jahadmy** (o/p), but some of Swahili's best-known classical compositions from the Lamu Archipelago are included, with pertinent background. There's a more enjoyable anthology of romantic and erotic verse, *A Choice of Flowers*, with **Jan Knappert's** idiosyncratic translations and inter-pretations (o/p), and the same linguist's *Four Centuries of Swahili Verse* (Darf, UK & US), which expounds and creatively interprets at much greater length. A translation of an exquisite poem from the latter is included on p.711.

Up-country poetry in the sense of written verse is a recent form. But oral folk literature was often relayed in the context of music, rhythm and dance.

Wole Soyinka (editor) *Poems of Black Africa* (Heinemann, UK). A hefty and catholic selection. Its Kenyan component includes the work of Abangira, Jared Angira, Jonathan Kariara and Amin Kassam.

Heinemann Book of African Poetry (Heinemann, UK/US). Includes the work of Kenyan poet Marjorie Oludhe Macgoye.

Kenya in modern western fiction

★ **Justin Cartwright** *Masai Dreaming* (Picador, UK/Random House, US). A com-pelling novel juxtaposing a film-maker's vision of Maasai-land with the barbarities of the Holocaust, linked by the tapes of a Jewish anthropologist.

Jeremy Gavron *Moon* (Penguin, UK). Vivid short novel about a white boy growing up on a farm during the Emergency.

Martha Gellhorn *The Weather in Africa* (Eland, UK). Three absorbing novellas, each dealing with aspects of the Europe–Africa relationship, set on the slopes of Kilimanjaro, in the "White Highlands" of Kenya and on the tourist coast north of Mombasa.

David Lambkin *The Hanging Tree* (Penguin, UK/Counterpoint, US). A human-nature-through-the-ages saga which makes a good yarn – in fact, several yarns.

★ **John Le Carré** *The Constant Gardener* (Hodder Headline, UK). The spymaster turns his hand to a whodunnit, in which a cam-paigner against the misdeeds of Western drug companies in Kenya is raped and murdered. Her husband, a British diplomat in Nairobi, fails to believe official explanations and starts his own investigation. Effectively banned in Kenya, the novel is brilliantly crafted, though not always convincing in its portrayal of today's expat society.

Paul Meyer *Herdsboy* (Northwest Publishing, US). American tourist "finds herself captive of a native tribe". A pacey first novel, set in Samburu-land, that overcomes the jacket description.

Maria Thomas *Come to Africa and Save Your Marriage* (Serpent's Tail, UK/Soho Press, US). Most of these tales are set in Kenya or Tanzania. Thomas's characters are solid, but the stories leave a wearying aftertaste as if there were nothing positive to be had from the expatriate experience. Her first novel, *Antonia Saw the Oryx First*, is painfully detailed – a good antidote to *Out of Africa*.

Barbara Wood *Green City in the Sun* (Pan, UK) A white settler family come into conflict with a Kikuyu medicine woman in one of the few credible novels about the realities of colonial Kenya by a *mzungu* writer.

History and peoples

Kenya in African history

Basil Davidson *Let Freedom Come: Africa in Modern History* (o/p). Lucidly argued and very readable summary of nineteenth- and twentieth-century events.

Christopher Hibbert *Africa Explored: Europeans in the Dark Continent 1769–1889* (o/p). Entertaining read, devoted in large part to the "discovery" of east and central Africa.

Alan Moorehead *The White Nile* (Penguin, UK/Adventure Library, US). a riveting account of the search for the source and European rivalries for control in the region.

Roland Oliver and J. D. Fage *A Short History of Africa* (Penguin, UK/US). Dated, but still the standard paperback introduction.

Thomas Pakenham *The Scramble for Africa* (Abacus, UK). The story of how the European powers rushed to conquer and exploit Africa in the name of commerce, Christianity and civilization, in the last two decades of the nineteenth century. Not specifically about Kenya, but extremely relevant to Kenyan history.

Kenya in general

Jeffrey A. Fadiman *When We Began There Were Witchmen* (California University Press, US). Recounts the story of the Meru people from their mythical origins in Shungwaya in northeastern Kenya to the decimation of Meru culture by a tiny handful of missionaries and colonial administrators.

Fedders and Salvadori *People and*

Cultures of Kenya (o/p). A useful tribe-by-tribe introduction.

Terry Hirst *The Struggle for Nairobi* (Mazingira Institute, Kenya). Sort of large-format "Nairobi for Beginners" that manages to make town planning (or the lack of it) fascinating, bringing together a mass of otherwise hard-to-get information about the city's growth.

Kenya's People (series of ten pamphlets, Evans, Kenya). Simple and reliable background on ten of Kenya's peoples. Aimed at Kenyan secondary schools, they're pitched just right for culturally uninitiated visitors.

Jomo Kenyatta *Facing Mount Kenya* (Vintage, UK). A traditional, functionalist, anthropological monograph, but written by a member of the society in question – in this case, the Kikuyu – under the supervision of Bronislaw Malinowski at the London School of Economics, shortly before World War II. One of the few scholarly works ever written on traditional Kikuyu culture, this is as interesting for the insights it offers on its author as for its quite readable content. Good Kikuyu glossary.

Maxon and Ofcansky *Historical Dictionary of Kenya* (Scarecrow Press, US). From a reliable series that covers nearly every African country, this is an A to Z of Kenya's history. Includes an extensive bibliography.

William R. Ochieng *A History of Kenya* (o/p). Somewhat pedestrian, but the best general overview from prehistory to 1980, with useful maps and photos to show the way. *A Modern History of Kenya 1895–1980* (o/p) covers the twentieth century in eight chapters – solid enough up to the middle of Kenyatta's reign.

William R. Ochieng (editor) *Themes in Kenyan History* (o/p). A new collection of writings by historians and other academics, all teaching in Kenyan universities.

Thomas Spear and Richard Waller (editors) *Being Maasai* (James Currey, UK/Ohio University Press, US). Articles about Maasai identity – a subtle and interesting field, and vital reading for anyone concerned with the ethnic politics of modern Kenya.

Coastal history

G. S. P. Freeman-Grenville *The East African Coast* (o/p). If you're heading for the coast, this is fascinating – a series of accounts from the first century to the nineteenth – vivid and often extraordinary.

Sarah Mirza and Margaret Strobel *Three Swahili Women* (Indiana University Press, US). Three histories of ritual, three women's lives. Born between 1890 and 1920 into different social backgrounds, these biographies document enormous changes from the most important of neglected viewpoints.

James de Vere Allen *Swahili Origins: Swahili Culture and the Shungwaya Phenomenon* (James Currey, UK/Ohio University Press, US). The life work of a challenging and readable scholar, bound to raise a fascinating field of study to new prominence.

Protectorate and colonial Kenya

James Fox *White Mischief* (Vintage, UK). Investigative romp through the events surrounding the notorious unsolved murder of Lord Errol, one of Kenya's most aristocratic settlers, at Karen in 1941. Well told and highly revealing of British Kenyan society of the time. Michael Radford's 1987 film version is equally enjoyable, and a good deal more stimulating than the *Out of Africa* movie.

Charles Miller *The Lunatic Express* (o/p). The story of *that* railway. Miller narrates the drama of one of the great feats of Victorian engineering – as bizarre and as madly magnificent as any Wild West epic – adding weight with a broad historical background of East Africa from the year dot. The same author's *The Battle for the Bundu* (o/p) follows a little-known corner of World War I, as fought out on the plains of Tsavo between British Kenya and German Tanganyika – immensely readable.

Errol Trzebinski *The Kenya Pioneers* (o/p). Despite academic pretensions, this is something of a paean to the early settlers.

The Mau Mau rebellion

Bruce Berman *Control and Crisis in Modern Kenya* (James Currey, UK/Ohio University Press, US). A study of the growth of state control, from the 1890s through to interwar crisis and postwar disintegration.

Donald L. Barnett and Karari Njama *Mau Mau from Within: Autobiography and Analysis of Kenya's Peasant Revolt* (o/p). An account based on personal recollections.

Robert B. Edgerton *Mau Mau: An African Crucible* (o/p). An account of the revolt based on guerrillas' testimonies. Includes explorations of the role of women and class formation in modern Kenya.

Frank Furedi *The Mau Mau War in Perspective* (James Currey, UK/Ohio University Press, US). Furedi analyses, using new archival sources, the continued struggle for land redistribution once the struggle for Independence had been won.

Tabitha Kanogo *Squatters and the Roots of Mau Mau 1905–63* (James Currey, UK/Ohio University Press, US). Delves into the early years of the "White Highlands" to show how resistance, and the conditions for revolt, were built into the relations between the settler land-grabbers and the peasant farmers and herders ("squatters") they usurped. Strong on the role of women in the Mau Mau movement.

J. M. Kariuki *Mau Mau Detainee: The Account by a Kenya African of His Experience in Detention Camps* (o/p). A remarkably forbearing account of life and death in the detention camps. Kariuki's vision for the future of Kenya and his loyalty to Kenyatta have a special irony after his assassination in 1975.

★ **David Throup** *Economic and Social Origins of Mau Mau* (James Currey, UK/Ohio University Press, US). An examination of the story from the end of World War II, covering the colonial mentality and differences in efficiency between peasant cash-cropping and more wasteful plantation agriculture.

Post Independence

Jean Davison *Voices from Mutira: Change in the Lives of Rural Gikuyu Women 1910–1995* (Lynne Rienner, US). Rich, unselfconsciously moving and particularly interesting for the attitudes it documents on brideprice and genital mutilation.

Anthony Howarth *Kenyatta: A Photographic Biography* (o/p). A roughly hewn biography composed of an amalgam of black-and-white photographs, news clippings and quotations. It doesn't pretend to be exhaustive, but manages to capture the spirit of the leader and the struggle for Independence.

Kenneth King *Jua Kali Kenya* (James Currey, UK/Ohio University Press, US). First serious study of Kenya's important informal sector – the self-employed fixers and manufacturers who work under the "hot sun" (the *jua kali*). Great photos.

Tom Mboya *The Challenge of Nationhood* (Heinemann, UK/US). The vision of Kenya's best-loved statesman – and a Luo – assassinated in 1969 for looking like a clear successor to Kenyatta.

Andrew Morton *Moi: the Making of an African Statesman* (Michael O'Mara, UK/US). Strange subject for the author of *Diana: Her True Story* and a strangely compelling book is the result. While it would be impossible to deny this is a sycophantic biography – Morton's reported conversations with Moi usually dry up just as the reader formulates the critical question – simply getting access to the notoriously defensive president was remarkable in itself. The research is here; there are insights, but also too many factual inaccuracies (including the notion that "the Kalenjin are a homogenous tribe", a political hot potato Morton swallows whole not to cast a shadow of doubt over the whole account.

Jeremy-Murray Brown *Kenyatta* (o/p), and David Goldsworthy *Tom Mboya: The Man Who Kenya Wanted to Forget* (Africana, US), are

the two big biographies: both weighty and deeply researched.

★ Ngugi wa Thiong'o *Detained – A Writer's Prison Diary* (Heinemann, UK). A retrospective of Kenya's history up to 1978, woven into the daily routine of political detention during Kenyatta's last year. Ngugi discourses widely and, while his reflections are occasionally pedantic or obscure and sometimes written with almost religious fervour, he hits home often. His *Barrel of a Pen: Resistance to Repression in Neo-Colonial Kenya* (Africa World Press, US) hones some of his points sharply (see also the box on p.692).

Oginga Odinga *Not Yet Uhuru* (o/p). The classic critique of Kenya's direction at the time it was written.

Bethuel Ogot and William Ochieng (editors) *Decolonization and Independence in Africa 1940–93* (James Currey, UK/Ohio University Press, US). The standard work on these years, asking how much Kenya's – and other countries' – difficulties are linked to the colonial past and the process of growing away from it.

★ Geoff Sayer *Kenya: Promised Land?* (Oxfam GB, UK/Humanities Press International, US). Concise, readable essays – newspaper-article length with good photography, properly captioned – that get right to the point about the issues that make Kenya the fascinatingly problematic place it is.

WorldFocus *Kenya* (Heinemann, UK). Children's introduction to the country – one of a series for the seven-plus age group – written with style and intelligence, and incorporating good photos and case studies of real people.

Arts

Jane Barbour and Simiyu Wandibba *Kenyan Pots and Potters* (o/p). This comprehensive description of pot-making communities includes techniques, training, marketing and sociological perspectives.

Roy Braverman *Islam and Tribal Art* (o/p). A useful paperback text for the dedicated.

Susan Denyer *African Traditional Architecture* (Holmes & Meier, UK). Useful and interesting, with hundreds of photos (most of them old) and detailed line drawings.

Frank Willett *African Art* (Thames & Hudson, UK/US). An accessible volume; good value, with a generous illustrations–text ratio.

Geoffrey Williams *African Designs from Traditional Sources* (Dover, UK/US). A designer's and enthusiast's sourcebook, from the copyright-free publishers.

Mountain, hiking and diving guides

Paul Clarke *Mountains of Kenya* (Mountain Club of Kenya). A detailed and practical guide, comprehensively updated since its earlier incarnation and well worth buying if you plan to do any Kenyan hiking.

David Else *Trekking in East Africa* (Lonely Planet, UK/US). Well-produced guide to hiking in the region, with good coverage of Mount Kenya and less extensive coverage of other areas.

Guide Book to Mount Kenya and Kilimanjaro (Mountain Club of Kenya). For fully equipped alpinism, this is indispensable.

Anton Koornhof *The Dive Sites of East Africa* (New Holland, UK). Highly recommended if you're at all taken by snorkelling or diving, with detailed text on each and every major site in Kenya, Tanzania and Zanzibar, beautifully illustrated and with thoughtful sections on environmental matters. One to make you dream.

Coffee-table books

Mohamed Amin *Cradle of Mankind* and *Portrait of Kenya* (Camerapix, UK). Stunning photographs of the Lake Turkana region, by the award-winning maverick photo-journalist Amin, killed in the Comoros plane hijack in 1997.

Anne Arthus-Bertrand and Anne Spoerry, photos by Yann Arthus-Bertrand *Kenya from the Air* (Thames and Hudson, UK/Vendome, US). Superb images of the country from the eagle's viewpoint.

★ **Mitsuaki Iwago** *Serengeti* (Chronicle, US). Stunning scenes and portraits from Serengeti (the Tanzanian continuation of the Maasai Mara) from a master photographer. Simply the best volume of wildlife photography ever assembled, this makes most glossies look feeble. If you're trying to persuade someone to visit East Africa – or if any aesthetic argument were needed to preserve the parks and animals – this is the book to use.

⭐ David Keith Jones *Shepherds of the Desert* (Hamish Hamilton, UK). Brilliant photos (many in black and white), with a text more lucid and less superficial than most glossies; this book concerns itself only with northern Kenya.

Brian Jackman and Jonathan Scott *The Marsh Lions* (o/p). Beautifully produced and painstakingly researched study of the lions and other animals around the Musiara Marsh in Maasai Mara.

Tepilit Ole Saitoti and Carol Beckwith *Maasai* (Harvill, UK/Abradale Press, US). *The* Maasai coffee-table book; some photos are too much to take at reading distance. Exquisite, but largely staged, portraits of Maasai culture (and even Beckwith's camera can't disguise the tourist souvenirs in the background). Variably interesting, chauvinistic text, which plays the cult value of the Maasai for all it's worth.

Writing from Kenya

Very little Kenyan literature appeared in print before World War II. But while East Africa has tended to lag behind the rest of the continent in modern forms – the novel, short stories, drama and modern poetry – there's a rich tradition of oral literature and a specifically coastal Swahili verse culture that put African stories into writing as long as three hundred years ago.

The oral tradition in print

With the exception of the coast, precolonial Kenyan literature was entirely oral, and stories were passed – and modified – from generation to generation. These **folk tales**, commonly told by the leaders of the community to the children, were very often "trickster" tales about animals. While they frequently contained a moral, their main purpose was to entertain.

The hare's practical joke

A long, long time ago, there were two people who were very good friends. One was Mr. Hare and the other Mr. Hyena. They used to visit each other and on each of these visits, the Hare used to carry in his bag some honey and sweetened meat. He used to put his little finger in the bag and give his friend to lick. Said the Hare: "Brother, I have something very, very sweet in my bag here. Take it and see for yourself." The Hyena liked it very much.

"Hi, Hi, Brother Hare, give me some more, more I say. It is very, very . . ."

"No, no, this is a sweetness that you must have a little at a time."

And the same thing happened day after day for many days. One day, the Hare came on as usual and said:

"Brother Hyena, may I give you something very, very sweet, sweeter than sweetness itself?"

"Yes, my good friend, I'd love some very, very much." And the Hare gave his sweetened finger to the Hyena to lick.

"Oh, Hare, my very good friend do give me more."

"No, no, old man, you cannot eat much of this sweetness. It is a sweetness that must be eaten sparingly."

"But brother, where do you get much much sweetness?"

"I get it from those mountains you see above our heads," pointing at the white clouds. "Once you eat this sweetness you should never pass piss or shit because then the sweetness gets lost."

"Then what do people do so that they do not pass out piss or shit after they have eaten this sweetness?"

"Ah, Mr. Hyena, that is very simple, they have their bottoms sewn up and if you want, I can do the sewing up for you."

"Yes, yes, do sew it up for me." And the Hare sewed the Hyena's bottom.

They took three bags each and the Hare led the way to the sweetness that never passes. Now the Hyena ate the honey, the honeycombs and the dead bees. Then the Hare said: "Now that we have filled our stomachs and our bags let us go home." Now when they were on the way, the Hyena went down to the stream to drink some water. And when he drank he just dropped down like a stump of a tree. He stayed and stayed and stayed there; his eyes popping out like sweet potatoes. He stayed there for so many days, until he thought he was going to die.

One day he saw the Eagle coming down to drink some water – said he: "Good Brother Eagle, help me."

"Hi, brother, how shall I help you?"

"Come round behind me at my bottom end. You will see a string going right through it, prick it and pull carefully because I feel pain. I was sewn up by the Hare and he did a very bad thing."

Now as soon as the Eagle touched this string a flood of piss and shit rushed out and covered the Eagle and the piss was like a mountain with the Eagle as the core.

One day there was a heavy rain which washed away the piss and shit, slowly by slowly until the Eagle emerged with a scratch on the neck. He flew away swearing revenge on the Hyena. For many days he and the Hyena played hide and seek until one day the Hyena, being the foolish person, forgot that he was the sworn enemy of the Eagle. The Eagle being clever did not want a physical contact with the Hyena. He knew very well that the Hyena was stronger than him. Now he started to show the Hyena the choice pieces of meat that he carried in his bag and every day he gave a little to the Hyena saying: "Brother, I carry this kind of meat, have a bite" and the Hyena said: "Brother Eagle, these delicacies, this choice meat you give me, where does it come from?"

"Now, Brother Hyena, these delicacies, the choice meats are very, very many. If you like, I can take you where they come from. But," continued the Eagle, "it is impossible to get that meat alone. You must come too. Now go and collect all your people. Let them bring bags, tins and drums. Then we shall bring as much meat as will last for three years."

The Hyena was very happy and he ran to collect all his people. Panting: "Do you see all that meat above? My friend brings it to me every day. Now this friend has told me to collect all my people so that we can go and fetch this meat. Let each one of you bring tins, bags or drums and I, with your permission, will ask the Eagle to mention the day on which we can go."

Said all Hyenas: "Hi, we also would like to eat the white choice meat."

All the Hyenas of that country had gathered together and when they saw the Eagle coming towards them they said: "Now, Brother Eagle, let us go to get this meat. Tell us when we can go".

The Eagle said, "We shall go on the third day from today. Be ready."

On that day the Hyena gathered and the Eagle arranged them in a line according to age, the smallest one being put at the back. The Eagle was right in front. He said to the Hyena behind him: "Now, Brother, hold tight to the feathers of my tail," and the Hyena held tight. "Everybody hold each other's tail," he shouted and then he flew up, up, up, and heading to the choice meats in the sky. Now when they had gone very high, the Eagle asked:

"Are you all clear off the ground?"

"No, no, some are still touching the ground." He flew, flew and flew.

"Can you see the earth?"

"Yes, yes, we can see it." The Eagle was waiting to hear that all the Hyenas could no longer see the earth.

"Can you see the earth?"

"We see it dimly now." The Eagle flew and flew.

"Do you still see the earth?"

"We see only black, black darkness, we cannot tell where the earth is."

The Eagle knew then that the distance from the earth was very, very great. Then he said to the Hyena behind him:

"Hi, hi, my friend, a scratch, a scratch on my back wing," and the Hyena behind let go the tail feathers of the Eagle. Suddenly the whole line of Hyenas went tumbling down. Kuru Kuru Kuru like the sound of thunder. Some Hyenas crushed their limbs, their bones and died instantly. Some died before they reached the earth. Only the last Hyena was left, but she acquired a limp in the leg which she carries to this day.

Reprinted from *Kikuyu Folktales*, edited and translated by Rose Gecau. By permission of Kenya Literature Bureau.

Hare and hornbill

Hare and Hornbill were great friends. One day Hare said: "My friend, we have looked for girls all over this land, and there are none that are good enough for you and me. Let us go up to Skyland, perhaps we will find some suitable ones."

Hornbill replied: "I know it is getting a bit late for us to get married, but you know my problem, you know I have this terrible thing!"

"You mean your chronic diarrhoea? But that is nothing to worry about." Hare produced a cork of the right size and blocked up Hornbill's anus.

The two friends made preparations for the journey, and after saying good-bye to their families, Hare got on Hornbill's back and they flew up through the clouds into Skyland. There was a big marriage dance. Hare and Hornbill put on their dancing costumes and went straight into the arena. Hornbill danced gracefully, touching the ground lightly and moving his wings up and down to the rhythm of the drums. His neck swayed this way and that way, and his eyes sparkled with love. Hare danced as best he could, but he could not follow the rhythm of the dance, and sang out of tune; moreover, his big ears looked funny. Beautiful girls fought to dance before Hornbill, but none came anywhere near Hare; and when he approached the girls they ran away from him. That night Hornbill slept with a very pretty girl. Hare slept cold.

The next day Hornbill won two girls; Hare again slept cold. The next night when Hornbill was asleep, resting beside his fourth lover, Hare tip-toed into the house and unhooked the cork. Three days' accumulation of diarrhoea spewed out and flooded the entire house. The stench rose like smoke and the dancers fled from the arena, and Hornbill woke up, and in great shame flew down through the clouds, leaving Hare behind.

There was much commotion as the Skylanders tried to find out what had happened. Hare denied all knowledge of the cause of the trouble.

"But where is your handsome friend?" they asked.

"I am also looking for him," said Hare, adding, "I must find him otherwise it will be a bit difficult to return to earth."

When they failed to find Hornbill the Skylanders decided to get rid of Hare by lowering him down to earth on a rope of plaited grass. The girls cut many heaps of grass. They made the rope and tied one end around Hare's waist and continued to plait the other end as Hare was lowered downwards. The Skylanders gave Hare a drum and told him, "As soon as you reach the earth beat this drum very hard so that the girls may stop plaiting the rope." Hare thanked the Skylanders, said good-bye and began his homeward journey.

Hare descended slowly through the clouds, but on seeing the faint tips of the highest mountain he hit the drum very hard. The skylanders stopped plaiting and dropped the rope. Hare came hurtling down like a falling stone. But just before hitting the ground he cried to the smallest black ants, "Collect me! Collect me! Collect . . ."

Hare hit the ground and broke up into many many very small pieces. The smallest black ants collected the pieces and put them together again, and Hare became alive. But today when Hare is running you hear his chest making crackling sounds, because the bones of his chest were not put together properly.

Reprinted from *Hare and Hornbill*, a collection of folk tales edited and translated by Okot p'Bitek. By permission of Heinemann Educational Books.

Petals of Blood

Ngugi wa Thiong'o is Kenya's best-known writer and one of the country's most consistently outspoken critics. The following extract from the satirical *Petals of Blood* has been taken from the middle of the book. The people of Ilmorog, a village in the Rift Valley, are beginning to appreciate the power and influence of the New Kenya.

Changes come to Ilmorog

Munira folded the newspaper and went to Wanja's place to break the news. He felt for her and Nyakinyua. He did not expect favours. He just wanted to take her the news. And to find out more about it. She was not at her Theng'eta premises. Abdulla told him that she had gone to Nyakinyua's hut. Munira walked there and found other people. News of the threatened sale must have reached them too. They had come to commiserate with her and others similarly affected, to weep with one another. They looked baffled: how could a bank sell their land? A bank was not a government: from whence then, its powers? Or maybe it was the government, an invisible government, some others suggested. They turned to Munira. But he could not answer their question. He only talked about a piece of paper, they had surrendered to the bank. But he could not answer, put to sleep, the bitter scepticism in their voices and looks. What kind of monster was this bank that was a power unto itself, that could uproot lives of a thousand years?

He went back and tried to drink Theng'eta, but it did not have the taste. He remembered that recently he had seen Wambui carting stones to earn bread for the day and he wondered what would happen to the old woman. She was too old to sell her labour and sweat in a market.

"The old woman? Nyakinyua?" Munira echoed Karega's question, slowly. "She died! She is dead!" he added quickly, almost aggressively, waking up from his memories.

Karega's face seemed to move.

Nyakinyua, the old woman, tried to fight back. She tramped from hut to hut calling upon the peasants of Ilmorog to get together and fight it out. They looked at her and they shook their heads: whom would they fight now? The Government? The Banks? KCO? The Party Nderi? Yes who would they really fight? But she tried to convince them that all these were one and that she would fight them. Her land would never be settled by strangers. There was something grand, and defiant, in the woman's action – she with her failing health and flesh trying to organise the dispossessed of Ilmorog into a protest. But there was pathos in the exercise. Those whose land had not yet been taken looked nervously aloof and distant. One or two even made disparaging remarks about an old woman not quite right in the head. Others genuinely not seeing the point of a march to Ruwaini or to the big City restrained her. She could not walk all the way, they told her. But she said: "I'll go alone . . . my man fought the white man. He paid for it with his blood . . . I'll struggle against these black oppressors . . . alone . . . alone . . ."

What would happen to her, Munira wondered.

He need not have worried about her. Nyakinyua died peacefully in her sleep a few days after the news of the bank threat. Rumour went that she had told Wanja about the impending journey: she had said that she could not even think of being buried in somebody else's land: for what would her man say to her when she met him on the other side? People waited for the bank to come and sell her land. But on the day of the sale Wanja redeemed the land and became the heroine of the new and the old Ilmorog.

Later Munira was to know.

But at that time only Abdulla really knew the cost: Wanja had offered to sell him her rights to their jointly owned New Building. He did not have the money and it was he who suggested that they sell the whole building to a third person and divide the income between them.

So Wanja was back to her beginnings.

And Mzigo was the new proud owner of the business premises in Ilmorog.

Wanja was not quite the same after her recent loss. For a time, she continued the proud proprietor of the old Theng'eta place. Her place still remained the meat-roasting centre. Dance steps in the hall could still raise dust to the roof, especially when people were moving to their favourite tunes:

How beautiful you are, my love!
How soft your round eyes are, my honey!
What a pleasant thing you are,
Lying here
Shaded by this cedar bush!
But oh, darling,
What poison you carry between your legs!

But Wanja's heart was not in it. She started building a huge wooden bungalow at the lower end of her shamba, some distance from the shanty town that was growing up around Abdulla's shop, the lodgings and the meat-roasting centre, almost as a natural growth complement to the more elegant new Ilmorog. People said that she was wise to invest in a building the money remaining after redeeming her grandmother's shamba: but what was it for? She already had a hut further up the shamba, hidden from the noise and inquisitive eyes of the New Ilmorog by a thick natural hedge. She went about her work without taking anybody into her confidence. But it was obvious that it was built in the style of a living house with several spacious rooms. Later she moved in: she planted flower gardens all around and had electric lights fixed there. It was beautiful: it was a brave effort so soon after her double loss, people said.

One night the band struck up a song they had composed on their first arrival. As they played, the tune and the words seemed to grow fresher and fresher and the audience clapped and whistled and shouted encouragement. The band added innovations and their voices seemed possessed of a wicked carefree devil.

This shamba girl
Was my darling
Told me she loved my sight.
I broke bank vaults for her,
I went to jail for her,
But when I came back
I found her a lady,
Kept by a wealthy roundbelly daddy,
And she told me,
This shamba-lady girl told me,
No, Gosh!
Sikujui

Serikali imebadilishwa
Coup d'état!

They stopped to thunderous handclaps and feet pounding on the floor. Wanja suddenly stood up and asked them to play it again. She started dancing to it, alone, in the arena. People were surprised. They watched the gyrations of her body, speaking pleasure and pain, memories and hopes, loss and gain, unfulfilled longing and desire. The band, responding to the many beating hearts, played with sad maddening intensity as if it were reaching out to her loneliness and solitary struggle. She danced slowly and deliberately toward Munira and he was remembering that time he had seen her dancing to a juke-box at Safari Bar in Kamiritho. As suddenly as she had started, she stopped. She walked to the stage at the bandstand. The "house" was hushed. The customers knew that something big was in the air.

"I am sorry, dear customers, to have to announce the end of the old Ilmorog Bar and meat-roasting centres, and the end of Ilmorog Bar's own Sunshine Band. Chiri County Council says we have to close."

She would not say more. And now they watched her as she walked across the dusty floor toward where Munira was sitting. She stopped, whirled back, and screamed at the band. "Play! Play! Play on. Everybody dance – Daaance!" And she sat down beside Munira.

"Munira, wouldn't you like to come and see my new place tomorrow night?"

Munira could hardly contain himself. So at long last. So the years of waiting were over. It was just like the old days before Karega and the roads and the changes had come to disturb the steamy peaceful rhythm in Ilmorog, when he was the teacher.

The next day he could not teach. He could not talk. He could hardly sit or stand still in one place. And when the time came, he walked to her place with tremulous hands and beating heart. He had not been inside the new house and he felt it an honour that she had chosen him out of all those faces.

He knocked at the door. She was in. She stood in the middle of the room lit by a blue light. For a second he thought himself in the wrong place with the wrong person.

She had on a miniskirt which revealed just about everything, and he felt his manhood rise of itself. On her lips was smudgy red lipstick: her eyebrows were pencilled and painted a luminous blue. What was the game, he wondered? He thought of one of the many advertisements he had earlier collected: Be a platinum blonde: be a whole new you in 100% imported hand-made human hair. Wanja was a really new her.

"You look surprised, Mwalimu. I thought you always wanted me," she said, with a false seductive blur in her voice. Then in a slightly changed voice, more natural, which he could recognise, she added: "That's why you had him dismissed, not so? Look now. They have even taken away my right, well, our right to brew. The County Council says our licence was sold away with the New Building. They also say our present premises are in any case unhygienic! There's going to be a tourist centre and such places might drive visitors away. Do you know the new owner of our Theng'eta breweries? Do you know the owner of the New Ilmorog Utamaduni Centre? Never mind!" She had, once again, changed her voice: "But come: what are you waiting for?" She walked backwards: he followed her and they went into another room – with a double bed and a reddish light. He was hypnotized. He was angry with himself for being tongue-tied and yet he was propelled toward her by the engine-power of his risen body and the drums in the heart. Yet below it all, deep inside, he felt a sensation of shame and disgust at his helplessness.

She removed everything, systematically, piece by piece, and then jumped into bed.

"Come, come, my darling!" she cooed from inside the sheets.

He was about to jump into bed beside her and clasp her to himself, when she suddenly turned cold and chilly, and her voice was menacing.

"No, Mwalimu. No free things in Kenya. A hundred shillings on the table if you want high-class treatment."

He thought she was joking, but as he was about to touch her she added more coldly:

"This is New Kenya. You want it, you pay for it, for the bed and the light and my time and the drink that I shall later give you and the breakfast tomorrow. And all for a hundred shillings. For you. Because of old times. For others it will be more expensive."

He was taken aback, felt the wound of this unexpected humiliation. But now he could not retreat. Her thighs called out to him.

He took out a hundred shillings and handed it to her. He watched her count it and put the money under the mattress. Now panic seized him. His thing had shrivelled. He stood there and tried to fix his mind on the old Wanja, on the one who had danced pain and ecstasy, on the one who had once cried under watchful moonbeams stealing into a hut. She watched him, coldly, with menace, and then suddenly she broke out in her put-on, blurred, seductive voice.

"Come, darling. I'll keep you warm. You are tonight a guest at *Sunshine Lodge*."

There was something pathetic, sad, painful in the tone. But Munira's thing obeyed her voice. Slowly he removed his clothes and joined her in bed. Even as the fire and thirst and hunger in his body were being quenched, the pathetic strain in her voice lingered in the air, in him, in the room everywhere.

It was New Kenya. It was New Ilmorog. Nothing was free. But for a long time, for years to come, he was not to forget the shock and the humiliation of the hour. It was almost like that first time, long ago, when he was only a boy.

Indeed, changes did come to Ilmorog, changes that drove the old one away and ushered a new era in our lives. And nobody could tell, really tell, how it had happened, except that it had happened. With a year or so of the new Ilmorog shopping centre being completed, wheatfields and ranches had sprung up all around the plains: the herdsmen had died or had been driven further afield into the drier parts, but a few had become workers on the wheatfields and ranches on the earth upon which they once roamed freely. The new owners, master-servants of bank power, money and cunning came over at weekends and drove in Landrovers or Range Rovers, depending on the current car fashion, around the farms whose running they had otherwise entrusted to paid managers. The peasants of Ilmorog had also changed. Some had somehow survived the onslaught. They could employ one or two hands on their small farms. Most of the others had joined the army of workers who had added to the growing population of the New Ilmorog. But which New Ilmorog?

There were several Ilmorogs. One was the residential area of the farm managers, County Council officials, public service officers, the managers of Barclays, Standard and African Economic Banks, and other servants of state and money power. This was called Cape Town. The other – called New Jerusalem – was a shanty town of migrant and floating workers, the unemployed, the prostitutes and small traders in tin and scrap metal. Between the New Jerusalem and Cape Town, not far from where Mwathi had once lived guarding the secrets of iron works and native medicine, was All Saints church, now led by

Rev. Jerrod Brown. Also somewhere between the two areas was Wanja's *Sunshine Lodge*, almost as famous as the church.

The shopping and business centre was dominated by two features. Just outside it was a tourist cultural (Utamaduni) village owned by Nderi wa Riera and a West German concern, appropriately called Ilmorog African Diamond Cultural and Educational Tours. Many tourists came for a cultural fiesta. A few hippies also came to look for the Theng'eta Breweries which, starting on the premises owned by Mzingo, had now grown into a huge factory employing six hundred workers with a number of research scientists and chemical engineers. The factory also owned an estate in the plains where they experimented with different types of Theng'eta plants and wheat. They brewed a variety of Theng'eta drinks: from the pure gin for export to cheap but potent drinks for workers and the unemployed. They put some in small plastic bags in different measures of one, two and five shillings' worth so that these bagfuls of poison could easily be carried in people's pockets. Most of the containers, whether plastic or glass bottles, carried the famous ad, now popularized in most parts of the country through their sales vans, newspapers and handbills: POTENCY – Theng'a Theng'a with Theng'eta. P=3T.

The breweries were owned by an Anglo-American international combine but of course with African directors and even shareholders. Three of the four leading local personalities were Mzingo, Chui and Kimeria.

Long live New Ilmorog! Long live Partnership in Trade and Progress!

Reprinted from *Petals of Blood*. By permission of Heinemann Educational Books.

Short story – Sam Kahiga

Short stories are immensely popular in Kenya and you'll find stacks of well-thumbed, short romantic novels at any second-hand bookstall. **Sam Kahiga**'s energetic, exasperatingly racy style, sprinkled with a combination of British and American idioms, is strange at first, but his stories are revealing about the values of modern, urban Kenya.

A high voltage affair

At school I was afflicted by that chronic laziness that is often the lot of young students who think they are especially clever and can pass any exam through sheer genius. After getting my "O" levels with nine points and no sweat at all, I went to Strathmore College for "A" levels. I remember my goal then – to be a nuclear physicist. And if that was too advanced for the Third World then I'd compromise gracefully, step down, and just be a bloody good research scientist. The Third World could do with some of those.

Well my "A" levels were a disaster. What could I blame it on? Girls, booze or drugs? I blame it on the lot – plus the sort of risky confidence that comes after you've been top of the class too many times. Of my days in Strathmore I remember the movies and the parties rather than what happened in the labs. Except for jokingly trying to invent a drug that could give one a trip I hardly applied myself. And when the final results came out I realized that I was on a bad trip that just wouldn't end up in the university. It was bad, shocking, in fact.

Guys whose IQs were nowhere near as high as mine got called up to the university. As for me I was bad news in academic circles. Trying to save face I applied feverishly to foreign universities. My daddy could afford to send me to one. But no foreign university seemed interested. I kept trying until my daddy casually let me know that if I was intending to go abroad I would have to get the dough myself. That's what is known as fatherly affection.

Let me explain his attitude, for I understood it perfectly. My daddy (his friends and enemies call him GM) was no kid-spoiler. Although he could afford to send me round the world seven times he wasn't going to help because I had proved I was a failure. If I had failed at home I would not succeed abroad. I realized from his acid comments that he knew about the kind of life I had led at Strathmore – girls, booze, drugs. Could he then seriously think of sending me to America, that modern Babylon and hippy headquarters.

"Go on your own," said GM. He had turned a blind eye to my mischief until I let him down and failed to make it to the university. And GM is not the kind of man you let down and get away with it. He himself had never failed. Where he couldn't work his way out smoothly he bulldozed. If the front door was closed he tried the back door. That was the way he made his millions in the construction business.

Sons of poor men were going to university, so why not GM's first-born? He felt betrayed. What was it that he had not done for me? My pocket money had been two hundred and fifty bob a month. And he had told me to buy any book that I wanted. So why had I not gone to university?

GM had never even been to high school because he had been born too many years before the fruit of independence ripened. When independence came he was just a mason grade three. We lived at Shauri Moyo. GM grabbed his share of the fruit and we moved off to Lavington where I had my own motor-cycle and a couple of rooms to myself which were a mess of wires, novels and beat music that made my mother ill. The smell of my strange "cigarettes" made her ill too, but mothers are like that. You have to be patient with them.

I agree that GM spoilt me. But all the money and stuff he showered on me was on the understanding that I would live up to his expectations, which I did until those hazy "A" levels. In fact I did more. For instance at seventeen I was the maintenance man around the place, the little genie who knew what was wrong with the TV, the fridge or even his car. GM couldn't even change his own spark plugs. He trusted me to tune and service his car and considered me the last word in wiring. Now you can begin to understand about the two hundred and fifty bob pocket money. I spent most of it on cocaine.

After I had failed GM didn't want to see me around. He is a very unforgiving man. He had dug up my Strathmore background and it had shocked him so much that he didn't want me to even touch his car.

What finally broke up our relationship was when the disciplinarian daddy in him came to the surface and he thought he could teach me a physical lesson just because my room smelt of something strange. He sniffed and realized that it was grass.

The rest is embarrassing. Let's just say that there was yet another side of me that he hadn't known. I had a panther's reflexes that had come from picking up all that one needs to know about judo and karate. I didn't hurt him at all but he stared at me from the floor with great surprise. Through his gaping mouth I saw a little film of blood on his small white teeth – nothing serious.

After that there was nothing else to do except pack. The mansion at Lavington was a bit too small for both of us.

Somehow I feel that this background is important before I tell the story that follows. When I went to the Power Institute to train as a technician for the Power Company I went on my own ticket. The exams accompanying the interview were tough and gruelling to most of the boys but I sailed through, although I was half-starving. They accepted me at the Power Institute on my own merit, not a millionaire's influential word. It is important that this is understood.

Every young boy carries in his heart the soft-focus image of a woman he could love, serve and die for. I'm still not sure whether she eventually turns up, this ever youthful, totally compliant dream girl whom you want to set on a pedestal and worship. She is mutable, changing with your fancy and experience, but something remains constant about her, whether you are twelve or forty.

This constancy I guess is the subservience to your ego. She will love you no matter what happens, no matter who else is there. She loves you when you are vomiting into the toilet bowl and sticks by your side as you piss into a dark alley. She will be petite and cuddlesome when you are in a gentle mood and you want her to be like that. She will have an Afro hairdo if that's what you want. She's a virgin, nobody ever touched her before. Sometimes her breasts are small, sometimes her breasts are large. Sometimes she's innocent, sometimes she's master of the Kama Sutra, a deep well of erotic knowledge.

The first time she came to me in the flesh (or was it her more mundane twin sister?) was at the Power Institute at the beginning of the second year. My thoughts were hardly on love but on electro-magnetic forces, watts, ohms and coulombs. Instead of breasts I was thinking of turbines and transformers and the only kick I ever got during those sober, sombre months was the flow of electrons through me whenever I was fool enough to step on a live wire. In short, I was immersed in electricity, my biggest love since childhood. I hadn't seen anybody for a year – nobody mattered. For companions I had watts, coils and ohm's law. If I needed a drink, coke was enough, thanks. The hostel supplied the grub. There wasn't much else I felt I needed.

Then during Easter we had a dance at the hostel and this chick came along with one of the boys. I remember I was pretty lonesome hanging around the stuffy room with my coke and yet expecting nothing from all the bull-shit. To make things worse it was raining badly outside and I couldn't walk back to the hostel even if I had wanted to.

What is dancing? I asked myself. Some hangover from some primitive era. Some sort of savage convolution totally outside the realm of scientific discipline. I wanted to go home but the damn rain was falling. When I looked out of the window the world was suddenly lit up by the taut gnarled roots of a devilish lightning flash. "Jupiter's thunder-bolt." "God's footstep." To scientists: atmospheric electric phenomena. I wanted to go to bed.

She was very pretty but couldn't have been with a worse man. Mbote was rude, coarse and argumentative. He was a slum child and he was proud of the fact. No efforts at all to be a gentleman. The girl he was with was a lady from the toe up to the rich mass of black hair. And if I wasn't wrong she was trying to catch my eye.

I put my ginger ale on the ledge of a window (tired of cokes by now). I singled her out from the rest of the clumsy humanity, forgave her for imperfections and danced with her to a slow number.

"What's your label?" I asked.

"I beg your pardon?"

"The name. What's your name?"

"Esther."

"Esther what?"

"Mbacia."

Esther Mbacia. I was a bit annoyed with her for looking like my dream girl while going around with a guy like Mbote. My dream girls are supposed to be my own. They shouldn't be wandering around among crude wolves. They might get eaten. I wouldn't have been surprised if she ended up in Mbote's cubicle.

"You didn't tell me your name, but I know you," she said. "You are GM's son, aren't you?"

"So?" I asked coldly.

"I used to see you when you were in Strathmore. I was then in Kenya High. You know, when you had that motor-cycle." I couldn't help grinning.

"Your girl-friend was my classmate, Edith." Edith, a grass addict.

"Mbacia," I said. "Is your father the Mbacia? Mbacia Enterprises?"

"Happens to be," she said.

"Oh."

"Oh, what?"

"Nothing."

We laughed together. And then I saw the livid angry eyes of Mbote staring at me over the rim of his glass of alcoholic poison. He was mixing everything, the only way he could get drunk cheaply. He had drunk changaa ever since he was a small boy in Majengo slums, so beer to him was mere water.

"Your boyfriend looks angry and dangerous," I said.

"He's not my boyfriend," said Mbacia's daughter.

There might have been a fight that night had I been just any other boy. But my reputation was good. They knew my reflexes. Mbote was a dreaded street fighter who bullied almost everybody else but he knew I could paralyse him by just touching a nerve. Neatly, with no glasses being broken. He didn't want that. I didn't want to be unfair so I gave her a date and went to bed.

So that's how the tragic triangle started. Poor slum boy grabs a rich girl, wants to make her happy in his own rude way. Rich boy comes along with polished karate and his father's millions behind him and poor boy has no chance. The fact that I was broke most of the time didn't worry her one bit. In fact it seemed to add to my attraction. GM's son, but always broke. How funny!

I liked serious movies but also liked seeing Chinese movies to improve on my karate. She liked ice-cream, chewing gum and I'm not quite sure what else. I liked her. A girl doesn't have to have a line of interest to be liked. I still don't know her line of interest. She doesn't share my passion for turbines and transformers but so what? So nothing. She was high voltage. There were electrostatic forces in her breasts. When she smiled at me the electrons flowed. She was my cathode and I was her anode.

She was Mbote's heartbreak. Poor slum boy, son of a Majengo prostitute, he had never had any love in his life. He thought he had found it in Esther. Esther thought she had found it in me. The eternal triangle.

He came to me one night when I was reading and knocked on the door of my cubicle. He was totally drunk. I threw him out. I threw him out because he called me a hybrid.

"Just because you are a hybrid and she's a hybrid you feel you must cross-breed. To keep the millions in one family."

"Get the hell out," I said. But I had to remove him physically.

What I think shattered him was my bringing Esther to the end of term dance. At first he was vulgar and insulting, though not talking to us directly. I heard the words "hybrid" and "cross-breeding" and tried to take no notice. Then I saw that he was staring at us silently, no longer speaking. The jilted lover: why not just find a girl? Why let this thing play on his complexes? I wished I could give him the girl but I was already in love with her. Or maybe there was this vacuum in my soul that she very conveniently filled. Sometimes it's difficult to distinguish love from the flight from loneliness.

Swahili poetry

Swahili poetry is Kenya's oldest written literature, recorded in Arabic script since the seventeenth century and in the Roman alphabet since the beginning of the twentieth century. The oldest poems are praise and wedding songs from the oral tradition and narrative epics relating the early years of Islam. There's a wide variety of forms, but the rhythms and rhymes are not too unfamiliar to Western ears. Swahili, with its infinite capacity for allusion and imagery, has produced some beautiful verse. **Shaaban Robert**, who died in 1962, is probably the greatest twentieth-century Swahili poet. This lament for his wife was written in the shairi metre of sixteen syllables to the line.

AMINA

Amina unmejitenga, kufa umetangulia,	Amina, you have withdrawn yourself, you led the way in dying,
Kama ua umefunga, baada ya kuchanua,	Like a flower you have closed, after having opened first,
Nukuombea mwanga, peponi kukubaliwa.	I pray for you, my light, that you may be welcomed in paradise.
Mapenzi tuliyofunga, hapana wa kufungua.	The love we made between us, no one ever will undo it.
Nilitaka unyanyuke, kwa kukuombea dua,	I had hoped that you would rise again, and I prayed for you,
Sikupenda ushindike, maradhi kukuchukua,	I did not want you to be defeated, and be carried away by the disease,
Ila kwa rehema yake, Mungu amekuchagua.	But by His mercy, God has chosen you.
Mapenzi tuliyofunga, hapana wa kufungua.	The love we made between us, no one ever will undo it.
Majonzi hayaneneki, kila nikikumbukia,	My grief is indescribable, every moment I remember,
Nawaza kile na hiki, naona kama ruia,	I keep thinking this and yonder I see things as if I were dreaming,
Mauti siyasadiki kuwa, mwisho wa dunia.	I did not believe in death first, that it was the end of the world, this life.
Mapenzi tuliyofunga, hapana wa kufungua.	The love we made between us, no one ever will undo it.
Nasadiki haziozi, roho hazitapotea,	I believe that souls don't perish, they cannot be lost forever,
Twafuata wokozi, kwa mauti kutujia,	We pursue salvation's pathway, when death's angel comes to meet us,
Nawe wangu mpenzi, Peponi utaingia.	And you, my beloved partner, you will enter heaven's gateway.
Mapenzi tuliyofunga, hapana wa kufungua.	The love we made between us, no one ever will undo it.
Jambo moja nakumbuka, sahihi ninalijua,	Just one thing I do remember, one I know for sure and truly,
Kuwa sasa umefika, ta'bu isikosumbua,	That you have now reached the place where no suffering can plague you,
Kwayo nimefurahika, nyuma nilikobakia.	Therefore do I still feel gladdened, here where I am left behind.
Mapenzi tuliyofunga, hapana wa kufungua.	The love we made between us, no one ever will undo it.
Ninamaliza kutunga, kwa kukuombea dua,	I have finished my composing, while for you I pray,
Vumbi tena likiunga, roho likirudishiwa,	When dust is rejoined together, when the soul returns into it,
Mauti yakijitenga, mapenzi yatarejea.	While the power of death retires, then our love will be returning.
Mapenzi tuliyofunga, hapana wa kufungua.	The love we made between us, no one ever will undo it.

Translated by Jan Knappert, 1979. Reprinted from *Four Centuries of Swahili Verse*, by permission of the translator.

The following morning was Sunday and that was when the nightmare began. Most of the boys had already gone home and the hostel was almost deserted.

With a towel around my loins I went into the shower room. Mbote who was waiting for that move came and locked the door with a key. Standing outside the door he told me a lot of things. How he had loved and how I had ruined his chances.

"What's the point of locking the door?"

"I want to kill you."

The shower was running, the warm water caressing my skin. He was going to kill me. He must be joking. And yet I knew how reckless he was, the kind of strange practical jokes he used to play on people. Better watch out.

"Look Mbote, Esther is mine," I said, wearily.

"You snatched her. You rich people think you can snatch everything. You think you are smart. You'll pay for it."

"How?"

"I want to make you dance. You like dancing I'll make you dance."

"Look, open the door and stop being stupid. What are you up to?"

"When you come out of there you won't be alive."

"Why?"

"The shower room is wired. I'm just about to give you a thousand volts." I got the idea. I broke into a sweat. I stared at the wet floor of my death cell. The water would conduct the electricity from wherever the terminals were.

"Open the door and don't be stupid," I cried and that was the last thing I said before the current shot up through my bare feet and shot me up to the ceiling. I screamed, then hit the floor unconscious.

Hospital. The first week was a blank. The next one I began to recognise people – chaps from the Power Institute, GM, Esther.

The third week I was fine and that was when they told me that Mbote had electrocuted himself when I was in a coma. The cops had come for him and rather than face the law he had taped electric wires to his head. He had turned on the switch, died instantly and made headlines for the first and last time.

I try to look on it all to see why and how it happened but I'm still not strong enough to sort out little psychological details. Or perhaps my mind just refuses to work. I saw a picture of Mbote's mother in the papers and she was wailing, saying he was a good boy. I take my own refuge behind public opinion for that's all I can do. Public opinion has it that Mbote was crazy to try and electrocute GM's son. He was quite right to electrocute himself, though. But he shouldn't go round trying to electrocute heirs to millions. (GM wants to know if I need bodyguards.)

It all depresses me. When my heart is really low I call up Esther on the phone.

"Doctor says I need lots of therapy, girl, and only you can give it to me. So come over quick."

She always does. I told you she's high voltage – if you see what I mean. Maybe she really *is* hybrid.

Reprinted from the collection *Flight to Juba*. By permission of Longman Kenya.

Music

Although its music is less well known abroad than that of a number of other African countries, Kenya's home-grown musical vitality is there if you listen, and Nairobi's audiences and recording facilities have long been a draw for musicians from all over east and central Africa, bringing to the city a pan-African musical flavour.

Traditional music

All the people of Kenya have **traditional musical cultures**, some of which have survived more intact than others into the twenty-first century. Music has always been used to accompany ceremonies, events and **rites of passage**, from celebrations at a baby's birth to songs of adolescence and warriorhood, and from marriage, harvests and solar and lunar cycles, to festivities, religious events and death.

Nowadays, the majority of Kenyans are Christian, and **gospel** music reigns supreme; sadly not the uplifting version of the southern United States, but a tinny, synthesized and homogenous form which in many areas has all but obliterated traditional music. Among the Kikuyu and the Kalenjin, for example, traditional music is almost extinct, and elsewhere, to hear anything at all, you need time, patience and local people's trust before being allowed to witness what can still be very sacred events.

The following is a brief tribe-by-tribe run-down of more easily encountered traditional music and instruments. Obviously, there's much more available if you know where to search and what to ask for: essential **reading** for this is George Senoga-Zake's *Folk Music of Kenya* (Uzima Press, Nairobi). Other works on music are thin on the ground, though most bookshops stock a reasonable selection of school textbooks, some of which provide a handy introduction to the subject. If you want to **buy** some recordings then, with a little perseverance, you can usually find cassettes locally, though the quality is often dire.

Akamba

Best known for their skill at drumming, the **Akamba** tradition has sadly now all but disappeared. To record anything, you'll have to go well off the beaten track in Ukambani, as there's next to nothing either in Machakos or Kitui. There's only one commercial cassette available (*Akamba Drums*, Tamasha), which covers many styles and has some interesting sleeve notes, which you can order from the Zanzibar Curio Shop in Nairobi.

Bajuni

The **Bajuni** are a small ethnic group living in the Lamu Archipelago and on the nearby mainland, and are known musically for an epic women's work song called *Mashindano Ni Matezo*. One of only very few easily available recordings of women singing in Kenya, this is gradually hypnotic counterpoint singing, punctuated by metallic rattles and supported by subdued drumming. You can find it in Lamu, Kilifi or Mombasa.

Borana

The **Borana**, who live between Marsabit and the Ethiopian border, have a rich musical tradition. The Arab influence is readily discernible, as are more typically Saharan rhythms, and most distinctive is their use of the *chamonge* guitar, nowadays a large cooking pot loosely strung with metal wires. Cassettes are difficult to obtain; spread the word in either Isiolo or Marsabit.

Chuka

Sadly almost extinct, **Chuka** music from the east side of Mount Kenya – like that of the Akamba – is drumming genius. Your only hope is to catch the one remaining band (which currently plays at the *Mount Kenya Safari Club* near Nanyuki), or pale imitations in coastal holiday resorts.

Gusii

Gusii music is certainly Kenya's oddest. The favoured instrument is the *obokano*, an enormous version of the Luo *nyatiti* lyre which is pitched at least an octave below the human voice, and which at times can sound like roaring thunder. They also use the ground bow, essentially a large hole dug in the ground over which an animal skin is tightly pegged. The skin has a small hole cut in the centre, into which a single-stringed bow is placed and plucked: the sound defies description. Ask around and you should be able to pick up recordings in Kisii easily enough.

Luhya

Luhya music has a clear Bantu flavour, easily discernible in the pre-eminence of drums. Of these, the *sukuti* is best known, sometimes played in ensembles, and still used in rites of passage such as circumcision. Tapes are easily available in Kakamega and Kitale, and in some River Road shops in Nairobi.

Luo

The **Luo** are best known as the originators of *benga* (see p.718). Their most distinctive musical instrument is the *nyatiti*, a double-necked eight-string lyre with a skin resonator which is also struck on one neck with a metal ring tied to the toe. It produces a tight, resonant sound, and is used to generate sometimes long and remarkably complex hypnotic rhythms. Originally used in the fields to relieve workers' tiredness, a typical piece begins at a moderate pace, and quickens progressively, the musician singing over the sound. The lyrics cover all manner of subjects, from politics and change since the *wazungu* arrived, to moral fables and age-old legends. Look out also for recordings of *onand* (accordion) and *orutu* (a single-stringed fiddle).

Maasai

The nomadic lifestyle of the **Maasai** tends to preclude the carrying of any large instruments, and as a result their music is one of the most distinctive in Kenya, characterized by a total lack of instruments, and some astonishing polyphonous multi-part singing – both call-and-response, sometimes with women included in the chorus, but most famously in the songs of the *morani* warriors, where each man sings part of a rhythm, more often than not from his throat (rather like a grunt), which together with the calls of his companions creates a pattern of rhythms. The songs are usually competitive (expressed through the singers alternately leaping as high as they can) or bragging – about how the singer killed a lion, or rustled cattle from a neighbouring community. The Maasai have retained much of their traditional culture, so singing is still very much used in traditional ceremonies, most spectacularly in the *eunoto* circumcision ceremony in which boys are initiated into manhood to begin their ten- to fifteen-year stint as *morani*.

Most tourists staying in big coastal hotels or in game park lodges in Amboseli and Maasai Mara will have a chance to sample Maasai music in the form of groups of *morani* playing at the behest of hotel management. Cassettes are difficult to find: there's a Maasai variant of gospel music (from Arusha in Tanzania) available in Narok, and an excellent little music store in Oloitokitok, but otherwise your only hope is to record the music yourself.

Mijikenda

The **Mijikenda** of the coast have a prolific musical tradition which has survived Christian conversion and is readily available on tape throughout the coastal region. Performances can occasionally be seen in the larger hotels. Most of the music available is from the Giriama section of the Mijikenda, who live inland of Malindi. Like the Akamba, the Mijikenda are superb drummers and athletic dancers. The music is generally light and overlaid with complex rhythms, impossible not to dance to. Look out also for the *kiringongo* music of the Chonyi people, which features the xylophone (an instrument otherwise unknown in Kenya).

Samburu

Despite its having been discovered by tourists and authors of glossy coffee-table books, there are no commercial recordings of **Samburu** music except on the occasional compilation. Like their Maasai cousins, whose singing it closely resembles, Samburu musicians make a point of not playing instruments – at least in theory. In practice, they do play small pipes, and also a kind of guitar with a box resonator and loose metal strings – which seems to be related to the *chamonge* of the Borana further north. But these are played purely for pleasure, or to soothe a crying baby, and are thus not deemed "music" by Samburu. Listen out also for the sinuously erotic rain songs sung by women in times of

---

Tape compilations of traditional music available in Kenya

Bomas of Kenya: Songs of our African Heritage (ZAIT 511). Includes pieces from the Kikuyu, Mijikenda (Digo and Giriama), Embu, Akamba, Samburu, Borana, Luo and Luhya tribes.

Folk Music of East Africa (Philips CPKLP 102). Accompanies the book (out of print) *Musical Instruments of East Africa* by Graham Hyslop. Includes music from the Luhya, Kuria, Mijikenda (Digo) and Swahili peoples.

Gonda Traditional Entertainment "Second Step" (Tamasha CPOLP 327). Music from the Mijikenda and Taita people.

Muziki Wa Kiasili (*Folk Music of Kenya*) (ZAIT 503). Contains Luo, Gusii, Luhya, Kuria and Mijikenda music.

Traditional Music of East Africa Vol.I (C/Trad Vol 1). Includes Kikuyu dances, *nyatiti* (Luo), *litungu* (Luhya), Akamba singing and drums, Giriama and Digo dances.

Traditional Music of East Africa Vol.II (C/Trad Vol 2). Includes Akamba, Luo, Kikuyu and Luhya music.

Traditional Musical Instruments of Kenya Vol 1 (Tamasha CPOLP 321). Melodic and percussive instruments including: *nyatiti* (Luo lyre), *chivoti* and *nzumari* (Mijikenda flutes), *marimba* (Mijikenda xylophone), *orutu* (single-string Luo fiddle), *sukuti* (Luhya drums), *sengenya* and *chakacha* (Mijikenda drums) and *mbeni* (Akamba drums).

drought. For cassettes, ask around at the lodges and campsites in Samburu/Buffalo Springs National Reserves, or – better still – in Maralal.

Turkana

Until the 1970s, the **Turkana** were one of Kenya's remotest tribes, and in large part are still untouched by Christian missionaries. Their traditional music is based loosely on a call-and-response pattern. The main instrument is a kudu antelope horn with or without finger holes, but most of their music is entirely vocal. A rarity to look out for are the women's rain songs, sung to the god Akuj during times of drought. As traditional music is still played on ceremonial occasions (and being nomadic, the Turkana have no electricity or tape recorders), finding cassettes is extremely difficult; it's a question of asking around in Loiyangalani. You're usually welcome to join performances in Loiyangalani for a small fee.

Ngoma, and the arrival of the guitar

Kenya's oldest musical tradition is **ngoma**, still the central term used to describe all the facets of a musical performance, including the accompanying dances. *Ngoma* in most Bantu languages of Kenya refers to a specific kind of **drum** and a related dance.

Although an inter-ethnic *ngoma* called *beni* (band) emerged on the coast at the beginning of the twentieth century and spread inland (you can still witness this anachronistic, marching-band form on special occasions in Lamu), *ngoma* music today is essentially ethnic, related to a specific language group and using the respective vernacular and local dance rhythms. *Ngoma* also provides most of the music used during the life-cycle festivities (birth, initiation and circumcision, marriage and death), whether in the town or the country. Look out for recordings by Luhya **sukuti** groups: the *sukuti* is the central drum of these ensembles.

From the early 1950s on, with the coming of recording and broadcasting, and the introduction of new instruments – especially the **guitar** – an acoustic guitar-based music developed as accompaniment to songs sung in **Swahili**. Perhaps the most important artist of this "first generation" of guitarists was **Fundi Konde**. A basis for Swahili-language popular music had already been laid by the *beni* groups flourishing in East African towns during the first half of the century. *Beni* songs, as well as the new guitar songs, featured the strong and critical social commentary so beloved of Kenyans. The songs are usually in the form of a short story and may comment on an actual political or social topic, or perhaps recount a personal experience of the musician. Romantic lyrics are almost non-existent, even in songs dealing with men and women.

The guitar styles themselves developed out of different instrumental techniques and musical perceptions, but they were influenced by the records available at the time, mainly from other parts of Africa. Kenyan musicians of the period cite the finger-picking style of **Jean Bosco Mwenda** and **Losta Abelo**, both from Katanga (today, Shaba Province in the Congo), and **George Sibanda**, from Bulawayo in Zimbabwe, as important inspirations. From this period, the notables of Kenya's acoustic guitar styles are **John Mwale**, **George Mukabi** (directly out of the Luhya *sukuti* tradition) and **Isaya Mwinamo**.

The 1960s saw the introduction of **electric guitars** as well as larger groups (of three to four guitars). **Kwela** and **twist** were the rage, coming from, or via, southern Africa. These were the days of the **Equator Sound Band** (Equator being the main record label), featuring the songs of **Daudi Kabaka**, **Fadhili William**, **Nashil Pichen** and **Peter Tsotsi**.

Tarabu music

Tarabu, the main popular music of the coastal Swahili people, deserves special mention. It has a long tradition in the festive life of the Swahili, especially at weddings, and is also the general music of entertainment of the coastal communities. Many of the lead singers and bandleaders of *tarabu* groups are women, almost unique in Kenyan traditional music. The music also has strong Arabic-Islamic overtones in instrumentation, especially in the haunting vocals. Earlier *tarabu* (*taarab*, *tarab*) groups used the full Arabic orchestra, including the lute-like *oud* and violins. Today, the main instruments are mandolin or guitar and either an Indian harmonium or a small electronic organ/piano, plus a variety of local, Arabic or Indian drums. Indian movies, with their strong musical component, are very popular among the coastal people and under their influence many features of Indian music have entered *tarabu*.

On Lamu island, the old centre of Swahili culture, most weddings today are served by a few amateur groups, with professional groups bussed up from Mombasa only for more well-to-do marriages. The **Zein Musical Party**, now based in Mombasa, is the heir of Lamu's *taarab* tradition. Zein l'Abdin was born in Lamu and hails from a family in which the Swahili arts were highly valued. Together with the Swahili poet Sheikh Nabhany, Zein has unearthed a number of poems, dating back to the nineteenth century, which he has included in his repertoire. But Zein is not just a fabulous singer and composer, he ranks as the finest *oud* player in East Africa and is well known throughout the Islamic world.

Maulidi Musical Party, **Zuhura & Party** and **Malika** have, for the past three decades, been Mombasa's main wedding favourites. Singer Maulidi Juma and group are at ease both with traditional Swahili wedding songs and the Hindi-style songs that are so characteristic of Mombasa *taarab*, in which Swahili words are set to tunes from the latest Bollywood movie. Maulidi Musical Party can stand as the prototype Mombasa ensemble, its sound being based on a keyboard, with fills by accordion, guitar, bass and percussion. Many rhythms are rooted in local *ngoma* traditions, and bandmaster Mohamed Shigoo's keyboard work stands out as especially original, with a strong flavour of harmonium (which he used to play earlier in his career) and *nzumari* (a local double-reed horn). Shigoo and the Maulidi Party used to back Malika (Asha Abdo Suleiman) when she was visiting from Somalia, where she lived for a while in the 1970s and 1980s. Since the civil war broke out, she has returned to Mombasa and now leads her own group: hers is still the female voice most in demand in Mombasa, and few can rival her stage aura. Mombasa's other female star is the enchanting **Zuhura Swaleh**, whose energetic songs have a firm base in the local *chakacha* rhythms and lyrics. The *taishokoto* is a prominent sound in her group.

The popularity of all three singers is currently falling. They are in their fifties now and their voices have somehow suffered from the pains of singing at weddings six hours in a row. Besides, the audience wants new stars: **Sitara**, second voice in Maulidi Musical Party for some years recently came out with her own group Diamond Star, taking half of Maulidi's band with her. She is popular with the young wedding audience who like her Swahili covers of some of the latest Western and Indian pop songs. And an up-and-coming male voice is **Yusuf Mohamed "Tenge"**, following in the steps of Maulidi and Juma Bhalo, who used to be the hero of Indian-style *taarab*.

Modern Kenyan styles

Kenyan pop is in the midst of a revolution. It's far too early to see the eventual outcome of this transition, but what is for sure is that there is a changing of the guard in Kenyan music. The ranks of the elder generation of pop musicians have thinned all too quickly in recent years, with a startling number of younger veteran musicians having also died; men in their forties or fifties with twenty or thirty years experience in the music business. One suspects that HIV/AIDS may be a factor in many of these cases, but it is rarely confirmed. Whatever the causes, the effects have been devastating not only for the loss of creative talent, but also because with these musicians goes the living memory of the historical context and evolution of Kenyan music. Indeed, the music scene in Kenya today has a very different landscape to that of only five or ten years ago. A new generation of musicians and producers with quite different backgrounds, training, and experience is beginning to make its imprint on the scene.

In Kenya's forty or so years of independence, it's never been very meaningful to speak of Kenyan pop as a genre. There have always been a number of styles competing with each other for the Kenyan audience with interest in particular styles rising and falling over time. There has also been considerable interchange between styles with musicians borrowing ideas and influencing each other in a cross-fertilization that gives the music an unmistakable Kenyan flavour. Most importantly, over this period, the fundamental element shared by all these styles has been the prominent role of guitars and guitar solos. This point is made delightfully clear in the unfortunately small number of CD compilations of Kenyan pop currently available on the world market (see, for example, various Earthworks releases and Rounder's *The Nairobi Beat*).

Another ingredient in the Kenyan mix is the **cavacha** rhythm popularized in the mid-1970s by Congolese groups such as Zaiko Langa Langa and Orchestra Shama Shama. A sense of this rhythm is conveyed by Bo Diddley's distinctive beat, the "shave-and-a-haircut, six-bits" rhythm which closely approximates *cavacha*. This rapid-fire percussion, usually on the snare or high hat, quickly took hold in Kenya and continues to underlie a great sweep of Kenyan music from the Kalambya Sisters to Les Wanyika and Orchestra Virunga. Many Kenyan musicians direct their efforts towards their own linguistic groups and perform most of their songs in one of Kenya's indigenous languages. Alongside this regional or ethnic orientation, at least three other local pop music varieties can be distinguished. The first consists of songs with lyrics in Swahili, or the Congolese language Lingala, aimed at a national and largely urban audience. Another is propelled by foreign tourism and Kenyans with a taste for international pop. The last category, and the one that is creating quite a stir among Kenya's youth, is music that fuses contemporary pop influences from hip hop, rap, reggae, or R&B with local Kenyan rhythms, melodies, and localized lyrics.

Benga bands

The late 1960s and early 1970s was another time of transition in Kenyan music. Lively, guitar-based, Swahili language music dominated the airwaves and the record stores. Finger-picking guitarists from western Kenya and the smoother, driving, electric guitar sound of groups like Equator Sound Band were on top. During the sixties, Daudi Kabaka reigned as the King of Twist with his "twist" rhythm, a beat similar to South African *kwela*. Entering the 1970s, while Kabaka's African Eagles and others continued to play their brands of Swahili music, many top Kenyan groups, such as the Ashantis, Air Fiesta and the Hodi Boys, were playing Congolese covers and international pop, especially soul music, in the Nairobi clubs. But it was also at this time that a number of musicians were beginning to define the direction of a new emerging form. More than any other Kenyan music, this style called *benga* became Kenya's most characteristic pop sound. Although it originated with the Luo people of western Kenya, *benga*'s transition to a popular style has been so pervasive that practically all the local bands, Luo or otherwise, play variants of it, and today most of the regional or ethnic pop groups refer generally to their music as *benga*. As a pop style, *benga* dates back to the 1950s when musicians began adapting traditional dance rhythms and the string sounds of the *nyatiti* and *orutu* to the acoustic guitar and later to electric instruments. During its heyday in the 1970s and into the 1980s, *benga* music dominated Kenya's recording industry and much of the early output was exported to west and southern Africa where it was very popular.

Luo

By any measure, the most famous **Luo** *benga* group is **Shirati Jazz** led by **D.O. (Daniel Owino) Misiani**. Born in Shirati, Tanzania, just south of the Kenyan border, he has been playing *benga* since the mid-1960s. His style is characterized by soft, flowing and melodic two-part vocal harmonies, a very active, pulsating bass line that derives at least in part from traditional *nyatiti* and drum rhythms, and stacks of invigorating guitar work, the lead alternating with the vocal. Other important *benga* artists include the pioneering Colella Mazee and Ochieng Nelly – either together or separately in various incarnations of **Victoria Jazz** and the **Victoria Kings** – as well as George Ramogi and his Continental Luo Sweet Band. The mid-1990s also saw the emergence of two more crowd pleasing *benga* groups: Okatch Biggy (Elly Otieno Okatch) and Heka Heka and Prince Jully (Julius Okumu) with the Jolly Boy's Band. Among these leaders, only Misiani is still alive and performing today. Ramogi, Okatch, and Jully passed away in 1997, Colella in 2000, and Nelly in 2001. Interestingly, Heka Heka and the Jolly Boys have continued to flourish, moving into new areas of more risqué *benga* performance. At the time of his death, Prince Jully and his group were already riding a wave of popularity, and with Jully's wife assuming control of the group and now fronting the Jolly Boys as Princess Jully, the subsequent response has been nothing short of phenomenal, drawing enthusiastic crowds wherever she performs.

One Luo name which doesn't fit neatly under the *benga* banner is **Ochieng Kabaselleh** and his **Luna Kidi Band**. His songs were mostly in Luo, but sometimes with a liberal seasoning of Swahili and English. Likewise, the melodies and harmonies are from the Luo *benga* realm but the rhythm, guitar work, and horns suggest influences from the Congolese/Swahili-dominated sound. Kabaselleh, who languished in prison for several years (for "subversion"), returned to the music world with a flood of new releases in the 1990s. In 1997, Kabaselleh and group toured the USA and recorded his first international CD release, *From Nairobi with Love*. In 1998, he suddenly died, a victim of complications related to diabetes. Some of his most interesting music of the 1980s is available in a collection called *Sanduku ya Mapendo* (A Loadful of Love) from Equator Heritage Sounds.

Luhya

The **Luhya** highlands to the north of Luoland are home to many of Kenya's most famous guitarists and vocalists. Daudi Kabaka, the King of Twist, died two days short of his sixty-second birthday in 2001. He is survived, however, by a number of fellow, story-telling, guitarists. One is Sukuma bin Ongaro who was doing the equivalent of Luhya rap music long before most of the world had ever heard American rap. The humorous social commentary of **Sukuma bin Ongaro** has made him a giant of the current scene, although mainly among his fellow Luhya-speakers. **Shem Tube**, however, is an artist who straddles both past and present in his music, though it's his back catalogue which has given him a popular following in Europe. In 1989, GlobeStyle Records released *Abana ba Nasery* (The Nursery Boys), a compilation of songs by Tube and his group in the *omutibo* style. Coming together as a trio in the early 1960s, Abana ba Nasery were innovators, using traditional Luhya rhythms and melody lines, their two-guitar line-up and three-part vocal harmonies (and a Fanta bottle). Abana's style from the 1960s contains the major elements of today's contemporary pop sound in Kenya: the central position of the solo guitar in Kenya's electric groups is anticipated in Shem Tube's solos of twenty-five years ago. Justo Osala's guitar parts in the lower ranges are like the rhythm and bass parts in today's electric bands. Even Enos Okola's Fanta rhythms are a precursor of the modern drum kit. While Abana's first CD release created tremendous interest – a rootsy but very accessible African sound – the compatibility of their music with strands of European folk tradition is clear in their second CD release, recorded by GlobeStyle in London: *Nursery Boys Go Ahead!* Guest artists included members of the Oyster Band and Mustaphas as well as Ron Kavana and Tomás Lynch.

Kikuyu

As Kenya's largest ethnic group, the **Kikuyu**-speaking people of Central Province and Nairobi are a major market force in Kenya's music industry. Perhaps because of this large "built-in" audience, few Kikuyu musicians have tried to cross over into the national Swahili or English-language markets. Kikuyu **melodies** are quite distinct from those of the Luo and Luhya of western Kenya, and their pop manifestations also differ significantly in harmonies and rhythm guitar parts. In contrast to Luo and Luhya pop, women vocalists play major roles as lead and backing singers for Kikuyu groups. Many of the top groups have women's auxiliaries – duos and trios invariably called the something-or-other sisters. While Kikuyu pop music has a traditional melodic structure, there is a good deal of stylistic variety and innovation. Most often, Kikuyu pop takes the form of the *benga/cavacha* style, but popular alternatives are also based on country and western, reggae and Congolese *soukous*. Since the late sixties, the king of Kikuyu pop has been Joseph Kamaru. He began making hit records in 1967 with the release of Celina, performed, on one guitar and maracas with his sister Catherine Muthoni. Since then he has carved a small empire with his **Njung'wa Stars** band and the Kamarulets dancers, two music shops and a recording studio. He sees himself as a teacher, expressing the traditional values of his culture, as well as contemporary social commentary. In the early 1990s, his recording, *Mahoya ma Bururi* (Prayers for the Country), gently criticized the Kenya government but resulted in his shop being raided and the banning of the song from the airwaves. Kamaru takes pride in his lyrics for going beyond trivial matters. "My songs are not like other peoples' 'I love you, I love you,' they keep on singing – No, no, no! My songs are not that way. I can compose a love song but very deep, a grown-up loving." In the period following

Mahoya ma Bururi, Kamaru's popularity was steadily on the rise: his band was fully booked, playing his regular and "X-rated, Adults Only" shows to packed nightclub crowds. Thus his announcement in 1993 that he had been "born again" came as a bombshell for his fans. Much to their disappointment, Kamaru abandoned the pop music scene to devote his efforts to evangelistic activities and gospel music promotion. Kamaru may not write songs for teenage lovers but someone who does, and who became famous in the process, is hit-maker **Daniel "DK" (Councillor) Kamau**. Kamau released his first three records in 1967 while still at school, and continued with a highly successful career through the 1970s. He is regarded as having brought Kikuyu music into the *benga* mainstream, but it wasn't until 1990 that he returned to the stage with a new **Lulus Band**. In Kenya's rapidly changing political climate, the councillor struck a responsive chord with his fans and the population at large with his Top Ten hit, FORD Fever (about the newly formed opposition party). DK has continued to address political and human rights issues, in partnership with singer-composer Albert Gacheru. With Kamaru's departure from the pop market, at least a part of the void has been filled by one of the rare female headliners in Kikuyu pop, **Jane Nyambura**. Known these days simply as Queen Jane, she's a staunch advocate for the inclusion of traditional folk forms and local languages within contemporary pop. The use of tribal languages in her music, has severely limited her radio exposure – and that of all musicians singing in local languages (such music is deemed "tribal" in official circles).

Akamba

East and southeast of Nairobi is a vast, semi-arid plateau, the home of the Akamba people, linguistically close relations of the Kikuyu. Akamba pop music is firmly entrenched in the *benga/cavacha* camp. Although distinctive melodies distinguish Akamba pop from other styles of *benga*, there are other special Akamba features. One is the delicate, flowing, **interlocking** rhythm guitar that underlies many Akamba arrangements. While the primary guitar plays chords in the lower range, the second guitar plays a fast pattern of notes that mesh with the rest of the instrumentation to fill in the holes. This gentle presence is discernible in many of the recordings of the three most famous Akamba groups who dominated Akamba music from the mid-1970s: the Kalambya Boys & Kalambya Sisters, Peter Mwambi and his Kyanganga Boys and Kakai Kilonzo's Les Kilimambogo Brothers. Mwambi has a following that comes largely from within the Akamba community: his musically simple, pulsing-bass drum style may not have enough musical variation to keep non-Akamba speakers interested. The Kalambya Sisters are a different story. Backed by Onesmus Musyoki's Kalambya Boys Band, the Sisters (now disbanded) were famous, even notorious, throughout Kenya and they even had a minor hit in Europe with *Katelina*. This relates the comic plight of a young woman, Katelina, who likes to drink the home-brew *uki*, but gets pregnant with annual regularity in the process. The soft, high-pitched, feline voices of the Sisters whine engagingly in unison over the delightfully sweet guitar work of Musyoki and the Boys (check out their style in *Kopulo Onesi* on *The Nairobi Beat* CD). After a ten-year absence from the studio, Musyoki returned to record *Sweet Sofia* in 1993, while founding sister, Mary Nduku, now leads the **Mitaboni Sisters**. To reach a larger audience, a number of local-language artists have turned to Swahili, which is widely spoken throughout east and central Africa. Kakai Kilonzo and Les Kilimambogo Brothers band were always identified as a "Akamba" band, but once Kakai started recording in Swahili, the group enjoyed widespread popularity in Kenya. With socially relevant lyrics, intricate guitar weaves and a solid dance-beat backing, Les Kilimambogo were national favourites until Kakai's death in 1987. These days, a new generation of musicians, relative newcomers to the Akamba hall of fame, is drawing most of the limelight away from the old guard. The **Katitu Boys Band** have come to dominate the Akamba cassette market. Leader David Kasyoki, a former guitarist with Mwambi's Kyanganga Boys, won the 1992 Singer of the Year award for *Cheza na Katitu* (Dance with Katitu). Other groups of the new Akamba generation include Kimangu Boys Band, Kiteta Boys and Mutituni Boys Band.

Big-name bands

The **big-name bands** in Kenya can usually muster sufficiently large audiences for shows in sprawling, ethnically diverse towns like Nairobi, Nakuru and Mombasa. Unlike the groups with a particular ethnic leaning, the national performers can appeal to a broad cross-section of the population with music which tends to be either a local variant of the **Congolese** sound or **Swahili music**, a Kenyan-Tanzanian hybrid sound unique to Kenya. In both Congolese and Swahili popular music, rumba has always been a major ingredient. Songs typically open with a slow-to-medium rumba that ambles through the verses, backed by a light percussion of gentle congas, snare and high hat. Then, three or four minutes into the song, there's a transition from verses and rolling rumba to much faster rhythms, highlighting the instrumental parts, especially solo guitar and brass. There are some significant points of divergence in the Swahili and Congolese styles. The tempo of Swahili music is generally slower, even in the fast section. Swahili music over the last twenty-five years has been particularly faithful to this two-part structure although, today, both Swahili and Congolese musicians often dispense with the slow rumba portion altogether.

While the Congolese musicians are famous for their vocals and their intricate harmonies, Swahili groups are renowned for their demon guitarists and crisp, clear guitar interplay. While "Swahili pop" is usually associated with Swahili lyrics, it isn't distinguished by the language. In fact one of the greatest Swahili hits of all time, *Charonyi Ni Wasi*, is not in Swahili but in the closely related Taita language. Similarly, Nairobi's Congolese scene has become less Lingala as it has moved from the near-exclusive use of that Congolese language twenty-five years ago to a preponderance of Swahili lyrics today. From the mid-1980s onwards, most of the lyrics from the immensely popular Samba Mapangala and Orchestra Virunga have been in Swahili, helping to guarantee popularity with a mass audience. As for Lingala songs, while few Kenyans understand the lyrics, their mysterious incomprehensibility and a veneer of Gallic sophistication gives them a certain sex appeal. Most of the Swahili and Congolese music produced in Kenya originated with the (now departed) multinational giants like Polygram and CBS/Sony or was put out by independent labels run by British or Asian Kenyans. When European and American interest in African music began to emerge in the early 1980s, it was these companies with their international connections that put out the first, tantalizing sounds from Nairobi. Although they were also involved in the vernacular language scene, the early Kenyan recordings released in London were drawn from the big names and featured artists such as Super Mazembe, Orchestra Makassy, Orchestra Virunga, Lessa Lassan, Issa Juma and Lovy Longomba. Of these, all but the Tanzania-born Issa Juma came from Congo (then Zaire) – there wasn't a Kenyan among them – and it wasn't until several years later, after Shirati Jazz had made their first British tour, that Kenya achieved an international reputation for its indigenous *benga* dance music.

The Congolese connection

Congolese musicians have been making musical waves in Kenya since the late 1950s. It was the Congolese OS Africa Band that opened Nairobi's famous *Starlight Club* on Nairobi Hill (now defunct) back in 1964. But it wasn't until the mid-1970s, after the passing of the American soul craze, that music from Congo began to dominate the city nightclubs. One of the first musicians to settle in Kenya during this period was **Baba Gaston**. The rotund Gaston had already been in the business for twenty years when he arrived in Nairobi with his group Baba National in 1975. A prolific musician and father (he had twelve children), he stole the scene until his retirement as a performer and recording artist in 1989. In the mid-1970s, at about the same time Baba Gaston was just getting settled in Nairobi, the Congolese group Boma Liwanza was already on the scene at the *Starlight Club* and the popular Bana Ngenge were about to leave Nairobi for a year in Tanzania. Super Mazembe had just completed their migration from (then) Zaire to Kenya by way of Zambia and Tanzania. And soon to follow were Samba Mapangala and Les Kinois, though they stopped along the way in Uganda for a couple of years before moving to Nairobi in 1977. With the break-up of Les Kinois in 1980, some members moved to Mazembe, while Samba began putting together his first version of **Orchestra Virunga**. The famous "Malako" recordings included several members of Bana Ngenge, including vocalist Fataki Lokassa and the late Lawi Somana, who went on to lead Tabu Ley's Afrisa.

Meanwhile, despite their rising popularity in 1982–83, Super Mazembe began to fragment. The group's versatile lead singers Lovy Longomba and Kasongo wa Kanema (of "Kasongo" and "Shauri Yako" fame) quit the band – Kasongo to team up with Virunga and Lovy to front his own group, Super Lovy, and later Bana Likasi. By 1984, Samba Mapangala's line-up had experienced a number of changes in personnel but was still going strong. It wasn't long, however, before Virunga also ran into the Kenya Immigration Department. With extensions to their work permits refused, Virunga were soon out of money and falling apart.

Out of Virunga's misfortune came **Ibeba System**. It was led by ex-Virunga guitarist Sammy Mansita and other Virunga/Kinois alumni including Siama Matuzungidi on guitar, Johnny-Ko Walengo on bass, and vocalists Kasongo wa Kanema and Coco Zigo Mike. Lovy Longomba also did a spell with Ibeba System before setting off to Dar es Salaam to join Afriso Ngoma. When Ibeba first took over from Virunga at the *Starlight*, the group was a virtual clone of the Virunga sound. Over several years performing at the *JKA Resort Club* they became one of Nairobi's most accomplished club acts with a good mix of their own *soukous* and covers of African pop.

The ultimate Congolese crossover band in Nairobi, and darlings of Kenya's young elite, were **Vundumuna**. The group formed in 1984 with guitarist **Tabu Frantal** of Boma Liwanza and Shika Shika, Ugandan vocalist Sammy Kasule, and bassist Nsilu wa Bansilu of Bana Ngenge and Virunga. Vundumuna quickly gained institutional status at the *Carnivore*, packing in the crowds with their Wednesday and Saturday night performances. With the best equipment in the city, they presented a clean, hi-tech sound fusing Congolese *soukous*, *benga* rhythms, and elements of Western jazz. Their flawless horn arrangements blended beautifully with leader **Botango Bedjil**'s (B.B. Mo-Franck) keyboards and Frantal's guitar. After three LPs and riding a crest of popularity, the future was looking bright until, once again, the Immigration Department struck. The group played its farewell concert at the *Carnivore* in 1986 and, since then, they have worked abroad in places as far afield as Japan and Oman. In between jobs, they returned to Kenya – several band members have Kenyan wives and children – and they have been allowed to play short stints as guest performers. The vacuum created by the loss of Vundumuna set the stage for the return of Orchestra Virunga to Nairobi in 1988. Kenyans were hungry for top-flight Congolese music. With work permits suddenly no longer a problem, Virunga made a triumphant entry into *Garden Square Nightclub*. They had no trouble immediately recapturing the abundant enthusiasm they left behind after their untimely departure from the music scene three years prior. With a captivating stage show, they played dazzling renditions of all their familiar hits. New compositions like *Safari* and *Vunja Mifupa* joined the list of favourites. Sadly, in 1993, Samba gave up on the local nightclub scene and disbanded the group. More recently, he has taken up residence in the United States though he still performs for special events in Kenya, tours abroad, and continues to record. Although his backing musicians continue to change, nothing has altered Samba Mapangala's formula for brilliant music – a catchy, not over-complex melody, faultless vocal harmonies, innovative, interlocking guitar lines and superbly crafted horns floating over light, high-tensile percussion. Samba Mapangala was not the only one disillusioned by the business of music in Nairobi. By the early 1990s, Nairobi's status as an island of opportunity for Congolese musicians had fallen flat. With harder economic times, a declining record industry, fewer live music venues and restrictive work rules for foreign musicians, Nairobi had become a departure point for greener pastures. Some musicians headed for neighbouring countries but others followed Vundumuna's lead and signed up to play abroad. Since the mid-1990s, however, the Congolese music scene has once again been on the upswing with a host of new names and new places to work. Some Congolese names on the current scene are **Senza Musica**, **Choc la Musica**, **Station Japan**, **Tshiakatumaba International** and **Bilenge Musica**. The latter have a CD release called *Rumba Is Rumba* (Kelele Records) that, in terms of quality, places them among the top *soukous* bands anywhere. The name of vocalist Coco Zigo Mike was originally included in this list as leader of Losako la Musica. Sadly, he died in 1998 at the age of 39. "Prince Cocozigo", as he was known, sang in the late-1970s band Viva Makale, and later in Orchestra Virunga, Ibeba System, and Moreno Batamba's Orchestra Moja One.

Swahili bands: the Tanzanian influence

Songs with **Swahili lyrics** are part of the common currency of East African musical culture. Kenya's own brand of Swahili pop music has its origin in the Tanzanian pop styles of the 1970s but, since that time, the Kenyan variety has followed a separate evolutionary path from the Tanzanian mainstream. In addition to the stylistic features it shares with the Congolese sound (light, high-hat-and-conga percussion and a delicate two/three-guitar interweave), the Kenyan Swahili sound is instrumentally sparse, allowing the bass to fill in gaps, often in syncopated rhythms. Trumpets and saxes are common in recorded arrangements but usually omitted in club performances because of the extra expense.

One of the first groups to migrate to Kenya was Arusha Jazz, the predecessor of what is now the legendary **Simba Wanyika Original** ("Simba Wanyika" means "Lion of the Savanna"). Founded by Wilson Peter Kinyonga and his brothers George and William, the group began performing in Mombasa in 1971. The following year, they began recording for Phonogram (Polygram), making a name for themselves with single releases such as *Eliza Wangu* (My Eliza), *Jose Twende Zaire* (Jose Let's Go to Zaire) and *Mama Suzie*. In 1975, the three brothers, along with Tanzanian recruit Omar Shabani on rhythm and Kenyan Tom Malanga on bass, shifted their base to Nairobi and released their first album, *Jiburudisheni na Simba Wanyika* (Chill Out with Simba Wanyika). Over their twenty-year history in Nairobi (to 1995), the group were favourites of the city's club scene and made scores of recordings. Despite George Kinyonga's death in 1992, the band continued to perform, but following the death of Wilson Kinyonga in 1995, Simba Wanyika rapidly collapsed.

Interestingly, their most widely circulated recordings outside Kenya present a rather different sound from their typical recordings for Polygram in Nairobi. In both their international releases, *Simba Wanyika Original: Kenya Vol I* and *Pepea*, the group has taken a page from the *benga* handbook and quickened the pace considerably – though the vocal and instrumental parts are indeed "original" Simba Wanyika of great guitars, creamy sax (on "Vol I") and pleasing, listener-friendly vocal lines. For purists interested in Simba Wanyika's Polygram sound, the albums *Haleluya* and *Mapenzi Ni Damu*, recorded before and after *Kenya Vol I*, are more representative of their local, "performance" sound.

The Wanyika name is famous in East Africa not only for Simba Wanyika, but for several other related bands that emerged from the Wanyika line. The first big split occurred in 1978 when the core of supporting musicians around the Kinyonga brothers left Simba Wanyika to form **Les Wanyika**. Among those who made the move were rhythm guitarist "Professor" Omari Shabani, bass player Tom Malanga, drummer Rashid Juma and vocalist Issa Juma, who had only joined Simba Wanyika a month before. The group added another crucial member in Tanzanian lead guitar player John Ngereza, who had been playing in Kenya with the Congolese group Bwambe Bwambe. After six months' practice, Les Wanyika began performing at *Garden Square* and soon found fame across Kenya with their massive hit *Sina Makosa* (It's Not My Fault).

Under Ngereza's leadership, Les Wanyika have remained one of Nairobi's top bands. While cut from the same mould as the Simbas, Les Wanyika distinguished themselves with imaginative compositions and arrangements, a typically lean, clean sound and the delicious blend of Professor Omari's rhythm-guitar mastery with Tom Malanga's bass. The sparse percussion majors on the high hat and a muted, pulsing kick drum. This lean instrumentation provides the backing for vocalist and lead guitar player Ngereza, who alternates between the two roles. During vocal choruses, there's solid vocal backing in multi-part harmonies from Mohamed Tika and other Swahili session vocalists. Some of the finest examples of their work are found on the *Dunia Kigeu-geu* compilation, released in Kenya in 1985.

In the early 1990s, as Kenyan tastes embraced disco music, Les Wanyika were there with a remake of their greatest hits into two disco medleys. *Les Les Non-Stop '90* was locally quite successful and carried over into their next album, *Kabibi* – an unfortunate departure into the dismal realm of international disco crossover. Mercifully, Ngereza abandoned this course on his following cassette releases and, in returning to classic Les Wanyika form, has consistently been in Kenya's Top Ten charts with each new release. His inclusion as a guest artist on Orchestra Virunga's 1997 US tour has finally brought him some international exposure outside Africa as well as his first international CD in 1998 entitled *Amigo*. Sadly, 1998 saw the death of Professor Omari, whose brilliant rhythm guitar was a mainstay of the Les Wanyika sound and who composed many of the group's early hits. John Ngereza followed, passing away in February 2000.

An important figure in the Wanyika story is Tanzania-born **Issa Juma**, who quickly established a name for himself in Kenya as a premier vocalist in the early days of Les Wanyika. Mention his name today and many Kenyans will immediately think of "Sigalame", a character from his 1983 single of the same name and now a part of Kenyan vocabulary. *Sigalame* is Issa Juma's most famous song, not because of the music, which is generic *cavacha*, but because of its entertaining lyrics. Sigalame is a mysterious character who has disappeared from family and friends but is rumoured to be living in Bungoma doing "business". What kind of business? ("Biashara gani?") With so many illegal activities to choose from, it was up to the listener to answer. As one of the most productive recording artists of the 1980s, Issa Juma released many numbers in the style of Swahili-*benga* fusion heard in *Sigalame*. Yet, he has been perhaps the most versatile and creative of the Swahili artists in his willingness to take his music in different directions.

Although the Wanyika bands have been dominant in Swahili music, it is not their exclusive domain. Foremost among other Tanzanians and Kenyans performing in the Swahili style are the **Maroon Commandos**. Still members of the Kenya Army, the Commandos are one of the oldest performing groups in the country. They first came together in 1970, and performed mainly covers, but by 1977 they had come out as a strong force in the Swahili style with the huge Taita-language *Charonyi Ni Wasi*, recently released again in Kenya. Within their genre, the Commandos do not limit themselves to any sort of rigid formula. Like many of the Swahili groups, they use trumpets and sax liberally but they're also quite experimental and have at various times added a keyboard and innovative guitar effects and, at their most creative, mingle Swahili and *benga* styles.

In Kenya today, the Swahili rumba sounds of groups like the Wanyikas and Maroons are nearly extinct. From time to time, new bands form but currently, the only serious exponents of the Swahili rumba sound are Abdul Muyonga and Everest Kings. The style, however, remains widely available in reissues in both cassette and CD.

Tourist and international pop

International influences have always been a part of Kenyan music, but where Kenyan pop meets the tourist industry, such as on the Kenyan coast, another distinct brand of music can be heard in all the hotels. Down on the coast, north and south of Mombasa, are the tourist resorts, where a successful band can make a living just playing hotel gigs. **Tourist pop bands** typically have highly competent musicians, relatively good equipment and, overall, a fairly polished sound. In live performances, they play an eclectic mix of old Congolese rumba tunes as warm-ups, popular international covers, a few Congolese favourites of the day, greatest hits from Kenya's past, and then some original material that leans heavily towards the American/Euro-pop sound but with lyrics relating to local topics.

The most successful Kenyan group in this realm has been a perennial favourite, the oddly named **Them Mushrooms**. Strictly speaking, the Mushrooms graduated from the coastal hotel circuit when they moved to Nairobi in 1987. Their music, however, lives on at the coast, highlighted by their crowning achievement, the tourist anthem *Jambo Bwana* with its refrain, *Hakuna Matata* – no problems. TM have several different versions of the song, and while they are proud to take credit for this insidiously infectious bit of fluff, they have much more serious intentions in the world of music.

At their inception, in 1972, the Mushrooms were a reggae band without an audience. However, as they gravitated toward the hotel circuit for work, they changed their style to a more "commercial" sound encompassing international covers, African pop standards, a little soca and reggae, and some Kenyan variants of *benga* and the coastal *chakacha* rhythm. As they moved to Nairobi and the famous *Carnivore* restaurant in 1987, their polished sound established them as a favourite among the affluent nightclub set.

Them Mushrooms are without doubt Kenya's most active band today, with at least fifteen albums to their credit. They now own and operate one of the better studios in Kenya. Over their thirty or so years, they have produced a series of highly successful collaborations, highlighting quite diverse artists, including pioneering musician Fundi Konde, *taarab* star Malika and the Kikuyu singer Queen Jane Nyambura. Their recent work has taken them back to their first love, reggae, with the CD *Kazi Ni Kazi* (Work Is Work), released internationally on the Kelele label.

The Mushrooms' long-time counterparts in the hotel circuit, **Safari Sound**, have also joined the reggae club with another Kelele release called *Mambo Jambo*. This group already has the distinction of having Kenya's best-selling album ever in *The Best of African Songs*, a veritable greatest hits of hotel classics that includes *Malaika* – a beautiful composition about ill-starred love, first sung by Fadhili William, and rarely given the soulful treatment it deserves (see box on p.732).

The evolving music scene

Although Kenya has a rich musical tradition, it's always been a struggle on the part of musicians to gain recognition and respect. Kenyans speak fondly of the great names in Kenyan pop, and relish the local music around them on the streets, but at the same time speak disparagingly about Kenyan music in comparison with music from neighbouring Tanzania, Congo, Europe or America. Institutionally, little has been done to help Kenyan musicians, with cassette piracy and lack of local sources for affordable instruments and supplies, two of the major **problems**. Nor does Kenyan radio give them much support either, especially if their songs are recorded in a local language.

These days, musicians playing *benga*, Swahili pop, or Congolese music face stiff competition on the airwaves and in the music shops. Many of Kenya's younger generation of musicians take their inspiration from rap, R&B, house, reggae and dancehall genres, not simply copying international styles but blending elements of Euro-American pop with local Kenyan melodies, lyrics and rhythms.

For the first time in several years, there seems to be some genuine enthusiasm for local music in this niche, along with a sense of anticipation of greater things to come. The 1998 CD, *Kenyan: The First Chapter*, seems to be an expression of such optimism, providing a showcase for several of the pioneers of this new music. Established artists such as Hardstone, Hart and Shadz O'Blak are represented, but so are another half-dozen newcomers, most receiving their first exposure on CD. *First Chapter* producer, Tedd Josiah, expanded his scope with the release of *Kenyan: The Second Chapter* in 1999. This collection contains the hit song from hip hop duo Gidi Gidi Maji Maji *Ting Badi Malo* (Throw Your Hands Up) and it prepared the groundwork for their solo release *Ismarwa*.

Josiah and other producers such as Bruce Odhiambo and Suzanne Kibukosya are working with a diverse set of artists with quite different interests. One song might be a hip hop cover of an African pop classic. Another might be a rhythm and blues gospel ballad, or a blend of traditional instruments with keyboards and rap. Eric Wainaina's *Sawa Sawa* CD (2001) mingles the cutting social commentary of the Redykyulass comedy team with songs about life in Kenya. In particular, Kenyans really connected with the song *Nchi ya Kitu Kidogo* (Nation of "a little something"), a song decrying the way bribery has permeated Kenyan society.

At this stage, it's hard to predict the direction of music and the music business in Kenya. The one thing that is certain is that we're in the midst of an interesting time, with lots of new players, many of them still learning the game. It will be fun to follow.

Discography

The following recordings are all available on CD.

Compilations

Guitar Paradise of East Africa; *Kenya Dance Mania* (Earthworks/Stern's, UK). These two CDs provide an excellent introduction to Kenya's various styles, although not always the best or most representative material from the artists. Highlights on *Guitar Paradise* include the classic hit *Shauri Yako* by Super Mazembe as well as Kabaselleh Ochieng's *Achi Maria*. On *Kenya Dance Mania* are some Kenyan classics of the 1970s and 1980s including Les Wanyika's *Sina Makosa* and Maroon Commandos' evergreen hit *Charonyi Ni Wasi*.

Luo Roots: Musical Currents from Western Kenya (GlobeStyle, UK). The Kapere Jazz Band and others perform versions of the traditional music of the Luo people, suggesting the foundations of the *benga* style.

The Most Beautiful Songs of Africa (ARC Music, UK). Quite a good collection of (largely) 1970s Kenyan and Tanzanian music. The mix is totally eclectic with the Congolese dance sounds of Super Mazembe (with *Kasongo* and *Shauri Yako*) and Bopol Mansiamina, *taarab* music of the coast, Tanzanian dance music from Afro 70 and Western jazz, not to mention one of Miriam Makeba's best versions of the Swahili song, *Malaika* (the version that served as the model for Angelique Kidjo's rendition).

The Nairobi Beat: Kenyan Pop Music Today (Rounder, US). This is a collection of mid-eighties music put together by the author of this article for Rounder Records. A fine cross-section of pop music varieties, it showcases some of the best examples of regional *benga* styles: Luo, Kikuyu, Akamba and Luhya, plus a couple of Swahili and Congolese dance tunes for good measure.

The Rough Guide to the Music of Kenya and Tanzania (World Music Network, UK). A superb collection of Kenyan and Tanzanian music, it samples traditional and popular styles, including *taarab* from the coastal region. Kenyan artists include Simba Wanyika (of Tanzanian origin), Victoria Kings, D.O. Misiani and Shirati Jazz, Abana ba Nasery, Henry Makobi, Ogwang Lelo Okoth with Paddy J. Onono and Zein Musical Party.

The Secret Museum of Mankind, Music of East Africa, Ethnic Music Classics: 1925–48 (Yazoo, US). This compilation, with selections from throughout East Africa, provides a fascinating window onto traditional and popular sounds reflecting local styles (mainly of the 1930s and 40s).

Artists

Abana Ba Nasery

From western Kenya, this trio keeps alive a style of music they pioneered in the 1960s and early 1970s.

Classic Acoustic Recordings from Western Kenya (GlobeStyle, UK). These are the original recordings made back in the late sixties and early seventies. A charming collection of finger-picking acoustic guitar music from Bunyore, Kenya.

!Nursery Boys Go Ahead! The Guitar and Bottle Kings of Kenya (GlobeStyle, UK/Xenophile, US). This CD captures the crisp ABN sound in new recordings made on their 1991 tour to the UK. It also places the trio in some interesting collaborations with European artists, some of which really get rockin'.

Bilenge Musica

This group of eight Congolese musicians came together in Nairobi in early 1996 under the leadership of Didie Double-weight. Individually, they've played with some of Congo's most famous musicians and groups including Sam Mangwana, Koffi Olomide, Viva la Musica and Tanzanian-based Maquis Original and Carnival Band.

Rumba is Rumba (Kelele, Germany). But for Swahili language lyrics in several of the songs, this is mainstream Congolese *soukous* all the way – and that's not bad. The sound is reminiscent of Wenge Musica and the production at Sync Sound Studios in Nairobi is first-rate, as usual.

Oguta Bobo

Not much is known about the late Oguta Bobo Otange, but that he's a compelling accordion player from among the Luo of western Kenya and his music covered the gamut of topics from serious social commentary to the lighter side of love.

Rujina Kalando (Equator Heritage Sounds, US). Squeeze-box fanatics: here's your chance to get some rare recordings of African accordion with Oguta Bobo singing and playing. The songs are traditional in melody and rhythm but contemporary in lyrics of the time (the 1960s). And, for those who understand Luo, the songs are filled with humour.

Hardstone

Born in 1977, Hardstone is a rapper in Kikuyu and Jamaican English, and one of the new breed of young Kenyan artists pursuing musical interests in international pop. He's recently relocated to the USA.

Nuting but de Stone (Kelele Records, Germany). This CD joins Caribbean ragga, American urban sounds, and

African lyrics and rhythms in a superbly produced package that ranges from ragga to R&B.

H.N. Ochieng' Kabaselleh & the Lunna Kidi band

From the area around Lake Victoria, Kabaselleh (died 1998) was one Kenyan bandleader whose music is always a little bit different – an interesting mix of Luo *benga*, Swahili rumba and Congolese influences.

Sanduku ya Mapendo; *Achi Maria* (Equator Heritage Sounds, US). Two collections of Kabaselleh's double-sided singles from the 1980s – fine examples of his fusion of *benga*, rumba and *soukous*.

Kakai Kilonzo

Kakai was at the top of Kamba language music in Kenya from the mid-1970s until his death in 1987. But with catchy Swahili lyrics and very together *benga* sound, Kakai had fans from all parts of the country and beyond.

Best of Kakai Vol 1 (Andy G Music Productions, Germany). This is a fine compilation of 45rpm singles from the mid-1980s. Interestingly, most of Kakai's singles split a song into two parts for the A and B sides of the record. Here we get parts 1 and 2 for six singles plus a one-side bonus.

Fundi Konde

One of Kenya's most renowned early guitarists and the creator of many of what Kenyans consider "the classics". His heyday was the 1950s, but he was rediscovered by Kenyans in the 1990s through his collaboration with Them Mushrooms in new releases of his music.

Fundi Konde Retrospective Vol. 1 (1947–56) (RetroAfric, UK). Many of the tunes are rumbas, though a couple sound as though they are precursors to reggae.

Samba Mapangala & Orchestra Virunga

Orchestra Virunga have long been one of Kenya's most exciting groups and Samba one of Kenya's most gifted talents.

Virunga Volcano (Earthworks/Stern's, UK). The first CD from Samba Mapangala and Orchestra Virunga. In a class all of its own, this is the perfect album, with each song like a story that develops over a ten-minute period, exploring different combinations of rhythm, melody and harmony right through to the finish. As fresh and enticing today as it was when created back in the early 1980s.

Feet On Fire (Stern's Africa, UK). First-rate Samba Mapangala in the East African groove, recorded on the 1991 UK tour.

Ujumbe (Earthworks/Stern's, UK). Samba's latest CD from 2001 picks up right where he left off; great melodies and harmonies, lush guitar, sublime sax, and that eminently danceable East African rumba beat.

D.O. Misiani & Shirati Band

One of the founding fathers of *benga* music, Daniel Owino Misiani is still playing after more than thirty years.

Benga Blast! (Earthworks/Stern's, UK); *Piny Ose Mer/The World Upside Down* (GlobeStyle, UK). Fine collections from the definitive name in Luo *benga*, the former (being the rough, unpolished sound of the old Pioneer House studios) in glorious mono.

Ayub Ogada

Ayub Ogada has been exploring and bridging cultural boundaries over the last two decades.

En Mana Kuoyo (Real World, UK). This begins with Luo tradition: the *nyatiti* harp, praise songs and indigenous rhythms. Then he infuses his own creative genius for a quiet, largely acoustic CD with beautiful melodies and captivating rhythms.

Simba Wanyika Original

One of Kenya's favourite Swahili rumba bands since the early 1970s, the deaths of both of the founding brothers, George and Wilson Peter Kinyonga recently wound up the band.

Pepea (Kameleon Records/Stern's, Netherlands/UK). Their only solo CD, this is superbly produced, allowing the band to shine on some of their biggest hits of the previous twenty years. Highly recommended.

Orchestra Super Mazembe

The Congolese group that made their way to Nairobi in the 1970s is still together, performing regularly, and sounding great. In songs such as *Kasongo* and *Shauri Yako*, they exemplify the definitive sound of Congolese rumba in East Africa.

Giants of East Africa (Earthworks/Stern's, UK) Mazembe's early-eighties LP, *Kaivaska*, kindled much of the mid-1980s enthusiasm for Afropop in the UK and Europe. This collection has five of the best songs off *Kaivaska*, plus *Shauri Yako*, and another five previously unavailable outside Kenya.

Them Mushrooms

Them Mushrooms have sprouted in several forms over their thirty-year history. Since 1993, they've returned to their reggae origins.

Them Mushrooms (Rags Music, UK). After the first two songs, *Jambo Bwana* and *Mushroom Soup*, the remainder of the CD is the Mushrooms' remakes of classic Kenyan tunes from the 1950s and 1960s.

Kazi Ni Kazi (Kelele Records, Germany). The Mushrooms have fully entered the reggae camp in this CD and they certainly sound at home.

Jambo Bwana (Kelele Records, Germany). Reggae for tourists in the beach hotels.

Victoria Kings

One of the great *benga* groups from Luo country, they started in the early 1970s with Ochieng Nelly as bandleader, soon joined by long-time musical partner Collela Mazee. One of the top-selling recording groups of the golden age of *benga* in the late 1970s and early 1980s.

The Mighty Kings of Benga (GlobeStyle, UK). A different perspective on *benga* (ie not Shirati Jazz) and a very good compilation.

Eric Wainaina

Although based in the US for his music studies, Wainaina is one of the stars of the new generation of younger Kenyan musicians. He brings together an innovative mix of Kenyan pop sounds with Euro/American influences.

Sawa Sawa (Wainaina/Kaufmann Prod, USA/Kenya). Contains the hit song *Nchi ya Kitu Kidogo* about corruption and bribery in Kenya, a subject that resonates with every Kenyan. The CD spans a broad range of styles from up-tempo African dance rhythms to ballads and "smooth jazz" sax. And for Swahili speakers, there are comedic interludes from the Kenyan troupe Redykyulass. It's a superb, well-crafted debut CD.

Zein Musical Party

Zein l'Abdin, a master of the *oud*, hails from Lamu but now lives in Mombasa. As befits a native of the old centre of Swahili culture and lit-

These are two songs you're almost certain to hear, sooner of later, regardless of where you stay or how you travel.

Jambo Bwana
by Teddy Kalanda Harrison

Jambo, jambo Bwana	Greetings, greetings Bwana
Habarai gani?	How are you doing?
Nzuri sana	Very well
Wageni, mwakaribishwa	Visitors, you are all welcomed
Kenya yetu	In our Kenya
Hakuna matata	There are no problems
Kenya ni nchi nzuri	Kenya's a beautiful country
Hakuna matata	There are no problems
Nchi ya kupendeza	A pleasing country
Hakuna matata	There are no problems
Nchi ya maajabu	A country of wonders
Hakuna matata	There are no problems
Nchi yenye amani	A country of peace
Hakuna matata	There are no problems

Malaika
Authorship disputed, first popularized by Fadhili William

Malaika, nakupenda malaika	Angel, I love you angel
Malaika, nakupenda malaika	Angel, I love you angel
Nami nifanyeje, kijana mwenzio?	And me, what shall I, your boyfriend, do?
Nashindwa na mali sina wee	If I weren't struggling for money
Ningekuoa malaika	I would marry you angel
Nashindwa na mali sina wee	If I weren't struggling for money
Ningekuoa malaika	I would marry you angel
Pesa zasumbuwa roho yangu	Money is the source of my heartache
Pesa zasumbuwa roho yangu	Money is the source of my heartache
Nami nifanyeje, kijana mwenzio?	And me, what shall I, your boyfriend, do?
Nashindwa na mali sina wee	If I weren't struggling for money
Ningekuoa malaika	I would marry you angel
Nashindwa na mali sina wee	If I weren't struggling for money
Ningekuoa malaika	I would marry you angel
Kidege, hukuwaza kidege	Little bird, I'm always dreaming of you, little bird
Kidege, hukuwaza kidege	Little bird, I'm always dreaming of you, little bird
Nami nifanyeje, kijana mwenzio?	And me, what shall I, your boyfriend, do?
Nashindwa na mali sina wee	If I weren't struggling for money
Ningekuoa malaika	I would marry you angel
Nashindwa na mali sina wee	If I weren't struggling for money
Ningekuoa malaika	I would marry you angel

erature, he is known for his research into old Swahili poetry.

Mtindo wa Mombasa: The Style of Mombasa (GlobeStyle, UK). Some great tunes here: just check out the tour-de-force on *Wanawake wa Kiamu*, just *oud*, dumbak and vocals.

The Swahili Song Book (Dizim, Germany). All-acoustic versions of timeless Swahili classics, like *Loho ya Kihindi, Maneno Tisiya* and *Mnazi Wangu*, along with some of Zein's own recent compositions. Highly recommended.

Zuhura & Party
Zuhura Swaleh, one of Mombasa's outstanding female singers has an energetic style firmly based in *chakacha ngoma* rhythms.

Jino la Pembe (GlobeStyle, UK). One of the best available introductions to *taarab* music, this is a compendium of Zuhura's most popular *chakacha* songs, notably *Parare* and the title tune *Jino la Pembe* recorded on a European tour with the Maulidi Musical Party.

Updated and expanded by Doug Paterson from his article in *The Rough Guide to World Music Vol 1*. Traditional music: Jens Finke. Tarabu Music: Werner Graebner. *Malaika* translated by Farouk Abdillah.

language

language

Language

S urprisingly, perhaps, Swahili is one of the easiest languages to learn. It's pronounced exactly as it's written, with the stress nearly always on the penultimate syllable. And it's satisfyingly regular, so even with limited knowledge you can make yourself understood and construct simple sentences.

In Kenya, you'd rarely be stuck without Swahili, but it makes a huge difference to your perceptions if you try to speak it. People are delighted if you make the effort (though they'll also tend to assume you understand more than you do). Don't forget that for many Kenyans Swahili is another foreign language they get by in, like English. For travels further afield in East Africa, and especially in Tanzania, some knowledge of Swahili is a very useful backup.

The language has spread widely from its coastal origins to become the lingua franca of east Africa and it has tended to lose its richness and complexity as a result. Up-country, it is often spoken as a second language with a minimum of grammar. On the coast, you'll hear it spoken with tremendous panache: oratorial skills and punning (to which it lends itself with great facility) are much appreciated. Swahili is a Bantu language (in fact one of the more mainstream of the family), but it has incorporated thousands of foreign words, the majority of them Arabic, but including Portuguese and English. Far more of this Arabic inheritance and borrowing is preserved on the coast. The "standard" dialect is derived from Zanzibar Swahili, which the early missionaries learned and first transcribed into the Roman alphabet. **Written Swahili** is still not completely uniform, and you'll come across slight variations in spelling, particularly on menus.

Books and courses

There are several published language **courses** around. *Teach Yourself Swahili* by Joan Russel (Teach Yourself Books, 1995) is an excellent book, with practical everyday Swahili that you can use from the beginning. For the analytical approach, the best book is probably *Simplified Swahili* by Peter M Wilson (Longman, 1985). *Kiswahili kwa Kitendo* ("Swahili by Action", US only, Africa World Press, 1988) is the best bet if you find ordinary grammars indigestible. The course by Joan Maw, *Swahili for Starters* (Oxford University Press, 1999), is good. As for phrasebooks, try the *Rough Guide Swahili Dictionary Phrasebook*.

Pronunciation

Once you get the hang of voicing every syllable, **pronunciation** is easy. Each vowel is syllabic. However, odd-looking combinations of consonants are often pronounced as one syllable. **Mzee**, for example, is pronounced "mz-ay-ay" (rhyming with "hey") and **shauri** (troubles, problem) is pronounced "sha-oo-ri" while **mgonjwa** ("ill") has just two syllables – "mgo-njwa". Nothing is silent.

You'll often come across an "**m**" where it looks out of place: this letter can precede any other. That is because it's a noun prefix (usually replaced in the plural with "wa-" or "mi-"), as in **mtoto** – child (plural: **watoto**) or **mti** – tree (plural: **miti**). Just add a bit of an "m" sound at the beginning; "mm-toto". Don't say "um-toto" or "ma-toto"– you'll be misunderstood. In one or two nouns beginning with "mb" or "mv" (with no change in the plural), the "m" merges into the "b" or "v", as in **mbuzi** – goat or goats. The letter "n" can precede a number of others and gives a nasal quality. "Ng" followed by an apostrophe makes a sound like the "ng" in banger (try saying it without the "ba", and then use it in a word like **ng'ombe** – cow or beef); without the apostrophe, it's like two separate letters as in "finger" (or as in **nguo** – garment, clothes).

For memorizing, it often helps to ignore the first letter or syllable. Thousands of nouns, for example, start with "ki" (singular) and "vi" (plural), and they're all in the same noun class.

A as in Arthur

B as in bed

C doesn't exist on its own

CH as in church, but often sounds like a "t", a "dj", or a "ky"

D as in donkey

DJ like the "j" in pyjamas

DH like a cross between dhow and thou

E between the "e" in Edward and "ai" in ailing

F as in fan

G as in good

GH at the back of the throat, like a gargle or a French "r"

H as in harmless

I like the "e" in evil

J as in jug

K as in kiosk, sometimes like soft "t" or "ch"

KH like the "ch" in loch

L as in lullaby, but often pronounced like an "r"

M as in Martian

N as in nonsense

NG as in finger or hunger, with a clear "g" sound

NG' as in wrong or banger, with no "g" sound

O as in orange, never as in "open" or "do"

P as in penguin

Q doesn't exist (except in early Romanized texts; now "k")

R as in rapid

S as in Samson

T as in tiny

TH as in thanks, never as in them

U as in lute

V as in victory

W as in wobble

X doesn't exist

Y as in you

Z as in zero

Elementary grammar

Noun classes put people off Swahili. They are something like the genders in French or Latin in that you alter each adjective according to the class of noun. In Swahili you add a **prefix** to the word. Each class covers certain areas of meaning and usually has a prefix letter associated with most of its nouns. For example, words beginning "m" in the singular and "wa" in the plural are almost always people (eg **mtu/watu** – person/people; **mtalii/watalii** – tourist/tourists). Words beginning "ki" or "ch" (singular), and "vi" or "vy" (plural) are in the general class of "things", notably smallish things (eg **kitabu/vitabu** – book/books; **chumba/vyumba** – room/rooms). Words beginning "m" (singular) and "mi" (plural) are often trees and plants (eg **mti/miti** – tree/trees), or have connections with life. One of the biggest classes of nouns (the "N class") has no prefix, though nouns in it often begin with "n", "mb" or "mv"; they do not change in the plural (eg **ndizi** – banana/bananas, **njui** – road/roads, **mbu** – mosquito/mosquitos). Most abstract nouns begin with "u" (eg **uhuru** – freedom, utoto – childhood). There are seven classes altogether, with singular and plural versions of each.

Prefixes get added to **adjectives**, so you get **kiti kizuri** – a good chair; **mtu mzuri** – a good person; **miti mizuri** – good trees. Really correct Swahili, with everything agreeing, isn't much spoken except on the coast, and you can get away with murder. But once you've grasped the essential building blocks – the root meanings and the prefixes, suffixes and infixes of one or two letters which turn them into words – it becomes a very creative language to learn. Swahili nouns don't have articles, either definite ("the") or indefinite ("a"or "an"), which makes the language a little easier, while losing nothing in richness.

Although Swahili nouns are relatively complicated compared to other languages, the **verb** system is reasonably simple. You begin with a prefix for the person, then a marker for the tense (or just "ku-" for the infinitive; we've added hyphens for clarification), and then the verb root. So from the verb **ku-taka** – to want, you get **ni-na-taka** – I want, **u-li-taka** – "you wanted", and **wa-ta-taka** - they will want. The present marker "na" isn't really a tense marker but a little connective the best translation of which is really "with". Negatives are a bit more difficult: in principle, you add "ha-" at the beginning, but in the present you take away the tense marker and change the last letter to "i", so the negative of **tu-na-jua** ("we know") is **ha-tu-ju-i** ("we don't know"); also, the "ha-" gets merged into the singular person prefixes, as shown below.

Personal prefixes

I - **ni-** (sometimes omitted in the present; negative **si-**). Eg: **najua** "I know", **sijui** "I don't know"
you (sing.) - **u-** (negative **hu-**)
he or she - **a-** (negative **ha-**)
we - **tu-** (negative **hatu-**)
you (pl) - **m-** (negative **ham-**)
they (people or animals) - **wa-** (negative **hawa-**)

Third person prefixes for inanimate objects are usually the same as their noun prefixes, but are **i-**(singular) and **zi-**(plural) for the common nouns in the N-class. However, for people and animals, regardless of the class, they are always **a-** and **wa-**

Pronouns

I, me - **mimi**
you (sing.) - **wewe**
he, she, him, her - **yeye**

we, us - **sisi**
you (pl.) - **ninyi**
they, them - **wao**

Tense markers

past ("did") - **-li-** (**-ku-** in negative)
perfect ("has done") - **-me-** (negative **-ja-**, with the implication "not yet")
present ("does or is doing") - **-na-** (omitted in negative)
future ("will do") - **-ta-**

infinitive ("to do") - **ku-**
One or two very common short verbs keep the "**ku-**" of the infinitive when making tenses (except negatives), for example **kuja** – to come, **kula** to eat

739

to be able (can) – **kuweza** (**mnaweza kusema Kiswahili** – you (plural) can speak Swahili)

to bring – **kuleta** (**tumeleta** – we've brought)

to buy – **kununua** (**walinunua** – they bought)

to come – **kuja** (keeps "**ku**-"; **walikuja** – they came)

to come from – **kutoka** (**unatoka wapi?** – where do you come from?)

to drink – **kunywa** (keeps "**ku**-"; **atakunywa** – s/he will drink)

to eat – **kula** (keeps "**ku**-"; **tumekula** – we have eaten)

to give – **kupa** (keeps "**ku**"; **alikupa** – s/he gave)

to go – **kwenda** (ie **ku-enda**; **unaenda** or **unaenda** – you are going)

to hear – **kusikia** (**hajasikia** – s/he hasn't heard yet)

to like/love – **kupenda** (**anapenda kulala** – s/he likes to sleep)

to look – **kutazama** (**utatazama** – you looked)

to meet – **kuonana** (**tutaonana** – we will meet, ie "see you")

to say, speak – **kusema** (**alisema** – s/he said)

to see – **kuona** (**niliona** – I saw)

to sleep – **kulala** (**hatukulala** – we didn't sleep)

to stay – **kukaa** (**mtakaa?** – will you (plural) stay?)

to think – **kufikiri** (**ninafikiri** or **nafikiri** – I think)

to be tired – **kuchoka** (**sichoki** – I'm not tired)

to understand – **kuelewa** (**sielewi** – I don't understand)

to want – **kutaka** (**ninataka** or **nataka** – I want)

To be – **kuwa** – is not used in the present. It keeps "**ku**-"; **watakuwa** – they will be. In the present, "to be" in the sense of "am" "are" or "is" is simply **ni** or, in the negative ("am not", "isn't", "aren't"), **si**. These very common constructions are often used with a personal pronoun as listed on p.739. For example: **Mimi si Mkenya, ni mtalii** – I'm not Kenyan, I'm a tourist, or **Yeye nimbaya** – S/he's bad.

To have – **kuwa na** – is literally "to be with", as in **nilikuwa na mbwa** – I had a dog, with a personal verb prefix in front. In the present it's simpler still: **nina**, **una**, **ana** – I have, you have s/he has; **tuna**, **mna**, **wana** – we have, you (plural) have, they have. Thus: **nina gari** (literally "I with car"– I have a car).

Also useful is the suffix -**ko**, which means to be in a place, and takes the same prefixes except that the prefix for "he" or "she" is **yu**- instead of **a**-. Hence **niko wapi?** – where am I? **John yuko wapi?** – where's John? **posta iko wapi?** – where's the post office?

Words and phrases

The words and phrases listed here are all in common usage, but Swahili (like English) is far from being a homogeneous language, so don't be surprised if you sometimes get some funny looks. And, for lack of space for explanation, there are a number of apparent inconsistencies; just ignore them unless you intend to learn the language seriously. These phrases should make you understood at least.

Jambo – Hello, good day, how are you? (multi-purpose greeting, means "Problems?")

Jambo – (the response) No problems

Hujambo? – (gramatically correct) Hello, good day, how are you?

Sijambo – (gramatically correct) No problems
Habari? – How are things? (literally "News?")
Mambo? – (informal, colloquial, literally "things?/issues?") How goes?/Hi!
Sasa? – (literally "now?") How goes?
Vipi? – (informal, colloquial, no literal translation) What's up?
Safi – (informal, colloquial, literally "pure") Cool, sweet
Fiti – (informal, colloquial, literally "fit") Cool, excellent
Hodi! – Hello? Anyone in? (said on knocking or entering)
Karibu – Come in, enter, welcome (also said on offering something)
Kwaheri/ni – Goodbye to one/many
Asante/ni – Thank you to one/many
sana – very (a common emphasis)
Bwana – Mister, the equivalent of Monsieur in French (mabwana is the plural)
Mama – like the French Madame or Mademoiselle, for adult women
kjana – youth, teenager (pl. vijana)
mtoto – child, kid (pl. watoto)
Jina lako nani? – What's your name?/What are you called?
-zungu – white, European (eg mzungu – white person; wazungu, white people)

Basics

My name is/I am called – Jina langu/Nina itwa
Where are you from? – Unatoka wapi?
Where are you staying? – Unakaa wapi?
I am from – Ninatoka
I am staying (at/in) – Ninakaa
See you! – Tutaonana! (lit. "We shall meet")
yes, that's right – ndiyo (denoting agreement, even with a negative)
no – hapana; siyo; la (Arabic heard mostly on the coast)
I don't understand – Sifahamu/Sielewi
I don't speak Swahili, but... – Sisemi kiswahili, lakini...
How do you say...in Swahili – Unasemaje kwa kiswahili...?
Could you repeat that? – Sema tena (lit. "speak again")
Speak slowly – Sema pole pole
I don't know – Sijui
where (is)? – wapi?
here – hapa
when? – lini?
now – sasa
soon – sasa hivi
why? – kwa nini?

because. . . – kwa sababu. . .
but – lakini
who? – nani?
what? – nini?
which? – gani?
true – kweli
and/with – na
or – au
isn't it? – siyo? (equivalent of French n'est-ce pas?)
I'm English (or British)/Scottish/Welsh/Irish/American/Canadian/Australian/a New Zealander/Kenyan – Mimi ni mwingereza/mskochi/mwelsh/muairish/mwamerika/mkanada/mwaustralia/mnyuziland/mkenya

The plural for nationalities will begin with "Wa-" instead of "M-". Scottish and Welsh readers will no doubt not be pleased to know that Mwingereza is used to mean "British" rather than just "English", and that Britain or the UK are usually referred to as Uingereza, which strictly speaking should mean England.

Signs

Hatari! – Danger
Angalia!/Onyo! – Warning
Mbwa mkali! – Fierce dog!
Hakuna njia! – No entry!

And two phrases you're more likely to hear than to ever say
Piga picha mimi! – Take a picture of me!
Saidia maskini! – Help the poor!

Adjectives and idioms

good – -zuri (with a prefix at the front)
bad – -baya (ditto)
big – -kubwa
small – -dogo
a lot of – -ingi
other/another – -ingine
not bad – si mbaya
OK, right, fine – sawa
fine, cool – safi
completely – kabisa
just, only – tu (kitanda kimoja tu – just one bed)
thing(s) – kitu (vitu)

No problem – Hakuna wasiwasi/Hakuna matata
problems, hassles – wasiwasi, matata
friend – rafiki
sorry, pardon – samahani
It's nothing – Si kitu
Excuse me, let me through – Hebu
What's up? – Namna gani?
If God wills it – Inshallah (heard often on the coast)
please – Tafadhali (rare up-country and not heard much on the coast either)

Daily needs

Where can I sleep? – Naweza kulala wapi?
Can I stay here? – Naweza kulala hapa?
room(s) – chumba (vyumba)
bed(s) – kitanda (vitanda)
chair(s) – kiti (viti)
table(s) – meza
toilet, bathroom – choo, bafu
men, women – wanaume, wanawakea
washing water – maji ya kuosha
hot/cold water – maji moto/baridi
I'm hungry – Nina njaa
I'm thirsty – Nina kiu
Is there any...? – Iko...? or Kuna...?
Yes there is... – Iko..., or Kuna...
No there isn't any – Haiko..., or Hakuna...
How much? – Ngapi?
money – pesa
What price...? – Bei gani...?
How much is...? – Pesa ngapi...?
I want... – Nataka...
I don't want... – Sitaki...

Give me/Bring me (can I have?) – Nipe/Niletee
again/more – tena
enough – tosha/basi
expensive – ghali sana
cheap (also "easy") – rahisi
fifty cents – sumni
Reduce the price, come down a little! – Punguza kidogo!
shop – duka
bank – benki
post office – posta
café, restaurant – hoteli
telephone – simu
cigarettes – sigara
I'm ill – Mimi mgonjwa
doctor – daktari
hospital – hospitali
police – polisi
tip, bribe – chai

Travel and directions

travel – kusafiri
journey – safari
bus(es) – bas, basi/mabasi
car(s), vehicle/s – gari (magari)
taxi – teksi
bicycle – baiskeli
train – treni
plane – ndege
boat/ship – chombo/meli
petrol – petroli
road, path – njia/ndia
highway – barabara

on foot/walking – kwa miguu (literally "by feet")
When does it leave? – Inaondoka lini?
When will we arrive? – Tutafika lini?
slowly – pole pole
fast, quickly – haraka
Wait!/Hang on a moment! – Ngoja!/Ngoja kidogo!
Stop! – Simama!
Where are you going? – Unaenda wapi?
To where? – Mpaka wapi?
From where? – Kutoka wapi?

How many kilometres? - Kilometa ngapi?
I'm going to... - Nenda...
Move along, squeeze up a little -
  Songa!/Songa kidogo
Let's go, carry on - Twende, endelea
straight ahead - moja kwa moja

right - kulia
left - kushoto
up - juu
down - chini
I want to get off here - Nataka kushuka hapa
The car has broken down - Gari imevunjika

Time, calendar and numbers

What time is it? - Saa ngapi?
four o'clock - saa nne (ie 4 hours past dawn
  or dusk, in other words 10am or 10pm; see
  p.78)
quarter past - na robo
half past - na nusu
quarter to - kasa robo
minutes - dakika
daytime - mchana
night time - usiku
dawn - alfajiri
morning - asubuhi
early - mapema
yesterday - jana
today - Ico
tomorrow - kesho
last week/this week/next week - wiki
  iliopita/wiki hii/wiki ijayo
this year - mwaka huu
this month (lit. "moon") - mwezi huu
Monday - jumatatu
Tuesday - jumanne
Wednesday - jumatano
Thursday - alhamisi
Friday - ijumaa
Saturday - jumamosi

Sunday - jumapili
1 - moja
2 - mbili
3 - tatu
4 - nne
5 - tano
6 - sita
7 - saba
8 - nane
9 - tisa
10 - kumi
11 - kumi na moja
12 - kumi na mbili
20 - ishirini
21 - ishirini na moja
30 - thelathini
40 - arobaini
50 - hamsini
60 - sitini
70 - sabini
80 - themanini
90 - tisini
100 - mia moja
121 - mia moja na ishirini na moja
1000 - elfu

Menu and food terms

The lists below should be adequate for translating most Swahili menus and
explaining what you want, though bear in mind that spelling may vary.

Basics

food - chakula
water, juice - maji
ice - barafu
table - meza
plate - sahani
spoon - kijiko
knife - kisu
fork - uma
bottle - chupa

bill - hesabu
salt - chumvi
pepper - piripiri
bread - mkate
butter, margarine - siagi
sugar - sukari
milk - maziwa
egg(s) - yal (mayai)
fish - samaki

meat – **nyama**
vegetables – **mboga**
sauce – **mchuzi**
fruit – **matunda**
more, another – **ingine**
half – **nusu**

roast– **choma** (**nyama choma** – roast meat, is the food for parties and celebrations)
boiled – **chemka**
fried – **kaanga**
hot – **moto**
cold – **baridi**

Snacks

chapa – unleavened, flat wheat bread, baked on a hot plate or in an oven (tandoor)
halwa – gelatinous sweetmeat, like turkish delight
keki – cake
kitumbuo – deep-fried rice bread
mandaazi – deep-fried sweet dough, sometimes flavoured with spices, known as

mahamri on the coast
maziwalala – yogurt (literally: "milk asleep")
mkate mayai – "egg-bread": soft thin dough wrapped around fried egg and minced meat
samosa – deep-fried triangular case of chopped meat and vegetables
tosti/slice – slice of bread

Dishes

frigisi – chicken giblets
githeri – kikuyu dish of beans and corn, sometimes with meat
irio/kienyeji – potato, cabbage and beans mashed together (mount kenya region)
kima – mince
matoke – green banana, usually boiled and mashed
mboga – vegetables: usually potatoes, carrots and onions in meaty gravy
mchele – plain white rice
michicha – spinach cooked with onions and

tomatoes
pilau – rice with spices and meat
sukuma wiki – boiled green leaves, usually a kind of spinach
ugali/sima – cornmeal boiled to a solid porridge with water, occasionally milk; yellow *ugali* is considered inferior to white but is more nutritious
uji – porridge or gruel made of millet; good for chilly mornings
wali – rice with added fat and spices; almost pilau

Meat

kondo – lamb
kuku – chicken
mbuzi – goat
mushkaki – kebab – small pieces of grilled,

marinated meat on or off the skewer
ng'ombe – beef
nguruwe – pork
steki – steak, grilled meat

Fruit

limau – lime
machungwa – oranges
madafu – green coconuts
maembe – mangoes
mastafeli – soursops
matopetope – custard apples
nanasi – pineapple

nazi – coconuts
ndimu – lemon
ndizi – bananas
papai – papaya/pawpaw
parachichi – avocado
pera – guava
sandara – mandarins

Vegetables

maharagwe – red kidney beans, often cooked with coconut

mahindi – corn
mbaazi – pigeon peas, small beans

mtama – millet (made into a gruel for breakfast)
muhogo – cassava
ndizi – bananas or plantains (often served with meat dishes)

nyanya – tomatoes (also means grandmother)
sukuma wiki – greens, usually kale or collard greens
viazi – potatoes
Vitunguu – Onions

Drinks

busaa – maize beer
chai, chai kavu, chai strungi – tea, black tea, strongly spiced tea
changa'a – hootch, illegal spirits
mnazi – coconut palm wine
muratina – porridgey kikuyu honey and millet

beer
mabziwalala – fermented milk/almost yoghurt (literally "sleeping milk")
kahawa – coffee
bia, tembo – beer
pombe – booze

Swahili animal names

Animal is **mnyama** (plural **wanyama**) but most species' names are the same in singular and plural.

Bweha – Jackal
Bweha masigio – Bat-eared fox
Choroa – Oryx
Chui – Leopard
Dondoo – Steinbok, grysbok
Duma – Cheetah
Faru – Rhinoceros
Fisi – Hyena
Fisi maji – Otter
Fungo – Civet
Kakukuona – Pangolin
Kalasinga – De Brazza's monkey
Kalunguyeye – Hedgehog
Kamandegere – Springhare
Kanu – Genet
Kiboko – Hippopotamus
Kima – Monkey (usually Sykes' monkey)
Kindi – Ground squirrel
Kobe – Tortoise
Komba – Bushbaby
Kongoni – Hartebeest
Korongo – Roan antelope
Kuru – Waterbuck
Mamba – Crocodile
Mbega – Colobus monkey
Mbuni – Ostrich
Mbuzi mawe – Klipspringer
Mbwa – Dog
Mbwa mwitu – Hunting dog
Mdudu – Insect, bug
Mjusi – Lizard

Mondo – Serval
Muhanga – Aardvark
Ndege – Bird (also means plane)
Ndeze – Cane rat
Ndovu – Elephant
Ngiri – Warthog
Nguchiro – Mongoose
Nguruwe – Pig, hog
Nsya – Duiker
Nungu – Porcupine
Nyamera – Topi
Nyani – Baboon
Nyati – Buffalo
Nyegere – Ratel
Nyoka – Snake
Nyumbu – Wildebeest
Paa – Suni antelope
Paka – Cat
Paka pori – Wild cat
Pala hala – Sable antelope
Papa – Shark
Pembere – Tree hyrax
Pimbi – Rock hyrax
Pofu – Eland
Punda – Horse, ass
Punda milia – Zebra
Sange – Elephant shrew
Simba – Lion
Simbamangu – Caracal
Soko – Chimpanzee
Sunguru – Hare, rabbit

Swala granti – Grant's gazelle
Swala pala – Impala
Swala tomi – Thomson's gazelle
Swala twiga – Gerenuk
Tandala – Kudu

Taya – Oribi
Tohe – Reedbuck
Tumbili – Vervet monkey
Twiga – Giraffe

Other languages

The following brief lists are intended only for introductions and as a spring-board for communication. If you'll be spending time in a particular linguistic region, you may be surprised at how difficult it is to track down usable primers and phrasebooks for these languages. Very little material exists for non-native speakers of African languages, though you can make some progress if you're prepared to struggle (with a dictionary) with short novels or the Bible and the like. Try the sources on p.23 for further ideas. However, even the prodigiously stocked library of London University's School of African and Oriental Studies is rather bereft of user-friendly material.

Luo (Lake Victoria)

How do you do? – Iriyo nade?
Response: – Ariyo maber!
Thank you – Erokamano
1 – Achiel
2 – Ariyo
3 – Adek
4 – Angwen

5 – Abich
6 – Auchiely
7 – Abiriyo
8 – Aboro
9 – Ochiko
10 – Apar

Maa (Maasai)

Greetings to a man: – Lo murrani! Supa!
Response: – Ipa!
Greetings to a woman: – Na kitok!
   Takuenya!
Response: – Iko!
Thank you (very much!) – Ashe (naleng!)
Goodbye! – Sere!
1 – Obo
2 – Aare

3 – Okuni
4 – Oonguan
5 – Imiet
6 – Ile
7 – Oopishana
8 – Isiet
9 – Ooudo
10 – Tomon

Kikuyu (Central Highlands)

How are things? – Kweruo atia?
Fine! – Ni kwega!
How are you? – Waigua atia?
Are you well? (pl.) – Wi mwega/Muri ega?
Response: ("Nothing wrong") – Asha, ndi
   mwega
Goodbye (when you're leaving) – Tigwo na
   wega
Goodbye (when you're staying) – Thii na
   wega

1 – Imwe
2 – Igiri
3 – Ithatu
4 – Inya
5 – Ithano
6 – Ithathatu
7 – Mugwanja
8 – Inyanya
9 – Kenda
10 – Ikumi

Glossary

These words are all in common usage. Remember, however, that plural forms often have different beginnings.

AFCO – Armed Forces Catering Ordnance

ASK – Agricultural Society of Kenya

Askari – Policeman, security guard

Banda – Any kind of hut, usually round and thatched

Bangi, Bhang – Marijuana

Baobab – Species of tree whose trunk retains water

Barabara – Main road

Boda-boda – Bicycle taxi

Boma – A fort or defensive stockade, often used to mean a small village or cluster of huts

Boriti – Mangrove poles, used on the coast for building and exported to the Gulf states for the same purpose

Buibui – The black cover-all cloak and scarf of Swahili women

Bwana – Mister, a polite form of address

Chai – Not just tea, but also the common term for a tip, or more often a small bribe or persuasion

Choo – Toilet (pronounced cho)

Duka – Shop, store

Duka la dawa – Chemist

Enkang – Maasai village

FORD – Forum for the Restoration of Democracy, opposition political party

Fundi – Mechanic, craftsman, expert

Gari – Car

Gema – The ethnic grouping of Gikuyu (Kikuyu), Embu and Meru

GK – Government of Kenya

Harambee – "Pull together" – the ideology of peaceable community development espoused by Jomo Kenyatta. *Harambee* meetings are local fund-raising gatherings – for schools, clinics, etc – but they've come in for some criticism in recent years as politicians vie to contribute the most money.

Hoteli – Small restaurant, chai shop, café, rarely with accommodation

Jua kali – "Hot sun" – open-air car repairer's yard or small workshop

Kanga – Printed cotton sheet used as a wrap, often incorporating a motto

Kanisa – Church

KANU – Kenya African National Union, Kenya's ruling political party

KBC – Kenya Broadcasting Corporation

Kikoi – Brightly coloured woven cloth

Laibon – Maasai spiritual leader, with the status of regional headman

Lugga – Dry river valley (usually in the north)

Maendeleo – Progress, development

Magendo – Corruption, bribery, abuse of power

Majimboism – The creation of federal blocks in formerly heterogeneous regions – these days associated with ethnic cleansing

Makonde – Beautifully worked Tanzanian wood carving, typically in ebony and representing entwined spirit families – much copied in the tourist markets

Makuti – Palm-leaf roof common on the coast

Malaika – Angel

Malaya – Prostitute

Mama – Common term of address for married women

Manamba – Matatu tout, "turnboy"

Manyatta – Temporary cattle camp, often loosely used for a village (Maasai)

Maskini – The poor, beggars (*Saidia maskini!* – "Help the poor!")

Matatu – Pick-up taxi, usually full to overflowing

Mbenzi – Member of the rich elite (presumed to have a Mercedes; plural *wabenzi*)

Miraa – Qat, a natural stimulant (see p.200)

Mkenya – Kenyan (pl. *wakenya*)

Moran – Man in the warrior age group of Maasai or Samburu (pl. *morani*)

Msikiti – Mosque

Mtalii – Tourist (pl. *watalii*)

Mtoto – Child (pl. *watoto*)

Mungiki – Anti-establishment Kikuyu youth cult that violently rejects western values

Mungu – God

Murram – Red or black clay soil, usually referring to a road

Mwananchi – Person, peasant, worker (pl. *wananchi*, "the people")

Mzee – Old man: "the Mzee" is Kenyatta
Mzungu – White person (pl. *wazungu*)
NCCK – National Christian Council of Kenya
NDP – National Development Party, mainly Luo
Ngai – Supreme god of the Kikuyu and other groups
NGO – Non-governmental organization
Ngoma – Dancing, drumming, party, celebration
Njia – Road, path
Nyayo – "Footsteps" – the follow-in-his-footsteps philosophy of post-Kenyatta Kenya propounded by President Moi
Panga – Multi-purpose short machete carried everywhere in the countryside

Pesa – Money, cash (lit. "silver")
Pombe – Booze
Safari – Journey of any kind
Shamba – Small farm, plot
Soda – Fizzy drink, but also a euphemism for a tip
Stage – Matatu stand
Uhuru – Freedom, independence
Ukimwi – AIDS
Ulaya – Europe
Watu – Literally "people", but often used slightly disparagingly by expats and Anglo-Kenyans, especially when referring to their staff

index

and small print

Index

Map entries are in green.

INDEX

INDEX

INDEX

I

INDEX

Twenty Years of Rough Guides

In the summer of 1981, Mark Ellingham, Rough Guides' founder, knocked out the first guide on a typewriter, with a group of friends. Mark had been travelling in Greece after university, and couldn't find a guidebook that really answered his needs. There were heavyweight cultural guides on the one hand – good on museums and classical sites but not on beaches and tavernas – and on the other hand student manuals that were so caught up with how to save money that they lost sight of the country's significance beyond its role as a place for a cool vacation. None of the guides began to address Greece as a country, with its natural and human environment, its politics and its contemporary life.

Having no urgent reason to return home, Mark decided to write his own guide. It was a guide to Greece that tried to combine some erudition and insight with a thoroughly practical approach to travellers' needs. Scrupulously researched listings of places to stay, eat and drink were matched by careful attention to detail on everything from Homer to Greek music, from classical sites to national parks and from nude beaches to monasteries. Back in London, Mark and his friends got their Rough Guide accepted by a farsighted commissioning editor at the publisher Routledge and it came out in 1982.

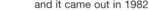

The Rough Guide to Greece was a student scheme that became a publishing phenomenon. The immediate success of the book – shortlisted for the Thomas Cook award – spawned a series that rapidly covered dozens of countries. The Rough Guides found a ready market among backpackers and budget travellers, but soon acquired a much broader readership that included older and less impecunious visitors. Readers relished the guides' wit and inquisitiveness as much as the enthusiastic, critical approach that acknowledges everyone wants value for money – but not at any price.

Rough Guides soon began supplementing the "rougher" information – the hostel and low-budget listings – with the kind of detail that independent-minded travellers on any budget might expect. These days, the guides – distributed worldwide by the Penguin group – include recommendations spanning the range from shoestring to luxury, and cover more than 200 destinations around the globe. Our growing team of authors, many of whom come to Rough Guides initially as outstandingly good letter-writers telling us about their travels, are spread all over the world, particularly in Europe, the USA and Australia. As well as the travel guides, Rough Guides publishes a series of dictionary phrasebooks covering two dozen major languages, an acclaimed series of music guides running the gamut from Classical to World Music, a series of music CDs in association with World Music Network, and a range of reference books on topics as diverse as the Internet, Pregnancy and Unexplained Phenomena. Visit **www.roughguides.com** to see what's cooking.

Rough Guide Credits

Text editor: Clifton Wilkinson
Series editor: Mark Ellingham
Editorial: Martin Dunford, Jonathan Buckley, Kate Berens, Ann-Marie Shaw, Helena Smith, Judith Bamber, Orla Duane, Olivia Eccleshall, Ruth Blackmore, Geoff Howard, Claire Saunders, Gavin Thomas, Alexander Mark Rogers, Polly Thomas, Joe Staines, Richard Lim, Duncan Clark, Peter Buckley, Lucy Ratcliffe, Alison Murchie, Matthew Teller, Andrew Dickson, Fran Sandham (UK); Andrew Rosenberg, Stephen Timblin, Yuki Takagaki, Richard Koss, Hunter Slaton, Julie Feiner (US)
Production: Susanne Hillen, Andy Hilliard, Link Hall, Helen Prior, Julia Bovis, Michelle Draycott, Katie Pringle, Mike Hancock, Zoë

Nobes, Rachel Holmes, Andy Turner
Cartography: Melissa Baker, Maxine Repath, Ed Wright, Katie Lloyd-Jones
Cover art direction: Louise Boulton
Picture research: Sharon Martins, Mark Thomas
Online: Kelly Cross, Anja Mutic-Blessing, Jennifer Gold, Audra Epstein, Suzanne Welles, Cree Lawson (US)
Finance: John Fisher, Gary Singh, Edward Downey, Mark Hall, Tim Bill
Marketing & Publicity: Richard Trillo, Niki Smith, David Wearn, Chloë Roberts, Demelza Dallow, Claire Southern (UK); Simon Carloss, David Wechsler, Kathleen Rushforth (US)
Administration: Tania Hummel, Julie Sanderson

Publishing Information

This seventh edition published May 2002 by **Rough Guides Ltd**,
62–70 Shorts Gardens, London WC2H 9AH.
Penguin Putnam, Inc. 375 Hudson Street, NY 10014, USA.
Distributed by the Penguin Group
Penguin Books Ltd,
80 Strand, London WC2R ORL
Penguin Putnam, Inc.
375 Hudson Street, NY 10014, USA
Penguin Books Australia Ltd,
487 Maroondah Highway, PO Box 257, Ringwood, Victoria 3134, Australia
Penguin Books Canada Ltd,
10 Alcorn Avenue, Toronto, Ontario, Canada M4V 1E4
Penguin Books (NZ) Ltd,
182–190 Wairau Road, Auckland 10, New Zealand
Typeset in Bembo and Helvetica to an original design by Henry Iles.

Printed in Italy by LegoPrint S.p.A

© Richard Trillo 2002

816pp includes index
A catalogue record for this book is available from the British Library
ISBN 1-85828-859-2

SMALL PRINT

Help us update

We've gone to a lot of effort to ensure that the seventh edition of **The Rough Guide to Kenya** is accurate and up-to-date. However, things change – places get "discovered", opening hours are notoriously fickle, restaurants and rooms raise prices or lower standards. If you feel we've got it wrong or left something out, we'd like to know, and if you can remember the address, the price, the time, the phone number, so much the better.

We'll credit all contributions, and send a copy of the next edition (or any other Rough Guide if you prefer) for the best letters.

Everyone who writes to us and isn't already a subscriber will receive a copy of our full-colour thrice-yearly newsletter. Please mark letters: "**Rough Guide Kenya Update**" and send to: Rough Guides, 62–70 Shorts Gardens, London WC2H 9AH, or Rough Guides, 4th Floor, 345 Hudson St, New York, NY 10014. Or send an email to: **mail@roughguides.co.uk** or **mail@roughguides.com**

Have your questions answered and tell others about your trip at
http://roughguides.atinfopop.com

Acknowledgements

The author thanks everyone who worked on this guide, especially Clifton Wilkinson for diligent editing, Katie Pringle once again for slick typesetting and kind patience, Jo Mead for astute proofreading, Maxine Repath's cartographic team for rising to the mapping challenge, Mark Thomas for inspired picture research, Louise Boulton for the gorgeous zebras, Michelle Draycott and Julia Bovis for doing production things so well and so sociably, Doug Paterson for being musically au courant and Isabelle Prondzynski and Jens Finke for their invaluable input. A special thanks to the hardworking updaters on this edition, Okigbo Ojukwu and Daniel Jacobs.

For aid, ideas and encouragement on the previous editions, continuing indebtedness goes to Jeremy Torr for the amazing English Cycles bike that got me round Kenya on the first trip, Bruce Buckland and Michelle Cox, Mark Dubin, David Else, Jens Finke, Emma Gregg, Rosie Mercer, Tony Stones, Jackie Switzer, Tony Zurbrugg, Robert Gordon and the Gordon family, and the Khan family in Kisii. Finally, as ever, to Teresa, Alex, David and Phoebe, all my love and thanks for putting up with a bit more for a bit longer (XXXX).

Okigbo would like to thank Sammy Murege Kamau, Rufus Mutakaa Carr at Mt Kenya Chogoria Guides & Porters Association, Fred Kaigua at KATO, Pineapple Dougy, Val and Brendan Black at Nairobi Park Services, Nelson "Smiley" Wambogu, Lorna Abungu at Arficom, Victoria Logan, Sarah Higgins at Lake Naivasha Riperian Association, Eunice Apiyo, Alan Dixson, Henry Kahuki, Dennis Mutua and Brenda Wood at Let's Go Travel, Malcolm Gascoigne at Yare Safaris in Maralal, David Chianda and John Bisley at Gametrackers, Michael Ngige, Joseph Gathu at Icetrek, Damian Davis at Aberdares Country Club and Ashwin Bhatt at Kenia Tours and Safaris.

Daniel would like to thank Sharon and Colin Forbes at *Kijiji Cottages*, Jane and Julia Barnley and Sammy Chepas at *Sirikwa Guest House*, Mr Hans at *Mwazaro Beach Resort*, Yasmin Mumbi, Jitu and Ajay Taylor, Peter Owino, Kiprotich Chemjor at the *Tea Hotel*, Kericho, Mbarak Omar at the Lamu Tourist Information Bureau, Ozi Dosaji, Elijah Kasati at the Malindi Tourist Office, Ashwin Bhatt and Bernard Kabuu at Kenia Tours, Asha Ochieng, Amina Kibiringoh at Mombasa and Coast Tourist Association, Amanda Mills and Steve Crawley at the Kenya Tourist Board, London, and the staff of *Kijiji Cottages* at Diani, *Ozi's Hotel* in Malindi, the *Iqbal Hotel* in Nairobi and the *New People's Hotel* in Mombasa.

Readers' letters

Many thanks to everyone who wrote in with comments and updates on the sixth edition. Keep 'em coming!

Pat Anderson and Margaret McCord, Dean and Anki Apel, Martin Bauer, Dave Caister, Dorothy Carson, Linda Cawley, Kevin Chisholm, Vicki Clements and Steve Scott, Peter Coghlan, Mica Collister, Ian Croft, Sean Crosson, Aretha Fiebig and Natalie Dean, Joukje Dam and Jacob Wiersma, Mieke and Marc Devigne, Steve Ernest, Arnold D Evans, Mark Fairweather, Linda Francis, Charlotte Hanratty, Niek Heering, Sharon Hockey, Lotte Hughes, Steffen Jensen and Kjell, Barbara Jones, Naomi Jones, Cathy Kim, Deborah Lewis, Jerry Liebowitz and Leah Thayer, James Litten, Maayke Lockefeer, Geoff Mason, James McCaldin, Peter Oestbirk, Arie van Oosterwyk and Ellen Bassett, Krista Peterson, Helen Poole, Lucy Robertson, Danielle Rodgers, Mandy Seal, Hank Selke, Graham Simons, Steve Smith, Lex Spahr, Poul Thisted, David and Louise Thums, Melissa Top, Rico Torriani, Roger W Warren, Michael Watkins.

And many thanks from the author to the following people who helped so generously on this edition, either on the ground or by replying to queries.

Terry Light at Africa Expeditions, Raymond Matiba and Clement Kiragu at Alliance Hotels, Fatma Muses at Block Hotels, Mohamed Shafi at Glory Car Hire, Chris Morris at Into Africa, Sharon and Colin Forbes at Kijiji, Tinu Mhajan at Mada Hotels, Lacty de Sousa at Rhino Safaris, Nishit Lakami at Suntrek, Jake Grieves-Cook and Donna Owen at Tropical Places, Sean Gavaghan at Travellers Hotels, Fayyaz Kasmani at Visit.Kenya.com.

Photo Credits

Cover
Front (small top image) giant euphorbia tree, Amboseli National Park © Robert Harding
Front (small bottom image) crowned crane © Robert Harding
Back (top) Mount Kenya © Trip
Back (lower) Dhow, Malindi © Stone

Colour introduction
p.i Maasai Mara landscape © Robert Harding

p.iv Ear and neck beads © Thomasin Magor/Robert Harding

p.v Samburu handshake © Richard Trillo

p.vi Maasai giraffe © Carla Signorini Jones/ Images of Africa

p.vii Samburu warrior © David Keith Jones/ Images of Africa

p.viii Baobab tree © David Keith Jones/ Images of Africa

Things not to miss
1. Balloon inflation at *Little Governor's Camp*, Maasai Mara © Richard Trillo

2. Hot spring, Lake Bogoria © Carla Signorini Jones/Images of Africa

3. Nile crocodile hatching © Nick Greaves/ Images of Africa

4. Turkana overland safari and flash flood © Richard Trillo

5. Tea-pickers near Kericho © David Keith Jones/Images of Africa

6. Kichwa Tembo airstrip, Maasai Mara © David Keith Jones/Images of Africa

7. Fort Jesus, Mombasa © David Keith Jones/Images of Africa

8. Angel fish © David Keith Jones/Images of Africa

9. Harambee Avenue, Lamu © David Keith Jones/Images of Africa

10. Hippos, Mzima Springs © David Keith Jones/Images of Africa

11. Hut Tarn, 4500m, Mount Kenya © Richard Trillo

12. Gedi ruins, near Watamu © David Keith Jones/Images of Africa

13. Cave of skulls, Wundanyi © Richard Trillo

14. Nairobi Agricultural Show © David Keith Jones/Images of Africa

15. Olorgasailie hand-axe site © David Keith Jones/Images of Africa

16. Kebab grill, Lake Victoria © Frank Connolly

17. Fischer's Tower, Hell's Gate National Park © David Keith Jones/Images of Africa

18. Makindu Crafts Co-op © Richard Trillo

19. Citrus swallowtail butterfly © David Keith Jones/Images of Africa

20. Twahir Mohamed and Golden Sounds Band © Twahir Mohamed

21. Saiwa Swamp National Park © Richard Trillo

22. Wildebeest migration, Mara River © David Keith Jones/Images of Africa

23. Maulidi festival © David Keith Jones/Images of Africa

24. Aerial walkway, *Shimba Lodge* © Ariadne Van Zandbergen

25. Kakamega Forest © Friedrich Von Horsten/Images of Africa

Wildlife section
All images © Bruce Coleman Library

Black and white photos
Langata Giraffe Centre © Richard Trillo (p.82)

Kenyatta Conference Centre, Nairobi © David Keith Jones/Images of Africa (p.116)

Lioness, Nairobi National Park © David Keith Jones/Images of Africa (p.162)

Maasai dancers, *Outspan Hotel* © Richard Trillo (p.164)

Chania Falls, Aberdares © David Keith Jones/Images of Africa (p.208)

Lake Bogoria © Richard Trillo (p.222)

Rift Valley © David Keith Jones/ Images of Africa (p.257)

Women at Simbi Lake © Richard Trillo (p.286)

Woman carrying clay pot © David Keith Jones/Images of Africa (p.308)

Grant's (Burchell's) zebra, Tsavo West National Park © Richard Trillo (p.362)

Hot air balloon trip, Maasai Mara © David Keith Jones/Images of Africa (p.387)

Low tide at Faza, Lamu archipelago © Richard Trillo (p.438)

Pillar tombs, Malindi © David Keith Jones/Images of Africa (p.536)

Bus breakdown © Richard Trillo (p.584)

Turkana overland trip © Richard Trillo (p.612)

around the world

Alaska ★ Algarve ★ Amsterdam ★ Andalucía ★ Antigua & Barbuda ★
Argentina ★ Auckland Restaurants ★ Australia ★ Austria ★ Bahamas ★
Bali & Lombok ★ Bangkok ★ Barbados ★ Barcelona ★ Beijing ★ Belgium &
Luxembourg ★ Belize ★ Berlin ★ Big Island of Hawaii ★ Bolivia ★ Boston
★ Brazil ★ Britain ★ Brittany & Normandy ★ Bruges & Ghent ★ Brussels ★
Budapest ★ Bulgaria ★ California ★ Cambodia ★ Canada ★ Cape Town ★
The Caribbean ★ Central America ★ Chile ★ China ★ Copenhagen ★
Corsica ★ Costa Brava ★ Costa Rica ★ Crete ★ Croatia ★ Cuba ★ Cyprus ★
Czech & Slovak Republics ★ Devon & Cornwall ★ Dodecanese & East
Aegean ★ Dominican Republic ★ The Dordogne & the Lot ★ Dublin ★
Ecuador ★ Edinburgh ★ Egypt ★ England ★ Europe ★ First-time Asia ★
First-time Europe ★ Florence ★ Florida ★ France ★ French Hotels &
Restaurants ★ Gay & Lesbian Australia ★ Germany ★ Goa ★ Greece ★
Greek Islands ★ Guatemala ★ Hawaii ★ Holland ★ Hong Kong & Macau ★
Honolulu ★ Hungary ★ Ibiza & Formentera ★ Iceland ★ India ★ Indonesia
★ Ionian Islands ★ Ireland ★ Israel & the Palestinian Territories ★ Italy ★
Jamaica ★ Japan ★ Jerusalem ★ Jordan ★ Kenya ★ The Lake District ★
Languedoc & Roussillon ★ Laos ★ Las Vegas ★ Lisbon ★ London ★

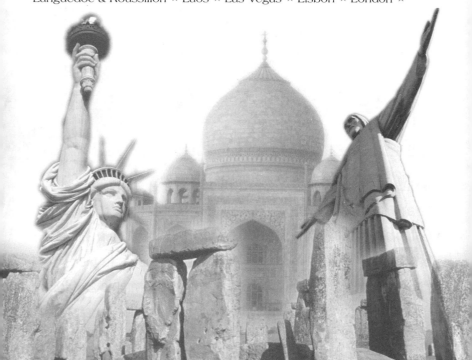

in twenty years

London Mini Guide ★ London Restaurants ★ Los Angeles ★ Madeira ★ Madrid ★ Malaysia, Singapore & Brunei ★ Mallorca ★ Malta & Gozo ★ Maui ★ Maya World ★ Melbourne ★ Menorca ★ Mexico ★ Miami & the Florida Keys ★ Montréal ★ Morocco ★ Moscow ★ Nepal ★ New England ★ New Orleans ★ New York City ★ New York Mini Guide ★ New York Restaurants ★ New Zealand ★ Norway ★ Pacific Northwest ★ Paris ★ Paris Mini Guide ★ Peru ★ Poland ★ Portugal ★ Prague ★ Provence & the Côte d'Azur ★ Pyrenees ★ The Rocky Mountains ★ Romania ★ Rome ★ San Francisco ★ San Francisco Restaurants ★ Sardinia ★ Scandinavia ★ Scotland ★ Scottish Highlands & Islands ★ Seattle ★ Sicily ★ Singapore ★ South Africa, Lesotho & Swaziland ★ South India ★ Southeast Asia ★ Southwest USA ★ Spain ★ St Lucia ★ St Petersburg ★ Sweden ★ Switzerland ★ Sydney ★ Syria ★ Tanzania ★ Tenerife and La Gomera ★ Thailand ★ Thailand's Beaches & Islands ★ Tokyo ★ Toronto ★ Travel Health ★ Trinidad & Tobago ★ Tunisia ★ Turkey ★ Tuscany & Umbria ★ USA ★ Vancouver ★ Venice & the Veneto ★ Vienna ★ Vietnam ★ Wales ★ Washington DC ★ West Africa ★ Women Travel ★ Yosemite ★ Zanzibar ★ Zimbabwe

also look out for our maps, phrasebooks, music guides and reference books

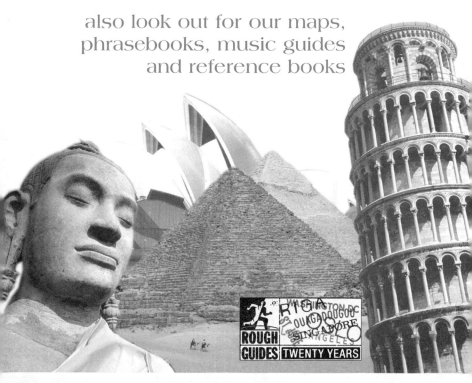

ROUGH GUIDES | TWENTY YEARS

EXCLUSIVE AFRICAN SAFARIS FROM TROPICAL PLACES

SAFARI PRICES FROM ONLY £200*

Tropical Places offer a wide selection of Road and Air safaris featuring many National Parks and Game Reserves including the Maasai Mara. Exclusive to Tropical Places in the UK is Porini Camp, situated in Kenya's Eselenkei Conservation Area. With only 8 tents in the whole camp, you are guaranteed an intimate and personal African adventure.

KENYA BEACH-ONLY
packages from as little as £579 for 7 nights

*price is for 2 nights full board accommodation at Taita Hills excluding flights.

- Tailor-made options
- Kenya and Tanzania safaris
- Dedicated specialist team open 9am - 9pm
- Optional beach extensions
- Multi-centres available including Dubai, Mauritius and Seychelles

Call 0870 444 0695 9am-9pm seven days a week.

See our latest special offers on -**www.tropicalplaces.co.uk**

ITV Teletext Page 259 Sky Active..Interactive TV on Sky Digital

For a Tropical Places brochure call **0870 444 0693** quoting 'Rough Guide'.

TROPICAL PLACES
THE DIRECT SELL SPECIALIST FOR EXOTIC HOLIDAYS

CARIBBEAN • AFRICA • INDIAN OCEAN • FAR EAST • MIDDLE EAST

Bill Bryson's next big adventure...

"I'm off on my travels again. This time, to east Africa with CARE International, one of the world's most effective aid and development charities.

I've long been an admirer - and supporter - of their work in poor communities around the world. Because by helping local people secure food, clean water, healthcare and an education, they really do change lives for good.

Of course, I'll be writing an account of the places I go and the people I meet. Read all about it in my exclusive diary and help me to support their incredible work."

Bill Bryson

Bill's diary will be published in early December 2002. Order your copy now for the chance to have it signed. The 20 lucky winners will be drawn in December 2002.

There's no other way to experience Kenya !
... keep trekking!

Short excursions

Extended safaris

Specialist and tailor made safaris

Car Hire, Hotel and Lodge

Bookings and much more

Safari Centre, Waiyaki Way
P O Box 48146, Nairobi, Kenya
tel: 442982, 442486, 443829 fax: 254-2-448351
email: safaris@suntreksafaris.com
web. www.suntreksafaris.com

CAR HIRE, TOURS & SAFARIS LTD.

Know what you require? Don't know what Kenya has to offer?
Rent a car from Glory Car Hire and explore Kenya the way you
want. A wide variety of cars to choose
from saloons to 4WD

Glory Villas is located in Nyali which is about 20 minutes drive
from Mombasa town. What's more, with its beautiful structure, you
are guaranteed to enjoy your vacation be it for pleasure or business.
We provide excellent service and to the best highest standard. When
looking for an ideal, secured and safe place. Always rely on Glory to
provide a peaceful vacation.

Glory Mombasa Palace hotel is situated in South Coast, in Diani. It
is a 30km drive from Mombasa town. When in Diani and looking
for a Luxurious stay ensure to visit and enjoy our grand service.

NAIROBI
Reinsurance Plaza
Taifa Road
PO Box 66969
Tel: 224428/213596/
225024
Fax: 02-331533

MOMBASA
Glory House
Moi Avenue
PO Box 85527
Tel: 221159/313561/
314284/315937
Fax: 22196

DIANI SHOPPING CTR
Tel: 0127-2276/3076/
3392
Fax: 0127-3076

MALINDI
Ngala Building
Lamu Road
PO Box 994
Tel: 20065/30309
Fax: 0123-20065

Nairobi email: glorycarhire@net200ke.com **Mombasa email:** glory@africaonline.co.ke